INTERNATIONAL BUSINESS

Competing in the Global Marketplace

10th Edition

INTERNATIONAL BUSINESS

Competing in the Global Marketplace

10th Edition

INTERNATIONAL BUSINESS

Competing in the Global Marketplace

10th Edition

Charles W. L. Hill

University of Washington

Arun Kumar Jain

Indian Institute of Management Lucknow

McGraw Hill Education (India) Private Limited

NEW DELHI

McGraw Hill Education Offices

New Delhi New York St Louis San Francisco Auckland Bogotá Caracas
Kuala Lumpur Lisbon London Madrid Mexico City Milan Montreal
San Juan Santiago Singapore Sydney Tokyo Toronto

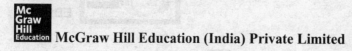

McGraw Hill Education (India) Private Limited

International Business: Competing in the Global Marketplace, 10/e (SIE)

Indian Adaptation done by arrangement with McGraw-Hill Global Education Holdings, LLC, New York.

Sales territories: India, Pakistan, Nepal, Bangladesh, Sri Lanka and Bhutan

Fifth reprint 2015
RQQCRRCVDRZRR

McGraw Hill Education (India) Edition 2014

ISBN (13 digit): 978-1-25-909803-1
ISBN (10 digit): 1-25-909803-6

Managing Director: *Kaushik Bellani*
Head—Higher Education Publishing and Marketing: *Vibha Mahajan*
Assistant Sponsoring Editor: *Anirudh Sharan*
Manager (Editorial Services): *Hema Razdan*
Senior Production Manager: *Manohar Lal*
Senior Production Executive: *Atul Gupta*
Assistant General Manager—Higher Education Marketing: *Vijay Sarathi*
Senior Product Specialist: *Navneet Kumar*
Senior Graphic Designer (Cover Design): *Meenu Raghav*
General Manager—Production: *Rajender P Ghansela*
Manager—Production: *Reji Kumar*

Published by McGraw Hill Education (India) Private Limited
P-24, Green Park Extension, New Delhi 110 016, typeset at The Composers, 260, C.A. Apt., Paschim Vihar New Delhi 110 063 and printed at Pashupati Printers, 1/429/16, Gali No. 1, Friends Colony, Industrial Area, G.T. Road, Shahdara, Delhi 110 095

Cover Printer: SDR

Visit us at: www.mheducation.co.in

For June and
***Mike Hill**, my parents*
and
***Nidhi** and **Kriti**, my family*

About the Authors

CHARLES W. L. HILL
University of Washington

Charles W. L. Hill is the Hughes M. and Katherine Blake Professor of Strategy and International Business at the School of Business, University of Washington. Professor Hill received his PhD from the University of Manchester in Britain. In addition to the University of Washington, he has served on the faculties of UMIST, Texas A&M University, and Michigan State University.

Professor Hill has published over 50 articles in peer reviewed academic journals including the *Academy of Management Journal, Academy of Management Review, Strategic Management Journal,* and *Organization Science.* His work is widely cited by other academics.

Professor Hill has published several college textbooks including *International Business* (McGraw-Hill) and *Global Business Today* (McGraw-Hill). Both texts have been translated into several languages and are worldwide market share leaders.

Professor Hill has taught in the MBA, Executive MBA, Technology Management MBA, Management, and PhD programs at the University of Washington. He has received numerous awards for teaching excellence, the majority in executive level programs.

Professor Hill works on a private basis with a number of organizations. His clients have included ATL, AT&T Wireless, Boeing, BF Goodrich, Group Health, Hexcel, Microsoft, Philips Healthcare, Seattle City Light, Swedish Health Services, Tacoma City Light, Thompson Financial Services, WRQ, and Wizards of the Coast.

Professor Hill has been teaching in-house executive education courses for Microsoft for 15 years. He has worked closely with the Leadership Development Group at Microsoft for most of that time.

Professor Hill has served on the advisory board of several start-up companies. For recreation, Professor Hill enjoys mountaineering, rock climbing, skiing, and sailing.

ARUN KUMAR JAIN

IIM Lucknow

Arun Kumar Jain is a globally traveled well-known strategy scholar. He is a Gold-medalist engineer (receiving 'All-Round Best Student' award) and a Ph. D from IIM-Ahmedabad (receiving the IFCI Outstanding Doctoral Research Award). Dr. Jain is a Professor-Researcher, Entrepreneur-Innovator, Author, Engineer, and TV Commentator.

He has published more than 100 research-based case studies and articles in international journals including Harvard Business Review. His all three general management books, viz., (a) *Corporate Excellence*, (b) *Managing Global Competition*, and (c) *Competitive Excellence* have received Best Management Book Awards. His two MBA textbooks on *Crafting and Executing Strategy (19 ed.)* and *International Business*—co-authored with US-based professors—are standard and largest selling textbooks in the sub-continent.

Dr. Jain has also advised Chief Ministers and State governments in India, and Boardroom adviser-facilitator to large businesses (including ABB-India, Bharat Electronics, GE-Healthcare, Maruti-Suzuki India, Engineers India Limited, SAIL, ONGC, L&T, NTPC, Tata-Group, State Bank, Indian Armed Forces, etc.).

Dr. Jain has taught at leading MBA institutions across the world including Bradford (UK), Connecticut (USA), Israel, and Kenya. In India prior to joining Indian Institute of Management - Lucknow, was a member of faculty at IIM-Bangalore. Received best teaching scores on several occasions.

He was invited by leading Institutions for lectures, keynotes and research—including Global Corporate Governance Forum at Washington, World Bank/IFC, Bundesbank (Germany), Global Forum for International Investment (Paris), OECD at Paris and Copenhagen, UNCTAD, MITI (Japan), European Union (Brussels and Strasbourg), Commonwealth Secretariat (UK), India-Germany Business Forum (Germany), etc.

In mid-1990s, taking a break from academics, he was Founder-Chairman of a strategy research consulting firm based in Delhi (India). Carried out path-breaking research on drivers of corporate excellence which was featured by Harvard Business Review (July-August 2005) as one of the ten most influential researches on Organizational Excellence across the world during last 25 years.

He is a visiting Research Chair Professor of International Business and Corporate Governance at the German Graduate School of Business and Law at Heilbronn (Germany). He was also Chairman and President of Centre for Accelerated Learning, Innovation, and Competitiveness (Germany) in 2008-09. Dr. Jain held honorary chairs as Distinguished Professor of Corporate Governance and Strategy, SP Jain Center for Global Management, Singapore-Dubai and Professor of Strategy, International Business, and Corporate Governance at EM Strasbourg School of Business, Strasbourg (France's largest University).

As a regular speaker on Business TV channels such as ET Now and Bloomberg, he provides strategic perspectives to issues. He is also a regular columnist for Financial Chronicle. His articles can be accessed at http://www.mydigitalfc.com/2009/arun-kumar-jain.

He is currently an Independent non-Executive Board member of Jain Irrigation Systems Limited—a $1 bn company with 12 factories worldwide, and on the advisory panel of Institute of Company Secretaries of India. He was a member of Primary Market Advisory Committee (PMAC) of Securities & Exchange Board of India.

The Proven Choice for International Business

CURRENT. APPLICATION RICH. RELEVANT. INTEGRATED.

In this Tenth Special Indian Edition, we have made some fundamental changes. The reason is the changing nature of Indian and World economy and its better integration with the outside world while at the same time being buffeted by entrenched forces. Therefore while there are huge opportunities for the global firm to invest in India, at the same time, such investments carry associated risks. These are highlighted in the cases of Wal-Mart attempts to secure a foothold in India, Vodafone's fight in the Supreme Court on retrospective taxes on assets transfer, and the losses incurred by many global telecom companies which invested in India in 2G licenses but lost due to Supreme Court order cancelling the sovereign agreements that the companies entered into with the Government of India. This edition highlights and describes all these cases. In the light of emerging opportunities and changes in taxation law, we have added Sections on Transfer pricing and advance pricing agreements (APA), India's taxation system including coming Goods and Service Tax (GST) regime, and Land Acquisition Act which is important for foreign companies making direct investments. Similarly we have included cases on the peculiar cultural and customer behavior issues faced by foreign firms in India highlighting the need for careful assessment of entry strategies and competitive approaches for stabilizing during downturns. The cases of Peugeot-Citroen's entry issues, Volkswagen's attempts to create a space for itself by bringing learnings from across the world, Adidas' problems with its subsidiary Reebok unit in India, are great for students to assimilate important concepts of how global companies dovetail investment decisions with ground realities.

COMPREHENSIVE AND UP-TO-DATE

To be comprehensive, an international business textbook must:

- Explain how and why the world's countries differ.
- Present a thorough review of the economics and politics of international trade and investment.
- Explain the functions and form of the global monetary system.
- Examine the strategies and structures of international businesses.
- Assess the special roles of an international business's various functions.

We have always endeavored to do all of these things in International Business. In our views, many other texts paid insufficient attention to the strategies and structures of international businesses and to the implications of international business for firms' various functions. This omission has been a serious deficiency. Many of the students in these international business courses will soon be working in international businesses, and they will be expected to understand the implications of international business for their organization's strategy, structure, and functions. This book pays close attention to these issues.

Comprehensiveness and relevance also require coverage of the major theories. It has always been our goal to incorporate the insights gleaned from recent academic work into the text. Consistent with this goal, over the last eight editions insights from the following research have been added:

- The new trade theory and strategic trade policy.
- The work of Nobel Prize–winning economist Amartya Sen on economic development.
- The work of Hernando de Soto on the link between property rights and economic development.
- Samuel Huntington's influential thesis on the "clash of civilizations."
- The new growth theory of economic development championed by Paul Romer and Gene Grossman.
- Empirical work by Jeffrey Sachs and others on the relationship between international trade and economic growth.
- Michael Porter's theory of the competitive advantage of nations.
- Robert Reich's work on national competitive advantage.
- The work of Nobel Prize–winner Douglas North and others on national institutional structures and the protection of property rights.
- The market imperfections approach to foreign direct investment that has grown out of Ronald Coase and Oliver Williamson's work on transaction cost economics.
- Bartlett and Ghoshal's research on the transnational corporation.
- The writings of C. K. Prahalad and Gary Hamel on core competencies, global competition, and global strategic alliances.
- Insights for international business strategy that can be derived from the resource-based view of the firm.
- Paul Samuelson's critique of free trade theory.

In addition to including leading-edge theory, in light of the fast-changing nature of the international business environment, every effort is being made to ensure that the book is as up-to-date as possible when it goes to press. Much has happened in the world since the first edition of this book was published in 1993. The Uruguay Round of GATT negotiations were successfully concluded and the World Trade Organization was established. In 2001 the WTO embarked upon another major round of talks aimed to reduce barriers to trade, the Doha Round. The European Union moved forward with its post-1992 agenda to achieve a closer economic and monetary union, including the establishment of a common currency in January 1999. The North American Free Trade Agreement passed into law. The former Communist states of Eastern Europe and Asia continued on the road to economic and political r e form. As they did, the euphoric mood that followed the collapse of communism in 1989 was slowly replaced with a growing sense of realism about the hard path ahead for many of these countries. The global money market continued its meteoric growth. By 2009 more than $2 trillion per day was flowing across national borders. The size of such flows fueled concern about the ability of short-term speculative shifts in global capital markets to destabilize the world economy. The World Wide Web emerged from nowhere to become the backbone of an emerging global ne t work for electronic commerce. The world continued to become more global. Several Asian Pacific economies, including most notably China, continued to grow their economies at a rapid rate. Outsourcing of service functions to places such as China and India emerged as a major issue in developed Western nations. New multinationals continued to emerge from developing nations in addition to the world's established industrial powers. Increasingly, the globalization of the world economy affected a wide range of firms of all sizes, from the very large to the very small.

Also, in the wake of the terrorist attacks on the United States that took place on September 11, 2001, global terrorism and the attendant geopolitical risks emerged as a threat to global economic integration and activity. This has been given due coverage.

What's New in the 10th Edition

The success of the first nine editions of International Business was based in part upon the incorporation of leading-edge research into the text, the use of the up-to-date examples and statistics to illustrate global trends and enterprise strategy, and the discussion of current events within the context of the appropriate theory. Building on these strengths, the goals for this revision have been threefold:

1. To incorporate new insights from recent scholarly research wherever appropriate.
2. To make sure the content of the text covers all appropriate issues.
3. To make sure the text is as up-to-date as possible with regard to current events, statistics, and examples.

As part of the overall revision process, changes have been made to every chapter in the book. All statistics have been updated to incorporate the most recently available data. New examples, cases, and boxes have been added and older examples updated to reflect new developments. Almost all of the chapter opening and closing cases are new to this edition. New material has been inserted wherever appropriate to reflect recent academic work or important current events.

Most notably for this edition, detailed discussion of the global financial crisis that occurred in 2008 and 2009, and its implications for international business, has been added to many chapters. For example, Chapter 7 opens with a case that discusses the impact of the global financial crisis on attitudes toward protectionism in many countries. Similarly, Chapter 11 closes with a case that profiles how the global financial crisis triggered economic turmoil and a currency crisis in Latvia.

Elsewhere, Chapter 7 has been updated to discuss progress on the current round of talks sponsored by the WTO aimed at reducing barriers to trade, particularly in agriculture (the Doha Round). Chapter 8 now discusses the slump in foreign direct investment flows that took place in 2008 and 2009, and explains how the global financial crisis of 2008 contributed to it. Chapter 10 discusses the weakness in the U.S. dollar between 2004 and 2008, and its paradoxical rebound in late 2008 in the midst of a severe financial crisis in the United States and elsewhere. Similarly, furtherdiscussion of the unrest that continues to sweep across the Middle East following the ArabSpring of 2011 and the ongoing turmoil in Egypt has been added to the book.

BEYOND UNCRITICAL PRESENTATION AND SHALLOW EXPLANATION

Many issues in international business are complex and thus necessitate considerations of pros and cons. To demonstrate both sides of issues to students, we have adopted a critical approach that presents the arguments for and against economic theories, government policies, business strategies, organizational structures, and so on.

Therefore, attempt is made to explain the complexities of the many theories and phenomena unique to international business so the student might comprehend the statements of a theory or the reasons a phenomenon is the way it is. These theories and phenomena are explained in more depth than they are in competing textbooks, the rationale being that a shallow explanation is little better than no explanation.

FOCUS ON RICH APPLICATIONS OF INTERNATIONAL BUSINESS CONCEPTS

We have always believed that it is important to show students how the material covered in the text is relevant to the actual practice of international business. This is explicit in the later chapters of the book, which focus on the practice of international business, but it is not always obvious in the first half of the book, which considers many macroeconomic and political issues, from international trade theory and foreign direct investment flows to the IMF and the influence of inflation rates on foreign exchange quotations. Accordingly, at the end of each chapter in Parts Two, Three, and Four—where the focus is on the environment of international business, as opposed to particular firms—there is a section titled **Implications for Managers**. In this section, the managerial implications of the material discussed in the chapter are clearly explained.

world's new market economies is large, the risks associated with any such investment are also substantial. It would be foolish to ignore these. The financial system in China, for example, is not transparent, and many suspect that Chinese banks hold a high proportion of nonperforming loans on their books. If true, these bad debts could trigger a significant financial crisis during the next decade in China, which would dramatically lower growth rates.

■ IMPLICATIONS FOR MANAGERS ▬▬▬▬▬▬▬▬ ▌O3-4

As noted in the previous chapter, the political, economic, and legal environments of a country clearly influence the attractiveness of that country as a market or investment site. In this chapter, we argued that countries with democratic regimes, market-based economic policies, and strong protection of property rights are more likely to attain high and sustained economic growth rates and are thus a more attractive location for international business. It follows that the benefits, costs, and risks associated with doing business in a country are a function of that country's political, economic, and legal systems. The overall attractiveness of a country as a market or investment site depends on balancing the likely long-term benefits of doing business in that country against the likely costs and risks. Here, we consider the determinants of benefits, costs, and risks.

BENEFITS

In the most general sense, the long-run monetary benefits of doing business in a country are a function of the size of the market, the present wealth (purchasing power) of consumers in that market, and the likely future wealth of consumers. While some markets are very large when measured by number of consumers (e.g., China and India), low living standards may imply limited purchasing power and therefore a relatively

Another tool is used to focus on managerial implications is the **Management Focus** box. Most chaptershave at least one Management Focus. Like the opening cases, the purpose of these boxes is to illustrate the relevanceof chapter material for the practice of international business.

Did Walmart Violate the Foreign Corrupt Practices Act?

In the early 2000s Walmart wanted to build a new store in San Juan Teotihuacan, Mexico, barely a mile from ancient pyramids that drew tourists from around the world. The owner of the land was happy to sell to Walmart, but one thing stood in the way of a deal—the city's new zoning laws. These prohibited commercial development in the historic area. Not to be denied, executives at the headquarters of Walmart de Mexico found a way around the problem; they paid a $52,000 bribe to a local official to redraw the zoning area so that the property Walmart wanted to purchase was placed *outside* the commercial-free zone. Walmart then went ahead and built the store, despite vigorous local opposition, opening it in late 2004.

A former lawyer for Walmart de Mexico subsequently contacted Walmart executives at the company's corporate headquarters in Bentonville, Arkansas. He told them that Walmart de Mexico routinely resorted to bribery, citing the altered zoning map as just one example. Alarmed, executives at Walmart started their own investigation. Faced with growing evidence of corruption in Mexico, top Walmart executives decided to engage in damage control, rather than coming clean. Walmart's top lawyer shipped the case files back to Mexico and handed responsibility for the investigation over to the general council of Walmart de Mexico. This was an interesting choice, since the very same general council was alleged to have authorized bribes. The general council quickly exonerated fellow Mexican executives, and the internal investigation was closed in 2006.

For several years nothing more happened; then in April 2012 *The New York Times* published an article detailing bribery by Walmart. *The Times* cited the changed zoning map and several

In addition, each chapter begins with an **opening case** that sets the stage for the chapter content and familiarizes students with how real international companies conduct business.

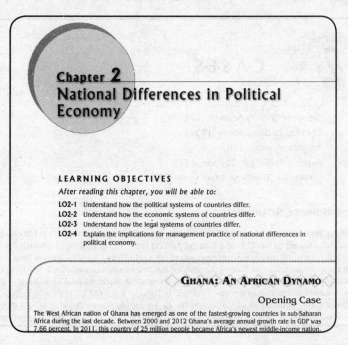

Chapter 2
National Differences in Political Economy

LEARNING OBJECTIVES

After reading this chapter, you will be able to:

LO2-1 Understand how the political systems of countries differ.
LO2-2 Understand how the economic systems of countries differ.
LO2-3 Understand how the legal systems of countries differ.
LO2-4 Explain the implications for management practice of national differences in political economy.

◇ **GHANA: AN AFRICAN DYNAMO** ◇

Opening Case

The West African nation of Ghana has emerged as one of the fastest-growing countries in sub-Saharan Africa during the last decade. Between 2000 and 2012 Ghana's average annual growth rate in GDP was 7.66 percent. In 2011, this country of 25 million people became Africa's newest middle-income nation.

A **closing case** to each chapter is designed to illustrate the relevance of chapter material for the practice of international business and provide continued insight into how real companies handle those issues.

Closing **CASE**

Poland's Economy

As the financial crisis of 2008 and 2009 unfolded, countries across Europe were hit hard. A notable exception was Poland, whose economy grew by 1.5 percent during 2009, while every other economy in the European Union contracted. Between 2010 and 2012 Poland's growth rate averaged 3.4 percent per annum, the best in Europe. How did Poland achieve this?

In 1989, Poland elected its first democratic government after more than four decades of Communist rule. Since then, like many other eastern European countries, Poland has embraced market-based economic policies, opened its markets to international trade and foreign investment, and privatized many state-owned businesses. In 2004, the country joined the European Union, giving it easy access to the large consumer markets of western Europe. All this helped transform Poland into a major exporter. Exports account for about 40 percent of gross domestic product (in contrast, they account for around 12 percent in the United States). As a consequence, between 1989 and 2010, Poland recorded the highest sustained growth in the region. Real GDP doubled over this period, compared to a 70 percent increase in neighboring Slovakia and 45 percent in the Czech Republic.

Poland's government has also been fiscally conservative, keeping public debt in check, not allowing it to expand during the recession as many other countries did. This led to investor confidence in the country. Consequently, there was no large outflow of funds during the 2008–2009 economic turmoil. This stands in stark contrast to what happened in the Baltic states, where investors pulled money out of those economies during 2008 and 2009, driving their currencies down, raising the cost of government debt, and precipitating a full-blown economic crisis that required the IMF and EU to step in with finan-

End-of-part cases are longer, allowing a more in-depth study of international companies.

P·A·R·T **2** C·A·S·E·S

SIEMENS BRIBERY SCANDAL

In December 2008 Siemens, the large German electronics firm, agreed to pay $1.6 billion in fines to settle legal suits bought by the U.S. and German governments. The governments asserted that Siemens had used bribes to win business in countries around the world. These were the largest fines ever levied against a company for bribes, reflecting the scale of the problem at Siemens. Since 1999, the company had apparently paid some $1.4 billion in bribes. In Bangladesh, Siemens paid $5 million to the son of the prime minister to win a mobile phone contract. In Nigeria, it paid $12.7 million to various officials to win government telecommunications contracts. In Argentina, Siemens paid at least $40 million in bribes to win a $1 billion contract to produce national identity cards. In Israel, the company "provided"

INTEGRATED PROGRESSION OF TOPICS

A weakness of many texts is that they lack a tight, integrated flow of topics from chapter to chapter. This book explains to students in Chapter 1 how the book's topics are related to each other. Integration has been achieved by organizing the material so that each chapter builds on the material of the previous ones in a logical fashion.

Part One

Chapter 1 provides an overview of the key issues to be addressed and explains the plan of the book.

Part Two

Chapters 2 and 4 focus on national differences in political economy and culture, and Chapter 5 on ethical issues in international business. Most international business textbooks place this material at a later point, but it is vital to discuss national differences first. After all, many of the central issues in international trade and investment, the global monetary system, international business strategy and structure, and international business operations arise out of national differences in political economy and culture. To fully understand these issues, students must first appreciate the differences in countries and cultures. We discuss ethical issues at this juncture primarily because many ethical dilemmas flow out of national differences in political systems, economic systems, and culture.

Part Three

Chapters 6 through 9 investigate the political economy of international trade and investment. The purpose of this part is to describe and explain the trade and investment environment in which international business occurs.

Part Four

Chapters 10 through 12 describe and explain the global monetary system, laying out in detail the monetary framework in which international business transactions are conducted.

Part Five

In Chapters 13 through 15 attention shifts from the environment to the firm. Here the book examines the strategies and structures that firms adopt to compete effectively in the international business environment.

Part Six

In Chapters 16 through 20 the focus narrows further to investigate business operations. These chapters explain how firms can perform their key functions—manufacturing, marketing, R&D, human resource management, accounting, and finance—to compete and succeed in the international business environment.

Throughout the book, the relationship of new material to topics discussed in earlier chapters is pointed out to the students to reinforce their understanding of how the material comprises an integrated whole.

ACCESSIBLE AND INTERESTING

The international business arena is fascinating and exciting, and we have tried to communicate our enthusiasm for it to the student. Learning is easier and better if the subject matter is communicated in an interesting, informative, and accessible manner. One technique used to achieve this is weaving interesting anecdotes into the narrative of the text, that is, stories that illustrate theory.

Most chapters have a **Country Focus** box that provides background on the political, economic, social, or cultural aspects of countries grappling with an international business issue.

COUNTRY FOCUS

Trade in Hormone-Treated Beef

In the 1970s, scientists discovered how to synthesize certain hormones and use them to accelerate the growth rate of livestock animals, reduce the fat content of meat, and increase milk production. Bovine somatotropin (BST), a growth hormone produced by cattle, was first synthesized by the biotechnology firm Genentech. Injections of BST could be used to supplement an animal's own hormone production and increase its growth rate. These hormones became popular among farmers, who found they could cut costs and help satisfy consumer demands for leaner meat. Although these hormones occurred naturally in animals, consumer groups in several countries soon raised concerns about the practice. They argued that the use of hormone supplements was unnatural and that the health consequences of consuming hormone-treated meat were unknown but might include hormonal irregularities and cancer.

The European Union responded to these concerns in 1989 by banning the importation of hormone-treated meat and the use of growth-promoting hormones in the production of livestock. The ban was controversial because a reasonable consensus existed among scientists that the hormones posed no health risk. Although the EU banned hormone-treated meat, many other countries did not, including big meat-producing countries such as Australia, Canada, New Zealand, and the United States. The use of hormones soon became widespread in these countries. According to trade officials outside the EU, the European ban constituted an unfair restraint on trade. As a result of this ban, exports of meat to the EU fell. For example, U.S. red meat exports to the EU declined from $231 million in 1988 to $98 million in 1994. The complaints of

---

ONLINE LEARNING CENTER (www.mhhe.com/sie-hill10e)

To enhance the both the teaching and learning experience, the tenth edition includes the following features:

Instructor Resources

Through our convenient Online Learning Center, you can access everything you need in preparation for your course. A secured resource site provides your essential course materials tosave you prep time before class. They are:

- Instructor's Manual **and Video Guide**
- PowerPoint Presentations
- Testbank/EZ Test Bank
- IB Newsletter

Student Resources

The student side contains chapter-wise MCQs which can be used individually as a refresher.

ACKNOWLEDGMENTS

Numerous people deserve to be thanked for their assistance in preparing this book. First, thank you to all the people at McGraw-Hill Education who have worked with us on this project:

Paul Ducham, Managing Director

Anke Braun Weekes, Senior Brand Manager

Kelly Delso, Senior Developmental Editor

Michael Gedatus, Marketing Manager

Elizabeth Steiner, Marketing Coordinator

Danielle Clement, Content Project Manager

Debra Sylvester, Senior Buyer

Srdjan Savanovic, Designer

Jeremy Cheshareck, Senior Content Licensing Specialist

David Ploskonka, Freelance Content Development Editor

Second, our thanks go to the reviewers who provided good feedback that helped shape this book.

Yeqing Bao, University of Alabama, Huntsville

Jacobus F. Boers, Georgia State University

Ken Chinen, California State University, Sacramento

Abiola O. Fanimokun, Pennsylvania State University, Fayette

John Finley, Columbus State University

Michael Harris, East Carolina University

Anthony C. Koh, University of Toledo

Steve Lawton, Oregon State University

Ruby Lee, Florida State University

Joseph W. Leonard, Miami University

David N. McArthur, Utah Valley University

Sunder Narayanan, New York University

Eydis Olsen, Drexel University

Daria Panina, Texas A&M University

Hoon Park, University of Central Florida

Dr. Mahesh Raisinghani, Texas Women's University

Brian Satterlee, EdD, DBA, Liberty University

Michael Volpe, University of Maryland

Macgorine A. Cassell, Fairmont State University

Ping Deng, Maryville University of St. Louis

Betty J. Diener, Barry University

Pat Fox, Marion Technical College

Connie Golden, Lakeland Community College

Laura Kozloski Hart, Barry University

Chip Izard, Richland College

Vishakha Maskey, West Liberty University

Shelly McCallum, Saint Mary's University of Minnesota

Emily A. Morad, Reading Area Community College

Tim Muth, Florida Institute of Technology

Dwight Shook, Catawba Valley Community College

James Whelan, Manhattan College

Man Zhang, Bowling Green State University

Martin Grossman, Bridgewater State University

Sara B. Kimmel, Mississippi College

Candida Johnson, Holyoke Community College

Kathy Hastings, Greenville Technical College

JibanMukhopadhyay, SP Jain Institute of Management Research, Mumbai

Satish Modh, NarseeMonji Institute of Management Studies, Mumbai

Prakash Mathure, Great Lakes Institute of Management, Chennai

Rahul Mishra, IILM Institute for Business & Management, Gurgaon

Shekhar Srivastava, International Institute For Special Education, Lucknow

D. Swamy, Jansons School of Business, Chennai

Brief Contents

Contents

Chapter 5   **Ethics in International Business**   **140**

Part 3
The Global Trade and Investment Environment

Part 4
The Global Monetary System

Chapter 15 Entry Strategy and Strategic Alliances   508

Part 6
International Business Functions

Chapter 18   Global Marketing and R&D   **627**

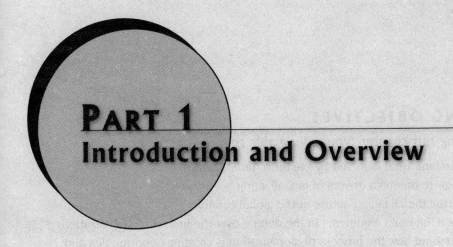

PART 1
Introduction and Overview

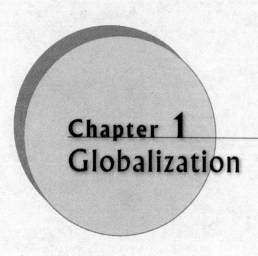

Chapter 1
Globalization

LEARNING OBJECTIVES

After reading this chapter, you will be able to:

LO1-1 Understand what is meant by the term *globalization*.

LO1-2 Recognize the main drivers of globalization.

LO1-3 Describe the changing nature of the global economy.

LO1-4 Explain the main arguments in the debate over the impact of globalization.

LO1-5 Understand how the process of globalization is creating opportunities and challenges for business managers.

◇ THE RISE OF ECUADOR'S ROSE INDUSTRY ◇

Opening Case

It is 6:20 a.m. on February 7 in the Ecuadorean town of Cayambe, and Maria Pacheco has just been dropped off for work by the company bus. She pulls on thick rubber gloves, wraps an apron over her dress, and grabs her clippers, ready for another long day. Any other time of year, Maria would work until 2 p.m., but it's a week before Valentine's Day, and Maria, along with her coworkers at the farm, are likely to be busy until 5 p.m. By then, Maria will have cut more than 1,000 rose stems. A few days later, after they have been refrigerated and shipped via aircraft, the roses Maria cut will be selling for premium prices in stores from New York to London.

Ecuadorean roses are acknowledged to be the best in the world. They have huge heads and unusually vibrant colors, including 10 different reds, from bleeding-heart crimson to a rosy lover's blush. Of the 200 million roses produced for American consumers on Valentine's Day, about 80 percent comes from Ecuador or neighboring Colombia. The rest are mostly grown in California. It used to be the case that many more were grown in the United States in places like New Jersey, once known as the nation's rose capital, but a combination of high costs, lower trade barriers, and rapid intercontinental transportation led to the migration of production to countries like Ecuador. The last commercial rose grower in New Jersey shut down in 1999.

Most of Ecuador's 400 or so rose farms are located in the Cayambe and Cotopaxi regions, 10,000 feet up in the Andes about an hour's drive from the capital, Quito. The rose bushes are planted in huge flat fields at the foot of snowcapped volcanoes that rise to more than 20,000 feet. The bushes are protected by 20-foot-high canopies of plastic sheeting. The combination of intense sunlight, fertile volcanic soil, an equatorial location, and high altitude makes for ideal growing conditions, allowing roses to flower almost year-round, giving Ecuador a comparative advantage in the production of roses.

Ecuador's rose industry started some 30 years ago and was spurred on in the early 1990s when the U.S. government reduced tariffs on some South American imports, including flowers, to steer the countries away from cocaine production. Ecuador is now the world's second-largest producer of roses, and roses are the nation's third-largest export. Rose farms support over 100,000 jobs in the country. The revenues and taxes from rose growers have helped to pave roads, build schools, and construct sophisticated irrigation systems.

Maria works Monday to Saturday and earns $400 a month, substantially above the country's $240-a-month minimum wage. The farm also provides her with health care and a pension. By employing women such as Maria, the industry has fostered a social revolution in which mothers and wives have more control over their family's spending, especially on schooling for their children.

For all of the benefits that roses have bought to Ecuador, the industry has come under fire from environmentalists. Large growers have been accused of misusing a toxic mixture of pesticides, fungicides, and fumigants to grow and export unblemished, pest-free flowers. Reports claim that workers often fumigate roses in street clothes without protective equipment. Some doctors and scientists claim that many of the industry's employees have serious health problems as a result of exposure to toxic chemicals. A study by the International Labor Organization claimed that women in the industry had more miscarriages than average and that some 60 percent of all workers suffered from headaches, nausea, blurred vision, and fatigue. Still, the critics acknowledge that their studies have been hindered by a lack of access to the farms, and they do not know what the true situation is.

In response, some Ecuadorean growers have joined a voluntary program aimed at helping customers identify responsible growers. Fair-trade certification signifies that the grower has distributed protective gear, trained workers in using chemicals, and hired doctors to visit workers at least weekly. Other environmental groups have pushed for stronger sanctions, including trade sanctions, against Ecuadorean rose growers that are not environmentally certified by a reputable agency. On February 14, however, most consumers are oblivious to these issues; they simply want to show their appreciation to their significant others with a perfect bunch of roses.[1]

INTRODUCTION

Over the past three decades a fundamental shift has been occurring in the world economy. We have been moving away from a world in which national economies were relatively self-contained entities, isolated from each other by barriers to cross-border trade and investment; by distance, time zones, and language; and by national differences in government regulation, culture, and business systems. We are moving toward a world in which barriers to cross-border trade and investment are declining; perceived distance is shrinking due to advances in transportation and telecommunications technology; material culture is starting to look similar the world over; and national economies are merging into an interdependent, integrated global economic system. The process by which this transformation is occurring is commonly referred to as *globalization*.

The rise of the Ecuadorian rose-growing industry, profiled in the opening case, is but one small example of the trend toward globalization. Thirty years ago the roses purchased by a New Yorker on Valentine's Day were probably grown in neighboring New Jersey. Now they are grown on another continent and cut, packed, and shipped to New York within 24 hours of being purchased. The same New Yorker might drive to work in a car that was designed in Germany and assembled in Mexico by Ford from components made in the United States and Japan, which were fabricated from Korean steel and Malaysian rubber. He may have filled the car with gasoline at a Shell service station owned by a British-Dutch multinational company. The gasoline could have been made from oil pumped out of a well off the coast of Africa by a French oil company that transported it to the United States in a ship owned by a Greek shipping line. While driving to work, the American might talk to his stockbroker (using a hands-free in-car speaker) on an Apple iPhone that was designed in California and assembled in China using chip sets produced in Japan and Europe, glass made by Corning in Kentucky, and memory chips from South Korea. He could tell the stockbroker to purchase shares in Lenovo, a multinational Chinese PC manufacturer whose operational headquarters is in North Carolina.

This is the world in which we live. It is a world where the volume of goods, services, and investments crossing national borders has expanded faster than world output for more than half a century. It is a world where more than $4 trillion in foreign exchange transactions are made every day, where $18.3 trillion of goods and $4.3 trillion of services were sold across national borders in 2012.[2] It is a world in which international institutions such as the World Trade Organization and gatherings of leaders from the world's most powerful economies have repeatedly called for even lower barriers to cross-border trade and investment. It is a world where the symbols of material and popular culture are increasingly global: from Coca-Cola and Starbucks to Sony PlayStations, Facebook, MTV shows, Disney films, IKEA stores, and Apple iPads and iPhones. It is also a world in which vigorous and vocal groups protest against globalization, which they blame for a list of ills, from unemployment in developed nations to environmental degradation and the Americanization of local culture.

For businesses, this globalization process has produced many opportunities. Firms can expand their revenues by selling around the world and/or reduce their costs by producing in nations where key inputs, including labor, are cheap. The global expansion of enterprises has been facilitated by favorable political and economic trends. Since the collapse of communism at the end of the 1980s, the pendulum of public policy in nation after nation has swung toward the free market end of the economic spectrum. Regulatory and administrative barriers to doing business in foreign nations have been reduced, while those nations have often transformed their economies, privatizing state-owned enterprises, deregulating markets, increasing competition, and welcoming investment by foreign businesses. This has allowed businesses both large and small, from both advanced nations and developing nations, to expand internationally.

As globalization unfolds, it is transforming industries and creating anxiety among those who believed their jobs were protected from foreign competition. Historically, while many workers in manufacturing industries worried about the impact foreign competition might have on their jobs, workers in service industries felt more secure. Now, this too is changing. Advances in technology, lower transportation costs, and the rise of skilled workers in developing countries imply that many services no longer need to be performed where they are delivered. The same is true of some accounting services. Today, many individual U.S. tax returns are compiled in India. Indian accountants, trained in U.S. tax rules, perform work for U.S. accounting firms.[3] They access individual tax returns stored on computers in the United States, perform routine calculations, and save their work so that it can be inspected by a U.S. accountant, who then bills clients. As the best-selling author Thomas Friedman has argued, the world is becoming flat.[4] People living in developed nations no longer have the playing field tilted in their favor. Increasingly, enterprising individuals based in India, China, or Brazil have the same opportunities to better themselves as those living in western Europe, the United States, or Canada.

In this book, we will take a close look at the issues introduced here and many more. We will explore how changes in regulations governing international trade and investment, when coupled with changes in political systems and technology, have dramatically altered the competitive playing field confronting many businesses. We will discuss the resulting opportunities and threats, and review the strategies that managers can pursue to exploit the opportunities and counter the threats. We will consider whether globalization benefits or harms national economies. We will look at what economic theory has to say about the outsourcing of manufacturing and service jobs to places such as India and China and look at the benefits and costs of outsourcing, not just to business firms and their employees but also to entire economies. First, though, we need to get a better overview of the nature and process of globalization, and that is the function of this first chapter.

WHAT IS GLOBALIZATION?

As used in this book, **globalization** refers to the shift toward a more integrated and interdependent world economy. Globalization has several facets, including the globalization of markets and the globalization of production.

The Globalization of Markets

The **globalization of markets** refers to the merging of historically distinct and separate national markets into one huge global marketplace. Falling barriers to cross-border trade have made it easier to sell internationally. It has been argued for some time that the tastes and preferences of consumers in different nations are beginning to converge on some global norm, thereby helping to create a global market.[5] Consumer products such as Citigroup credit cards, Coca-Cola soft drinks, video games, McDonald's hamburgers, Starbucks coffee, IKEA furniture, and Apple iPhones are frequently held up as prototypical examples of this trend. The firms that produce these products are more than just benefactors of this trend; they are also facilitators of it. By offering the same basic product worldwide, they help create a global market.

A company does not have to be the size of these multinational giants to facilitate, and benefit from, the globalization of markets. In the United States, for example, according to the International Trade Administration, more than 286,000 small and medium-size firms exported in 2010, accounting for 98 percent of the companies that exported that year. More generally, exports from small and medium-size companies accounted for 34 percent of all U.S. exports in 2010.[6] Typical of these is B&S Aircraft Alloys, a New York company whose exports account for 40 percent of its $8 million annual revenues.[7] The situation is similar in several other nations. For example, in Germany, the world's largest exporter, a staggering 98 percent of small and midsize companies have exposure to international markets, via either exports or international production.[8]

Despite the global prevalence of Citigroup credit cards, McDonald's hamburgers, Starbucks coffee, and IKEA stores, it is important not to push too far the view that national markets are giving way to the global market. As we shall see in later chapters, significant differences still exist among national markets along many relevant dimensions, including consumer tastes and preferences, distribution channels, culturally embedded value systems, business systems, and legal regulations. These differences frequently require companies to customize marketing strategies, product features, and operating practices to best match conditions in a particular country.

The most global of markets are not typically markets for consumer products—where national differences in tastes and preferences can still be important enough to act as a brake on globalization—but markets for industrial goods and materials that serve universal needs the world over. These include the markets for commodities such as aluminum, oil, and wheat; for industrial products such as microprocessors, DRAMs (computer memory chips), and commercial jet aircraft; for computer software; and for financial assets from U.S. Treasury bills to Eurobonds and futures on the Nikkei index or the euro. That being said, it is increasingly evident that many newer high-technology consumer products, such as Apple's iPhone, are being successfully sold the same way the world over.

In many global markets, the same firms frequently confront each other as competitors in nation after nation. Coca-Cola's rivalry with PepsiCo is a global one, as are the rivalries between Ford and Toyota; Boeing and Airbus; Caterpillar and Komatsu in earthmoving equipment; General Electric and Rolls-Royce in aero engines; and Sony, Nintendo, and Microsoft in video-game consoles. If a firm moves into a nation not currently served by its rivals, many of those rivals are sure to follow to prevent their competitor from gaining an advantage.[9] As firms follow each other around the world, they bring with them many of the assets that served them well in other national markets—their products, operating strategies, marketing strategies, and brand names—creating some homogeneity across markets. Thus, greater uniformity replaces diversity. In an increasing number of industries, it is no longer meaningful to talk about "the German market," "the American market," "the Brazilian market," or "the Japanese market"; for many firms there is only the global market.

The Globalization of Production

The **globalization of production** refers to the sourcing of goods and services from locations around the globe to take advantage of national differences in the cost and quality of **factors of production** (such as labor, energy, land, and capital). By doing this, companies hope to lower their overall cost structure or improve the quality or functionality of their product offering, thereby allowing them to compete more effectively. Consider Boeing's 777, a commercial jet airliner. Eight Japanese suppliers make parts for the fuselage, doors, and wings; a supplier in Singapore makes the doors for the nose landing gear; three suppliers in Italy manufacture wing flaps; and so on.[10] In total, some 30 percent of the 777, by value, is built by foreign companies. For its most recent jet airliner, the 787, Boeing has pushed this trend even further; some 65 percent of the total value of the aircraft is outsourced to foreign companies, 35 percent of which goes to three major Japanese companies.

Part of Boeing's rationale for outsourcing so much production to foreign suppliers is that these suppliers are the best in the world at their particular activity. A global web of suppliers yields a better final product, which enhances the chances of Boeing winning a greater share of total orders for aircraft than its global rival Airbus. Boeing also outsources some production to foreign countries to increase the chance that it will win significant orders from airlines based in that country. For another example of a global web of activities, consider the example of Vizio profiled in the accompanying Management Focus.

Early outsourcing efforts were primarily confined to manufacturing activities, such as those undertaken by Boeing, Apple, and Vizio; increasingly, however, companies are taking advantage of modern communications technology, particularly the Internet, to outsource service activities to low-cost producers in other nations. The Internet has allowed hospitals to outsource some radiology work to India, where images from MRI scans and the like are read at night while U.S. physicians sleep and the

Vizio and the Market for Flat-Panel TVs

Operating sophisticated tooling in environments that must be kept absolutely clean, fabrication centers in South Korea, Taiwan, and Japan produce sheets of glass twice as large as king-size beds to exacting specifications. From there, the glass panels travel to Mexican plants located alongside the U.S. border. There they are cut to size, combined with electronic components shipped in from Asia and the United States, assembled into finished flat-panel TVs, and loaded onto trucks bound for retail stores in the United States, where consumers spend more than $35 billion a year on flat-panel TVs.

The underlying technology for flat-panel displays was invented in the United States in the late 1960s by RCA. But after RCA and rivals Westinghouse and Xerox opted not to pursue the technology, the Japanese company Sharp made aggressive investments in flat-panel displays. By the early 1990s Sharp was selling the first flat-panel screens, but as the Japanese economy plunged into a decade-long recession, investment leadership shifted to South Korean companies such as Samsung. Then the 1997 Asian crisis hit Korea hard, and Taiwanese companies seized leadership. Today, Chinese companies are elbowing their way into the flat-panel display manufacturing business.

As production for flat-panel displays migrates its way around the globe to low-cost locations, there are clear winners and losers. U.S. consumers have benefited from the falling prices of flat-panel TVs and are snapping them up. Efficient manufacturers have taken advantage of globally dispersed supply chains to make and sell low-cost, high-quality, flat-panel TVs. Foremost among these has been the California-based company Vizio, founded by a Taiwanese immigrant. In just eight years, sales of Vizio flat-panel TVs ballooned from nothing to around $3 billion by 2012. The privately held company is the largest provider to the U.S. market with an 18–19 percent share. Vizio, however, has reportedly fewer than 500 employees. Their focus is on final product design, sales, and customer service. Vizio outsources most of its engineering work, all of its manufacturing, and much of its logistics. For each of its models, Vizio assembles a team of supplier partners strung across the globe. Its 42-inch flat-panel TV, for example, contains a panel from South Korea, electronic components from China, and processors from the United States, and it is assembled in Mexico. Vizio's managers scour the globe continually for the cheapest manufacturers of flat-panel displays and electronic components. They sell most of their TVs to large discount retailers such as Costco and Sam's Club. Good order visibility from retailers, coupled with tight management of global logistics, allows Vizio to turn over its inventory every three weeks, twice as fast as many of its competitors, which allows major cost savings in a business where prices are falling continually.[13]

results are ready for them in the morning. Many software companies, including IBM and Microsoft, now use Indian engineers to perform test functions on software designed in the United States. The time difference allows Indian engineers to run debugging tests on software written in the United States when U.S. engineers sleep, transmitting the corrected code back to the United States over secure Internet connections so it is ready for U.S. engineers to work on the following day. Dispersing value-creation activities in this way can compress the time and lower the costs required to develop new software programs. Other companies, from computer makers to banks, are outsourcing customer service functions, such as customer call centers, to developing nations where labor is cheaper. In another example from health care, workers in the Philippines transcribe American medical files (such as audio files from doctors seeking approval from insurance companies for performing a procedure). Some estimates suggest the outsourcing of many administrative procedures in health care, such as customer service and claims processing, could reduce health care costs in America by as much as $70 billion.[11]

Robert Reich, who served as secretary of labor in the Clinton administration, has argued that as a consequence of the trend exemplified by companies such as Boeing, Apple, IBM, and Vizio, in many cases it is becoming irrelevant to talk about American products, Japanese products, German products, or Korean products. Increasingly, according to Reich, the outsourcing of productive activities to different suppliers results in the creation of products that are global in nature, that is, "global products."[12] But as with the globalization of markets, companies must be careful not to push the globalization of production too far. As we will see in later chapters, substantial impediments still make it difficult for firms to achieve the optimal dispersion of their productive activities to locations around the globe. These impediments include formal and informal barriers to trade between countries, barriers to foreign direct investment, transportation costs, and issues associated with economic and political risk. For example, government regulations ultimately limit the ability of hospitals to outsource the process of interpreting MRI scans to developing nations where radiologists are cheaper.

Nevertheless, the globalization of markets and production will continue. Modern firms are important actors in this trend, their very actions fostering increased globalization. These firms, however, are merely responding in an efficient manner to changing conditions in their operating environment—as well they should.

THE EMERGENCE OF GLOBAL INSTITUTIONS

As markets globalize and an increasing proportion of business activity transcends national borders, institutions are needed to help manage, regulate, and police the global marketplace and to promote the establishment of multinational treaties to govern the global business system. Over the past half century, a number of important global institutions have been created to help perform these functions, including the **General Agreement on Tariffs and Trade (GATT)** and its successor, the World Trade Organization (WTO); the International Monetary Fund (IMF) and its sister institution, the World Bank; and the United Nations (UN). All these institutions were created by voluntary agreement between individual nation-states, and their functions are enshrined in international treaties.

The **World Trade Organization** (like the GATT before it) is primarily responsible for policing the world trading system and making sure nation-states adhere to the rules laid down in trade treaties signed by WTO member states. As of early 2013, 159 nations that collectively accounted for 98 percent of world trade were WTO members, thereby giving the organization enormous scope and influence. The WTO is also responsible for facilitating the establishment of additional multinational agreements between WTO member states. Over its entire history, and that of the GATT before it, the WTO has promoted the lowering of barriers to cross-border trade and investment. In doing so, the WTO has been the instrument of its member states, which have sought to create a more open global business system unencumbered by barriers to trade and investment between countries. Without an institution such as the WTO, the globalization of markets and production is unlikely to have proceeded as far as it has. However, as we shall see in this chapter and in Chapter 7 when we look closely at the WTO, critics charge that the organization is usurping the national sovereignty of individual nation-states.

The **International Monetary Fund** and the **World Bank** were both created in 1944 by 44 nations that met at Bretton Woods, New Hampshire. The IMF was established to maintain order in the international monetary system; the World Bank was set up to promote economic development. In the more than six decades since their creation, both institutions have emerged as significant players in the global economy. The World Bank is the less controversial of the two sister institutions. It has focused on making low-interest loans to cash-strapped governments in poor nations that wish to undertake significant infrastructure investments (such as building dams or roads).

The IMF is often seen as the lender of last resort to nation-states whose economies are in turmoil and whose currencies are losing value against those of other nations. During the past two decades, for example, the IMF has lent money to the governments of troubled states, including Argentina, Indonesia, Mexico, Russia, South Korea, Thailand, and Turkey. More recently, the IMF has taken a proactive role in helping countries cope with some of the effects of the 2008–2009 global financial crisis. IMF loans come with strings attached, however; in return for loans, the IMF requires nation-states to adopt specific economic policies aimed at returning their troubled economies to stability and growth. These requirements have sparked controversy. Some critics charge that the IMF's policy recommendations are often inappropriate; others maintain that by telling national governments what economic policies they must adopt, the IMF, like the WTO, is usurping the sovereignty of nation-states. We will look at the debate over the role of the IMF in Chapter 11.

The **United Nations** was established October 24, 1945, by 51 countries committed to preserving peace through international cooperation and collective security. Today, nearly every nation in the world belongs to the United Nations; membership now totals 193 countries. When states become members of the United Nations, they agree to accept the obligations of the UN Charter, an international treaty that establishes basic principles of international relations. According to the charter, the UN has four purposes: to maintain international peace and security, to develop friendly relations among nations, to cooperate in solving international problems and in promoting respect for human rights, and to be a center for harmonizing the actions of nations. Although the UN is perhaps best known for its peacekeeping role, one of the organization's central mandates is the promotion of higher standards of living, full employment, and conditions of economic and social progress and development—all issues that are central to the creation of a vibrant global economy. As much as 70 percent of the work of the UN system is devoted to accomplishing this mandate. To do so, the UN works closely with other international institutions such as the World Bank. Guiding the work is the belief that eradicating poverty and improving the well-being of people everywhere are necessary steps in creating conditions for lasting world peace.[14]

Another institution in the news is the **G20**. Established in 1999, the G20 comprises the finance ministers and central bank governors of the 19 largest economies in the world, plus representatives from the European Union and the European Central Bank. Collectively, the G20 represents 90 percent of global GDP and 80 percent of international global trade. Originally established to formulate a coordinated policy response to financial crises in developing nations, in 2008 and 2009 it became the forum though which major nations attempted to launch a coordinated policy response to the global financial crisis that started in America and then rapidly spread around the world, ushering in the first serious global economic recession since 1981.

DRIVERS OF GLOBALIZATION

Two macro factors underlie the trend toward greater globalization.[15] The first is the decline in barriers to the free flow of goods, services, and capital that has occurred since the end of World War II. The second factor is technological change, particularly the dramatic developments in recent decades in communication, information processing, and transportation technologies.

Declining Trade and Investment Barriers

During the 1920s and 1930s, many of the world's nation-states erected formidable barriers to international trade and foreign direct investment. **International trade** occurs when a firm exports goods or services to consumers in another country. **Foreign direct investment (FDI)** occurs when a firm invests resources in business activities outside its home country. Many of the barriers to international trade took the form of high tariffs on imports of manufactured goods. The typical aim of such tariffs was to protect domestic industries from foreign competition. One consequence, however, was "beggar thy neighbor" retaliatory trade policies, with countries progressively raising trade barriers against each other. Ultimately, this depressed world demand and contributed to the Great Depression of the 1930s.

Having learned from this experience, the advanced industrial nations of the West committed themselves after World War II to removing barriers to the free flow of goods, services, and capital among nations.[16] This goal was enshrined in the General Agreement on Tariffs and Trade. Under the umbrella of GATT, eight rounds of negotiations among member states worked to lower barriers to the free flow of goods and services. The most recent negotiations to be completed, known as the Uruguay Round, were finalized in December 1993. The Uruguay Round further reduced trade barriers; extended GATT to cover services as well as manufactured goods; provided enhanced protection for patents, trademarks, and copyrights; and established the World Trade Organization to police the international trading system.[17] Table 1.1 summarizes the impact of GATT agreements on average tariff rates for manufactured goods. As can be seen, average tariff rates have fallen significantly since 1950 and now stand at about 4 percent.

TABLE 1.1 Average Tariff Rates on Manufactured Products as Percent of Value

	1913	1950	1990	2010
France	21%	18%	5.9%	3.9%
Germany	20	26	5.9	3.9
Italy	18	25	5.9	3.9
Japan	30	—	5.3	2.3
Holland	5	11	5.9	3.9
Sweden	20	9	4.4	3.9
Great Britain	—	23	5.9	3.9
United States	44	14	4.8	3.2

Sources: The 1913–1990 data are from "Who Wants to Be a Giant?" *The Economist: A Survey of the Multinationals,* June 24, 1995, pp. 3–4. Copyright © The Economist Books, Ltd. The 2010 data are from World Trade Organization, *The World Trade Report 2011* (Geneva: WTO, 2011).

In late 2001, the WTO launched a new round of talks aimed at further liberalizing the global trade and investment framework. For this meeting, it picked the remote location of Doha in the Persian Gulf state of Qatar. At Doha, the member states of the WTO staked out an agenda. The talks were scheduled to last three years, but, as of 2013, the talks are effectively stalled due to opposition from several key nations. The Doha agenda includes cutting tariffs on industrial goods, services, and agricultural products; phasing out subsidies to agricultural producers; reducing barriers to cross-border investment; and limiting the use of antidumping laws. If the Doha talks are ever completed, the biggest gain may come from discussion on agricultural products; average agricultural tariff rates are still about 40 percent, and rich nations spend some $300 billion a year in subsidies to support their farm sectors. The world's poorer nations have the most to gain from any reduction in agricultural tariffs and subsidies; such reforms would give them access to the markets of the developed world.[18]

In addition to reducing trade barriers, many countries have also been progressively removing restrictions to foreign direct investment. According to the United Nations, some 90 percent of the 2,700 changes made worldwide between 1992 and 2009 in the laws governing foreign direct investment created a more favorable environment for FDI.[19]

Such trends have been driving both the globalization of markets and the globalization of production. The lowering of barriers to international trade enables firms to view the world, rather than a single country, as their market. The lowering of trade and investment barriers also allows firms to base production at the optimal location for that activity. Thus, a firm might design a product in one country, produce component parts in two other countries, assemble the product in yet another country, and then export the finished product around the world.

According to WTO, the volume world trade in merchandised goods has grown at *twice* the rate of the world economy since 1950. As a consequence, by 2012 the volume of world trade was 31 times larger than in 1950, whereas the world economy was 8.7 times larger (these figures are in *real* terms, adjusted for inflation). This trend has continued into the modern era. Between 1992 and 2012 world trade grew at 5.3 percent per annum, whereas the world economy grew at 2.15 percent per annum after adjusting for inflation. Consequently, the volume of world merchandised trade was three times larger in 2012 than it was in 1990, whereas the world economy was 1.62 times larger in real terms.[20] Since the mid-1980s, the value of international trade in services has also grown robustly and now accounts for about 19 percent of the value of all international trade. Increasingly, international trade in services has been driven by advances in communications, which allow corporations to outsource service activities to different locations around the globe. For example, many corporations in the developed world outsource customer service functions, from software testing to customer call centers, to developing nations where labor costs are lower.

The fact that the volume of world trade has been growing faster than world GDP implies several things. First, more firms are doing what Boeing does with the 777 and 787, and Apple with the iPhone: dispersing parts of their production process to different locations around the globe to drive down production costs and increase product quality. Second, the economies of the world's nation-states are becoming ever more intertwined. As trade expands, nations are becoming increasingly dependent on each other for important goods and services. Third, the world has become significantly wealthier since 1990. The implication is that rising trade is the engine that has helped pull the global economy along.

Evidence also suggests that foreign direct investment is playing an increasing role in the global economy as firms increase their cross-border investments. The average yearly outflow of FDI increased from $26.6 billion in 1975 to $1.3 trillion in 2012.[21] Even though the 2012 figure was significantly below the peak of $2 billion in foreign direct investment recorded in 2007, the long-term trends remain positive. As a result of the strong FDI flow, by 2011 the global stock of FDI was about $20.4 trillion. At least 82,000 parent companies had 810,000 affiliates in foreign markets that collectively employed more than 77 million people abroad and generated value accounting for about 11 percent of global GDP. The foreign affiliates of multinationals had more than $32 trillion in global sales, higher than the value of global exports of goods and services, which stood at close to $20 trillion.[22]

The globalization of markets and production and the resulting growth of world trade, foreign direct investment, and imports all imply that firms are finding their home markets under attack from foreign competitors. This is true in China, where U.S. companies such as Apple, General Motors, and Starbucks are expanding their presence. It is true in the United States, where Japanese automobile firms have taken market share away from General Motors and Ford (although there are signs that this trend is reversing). And it is true in Europe, where the once-dominant Dutch company Philips has seen its market share in the consumer electronics industry taken by Japan's Panasonic and Sony and Korea's Samsung and LG. The growing integration of the world economy into a single, huge marketplace is increasing the intensity of competition in a range of manufacturing and service industries.

However, declining barriers to cross-border trade and investment cannot be taken for granted. As we shall see in subsequent chapters, demands for "protection" from foreign competitors are still often heard in countries around the world, including the United States. Although a return to the restrictive trade policies of the 1920s and 1930s is unlikely, it is not clear whether the political majority in the industrialized world favors further reductions in trade barriers. Indeed, the global financial crisis of 2008–2009 and the associated drop in global output that occurred led to more calls for trade barriers to protect jobs at home. If trade barriers decline no further, this may slow the rate of globalization of both markets and production.

The Role of Technological Change

The lowering of trade barriers made globalization of markets and production a theoretical possibility. Technological change has made it a tangible reality. Since the end of World War II, the world has seen major advances in communication, information processing, and transportation technology, including the explosive emergence of the Internet.

Microprocessors and Telecommunications

Perhaps the single most important innovation has been development of the microprocessor, which enabled the explosive growth of high-power, low-cost computing, vastly increasing the amount of information that can be processed by individuals and firms. The microprocessor also underlies many recent advances in telecommunications technology. Over the past 30 years, global communications have been revolutionized by developments in satellite, optical fiber, wireless technologies, and the Internet. These technologies rely on the microprocessor to encode, transmit, and decode the vast amount of information that flows along these electronic highways. The cost of microprocessors continues to fall, while their power increases (a phenomenon known as **Moore's law**, which predicts that the power of microprocessor technology doubles and its cost of production falls in half every 18 months).[23]

The Internet

The explosive growth of the Internet since 1994 when the first web browser was introduced is the latest expression of this development. In 1990, fewer than 1 million users were connected to the Internet. By 1995, the figure had risen to 50 million. By 2012, the Internet had 2.4 billion users.[24] The Internet has developed into the information backbone of the global economy. In North America alone, e-commerce retail sales reached $365 billion in 2012 (up from almost nothing in 1998), while global e-commerce sales surpassed $1 trillion for the first time in 2012.[25] Viewed globally, the Internet has emerged as an equalizer. It rolls back some of the constraints of location, scale, and time zones.[26] The Internet makes it much easier for buyers and sellers to find each other, wherever they may be located and whatever their size. It allows businesses, both small and large, to expand their global presence at a lower cost than ever before. It enables enterprises to coordinate and control a globally dispersed production system in a way that was not possible 20 years ago.

Transportation Technology

In addition to developments in communications technology, several major innovations in transportation technology have occurred since World War II. In economic terms, the most important are probably the development of commercial jet aircraft and superfreighters and the introduction of containerization, which simplifies transshipment from one mode of transport to another. The advent of commercial jet travel, by reducing the time needed to get from one location to another, has effectively shrunk the globe. In terms of travel time, New York is now "closer" to Tokyo than it was to Philadelphia in the colonial days.

Containerization has revolutionized the transportation business, significantly lowering the costs of shipping goods over long distances. Before the advent of containerization, moving goods from one mode of transport to another was very labor intensive, lengthy, and costly. It could take days and several hundred longshoremen to unload a ship and reload goods onto trucks and trains. With the advent of widespread containerization in the 1970s and 1980s, the whole process can now be executed by a handful of longshoremen in a couple of days. As a result of the efficiency gains associated with containerization, transportation costs have plummeted, making it much more economical to ship goods around the globe, thereby helping drive the globalization of markets and production. Between 1920 and 1990, the average ocean freight and port charges per ton of U.S. export and import cargo fell from $95 to $29 (in 1990 dollars).[27] The cost of shipping freight per ton-mile on railroads in the United States fell from 3.04 cents in 1985 to 2.3 cents in 2000, largely as a result of efficiency gains from the widespread use of containers.[28] An increased share of cargo now goes by air. Between 1955 and 1999, average air transportation revenue per ton-kilometer fell by more than 80 percent.[29] Reflecting the falling cost of airfreight, by the early 2000s air shipments accounted for 28 percent of the value of U.S. trade, up from 7 percent in 1965.[30]

Implications for the Globalization of Production

As transportation costs associated with the globalization of production have declined, dispersal of production to geographically separate locations became more economical. As a result of the technological innovations discussed earlier, the real costs of information processing and communication have fallen dramatically in the past two decades. These developments make it possible for a firm to create and then manage a globally dispersed production system, further facilitating the globalization of production. A worldwide communications network has become essential for many international businesses. For example, Dell uses the Internet to coordinate and control a globally dispersed production system to such an extent that it holds only three days' worth of inventory at its assembly locations. Dell's Internet-based system records orders for computer equipment as they are submitted by customers via the company's website and then immediately transmits the resulting orders for components to various suppliers around the world, which have a real-time look at Dell's order flow and can adjust their production schedules accordingly. Given the low cost of airfreight, Dell can use air transportation to speed up the delivery of critical components to meet unanticipated demand shifts without delaying the shipment of final product to consumers. Dell has also used modern communications technology to outsource its customer service operations to India. When U.S. customers call Dell with a service inquiry, they are routed to Bangalore in India, where English-speaking service personnel handle the call.

Implications for the Globalization of Markets

In addition to the globalization of production, technological innovations have facilitated the globalization of markets. Low-cost global communications networks such as the Internet are helping to create electronic global marketplaces. As noted earlier, low-cost transportation has made it more economical to ship products around the world, thereby helping create global markets (roses grown in and exported by Ecuador, for example; see the opening case). In addition, low-cost jet travel has resulted in the mass movement of people between countries. This has reduced the cultural distance between countries and is bringing about some convergence of consumer tastes and preferences. At the same time, global communications networks and global media are creating a worldwide culture. U.S. television networks such as CNN, MTV, and HBO are now received in many countries, and Hollywood films are shown the world over. In any society, the media are primary conveyors of culture; as global media develop, we must expect the evolution of something akin to a global culture. A logical result of this evolution is the emergence of global markets for consumer products. The first signs of this are already apparent. It is now as easy to find a McDonald's restaurant in Tokyo as it is in New York, to buy an iPad in Rio as it is in Berlin, and to buy Gap jeans in Paris as it is in San Francisco.

Despite these trends, we must be careful not to overemphasize their importance. While modern communications and transportation technologies are ushering in the "global village," significant national differences remain in culture, consumer preferences, and business practices. A firm that ignores differences between countries does so at its peril. We shall stress this point repeatedly throughout this book and elaborate on it in later chapters.

THE CHANGING DEMOGRAPHICS OF THE GLOBAL ECONOMY

LO1-3

Hand in hand with the trend toward globalization has been a fairly dramatic change in the demographics of the global economy over the past 30 years. As late as the 1960s, four stylized facts described the demographics of the global economy. The first was U.S. dominance in the world economy and world trade picture. The second was U.S. dominance in world foreign direct investment. Related to this, the third fact was the dominance of large, multinational U.S. firms on the international business scene. The fourth was that roughly half the globe—the centrally planned economies of the Communist world—was off-limits to Western international businesses. As will be explained here, all four of these qualities either have changed or are now changing rapidly.

The Changing World Output and World Trade Picture

In the early 1960s, the United States was still by far the world's dominant industrial power. In 1960 the United States accounted for 38.3 percent of world output, measured by gross domestic product (GDP). By 2012, the United States accounted for 23.1 percent of world output, still the world's largest industrial power but down significantly in relative size (see Table 1.2). Nor was the United States the only developed nation to see its relative standing slip. The same occurred to Germany, France, and the United Kingdom, all nations that were among the first to industrialize. This change in the U.S. position was not an absolute decline, because the U.S. economy grew significantly between 1960 and 2010 (the economies of

TABLE 1.2 The Changing Demographics of World Output and Trade

Country	Share of World Output, 1960 (%)	Share of World Output, 2011 (%)	Share of World Exports, 2012 (%)
United States	38.3	21.4	8.7
Germany	8.7	5.1	7.9
France	4.6	4.0	3.3
Italy	3.0	3.1	2.8
United Kingdom	5.3	3.5	2.6
Canada	3.0	2.5	2.5
Japan	3.3	8.4	4.5
China	NA	10.5	11.4

Sources: Output data from World Bank database, April 2013. Export data from WTO press release, "Trade to remain subdued in 2013," April 10, 2013.

Germany, France, and the United Kingdom also grew during this time). Rather, it was a relative decline, reflecting the faster economic growth of several other economies, particularly in Asia. For example, as can be seen from Table 1.2, from 1960 to 2010, China's share of world output increased from a trivial amount to 9.4 percent, making it the world's second-largest economy. Other countries that markedly increased their share of world output included Japan, Thailand, Malaysia, Taiwan, and South Korea.

By the end of the 1980s, the U.S. position as the world's leading exporter was threatened. Over the past 30 years, U.S. dominance in export markets has waned as Japan, Germany, and a number of newly industrialized countries such as South Korea and China have taken a larger share of world exports. During the 1960s, the United States routinely accounted for 20 percent of world exports of manufactured goods. But as Table 1.2 shows, the U.S. share of world exports of goods and services had slipped to 8.7 percent by 2012, behind that of China.

As emerging economies such as China, India, Russia, and Brazil continue to grow, a further relative decline in the share of world output and world exports accounted for by the United States and other long-established developed nations seems likely. By itself, this is not bad. The relative decline of the United States reflects the growing economic development and industrialization of the world economy, as opposed to any absolute decline in the health of the U.S. economy.

Most forecasts now predict a rapid rise in the share of world output accounted for by developing nations such as China, India, Russia, Indonesia, Thailand, South Korea, Mexico, and Brazil, and a commensurate decline in the share enjoyed by rich industrialized countries such as Great Britain, Germany, Japan, and the United States. If current trends continue, the Chinese economy could ultimately be larger than that of the United States on a purchasing power parity basis, while the economy of India will approach that of Germany. The World Bank has estimated that today's developing nations may account for more than 60 percent of world economic activity by 2020, while today's rich nations, which currently account for more than 55 percent of world economic activity, may account for only about 38 percent. Forecasts are not always correct, but these suggest that a shift in the economic geography of the world is now under way, although the magnitude of that shift is not totally evident. For international businesses, the implications of this changing economic geography are clear: Many of tomorrow's

India's Software Sector

Some 25 years ago, a number of small software enterprises were established in Bangalore, India. Typical of these enterprises was Infosys Technologies, which was started by seven Indian entrepreneurs with about $1,000 among them. Infosys now has annual revenues of $7.4 billion and some 155,600 employees, but it is just one of more than a hundred software companies clustered around Bangalore, which has become the epicenter of India's fast-growing information technology sector. From a standing start in the mid-1980s, by 2012 this sector was generating export sales of $68 billion in 2011–2012.

The growth of the Indian software sector has been based on four factors. First, the country has an abundant supply of engineering talent. Every year, Indian universities graduate some 400,000 engineers. Second, labor costs in India have historically been low. As recently as 2008 the cost to hire an Indian graduate was roughly 12 percent of the cost of hiring an American graduate (this is now changing, with salaries increasing in India). Third, many Indians are fluent in English, which makes coordination between Western firms and India easier. Fourth, due to time differences, Indians can work while Americans sleep.

Initially, Indian software enterprises focused on the low end of the software industry, supplying basic software development and testing services to Western firms. But as the industry has grown in size and sophistication, Indian firms have moved up the market. Today, the leading Indian companies compete directly with the likes of IBM and EDS for large software development projects, business process outsourcing contracts, and information technology consulting services. Over the last 15 years these markets have boomed, with Indian enterprises capturing a large slice of the pie. One response of Western firms to this emerging competitive threat has been to invest in India to garner the same kind of economic advantages that Indian firms enjoy. IBM, for example, has invested $2 billion in its Indian operations and now has 150,000 employees located there, more than in any other country. Microsoft, too, has made major investments in India, including a research and development (R&D) center in Hyderabad that employs 4,000 people and was located there specifically to tap into talented Indian engineers who did not want to move to the United States.[31]

economic opportunities may be found in the developing nations of the world, and many of tomorrow's most capable competitors will probably also emerge from these regions. A case in point has been the dramatic expansion of India's software sector, which is profiled in the accompanying Country Focus.

The Changing Foreign Direct Investment Picture

Reflecting the dominance of the United States in the global economy, U.S. firms accounted for 66.3 percent of worldwide foreign direct investment flows in the 1960s. British firms were second, accounting for 10.5 percent, while Japanese firms were a distant eighth, with only 2 percent. The dominance of U.S. firms was so great that books were written about the economic threat posed to Europe by U.S. corporations.[32] Several European governments, most notably France, talked of limiting inward investment by U.S. firms.

However, as the barriers to the free flow of goods, services, and capital fell, and as other countries increased their shares of world output, non-U.S. firms increasingly began to invest across national borders. The motivation for much of this foreign direct investment by non-U.S. firms was the desire to disperse production activities to optimal locations and to build a direct presence in major foreign markets. Thus, beginning in the 1970s, European and Japanese firms began to shift labor-intensive manufacturing operations from their home markets to developing nations where labor costs were lower. In addition, many Japanese firms invested in North America and Europe—often as a hedge against unfavorable currency movements and the possible imposition of trade barriers. For example, Toyota, the Japanese automobile company, rapidly increased its investment in automobile production facilities in the United States and Europe during the late 1980s and early 1990s. Toyota executives believed that an increasingly strong Japanese yen would price Japanese automobile exports out of foreign markets; therefore, production in the most important foreign markets, as opposed to exports from Japan, made sense. Toyota also undertook these investments to head off growing political pressures in the United States and Europe to restrict Japanese automobile exports into those markets.

One consequence of these developments is illustrated in Figure 1.1, which shows how the stock of foreign direct investment by the world's six most important national sources—the United States, the United Kingdom, Germany, the Netherlands, France, and Japan—changed between 1980 and 2011. (The **stock of foreign direct investment (FDI)** refers to the total cumulative value of foreign investments.) Figure 1.1 also shows the stock accounted for by firms from developing economies. The share of the total stock accounted for by U.S. firms declined from about 38 percent in 1980 to 21 percent in 2011. Meanwhile, the shares accounted for by France and the world's developing nations increased markedly. The rise in the share of FDI stock accounted for by developing nations reflects a growing trend for firms from these countries to invest outside their borders. In 2011, firms based in developing nations accounted for 17.5 percent of the stock of foreign direct investment, up from around 1 percent in 1980. Firms based in Hong Kong, South Korea, Singapore, Taiwan, India, and mainland China accounted for much of this investment.

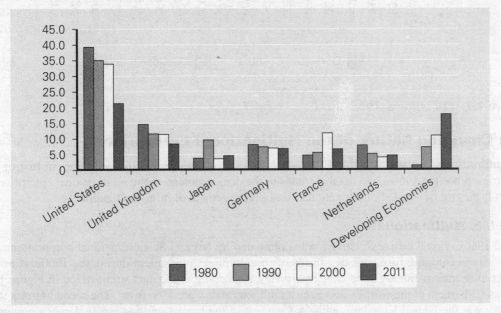

Figure 1.1 *Percentage Share of Total FDI Stock, 1980–2011*

Figure 1.2 illustrates two other important trends—the sustained growth in cross-border flows of foreign direct investment that occurred during the 1990s and the importance of developing nations as the destination of foreign direct investment. Throughout the 1990s, the amount of investment directed at both developed and developing nations increased dramatically, a trend that reflects the increasing internationalization of business corporations. A surge in foreign direct investment from 1998 to 2000 was followed by a slump from 2001 to 2003 associated with a slowdown in global economic activity after the collapse of the financial bubble of the late 1990s and 2000. However, the growth of foreign direct investment resumed in 2004 and continued through 2007, when it hit record levels, only to slow again in 2008 and 2009 as the global financial crisis took hold. Among developing nations, the largest recipient of foreign direct investment has been China, which in 2004–2011 received $60 billion to $100 billion a year in inflows. As we shall see later in this book, the sustained flow of foreign investment into developing nations is an important stimulus for economic growth in those countries, which bodes well for the future of countries such as China, Mexico, and Brazil—all leading beneficiaries of this trend.

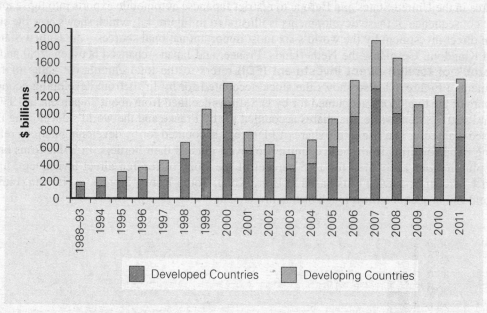

Figure 1.2 *FDI Inflows, 1988–2011*

The Changing Nature of the Multinational Enterprise

A **multinational enterprise (MNE)** is any business that has productive activities in two or more countries. Since the 1960s, two notable trends in the demographics of the multinational enterprise have been (1) the rise of non-U.S. multinationals and (2) the growth of mini-multinationals.

Non-U.S. Multinationals

In the 1960s, global business activity was dominated by large U.S. multinational corporations. With U.S. firms accounting for about two-thirds of foreign direct investment during the 1960s, one would expect most multinationals to be U.S. enterprises. According to the data summarized in Figure 1.3, in 1973, 48.5 percent of the world's 260 largest multinationals were U.S. firms. The second-largest source country was the United Kingdom, with 18.8 percent of the largest multinationals. Japan accounted for

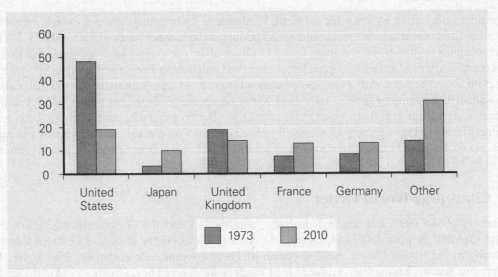

Figure 1.3 *National Origin of Largest Multinational Enterprises, 1973 and 2010*

3.5 percent of the world's largest multinationals at the time. The large number of U.S. multinationals reflected U.S. economic dominance in the three decades after World War II, while the large number of British multinationals reflected that country's industrial dominance in the early decades of the twentieth century.

By 2010, things had shifted significantly. Some 21 of the world's 100 largest nonfinancial multinationals were U.S. enterprises; 15 were French; 11, German; 15, British; and 8, Japanese.[33] Although the 1973 data are not strictly comparable with the later data, they illustrate the trend (the 1973 figures are based on the largest 260 firms, whereas the later figures are based on the largest 100 multinationals). The globalization of the world economy has resulted in a relative decline in the dominance of U.S. firms in the global marketplace.

According to UN data, the ranks of the world's largest 100 multinationals are still dominated by firms from developed economies.[34] However, seven firms from developing economies had entered the UN's list of the 100 largest multinationals by 2010. The largest was Hutchison Whampoa of Hong Kong, China, which ranked twenty-third.[35] Firms from developing nations can be expected to emerge as important competitors in global markets, further shifting the axis of the world economy away from North America and western Europe and threatening the long dominance of Western companies. One such rising competitor, Hisense, one of China's premier manufacturers of consumer appliances and telecommunications equipment, is profiled in the accompanying Management Focus.

The Rise of Mini-multinationals

Another trend in international business has been the growth of medium-size and small multinationals (mini-multinationals).[36] When people think of international businesses, they tend to think of firms such as ExxonMobil, General Motors, Ford, Panasonic, Procter & Gamble, Sony, and Unilever—large, complex multinational corporations with operations that span the globe. Although most international trade and investment are still conducted by large firms, many medium-size and small businesses are becoming increasingly involved in international trade and investment. The rise of the Internet is lowering the barriers that small firms face in building international sales.

Consider Lubricating Systems Inc. of Kent, Washington. Lubricating Systems, which manufactures lubricating fluids for machine tools, employs 25 people and generates sales of $6.5 million. It's hardly a large, complex multinational, yet more than $2 million of the company's sales are generated by exports to a score of countries, including Japan, Israel, and the United Arab Emirates. Lubricating Systems has also set up a joint venture with a German company to serve the European market.[37] Consider also Lixi Inc., a small U.S. manufacturer of industrial X-ray equipment; 70 percent of Lixi's $4.5 million in revenues comes from exports to Japan.[38] Or take G. W. Barth, a manufacturer of cocoa-bean roasting machinery based in Ludwigsburg, Germany. Employing just 65 people, this small company has captured 70 percent of the global market for cocoa-bean roasting machines.[39] International business is conducted not just by large firms but also by medium-size and small enterprises.

The Changing World Order

Between 1989 and 1991, a series of democratic revolutions swept the Communist world. For reasons that are explored in more detail in Chapter 3, in country after country throughout eastern Europe and eventually in the Soviet Union itself, Communist Party governments collapsed. The Soviet Union receded into history, having been replaced by 15 independent republics. Czechoslovakia divided itself into two states, while Yugoslavia dissolved into a bloody civil war, now thankfully over, among its five successor states.

Many of the former Communist nations of Europe and Asia seem to share a commitment to democratic politics and free market economics. For half a century, these countries were essentially closed to Western international businesses. Now, they present a host of export and investment opportunities. Two decades later, the economies of many of the former Communist states are still relatively undeveloped, and their continued commitment to democracy and market-based economic systems cannot be taken for granted. Disturbing signs of growing unrest and totalitarian tendencies continue to be seen in several eastern European and central Asian states, including Russia, which has shown signs of shifting back toward greater state involvement in economic activity and authoritarian government.[40] Thus, the risks involved in doing business in such countries are high, but so may be the returns.

In addition to these changes, quieter revolutions have been occurring in China, other states in Southeast Asia, and Latin America. Their implications for international businesses may be just as profound as the collapse of communism in eastern Europe. China suppressed its own pro-democracy movement in the bloody Tiananmen Square massacre of 1989. Despite this, China continues to move progressively toward greater free market reforms. If what is occurring in China continues for two more decades, China may move from third-world to industrial superpower status even more rapidly than Japan did. If China's GDP per capita grows by an average of 6 to 7 percent, which is slower than the 8 to 10 percent growth rate achieved during the past decade, then by 2020 this nation of 1.3 billion people could boast an average income per capita of about $13,000, roughly equivalent to that of Spain's today.

The potential consequences for international business are enormous. On the one hand, China represents a huge and largely untapped market. Reflecting this, between 1983 and 2010, annual foreign direct investment in China increased from less than $2 billion to $100 billion annually. On the other hand, China's new firms are proving to be very capable competitors, and they could take global market share away from Western and Japanese enterprises (e.g., see the Management Focus about Hisense). Thus, the changes in China are creating both opportunities and threats for established international businesses.

As for Latin America, both democracy and free market reforms have been evident there too. For decades, most Latin American countries were ruled by dictators, many of whom seemed to view Western

China's Hisense—An Emerging Multinational

Hisense is rapidly emerging as one of China's leading multinationals. Like many other Chinese corporations, Hisense traces its origins back to a state-owned manufacturer, in this case Qingdao No. 2 Radio Factory, which was established in 1969 with just 10 employees. In the 1970s, the state-owned factory diversified into the manufacture of TV sets; by the 1980s, it was one of China's leading manufacturers of color TVs, making sets designed by Matsushita under license. In 1992, a 35-year-old engineer named Zhou Houjian was appointed head of the enterprise. In 1994, the shackles of state ownership were relaxed when the Hisense Company Ltd. was established with Zhou as CEO (he is now chairman of the board).

Under Zhou's leadership, Hisense entered a period of rapid growth, product diversification, and global expansion. By 2012, the company had sales of more than $13 billion and had emerged as one of China's premier makers of TV sets, air conditioners, refrigerators, personal computers, and telecommunications equipment. Hisense sold around 10 million TV sets, 3 million air conditioners, 4 million CDMA wireless phones, 6 million refrigerators, and 1 million personal computers. International sales accounted for more than 15 percent of total revenue. The company had established overseas manufacturing subsidiaries in Algeria, Hungary, Iran, Pakistan, and South Africa and was growing rapidly in developing markets, where it was taking share away from long-established consumer electronics and appliance makers.

Hisense's ambitions are grand. It seeks to become a global enterprise with a world-class consumer brand. Although it is without question a low-cost manufacturer, Hisense believes its core strength is in rapid product innovation. The company believes that the only way to gain leadership in the highly competitive markets in which it competes is to continuously launch advanced, high-quality, and competitively priced products.

To this end, Hisense established its first R&D center in China in the mid-1990s. This was followed by a South African R&D center in 1997 and a European R&D center in 2007. The company also has plans for an R&D center in the United States. By 2008, these R&D centers filed for more than 600 patents.

Hisense's technological prowess is evident in its digital TV business. It introduced set-top boxes in 1999, making it possible to browse the Internet from a TV. In 2002, Hisense introduced its first interactive digital TV set, and in 2005 it developed China's first core digital processing chip for digital TVs, breaking the country's reliance on foreign chip makers for this core technology. In 2006, Hisense launched an innovative line of multimedia TV sets that integrated digital high-definition technology, network technology, and flat-panel displays.[41]

international businesses as instruments of imperialist domination. Accordingly, they restricted direct investment by foreign firms. In addition, the poorly managed economies of Latin America were characterized by low growth, high debt, and hyperinflation—all of which discouraged investment by international businesses. In the past two decades, much of this has changed. Throughout most of Latin America, debt and inflation are down, governments have sold state-owned enterprises to private investors, foreign investment is welcomed, and the region's economies have expanded. Brazil, Mexico, and Chile have led the way. These changes have increased the attractiveness of Latin America, both as a market for exports and as a site for foreign direct investment. At the same time, given the long history of economic mismanagement in Latin America, there is no guarantee that these favorable trends will continue. Indeed, Bolivia, Ecuador, and most notably Venezuela have seen shifts back toward greater state involvement in industry in the past few years, and foreign investment is now less welcome than it was during the 1990s. In these nations, the government has seized control of oil and gas fields from foreign investors and has limited the rights of foreign energy companies to extract oil and gas from their nations. Thus, as in the case of eastern Europe, substantial opportunities are accompanied by substantial risks.

The Global Economy of the Twenty-First Century

As discussed, the past quarter century has seen rapid changes in the global economy. Barriers to the free flow of goods, services, and capital have been coming down. As their economies advance, more nations are joining the ranks of the developed world. A generation ago, South Korea and Taiwan were viewed as second-tier developing nations. Now they boast large economies, and their firms are major players in many global industries, from shipbuilding and steel to electronics and chemicals. The move toward a global economy has been further strengthened by the widespread adoption of liberal economic policies by countries that had firmly opposed them for two generations or more. In short, current trends indicate the world is moving toward an economic system that is more favorable for international business.

But it is always hazardous to use established trends to predict the future. The world may be moving toward a more global economic system, but globalization is not inevitable. Countries may pull back from the recent commitment to liberal economic ideology if their experiences do not match their expectations. There are clear signs, for example, of a retreat from liberal economic ideology in Russia. If Russia's hesitation were to become more permanent and widespread, the liberal vision of a more prosperous global economy based on free market principles might not occur as quickly as many hope. Clearly, this would be a tougher world for international businesses.

Also, greater globalization brings with it risks of its own. This was starkly demonstrated in 1997 and 1998 when a financial crisis in Thailand spread first to other East Asian nations and then to Russia and Brazil. Ultimately, the crisis threatened to plunge the economies of the developed world, including the United States, into a recession. We explore the causes and consequences of this and other similar global financial crises in Chapter 11. Even from a purely economic perspective, globalization is not all good. The opportunities for doing business in a global economy may be significantly enhanced, but as we saw in 1997–1998, the risks associated with global financial contagion are also greater. Indeed, during 2008–2009 a crisis that started in the financial sector of America, where banks had been too liberal in their lending policies to homeowners, swept around the world and plunged the global economy into its deepest recession since the early 1980s, illustrating once more that in an interconnected world a severe crisis in one region can affect the entire globe. Still, as explained later in this book, firms can exploit the opportunities associated with globalization while reducing the risks through appropriate hedging strategies.

THE GLOBALIZATION DEBATE

Is the shift toward a more integrated and interdependent global economy a good thing? Many influential economists, politicians, and business leaders seem to think so.[42] They argue that falling barriers to international trade and investment are the twin engines driving the global economy toward greater prosperity. They say increased international trade and cross-border investment will result in lower prices for goods and services. They believe that globalization stimulates economic growth, raises the incomes of consumers, and helps create jobs in all countries that participate in the global trading system. The arguments of those who support globalization are covered in detail in Chapters 6, 7, and 8. As we shall see, there are good theoretical reasons for believing that declining barriers to international trade and investment do stimulate economic growth, create jobs, and raise income levels. As described in Chapters 6, 7 and 8, empirical evidence lends support to the predictions of this theory. However, despite the existence of a compelling body of theory and evidence, globalization has its critics.[43] Some of these critics have become increasingly vocal and active, taking to the streets to demonstrate their opposition to globalization. Here, we look at the nature of protests against globalization and briefly review the main themes of the debate concerning the merits of globalization. In later chapters, we elaborate on many of these points.

Antiglobalization Protests

Demonstrations against globalization date to December 1999, when more than 40,000 protesters blocked the streets of Seattle in an attempt to shut down a World Trade Organization meeting being held in the city. The demonstrators were protesting against a wide range of issues, including job losses in industries under attack from foreign competitors, downward pressure on the wage rates of unskilled workers, environmental degradation, and the cultural imperialism of global media and multinational enterprises, which was seen as being dominated by what some protesters called the "culturally impoverished" interests and values of the United States. All of these ills, the demonstrators claimed, could be laid at the feet of globalization. The World Trade Organization was meeting to try to launch a new round of talks to cut barriers to cross-border trade and investment. As such, it was seen as a promoter of globalization and a target for the protesters. The protests turned violent, transforming the normally placid streets of Seattle into a running battle between "anarchists" and Seattle's bemused and poorly prepared police department. Pictures of brick-throwing protesters and armored police wielding their batons were duly recorded by the global media, which then circulated the images around the world. Meanwhile, the WTO meeting failed to reach agreement, and although the protests outside the meeting halls had little to do with that failure, the impression took hold that the demonstrators had succeeded in derailing the meetings.

Emboldened by the experience in Seattle, antiglobalization protesters now often turn up at major meetings of global institutions. Smaller-scale protests have occurred in several countries, such as France, where antiglobalization activists destroyed a McDonald's restaurant in 1999 to protest the impoverishment of French culture by American imperialism (see the accompanying Country Focus for details). While violent protests may give the antiglobalization effort a bad name, it is clear from the scale of the demonstrations that support for the cause goes beyond a core of anarchists. Large segments of the population in many countries believe that globalization has detrimental effects on living standards and the environment, and the media have often fed on this fear. For example, former CNN news anchor Lou Dobbs ran TV shows that were highly critical of the trend by American companies to take advantage of globalization and "export jobs" overseas. As the world slipped into a recession in 2008, Dobbs stepped up his antiglobalization rhetoric (Dobbs left CNN in 2009).

Both theory and evidence suggest that many of these fears are exaggerated; both politicians and businesspeople need to do more to counter these fears. Many protests against globalization are tapping into a general sense of loss at the passing of a world in which barriers of time and distance, and vast differences in economic institutions, political institutions, and the level of development of different nations, produced a world rich in the diversity of human cultures. However, while the rich citizens of the developed world may have the luxury of mourning the fact that they can now see McDonald's restaurants

Protesting Globalization in France

One night in August 1999, 10 men under the leadership of local sheep farmer and rural activist José Bové crept into the town of Millau in central France and vandalized a McDonald's restaurant under construction, causing an estimated $150,000 in damage. These were no ordinary vandals, however, at least according to their supporters, for the "symbolic dismantling" of the McDonald's outlet had noble aims, or so it was claimed. The attack was initially presented as a protest against unfair American trade policies. The European Union had banned imports of hormone-treated beef from the United States, primarily because of fears that it might lead to health problems (although EU scientists had concluded there was no evidence of this). After a careful review, the World Trade Organization stated the EU ban was not allowed under trading rules that the EU and United States were party to and that the EU would have to lift it or face retaliation. The EU refused to comply, so the U.S. government imposed a 100 percent tariff on imports of certain EU products, including French staples such as foie gras, mustard, and Roquefort cheese. On farms near Millau, Bové and others raised sheep whose milk was used to make Roquefort. They felt incensed by the American tariff and decided to vent their frustrations on McDonald's.

Bové and his compatriots were arrested and charged. About the same time in the Languedoc region of France, California winemaker Robert Mondavi had reached agreement with the mayor and council of the village of Aniane and regional authorities to turn 125 acres of wooded hillside belonging to the village into a vineyard. Mondavi planned to invest $7 million in the project and hoped to produce top-quality wine that would sell in Europe and the United States for $60 a bottle. However, local environmentalists objected to the plan, which they claimed would destroy the area's unique ecological heritage. José Bové, basking in sudden fame, offered his support to the opponents, and the protests started. In May 2001, the Socialist mayor who had approved the project was defeated in local elections in which the Mondavi project had become the major issue. He was replaced by a Communist, Manuel Diaz, who denounced the project as a capitalist plot designed to enrich wealthy U.S. shareholders at the cost of his villagers and the environment. Following Diaz's victory, Mondavi announced he would pull out of the project. A spokesman noted, "It's a huge waste, but there are clearly personal and political interests at play here that go way beyond us."

So are the French opposed to foreign investment? The experience of McDonald's and Mondavi seems to suggest so, as does the associated news coverage, but look closer and a different reality seems to emerge. McDonald's has more than 1,200 restaurants in France and continues to do very well there. In fact, France is one of the most profitable markets for McDonald's. France has long been one of the most favored locations for inward foreign direct investment, receiving more than $385 billion of foreign investment between 2005 and 2010, more than any other European nation with the exception of Britain. American companies have always accounted for a significant percentage of this investment. Moreover, French enterprises have also been significant foreign investors; some 1,100 French multinationals account for about 8 percent of the global stock of foreign direct investment.[44]

Indian *Chaat* in the USA[45]

WHERE FLAVORS MEET: Chutneys accompany a platter of *sev* (fried noodles) at a *chaat* station at Sukhadia's in Midtown, New York.

In Manhattan, New York, one can perceive a liking for Indian street food, with upscale new places like Spice Market, Bombay Talkie, Von Singh's, Devi, Lassi and Babu; all claiming authentic Indian snacks. New York-style habits are well known, eating on the run, especially flatbreads like *parathas* and *chapatis* and wraps like *dosas*, *kati rolls* and Bombay frankies (a roti wrapped around tandoori chicken).

Asking Indians in America about *chaat*, India's national snack, is like asking Americans in India about burgers: the word unleashes unbearable cravings, nostalgia and homesickness. "I remember going to Kwality Snacks for *papri chaat* when I was a boy," said Gandar Nasri, 74, a retired New York City taxi driver, who moved from Delhi in 1955. "Nothing will ever taste like that again." Taste a good *chaat*, and you understand why it is not soon forgotten.

Chaats are jumbles of flavor and texture: sweet, sour, salty, spicy, crunchy, soft, nutty, fried and flaky tidbits doused with cool yogurt, fresh cilantro and tangy tamarind and sprinkled with *chaat masala*, a spice mixture that is wildly eventful. The contrasts are, as one fan said, "a steeplechase for your mouth," with different sensations galloping faster than you can track them.

All Indians in the US are homesick for the same thing, said Mitra Choudhuri, a software engineer from Gujarat, who lives in Fort Collins, Colo. "There is no *chaat* here, only curries," he said. But in the New York region, that has finally changed. In Jersey City, the Little India strip on Newark Avenue is lined with places for *chaats* and sweets, while only one restaurant serves the rich curries familiar to most Americans as Indian food. (Indians call those dishes Punjabi, after the northern state of Punjab, where they originated.) In Jackson Heights, Queens, signs for new *chaat* menus flutter from many awnings, reflecting, according to Sanjiv Mody, an owner of Rajbhog Foods, a growing insistence by Indians in America on the authentic foods of home.

Chaats are mixed to one's specifications (spicier, not so much cilantro, extra chickpeas), handed over on a banana leaf and devoured instantly. "*Chaats* are like every flavor of chips and every kind of pizza you have here," said Dave Sharma, an owner of Amma, a Midtown restaurant, who is from Mumbai. "We eat *chaat* whenever we have a small hunger, but we will travel miles to get a good one. And people are loyal to their favorites."

Chaats can be made with almost anything crispy: fried bits of chickpeas, puffed rice, peanuts, browned mashed-potato patties, fresh ginger, *mung* bean sprouts and spice-dusted toasted lentils. *Chaat masala* usually includes *aamchoor*, a tangy powder made from green mangoes, mint, cumin and pomegranate, but it must always include *kala namak*, black salt with a pleasant whiff of sulfur, vital to *chaat* lovers.

Going for a *chaat*, Mr. Sharma says, is a social act with the same casual sociability as going for a beer. (Most Indians are Hindus and Muslims and drink little or no alcohol.) "After work, a group of men will buy each other rounds of *chaat* on the way to the train and sometimes even have competitions over who can eat more." Piyush Sukhadia, an owner of chaat-and-sweet stores, said. "In India, a guy might have a Mercedes and live in a house on a hill, but he still puts on his slippers and goes to eat *chaat*."

The word *chaat* means 'to lick', in Hindi, said Mr. Sukhadia, whose family business was established in 1890, when his great-great-grandfather received the title of official sweetmaker to the nawab of Cambay in southern Gujarat. He said that although *chaats* used to be considered humble food with a taint of the street, the concept is gradually changing and can be witnessed as one of the food menus in elegant weddings.

To that end Sandip Patel, the owner of Chowpatty Foods, one of the first *chaat* houses in the United States, has just imported a *chaat* cart from India in the red-and-white color scheme of the Chowpatty *chaatwallahs*. Chowpatty is the biggest chaat-and-sweet specialist in the Oak Tree Road neighborhood of Iselin, New Jersey, which lures thousands of Indian-Americans from as far as Philadelphia and Boston to shop and snack every weekend. Oak Tree Road serves a knowledgeable clientele and has the best-quality sweets and *chaats* in the region: all the major manufacturers have shops there, and even amateurs like Shalimar and the Galaxy food court serve lively *chaats* with startlingly fresh flavors.

On Oak Tree Road, you can see the ingredients for *chaats* divided in rows of stainless-steel bins, but a traditional *chaatwallah* sits surrounded by his mounds of dry ingredients and bowls of yogurt, *chaat masala*, cilantro or mint chutney and tamarind chutney and his own mix of *jaljeera*, the "firewater" that is used to fill the habit-forming *pani puri*. "I just got back from India, and I ate 60 or 70 *pani puris* a day," Mr. Patel said.

A fine tribute to *pani puri* appears in a 1991 memoir about Mumbai by Gopal Gadgil. After several thousand words describing the process of eating and experiencing *pani puri*, he concludes with this tribute to the afterglow that, as I can attest, follows a *pani puri* binge: "In that state of beatitude, the Maharashtrians stop being surly, the *Marwaris* look at the millions of stars without being reminded of their own millions, the *Sindhis* admire the horizon without any intention of selling it, the *Gujaratis* speculate on the moon instead of the scrips they should have sold, the North Indians dream of things other than Hindi as the official language of the United Nations, and even the Parsi ladies stop nagging their husbands."

and Starbucks coffeehouses on their vacations to exotic locations such as Thailand, fewer complaints are heard from the citizens of those countries, who welcome the higher living standards that progress brings.

Globalization, Jobs, and Income

One concern frequently voiced by globalization opponents is that falling barriers to international trade destroy manufacturing jobs in wealthy advanced economies such as the United States and western Europe. The critics argue that falling trade barriers allow firms to move manufacturing activities to countries where wage rates are much lower.[46] Indeed, due to the entry of China, India, and states from eastern Europe into the global trading system, along with global population growth, estimates suggest that the pool of global labor may have quadrupled between 1985 and 2005, with most of the increase occurring after 1990.[47] Other things being equal, one might conclude that this enormous expansion in the global labor force, when coupled with expanding international trade, would have depressed wages in developed nations.

This fear is supported by anecdotes. For example, D. L. Bartlett and J. B. Steele, two journalists for the *Philadelphia Inquirer* who gained notoriety for their attacks on free trade, cite the case of Harwood Industries, a U.S. clothing manufacturer that closed its U.S. operations, where it paid workers $9 per hour, and shifted manufacturing to Honduras, where textile workers received 48 cents per hour.[48] Because of moves such as this, argue Bartlett and Steele, the wage rates of poorer Americans have fallen significantly over the past quarter of a century.

In the past few years, the same fears have been applied to services, which have increasingly been outsourced to nations with lower labor costs. The popular feeling is that when corporations such as Dell, IBM, or Citigroup outsource service activities to lower-cost foreign suppliers—as all three have done—they are "exporting jobs" to low-wage nations and contributing to higher unemployment and lower living standards in their home nations (in this case, the United States). Some lawmakers in the United States have responded by calling for legal barriers to job outsourcing.

Supporters of globalization reply that critics of these trends miss the essential point about free trade—the benefits outweigh the costs.[49] They argue that free trade will result in countries specializing in the production of those goods and services that they can produce most efficiently, while importing goods and services that they cannot produce as efficiently. When a country embraces free trade, there is always some dislocation—lost textile jobs at Harwood Industries, or lost call-center jobs at Dell—but the whole economy is better off as a result. According to this view, it makes little sense for the United States to produce textiles at home when they can be produced at a lower cost in Honduras or China (which, unlike Honduras, is a major source of U.S. textile imports). Importing textiles from China leads to lower prices for clothes in the United States, which enables consumers to spend more of their money on other items. At the same time, the increased income generated in China from textile exports increases income levels in that country, which helps the Chinese to purchase more products produced in the United States, such as pharmaceuticals from Amgen, Boeing jets, Intel-based computers, Microsoft software, and Cisco routers.

The same argument can be made to support the outsourcing of services to low-wage countries. By outsourcing its customer service call centers to India, Dell can reduce its cost structure, and thereby its prices for PCs. U.S. consumers benefit from this development. As prices for PCs fall, Americans can spend more of their money on other goods and services. Moreover, the increase in income levels in India allows Indians to purchase more U.S. goods and services, which helps create jobs in the United States. In this manner, supporters of globalization argue that free trade benefits *all* countries that adhere to a free trade regime.

If the critics of globalization are correct, three things must be shown. First, the share of national income received by labor, as opposed to the share received by the owners of capital (e.g., stockholders and bondholders), should have declined in advanced nations as a result of downward pressure on wage rates. Second, even though labor's share of the economic pie may have declined, this does not mean lower living standards if the size of the total pie has increased sufficiently to offset the decline in labor's share—in other words, if economic growth and rising living standards in advanced economies have offset declines in labor's share (this is the position argued by supporters of globalization). Third, the decline in labor's share of national income must be due to moving production to low-wage countries, as opposed to improvement in production technology and productivity.

Several studies shed light on these issues.[50] First, the data suggest that over the past two decades, the share of labor in national income has declined. The decline in share is much more pronounced in Europe and Japan (about 10 percentage points) than in the United States and the United Kingdom (where it is 3 to 4 percentage points). However, detailed analysis suggests the share of national income enjoyed by *skilled labor* has actually *increased,* suggesting that the fall in labor's share has been due to a fall in the share taken by *unskilled labor*. A study by the IMF suggested the earnings gap between workers in skilled and unskilled sectors has widened by 25 percent over the past two decades.[51] The average income level of the richest 10 percent of the population in developed economies was nine times that of the poorest 10 percent, according to 2010 data. The ratio in the United States was among the highest, with the top 10 percent earning 14 times as much as the bottom 10 percent.[52] These figures strongly suggest that unskilled labor in developed nations has seen its share of national income decline over the past two decades.

However, this does not mean that the *living standards* of unskilled workers in developed nations have declined. It is possible that economic growth in developed nations has offset the fall in the share of national income enjoyed by unskilled workers, raising their living standards. Evidence suggests that real labor compensation has expanded in most developed nations since the 1980s, including the United States. Several studies by the Organization for Economic Cooperation and Development (OECD), whose members include the 34 richest economies in the world, conclude that while the gap between the poorest and richest segments of society in OECD countries has widened, in *most* countries real income levels have increased for all, including the poorest segment. In a study published in 2011, the OECD found that between 1985 and 2008 real household income (adjusted for inflation) increased by 1.7 percent annually among its member states. The real income level of the poorest 10 percent of the population increased at 1.4 percent on average, while that of the richest 10 percent increased by 2 percent annually (i.e., while everyone got richer, the gap between the most affluent and the poorest sectors of society widened). The differential in growth rates was more extreme in the United States than most other countries. The study found that the real income of the poorest 10 percent of the population grew by just 0.5 percent a year in the United States between 1985 and 2008, while that of the richest 10 percent grew by 1.9 percent annually.[53]

As noted earlier, globalization critics argue that the decline in unskilled wage rates is due to the migration of low-wage manufacturing jobs offshore and a corresponding reduction in demand for unskilled workers. However, supporters of globalization see a more complex picture. They maintain that the weak growth rate in real wage rates for unskilled workers owes far more to a technology-induced shift within advanced economies away from jobs where the only qualification was a willingness to turn up for work every day and toward jobs that require significant education and skills. They point out that many advanced economies report a shortage of highly skilled workers and an excess supply of unskilled workers. Thus, growing income inequality is a result of the wages for skilled workers being bid up by the labor market and the wages for unskilled workers being discounted. In fact, evidence suggests that technological change has had a bigger impact than globalization on the declining share of national income enjoyed by labor.[54] This suggests that a solution to the problem of slow real income growth among the unskilled is to be found not in limiting free trade and globalization, but in increasing society's investment in education to reduce the supply of unskilled workers.[55]

Finally, it is worth noting that the wage gap between developing and developed nations is closing as developing nations experience rapid economic growth. For example, one estimate suggests that wages in China will approach Western levels in about 30 years.[56] To the extent that this is the case, any migration of unskilled jobs to low-wage countries is a temporary phenomenon representing a structural adjustment on the way to a more tightly integrated global economy.

Globalization, Labor Policies, and the Environment

A second source of concern is that free trade encourages firms from advanced nations to move manufacturing facilities to less developed countries that lack adequate regulations to protect labor and the environment from abuse by the unscrupulous.[57] Globalization critics often argue that adhering to labor and environmental regulations significantly increases the costs of manufacturing enterprises and puts them at a competitive disadvantage in the global marketplace vis-à-vis firms based in developing nations that do not have to comply with such regulations. Firms deal with this cost disadvantage, the theory goes, by moving their production facilities to nations that do not have such burdensome regulations or that fail to enforce the regulations they have.

If this were the case, one might expect free trade to lead to an increase in pollution and result in firms from advanced nations exploiting the labor of less developed nations.[58] This argument was used repeatedly by those who opposed the 1994 formation of the North American Free Trade Agreement (NAFTA) among Canada, Mexico, and the United States. They painted a picture of U.S. manufacturing firms moving to Mexico in droves so that they would be free to pollute the environment, employ child labor, and ignore workplace safety and health issues, all in the name of higher profits.[59]

Supporters of free trade and greater globalization express doubts about this scenario. They argue that tougher environmental regulations and stricter labor standards go hand in hand with economic progress.[60] In general, as countries get richer, they enact tougher environmental and labor regulations.[61] Because free trade enables developing countries to increase their economic growth rates and become richer, this should lead to tougher environmental and labor laws. In this view, the critics of free trade have got it backward—free trade does not lead to more pollution and labor exploitation; it leads to less. By creating wealth and incentives for enterprises to produce technological innovations, the free market system and free trade could make it easier for the world to cope with pollution and population growth. Indeed, while pollution levels are rising in the world's poorer countries, they have been falling in developed nations. In the United States, for example, the concentration of carbon monoxide and sulfur dioxide pollutants in the atmosphere decreased by 60 percent between 1978 and 1997, while lead concentrations decreased by 98 percent—and these reductions have occurred against a background of sustained economic expansion.[62]

A number of econometric studies have found consistent evidence of a hump-shaped relationship between income levels and pollution levels (see Figure 1.4).[63] As an economy grows and income levels rise, initially pollution levels also rise. However, past some point, rising income levels lead to demands for greater environmental protection, and pollution levels then fall. A seminal study by Grossman and Krueger found that the turning point generally occurred before per capita income levels reached $8,000.[64]

While the hump-shaped relationship depicted in Figure 1.4 seems to hold across a wide range of pollutants—from sulfur dioxide to lead concentrations and water quality—carbon dioxide emissions are

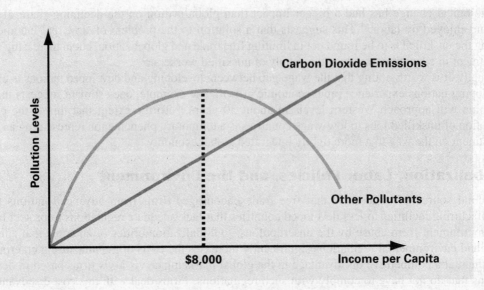

Figure 1.4 *Income Levels and Environmental Pollution*

an important exception, rising steadily with higher-income levels. Given that increased atmospheric carbon dioxide concentrations are a cause of global warming, this should be of serious concern. The solution to the problem, however, is probably not to roll back the trade liberalization efforts that have fostered economic growth and globalization, but to get the nations of the world to agree to policies designed to limit carbon emissions. Although UN-sponsored talks have had this as a central aim since the 1992 Earth Summit in Rio de Janeiro, there has been little success in moving toward the ambitious goals for reducing carbon emissions laid down in the Earth Summit and subsequent talks in Kyoto, Japan, in 1997 and in Copenhagen in 2009. In part this is because the largest emitters of carbon dioxide, the United States and China, have failed to reach agreements about how to proceed. China, a country whose carbon emissions are increasing at an alarming rate, has so far shown little appetite to adopt tighter pollution controls. As for the United States, political divisions in Congress have made it difficult for even a progressive administration such as that of Barack Obama to move forward with tight legislation on climate change.

Notwithstanding this, supporters of free trade point out that it is possible to tie free trade agreements to the implementation of tougher environmental and labor laws in less developed countries. NAFTA, for example, was passed only after side agreements had been negotiated that committed Mexico to tougher enforcement of environmental protection regulations. Thus, supporters of free trade argue that factories based in Mexico are now cleaner than they would have been without the passage of NAFTA.[65]

They also argue that business firms are not the amoral organizations that critics suggest. While there may be some rotten apples, most business enterprises are staffed by managers who are committed to behave in an ethical manner and would be unlikely to move production offshore just so they could pump more pollution into the atmosphere or exploit labor. Furthermore, the relationship between pollution, labor exploitation, and production costs may not be that suggested by critics. In general, a well-treated labor force is productive, and it is productivity rather than base wage rates that often has the greatest influence on costs. The vision of greedy managers who shift production to low-wage countries to exploit their labor force may be misplaced.

Globalization and National Sovereignty

Another concern voiced by critics of globalization is that today's increasingly interdependent global economy shifts economic power away from national governments and toward supranational organizations such as the World Trade Organization, the European Union, and the United Nations. As perceived by critics, unelected bureaucrats now impose policies on the democratically elected governments of nation-states, thereby undermining the sovereignty of those states and limiting the nation's ability to control its own destiny.[66]

The World Trade Organization is a favorite target of those who attack the headlong rush toward a global economy. As noted earlier, the WTO was founded in 1995 to police the world trading system established by the General Agreement on Tariffs and Trade. The WTO arbitrates trade disputes between the 159 states that are signatories to the GATT. The arbitration panel can issue a ruling instructing a member state to change trade policies that violate GATT regulations. If the violator refuses to comply with the ruling, the WTO allows other states to impose appropriate trade sanctions on the transgressor. As a result, according to one prominent critic, U.S. environmentalist, consumer rights advocate, and sometime presidential candidate Ralph Nader:

> Under the new system, many decisions that affect billions of people are no longer made by local or national governments but instead, if challenged by any WTO member nation, would be deferred to a group of unelected bureaucrats sitting behind closed doors in Geneva (which is where the headquarters of the WTO are located). The bureaucrats can decide whether or not people in California can prevent the destruction of the last virgin forests or determine if carcinogenic pesticides can be banned from their foods; or whether European countries have the right to ban dangerous biotech hormones in meat. . . . At risk is the very basis of democracy and accountable decision making.[67]

In contrast to Nader, many economists and politicians maintain that the power of supranational organizations such as the WTO is limited to what nation-states collectively agree to grant. They argue that bodies such as the United Nations and the WTO exist to serve the collective interests of member states, not to subvert those interests. Supporters of supranational organizations point out that the power of these bodies rests largely on their ability to persuade member states to follow a certain action. If these bodies fail to serve the collective interests of member states, those states will withdraw their support and the supranational organization will quickly collapse. In this view, real power still resides with individual nation-states, not supranational organizations.

Globalization and the World's Poor

Critics of globalization argue that despite the supposed benefits associated with free trade and investment, over the past hundred years or so the gap between the rich and poor nations of the world has gotten wider. In 1870, the average income per capita in the world's 17 richest nations was 2.4 times that of all other countries. In 1990, the same group was 4.5 times as rich as the rest.[68] While recent history has shown that some of the world's poorer nations are capable of rapid periods of economic growth— witness the transformation that has occurred in some Southeast Asian nations such as South Korea, Thailand, and Malaysia—there appear to be strong forces for stagnation among the world's poorest nations. A quarter of the countries with a GDP per capita of less than $1,000 in 1960 had growth rates of less than zero from 1960 to 1995, and a third had growth rates of less than 0.05 percent.[69] Critics argue that if globalization is such a positive development, this divergence between the rich and poor should not have occurred.

Although the reasons for economic stagnation vary, several factors stand out, none of which has anything to do with free trade or globalization.[70] Many of the world's poorest countries have suffered from totalitarian governments, economic policies that destroyed wealth rather than facilitated its creation, endemic corruption, scant protection for property rights, and war. Such factors help explain why countries such as Afghanistan, Cambodia, Cuba, Haiti, Iraq, Libya, Nigeria, Sudan, Vietnam, and Zaire have failed to improve the economic lot of their citizens during recent decades. A complicating factor is the rapidly expanding populations in many of these countries. Without a major change in government, population growth may exacerbate their problems. Promoters of free trade argue that the best way for these countries to improve their lot is to lower their barriers to free trade and investment and to implement economic policies based on free market economics.[71]

Many of the world's poorer nations are being held back by large debt burdens. Of particular concern are the 40 or so "highly indebted poorer countries" (HIPCs), which are home to some 700 million people. Among these countries, the average government debt burden has been as high as 85 percent of the value of the economy, as measured by gross domestic product, and the annual costs of serving government debt consumed 15 percent of the country's export earnings.[72] Servicing such a heavy debt load leaves the governments of these countries with little left to invest in important public infrastructure projects, such as education, health care, roads, and power. The result is the HIPCs are trapped in a cycle of poverty and debt that inhibits economic development. Free trade alone, some argue, is a necessary but not sufficient prerequisite to help these countries bootstrap themselves out of poverty. Instead, large-scale debt relief is needed for the world's poorest nations to give them the opportunity to restructure their economies and start the long climb toward prosperity. Supporters of debt relief also argue that new democratic governments in poor nations should not be forced to honor debts that were incurred and mismanaged long ago by their corrupt and dictatorial predecessors.

In the late 1990s, a debt relief movement began to gain ground among the political establishment in the world's richer nations.[73] Fueled by high-profile endorsements from Irish rock star Bono (who has been a tireless and increasingly effective advocate for debt relief), the Dalai Lama, and influential Harvard economist Jeffrey Sachs, the debt relief movement was instrumental in persuading the United States to enact legislation in 2000 that provided $435 million in debt relief for HIPCs. More important perhaps, the United States also backed an IMF plan to sell some of its gold reserves and use the proceeds to help with debt relief. The IMF and World Bank have now picked up the banner and have embarked on a systematic debt relief program.

For such a program to have a lasting effect, however, debt relief must be matched by wise investment in public projects that boost economic growth (such as education) and by the adoption of economic policies that facilitate investment and trade. The rich nations of the world also can help by reducing barriers to the importation of products from the world's poorer nations, particularly tariffs on imports of agricultural products and textiles. High-tariff barriers and other impediments to trade make it difficult for poor countries to export more of their agricultural production. The World Trade Organization has estimated that if the developed nations of the world eradicated subsidies to their agricultural producers and removed tariff barriers to trade in agriculture, this would raise global economic welfare by $128 billion, with $30 billion of that going to developing nations, many of which are highly indebted. The faster growth associated with expanded trade in agriculture could reduce the number of people living in poverty by as much as 13 percent by 2015, according to the WTO.[74]

MANAGING IN THE GLOBAL MARKETPLACE   **LO1-5**

Much of this book is concerned with the challenges of managing in an international business. An **international business** is any firm that engages in international trade or investment. A firm does not have to become a multinational enterprise, investing directly in operations in other countries, to engage in international business, although multinational enterprises are international businesses. All a firm has to do is export or import products from other countries. As the world shifts toward a truly integrated global economy, more firms—both large and small—are becoming international businesses. What does this shift toward a global economy mean for managers within an international business?

As their organizations increasingly engage in cross-border trade and investment, managers need to recognize that the task of managing an international business differs from that of managing a purely domestic business in many ways. At the most fundamental level, the differences arise from the simple fact that countries are different. Countries differ in their cultures, political systems, economic systems, legal systems, and levels of economic development. Despite all the talk about the emerging global village, and despite the trend toward globalization of markets and production, as we shall see in this book, many of these differences are very profound and enduring.

Differences among countries require that an international business vary its practices country by country. Marketing a product in Brazil may require a different approach from marketing the product in Germany; managing U.S. workers might require different skills from managing Japanese workers; maintaining close relations with a particular level of government may be very important in Mexico and irrelevant in Great Britain; the business strategy pursued in Canada might not work in South Korea; and so on. Managers in an international business must not only be sensitive to these differences but also adopt the appropriate policies and strategies for coping with them. Much of this book is devoted to explaining the sources of these differences and the methods for successfully coping with them.

A further way in which international business differs from domestic business is the greater complexity of managing an international business. In addition to the problems that arise from the differences between countries, a manager in an international business is confronted with a range of other issues that the manager in a domestic business never confronts. The managers of an international business must decide where in the world to site production activities to minimize costs and to maximize value added. They must decide whether it is ethical to adhere to the lower labor and environmental standards found in many less developed nations. Then they must decide how best to coordinate and control globally dispersed production activities (which, as we shall see later in the book, is not a trivial problem). The managers in an international business also must decide which foreign markets to enter and which to avoid. They must choose the appropriate mode for entering a particular foreign country. Is it best to export its product to the foreign country? Should the firm allow a local company to produce its product under license in that country? Should the firm enter into a joint venture with a local firm to produce its product in that country? Or should the firm set up a wholly owned subsidiary to serve the market in that country? As we shall see, the choice of entry mode is critical because it has major implications for the long-term health of the firm.

Conducting business transactions across national borders requires understanding the rules governing the international trading and investment system. Managers in an international business must also deal with government restrictions on international trade and investment. They must find ways to work within the limits imposed by specific governmental interventions. As this book explains, even though many governments are nominally committed to free trade, they often intervene to regulate cross-border trade and investment. Managers within international businesses must develop strategies and policies for dealing with such interventions.

Cross-border transactions also require that money be converted from the firm's home currency into a foreign currency and vice versa. Because currency exchange rates vary in response to changing economic conditions, managers in an international business must develop policies for dealing with exchange rate movements. A firm that adopts the wrong policy can lose large amounts of money, whereas one that adopts the right policy can increase the profitability of its international transactions.

In sum, managing an international business is different from managing a purely domestic business for at least four reasons: (1) countries are different, (2) the range of problems confronted by a manager in an international business is wider and the problems themselves more complex than those confronted by a manager in a domestic business, (3) an international business must find ways to work within the limits imposed by government intervention in the international trade and investment system, and (4) international transactions involve converting money into different currencies.

In this book, we examine all these issues in depth, paying close attention to the different strategies and policies that managers pursue to deal with the various challenges created when a firm becomes an international business. Chapters 2, 3, and 4 explore how countries differ from each other with regard to their political, economic, legal, and cultural institutions. Chapter 5 takes a detailed look at the ethical issues that arise in international business. Chapters 6 through 9 look at the international trade and investment environment within which international businesses must operate. Chapters 10 and 11 review the international monetary system. These chapters focus on the nature of the foreign exchange market and the emerging global monetary system. Chapters 12 and 13 explore the strategy of international businesses. Chapters 14 through 17 look at the management of various functional operations within an international business, including production, marketing, and human relations. By the time you complete this book, you should have a good grasp of the issues that managers working within international business have to grapple with on a daily basis, and you should be familiar with the range of strategies and operating policies available to compete more effectively in today's rapidly emerging global economy.

Chapter Summary

This chapter has shown how the world economy is becoming more global and reviewed the main drivers of globalization, arguing that they seem to be thrusting nation-states toward a more tightly integrated global economy. It looked at how the nature of international business is changing in response to the changing global economy, discussed concerns raised by rapid globalization, and reviewed implications of rapid globalization for individual managers. The chapter made the following points:

1. Over the past three decades, we have witnessed the globalization of markets and production.
2. The globalization of markets implies that national markets are merging into one huge marketplace. However, it is important not to push this view too far.
3. The globalization of production implies that firms are basing individual productive activities at the optimal world locations for the particular activities. As a consequence, it is increasingly irrelevant to talk about American products, Japanese products, or German products, because these are being replaced by "global" products.
4. Two factors seem to underlie the trend toward globalization: declining trade barriers and changes in communication, information, and transportation technologies.
5. Since the end of World War II, barriers to the free flow of goods, services, and capital have been lowered significantly. More than anything else, this has facilitated the trend toward the globalization of production and has enabled firms to view the world as a single market.
6. As a consequence of the globalization of production and markets, in the last decade world trade has grown faster than world output, foreign direct investment has surged, imports have penetrated more deeply into the world's industrial nations, and competitive pressures have increased in industry after industry.

7. The development of the microprocessor and related developments in communication and information processing technology have helped firms link their worldwide operations into sophisticated information networks. Jet air travel, by shrinking travel time, has also helped link the worldwide operations of international businesses. These changes have enabled firms to achieve tight coordination of their worldwide operations and to view the world as a single market.

8. In the 1960s, the U.S. economy was dominant in the world, U.S. firms accounted for most of the foreign direct investment in the world economy, U.S. firms dominated the list of large multinationals, and roughly half the world—the centrally planned economies of the Communist world—was closed to Western businesses.

9. By the mid-1990s, the U.S. share of world output had been cut in half, with major shares now being accounted for by western European and Southeast Asian economies. The U.S. share of worldwide foreign direct investment had also fallen, by about two-thirds. U.S. multinationals were now facing competition from a large number of Japanese and European multinationals. In addition, the emergence of mini-multinationals was noted.

10. One of the most dramatic developments of the past 20 years has been the collapse of communism in eastern Europe, which has created enormous opportunities for international businesses. In addition, the move toward free market economies in China and Latin America is creating opportunities (and threats) for Western international businesses.

11. The benefits and costs of the emerging global economy are being hotly debated among businesspeople, economists, and politicians. The debate focuses on the impact of globalization on jobs, wages, the environment, working conditions, and national sovereignty.

12. Managing an international business is different from managing a domestic business for at least four reasons: (*a*) countries are different, (*b*) the range of problems confronted by a manager in an international business is wider and the problems themselves more complex than those confronted by a manager in a domestic business, (*c*) managers in an international business must find ways to work within the limits imposed by governments' intervention in the international trade and investment system, and (*d*) international transactions involve converting money into different currencies.

Critical Thinking and Discussion Questions

1. Describe the shifts in the world economy over the past 30 years. What are the implications of these shifts for international businesses based in Great Britain? North America? Hong Kong?

2. "The study of international business is fine if you are going to work in a large multinational enterprise, but it has no relevance for individuals who are going to work in small firms." Evaluate this statement.

3. How have changes in technology contributed to the globalization of markets and production? Would the globalization of production and markets have been possible without these technological changes?

4. "Ultimately, the study of international business is no different from the study of domestic business. Thus, there is no point in having a separate course on international business." Evaluate this statement.

5. How does the Internet affect international business activity and the globalization of the world economy?

6. If current trends continue, China may be the world's largest economy by 2020. Discuss the possible implications of such a development for (*a*) the world trading system, (*b*) the world mone-

tary system, (*c*) the business strategy of today's European and U.S.-based global corporations, and (*d*) global commodity prices.

7. Reread the Management Focus on Vizio and answer the following questions:

a. Why is the manufacturing of flat-panel TVs migrating to different locations around the world?

b. Who benefits from the globalization of the flat-panel display industry? Who are the losers?

c. What would happen if the U.S. government required that flat-panel displays sold in the United States had to also be made in the United States? On balance, would this be a good or a bad thing?

d. What does the example of Vizio tell you about the future of production in an increasingly integrated global economy? What does it tell you about the strategies that enterprises must adopt to thrive in highly competitive global markets?

Research Task ⬡ globalEDGE globaledge.msu.edu

The High End of Technology—Animation Skills[75]

When children in the US tune into the popular cartoon programme, "Jakers! The Adventures of Piggley Winks" on PBS, few are aware that the adorable pig and his friends have been created in India. Mumbai-based Crest Communications, the creator of Piggley Winks, has tie-ups with television networks in the US to produce animated content. So does Chennai-based Pentamedia Graphics, which has produced the most number of 3D animated movies in the world—six—and has a few more under production. One of the company's movies, the USD 6-million "Buddha", was released in 2005.

India's software success story is graduating to the creative space. It is now blending its IT skills with its legendary prowess in story telling to cook up an immensely entertaining broth. Cashing in on its English-educated manpower, which is conversant with English humor, and cost effectiveness, India is now on the fast lane to becoming a key player in the animation world. While animation is just one niche of the entertainment industry, it is still big business—the worldwide market for digital animation is estimated to reach USD 600 billion in 2015. Of this, India is said to have earned revenues ranging between USD 200 and USD 800 million—a growth of over 20 percent.

While India's share in the world animation market is fairly small, the potential is huge, as the needs of the film and television industry are growing worldwide. The appetite for animation is on a surge. It is not only because of the commercial success of completely animated films and television programmes such as Princess Mononoke, Final Fantasy, Toy Story, Star Wars, or the popularity of special effects in feature films, ad films and the like but also because the world has begun to acknowledge the contribution of technology beyond the film theatre. Be it mobile phones, games, PDAs, the demand for audiovisual content can only grow in one direction—skywards. Producers have realized that computer animation can fill in gaps that could be caused by external factors such as uncertain weather conditions, unavailability of conducive locations, etc.

Another factor that is working in India's favor is the global need to cut production costs. According to a CNN report, the margins in animation work have tightened in the last three or four years, with more money being spent on branding and marketing. Now, large US and European studios are looking for partners who are willing to share risks, budgets and future developments—an advantage that can be easily leveraged by Indian companies.

The co-production model also allows the Indian animation companies to work with film-makers from Japan, North America, Europe and other parts of Asia, thus, enriching the experience. Maya Entertainment, based in Mumbai and promoted by the director and actress duo Ketan and Deepa Mehta, had contributed to the special effects of Hollywood blockbusters such as Star Wars, The Phantom Menace,

The Mummy and Stuart Little. The Kerala-based Toonz Animation, which was set up with an investment of USD 7 million in 1999, caters to clients from across the globe—from the US, France and Belgium to South Korea.

Best known for its popular television series "The Adventures of Tenali Raman", Toonz has produced many acclaimed television programmes such as "Katya and Nutcracker", "Prezzy", "Tommy and Oscar", "Turtle Island" and "The Land of Gnoo". The Tenali Raman series, which is based on age-old stories about a clever court jester of King Krishnadeva Raya of the Vijayanagar Empire, has been a massive hit on Cartoon Network and is also being telecast on the Indian television channel, ETV. Cartoon Network is planning to launch a series of programmes from adaptations of Indian fables and mythology. Rising to the occasion, many companies such as Toonz, Maya and Pentamedia have got into the production of animated versions of Indian fables and folk tales. There is definitely no dearth of stories—Tata Elxsi recently released "Krishna Leela", Maya completed a 54-part science fiction series titled "Captain Vyom—The Sky Warrior", while Toonz is working on its "Hanuman" series. Apart from leveraging relationships with foreign partners, Indian companies have a huge cost advantage to their benefit. The cost of animation production services in India can cost just about 10–20 percent of what it would cost in the US. A 22-minute episode that may cost about USD 200,000 in the US and Canada, and between USD 250,000 and USD 300,000 in Europe, can work out to be about USD 50,000 in India.

However, the story of Indian animation is not only about cost effectiveness but also about quality, along with a cost advantage. The Indian animation industry owes much of its quality to the domestic advertising sector, which has been a key growth driver in the industry long before the technique was used to create television serials or for special effects in films. The success of ad characters such as the Amul Girl, Gattoo (the Asian Paints mascot), the Handiplast Boy, the Bata Bubble Gum, or of 30-second 'animercials' for brands like Hutch, Amaron, Orange, All-Out Mosquito Repellent, 7-Up, Kellogg's, ICICI, Mortein, Good Night, and Vicks are cases in point.

The Indian film industry is purportedly the largest in the world in terms of the number of movies produced annually. And if the trend in Hollywood is anything to go by, special effect is bound to play an important role in forthcoming movies. In India, this transition is already apparent as more and more Indian studios are opting for special effects to draw the crowds in.

NO LAUGHING MATTER

The 3D animation skills of Indian studios have earned high praise from their international clients for the quality of their animation output.

One of the first among Indian companies to bag an international contract was Crest Communications. The firm's 3D animation contract with Mike Young Productions in 2002, for 26 episodes of a TV serial, "Jakers! The Adventures Of Piggly Winks", broke the initial ground for Indian companies. This was televised on 17 channels across the US, Canada and Europe. Its nomination alongside top-rung global producers (Warner Bros, DNA Productions and Nickelodeon), gave Crest the exposure it had been craving for. But more importantly, it half opened the door for others. More recently, Maya Entertainment's "Jack Frost", a Christmas Special for BBC, was put at number one slot by the channel during its Christmas Week programmes in December 2004.

Crest's recent co-production, "Pet Alien", with Mike Young Productions and a French company, has also received rave reviews from the czars of the US animation industry. After seeing it, Pixar's John Lasseter is known to have remarked, "The colours are rich, the designs are appealing, the characters are funny and the animation approximates feature quality (as in the Incredibles) on a television budget and schedule."

Though Crest is at the forefront, there are others as well who have made a mark with prestigious assignments. Tata Elxsi's Visual Computing Lab, for example, designed the "Liquid Gold" credits at last year's Oscars. A Bangalore-based gaming company, Dhruva Interactive, won global deals with Microsoft Games Studios to work on its latest releases, and with mobile handset vendor Nokia to develop Javabased games. Maya did "Golden Eye", a 15-minute game, for Game Cinematics of the US, modelling, props and background for the 26 episodes of Monster by Mistake made by a Canadian-Israeli company, DPSI.

Similarly, Color Chips completed a 13-episode animation series for Benz Production of France and it is now working on a 26-episode TV series for a German production, BKN International AG.

Though Indian companies have a modest share of the world market, most of the top-rung companies are growing at more than 100 per cent a year. Crest, after its acquisiton of Rich Animation Studio in 2001, in the US, has positioned itself across the computer animation value chain spanning pre-production, production and post-production segments of 3D animation.

While there is no shortage of creative talent, the biggest hurdle to growth of animation firms is the acute shortage of trained animators. The industry needs 10,000 animators but only 3,000 are available. It took several years for Crest to build its animator strength to 270. And when Maya was raising its animator strength from five to 50, it set up its own academy, Maya Academy of Advanced Cinematics. It now has 35 centres with 3,500 seats in India.

Possibilities of 3D animations

- Enormous sets that would take millions to create can be hand-drawn in a studio and fed into a computer. In fact, many animation companies have large banks of BGs (backgrounds), which a producer may just choose from.
- Danger to life and property can be minimised, or, indeed eleminated, providing to be a big help in saving insurance premia.
- The costs of taking normal shots can be drastically minimised. For example, if a producer wants to take an aerial shot of, say, a temple tower in such a way that a view of the tower slowly turns around, the only traditional way is to hire a helicopter. But now, you simply take a picture of the tower and turn it around in the computer.
- Actors need never die. Even today, it is possible to produce movies of yesteryear heroes like Sivaji Ganesan or a Raj Kapoor by just using a picture of the actor and animating it as required.
- It is possible to 'set' actors and actresses against exotic backgrounds without having to take them there.

Source: IBEF bimonthly publication, India Now - a perspective, Volume 2, Issue 2.

Globalization

Use the globalEDGE website (globaledge.msu.edu) to complete the following exercises:

Exercise 1

As the drivers of the globalization continue to pressure both the globalization of markets and globalization of production, we continue to see the impact of greater globalization on trade patterns. HSBC, a global bank, analyzes these pressures and trends to identify opportunities across markets and sectors, through its *trade forecasts*. Visit the HSBC Global Connections site, and use the trade forecast tool to identify which export routes are forecasted to see the greatest growth over the next 15–20 years. What patterns do you see? What types of countries dominate these routes?

Exercise 2

You are working for a company that is considering investing in a foreign country. Investing in countries with different traditions is an important element of your company's long-term strategic goals. As such, management has requested a report regarding the attractiveness of alternative countries based on the potential return of FDI. Accordingly, the ranking of the top 25 countries in terms of FDI attractiveness is a crucial ingredient for your report. A colleague mentioned a potentially useful tool called the "FDI Confidence Index" which is updated periodically. Find this index, and provide additional information regarding how the index is constructed.

Closing **CASE**

Who Makes the Apple iPhone?

In its early days, Apple usually didn't look beyond its own backyard to manufacture its devices. A few years after Apple started to make the Macintosh computer back in 1983, Steve Jobs bragged that it was "a machine that was made in America." As late as the early 2000s, Apple still manufactured many of its computers at the company's iMac plant in Elk Grove, California. Jobs often said that he was as proud of the Apple's manufacturing plants as he was of the devices themselves.

By 2004, however, Apple had largely turned to foreign manufacturing. The shift to offshore manufacturing reached its peak with the iconic iPhone, which Apple first introduced in 2007. All iPhones contain hundreds of parts, an estimated 90 percent of which are manufactured abroad. Advanced semiconductors come from Germany and Taiwan, memory from Korea and Japan, display panels and circuitry from Korea and Taiwan, chip sets from Europe, and rare metals from Africa and Asia. Apple's major subcontractor, the Taiwanese multinational firm, Foxconn, performs final assembly in China.

Apple still employees some 43,000 people in the United States, and it has kept important activities at home, including product design, software engineering, and marketing. Furthermore, Apple claims that its business supports another 254,000 jobs in the United States in engineering, manufacturing, and transportation. For example, the glass for the iPhone is manufactured at Corning's U.S. plants in Kentucky and New York. But an additional 700,000 people are involved in the engineering, building, and final assembly of its products *outside* of the United States, and most of them work at subcontractors like Foxconn.

When explaining its decision to assemble the iPhone in China, Apple cites a number of factors. While it is true that labor costs are much lower in China, Apple executives point out that labor costs only account for a very small proportion of the total value of its products and are not the main driver of location decisions. Far more important, according to Apple, is the ability of its Chinese subcontractors to respond very quickly to requests from Apple to scale production up and down. In a famous illustration of this capability, back in 2007 Steve Jobs demanded that a glass screen replace the plastic screen on his prototype iPhone. Jobs didn't like the look and feel of plastic screens, which at the time were standard in the industry, nor did he like the way they scratched easily. This last-minute change in the design of the iPhone put Apple's market introduction date at risk. Apple had selected Corning to manufacture large panes of strengthened glass, but finding a manufacturer that could cut those panes into millions of iPhone screens wasn't easy. Then a bid arrived from a Chinese factory. When the Apple team visited the factory, they found that the plant's owners were already constructing a new wing to cut the glass and installing equipment. "This is in case you give us the contract," the manager said. The plant also had a warehouse full of glass samples for Apple, and a team of engineers available to work with Apple. They had built on-site dormitories, so that the factory could run three shifts seven days a week in order to meet Apple's demanding production schedule. The Chinese company got the bid.

Another critical advantage of China for Apple was that it was much easier to hire engineers there. Apple calculated that about 8,700 industrial engineers were needed to oversee and guide the 200,000 assembly-line workers involved in manufacturing the iPhone. The company had estimated that it would take as long as nine months to find that many engineers in the United States. In China it took 15 days.

Also important is the clustering together of factories in China. Many of the factories providing components for the iPhone are located close to Foxconn's assembly plant. As one executive noted, "The entire supply chain is in China. You need a thousand rubber gaskets? That's the factory next door. You need a million screws? That factory is a block away. You need a screw made a little bit different? That will take three hours."

All this being said, there are drawbacks to outsourcing to China. Several of Apple's subcontractors have been targeted for their poor working conditions. Criticisms include low pay of line workers, long hours, mandatory overtime for little or no additional pay, and poor safety records. Some former Apple executives say that there is an unresolved tension within the company; executives want to improve working conditions within the factories of subcontractors such as Foxconn, but that dedication falters when it conflicts with crucial supplier relationships or the fast delivery of new products.[76]

Case Discussion Questions

1. What are the benefits to Apple of outsourcing the assembly of the iPhone to foreign countries, and particularly China? What are the potential costs and risks to Apple?

2. In addition to Apple, who else benefits from Apple's decision to outsource assembly to China? Who are the potential losers here?

3. What are the potential ethical problems associated with outsourcing assembly jobs to Foxconn in China? How might Apple deal with these?

4. On balance, do you think that the kind of outsourcing undertaken by Apple is a good thing or a bad thing for the American economy? Explain your reasoning?

Endnotes

1. G. Thompson, "Behind Roses' Beauty, Poor and Ill Workers," *The New York Times,* February 13, 2003, pp. A1, A27; V. Marino, "By Any Other Name, It's Usually a Rosa," *The New York Times,* May 11, 2003, p. A9; "The Search for Roses without Thorns," *The Economist,* February 18, 2006, p. 38; L. Kwoh, "Rose Growing Industry Wilts in U.S. as South America's Blossoms," *The Star Ledger,* February 6, 2011; and R. Nevado and J. Nevado, "When a Rose Is more than Just a Rose," *The Washington Post,* November 11, 2002.

2. Figures from World Trade Organization, Statistics Database, 2013.

3. Thomas L. Friedman, *The World Is Flat* (New York: Farrar, Straus and Giroux, 2005).

4. Ibid.

5. T. Levitt, "The Globalization of Markets," *Harvard Business Review,* May–June 1983, pp. 92–102.

6. U.S. Department of Commerce, Internal Trade Administration, "U.S. Export Fact Sheet," May 10, 2012.

7. C. M. Draffen, "Going Global: Export Market Proves Profitable for Region's Small Businesses," *Newsday,* March 19, 2001, p. C18.

8. B. Benoit and R. Milne, "Germany's Best Kept Secret, How Its Exporters Are Betting the World," *Financial Times,* May 19, 2006, p. 11.

9. See F. T. Knickerbocker, *Oligopolistic Reaction and Multinational Enterprise* (Boston: Harvard Business School Press, 1973); and R. E. Caves, "Japanese Investment in the U.S.: Lessons for the Economic Analysis of Foreign Investment," *The World Economy* 16 (1993), pp. 279–300.

10. I. Metthee, "Playing a Large Part," *Seattle Post-Intelligencer,* April 9, 1994, p. 13.

11. "Operating Profit," *The Economist,* August 16, 2008, pp. 74–76.

12. R. B. Reich, *The Work of Nations* (New York: A. A. Knopf, 1991).

13. D. J. Lynch, "Flat Panel TVs Display Effects of Globalization," *USA Today,* May 8, 2007, pp. 1B, 2B; P. Engardio and E. Woyke, "Flat Panels, Thin Margins," *BusinessWeek,* February 26, 2007, p. 50; B. Womack, "Flat TV Seller Vizio Hits $600 Million in Sales, Growing," *Orange County Business Journal,* September 4, 2007, pp. 1, 64; E. Taub, "Vizio's Flat Panel Display Sales Are Anything but Flat," *The New York Times Online,* May 12, 2009; and Greg Tarr, "HIS: Samsung Dusts Vizio in Q4 LCD TV Share in the U.S.," *This Week in Consumer Electronics,* April 12, 2012, p. 12.

14. United Nations, "The UN in Brief," www.un.org/Overview/brief.html.

15. J. A. Frankel, "Globalization of the Economy," National Bureau of Economic Research, working paper no. 7858, 2000.

16. J. Bhagwati, *Protectionism* (Cambridge, MA: MIT Press, 1989).

17. F. Williams, "Trade Round Like This May Never Be Seen Again," *Financial Times,* April 15, 1994, p. 8.

18. W. Vieth, "Major Concessions Lead to Success for WTO Talks," *Los Angeles Times,* November 14, 2001, p. A1; and "Seeds Sown for Future Growth," *The Economist,* November 17, 2001, pp. 65–66.

19. Ibid.

20. World Trade Organization Press release, "Trade to Remain Subdued in 2013 after Sluggish Growth in 2012 as European Economies Continue to Struggle," April 10, 2013; World Trade Organization, *International Trade Statistics 2012* (Geneva: WTO 2012).

21. United Nations Conference on Trade and Investment, "Global FDI Recovery Derails," *Global Investment Trends Monitor,* January 23, 2013.

22. United Nations, *World Investment Report, 2012* (New York and Geneva: United Nations, 2012).

23. Moore's law is named after Intel founder Gordon Moore.

24. Data compiled from various sources and listed at www.internetworldstats.com/stats.htm.

25. From www.census.gov/mrts/www/ecomm.html. See also S. Fiegerman, "Ecommerce Is Now a Trillion Dollar Industry," *Mashable Business*, February 5, 2013.

26. For a counterpoint, see "Geography and the Net: Putting It in Its Place," *The Economist,* August 11, 2001, pp. 18–20.

27. Frankel, "Globalization of the Economy."

28. Data from Bureau of Transportation Statistics, 2001.

29. Fernald and Greenfield, "The Fall and Rise of the Global Economy."

30. Data located at www.bts.gov/publications/us_international_trade_and_freight_transportation_trends/2003/index.html.

31. "America's Pain, India's Gain: Outsourcing," *The Economist,* January 11, 2003, p. 59; "The World Is Our Oyster," *The Economist,* October 7, 2006, pp. 9–10; "IBM and Globalization: Hungry Tiger, Dancing Elephant," *The Economist,* April 7, 2007, pp. 67–69; P. Mishra, "New Billing Model May Hit India's Software Exports," *Live Mint,* February 14, 2013; and "India's Outsourcing Business: On the Turn," *The Economist,* January 19, 2013.

32. N. Hood and J. Young, *The Economics of the Multinational Enterprise* (New York: Longman, 1973).

33. United Nations, *World Investment Report, 2012.*

34. Ibid.

35. Ibid.

36. S. Chetty, "Explosive International Growth and Problems of Success among Small and Medium Sized Firms," *International Small Business Journal,* February 2003, pp. 5–28.

37. R. A. Mosbacher, "Opening Up Export Doors for Smaller Firms," *Seattle Times,* July 24, 1991, p. A7.

38. "Small Companies Learn How to Sell to the Japanese," *Seattle Times,* March 19, 1992.

39. Holstein, "Why Johann Can Export, but Johnny Can't." *BusinessWeek,* November 3, 1991.

40. N. Buckley and A. Ostrovsky, "Back to Business—How Putin's Allies Are Turning Russia into a Corporate State," *Financial Times,* June 19, 2006, p. 11.

41. Harold L. Sirkin, "Someone May Be Gaining on Us," *Barron's,* February 5, 2007, p. 53; "Hisense Plans to Grab More International Sales," *Sino Cast China IT Watch,* November 30, 2006; "Hisense's Wonder Chip," *Financial Times Information Limited—Asian Intelligence Wire,* October 30, 2006; and Hisense's website, www.hisense.com/en/index.jsp.

42. J. E. Stiglitz, *Globalization and Its Discontents* (New York: W. W. Norton, 2003); J. Bhagwati, *In Defense of Globalization* (New York: Oxford University Press, 2004); and Friedman, *The World Is Flat.*

43. See, for example, Ravi Batra, *The Myth of Free Trade* (New York: Touchstone Books, 1993); William Greider, *One World, Ready or Not: The Manic Logic of Global Capitalism* (New York: Simon & Schuster, 1997); and D. Radrik, *Has Globalization Gone Too Far?* (Washington, DC: Institution for International Economics, 1997).

44. "Behind the Bluster," *The Economist,* May 26, 2001; "The French Farmers' Anti-global Hero," *The Economist,* July 8, 2000; C. Trueheart, "France's Golden Arch Enemy?" *Toronto Star,* July 1, 2000; J. Henley, "Grapes of Wrath Scare Off U.S. Firm," *The Economist,* May 18, 2001, p. 11; and United Nations, *World Investment Report, 2011* (New York and Geneva: United Nations, 2011).

45. Moskin J., 'Mumbai To Midtown, Chaat Hits The Spot', New York Times, March 9, 2003.

46. James Goldsmith, "The Winners and the Losers," in *The Case against the Global Economy*, eds. J. Mander and E. Goldsmith (San Francisco: Sierra Club, 1996); and Lou Dobbs, *Exporting America* (New York: Time Warner Books, 2004).

47. For an excellent summary, see "The Globalization of Labor," Chapter 5 in *IMF, World Economic Outlook 2007* (Washington, DC: IMF, April 2007). Also see R. Freeman, "Labor Market Imbalances," Harvard University working paper, www.bos.frb.org/economic/conf/conf51/conf51d.pdf.

48. D. L. Bartlett and J. B. Steele, "America: Who Stole the Dream," *Philadelphia Inquirer,* September 9, 1996.

49. For example, see Paul Krugman, *Pop Internationalism* (Cambridge, MA: MIT Press, 1996).

50. For example, see B. Milanovic and L. Squire, "Does Tariff Liberalization Increase Wage Inequality?" *National Bureau of Economic Research,* working paper no. 11046, January 2005; and B. Milanovic, "Can We Discern the Effect of Globalization on Income Distribution?" *World Bank Economic Review* 19 (2005), pp. 21–44. Also see the summary in "The Globalization of Labor."

51. See "The Globalization of Labor."

52. The 2010 data are from an unpublished OECD study cited in S. Moffett, "Income Inequality Increases," *The Wall Street Journal,* May 3, 2011.

53. M. Forster and M. Pearson, "Income Distribution and Poverty in the OECD Area," *OECD Economic Studies* 34 (2002); Moffett, "Income Inequality Increases"; and OECD, "Growing Income Inequality in OECD Countries," *OECD Forum,* May 2, 2011.

54. See "The Globalization of Labor."

55. See Krugman, *Pop Internationalism;* and D. Belman and T. M. Lee, "International Trade and the Performance of U.S. Labor Markets," in *U.S. Trade Policy and Global Growth*, ed. R. A. Blecker (New York: Economic Policy Institute, 1996).

56. Freeman, "Labor Market Imbalances."

57. E. Goldsmith, "Global Trade and the Environment," in *The Case against the Global Economy*, eds. J. Mander and E. Goldsmith (San Francisco: Sierra Club, 1996).

58. P. Choate, *Jobs at Risk: Vulnerable U.S. Industries and Jobs under NAFTA* (Washington, DC: Manufacturing Policy Project, 1993).

59. Ibid.

60. B. Lomborg, *The Skeptical Environmentalist* (Cambridge, UK: Cambridge University Press, 2001).

61. H. Nordstrom and S. Vaughan, *Trade and the Environment, World Trade Organization Special Studies No. 4* (Geneva: WTO, 1999).

62. Figures are from "Freedom's Journey: A Survey of the 20th Century. Our Durable Planet," *The Economist,* September 11, 1999, p. 30.

63. For an exhaustive review of the empirical literature, see B. R. Copeland and M. Scott Taylor, "Trade, Growth and the Environment," *Journal of Economic Literature,* March 2004, pp. 7–77.

64. G. M. Grossman and A. B. Krueger, "Economic Growth and the Environment," *Quarterly Journal of Economics* 110 (1995), pp. 353–78.

65. Krugman, *Pop Internationalism.*

66. R. Kuttner, "Managed Trade and Economic Sovereignty," in *U.S. Trade Policy and Global Growth,* ed. R. A. Blecker (New York: Economic Policy Institute, 1996).

67. Ralph Nader and Lori Wallach, "GATT, NAFTA, and the Subversion of the Democratic Process," in *U.S. Trade Policy and Global Growth,* ed. R. A. Blecker (New York: Economic Policy Institute, 1996), pp. 93–94.

68. Lant Pritchett, "Divergence, Big Time," *Journal of Economic Perspectives* 11, no. 3 (Summer 1997), pp. 3–18.

69. Ibid.

70. W. Easterly, "How Did Heavily Indebted Poor Countries Become Heavily Indebted?" *World Development,* October 2002, pp. 1677–96; and J. Sachs, *The End of Poverty* (New York, Penguin Books, 2006).

71. See D. Ben-David, H. Nordstrom, and L. A. Winters, *Trade, Income Disparity and Poverty. World Trade Organization Special Studies No. 5* (Geneva: WTO, 1999).

72. William Easterly, "Debt Relief," *Foreign Policy,* November–December 2001, pp. 20–26.

73. Jeffrey Sachs, "Sachs on Development: Helping the World's Poorest," *The Economist,* August 14, 1999, pp. 17–20.

74. World Trade Organization, *Annual Report 2003* (Geneva: WTO, 2004).

75. Reproduced with permission from a write-up by India Band Equity Foundation.

76. Gu Huini, "Human Costs Are Built into iPad in China," *The New York Times,* January 26, 2012; C. Duhigg and K. Bradsher, "How U.S. Lost Out on iPhone Work," *The New York Times,* January 22, 2012; and "Apple Takes Credit for Over Half a Million U.S. Jobs," *Apple Intelligence,* March 2, 2012, http://9to5mac.com/2012/03/02/apple-takes-credit-for-514000-u-s-jobs/#more-142766.

PART 2
Country Differences

Chapter 2
National Differences in Political Economy

LEARNING OBJECTIVES

After reading this chapter, you will be able to:

LO2-1 Understand how the political systems of countries differ.

LO2-2 Understand how the economic systems of countries differ.

LO2-3 Understand how the legal systems of countries differ.

LO2-4 Explain the implications for management practice of national differences in political economy.

◇ **GHANA: AN AFRICAN DYNAMO** ◇

Opening Case

The West African nation of Ghana has emerged as one of the fastest-growing countries in sub-Saharan Africa during the last decade. Between 2000 and 2012 Ghana's average annual growth rate in GDP was 7.66 percent. In 2011, this country of 25 million people became Africa's newest middle-income nation. Driving this growth has been strong demand for two of Ghana's major exports—gold and cocoa—as well as the start of oil production in 2010. Indeed, due to recent oil discoveries, Ghana is set to become one of the biggest oil producers in sub-Saharan Africa, a fact that could fuel strong economic expansion for years to come.

It wasn't always this way. Originally a British colony, Ghana gained independence in 1957. For the next three decades, the country suffered from a long series of military coups that killed any hope for stable democratic government. Successive governments adopted a socialist ideology, often as a reaction to their colonial past. As a result, large portions of the Ghana economy were dominated by state-owned enterprises. Corruption was rampant and inflation often a problem, while the country's dependence on cash crops for foreign currency earnings made it vulnerable to swings in commodity prices. It seemed like yet another failed state.

In 1981 an air force officer, Jerry Rawlings, led a military coup that deposed the president and put Rawlings in power. Rawlings started a vigorous anticorruption drive that made him very popular among ordinary Ghanaians. Rawlings initially pursued socialist policies and banned political parties, but in the early 1990s, he changed his views. He may well have been influenced by the wave of democratic change and economic liberalization that was then sweeping the formally Communist states of eastern Europe. In addition, he was pressured by Western governments and the International Monetary Fund to embrace democratic reforms and economic liberalization policies (the IMF was lending money to Ghana).

Presidential elections were held in 1992. Prior to the elections, the ban on political parties was lifted, restrictions on the press were removed, and all parties were given equal access to the media. Rawlings won the election, which foreign observers declared to be "free and fair." Ghana has had a functioning democratic system since then. Rawlings won again in 1996 and retired in 2001. Beginning in 1992, Rawlings started to liberalize the economy, privatizing state-owned enterprises, instituting market-based reforms, and opening Ghana up to foreign investors. Over the next decade more than 300 state-owned enterprises were privatized, and the now, largely privately held economy was booming.

Following the discovery of oil in 2007, Ghana's' politicians studied oil revenue laws from other countries, including Norway and Trinidad. They put in place laws designed to limit the ability of corrupt officials to siphon off oil revenues from royalties to enrich themselves; something that has been a big problem in oil-rich Nigeria. Some oil revenues are slated to go directly into the national budget, while the rest will be split between a "stabilization fund" to support the budget should oil prices drop and a "heritage fund" to be spent only when the oil starts to run out.[1]

INTRODUCTION

International business is much more complicated than domestic business because countries differ in many ways. Countries have different political, economic, and legal systems. They vary significantly in their level of economic development and future economic growth trajectory. Cultural practices can vary dramatically, as can the education and skill level of the population. All these differences can and do have major implications for the practice of international business. They have a profound impact on the benefits, costs, and risks associated with doing business in different countries; the way in which operations in different countries should be managed; and the strategy international firms should pursue in different countries. The main function of this chapter and the next two is to develop an awareness of and appreciation for the significance of country differences in political systems, economic systems, legal systems, economic development, and societal culture. Another function of the three chapters is to describe how the political, economic, legal, and cultural systems of many of the world's nation-states are evolving and to draw out the implications of these changes for the practice of international business.

The opening case illustrates some of the issues covered in this chapter and the next. From its independence from Britain in 1957 until the early 1990s, Ghana was not a democracy; its economy was run on socialist principles, and corruption was rampant. This was not a recipe for economic development, and indeed, Ghana was among the world's poorest nations. Starting with the introduction of a multiparty democracy in 1992, and subsequent economic reforms, Ghana has been transformed into one of Africa's more dynamic economies. To be sure, booming demand for its three main exports—cocoa, gold, and, since 2010, oil—has been a major contributor to Ghana's success. But other developing nations have experienced commodity booms only to see the revenues siphoned off by corrupt politicians. So far, this does not seem to be happening in Ghana, which holds out the promise that the nation will experience sustainable economic growth, transforming it into an attractive place for foreign firms to do business.

This chapter focuses on how the political, economic, and legal systems of countries differ. Collectively we refer to these systems as constituting the political economy of a country. We use the term **political economy** to stress that the political, economic, and legal systems of a country are interdependent; they interact and influence each other, and in doing so, they affect the level of economic well-being. In Chapter 3, we build on the concepts discussed here to explore in detail how differences in political, economic, and legal systems influence the economic development of a nation-state and its likely future growth trajectory. In Chapter 4, we look at differences in societal culture and at how these differences influence the practice of international business. Moreover, as we will see in Chapter 4, societal culture has an influence on the political, economic, and legal systems in a nation, and thus its level of economic well-being. We also discuss how the converse may also occur—how political, economic, and legal systems may also shape societal culture.

POLITICAL SYSTEMS

The political system of a country shapes its economic and legal systems.[2] As such, we need to understand the nature of different political systems before discussing economic and legal systems. By **political system** we mean the system of government in a nation. Political systems can be assessed according to two dimensions. The first is the degree to which they emphasize collectivism as opposed to individualism. The second is the degree to which they are democratic or totalitarian. These dimensions are interrelated; systems that emphasize collectivism tend to lean toward totalitarianism, whereas those that place a high value on individualism tend to be democratic. However, a large gray area exists in the middle. It is possible to have democratic societies that emphasize a mix of collectivism and individualism. Similarly, it is possible to have totalitarian societies that are not collectivist.

Collectivism and Individualism

Collectivism refers to a political system that stresses the primacy of collective goals over individual goals.[3] When collectivism is emphasized, the needs of society as a whole are generally viewed as being more important than individual freedoms. In such circumstances, an individual's right to do something may be restricted on the grounds that it runs counter to "the good of society" or to "the common good." Advocacy of collectivism can be traced to the ancient Greek philosopher Plato (427–347 B.C.), who in *The Republic* argued that individual rights should be sacrificed for the good of the majority and that property should be owned in common. Plato did not equate collectivism with equality; he believed that society should be stratified into classes, with those best suited to rule (which for Plato, naturally, were philosophers and soldiers) administering society for the benefit of all. In modern times, the collectivist mantle has been picked up by socialists.

Socialism

Modern **socialists** trace their intellectual roots to Karl Marx (1818–1883), although socialist thought clearly predates Marx (elements of it can be traced to Plato). Marx argued that the few benefit at the expense of the many in a capitalist society where individual freedoms are not restricted. While successful capitalists accumulate considerable wealth, Marx postulated that the wages earned by the majority of workers in a capitalist society would be forced down to subsistence levels. He argued that capitalists expropriate for their own use the value created by workers, while paying workers only subsistence wages in return. According to Marx, the pay of workers does not reflect the full value of their labor. To correct this perceived wrong, Marx advocated state ownership of the basic means of production, distribution, and exchange (i.e., businesses). His logic was that if the state owned the means of production, the state could ensure that workers were fully compensated for their labor. Thus, the idea is to manage state-owned enterprise to benefit society as a whole, rather than individual capitalists.[4]

In the early twentieth century, the socialist ideology split into two broad camps. The **Communists** believed that socialism could be achieved only through violent revolution and totalitarian dictatorship, whereas the **social democrats** committed themselves to achieving socialism by democratic means, turning their backs on violent revolution and dictatorship. Both versions of socialism waxed and waned during the twentieth century. The Communist version of socialism reached its high point in the late 1970s, when the majority of the world's population lived in Communist states. The countries under Communist Party rule at that time included the former Soviet Union; its eastern European client nations (e.g., Poland, Czechoslovakia, Hungary); China; the Southeast Asian nations of Cambodia, Laos, and Vietnam; various African nations (e.g., Angola and Mozambique); and the Latin American nations of Cuba and Nicaragua. By the mid-1990s, however, communism was in retreat worldwide. The Soviet Union had collapsed and had been replaced by a collection of 15 republics, many of which were at least nominally structured as democracies. Communism was swept out of eastern Europe by the largely bloodless revolutions of 1989. Although China is still nominally a Communist state with substantial limits to individual political freedom, in the economic sphere the country has moved sharply away from strict adherence to Communist ideology. Other than China, communism hangs on only in a handful of small fringe states, such as North Korea and Cuba.

Social democracy also seems to have passed a high-water mark, although the ideology may prove to be more enduring than communism. Social democracy has had perhaps its greatest influence in a number of democratic Western nations, including Australia, France, Germany, Great Britain, Norway, Spain, and Sweden, where social democratic parties have often held political power. Other countries where social democracy has had an important influence include India and Brazil. Consistent with their Marxist roots, many social democratic governments after World War II nationalized private companies in certain industries, transforming them into state-owned enterprises to be run for the "public good rather than private profit." In Great Britain by the end of the 1970s, for example, state-owned companies had a monopoly in the telecommunications, electricity, gas, coal, railway, and shipbuilding industries, as well as substantial interests in the oil, airline, auto, and steel industries.

However, experience demonstrated that state ownership of the means of production ran counter to the public interest. In many countries, state-owned companies performed poorly. Protected from competition by their monopoly position and guaranteed government financial support, many became increasingly inefficient. Individuals paid for the luxury of state ownership through higher prices and higher taxes. As a consequence, a number of Western democracies voted many social democratic parties out of office in the late 1970s and early 1980s. They were succeeded by political parties, such as Britain's Conservative Party and Germany's Christian Democratic Party, that were more committed to free market economics. These parties sold state-owned enterprises to private investors (a process referred to as **privatization**). Even where social democratic parties regained the levers of power, as in Great Britain in 1997 when the left-leaning Labor Party won control of the government, they too now seem committed to continued private ownership.

Individualism

The opposite of collectivism, **individualism** refers to a philosophy that an individual should have freedom in his or her economic and political pursuits. In contrast to collectivism, individualism stresses that the interests of the individual should take precedence over the interests of the state. Like collectivism, individualism can be traced to an ancient Greek philosopher, in this case Plato's disciple Aristotle (384–322 B.C.). In contrast to Plato, Aristotle argued that individual diversity and private ownership are desirable. In a passage that might have been taken from a speech by contemporary politicians who adhere to a free market ideology, he argued that private property is more highly productive than communal property and will thus stimulate progress. According to Aristotle, communal property receives little care, whereas property that is owned by an individual will receive the greatest care and therefore be most productive.

Individualism was reborn as an influential political philosophy in the Protestant trading nations of England and the Netherlands during the sixteenth century. The philosophy was refined in the work of a number of British philosophers, including David Hume (1711–1776), Adam Smith (1723–1790), and John Stuart Mill (1806–1873). Individualism exercised a profound influence on those in the American colonies who sought independence from Great Britain. Indeed, the concept underlies the ideas expressed in the Declaration of Independence. In the twentieth century, several Nobel Prize–winning economists, including Milton Friedman, Friedrich von Hayek, and James Buchanan, have championed the philosophy.

Individualism is built on two central tenets. The first is an emphasis on the importance of guaranteeing individual freedom and self-expression. The second tenet of individualism is that the welfare of society is best served by letting people pursue their own economic self-interest, as opposed to some collective body (such as government) dictating what is in society's best interest. Or as Adam Smith put it in a famous passage from *The Wealth of Nations,* an individual who intends his own gain is

> led by an invisible hand to promote an end which was no part of his intention. Nor is it always worse for the society that it was no part of it. By pursuing his own interest he frequently promotes that of the society more effectually than when he really intends to promote it. I have never known much good done by those who effect to trade for the public good.[5]

The central message of individualism, therefore, is that individual economic and political freedoms are the ground rules on which a society should be based. This puts individualism in conflict with collectivism. Collectivism asserts the primacy of the collective over the individual; individualism asserts the opposite. This underlying ideological conflict shaped much of the recent history of the world. The Cold War, for example, was in many respects a war between collectivism, championed by the former Soviet Union, and individualism, championed by the United States. From the late 1980s until about 2005, the waning of collectivism was matched by the ascendancy of individualism. Democratic ideals and market economics replaced socialism and communism in many states. Since 2005, there have been some signs of a swing back toward left-leaning socialist ideas in several countries, including several Latin America nations such as Venezuela, Bolivia, and Paraguay, along with Russia (see the accompanying Country Focus, which details what has been occurring in Venezuela). Also, the global financial crisis of 2008–2009 may cause some reevaluation of the trends of the past two decades, and the pendulum might tilt back the other way for a while.

Democracy and Totalitarianism

Democracy and totalitarianism are at different ends of a political dimension. **Democracy** refers to a political system in which government is by the people, exercised either directly or through elected representatives. **Totalitarianism** is a form of government in which one person or political party exercises absolute control over all spheres of human life and prohibits opposing political parties. The

Venezuela under Hugo Chávez, 1999–2013

COUNTRY FOCUS

On March 5, 2013, Hugo Chávez, the president of Venezuela, died after losing a battle against cancer. Chávez had been president of Venezuela since 1999. A former military officer who was once jailed for engineering a failed coup attempt, Chávez was a self-styled democratic socialist who won the presidential election by campaigning against corruption, economic mismanagement, and the "harsh realities" of global capitalism. When he took office in February 1999, Chávez claimed he had inherited the worst economic situation in the country's recent history. He wasn't far off the mark. A collapse in the price of oil, which accounted for 70 percent of the country's exports, left Venezuela with a large budget deficit and forced the economy into a deep recession.

Soon after taking office, Chávez worked to consolidate his hold over the apparatus of government. By 2012, Freedom House, which annually assesses political and civil liberties worldwide, concluded Venezuela was only "partly free" and that freedoms were being progressively curtailed.

On the economic front, things remained rough. The economy shrank in the early 2000s while unemployment remained persistently high at 15 to 17 percent and the poverty rate rose to more than 50 percent of the population. A 2003 study by the World Bank concluded Venezuela was one of the most regulated economies in the world and that state controls over business activities gave public officials ample opportunities to enrich themselves by demanding bribes in return for permission to expand operations or enter new lines of business. Indeed, despite Chávez's anti-corruption rhetoric, Transparency International, which ranks the world's nations according to the extent of public corruption, has noted that corruption has increased under Chávez. In 2012, Transparency International ranked Venezuela 165 out of 174 nations. Consistent with his socialist rhetoric, Chávez progressively took various enterprises into state ownership and has required that other enterprises be restructured as "workers' cooperatives" in return for government loans. In addition, the government has taken over large rural farms and ranches that Chávez claimed were not sufficiently productive and turned them into state-owned cooperatives.

In mid-2000, the world oil market bailed Chávez out of mounting economic difficulties. Oil prices started to surge from the low $20s in 2003, reaching $150 a barrel by mid-2008. Venezuela, the world's fifth-largest producer, reaped a bonanza. On the back of surging oil exports, the economy grew at a robust rate. Chávez used the oil revenues to boost government spending on social programs, many of them modeled after programs in Cuba. In 2006, he announced plans to reduce the stakes held by foreign companies in oil projects in the Orinoco regions and to give the state-run oil company a majority position.

Riding a wave of popularity at home, in December 2006 Chávez won reelection as president. He celebrated his victory by stepping on the revolutionary accelerator. Parliament gave him the power to legislate by decree for 18 months. In late 2010, Chávez yet again persuaded the National Assembly, where his supporters dominated, to once more grant him the power to rule by decree for another 18 months.

Notwithstanding his ability to consolidate political power, on the economic front Venezuela's performance under Chávez was decidedly mixed. His main achievements were to reduce poverty, which fell from 50 percent to 28 percent by 2012, and to bring down unemployment from

14.5 percent at the start of his rule to 7.6 percent in February 2013. State-owned enterprises helped Chávez achieve both these goals.

However, despite strong global demand and massive reserves, oil production in Venezuela fell by a third between 2000 and 2012 as foreign oil companies exited the country. Inflation surged and was running at around 28 percent per annum between 2008 and 2012, one of the highest rates in the world. To compound matters, the budget deficit expanded to 17 percent of GDP in 2012 as the government spent heavily to support its social programs and various subsidies.[6]

democratic–totalitarian dimension is not independent of the individualism–collectivism dimension. Democracy and individualism go hand in hand, as do the Communist version of collectivism and totalitarianism. However, gray areas exist; it is possible to have a democratic state in which collective values predominate, and it is possible to have a totalitarian state that is hostile to collectivism and in which some degree of individualism—particularly in the economic sphere—is encouraged. For example, China has seen a move toward greater individual freedom in the economic sphere, but the country is still ruled by a totalitarian dictatorship that constrains political freedom.

Democracy

The pure form of democracy, as originally practiced by several city-states in ancient Greece, is based on a belief that citizens should be directly involved in decision making. In complex, advanced societies with populations in the tens or hundreds of millions, this is impractical. Most modern democratic states practice **representative democracy.** In a representative democracy, citizens periodically elect individuals to represent them. These elected representatives then form a government, whose function is to make decisions on behalf of the electorate. In a representative democracy, elected representatives who fail to perform this job adequately will be voted out of office at the next election.

To guarantee that elected representatives can be held accountable for their actions by the electorate, an ideal representative democracy has a number of safeguards that are typically enshrined in constitutional law. These include (1) an individual's right to freedom of expression, opinion, and organization; (2) a free media; (3) regular elections in which all eligible citizens are allowed to vote; (4) universal adult suffrage; (5) limited terms for elected representatives; (6) a fair court system that is independent from the political system; (7) a nonpolitical state bureaucracy; (8) a nonpolitical police force and armed service; and (9) relatively free access to state information.[7]

Totalitarianism

In a totalitarian country, all the constitutional guarantees on which representative democracies are built—an individual's right to freedom of expression and organization, a free media, and regular elections—are denied to the citizens. In most totalitarian states, political repression is widespread, free and fair elections are lacking, media are heavily censored, basic civil liberties are denied, and those who question the right of the rulers to rule find themselves imprisoned, or worse.

Four major forms of totalitarianism exist in the world today. Until recently, the most widespread was **Communist totalitarianism**. Communism, however, is in decline worldwide, and most of the Communist Party dictatorships have collapsed since 1989. Exceptions to this trend (so far) are China, Vietnam, Laos, North Korea, and Cuba, although most of these states exhibit clear signs that the Communist Party's monopoly on political power is retreating. In many respects, the governments of China, Vietnam, and Laos are Communist in name only because those nations have adopted wide-ranging, market-based economic reforms. They remain, however, totalitarian states that deny many basic civil liberties to their populations. On the other hand, there are signs of a swing back toward Communist totalitarian ideas in some states, such as Venezuela, where the late Hugo Chávez's government displayed totalitarian tendencies (see the Country Focus).

A second form of totalitarianism might be labeled **theocratic totalitarianism**. Theocratic totalitarianism is found in states where political power is monopolized by a party, group, or individual that governs according to religious principles. The most common form of theocratic totalitarianism is based on Islam and is exemplified by states such as Iran and Saudi Arabia. These states limit freedom of political and religious expression with laws based on Islamic principles.

A third form of totalitarianism might be referred to as **tribal totalitarianism**. Tribal totalitarianism has arisen from time to time in African countries such as Zimbabwe, Tanzania, Uganda, and Kenya. The borders of most African states reflect the administrative boundaries drawn by the old European colonial powers rather than tribal realities. Consequently, the typical African country contains a number of tribes (e.g., in Kenya there are more than 40 tribes). Tribal totalitarianism occurs when a political party that represents the interests of a particular tribe (and not always the majority tribe) monopolizes power. In Kenya, for example, politicians from the Kikuyu tribe long dominated the political system.

A fourth major form of totalitarianism might be described as **right-wing totalitarianism.** Right-wing totalitarianism generally permits some individual economic freedom but restricts individual political freedom, frequently on the grounds that it would lead to the rise of communism. A common feature of many right-wing dictatorships is an overt hostility to socialist or Communist ideas. Many right-wing totalitarian governments are backed by the military, and in some cases the government may be made up of military officers. The fascist regimes that ruled Germany and Italy in the 1930s and 1940s were right-wing totalitarian states. Until the early 1980s, right-wing dictatorships, many of which were military dictatorships, were common throughout Latin America. They were also found in several Asian countries, particularly South Korea, Taiwan, Singapore, Indonesia, and the Philippines. Since the early 1980s, however, this form of government has been in retreat. Most Latin American countries are now genuine multiparty democracies. Similarly, South Korea, Taiwan, and the Philippines have all become functioning democracies, as has Indonesia.

ECONOMIC SYSTEMS

It should be clear from the previous section that political ideology and economic systems are connected. In countries where individual goals are given primacy over collective goals, we are more likely to find market-based economic systems. In contrast, in countries where collective goals are given preeminence, the state may have taken control over many enterprises; markets in such countries are likely to be restricted rather than free. We can identify three broad types of economic systems—a market economy, a command economy, and a mixed economy.

Market Economy

In the archetypal pure **market economy**, all productive activities are privately owned, as opposed to being owned by the state. The goods and services that a country produces are not planned by anyone. Production is determined by the interaction of supply and demand and signaled to producers through the price system. If demand for a product exceeds supply, prices will rise, signaling producers to produce more. If supply exceeds demand, prices will fall, signaling producers to produce less. In this system consumers are sovereign. The purchasing patterns of consumers, as signaled to producers through the mechanism of the price system, determine what is produced and in what quantity.

For a market to work in this manner, supply must not be restricted. A supply restriction occurs when a single firm monopolizes a market. In such circumstances, rather than increase output in response to increased demand, a monopolist might restrict output and let prices rise. This allows the monopolist to take a greater profit margin on each unit it sells. Although this is good for the monopolist, it is bad for the consumer, who has to pay higher prices. It also is probably bad for the welfare of society. Because a monopolist has no competitors, it has no incentive to search for ways to lower production costs. Rather, it can simply pass on cost increases to consumers in the form of higher prices. The net result is that the monopolist is likely to become increasingly inefficient, producing high-priced, low-quality goods, and society suffers as a consequence.

Given the dangers inherent in monopoly, the role of government in a market economy is to encourage vigorous free and fair competition between private producers. Governments do this by outlawing restrictive business practices designed to monopolize a market (antitrust laws serve this function in the United States). Private ownership also encourages vigorous competition and economic efficiency. Private ownership ensures that entrepreneurs have a right to the profits generated by their own efforts. This gives entrepreneurs an incentive to search for better ways of serving consumer needs. That may be through introducing new products, by developing more efficient production processes, by pursuing better marketing and after-sale service, or simply through managing their businesses more efficiently than their competitors. In turn, the constant improvement in product and process that results from such an incentive has been argued to have a major positive impact on economic growth and development.[8]

Command Economy

In a pure **command economy**, the government plans the goods and services that a country produces, the quantity in which they are produced, and the prices at which they are sold. Consistent with the collectivist ideology, the objective of a command economy is for government to allocate resources for "the good of society." In addition, in a pure command economy, all businesses are state-owned, the rationale being that the government can then direct them to make investments that are in the best interests of the nation as a whole rather than in the interests of private individuals. Historically, command economies were found in Communist countries where collectivist goals were given priority over individual goals. Since the demise of communism in the late 1980s, the number of command economies has fallen dramatically. Some elements of a command economy were also evident in a number of democratic nations led by socialist-inclined governments. France and India both experimented with extensive government planning and state ownership, although government planning has fallen into disfavor in both countries.

While the objective of a command economy is to mobilize economic resources for the public good, the opposite often seems to have occurred. In a command economy, state-owned enterprises have little incentive to control costs and be efficient, because they cannot go out of business. Also, the abolition of private ownership means there is no incentive for individuals to look for better ways to serve consumer needs; hence, dynamism and innovation are absent from command economies. Instead of growing and becoming more prosperous, such economies tend to stagnate.

Mixed Economy

Between market economies and command economies can be found mixed economies. In a mixed economy, certain sectors of the economy are left to private ownership and free market mechanisms, while other sectors have significant state ownership and government planning. Mixed economies were once common throughout much of the world, although they are becoming much less so. Until the 1980s, Great Britain, France, and Sweden were mixed economies, but extensive privatization has reduced state ownership of businesses in all three nations. A similar trend occurred in many other countries where there was once a large state-owned sector, such as Brazil, Italy, and India (although there are still state-owned enterprises in all of these nations).

In mixed economies, governments also tend to take into state ownership troubled firms whose continued operation is thought to be vital to national interests. For example, in 2008 and early 2009, the U.S. government took an 80 percent stake in AIG to stop that financial institution from collapsing, the theory being that if AIG did collapse, it would have very serious consequences for the entire financial system. The U.S. government usually prefers market-oriented solutions to economic problems, and in the AIG case the intention was to sell the institution back to private investors as soon as possible. The United States also took similar action with respect to a number of other troubled private enterprises, including Citigroup and General Motors. In all these cases, the government stake was seen as nothing more than a short-term action designed to stave off economic collapse by injecting capital into troubled enterprises. As soon as it was able to, the government sold these stakes. (In early 2010, for example, it sold its stake in Citigroup, for a profit; in late 2010, it sold some of its stake in GM to public investors.)

LEGAL SYSTEMS

The **legal system** of a country refers to the rules, or laws, that regulate behavior along with the processes by which the laws are enforced and through which redress for grievances is obtained. The legal system of a country is of immense importance to international business. A country's laws regulate business practice, define the manner in which business transactions are to be executed, and set down the rights and obligations of those involved in business transactions. The legal environments of countries differ in significant ways. As we shall see, differences in legal systems can affect the attractiveness of a country as an investment site or market.

Like the economic system of a country, the legal system is influenced by the prevailing political system (although it is also strongly influenced by historical tradition). The government of a country defines the legal framework within which firms do business, and often the laws that regulate business reflect the rulers' dominant political ideology. For example, collectivist-inclined totalitarian states tend to enact laws that severely restrict private enterprise, whereas the laws enacted by governments in democratic states where individualism is the dominant political philosophy tend to be pro-private enterprise and pro-consumer.

Here, we focus on several issues that illustrate how legal systems can vary—and how such variations can affect international business. First, we look at some basic differences in legal systems. Next we look at contract law. Third, we look at the laws governing property rights with particular reference to patents, copyrights, and trademarks. Then we discuss protection of intellectual property. Finally, we look at laws covering product safety and product liability.

Different Legal Systems

There are three main types of legal systems—or legal tradition—in use around the world: common law, civil law, and theocratic law.

Common Law

The common law system evolved in England over hundreds of years. It is now found in most of Great Britain's former colonies, including the United States. **Common law** is based on tradition, precedent, and custom. *Tradition* refers to a country's legal history, *precedent* to cases that have come before the courts in the past, and *custom* to the ways in which laws are applied in specific situations. When law courts interpret common law, they do so with regard to these characteristics. This gives a common law system a degree of flexibility that other systems lack. Judges in a common law system have the power to interpret the law so that it applies to the unique circumstances of an individual case. In turn, each new interpretation sets a precedent that may be followed in future cases. As new precedents arise, laws may be altered, clarified, or amended to deal with new situations.

Civil Law

A **civil law system** is based on a detailed set of laws organized into codes. When law courts interpret civil law, they do so with regard to these codes. More than 80 countries, including Germany, France, Japan, and Russia, operate with a civil law system. A civil law system tends to be less adversarial than a common law system, because the judges rely upon detailed legal codes rather than interpreting tradition, precedent, and custom. Judges under a civil law system have less flexibility than those under a common law system. Judges in a common law system have the power to interpret the law, whereas judges in a civil law system have the power only to apply the law.

Theocratic Law

A **theocratic law system** is one in which the law is based on religious teachings. Islamic law is the most widely practiced theocratic legal system in the modern world, although usage of both Hindu and Jewish law persisted into the twentieth century. Islamic law is primarily a moral rather than a commercial law and is intended to govern all aspects of life.[9] The foundation for Islamic law is the holy book of Islam, the Koran, along with the Sunnah, or decisions and sayings of the Prophet Muhammad, and the writings of Islamic scholars who have derived rules by analogy from the principles established in the Koran and the Sunnah. Because the Koran and Sunnah are holy documents, the basic foundations of Islamic law cannot be changed. However, in practice Islamic jurists and scholars are constantly debating the application of Islamic law to the modern world. In reality, many Muslim countries have legal systems that are a blend of Islamic law and a common or civil law system.

Although Islamic law is primarily concerned with moral behavior, it has been extended to cover certain commercial activities. An example is the payment or receipt of interest, which is considered usury and outlawed by the Koran. To the devout Muslim, acceptance of interest payments is seen as a grave sin; the giver and the taker are equally damned. This is not just a matter of theology; in several Islamic states it has also become a matter of law. In the 1990s, for example, Pakistan's Federal Shariat Court, the highest Islamic lawmaking body in the country, pronounced interest to be un-Islamic and therefore illegal and demanded that the government amend all financial laws accordingly. In 1999, Pakistan's Supreme Court ruled that Islamic banking methods should be used in the country after July 1, 2001.[10] By the late 2000s, some 500 Islamic financial institutions in the world collectively managed more than $500 billion in assets. In addition to Pakistan, Islamic financial institutions are found in many of the Gulf states, Egypt, and Malaysia.[11]

Differences In Contract Law

The difference between common law and civil law systems can be illustrated by the approach of each to contract law (remember, most theocratic legal systems also have elements of common or civil law). A **contract** is a document that specifies the conditions under which an exchange is to occur and details the rights and obligations of the parties involved. Some form of contract regulates many business transactions. **Contract law** is the body of law that governs contract enforcement. The parties to an agreement normally resort to contract law when one party feels the other has violated either the letter or the spirit of an agreement.

Because common law tends to be relatively ill specified, contracts drafted under a common law framework tend to be very detailed with all contingencies spelled out. In civil law systems, however, contracts tend to be much shorter and less specific because many of the issues are already covered in a civil code. Thus, it is more expensive to draw up contracts in a common law jurisdiction, and resolving contract disputes can be very adversarial in common law systems. But common law systems have the advantage of greater flexibility and allow judges to interpret a contract dispute in light of the prevailing situation. International businesses need to be sensitive to these differences; approaching a contract dispute in a state with a civil law system as if it had a common law system may backfire, and vice versa.

When contract disputes arise in international trade, there is always the question of which country's laws to apply. To resolve this issue, a number of countries, including the United States, have ratified the **United Nations Convention on Contracts for the International Sale of Goods (CIGS)**. The CIGS establishes a uniform set of rules governing certain aspects of the making and performance of everyday commercial contracts between sellers and buyers who have their places of business in different nations. By adopting the CIGS, a nation signals to other adopters that it will treat the convention's rules as part of its law. The CIGS applies automatically to all contracts for the sale of goods between different firms based in countries that have ratified the convention, unless the parties to the contract explicitly opt out. One problem with the CIGS, however, is that fewer than 70 nations have ratified the convention (the CIGS went into effect in 1988).[12] Many of the world's larger trading nations, including Japan and the United Kingdom, have not ratified the CIGS.

When firms do not wish to accept the CIGS, they often opt for arbitration by a recognized arbitration court to settle contract disputes. The most well known of these courts is the International Court of Arbitration of the International Chamber of Commerce in Paris, which handles more than 500 requests per year from more than 100 countries.[13]

Property Rights and Corruption

In a legal sense, the term *property* refers to a resource over which an individual or business holds a legal title, that is, a resource that it owns. Resources include land, buildings, equipment, capital, mineral rights, businesses, and intellectual property (ideas, which are protected by patents, copyrights, and trademarks). **Property rights** refer to the legal rights over the use to which a resource is put and over the use made of any income that may be derived from that resource.[14] Countries differ in the extent to which their legal systems define and protect property rights. Almost all countries now have laws on their books that protect property rights. Even China, still nominally a Communist state despite its booming market economy, finally enacted a law to protect the rights of private property holders in 2007 (the law gives individuals the same legal protection for their property as the state has).[15] However, in many countries, these laws are not enforced by the authorities, and property rights are violated. Property rights can be violated in two ways—through private action and through public action.

Private Action

In terms of violating property rights, **private action** refers to theft, piracy, blackmail, and the like by private individuals or groups. Although theft occurs in all countries, a weak legal system allows a much higher level of criminal action. For example, in Russia in the chaotic period following the collapse of communism, an outdated legal system, coupled with a weak police force and judicial system, offered both domestic and foreign businesses scant protection from blackmail by the "Russian Mafia." Successful business owners in Russia often had to pay "protection money" to the Mafia or face violent retribution, including bombings and assassinations (about 500 contract killings of businessmen occurred per year in the 1990s).[16]

Russia is not alone in having Mafia problems (and the situation in Russia has improved significantly since the 1990s). The Mafia has a long history in the United States (Chicago in the 1930s was similar to Moscow in the 1990s). In Japan, the local version of the Mafia, known as the *yakuza,* runs protection rackets, particularly in the food and entertainment industries.[17] However, there was a big difference between the magnitude of such activity in Russia in the 1990s and its limited impact in Japan and the United States. The difference arose because the legal enforcement apparatus, such as the police and court system, was weak in Russia following the collapse of communism. Many other countries from time to time have had problems similar to or even greater than those experienced by Russia.

Public Action and Corruption

Public action to violate property rights occurs when public officials, such as politicians and government bureaucrats, extort income, resources, or the property itself from property holders. This can be done through legal mechanisms such as levying excessive taxation, requiring expensive licenses or permits from property holders, taking assets into state ownership without compensating the owners, or redistributing assets without compensating the prior owners. It can also be done through illegal means, or corruption, by demanding bribes from businesses in return for the rights to operate in a country, industry, or location.[18]

Corruption has been well documented in every society, from the banks of the Congo River to the palace of the Dutch royal family, from Japanese politicians to Brazilian bankers, and from Indonesian government officials to the New York City Police Department. The government of the late Ferdinand Marcos in the Philippines was famous for demanding bribes from foreign businesses wishing to set up operations in that country. The same was true of government officials in Indonesia under the rule of former president Suharto. No society is immune to corruption. However, there are systematic differences in the extent of corruption. In some countries, the rule of law minimizes corruption. Corruption is seen and treated as illegal, and when discovered, violators are punished by the full force of the law. In other countries, the rule of law is weak and corruption by bureaucrats and politicians is rife. Corruption is so endemic in some countries that politicians and bureaucrats regard it as a perk of office and openly flout laws against corruption.

According to Transparency International, an independent nonprofit organization dedicated to exposing and fighting corruption, businesses and individuals spend some $400 billion a year worldwide on bribes related to government procurement contracts alone.[19] Transparency International has also measured the level of corruption among public officials in different countries.[20] As can be seen in Figure 2.1, the organization rated countries such as Finland and New Zealand as clean; it rated others, such as Russia, India, and Indonesia, as corrupt. Somalia ranked last out of all 174 countries in the survey (the country is often described as a "failed state").

Economic evidence suggests that high levels of corruption significantly reduce the foreign direct investment, level of international trade, and economic growth rate in a country.[21] By siphoning off profits, corrupt politicians and bureaucrats reduce the returns to business investment and, hence, reduce the incentive of both domestic and foreign businesses to invest in that country. The lower level of investment that results hurts economic growth. Thus, we would expect countries with high levels of corruption such as Indonesia, Nigeria, and Russia to have a much lower rate of economic growth than might otherwise have been the case. A detailed example of the negative effect that corruption can have on economic progress is given in the accompanying Country Focus, which looks at the impact of corruption on economic growth in Nigeria.

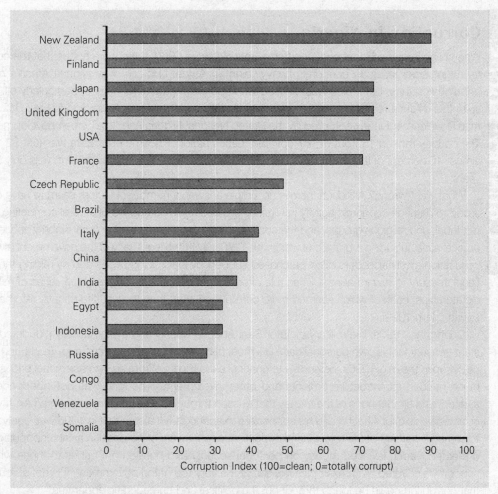

Figure 2.1 *Rankings of Corruption by Country, 2012*

Source: Constructed by the author from raw data in Transparency International, *Corruption Perceptions Index 2012,* 2012.

Foreign Corrupt Practices Act

In the 1970s, the United States passed the **Foreign Corrupt Practices Act** following revelations that U.S. companies had bribed government officials in foreign countries in an attempt to win lucrative contracts. This law makes it illegal to bribe a foreign government official to obtain or maintain business over which that foreign official has authority, and it requires all publicly traded companies (whether or not they are involved in international trade) to keep detailed records that would reveal whether a violation of the act has occurred. In 2012 evidence emerged that in its eagerness to expand in Mexico, Walmart may have run afoul of the Foreign Corrupt Practices Act (for details, see the next Management Focus feature).

In 1997 trade and finance ministers from the member states of the Organization for Economic Cooperation and Development (OECD), an association of the world's 34 most powerful economies, adopted the Convention on Combating Bribery of Foreign Public Officials in International Business

Corruption in Nigeria

When Nigeria gained independence from Great Britain in 1960, there were hopes that the country might emerge as an economic heavyweight in Africa. Not only was Nigeria Africa's most populous country, but it also was blessed with abundant natural resources, particularly oil. Despite this, Nigeria remains one of the poorest countries in the world. According to the 2012 Human Development Index compiled by the United Nations, Nigeria had "low human development." The country ranked 153 out of 187 covered. Gross national income per capita was just $2,102; almost 40 percent of the adult population was illiterate; and life expectancy at birth was only 52.3 years.

What went wrong? Although there is no simple answer, a number of factors seem to have conspired to damage economic activity in Nigeria. The country is composed of several competing ethnic, tribal, and religious groups, and the conflict among them has limited political stability and led to political strife, including a brutal civil war in the 1970s. With the legitimacy of the government always in question, political leaders often purchased support by legitimizing bribes and by raiding the national treasury to reward allies. Civilian rule after independence was followed by a series of military dictatorships, each of which seemed more corrupt and inept than the last (the country returned to civilian rule in 1999).

During the 1990s, the military dictator Sani Abacha openly and systematically plundered the state treasury for his own personal gain. His most blatant scam was the Petroleum Trust Fund that he set up in the mid-1990s, ostensibly to channel extra revenue from an increase in fuel prices into much-needed infrastructure projects and other investments. The fund was not independently audited, and almost none of the money that passed through it was properly accounted for. It was, in fact, a vehicle for Abacha and his supporters to spend at will a sum that in 1996 was equivalent to some 25 percent of the total federal budget. Abacha, aware of his position as an unpopular and unelected leader, lavished money on personal security and handed out bribes to those whose support he coveted. With examples like this at the very top of the government, it is not surprising that corruption could be found throughout the political and bureaucratic apparatus.

Has the situation in Nigeria improved since the country returned to civilian rule in 1999? In 2003, Olusegun Obasanjo was elected president on a platform that included a promise to fight corruption. By some accounts, progress has been seen. His anticorruption chief, Nuhu Ribadu, claimed that whereas 70 percent of the country's oil revenues were being stolen or wasted in 2002, by the mid-2000s the figure was "only" 40 percent. But in its most recent survey (2012), Transparency International still ranked Nigeria 139 out of 174, suggesting that the country still has a long way to go.[22]

Transactions.[24] The convention obliges member states to make the bribery of foreign public officials a criminal offense.

Both the U.S. law and OECD convention include language that allows exceptions known as facilitating or expediting payments (also called *grease payments* or *speed money*), the purpose of which is to expedite or to secure the performance of a routine governmental action.[25] For example, they allow small payments made to speed up the issuance of permits or licenses, process paperwork, or just get vegetables off the

Did Walmart Violate the Foreign Corrupt Practices Act?

In the early 2000s Walmart wanted to build a new store in San Juan Teotihuacan, Mexico, barely a mile from ancient pyramids that drew tourists from around the world. The owner of the land was happy to sell to Walmart, but one thing stood in the way of a deal—the city's new zoning laws. These prohibited commercial development in the historic area. Not to be denied, executives at the headquarters of Walmart de Mexico found a way around the problem; they paid a $52,000 bribe to a local official to redraw the zoning area so that the property Walmart wanted to purchase was placed *outside* the commercial-free zone. Walmart then went ahead and built the store, despite vigorous local opposition, opening it in late 2004.

A former lawyer for Walmart de Mexico subsequently contacted Walmart executives at the company's corporate headquarters in Bentonville, Arkansas. He told them that Walmart de Mexico routinely resorted to bribery, citing the altered zoning map as just one example. Alarmed, executives at Walmart started their own investigation. Faced with growing evidence of corruption in Mexico, top Walmart executives decided to engage in damage control, rather than coming clean. Walmart's top lawyer shipped the case files back to Mexico and handed responsibility for the investigation over to the general council of Walmart de Mexico. This was an interesting choice, since the very same general council was alleged to have authorized bribes. The general council quickly exonerated fellow Mexican executives, and the internal investigation was closed in 2006.

For several years nothing more happened; then in April 2012 *The New York Times* published an article detailing bribery by Walmart. *The Times* cited the changed zoning map and several other examples of bribery by Walmart. For example, eight bribes totaling $341,000 enabled Walmart to build a Sam's Club in one of Mexico City's most densely populated neighborhoods without a construction license, or an environmental permit, or an urban impact assessment, or even a traffic permit. Similarly, thanks to nine bribe payments totaling $765,000, Walmart built a vast refrigerated distribution center in an environmentally fragile flood basin north of Mexico City, in an area where electricity was so scarce that many smaller developers were turned away.

Walmart responded to *The New York Times* article by ramping up a second internal investigation into bribery that it had initiated in 2011. As of late 2012, there were reportedly more than 300 outside lawyers working on the investigation, and it had cost over $100 million in fees. In addition, the U.S. Department of Justice and the Securities and Exchange Commission both announced that they had started investigations into Walmart's practices. In November 2012, Walmart reported that its own investigation into violations had extended beyond Mexico to include China and India. Among other things, they were looking into the allegations by *The Times* that top executives at Walmart, including former CEO Lee Scott Jr., had deliberately squashed earlier investigations.[23]

dock and on their way to market. The explanation for this exception to general antibribery provisions is that while grease payments are, technically, bribes, they are distinguishable from (and, apparently, less offensive than) bribes used to obtain or maintain business because they merely facilitate performance of duties that the recipients are already obligated to perform.

The Protection of Intellectual Property

Intellectual property refers to property that is the product of intellectual activity, such as computer software, a screenplay, a music score, or the chemical formula for a new drug. Patents, copyrights, and trademarks establish ownership rights over intellectual property. A **patent** grants the inventor of a new product or process exclusive rights for a defined period to the manufacture, use, or sale of that invention. **Copyrights** are the exclusive legal rights of authors, composers, playwrights, artists, and publishers to publish and disperse their work as they see fit. **Trademarks** are designs and names, officially registered, by which merchants or manufacturers designate and differentiate their products (e.g., Christian Dior clothes). In the high-technology "knowledge" economy of the twenty-first century, intellectual property has become an increasingly important source of economic value for businesses. Protecting intellectual property has also become increasingly problematic, particularly if it can be rendered in a digital form and then copied and distributed at very low cost via pirated DVDs or over the Internet (e.g., computer software, music, and video recordings).[26]

The philosophy behind intellectual property laws is to reward the originator of a new invention, book, musical record, clothes design, restaurant chain, and the like, for his or her idea and effort. Such laws stimulate innovation and creative work. They provide an incentive for people to search for novel ways of doing things, and they reward creativity. For example, consider innovation in the pharmaceutical industry. A patent will grant the inventor of a new drug a 20-year monopoly in production of that drug. This gives pharmaceutical firms an incentive to undertake the expensive, difficult, and time-consuming basic research required to generate new drugs (it can cost $800 million in R&D and take 12 years to get a new drug on the market). Without the guarantees provided by patents, companies would be unlikely to commit themselves to extensive basic research.[27]

The protection of intellectual property rights differs greatly from country to country. Although many countries have stringent intellectual property regulations on their books, the enforcement of these regulations has often been lax. This has been the case even among many of the 185 countries that are now members of the **World Intellectual Property Organization**, all of which have signed international treaties designed to protect intellectual property, including the oldest such treaty, the **Paris Convention for the Protection of Industrial Property,** which dates to 1883 and has been signed by some 174 nations. Weak enforcement encourages the piracy (theft) of intellectual property. China and Thailand have recently been among the worst offenders in Asia. Pirated computer software is widely available in China. Similarly, the streets of Bangkok, Thailand's capital, are lined with stands selling pirated copies of Rolex watches, Levi's jeans, DVDs, and computer software.

The computer software industry is an example of an industry that suffers from lax enforcement of intellectual property rights. Estimates suggest that violations of intellectual property rights cost personal computer software firms revenues equal to $63 billion in 2011.[28] According to the Business Software Alliance, a software industry association, in 2011 some 42 percent of all software applications used in the world were pirated. One of the worst countries was China, where the piracy rate in 2011 ran at 77 percent and cost the industry more than $9.8 billion in lost sales, up from $444 million in 1995. The piracy rate in the United States was much lower at 19 percent; however, the value of sales lost was significant because of the size of the U.S. market, reaching an estimated $9.8 billion in 2011.[29]

International businesses have a number of possible responses to violations of their intellectual property. They can lobby their respective governments to push for international agreements to ensure that intellectual property rights are protected and that the law is enforced. Partly as a result of such actions, international laws are being strengthened. As we shall see in Chapter 7, the most recent world trade agreement, signed in 1994, for the first time extends the scope of the General Agreement on Tariffs

Starbucks Wins Key Trademark Case in China

MANAGEMENT FOCUS

Starbucks has big plans for China. It believes the fast-growing nation will become the company's second-largest market after the United States. Starbucks entered the country in 1999, and by the end of 2012 it had opened more than 400 stores. But in China, copycats of well-established Western brands are common. Starbucks faced competition from a look-alike, Shanghai Xing Ba Ke Coffee Shop, whose stores closely matched the Starbucks format, right down to a green-and-white Xing Ba Ke circular logo that mimics Starbucks' ubiquitous logo. The name also mimics the standard Chinese translation for Starbucks. *Xing* means "star," and *Ba Ke* sounds like "bucks."

In 2003, Starbucks decided to sue Xing Ba Ke in Chinese court for trademark violations. Xing Ba Ke's general manager responded by claiming it was just an accident that the logo and name were so similar to that of Starbucks. He claimed the right to use the logo and name because Xing Ba Ke had registered as a company in Shanghai in 1999, before Starbucks entered the city. "I hadn't heard of Starbucks at the time," claimed the manager, "so how could I imitate its brand and logo?"

However, in January 2006 a Shanghai court ruled that Starbucks had precedence, in part because it had registered its Chinese name in 1998. The court stated that Xing Ba Ke's use of the name and similar logo was "clearly malicious" and constituted improper competition. The court ordered Xing Ba Ke to stop using the name and to pay Starbucks $62,000 in compensation. While the money involved here may be small, the precedent is not. In a country where violation of trademarks has been common, the courts seem to be signaling a shift toward greater protection of intellectual property rights. This is perhaps not surprising, because foreign governments and the World Trade Organization have been pushing China hard recently to start respecting intellectual property rights.[31]

and Trade to cover intellectual property. Under the new agreement, known as the Trade-Related Aspects of Intellectual Property Rights (TRIPS), as of 1995 a council of the World Trade Organization is overseeing enforcement of much stricter intellectual property regulations. These regulations oblige WTO members to grant and enforce patents lasting at least 20 years and copyrights lasting 50 years after the death of the author. Rich countries had to comply with the rules within a year. Poor countries, in which such protection generally was much weaker, had five years of grace, and the very poorest have 10 years.[30] (For further details of the TRIPS agreement, see Chapter 7.)

In addition to lobbying governments, firms can file lawsuits on their own behalf. For example, Starbucks won a landmark trademark copyright case in China against a copycat that signaled a change in the approach in China (see the accompanying Management Focus for details). Firms may also choose to stay out of countries where intellectual property laws are lax, rather than risk having their ideas stolen by local entrepreneurs. Firms also need to be on the alert to ensure that pirated copies of their products produced in countries with weak intellectual property laws don't turn up in their home market or in third countries. U.S. computer software giant Microsoft, for example, discovered that pirated Microsoft software, produced illegally in Thailand, was being sold worldwide as the real thing.

Product Safety and Product Liability

Product safety laws set certain safety standards to which a product must adhere. **Product liability** involves holding a firm and its officers responsible when a product causes injury, death, or damage. Product liability can be much greater if a product does not conform to required safety standards. Both civil and criminal product liability laws exist. Civil laws call for payment and monetary damages. Criminal liability laws result in fines or imprisonment. Both civil and criminal liability laws are probably more extensive in the United States than in any other country, although many other Western nations also have comprehensive liability laws. Liability laws are typically least extensive in less developed nations. A boom in product liability suits and awards in the United States resulted in a dramatic increase in the cost of liability insurance. Many business executives argue that the high costs of liability insurance make American businesses less competitive in the global marketplace.

In addition to the competitiveness issue, country differences in product safety and liability laws raise an important ethical issue for firms doing business abroad. When product safety laws are tougher in a firm's home country than in a foreign country or when liability laws are more lax, should a firm doing business in that foreign country follow the more relaxed local standards or should it adhere to the standards of its home country? While the ethical thing to do is undoubtedly to adhere to home-country standards, firms have been known to take advantage of lax safety and liability laws to do business in a manner that would not be allowed at home.

■ IMPLICATIONS FOR MANAGERS ▨▨▨▨ ▨LO2-4▨

The material discussed in this chapter has two broad implications for international business. First, the political, economic, and legal systems of a country raise important ethical issues that have implications for the practice of international business. For example, what ethical implications are associated with doing business in totalitarian countries where citizens are denied basic human rights, corruption is rampant, and bribes are necessary to gain permission to do business? Is it right to operate in such a setting? A full discussion of the ethical implications of country differences in political economy is reserved for Chapter 5, where we explore ethics in international business in much greater depth.

Second, the political, economic, and legal environments of a country clearly influence the attractiveness of that country as a market or investment site. The benefits, costs, and risks associated with doing business in a country are a function of that country's political, economic, and legal systems. The overall attractiveness of a country as a market or investment site depends on balancing the likely long-term benefits of doing business in that country against the likely costs and risks. Because this chapter is the first of two dealing with issues of political economy, we will delay a detailed discussion of how political economy impacts the benefits, costs, and risks of doing business in different nation-states until the end of the next chapter, when we have a full grasp of all the relevant variables that are important for assessing benefits, costs, and risks.

For now, other things being equal, a nation with democratic political institutions, a market-based economic system, and strong legal system that protects property rights and limits corruption is clearly more attractive as a place in which to do business than a nation that lacks democratic institutions, where economic activity is heavily regulated by the state, and where corruption is rampant and the rule of law is not respected. On this basis, for example, Poland is a better place in which to do business than the Venezuela of Hugo Chávez (see the Country Focus on Venezuela and Closing Case on Poland). That being said, the reality is often more nuanced and complex. For example, China lacks democratic institutions, corruption is widespread, property rights are not always respected, and even though the country has embraced many market-based economic reforms, there are still large numbers of state-owned enterprises, yet many Western businesses feel that they must invest in China. They do so despite the risks because the market is large, the nation is moving toward a market-based system, economic growth is strong, legal protection of property rights has been improving, and in the not too distant future China may become the largest economy in the world. Thus, China is becoming increasingly attractive as a place in which to do business, and given the future growth trajectory, significant opportunities may be lost by not investing in the country. We will explore how changes in political economy impact the attractiveness of a nation as a place in which to do business in the next chapter.

Chapter Summary

This chapter has reviewed how the political, economic, and legal systems of countries vary. The potential benefits, costs, and risks of doing business in a country are a function of its political, economic, and legal systems. The chapter made the following points:

1. Political systems can be assessed according to two dimensions: the degree to which they emphasize collectivism as opposed to individualism and the degree to which they are democratic or totalitarian.
2. Collectivism is an ideology that views the needs of society as being more important than the needs of the individual. Collectivism translates into an advocacy for state intervention in economic activity and, in the case of communism, a totalitarian dictatorship.
3. Individualism is an ideology that is built on an emphasis of the primacy of the individual's freedoms in the political, economic, and cultural realms. Individualism translates into an advocacy for democratic ideals and free market economics.
4. Democracy and totalitarianism are at different ends of the political spectrum. In a representative democracy, citizens periodically elect individuals to represent them, and political freedoms are guaranteed by a constitution. In a totalitarian state, political power is monopolized by a party, group, or individual, and basic political freedoms are denied to citizens of the state.
5. There are three broad types of economic systems: a market economy, a command economy, and a mixed economy. In a market economy, prices are free of controls, and private ownership is predominant. In a command economy, prices are set by central planners, productive assets are owned by the state, and private ownership is forbidden. A mixed economy has elements of both a market economy and a command economy.
6. Differences in the structure of law between countries can have important implications for the practice of international business. The degree to which property rights are protected can vary dramatically from country to country, as can product safety and product liability legislation and the nature of contract law.

Critical Thinking and Discussion Questions

1. Free market economies stimulate greater economic growth, whereas state-directed economies stifle growth. Discuss.

2. A democratic political system is an essential condition for sustained economic progress. Discuss.

3. What is the relationship between corruption in a country (i.e., government officials taking bribes) and economic growth? Is corruption always bad?

4. You are the CEO of a company that has to choose between making a $100 million investment in Russia or Poland. Both investments promise the same long-run return, so your choice is driven by risk considerations. Assess the various risks of doing business in each of these nations. Which investment would you favor and why?

5. Read the Country Focus on Venezuela under the leadership of Hugo Chávez; then answer the following questions:

   a. Under Chávez's leadership, what kind of economic system was put in place in Venezuela? How would you characterize the political system?

   b. How do you think that Chávez's unilateral changes to contracts with foreign oil companies will affect future investment by foreigners in Venezuela?

   c. How will the high level of public corruption in Venezuela affect future growth rates?

   d. Currently, Venezuela is benefiting from a boom in oil prices. What do you think might happen if oil prices retreat from their current high level?

   e. In your estimation, what is the long-run prognosis for the Venezuelan economy? Is this a country that is attractive to international businesses?

6. Read the Management Focus feature: Did Walmart violate the Foreign Corrupt Practices Act? What is your opinion? If you think it did, what do you think the consequences will be for Walmart?

Research Task ◯ globalEDGE | globaledge.msu.edu

National Differences in Political Economy

Use the globalEDGE website (globaledge.msu.edu) to complete the following exercises:

Exercise 1

The definition of words and political ideas can have different meanings in different contexts worldwide. In fact, the *Freedom in the World* survey published by Freedom House evaluates the state of political rights and civil liberties around the world. Provide a description of this survey and a ranking (in terms of "freedom") of the world's leaders and laggards. What factors are taken into consideration in this survey?

Exercise 2

As the chapter discusses, differences in political, economic, and legal systems have considerable impact on the benefits, costs, and risks of doing business in countries around the world. The *World Bank Doing Business indicators* measure the extent of business regulations in countries around the world. Compare the United States, France, Japan, Brazil, and Nigeria in terms of how easily contracts are enforced, how property can be registered, and how investors can be protected. Identify in which area you see the greatest variation from one country to the next.

Closing CASE

Poland's Economy

As the financial crisis of 2008 and 2009 unfolded, countries across Europe were hit hard. A notable exception was Poland, whose economy grew by 1.5 percent during 2009, while every other economy in the European Union contracted. Between 2010 and 2012 Poland's growth rate averaged 3.4 percent per annum, the best in Europe. How did Poland achieve this?

In 1989, Poland elected its first democratic government after more than four decades of Communist rule. Since then, like many other eastern European countries, Poland has embraced market-based economic policies, opened its markets to international trade and foreign investment, and privatized many state-owned businesses. In 2004, the country joined the European Union, giving it easy access to the large consumer markets of western Europe. All this helped transform Poland into a major exporter. Exports account for about 40 percent of gross domestic product (in contrast, they account for around 12 percent in the United States). As a consequence, between 1989 and 2010, Poland recorded the highest sustained growth in the region. Real GDP doubled over this period, compared to a 70 percent increase in neighboring Slovakia and 45 percent in the Czech Republic.

Poland's government has also been fiscally conservative, keeping public debt in check, not allowing it to expand during the recession as many other countries did. This led to investor confidence in the country. Consequently, there was no large outflow of funds during the 2008–2009 economic turmoil. This stands in stark contrast to what happened in the Baltic states, where investors pulled money out of those economies during 2008 and 2009, driving their currencies down, raising the cost of government debt, and precipitating a full-blown economic crisis that required the IMF and EU to step in with financial assistance.

Poland got lucky. A tight monetary squeeze in the early 2000s, which was designed to curb inflation and ease Poland's entry into the European Union, headed off the asset price bubble, particularly surging home prices that hurt so many other economies around the world. Ironically, the Polish government had been criticized for its tight monetary policy earlier in the decade, but in 2008 and 2009 it served the country well. Moreover, in 2009 Poland benefited from the economic stimulus in neighboring Germany, its largest trading partner. A scheme to boost demand for German automobile companies by giving cash grants to people who exchanged old cars for new ones (a "cash for clunkers" program) helped Poland because the country has several automobile plants and was selling many cars and components to Germany.

None of this is to say that Poland is a model state. The country still has substantial problems. Migrant workers returning from western Europe have swelled the ranks of the unemployed, which was over 12 percent at the end of 2012. The tax system is complex and archaic. A study by the World Bank put the Polish tax system at 151st out of the 183 countries it surveyed. Extensive regulations can still make it difficult to do business in Poland: The World Bank ranked Poland 62nd in ease of doing business. Even after 20 years, the transition from a socialist economy to a market-based system is still not complete, and many state-owned enterprises remain.

On the other hand, the Polish government has committed itself to changing much of this. Steps are being taken to simplify tax laws, reduce tax rates, and remove bureaucratic hurdles to doing business in the country. An example was the Entrepreneurship Law passed in March 2009, which dramatically reduced the number of health, labor, and tax controls that companies had to comply with, making it much easier to start a business in the country. Also, after a six-year standstill, Poland privatized state-owned enterprises that accounted for 0.6 percent of GDP in 2009 and those accounting for another 2.5 percent of GDP in 2010.[32]

Case Discussion Questions

1. How was Poland able to avoid the worst effects of the economic crisis that gripped most of Europe during 2008–2009?

2. What lessons can be derived from the Polish experience during 2008–2009?

3. From the perspective of international business, what is attractive about the Polish economy? What are the weaknesses and risks associated with doing business there?

4. Even though Poland has been committed to liberalizing its economy since the collapse of communism in 1989, significant vestiges of the old system still remain. Why do you think it has taken Poland so long to transform its economic, political, and legal system?

Endnotes

1. D. Hinshaw, "In an African Dynamo's Expansion, the Perils of Prosperity," *The Wall Street Journal,* December 30, 2011, p. A9; "Dangerously Hopeful," *The Economist,* January 2, 2010, p. 36; "Carats and Sticks," *The Economist,* March 3, 2010, p. 68; and "Rawlings: The Legacy," *BBC News,* December 1, 2000, http://news.bbc.co.uk/2/hi/africa/1050310.stm; and "Ghana GDP expands 2.1% in Q4 2012," Ghana Statistical Service, April 12, 2013.

2. As we shall see, there is not a strict one-to-one correspondence between political systems and economic systems. A. O. Hirschman, "The On-and-Off Again Connection between Political and Economic Progress," *American Economic Review* 84, no. 2 (1994), pp. 343–48.

3. For a discussion of the roots of collectivism and individualism, see H. W. Spiegel, *The Growth of Economic Thought* (Durham, NC: Duke University Press, 1991). A discussion of collectivism and individualism can be found in M. Friedman and R. Friedman, *Free to Choose* (London: Penguin Books, 1980).

4. For a classic summary of the tenets of Marxism, see A. Giddens, *Capitalism and Modern Social Theory* (Cambridge: Cambridge University Press, 1971).

5. A. Smith, *The Wealth of Nations, Vol. 1* (London: Penguin Book), p. 325.

6. D. Luhnow and P. Millard, "Chavez Plans to Take More Control of Oil away from Foreign Firms," *The Wall Street Journal,* April 24, 2006, p. A1; R. Gallego, "Chavez's Agenda Takes Shape," *The Wall Street Journal,* December 27, 2005, p. A12; "The Sickly Stench of Corruption: Venezuela," *The Economist,* April 1, 2006, p. 50; "Chavez Squeezes the Oil Firms," *The Economist,* November 12, 2005, p. 61; "Glimpsing the Bottom of the Barrel: Venezuela," *The Economist,* February 3, 2007, p. 51; "The Wind Goes Out of the Revolution—Defeat for Hugo Chavez," *The Economist,* December 8, 2007, pp. 30–32; "Oil Leak," *The Economist,* February 26, 2011, p. 43; "Medieval Policies," *The Economist,* August 8, 2011, p. 38; and "Now for the Reckoning," *The Economist,* May 5, 2013.

7. R. Wesson, *Modern Government—Democracy and Authoritarianism,* 2nd ed. (Englewood Cliffs, NJ: Prentice Hall, 1990).

8. For a detailed but accessible elaboration of this argument, see Friedman and Friedman, *Free to Choose.* Also see P. M. Romer, "The Origins of Endogenous Growth," *Journal of Economic Perspectives* 8, no. 1 (1994), pp. 2–32.

9. T. W. Lippman, *Understanding Islam* (New York: Meridian Books, 1995).

10. "Islam's Interest," *The Economist,* January 18, 1992, pp. 33–34.

11. M. El Qorchi, "Islamic Finance Gears Up," *Finance and Development,* December 2005, pp. 46–50; and S. Timewell, "Islamic Finance—Virtual Concept to Critical Mass," *The Banker,* March 1, 2008, pp. 10–16.

12. This information can be found on the UN's treaty website at http://www.uncitral.org/uncitral/en/uncitral_texts/sale_goods/1980CISG.html.

13. International Court of Arbitration, www.iccwbo.org/index_court.asp.

14. D. North, *Institutions, Institutional Change, and Economic Performance* (Cambridge, UK: Cambridge University Press, 1991).

15. "China's Next Revolution," *The Economist,* March 10, 2007, p. 9.

16. P. Klebnikov, "Russia's Robber Barons," *Forbes,* November 21, 1994, pp. 74–84; C. Mellow, "Russia: Making Cash from Chaos," *Fortune,* April 17, 1995, pp. 145–51; and "Mr Tatum Checks Out," *The Economist,* November 9, 1996, p. 78.

17. K. van Wolferen, *The Enigma of Japanese Power* (New York: Vintage Books, 1990), pp. 100–105.

18. P. Bardhan, "Corruption and Development: A Review of the Issues," *Journal of Economic Literature,* September 1997, pp. 1320–46.

19. Transparency International, "Global Corruption Report, 2009," www.transparency.org, 2009.

20. www.transparency.org.

21. J. Coolidge and S. Rose Ackerman, "High Level Rent Seeking and Corruption in African Regimes," World Bank policy research working paper no. 1780, June 1997; Murphy et al., "Why Is Rent Seeking So Costly to Growth?"; M. Habib and L. Zurawicki, "Corruption and Foreign Direct Investment," *Journal of International Business Studies* 33 (2002), pp. 291–307; J. E. Anderson and D. Marcouiller, "Insecurity and the Pattern of International Trade," *Review of Economics and Statistics* 84 (2002), pp. 342–52; T. S. Aidt, "Economic Analysis of Corruption: A Survey," *The Economic Journal* 113 (November 2003), pp. 632–53; and D. A. Houston, "Can Corruption Ever Improve an Economy?" *Cato Institute* 27 (2007), pp. 325–43.

22. "A Tale of Two Giants," *The Economist,* January 15, 2000, p. 5; J. Coolidge and S. Rose Ackerman, "High Level Rent Seeking and Corruption in African Regimes," World Bank policy research working paper no. 1780, June 1997; D. L. Bevan, P. Collier, and J. W. Gunning, *Nigeria and Indonesia: The Political Economy of Poverty, Equity and Growth* (Oxford: Oxford University Press, 1999); "Democracy and Its Discontents," *The Economist,* January 29, 2005, p. 55; A. Field, "Can Reform Save Nigeria?" *Journal of Commerce,* November 21, 2005, p. 1; "A Blacklist to Bolster Democracy," *The Economist,* February 17, 2007, p. 59; J. P. Luna, "Back on Track: Nigeria's Hard Path towards Reform," *Harvard International Review* 29, no. 3 (2007), p. 7; and Transparency International, *Corruption Perceptions Index, 2012.*

23. David Barstow, "Vast Mexican Bribery Case Hushed Up by Wal-Mart after Top Level Struggle," *The New York Times,* April 21, 2012; Stephanie Clifford and David Barstow, "Wal-Mart Inquiry Reflects Alarm on Corruption," *The New York Times,* November 15, 2012; and Nathan Vardi, "Why Justice Department Could Hit Wal-Mart Hard over Mexican Bribery Allegations," *Forbes,* April 22, 2012.

24. Details can be found at http://www.oecd.org/corruption/oecdantibriberyconvention.htm.

25. Dale Stackhouse and Kenneth Ungar, "The Foreign Corrupt Practices Act: Bribery, Corruption, Record Keeping and More," *Indiana Lawyer,* April 21, 1993.

26. For an interesting discussion of strategies for dealing with the low cost of copying and distributing digital information, see the chapter on rights management in C. Shapiro and H. R. Varian, *Information Rules* (Boston: Harvard Business School Press, 1999). Also see Charles W. L. Hill, "Digital Piracy," *Asian Pacific Journal of Management,* 2007, pp 9–25.

27. Douglass North has argued that the correct specification of intellectual property rights is one factor that lowers the cost of doing business and, thereby, stimulates economic growth and development. See North, *Institutions, Institutional Change, and Economic Performance.*

28. Business Software Alliance, "Ninth Annual BSA Global Software Piracy Study," May 2012, www.bsa.org.

29. Ibid.

30. "Trade Tripwires," *The Economist,* August 27, 1994, p. 61.

31. M. Dickie, "Starbucks Wins Case against Chinese Copycat," *Financial Times,* January 3, 2006, p. 1; "Starbucks: Chinese Court Backs Company over Trademark Infringement," *The Wall Street Journal,* January 2, 2006, p. A11; and "Starbucks Calls China Its Top Growth Focus," *The Wall Street Journal,* February 14, 2006, p. 1.

32. J. Rostowski, "The Secret of Poland's Success," *The Wall Street Journal,* February 1, 2010, p. 15; "Not Like the Neighbors," *The Economist,* April 25, 2009, p. 55; "Horse Power to Horsepower," *The Economist,* January 30, 2010, pp. 60–61; "Get a Move On," *The Economist,* January 8, 2011, p. 52: and J. Cienski, "Poland Faces Rising Unemployment as Slowdown Bites," *Financial Times,* December 10, 2012.

Chapter 3
Political Economy and Economic Development

LEARNING OBJECTIVES

After reading this chapter, you will be able to:

LO3-1 Explain what determines the level of economic development of a nation.

LO3-2 Identify the macro-political and economic changes occurring worldwide.

LO3-3 Describe how transition economies are moving toward market-based systems.

LO3-4 Explain the implications for management practice of national difference in political economy.

POLITICAL AND ECONOMIC REFORM IN MYANMAR (BURMA)

Opening Case

For decades the Southeast Asian nation of Myanmar was an international pariah. Ruled by a brutal military dictatorship since the 1960s, political dissent was not tolerated, the press was tightly controlled, and opposition parties were shut down. Much economic activity was placed in the hands of the state, which effectively meant the hands of the military elite, who siphoned off economic profits for their own benefit. Corruption was rampant. In the 1990s America and the European Union imposed sweeping economic sanctions on the country to punish the military junta for stealing elections and jailing opponents. The de facto leader of the country's democratic opposition movement, Nobel Peace Prize winner Aung San Suu Kyi, was repeatedly placed under house arrest from 1989 through 2010.

None of this was good for the country's economy. Despite having a wealth of natural resources, including timber, minerals, oil, and gas, the economy stagnated while its Southeast Asian neighbors flourished. By 2012, Myanmar's GDP per capita was $1,400. In neighboring Thailand it was $10,000 per capita. The economy was still largely rural, with 70 percent of the country's nearly 60 million people involved in agriculture. This compares to 8.6 percent in Thailand. Few people own cars or cell phones, and there are no major road or rail links between Myanmar and its neighbors—China, India, and Thailand.

In 2010, the military again won elections that were clearly rigged. Almost no one expected any changes, but the new president, Thein Sein, was to defy expectations. The government released hundreds of political prisoners, removed restrictions on the press, freed Aung San Suu Kyi, and allowed opposition parties to contest seats in a series of by-elections. When Aung San Suu Kyi won a by-election, thrashing her military-backed opponent, they let her take the seat, raising hopes that Myanmar was at last joining the modern world. In response, both America and the European Union began to lift their sanctions.

Thein Sein also started to initiate much-needed economic reforms. Even before the 2010 elections, the military had begun to quietly privatize state-owned enterprises, although many were placed in the hands of cronies of the regime. In 2012, Thein Sein stated that the government would continue to reduce its role in a wide range of sectors, including energy, forestry, health care, finance, and telecommunications. The government also abandoned the official fixed exchange rate for the Myanmar currency, the *kyat*, replacing it with a managed float. From 2001 to 2012 the official exchange rate for the kyat varied between 5.75 and 6.70 per U.S. dollar, while the black-market rate was between 750 and 1,335 per U.S. dollar. The official fixed exchange rate had effectively priced Myanmar's exports out of the world market, although it did benefit the military elite who were able to exchange their worthless kyat for valuable U.S. dollars on very favorable terms. Implemented in April 2012, the managed float valued the kyat at 818 per U.S. dollar. The dramatic fall in the value of the kyat is expected to stimulate demand for exports from Myanmar, and help the economy grow.

To further encourage economic growth, the government has signaled that it will now welcome foreign direct investment, and is encouraging foreign enterprises to enter into partnerships with domestic enterprises in its underdeveloped telecommunications sector. General Electric and IBM are among the companies stating that they may invest in the country. Land reforms are also under way.

Much clearly remains to be done. Observers predict that it will be decades before Myanmar catches up with its Southeast Asian neighbors. The next big test for the government of Thein Sein will occur in 2015, when general elections are scheduled to be held. If current trends hold, the military-backed government could be swept out of power, losing most of its parliamentary seats. It's an open question as to whether the military will allow this to happen. If it does, and power is passed on to the democratic opposition, Myanmar may finally emerge from its isolation.[1]

INTRODUCTION

In the previous chapter, we described how countries differ with regard to their political systems, economic systems, and legal systems. In this chapter, we build on this material to explain how these differences in political economy influence the level of economic development of a nation and, thus, how attractive it is as a place for doing business. We also look at how political economy is changing around the world and what the implications of this are for the future rate of economic development of nations and regions. The past three decades have seen a general move toward more democratic forms of government, market-based economic reforms, and adoption of legal systems that better enforce property rights. Taken together, these trends have helped foster greater economic development around the world and have created a more favorable environment for international business. In the final section of this chapter, we pull all this material together to explore how differences in political economy affect the benefits, costs, and risks of doing business in different nations.

The opening case, which looks at recent changes in Myanmar, highlights many of the issues that we discuss here. For 50 years Myanmar was run by military dictatorship that systematically plundered the country in the name of socialist ideology. The end result was that a country rich in natural resources, and located in one of the most economically dynamic regions of the world, became one of the poorest nations on the planet. Things are now shifting in Myanmar. Since 2011 the country has moved toward becoming a functioning democracy. The economy is also being liberalized to allow for greater free enterprise, state-owned businesses are being privatization, and foreign investment is now encouraged. If the evidence from a wide range of other countries is any guide, the long-term consequences of such reforms should include greater economic growth, rising living standards, and a more welcoming environment for international businesses.

DIFFERENCES IN ECONOMIC DEVELOPMENT

Different countries have dramatically different levels of economic development. One common measure of economic development is a country's **gross national income (GNI)** per head of population. GNI is regarded as a yardstick for the economic activity of a country; it measures the total annual income received by residents of a nation. Map 3.1 summarizes the GNI per capita of the world's nations in 2011. As can be seen, countries such as Japan, Sweden, Switzerland, the United States and Australia are

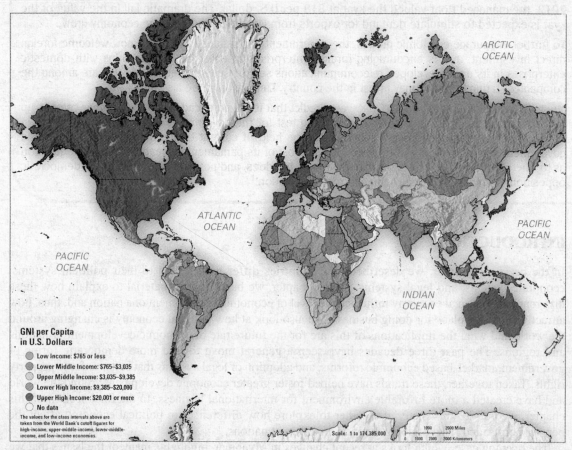

GNI per Capita in U.S. Dollars

- Low Income: $765 or less
- Lower Middle Income: $765–$3,035
- Upper Middle Income: $3,035–$9,385
- Lower High Income: $9,385–$20,000
- Upper High Income: $20,001 or more
- No data

The values for the class intervals above are taken from the World Bank's cutoff figures for high-income, upper-middle-income, lower-middle-income, and low-income economies.

Scale: 1 to 174,385,000

MAP 3.1 GNI per Capita, 2011

among the richest on this measure, whereas the large developing countries of China and India are significantly poorer. Japan, for example, had a 2011 GNI per capita of $44,900, but China achieved only $4,940 and India just $1,420.[2]

GNI per person figures can be misleading because they don't consider differences in the cost of living. For example, although the 2011 GNI per capita of Switzerland at $76,350 exceeded that of the United States, which was $48,620, the higher cost of living in Switzerland meant that U.S. citizens could actually afford almost as many goods and services as the average Swiss citizen. To account for differences in the cost of living, one can adjust GNI per capita by purchasing power. Referred to as a **purchasing power parity (PPP)** adjustment, it allows a more direct comparison of living standards in different countries. The base for the adjustment is the cost of living in the United States. The PPP for different countries is then adjusted (up or down) depending upon whether the cost of living is lower or higher than in the United States. For example, in 2011 the GNI per capita for China was $4,940, but the PPP per capita was $8,390, suggesting that the cost of living was lower in China and that $4,270 in China would buy as much as $8,390 in the United States. Table 3.1 gives the GNI per capita measured at PPP in 2011 for a selection of countries, along with their GNI per capita and their growth rate in gross domestic product (GDP) from 2002 to 2011. Map 3.2 summarizes the GNI PPP per capita in 2011 for the nations of the world.

TABLE 3.1   Economic Data for Select Countries

Country	GNI per Capita, 2011 ($)	GNI PPP per Capita, 2011 ($)	Annual Average GDP Growth Rate, 2002– 2011 (%)	Size of Economy GDP, 2011 ($ billions)
Brazil	11,420	10,720	3.78	2,477
China	4,940	8,390	10.59	7,319
Germany	44,230	40,190	1.16	3,601
India	1,420	3,620	7.73	1,873
Japan	44,900	34,670	0.67	5,867
Nigeria	1,280	2,290	6.88	244
Poland	12,380	20,260	4.23	514
Russia	10,650	21,210	4.84	1,858
Switzerland	76,340	52,530	1.81	659
United Kingdom	37,780	35,590	1.58	2,445
United States	48,620	48,620	1.63	14,991

Source: World Development Indicators Online, 2013.

As can be seen, there are striking differences in the standards of living among countries. Table 3.1 suggests the average Indian citizen can afford to consume only about 7.4 percent of the goods and services consumed by the average U.S. citizen on a PPP basis. Given this, one might conclude that despite having a population of 1.2 billion, India is unlikely to be a very lucrative market for the consumer

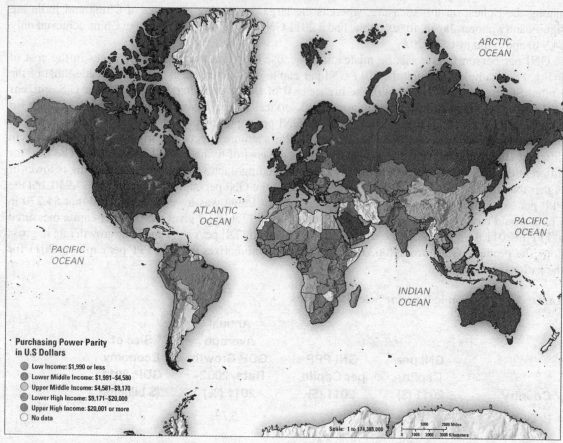

MAP 3.2 GNI PPP per Capita, 2011

products produced by many Western international businesses. However, this would be incorrect because India has a fairly wealthy middle class of close to 250 million people, despite its large number of poor citizens. In absolute terms, the Indian economy now rivals that of Russia and it is catching up with Brazil (see Table 3.1).

To complicate matters, in some countries the "official" figures do not tell the entire story. Large amounts of economic activity may be in the form of unrecorded cash transactions, or barter agreements. People engage in such transactions to avoid paying taxes, and although the share of total economic activity accounted for by such transactions may be small in developed economies such as the United States, in some countries (India being an example), they are reportedly very significant. Known as the *black economy,* estimates suggest that in India it may be around 50 percent of GDP, which implies that the Indian economy is half as big again as the figures reported in Table 3.1.[3]

The GNI and PPP data give a static picture of development. They tell us, for example, that China is much poorer than the United States, but they do not tell us if China is closing the gap. To assess this, we have to look at the economic growth rates achieved by countries. Table 3.1 gives the rate of growth in gross domestic product (GDP) achieved by a number of countries between 2002 and 2011. Map 3.3 summarizes the annual average percentage growth rate in GDP from 2002 to 2011. Although countries

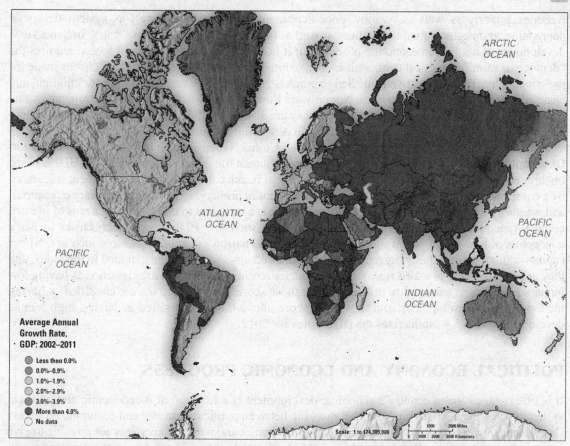

MAP 3.3   Average Annual Growth Rate in GDP, 2002-2011

such as China and India are currently relatively poor, their economies are already large in absolute terms and growing far more rapidly than those of many advanced nations. They are already huge markets for the products of international businesses. In 2010, China overtook Japan to become the second-largest economy in the world after the United States. Indeed, if both China and the United States maintain their current economic growth rates, China will become the world's largest economy sometime between 2020 and 2025. On current trends, India too will be among the largest economies in the world. Given that potential, many international businesses are trying to establish a strong presence in these markets.

Broader Conceptions of Development: Amartya Sen

The Nobel Prize–winning economist Amartya Sen has argued that development should be assessed less by material output measures such as GNI per capita and more by the capabilities and opportunities that people enjoy.[4] According to Sen, development should be seen as a process of expanding the real freedoms that people experience. Hence, development requires the removal of major impediments to freedom: poverty as well as tyranny, poor economic opportunities as well as systematic social deprivation, and neglect of public facilities as well as the intolerance of repressive states. In Sen's view, development is not just an economic process, but it is a political one too, and to succeed requires the "democratization" of political communities to give citizens a voice in the important decisions made for the community. This perspective leads Sen to emphasize basic health care, especially for children, and basic education, especially for women. Not only are these factors desirable for their instrumental value in helping to achieve higher income levels, but they are also beneficial in their own right. People cannot develop their capabilities if they are chronically ill or woefully ignorant.

Sen's influential thesis has been picked up by the United Nations, which has developed the **Human Development Index (HDI)** to measure the quality of human life in different nations. The HDI is based on three measures: life expectancy at birth (a function of health care); educational attainment (measured by a combination of the adult literacy rate and enrollment in primary, secondary, and tertiary education); and whether average incomes, based on PPP estimates, are sufficient to meet the basic needs of life in a country (adequate food, shelter, and health care). As such, the HDI comes much closer to Sen's conception of how development should be measured than narrow economic measures such as GNI per capita—although Sen's thesis suggests that political freedoms should also be included in the index, and they are not. The HDI is scaled from 0 to 1. Countries scoring less than 0.5 are classified as having low human development (the quality of life is poor); those scoring from 0.5 to 0.8 are classified as having medium human development; and those that score above 0.8 are classified as having high human development. Map 3.4 summarizes the HDI scores for 2012.

POLITICAL ECONOMY AND ECONOMIC PROGRESS

It is often argued that a country's economic development is a function of its economic and political systems. What then is the nature of the relationship between political economy and economic progress? Despite the long debate over this question among academics and policymakers, it is not possible to give an unambiguous answer. However, it is possible to untangle the main threads of the arguments and make a few generalizations as to the nature of the relationship between political economy and economic progress.

Innovation and Entrepreneurship are the Engines of Growth

There is substantial agreement among economists that innovation and entrepreneurial activity are the engines of long-run economic growth.[5] Those who make this argument define **innovation** broadly to include not just new products but also new processes, new organizations, new management practices, and new strategies. Thus, the Toys "R" Us strategy of establishing large warehouse-style toy stores and then engaging in heavy advertising and price discounting to sell the merchandise can be classified as an innovation because it was the first company to pursue this strategy. Similarly, the development of mass-market online retailing by Amazon.com can be seen as an innovation. Innovation and entrepreneurial activity help increase economic activity by creating new products and markets that did not previously exist. Moreover, innovations in production and business processes lead to an increase in the productivity of labor and capital, which further boosts economic growth rates.[6]

Innovation is also seen as the product of entrepreneurial activity. Often, **entrepreneurs** first commercialize innovative new products and processes, and entrepreneurial activity provides much of

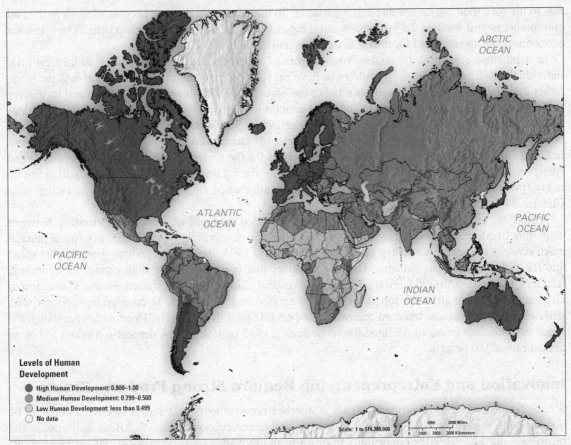

ARCTIC
OCEAN

ATLANTIC
OCEAN

PACIFIC
OCEAN

PACIFIC
OCEAN

INDIAN
OCEAN

**Levels of Human
Development**

● High Human Development: 0.800–1.00
● Medium Human Development: 0.799–0.500
○ Low Human Development: less than 0.499
○ No data

Scale: 1 to 174,385,000

0   1000   2000 Miles
0   1000   2000   3000 Kilometers

MAP 3.4   Human Development Index, 2012.

the dynamism in an economy. For example, the U.S. economy has benefited greatly from a high level of entrepreneurial activity, which has resulted in rapid innovation in products and process. Firms such as Google, Facebook, Amazon, Cisco Systems, Dell, Microsoft, and Oracle were all founded by entrepreneurial individuals to exploit new technology. All these firms created significant economic value and boosted productivity by helping commercialize innovations in products and processes. Thus, one can conclude that if a country's economy is to sustain long-run economic growth, the business environment must be conducive to the consistent production of product and process innovations and to entrepreneurial activity.

Innovation and Entrepreneurship Require a Market Economy

This leads logically to a further question: What is required for the business environment of a country to be conducive to innovation and entrepreneurial activity? Those who have considered this issue highlight the advantages of a market economy.[7] It has been argued that the economic freedom associated with a market economy creates greater incentives for innovation and entrepreneurship than either a planned or a mixed economy. In a market economy, any individual who has an innovative idea is free to try to make money out of that idea by starting a business (by engaging in entrepreneurial activity). Similarly, existing businesses are free to improve their operations through innovation. To the extent that they are successful, both individual entrepreneurs and established businesses can reap rewards in the form of high profits. Thus, market economies contain enormous incentives to develop innovations.

In a planned economy, the state owns all means of production. Consequently, entrepreneurial individuals have few economic incentives to develop valuable new innovations, because it is the state, rather than the individual, that captures most of the gains. The lack of economic freedom and incentives for innovation was probably a main factor in the economic stagnation of many former Communist states and led ultimately to their collapse at the end of the 1980s. Similar stagnation occurred in many mixed economies in those sectors where the state had a monopoly (such as coal mining and telecommunications in Great Britain). This stagnation provided the impetus for the widespread privatization of state-owned enterprises that we witnessed in many mixed economies during the mid-1980s and that is still going on today (privatization refers to the process of selling state-owned enterprises to private investors—see Chapter 2 for details).

A study of 102 countries over a 20-year period provided evidence of a strong relationship between economic freedom (as provided by a market economy) and economic growth.[8] The study found that the more economic freedom a country had between 1975 and 1995, the more economic growth it achieved and the richer its citizens became. The six countries that had persistently high ratings of economic freedom from 1975 to 1995 (Hong Kong, Switzerland, Singapore, the United States, Canada, and Germany) were also all in the top 10 in terms of economic growth rates. In contrast, no country with persistently low economic freedom achieved a respectable growth rate. In the 16 countries for which the index of economic freedom declined the most during 1975 to 1995, gross domestic product fell at an annual rate of 0.6 percent.

Innovation and Entrepreneurship Require Strong Property Rights

Strong legal protection of property rights is another requirement for a business environment to be conducive to innovation, entrepreneurial activity, and hence economic growth.[9] Both individuals and businesses must be given the opportunity to profit from innovative ideas. Without strong property rights protection, businesses and individuals run the risk that the profits from their innovative efforts will be expropriated, either by criminal elements or by the state. The state can expropriate the profits from innovation through legal means, such as excessive taxation, or through illegal means, such as demands from state bureaucrats for kickbacks in return for granting an individual or firm a license to do business in a certain area (i.e., corruption). According to the Nobel Prize–winning economist Douglass North, throughout history many governments have displayed a tendency to engage in such behavior. Inadequately enforced property rights reduce the incentives for innovation and entrepreneurial activity—because the profits from such activity are "stolen"—and hence reduce the rate of economic growth.

The influential Peruvian development economist Hernando de Soto has argued that much of the developing world will fail to reap the benefits of capitalism until property rights are better defined and protected.[10] De Soto's arguments are interesting because he says the key problem is not the risk of expropriation but the chronic inability of property owners to establish legal title to the property they own. As an example of the scale of the problem, he cites the situation in Haiti, where individuals must take 176 steps over 19 years to own land legally. Because most property in poor countries is informally "owned," the absence of legal proof of ownership means that property holders cannot convert their assets into capital, which could then be used to finance business ventures. Banks will not lend money to the poor to start businesses because the poor possess no proof that they own property, such as farmland, that can be used as collateral for a loan. By de Soto's calculations, the total value of real estate held by

Emerging Property Rights in China

On October 1, 2007, a new property law took effect in China, granting rural and urban landholders far more secure property rights. The law was a much-needed response to how China's economy has changed over the past 30 years as it transitions from a centrally planned system to a more dynamic market-based economy where two-thirds of economic activity is in the hands of private enterprises.

Although all land in China still technically belongs to the state—an ideological necessity in a country where the government still claims to be guided by Marxism—urban landholders had been granted 40- to 70-year leases to use the land, while rural farmers had 30-year leases. However, the lack of legal title meant that landholders were at the whim of the state. Large-scale appropriation of rural land for housing and factory construction had rendered millions of farmers landless. Many were given little or no compensation, and they drifted to the cities where they added to a growing underclass. In both urban and rural areas, property and land disputes had become a leading cause of social unrest. According to government sources, in 2006 there were about 23,000 "mass incidents" of social unrest in China, many related to disputes over property rights.

The 2007 law, which was 14 years in gestation due to a rearguard action fought by left-wing Communist Party activists who objected to it on ideological grounds, gives urban and rural land users the right to automatic renewal of their leases after the expiration of the 30- to 70-year terms. In addition, the law requires that land users be fairly compensated if the land is required for other purposes, and it gives individuals the same legal protection for their property as the state. Taken together with a 2004 change in China's constitution, which stated that private property "was not to be encroached upon," the new law significantly strengthens property rights in China.

Nevertheless, the law has its limitations; most notably it still falls short of giving peasants marketable ownership rights to the land they farm. If they could sell their land, tens of millions of underemployed farmers might find more productive work elsewhere. Those that stayed could acquire bigger land holdings that could be used more efficiently. Also, farmers might be able to use their land holdings as security against which they could borrow funds for investments to boost productivity.[13]

the poor in third-world and former Communist states amounted to more than $9.3 trillion in 2000. If those assets could be converted into capital, the result could be an economic revolution that would allow the poor to bootstrap their way out of poverty. Interestingly enough, the Chinese seem to have taken de Soto's arguments to heart. Despite still being nominally a Communist country, in October 2007 the government passed a law that gave private property owners the same rights as the state, which significantly improved the rights of urban and rural landowners to the land that they use (see the accompanying Country Focus).

The Required Political System

Much debate surrounds which kind of political system best achieves a functioning market economy with strong protection for property rights.[11] People in the West tend to associate a representative democracy with a market economic system, strong property rights protection, and economic progress. Building on this, we tend to argue that democracy is good for growth. However, some totalitarian regimes have fostered a market economy and strong property rights protection and have experienced rapid economic growth. Five of the fastest growing economies of the past 30 years—China, South Korea, Taiwan, Singapore, and Hong Kong—had one thing in common at the start of their economic growth: undemocratic governments. At the same time, countries with stable democratic governments, such as India, experienced sluggish economic growth for long periods. In 1992, Lee Kuan Yew, Singapore's leader for many years, told an audience, "I do not believe that democracy necessarily leads to development. I believe that a country needs to develop discipline more than democracy. The exuberance of democracy leads to undisciplined and disorderly conduct which is inimical to development."[12]

However, those who argue for the value of a totalitarian regime miss an important point: If dictators made countries rich, then much of Africa, Asia, and Latin America should have been growing rapidly during 1960 to 1990, and this was not the case. Only a totalitarian regime that is committed to a market system and strong protection of property rights is capable of promoting economic growth. Also, there is no guarantee that a dictatorship will continue to pursue such progressive policies. Dictators are rarely benevolent. Many are tempted to use the apparatus of the state to further their own private ends, violating property rights and stalling economic growth (as may have occurred in Myanmar—see the opening case). Given this, it seems likely that democratic regimes are far more conducive to long-term economic growth than are dictatorships, even benevolent ones. Only in a well-functioning, mature democracy are property rights truly secure.[14] Nor should we forget Amartya Sen's arguments reviewed earlier. Totalitarian states, by limiting human freedom, also suppress human development and therefore are detrimental to progress.

Economic Progress Begets Democracy

While it is possible to argue that democracy is not a necessary precondition for a free market economy in which property rights are protected, subsequent economic growth often leads to establishment of a democratic regime. Several of the fastest-growing Asian economies adopted more democratic governments during the past three decades, including South Korea and Taiwan. Thus, although democracy may not always be the cause of initial economic progress, it seems to be one consequence of that progress.

A strong belief that economic progress leads to adoption of a democratic regime underlies the fairly permissive attitude that many Western governments have adopted toward human rights violations in China. Although China has a totalitarian government in which human rights are violated, many Western countries have been hesitant to criticize the country too much for fear that this might hamper the country's march toward a free market system. The belief is that once China has a free market system, greater individual freedoms and democracy will follow. Whether this optimistic vision comes to pass remains to be seen.

Geography, Education, and Economic Development

While a country's political and economic systems are probably the big engine driving its rate of economic development, other factors are also important. One that has received attention is geography.[15] But the belief that geography can influence economic policy, and hence economic growth rates, goes back to Adam Smith. The influential economist Jeffrey Sachs argues throughout history, coastal states, with their long engagements in international trade, have been more supportive of market institutions than landlocked states, which have tended to organize themselves as hierarchical (and often militarised) societies. Mountainous states, as a result of physical isolation, have often neglected market-based trade. Temperate climes have generally supported higher densities of population and thus a more extensive division of labour than tropical regions.[16]

Sachs's point is that by virtue of favorable geography, certain societies are more likely to engage in trade than others and are thus more likely to be open to and develop market-based economic systems, which in turn promotes faster economic growth. He also argues that, irrespective of the economic and political institutions a country adopts, adverse geographic conditions—such as the high rate of disease, poor soils, and hostile climate that afflict many tropical countries—can have a negative impact on development. Together with colleagues at Harvard's Institute for International Development, Sachs tested for the impact of geography on a country's economic growth rate between 1965 and 1990. He found that landlocked countries grew more slowly than coastal economies and that being entirely landlocked reduced a country's growth rate by roughly 0.7 percent per year. He also found that tropical countries grew 1.3 percent more slowly each year than countries in the temperate zone.

Education emerges as another important determinant of economic development (a point that Amartya Sen emphasizes). The general assertion is that nations that invest more in education will have higher growth rates because an educated population is a more productive population. Anecdotal comparisons suggest this is true. In 1960, Pakistanis and South Koreans were on equal footing economically. However, just 30 percent of Pakistani children were enrolled in primary schools, while 94 percent of South Koreans were. By the mid-1980s, South Korea's GNP per person was three times that of Pakistan.[17] A survey of 14 statistical studies that looked at the relationship between a country's investment in education and its subsequent growth rates concluded investment in education did have a positive and statistically significant impact on a country's rate of economic growth.[18] Similarly, the work by Sachs discussed earlier suggests that investments in education help explain why some countries in Southeast Asia, such as Indonesia, Malaysia, and Singapore, have been able to overcome the disadvantages associated with their tropical geography and grow far more rapidly than tropical nations in Africa and Latin America.

STATES IN TRANSITION

The political economy of many of the world's nation-states has changed radically since the late 1980s. Two trends have been evident. First, during the late 1980s and early 1990s, a wave of democratic revolutions swept the world. Totalitarian governments collapsed and were replaced by democratically elected governments that were typically more committed to free market capitalism than their predecessors had been. Second, there has been a strong move away from centrally planned and mixed economies and toward a more free market economic model.

The Spread of Democracy

One notable development of the past 25 years has been the spread of democracy (and, by extension, the decline of totalitarianism). Map 3.5 reports on the extent of totalitarianism in the world as determined by Freedom House.[19] This map charts political freedom in 2012, grouping countries into three broad groupings: free, partly free, and not free. In "free" countries, citizens enjoy a high degree of political and civil freedoms. "Partly free" countries are characterized by some restrictions on political rights and

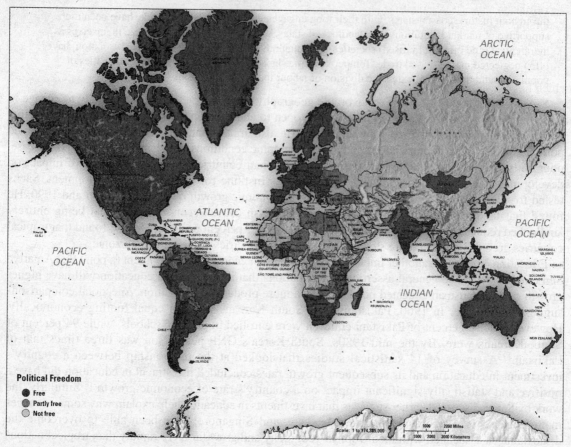

MAP 3.5 Political Freedom in 2012

Source: The Freedom House Survey Team, "Freedom in the World: 2013," www.freedomhouse.org.

civil liberties, often in the context of corruption, weak rule of law, ethnic strife, or civil war. In "not free" countries, the political process is tightly controlled and basic freedoms are denied.

Freedom House classified some 90 countries as free in 2012, accounting for about 46 percent of the world's nations and 43 percent of the global population. These countries respect a broad range of political rights. Another 58 countries accounting for 30 percent of the world's nations and 23 percent of the world's population were classified as partly free, while 47 countries representing approximately 24 percent of the world's nations and 34 percent of the global population were classified as not free. The number of democracies in the world has increased from 69 nations in 1987 to 117 in 2012, slightly below the 2006 total of 123. But not all democracies are free, according to Freedom House, because some democracies still restrict certain political and civil liberties. For example, Russia has consistently been rated "not free" since the early 2000s. According to Freedom House,

> Russia's step backwards into the Not Free category is the culmination of a growing trend . . . to concentrate political authority, harass and intimidate the media, and politicize the country's law-enforcement system.[20]

Similarly, Freedom House argues that democracy has been restricted in Venezuela under the leadership of the late Hugo Chávez.

Many of the newer democracies are to be found in eastern Europe and Latin America, although there also have been notable gains in Africa during this time, such as in South Africa and more recently Libya. Entrants into the ranks of the world's democracies during the last 25 years include Mexico, which held its first fully free and fair presidential election in 2000 after free and fair parliamentary and state elections in 1997 and 1998; Senegal, where free and fair presidential elections led to a peaceful transfer of power; Ukraine, where popular unrest following widespread ballot fraud in the 2004 presidential election resulted in a second election, the victory of a reform candidate, and a marked improvement in civil liberties (although sadly, the reform candidate also proved to be corrupt); and Libya, which held successful elections in 2012 after the removal by popular revolt of that country's long-standing dictator, Muammar Gaddafi.

Three main reasons account for the spread of democracy.[21] First, many totalitarian regimes failed to deliver economic progress to the vast bulk of their populations. The collapse of communism in eastern Europe, for example, was precipitated by the growing gulf between the vibrant and wealthy economies of the West and the stagnant economies of the Communist East. In looking for alternatives to the socialist model, the populations of these countries could not have failed to notice that most of the world's strongest economies were governed by representative democracies. Today, the economic success of many of the newer democracies, such as Poland and the Czech Republic in the former Communist bloc, the Philippines and Taiwan in Asia, and Chile in Latin America, has strengthened the case for democracy as a key component of successful economic advancement.

Second, new information and communication technologies, including satellite television, fax machines, desktop publishing, and, most important, the Internet, have reduced a state's ability to control access to uncensored information. These technologies have created new conduits for the spread of democratic ideals and information from free societies. Today, the Internet is allowing democratic ideals to penetrate closed societies as never before.[22] The demonstrations that led to the overthrow of the Egyptian government were organized by young people who utilized Facebook and Twitter to reach large numbers of people very quickly and coordinate their actions.

Third, in many countries economic advances have led to the emergence of increasingly prosperous middle and working classes that have pushed for democratic reforms. This was certainly a factor in the democratic transformation of South Korea. Entrepreneurs and other business leaders, eager to protect their property rights and ensure the dispassionate enforcement of contracts, are another force pressing for more accountable and open government.

Despite this, it would be naive to conclude that the global spread of democracy will continue unchallenged. Democracy is still rare in large parts of the world. In sub-Saharan Africa in 2012, only 11 countries were considered free, 18 were partly free, and 20 were not free. Among the post-Communist countries in eastern and central Europe and the former Soviet Union only 13 are classified as free (primarily in eastern Europe). And there is only 1 free state among the 18 nations of the Middle East and North Africa—although it remains to be seen how the wave of unrest that spread across the Middle East during 2012 and 2013 will change this.

The New World Order and Global Terrorism

The end of the Cold War and the "new world order" that followed the collapse of communism in eastern Europe and the former Soviet Union, taken together with the demise of many authoritarian regimes in Latin America, have given rise to intense speculation about the future shape of global geopolitics.

Author Francis Fukuyama has argued, "We may be witnessing . . . the end of history as such: that is, the end point of mankind's ideological evolution and the universalization of Western liberal democracy as the final form of human government."[23] Fukuyama goes on to say that the war of ideas may be at an end and that liberal democracy has triumphed.

Others question Fukuyama's vision of a more harmonious world dominated by a universal civilization characterized by democratic regimes and free market capitalism. In a controversial book, the late influential political scientist Samuel Huntington argued there is no "universal" civilization based on widespread acceptance of Western liberal democratic ideals.[24] Huntington maintained that while many societies may be modernizing—they are adopting the material paraphernalia of the modern world, from automobiles to Coca-Cola and MTV—they are not becoming more Western. On the contrary, Huntington theorized that modernization in non-Western societies can result in a retreat toward the traditional, such as the resurgence of Islam in many traditionally Muslim societies. He wrote,

> The Islamic resurgence is both a product of and an effort to come to grips with modernization. Its underlying causes are those generally responsible for indigenization trends in non-Western societies: urbanization, social mobilization, higher levels of literacy and education, intensified communication and media consumption, and expanded interaction with Western and other cultures. These developments undermine traditional village and clan ties and create alienation and an identity crisis. Islamist symbols, commitments, and beliefs meet these psychological needs, and Islamist welfare organizations, the social, cultural, and economic needs of Muslims caught in the process of modernization. Muslims feel a need to return to Islamic ideas, practices, and institutions to provide the compass and the motor of modernization.[25]

Thus, the rise of Islamic fundamentalism is portrayed as a response to the alienation produced by modernization.

In contrast to Fukuyama, Huntington envisioned a world split into different civilizations, each of which has its own value systems and ideology. Huntington predicted conflict between the West and Islam and between the West and China. While some commentators originally dismissed Huntington's thesis, in the aftermath of the terrorist attacks on the United States on September 11, 2001, Huntington's views received new attention.

If Huntington's views are even partly correct, they have important implications for international business. They suggest many countries may be increasingly difficult places in which to do business, either because they are shot through with violent conflicts or because they are part of a civilization that is in conflict with an enterprise's home country. Huntington's views are speculative and controversial. More likely than his predictions coming to pass is the evolution of a global political system that is positioned somewhere between Fukuyama's universal global civilization based on liberal democratic ideals and Huntington's vision of a fractured world. That would still be a world, however, in which geopolitical forces periodically limit the ability of business enterprises to operate in certain foreign countries.

In Huntington's thesis, global terrorism is a product of the tension between civilizations and the clash of value systems and ideology. Others point to terrorism's roots in long-standing conflicts that seem to defy political resolution—the Palestinian, Kashmir, and Northern Ireland conflicts being obvious examples. It should also be noted that a substantial amount of terrorist activity in some parts of the world, such as Colombia, has been interwoven with the illegal drug trade. As former U.S. Secretary of State Colin Powell has maintained, terrorism represents one of the major threats to world peace and economic progress in the twenty-first century.[26]

The Spread of Market-Based Systems

Paralleling the spread of democracy since the 1980s has been the transformation from centrally planned command economies to market-based economies. More than 30 countries that were in the former Soviet Union or the eastern European Communist bloc have changed their economic systems. A complete list of countries where change is now occurring also would include Asian states such as China and Vietnam, as well as African countries such as Angola, Ethiopia, and Mozambique.[27] There has been a similar shift away from a mixed economy. Many states in Asia, Latin America, and western Europe have sold state-owned businesses to private investors (privatization) and deregulated their economies to promote greater competition.

The rationale for economic transformation has been the same the world over. In general, command and mixed economies failed to deliver the kind of sustained economic performance that was achieved by countries adopting market-based systems, such as the United States, Switzerland, Hong Kong, and Taiwan. As a consequence, even more states have gravitated toward the market-based model. Map 3.6, based on data from the Heritage Foundation, a politically conservative U.S. research foundation, gives

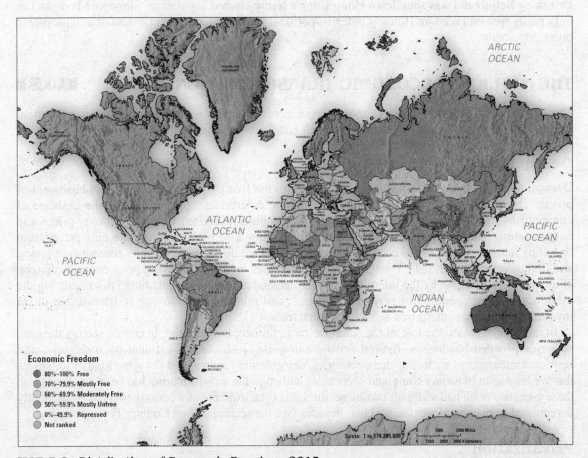

MAP 3.6 Distribution of Economic Freedom, 2013

Source: *2013 Index of Economic Freedom* (Washington, DC: Heritage Foundation, 2013). Reprinted with permission of The Heritage Foundation, www.heritage.org.

some idea of the degree to which the world has shifted toward market-based economic systems (given that the Heritage Foundation has a political agenda, its work should be viewed with caution). The Heritage Foundation's index of economic freedom is based on 10 indicators, including the extent to which the government intervenes in the economy, trade policy, the degree to which property rights are protected, foreign investment regulations, and taxation rules. A country can score between 100 (most free) and 0 (least free) on each of these indicators. The higher a country's average score across all 10 indicators, the more closely its economy represents the pure market model. According to the 2013 index, which is summarized in Map 3.6, the world's freest economies are (in rank order) Hong Kong, Singapore, Australia, New Zealand, Switzerland, Canada, Chile, Mauritius, Denmark, and the United States. Japan came in at 24, Mexico at 50, France at 62, Brazil at 100, India at 119, China at 136, and Russia at 139. The economies of Cuba, Iran, Venezuela, Zimbabwe, and North Korea are to be found near the bottom of the rankings.[28]

Economic freedom does not necessarily equate with political freedom, as detailed in Map 3.6. For example, the two top states in the Heritage Foundation index, Hong Kong and Singapore, cannot be classified as politically free. Hong Kong was reabsorbed into Communist China in 1997, and the first thing Beijing did was shut down Hong Kong's freely elected legislature. Singapore is ranked as only partly free on Freedom House's index of political freedom due to practices such as widespread press censorship.

THE NATURE OF ECONOMIC TRANSFORMATION ██ LO3-3

The shift toward a market-based economic system often entails a number of steps: deregulation, privatization, and creation of a legal system to safeguard property rights.[29]

Deregulation

Deregulation involves removing legal restrictions to the free play of markets, the establishment of private enterprises, and the manner in which private enterprises operate. Before the collapse of communism, the governments in most command economies exercised tight control over prices and output, setting both through detailed state planning. They also prohibited private enterprises from operating in most sectors of the economy, severely restricted direct investment by foreign enterprises, and limited international trade. Deregulation in these cases involved removing price controls, thereby allowing prices to be set by the interplay between demand and supply; abolishing laws regulating the establishment and operation of private enterprises; and relaxing or removing restrictions on direct investment by foreign enterprises and international trade.

In mixed economies, the role of the state was more limited; but here too, in certain sectors the state set prices, owned businesses, limited private enterprise, restricted investment by foreigners, and restricted international trade. For these countries, deregulation has involved the same kind of initiatives that we have seen in former command economies, although the transformation has been easier because these countries often had a vibrant private sector. India is an example of a country that has substantially deregulated its economy over the past two decades (see the accompanying Country Focus on India).

Privatization

Hand in hand with deregulation has come a sharp increase in privatization. Privatization, as we discussed in Chapter 2, transfers the ownership of state property into the hands of private individuals, frequently

India's Economic Transformation

After gaining independence from Britain in 1947, India adopted a democratic system of government. The economic system that developed in India after 1947 was a mixed economy characterized by a large number of state-owned enterprises, centralized planning, and subsidies. This system constrained the growth of the private sector. Private companies could expand only with government permission. It could take years to get permission to diversify into a new product. Much of heavy industry, such as auto, chemical, and steel production, was reserved for state-owned enterprises. Production quotas and high tariffs on imports also stunted the development of a healthy private sector, as did labor laws that made it difficult to fire employees.

By the early 1990s, it was clear this system was incapable of delivering the kind of economic progress that many Southeast Asian nations had started to enjoy. In 1994, India's economy was still smaller than Belgium's, despite having a population of 950 million. Its GDP per capita was a paltry $310, less than half the population could read, only 6 million had access to telephones, only 14 percent had access to clean sanitation; the World Bank estimated that some 40 percent of the world's desperately poor lived in India, and only 2.3 percent of the population had a household income in excess of $2,484.

The lack of progress led the government to embark on an ambitious economic reform program. Starting in 1991, much of the industrial licensing system was dismantled, and several areas once closed to the private sector were opened, including electricity generation, parts of the oil industry, steelmaking, air transport, and some areas of the telecommunications industry. Investment by foreign enterprises, formerly allowed only grudgingly and subject to arbitrary ceilings, was suddenly welcomed. Approval was made automatic for foreign equity stakes of up to 51 percent in an Indian enterprise, and 100 percent foreign ownership was allowed under certain circumstances. Raw materials and many industrial goods could be freely imported, and the maximum tariff that could be levied on imports was reduced from 400 percent to 65 percent. The top income tax rate was also reduced, and corporate tax fell from 57.5 percent to 46 percent in 1994, and then to 35 percent in 1997. The government also announced plans to start privatizing India's state-owned businesses, some 40 percent of which were losing money in the early 1990s.

Judged by some measures, the response to these economic reforms has been impressive. The economy expanded at an annual rate of about 6.3 percent from 1994 to 2004, and then accelerated to 7 to 8 percent annually during 2005–2012. Foreign investment, a key indicator of how attractive foreign companies thought the Indian economy was, jumped from $150 million in 1991 to $27.3 billion in 2012. Some economic sectors have done particularly well, such as the information technology sector where India has emerged as a vibrant global center for software development with sales of $100 billion in 2012, up from $150 million in 1990. In pharmaceuticals, too, Indian companies are emerging as credible players in the global marketplace, primarily by selling low-cost, generic versions of drugs that have come off patent in the developed world.

However, the country still has a long way to go. Attempts to further reduce import tariffs have been stalled by political opposition from employers, employees, and politicians, who fear that if barriers come down, a flood of inexpensive Chinese products will enter India. The privatization program continues to hit speed bumps—the latest in September 2003 when the Indian Supreme Court ruled that the government could not privatize two state-owned oil companies without explicit approval from the parliament. State-owned firms still account for 38 percent of national output in the nonfarm sector, yet India's private firms are 30 to 40 percent more productive than state-owned enterprises. There has also been strong resistance to reforming many of India's laws that make it difficult for private business to operate efficiently. For example, labor laws make it almost impossible for firms with more than 100 employees to fire workers, creating a disincentive for entrepreneurs to increase their enterprises beyond 100 employees. Other laws mandate that certain products can be manufactured only by small companies, effectively making it impossible for companies in these industries to attain the scale required to compete internationally.[36]

by the sale of state assets through an auction.[30] Privatization is seen as a way to stimulate gains in economic efficiency by giving new private owners a powerful incentive—the reward of greater profits—to search for increases in productivity, to enter new markets, and to exit losing ones.[31]

The privatization movement started in Great Britain in the early 1980s when then Prime Minister Margaret Thatcher started to sell state-owned assets such as the British telephone company, British Telecom (BT). In a pattern that has been repeated around the world, this sale was linked with the deregulation of the British telecommunications industry. By allowing other firms to compete head to head with BT, deregulation ensured that privatization did not simply replace a state-owned monopoly with a private monopoly. Since the 1980s, privatization has become a worldwide phenomenon. More than 8,000 acts of privatization were completed around the world between 1995 and 1999.[32] Some of the most dramatic privatization programs occurred in the economies of the former Soviet Union and its eastern European satellite states. In the Czech Republic, for example, three-quarters of all state-owned enterprises were privatized between 1989 and 1996, helping push the share of gross domestic product accounted for by the private sector up from 11 percent in 1989 to 60 percent in 1995.[33]

Despite this three-decade trend, large amounts of economic activity are still in the hands of state-owned enterprises in many nations. In China, for example, state-owned companies still dominate the banking, energy, telecom, health care, and technology sectors. Overall, they account for about 40 percent of the country's GDP. In a report released in early 2012, the World Bank cautioned China that unless it reformed these sectors—liberalizing them and privatizing many state-owned enterprises—the country runs the risk of experiencing a serious economic crisis.[34]

As privatization has proceeded, it has become clear that simply selling state-owned assets to private investors is not enough to guarantee economic growth. Studies of privatization in central Europe have shown that the process often fails to deliver predicted benefits if the newly privatized firms continue to receive subsidies from the state and if they are protected from foreign competition by barriers to international trade and foreign direct investment.[35] In such cases, the newly privatized firms are sheltered from competition and continue acting like state monopolies. When these circumstances prevail, the newly privatized entities often have little incentive to restructure their operations to become more efficient. For privatization to work, it must also be accompanied by a more general deregulation and opening of the economy. Thus, when Brazil decided to privatize the state-owned telephone monopoly, Telebrás Brazil, the government also split the company into four independent units that were to compete with each other and removed barriers to foreign direct investment in telecommunications services. This action ensured that the newly privatized entities would face significant competition and thus would have to improve their operating efficiency to survive.

Legal Systems

As noted in Chapter 2, a well-functioning market economy requires laws protecting private property rights and providing mechanisms for contract enforcement. Without a legal system that protects property rights, and without the machinery to enforce that system, the incentive to engage in economic activity can be reduced substantially by private and public entities, including organized crime, that expropriate the profits generated by the efforts of private-sector entrepreneurs. For example, when communism collapsed in eastern Europe, many countries lacked the legal structure required to protect property rights, all property having been held by the state. Although many nations have made big strides toward instituting the required system, it may be years before the legal system is functioning as smoothly as it does in the West. For example, in most eastern European nations, the title to urban and agricultural property is often uncertain because of incomplete and inaccurate records, multiple pledges on the same property, and unsettled claims resulting from demands for restitution from owners in the pre-Communist era. Also, although most countries have improved their commercial codes, institutional weaknesses still undermine contract enforcement. Court capacity is often inadequate, and procedures for resolving contract disputes out of court are often lacking or poorly developed.[37] Nevertheless, progress is being made. In 2004, for example, China amended its constitution to state that "private property was not to be encroached upon," and in 2007 it enacted a new law on property rights that gave property holders many of the same protections as those enjoyed by the state (see the earlier Country Focus on China's emerging property rights).[38]

IMPLICATIONS OF CHANGING POLITICAL ECONOMY

The global changes in political and economic systems discussed earlier have several implications for international business. The long-standing ideological conflict between collectivism and individualism that defined the twentieth century is less in evidence today. The West won the Cold War, and Western ideology is now widespread. Although command economies remain and totalitarian dictatorships can still be found around the world, the tide has been running in favor of free markets and democracy. It remains to be seen, however, whether the global financial crisis of 2008–2009, and the recession that followed, will lead to a retrenchment. Certainly many commentators have blamed the problems that led to this crisis on a lack of regulation, and some reassessment of Western political ideology seems likely.

Notwithstanding the crisis of 2008–2009, the trends of the past 25 years have enormous implications for business. For nearly 50 years, half of the world was off-limits to Western businesses. Now much of that has changed. Many of the national markets of eastern Europe, Latin America, Africa, and Asia may still be underdeveloped, but they are potentially enormous. With a population of more than 1.3 billion, the Chinese market alone is potentially bigger than that of the United States, the European Union, and Japan combined. Similarly, India, with about 1.2 billion people, is a potentially huge market. Latin America has another 600 million potential consumers. It is unlikely that China, Russia, Vietnam, or any of the other states now moving toward a market system will attain the living standards of the West soon. Nevertheless, the upside potential is so large that companies need to consider making inroads now. For example, if China and the United States continue to grow at the rates they did during 1996–2012, China will surpass the United States to become the world's largest national economy within the next 15 years.

Just as the potential gains are large, so are the risks. There is no guarantee that democracy will thrive in many of the world's newer democratic states, particularly if these states have to grapple with severe economic setbacks. Totalitarian dictatorships could return, although they are unlikely to be of the Communist variety. Although the bipolar world of the Cold War era has vanished, it may be replaced by a multipolar world dominated by a number of civilizations. In such a world, much of the economic promise inherent in the global shift toward market-based economic systems may stall in the face of conflicts between civilizations. While the long-term potential for economic gain from investment in the world's new market economies is large, the risks associated with any such investment are also substantial. It would be foolish to ignore these. The financial system in China, for example, is not transparent, and many suspect that Chinese banks hold a high proportion of nonperforming loans on their books. If true, these bad debts could trigger a significant financial crisis during the next decade in China, which would dramatically lower growth rates.

■ IMPLICATIONS FOR MANAGERS ▮ LO3-4

As noted in the previous chapter, the political, economic, and legal environments of a country clearly influence the attractiveness of that country as a market or investment site. In this chapter, we argued that countries with democratic regimes, market-based economic policies, and strong protection of property rights are more likely to attain high and sustained economic growth rates and are thus a more attractive location for international business. It follows that the benefits, costs, and risks associated with doing business in a country are a function of that country's political, economic, and legal systems. The overall attractiveness of a country as a market or investment site depends on balancing the likely long-term benefits of doing business in that country against the likely costs and risks. Here, we consider the determinants of benefits, costs, and risks.

BENEFITS

In the most general sense, the long-run monetary benefits of doing business in a country are a function of the size of the market, the present wealth (purchasing power) of consumers in that market, and the likely future wealth of consumers. While some markets are very large when measured by number of consumers (e.g., China and India), low living standards may imply limited purchasing power and therefore a relatively small market when measured in economic terms. International businesses need to be aware of this distinction, but they also need to keep in mind the likely future prospects of a country. In 1960, South Korea was viewed as just another impoverished third-world nation. By 2011 it had the world's 15th-largest economy. International firms that recognized South Korea's potential in 1960 and began to do business in that country may have reaped greater benefits than those that wrote off South Korea.

By identifying and investing early in a potential future economic star, international firms may build brand loyalty and gain experience in that country's business practices. These will pay back substantial dividends if that country achieves sustained high economic growth rates. In contrast, late entrants may find that they lack the brand loyalty and experience necessary to achieve a significant presence in the market. In the language of business strategy, early entrants into potential future economic stars may be able to reap substantial first-mover advantages, while late entrants may fall victim to late-mover disadvantages.[39] (**First-mover advantages** are the advantages that accrue to early entrants into a market. **Late-mover**

disadvantages are the handicaps that late entrants might suffer.) This kind of reasoning has been driving significant inward investment into China, which may become the world's first-largest economy by the mid-2020s if it continues growing at current rates (China is already the world's second-largest national economy). For more than two decades, China has been the largest recipient of foreign direct investment in the developing world as international businesses including General Motors, Volkswagen, Coca-Cola, and Unilever try to establish a sustainable advantage in this nation.

A country's economic system and property rights regime are reasonably good predictors of economic prospects. Countries with free market economies in which property rights are protected tend to achieve greater economic growth rates than command economies or economies where property rights are poorly protected. It follows that a country's economic system, property rights regime, and market size (in terms of population) probably constitute reasonably good indicators of the potential long-run benefits of doing business in a country. In contrast, countries where property rights are not well respected and where corruption is rampant tend to have lower levels of economic growth. One must be careful about generalizing too much from this, however, because both China and India have achieved high growth rates despite relatively weak property rights regimes and high levels of corruption. In both countries, the shift toward a market-based economic system has produced large gains despite weak property rights and endemic corruption.

Costs

A number of political, economic, and legal factors determine the costs of doing business in a country. With regard to political factors, a company may have to pay off politically powerful entities in a country before the government allows it to do business there. The need to pay what are essentially bribes is greater in closed totalitarian states than in open democratic societies where politicians are held accountable by the electorate (although this is not a hard-and-fast distinction). Whether a company should actually pay bribes in return for market access should be determined on the basis of the legal and ethical implications of such action. We discuss this consideration in Chapter 5, when we look closely at the issue of business ethics.

With regard to economic factors, one of the most important variables is the sophistication of a country's economy. It may be more costly to do business in relatively primitive or undeveloped economies because of the lack of infrastructure and supporting businesses. At the extreme, an international firm may have to provide its own infrastructure and supporting business, which obviously raises costs. When McDonald's decided to open its first restaurant in Moscow, it found that to serve food and drink indistinguishable from that served in McDonald's restaurants elsewhere, it had to vertically integrate backward to supply its own needs. The quality of Russian-grown potatoes and meat was too poor. Thus, to protect the quality of its product, McDonald's set up its own dairy farms, cattle ranches, vegetable plots, and food processing plants within Russia. This raised the cost of doing business in Russia, relative to the cost in more sophisticated economies where high-quality inputs could be purchased on the open market.

As for legal factors, it can be more costly to do business in a country where local laws and regulations set strict standards with regard to product safety, safety in the workplace, environmental pollution, and the like (because adhering to such regulations is costly). It can also be more costly to do business in a country like the United States, where the absence of a cap on damage awards has meant spiraling liability insurance rates. It can be more costly to do business in a country that lacks well-established laws for regulating business practice (as is the case in many of the former Communist nations). In the absence of a well-developed body of business contract law, international firms may find no satisfactory way to resolve contract disputes and, consequently, routinely face large losses from contract violations. Similarly, local laws that fail to adequately protect intellectual property can lead to the theft of an international business's intellectual property and lost income.

RISKS

As with costs, the risks of doing business in a country are determined by a number of political, economic, and legal factors. **Political risk** has been defined as the likelihood that political forces will cause drastic changes in a country's business environment that adversely affect the profit and other goals of a business enterprise.[40] So defined, political risk tends to be greater in countries experiencing social unrest and disorder or in countries where the underlying nature of a society increases the likelihood of social unrest. Social unrest typically finds expression in strikes, demonstrations, terrorism, and violent conflict. Such unrest is more likely to be found in countries that contain more than one ethnic nationality, in countries where competing ideologies are battling for political control, in countries where economic mismanagement has created high inflation and falling living standards, or in countries that straddle the "fault lines" between civilizations.

Social unrest can result in abrupt changes in government and government policy or, in some cases, in protracted civil strife. Such strife tends to have negative economic implications for the profit goals of business enterprises. For example, in the aftermath of the 1979 Islamic revolution in Iran, the Iranian assets of numerous U.S. companies were seized by the new Iranian government without compensation. Similarly, the violent disintegration of the Yugoslavian federation into warring states, including Bosnia, Croatia, and Serbia, precipitated a collapse in the local economies and in the profitability of investments in those countries.

More generally, a change in political regime can result in the enactment of laws that are less favorable to international business. In Venezuela, for example, the populist socialist politician Hugo Chávez held power from 1998 until his death in 2013. Chávez declared himself to be a "Fidelista," a follower of Cuba's Fidel Castro. He pledged to improve the lot of the poor in Venezuela through government intervention in private business and frequently railed against American imperialism, all of which is of concern to Western enterprises doing business in the country. Among other actions, he increased the royalties that foreign oil companies operating in Venezuela have to pay the government from 1 to 30 percent of sales.

Other risks may arise from a country's mismanagement of its economy. An **economic risk** can be defined as the likelihood that economic mismanagement will cause drastic changes in a country's business environment that hurt the profit and other goals of a particular business enterprise. Economic risks are not independent of political risk. Economic mismanagement may give rise to significant social unrest and hence political risk. Nevertheless, economic risks are worth emphasizing as a separate category because there is not always a one-to-one relationship between economic mismanagement and social unrest. One visible indicator of economic mismanagement tends to be a country's inflation rate. Another is the level of business and government debt in the country.

In Asian states such as Indonesia, Thailand, and South Korea, businesses increased their debt rapidly during the 1990s, often at the behest of the government, which was encouraging them to invest in industries deemed to be of "strategic importance" to the country. The result was overinvestment, with more industrial (factories) and commercial capacity (office space) being built than could be justified by demand conditions. Many of these investments turned out to be uneconomic. The borrowers failed to generate the profits necessary to service their debt payment obligations. In turn, the banks that had lent money to these businesses suddenly found that they had rapid increases in nonperforming loans on their books. Foreign investors, believing that many local companies and banks might go bankrupt, pulled their money out of these countries, selling local stock, bonds, and currency. This action precipitated the 1997–1998 financial crises in Southeast Asia. The crises included a precipitous decline in the value of Asian stock markets, which in some cases exceeded 70 percent; a similar collapse in the value of many Asian currencies against the U.S. dollar; an implosion of local demand; and a severe economic recession that will affect many Asian countries for years. In short, economic risks were rising throughout Southeast Asia during the 1990s.

Astute foreign businesses and investors limited their exposure in this part of the world. More naive businesses and investors lost their shirts.

On the legal front, risks arise when a country's legal system fails to provide adequate safeguards in the case of contract violations or to protect property rights. When legal safeguards are weak, firms are more likely to break contracts or steal intellectual property if they perceive it as being in their interests to do so. Thus, a **legal risk** can be defined as the likelihood that a trading partner will opportunistically break a contract or expropriate property rights. When legal risks in a country are high, an international business might hesitate entering into a long-term contract or joint-venture agreement with a firm in that country. For example, in the 1970s when the Indian government passed a law requiring all foreign investors to enter into joint ventures with Indian companies, U.S. companies such as IBM and Coca-Cola closed their investments in India. They believed that the Indian legal system did not provide adequate protection of intellectual property rights, creating the very real danger that their Indian partners might expropriate the intellectual property of the American companies—which for IBM and Coca-Cola amounted to the core of their competitive advantage.

OVERALL ATTRACTIVENESS

The overall attractiveness of a country as a potential market or investment site for an international business depends on balancing the benefits, costs, and risks associated with doing business in that country (see Figure 3.1). Generally, the costs and risks associated with doing business in a foreign country are typically lower in economically advanced and politically stable democratic nations and greater in less developed and politically unstable nations. The calculus is complicated, however, because the potential long-run benefits are dependent not only on a nation's current stage of economic development or political stability but also

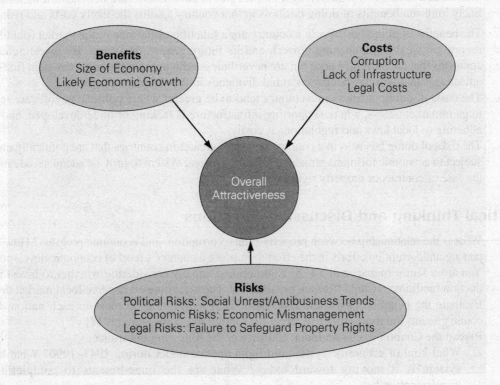

Figure 3.1   *Country Attractiveness*

on likely future economic growth rates. Economic growth appears to be a function of a free market system and a country's capacity for growth (which may be greater in less developed nations). This leads one to conclude that, other things being equal, the benefit–cost–risk trade-off is likely to be most favorable in politically stable developed and developing nations that have free market systems and no dramatic upsurge in either inflation rates or private-sector debt. It is likely to be least favorable in politically unstable developing nations that operate with a mixed or command economy or in developing nations where speculative financial bubbles have led to excess borrowing.

Chapter Summary

This chapter reviewed how the political, economic, and legal systems of countries vary. The potential benefits, costs, and risks of doing business in a country are a function of its political, economic, and legal systems. The chapter made the following points:

1. The rate of economic progress in a country seems to depend on the extent to which that country has a well-functioning market economy in which property rights are protected.

2. Many countries are now in a state of transition. There is a marked shift away from totalitarian governments and command or mixed economic systems and toward democratic political institutions and free market economic systems.

3. The attractiveness of a country as a market and/or investment site depends on balancing the likely long-run benefits of doing business in that country against the likely costs and risks.

4. The benefits of doing business in a country are a function of the size of the market (population), its present wealth (purchasing power), and its future growth prospects. By investing early in countries that are currently poor but are nevertheless growing rapidly, firms can gain first-mover advantages that will pay back substantial dividends in the future.

5. The costs of doing business in a country tend to be greater where political payoffs are required to gain market access, where supporting infrastructure is lacking or underdeveloped, and where adhering to local laws and regulations is costly.

6. The risks of doing business in a country tend to be greater in countries that are politically unstable, subject to economic mismanagement, and lacking a legal system to provide adequate safeguards in the case of contract or property rights violations.

Critical Thinking and Discussion Questions

1. What is the relationship between property rights, corruption, and economic progress? How important are anticorruption efforts in the effort to improve a country's level of economic development?

2. You are a senior manager in a U.S. automobile company considering whether to invest in production facilities in China, Russia, or Germany. These facilities will serve local market demand. Evaluate the benefits, costs, and risks associated with doing business in each nation. Which country seems the most attractive target for foreign direct investment? Why?

3. Reread the Country Focus on India, and answer the following questions:

    a. What kind of economic system did India operate under during 1947–1990? What kind of system is it moving toward today? What are the impediments to completing this transformation?

b. How might widespread public ownership of businesses and extensive government regulations have affected (*i*) the efficiency of state and private businesses and (*ii*) the rate of new business formation in India during the 1947–1990 time frame? How do you think these factors affected the rate of economic growth in India during this time frame?

c. How would privatization, deregulation, and the removal of barriers to foreign direct investment affect the efficiency of business, new business formation, and the rate of economic growth in India during the post-1990 time period?

d. India now has pockets of strengths in key high-technology industries such as software and pharmaceuticals. Why do you think India is developing strength in these areas? How might success in these industries help generate growth in the other sectors of the Indian economy?

e. Given what is now occurring in the Indian economy, do you think the country represents an attractive target for inward investment by foreign multinationals selling consumer products? Why?

Research Task ◯ globalEDGE globaledge.msu.edu

Political Economy and Economic Development

Use the globalEDGE website (globaledge.msu.edu) to complete the following exercises:

Exercise 1

Increased instability in the global marketplace can introduce unanticipated risks in a company's daily transactions. As such, your company must evaluate these *commercial transaction* risks for its foreign operations in Argentina, China, Indonesia, Poland, and South Africa. A risk analyst at your firm said that you could evaluate both the political and commercial risk of these countries simultaneously. Provide a commercial transaction risk overview of all six countries for top management. In your evaluation, indicate possible corrective measures in the countries with considerably high political and/or commercial risk.

Exercise 2

Managers at your firm are very concerned about the influence of terrorism on its long-term strategy. To counter this issue, the CEO has indicated you must identify the countries where *terrorism threat* and political risk are minimal. This will provide the basis for the development of future company facilities, which need to be built in all major continents in the world. Include recommendations on which countries in each continent would serve as a good candidate for your company to further analyze.

Closing **CASE**

Revolution in Egypt

With 83 million people, Egypt is the most populous Arab state. On the face of it, Egypt made significant economic progress during the 2000s. In 2004, the government of Hosni Mubarak enacted a series of economic reforms that included trade liberalization, cuts in import tariffs, tax cuts, deregulation, and changes in investment regulations that allowed for more foreign direct investment in the Egyptian economy. As a consequence, economic growth, which had been in the 2 to 4 percent range during the early 2000s, accelerated to around 7 percent a year. Exports almost tripled, from $9 billion in 2004 to more than $25 billion by 2010. Foreign direct investment increased from $4 billion in 2004 to $11 billion in 2008, while unemployment fell from 11 percent to 8 percent.

By 2008, Egypt seemed to be displaying many of the features of other emerging economies. On Cairo's outskirts, clusters of construction cranes could be seen where gleaming new offices were being built for companies such as Microsoft, Oracle, and Vodafone. Highways were being constructed, hypermarkets were opening their doors, and sales of private cars quadrupled between 2004 and 2008. Things seemed to be improving.

But appearances can be deceiving. Underneath the surface, Egypt had major economic and political problems. Inflation, long a concern, remained high at 12.8 percent. As the global economic crisis took hold in 2008–2009, Egypt saw many of its growth drivers slow. In 2008, tourism brought some $11 billion into the country, accounting for 8.5 percent of gross domestic product, but it fell sharply in 2009 and 2010. Remittances from Egyptian expatriates working overseas, which amounted to $8.5 billion in 2008, declined sharply as construction projects in the Gulf, where many of them worked, were cut back or shut down. Earnings from the Suez Canal, which stood at $5.2 billion in 2008, declined by 25 percent in 2009 as the volume of world shipping slumped in the wake of the global economic slowdown.

Moreover, Egypt remained a country with a tremendous gap between the rich and the poor. Some 44 percent of Egyptians are classified as poor or extremely poor; the average wage is less than $100 a month. Some 2.6 million people are so destitute that their entire income cannot cover their basic food needs.

The gap between rich and poor, when coupled with a sharp economic slowdown, became a toxic mix. Nominally a stable democracy with a secular government, Egypt was in fact an autocratic state. By 2011, President Hosni Mubarak had been in power for more than a quarter of a century. The government was highly corrupt. Mubarak and his family reportedly amassed personal fortunes amounting to billions of U.S. dollars, most of which were banked outside Egypt. Although elections were held, they were hardly free and fair. Opposition parties were kept in check by constant police harassment, their leaders often jailed on trumped-up charges.

Given all of this, it is perhaps not surprising that in January 2011 popular discontent spilled over into the streets. Led by technologically savvy young Egyptians—who harnessed the power of the Internet and social network media such as Facebook and Twitter to organize mass demonstrations—hundreds of thousands of Egyptians poured into Cairo's Tahrir Square and demanded the resignation of the Mubarak government. There they stayed, their numbers only growing over time. For weeks, Mubarak refused to step down, while the demonstrations gained momentum and Egypt's powerful military establishment stood on the sidelines. Foreign governments, including the Obama administration in the United States, long one of Egypt's most important Western allies, joined the chorus of voices calling for Mubarak to resign. In the end, his position became untenable, and he stepped down on February 11, 2011. The Egyptian military took the reins of power, vowing to do so for a short time while it organized a transition to democratic elections in the fall of 2011. In March 2011, Egyptians voted on a set of proposed constitutional amendments designed to pave the way for the elections in late 2011. This was the first time in six decades that Egyptians had been offered a free choice on any public issues.

Does this mean that Egypt is now on the road to becoming a democratic state with a vibrant economy? That is still far from clear. In mid 2012 moderate Islamists from the Muslim Brotherhood won the most seats in the country's first democratic election, and the Brotherhood candidate Mohamed Morsi won the presidential election. However, the Morsi government struggled. By early 2013 the economy was in deep trouble. Unemployment was as high as 20 percent, the Egyptian currency was steadily losing value on foreign exchange markets, and inflation was increasing again. Tourism, which used to account for 8–12 percent of GDP, evaporated. Foreign investment stalled, and the country's foreign reserves were falling fast. Meanwhile, the Morsi government failed to enact any meaningful economic reforms. It was unwilling to remove politically popular food and fuel subsidies totaling $20 billion a year, even though the country clearly cannot afford to pay for them. Government debt was increasing, and the annual budget deficit now accounted for over 12 percent of GDP. Many successful businesspeople have left the country, fearing reprisals for their role under the Mubarak regime. Court rulings overturned privatization deals from more than a decade ago, effectively moving several enterprises back into state hands. In June 2013 protestors again took to the streets, and with the backing of the still powerful Egyptian military, Morsi was removed from office in early July 2013. An interim government is now running the country.[41]

Case Discussion Questions

1. What were the underlying causes, economic and political, of the collapse of the Mubarak regime?
2. What do you think the Egyptian government needs to do in order to get the economy growing again and to attract foreign capital? What are the risks to the government of taking such actions?
3. What dangers do you see in the current trajectory of the Egyptian economy? What are the implications of these dangers for foreign companies considering doing business in Egypt? What do you think it would take to encourage more foreigners to visit, invest, and do business in Egypt? Would such inward investment be good for the Egyptian economy?

Vodafone Tax Woes in India

In December 2006, Hutchison Telecommunications International Ltd. (HTIL), a company incorporated in Cayman Islands and having its principal executive office at Hong Kong, held 66.9848 percent interest in an Indian company, Hutchison Essar Ltd. (HEL) through a maze of subsidiaries in British Virgin Islands, Cayman Islands and Mauritius (around 15 offshore companies) and through complicated 'option' agreements with a number of Indian companies. HEL along with its Indian subsidiaries held licenses for providing cellular services in 23 telecom circles in India. The balance 33.0152 percent interest in HEL was held by the Essar Group of Companies.[42]

Vodafone (through its Netherlands entity) entered into a share purchase agreement with HTIL in February 2007 to acquire the holdings of Hutchison Essar and claimed to have acquired the same through purchase of the solitary share of a Cayman Island company of the Hutch Group [viz., CGP Investments Holdings Ltd. (CGP)].

In this manner, the controlling interest of Hutchison Essar was held by HTIL, Hong Kong through the intermediary CGP. Since CGP was holding directly and indirectly 67 percent shares of Hutchison Essar (India), the above transaction resulted in transfer of shares and controlling interest of Hutchison Essar (India) from HTIL, Hong Kong to Vodafone International Holding, Netherland. The consideration for transfer was stated to be USD 11.1 billion.[43]

Tax Issues

The Indian Revenue Authorities alleged that Vodafone International Holdings B.V., Netherlands (Vodafone BV) had failed to withhold income tax on the payment of consideration made to HTIL and, hence, sought to assess tax in its hands as a taxpayer in default and issued a notice to Vodafone.[44]

Vodafone BV challenged the issue of this notice before the Bombay High Court and the case was decided against it. Vodafone filed a petition before the Supreme Court (SC); however, the same was dismissed by the SC and it directed the Revenue Authorities to decide whether it had jurisdiction to tax the transaction. It also said that if the issue was decided against Vodafone BV, Vodafone BV was entitled to challenge it as a question of law before the High Court. The Revenue Authorities by an order in May 2010 held that it had jurisdiction to treat Vodafone BV as an assessee in default u/s. 201 of the Income Tax Act, 1961 for failure to deduct tax at source.

This order was challenged by Vodafone BV before the Bombay High Court, by a writ petition. The key issue before the HC was whether the Indian Revenue Authorities have the jurisdiction to proceed against Vodafone BV and tax the transaction.

The High Court held that 'the very purpose of entering into agreements between the two foreigners is to acquire the controlling interest which one foreign company held in the Indian Company, by other foreign company. This being the dominant purpose of the transaction, the transaction would certainly be subject to municipal law of India, including the Indian Income Tax Act'. The Indian Law does not permit use of any "colorable" device by any taxpayer for perpetuating tax evasion in India. The High Court remarked that the present is a case of tax evasion and not tax avoidance.[45]

Thereafter, Vodafone approached the Supreme Court for stay of Mumbai High Court's decision. The Supreme Court on September 27th, 2010, ordered that Vodafone had to deposit a part of the amount in dispute, before its case is heard by the Court. Finally, the Supreme Court gave its verdict on January 01, 2012 and had decided the issue in favor of Vodafone.

GAAR and Vodafone Issue

General Anti-Avoidance Rule (GAAR) is a concept which generally empowers the Revenue Authorities in a country to deny the tax benefits of transactions or arrangements which do not have any commercial substance or consideration other than achieving tax benefit. Denial of tax benefits by the Revenue Authorities in different countries, often by disregarding the form of the transaction, has been a matter of conflict between the Revenue Authorities and the taxpayers.[46]

On August 12th, 2009, the Indian Government released the draft Direct Taxes Code Bill (DTC 2009) and discussion paper for public debate. Subsequently, a Revised Discussion Paper was released in June 2010. A formal bill to enact a law known as the Direct Taxes Code, 2010 (the Code) tabled in the Parliament on August 30th, 2010, was an outcome of this process. The Code is meant to replace the current Income Tax Act, 1961 (the Act). The Code is pending consideration before the Standing Committee of Finance and the report of the Committee is still awaited. The stated effective date of the Code was April 01st, 2012. For the first time, the introduction of GAAR into the Income tax law of India was proposed.

Facts	Issue
• The Hutchison Group (Hong Kong) had acquired interests in mobile telecommunications industry in India from 1992 onwards and over a long period of time, a large and complicated ownership structure evolved. The Hutchison Group had an interest in the Indian operating company Hutchison Essar Ltd (HEL) through a number of overseas holding companies. HEL had further step down operating subsidiaries in India.	The controversy in this case centred on the taxability in India of the offshore transfer of shares in CGP, a Cayman Islands Company by the Hutchison Group to the Vodafone Group.
• The majority of the share capital of HEL, which was under the direct or indirect control of Hutchison Group, was held by various Mauritius/Indian companies, which in turn were held by Mauritian/ Cayman Islands companies.	The Indian Revenue Authorities contended that in view of substantial underlying assets in India, in the form of HEL and its business, the transfer was not of the share of CGP but in substance that of the underlying Indian assets. Accordingly, capital gain arising from transfer of assets was taxable in India and VIH was liable to withhold tax from the consideration payable to HTIL.

- Hutchison held certain call and put options (representing 15 percent of the shareholding of HEL) over companies controlled by other persons. These options were in favor of 3Global Services Pvt. Ltd. (3GSPL), an Indian company, against consideration of credit support.

- In late 2006, Hutchison Telecommunications International Ltd., Cayman Islands (HTiL) received various offers from potential buyers to acquire its equity interest in HEL including one from Vodafone Group plc, who made a non-binding offer for 67 percent of HEL for a sum of USD 11.076 billion, based on an enterprise value of USD 18.8 billion of HEL.

- A sale purchase agreement (SPA) was entered into on 11 February, 2007 between VIH and HTIL, under which VIH was to acquire the sole share of CGP Investment (Holdings) Ltd., a Cayman Islands company (CGP).

- Subsequently, on 20 February, 2007 VIH filed an application under Press Note 1 of 2005 for an approval from Foreign Investment Promotion Board (FIPB) and for FIPB to make a noting of the transaction. On May 07th, 2007, FIPB granted approval to VIH and on 8 May, 2007, VIH paid over the consideration.

The issues before the Supreme Court were as follows:

- Were the gains arising on the sale of CGP taxable in India?
  - What was the status of shares of CGP?
  - Did the transaction result in transfer of any asset in India?
- Was VTIL liable to withhold Indian tax from the consideration?

The Ruling

The Supreme Court held as follows:

- Gains arising on sale of the share of CGP were not taxable in India
  - The share of CGP was situated outside India (i.e., in the Cayman Islands)
  - The transaction did not result in transfer of any asset in India
- VTIL was not liable to withhold tax from payment of the sale consideration for acquisition of CGP.

Indian Government Reactions and Moves on Vodafone Tax Issues

In April 2012, Prime Minister Manmohan Singh had asked for an explanatory note from the finance ministry on the Vodafone taxation issue. He wanted to be prepared when it comes up for discussion in the forthcoming second phase of the budget session in Parliament.[47]

It may be recalled that income tax authorities had asked Vodafone Holding to pay INR 11,000 crores in tax for having acquired majority shares in Hutchison-Essar in the year 2007. After a protracted legal battle, the Supreme Court had set aside the IT authorities' demand. In his budget proposal, the then finance minister Pranab Mukherjee sought to bring the deal under tax purview by proposing a retrospective effect to a clause in the taxation law.

It has been suggested that the request was an indicator of the PM's unease over the developments and moves initiated by the finance ministry in this regard. The PM did not want foreign investors to shy away from India and was doubtful if retrospective legislation to enforce a long-pending tax sent out the right signal in a competitive global environment.

However, he did understand the logic behind the finance ministry's move given the fact that the Indian authorities had kept the Vodafone management informed of a possible taxation in March 2007, even before the company finalized its deal with Hutchison-Essar. Later, the SC judgment prevented the imposition of the tax, but it was not as if the tax burden had not been anticipated by the company.

There was another issue of concern. In his letter to former Britain PM, Gordon Brown, Singh assured him that nothing would be done outside the purview of Indian law. Though finance ministry sources insisted that levying of the tax with the backing of retrospective legislation did not necessarily imply that the PM was going back on his word, there were others who pointed out that the Vodafone authorities used Singh's letter to strengthen their case in international forums.

Further in June 2012, Prime Minister Manmohan Singh had asked for a fresh appraisal of the General Anti-Avoidance Rules (GAAR), the controversial measure that became the highlight of former finance minister Pranab Mukherjee's last budget.[48]

"Prime Minister's Office sought clarifications on taxation issues and Section 9 of Income Tax Act (related to tax on indirect transfer of assets).... We asked them to give us two–three weeks' time," Finance Secretary R S Gujral told reporters.[49]

Vodafone Reaction to Indian IT Tax Issues

Vittorio Colao, Chief Executive of Vodafone Group Plc, met the then finance minister Pranab Mukherjee and finance secretary R S Gujral in May 2012 to try and persuade the Indian government to withdraw provisions of the finance Bill that would reverse a Supreme Court verdict that had gone in the company's favor.[50]

"It is time for India to get their machinery under control," said Colao. "I have had really good meetings with very senior people in the Indian government, including the prime minister, and they look sensible, but then something happens. The policymakers become hostage of their own people in the ministries". He further stated, "I really think the bureaucrats, the unelected officials, corner the ministers, the government and the policy makers with a series of complexities which even the policymakers don't know how to get out of. There are rumblings that the Indian government might be starting to shift its position behind the scenes and that it has started to put the brakes on its apparent collision course with Vodafone. But if there is no agreement, the mobile operator's plans for an initial public offering in the territory are on hold."[51]

British Ministry Views on Vodafone Tax Issues in India

British Finance Minister George Osborne in April 2012 raised the INR 11,000 crore Vodafone tax issue with the Indian government which was proposing to amend the Income Tax Act to bring into net overseas mergers and acquisitions involving domestic assets and said the Indian government's proposal to change tax laws retrospectively will damage its investment climate.[52] The UK Exchequer, George Osbourne, raised the issue of Vodafone tax case with India's Finance Minister. He also addressed the concern over the unpredictability of tax regime in India.[53]

A day before, global industry associations had written to Prime Minister Manmohan Singh seeking reconsideration of the retrospective amendment to the tax laws warning that the proposed change had prompted widespread review of costs and benefits of investing in India.

Osborne said both India and the UK were keen to enhance their two-way economic partnership. "What we want to see happen is more investment, more trade, more Indian businesses doing businesses in Britain, more British businesses doing business in India," he said.

Vodafone and British reaction[54]

UK categorically conveyed to India that its proposed move would hurt the overall investment climate in the country. Vodafone's chief executive Vittorio Colao was prompt in expressing his concern, and said that the retrospective taxation could tarnish India's image as an investment destination in a letter written to the Prime Minster Manmohan Singh. "We are concerned about the proposed Budget measure...Not just because of its impact on one company, Vodafone, but because we think, it might damage the overall climate for investment in India," UK's Chancellor of the exchequer, George Osborne told reporters.

Government Views on GAAR and its Retrospective Amendments

"We have been told, do not worry." Those were the words of Vodafone India non-Executive Chairman, Mr Analjit Singh, after his meeting with the Deputy Chairman of the Planning Commission, Mr Montek

Singh Ahluwalia in June 2012.[55] Prime Minister Manmohan Singh declared in November 2012 that government will soon announce steps to stave off investors' fears ensuing from measures like anti-tax avoidance rule and retrospective amendments and hinted at a fast track mechanism to speed up clearance of infrastructure projects.[56]

Admitting that certain tax measures like GAAR (General Anti-Avoidance Rules) and retrospective tax amendments in the Budget had led to "a very negative" reaction from the investors, he said. "We hope to announce decisions on all these issues within the next few weeks", he added.

General Reaction from the Industrial Groups and Associations

The government claimed INR 12,000 crore tax liabilities from Vodafone after the Income Tax Act was amended, bringing in the retrospective clause in the budget. Several global business associations, including Confederation of British Industry and Japan Foreign Trade Council, had already written to Prime Minister Manmohan Singh seeking reconsideration of the amendment.[57]

In August 2012, Adi Godrej, President of the Confederation of Indian Industry (CII) —India had to accelerate reforms and strengthen governance to improve investor sentiment that had turned negative in the wake of serial scams that virtually paralyzed decision-making, retrospective tax changes and labor unrest.[58]

In October 2012, CII wanted the Partha Sarathi Shome Committee to recommend that controversial amendments to the Income Tax Act be made effective prospectively instead of retrospectively from 1962, as had been enacted through year 2012 Union Budget, in the Finance Act.[59]

"If implemented, GAAR would open up a Pandora's Box of uncertainty and litigation, and investors might be forced to think twice before considering opportunities in India," said Nishith Desai, founder of law firm, Nishith Desai Associates. "Several genuine legitimate tax planning arrangements and investments through popular jurisdictions such as Mauritius, Singapore and Cyprus might be hit by GAAR," he added.

GAAR provisions give wide discretionary powers to revenue authorities in taxing transactions on grounds of tax avoidance. "GAAR is indeed going to haunt us in times to come. What do the provisions mean to the India–Mauritius tax treaty? The safeguard of dispute resolution panel is not at all sufficient. These provisions are likely to result in huge tax litigation," said Dinesh Kanabar, deputy CEO & chairman, Tax, KPMG India.

Echoing similar views, Vipul Jhaveri, partner-M&A, Deloitte India said, "Introduction of GAAR, albeit with checks to prevent its abuse would add to uncertainty on tax positions regarding prevailing arrangements and structures. In cross-border M&A, one would have to watch out for the tool box of counter measures for tax avoidance in respect of transactions with persons located in notified jurisdictions that do not effectively exchange information with India."

Effect of Retrospective Tax on Indian Trade

The provision is likely to have an impact on foreign investor sentiment in India. The changes in the Income Tax Act, will also have a bearing on approximately 500 overseas deals of similar kind. Sanofi Aventis' acquisition of Shanta Biotech and Vedanta's takeover of Cairn India are similar transactions of foreign companies acquiring Indian assets.[60]

Apart from making transactions such as the USD 11.1 billion Vodafone–Hutchinson deal in 2007 liable to tax, this amendment would have serious ramifications on deals such as Aditya Birla Nuvo's USD 150 million buyout of 16 percent stake in Idea Cellular India from AT&T Mauritius, SAB Miller's acquisition of Foster and Vedanta's deal to buy a 51 percent stake in Sesa Goa from Mitsui. Similarly, Tata Industries' acquisition of 17 percent stake in Idea Cellular India from AT&T is also likely to be in trouble.[61]

The country witnessed 644 M&A deals worth USD 45 billion in 2011, against 662 deals worth USD 50 billion in 2010, according to report from Grant Thornton. The budget had also proposed to introduce comprehensive General Anti-Avoidance Rules (GAAR), effective from April 01, 2013. These new norms, which would override the provisions of tax treaties signed by India, would capture most conventional structures for M&As and investments into the country.

Endnotes

1. Lex Rieffel, "Myanmar's Economy Confronts Tough Policy Challenges," *East Asian Forum*, July 31, 2012; "Opening Soon: Myanmar Gets Ready for Business," *The Economist*, March 3, 2012; "Myanmar on the Move," *The Economist*, November 21, 2012; and *The World Factbook* (Washington, DC, CIA), https://www.cia.gov/library/publications/the-world-factbook/geos/bm.html.
2. World Bank, *World Development Indicators Online*, 2013.
3. P. Sinha and N. Singh, "The Economy's Black Hole," *The Times of India*, March 22, 2010.
4. A. Sen, *Development as Freedom* (New York: Alfred A. Knopf, 1999).
5. G. M. Grossman and E. Helpman, "Endogenous Innovation in the Theory of Growth," *Journal of Economic Perspectives* 8, no. 1 (1994), pp. 23–44; and P. M. Romer, "The Origins of Endogenous Growth," *Journal of Economic Perspectives* 8, no. 1 (1994), pp. 2–22.
6. W. W. Lewis, *The Power of Productivity* (Chicago: University of Chicago Press, 2004).
7. F. A. Hayek, *The Fatal Conceit: Errors of Socialism* (Chicago: University of Chicago Press, 1989).
8. James Gwartney, Robert Lawson, and Walter Block, *Economic Freedom of the World: 1975–1995* (London: Institute of Economic Affairs, 1996).
9. D. North, *Institutions, Institutional Change, and Economic Performance* (Cambridge, UK: Cambridge University Press, 1991). See also K. M. Murphy, A. Shleifer, and R. Vishney, "Why Is Rent Seeking So Costly to Growth?" *American Economic Review* 83, no. 2 (1993), pp. 409–14; and K. E. Maskus, "Intellectual Property Rights in the Global Economy," Institute for International Economics, 2000.
10. Hernando de Soto, *The Mystery of Capital: Why Capitalism Triumphs in the West and Fails Everywhere Else* (New York: Basic Books, 2000).
11. A. O. Hirschman, "The On-and-Off Again Connection between Political and Economic Progress," *American Economic Review* 84, no. 2 (1994), pp. 343–48; and A. Przeworski and F. Limongi, "Political Regimes and Economic Growth," *Journal of Economic Perspectives* 7, no. 3 (1993), pp. 51–59.
12. Ibid.
13. "China's Next Revolution—Property Rights in China," *The Economist*, March 10, 2007, p. 11; "Caught between the Right and Left," *The Economist*, March 10, 2007, pp. 25–27; and Z. Keliang and L. Ping, "Rural Land Rights under the PRC Property Law," *China Law and Practice*, November 2007, pp. 10–15.
14. For details of this argument, see M. Olson, "Dictatorship, Democracy, and Development," *American Political Science Review*, September 1993.
15. For example, see Jared Diamond's Pulitzer Prize–winning book, *Guns, Germs, and Steel* (New York: W. W. Norton, 1997). Also see J. Sachs, "Nature, Nurture and Growth," *The Economist*, June 14, 1997, pp. 19–22; and J. Sachs, *The End of Poverty* (New York: Penguin Books, 2005).
16. Sachs, "Nature, Nurture and Growth."
17. "What Can the Rest of the World Learn from the Classrooms of Asia?" *The Economist*, September 21, 1996, p. 24.
18. J. Fagerberg, "Technology and International Differences in Growth Rates," *Journal of Economic Literature* 32 (September 1994), pp. 1147–75.
19. See The Freedom House Survey Team, "Freedom in the World: 2013" and associated materials, www.freedomhouse.org.
20. "Russia Downgraded to Not Free," Freedom House press release, December 20, 2004, www.freedomhouse.org.
21. Freedom House, "Democracies Century: A Survey of Political Change in the Twentieth Century, 1999," www.freedomhouse.org.
22. L. Conners, "Freedom to Connect," *Wired*, August 1997, pp. 105–6.
23. F. Fukuyama, "The End of History," *The National Interest* 16 (Summer 1989), p. 18.
24. S. P. Huntington, *The Clash of Civilizations and the Remaking of World Order* (New York: Simon & Schuster, 1996).
25. Ibid., p. 116.
26. United States National Counterterrorism Center, *Reports on Incidents of Terrorism*, 2005, April 11, 2006.
27. S. Fisher, R. Sahay, and C. A. Vegh, "Stabilization and the Growth in Transition Economies: The Early Experience," *Journal of Economic Perspectives* 10 (Spring 1996), pp. 45–66.

28. M. Miles et al., *2013 Index of Economic Freedom* (Washington, DC: Heritage Foundation, 2013).

29. International Monetary Fund, *World Economic Outlook: Focus on Transition Economies* (Geneva: IMF, October 2000).

30. J. C. Brada, "Privatization Is Transition—Is It?" *Journal of Economic Perspectives,* Spring 1996, pp. 67–86.

31. See S. Zahra et al., "Privatization and Entrepreneurial Transformation," *Academy of Management Review* 3, no. 25 (2000), pp. 509–24.

32. N. Brune, G. Garrett, and B. Kogut, "The International Monetary Fund and the Global Spread of Privatization," IMF Staff Papers 51, no. 2 (2003), pp. 195–219.

33. Fischer et al., "Stabilization and Growth in Transition Economies." Journal of Economic Perspectives, 1996, Spring, pp 45–66.

34. "China 2030" (Washington, DC: The World Bank, 2012).

35. J. Sachs, C. Zinnes, and Y. Eilat, "The Gains from Privatization in Transition Economies: Is Change of Ownership Enough?" CAER discussion paper no. 63 (Cambridge, MA: Harvard Institute for International Development, 2000).

36. "India's Breakthrough Budget?" *The Economist,* March 3, 2001; Shankar Aiyar, "Reforms: Time to Just Do It," *India Today,* January 24, 2000, p. 47; "America's Pain, India's Gain," *The Economist,* January 11, 2003, p. 57; Joanna Slater, "In Once Socialist India, Privatizations Are Becoming More Like Routine Matters," *The Wall Street Journal,* July 5, 2002, p. A8; "India's Economy: Ready to Roll Again?" *The Economist,* September 20, 2003, pp. 39–40; Joanna Slater, "Indian Pirates Turned Partners," *The Wall Street Journal,* November 13, 2003, p. A14; "The Next Wave: India," *The Economist,* December 17, 2005, p. 67; M. Dell, "The Digital Sector Can Make Poor Nations Prosper," *Financial Times,* May 4, 2006, p. 17; "What's Holding India Back," *The Economist,* March 8, 2008, p. 11; and "Battling the Babu Raj," *The Economist,* March 8, 2008, pp. 29–31.

37. M. S. Borish and M. Noel, "Private Sector Development in the Visegrad Countries," World Bank, March 1997.

38. "Caught between Right and Left," *The Economist,* March 8, 2007.

39. For a discussion of first-mover advantages, see M. Liberman and D. Montgomery, "First-Mover Advantages," *Strategic Management Journal* 9 (Summer Special Issue, 1988), pp. 41–58.

40. S. H. Robock, "Political Risk: Identification and Assessment," *Columbia Journal of World Business,* July–August 1971, pp. 6–20.

41. D. C. Kurtzer, "Where Is Egypt Headed?" *Spero Forum,* April 4, 2009, www.speroforum.com; "Yes They Can," *The Economist,* March 26, 2011, pp. 55–56; "A Long March," *The Economist,* February 18, 2012, pp. 49–51; and "Going to the Dogs," *The Economist*, March 30, 2013.

42. http://www.bcasonline.org/articles/artin.asp?961

43. http://www.hlbi.com/index.php?option=com_content&view=article&id=668:india-vodafone-tax-ruling-a-legal-analysis-of-the-triumph&catid=162:tax-updates

44. http://www.bcasonline.org/articles/artin.asp?961

45. http://www.hlbi.com/index.php?option=com_content&view=article&id=668:india-vodafone-tax-ruling-a-legal-analysis-of-the-triumph&catid=162:tax-updates

46. http://www.pwc.com/in/en/assets/pdfs/publications-2012/pwc-white-paper-on-gaar.pdf

47. http://www.dnaindia.com/india/report_pm-asks-finance-ministry-to-explain-vodafone-issue_1678289

48. http://timesofindia.indiatimes.com/business/india-business/After-Vodafone-GAAR-PM-takes-charge-of-finance-ministry/articleshow/14513903.cms

49. http://www.businessworld.in/en/storypage/-/bw/govt-to-post-clarifications-on-retro-tax-amendments/423659.0/page/0

50. http://www.livemint.com/Companies/LuPfa6DXMXOmIShI2p423O/Vodafone-CEO-meets-Mukherjee-over-retrospective-tax-issue.html

51. http://www.telegraph.co.uk/finance/newsbysector/mediatechnologyandtelecoms/telecoms/9366967/Vodafone-chief-Vittorio-Colao-Am-I-paid-too-much-Thats-a-tough-call.html

52. http://indiatoday.intoday.in/story/vodafone-tax-change-george-osborne/1/182725.html

53. http://ibnlive.in.com/news/uk-discusses-vodafone-tax-issue-with-india/245125-7.html

54. http://www.business-standard.com/india/news/retrospective-taxtimelineflip-flops-/190546/on

55. http://www.thehindubusinessline.com/industry-and-economy/will-manmohan-roll-back-pranabs-tax-amendment/article3581233.ece

56. http://www.moneycontrol.com/news/economy/decisiongaarretro-tax-soon-says-pm_781003.html

57. http://ibnlive.in.com/news/uk-discusses-vodafone-tax-issue-with-india/245125-7.html

58. http://www.thehindu.com/business/cii-calls-for-transparency-in-governance-to-return-to-high-gdp-rates-of-growth/article3816266.ece

59. http://www.business-standard.com/india/news/shome-panels-final-report-likely-today/488150/

60. http://www.theoffshoreonline.com/node/86

61. http://www.business-standard.com/india/news/taxoffshore-share-transfers-may-hit-cross-border-ma-deals/468210/

Chapter 4
Differences in Culture

WHY DID WALMART FAIL IN GERMANY?

Opening Case

Walmart is one of the world's most successful retailers. In the United States, its formula of everyday low prices, tight cost controls, nonunion employees, and superb inventory management helped propel the company to retailing dominance. By the mid-1990s, with the U.S. market starting to look saturated, Walmart began to turn its attention to other nations. While it has certainly had some successes outside the United States, most notably in Mexico where it is now that country's largest retailer, it has slipped up badly in some other nations. Germany, in particular, proved to be a particularly tough market for Walmart to address. After 10 difficult years in Germany, during which time it never turned a profit, Walmart exited in 2007.

Walmart entered Germany by purchasing two German retailers. In 1997, it acquired Wertkauf, a profitable chain of 21 stores. In 1998, it acquired the Spar chain, which had 74 hypermarkets and was perhaps the weakest of Germany's major retailers. Right from the start, Walmart made a number of missteps. The first CEO, Ron Tiarks, was a U.S. citizen who had previously supervised 200 U.S. super-centers from the company's headquarters in Bentonville. Tiarks brought a number of U.S. managers with him. He did not speak German and made no attempt to learn the language. Instead, he decreed that English would be the official language in Germany at the management level. If this act of hubris wasn't enough, he reportedly displayed a high degree of ignorance concerning the complexities of retailing in Germany, particularly with regard to the different legal and institutional framework in the nation. Nor did he understand how German shopping culture differed from that in the United States. He ignored strategic advice presented to him by former Wertkauf executives, encouraging three of the top six to leave within six months.

After a rocky tenure, an Englishman, Allan Leighton, replaced Tiarks. Leighton also spoke no German, and elected to run the German unit from his office in the United Kingdom! Not surprisingly, this too didn't work. After six months, a German, Volker Barth, replaced Leighton. Barth, and his German successor, Kay Hafner, who took over in 2001, struggled to make the unit profitable, but they were hamstrung by the requirement that they impose the Walmart way of doing things on German stores.

At the management level, there was widespread dissatisfaction with the relatively low base pay at Walmart and the practice of transferring managers after one or two years—something that is not normal in Germany. Managers also complained about the company's frugal regulations for business trips—in particular, the decree that executives had to share rooms, a practice unheard of in any other major German company. Moreover, Walmart failed to get its head around the fact that unions still had a strong influence in Germany. The company refused to acknowledge the outcome of a sector-specific, centralized, wage-bargaining process between unions and retailers and was then surprised when the union organized a walkout at 30 Walmart stores. This not only resulted in lost sales but also tarnished Walmart with an image of union bashing, something that hurt it with many of its customers.

Many shoppers perceived Walmart to be offering low-value, low-priced merchandise. Some rivals charac-terized it as "American junk." This mattered in a culture where quality is valued, and where the most suc-cessful German retailer, Aldi, had a reputation for offering low-priced but high-quality merchandise. Nor did German shoppers like Walmart's greeters, who stood at the store entrance and "greeted" shoppers as they entered and exited the store. Germans typically do not greet strangers, and shoppers soon started to complain about being harassed by greeters! Initially Walmart offered a grocery bagging service, standard practice in the United States, but it turned out that Germans don't want strangers handling their groceries. When checkout clerks followed company orders to smile at a shopper, many male customers took it as a turn on. German people don't usually smile at strangers. Walmart employees also reportedly found the practice of starting their shifts by engaging in the Walmart chant, and stretching exercises, to be embar-rassing and silly. When Walmart distributed its newly translated ethics code to German employees in 2005, it caused an uproar. The code cautioned against supervisor–employee relationships and called on employ-ees to report any improper behavior. While this might seem reasonable to an American executive sitting in Arkansas schooled in American ethics on sexual harassment, Germans interpreted it as a ban on interoffice romance by puritanical Americans and an invitation to rat on coworkers.[1]

INTRODUCTION

In Chapters 2 and 3, we saw how national differences in political, economic, and legal systems influence the benefits, costs, and risks associated with doing business in different countries. In this chapter, we explore how differences in culture across and within countries can affect international business. Several themes run through this chapter. The first is that business success in a variety of countries requires cross-cultural literacy. By **cross-cultural literacy**, we mean an understanding of how cultural differences across and within nations can affect the way business is practiced. In these days of global communications, rapid transportation, worldwide markets, and global brands, when the era of the global village seems just around the corner, it is easy to forget just how different various cultures really are. Underneath the veneer of modernism, deep cultural differences often remain.[2]

The opening case deals with precisely this point. Walmart's failure in Germany was due in large part to its inability to come to grips with the cultural differences between Germany and the United States. Walmart displayed a remarkable lack of cross-cultural literacy when it appointed an American manager with no international experience, no German language capability, and apparently no interest in learning about cultural differences to run its German operation. It compounded its mistake by trying to impose the Walmart way of managing on its German employees, without making adjustments to account for nontrivial differences in national culture. As Walmart soon found, management practices that seemed reasonable in the United States did not sit well with German employees. Generalizing from this example, in this chapter, we argue that it is important for foreign businesses to gain an understanding of the culture that prevails in those countries where they do business and that success requires a foreign enterprise to adapt to the culture of its host country.[3]

Another theme developed in this chapter is that a relationship may exist between culture and the cost of doing business in a country or region. Different cultures are more or less supportive of the capitalist mode of production and may increase or lower the costs of doing business. For example, some observers have argued that cultural factors lowered the costs of doing business in Japan and helped explain Japan's rapid economic ascent during the 1960s, 1970s, and 1980s.[4] Similarly, cultural factors can sometimes raise the costs of doing business. Historically, class divisions were an important aspect of British culture, and for a long time, firms operating in Great Britain found it difficult to achieve cooperation between management and labor. Class divisions led to a high level of industrial disputes in that country during the 1960s and 1970s and raised the costs of doing business relative to the costs in countries such as Switzerland, Norway, Germany, or Japan, where class conflict was historically less prevalent.

The British example, however, brings us to another theme we explore in this chapter. Culture is not static. It can and does evolve, although the rate at which culture can change is the subject of some dispute. Important aspects of British culture have changed significantly over the past 30 years, and this has been reflected in weaker class distinctions and a lower level of industrial disputes.[5] Finally, it is important to note that multinational enterprises can themselves be engines of cultural change. In India, for example, McDonald's and other Western fast-food companies may help change the dining culture of that nation, drawing them away from traditional restaurants and toward fast-food outlets.

WHAT IS CULTURE?

Scholars have never been able to agree on a simple definition of *culture*. In the 1870s, the anthropologist Edward Tylor defined culture as "that complex whole which includes knowledge, belief, art, morals, law, custom, and other capabilities acquired by man as a member of society."[6] Since then hundreds of other definitions have been offered. Geert Hofstede, an expert on cross-cultural differences and management, defined culture as "the collective programming of the mind which distinguishes the members of one human group from another. . . . Culture, in this sense, includes systems of values; and values are among the building blocks of culture."[7] Another definition of culture comes from sociologists Zvi Namenwirth and Robert Weber, who see culture as a system of ideas and argue that these ideas constitute a design for living.[8]

Here, we follow both Hofstede and Namenwirth and Weber by viewing **culture** as a system of values and norms that are shared among a group of people and that when taken together constitute a design for living. By **values**, we mean abstract ideas about what a group believes to be good, right, and desirable.

Put differently, values are shared assumptions about how things ought to be.[9] By **norms**, we mean the social rules and guidelines that prescribe appropriate behavior in particular situations. We shall use the term **society** to refer to a group of people sharing a common set of values and norms. While a society may be equivalent to a country, some countries harbor several societies (i.e., they support multiple cultures), and some societies embrace more than one country.

Values and Norms

Values form the bedrock of a culture. They provide the context within which a society's norms are established and justified. They may include a society's attitudes toward such concepts as individual freedom, democracy, truth, justice, honesty, loyalty, social obligations, collective responsibility, the role of women, love, sex, marriage, and so on. Values are not just abstract concepts; they are invested with considerable emotional significance. People argue, fight, and even die over values such as freedom. Values are also often reflected in the political and economic systems of a society. As we saw in Chapter 2, democratic free market capitalism is a reflection of a philosophical value system that emphasizes individual freedom.

Norms are the social rules that govern people's actions toward one another. Norms can be subdivided further into two major categories: folkways and mores. **Folkways** are the routine conventions of everyday life. Generally, folkways are actions of little moral significance. Rather, they are social conventions concerning things such as the appropriate dress code in a particular situation, good social manners, eating with the correct utensils, neighborly behavior, and the like. Although folkways define the way people are expected to behave, violation of them is not normally a serious matter. People who violate folkways may be thought of as eccentric or ill-mannered, but they are not usually considered to be evil or bad. In many countries, foreigners may initially be excused for violating folkways.

A good example of folkways concerns attitudes toward time in different countries. People are keenly aware of the passage of time in the United States and northern European cultures such as Germany and Britain. Businesspeople are very conscious about scheduling their time and are quickly irritated when their time is wasted because a business associate is late for a meeting or if they are kept waiting. They talk about time as though it were money, as something that can be spent, saved, wasted, and lost.[10] Alternatively, in many Arabic, Latin, and African cultures, time has a more elastic character. Keeping to a schedule is viewed as less important than finishing an interaction with people. For example, an American businesswoman might feel slighted if she is kept waiting for 30 minutes outside the office of a Latin American executive before a meeting, but the Latin American may simply be completing an interaction with an associate and view the information gathered from this as more important than sticking to a rigid schedule. The Latin American executive intends no disrespect, but due to a mutual misunderstanding about the importance of time, the American may see things differently. Similarly, Saudi attitudes toward time have been shaped by their nomadic Bedouin heritage, in which precise time played no real role and arriving somewhere tomorrow might mean next week. Like Latin Americans, many Saudis are unlikely to understand the American obsession with precise time and schedules, and Americans need to adjust their expectations accordingly.

Folkways include rituals and symbolic behavior. Rituals and symbols are the most visible manifestations of a culture and constitute the outward expression of deeper values. For example, upon meeting a foreign business executive, a Japanese executive will hold his business card in both hands and bow while presenting the card to the foreigner.[11] This ritual behavior is loaded with deep cultural symbolism. The card specifies the rank of the Japanese executive, which is a very important piece of information in a hierarchical society such as Japan. The bow is a sign of respect, and the deeper the angle of the bow, the greater the reverence one person shows for the other. The person receiving the card is expected to examine it carefully (Japanese often have business cards with Japanese printed on one side and English printed on the other), which is a way of returning respect and acknowledging the card giver's position in the hierarchy. The foreigner is also expected to bow when taking the card and to return the greeting by presenting the Japanese executive with his or her own card, similarly bowing in the process. To not do so, and to fail to read the card that he has been given, instead casually placing it in a jacket, pocket, or purse, violates this important folkway and is considered rude.

Mores are norms that are seen as central to the functioning of a society and to its social life. They have much greater significance than folkways. Accordingly, violating mores can bring serious retribution. Mores include such factors as indictments against theft, adultery, incest, and cannibalism. In many societies, certain mores have been enacted into law. Thus, all advanced societies have laws against theft, incest, and cannibalism. However, there are also many differences among cultures. In America, for example, drinking alcohol is widely accepted, whereas in Saudi Arabia the consumption of alcohol is viewed as violating important social mores and is punishable by imprisonment (as some Western citizens working in Saudi Arabia have discovered).

Culture, Society, and the Nation-State

We have defined a society as a group of people that share a common set of values and norms, that is, people who are bound together by a common culture. There is not a strict one-to-one correspondence between a society and a nation-state. Nation-states are political creations. They may contain a single culture or several cultures. While the French nation can be thought of as the political embodiment of French culture, the nation of Canada has at least three cultures—an Anglo culture, a French-speaking "Quebecois" culture, and a Native American culture. Similarly, many African nations have important cultural differences between tribal groups, as exhibited in the early 1990s when Rwanda dissolved into a bloody civil war between two tribes, the Tutsis and Hutus. Africa is not alone in this regard. India, for example, is composed of many distinct cultural groups with their own rich history and traditions.

At the other end of the scale are cultures that embrace several nations. Several scholars argue that we can speak of an Islamic society or culture that is shared by the citizens of many different nations in the Middle East, Asia, and Africa. As you will recall from the previous chapter, this view of expansive cultures that embrace several nations underpins Samuel Huntington's view of a world that is fragmented into different civilizations, including Western, Islamic, and Sinic (Chinese).[12]

To complicate things further, it is also possible to talk about culture at different levels. It is reasonable to talk about "American society" and "American culture," but there are several societies within America, each with its own culture. One can talk about African American culture, Cajun culture, Chinese American culture, Hispanic culture, Indian culture, Irish American culture, and Southern culture. The relationship between culture and country is often ambiguous. Even if a country can be characterized as having a single homogeneous culture, often that national culture is a mosaic of subcultures.

The Determinants of Culture

LO4-2

The values and norms of a culture do not emerge fully formed. They evolve over time in response to a number of factors, including prevailing political and economic philosophies, the social structure of a society, and the dominant religion, language, and education (see Figure 4.1). We discussed political and economic philosophies in Chapter 2. Such philosophies clearly influence the value systems of a society. For example, the values found in Communist North Korea toward freedom, justice, and individual achievement are clearly different from the values found in the United States, precisely because each society operates according to different political and economic philosophies. In the rest of this chapter,

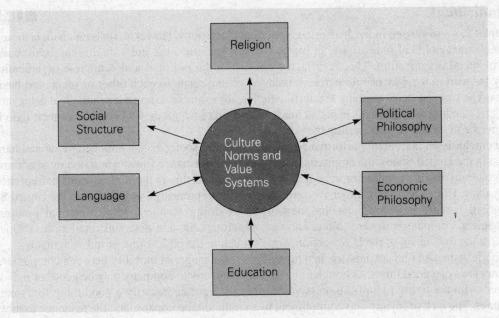

Figure 4.1 *The Determinants of Culture*

we discuss the influence of social structure, religion, language, and education. The chain of causation runs both ways. While factors such as social structure and religion clearly influence the values and norms of a society, the values and norms of a society can influence social structure and religion.

SOCIAL STRUCTURE

A society's **social structure** refers to its basic social organization. Although social structure consists of many different aspects, two dimensions are particularly important when explaining differences among cultures. The first is the degree to which the basic unit of social organization is the individual, as opposed to the group. In general, Western societies tend to emphasize the primacy of the individual, whereas groups tend to figure much larger in many other societies. The second dimension is the degree to which a society is stratified into classes or castes. Some societies are characterized by a relatively high degree of social stratification and relatively low mobility between strata (e.g., Indian); other societies are characterized by a low degree of social stratification and high mobility between strata (e.g., American).

Individuals and Groups

A **group** is an association of two or more individuals who have a shared sense of identity and who interact with each other in structured ways on the basis of a common set of expectations about each other's behavior.[13] Human social life is group life. Individuals are involved in families, work groups, social groups, recreational groups, and so on. However, while groups are found in all societies, societies differ according to the degree to which the group is viewed as the primary means of social organization.[14] In some societies, individual attributes and achievements are viewed as being more important than group membership; in others the reverse is true.

The Individual

LO4-3

In Chapter 2, we discussed individualism as a political philosophy. However, individualism is more than just an abstract political philosophy. In many Western societies, the individual is the basic building block of social organization. This is reflected not just in the political and economic organization of society but also in the way people perceive themselves and relate to each other in social and business settings. The value systems of many Western societies, for example, emphasize individual achievement. The social standing of individuals is not so much a function of whom they work for as of their individual performance in whatever work setting they choose.

The emphasis on individual performance in many Western societies has both beneficial and harmful aspects. In the United States, the emphasis on individual performance finds expression in an admiration of rugged individualism and entrepreneurship. One benefit of this is the high level of entrepreneurial activity in the United States and other Western societies. Entrepreneurial individuals in the United States have created many new products and new ways of doing business (e.g., personal computers, photocopiers, computer software, biotechnology, supermarkets, and discount retail stores). One can argue that the dynamism of the U.S. economy owes much to the philosophy of individualism.

Individualism also finds expression in a high degree of managerial mobility between companies, and this is not always a good thing. Although moving from company to company may be good for individual managers who are trying to build impressive résumés, it is not necessarily a good thing for American companies. The lack of loyalty and commitment to an individual company, and the tendency to move on for a better offer, can result in managers who have good general skills but lack the knowledge, experience, and network of interpersonal contacts that come from years of working within the same company. An effective manager draws on company-specific experience, knowledge, and a network of contacts to find solutions to current problems, and American companies may suffer if their managers lack these attributes. One positive aspect of high managerial mobility is that executives are exposed to different ways of doing business. The ability to compare business practices helps U.S. executives identify how good practices and techniques developed in one firm might be profitably applied to other firms.

The Group

In contrast to the Western emphasis on the individual, the group is the primary unit of social organization in many other societies. For example, in Japan, the social status of an individual has traditionally been determined as much by the standing of the group to which he or she belongs as by his or her individual performance.[15] In traditional Japanese society, the group was the family or village to which an individual belonged. Today, the group has frequently come to be associated with the work team or business organization to which an individual belongs. In a now-classic study of Japanese society, Nakane noted how this expresses itself in everyday life:

> When a Japanese faces the outside (confronts another person) and affixes some position to himself socially he is inclined to give precedence to institution over kind of occupation. Rather than saying, "I am a typesetter" or "I am a filing clerk," he is likely to say, "I am from B Publishing Group" or "I belong to S company."[16]

Nakane goes on to observe that the primacy of the group to which an individual belongs LO4-3 often evolves into a deeply emotional attachment in which identification with the group becomes all-important in one's life. One central value of Japanese culture is the importance attached to group membership. This may have beneficial implications for business firms. Strong identification with the group is argued to create pressures for mutual self-help and collective action. If the worth of an individual is closely linked to the achievements of the group (e.g., firm), as Nakane maintains is the case in Japan, this creates a strong incentive for individual members of the group to work together for the common good. Some argue that the success of some Japanese enterprises in the global economy has been based partly on their ability to achieve close cooperation between individuals within a company and between companies. This has found expression in the widespread diffusion of self-managing work teams within Japanese organizations; the close cooperation among different functions within Japanese companies (e.g., among manufacturing, marketing, and R&D); and the cooperation between a company and its suppliers on issues such as design, quality control, and inventory reduction.[17] In all these cases, cooperation is driven by the need to improve the performance of the group (i.e., the business firm).

The primacy of the value of group identification also discourages managers and workers from moving from company to company. Lifetime employment in a particular company was long the norm in certain sectors of the Japanese economy (estimates suggest that between 20 and 40 percent of all Japanese employees have formal or informal lifetime employment guarantees). Over the years, managers and workers build up knowledge, experience, and a network of interpersonal business contacts. All these things can help managers perform their jobs more effectively and achieve cooperation with others.

However, the primacy of the group is not always beneficial. Just as U.S. society is characterized by a great deal of dynamism and entrepreneurship, reflecting the primacy of values associated with individualism, some argue that Japanese society is characterized by a corresponding lack of dynamism and entrepreneurship. Although the long-run consequences are unclear, the United States could continue to create more new industries than Japan and continue to be more successful at pioneering radically new products and new ways of doing business.

Social Stratification

All societies are stratified on a hierarchical basis into social categories—that is, into **social strata**. These strata are typically defined on the basis of characteristics such as family background, occupation, and income. Individuals are born into a particular stratum. They become a member of the social category to which their parents belong. Individuals born into a stratum toward the top of the social hierarchy tend to have better life chances than those born into a stratum toward the bottom of the hierarchy. They are likely to have better education, health, standard of living, and work opportunities. Although all societies are stratified to some degree, they differ in two related ways. First, they differ from each other with regard to the degree of mobility between social strata; second, they differ with regard to the significance attached to social strata in business contexts.

Social Mobility

The term **social mobility** refers to the extent to which individuals can move out of the strata into which they are born. Social mobility varies significantly from society to society. The most rigid system of stratification is a caste system. A **caste system** is a closed system of stratification in which social position is determined by the family into which a person is born, and change in that position is usually not possible during an individual's lifetime. Often a caste position carries with it a specific occupation. Members of one caste might be shoemakers, members of another might be butchers, and so on. These occupations are embedded in the caste and passed down through the family to succeeding generations. Although the number of societies with caste systems diminished rapidly during the twentieth century, one partial example still remains. India has four main castes and several thousand subcastes. Even though the caste system was officially abolished in 1949, two years after India became independent, it

Breaking India's Caste System

Modern India is a country of dramatic contrasts. Its information technology sector is among the most vibrant in the world with companies such as Infosys and Wipro emerging as powerful global players. India's caste system, long an impediment to social mobility, is a fading memory among the educated, urban middle-class Indians who make up the majority of employees in the high-tech economy. However, the same is not true in rural India, where 70 percent of the nation's population still resides. There caste remains a pervasive influence.

For example, a young female engineer at Infosys who grew up in a small rural village and is a *dalit* recounts how she never entered the house of a *Brahmin,* India's elite priestly caste, even though half of her village was *Brahmins.* When a *dalit* was hired to cook at the school in her native village, *Brahmins* withdrew their children from the school. The engineer herself is the beneficiary of a charitable training scheme that Infosys launched in 2006. Her caste is among the poorest in India, with some 91 percent making less than $100 a month, compared to 65 percent of *Brahmins.*

To try to correct this historic inequality, politicians have talked for years about extending the employment quota system to private enterprises. The government has told private companies to hire more *dalits* and members of tribal communities and warned that "strong measures" will be taken if companies do not comply. Private employers are resisting attempts to impose quotas, arguing with some justification that people who are guaranteed a job by a quota system are unlikely to work very hard. At the same time, progressive employers realize they need to do something to correct the inequalities, and unless India taps into the lower castes, it may not be able to find the employees required to staff rapidly growing high-technology enterprises. Thus, the Confederation of Indian Industry recently introduced a package of *dalit*-friendly measures, including scholarships for bright lower-caste children. Building on this, Infosys is leading the way among high-tech enterprises. The company provides special training to low-caste engineering graduates who have failed to get a job in industry after graduation. While the training does not promise employment, so far almost all graduates who completed the seven-month training program have been hired by Infosys and other enterprises.[18]

is still a force in rural Indian society where occupation and marital opportunities are still partly related to caste (for more details, see the accompanying Country Focus on the caste system in India today).[19]

A **class system** is a less rigid form of social stratification in which social mobility is possible. It is a form of open stratification in which the position a person has by birth can be changed through his or her own achievements or luck. Individuals born into a class at the bottom of the hierarchy can work their way up; conversely, individuals born into a class at the top of the hierarchy can slip down.

While many societies have class systems, social mobility within a class system varies from society to society. For example, some sociologists have argued that Britain has a more rigid class structure than certain other Western societies, such as the United States.[20] Historically, British society was divided into three main classes: the upper class, which was made up of individuals whose families for generations had wealth, prestige, and occasionally power; the middle class, whose members were involved in professional, managerial, and clerical occupations; and the working class, whose members earned their living from manual occupations. The middle class was further subdivided into the upper-middle class, whose members were involved in important managerial occupations and the prestigious professions (e.g., lawyers, accountants, doctors), and the lower-middle class, whose members were involved in clerical work (e.g., bank tellers) and the less prestigious professions (e.g., schoolteachers).

The British class system exhibited significant divergence between the life chances of members of different classes. The upper and upper-middle classes typically sent their children to a select group of private schools, where they wouldn't mix with lower-class children and where they picked up many of the speech accents and social norms that marked them as being from the higher strata of society. These same private schools also had close ties with the most prestigious universities, such as Oxford and Cambridge. Until fairly recently, Oxford and Cambridge guaranteed a certain number of places for the graduates of these private schools. Having been to a prestigious university, the offspring of the upper and upper-middle classes then had an excellent chance of being offered a prestigious job in companies, banks, brokerage firms, and law firms run by members of the upper and upper-middle classes.

In contrast, the members of the British working and lower-middle classes typically went to state schools. The majority left at age 16, and those who went on to higher education found it more difficult to get accepted at the best universities. When they did, they found that their lower-class accent and lack of social skills marked them as being from a lower social stratum, which made it more difficult for them to get access to the most prestigious jobs.

Because of this, the class system in Britain perpetuated itself from generation to generation, and mobility was limited. Although upward mobility was possible, it could not normally be achieved in one generation. While an individual from a working-class background may have established an income level that was consistent with membership in the upper-middle class, he or she may not have been accepted as such by others of that class due to accent and background. However, by sending his or her offspring to the "right kind of school," the individual could ensure that his or her children were accepted.

According to some commentators, modern British society is now rapidly leaving this class structure behind and moving toward a classless society. However, sociologists continue to dispute this finding and present evidence that this is not the case. For example, one study reported that state schools in the London suburb of Islington, which has a population of 175,000, had only 79 candidates for university, while one prestigious private school alone, Eton, sent more than that number to Oxford and Cambridge.[21] This, according to the study's authors, implies that "money still begets money." They argue that a good school means a good university, a good university means a good job, and merit has only a limited chance of elbowing its way into this tight little circle. In another recent survey of the empirical literature, a sociologist noted that class differentials in educational achievement have changed surprisingly little over the last few decades in many societies, despite assumptions to the contrary.[22]

The class system in the United States is less pronounced than in Britain and mobility is greater. Like Britain, the United States has its own upper, middle, and working classes. However, class membership is determined to a much greater degree by individual economic achievements, as opposed to background and schooling. Thus, an individual can, by his or her own economic achievement, move smoothly from the working class to the upper class in a lifetime. Successful individuals from humble origins are highly respected in American society.

Another society for which class divisions have historically been of some importance has been China, where there has been a long-standing difference between the life chances of the rural peasantry and urban dwellers. Ironically, this historic division was strengthened during the high point of Communist rule because of a rigid system of household registration that restricted most Chinese to the place of their birth for their lifetime. Bound to collective farming, peasants were cut off from many urban privileges—compulsory education, quality schools, health care, public housing, varieties of foodstuffs, to name only a few—and they largely lived in poverty. Social mobility was thus very limited. This system crumbled following reforms of the late 1970s and early 1980s, and as a consequence, migrant peasant laborers have flooded into China's cities looking for work. Sociologists now hypothesize that a new class system is emerging in China based less on the rural–urban divide and more on urban occupation.[23]

Significance

L04-3

From a business perspective, the stratification of a society is significant if it affects the operation of business organizations. In American society, the high degree of social mobility and the extreme emphasis on individualism limit the impact of class background on business operations. The same is true in Japan, where most of the population perceives itself to be middle class. In a country such as Great Britain, however, the relative lack of class mobility and the differences between classes have resulted in the emergence of class consciousness. **Class consciousness** refers to a condition by which people tend to perceive themselves in terms of their class background, and this shapes their relationships with members of other classes.

This has been played out in British society in the traditional hostility between upper-middle-class managers and their working-class employees. Mutual antagonism and lack of respect historically made it difficult to achieve cooperation between management and labor in many British companies and resulted in a relatively high level of industrial disputes. However, the past two decades have seen a dramatic reduction in industrial disputes, which bolsters the arguments of those who claim that the country is moving toward a classless society. Alternatively, as noted earlier, class consciousness may be reemerging in urban China, and it may ultimately prove to be significant there.

An antagonistic relationship between management and labor classes, and the resulting lack of cooperation and high level of industrial disruption, tends to raise the costs of production in countries characterized by significant class divisions. In turn, this can make it more difficult for companies based in such countries to establish a competitive advantage in the global economy.

RELIGIOUS AND ETHICAL SYSTEMS

L04-2

Religion may be defined as a system of shared beliefs and rituals that are concerned with the realm of the sacred.[24] **Ethical systems** refer to a set of moral principles, or values, that are used to guide and shape behavior. Most of the world's ethical systems are the product of religions. Thus, we can talk about Christian ethics and Islamic ethics. However, there is a major exception to the principle that ethical systems are grounded in religion. Confucianism and Confucian ethics influence behavior and shape culture in parts of Asia, yet it is incorrect to characterize Confucianism as a religion.

The relationship between religion, ethics, and society is subtle and complex. Among the thousands of religions in the world today, four dominate in terms of numbers of adherents: Christianity with roughly 2–2.2 billion adherents, Islam with around 1.6 billion adherents, Hinduism with 800–950 million adherents (primarily in India), and Buddhism with 400–500 (see Map 4.1). Although many other religions have an important influence in certain parts of the modern world (e.g., Shintoism in Japan, with roughly 40 million followers, and Judaism, which has 18 million adherents and accounts for 75 percent of the population of Israel), their numbers pale in comparison with these dominant religions

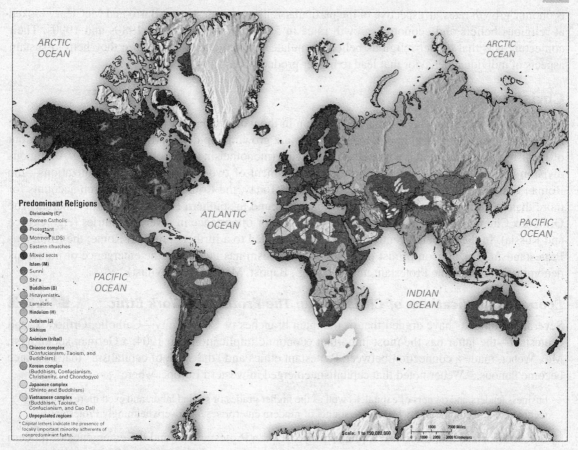

MAP 4.1 World Religions

Source: From John L. Allen, *Student Atlas of World Politics* 9th edition, 2008, Map 13. Copyright © 2008 by The McGraw-Hill Companies. Reproduced by permission of McGraw-Hill Contemporary Learning Series.

(although as the precursor of both Christianity and Islam, Judaism has an indirect influence that goes beyond its numbers). We review these four religions, along with Confucianism, focusing on their potential economic and business implications.

Some scholars have theorized that the most important business implications of religion center on the extent to which different religions shape attitudes toward work and entrepreneurship and the degree to which the religious ethics affects the costs of doing business in a country. However, it is hazardous to make sweeping generalizations about the nature of the relationship between religion and ethical systems and business practice. While some scholars argue that there is a relationship between religious and ethical systems and business practice in a society, in a world where nations with Catholic, Protestant, Muslim, Hindu, and Buddhist majorities all show evidence of entrepreneurial activity and sustainable economic growth, it is important to view such proposed relationships with a degree of skepticism. The proposed relationships may exist, but their impact may be small compared with the impact of economic policy. On the other hand, research by economists Robert Barro and Rachel McCleary does suggest that strong religious beliefs, particularly beliefs in heaven, hell, and an afterlife, have a positive impact on economic growth rates, irrespective of the particular religion in question.[25] Barro and McCleary looked at religious beliefs and economic growth rates in 59 countries during the 1980s and 1990s. Their conjecture was that higher religious beliefs stimulate economic growth because they help to sustain aspects of individual behavior that lead to higher productivity.

Christianity

Christianity is the most widely practiced religion in the world. The vast majority of Christians live in Europe and the Americas, although their numbers are growing rapidly in Africa. Christianity grew out of Judaism. Like Judaism, it is a monotheistic religion (monotheism is the belief in one God). A religious division in the eleventh century led to the establishment of two major Christian organizations—the Roman Catholic Church and the Orthodox Church. Today, the Roman Catholic Church accounts for more than half of all Christians, most of whom are found in southern Europe and Latin America. The Orthodox Church, while less influential, is still of major importance in several countries (e.g., Greece and Russia). In the sixteenth century, the Reformation led to a further split with Rome; the result was Protestantism. The nonconformist nature of Protestantism has facilitated the emergence of numerous denominations under the Protestant umbrella (e.g., Baptist, Methodist, Calvinist).

Economic Implications of Christianity: The Protestant Work Ethic   **LO4-3**

Several sociologists have argued that of the main branches of Christianity—Catholic, Orthodox, and Protestant—the latter has the most important economic implications. In 1904, a German sociologist, Max Weber, made a connection between Protestant ethics and "the spirit of capitalism" that has since become famous.[26] Weber noted that capitalism emerged in western Europe, where

> business leaders and owners of capital, as well as the higher grades of skilled labor, and even more the higher technically and commercially trained personnel of modern enterprises, are overwhelmingly Protestant.[27]

Weber theorized that there was a relationship between Protestantism and the emergence of modern capitalism. He argued that Protestant ethics emphasizes the importance of hard work and wealth creation (for the glory of God) and frugality (abstinence from worldly pleasures). According to Weber, this kind of value system was needed to facilitate the development of capitalism. Protestants worked hard and systematically to accumulate wealth. However, their ascetic beliefs suggested that rather than consuming this wealth by indulging in worldly pleasures, they should invest it in the expansion of capitalist enterprises. Thus, the combination of hard work and the accumulation of capital, which could be used to finance investment and expansion, paved the way for the development of capitalism in western Europe and subsequently in the United States. In contrast, Weber argued that the Catholic promise of salvation in the next world, rather than this world, did not foster the same kind of work ethic.

Protestantism also may have encouraged capitalism's development in another way. By breaking away from the hierarchical domination of religious and social life that characterized the Catholic Church for much of its history, Protestantism gave individuals significantly more freedom to develop their own relationship with God. The right to freedom of form of worship was central to the nonconformist nature of early Protestantism. This emphasis on individual religious freedom may have paved the way for the subsequent emphasis on individual economic and political freedoms and the development of individualism as an economic and political philosophy. As we saw in Chapter 2, such a philosophy forms the bedrock on which entrepreneurial free market capitalism is based. Building on this, some scholars claim there is a connection between individualism, as inspired by Protestantism, and the extent of entrepreneurial activity in a nation.[28] Again, one must be careful not to generalize too much from this historical sociological view. While nations with a strong Protestant tradition such as Britain, Germany, and the United States were early leaders in the industrial revolution, nations with Catholic or Orthodox majorities show significant and sustained entrepreneurial activity and economic growth in the modern world.

Islam

With about 1.6 billion adherents, Islam is the second largest of the world's major religions. Islam dates back to A.D. 610 when the Prophet Muhammad began spreading the word, although the Muslim calendar begins in A.D. 622 when, to escape growing opposition, Muhammad left Mecca for the oasis settlement of Yathrib, later known as Medina. Adherents of Islam are referred to as Muslims. Muslims constitute a majority in more than 40 countries and inhabit a nearly contiguous stretch of land from the northwest coast of Africa, through the Middle East, to China and Malaysia in the Far East.

Islam has roots in both Judaism and Christianity (Islam views Jesus Christ as one of God's prophets). Like Christianity and Judaism, Islam is a monotheistic religion. The central principle of Islam is that there is but the one true omnipotent God (Allah). Islam requires unconditional acceptance of the uniqueness, power, and authority of God and the understanding that the objective of life is to fulfill the dictates of his will in the hope of admission to paradise. According to Islam, worldly gain and temporal power are an illusion. Those who pursue riches on earth may gain them, but those who forgo worldly ambitions to seek the favor of Allah may gain the greater treasure—entry into paradise. Other major principles of Islam include (1) honoring and respecting parents, (2) respecting the rights of others, (3) being generous but not a squanderer, (4) avoiding killing except for justifiable causes, (5) not committing adultery, (6) dealing justly and equitably with others, (7) being of pure heart and mind, (8) safeguarding the possessions of orphans, and (9) being humble and unpretentious.[29] Obvious parallels exist with many of the central principles of both Judaism and Christianity.

Islam is an all-embracing way of life governing the totality of a Muslim's being.[30] As God's surrogate in this world, a Muslim is not a totally free agent but is circumscribed by religious principles—by a code of conduct for interpersonal relations—in social and economic activities. Religion is paramount in all areas of life. The Muslim lives in a social structure that is shaped by Islamic values and norms of moral conduct. The ritual nature of everyday life in a Muslim country is striking to a Western visitor. Among other things, orthodox Muslim ritual requires prayer five times a day (business meetings may be put on hold while the Muslim participants engage in their daily prayer ritual), demands that women should be dressed in a certain manner, and forbids the consumption of pork and alcohol.

Islamic Fundamentalism

The past three decades have witnessed the growth of a social movement often referred to as Islamic fundamentalism.[31] In the West, Islamic fundamentalism is associated in the media with militants, terrorists, and violent upheavals, such as the bloody conflict occurring in Algeria, the killing of foreign tourists in Egypt, and the September 11, 2001 attacks on the World Trade Center and Pentagon in the United States. This characterization is misleading. Just as Christian fundamentalists are motivated by sincere and deeply held religious values firmly rooted in their faith, so are Islamic fundamentalists. The violence that the Western media associates with Islamic fundamentalism is perpetrated by a small minority of radical "fundamentalists" who have hijacked the religion to further their own political and violent ends. (Some Christian "fundamentalists" have done exactly the same, including Jim Jones and David Koresh.) The vast majority of Muslims point out that Islam teaches peace, justice, and tolerance, not violence and intolerance, and that Islam explicitly repudiates the violence that a radical minority practices.

The rise of Islamic fundamentalism has no one cause. In part, it is a response to the social pressures created in traditional Islamic societies by the move toward modernization and by the influence of Western ideas, such as liberal democracy, materialism, equal rights for women, and attitudes toward sex, marriage, and alcohol. In many Muslim countries, modernization has been accompanied by a growing gap between a rich urban minority and an impoverished urban and rural majority. For the impoverished majority, modernization has offered little in the way of tangible economic progress, while threatening the traditional value system. Thus, for a Muslim who cherishes his or her traditions and feels that his or her identity is jeopardized by the encroachment of alien Western values, Islamic fundamentalism has become a cultural anchor.

Fundamentalists demand commitment to traditional religious beliefs and rituals. The result has been a marked increase in the use of symbolic gestures that confirm Islamic values. In areas where fundamentalism is strong, women have resumed wearing floor-length, long-sleeved dresses and covering their hair; religious studies have increased in universities; the publication of religious tracts has increased; and public religious orations have risen.[32] Also, the sentiments of some fundamentalist groups are often anti-Western. Rightly or wrongly, Western influence is blamed for a range of social ills, and many fundamentalists' actions are directed against Western governments, cultural symbols, businesses, and even individuals.

In several Muslim countries, fundamentalists have gained political power and have used this to try to make Islamic law (as set down in the Koran, the bible of Islam) the law of the land. There are grounds for this in Islam doctrine. Islam makes no distinction between church and state. It is not just a religion; Islam is also the source of law, a guide to statecraft, and an arbiter of social behavior. Muslims believe that every human endeavor is within the purview of the faith—and this includes political activity—because the only purpose of any activity is to do God's will.[33] (Some Christian fundamentalists also share this view.) Muslim fundamentalists have been most successful in Iran, where a fundamentalist party has held power since 1979, but they also have had an influence in many other countries, such as Afghanistan (where the Taliban established an extreme fundamentalist state until removed by the U.S.-led coalition in 2002), Algeria, Egypt, Pakistan, Saudi Arabia, and the Sudan.

Economic Implications of Islam

LO4-3

The Koran establishes some explicit economic principles, many of which are pro–free enterprise.[34] The Koran speaks approvingly of free enterprise and of earning legitimate profit through trade and commerce (the Prophet Muhammad himself was once a trader). The protection of the right to private property is also embedded within Islam, although Islam asserts that all property is a favor from Allah (God), who created and so owns everything. Those who hold property are regarded as trustees rather than owners in the Western sense of the word. As trustees they are entitled to receive profits from the property but are admonished to use it in a righteous, socially beneficial, and prudent manner. This reflects Islam's concern with social justice. Islam is critical of those who earn profit through the exploitation of others. In the Islamic view of the world, humans are part of a collective in which the wealthy and successful have obligations to help the disadvantaged. Put simply, in Muslim countries, it is fine to earn a profit, so long as that profit is justly earned and not based on the exploitation of others for one's own advantage. It also helps if those making profits undertake charitable acts to help the poor. Furthermore, Islam stresses the importance of living up to contractual obligations, of keeping one's word, and of abstaining from deception. For a closer look at how Islam, capitalism, and globalization can coexist, see the accompanying Country Focus about the region around Kayseri in central Turkey.

Islamic Capitalism in Turkey

For years now, Turkey has been lobbying the European Union to allow it to join the free trade bloc as a member state. If the EU says yes, it will be the first Muslim state in the union. Many critics in the EU worry that Islam and Western-style capitalism do not mix well and that, as a consequence, allowing Turkey into the EU would be a mistake. However, a close look at what is going on in Turkey suggests this view may be misplaced. Consider the area around the city of Kayseri in central Turkey. Many dismiss this poor, largely agricultural region of Turkey as a non-European backwater, far removed from the secular bustle of Istanbul. It is a region where traditional Islamic values hold sway. And yet, it is also a region that has produced so many thriving Muslim enterprises that it is sometimes called the "Anatolian Tiger." Businesses based here include large food manufacturers, textile companies, furniture manufacturers, and engineering enterprises, many of which export a substantial percentage of their production.

Local business leaders attribute the success of companies in the region to an entrepreneurial spirit that they say is part of Islam. They point out that the Prophet Muhammad, who was himself a trader, preached merchant honor and commanded that 90 percent of a Muslim's life be devoted to work in order to put food on the table. Outside observers have gone further, arguing that what is occurring around Kayseri is an example of Islamic Calvinism, a fusion of traditional Islamic values and the work ethic often associated with Protestantism in general and Calvinism in particular.

However, not everyone agrees that Islam is the driving force behind the region's success. Saffet Arslan, the managing director of Ipek, the largest furniture producer in the region (which exports to more than 30 countries), says another force is at work—globalization! According to Arslan, over the past three decades local Muslims who once eschewed making money in favor of focusing on religion are now making business a priority. They see the Western world, and Western capitalism, as a model, not Islam, and because of globalization and the opportunities associated with it, they want to become successful.

If there is a weakness in the Islamic model of business that is emerging in places such as Kayseri, some say it can be found in traditional attitudes toward the role of women in the workplace, and the low level of female employment in the region. According to a report by the European Stability Initiative, the same group that holds up the Kayseri region as an example of Islamic Calvinism, the low participation of women in the local workforce is the Achilles' heel of the economy and may stymie the attempts of the region to catch up with the countries of the European Union.[35]

Given the Islamic proclivity to favor market-based systems, Muslim countries are likely to be receptive to international businesses as long as those businesses behave in a manner that is consistent with Islamic ethics. Businesses that are perceived as making an unjust profit through the exploitation of others, by deception, or by breaking contractual obligations are unlikely to be welcomed in an Islamic country. In addition, in Islamic countries where fundamentalism is on the rise, hostility toward Western-owned businesses is likely to increase.

One economic principle of Islam prohibits the payment or receipt of interest, which is considered usury. This is not just a matter of theology; in several Islamic states, it is also a matter of law. The Koran clearly condemns interest, which is called *riba* in Arabic, as exploitative and unjust. For many years, banks operating in Islamic countries conveniently ignored this condemnation, but starting about 40 years ago with the establishment of an Islamic bank in Egypt, Islamic banks started to open in predominantly Muslim countries. By 2009, more than 400 Islamic banks in more than 50 countries had assets of around $400 billion, while another $800 billion was managed by mutual funds that adhered to Islamic principles.[36] Even conventional banks are entering the market—both Citigroup and HSBC, two of the world's largest financial institutions, now offer Islamic financial services. While only Iran and the Sudan enforce Islamic banking conventions, in an increasing number of countries customers can choose between conventional banks and Islamic banks.

Conventional banks make a profit on the spread between the interest rate they have to pay to depositors and the higher interest rate they charge borrowers. Because Islamic banks cannot pay or charge interest, they must find a different way of making money. Islamic banks have experimented with two different banking methods—the *mudarabah* and the *murabaha*.[37]

A *mudarabah* contract is similar to a profit-sharing scheme. Under *mudarabah,* when an Islamic bank lends money to a business, rather than charging that business interest on the loan, it takes a share in the profits that are derived from the investment. Similarly, when a business (or individual) deposits money at an Islamic bank in a savings account, the deposit is treated as an equity investment in whatever activity the bank uses the capital for. Thus, the depositor receives a share in the profit from the bank's investment (as opposed to interest payments) according to an agreed-on ratio. Some Muslims claim this is a more efficient system than the Western banking system, because it encourages both long-term savings and long-term investment. However, there is no hard evidence of this, and many believe that a *mudarabah* system is less efficient than a conventional Western banking system.

The second Islamic banking method, the *murabaha* contract, is the most widely used among the world's Islamic banks, primarily because it is the easiest to implement. In a *murabaha* contract, when a firm wishes to purchase something using a loan—let's say a piece of equipment that costs $1,000—the firm tells the bank after having negotiated the price with the equipment manufacturer. The bank then buys the equipment for $1,000, and the borrower buys it back from the bank at some later date for, say, $1,100, a price that includes a $100 markup for the bank. A cynic might point out that such a markup is functionally equivalent to an interest payment, and it is the similarity between this method and conventional banking that makes it so much easier to adopt.

Hinduism

LO4-2

Hinduism has approximately 750 million adherents, most of them on the Indian subcontinent. Hinduism began in the Indus Valley in India more than 4,000 years ago, making it the world's oldest major religion. Unlike Christianity and Islam, its founding is not linked to a particular person. Nor does it have an officially sanctioned sacred book such as the Bible or the Koran. Hindus believe that a moral force in society requires the acceptance of certain responsibilities, called *dharma*. Hindus believe in reincarnation, or rebirth into a different body, after death. Hindus also believe in *karma,* the spiritual progression of each person's soul. A person's karma is affected by the way he or she lives. The moral state of an individual's karma determines the challenges he or she will face in the next life. By perfecting the soul in each new life, Hindus believe that an individual can eventually achieve *nirvana,* a state of complete spiritual perfection that renders reincarnation no longer necessary. Many Hindus believe that the way to achieve nirvana is to lead a severe ascetic lifestyle of material and physical self-denial, devoting life to a spiritual rather than material quest.

Economic Implications of Hinduism　　　■**LO4-3**

Max Weber, famous for expounding on the Protestant work ethic, also argued that the ascetic principles embedded in Hinduism do not encourage the kind of entrepreneurial activity in pursuit of wealth creation that we find in Protestantism.[38] According to Weber, traditional Hindu values emphasize that individuals should be judged not by their material achievements but by their spiritual achievements. Hindus perceive the pursuit of material well-being as making the attainment of nirvana more difficult. Given the emphasis on an ascetic lifestyle, Weber thought that devout Hindus would be less likely to engage in entrepreneurial activity than devout Protestants.

Mahatma Gandhi, the famous Indian nationalist and spiritual leader, was certainly the embodiment of Hindu asceticism. It has been argued that the values of Hindu asceticism and self-reliance that Gandhi advocated had a negative impact on the economic development of post independence India.[39] But one must be careful not to read too much into Weber's arguments. Modern India is a very dynamic entrepreneurial society, and millions of hardworking entrepreneurs form the economic backbone of the country's rapidly growing economy.

Historically, Hinduism also supported India's caste system. The concept of mobility between castes within an individual's lifetime makes no sense to traditional Hindus. Hindus see mobility between castes as something that is achieved through spiritual progression and reincarnation. An individual can be reborn into a higher caste in his or her next life if he or she achieves spiritual development in this life. Although the caste system has been abolished in India, as discussed earlier in the chapter, it still casts a long shadow over Indian life.

Buddhism　　　■**LO4-2**

Buddhism was founded in the sixth century B.C. by Siddhartha Gautama, in what is now Nepal. Siddhartha renounced his wealth to pursue an ascetic lifestyle and spiritual perfection. His adherents claimed he achieved nirvana but decided to remain on earth to teach his followers how they too could achieve this state of spiritual enlightenment. Siddhartha became known as the Buddha (which means "the awakened one"). Today, most Buddhists are found in Central and Southeast Asia, China, Korea, and Japan. According to Buddhism, suffering originates in people's desires for pleasure. Cessation of suffering can be achieved by following a path for transformation. Siddhartha offered the Noble Eightfold Path as a route for transformation. This emphasizes right seeing, thinking, speech, action, living, effort, mindfulness, and meditation. Unlike Hinduism, Buddhism does not support the caste system. Nor does Buddhism advocate the kind of extreme ascetic behavior that is encouraged by Hinduism. Nevertheless, like Hindus, Buddhists stress the afterlife and spiritual achievement rather than involvement in this world.

Economic Implications of Buddhism　　　■**LO4-3**

The emphasis on wealth creation that is embedded in Protestantism is not found in Buddhism. Thus, in Buddhist societies, we do not see the same kind of historical cultural stress on entrepreneurial behavior that Weber claimed could be found in the Protestant West. But unlike Hinduism, the lack of support for the caste system and extreme ascetic behavior suggests that a Buddhist society may represent a more fertile ground for entrepreneurial activity than a Hindu culture.

Confucianism　　　■**LO4-2**

Confucianism was founded in the fifth century B.C. by K'ung-Fu-tzu, more generally known as Confucius. For more than 2,000 years until the 1949 Communist revolution, Confucianism was the official ethical system of China. While observance of Confucian ethics has been weakened in China since 1949, many people still follow the teachings of Confucius, principally in China, Korea, and Japan. Confucianism teaches the importance of attaining personal salvation through right action. Although not a religion, Confucian ideology has become deeply embedded in the culture of these countries over the centuries and, through that, has an impact on the lives of many millions more. Confucianism is built around a comprehensive ethical code that sets down guidelines for relationships with others. High moral and ethical conduct and loyalty to others are central to Confucianism. Unlike religions, Confucianism is not concerned with the supernatural and has little to say about the concept of a supreme being or an afterlife.

Economic Implications of Confucianism

LO4-3

Some scholars maintain that Confucianism may have economic implications as profound as those Weber argued were to be found in Protestantism, although they are of a different nature.[40] Their basic thesis is that the influence of Confucian ethics on the culture of China, Japan, South Korea, and Taiwan, by lowering the costs of doing business in those countries, may help explain their economic success. In this regard, three values central to the Confucian system of ethics is of particular interest: loyalty, reciprocal obligations, and honesty in dealings with others.

In Confucian thought, loyalty to one's superiors is regarded as a sacred duty—an absolute obligation. In modern organizations based in Confucian cultures, the loyalty that binds employees to the heads of their organization can reduce the conflict between management and labor that we find in more class-conscious societies. Cooperation between management and labor can be achieved at a lower cost in a culture where the virtue of loyalty is emphasized in the value systems.

However, in a Confucian culture, loyalty to one's superiors, such as a worker's loyalty to management, is not blind loyalty. The concept of reciprocal obligations is important. Confucian ethics stresses that superiors are obliged to reward the loyalty of their subordinates by bestowing blessings on them. If these "blessings" are not forthcoming, then neither will be the loyalty. This Confucian ethic is central to the Chinese concept of *guanxi,* which refers to relationship networks supported by reciprocal obligations.[41] *Guanxi* means relationships, although in business settings it can be better understood as connections. Today, Chinese will often cultivate a *guanxiwang,* or "relationship network," for help. Reciprocal obligations are the glue that holds such networks together. If those obligations are not met— if favors done are not paid back or reciprocated—the reputation of the transgressor is tarnished and the person will be less able to draw on his or her *guanxiwang* for help in the future. Thus, the implicit threat of social sanctions is often sufficient to ensure that favors are repaid, obligations are met, and relationships are honored. In a society that lacks a rule-based legal tradition, and thus legal ways of redressing wrongs such as violations of business agreements, *guanxi* is an important mechanism for building long-term business relationships and getting business done in China. For an example of the importance of *guanxi,* read the Management Focus on DMG-Shanghai.

A third concept found in Confucian ethics is the importance attached to honesty. Confucian thinkers emphasize that although dishonest behavior may yield short-term benefits for the transgressor, dishonesty does not pay in the long run. The importance attached to honesty has major economic implications. When companies can trust each other not to break contractual obligations, the costs of doing business are lowered. Expensive lawyers are not needed to resolve contract disputes. In a Confucian society, people may be less hesitant to commit substantial resources to cooperative ventures than in a society where honesty is less pervasive. When companies adhere to Confucian ethics, they can trust each other not to violate the terms of cooperative agreements. Thus, the costs of achieving cooperation between companies may be lower in societies such as Japan relative to societies where trust is less pervasive.

DMG-Shanghai

In 1993, New Yorker Dan Mintz moved to China as a freelance film director with no contacts, no advertising experience, and no Mandarin skills. By 2009, the company he subsequently founded in China, DMG, had emerged as one of China's fastest-growing advertising agencies with a client list that includes Budweiser, Unilever, Sony, Nabisco, Audi, Volkswagen, China Mobile, and dozens of other Chinese brands. Mintz attributes his success in part to what the Chinese call *guanxi.*

Guanxi literally means relationships, although in business settings it can be better understood as connections. *Guanxi* has its roots in the Confucian philosophy of valuing social hierarchy and reciprocal obligations. Confucian ideology has a 2,000-year-old history in China. Confucianism stresses the importance of relationships, both within the family and between master and servant. Confucian ideology teaches that people are not created equal. In Confucian thought, loyalty and obligations to one's superiors (or to family) is regarded as a sacred duty, but at the same time, this loyalty has its price. Social superiors are obligated to reward the loyalty of their social inferiors by bestowing "blessings" upon them; thus, the obligations are reciprocal. Chinese will often cultivate a *guanxiwang,* or "relationship network," for help. There is a tacit acknowledgment that if you have the right *guanxi,* legal rules can be broken, or at least bent.

Mintz, who is now fluent in Mandarin, cultivated his *guanxiwang* by going into business with two young Chinese who had connections, Bing Wu and Peter Xiao. Wu, who works on the production side of the business, was a former national gymnastics champion, which translates into prestige and access to business and government officials. Xiao comes from a military family with major political connections. Together, these three have been able to open doors that long-established Western advertising agencies could not. They have done it in large part by leveraging the contacts of Wu and Xiao, and by backing up their connections with what the Chinese call *Shi li,* the ability to do good work.

A case in point was DMG's campaign for Volkswagen, which helped the German company become ubiquitous in China. The ads used traditional Chinese characters, which had been banned by Chairman Mao during the cultural revolution in favor of simplified versions. To get permission to use the characters in film and print ads—a first in modern China—the trio had to draw on high-level government contacts in Beijing. They won over officials by arguing that the old characters should be thought of not as "characters" but as art. Later, they shot TV spots for the ad on Shanghai's famous Bund, a congested boulevard that runs along the waterfront of the old city. Drawing again on government contacts, they were able to shut down the Bund to make the shoot. Steven Spielberg had been able to close down only a portion of the street when he filmed *Empire of the Sun* there in 1986. DMG has also filmed inside Beijing's Forbidden City, even though it is against the law to do so. Using his contacts, Mintz persuaded the government to lift the law for 24 hours. As Mintz has noted, "We don't stop when we come across regulations. There are restrictions everywhere you go. You have to know how get around them and get things done."[42]

For example, it has been argued that the close ties between the automobile companies and their component parts suppliers in Japan are facilitated by a combination of trust and reciprocal obligations. These close ties allow the auto companies and their suppliers to work together on a range of issues, including inventory reduction, quality control, and design. The competitive advantage of Japanese auto companies such as Toyota may in part be explained by such factors.[43] Similarly, the combination of trust and reciprocal obligations is central to the workings and persistence of *guanxi* networks in China.

LANGUAGE

One obvious way in which countries differ is language. By language, we mean both the spoken and the unspoken means of communication. Language is one of the defining characteristics of a culture.

Spoken Language

Language does far more than just enable people to communicate with each other. The nature of a language also structures the way we perceive the world. The language of a society can direct the attention of its members to certain features of the world rather than others. The classic illustration of this phenomenon is that whereas the English language has but one word for snow, the language of the Inuit (Eskimos) lacks a general term for it. Instead, because distinguishing different forms of snow is so important in the lives of the Inuit, they have 24 words that describe different types of snow (e.g., powder snow, falling snow, wet snow, drifting snow).[44]

Because language shapes the way people perceive the world, it also helps define culture. Countries with more than one language often have more than one culture. Canada has an English-speaking culture and a French-speaking culture. Tensions between the two can run quite high, with a substantial proportion of the French-speaking minority demanding independence from a Canada "dominated by English speakers." The same phenomenon can be observed in many other countries. Belgium is divided into Flemish and French speakers, and tensions between the two groups exist; in Spain, a Basque-speaking minority with its own distinctive culture has been agitating for independence from the Spanish-speaking majority for decades; on the Mediterranean island of Cyprus, the culturally diverse Greek- and Turkish-speaking populations of the island engaged in open conflict in the 1970s, and the island is now partitioned into two parts. While it does not necessarily follow that language differences create differences in culture and, therefore, separatist pressures (e.g., witness the harmony in Switzerland, where four languages are spoken), there certainly seems to be a tendency in this direction.[45]

Chinese is the mother tongue of the largest number of people, followed by English and ▮ **04-2** ▮ Hindi, which is spoken in India. However, the most widely spoken language in the world is English, followed by French, Spanish, and Chinese (i.e., many people speak English as a second language). English is increasingly becoming the language of international business. When a Japanese and a German businessperson get together to do business, it is almost certain that they will communicate in English. However, although English is widely used, learning the local language yields considerable advantages. Most people prefer to converse in their own language, and being able to speak the local language can build rapport, which may be very important for a business deal. International businesses that do not understand the local language can make major blunders through improper translation. For example, the Sunbeam Corporation used the English words for its "Mist-Stick" mist-producing hair-curling iron when it entered the German market, only to discover after an expensive advertising campaign that *mist* means excrement in German. General Motors was troubled by the lack of enthusiasm among Puerto Rican dealers for its new Chevrolet Nova. When literally translated into Spanish, *nova* means star. However, when spoken it sounds like "no va," which in Spanish means "it doesn't go." General Motors changed the name of the car to Caribe.[46]

Unspoken Language

Unspoken language refers to nonverbal communication. We all communicate with each other by a host of nonverbal cues. The raising of eyebrows, for example, is a sign of recognition in most cultures, while a smile is a sign of joy. Many nonverbal cues, however, are culturally bound. A failure to understand the nonverbal cues of another culture can lead to a communication failure. For example, making a circle with the thumb and the forefinger is a friendly gesture in the United States, but it is a vulgar sexual invitation in Greece and Turkey. Similarly, while most Americans and Europeans use the thumbs-up gesture to indicate that "it's all right," in Greece the gesture is obscene.

Another aspect of nonverbal communication is personal space, which is the comfortable amount of distance between you and someone you are talking with. In the United States, the customary distance apart adopted by parties in a business discussion is five to eight feet. In Latin America, it is three to five feet. Consequently, many North Americans unconsciously feel that Latin Americans are invading their personal space and can be seen backing away from them during a conversation. Indeed, the American may feel that the Latin is being aggressive and pushy. In turn, the Latin American may interpret such backing away as aloofness. The result can be a regrettable lack of rapport between two businesspeople from different cultures.

EDUCATION

Formal education plays a key role in a society. Formal education is the medium through which individuals learn many of the language, conceptual, and mathematical skills that are indispensable in a modern society. Formal education also supplements the family's role in socializing the young into the values and norms of a society. Values and norms are taught both directly and indirectly. Schools generally teach basic facts about the social and political nature of a society. They also focus on the fundamental obligations of citizenship. Cultural norms are also taught indirectly at school. Respect for others, obedience to authority, honesty, neatness, being on time, and so on, are all part of the "hidden curriculum" of schools. The use of a grading system also teaches children the value of personal achievement and competition.[47]

From an international business perspective, one important aspect of education is its role as a determinant of national competitive advantage.[48] The availability of a pool of skilled and educated workers seems to be a major determinant of the likely economic success of a country. In analyzing the competitive success of Japan since 1945, for example, Michael Porter notes that after the war, Japan had almost nothing except for a pool of skilled and educated human resources.

> With a long tradition of respect for education that borders on reverence, Japan possessed a large pool of literate, educated, and increasingly skilled human resources. . . . Japan has benefited from a large pool of trained engineers. Japanese universities graduate many more engineers per capita than in the United States. . . . A first-rate primary and secondary education system in Japan operates based on high standards and emphasizes math and science. Primary and secondary education is highly competitive. . . . Japanese education provides most students all over Japan with a sound education for later education and training. A Japanese high school graduate knows as much about math as most American college graduates.[49]

Porter's point is that Japan's excellent education system is an important factor explaining the country's postwar economic success. Not only is a good education system a determinant of national competitive advantage, but it is also an important factor guiding the location choices of international businesses. The recent trend to outsource information technology jobs to India, for example, is partly due to the presence of significant numbers of trained engineers in India, which in turn is a result of the Indian education system. By the same token, it would make little sense to base production facilities that require highly skilled labor in a country where the education system was so poor that a skilled labor pool wasn't available, no matter how attractive the country might seem on other dimensions. It might make sense to base production operations that require only unskilled labor in such a country.

The general education level of a country is also a good index of the kind of products that might sell in a country and of the type of promotional material that should be used. For example, a country where more than 70 percent of the population is illiterate is unlikely to be a good market for popular books. Promotional material containing written descriptions of mass-marketed products is unlikely to have an effect in a country where almost three-quarters of the population cannot read. It is far better to use pictorial promotions in such circumstances.

CULTURE AND THE WORKPLACE   █ LO4-4 █

Of considerable importance for an international business with operations in different countries is how a society's culture affects the values found in the workplace. Management process and practices may need to vary according to culturally determined work-related values. For example, if the cultures of the United States and France result in different work-related values, an international business with operations in both countries should vary its management process and practices to account for these differences.

Probably the most famous study of how culture relates to values in the workplace was undertaken by Geert Hofstede.[50] As part of his job as a psychologist working for IBM, Hofstede collected data on employee attitudes and values for more than 100,000 individuals from 1967 to 1973. These data enabled him to compare dimensions of culture across 40 countries. Hofstede isolated four dimensions that he claimed summarized different cultures—power distance, uncertainty avoidance, individualism versus collectivism, and masculinity versus femininity.

Hofstede's **power distance** dimension focused on how a society deals with the fact that people are unequal in physical and intellectual capabilities. According to Hofstede, high power distance cultures were found in countries that let inequalities grow over time into inequalities of power and wealth. Low power distance cultures were found in societies that tried to play down such inequalities as much as possible.

The **individualism versus collectivism** dimension focused on the relationship between the individual and his or her fellows. In individualistic societies, the ties between individuals were loose, and individual achievement and freedom were highly valued. In societies where collectivism was emphasized, the ties between individuals were tight. In such societies, people were born into collectives, such as extended families, and everyone was supposed to look after the interest of his or her collective.

Hofstede's **uncertainty avoidance** dimension measured the extent to which different cultures socialized their members into accepting ambiguous situations and tolerating uncertainty. Members of high uncertainty avoidance cultures placed a premium on job security, career patterns, retirement benefits, and so on. They also had a strong need for rules and regulations; the manager was expected to issue clear instructions, and subordinates' initiatives were tightly controlled. Lower uncertainty avoidance cultures were characterized by a greater readiness to take risks and less emotional resistance to change.

Hofstede's **masculinity versus femininity** dimension looked at the relationship between gender and work roles. In masculine cultures, sex roles were sharply differentiated, and traditional "masculine values," such as achievement and the effective exercise of power, determined cultural ideals. In feminine cultures, sex roles were less sharply distinguished, and little differentiation was made between men and women in the same job.

Hofstede created an index score for each of these four dimensions that ranged from 0 to 100 and scored high for high individualism, high power distance, high uncertainty avoidance, and high masculinity. He averaged the score for all employees from a given country. Table 4.1 summarizes these data for 20 selected countries. Western nations such as the United States, Canada, and Britain score high on the individualism scale and low on the power distance scale. At the other extreme are a group of Latin American and Asian countries that emphasize collectivism over individualism and score high on the power distance scale. Table 4.1 also reveals that Japan's culture has strong uncertainty avoidance and high masculinity. This characterization fits the standard stereotype of Japan as a country that is male dominant and where uncertainty avoidance exhibits itself in the institution of lifetime employment. Sweden and Denmark stand out as countries that have both low uncertainty avoidance and low masculinity (high emphasis on "feminine" values).

TABLE 4.1 Work-Related Values for 20 Selected Countries

	Power Distance	Uncertainty Avoidance	Individualism	Masculinity
Argentina	49	86	46	56
Australia	36	51	90	61
Brazil	69	76	38	49
Canada	39	48	80	52
Denmark	18	23	74	16
France	68	86	71	43
Germany (F.R.)	35	65	67	66
Great Britain	35	35	89	66
India	77	40	48	56
Indonesia	78	48	14	46
Israel	13	81	54	47
Japan	54	92	46	95
Mexico	81	82	30	69
Netherlands	38	53	80	14
Panama	95	86	11	44
Spain	57	86	51	42
Sweden	31	29	71	5
Thailand	64	64	20	34
Turkey	66	85	37	45
United States	40	46	91	62

Source: Cited in G. Hofstede, "The Cultural Relativity of Organizational Practices and Theories," *Journal of International Business Studies* 14 (Fall 1983), pp. 75–89. Reprinted by permission of Dr. Hofstede.

Hofstede's results are interesting for what they tell us in a very general way about differences between cultures. Many of Hofstede's findings are consistent with standard Western stereotypes about cultural differences. For example, many people believe Americans are more individualistic and egalitarian than the Japanese (they have a lower power distance), who in turn are more individualistic and egalitarian than Mexicans. Similarly, many might agree that Latin countries such as Mexico place a higher emphasis on masculine value—they are machismo cultures—than the Nordic countries of Denmark and Sweden.

However, one should be careful about reading too much into Hofstede's research. It has been criticized on a number of points.[51] First, Hofstede assumes there is a one-to-one correspondence between culture and the nation-state, but as we saw earlier, many countries have more than one culture. Hofstede's results do not capture this distinction. Second, the research may have been culturally bound. The research team was composed of Europeans and Americans. The questions they asked of IBM employees and their analysis of the answers may have been shaped by their own cultural biases and concerns. So it is not surprising that Hofstede's results confirm Western stereotypes, because it was Westerners who undertook the research.

Third, Hofstede's informants worked not only within a single industry, the computer industry, but also within one company, IBM. At the time, IBM was renowned for its own strong corporate culture and employee selection procedures, making it possible that the employees' values were different in important respects from the values of the cultures from which those employees came. Also, certain social classes (such as unskilled manual workers) were excluded from Hofstede's sample. A final caution is that Hofstede's work is now beginning to look dated. Cultures do not stand still; they evolve, albeit slowly. What was a reasonable characterization in the 1960s and 1970s may not be so today.

Still, just as it should not be accepted without question, Hofstede's work should not be dismissed either. It represents a starting point for managers trying to figure out how cultures differ and what that might mean for management practices. Also, several other scholars have found strong evidence that differences in culture affect values and practices in the workplace, and Hofstede's basic results have been replicated using more diverse samples of individuals in different settings.[52] Nevertheless, managers should use the results with caution, for they are not necessarily accurate.

Hofstede subsequently expanded his original research to include a fifth dimension that he argued captured additional cultural differences not brought out in his earlier work.[53] He referred to this dimension as "Confucian dynamism" (sometimes called *long-term orientation*). According to Hofstede, **Confucian dynamism** captures attitudes toward time, persistence, ordering by status, protection of face, respect for tradition, and reciprocation of gifts and favors. The label refers to these "values" being derived from Confucian teachings. As might be expected, East Asian countries such as Japan, Hong Kong, and Thailand scored high on Confucian dynamism, while nations such as the United States and Canada scored low. Hofstede and his associates went on to argue that their evidence suggested that nations with higher economic growth rates scored high on Confucian dynamism and low on individualism—the implication being Confucianism is good for growth. However, subsequent studies have shown that this finding does not hold up under more sophisticated statistical analysis.[54] During the past decade, countries with high individualism and low Confucian dynamics such as the United States have attained high growth rates, while some Confucian cultures such as Japan have had stagnant economic growth. In reality, while culture might influence the economic success of a nation, it is just one of many factors, and while its importance should not be ignored, it should not be overstated either. The factors discussed in Chapters 2 and 3—economic, political, and legal systems—are probably more important than culture in explaining differential economic growth rates over time.

CULTURAL CHANGE   LO4-5

Culture is not a constant; it evolves over time.[55] Changes in value systems can be slow and painful for a society. In the 1960s, for example, American values toward the role of women, love, sex, and marriage underwent significant changes. Much of the social turmoil of that time reflected these changes. Change, however, does occur and can often be quite profound. For example, at the beginning of the 1960s, the idea that women might hold senior management positions in major corporations was not widely accepted. Many scoffed at the idea. Today, it is a reality. For example, in 2012 Virginia Rometty became the CEO of IBM. No one in the mainstream of American society now questions the development or the capability of women in the business world. American culture has changed (although it is still more difficult for women than men to gain senior management positions).

For another illustration of cultural change, consider Japan. Some academics argue that a major cultural shift has been occurring in Japan, with a move toward greater individualism.[56] The model Japanese office worker, or "salaryman," is characterized as being loyal to his boss and the organization to the point of giving up evenings, weekends, and vacations to serve the organization, which is the collective of which the employee is a member. However, a new generation of office workers may not fit this model. An individual from the new generation is likely to be more direct than the traditional Japanese. He acts more like a Westerner, a *gaijin*. He does not live for the company and will move on if he gets the offer of a better job. He is not keen on overtime, especially if he has a date. He has his own plans for his free time, and they may not include drinking or playing golf with the boss.[57]

Several studies have suggested that economic advancement and globalization may be important factors in societal change.[58] There is evidence that economic progress is accompanied by a shift in values away from collectivism and toward individualism.[59] Thus, as Japan has become richer, the cultural emphasis on collectivism has declined and greater individualism is being witnessed. One reason for this shift may be that richer societies exhibit less need for social and material support structures built on collectives, whether the collective is the extended family or the paternalistic company. People are better able to take care of their own needs. As a result, the importance attached to collectivism declines, while greater economic freedoms lead to an increase in opportunities for expressing individualism.

The culture of societies may also change as they become richer because economic progress affects a number of other factors, which in turn influence culture. For example, increased urbanization and improvements in the quality and availability of education are both a function of economic progress, and both can lead to declining emphasis on the traditional values associated with poor rural societies. A 25-year study of values in 78 countries, known as the World Values Survey, coordinated by the University of Michigan's Institute for Social Research, has documented how values change. The study linked these changes in values to changes in a country's level of economic development.[60] According to this research, as countries get richer, a shift occurs away from "traditional values" linked to religion, family, and country, and toward "secular rational" values. Traditionalists say religion is important in their lives. They have a strong sense of national pride; they also think that children should be taught to obey and that the first duty of a child is to make his or her parents proud. They say abortion, euthanasia, divorce, and suicide are never justified. At the other end of this spectrum are secular rational values.

Another category in the World Values Survey is quality of life attributes. At one end of this spectrum are "survival values," the values people hold when the struggle for survival is of paramount importance. These values tend to stress that economic and physical security are more important than self-expression. People who cannot take food or safety for granted tend to be xenophobic, are wary of political activity, have authoritarian tendencies, and believe that men make better political leaders than women. "Self-expression" or "well-being" values stress the importance of diversity, belonging, and participation in political processes.

As countries get richer, there seems to be a shift from "traditional" to "secular rational" values, and from "survival values" to "well-being" values. The shift, however, takes time, primarily because individuals are socialized into a set of values when they are young and find it difficult to change as they grow older. Substantial changes in values are linked to generations, with younger people typically being in the vanguard of a significant change in values.

With regard to globalization, some have argued that advances in transportation and communication technologies, the dramatic increase in trade that we have witnessed since World War II, and the rise of global corporations such as Hitachi, Disney, Microsoft, IBM, Google, and Levi Strauss, whose products and operations can be found around the globe, are helping create conditions for the merging or convergence of cultures.[61] With McDonald's hamburgers in China, The Gap in India, iPods in South Africa, and MTV everywhere helping foster a ubiquitous youth culture, and with countries around the world climbing the ladder of economic progress, some argue that the conditions for less cultural variation have been created. There may be, in other words, a slow but steady convergence occurring across different cultures toward some universally accepted values and norms: This is known as the *convergence* hypothesis.[62]

Having said this, one must not ignore important countertrends, such as the shift toward Islamic fundamentalism in several countries; the separatist movement in Quebec, Canada; or ethnic strains and separatist movements in Russia. Such countertrends in many ways are a reaction to the pressures for cultural convergence. In an increasingly modern and materialistic world, some societies are trying to reemphasize their cultural roots and uniqueness. Cultural change is not unidirectional, with national cultures converging toward some homogeneous global entity. It is also important to note that while some elements of culture change quite rapidly—particularly the use of material symbols—other elements change slowly if at all. Thus, just because people the world over wear jeans, eat at McDonald's, use smartphones, watch their national version of *American Idol,* and drive Ford cars to work down freeways, one should not assume that they have also adopted American (or Western) values —for often they have not.[63] To illustrate, consider that many Westerners eat Chinese food, watch Chinese martial arts movies, and take classes in kung fu, but their values are still those of Westerners. Thus, a distinction needs to be made between the visible material aspects of culture and the deep structure, particularly core social values and norms. The deep structure changes only slowly, and differences here are often far more persistent than one might suppose.

■ IMPLICATIONS FOR MANAGERS ■

International business is different from national business because countries and societies are different. In this chapter, we have seen just how different societies can be. Societies differ because their cultures vary. Their cultures vary because of profound differences in social structure, religion, language, education, economic philosophy, and political philosophy. Three important implications for international business flow from these differences. The first is the need to develop cross-cultural literacy. There is a need not only to appreciate that cultural differences exist but also to appreciate what such differences mean for international business. A second implication centers on the connection between culture and national competitive advantage. A third implication looks at the connection between culture and ethics in decision making. In this section, we explore the first two of these issues in depth. The connection between culture and ethics is explored in the next chapter.

CROSS-CULTURAL LITERACY

One of the biggest dangers confronting a company that goes abroad for the first time is the danger of being ill-informed. International businesses that are ill-informed about the practices of another culture are likely to fail. Doing business in different cultures requires adaptation to conform with the value systems and norms of that culture. Adaptation can embrace all aspects of an international firm's operations in a foreign country. The way in which deals are negotiated, the appropriate incentive pay systems for salespeople, the structure of the organization, the name of a product, the tenor of relations between management and labor, the manner in which the product is promoted, and so on, are all sensitive to cultural differences. What works in one culture might not work in another (see the opening case on Walmart in Germany for an example).

To combat the danger of being ill-informed, international businesses should consider employing local citizens to help them do business in a particular culture. They must also ensure that home-country executives are cosmopolitan enough to understand how differences in culture affect the practice of business. Transferring executives overseas at regular intervals to expose them to different cultures will help build a cadre of cosmopolitan executives. An international business must also be constantly on guard against the dangers of *ethnocentric behavior.* **Ethnocentrism** is a belief in the superiority of one's own ethnic group or culture. Hand in hand with ethnocentrism goes a disregard or contempt for the culture of other countries. Unfortunately, ethnocentrism is all too prevalent; many Americans are guilty of it, as are many French people, Japanese people, British people, and so on. Ugly as it is, ethnocentrism is a fact of life, one that international businesses must be on guard against.

Simple examples illustrate how important cross-cultural literacy can be. Anthropologist Edward T. Hall has described how Americans, who tend to be informal in nature, react strongly to being corrected or reprimanded in public.[64] This can cause problems in Germany, where a cultural tendency toward correcting strangers can shock and offend most Americans. For their part, Germans can be a bit taken aback by the tendency of Americans to call people by their first name. This is uncomfortable enough among executives of the same rank, but it can be seen as insulting when a young and junior American executive addresses an older and more senior German manager by his first name without having been invited to do so. Hall concludes it can take a long time to get on a first-name basis with a German; if you rush the process, you will be perceived as overfriendly and rude, and that may not be good for business.

Hall also notes that cultural differences in attitude to time can cause a myriad problems. He notes that in the United States, giving a person a deadline is a way of increasing the urgency or relative importance of a task. However, in the Middle East, giving a deadline can have exactly the opposite effect. The American who insists an Arab business associate make his mind up in a hurry is likely to be perceived as overly demanding and exerting undue pressure. The result may be exactly the opposite of what the American intended, with the Arab going slow as a reaction to the American's arrogance and rudeness. For his part, the American may believe that an Arab associate is being rude if he shows up late to a meeting because he met a friend in the street and stopped to talk. The American, of course, is very concerned about time and scheduling. But for the Arab, who lives in a society where social networks are a major source of information, and maintaining relationships is important, finishing the discussion with a friend is more important than adhering to a strict schedule. Indeed, the Arab may be puzzled as to why the American attaches so much importance to time and schedule.

CULTURE AND COMPETITIVE ADVANTAGE

One theme that surfaces in this chapter is the relationship between culture and national competitive advantage. Put simply, the value systems and norms of a country influence the costs of doing business in that country. The costs of doing business in a country influence the ability of firms to establish a competitive advantage in the global marketplace. We have seen how attitudes toward cooperation between management and labor, toward work, and toward the payment of interest are influenced by social structure and religion. It can be argued that the class-based conflict between workers and management in class-conscious societies, when it leads to industrial disruption, raises the costs of doing business in that society. Similarly, we have seen how some sociologists have argued that the ascetic "other-worldly" ethics of Hinduism may not be as supportive of capitalism as the ethics embedded in Protestantism and Confucianism. Also, Islamic laws banning interest payments may raise the costs of doing business by constraining a country's banking system.

Japan presents an interesting case study of how culture can influence competitive advantage. Some scholars have argued that the culture of modern Japan lowers the costs of doing business relative to the costs in most Western nations. Japan's emphasis on group affiliation, loyalty, reciprocal obligations, honesty, and education all boost the competitiveness of Japanese companies. The emphasis on group affiliation and loyalty encourages individuals to identify strongly with the companies in which they work. This tends to foster an ethic of hard work and cooperation between management and labor "for the good of the company." Similarly, reciprocal obligations and honesty help foster an atmosphere of trust between companies and their suppliers. This encourages them to enter into long-term relationships with each other to work on inventory reduction, quality control, and design—all of which have been shown to improve an organization's competitiveness. This level of cooperation has often been lacking in the West, where the relationship between a company and its suppliers tends to be a short-term one structured around competitive bidding rather than one based on long-term mutual commitments. In addition, the availability of a pool of highly skilled labor, particularly engineers, has helped Japanese enterprises develop cost-reducing process innovations that have boosted their productivity.[65] Thus, cultural factors may help explain the success enjoyed by many Japanese businesses in the global marketplace. Most notably, it has been argued that the rise of Japan as an economic power during the second half of the twentieth century may be in part attributed to the economic consequences of its culture.[66]

It also has been argued that the Japanese culture is less supportive of entrepreneurial activity than, say, American society. In many ways, entrepreneurial activity is a product of an individualistic mindset, not a classic characteristic of the Japanese. This may explain why American enterprises, rather than Japanese corporations, dominate industries where entrepreneurship and innovation are highly valued, such as computer software and biotechnology. Of course, obvious and significant exceptions to this generalization exist. Masayoshi Son recognized the potential of software far faster than any of Japan's corporate giants; set up his company, Softbank, in 1981; and over the past 30 years has built it into Japan's top software distributor. Similarly, dynamic entrepreneurial individuals established major Japanese companies such as Sony and Matsushita. But these examples may be the exceptions that prove the rule, for as yet there has been no surge in entrepreneurial high-technology enterprises in Japan equivalent to what has occurred in the United States.

For the international business, the connection between culture and competitive advantage is important for two reasons. First, the connection suggests which countries are likely to produce the most viable competitors. For example, one might argue that U.S. enterprises are likely to see continued growth in aggressive, cost-efficient competitors from those Pacific Rim nations where a combination of free market economics, Confucian ideology, group-oriented social structures, and advanced education systems can all be found (e.g., South Korea, Taiwan, Japan, and, increasingly, China).

Second, the connection between culture and competitive advantage has important implications for the choice of countries in which to locate production facilities and do business. Consider a hypothetical case when a company has to choose between two countries, A and B, for locating a production facility. Both countries are characterized by low labor costs and good access to world markets. Both countries are of roughly the same size (in terms of population), and both are at a similar stage of economic development. In country A, the education system is undeveloped, the society is characterized by a marked stratification between the upper and lower classes, and there are six major linguistic groups. In country B, the education system is well developed, social stratification is lacking, group identification is valued by the culture, and there is only one linguistic group. Which country makes the best investment site?

Country B probably does. In country A, conflict between management and labor, and between different language groups, can be expected to lead to social and industrial disruption, thereby raising the costs of doing business.[67] The lack of a good education system also can be expected to work against the attainment of business goals.

The same kind of comparison could be made for an international business trying to decide where to push its products, country A or B. Again, country B would be the logical choice because cultural factors suggest that in the long run, country B is the nation most likely to achieve the greatest level of economic growth.

But as important as culture is, it is probably less important than economic, political, and legal systems in explaining differential economic growth between nations. Cultural differences are significant, but we should not overemphasize their importance in the economic sphere. For example, earlier we noted that Max Weber argued that the ascetic principles embedded in Hinduism do not encourage entrepreneurial activity. While this is an interesting academic thesis, recent years have seen an increase in entrepreneurial activity in India, particularly in the information technology sector, where India is rapidly becoming an important global player. The ascetic principles of Hinduism and caste-based social stratification have apparently not held back entrepreneurial activity in this sector.

STARBUCKS–TATA JOINT VENTURE IN INDIA

Tata Global Beverages (TGB) is a part of the global Tata Group, and is the world's second largest tea company with group annual turnover of USD 1.5 billion and employee strength of around 3000 worldwide. The company focuses on 'good for you' beverages and has a stable of innovative regional and global beverage brands, including Tata Tea, Tetley, Himalayan natural mineral water and Eight O' Clock Coffee.

Tata Coffee is a subsidiary of TGB. It is Asia's largest coffee plantation company and the third largest exporter of instant coffee in the country. The company produces more than 10,000 metric tonnes of shade grown Arabica and Robusta coffees at its 19 estates in South India and its two Instant Coffee manufacturing facilities have a combined installed capacity of 6000 metric tonnes. It exports green coffee to countries in Europe, Asia, Middle East and North America. Tata Coffee's farms are triple certified: Utz, Rainforest Alliance and SA8000, reinforcing its commitment to the people and the environment.

TGB and Starbucks Coffee Company announced the strategic joint venture partnership—Tata Starbucks Limited (TSL), to open Starbucks stores in India in January 2012. TSL, the 50-50 joint venture between Starbucks Coffee Company and TGB, opened the doors to the first Starbucks store in India on October 19, 2012. This flagship store is located at the historic Elphinstone Building, Horniman Circle, in Mumbai and marks the beginning of the iconic brand's journey to India. In addition to the flagship store at Horniman Circle, TSL launched two more stores at Oberoi Mall and the Taj Mahal Palace Annexe in Mumbai. Starbucks claimed to have similar values as Tata Global Beverages. The CEO and Chairman, Mr Schultz stated, "when we met Ratan Tata and (R.K.) Krishnakumar it was clear that both the humanity of the company and the scale and reputation of the Tata's and what they could bring to us… there was a clear distinction in our mind that they were the company for us".[68]

In addition to the exceptional experience Starbucks is known for globally, the two companies offered Indian Espresso Roast, sourced locally through the coffee sourcing and roasting agreement with Tata Coffee. The Indian Espresso Roast will be a hallmark feature of all Starbucks stores in the market and highlights the quality espresso available in India. As part of the agreement, Starbucks and Tata Coffee Limited will work for developing and improving the profile of Indian-grown Arabica coffees around the world by elevating the stature of Indian coffee, as well as improving the quality of coffee through sustainable practices and advanced agronomy solutions.

STARBUCKS ON INDIAN CONSUMER

Just before launching Starbucks in India, Howard Schultz, Chairman and CEO stated, "Having Tata as a partner and visiting coffee stores has given us all the insight we need. The number of people who have been to Starbucks (overseas) and live in India is a very large number and the awareness of the brand is huge. The fact that Indians are drinking a lot of coffee despite quality being not so good gives us a lot of confidence. We're doing something here that we have never done before—we're sourcing and roasting Indian coffee… The core product is sourced and roasted here. It is going to be ultra fresh. We have taken a lot of effort to produce the perfect blend".[69]

Starbucks India Facebook Page

India's first Starbucks' coffee shop opened in Mumbai's upscale Horniman Circle[70]

INDIA IS A PRICE SENSITIVE MARKET

Starbucks decided to be 'highly accessible and approachable from a price value proposition' in Indian market. CEO expressed that 'the pricing that reflects the experience' to be followed in India.[71]

Schultz, the Chairman and CEO declared, "We recognize in the pricing architecture of opening a market and we did not want to price Starbucks in a manner that would be off-putting or intimidating. Some of that leverage comes from the fact that we are doing local sourcing but we would have not come to this market and used price as a barrier. We want to appeal to a broad base of people". He further added, "We've never built stores for the purpose of intercepting traffic. In my many visits to coffee stores in India, it appears to me that they are intercepting traffic. The Starbucks stores are built in many different ways—the quality of the coffee, the quality of the people, the 'third place', the sense of design and community, and the non-verbal cues that exist. All the stores will have a sense of style and elegance".[72]

"Asia and the entire Pacific Rim present one of the most significant growth opportunities within Starbucks Coffee Company", Schultz said. "India is at the core, along with China. India represents one of the most significant opportunities that we have in all of Starbucks. India should be one of the largest markets in the world for Starbucks. I would say one of the top five over time".[73]

COMMITMENT TO COMMUNITY

Deepening its commitment to community, Tata Starbucks Limited proposed to work towards improving the lives of coffee growing communities in the State of Karnataka. The joint venture, through an initial financial commitment, would work to support 'Swastha', a school for children with special needs (in partnership with the Coorg Foundation). Additionally, Tata Starbucks Limited would work on initiatives including the promotion of responsible agronomy practices and training of local farmers, technicians and agronomists to improve their coffee-growing and milling skills.

FAIRTRADE FOR A BETTER QUALITY OF LIFE BY STARBUCKS

Fairtrade coffee empowers small-scale farmers organized in democratically-run cooperatives to invest in their farms and communities, protect the environment, and develop the business skills necessary to compete in the global marketplace.[74]

Starbucks began purchasing Fairtrade coffee in 2000. Since then, the company has paid over USD 16 million in Fairtrade premiums (on top of the purchase price of green coffee), which are used by producer organizations for social and economic investments at the community and organizational level. In addition, over USD 10 million was paid to Fairtrade licensing initiatives that support the international certification system (FLO-Cert), producer services and awareness building around the benefits of Fairtrade.[75]

Chapter Summary

This chapter looked at the nature of social culture and studied some implications for business practice. The chapter made the following points:

1. Culture is a complex whole that includes knowledge, beliefs, art, morals, law, customs, and other capabilities acquired by people as members of society.
2. Values and norms are the central components of a culture. Values are abstract ideals about what a society believes to be good, right, and desirable. Norms are social rules and guidelines that prescribe appropriate behavior in particular situations.
3. Values and norms are influenced by political and economic philosophy, social structure, religion, language, and education.
4. The social structure of a society refers to its basic social organization. Two main dimensions along which social structures differ are the individual–group dimension and the stratification dimension.
5. In some societies, the individual is the basic building block of social organization. These societies emphasize individual achievements above all else. In other societies, the group is the basic building block of social organization. These societies emphasize group membership and group achievements above all else.
6. All societies are stratified into different classes. Class-conscious societies are characterized by low social mobility and a high degree of stratification. Less class-conscious societies are characterized by high social mobility and a low degree of stratification.
7. Religion may be defined as a system of shared beliefs and rituals that is concerned with the realm of the sacred. Ethical systems refer to a set of moral principles, or values, that are used to guide and shape behavior. The world's major religions are Christianity, Islam, Hinduism, and

Buddhism. Although not a religion, Confucianism has an impact on behavior that is as profound as that of many religions. The value systems of different religious and ethical systems have different implications for business practice.

8. Language is one defining characteristic of a culture. It has both spoken and unspoken dimensions. In countries with more than one spoken language, we tend to find more than one culture.

9. Formal education is the medium through which individuals learn skills and are socialized into the values and norms of a society. Education plays an important role in the determination of national competitive advantage.

10. Geert Hofstede studied how culture relates to values in the workplace. He isolated four dimensions that he claimed summarized different cultures: power distance, uncertainty avoidance, individualism versus collectivism, and masculinity versus femininity.

11. Culture is not a constant; it evolves. Economic progress and globalization seem to be two important engines of cultural change.

12. One danger confronting a company that goes abroad for the first time is being ill-informed. To develop cross-cultural literacy, international businesses need to employ host-country nationals, build a cadre of cosmopolitan executives, and guard against the dangers of ethnocentric behavior.

13. The value systems and norms of a country can affect the costs of doing business in that country.

Critical Thinking and Discussion Questions

1. Outline why the culture of a country might influence the costs of doing business in that country. Illustrate your answer with examples.

2. Do you think that business practices in an Islamic country are likely to differ from business practices in the United States? If so, how?

3. What are the implications for international business of differences in the dominant religion or ethical system of a country?

4. Choose two countries that appear to be culturally diverse. Compare the cultures of those countries, and then indicate how cultural differences influence (*a*) the costs of doing business in each country, (*b*) the likely future economic development of that country, and (*c*) business practices.

5. Reread the Country Focus about Islamic capitalism in Turkey. Then answer the following questions:
   a. Can you see anything in the value of Islam that is hostile to business?
   b. What does the experience of the region around Kayseri teach about the relationship between Islam and business?
   c. What are the implications of Islamic values toward business for the participation of a country such as Turkey in the global economy?

6. Reread the Management Focus on DMG-Shanghai and answer the follow questions:
   a. Why do you think it is so important to cultivate *guanxi* and *guanxiwang* in China?
   b. What does the experience of DMG tells us about the way things work in China? What would likely happen to a business that obeyed all the rules and regulations, rather than trying to find a way around them as Dan Mintz apparently does?
   c. What ethical issues might arise when drawing upon *guanxiwang* to get things done in China? What does this suggest about the limits of using *guanxiwang* for a Western business committed to high ethical standards?

Research Task ⊕ globalEDGE | globaledge.msu.edu

Differences in Culture

Use the globalEDGE website (globaledge.msu.edu) to complete the following exercises:

Exercise 1

You are preparing for a business trip to Chile where you will need to interact extensively with local professionals. Therefore, you would like to collect information regarding local culture and business practices prior to your departure. A colleague from Latin America recommends you visit the "Centre for Intercultural Learning" and read through the country insights provided for Chile. Prepare a short description of the most striking cultural characteristics that may affect business interactions in this country.

Exercise 2

Typically, cultural factors drive the differences in business etiquette encountered during international business travel. In fact, Middle Eastern cultures exhibit significant differences in business etiquette when compared to Western cultures. Prior to leaving for your first business trip to the region, a colleague informed you that a guide named *Business Etiquette around the World* may help you. Using this guide, identify five tips regarding business etiquette in the Middle Eastern country of your choice.

Closing **CASE**

Culture and Business in Saudi Arabia

Saudi Arabia is not the easiest place in the world for Western enterprises to do business. On the one hand, the oil-rich kingdom offers many opportunities for enterprising businesses. Western construction companies have long played a role in building infrastructure in the kingdom. Western brands from Coca-Cola, Nike, and McDonald's to The Body Shop, Next, and Benetton have a significant presence. Western aerospace companies such as Boeing and Lockheed have sold a significant number of aircraft to Saudi Arabia over the years. The Saudi market is one of the larger in the Middle East. For more than a decade now, the government has signaled that it is more open to foreign investment in certain sectors of the economy, although oil and gas extraction is still reserved for state-owned enterprises.

On the other hand, Saudi Arabia is a historically conservative country where a large segment of the population desires to preserve the religious values and ancient traditions of the region. This can and does spill over into the business sector. The culture of the country has been shaped by a combination of Islam and Bedouin traditions. In 1744 when desert nomads populated the Arabian Peninsula, the oasis-dwelling al Saud clan made a pact with Ibn Abd-al-Wahhab. Wahhab was an influential Islamic scholar who sought to purify Islam and return it to its traditional roots through strict adherence to what he believed were the original principles of Islam, as expressed in the Koran. In exchange for protecting Wahhab and following his teachings, Wahhab offered his backing to the ambitious al Saud family. One hundred and forty years later, the family united the nomadic desert tribes under its rule, and in 1922 the Saudi kingdom was born.

Today, the strict Wahhab sect of Islam still has a profound influence on Saudi culture, something that is very visible to foreign travelers. For example, stores and restaurants close at the five daily prayer times, and many restaurants, including Western ones such as McDonald's, have separate dining areas for men and women. Women in Saudi Arabia are not allowed to drive a car, sail a boat, or fly a plane or to appear outdoors with hair, wrists, or ankles exposed—something that Western companies need to keep in mind when doing business in the country or with Saudis elsewhere. Indeed, women traveling on their own have generally needed government minders or permission slips.

Saudi adherence to Islamic values has also given rise to anti-American sentiment, which increased following the American-led invasion of another Muslim nation, Iraq. Cultural solidarity expressed itself in consumer boycotts of American products. More disturbing than consumer boycotts have been terrorist attacks against Western expatriates in Saudi Arabia during the past decade, significantly increasing the perceived risks of doing business in the kingdom.

Bedouin traditions have been just as strong as Islamic values in shaping Saudi culture. Values that were important to those proud nomads—and that have enabled them to survive in their harsh desert landscape—are still found in modern Saudi society. They include loyalty, status, an emphasis on interpersonal relationships, the idea of approximate rather than precise time, and an aversion to any behavior that might seem menial or servile (including manual labor).

Reflecting Bedouin traditions, Saudis will often conduct business only after trust has been well established—a process that might require (by Western standards) a large number of face-to-face meetings. Saudis may resent being rushed into a business decision, preferring to let discussions proceed in a more relaxed fashion—something that Westerners with their attachment to precise rather than approximate time might find taxing. Business meetings may be long because many Saudis maintain an "open office" and will interrupt a meeting to conduct other business, which can be traced back to the Bedouin tradition where all tribal members have a right to visit and petition their leaders without an appointment. Given the cultural importance attached to status, Saudi executives will not react well if a foreign company sends a junior executive to transact business.

Loyalty to family and friends is a powerful force, and job security and advancement may be based on family and friendship ties, rather than, or in addition to, demonstrated technical or managerial competence. Westerners might construe this negatively as nepotism, but it reflects a nomadic culture where trust in family and tribe was placed above all else. Saudi executives will also consult with family and friends before making a business decision, and they may place more weight on their opinions than that of experts whom they do not know as well.

The Bedouin aversion to menial work has produced a chronic labor problem in the kingdom, and foreign companies will quickly discover that it is difficult to find Saudi nationals who will undertake manual labor or basic service work. Consequently, some 6 million foreign nationals reside in Saudi Arabia. These expatriates, who are primarily from other Muslim nations, such as Pakistan and Indonesia, undertake many of the menial occupations that Saudis disdain. Although oil revenues have made this social stratification possible, the Saudi government sees it as a potential long-term problem—almost 90 percent of all private-sector jobs in Saudi Arabia are filled by foreign nationals—and it has launched a program of "Saudization." The aim is to change cultural values toward work perceived as menial and, by doing so, to help build a modern economy. So far success had been halting at best.

Saudi society is starting to change in other important ways. Slowly the rights of Saudi women are being expanded. In 1964, Saudi girls were not allowed to go to school; today, more than half of university students in the kingdom are women. In 2004, Saudi women were granted the right to hold commercial business licenses, a significant advance considering the women held some $25 billion in deposits in Saudi banks and had little opportunity to use them. As Saudi society evolves, women may come to play a greater role in business.[76]

Case Discussion Questions

1. What forces shaped modern Saudi culture? How similar or different are these forces from those that shaped the culture of Western nations?

2. What kinds of misunderstanding are likely to arise between an American company and a Saudi enterprise, if neither of which has experience dealing with the other?

3. If you were in a position to advise a Western company that was considering doing business in Saudi Arabia for the first time, what would your advice be?

Endnotes

1. A. Knorr and A. Arndt, "Why Did Walmart Fail in Germany?" Institute for World Economics and International Management, University of Bremen, 2003; K. Norton, "Walmart's German Retreat," *Bloomberg BusinessWeek,* July 28, 2006; and D. Macaray, "Why Did Walmart Leave Germany?" *Huffington Post,* August 29, 2011.

2. This is a point made forcibly by K. Leung, R. S. Bhagat, N. R. Buchan, M. Erez, and C. B. Gibson, "Culture and International Business: Recent Advances and Their Implications for Future Research," *Journal of International Business Studies,* 2005, pp. 357–78.

3. Mary Yoko Brannen, "When Micky Loses Face: Recontextualization, Semantic Fit, and the Semiotics of Foreignness," *Academy of Management Review,* 2004, pp. 593–616.

4. See R. Dore, *Taking Japan Seriously* (Stanford, CA: Stanford University Press, 1987).

5. Data come from J. Monger, "International Comparison of Labor Disputes in 2004," *Labor Market Trends,* April 2006, pp. 117–28.

6. E. B. Tylor, *Primitive Culture* (London: Murray, 1871).

7. Geert Hofstede, *Culture's Consequences: International Differences in Work-Related Values* (Beverly Hills, CA: Sage Publications, 1984), p. 21.

8. J. Z. Namenwirth and R. B. Weber, *Dynamics of Culture* (Boston: Allen & Unwin, 1987), p. 8.

9. R. Mead, *International Management: Cross-Cultural Dimensions* (Oxford: Blackwell Business, 1994), p. 7.

10. Edward T. Hall and M. R. Hall, *Understanding Cultural Differences* (Yarmouth, ME: Intercultural Press, 1990).

11. Edward T. Hall and M. R. Hall, *Hidden Differences: Doing Business with the Japanese* (New York: Doubleday, 1987).

12. S. P. Huntington, *The Clash of Civilizations* (New York: Simon & Schuster, 1996).

13. M. Thompson, R. Ellis, and A. Wildavsky, *Cultural Theory* (Boulder, CO: Westview Press, 1990).

14. M. Douglas, *In the Active Voice* (London: Routledge, 1982), pp. 183–254.

15. C. Nakane, *Japanese Society* (Berkeley: University of California Press, 1970).

16. Ibid.

17. For details, see M. Aoki, *Information, Incentives, and Bargaining in the Japanese Economy* (Cambridge, UK: Cambridge University Press, 1988); and M. L. Dertouzos, R. K. Lester, and R. M. Solow, *Made in America* (Cambridge, MA: MIT Press, 1989).

18. "With Reservations: Business and Caste in India," *The Economist,* October 6, 2007, pp. 81–83; and Eric Bellman, "Reversal of Fortune Isolates India's Brahmins," *The Wall Street Journal,* December 24, 2007, p. 4.

19. E. Luce, *The Strange Rise of Modern India* (Boston: Little Brown, 2006); and D. Pick and K. Dayaram, "Modernity and Tradition in the Global Era: The Re-invention of Caste in India," *International Journal of Sociology and Social Policy,* 2006, pp. 284–301.

20. For an excellent historical treatment of the evolution of the English class system, see E. P. Thompson, *The Making of the English Working Class* (London: Vintage Books, 1966). See also R. Miliband, *The State in Capitalist Society* (New York: Basic Books, 1969), especially Chapter 2. For more recent studies of class in British societies, see Stephen Brook, *Class: Knowing Your Place in Modern Britain* (London: Victor Gollancz, 1997); A. Adonis and S. Pollard, *A Class Act: The Myth of Britain's Classless Society* (London: Hamish Hamilton, 1997); and J. Gerteis and M. Savage, "The Salience of Class in Britain and America: A Comparative Analysis," *British Journal of Sociology,* June 1998.

21. Adonis and Pollard, *A Class Act.*

22. J. H. Goldthorpe, "Class Analysis and the Reorientation of Class Theory: The Case of Persisting Differentials in Education Attainment," *British Journal of Sociology,* 2010, pp. 311–35.

23. Y. Bian, "Chinese Social Stratification and Social Mobility," *Annual Review of Sociology* 28 (2002), pp. 91–117.

24. N. Goodman, *An Introduction to Sociology* (New York: HarperCollins, 1991).

25. R. J. Barro and R. McCleary, "Religion and Economic Growth across Countries," *American Sociological Review,* October 2003, pp. 760–82; and R. McCleary and R. J. Barro, "Religion and Economy," *Journal of Economic Perspectives,* Spring 2006, pp. 49–72.

26. M. Weber, *The Protestant Ethic and the Spirit of Capitalism* (New York: Charles Scribner's Sons, 1958, original 1904–1905). For an excellent review of Weber's work, see A. Giddens, *Capitalism and Modern Social Theory* (Cambridge, UK: Cambridge University Press, 1971).

27. Weber, *The Protestant Ethic and the Spirit of Capitalism,* p. 35.

28. A. S. Thomas and S. L. Mueller, "The Case for Comparative Entrepreneurship," *Journal of International Business Studies* 31, no. 2 (2000), pp. 287–302; and S. A. Shane, "Why Do Some Societies Invent More than Others?" *Journal of Business Venturing* 7 (1992), pp. 29–46.

29. See S. M. Abbasi, K. W. Hollman, and J. H. Murrey, "Islamic Economics: Foundations and Practices," *International Journal of Social Economics* 16, no. 5 (1990), pp. 5–17; and R. H. Dekmejian, *Islam in Revolution: Fundamentalism in the Arab World* (Syracuse, NY: Syracuse University Press, 1995).

30. T. W. Lippman, *Understanding Islam* (New York: Meridian Books, 1995).

31. Dekmejian, *Islam in Revolution.*

32. M. K. Nydell, *Understanding Arabs* (Yarmouth, ME: Intercultural Press, 1987).

33. Lippman, *Understanding Islam.*

34. The material in this section is based largely on Abbasi et al., "Islamic Economics."

35. D. Bilefsky, "Turks Knock on Europe's Door with Evidence That Islam and Capitalism Can Coexist," *The New York Times,* August 27, 2006, p. 4; and European Stability Initiative, *Islamic Calvinists,* September 19, 2005, archived at www.esiweb.org.

36. "Sharia Calling," *The Economist,* November 12, 2010.

37. "Forced Devotion," *The Economist,* February 17, 2001, pp. 76–77.

38. For details of Weber's work and views, see Giddens, *Capitalism and Modern Social Theory.*

39. See, for example, the views expressed in "A Survey of India: The Tiger Steps Out," *The Economist,* January 21, 1995.

40. See Dore, *Taking Japan Seriously;* and C. W. L. Hill, "Transaction Cost Economizing as a Source of Comparative Advantage: The Case of Japan," *Organization Science* 6 (1995).

41. C. C. Chen, Y. R. Chen, and K. Xin, "Guanxi Practices and Trust in Management," *Organization Science* 15, no. 2 (March–April 2004), pp. 200–10.

42. J. Bryan, "The Mintz Dynasty," *Fast Company,* April 2006, pp. 56–62; and M. Graser, "Featured Player," *Variety,* October 18, 2004, p. 6.

43. See Aoki, *Information, Incentives, and Bargaining*; and J. P. Womack, D. T. Jones, and D. Roos, *The Machine That Changed the World* (New York: Rawson Associates, 1990).

44. This hypothesis dates back to two anthropologists, Edward Sapir and Benjamin Lee Whorf. See E. Sapir, "The Status of Linguistics as a Science," *Language* 5 (1929), pp. 207–14; and B. L. Whorf, *Language, Thought, and Reality* (Cambridge, MA: MIT Press, 1956).

45. The tendency has been documented empirically. See A. Annett, "Social Fractionalization, Political Instability, and the Size of Government," *IMF Staff Papers* 48 (2001), pp. 561–92.

46. D. A. Ricks, *Big Business Blunders: Mistakes in Multinational Marketing* (Homewood, IL: Dow Jones–Irwin, 1983).

47. Goodman, *An Introduction to Sociology.*

48. M. E. Porter, *The Competitive Advantage of Nations* (New York: Free Press, 1990).

49. Ibid., pp. 395–97.

50. G. Hofstede, "The Cultural Relativity of Organizational Practices and Theories," *Journal of International Business Studies,* Fall 1983, pp. 75–89; and G. Hofstede, *Cultures and Organizations: Software of the Mind* (New York: McGraw-Hill, 1997).

51. For a more detailed critique, see R. Mead, *International Management: Cross-Cultural Dimensions* (Oxford: Blackwell, 1994), pp. 73–75.

52. For example, see W. J. Bigoness and G. L. Blakely, "A Cross-National Study of Managerial Values," *Journal of International Business Studies,* December 1996, p. 739; D. H. Ralston, D. H. Holt, R. H. Terpstra, and Y. Kai-Cheng, "The Impact of National Culture and Economic Ideology on Managerial Work Values," *Journal of International Business Studies* 28, no. 1 (1997), pp. 177–208; P. B. Smith, M. F. Peterson, and Z. Ming Wang, "The Manager as a Mediator of Alternative Meanings," *Journal of International Business Studies* 27, no. 1 (1996), pp. 115–37; and L. Tang and P. E. Koves, "A Framework to Update Hofstede's Cultural Value Indices," *Journal of International Business Studies* 39 (2008), pp. 1045–63.

53. G. Hofstede and M. H. Bond, "The Confucius Connection," *Organizational Dynamics* 16, no. 4 (1988), pp. 5–12; and G. Hofstede, *Culture's Consequences: Comparing Values, Behaviors, Institutions and Organizations across Nations* (Thousand Oaks, CA: Sage, 2001).

54. R. S. Yeh and J. J. Lawrence, "Individualism and Confucian Dynamism," *Journal of International Business Studies* 26, no. 3 (1995), pp. 655–66.

55. For evidence of this, see R. Inglehart, "Globalization and Postmodern Values," *The Washington Quarterly,* Winter 2000, pp. 215–28.

56. Mead, *International Management,* chap. 17.

57. "Free, Young, and Japanese," *The Economist,* December 21, 1991.

58. Namenwirth and Weber, *Dynamics of Culture;* and Inglehart, "Globalization and Postmodern Values."

59. G. Hofstede, "National Cultures in Four Dimensions," *International Studies of Management and Organization* 13, no. 1 (1983), pp. 46–74; and Tang and Koves, "A Framework to Update Hofstede's Cultural Value Indices."

60. See Inglehart, "Globalization and Postmodern Values." For updates, go to http://wvs.isr.umich.edu/index.html.

61. Hofstede, "National Cultures in Four Dimensions."

62. D. A. Ralston, D. H. Holt, R. H. Terpstra, and Y. Kai-Chung, "The Impact of National Culture and Economic Ideology on Managerial Work Values," *Journal of International Business Studies,* 2007, pp. 1–19.

63. See Leung, et al., "Culture and International Business."

64. Hall and Hall, *Understanding Cultural Differences.*

65. See Aoki, *Information, Incentives, and Bargaining;* Dertouzos et al., *Made in America;* and Porter, *The Competitive Advantage of Nations,* pp. 395–97.

66. See Dore, *Taking Japan Seriously;* and C. W. L. Hill, "Transaction Cost Economizing as a Source of Comparative Advantage: The Case of Japan," *Organization Science* 6 (1995).

67. For empirical work supporting such a view, see Annett, "Social Fractionalization, Political Instability, and the Size of Government."

68. http://www.tataglobalbeverages.com/media-centre/news/news-detail/2012/10/19/starbucks-opens-spectacular-flagship-store-in-mumbai-honoring-the-dynamic-culture-of-india

69. http://forbesindia.com/printcontent/33971

70. http://www.coolage.in/2012/10/21/starbucks-in-india/

71. http://forbesindia.com/printcontent/33971

72. http://forbesindia.com/printcontent/33971

73. http://articles.timesofindia.indiatimes.com/keyword/cafe-coffee-day/recent/2

74. http://www.starbucks.co.th/responsibility/ethical-sourcing/coffee-sourcing

75. Op-cit

76. G. Rice, "Doing Business in Saudi Arabia," *Thunderbird International Business Review,* January–February 2004, pp. 59–84; A. Kronemer, "Inventing a Working Class in Saudi Arabia," *Monthly Labor Review,* May 1997, pp. 29–30; "Out of the Shadows, into the World—Arab Women," *The Economist,* June 19, 2004, pp. 28–30; B. Mroue, "Arab Countries Boycott U.S. Goods over Mideast Policies," *Los Angeles Times,* July 29, 2002, p. C3; and Maureen Dowd, "A Girl's Guide to Saudi Arabia," *Vanity Fair,* August 2010.

Chapter 5
Ethics in International Business

LEARNING OBJECTIVES

After reading this chapter, you will be able to:

LO5-1 Understand the ethical issues faced by international businesses.

LO5-2 Recognize an ethical dilemma.

LO5-3 Identify the causes of unethical behavior by managers.

LO5-4 Describe the different philosophical approaches to ethics.

LO5-5 Explain how managers can incorporate ethical considerations into their decision making.

EXPORTING USED BATTERIES TO MEXICO

Opening Case

Lead is a highly toxic metal. Elevated levels of lead in the human body have been associated with damage to many organs and tissues, including the heart, bones, intestines, kidneys, and reproductive and nervous systems. High lead exposure in young children is particularly worrying. It can result in lower intelligence and learning disabilities, impaired hearing, reduced attention span, hyperactivity, and antisocial behavior. It is not surprising then that exposure to lead has been highly regulated in developed nations. In the United States, the Environmental Protection Agency (EPA) has mandated tough rules designed to limit lead pollution. One consequence of these rules has been to increase the cost of recycling lead batteries. These rules, however, do not prohibit companies from exporting used batteries to other nations where standards are lower and enforcement is lax.

A study conducted by reporters from *The New York Times* found that about 20 percent of used vehicle and industrial batteries in the United States were exported to Mexico in 2011, up from 6 percent in 2007.

The lead is then extracted from these batteries and resold on commodities markets. It's a booming business. Lead scrap prices stood at $0.42 a pound in January 2012, up from $0.05 a pound a decade earlier. Recycling in Mexico is also a dirty business. While Mexico does have some regulation for smelting and recycling lead, the laws are weak by American standards, allowing plants to release about 20 times as much as their American equivalents. To make matters worse, enforcement is lax due to a lack of funds. A recent government study in Mexico found that 19 out of 20 recycling plants did not have proper authorization for importing dangerous waste, including lead batteries.

At some plants in Mexico, batteries are dismantled by men wielding hammers and their lead smelted in furnaces whose smokestacks vent into the air. A sample of soil collected from a schoolyard next to one such recycling plant showed a lead level of 2,000 parts per million, five times the limit for children's play areas in the United States, as set by the EPA. *The New York Times* reporters documented several cases of children living close to this plant and who had elevated levels of lead in their bodies. One 4-month-old had 24.8 micrograms of lead per deciliter of blood, almost two and a half times as much as the level typically associated with serious mental retardation.

Much of the exporting of lead batteries to Mexico is done by middle people in the United States who buy up old batteries and then ship them over the border to the cheapest processor, typically a Mexican company. Some large companies are also in this business, although they mostly try and adhere to higher standards. One large U.S. battery company, Exide, has five recycling plants in the United States, but it does no recycling in Mexico. According to an Exide official, it was not in the company's interests to skirt regulations. Another large U.S. battery manufacturer, Johnson Controls, does ship a significant number of batteries to Mexico, but it has its own recycling plant there and will open another in 2013. Johnson Controls states that its Mexican facilities abide by the stricter U.S. regulations, rather than Mexican standards, and that its recycling operations in Mexico are well below current U.S. standards for employee blood levels and substantially better than average.[1]

INTRODUCTION

The opening case describes the thriving business of exporting used lead batteries from the United States to Mexico, where the lead is extracted and sold for a profit. Because environmental regulations are weaker and enforcement is lax in Mexico, this practice can result in much higher levels of lead pollution than would be allowed in the United States. Is it ethical to engage in such practices? Most would argue that it is not, and yet the practice is widespread, with 20 percent of all U.S. lead batteries ending up at Mexican recyclers. What should a company engaged in the lead recycling business do about this? One approach, championed by Exide, is to refuse to export used batteries to Mexico, even though doing so penalizes Exide with higher costs. Another U.S. producer, Johnson Controls, does recycle in Mexico, but it has its own plants there that adhere to U.S. environmental standards. Both Exide and Johnson Controls appear to be acting in an ethical manner when they are conducting their business, but many other producers apparently are not.

Ethical issues arise frequently in international business, often because business practices and regulations differ from nation to nation. With regard to lead pollution, for example, what is allowed in Mexico is outlawed in the United States. These differences can create ethical dilemmas for businesses. Understanding the nature of an ethical dilemma, and deciding the course of action to pursue when confronted with one, is a central theme in this chapter.

The term *ethics* refers to accepted principles of right or wrong that govern the conduct of a person, the members of a profession, or the actions of an organization. **Business ethics** are the accepted principles of right or wrong governing the conduct of businesspeople, and an **ethical strategy** is a strategy, or course of action, that does not violate these accepted principles. This chapter looks at how ethical issues should be incorporated into decision making in an international business. The chapter also reviews the reasons for poor ethical decision making and discusses different philosophical approaches to business ethics. The chapter closes by reviewing the different processes that managers can adopt to make sure that ethical considerations are incorporated into decision making in an international business.

ETHICAL ISSUES IN INTERNATIONAL BUSINESS   ▌LO5▐

Many of the ethical issues in international business are rooted in the fact that political systems, law, economic development, and culture vary significantly from nation to nation. What is considered normal practice in one nation may be considered unethical in another. Because they work for an institution that transcends national borders and cultures, managers in a multinational firm need to be particularly sensitive to these differences. In the international business setting, the most common ethical issues involve employment practices, human rights, environmental regulations, corruption, and the moral obligation of multinational corporations.

Employment Practices

When work conditions in a host nation are clearly inferior to those in a multinational's home nation, which standards should be applied? Those of the home nation, those of the host nation, or something in between? While few would suggest that pay and work conditions should be the same across nations, how much divergence is acceptable? For example, while 12-hour workdays, extremely low pay, and a failure to protect workers against toxic chemicals may be common in some developing nations, does this mean that it is okay for a multinational to tolerate such working conditions in its subsidiaries there, or to condone it by using local subcontractors (the opening case gives an example of such a situation)?

In the 1990s, Nike found itself the center of a storm of protests when news reports revealed that working conditions at many of its subcontractors were very poor. Typical of the allegations were those detailed in a *48 Hours* program that aired in 1996. The report painted a picture of young women who worked with toxic materials six days a week in poor conditions for only 20 cents an hour at a Vietnamese subcontractor. The report also stated that a living wage in Vietnam was at least $3 a day, an income that could not be achieved at the subcontractor without working substantial overtime. Nike and its subcontractors were not breaking any laws, but this report, and others like it, raised questions about the ethics of using sweatshop labor to make what were essentially fashion accessories. It may have been legal, but was it ethical to use subcontractors who, by Western standards, clearly exploited their workforce? Nike's critics thought not, and the company found itself the focus of a wave of demonstrations and consumer boycotts. These exposés surrounding Nike's use of subcontractors forced the company to reexamine its policies. Realizing that even though it was breaking no law, its subcontracting policies were perceived as unethical, Nike's management established a code of conduct for Nike subcontractors and instituted annual monitoring by independent auditors of all subcontractors.[2]

As the Nike case demonstrates, a strong argument can be made that it is not okay for a multinational firm to tolerate poor working conditions in its foreign operations or those of subcontractors. However, this still leaves unanswered the question of which standards should be applied. We shall return to and consider this issue in more detail later in the chapter. For now, note that establishing minimal acceptable standards that safeguard the basic rights and dignity of employees, auditing foreign subsidiaries and subcontractors on a regular basis to make sure those standards are met, and taking corrective action if they are not up to standards are a good way to guard against ethical abuses. For another example of problems with working practices among suppliers, read the accompanying Management Focus, which looks at working conditions in a factory that supplied Apple with iPods.

Making Apple's iPod

In mid-2006, news reports surfaced suggesting there were systematic labor abuses at a factory in China that makes the iconic iPod for Apple Computer. According to the reports, workers at Hongfujin Precision Industry were paid as little as $50 a month to work 15-hour shifts making the iPod. There were also reports of forced overtime and poor living conditions for the workers, many of them young women who had migrated from the countryside to work at the plant and lived in company-owned dormitories. The articles were the work of two Chinese journalists, Wang You and Weng Bao, employed by *China Business News,* a state-run newspaper. The target of the reports, Hongfujin Precision Industry, was reportedly China's largest export manufacturer in 2005 with overseas sales totaling $14.5 billion. Hongfujin is owned by Foxconn, a large Taiwanese conglomerate, whose customers (in addition to Apple) include Intel, Dell, and Sony Corporation. The Hongfujin factory is a small city in its own right, with clinics, recreational facilities, buses, and 13 restaurants that serve the 200,000 employees.

Upon hearing the news, Apple management responded quickly, pledging to audit the operations to make sure Hongfujin was complying with Apple's code on labor standards for subcontractors. Managers at Hongfujin took a somewhat different tack; they filed a defamation suit against the two journalists, suing them for $3.8 million in a local court, which promptly froze the journalists' personal assets pending a trial. Clearly, the management of Hongfujin was trying to send a message to the journalist community—criticism would be costly. The suit sent a chill through the Chinese journalist community because Chinese courts have shown a tendency to favor powerful, locally based companies in legal proceedings.

Within six weeks, Apple had completed its audit. The company's report suggested that although workers had not been forced to work overtime and were earning at least the local minimum wage, many had worked more than the 60 hours a week allowed for by Apple, and their housing was substandard. Under pressure from Apple, management at Hongfujin agreed to bring practices in line with Apple's code, committing to building new housing for employees and limiting work to 60 hours a week.

However, Hongfujin did not immediately withdraw the defamation suit. In an unusually bold move in a country where censorship is still common, *China Business News* gave its unconditional backing to Wang and Weng. The Shanghai-based news organization issued a statement arguing that what the two journalists did "was not a violation of any rules, laws, or journalistic ethics." The Paris-based Reporters Without Borders also took up the case of Wang and Weng, writing a letter to Apple's CEO Steve Jobs stating, "We believe that all Wang and Weng did was to report the facts and we condemn Foxconn's reaction. We therefore ask you to intercede on behalf of these two journalists so that their assets are unfrozen and the lawsuit is dropped."

Once again, Apple moved quickly, pressuring Foxconn behind the scenes to drop the suit. In early September, Foxconn agreed to do so and issued a "face-saving" statement saying the two sides had agreed to end the dispute after apologizing to each other "for the disturbances brought to both of them by the lawsuit." While the dispute is now over, the experience shed a harsh light on labor conditions in China. At the same time, the response of the Chinese media, and *China Business News* in particular, point toward the emergence of some journalistic freedoms in a nation that has historically seen news organizations as a mouthpiece for the state.[4]

Human Rights

Questions of human rights can arise in international business. Basic human rights still are not respected in many nations. Rights taken for granted in developed nations, such as freedom of association, freedom of speech, freedom of assembly, freedom of movement, freedom from political repression, and so on, are by no means universally accepted (see Chapter 2 for details). One of the most obvious historic examples was South Africa during the days of white rule and apartheid, which did not end until 1994. The apartheid system denied basic political rights to the majority nonwhite population of South Africa, mandated segregation between whites and nonwhites, reserved certain occupations exclusively for whites, and prohibited blacks from being placed in positions where they would manage whites. Despite the odious nature of this system, Western businesses operated in South Africa. By the 1980s, however, many questioned the ethics of doing so. They argued that inward investment by foreign multinationals, by boosting the South African economy, supported the repressive apartheid regime.

Several Western businesses started to change their policies in the late 1970s and early 1980s.[3] General Motors, which had significant activities in South Africa, was at the forefront of this trend. GM adopted what came to be called the *Sullivan principles,* named after Leon Sullivan, a black Baptist minister and a member of GM's board of directors. Sullivan argued that it was ethically justified for GM to operate in South Africa so long as two conditions were fulfilled. First, the company should not obey the apartheid laws in its own South African operations (a form of passive resistance). Second, the company should do everything within its power to promote the abolition of apartheid laws. Sullivan's principles were widely adopted by U.S. firms operating in South Africa. Their violation of the apartheid laws was ignored by the South African government, which clearly did not want to antagonize important foreign investors.

After 10 years, Leon Sullivan concluded that simply following the principles was not sufficient to break down the apartheid regime and that any American company, even those adhering to his principles, could not ethically justify their continued presence in South Africa. Over the next few years, numerous companies divested their South African operations, including Exxon, General Motors, Kodak, IBM, and Xerox. At the same time, many state pension funds signaled they would no longer hold stock in companies that did business in South Africa, which helped persuade several companies to divest their South African operations. These divestments, coupled with the imposition of economic sanctions from the United States and other governments, contributed to the abandonment of white minority rule and apartheid in South Africa and the introduction of democratic elections in 1994. Thus, adopting an ethical stance was argued to have helped improve human rights in South Africa.[5]

Although change has come in South Africa, many repressive regimes still exist in the world. Is it ethical for multinationals to do business in them? It is often argued that inward investment by a multinational can be a force for economic, political, and social progress that ultimately improves the rights of people in repressive regimes. This position was first discussed in Chapter 2, when we noted that economic progress in a nation could create pressure for democratization. In general, this belief suggests it is ethical for a multinational to do business in nations that lack the democratic structures and human rights records of developed nations. Investment in China, for example, is frequently justified on the grounds that although China's human rights record is often questioned by human rights groups, and although the country is not a democracy, continuing inward investment will help boost economic growth and raise living standards. These developments will ultimately create pressures from the Chinese people for more participative government, political pluralism, and freedom of expression and speech.

There is a limit to this argument. As in the case of South Africa, some regimes are so repressive that investment cannot be justified on ethical grounds. Another example would be Myanmar (formerly known as Burma). Ruled by a military dictatorship for more than 45 years, Myanmar has one of the worst human rights records in the world. Beginning in the mid-1990s, many Western companies exited Myanmar, judging the human rights violations to be so extreme that doing business there cannot be justified on ethical grounds. (In contrast, the accompanying Management Focus looks at the controversy surrounding one company, Unocal, which chose to stay in Myanmar.) However, a cynic might note that Myanmar has a small economy and that divestment carries no great economic penalty for Western firms, unlike, for example, divestment from China. Interestingly, after decades of pressure from the international community, in 2012 the military government of Myanmar finally acquiesced and allowed limited democratic elections to be held.

MANAGEMENT FOCUS

Unocal in Myanmar

In 1995, Unocal, an oil and gas enterprise based in California, took a 29 percent stake in a partnership with the French oil company Total and state-owned companies from both Myanmar and Thailand to build a gas pipeline from Myanmar to Thailand. At the time, the $1 billion project was expected to bring Myanmar about $200 million in annual export earnings, a quarter of the country's total. The gas used domestically would increase Myanmar's generating capacity by 30 percent. This investment was made when a number of other American companies were exiting Myanmar. Myanmar's government, a military dictatorship, had a reputation for brutally suppressing internal dissent. Citing the political climate, the apparel companies Levi Strauss and Eddie Bauer had both withdrawn from the country. However, as far as Unocal's management was concerned, the giant infrastructure project would generate healthy returns for the company and, by boosting economic growth, a better life for Myanmar's 43 million people. Moreover, while Levi Strauss and Eddie Bauer could easily shift production of clothes to another low-cost location, Unocal argued it had to go where the oil and gas were located.

However, Unocal's investment quickly became highly controversial. Under the terms of the contract, the government of Myanmar was contractually obliged to clear a corridor for the pipeline through Myanmar's tropical forests and to protect the pipeline from attacks by the government's enemies. According to human rights groups, the Myanmar army forcibly moved villages and ordered hundreds of local peasants to work on the pipeline in conditions that were no better than slave labor. Those who refused suffered retaliation. News reports cite the case of one woman who was thrown into a fire, along with her baby, after her husband tried to escape from troops forcing him to work on the project. The baby died and she suffered burns. Other villagers report being beaten, tortured, raped, and otherwise mistreated when the alleged slave labor conditions were occurring.

In 1996, human rights activists brought a lawsuit against Unocal in the United States on behalf of 15 Myanmar villagers who had fled to refugee camps in Thailand. The suit claimed that Unocal was aware of what was going on, even if it did not participate or condone it, and that awareness was enough to make Unocal in part responsible for the alleged crimes. The presiding judge dismissed the case, arguing that Unocal could not be held liable for the actions of a foreign government against its own people—although the judge did note that Unocal was indeed aware of what was going on in Myanmar. The plaintiffs appealed, and in late 2003 the case wound up at a superior court. In 2005, the case was settled out of court for an undisclosed amount. Unocal itself was acquired by Chevron in 2005.[7]

Environmental Pollution

Ethical issues arise when environmental regulations in host nations are inferior to those in the home nation (see the opening case for an example). Many developed nations have substantial regulations governing the emission of pollutants, the dumping of toxic chemicals, the use of toxic materials in the workplace, and so on. Those regulations are often lacking in developing nations, and according to critics, the result can be higher levels of pollution from the operations of multinationals than would be allowed at home.

Should a multinational feel free to pollute in a developing nation? To do so hardly seems ethical. Is there a danger that amoral management might move production to a developing nation precisely because costly pollution controls are not required, and the company is therefore free to despoil the environment and perhaps endanger local people in its quest to lower production costs and gain a competitive advantage? What is the right and moral thing to do in such circumstances: pollute to gain an economic advantage, or make sure that foreign subsidiaries adhere to common standards regarding pollution controls?

These questions take on added importance because some parts of the environment are a public good that no one owns but anyone can despoil. No one owns the atmosphere or the oceans, but polluting both, no matter where the pollution originates, harms all.[6] The atmosphere and oceans can be viewed as a global commons from which everyone benefits but for which no one is specifically responsible. In such cases, a phenomenon known as the *tragedy of the commons* becomes applicable. The tragedy of the commons occurs when a resource held in common by all, but owned by no one, is overused by individuals, resulting in its degradation. The phenomenon was first named by Garrett Hardin when describing a particular problem in sixteenth-century England. Large open areas, called commons, were free for all to use as pasture. The poor put out livestock on these commons and supplemented their meager incomes. It was advantageous for each to put out more and more livestock, but the social consequence was far more livestock than the commons could handle. The result was overgrazing, degradation of the commons, and the loss of this much-needed supplement.[8]

Corporations can contribute to the *global tragedy of the commons* by moving production to locations where they are free to pump pollutants into the atmosphere or dump them in oceans or rivers, thereby harming these valuable global commons. While such action may be legal, is it ethical? Again, such actions seem to violate basic societal notions of ethics and social responsibility. This issue is taking on greater importance as concerns about human-induced global warming move to center stage. Most climate scientists argue that human industrial and commercial activity is increasing the amount of carbon dioxide in the atmosphere; carbon dioxide is a greenhouse gas, which reflects heat back to the earth's surface, warming the globe; and as a result, the average temperature of the earth is increasing. The accumulated scientific evidence from numerous databases supports this argument.[9] Consequently, societies around the world are starting to restrict the amount of carbon dioxide that can be emitted into the atmosphere as a by-product of industrial and commercial activity. However, regulations differ from nation to nation. Given this, is it ethical for a company to try to escape tight emission limits by moving production to a country with lax regulations, given that doing so will contribute to global warming? Again, many would argue that doing so violates basic ethical principles.

Corruption

As noted in Chapter 2, corruption has been a problem in almost every society in history, and it continues to be one today.[10] There always have been and always will be corrupt government officials. International businesses can and have gained economic advantages by making payments to those officials. A classic example concerns a well-publicized incident in the 1970s. Carl Kotchian, the president of Lockheed, made a $12.6 million payment to Japanese agents and government officials to secure a large order for Lockheed's TriStar jet from Nippon Air. When the payments were discovered, U.S. officials charged Lockheed with falsification of its records and tax violations. Although such payments were supposed to be an accepted business practice in Japan (they might be viewed as an exceptionally lavish form of gift giving), the revelations created a scandal there too. The government ministers in question were criminally charged, one committed suicide, the government fell in disgrace, and the Japanese people were outraged. Apparently, such a payment was not an accepted way of doing business in Japan! The payment was nothing more than a bribe, paid to corrupt officials, to secure a large order that might otherwise have gone to another manufacturer, such as Boeing. Kotchian clearly engaged in unethical behavior—and to argue that the payment was an "acceptable form of doing business in Japan" was self-serving and incorrect.

The Lockheed case was the impetus for the 1977 passage of the Foreign Corrupt Practices Act in the United States, discussed in Chapter 2. The act outlawed the paying of bribes to foreign government officials to gain business. Some U.S. businesses immediately objected that the act would put U.S. firms at a competitive disadvantage (there is no evidence that had occurred).[11] The act was subsequently amended to allow for "facilitating payments." Sometimes known as *speed money* or *grease payments*, facilitating payments are *not* payments to secure contracts that would not otherwise be secured, nor are they payments to obtain exclusive preferential treatment. Rather they are payments to ensure receiving the standard treatment that a business ought to receive from a foreign government, but might not due to the obstruction of a foreign official. The accompanying Management Focus looks at what happened when the German company Daimler ran afoul of the Foreign Corrupt Practices Act.

In 1997, the trade and finance ministers from the member states of the Organization for Economic Cooperation and Development (OECD) followed the U.S. lead and adopted the **Convention on Combating Bribery of Foreign Public Officials in International Business Transactions**.[12] The convention, which went into force in 1999, obliges member states and other signatories to make the bribery of foreign public officials a criminal offense. The convention excludes facilitating payments made to expedite routine government action from the convention.

While facilitating payments, or *speed money,* are excluded from both the Foreign Corrupt Practices Act and the OECD convention on bribery, the ethical implications of making such payments are unclear. From a pragmatic standpoint, giving bribes, although a little evil, might be the price that must be paid to do a greater good (assuming the investment creates jobs where none existed and assuming the practice is not illegal). Several economists advocate this reasoning, suggesting that in the context of pervasive and cumbersome regulations in developing countries, corruption may improve efficiency and help growth! These economists theorize that in a country where preexisting political structures distort or limit the workings of the market mechanism, corruption in the form of black-marketeering, smuggling, and side payments to government bureaucrats to "speed up" approval for business investments may enhance welfare.[14] Arguments such as this persuaded the U.S. Congress to exempt facilitating payments from the Foreign Corrupt Practices Act.

In contrast, other economists have argued that corruption reduces the returns on business investment and leads to low economic growth.[15] In a country where corruption is common, unproductive bureaucrats who demand side payments for granting the enterprise permission to operate may siphon off the profits from a business activity. This reduces businesses' incentive to invest and may retard a country's

Corruption at Daimler

In 1998 Daimler, one of the world's largest manufacturers of automobiles, purchased the Chrysler Corporation. Soon afterward, a former Chrysler auditor identified suspicious payments being made by subsidiaries. For example, in 2002 Daimler's Chinese subsidiary paid $25,000 to a Texas company listed at a residential apartment complex in Houston. The auditor suspected that such payments were bribes and reported the issue to the Securities and Exchange Commission (SEC), which then teamed up with the U.S. Department of Justice (DOJ) and began an investigation.

The investigation took eight years. During that time, investigators uncovered a pattern of corruption so widespread that an SEC official described it as "standard operating practice at Daimler." In the case of the $25,000 payment, the Texas company was a shell organization established to launder the money, and the payment was to be passed on to the wife of a Chinese government official who was involved in contract negotiations for about $1.3 million in commercial vehicles. In another case, bribes were given to secure the sale of passenger and commercial vehicles to government entities in Russia. Daimler overcharged for the cars on invoices and passed the overpayments to bank accounts in Latvia controlled by the Russian officials responsible for the purchase decision. In certain cases, Daimler made bribes from "cash desks," allowing employees to take out large amounts of currency to make payments to foreign officials.

In total, the investigation uncovered hundreds of such payments in at least 22 countries that were linked to the sale of vehicles valued at $1.9 billion. The SEC stated, "The bribery was so pervasive in Daimler's decentralized corporate structure that it extended outside of the sales organization to internal audit, legal, and finance departments. These departments should have caught and stopped the illegal sales practices, but instead they permitted or were directly involved in the company's bribery practices."

Threatened with court proceedings in the United States, in 2010 Daimler entered into a consent decree with the SEC under which it agreed to pay $185 million in criminal and civil fines. While subsidiaries of Daimler in Germany and Russia pleaded guilty to corruption charges, the corporate parent and the Chinese subsidiary will avoid indictment so long as they live up to an agreement to halt such practices.[13]

economic growth rate. One study of the connection between corruption and economic growth in 70 countries found that corruption had a significant negative impact on a country's growth rate.[16] Another study found that firms that paid more in bribes are likely to spend more, not less, management time with bureaucrats negotiating regulations, and that this tended to raise the costs of the firm.[17]

Given the debate and the complexity of this issue, one again might conclude that generalization is difficult and the demand for speed money creates a genuine ethical dilemma. Yes, corruption is bad, and yes, it may harm a country's economic development, but yes, there are also cases where side payments to government officials can remove the bureaucratic barriers to investments that create jobs. However, this pragmatic stance ignores the fact that corruption tends to corrupt both the bribe giver and the bribe taker. Corruption feeds on itself, and once an individual starts down the road of corruption, pulling back may be difficult if not impossible. This argument strengthens the ethical case for never engaging in corruption, no matter how compelling the benefits might seem.

Many multinationals have accepted this argument. The large oil multinational BP, for example, has a zero-tolerance approach toward facilitating payments. Other corporations have a more nuanced approach. For example, consider the following from the code of ethics at Dow Corning:

> Dow Corning employees will not authorize or give payments or gifts to government employees or their beneficiaries or anyone else in order to obtain or retain business. Facilitating payments to expedite the performance of routine services are strongly discouraged. In countries where local business practice dictates such payments and there is no alternative, facilitating payments are to be for the minimum amount necessary and must be accurately documented and recorded.[18]

This statement allows for facilitating payments when "there is no alternative," although they are strongly discouraged.

Moral Obligations

Multinational corporations have power that comes from their control over resources and their ability to move production from country to country. Although that power is constrained not only by laws and regulations but also by the discipline of the market and the competitive process, it is substantial. Some moral philosophers argue that with power comes the social responsibility for multinationals to give something back to the societies that enable them to prosper and grow. The concept of **social responsibility** refers to the idea that businesspeople should consider the social consequences of economic actions when making business decisions and that there should be a presumption in favor of decisions that have both good economic and social consequences.[19] In its purest form, social responsibility can be supported for its own sake simply because it is the right way for a business to behave. Advocates of this approach argue that businesses, particularly large successful businesses, need to recognize their *noblesse oblige* and give something back to the societies that have made their success possible. *Noblesse oblige* is a French term that refers to honorable and benevolent behavior considered the responsibility of people of high (noble) birth. In a business setting, it is taken to mean benevolent behavior that is the responsibility of *successful* enterprises. This has long been recognized by many businesspeople, resulting in a substantial and venerable history of corporate giving to society, with businesses making social investments designed to enhance the welfare of the communities in which they operate.

Power itself is morally neutral; how power is used is what matters. It can be used in a positive way to increase social welfare, which is ethical, or it can be used in a manner that is ethically and morally suspect. Some multinationals have acknowledged a moral obligation to use their power to enhance social welfare in the communities where they do business. BP, one of the world's largest oil companies, has made it part of the company policy to undertake "social investments" in the countries where it does business.[20] In Algeria, BP has been investing in a major project to develop gas fields near the desert town of Salah. When the company noticed the lack of clean water in Salah, it built two desalination plants to provide drinking water for the local community and distributed containers to residents so they could take water from the plants to their homes. There was no economic reason for BP to make this social investment, but the company believes it is morally obligated to use its power in constructive ways. The action, while a small thing for BP, is a very important thing for the local community.

ETHICAL DILEMMAS

The ethical obligations of a multinational corporation toward employment conditions, human rights, corruption, environmental pollution, and the use of power are not always clear-cut. There may be no agreement about accepted ethical principles. From an international business perspective, some argue that what is ethical depends on one's cultural perspective.[21] In the United States, it is considered acceptable to execute murderers, but in many cultures this is not acceptable—execution is viewed as an affront to human dignity, and the death penalty is outlawed. Many Americans find this attitude very strange, but many Europeans find the American approach barbaric. For a more business-oriented example, consider the practice of "gift giving" between the parties to a business negotiation. While this is considered right and proper behavior in many Asian cultures, some Westerners view the practice as a form of bribery, and therefore unethical, particularly if the gifts are substantial.

Managers often confront very real ethical dilemmas where the appropriate course of action is not clear. For example, imagine that a visiting American executive finds that a foreign subsidiary in a poor nation has hired a 12-year-old girl to work on a factory floor. Appalled to find that the subsidiary is using child labor in direct violation of the company's own ethical code, the American instructs the local manager to replace the child with an adult. The local manager dutifully complies. The girl, an orphan, who is the only breadwinner for herself and her 6-year-old brother, is unable to find another job, so in desperation she turns to prostitution. Two years later she dies of AIDS.

Had the visiting American understood the gravity of the girl's situation, would he still have requested her replacement? Perhaps not! Would it have been better, therefore, to stick with the status quo and allow the girl to continue working? Probably not, because that would have violated the reasonable prohibition against child labor found in the company's own ethical code. What then would have been the right thing to do? What was the obligation of the executive given this ethical dilemma?

There are no easy answers to these questions. That is the nature of **ethical dilemmas**—they are situations in which none of the available alternatives seems ethically acceptable.[22] In this case, employing child labor was not acceptable, but given that she was employed, neither was denying the child her only source of income. What this American executive needs, what all managers need, is a moral compass, or perhaps an ethical algorithm, to guide them through such an ethical dilemma to find an acceptable solution. Later, we will outline what such a moral compass, or ethical algorithm, might look like. For now, it is enough to note that ethical dilemmas exist because many real-world decisions are complex, difficult to frame, and involve first-, second-, and third-order consequences that are hard to quantify. Doing the right thing, or even knowing what the right thing might be, is often far from easy.[23]

THE ROOTS OF UNETHICAL BEHAVIOR ■ 05-3 ■

Examples abound of managers behaving in a manner that might be judged unethical in an international business setting. Why do managers behave in an unethical manner? There is no simple answer to this question, because the causes are complex, but some generalizations can be made (see Figure 5.1).[24]

Personal Ethics

Societal business ethics are not divorced from *personal ethics*, which are the generally accepted principles of right and wrong governing the conduct of individuals. As individuals, we are typically taught that it is wrong to lie and cheat—it is unethical—and that it is right to behave with integrity and honor and to stand up for what we believe to be right and true. This is generally true across societies. The personal ethical code that guides our behavior comes from a number of sources, including our parents, our schools, our religion, and the media. Our personal ethical code exerts a profound influence on the way we behave as businesspeople. An individual with a strong sense of personal ethics is less

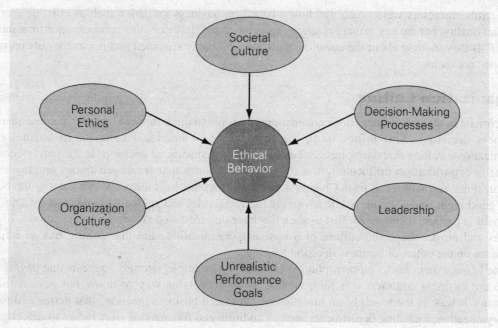

Figure 5.1 *Determinants of Ethical Behavior*

likely to behave in an unethical manner in a business setting. It follows that the first step to establishing a strong sense of business ethics is for a society to emphasize strong personal ethics.

Home-country managers working abroad in multinational firms (expatriate managers) may experience more than the usual degree of pressure to violate their personal ethics. They are away from their ordinary social context and supporting culture, and they are psychologically and geographically distant from the parent company. They may be based in a culture that does not place the same value on ethical norms important in the manager's home country, and they may be surrounded by local employees who have less rigorous ethical standards. The parent company may pressure expatriate managers to meet unrealistic goals that can only be fulfilled by cutting corners or acting unethically. For example, to meet centrally mandated performance goals, expatriate managers might give bribes to win contracts or might implement working conditions and environmental controls that are below minimal acceptable standards. Local managers might encourage the expatriate to adopt such behavior. Due to its geographic distance, the parent company may be unable to see how expatriate managers are meeting goals or may choose not to see how they are doing so, allowing such behavior to flourish and persist.

Decision-Making Processes

Several studies of unethical behavior in a business setting have concluded that businesspeople sometimes do not realize they are behaving unethically, primarily because they simply fail to ask, "Is this decision or action ethical?"[25] Instead, they apply a straightforward business calculus to what they perceive to be a business decision, forgetting that the decision may also have an important ethical dimension. The fault lies in processes that do not incorporate ethical considerations into business decision making. This may have been the case at Nike when managers originally made subcontracting decisions (see the earlier discussion). Those decisions were probably made based on good economic logic. Subcontractors were probably chosen based on business variables such as cost, delivery, and product quality, but the key managers simply failed to ask, "How does this subcontractor treat its workforce?" If they thought about the question at all, they probably reasoned that it was the subcontractor's concern, not theirs.

Organization Culture

The climate in some businesses does not encourage people to think through the ethical consequences of business decisions. This brings us to the third cause of unethical behavior in businesses—an organizational culture that deemphasizes business ethics, reducing all decisions to the purely economic. The term **organization culture** refers to the values and norms that are shared among employees of an organization. You will recall from Chapter 4 that *values* are abstract ideas about what a group believes to be good, right, and desirable, while *norms* are the social rules and guidelines that prescribe appropriate behavior in particular situations. Just as societies have cultures, so do business organizations. Together, values and norms shape the culture of a business organization, and that culture has an important influence on the ethics of business decision making.

The Management Focus on corruption at Daimler, for example, strongly suggests that paying bribes to secure business contracts was long viewed as an acceptable way of doing business within that company. It was, in the words of an investigator, "standard business practice" that permeated much of the organization, including departments such as auditing and finance that were meant to detect and halt such behavior. One can argue that such a widespread practice could have persisted only if the values and norms of the organization implicitly approved of paying bribes to secure business.

Unrealistic Performance Expectations

A fourth cause of unethical behavior has already been hinted at—pressure from the parent company to meet unrealistic performance goals that can be attained only by cutting corners or acting in an unethical manner. In the Daimler case, for example, bribery may have been viewed as a way to hit challenging performance goals. The combination of an organizational culture that legitimizes unethical behavior, or at least turns a blind eye to such behavior, and unrealistic performance goals may be particularly toxic. In such circumstances, there is a greater than average probability that managers will violate their own personal ethics and engage in unethical behavior. Conversely, an organization culture can do just the opposite and reinforce the need for ethical behavior. At Hewlett-Packard, for example, Bill Hewlett and David Packard, the company's founders, propagated a set of values known as The HP Way. These values, which shape the way business is conducted both within and by the corporation, have an important ethical component. Among other things, they stress the need for confidence in and respect for people, open communication, and concern for the individual employee.

Leadership

The Hewlett-Packard example suggests a fifth root cause of unethical behavior—leadership. Leaders help to establish the culture of an organization, and they set the example that others follow. Other employees in a business often take their cue from business leaders, and if those leaders do not behave in an ethical manner, they might not either. It is not just what leaders say that matters, but what they do or do not do. One wonders, for example, what message the leaders at Daimler sent about corrupt practices. Presumably, they did very little to discourage it and may well have encouraged such behavior.

Societal Culture

Societal culture may well have an impact on the propensity of people, and organizations, to behave in an unethical manner. One study of 2,700 firms in 24 countries found that there were significant differences among the ethical policies of firms headquartered in different countries.[26] Using Hofstede's dimensions of social culture (see the previous chapter), the study found that enterprises headquartered in cultures where individualism and uncertainty avoidance are strong were more likely to emphasize the importance of behaving ethically than firms headquartered in cultures where masculinity and power distance are important cultural attributes. Such analysis suggests that enterprises headquartered in a country such as Russia, which scores high on masculinity and power distance measures, and where corruption is endemic, are more likely to engage in unethical behavior than enterprises headquartered in Scandinavia.

PHILOSOPHICAL APPROACHES TO ETHICS   L05-4

We look at several different approaches to business ethics here, beginning with some that can best be described as straw men, which either deny the value of business ethics or apply the concept in a very unsatisfactory way. Having discussed, and dismissed the straw men, we then move on to consider approaches that are favored by most moral philosophers and form the basis for current models of ethical behavior in international businesses.

Straw Men

Straw men approaches to business ethics are raised by business ethics scholars primarily to demonstrate that they offer inappropriate guidelines for ethical decision making in a multinational enterprise. Four such approaches to business ethics are commonly discussed in the literature. These approaches can be characterized as the Friedman doctrine, cultural relativism, the righteous moralist, and the naive immoralist. All these approaches have some inherent value, but all are unsatisfactory in important ways. Nevertheless, sometimes companies adopt these approaches.

The Friedman Doctrine

The Nobel Prize–winning economist Milton Friedman wrote an article in 1970 that has since become a classic straw man example that business ethics scholars outline only to then tear down.[27] Friedman's basic position is that the only social responsibility of business is to increase profits, so long as the company stays within the rules of law. He explicitly rejects the idea that businesses should undertake social expenditures beyond those mandated by the law and required for the efficient running of a business. For example, his arguments suggest that improving working conditions beyond the level required by the law *and* necessary to maximize employee productivity will reduce profits and are therefore not appropriate. His belief is that a firm should maximize its profits because that is the way to maximize the returns that accrue to the owners of the firm, its stockholders. If stockholders then wish to use the proceeds to make social investments, that is their right, according to Friedman, but managers of the firm should not make that decision for them.

Although Friedman is talking about social responsibility, rather than business ethics per se, many business ethics scholars equate social responsibility with ethical behavior and thus believe Friedman is also arguing against business ethics. However, the assumption that Friedman is arguing against ethics is not quite true, for Friedman does state,

There is one and only one social responsibility of business—to use its resources and engage in activities designed to increase its profits so long as it stays within the rules of the game, which is to say that it engages in open and free competition without deception or fraud.[28]

In other words, Friedman states that businesses should behave in an ethical manner and not engage in deception and fraud.

Critics charge that Friedman's arguments do break down under examination. This is particularly true in international business, where the "rules of the game" are not well established and differ from country to county. Consider again the case of sweatshop labor. Child labor may not be against the law in a developing nation, and maximizing productivity may not require that a multinational firm stop using child labor in that country, but it is still immoral to use child labor because the practice conflicts with widely held views about what is the right and proper thing to do. Similarly, there may be no rules against pollution in a less developed nation and spending money on pollution control may reduce the profit rate of the firm, but generalized notions of morality would hold that it is still unethical to dump toxic pollutants into rivers or foul the air with gas releases. In addition to the local consequences of such pollution, which may have serious health effects for the surrounding population, there is also a global consequence as pollutants degrade those two global commons so important to us all—the atmosphere and the oceans.

Cultural Relativism

Another straw man often raised by business ethics scholars is **cultural relativism**, which is the belief that ethics are nothing more than the reflection of a culture—all ethics are culturally determined—and that accordingly, a firm should adopt the ethics of the culture in which it is operating.[29] This approach is often summarized by the maxim *when in Rome do as the Romans*. As with Friedman's approach, cultural relativism does not stand up to a closer look. At its extreme, cultural relativism suggests that if a culture supports slavery, it is okay to use slave labor in a country. Clearly, it is not! Cultural relativism implicitly rejects the idea that universal notions of morality transcend different cultures, but, as we argue later in the chapter, some universal notions of morality are found across cultures.

While dismissing cultural relativism in its most sweeping form, some ethicists argue there is residual value in this approach.[30] As we noted in Chapter 3, societal values and norms do vary from culture to culture, customs do differ, so it might follow that certain business practices are ethical in one country but not another. Indeed, the facilitating payments allowed in the Foreign Corrupt Practices Act can be seen as an acknowledgment that in some countries, the payment of speed money to government officials is necessary to get business done, and if not ethically desirable, it is at least ethically acceptable.

The Righteous Moralist

A **righteous moralist** claims that a multinational's home-country standards of ethics are the appropriate ones for companies to follow in foreign countries. This approach is typically associated with managers from developed nations. While this seems reasonable at first blush, the approach can create problems. Consider the following example: An American bank manager was sent to Italy and was appalled to learn that the local branch's accounting department recommended grossly underreporting the bank's profits for income tax purposes.[31] The manager insisted that the bank report its earnings accurately, American style. When he was called by the Italian tax department to the firm's tax hearing, he was told the firm owed three times as much tax as it had paid, reflecting the department's standard assumption that each firm underreports its earnings by two-thirds. Despite his protests, the new assessment stood. In this case, the righteous moralist has run into a problem caused by the prevailing cultural norms in the country where he was doing business. How should he respond? The righteous moralist would argue for maintaining the position, while a more pragmatic view might be that in this case, the right thing to do is to follow the prevailing cultural norms, because there is a big penalty for not doing so.

The main criticism of the righteous moralist approach is that its proponents go too far. While there are some universal moral principles that should not be violated, it does not always follow that the appropriate thing to do is adopt home-country standards. For example, U.S. laws set down strict guidelines with regard to minimum wage and working conditions. Does this mean it is ethical to apply the same guidelines in a foreign country, paying people the same as they are paid in the United States, providing the same benefits and working conditions? Probably not, because doing so might nullify the reason for investing in that country and therefore deny locals the benefits of inward investment by the multinational. Clearly, a more nuanced approach is needed.

The Naive Immoralist

A **naive immoralist** asserts that if a manager of a multinational sees that firms from other nations are not following ethical norms in a host nation, that manager should not either. The classic example to illustrate the approach is known as the drug lord problem. In one variant of this problem, an American manager in Colombia routinely pays off the local drug lord to guarantee that her plant will not be bombed and that none of her employees will be kidnapped. The manager argues that such payments are ethically defensible because everyone is doing it.

The objection is twofold. First, to say that an action is ethically justified if everyone is doing it is not sufficient. If firms in a country routinely employ 12-year-olds and make them work 10-hour days, is it therefore ethically defensible to do the same? Obviously not, and the company does have a clear choice. It does not have to abide by local practices, and it can decide not to invest in a country where the practices are particularly odious. Second, the multinational must recognize that it does have the ability to change the prevailing practice in a country. It can use its power for a positive moral purpose. This is what BP is doing by adopting a zero-tolerance policy with regard to facilitating payments. BP is stating that the prevailing practice of making facilitating payments is ethically wrong, and it is incumbent upon the company to use its power to try to change the standard. While some might argue that such an approach smells of moral imperialism and a lack of cultural sensitivity, if it is consistent with widely accepted moral standards in the global community, it may be ethically justified.

Utilitarian and Kantian Ethics

In contrast to the straw men just discussed, most moral philosophers see value in utilitarian and Kantian approaches to business ethics. These approaches were developed in the eighteenth and nineteenth centuries, and although they have been largely superseded by more modern approaches, they form part of the tradition upon which newer approaches have been constructed.

The utilitarian approach to business ethics dates to philosophers such as David Hume (1711–1776), Jeremy Bentham (1748–1832), and John Stuart Mill (1806–1873). **Utilitarian approaches** to ethics hold that the moral worth of actions or practices is determined by their consequences.[32] An action is judged desirable if it leads to the best possible balance of good consequences over bad consequences. Utilitarianism is committed to the maximization of good and the minimization of harm. Utilitarianism recognizes that actions have multiple consequences, some of which are good in a social sense and some of which are harmful. As a philosophy for business ethics, it focuses attention on the need to weigh carefully all the social benefits and costs of a business action and to pursue only those actions where the benefits outweigh the costs. The best decisions, from a utilitarian perspective, are those that produce the greatest good for the greatest number of people.

Many businesses have adopted specific tools such as cost–benefit analysis and risk assessment that are firmly rooted in a utilitarian philosophy. Managers often weigh the benefits and costs of an action before deciding whether to pursue it. An oil company considering drilling in the Alaskan wildlife preserve must weigh the economic benefits of increased oil production and the creation of jobs against the costs of environmental degradation in a fragile ecosystem. An agricultural biotechnology company such as Monsanto must decide whether the benefits of genetically modified crops that produce natural pesticides outweigh the risks. The benefits include increased crop yields and reduced need for chemical fertilizers. The risks include the possibility that Monsanto's insect-resistant crops might make matters worse over time if insects evolve a resistance to the natural pesticides engineered into Monsanto's plants, rendering the plants vulnerable to a new generation of superbugs.

The utilitarian philosophy does have some serious drawbacks as an approach to business ethics. One problem is measuring the benefits, costs, and risks of a course of action. In the case of an oil company considering drilling in Alaska, how does one measure the potential harm done to the region's ecosystem? The second problem with utilitarianism is that the philosophy omits the consideration of justice. The action that produces the greatest good for the greatest number of people may result in the unjustified treatment of a minority. Such action cannot be ethical, precisely because it is unjust. For example, suppose that in the interests of keeping down health insurance costs, the government decides to screen people for the HIV virus and deny insurance coverage to those who are HIV positive. By reducing health costs, such action might produce significant benefits for a large number of people, but the action is unjust because it discriminates unfairly against a minority.

Kantian ethics is based on the philosophy of Immanuel Kant (1724–1804). **Kantian ethics** holds that people should be treated as ends and never purely as *means* to the ends of others. People are not instruments, like a machine. People have dignity and need to be respected as such. Employing people in sweatshops, making them work long hours for low pay in poor work conditions, is a violation of ethics, according to Kantian philosophy, because it treats people as mere cogs in a machine and not as conscious moral beings that have dignity. Although contemporary moral philosophers tend to view Kant's ethical philosophy as incomplete—for example, his system has no place for moral emotions or sentiments such as sympathy or caring—the notion that people should be respected and treated with dignity resonates in the modern world.

Rights Theories

Developed in the twentieth century, **rights theories** recognize that human beings have fundamental rights and privileges that transcend national boundaries and cultures. Rights establish a minimum level of morally acceptable behavior. One well-known definition of a fundamental right construes it as something that takes precedence over or "trumps" a collective good. Thus, we might say that the right to free speech is a fundamental right that takes precedence over all but the most compelling collective goals and overrides, for example, the interest of the state in civil harmony or moral consensus.[33] Moral theorists argue that fundamental human rights form the basis for the *moral compass* that managers should navigate by when making decisions that have an ethical component. More precisely, they should not pursue actions that violate these rights.

The notion that there are fundamental rights that transcend national borders and cultures was the underlying motivation for the United Nations **Universal Declaration of Human Rights**, adopted in 1948, which has been ratified by almost every country on the planet and lays down basic principles that should always be adhered to irrespective of the culture in which one is doing business.[34] Echoing Kantian ethics, Article 1 of this declaration states:

All human beings are born free and equal in dignity and rights. They are endowed with reason and conscience and should act towards one another in a spirit of brotherhood.

Article 23 of this declaration, which relates directly to employment, states:

(1) Everyone has the right to work, to free choice of employment, to just and favorable conditions of work, and to protection against unemployment.
(2) Everyone, without any discrimination, has the right to equal pay for equal work.
(3) Everyone who works has the right to just and favorable remuneration ensuring for himself and his family an existence worthy of human dignity, and supplemented, if necessary, by other means of social protection.
(4) Everyone has the right to form and to join trade unions for the protection of his interests.

Clearly, the rights to "just and favorable conditions of work," "equal pay for equal work," and remuneration that ensures an "existence worthy of human dignity" embodied in Article 23 imply that it is unethical to employ child labor in sweatshop settings and pay less than subsistence wages, even if that happens to be common practice in some countries. These are fundamental human rights that transcend national borders.

It is important to note that along with *rights* come *obligations*. Because we have the right to free speech, we are also obligated to make sure that we respect the free speech of others. The notion that people have obligations is stated in Article 29 of the Universal Declaration of Human Rights:

(1) Everyone has duties to the community in which alone the free and full development of his personality is possible.

Within the framework of a theory of rights, certain people or institutions are obligated to provide benefits or services that secure the rights of others. Such obligations also fall on more than one class of moral agent (a *moral agent* is any person or institution that is capable of moral action such as a government or corporation).

For example, to escape the high costs of toxic waste disposal in the West, in the late 1980s several firms shipped their waste in bulk to African nations, where it was disposed of at a much lower cost. In 1987, five European ships unloaded toxic waste containing dangerous poisons in Nigeria. Workers wearing sandals and shorts unloaded the barrels for $2.50 a day and placed them in a dirt lot in a residential area. They were not told about the contents of the barrels.[35] Who bears the obligation for protecting the rights of workers and residents to safety in a case like this? According to rights theorists, the obligation rests not on the shoulders of one moral agent, but on the shoulders of all moral agents whose actions might harm or contribute to the harm of the workers and residents. Thus, it was the obligation not just of the Nigerian government but also of the multinational firms that shipped the toxic waste to make sure it did no harm to residents and workers. In this case, both the government and the multinationals apparently failed to recognize their basic obligation to protect the fundamental human rights of others.

Justice Theories

Justice theories focus on the attainment of a just distribution of economic goods and services. A **just distribution** is one that is considered fair and equitable. There is no one theory of justice, and several theories of justice conflict with each other in important ways.[36] Here, we focus on one particular theory of justice that is both very influential and has important ethical implications. The theory is attributed to philosopher John Rawls.[37] Rawls argues that all economic goods and services should be distributed equally except when an unequal distribution would work to everyone's advantage.

According to Rawls, valid principles of justice are those with which all persons would agree if they could freely and impartially consider the situation. Impartiality is guaranteed by a conceptual device that Rawls calls the *veil of ignorance*. Under the veil of ignorance, everyone is imagined to be ignorant of all of his or her particular characteristics, for example, race, sex, intelligence, nationality, family background, and special talents. Rawls then asks what system people would design under a veil of ignorance. Under these conditions, people would unanimously agree on two fundamental principles of justice.

The first principle is that each person be permitted the maximum amount of basic liberty compatible with a similar liberty for others. Rawls takes these to be political liberty (e.g., the right to vote), freedom of speech and assembly, liberty of conscience and freedom of thought, the freedom and right to hold personal property, and freedom from arbitrary arrest and seizure.

The second principle is that once equal basic liberty is ensured, inequality in basic social goods—such as income and wealth distribution, and opportunities—is to be allowed *only* if such inequalities benefit everyone. Rawls accepts that inequalities can be just if the system that produces inequalities is to the advantage of everyone. More precisely, he formulates what he calls the *difference principle,* which is that inequalities are justified if they benefit the position of the least-advantaged person. So, for example, wide variations in income and wealth can be considered just if the market-based system that produces this unequal distribution also benefits the least-advantaged members of society. One can argue that a well-regulated, market-based economy and free trade, by promoting economic growth, benefit the least-advantaged members of society. In principle at least, the inequalities inherent in such systems are therefore just (in other words, the rising tide of wealth created by a market-based economy and free trade lifts all boats, even those of the most disadvantaged).

In the context of international business ethics, Rawls's theory creates an interesting perspective. Managers could ask themselves whether the policies they adopt in foreign operations would be considered just under Rawls's veil of ignorance. Is it just, for example, to pay foreign workers less than workers in the firm's home country? Rawls's theory would suggest it is, so long as the inequality benefits the least-advantaged members of the global society (which is what economic theory suggests). Alternatively, it is difficult to imagine that managers operating under a veil of ignorance would design a system where foreign employees were paid subsistence wages to work long hours in sweatshop conditions and where they were exposed to toxic materials. Such working conditions are clearly unjust in Rawls's framework, and therefore, it is unethical to adopt them. Similarly, operating under a veil of ignorance, most people would probably design a system that imparts some protection from environmental degradation to important global commons, such as the oceans, atmosphere, and tropical rain forests. To the extent that this is the case, it follows that it is unjust, and by extension unethical, for companies to pursue actions that contribute toward extensive degradation of these commons. Thus, Rawls's veil of ignorance is a conceptual tool that contributes to the moral compass that managers can use to help them navigate through difficult ethical dilemmas.

IMPLICATIONS FOR MANAGERS · LO5-5

What, then, is the best way for managers in a multinational firm to make sure that ethical considerations figure into international business decisions? How do managers decide on an ethical course of action when confronted with decisions pertaining to working conditions, human rights, corruption, and environmental pollution? From an ethical perspective, how do managers determine the moral obligations that flow from the power of a multinational? In many cases, there are no easy answers to these questions, for many of the most vexing ethical problems arise because there are very real dilemmas inherent in them and

no obvious correct action. Nevertheless, managers can and should do many things to make sure that basic ethical principles are adhered to and that ethical issues are routinely inserted into international business decisions.

Here, we focus on five things that an international business and its managers can do to make sure ethical issues are considered in business decisions: (1) Favor hiring and promoting people with a well-grounded sense of personal ethics; (2) build an organizational culture that places a high value on ethical behavior; (3) make sure that leaders within the business not only articulate the rhetoric of ethical behavior but also act in a manner that is consistent with that rhetoric; (4) put decision-making processes in place that require people to consider the ethical dimension of business decisions; and (5) develop moral courage.

HIRING AND PROMOTION

It seems obvious that businesses should strive to hire people who have a strong sense of personal ethics and would not engage in unethical or illegal behavior. Similarly, you would not expect a business to promote people, and perhaps to fire people, whose behavior does not match generally accepted ethical standards. However, actually doing so is very difficult. How do you know that someone has a poor sense of personal ethics? In our society, we have an incentive to hide a lack of personal ethics from public view. Once people realize that you are unethical, they will no longer trust you.

Is there anything that businesses can do to make sure they do not hire people who subsequently turn out to have poor personal ethics, particularly given that people have an incentive to hide this from public view (indeed, the unethical person may lie about his or her nature)? Businesses can give potential employees psychological tests to try to discern their ethical predispositions, and they can check with prior employees regarding someone's reputation (e.g., by asking for letters of reference and talking to people who have worked with the prospective employee). The latter is common and does influence the hiring process. Promoting people who have displayed poor ethics should not occur in a company where the organization culture values the need for ethical behavior and where leaders act accordingly.

Not only should businesses strive to identify and hire people with a strong sense of personal ethics, but it also is in the interests of prospective employees to find out as much as they can about the ethical climate in an organization. Who wants to work at a multinational such as Enron, which ultimately entered bankruptcy because unethical executives had established risky partnerships that were hidden from public view and that existed in part to enrich those same executives? Table 5.1 lists some questions job seekers might want to ask a prospective employer.

ORGANIZATION CULTURE AND LEADERSHIP

To foster ethical behavior, businesses need to build an organization culture that values ethical behavior. Three things are particularly important in building an organization culture that emphasizes ethical behavior. First, the businesses must explicitly articulate values that emphasize ethical behavior. Many companies now do this by drafting a **code of ethics**, which is a formal statement of the ethical priorities a business adheres to. Often, the code of ethics draws heavily upon documents such as the UN Universal Declaration of Human Rights, which itself is grounded in Kantian and rights-based theories of moral philosophy. Others have incorporated ethical statements into documents that articulate the values or mission of the business. For example, the food and consumer products multinational Unilever has a code of ethics that includes the following points:[38]

> **Employees:** Unilever is committed to diversity in a working environment where there is mutual trust and respect and where everyone feels responsible for the performance and reputation of our company. We will recruit, employ, and promote employees on the sole basis of the qualifications and

abilities needed for the work to be performed. We are committed to safe and healthy working conditions for all employees. We will not use any form of forced, compulsory, or child labor. We are committed to working with employees to develop and enhance each individual's skills and capabilities. We respect the dignity of the individual and the right of employees to freedom of association. We will maintain good communications with employees through company-based information and consultation procedures.

Business Integrity: Unilever does not give or receive, whether directly or indirectly, bribes or other improper advantages for business or financial gain. No employee may offer, give, or receive any gift or payment which is, or may be construed as being, a bribe. Any demand for, or offer of, a bribe must be rejected immediately and reported to management. Unilever accounting records and supporting documents must accurately describe and reflect the nature of the underlying transactions. No undisclosed or unrecorded account, fund, or asset will be established or maintained.

It is clear from these principles that among other things, Unilever will not tolerate substandard working conditions, use child labor, or give bribes under any circumstances. Note also the reference to respecting the dignity of employees, a statement that is grounded in Kantian ethics. Unilever's principles send a very clear message about appropriate ethics to managers and employees.

Having articulated values in a code of ethics or some other document, leaders in the business must give life and meaning to those words by repeatedly emphasizing their importance *and then acting on them.* This means using every relevant opportunity to stress the importance of business ethics and making sure that key business decisions not only make good economic sense but also are ethical. Many companies have gone a step further, hiring independent auditors to make sure they are behaving in a manner consistent with their ethical codes. Nike, for example, has hired independent auditors to make sure that subcontractors used by the company are living up to Nike's code of conduct.

Finally, building an organization culture that places a high value on ethical behavior requires incentive and reward systems, including promotions that reward people who engage in ethical behavior and sanction those who do not. At General Electric, for example, the former CEO Jack Welch has described how he reviewed the performance of managers, dividing them into several different groups. These included over-performers who displayed the right values and were singled out for advancement and bonuses and over-performers who displayed the wrong values and were let go. Welch was not willing to tolerate leaders within the company who did not act in accordance with the central values of the company, even if they were in all other respects skilled managers.[39]

DECISION-MAKING PROCESSES

In addition to establishing the right kind of ethical culture in an organization, businesspeople must be able to think through the ethical implications of decisions in a systematic way. To do this, they need a moral compass, and both rights theories and Rawls's theory of justice help provide such a compass. Beyond these theories, some experts on ethics have proposed a straightforward practical guide—or ethical algorithm—to determine whether a decision is ethical.[40] According to these experts, a decision is acceptable on ethical grounds if a businessperson can answer yes to each of these questions:

- Does my decision fall within the accepted values or standards that typically apply in the organizational environment (as articulated in a code of ethics or some other corporate statement)?

- Am I willing to see the decision communicated to all stakeholders affected by it—for example, by having it reported in newspapers or on television?

- Would the people with whom I have a significant personal relationship, such as family members, friends, or even managers in other businesses, approve of the decision?

Others have recommended a five-step process to think through ethical problems (this is another example of an ethical algorithm).[41] In step 1, businesspeople should identify which stakeholders a decision would affect and in what ways. A firm's **stakeholders** are individuals or groups that have an interest, claim, or stake in the company, in what it does, and in how well it performs.[42] They can be divided into internal stakeholders and external stakeholders. **Internal stakeholders** are individuals or groups who work for or own the business. They include all employees, the board of directors, and stockholders. **External stakeholders** are all the other individuals and groups that have some claim on the firm. Typically, this group comprises customers, suppliers, lenders, governments, unions, local communities, and the general public.

All stakeholders are in an exchange relationship with the company. Each stakeholder group supplies the organization with important resources (or contributions), and in exchange each expects its interests to be satisfied (by inducements).[43] For example, employees provide labor, skills, knowledge, and time and in exchange expect commensurate income, job satisfaction, job security, and good working conditions. Customers provide a company with its revenues and in exchange want quality products that represent value for money. Communities provide businesses with local infrastructure and in exchange want businesses that are responsible citizens and seek some assurance that the quality of life will be improved as a result of the business firm's existence.

Stakeholder analysis involves a certain amount of what has been called *moral imagination*.[44] This means standing in the shoes of a stakeholder and asking how a proposed decision might impact that stakeholder. For example, when considering outsourcing to subcontractors, managers might need to ask themselves how it might feel to be working under substandard health conditions for long hours.

Step 2 involves judging the ethics of the proposed strategic decision, given the information gained in step 1. Managers need to determine whether a proposed decision would violate the *fundamental rights* of any stakeholders. For example, we might argue that the right to information about health risks in the workplace is a fundamental entitlement of employees. Similarly, the right to know about potentially dangerous features of a product is a fundamental entitlement of customers (something tobacco companies violated when they did not reveal to their customers what they knew about the health risks of smoking). Managers might also want to ask themselves whether they would allow the proposed strategic decision if they were designing a system under Rawls's veil of ignorance. For example, if the issue under consideration was whether to outsource work to a subcontractor with low pay and poor working conditions, managers might want to ask themselves whether they would allow such action if they were considering it under a veil of ignorance, where they themselves might ultimately be the ones to work for the subcontractor.

The judgment at this stage should be guided by various moral principles that should not be violated. The principles might be those articulated in a corporate code of ethics or other company documents. In addition, certain moral principles that we have adopted as members of society—for instance, the prohibition on stealing—should not be violated. The judgment at this stage will also be guided by the decision rule that is chosen to assess the proposed strategic decision. Although maximizing long-run profitability is the decision rule that most businesses stress, it should be applied subject to the constraint that no moral principles are violated—that the business behaves in an ethical manner.

Step 3 requires managers to establish moral intent. This means the business must resolve to place moral concerns ahead of other concerns in cases where either the fundamental rights of stakeholders or key moral principles have been violated. At this stage, input from top management might be particularly valuable. Without the proactive encouragement of top managers, middle-level managers might tend to place the narrow economic interests of the company before the interests of stakeholders. They might do so in the (usually erroneous) belief that top managers favor such an approach.

Step 4 requires the company to engage in ethical behavior. Step 5 requires the business to audit its decisions, reviewing them to make sure they were consistent with ethical principles, such as those stated in the company's code of ethics. This final step is critical and often overlooked. Without auditing past decisions, businesspeople may not know if their decision process is working and if changes should be made to ensure greater compliance with a code of ethics.

ETHICS OFFICERS

To make sure that a business behaves in an ethical manner, a number of firms now have ethics officers. These individuals are responsible for making sure that all employees are trained to be ethically aware, that ethical considerations enter the business decision-making process, and that the company's code of ethics is followed. Ethics officers may also be responsible for auditing decisions to make sure they are consistent with this code. In many businesses, ethics officers act as an internal ombudsperson with responsibility for handling confidential inquiries from employees, investigating complaints from employees or others, reporting findings, and making recommendations for change.

For example, United Technologies, a multinational aerospace company with worldwide revenues of more than $30 billion, has had a formal code of ethics since 1990.[45] United Technologies has some 450 business practices officers (the company's name for ethics officers). They are responsible for making sure the code is followed. United Technologies also established an ombudsperson program in 1986 that lets employees inquire anonymously about ethics issues. The program has received some 60,000 inquiries since 1986, and over 10,000 cases have been handled by an ombudsperson.

MORAL COURAGE

Finally, it is important to recognize that employees in an international business may need significant *moral courage*. Moral courage enables managers to walk away from a decision that is profitable but unethical. Moral courage gives an employee the strength to say no to a superior who instructs her to pursue actions that are unethical. Moral courage gives employees the integrity to go public to the media and blow the whistle on persistent unethical behavior in a company. Moral courage does not come easily; there are well-known cases where individuals have lost their jobs because they blew the whistle on corporate behaviors they thought unethical, telling the media about what was occurring.[46]

However, companies can strengthen the moral courage of employees by committing themselves to not retaliate against employees who exercise moral courage, say no to superiors, or otherwise complain about unethical actions. For example, consider the following extract from Unilever's code of ethics:

Any breaches of the Code must be reported in accordance with the procedures specified by the Joint Secretaries. The Board of Unilever will not criticize management for any loss of business resulting from adherence to these principles and other mandatory policies and instructions. The Board of Unilever expects employees to bring to their attention, or to that of senior management, any breach or suspected breach of these principles. Provision has been made for employees to be able to report in confidence and no employee will suffer as a consequence of doing so.[47]

This statement gives permission to employees to exercise moral courage. Companies can also set up ethics hotlines, which allow employees to anonymously register a complaint with a corporate ethics officer.

SUBSIDIARY CONTROL ISSUES: REEBOK INDIA

In April 2012, Adidas told BBC that 'commercial irregularities' at its Reebok unit in India could cost the firm up to €125 million ($165m, £101m).[48] The executive also mentioned of an internal investigation, and also said that 'we will take further steps' when that process has been completed. Adidas admitted in March 2012 that the irregularities have resulted in a change of leadership at its India business.[49] Adidas had sacked the then-CEO Mr. Subhinder Singh Prem, and Vishnu Bhagat, COO.[50]

In May 2012, fraud at Reebok India unit was discovered by Adidas. Reebok India filed an FIR on May 21, 2012 against Prem and Bhagat, charging them with misappropriation of funds, inventory diversion, and fictitious inflation of sales revenue.[51] The financial accounts of both Adidas India and Reebok India are consolidated with Adidas' global account. KPMG, its global auditor, prepares a report on the financials of both subsidiaries as per international financial reporting standards (IFRS). KPMG had not flagged any financial misappropriations in its report on Reebok India. This IFRS report was signed by Reebok India executives including Shahin Padath, CFO. Incidentally, the FIR accusing Prem and Bhagat of financial bungling had been filed by Padath on behalf of Reebok.

While KPMG was involved in the consolidation of accounts of Indian subsidiaries of Adidas, Delhi-based N Narasimhan & Co was the auditor of Reebok India. Adidas AG in Germany had in 2011 tasked a forensics team from KPMG to probe into any instance of financial irregularities in Reebok and by its senior executives. The forensic audit was not carried out because of some specific allegations. The integration of the Indian units of Adidas and Reebok happened in 2011. It is a standard operating procedure for MNCs to conduct audits and the charges of financial bungling leveled by the company pertained to the period prior to December 2011.

Adidas in July 2012 had disclosed to the Serious Fraud Investigation Office (SFIO) that it lost around INR 170 crore (INR 1.7 billion) because of "goodwill impairment" after it bought Reebok. The company had said it lost INR 870 crore (INR 8.7 billion) due to alleged misappropriation by former employees Prem and Vishnu Bhagat.[52]

Accused executives blame Adidas for instructing them to do irregularities[53] In June 2012 another twist to the INR 870-crore Reebok fraud, two former company executives accused of fudging company accounts and operating secret warehouses, have blamed Adidas for hammering down the valuation of the Indian unit, as part of a strategy to reduce the payout to the minority shareholder in the company (Reebok).

According to an *Economic Times* report of June 2012, Prem and Vishnu Bhagat had alleged that Adidas asked them to manipulate company accounts, "to ensure that the market value of Reebok India fell so that a significantly lower amount becomes payable to the exiting Indian joint venture partner." In other words, Adidas wanted to make a minimum payout to buy out Focus Energy's 6.85 percent stake in Reebok India.

Adidas had sacked the two officials in March 2012, and in May, the duo was accused of financial embezzlement. However, the two officials told the Delhi high Court that their refusal to 'carry out unethical and illegitimate requests' by Adidas was what led to bitterness between them and the management.

It was in 2010—one year before Adidas merged its India operations with Reebok—that the parent firm first brought in KPMG India's forensic team to look into possible manipulation in the accounts of Reebok by two of its senior-most employees. However, KPMG gave Prem and Bhagat a near clean chit concluding that there was, "no evidence to prove allegations of possible fraudulent behavior" by either of them.

Adidas's Reebok financial irregularities handed over to SFIO by Indian Government[54] By June 2012, the case of financial irregularities was referred to three different agencies—the I-T department under Finance Ministry, the Serious Fraud Investigation Office (SFIO) under Corporate Affairs Ministry and the Economic Offences Wing of Gurgaon police.

In July 2012, the SFIO had found some anomalies in the business transactions between the subsidiary company Reebok India and its parent firm. "Preliminary scrutiny has thrown up some dubious transactions with the global company which needs to be looked into. We will be asking for details from Adidas AG," a senior official of the corporate affairs ministry told.

In September 2012, all the three agencies detected a systemic "mismanagement" in the business planning and running of the company[55] while recording the findings almost four months after a criminal case was filed by Reebok India against two of its former employees. The agencies reported, "The governance and operations in the company were mismanaged. The bills were inflated and not recorded correctly. So, the probe clearly indicates that it was not a corporate scam in the apparel manufacturing firm but it was non-adherence to the rules and guidelines of business procedures in the firm."

The Serious Fraud Investigation Office (SFIO), the country's corporate fraud investigation body, by November 2012 had arrested 12 accused including two main accused—ex-MD Prem and ex-COO Vishnu Bhagat—in the Reebok India scam. The agency claimed to have found evidence related to falsified documents for sundry debtor charges amounting to INR 500 crore. The court rejected the anticipatory bail application of two main accused Prem and Bhagat.[56]

Adidas Group unveiled a three-pronged strategy in India[57] In August 2012, Adidas Group unveiled a three-pronged strategy in India that included the closure of nearly a third of its 900 Reebok stores, a voluntary retirement scheme (VRS) for the 200-odd Reebok employees and integration of the two brands' suppliers. The German sportswear giant felt the financial irregularities discovered for financial year 2011 might have started much earlier and the company would not hesitate to open the accounts of previous years for investigation, if required.

Speaking after the group announced taking a hit of INR 870 crore as a result of alleged financial irregularities committed in Reebok India in 2011, Claus Heckerott, managing director of Adidas, group-market India, said, "We are changing our model from a minimum guarantee scheme (rent plus model) offered to franchisees, which is not sustainable for a cash-and-carry model. One-third of the franchisees are ready to go with this model. The others are not sure or will not go. However, we'll be happy with 300 outlets, provided they are profitable. We had started slowing down the opening of new stores from 2010."

Heckerott said a VRS scheme would be offered to all Reebok employees at generous terms. He said the terms would be much more attractive than market standards, without divulging the numbers. On asking as to why the offer was only to Reebok and not Adidas employees, Heckerott said, "Adidas is still running as a robust business and we are not expecting a big change there. However, in Reebok we had to take corrective action because of the financial irregularity. We want to make a fresh start in Reebok." The company is planning to integrate suppliers, which would include manufacturers making products of both the brands to bring in economies of scale.[58]

TRACKING THE CONTROVERSY: Year 2012

May 1–12: Adidas says 'commercial irregularities' at Reebok India; seeks criminal probe; turns heat on former MD Subhinder Singh Prem.

May 21: Reebok India files an FIR with Gurgaon police, accusing Prem and former COO Vishnu Bhagat of 'criminal conspiracy' and 'fraudulent' practices.

May 23: Ministry of Corporate Affairs (MCA) orders scrutiny of Reebok India's books.

May 24: Gurgaon police say Reebok fraud amount 'far from reality'; I-T dept issues notices to executives.

May 26: Prem, Bhagat denied anticipatory bail.

May 29: MCA refers the case to Serious Fraud Investigation Office (SFIO), blames the company for not cooperating.

June 1–6: Prem, Bhagat deny fraud charges; SFIO says fraud figure inflated; I-T dept, Institute of Chartered Accountants (ICAI) start probe.

July 2: Adidas values goodwill impairment at INR 170 crore; auditor N Narasimhan & Co says no accounting wrongdoing in Reebok.

July 9: Reebok refuses to give 'scam' details to ICAI.

July 15–18: I-T finds no signs of corporate fraud; summons auditors.

Chapter Summary

This chapter discussed the source and nature of ethical issues in international businesses, the different philosophical approaches to business ethics, and the steps managers can take to ensure that ethical issues are respected in international business decisions. The chapter made the following points:

1. The term *ethics* refers to accepted principles of right or wrong that govern the conduct of a person, the members of a profession, or the actions of an organization. Business ethics are the accepted principles of right or wrong governing the conduct of businesspeople, and an ethical strategy is one that does not violate these accepted principles.

2. Ethical issues and dilemmas in international business are rooted in the variations among political systems, law, economic development, and culture from nation to nation.

3. The most common ethical issues in international business involve employment practices, human rights, environmental regulations, corruption, and the moral obligation of multinational corporations.

4. Ethical dilemmas are situations in which none of the available alternatives seems ethically acceptable.

5. Unethical behavior is rooted in poor personal ethics, societal culture, the psychological and geographic distances of a foreign subsidiary from the home office, a failure to incorporate ethical issues into strategic and operational decision making, a dysfunctional culture, and failure of leaders to act in an ethical manner.

6. Moral philosophers contend that approaches to business ethics such as the Friedman doctrine, cultural relativism, the righteous moralist, and the naive immoralist are unsatisfactory in important ways.

7. The Friedman doctrine states that the only social responsibility of business is to increase profits, as long as the company stays within the rules of law. Cultural relativism contends that one should adopt the ethics of the culture in which one is doing business. The righteous moralist monolithically applies home-country ethics to a foreign situation, while the naive immoralist believes that if a manager of a multinational sees that firms from other nations are not following ethical norms in a host nation, that manager should not either.

8. Utilitarian approaches to ethics hold that the moral worth of actions or practices is determined by their consequences, and the best decisions are those that produce the greatest good for the greatest number of people.

9. Kantian ethics state that people should be treated as ends and never purely as *means* to the ends of others. People are not instruments, like a machine. People have dignity and need to be respected as such.

10. Rights theories recognize that human beings have fundamental rights and privileges that transcend national boundaries and cultures. These rights establish a minimum level of morally acceptable behavior.

11. The concept of justice developed by John Rawls suggests that a decision is just and ethical if people would allow it when designing a social system under a veil of ignorance.

12. To make sure that ethical issues are considered in international business decisions, managers should (*a*) favor hiring and promoting people with a well-grounded sense of personal ethics; (*b*) build an organization culture that places a high value on ethical behavior; (*c*) make sure that leaders within the business not only articulate the rhetoric of ethical behavior but also act in a manner that is consistent with that rhetoric; (*d*) put decision-making processes in place that re-

quire people to consider the ethical dimension of business decisions; and (*e*) be morally coura-
geous and encourage others to do the same.

Critical Thinking and Discussion Questions

1. A visiting American executive finds that a foreign subsidiary in a poor nation has hired a 12-year-old girl to work on a factory floor, in violation of the company's prohibition on child labor. He tells the local manager to replace the child and tell her to go back to school. The local manager tells the American executive that the child is an orphan with no other means of support, and she will probably become a street child if she is denied work. What should the American executive do?

2. Drawing upon John Rawls's concept of the veil of ignorance, develop an ethical code that will (*a*) guide the decisions of a large oil multinational toward environmental protection and (*b*) influence the policies of a clothing company to outsourcing of manufacturing process.

3. Under what conditions is it ethically defensible to outsource production to the developing world where labor costs are lower when such actions also involve laying off long-term employees in the firm's home country?

4. Are facilitating payments (*speed payments*) ethical?

5. A manager from a developing country is overseeing a multinational's operations in a country where drug trafficking and lawlessness are rife. One day, a representative of a local "big man" approaches the manager and asks for a "donation" to help the big man provide housing for the poor. The representative tells the manager that in return for the donation, the big man will make sure that the manager has a productive stay in his country. No threats are made, but the manager is well aware that the big man heads a criminal organization that is engaged in drug trafficking. He also knows that that the big man does indeed help the poor in the run-down neighborhood of the city where he was born. What should the manager do?

6. Reread the Management Focus on Unocal, and answer the following questions:
   a. Was it ethical for Unocal to enter into a partnership with a brutal military dictatorship for financial gain?
   b. What actions could Unocal have taken, short of not investing at all, to safeguard the human rights of people affected by the gas pipeline project?

Research Task ⓔ globalEDGE | globaledge.msu.edu

Ethics in International Business

Use the globalEDGE website (globaledge.msu.edu) to complete the following exercises:

Exercise 1

Promoting respect for universal human rights is a central dimension of many countries' foreign policy. As history has shown, human rights abuses are an important concern worldwide. Some countries are more ready to work with other governments and civil society organizations to prevent abuses of power. Begun in 1977, the annual *Country Reports on Human Rights Practices* are designed to assess the state of democracy and human rights around the world, call attention to violations, and—where needed—prompt needed changes in U.S. policies toward particular countries. Find the latest annual *Country Reports on Human Right Practices* for the BRIC countries (Brazil, China, India, and Russia), and create a table to compare the findings under the "Worker Rights" sections. What commonalities do you see? What differences are there?

Exercise 2

The use of bribery in the business setting is an important ethical dilemma many companies face both domestically and abroad. The *Bribe Payers Index* is a study published every three years to assess the likelihood of firms from 28 leading economies to win business overseas by offering bribes. It also ranks industry sectors based on the prevalence of bribery. Compare the five industries thought to have the largest problems with bribery with those five that have the least problems. What patterns do you see? What factors make some industries more conducive to bribery than others?

Closing **CASE**

Working Conditions in a Chinese Factory

In 2008, the National Labor Committee sponsored an investigation into working conditions in two factories in China that make computer equipment, including keyboards and printer cases, for Hewlett-Packard, Dell, Lenovo, and Microsoft. The report, which was published in early 2009, describes working conditions that are extremely harsh by Western standards.

According to the report, in the Metai factory in Guangdong, the workers sit on wooden stools, without backrests, as 500 computer keyboards an hour move down the assembly line, 12 hours a day, 7 days a week, with just 2 days off a month. Every 7.2 seconds a keyboard passes each worker, who has to snap six or seven keys into place—one key every 1.1 seconds. The assembly line never stops. The workplace is frantic, monotonous, numbing, and relentless. Each worker inserts 3,250 keys an hour; 35,750 keys during their shift; 250,250 a week, performing more than 1 million operations a month. Workers are paid 1/50th of a cent for each operation they complete. While working, employees cannot talk, listen to music, or even lift their heads to look around. Workers needing to use the bathroom must hold it until there is a break. Security guards spy on the workers, who are prohibited from putting their hands in their pockets and are searched when they enter and leave the factory. The factory operates 24 hours a day on two 12-hour shifts, with the workers rotating between day and night shifts each month. The workers are at the factory for up to 87 hours a week, and all overtime is mandatory. There are two half-hour meal breaks per shift, but after racing to the cafeteria and lining up to get food, the workers have only about 15 minutes to eat. The base wage is 64 cents an hour, which after deductions for primitive room and board drops to a take-home wage of just 41 cents an hour. The workers get up about 6:00 a.m. When they return to their dorm, sometime between 9:00 and 9:30 p.m., they bathe using a small plastic bucket. Summer temperatures routinely reach into the high 90s. During the winter, workers have to walk down several flights of stairs to fetch hot water in their buckets. Ten to twelve workers share each crowded dorm room, sleeping on narrow metal bunk beds that line the walls. Workers drape old sheets over their cubicle openings for privacy.

Comments from the workers at this factory, most of whom are young women between 18 and their mid-20s, reinforce how harsh the conditions are. One stated, "Every day I enter the factory and I assemble keyboards. My hands are moving constantly and I can't stop for a second. Our fingers, hands and arms are swollen and sore. Every day I do this for 12 hours. What makes it even worse is the constant pressure and boring monotony of the work." Another notes, "The factory rules are really like a private law. We are forced to obey and endure management's harsh treatment. Some young workers have boyfriends and girlfriends outside the factory and if they want to go on a date, we have to beg the boss for mercy to be able to leave the factory compound." Another said simply, "We feel like we are serving prison sentences."

When informed of these findings, a spokesman for Microsoft said the factory supplied one of its contract manufacturers, but Microsoft would investigate. Representatives from Hewlett-Packard and Lenovo also stated the factory was not a direct supplier, but supplied their suppliers. However, they too said they would look into the issue. A spokesman for Dell, for which the factory is a direct supplier, said it was actively investigating conditions. The spokesman went on to say, "I can tell you that any reports of poor working conditions in Dell's supply chain are investigated and appropriate action is taken."[59]

Case Discussion Questions

1. What enables the owners of the Metai factory profiled in this case to get away with such awful working conditions?
2. Should U.S. companies like Microsoft, Dell, and Hewlett-Packard be held responsible for working conditions in foreign factories that they do not own, but where subcontractors make products for them?
3. What labor standards regarding safety, working conditions, overtime, and the like should U.S. companies hold foreign factories to: those prevailing in that country or those prevailing in the United States?
4. Do you think the U.S. companies mentioned in this case need to make any changes to their current policies? If so, what? Should they make changes even if they hinder their ability to compete in the marketplace?

Endnotes

1. E. Rosenthal, "Used Batteries from U.S. Expose Mexicans to Risk," *The New York Times,* December 9, 2011, pp. A1, A12; "New Report Detailing Failures of Mexican Battery Recyclers Proves the Exportation of SLABs Must Be Stopped," *Business Wire,* June 15, 2011; and "Johnson Controls Announces Planned Investment in Its Automotive Battery Recycling Center in Mexico," *PR Newswire,* August 30, 2011.
2. S. Greenhouse, "Nike Shoe Plant in Vietnam Is Called Unsafe for Workers," *The New York Times,* November 8, 1997; and V. Dobnik, "Chinese Workers Abused Making Nikes, Reeboks," *Seattle Times,* September 21, 1997, p. A4.
3. Robert Kinloch Massie, *Loosing the Bonds: The United States and South Africa in the Apartheid Years* (New York: Doubleday, 1997).
4. E. Kurtenbach, "The Foreign Factory Factor," *Seattle Times,* August 31, 2006, pp. C1, C3; Elaine Kurtenbach, "Apple Says It's Trying to Resolve Dispute over Labor Conditions at Chinese iPod Factory," *Associated Press Financial Wire,* August 30, 2006; and "Chinese iPod Supplier Pulls Suit," *Associated Press Financial Wire,* September 3, 2006.
5. Not everyone agrees that the divestment trend had much influence on the South African economy. For a counterview see Siew Hong Teoh, Ivo Welch, and C. Paul Wazzan, "The Effect of Socially Activist Investing on the Financial Markets: Evidence from South Africa," *The Journal of Business* 72, no. 1 (January 1999), pp. 35–60.
6. Peter Singer, *One World: The Ethics of Globalization* (New Haven, CT: Yale University Press, 2002).
7. Jim Carlton, "Unocal Trial for Slave Labor Claims Is Set to Start Today," *The Wall Street Journal,* December 9, 2003, p. A19; Seth Stern, "Big Business Targeted for Rights Abuse," *Christian Science Monitor,* September 4, 2003, p. 2; "Trouble in the Pipeline," *The Economist,* January 18, 1997, p. 39; Irtani Evelyn, "Feeling the Heat: Unocal Defends Myanmar Gas Pipeline Deal," *Los Angeles Times,* February 20, 1995, p. D1; and "Unocal Settles Myanmar Human Rights Cases," *Business and Environment,* February 16, 2005, pp. 14–16.
8. Garrett Hardin, "The Tragedy of the Commons," *Science* 162, no. 1, pp. 243–48, 1968.
9. For a summary of the evidence, see S. Solomon, D. Qin, M. Manning, Z. Chen, M. Marquis, K. B. Averyt, M. Tignor, and H. L. Miller, eds., *Contribution of Working Group I to the Fourth Assessment Report of the Intergovernmental Panel on Climate Change* (Cambridge, UK: Cambridge University Press, 2007).
10. J. Everett, D. Neu and A. S. Rahaman, "The Global Fight against Corruption," *Journal of Business Ethics* 65 (2006), pp. 1–18.

11. Richard T. De George, *Competing with Integrity in International Business* (Oxford, UK: Oxford University Press, 1993).

12. Details can be found at http://www.oecd.org/corruption/oecdantibriberyconvention.

13. A. R. Sorkin, "Daimler to Pay $185 Million to Settle Corruption Charges," *The New York Times,* March 24, 2010; and "Corruption: Daimler Settles with DoJ; SEC Wades in: Germany Next," *Chiefofficers.net,* March 25, 2010.

14. Bardhan Pranab, "Corruption and Development," *Journal of Economic Literature* 36 (September 1997), pp. 1320–46.

15. A. Shleifer and R. W. Vishny, "Corruption," *Quarterly Journal of Economics,* no. 108 (1993), pp. 599–617; and I. Ehrlich and F. Lui, "Bureaucratic Corruption and Endogenous Economic Growth," *Journal of Political Economy* 107 (December 1999), pp. 270–92.

16. P. Mauro, "Corruption and Growth," *Quarterly Journal of Economics,* no. 110 (1995), pp. 681–712.

17. D. Kaufman and S. J. Wei, "Does Grease Money Speed up the Wheels of Commerce?" World Bank policy research working paper, January 11, 2000.

18. Detailed at http://ethics.iit.edu/ecodes/node/3436/.

19. S. A. Waddock and S. B. Graves, "The Corporate Social Performance–Financial Performance Link," *Strategic Management Journal* 8 (1997), pp. 303–19.

20. Details can be found at BP's website, www.bp.com.

21. This is known as the "when in Rome perspective." Donaldson, "Values in Tension: Ethics Away from Home," *Harvard Business Review,* September–October 1996.

22. De George, *Competing with Integrity in International Business.*

23. For a discussion of the ethics of using child labor, see J. Isern, "Bittersweet Chocolate: The Legacy of Child Labor in Cocoa Production in Cote d'Ivoire," *Journal of Applied Management and Entrepreneurship* 11 (2006), pp. 115–32.

24. Saul W. Gellerman, "Why Good Managers Make Bad Ethical Choices," in *Ethics in Practice: Managing the Moral Corporation,* ed. Kenneth R. Andrews (Cambridge, MA: Harvard Business School Press, 1989).

25. David Messick and Max H. Bazerman, "Ethical Leadership and the Psychology of Decision Making," *Sloan Management Review* 37 (Winter 1996), pp. 9–20.

26. B. Scholtens and L. Dam, "Cultural Values and International Differences in Business Ethics," *Journal of Business Ethics,* 2007.

27. Milton Friedman, "The Social Responsibility of Business Is to Increase Profits," *The New York Times Magazine,* September 13, 1970. Reprinted in Tom L. Beauchamp and Norman E. Bowie, *Ethical Theory and Business,* 7th ed. (Englewood Cliffs, NJ: Prentice Hall, 2001).

28. Ibid., p. 55.

29. For example, see Donaldson, "Values in Tension: Ethics Away from Home." See also Norman Bowie, "Relativism and the Moral Obligations of Multination Corporations," in Tom L. Beauchamp and Norman E. Bowie, *Ethical Theory and Business,* 7th ed. (Englewood Cliffs, NJ: Prentice Hall, 2001).

30. For example, see De George, *Competing with Integrity in International Business.*

31. This example is often repeated in the literature on international business ethics. It was first outlined by Arthur Kelly in "Case Study—Italian Style Mores." Printed in Thomas Donaldson and Patricia Werhane, *Ethical Issues in Business* (Englewood Cliffs, NJ: Prentice Hall, 1979).

32. See Beauchamp and Bowie, *Ethical Theory and Business.*

33. Thomas Donaldson, *The Ethics of International Business* (Oxford: Oxford University Press, 1989).

34. Found at www.un.org/Overview/rights.html.

35. Donaldson, *The Ethics of International Business.*

36. See Chapter 10 in Beauchamp and Bowie, *Ethical Theory and Business.*

37. John Rawls, *A Theory of Justice,* rev. ed. (Cambridge, MA: Belknap Press, 1999).

38. Found on Unilever's website at www.unilever.com/aboutus/purposeandprinciples/ourprinciples/default.aspx.

39. Joseph Bower and Jay Dial, "Jack Welch: General Electrics Revolutionary," Harvard Business School Case 9-394-065, April 1994.

40. For example, see R. Edward Freeman and Daniel Gilbert, *Corporate Strategy and the Search for Ethics* (Englewood Cliffs, NJ: Prentice Hall, 1988); Thomas Jones, "Ethical Decision Making by Individuals in Organizations," *Academy of Management Review* 16 (1991), pp. 366–95; and J. R. Rest, *Moral Development: Advances in Research and Theory* (New York: Praeger, 1986).

41. Ibid.

42. See E. Freeman, *Strategic Management: A Stakeholder Approach* (Boston: Pitman Press, 1984); C. W. L. Hill and T. M. Jones, "Stakeholder-Agency Theory," *Journal of Management Studies* 29 (1992), pp. 131–54; and J. G. March and H. A. Simon, *Organizations* (New York: John Wiley & Sons, 1958).

43. Hill and Jones, "Stakeholder-Agency Theory"; and March and Simon, *Organizations.*

44. De George, *Competing with Integrity in International Business.*

45. The code can be accessed at United Technologies website, www.utc.com/profile/ethics/index.htm.

46. Colin Grant, "Whistle Blowers: Saints of Secular Culture," *Journal of Business Ethics,* September 2002, pp. 391–400.

47. Found on Unilever's website at www.unilever.com/aboutus/purposeandprinciples/ourprinciples/default.aspx.

48. http://www.bbc.co.uk/news/business-17892602

49. op.cit 1 above

50. http://www.firstpost.com/business/reebok-scam-did-adidas-ask-accused-officials-to-fudge-accounts-332452.html

51. This part Is based on article published in Economic Times, http://articles.economictimes.indiatimes.com/2012-06-01/news/31959142_1_reebok-india-subhinder-singh-prem-shahin-padath

52. http://www.rediff.com/business/slide-show/slide-show-1-how-reebok-fraud-cost-adidas-rs-170-crore/20120703.htm

53. This part is from article published at http://www.firstpost.com/business/reebok-scam-did-adidas-ask-accused-officials-to-fudge-accounts-332452.html

54. This part is from article published at http://articles.economictimes.indiatimes.com/2012-07-18/news/32730669_1_vishnu-bhagat-ceo-subhinder-singh-prem-reebok-india

55. http://www.firstpost.com/business/reebok-india-scam-is-really-financial-mismanagement-465251.html

56. http://timesofindia.indiatimes.com/city/gurgaon/One-of-12-Reebok-case-accused-gets-bail/articleshow/17395661.cms

57. This part is from article published at http://www.business-standard.com/india/news/adidas-may-open-old-accounts-to-probe-india-irregularities/483214/

58. http://www.business-standard.com/india/news/adidas-may-open-old-accounts-to-probe-india-irregularities/483214/

59. "The Dehumanization of Young Workers Producing Our Computer Keyboards," The National Labor Committee, February 2009, accessed at www.globallabourrights.org/admin/reports/files/HIGHTECH_MISERY_CHINA_WEB.pdf; A. Butler, "29p-an-Hour Slaves Make Our Cut-Price Computers," *Sunday Mirror,* February 22, 2009, p. 34; and R. Thompson, "Prison-like Conditions for Workers Making IBM, Dell, HP, Microsoft and Lenovo Products," *Computer Weekly.com,* February 17, 2009.

P·A·R·T 2 C·A·S·E·S

SIEMENS BRIBERY SCANDAL

In December 2008 Siemens, the large German electronics firm, agreed to pay $1.6 billion in fines to settle legal suits bought by the U.S. and German governments. The governments asserted that Siemens had used bribes to win business in countries around the world. These were the largest fines ever levied against a company for bribes, reflecting the scale of the problem at Siemens. Since 1999, the company had apparently paid some $1.4 billion in bribes. In Bangladesh, Siemens paid $5 million to the son of the prime minister to win a mobile phone contract. In Nigeria, it paid $12.7 million to various officials to win government telecommunications contracts. In Argentina, Siemens paid at least $40 million in bribes to win a $1 billion contract to produce national identity cards. In Israel, the company "provided" $20 million to senior government officials in order to win a contract to build power plants. In China, it paid $14 million to government officials to win a contract to supply medical equipment. And so on.

Corruption at Siemens was apparently deeply embedded in the business culture. Before 1999, bribery of foreign officials was not illegal in Germany, and bribes could be deducted as a business expense under the German tax code. In this permissive environment, Siemens subscribed to the straightforward rule of adhering to local practices. If bribery was common in a country, Siemens would routinely use bribes to win business. Inside Siemens, bribes were referred to as "useful money."

When the German law changed in 1999, Siemens carried on as before, but put in place elaborate mechanisms to hide what it was doing. Money was transferred into hard-to-trace bank accounts in Switzerland. These funds were then used to hire an outside "consultant" to help win a contract. The consultant would in turn deliver the cash to the ultimate recipient, typically a government official. Siemens apparently had more than 2,700 such consultants worldwide. Bribes, which were viewed as a cost of doing business, typically ranged between 5 and 6 percent of a contract's value, although in corrupt countries bribes could be as much as 40 percent of the value of a contract. In justifying this behavior, one former Siemens employee stated, "It was about keeping the business alive and not jeopardizing thousands of jobs overnight." But the practice left behind angry competitors who were shut out of contracts and local residents in poor countries who paid too much for government services because of rigged deals. Also, by engaging in bribery, Siemens helped foster a culture of corruption in those countries where it made illegal payouts.

During this time period, in a cynical move, Siemens put in place a formal process for monitoring payments to make sure that no illegal payments were made. Senior executives even made some of the individuals responsible for managing the bribery funds sign compliance forms stating that they had not engaged in any such activity, while knowing full well that this was not the case.

This scheme began to collapse at Siemens when investigators in several countries began to examine suspicious transactions. Prosecutors in Italy, Liechtenstein, and Switzerland sent requests for help to counterparts in Germany, providing a list of Siemens employees who were implicated in making illegal payments. In late 2006 the German police acted, raiding the company, seizing data, and arresting several executives. Shortly afterward, the United States started to look into these charges. Since Siemens had a listing on the New York Stock Exchange, it had to adhere to the Foreign Corrupt Practices Act, which outlaws payments to government officials to win contracts. At the end of the day, Siemens had to not only pay $1.6 billion in fines but also commit to spending another $1 billion to improve its internal compliance process while several executives went to jail.

Case Discussion Questions

1. What explains the high level of corruption at Siemens? How did managers engaged in corruption rationalize it?
2. What do you think would have happened to a manager at Siemens if he or she had taken a stand against corrupt practices?
3. How does the kind of corruption Siemens engaged in distort competition?
4. What is the impact of corrupt behavior by Siemens on the countries where it does business?
5. If you were a manager at Siemens, and you became aware of these activities, what would you have done?

Sources

S. Schubert and C. Miller, "Where Bribery Was Just a Line Item," *The New York Times,* December 21, 2008, p. B1; J. Ewing, "Siemens Braces for a Slap from Uncle Sam," *BusinessWeek,* November 11, 2007, pp. 78–79; and J. Ewing, "Siemens Settlement: Relief, but Is It Over?" *BusinessWeek,* December 12, 2008, p. 8.

DISASTER IN BANGLADESH: THE COLLAPSE OF THE RANA PLAZA BUILDING

On the morning of Wednesday April 24, 2013, an eight-story industrial and commercial building in Bangladesh collapsed, killing over 1,100 people, most of them workers in one of the five garment factories that occupied six floors of the building. This was not the first high-profile accident in the Bangladesh garment industry. The prior November, a factory fire had killed 112 garment workers. Just days after the building collapse, a fire in another garment factory killed eight people. The spat of accidents led to calls for Western clothing retailers to do more to improve working conditions and safety in Bangladesh and other poor nations from which they source production. Some interest groups went further, arguing that Western companies should refuse to source production from countries where working conditions were so bad. One high-profile Western company, Walt Disney, had already made this decision. In March 2013, Disney removed Bangladesh from the list of countries where it authorized partners to produce clothing and other merchandise for Disney. Politicians in Bangladesh responded to the Disney announcement with dismay. They argued that the economy of Bangladesh was very dependent on the garment industry and that "the whole nation should not be made to suffer" because of these accidents.

The Garment Industry in Bangladesh

Bangladesh, one of the world's poorest countries, has long depended heavily on exports of textile products to generate income, employment, and economic growth. Most of these exports are low-cost finished garments sold to a wide range of retailers in the West, such as Walmart, The Gap, H&M, and Zara. For decades, Bangladesh was able to take advantage of a quota system for textile exports that gave it, and other poor countries, preferential access to rich markets such as the United States and the European Union. On January 1, 2005, that system was scrapped in favor of one that was based on free trade principles. From 2005 on, exporters in Bangladesh would have to compete for business against producers from other nations such as China and Indonesia. Many analysts foresaw the quick collapse of Bangladesh's textile industry. They predicted a sharp jump in unemployment, a decline in the country's balance of payments accounts, and a negative impact on economic growth.

The collapse didn't happen. Bangladesh's exports of textiles continued to grow, even as the rest of the world plunged into an economic crisis in 2008. Bangladesh's exports of garments rose to around $20 billion in 2012, up from $8.9 billion in 2006, making it the largest export industry in the country and a primary driver of economic growth. By 2012 the textile industry in Bangladesh comprised some 5,000 factories which were the source of employment for 3 million people, 85 percent of whom were women with few alternative employment opportunities.

As a deep economic recession took hold in developed nations during 2008–2009, big importers such as Walmart increased their purchases of low-cost garments from Bangladesh to better serve their customers, who were looking for low prices. Li & Fung, a Hong Kong company that handles sourcing and apparel manufacturing, stated its production in Bangladesh jumped 25 percent in 2009, while production in China, its biggest supplier, slid 5 percent.

Bangladesh's advantage is based on a number of factors. First, labor costs are low, in part due to low hourly wage rates and in part due to investments by textile manufacturers in productivity-boosting technology during the past decade. The minimum wage rate in Bangladesh is currently $38 a month, compared to a minimum wage in China of $138 a month. Wage rates in the textile industry are about $50 to $60 a month, less than a fifth of the going rate in China. Textile workers may have to work 12-hour shifts and can work 7 days a week during busy periods. While the pay rate is dismally low by Western standards, in a country where the gross national income per capita is only $850 a year, the pay is better than that available in many other unskilled and low-skilled occupations.

Second, there are few regulations in Bangladesh, and as one foreign buyer says, "There are no rules whatsoever that cannot be bent." The lack of effective regulations keeps costs down. Another source of advantage for Bangladesh is that it has an established network of supporting industries that supply inputs to its garment manufacturers. Some three-quarters of all inputs are made locally. This saves garment manufacturers transport and storage costs, import duties, and the long lead times that come with the imported woven fabrics used to make shirts and trousers.

Bangladesh also has the advantage of not being China. Many importers in the West have grown cautious about becoming too dependent on China for imports of specific goods for fear that if there was disruption, economic or other, their supply chains would be decimated unless they had an alternative source of supply. Thus, Bangladesh has benefited from the trend by Western importers to diversify their supply sources. Although China remains the world's largest exporter of garments, Bangladesh is now second. Moreover, Chinese wage rates are now rising fast, suggesting the trend to shift textile production away from China may continue.

Bangladesh, however, does have some negatives; most notable are the constant disruptions in electricity because the government has underinvested in power generation and distribution infrastructure. Roads and ports are also inferior to those found in China.

The demand for garments from low-cost sources such as Bangladesh has been driven by intense competition among Western clothing retailers. U.S. consumers, for example, have become accustomed to spending relatively little on clothing. In 2012 U.S. consumers devoted just 3 percent of their annual spending to clothing and footwear, compared to around 7 percent in 1970. One reason Americans now spend so little on clothing is that real prices have fallen significantly over the last two decades. Since 1990, clothing prices in the United States have risen by just 10 percent in nominal terms, compared to an 82 percent jump in nominal food prices during the same period. Adjusted for price inflation, clothing prices have fallen. The sluggish U.S. economy and stagnant wage growth have increased pressure on clothing retailers by capping consumers' disposable income. At the same time, the desire to shop for fashionable new outfits remains strong. The result has been strong price competition among retail apparel chains.

Factory Collapse

The building that collapsed on April 24 was an eight-story complex called the Rana Plaza after its owner, Sohel Rana, a local politician and member of the ruling political party. The builders of the Rana Plaza only had approval for the construction of a five-story structure, but in Bangladesh rules can be bent, so the builders added three extra floors. Five garment factories occupied six floors in the building. At the time of the collapse, it is estimated that they were making clothes for some 30 Western apparel brands.

In retrospect, the building collapse should not have been a total surprise. Parts of the complex had been built on a pond filled with sand, making for an unstable foundation. The entire building vibrated whenever its diesel generator was working. The day before the collapse, visible cracks had appeared in the building, promoting some workers to run out. Both the local police and the Bangladesh Garment Manufacturers and Exporters Association warned Sohel Rana that the building was unsafe. Rana disagreed, and the complex stayed open for business. Two inspectors were in the building when it collapsed. Both died. Some survivors stated that their employers had pressured them to turn up for work as usual on Wednesday. After the collapse Sohel Rana fled. He was found and arrested four days later on the border with India and charged with criminal negligence.

The death toll from the factory collapse was initially pegged at 250, but over the following days and weeks it kept increasing. By mid-May it was clear that over 1,100 people had died in the collapsed building, making it the second-worst industrial disaster in the history of South Asia after the infamous Bhopal disaster in 1984. The Bangladesh government stated that it would pay $250 in compensation to each family that lost a member in the building collapse.

Aftermath

The building collapse prompted some soul searching on the part of Western retailers who sourced production from Bangladesh. Critics were quick to point out that desires to drive prices down may have contributed to the situation in Bangladesh. Factory owners might bid low to get business from Western companies. While these factories themselves might meet the standards required by Western companies, such as they are, it is commonplace for them to outsource production to a shadow economy of subcontractors where regulations are routinely ignored and workers are paid less than the legal minimum wage. Indeed, this is how they make a profit. That being said, all the factories operating in the Rana Plaza seem to have been among the country's 1,500 or so regular exporters.

Some Western companies had already taken steps to improve working conditions in Bangladesh prior to the collapse of the Rana Plaza building. In October 2012, The Gap announced a $22 million fire and building safety plan with its suppliers in Bangladesh, without identifying which factories it was using there or how many factories would be improved under the plan. In early April, in response to the factory fire the prior November that had killed 112 people, Walmart pledged $1.8 million to train 2,000 Bangladesh factory managers about fire safety. Critics noted that these commitments represented a drop in the bucket. Some nongovernmental organizations estimated that it would cost some $3 billion to make the needed fire safety and building improvements to ensure that Bangladesh's 5,000 garment factories were safe.

Three weeks after the building collapse several of the world's largest apparel retailers—including the retailer H&M, Inditex (the owner of the Zara chain), Benetton, Marks & Spencer, and Tesco—agreed to sign a legally binding agreement designed to improve safety conditions in Bangladesh's garment factories. Under the five-year agreement, the signatories agreed not to hire manufacturers whose factories fail to meet safety standards and committed to help pay for necessary repairs and renovations. Signatories will form a governing board to oversee safety inspections of up to 5,000 factories over two years, with results being made public. The governing board will include three representatives from retailers, three labor representatives, and a chairperson chosen by the UN International Labor Organization. Participation will cost each company a maximum of $2.5 million each over the five-year period of the agreement.

Several major U.S. retailers, including Walmart, Gap, Sears, and JC Penny, did not initially sign the pact. Gap Inc. stated that it would not sign the pact because the language makes it legally binding in the United States, and if they failed to comply, they could be sued in U.S. courts. Instead Gap Inc. put forward an amendment calling for retailers to be publically expelled from the group if they fail to comply with arbitration. Walmart too cited the legally binding language as a reason for not signing the pact. Instead Walmart said that it would hire an outside auditor to inspect 279 Bangladesh factories and publish results on its website by June 1, 2013. When fire or building issues are found, Walmart said that it would require factory owners to make necessary renovations or risk being removed from its list of authorized suppliers. Walmart stated that it would not pay for factory renovations, but expected the cost of improvements to be reflected in the costs of goods it purchased. Walmart will also set up an independent call center for garment workers to report unsafe working conditions. For its part, the government of Bangladesh stated that it would raise the minimum wage for garment workers in the country and tighten building and fire regulations.

Case Discussion Questions

1. From an economic perspective, was the shift to a free trade regime in the textile industry good for Bangladesh?
2. Economically who benefits when retailers in Europe and the United States source textiles from low-wage countries such as Bangladesh? Who might lose? Do the gains outweigh the losses?
3. What are the causes of the weak safety record of the Bangladesh garment industry? Do Western companies that import garments from Bangladesh bear any responsibility for what happened at the Rana Plaza and other workplace accidents?
4. Do you think the legally binding agreement signed by H&M, Zara, Tesco, and others will make a difference? Does it go far enough? What else might be done?
5. What do you think about Walt Disney's decision not to purchase merchandise from Bangladesh? Is this an appropriate way of dealing with the problem?
6. What do you think of Walmart's approach to this problem? Is the company doing enough? What else could it do?

Sources

S. Banjo, "Promises in Bangladesh", *Wall Street Journal*, May 14, 2013; S. Banjo, "Wal-Mart Crafts own Bangladesh Safety Plan," *Wall Street Journal,* May 15, 2013; K. Bradsher, "Jobs Vanish as Exports Fall in Asia," *The New York Times,* January 22, 2009, p. B1; "Knitting Pretty," *The Economist,* July 18, 2008, p. 54; "The New Collapsing Building," *The Economist,* April 25, 2013; "Rags in the Ruins," *The Economist,* May 4, 2013; K. Bradsher, "Competition Means Learning to Offer More Than Just Low Wages," *The New York Times,* December 14, 2004, p. C1; V. Bajaj, "As Labor Costs Rise in China, Textile Jobs Shift Elsewhere," *The New York Times,* July 17, 2010, pp. 1, 3; S. Greenhouse, "Bangladesh Fears Exodus of Apparel Firms," *The New York Times,* May 2, 2013; S. Greenhouse, "Major Retailers join Bangladesh Safety Plan," *The New York Times,* May 13, 2013; and A. Zimmerman and N. Shah, "American Tastes Fuel Boom in Bangladesh," *Wall Street Journal,* May 13, 2013.

KNIGHTS APPAREL

Some years ago Joseph Bozich was watching his son play in a high school basketball game when his vision started to become blurred. A day later he couldn't read. His doctor suspected that Bozich had a brain tumor, but tests revealed that the cause was multiple sclerosis. Luckily for Bozich, his vision improved, and he has not suffered another attack, but the incident left him with a desire to do something important in life—to somehow make a contribution to humanity.

As founder and CEO of Knights Apparel, a privately held company, Bozich realized he had the power to make such a contribution. A former U.S. collegiate bodybuilding champion, Bozich got his start in apparel working for Gold's Gym, selling branded clothing to outside retailers. In 2000 he founded Knights Apparel and started to build a business selling athletic clothing with college logos to universities around America. Like most organizations in the apparel industry, Bozich relied on a network of foreign suppliers to manufacture his products. The apparel industry is often accused of using sweatshop suppliers based in poor nations where pay is low, hours are long, and working conditions are awful. In 2005, Bozich wondered if it might be possible to change this—to source product from less developed nations but to do so in a more ethical way, paying employees a decent wage and providing them with good working conditions.

After some investigation, Bozich decided to establish his own "model factory" in the Dominican Republic. He purchased a factory that had previously been used by a Korean company to make baseball caps for Nike and Reebok. The Korean company had moved production to a lower-wage country in 2007, throwing some 1,200 people out of work. The factory now produces under a new label, Alta Gracia, which is derived from the name of the local town, Ville Altagracia, and means "exalted grace." The minimum wage in the area is $147 a month, a figure so low that it is insufficient to live on. Bozich's factory pays its workers more than 3.5 times this amount. According a study done by a workers' rights group, this is the pay level required to support a family of four in the region. Bozich has allowed his employees to unionize and has made investments in safety and good working conditions a priority. Knights Apparel invested some $500,000 in upgrading the factory with features that include bright lights, five new sewing lines, and ergonomic chairs for employees, which many seamstresses thought were for the managers.

Clearly the higher pay translates into higher costs. Bozich calculates that the factory's cost per unit of clothing is 20 percent higher than if it paid the minimum wage. Given the competitive nature of the market for apparel, Knights cannot pass this cost increase onto wholesalers and retailers in the form of higher prices, so Bozich has elected to take smaller profit margins. For a product such as a basic T-shirt with a logo, the manufacturing cost at Alta Gracia is $4.80, about 80 cents more than if the pay were minimum wage. The shirt is sold for $8 to wholesalers, with most retailers marking them up to about $18.

Bozich realizes he has a strong marketing message built around "fair labor." This is particularly useful selling into colleges. Student groups have often agitated for boycotts against companies such as Nike and Reebok for using sweatshop labor. (Since being the target of protests in the 1990s, Nike has put rigorous procedures in place for auditing the operations of suppliers to make sure they adhere to Nike's own code of ethics for suppliers.) The "fair labor" marketing message seems to be resonating with colleges. Several universities have backed the project. Duke University's bookstore, for example, placed an initial order for $25,000 of merchandise. Barnes & Noble College Booksellers planned to have Alta Gracia products at some 350 stores in college campuses by early 2011. Barnes & Noble plans to promote the product heavily and expects to take lower margins to begin with. The United Students Against Sweatshops, a nationwide student group that often attacks apparel manufacturers, has also backed the project and has been distributing flyers at college bookstores urging students to purchase the Alta Gracia shirts. Companies such as Nike and Reebok that also serve the college market are reportedly watching what happens carefully.

Case Discussion Questions

1. The case states that higher wage rates at the Alta Gracia factory have raised the cost per item by 20 percent. Can you see any way in which the philosophy with regard to pay and working conditions at Alta Gracia might lower costs in the long run?
2. Do you think Joseph Bozich would have been able to try the Alta Gracia experiment if Knights Apparel were a publicly traded enterprise?
3. What do you think might stand in the way of Alta Gracia becoming successful? What strategies might Bozich adopt to minimize the risk of failure while still adhering to his high ethical standards?
4. Alta Gracia serves a niche market, colleges, where there is higher awareness of ethical issues in apparel production. Do you think the strategy would work if the company tried to sell to the mass market through retailers such as Walmart?
5. Is it ethical for apparel companies to move production around the world in pursuit of the lowest possible labor costs, even if that means paying wage rates that are below a living wage? What if the alternative is not to produce at all?
6. To what extent does the Alta Gracia experiment suggest that good ethics are also good business practice?

Sources

S. Greenhouse, "A Factory Defies Stereotypes, but Can It Survive?" *The New York Times,* July 18, 2010; G. Brown, "No Sweat: In the Dominican Republic," *Industrial Safety and Hygiene News,* September 13, 2010; and S. Furrow, "Alta Gracia Comes to College Campuses," *The Collegian,* January 19, 2011.

JAPAN'S ECONOMIC MALAISE

In 1989, Japan was widely viewed as an economic superpower. After three decades of robust economic growth, it had risen to become the world's second-largest economy. Japanese companies seemed to be obliterating entire American industries, from automobiles and semiconductors to earthmoving equipment and consumer electronics. Japanese companies were buying assets in the United States, including movie studios (Universal Studios and Columbia Pictures), golf courses (Pebble Beach), and real estate (the Rockefeller Center in New York). The stock market was booming, the Nikkei index hitting an all-time high of 38,915.87 in December 1989, an increase of more than 600 percent since 1980. Property prices had risen so much that 1 square mile of Tokyo was said to be worth more than the entire United States. Books were written about the Japanese threat to American dominance. Management theorists praised Japanese companies for their strategic savvy and management excellence. Economists were predicting that Japan would overtake America to become the world's largest economy by 2010.

It didn't happen. In quick succession the stock market collapsed and property prices rapidly followed it down. Japanese banks, which had financed much of the boom in asset prices with easy money, now found their balance sheets loaded with bad debt, and they sharply contracted lending. As the stock market plunged and property prices imploded, individuals saw their net worth shrink. Japanese consumers responded by sharply reducing spending, depressing domestic demand and sending the economy into a recession. And there it stayed—for most of the next two decades. Today, the Japanese economy is barely larger in real terms than it was in 1989. In 2010, China passed Japan to become the world's second-largest economy. The average price of a home in Japan is the same as it was in 1983, way below the 1989 peak. The Nikkei stock market index stood at 9,600 in early 2012, 75 percent below its 1989 high. And worst of all, Japan has been gripped by deflation for the best part of two decades.

Deflation is a situation in which prices are falling. When consumers and businesses expect prices to be lower tomorrow than they are today, they react by putting off spending, by hoarding cash, because that cash will buy more tomorrow than it will today. Such behavior can result in a negative cycle. Expectations that prices will fall can lead to reduced demand. Businesses respond by cutting prices further to try to get consumers to spend. Seeing this, consumers react by waiting to buy in expectation that prices will again fall in the future, and so demand continues to decline, which results in additional price cuts to try to stimulate demand, and so on. As businesses see their revenues and margins fall, they reduce employment and cut wages and salaries. This further reduces spending power and adds to the deflationary cycle. To make matters worse, in a deflationary environment, the real cost of debt goes up over time. While prices and wages fall, people still have to make fixed payments on their mortgages and car loans. Over time, this takes up an ever-greater proportion of their income, further limiting their ability to spend more on other goods and services.

All of this has happened in Japan over the past 20 years. For its part, after initially being slow to respond to falling asset prices, during the past 15 years the Japanese government has repeatedly tried to stimulate the economy and reignite consumer spending. Interest rates have been cut to zero, and major investments have been made in public infrastructure. Not only has this not worked, but it has also left Japan with the highest level of government debt as a percentage of GDP in the world, amounting to some 228 percent of GDP (in contrast, the figure for the United States in 2011 was about 97 percent of GDP). The high debt load is now a limit on the ability of the Japanese government to adopt additional expansionary policies.

In seeking to explain Japan's prolonged malaise, many economists also point to demographic factors. In the 1970s and 1980s, birthrates in Japan fell below replacement levels, leaving it with one of the oldest populations in the world. The working age population peaked at 87 million in 1995 and has been falling since. On current trends, by 2030 it will be 67 million. Every year there are fewer and fewer working age people to support ever more retired people—and Japan's retired people are notorious for not spending. Japan could reverse this trend by increasing immigration or boosting the birthrate, but neither of these seems likely at the moment. Increasingly, young people are pessimistic about the future. All they have known is a world where prices for everything, including the price of labor, have fallen. They have diminished expectations.

Case Discussion Questions

1. In the 1980s, Japan was viewed as one of the world's most dynamic economies. Today, it is viewed as one of its most stagnant. Why has the Japanese economy stagnated?

2. What lessons does the history of Japan over the past 20 years hold for other nations? What can countries do to avoid the kind of deflationary spiral that has gripped Japan?
3. What do you think would be required to get the Japanese economy moving again?
4. What are the implications of Japan's economic stagnation for the benefits, costs, and risks of doing business in this nation?
5. As an international business, which economy would you rather invest in, that of Japan or that of India? Explain your answer.

Sources

A. Ahearne et al, "Preventing Deflation: Lessons from Japan's Experience in the 1990s," U.S. Federal Reserve, International Finance Discussion Papers, Number 79, June 2002; "Ending deflation in Japan," *The Economist,* February 10, 2011; M. Fackler, "Japan Goes from Dynamic to Disheartened," *The New York Times,* October 16, 2010; and Paul Krugman, "Inflation, Deflation, Japan," *The New York Times,* May 25, 2010.

INDONESIA—THE NEXT ASIAN GIANT?

Indonesia is a vast country. Its 250 million people are spread out over some 17,000 islands that span an arc 3,200 miles long from Sumatra in the west to Irian Jaya in the east. It is the world's most populous Muslim nation—some 86 percent of the population count themselves as Muslims—but also one of the most ethnically diverse. More than 500 languages are spoken in the country, and separatists are active in a number of provinces. For 30 years the strong arm of President Suharto held this sprawling nation together. Suharto was a virtual dictator who was backed by the military establishment. Under his rule, the Indonesian economy grew steadily, but there was a cost. Suharto brutally repressed internal dissent. He was also famous for "crony capitalism," using his command of the political system to favor the business enterprises of his supporters and family.

In the end, Suharto was overtaken by massive debts that Indonesia had accumulated during the 1990s. In 1997, the Indonesian economy went into a tailspin. The International Monetary Fund stepped in with a $43 billion rescue package. When it was revealed that much of this money found its way into the personal coffers of Suharto and his cronies, people took to the streets in protest and he was forced to resign.

After Suharto, Indonesia moved rapidly toward a vigorous democracy, culminating in October 2004 with the inauguration of Susilo Bambang Yudhoyono, the country's first directly elected president (he was elected to a second term in 2009). The economic front has also seen progress. Public debt as a percentage of GDP fell from close to 100 percent in 2000 to around 25 percent by 2012. Inflation declined from 12 percent annually in 2001 to 4.5 percent in 2012. The economy grew at between 4 and 6.5 percent per annum during 2001–12.

Despite progress, Indonesia lags behind its Southeast Asian neighbors. Its economic growth has long trailed that of China, Malaysia, and Thailand. Unemployment was at about 6.1 percent of the working population in 2012. More than 32 million Indonesians still live below the poverty line. Growth in labor productivity has been sluggish. Worse still, significant foreign capital has left the country. Sony made headlines by shutting down an audio equipment factory in 2003, and a number of apparel enterprises have left Indonesia for China and Vietnam. Between 2001 and 2004 the stock of foreign direct investment in Indonesia fell from $24.8 billion to $11.4 billion. It has since increased to more than $80 billion, largely as a result of investment in Indonesia's natural resources, including mining, oil and gas production, and forestry, but outside of extractive industries, foreign investment has remained low.

Looking forward, there are signs of a rise of economic nationalism in Indonesia that might make it more difficult for foreign oil, gas, and mining firms to do business there in the future. In late 2012

Indonesia's Constitutional Court ruled that the country's 2001 oil and gas laws were unconstitutional. These laws had allowed the state to sell exploration and extraction licenses to foreign producers. The court recommended that oil and gas operations run by foreigners should be handed over to the state-run energy company after existing contracts expire. This followed a government ruling in March 2012 that foreign miners must sell 51 percent of their Indonesian operations to locals after operating for 10 years. Previously they were obliged to sell only 20 percent, albeit after only five years.

Some observers feel that Indonesia is hobbled by its poor infrastructure. Public infrastructure investment has been low for years. The road system is a mess, half of the country's population has no access to electricity, the electric grid needs investment to update it, and over 30 percent of the population still lacks access to modern sewerage facilities. The tsunami that ravaged the coast of Sumatra in late 2004 only made matters worse. Mirroring the decline in public investment has been a slump in private investment. Investment in the country's all-important oil industry fell from $3.8 billion in 1996 to just $187 million in 2002, although it has picked up since. Oil production, which peaked at 1.7 million barrels a day in the mid-1990s, declined to around 830,000 barrels a day by 2013, even though oil prices were strong. Once a net exporter of oil, Indonesia is now an importer.

According to a World Bank study, business activity in Indonesia is hurt by excessive red tape. It takes 151 days on average to complete the paperwork necessary to start a business, compared to 30 days in Malaysia and just 8 days in Singapore. Another problem is the endemically high level of corruption. Transparency International, which studies corruption around the world, ranks Indonesia among the most corrupt, listing it 118 out of the 178 countries it tracked in 2012. Government bureaucrats, whose salaries are very low, inevitably demand bribes from any company that crosses their path—and Indonesia's penchant for bureaucratic red tape means a long line of officials might require bribes. Abdul Rahman Saleh, the former attorney general in Indonesia, has stated that the entire legal system, including the police and the prosecutors, is mired in corruption. The police have been known to throw the executives of foreign enterprises into jail on the flimsiest of pretexts, although some well-placed bribes can secure their release. Even though Indonesia has launched an anticorruption drive, critics claim it lacks teeth. The political elite are reportedly so corrupt that it is not in their interests to do anything meaningful to fix the system.

Case Discussion Questions

1. What political factors explain Indonesia's relative sluggish economic performance when compared to some of its Southeast Asian neighbors? What economic factors? Are these two related?
2. Why do you think foreign firms exited Indonesia in the early 2000s? What are the implications for the country? What is required to reverse this trend?
3. Why is corruption so endemic in Indonesia? What are its consequences?
4. What are the risks facing foreign firms that do business in Indonesia? What is required to reduce these risks?

Sources

"A Survey of Indonesia: Time to Deliver," *The Economist,* December 11, 2004; "A Survey of Indonesia: Enemies of Promise," *The Economist,* December 11, 2004, pp. 4–5; "A Survey of Indonesia: The Importance of Going Straight," *The Economist,* December 11, 2004, pp. 6–7; World Bank, *World Development Indicators Online,* 2013; Transparency International, *Global Corruption Report,* 2012; S. Donnan, "Indonesian Workers Mark May Day with Protests at Planned Changes to Labor Laws," *Financial Times,* May 2, 2006, p. 4; "Feet of Clay," *The Economist,* February 19, 2011, pp. 43–44; and "Foreigners Beware," *The Economist*, November 24, 2012.

PART 3
The Global Trade and Investment Environment

Chapter 6
International Trade Theory

LEARNING OBJECTIVES

After reading this chapter, you will be able to:

LO6-1 Understand why nations trade with each other.

LO6-2 Summarize the different theories explaining trade flows between nations.

LO6-3 Recognize why many economists believe that unrestricted free trade between nations will raise the economic welfare of countries that participate in a free trade system.

LO6-4 Explain the arguments of those who maintain that government can play a proactive role in promoting national competitive advantage in certain industries.

LO6-5 Understand the important implications that international trade theory holds for business practice.

◇ CREATING THE WORLD'S BIGGEST FREE TRADE ZONE ◇

Opening Case

In his February 12, 2013, State of the Union address, President Barack Obama committed the United States to negotiating a free trade deal with the European Union (EU). The United States and the 27 countries that are members of the EU already make up the world's largest and richest trading partnership, accounting for about half of global GDP and one-third of all international trade. Nevertheless, the announcement was greeted with approval on both sides of the Atlantic and, unusually for this president, from both sides of the political divide in the United States.

The reason for the enthusiasm can be traced to widespread acceptance of the key axiom of international trade theory—trade is a good thing for *all* countries involved in a free trade agreement. Free trade is a *positive sum game;* it is equivalent to the rising tide that lifts all boats. Both the United States and the EU are struggling with low economic growth, persistently high unemployment, and large government deficits. A new free trade deal could help economies on both sides of the Atlantic grow faster, thereby reducing unemployment, without costing another dime in government spending. A trade deal is in effect a cost-free stimulus package.

How big the economic impact will be remains to be seen. For both the United States and the EU average tariffs (taxes) on imported goods are already low, close to 3 percent by most measures. Further reduction could nonetheless stimulate additional trade, and there are some areas where tariffs are much higher, notably on agricultural goods. Beyond tariff reductions, there are many nontariff barriers to international trade that could be reduced or eliminated as the result of a deal. One example is found in the automobile industry, where the EU and United States both employ equally strict but different safety standards. This means that to sell in both the EU and United States, automobile manufacturers must adhere to two different sets of regulations. Similarly, pharmaceutical firms currently have to submit new drugs to two sets of safety tests, one in the United States and one in the EU. Such regulatory requirements are functionally equivalent to an import tariff insofar as they raise the costs of business and international trade. By some calculations, nontariff barriers such as these are equivalent to a traditional import tariff of 10–20 percent. Initial estimates suggest that a comprehensive and ambitious agreement that covers both tariff and nontariff barriers to trade will boost annual GDP growth by about 0.5 percent per annum on both sides of the Atlantic, producing an additional $200 billion a year in economic activity.[1]

INTRODUCTION

The proposed free trade deal between the United States and the European Union is an example of the benefits of free trade. If an agreement can be reached, a reduction in tariff and nontariff barriers to the free flow of goods and services between the United States and the EU could boost economic growth rates and help bring down persistently high unemployment rates, without costing anything in additional government spending.

Economists have long argued that free trade stimulates economic growth and raises living standards across the board. As the opening case illustrates, the economic arguments concerning the benefits of free trade in goods and services are not abstract academic ones. International trade theories have shaped the economic policy of many nations for the past 60 years. They have been the driver behind the formation of the World Trade Organization and regional trade blocs such as the European Union and the North American Free Trade Agreement (NAFTA), and they underlie the current push for a free trade deal between the United States and EU. It is important to understand, therefore, what these theories are and why they have been so successful in shaping the economic policy of so many nations and the competitive environment in which international businesses compete.

This chapter has two goals that go to the heart of the debate over the benefits—and the costs—of free trade. The first is to review a number of theories that explain why it is beneficial for a country to engage in international trade. The second goal is to explain the pattern of international trade that we observe in the world economy. With regard to the pattern of trade, we will be primarily concerned with explaining the pattern of exports and imports of goods and services between countries. The pattern of foreign direct investment between countries is discussed in Chapter 8.

AN OVERVIEW OF TRADE THEORY

We open this chapter with a discussion of mercantilism. Propagated in the sixteenth and seventeenth centuries, mercantilism advocated that countries should simultaneously encourage exports and discourage imports. Although mercantilism is an old and largely discredited doctrine, its echoes remain in modern political debate and in the trade policies of many countries. Next, we will look at Adam Smith's theory of absolute advantage. Proposed in 1776, Smith's theory was the first to explain why unrestricted free trade is beneficial to a country. **Free trade** refers to a situation in which a government does not attempt to influence through quotas or duties what its citizens can buy from another country, or what they can produce and sell to another country. Smith argued that the invisible hand of the market mechanism, rather than government policy, should determine what a country imports and what it exports. His arguments imply that such a laissez-faire stance toward trade was in the best interests of a country. Building on Smith's work are two additional theories that we review. One is the theory of comparative advantage, advanced by the nineteenth-century English economist David Ricardo. This theory is the intellectual basis of the modern argument for unrestricted free trade. In the twentieth century, Ricardo's work was refined by two Swedish economists, Eli Heckscher and Bertil Ohlin, whose theory is known as the Heckscher-Ohlin theory.

The Benefits of Trade   **LO6-1**

The great strength of the theories of Smith, Ricardo, and Heckscher-Ohlin is that they identify with precision the specific benefits of international trade. Common sense suggests that some international trade is beneficial. For example, nobody would suggest that Iceland should grow its own oranges. Iceland can benefit from trade by exchanging some of the products that it can produce at a low cost (fish) for some products that it cannot produce at all (oranges). Thus, by engaging in international trade, Icelanders are able to add oranges to their diet of fish.

The theories of Smith, Ricardo, and Heckscher-Ohlin go beyond this commonsense notion, however, to show why it is beneficial for a country to engage in international trade *even for products it is able to produce for itself.* This is a difficult concept for people to grasp. For example, many people in the United States believe that American consumers should buy products made in the United States by American companies whenever possible to help save American jobs from foreign competition. The same kind of nationalistic sentiments can be observed in many other countries.

However, the theories of Smith, Ricardo, and Heckscher-Ohlin tell us that a country's economy may gain if its citizens buy certain products from other nations that could be produced at home. The gains arise because international trade allows a country to *specialize* in the manufacture and export of products that can be produced most efficiently in that country, while importing products that can be produced more efficiently in other countries. Thus, it may make sense for the United States to specialize in the production and export of commercial jet aircraft, because the efficient production of commercial jet aircraft requires resources that are abundant in the United States, such as a highly skilled labor force and cutting-edge technological know-how. On the other hand, it may make sense for the United States to import textiles from Bangladesh because the efficient production of textiles requires a relatively cheap labor force—and cheap labor is not abundant in the United States.

Of course, this economic argument is often difficult for segments of a country's population to accept. With their future threatened by imports, U.S. textile companies and their employees have tried hard to persuade the government to limit the importation of textiles by demanding quotas and tariffs. Although such import controls may benefit particular groups, such as textile businesses and their employees, the theories of Smith, Ricardo, and Heckscher-Ohlin suggest that the economy as a whole is hurt by such action. One of the key insights of international trade theory is that limits on imports are often in the interests of domestic producers, but not domestic consumers.

The Pattern of International Trade

The theories of Smith, Ricardo, and Heckscher-Ohlin help explain the pattern of international trade that we observe in the world economy. Some aspects of the pattern are easy to understand. Climate and natural resource endowments explain why Ghana exports cocoa, Brazil exports coffee, Saudi Arabia exports oil, and China exports crawfish. However, much of the observed pattern of international trade is more difficult to explain. For example, why does Japan export automobiles, consumer electronics, and machine tools? Why does Switzerland export chemicals, pharmaceuticals, watches, and jewelry? Why does Bangladesh export garments? David Ricardo's theory of comparative advantage offers an explanation in terms of international differences in labor productivity. The more sophisticated Heckscher-Ohlin theory emphasizes the interplay between the proportions in which the factors of production (such as land, labor, and capital) are available in different countries and the proportions in which they are needed for producing particular goods. This explanation rests on the assumption that countries have varying endowments of the various factors of production. Tests of this theory, however, suggest that it is a less powerful explanation of real-world trade patterns than once thought.

One early response to the failure of the Heckscher-Ohlin theory to explain the observed pattern of international trade was the product life-cycle theory. Proposed by Raymond Vernon, this theory suggests that early in their life cycle, most new products are produced in and exported from the country in which they were developed. As a new product becomes widely accepted internationally, however, production starts in other countries. As a result, the theory suggests, the product may ultimately be exported back to the country of its original innovation.

In a similar vein, during the 1980s economists such as Paul Krugman developed what has come to be known as the new trade theory. **New trade theory** (for which Krugman won the Nobel Prize in 2008) stresses that in some cases countries specialize in the production and export of particular products not because of underlying differences in factor endowments, but because in certain industries the world market can support only a limited number of firms. (This is argued to be the case for the commercial aircraft industry.) In such industries, firms that enter the market first are able to build a competitive advantage that is subsequently difficult to challenge. Thus, the observed pattern of trade between nations may be due in part to the ability of firms within a given nation to capture first-mover advantages. The United States is a major exporter of commercial jet aircraft because American firms such as Boeing were first movers in the world market. Boeing built a competitive advantage that has subsequently been difficult for firms from countries with equally favorable factor endowments to challenge (although Europe's Airbus has succeeded in doing that). In a work related to the new trade theory, Michael Porter developed a theory referred to as the theory of national competitive advantage. This attempts to explain why particular nations achieve international success in particular industries. In addition to factor endowments, Porter points out the importance of country factors such as domestic demand and domestic rivalry in explaining a nation's dominance in the production and export of particular products.

Trade Theory and Government Policy

Although all these theories agree that international trade is beneficial to a country, they lack agreement in their recommendations for government policy. Mercantilism makes a crude case for government involvement in promoting exports and limiting imports. The theories of Smith, Ricardo, and Heckscher-Ohlin form part of the case for unrestricted free trade. The argument for unrestricted free trade is that both import controls and export incentives (such as subsidies) are self-defeating and result in wasted resources. Both the new trade theory and Porter's theory of national competitive advantage can be interpreted as justifying some limited government intervention to support the development of certain export-oriented industries. We discuss the pros and cons of this argument, known as strategic trade policy, as well as the pros and cons of the argument for unrestricted free trade, in Chapter 7.

MERCANTILISM

LO6-2

The first theory of international trade, mercantilism, emerged in England in the mid-sixteenth century. The principle assertion of mercantilism was that gold and silver were the mainstays of national wealth and essential to vigorous commerce. At that time, gold and silver were the currency of trade between countries; a country could earn gold and silver by exporting goods. Conversely, importing goods from other countries would result in an outflow of gold and silver to those countries. The main tenet of **mercantilism** was that it was in a country's best interests to maintain a trade surplus, to export more than it imported. By doing so, a country would accumulate gold and silver and, consequently, increase its national wealth, prestige, and power. As the English mercantilist writer Thomas Mun put it in 1630:

> The ordinary means therefore to increase our wealth and treasure is by foreign trade, wherein we must ever observe this rule: to sell more to strangers yearly than we consume of theirs in value.[2]

Consistent with this belief, the mercantilist doctrine advocated government intervention to achieve a surplus in the balance of trade. The mercantilists saw no virtue in a large volume of trade. Rather, they recommended policies to maximize exports and minimize imports. To achieve this, imports were limited by tariffs and quotas, while exports were subsidized.

The classical economist David Hume pointed out an inherent inconsistency in the mercantilist doctrine in 1752. According to Hume, if England had a balance-of-trade surplus with France (it exported more than it imported), the resulting inflow of gold and silver would swell the domestic money supply and generate inflation in England. In France, however, the outflow of gold and silver would have the opposite effect. France's money supply would contract, and its prices would fall. This change in relative prices between France and England would encourage the French to buy fewer English goods (because they were becoming more expensive) and the English to buy more French goods (because they were becoming cheaper). The result would be a deterioration in the English balance of trade and an improvement in France's trade balance, until the English surplus was eliminated. Hence, according to Hume, in the long run no country could sustain a surplus on the balance of trade and so accumulate gold and silver as the mercantilists had envisaged.

The flaw with mercantilism was that it viewed trade as a zero-sum game. (A **zero-sum game** is one in which a gain by one country results in a loss by another.) It was left to Adam Smith and David Ricardo to show the shortsightedness of this approach and to demonstrate that trade is a positive-sum game, or a situation in which all countries can benefit. Unfortunately, the mercantilist doctrine is by no means dead. Neo-mercantilists equate political power with economic power and economic power with a balance-of-trade surplus. Critics argue that many nations have adopted a neo-mercantilist strategy that is designed to simultaneously boost exports and limit imports.[3] For example, critics charge that China is pursuing a neo-mercantilist policy, deliberately keeping its currency value low against the U.S. dollar in order to sell more goods to the United States and other developed nations, and thus amass a trade surplus and foreign exchange reserves (see the accompanying Country Focus).

Is China a Neo-mercantilist Nation?

COUNTRY FOCUS

China's rapid rise in economic power (it is now the world's second-largest economy) has been built on export-led growth. The country takes raw material imports and, using its cheap labor, converts them into products that it sells to developed nations. For years, the country's exports have been growing faster than its imports, leading some critics to claim that China is pursuing a neo-mercantilist policy, trying to amass record trade surpluses and foreign currency that will give it economic power over developed nations. In 2012 its foreign exchange reserves exceeded $3.3 trillion, some 60 percent of which were held in U.S. dollars. Observers worry that if China ever decides to sell its holdings of U.S. currency, this could depress the value of the dollar against other currencies and increase the price of imports into America.

Throughout most of the 2000s China's exports have grown faster than its imports, leading some to argue that China has been limiting imports by pursuing an import substitution policy, encouraging domestic investment in the production of products such as steel, aluminum, and paper, which it had historically imported from other nations. The trade deficit with America has been a particular cause for concern. In 2011, this reached a record $295 billion before falling to $231 billion in 2012. At the same time, China long resisted attempts to let its currency float freely against the U.S. dollar. Many claim that China's currency is too cheap, and that this keeps the prices of China's goods artificially low, which fuels the country's exports.

So is China a neo-mercantilist nation that is deliberately discouraging imports and encouraging exports in order to increase its trade surplus and accumulate foreign exchange reserves, which might give it economic power? The jury is out on this issue. Skeptics suggest that going forward, the country will have no choice but to increase its imports of commodities that it lacks, such as oil. They also note that China did start allowing the value of the *yuan* (China's currency) to appreciate against the dollar in July 2005, albeit at a slow pace. In July 2005 one U.S. dollar purchased 8.11 yuan. By January 2013, one U.S. dollar purchased 6.23 yuan, a decline of 23 percent. As a result, China's trade surplus has started to contract as export growth has slowed and imports have increased. The 2012 the surplus of $231 billion was down significantly from the record $295 billion surplus in 2011. While this suggests that China's trade surplus may have peaked for now, it is still a cause for concern in many developed nations, and particularly the United States.[4]

ABSOLUTE ADVANTAGE

In his 1776 landmark book *The Wealth of Nations,* Adam Smith attacked the mercantilist assumption that trade is a zero-sum game. Smith argued that countries differ in their ability to produce goods efficiently. In his time, the English, by virtue of their superior manufacturing processes, were the world's most efficient textile manufacturers. Due to the combination of favorable climate, good soils, and accumulated expertise, the French had the world's most efficient wine industry. The English had an *absolute advantage* in the production of textiles, while the French had an *absolute advantage* in the production of wine. Thus, a country has an **absolute advantage** in the production of a product when it is more efficient than any other country in producing it.

According to Smith, countries should specialize in the production of goods for which they have an absolute advantage and then trade these goods for those produced by other countries. In Smith's time, this suggested the English should specialize in the production of textiles, while the French should specialize in the production of wine. England could get all the wine it needed by selling its textiles to France and buying wine in exchange. Similarly, France could get all the textiles it needed by selling wine to England and buying textiles in exchange. Smith's basic argument, therefore, is that a country should never produce goods at home that it can buy at a lower cost from other countries. Smith demonstrates that, by specializing in the production of goods in which each has an absolute advantage, both countries benefit by engaging in trade.

Consider the effects of trade between two countries, Ghana and South Korea. The production of any good (output) requires resources (inputs) such as land, labor, and capital. Assume that Ghana and South Korea both have the same amount of resources and that these resources can be used to produce either rice or cocoa. Assume further that 200 units of resources are available in each country. Imagine that in Ghana it takes 10 resources to produce 1 ton of cocoa and 20 resources to produce 1 ton of rice. Thus, Ghana could produce 20 tons of cocoa and no rice, 10 tons of rice and no cocoa, or some combination of rice and cocoa between these two extremes. The different combinations that Ghana could produce are represented by the line GG' in Figure 6.1. This is referred to as Ghana's *production possibility frontier* (PPF). Similarly, imagine that in South Korea it takes 40 resources to produce 1

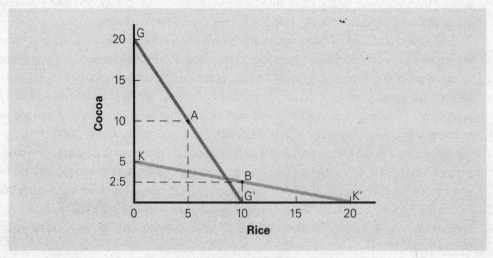

Figure 6.1 *The Theory of Absolute Advantage*

ton of cocoa and 10 resources to produce 1 ton of rice. Thus, South Korea could produce 5 tons of cocoa and no rice, 20 tons of rice and no cocoa, or some combination between these two extremes. The different combinations available to South Korea are represented by the line KK′ in Figure 6.1, which is South Korea's PPF. Clearly, Ghana has an absolute advantage in the production of cocoa. (More resources are needed to produce a ton of cocoa in South Korea than in Ghana.) By the same token, South Korea has an absolute advantage in the production of rice.

Now consider a situation in which neither country trades with any other. Each country devotes half its resources to the production of rice and half to the production of cocoa. Each country must also consume what it produces. Ghana would be able to produce 10 tons of cocoa and 5 tons of rice (point A in Figure 6.1), while South Korea would be able to produce 10 tons of rice and 2.5 tons of cocoa (point B in Figure 6.1). Without trade, the combined production of both countries would be 12.5 tons of cocoa (10 tons in Ghana plus 2.5 tons in South Korea) and 15 tons of rice (5 tons in Ghana and 10 tons in South Korea). If each country were to specialize in producing the good for which it had an absolute advantage and then trade with the other for the good it lacks, Ghana could produce 20 tons of cocoa, and South Korea could produce 20 tons of rice. Thus, by specializing, the production of both goods could be increased. Production of cocoa would increase from 12.5 tons to 20 tons, while production of rice would increase from 15 tons to 20 tons. The increase in production that would result from specialization is therefore 7.5 tons of cocoa and 5 tons of rice. Table 6.1 summarizes these figures.

TABLE 6.1 Absolute Advantage and the Gains from Trade

Resources Required to Produce 1 Ton of Cocoa and Rice

	Cocoa	Rice
Ghana	10	20
South Korea	40	10

Production and Consumption without Trade

Ghana	10.0	5.0
South Korea	2.5	10.0
Total production	12.5	15.0

Production with Specialization

Ghana	20.0	0.0
South Korea	0.0	20.0
Total production	20.0	20.0

Consumption after Ghana Trades 6 Tons of Cocoa for 6 Tons of South Korean Rice

Ghana	14.0	6.0
South Korea	6.0	14.0

Increase in Consumption as a Result of Specialization and Trade

Ghana	4.0	1.0
South Korea	3.5	4.0

By engaging in trade and swapping 1 ton of cocoa for 1 ton of rice, producers in both countries could consume more of both cocoa and rice. Imagine that Ghana and South Korea swap cocoa and rice on a one-to-one basis; that is, the price of 1 ton of cocoa is equal to the price of 1 ton of rice. If Ghana decided to export 6 tons of cocoa to South Korea and import 6 tons of rice in return, its final consumption after trade would be 14 tons of cocoa and 6 tons of rice. This is 4 tons more cocoa than it could have consumed before specialization and trade and 1 ton more rice. Similarly, South Korea's final consumption after trade would be 6 tons of cocoa and 14 tons of rice. This is 3.5 tons more cocoa than it could have consumed before specialization and trade and 4 tons more rice. Thus, as a result of specialization and trade, output of both cocoa and rice would be increased, and consumers in both nations would be able to consume more. Thus, we can see that trade is a positive-sum game; it produces net gains for all involved.

COMPARATIVE ADVANTAGE

LO6-2

David Ricardo took Adam Smith's theory one step further by exploring what might happen when one country has an absolute advantage in the production of all goods.[5] Smith's theory of absolute advantage suggests that such a country might derive no benefits from international trade. In his 1817 book *Principles of Political Economy,* Ricardo showed that this was not the case. According to Ricardo's theory of comparative advantage, it makes sense for a country to specialize in the production of those goods that it produces most efficiently and to buy the goods that it produces less efficiently from other countries, even if this means buying goods from other countries that it could produce more efficiently itself.[6] While this may seem counterintuitive, the logic can be explained with a simple example.

Assume that Ghana is more efficient in the production of both cocoa and rice; that is, Ghana has an absolute advantage in the production of both products. In Ghana it takes 10 resources to produce 1 ton of cocoa and 13½ resources to produce 1 ton of rice. Thus, given its 200 units of resources, Ghana can produce 20 tons of cocoa and no rice, 15 tons of rice and no cocoa, or any combination in between on its PPF (the line GG′ in Figure 6.2). In South Korea it takes 40 resources to produce 1 ton of cocoa and 20 resources to produce 1 ton of rice. Thus, South Korea can produce 5 tons of cocoa and no rice, 10 tons of rice and no cocoa, or any combination on its PPF (the line KK′ in Figure 6.2). Again assume

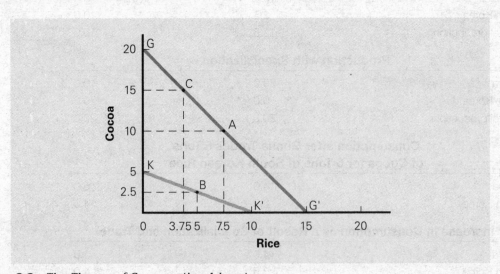

Figure 6.2   *The Theory of Comparative Advantage*

that without trade, each country uses half its resources to produce rice and half to produce cocoa. Thus, without trade, Ghana will produce 10 tons of cocoa and 7.5 tons of rice (point A in Figure 6.2), while South Korea will produce 2.5 tons of cocoa and 5 tons of rice (point B in Figure 6.2).

In light of Ghana's absolute advantage in the production of both goods, why should it trade with South Korea? Although Ghana has an absolute advantage in the production of both cocoa and rice, it has a comparative advantage only in the production of cocoa: Ghana can produce 4 times as much cocoa as South Korea, but only 1.5 times as much rice. Ghana is *comparatively* more efficient at producing cocoa than it is at producing rice.

Without trade the combined production of cocoa will be 12.5 tons (10 tons in Ghana and 2.5 in South Korea), and the combined production of rice will also be 12.5 tons (7.5 tons in Ghana and 5 tons in South Korea). Without trade each country must consume what it produces. By engaging in trade, the two countries can increase their combined production of rice and cocoa, and consumers in both nations can consume more of both goods.

The Gains From Trade

Imagine that Ghana exploits its comparative advantage in the production of cocoa to increase its output from 10 tons to 15 tons. This uses up 150 units of resources, leaving the remaining 50 units of resources to use in producing 3.75 tons of rice (point C in Figure 6.2). Meanwhile, South Korea specializes in the

TABLE 6.2 Comparative Advantage and the Gains from Trade

Resources Required to Produce 1 Ton of Cocoa and Rice		
	Cocoa	**Rice**
Ghana	10	13.33
South Korea	40	20
Production and Consumption without Trade		
Ghana	10.0	7.5
South Korea	2.5	5.0
Total production	12.5	12.5
Production with Specialization		
Ghana	15.0	3.75
South Korea	0.0	10.0
Total production	15.0	13.75
Consumption after Ghana Trades 4 Tons of Cocoa for 4 Tons of South Korean Rice		
Ghana	11.0	7.75
South Korea	4.0	6.0
Increase in Consumption as a Result of Specialization and Trade		
Ghana	1.0	0.25
South Korea	1.5	1.0

production of rice, producing 10 tons. The combined output of both cocoa and rice has now increased. Before specialization, the combined output was 12.5 tons of cocoa and 12.5 tons of rice. Now it is 15 tons of cocoa and 13.75 tons of rice (3.75 tons in Ghana and 10 tons in South Korea). The source of the increase in production is summarized in Table 6.2.

Not only is output higher, but both countries also can now benefit from trade. If Ghana and South Korea swap cocoa and rice on a one-to-one basis, with both countries choosing to exchange 4 tons of their export for 4 tons of the import, both countries are able to consume more cocoa and rice than they could before specialization and trade (see Table 6.2). Thus, if Ghana exchanges 4 tons of cocoa with South Korea for 4 tons of rice, it is still left with 11 tons of cocoa, which is 1 ton more than it had before trade. The 4 tons of rice it gets from South Korea in exchange for its 4 tons of cocoa, when added to the 3.75 tons it now produces domestically, leave it with a total of 7.75 tons of rice, which is 0.25 of a ton more than it had before specialization. Similarly, after swapping 4 tons of rice with Ghana, South Korea still ends up with 6 tons of rice, which is more than it had before specialization. In addition, the 4 tons of cocoa it receives in exchange is 1.5 tons more than it produced before trade. Thus, consumption of cocoa and rice can increase in both countries as a result of specialization and trade.

The basic message of the theory of comparative advantage is that *potential world production is greater with unrestricted free trade than it is with restricted trade.* Ricardo's theory suggests that consumers in all nations can consume more if there are no restrictions on trade. This occurs even in countries that lack an absolute advantage in the production of any good. In other words, to an even greater degree than the theory of absolute advantage, *the theory of comparative advantage suggests that trade is a positive-sum game in which all countries that participate realize economic gains.* As such, this theory provides a strong rationale for encouraging free trade. So powerful is Ricardo's theory that it remains a major intellectual weapon for those who argue for free trade.

Qualifications and Assumptions   ■ LO6-3 ■

The conclusion that free trade is universally beneficial is a rather bold one to draw from such a simple model. Our simple model includes many unrealistic assumptions:

1. We have assumed a simple world in which there are only two countries and two goods. In the real world, there are many countries and many goods.
2. We have assumed away transportation costs between countries.
3. We have assumed away differences in the prices of resources in different countries. We have said nothing about exchange rates, simply assuming that cocoa and rice could be swapped on a one-to-one basis.
4. We have assumed that resources can move freely from the production of one good to another within a country. In reality, this is not always the case.
5. We have assumed constant returns to scale; that is, that specialization by Ghana or South Korea has no effect on the amount of resources required to produce one ton of cocoa or rice. In reality, both diminishing and increasing returns to specialization exist. The amount of resources required to produce a good might decrease or increase as a nation specializes in production of that good.
6. We have assumed that each country has a fixed stock of resources and that free trade does not change the efficiency with which a country uses its resources. This static assumption makes no allowances for the dynamic changes in a country's stock of resources and in the efficiency with which the country uses its resources that might result from free trade.
7. We have assumed away the effects of trade on income distribution within a country.

Given these assumptions, can the conclusion that free trade is mutually beneficial be extended to the real world of many countries, many goods, positive transportation costs, volatile exchange rates, immobile domestic resources, nonconstant returns to specialization, and dynamic changes? Although a detailed extension of the theory of comparative advantage is beyond the scope of this book, economists have shown that the basic result derived from our simple model can be generalized to a world composed of many countries producing many different goods.[7] Despite the shortcomings of the Ricardian model, research suggests that the basic proposition that countries will export the goods that they are most efficient at producing is borne out by the data.[8]

However, once all the assumptions are dropped, the case for unrestricted free trade, while still positive, has been argued by some economists associated with the "new trade theory" to lose some of its strength.[9] We return to this issue later in this chapter and in the next when we discuss the new trade theory. In a recent and widely discussed analysis, the Nobel Prize–winning economist Paul Samuelson argued that contrary to the standard interpretation, in certain circumstances the theory of comparative advantage predicts that a rich country might actually be *worse* off by switching to a free trade regime with a poor nation.[10] We consider Samuelson's critique in the next section.

Extensions of the Ricardian Model

Let us explore the effect of relaxing three of the assumptions identified earlier in the simple comparative advantage model. Next, we relax the assumptions that resources move freely from the production of one good to another within a country, that there are constant returns to scale, and that trade does not change a country's stock of resources or the efficiency with which those resources are utilized.

Immobile Resources

In our simple comparative model of Ghana and South Korea, we assumed that producers (farmers) could easily convert land from the production of cocoa to rice and vice versa. While this assumption may hold for some agricultural products, resources do not always shift quite so easily from producing one good to another. A certain amount of friction is involved. For example, embracing a free trade regime for an advanced economy such as the United States often implies that the country will produce less of some labor-intensive goods, such as textiles, and more of some knowledge-intensive goods, such as computer software or biotechnology products. Although the country as a whole will gain from such a shift, textile producers will lose. A textile worker in South Carolina is probably not qualified to write software for Microsoft. Thus, the shift to free trade may mean that she becomes unemployed or has to accept another less attractive job, such as working at a fast-food restaurant.

Resources do not always move easily from one economic activity to another. The process creates friction and human suffering too. While the theory predicts that the benefits of free trade outweigh the costs by a significant margin, this is of cold comfort to those who bear the costs. Accordingly, political opposition to the adoption of a free trade regime typically comes from those whose jobs are most at risk. In the United States, for example, textile workers and their unions have long opposed the move toward free trade precisely because this group has much to lose from free trade. Governments often ease the transition toward free trade by helping retrain those who lose their jobs as a result. The pain caused by the movement toward a free trade regime is a short-term phenomenon, while the gains from trade once the transition has been made are both significant and enduring.

Diminishing Returns

The simple comparative advantage model developed above assumes constant returns to specialization. By **constant returns to specialization** we mean the units of resources required to produce a good (cocoa or rice) are assumed to remain constant no matter where one is on a country's production possibility frontier (PPF). Thus, we assumed that it always took Ghana 10 units of resources to produce 1 ton of cocoa. However, it is more realistic to assume diminishing returns to specialization. Diminishing returns to specialization occur when more units of resources are required to produce each additional unit. While 10 units of resources may be sufficient to increase Ghana's output of cocoa from 12 tons to 13 tons, 11 units of resources may be needed to increase output from 13 to 14 tons, 12 units of resources to increase output from 14 tons to 15 tons, and so on. Diminishing returns imply a convex PPF for Ghana (see Figure 6.3), rather than the straight line depicted in Figure 6.2.

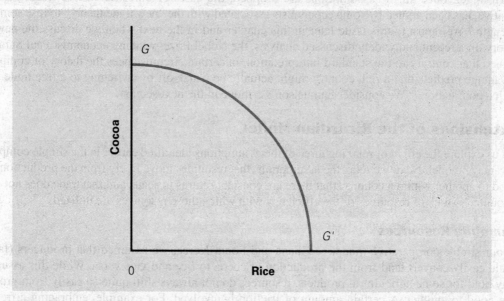

Figure 6.3 *Ghana's PPF under Diminishing Returns*

It is more realistic to assume diminishing returns for two reasons. First, not all resources are of the same quality. As a country tries to increase its output of a certain good, it is increasingly likely to draw on more marginal resources whose productivity is not as great as those initially employed. The result is that it requires ever more resources to produce an equal increase in output. For example, some land is more productive than other land. As Ghana tries to expand its output of cocoa, it might have to utilize increasingly marginal land that is less fertile than the land it originally used. As yields per acre decline, Ghana must use more land to produce 1 ton of cocoa.

A second reason for diminishing returns is that different goods use resources in different proportions. For example, imagine that growing cocoa uses more land and less labor than growing rice and that Ghana tries to transfer resources from rice production to cocoa production. The rice industry will release proportionately too much labor and too little land for efficient cocoa production. To absorb the additional resources of labor and land, the cocoa industry will have to shift toward more labor-intensive methods of production. The effect is that the efficiency with which the cocoa industry uses labor will decline, and returns will diminish.

Diminishing returns show that it is not feasible for a country to specialize to the degree suggested by the simple Ricardian model outlined earlier. Diminishing returns to specialization suggest that the gains from specialization are likely to be exhausted before specialization is complete. In reality, most countries do not specialize, but instead produce a range of goods. However, the theory predicts that it is worthwhile to specialize until that point where the resulting gains from trade are outweighed by diminishing returns. Thus, the basic conclusion that unrestricted free trade is beneficial still holds, although because of diminishing returns, the gains may not be as great as suggested in the constant returns case.

Dynamic Effects and Economic Growth

LO6-3

The simple comparative advantage model assumed that trade does not change a country's stock of resources or the efficiency with which it utilizes those resources. This static assumption makes no allowances for the dynamic changes that might result from trade. If we relax this assumption, it becomes apparent that opening an economy to trade is likely to generate dynamic gains of two sorts.[11] First, free trade might increase a country's stock of resources as increased supplies of labor and capital from abroad become available for use within the country. For example, this has been occurring in eastern Europe since the early 1990s, with many Western businesses investing significant capital in the former Communist countries.

Second, free trade might also increase the efficiency with which a country uses its resources. Gains in the efficiency of resource utilization could arise from a number of factors. For example, economies of large-scale production might become available as trade expands the size of the total market available to domestic firms. Trade might make better technology from abroad available to domestic firms; better technology can increase labor productivity or the productivity of land. (The so-called green revolution had this effect on agricultural outputs in developing countries.) Also, opening an economy to foreign competition might stimulate domestic producers to look for ways to increase their efficiency. Again, this phenomenon has arguably been occurring in the once-protected markets of eastern Europe, where many former state monopolies have had to increase the efficiency of their operations to survive in the competitive world market.

Dynamic gains in both the stock of a country's resources and the efficiency with which resources are utilized will cause a country's PPF to shift outward. This is illustrated in Figure 6.4, where the shift from PPF_1 to PPF_2 results from the dynamic gains that arise from free trade. As a consequence of this outward shift, the country in Figure 6.4 can produce more of both goods than it did before introduction

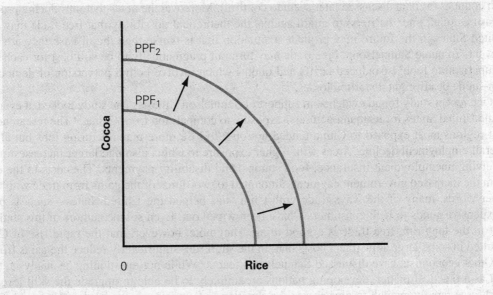

Figure 6.4 *The Influence of Free Trade on the PPF*

of free trade. The theory suggests that opening an economy to free trade not only results in static gains of the type discussed earlier but also results in dynamic gains that stimulate economic growth. If this is so, then one might think that the case for free trade becomes stronger still, and in general it does. However, as noted above, in a recent article one of the leading economic theorists of the twentieth century, Paul Samuelson, argued that in some circumstances, dynamic gains can lead to an outcome that is not so beneficial.

The Samuelson Critique

Paul Samuelson's critique looks at what happens when a rich country—the United States—enters into a free trade agreement with a poor country—China—that rapidly improves its productivity after the introduction of a free trade regime (i.e., there is a dynamic gain in the efficiency with which resources are used in the poor country). Samuelson's model suggests that in such cases, the lower prices that U.S. consumers pay for goods imported from China following the introduction of a free trade regime *may* not be enough to produce a net gain for the U.S. economy if the dynamic effect of free trade is to lower real wage rates in the United States. As he stated in a *New York Times* interview, "Being able to purchase groceries 20 percent cheaper at Wal-Mart (due to international trade) does not necessarily make up for the wage losses (in America)."[12]

Samuelson goes on to note that he is particularly concerned about the ability to offshore service jobs that traditionally were not internationally mobile, such as software debugging, call-center jobs, accounting jobs, and even medical diagnosis of MRI scans (see the accompanying Country Focus for details). Recent advances in communications technology have made this possible, effectively expanding the labor market for these jobs to include educated people in places such as India, the Philippines, and China. When coupled with rapid advances in the productivity of foreign labor due to better education, the effect on middle-class wages in the United States, according to Samuelson, may be similar to mass inward migration into the country: It will lower the market clearing wage rate, *perhaps* by enough to outweigh the positive benefits of international trade.

Having said this, it should be noted that Samuelson concedes that free trade has historically benefited rich counties (as data discussed later seem to confirm). Moreover, he notes that introducing protectionist measures (e.g., trade barriers) to guard against the theoretical possibility that free trade may harm the United States in the future may produce a situation that is worse than the disease they are trying to prevent. To quote Samuelson: "Free trade may turn out pragmatically to be still best for each region in comparison to lobbyist-induced tariffs and quotas which involve both a perversion of democracy and non-subtle deadweight distortion losses."[14]

One recent study found evidence in support of Samuelson's thesis. The study looked at every county in the United States for its manufacturers' exposure to competition from China.[15] The researchers found that regions most exposed to China tended not only to lose more manufacturing jobs but also to see overall employment decline. Areas with higher exposure to China also had larger increases in workers receiving unemployment insurance, food stamps, and disability payments. The costs to the economy from the increased government payments amounted to two-thirds of the gains from trade with China. In other words, many of the ways trade with China has helped the United States—such as providing inexpensive goods to U.S. consumers—have been wiped out. Even so, the authors of this study argued that in the long run, free trade is a good thing. They note, however, that the rapid rise of China has resulted in some large adjustment costs that, in the short run, significantly reduce the gains from trade.

Other economists have dismissed Samuelson's fears.[16] While not questioning his analysis, they note that as a practical matter, developing nations are unlikely to be able to upgrade the skill level of their workforce rapidly enough to give rise to the situation in Samuelson's model. In other words, they will

Moving U.S. White-Collar Jobs Offshore

Economists have long argued that free trade produces gains for all countries that participate in a free trading system. As the next wave of globalization sweeps through the U.S. economy, many people are wondering if this is true. During the 1980s and 1990s, free trade was associated with the movement of low-skill, blue-collar manufacturing jobs out of rich countries such as the United States and toward low-wage countries—textiles to Costa Rica, athletic shoes to the Philippines, steel to Brazil, electronic products to Thailand, and so on. While many observers bemoaned the "hollowing out" of U.S. manufacturing, economists stated that high-skill and high-wage white-collar jobs associated with the knowledge-based economy would stay in the United States. Computers might be assembled in Thailand, so the argument went, but they would continue to be designed in Silicon Valley by highly skilled U.S. engineers, and software applications would be written in the United States by programmers at Microsoft, Adobe, Oracle, and the like.

Developments over the past several decades have people questioning this assumption. Many American companies have been moving white-collar, "knowledge-based" jobs to developing nations where they can be performed for a fraction of the cost. During the long economic boom of the 1990s, Bank of America had to compete with other organizations for the scarce talents of information technology specialists, driving annual salaries to more than $100,000. However, with business under pressure during the 2000s, the bank cut nearly 5,000 jobs from its 25,000-strong, U.S.-based information technology workforce. Some of these jobs were transferred to India, where work that costs $100 an hour in the United States could be done for $20 an hour.

One beneficiary of Bank of America's downsizing is Infosys Technologies Ltd., a Bangalore, India, information technology firm where 250 engineers now develop information technology applications for the bank. Other Infosys employees are busy processing home loan applications for U.S. mortgage companies. Nearby in the offices of another Indian firm, Wipro Ltd., radiologists interpret 30 CT scans a day for Massachusetts General Hospital that are sent over the Internet. At yet another Bangalore business, engineers earn $10,000 a year designing leading-edge semiconductor chips for Texas Instruments. Nor is India the only beneficiary of these changes.

Some architectural work also is being outsourced to lower-cost locations. Flour Corp., a California-based construction company, employs some 1,200 engineers and draftsmen in the Philippines, Poland, and India to turn layouts of industrial facilities into detailed specifications. For a Saudi Arabian chemical plant Flour is designing, 200 young engineers based in the Philippines earning less than $3,000 a year collaborate in real time over the Internet with elite U.S. and British engineers who make up to $90,000 a year. Why does Flour do this? According to the company, the answer is simple. Doing so reduces the prices of a project by 15 percent, giving the company a cost-based competitive advantage in the global market for construction design. Most disturbing of all for future job growth in the United States, some high-tech start-ups are outsourcing significant work right from inception. For example, Zoho Corporation, a California-based start-up offering online web applications for small businesses, has about 20 employees in the United States and more than 1,000 in India![13]

quickly run into diminishing returns. However, such rebuttals are at odds with recent data suggesting that Asian countries are rapidly upgrading their educational systems. For example, about 56 percent of the world's engineering degrees awarded in 2008 were in Asia, compared with 4 percent in the United States![17]

Evidence for the Link between Trade and Growth

Many economic studies have looked at the relationship between trade and economic growth.[18] In general, these studies suggest that as predicted by the standard theory of comparative advantage, countries that adopt a more open stance toward international trade enjoy higher growth rates than those that close their economies to trade. Jeffrey Sachs and Andrew Warner created a measure of how "open" to international trade an economy was and then looked at the relationship between "openness" and economic growth for a sample of more than 100 countries from 1970 to 1990.[19] Among other findings, they reported:

> We find a strong association between openness and growth, both within the group of developing and the group of developed countries. Within the group of developing countries, the open economies grew at 4.49 percent per year, and the closed economies grew at 0.69 percent per year. Within the group of developed economies, the open economies grew at 2.29 percent per year, and the closed economies grew at 0.74 percent per year.[20]

A study by Wacziarg and Welch updated the Sachs and Warner data through the late 1990s. They found that over the period 1950–1998, countries that liberalized their trade regimes experienced, on average, increases in their annual growth rates of 1.5 percent compared to pre-liberalization times.[21] An exhaustive survey of 61 studies published between 1967 and 2009 concluded: "The macroeconomic evidence provides dominant support for the positive and significant effects of trade on output and growth."[22]

The message seems clear: Adopt an open economy and embrace free trade, and your nation will be rewarded with higher economic growth rates. Higher growth will raise income levels and living standards. This last point has been confirmed by a study that looked at the relationship between trade and growth in incomes. The study, undertaken by Jeffrey Frankel and David Romer, found that on average, a 1 percentage point increase in the ratio of a country's trade to its gross domestic product increases income per person by at least 0.5 percent.[23] For every 10 percent increase in the importance of international trade in an economy, average income levels will rise by at least 5 percent. Despite the short-term adjustment costs associated with adopting a free trade regime, trade would seem to produce greater economic growth and higher living standards in the long run, just as the theory of Ricardo would lead us to expect.[24]

HECKSCHER-OHLIN THEORY

Ricardo's theory stresses that comparative advantage arises from differences in productivity. Thus, whether Ghana is more efficient than South Korea in the production of cocoa depends on how productively it uses its resources. Ricardo stressed labor productivity and argued that differences in labor productivity between nations underlie the notion of comparative advantage. Swedish economists Eli Heckscher (in 1919) and Bertil Ohlin (in 1933) put forward a different explanation of comparative advantage. They argued that comparative advantage arises from differences in national factor endowments.[25] By **factor endowments** they meant the extent to which a country is endowed with such resources as land, labor, and capital. Nations have varying factor endowments, and different factor endowments explain differences in factor costs; specifically, the more abundant a factor, the lower its cost. The Heckscher-Ohlin theory predicts that countries will export those goods that make intensive use of factors that are locally abundant, while importing goods that make intensive use of factors that are locally scarce. Thus, the Heckscher-Ohlin theory attempts to explain the pattern of international trade that we observe in the world economy. Like Ricardo's theory, the Heckscher-Ohlin theory argues that free trade is beneficial. Unlike Ricardo's theory, however, the Heckscher-Ohlin theory argues that the pattern of international trade is determined by differences in factor endowments, rather than differences in productivity.

The Heckscher-Ohlin theory has commonsense appeal. For example, the United States has long been a substantial exporter of agricultural goods, reflecting in part its unusual abundance of arable land. In contrast, China has excelled in the export of goods produced in labor-intensive manufacturing industries. This reflects China's relative abundance of low-cost labor. The United States, which lacks abundant low-cost labor, has been a primary importer of these goods. Note that it is relative, not absolute, endowments that are important; a country may have larger absolute amounts of land and labor than another country, but be relatively abundant in one of them.

The Leontief Paradox

The Heckscher-Ohlin theory has been one of the most influential theoretical ideas in international economics. Most economists prefer the Heckscher-Ohlin theory to Ricardo's theory because it makes fewer simplifying assumptions. Because of its influence, the theory has been subjected to many empirical tests. Beginning with a famous study published in 1953 by Wassily Leontief (winner of the Nobel Prize in economics in 1973), many of these tests have raised questions about the validity of the Heckscher-Ohlin theory.[26] Using the Heckscher-Ohlin theory, Leontief postulated that because the United States was relatively abundant in capital compared to other nations, the United States would be an exporter of capital-intensive goods and an importer of labor-intensive goods. To his surprise, however, he found that U.S. exports were less capital-intensive than U.S. imports. Because this result was at variance with the predictions of the theory, it has become known as the *Leontief paradox.*

No one is quite sure why we observe the Leontief paradox. One possible explanation is that the United States has a special advantage in producing new products or goods made with innovative technologies. Such products may be less capital-intensive than products whose technology has had time to mature and become suitable for mass production. Thus, the United States may be exporting goods that heavily use skilled labor and innovative entrepreneurship, such as computer software, while importing heavy manufacturing products that use large amounts of capital. Some empirical studies tend to confirm this.[27] Still, tests of the Heckscher-Ohlin theory using data for a large number of countries tend to confirm the existence of the Leontief paradox.[28]

This leaves economists with a difficult dilemma. They prefer the Heckscher-Ohlin theory on theoretical grounds, but it is a relatively poor predictor of real-world international trade patterns. On the other hand, the theory they regard as being too limited, Ricardo's theory of comparative advantage, actually predicts trade patterns with greater accuracy. The best solution to this dilemma may be to return to the Ricardian idea that trade patterns are largely driven by international differences in productivity. Thus, one might argue that the United States exports commercial aircraft and imports textiles not because its factor endowments are especially suited to aircraft manufacture and not suited to textile manufacture, but because the United States is relatively more efficient at producing aircraft than textiles. A key assumption in the Heckscher-Ohlin theory is that technologies are the same across countries. This may not be the case. Differences in technology may lead to differences in productivity, which in turn, drives international trade patterns.[29] Thus, Japan's success in exporting automobiles from the 1970s onward has been based not only on the relative abundance of capital but also on its development of innovative manufacturing technology that enabled it to achieve higher productivity levels in automobile production than other countries that also had abundant capital. More recent empirical work suggests that this theoretical explanation may be correct.[30] The new research shows that once differences in technology across countries are controlled for, countries do indeed export those goods that make intensive use of factors that are locally abundant, while importing goods that make intensive use of factors that are locally scarce. In other words, once the impact of differences of technology on productivity is controlled for, the Heckscher-Ohlin theory seems to gain predictive power.

THE PRODUCT LIFE-CYCLE THEORY ■ LO6-2

Raymond Vernon initially proposed the product life-cycle theory in the mid-1960s.[31] Vernon's theory was based on the observation that for most of the twentieth century a very large proportion of the world's new products had been developed by U.S. firms and sold first in the U.S. market (e.g., mass-produced automobiles, televisions, instant cameras, photocopiers, personal computers, and semiconductor chips). To explain this, Vernon argued that the wealth and size of the U.S. market gave U.S. firms a strong incentive to develop new consumer products. In addition, the high cost of U.S. labor gave U.S. firms an incentive to develop cost-saving process innovations.

Just because a new product is developed by a U.S. firm and first sold in the U.S. market, it does not follow that the product must be produced in the United States. It could be produced abroad at some low-cost location and then exported back into the United States. However, Vernon argued that most new products were initially produced in America. Apparently, the pioneering firms believed it was better to keep production facilities close to the market and to the firm's center of decision making, given the uncertainty and risks inherent in introducing new products. Also, the demand for most new products tends to be based on nonprice factors. Consequently, firms can charge relatively high prices for new products, which obviates the need to look for low-cost production sites in other countries.

Vernon went on to argue that early in the life cycle of a typical new product, while demand is starting to grow rapidly in the United States, demand in other advanced countries is limited to high-income groups. The limited initial demand in other advanced countries does not make it worthwhile for firms in those countries to start producing the new product, but it does necessitate some exports from the United States to those countries.

Over time, demand for the new product starts to grow in other advanced countries (e.g., Great Britain, France, Germany, and Japan). As it does, it becomes worthwhile for foreign producers to begin producing for their home markets. In addition, U.S. firms might set up production facilities in those advanced countries where demand is growing. Consequently, production within other advanced countries begins to limit the potential for exports from the United States.

As the market in the United States and other advanced nations matures, the product becomes more standardized, and price becomes the main competitive weapon. As this occurs, cost considerations start to play a greater role in the competitive process. Producers based in advanced countries where labor costs are lower than in the United States (e.g., Italy and Spain) might now be able to export to the United States. If cost pressures become intense, the process might not stop there. The cycle by which the United States lost its advantage to other advanced countries might be repeated once more, as developing countries (e.g., Thailand) begin to acquire a production advantage over advanced countries. Thus, the locus of global production initially switches from the United States to other advanced nations and then from those nations to developing countries.

The consequence of these trends for the pattern of world trade is that over time the United States switches from being an exporter of the product to an importer of the product as production becomes concentrated in lower-cost foreign locations. Figure 6.5 shows the growth of production and consumption over time in the United States, other advanced countries, and developing countries.

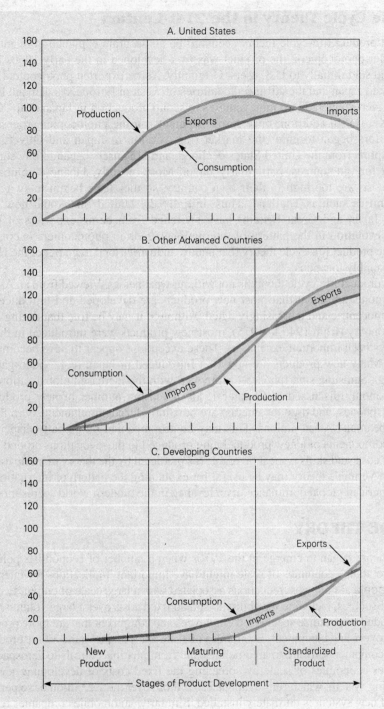

A. United States

B. Other Advanced Countries

C. Developing Countries

New
Product

Maturing
Product

Standardized
Product

Stages of Product Development

Figure 6.5 *The Product Life-Cycle Theory*

Source: Adapted from Raymond Vernon and Louis T. Wells, *The Economic Environment of International Business,* 5th edition © 1991.
Reproduced by permission of Pearson Education, Inc., Upper Saddle River, New Jersey.

Product Life-Cycle Theory in the 21st Century

Historically, the product life-cycle theory seems to be an accurate explanation of international trade patterns. Consider photocopiers; the product was first developed in the early 1960s by Xerox in the United States and sold initially to U.S. users. Originally, Xerox exported photocopiers from the United States, primarily to Japan and the advanced countries of western Europe. As demand began to grow in those countries, Xerox entered into joint ventures to set up production in Japan (Fuji-Xerox) and Great Britain (Rank-Xerox). In addition, once Xerox's patents on the photocopier process expired, other foreign competitors began to enter the market (e.g., Canon in Japan and Olivetti in Italy). As a consequence, exports from the United States declined, and U.S. users began to buy some photocopiers from lower-cost foreign sources, particularly Japan. More recently, Japanese companies found that manufacturing costs are too high in their own country, so they have begun to switch production to developing countries such as Thailand. Thus, initially the United States and now other advanced countries (e.g., Japan and Great Britain) have switched from being exporters of photocopiers to importers. This evolution in the pattern of international trade in photocopiers is consistent with the predictions of the product life-cycle theory that mature industries tend to go out of the United States and into low-cost assembly locations.

However, the product life-cycle theory is not without weaknesses. Viewed from an Asian or European perspective, Vernon's argument that most new products are developed and introduced in the United States seems ethnocentric and increasingly dated. Although it may be true that during U.S. dominance of the global economy (from 1945 to 1975), most new products were introduced in the United States, there have always been important exceptions. These exceptions appear to have become more common in recent years. Many new products are now first introduced in Japan (e.g., video-game consoles) or South Korea (e.g., Samsung smartphones). Moreover, with the increased globalization and integration of the world economy discussed in Chapter 1, an increasing number of new products (e.g., tablet computers, smartphones, and digital cameras) are now introduced simultaneously in the United States and many European and Asian nations. This may be accompanied by globally dispersed production, with particular components of a new product being produced in those locations around the globe where the mix of factor costs and skills is most favorable (as predicted by the theory of comparative advantage). In sum, although Vernon's theory may be useful for explaining the pattern of international trade during the period of American global dominance, its relevance in the modern world seems more limited.

NEW TRADE THEORY   ▮ LO6-2 ▮

The new trade theory began to emerge in the 1970s when a number of economists pointed out that the ability of firms to attain economies of scale might have important implications for international trade.[32] **Economies of scale** are unit cost reductions associated with a large scale of output. Economies of scale have a number of sources, including the ability to spread fixed costs over a large volume and the ability of large-volume producers to utilize specialized employees and equipment that are more productive than less specialized employees and equipment. Economies of scale are a major source of cost reductions in many industries, from computer software to automobiles and from pharmaceuticals to aerospace. For example, Microsoft realizes economies of scale by spreading the fixed costs of developing new versions of its Windows operating system, which runs to about $10 billion, over the 1.2 billion or so personal computers upon which each new system is ultimately installed. Similarly, automobile companies realize economies of scale by producing a high volume of automobiles from an assembly line where each employee has a specialized task.

New trade theory makes two important points: First, through its impact on economies of scale, trade can increase the variety of goods available to consumers and decrease the average cost of those goods. Second, in those industries when the output required to attain economies of scale represents a significant proportion of total world demand, the global market may be able to support only a small number of enterprises. Thus, world trade in certain products may be dominated by countries whose firms were first movers in their production.

Increasing Product Variety and Reducing Costs ■ L06-3 ■

Imagine first a world without trade. In industries where economies of scale are important, both the variety of goods that a country can produce and the scale of production are limited by the size of the market. If a national market is small, there may not be enough demand to enable producers to realize economies of scale for certain products. Accordingly, those products may not be produced, thereby limiting the variety of products available to consumers. Alternatively, they may be produced, but at such low volumes that unit costs and prices are considerably higher than they might be if economies of scale could be realized.

Now consider what happens when nations trade with each other. Individual national markets are combined into a larger world market. As the size of the market expands due to trade, individual firms may be able to better attain economies of scale. The implication, according to new trade theory, is that each nation may be able to specialize in producing a narrower range of products than it would in the absence of trade, yet by buying goods that it does not make from other countries, each nation can simultaneously increase the *variety* of goods available to its consumers and *lower the costs* of those goods—thus trade offers an opportunity for mutual gain even when countries do not differ in their resource endowments or technology.

Suppose there are two countries, each with an annual market for 1 million automobiles. By trading with each other, these countries can create a combined market for 2 million cars. In this combined market, due to the ability to better realize economies of scale, more varieties (models) of cars can be produced, and cars can be produced at a lower average cost, than in either market alone. For example, demand for a sports car may be limited to 55,000 units in each national market, while a total output of at least 100,000 per year may be required to realize significant scale economies. Similarly, demand for a minivan may be 80,000 units in each national market, and again a total output of at least 100,000 per year may be required to realize significant scale economies. Faced with limited domestic market demand, firms in each nation may decide not to produce a sports car, because the costs of doing so at such low volume are too great. Although they may produce minivans, the cost of doing so will be higher, as will prices, than if significant economies of scale had been attained. Once the two countries decide to trade, however, a firm in one nation may specialize in producing sports cars, while a firm in the other nation may produce minivans. The combined demand for 110,000 sports cars and 160,000 minivans allows each firm to realize scale economies. Consumers in this case benefit from having access to a product (sports cars) that was not available before international trade and from the lower price for a product (minivans) that could not be produced at the most efficient scale before international trade. Trade is thus mutually beneficial because it allows the specialization of production, the realization of scale economies, the production of a greater variety of products, and lower prices.

Economies of Scale, First-Mover Advantages, and the Pattern of Trade

A second theme in new trade theory is that the pattern of trade we observe in the world economy may be the result of economies of scale and first-mover advantages. **First-mover advantages** are the economic and strategic advantages that accrue to early entrants into an industry.[33] The ability to capture scale economies ahead of later entrants, and thus benefit from a lower cost structure, is an important first-mover advantage. New trade theory argues that for those products where economies of scale are significant and represent a substantial proportion of world demand, the first movers in an industry can gain a scale-based cost advantage that later entrants find almost impossible to match. Thus, the pattern of trade that we observe for such products may reflect first-mover advantages. Countries may dominate in the export of certain goods because economies of scale are important in their production, and because firms located in those countries were the first to capture scale economies, giving them a first-mover advantage.

For example, consider the commercial aerospace industry. In aerospace there are substantial scale economies that come from the ability to spread the fixed costs of developing a new jet aircraft over a large number of sales. It has cost Airbus some $15 billion to develop its new superjumbo jet, the 550-seat A380. To recoup those costs and break even, Airbus will have to sell at least 250 A380 planes. If Airbus can sell more than 350 A380 planes, it will apparently be a profitable venture. Total demand over the next 20 years for this class of aircraft is estimated to be between 400 and 600 units. Thus, the global market can probably profitably support only one producer of jet aircraft in the superjumbo category. It follows that the European Union might come to dominate in the export of very large jet aircraft, primarily because a European-based firm, Airbus, was the first to produce a superjumbo jet aircraft and realize scale economies. Other potential producers, such as Boeing, might be shut out of the market because they will lack the scale economies that Airbus will enjoy. By pioneering this market category, Airbus may have captured a *first-mover advantage* based on *scale economies* that will be difficult for rivals to match, and that will result in the European Union becoming the *leading exporter* of very large jet aircraft.

Implications of New Trade Theory
██ L06-3 ██

New trade theory has important implications. The theory suggests that nations may benefit from trade even when they do not differ in resource endowments or technology. Trade allows a nation to specialize in the production of certain products, attaining scale economies and lowering the costs of producing those products, while buying products that it does not produce from other nations that specialize in the production of other products. By this mechanism, the variety of products available to consumers in each nation is increased, while the average costs of those products should fall, as should their price, freeing resources to produce other goods and services.

The theory also suggests that a country may predominate in the export of a good simply because it was lucky enough to have one or more firms among the first to produce that good. Because they are able to gain economies of scale, the first movers in an industry may get a lock on the world market that discourages subsequent entry. First movers' ability to benefit from increasing returns creates a barrier to entry. In the commercial aircraft industry, the fact that Boeing and Airbus are already in the industry and have the benefits of economies of scale discourages new entry and reinforces the dominance of America and Europe in the trade of midsize and large jet aircraft. This dominance is further reinforced because global demand may not be sufficient to profitably support another producer of midsize and large jet aircraft in the industry. So although Japanese firms might be able to compete in the market, they have decided not to enter the industry but to ally themselves as major subcontractors with primary producers (e.g., Mitsubishi Heavy Industries is a major subcontractor for Boeing on the 777 and 787 programs).

New trade theory is at variance with the Heckscher-Ohlin theory, which suggests a country will predominate in the export of a product when it is particularly well endowed with those factors used intensively in its manufacture. New trade theorists argue that the United States is a major exporter of commercial jet aircraft not because it is better endowed with the factors of production required to manufacture aircraft, but because one of the first movers in the industry, Boeing, was a U.S. firm. The new trade theory is not at variance with the theory of comparative advantage. Economies of scale increase productivity. Thus, the new trade theory identifies an important source of comparative advantage.

This theory is quite useful in explaining trade patterns. Empirical studies seem to support the predictions of the theory that trade increases the specialization of production within an industry, increases the variety of products available to consumers, and results in lower average prices.[34] With regard to first-mover advantages and international trade, a study by Harvard business historian Alfred Chandler suggests the existence of first-mover advantages is an important factor in explaining the dominance of firms from certain nations in specific industries.[35] The number of firms is very limited in many global industries, including the chemical industry, the heavy construction-equipment industry, the heavy truck industry, the tire industry, the consumer electronics industry, the jet engine industry, and the computer software industry.

Perhaps the most contentious implication of the new trade theory is the argument that it   **LO6-4** generates for government intervention and strategic trade policy.[36] New trade theorists stress the role of luck, entrepreneurship, and innovation in giving a firm first-mover advantages. According to this argument, the reason Boeing was the first mover in commercial jet aircraft manufacture—rather than firms such as Great Britain's De Havilland and Hawker Siddeley, or Holland's Fokker, all of which could have been—was that Boeing was both lucky and innovative. One way Boeing was lucky is that De Havilland shot itself in the foot when its Comet jet airliner, introduced two years earlier than Boeing's first jet airliner, the 707, was found to be full of serious technological flaws. Had De Havilland not made some serious technological mistakes, Great Britain might have become the world's leading exporter of commercial jet aircraft. Boeing's innovativeness was demonstrated by its independent development of the technological know-how required to build a commercial jet airliner. Several new trade theorists have pointed out, however, that Boeing's R&D was largely paid for by the U.S. government; the 707 was a spin-off from a government-funded military program (the entry of Airbus into the industry was also supported by significant government subsidies). Herein is a rationale for government intervention; by the sophisticated and judicious use of subsidies, could a government increase the chances of its domestic firms becoming first movers in newly emerging industries, as the U.S. government apparently did with Boeing (and the European Union did with Airbus)? If this is possible, and the new trade theory suggests it might be, we have an economic rationale for a proactive trade policy that is at variance with the free trade prescriptions of the trade theories we have reviewed so far. We consider the policy implications of this issue in Chapter 7.

NATIONAL COMPETITIVE ADVANTAGE: PORTER'S DIAMOND   **LO6-2**

In 1990, Michael Porter published the results of an intensive research effort that attempted to determine why some nations succeed and others fail in international competition.[37] Porter and his team looked at 100 industries in 10 nations. Like the work of the new trade theorists, Porter's work was driven by a belief that existing theories of international trade told only part of the story. For Porter, the essential task was to explain why a nation achieves international success in a particular industry. Why does Japan do so well in the automobile industry? Why does Switzerland excel in the production and export of precision instruments and pharmaceuticals? Why do Germany and the United States do so well in the chemical industry? These questions cannot be answered easily by the Heckscher-Ohlin theory, and the theory of comparative advantage offers only a partial explanation. The theory of comparative advantage would say that Switzerland excels in the production and export of precision instruments because it uses its resources very productively in these industries. Although this may be correct, this does not explain why Switzerland is more productive in this industry than Great Britain, Germany, or Spain. Porter tries to solve this puzzle.

Porter theorizes that four broad attributes of a nation shape the environment in which local firms compete, and these attributes promote or impede the creation of competitive advantage (see Figure 6.6). These attributes are:

- *Factor endowments*—a nation's position in factors of production, such as skilled labor or the infrastructure necessary to compete in a given industry.
- *Demand conditions*—the nature of home demand for the industry's product or service.
- *Related and supporting industries*—the presence or absence of supplier industries and related industries that are internationally competitive.
- *Firm strategy, structure, and rivalry*—the conditions governing how companies are created, organized, and managed and the nature of domestic rivalry.

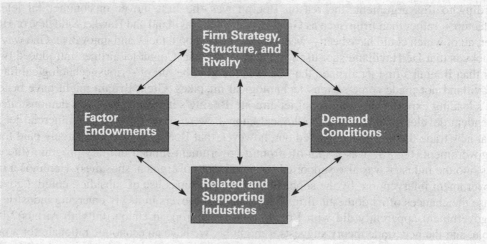

Figure 6.6 *Determinants of National Competitive Advantage: Porter's Diamond*

Source: Reprinted by permission of *Harvard Business Review.* Exhibit from "The Competitive Advantage of Nations," by Michael E. Porter, March–April 1990, p. 77. Copyright 1990 by the Harvard Business School Publishing Corporation; all rights reserved.

Porter speaks of these four attributes as constituting the *diamond.* He argues that firms are most likely to succeed in industries or industry segments where the diamond is most favorable. He also argues that the diamond is a mutually reinforcing system. The effect of one attribute is contingent on the state of others. For example, Porter argues favorable demand conditions will not result in competitive advantage unless the state of rivalry is sufficient to cause firms to respond to them.

Porter maintains that two additional variables can influence the national diamond in important ways: chance and government. Chance events, such as major innovations, can reshape industry structure and provide the opportunity for one nation's firms to supplant another's. Government, by its choice of policies, can detract from or improve national advantage. For example, regulation can alter home demand conditions, antitrust policies can influence the intensity of rivalry within an industry, and government investments in education can change factor endowments.

Factor Endowments

Factor endowments lie at the center of the Heckscher-Ohlin theory. While Porter does not propose anything radically new, he does analyze the characteristics of factors of production. He recognizes hierarchies among factors, distinguishing between *basic factors* (e.g., natural resources, climate, location, and demographics) and *advanced factors* (e.g., communication infrastructure, sophisticated and skilled labor, research facilities, and technological know-how). He argues that advanced factors are the most significant for competitive advantage. Unlike the naturally endowed basic factors, advanced factors are a product of investment by individuals, companies, and governments. Thus, government investments in basic and higher education, by improving the general skill and knowledge level of the population and by stimulating advanced research at higher education institutions, can upgrade a nation's advanced factors.

The relationship between advanced and basic factors is complex. Basic factors can provide an initial advantage that is subsequently reinforced and extended by investment in advanced factors. Conversely, disadvantages in basic factors can create pressures to invest in advanced factors. An obvious example of this phenomenon is Japan, a country that lacks arable land and mineral deposits and yet through investment has built a substantial endowment of advanced factors. Porter notes that Japan's large pool of engineers (reflecting a much higher number of engineering graduates per capita than almost any other nation) has been vital to Japan's success in many manufacturing industries.

Demand Conditions

Porter emphasizes the role home demand plays in upgrading competitive advantage. Firms are typically most sensitive to the needs of their closest customers. Thus, the characteristics of home demand are particularly important in shaping the attributes of domestically made products and in creating pressures for innovation and quality. Porter argues that a nation's firms gain competitive advantage if their domestic consumers are sophisticated and demanding. Such consumers pressure local firms to meet high standards of product quality and to produce innovative products. For example, Porter notes that Japan's sophisticated and knowledgeable buyers of cameras helped stimulate the Japanese camera industry to improve product quality and to introduce innovative models.

Related and Supporting Industries

The third broad attribute of national advantage in an industry is the presence of suppliers or related industries that are internationally competitive. The benefits of investments in advanced factors of production by related and supporting industries can spill over into an industry, thereby helping it achieve a strong competitive position internationally. Swedish strength in fabricated steel products (e.g., ball bearings and cutting tools) has drawn on strengths in Sweden's specialty steel industry. Technological leadership in the U.S. semiconductor industry provided the basis for U.S. success in personal computers and several other technically advanced electronic products. Similarly, Switzerland's success in pharmaceuticals is closely related to its previous international success in the technologically related dye industry.

One consequence of this process is that successful industries within a country tend to be grouped into clusters of related industries. This was one of the most pervasive findings of Porter's study. One such cluster Porter identified was in the German textile and apparel sector, which included high-quality cotton, wool, synthetic fibers, sewing machine needles, and a wide range of textile machinery. Such clusters are important because valuable knowledge can flow between the firms within a geographic cluster, benefiting all within that cluster. Knowledge flows occur when employees move between firms within a region and when national industry associations bring employees from different companies together for regular conferences or workshops.[38]

Firm Strategy, Structure, and Rivalry

The fourth broad attribute of national competitive advantage in Porter's model is the strategy, structure, and rivalry of firms within a nation. Porter makes two important points here. First, different nations are characterized by different management ideologies, which either help them or do not help them build national competitive advantage. For example, Porter noted the predominance of engineers in top management at German and Japanese firms. He attributed this to these firms' emphasis on improving manufacturing processes and product design. In contrast, Porter noted a predominance of people with finance backgrounds leading many U.S. firms. He linked this to U.S. firms' lack of attention to improving manufacturing processes and product design. He argued that the dominance of finance led to an overemphasis on maximizing short-term financial returns. According to Porter, one consequence of these different management ideologies was a relative loss of U.S. competitiveness in those engineering-based industries where manufacturing processes and product design issues are all-important (e.g., the automobile industry).

Porter's second point is that there is a strong association between vigorous domestic rivalry and the creation and persistence of competitive advantage in an industry. Vigorous domestic rivalry induces firms to look for ways to improve efficiency, which makes them better international competitors. Domestic rivalry creates pressures to innovate, to improve quality, to reduce costs, and to invest in upgrading advanced factors. All this helps create world-class competitors. Porter cites the case of Japan:

> Nowhere is the role of domestic rivalry more evident than in Japan, where it is all-out warfare in which many companies fail to achieve profitability. With goals that stress market share, Japanese companies engage in a continuing struggle to outdo each other. Shares fluctuate markedly. The process is prominently covered in the business press. Elaborate rankings measure which companies are most popular with university graduates. The rate of new product and process development is breathtaking.[39]

Evaluating Porter's Theory   `L06-4`

Porter contends that the degree to which a nation is likely to achieve international success in a certain industry is a function of the combined impact of factor endowments, domestic demand conditions, related and supporting industries, and domestic rivalry. He argues that the presence of all four components is usually required for this diamond to boost competitive performance (although there are exceptions). Porter also contends that government can influence each of the four components of the diamond—either positively or negatively. Factor endowments can be affected by subsidies, policies toward capital markets, policies toward education, and so on. Government can shape domestic demand through local product standards or with regulations that mandate or influence buyer needs. Government policy can influence supporting and related industries through regulation and influence firm rivalry through such devices as capital market regulation, tax policy, and antitrust laws.

If Porter is correct, we would expect his model to predict the pattern of international trade that we observe in the real world. Countries should be exporting products from those industries where all four components of the diamond are favorable, while importing in those areas where the components are not favorable. Is he correct? We simply do not know. Porter's theory has not been subjected to detailed empirical testing. Much about the theory rings true, but the same can be said for the new trade theory, the theory of comparative advantage, and the Heckscher-Ohlin theory. It may be that each of these theories, which complement each other, explains something about the pattern of international trade.

■ IMPLICATIONS FOR MANAGERS ▓▓▓▓▓▓▓ ▐ L06-5 ▌

Why does all this matter for business? There are at least three main implications for international businesses of the material discussed in this chapter: location implications, first-mover implications, and policy implications.

LOCATION

Underlying most of the theories we have discussed is the notion that different countries have particular advantages in different productive activities. Thus, from a profit perspective, it makes sense for a firm to disperse its productive activities to those countries where, according to the theory of international trade, they can be performed most efficiently. If design can be performed most efficiently in France, that is where design facilities should be located; if the manufacture of basic components can be performed most efficiently in Singapore, that is where they should be manufactured; and if final assembly can be performed most efficiently in China, that is where final assembly should be performed. The result is a global web of productive activities, with different activities being performed in different locations around the globe depending on considerations of comparative advantage, factor endowments, and the like. If the firm does not do this, it may find itself at a competitive disadvantage relative to firms that do.

FIRST-MOVER ADVANTAGES

According to the new trade theory, firms that establish a first-mover advantage with regard to the production of a particular new product may subsequently dominate global trade in that product. This is particularly true in industries where the global market can profitably support only a limited number of firms, such as the aerospace market, but early commitments may also seem to be important in less concentrated industries. For the individual firm, the clear message is that it pays to invest substantial financial resources in trying to build a first-mover, or early-mover, advantage, even if that means several years of losses before a new venture becomes profitable. The idea is to preempt the available demand, gain cost advantages related to volume, build an enduring brand ahead of later competitors, and, consequently, establish a long-term sustainable competitive advantage. Although the details of how to achieve this are beyond the scope of this book, many publications offer strategies for exploiting first-mover advantages and for avoiding the traps associated with pioneering a market (first-mover disadvantages).[40]

GOVERNMENT POLICY

The theories of international trade also matter to international businesses because firms are major players on the international trade scene. Business firms produce exports, and business firms import the products of other countries. Because of their pivotal role in international trade, businesses can exert a strong influence on government trade policy, lobbying to promote free trade or trade restrictions. The theories of international trade claim that promoting free trade is generally in the best interests of a country, although it may not always be in the best interest of an individual firm. Many firms recognize this and lobby for open markets.

For example, when the U.S. government announced its intention to place a tariff on Japanese imports of liquid crystal display (LCD) screens in the 1990s, IBM and Apple Computer protested strongly. Both IBM and Apple pointed out that (1) Japan was the lowest-cost source of LCD screens, (2) they used these screens in their own laptop computers, and (3) the proposed tariff, by increasing the cost of LCD screens, would increase the cost of laptop computers produced by IBM and Apple, thus making them less competitive in the world market. In other words, the tariff, designed to protect U.S. firms, would be self-defeating. In response to these pressures, the U.S. government reversed its posture.

Unlike IBM and Apple, however, businesses do not always lobby for free trade. In the United States, for example, restrictions on imports of steel have periodically been put into place in response to direct pressure by U.S. firms on the government. In some cases, the government has responded to pressure by getting foreign companies to agree to "voluntary" restrictions on their imports, using the implicit threat of more comprehensive formal trade barriers to get them to adhere to these agreements (historically, this has occurred in the automobile industry). In other cases, the government used what are called "antidumping" actions to justify tariffs on imports from other nations (these mechanisms will be discussed in detail in the next chapter).

As predicted by international trade theory, many of these agreements have been self-defeating, such as the voluntary restriction on machine tool imports agreed to in 1985. Shielded from international competition by import barriers, the U.S. machine tool industry had no incentive to increase its efficiency. Consequently, it lost many of its export markets to more efficient foreign competitors. Because of this misguided action, the U.S. machine tool industry shrunk during the period when the agreement was in force. For anyone schooled in international trade theory, this was not surprising.[41]

Finally, Porter's theory of national competitive advantage also contains policy implications. Porter's theory suggests that it is in the best interest of business for a firm to invest in upgrading advanced factors of production, for example, to invest in better training for its employees and to increase its commitment to research and development. It is also in the best interests of business to lobby the government to adopt policies that have a favorable impact on each component of the national diamond. Thus, according to Porter, businesses should urge government to increase investment in education, infrastructure, and basic research (since all these enhance advanced factors) and to adopt policies that promote strong competition within domestic markets (since this makes firms stronger international competitors, according to Porter's findings).

GLOBAL COMPETITIVENESS ALIGNMENT MATRIX*

While the various economic theories partially explain the developments in international trade, most fail to provide a framework for understanding the level of global competitiveness of a nation and the shifting positions of firms in this regard.

Mapping Competitiveness Shifts It is useful to try to capture complex phenomena through the use of frameworks that allow us to place the information in easy to understand and remember slots. Accordingly, while researching the levers of excellence in Indian companies under conditions of systemic constraints in the mid and late 1990s, the author developed a Country Competitiveness Alignment Matrix[42] to understand the opportunities and challenges that a nation, its firms and the people faced. This framework allows foreseeing the structural platforms for policy interventions and strategic actions (Figure 6.7).

Those ingredients of business environment that impact directly or indirectly on business performance are termed Macro types. These constraints or opportunities can either be in the domain of government (policy choice) affecting the entire industry structure, or as softer issues ('ethos') that reflect the core values and behavior of the people. Similarly, choices at the Micro-level would effect firm-level decisions and could be categorized as 'strategic' or 'cultural' (*hard* and *soft* respectively). Conceptually, soft constraints require people-based solutions, education and training, and a strong and exemplary leadership to bring about worthwhile attitudinal change. Hard constraints require planning based solutions through strong analytical and techno-economic approaches.

Based on the above research, another set of frameworks is created for further understanding the degree of alignment. A three-dimensional framework is conceptualized, which forms the basis for action for promoting sustainable national competitiveness and industry-wide excellence (Figure 6.8). The government's role in the creation and preservation of democratic and fair-competition inducing institutions is discussed later in the section.[43]

---

*This section has been developed by professor Arun Kumar Jain and taken from his book, *Competitive Excellence-Critical Success Factors*, Vikas Publishing, 2005.

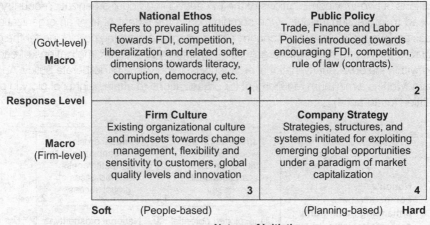

Figure 6.7 - Macro (Govt-level) / Macro (Firm-level), Response Level vs Nature of Initiatives (Soft People-based / Hard Planning-based):

	Soft (People-based)	Hard (Planning-based)
Macro (Govt-level)	**National Ethos** — Refers to prevailing attitudes towards FDI, competition, liberalization and related softer dimensions towards literacy, corruption, democracy, etc. (1)	**Public Policy** — Trade, Finance and Labor Policies introduced towards encouraging FDI, competition, rule of law (contracts). (2)
Macro (Firm-level)	**Firm Culture** — Existing organizational culture and mindsets towards change management, flexibility and sensitivity to customers, global quality levels and innovation (3)	**Company Strategy** — Strategies, structures, and systems initiated for exploiting emerging global opportunities under a paradigm of market capitalization (4)

Figure 6.7 *Country Global Competitiveness Alignment Matrix*

Framework for understanding government-industry linkages for corporate excellence

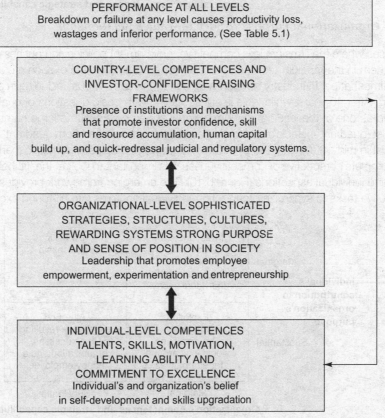

LEVELS OF EXCELLENCE FOR SUSTAINED SUPERIOR PERFORMANCE AT ALL LEVELS
Breakdown or failure at any level causes productivity loss, wastages and inferior performance. (See Table 5.1)

COUNTRY-LEVEL COMPETENCES AND INVESTOR-CONFIDENCE RAISING FRAMEWORKS
Presence of institutions and mechanisms that promote investor confidence, skill and resource accumulation, human capital build up, and quick-redressal judicial and regulatory systems.

ORGANIZATIONAL-LEVEL SOPHISTICATED STRATEGIES, STRUCTURES, CULTURES, REWARDING SYSTEMS STRONG PURPOSE AND SENSE OF POSITION IN SOCIETY
Leadership that promotes employee empowerment, experimentation and entrepreneurship

INDIVIDUAL-LEVEL COMPETENCES TALENTS, SKILLS, MOTIVATION, LEARNING ABILITY AND COMMITMENT TO EXCELLENCE
Individual's and organization's belief in self-development and skills upgradation

Figure 6.8 *Parameters for Sustaining Nation's Excellence*

The implications of two-way combinations of the three-level (individual-organization-country) framework in Figure 6.8 lead to interesting insights. One combination is the extent of fit of an organization's existing competitiveness and work culture with the country's competence-enhancing policies under the globalization paradigm (Figure 6.9). The framework is largely self-explanatory and some implications of each quadrant are mentioned within the box. Clearly, national prosperity is an outcome of deliberate policy. An appropriate institutional framework is a minimum requirement for organizations to attain heights of glory in conditions of global competition (quadrant 4).

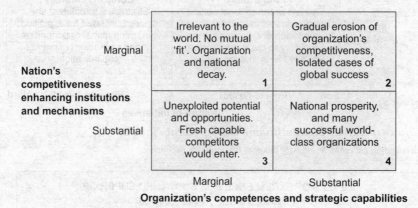

Figure 6.9 *Organizational Purpose & Societal Values Relationship*

Even in cases where the firms are less competitive, government policies and pushes can lead to substantial gains for them in the medium term (quadrant 3). Japan is an example of such a combination. India and Japan were almost at par in industry development during the early 1950s, including in automobile and steel manufacturing. After 40 years, while India is still struggling with basic questions of quality of life, Japan has spurted ahead as one of the leading economic global superpowers with a large number of its firms in the Fortune 500 list (quadrant 4). India's economic development has shifted from quadrant 1 (just one firm in the Fortune 500 list in mid-1990s, that too by virtue of monopoly holdings in domestic markets) to quadrant 4.

To get a complete perspective of competitiveness, it is important to look at the 'fit' between organizational work values and individual aspirations (Figure 6.10). The emerging framework provides managerial insights into the executive tasks to synergize organization-individual energies into all-round excellence.

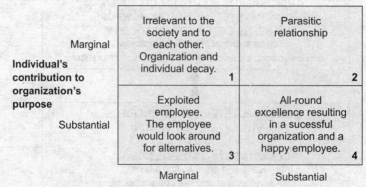

Figure 6.10 *Organizational Purpose & Individual Values Relationship*

The frameworks make the basic premise that a happy employee is the basic condition for organizational excellence. An unsatisfied and unmotivated employee can hardly contribute towards achievement of lofty organizational goals. Simultaneously, organizations need competent and skilled professionals to manage environmental complexities. A synergistic relationship calls for an organization to contribute towards employee self-development and growth, who, in turn, applies the new learnings and skills for creating superior advantages in the market-place for the firm (quadrant 4). In the absence or withdrawal of matching contributions from either of the participants, either a parasitic relationship (quadrant 2) or an exploitative relationship (quadrant 3) would result. None of these is sustainable in the medium-term. The exploited employee just bides his/her time and at the first opportunity shifts allegiance. Vice versa, the organization would not tolerate a non-value contributing member for long.

To understand the combinative implications of our frameworks 5.3 and 5.4, another three-dimensional structure was created where the three conditions of excellence were conceptualized on the three dimensions. The result is a framework which enables us to view several scenarios and make appropriate recommendations for each scenario and reinforces a compelling need for innovation (Figure 6.11). The implications of each octant is explained in a nutshell in Table 6.1. The important message from each octant is that protectionist policies are no solution for firms' quest for global competitiveness; at best such policies could only be for a short term and a specific purpose. India has steadily moved from octant 7 (in mid-1970s) to octant 6 (LHH) in mid-1990s and trying hard to move to octant 4 (HHH in mid-2000s). The result is that several Indian firms are competing successfully globally and India is emerging as a leading economic power.[44]

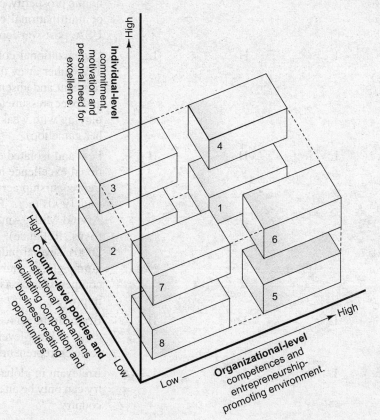

Figure 6.11 *3-D Template showing why some nations are great while others are not, and how organizations can excel Three interlinked dimensions for firmlevel excellence*

TABLE 6.3 Template for Country-Organizational-Individual Excellences

Octant	Country Factors	Organization Competence	Individual Talent & Skill	Outcomes and Responses
1	H	H	L	Invest in employee training and technology development, hire new talent, develop cross-functional teams.
2	H	L	L	Encourage competition, remove bottlenecks to foreign investments (e.g., Andhra Pradesh government's approach).
3	H	L	H	Encourage FDI and competition, emphasize need for competitiveness. (Some stakeholders may cry for state protection, many others see this situation as an opportunity to globalize.)
4	H	H	H	Excellence in several industries simultaneously, nation basks in economic prosperity, chance for creation of multinational corporations (e.g., USA, post-war Japan).
5	L	H	L	Organizational competences gradually wither away due to hostile environment and absence of competition and peer pressure (e.g., a good player playing with weak players ruins his/her game too).
6	L	H	H	Few and isolated cases of organizational excellence and innovative entrepreneurship across history till the mid-1990s (e.g., Tata, Nirma, Titan, Arvind Mills, Ambuja Cements, Infosys, Reliance). Now in the mid-2000s, several Indian companies are going global and achieving global competitiveness as the alignment has improved.
7	L	L	H	Brain drain, may be some isolated cases of local-level successful small-scale entrepreneurship.
8	L	L	L	Irrelevant in global arena. The country can only be an appendage to a big country.

H: High presence of enabling factors
L: Low presence of enabling factors.

Application of CAN and GCM Frameworks in case of India's IT-BPO Industry and Wipro

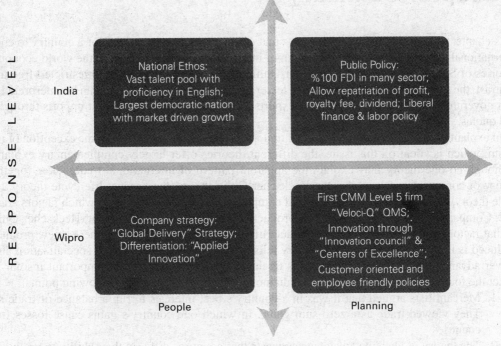

R E S P O N S E L E V E L

India

National Ethos:
Vast talent pool with
proficiency in English;
Largest democratic nation
with market driven growth

Public Policy:
%100 FDI in many sector;
Allow repatriation of profit,
royalty fee, dividend; Liberal
finance & labor policy

Wipro

Company strategy:
"Global Delivery" Strategy;
Differentiation: "Applied
Innovation"

First CMM Level 5 firm
"Veloci-Q" QMS;
Innovation through
"Innovation council" &
"Centers of Excellence";
Customer oriented and
employee friendly policies

People

Planning

Nature of Initiative

Competitive Advantage of Nations

The Diamond of National Advantage

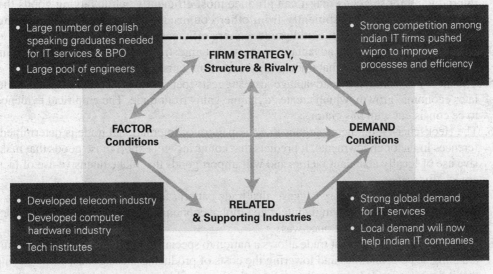

- Large number of english
  speaking graduates needed
  for IT services & BPO
- Large pool of engineers

**FIRM STRATEGY,
Structure & Rivalry**

- Strong competition among
  indian IT firms pushed
  wipro to improve
  processes and efficiency

**FACTOR
Conditions**

**DEMAND
Conditions**

**RELATED
& Supporting Industries**

- Developed telecom industry
- Developed computer
  hardware industry
- Tech institutes

- Strong global demand
  for IT services
- Local demand will now
  help indian IT companies

Chapter Summary

This chapter reviewed a number of theories that explain why it is beneficial for a country to engage in international trade and explained the pattern of international trade observed in the world economy. The theories of Smith, Ricardo, and Heckscher-Ohlin all make strong cases for unrestricted free trade. In contrast, the mercantilist doctrine and, to a lesser extent, the new trade theory can be interpreted to support government intervention to promote exports through subsidies and to limit imports through tariffs and quotas.

In explaining the pattern of international trade, this chapter shows that, with the exception of mercantilism, which is silent on this issue, the different theories offer largely complementary explanations. Although no one theory may explain the apparent pattern of international trade, taken together, the theory of comparative advantage, the Heckscher-Ohlin theory, the product life-cycle theory, the new trade theory, and Porter's theory of national competitive advantage do suggest which factors are important. Comparative advantage tells us that productivity differences are important; Heckscher-Ohlin tells us that factor endowments matter; the product life-cycle theory tells us that where a new product is introduced is important; the new trade theory tells us that increasing returns to specialization and first-mover advantages matter; and Porter tells us that all these factors may be important insofar as they affect the four components of the national diamond. The chapter made the following points:

1. Mercantilists argued that it was in a country's best interests to run a balance-of-trade surplus. They viewed trade as a zero-sum game, in which one country's gains cause losses for other countries.

2. The theory of absolute advantage suggests that countries differ in their ability to produce goods efficiently. The theory suggests that a country should specialize in producing goods in areas where it has an absolute advantage and import goods in areas where other countries have absolute advantages.

3. The theory of comparative advantage suggests that it makes sense for a country to specialize in producing those goods that it can produce most efficiently, while buying goods that it can produce relatively less efficiently from other countries—even if that means buying goods from other countries that it could produce more efficiently itself.

4. The theory of comparative advantage suggests that unrestricted free trade brings about increased world production, that is, that trade is a positive-sum game.

5. The theory of comparative advantage also suggests that opening a country to free trade stimulates economic growth, which creates dynamic gains from trade. The empirical evidence seems to be consistent with this claim.

6. The Heckscher-Ohlin theory argues that the pattern of international trade is determined by differences in factor endowments. It predicts that countries will export those goods that make intensive use of locally abundant factors and will import goods that make intensive use of factors that are locally scarce.

7. The product life-cycle theory suggests that trade patterns are influenced by where a new product is introduced. In an increasingly integrated global economy, the product life-cycle theory seems to be less predictive than it once was.

8. New trade theory states that trade allows a nation to specialize in the production of certain goods, attaining scale economies and lowering the costs of producing those goods, while buying goods that it does not produce from other nations that are similarly specialized. By this mechanism, the

variety of goods available to consumers in each nation is increased, while the average costs of those goods should fall.

9. New trade theory also states that in those industries where substantial economies of scale imply that the world market will profitably support only a few firms, countries may predominate in the export of certain products simply because they had a firm that was a first mover in that industry.

10. Some new trade theorists have promoted the idea of strategic trade policy. The argument is that government, by the sophisticated and judicious use of subsidies, might be able to increase the chances of domestic firms becoming first movers in newly emerging industries.

11. Porter's theory of national competitive advantage suggests that the pattern of trade is influenced by four attributes of a nation: *(a)* factor endowments, *(b)* domestic demand conditions, *(c)* related and supporting industries, and *(d)* firm strategy, structure, and rivalry.

12. Theories of international trade are important to an individual business firm primarily because they can help the firm decide where to locate its various production activities.

13. Firms involved in international trade can and do exert a strong influence on government policy toward trade. By lobbying government, business firms can promote free trade or trade restrictions.

Critical Thinking and Discussion Questions

1. Mercantilism is a bankrupt theory that has no place in the modern world. Discuss.
2. Is free trade fair? Discuss!
3. Unions in developed nations often oppose imports from low-wage countries and advocate trade barriers to protect jobs from what they often characterize as "unfair" import competition. Is such competition "unfair"? Do you think that this argument is in the best interests of (a) the unions, (b) the people they represent, and/or (c) the country as a whole?
4. What are the potential costs of adopting a free trade regime? Do you think governments should do anything to reduce these costs? What?
5. Reread the Country Focus "Is China a Neo-mercantilist Nation?"
   a. Do you think China is pursuing an economic policy that can be characterized as neo-mercantilist?
   b. What should the United States, and other countries, do about this?
6. Reread the Country Focus on moving white-collar jobs offshore.
   a. Who benefits from the outsourcing of skilled white-collar jobs to developing nations? Who are the losers?
   b. Will developed nations like the United States suffer from the loss of high-skilled and high-paying jobs?
   c. Is there a difference between the transference of high-paying white-collar jobs, such as computer programming and accounting, to developing nations, and low-paying blue-collar jobs? If so, what is the difference, and should government do anything to stop the flow of white-collar jobs out of the country to countries such as India?
7. Drawing upon the new trade theory and Porter's theory of national competitive advantage, outline the case for government policies that would build national competitive advantage in biotechnology. What kinds of policies would you recommend that the government adopt? Are these policies at variance with the basic free trade philosophy?
8. The world's poorest countries are at a competitive disadvantage in every sector of their economies. They have little to export. They have no capital; their land is of poor quality; they often have too many people given available work opportunities; and they are poorly educated. Free trade cannot possibly be in the interests of such nations. Discuss.

Research Task ○ globalEDGE globaledge.msu.edu

International Trade Theory

Use the globalEDGE website (globaledge.msu.edu) to complete the following exercises:

Exercise 1

The *World Trade Organization International Trade Statistics* is an annual report that provides comprehensive, comparable, and updated statistics on trade in merchandise and commercial services. The report allows an assessment of world trade flows by country, region, and main product or service categories. Using the most recent statistics available, identify the top 10 countries that lead in the export and import of merchandise trade, respectively. Which countries appear in the top 10 in both exports and imports? Can you explain why these countries appear at the top of both lists?

Exercise 2

Food in an integral part of understanding different countries, cultures, and lifestyles. You run a chain of high-end premium restaurants in the United States, and you are looking for unique Australian wines you can import. However, you must first identify which *Australian suppliers* can provide you with premium wines. After searching through the Australian supplier directory, identify three to four companies that can be potential suppliers. Then develop a list of criteria you would need to ask these companies to select which one to work with.

Read also about "India's Globally Competitive Two-Wheeler Industry" on page 621 (chap 17).

Closing CASE

The Rise of India's Drug Industry

One of the great success stories in international trade in recent years has been the strong growth of India's pharmaceutical industry. The country used to be known for producing cheap knockoffs of patented drugs discovered by Western and Japanese pharmaceutical companies. This made the industry something of an international pariah. Because they made copies of patented products, and therefore violated intellectual property rights, Indian companies were not allowed to sell these products in developed markets. With no assurance that their intellectual property would be protected, foreign drug companies refused to invest in, partner with, or buy from their Indian counterparts, further limiting the business opportunities of Indian companies. In developed markets such as the United States, the best that Indian companies could do was to sell low-cost generic pharmaceuticals (generic pharmaceuticals are products whose patents have expired).

In 2005, however, India signed an agreement with the World Trade Organization that brought the country into compliance with WTO rules on intellectual property rights. Indian companies stopped producing counterfeit products. Secure in knowledge that their patents would be respected, foreign companies started to do business with their Indian counterparts. For India, the result has been dramatic growth in its pharmaceutical sector. The sector generated sales of close to $30 billion in 2012, more than two and a half times the figure of 2005. Driving this growth have been surging exports, which grew at 15 percent per annum between 2006 and 2012. In 2000, pharmaceutical exports from India amounted to around $1 billion. By 2012, the figure was around $14 billion!

Much of this growth has been the result of partnerships between Western and Indian firms. Western companies have been increasingly outsourcing manufacturing and packaging activities to India while scaling back some of these activities at home and in places such as Puerto Rico, which historically has been a major manufacturing hub for firms serving the U.S. market. India's advantages in manufacturing and packaging include relatively low wage rates, an educated workforce, and the widespread use of English as a business language. Western companies have continued to perform high value-added R&D, marketing, and sales activities, and these remain located in their home markets.

During India's years as an international pariah in the drug business, its nascent domestic industry set the foundations for today's growth. Local start-ups invested in the facilities required to discover and produce pharmaceuticals, creating a market for pharmaceutical scientists and workers in India. In turn, this drove the expansion of pharmaceutical programs in the country's universities, thereby increasing the supply of talent. Moreover, the industry's experience in the generic drug business during the 1990s and early 2000s has given it expertise in dealing with regulatory agencies in the United States and European Union. After 2005, this know-how made Indian companies more attractive as partners for Western enterprises. Combined with low labor costs, all these factors came together to make India an increasingly attractive location for the manufacturing of pharmaceuticals.

The U.S. Federal Drug Administration (FDA) responded to the shift of manufacturing to India by opening two offices there to oversee manufacturing compliance and make sure safety was consistent with FDA-mandated standards. Today, the FDA has issued approvals to produce pharmaceuticals for sale in the United States to some 900 plants in India, giving Indian companies a legitimacy that potential rivals in places such as China lack.

For Western enterprises, the obvious attraction of outsourcing drug manufacturing to India is that it lowers their costs, enabling them to protect their earnings in an increasingly difficult domestic environment where government health care regulation and increased competition have put pressure on the pricing of many pharmaceuticals. Arguably, this also benefits consumers in the United States because lower pharmaceutical prices mean lower insurance costs, smaller copays, and ultimately lower out-of-pocket expenses than if those pharmaceuticals were still manufactured domestically. Offset against this economic benefit, of course, must be the cost of jobs lost in U.S. pharmaceutical manufacturing. Indicative of this trend, total manufacturing employment in this sector fell by 5 percent between 2008 and 2010.[45]

Case Discussion Questions

1. How might (a) U.S. pharmaceutical companies and (b) U.S. consumers benefit from the rise of the Indian pharmaceutical industry?
2. Who might have lost out as a result of the recent rise of the Indian pharmaceutical industry?
3. Do the benefits from trade with the Indian pharmaceutical sector outweigh the losses?
4. What international trade theory (or theories) best explain the rise of India as a major exporter of pharmaceuticals?

APPENDIX: International Trade and the Balance of Payments

International trade involves the sale of goods and services to residents in other countries (exports) and the purchase of goods and services from residents in other countries (imports). A country's **balance-of-payments accounts** keep track of the payments to and receipts from other countries for a particular time period. These include payments to foreigners for imports of goods and services, and receipts from foreigners for goods and services exported to them. A summary copy of the U.S. balance-of-payments accounts for 2011 is given in Table A.1. Any transaction resulting in a payment to other countries is entered in the balance-of-payments accounts as a debit and given a negative ($-$) sign. Any transaction resulting in a receipt from other countries is entered as a credit and given a positive ($+$) sign. In this appendix, we briefly describe the form of the balance-of-payments accounts, and we discuss whether a current account deficit, often a cause of much concern in the popular press, is something to worry about.

BALANCE-OF-PAYMENTS ACCOUNTS

Balance-of-payments accounts are divided into three main sections: the current account, the capital account, and the financial account (to confuse matters, what is now called the *capital account* was until recently part of the current account, and the *financial account* used to be called the capital account). The **current account** records transactions that pertain to three categories, all of which can be seen in Table A.1. The first category, *goods,* refers to the export or import of physical goods (e.g., agricultural foodstuffs, autos, computers, and chemicals). The second category is the export or import of *services* (e.g., intangible products such as banking and insurance services). The third category, *income receipts and payments,* refers to income from foreign investments and payments that have to be made to foreigners investing in a country. For example, if a U.S. citizen owns a share of a Finnish company and receives a dividend payment of $5, that payment shows up on the U.S. current account as the receipt of $5 of investment income. Also included in the current account are unilateral current transfers, such as U.S. government grants to foreigners (including foreign aid) and private payments to foreigners (such as when a foreign worker in the United States sends money to his or her home country).

A **current account deficit** occurs when a country imports more goods, services, and income than it exports. A **current account surplus** occurs when a country exports more goods, services, and income than it imports. Table A.1 shows that in 2011 the United States ran a current account deficit of $465.9 billion. This is often a headline-grabbing figure and is widely reported in the news media. In recent years, the U.S. current account deficit has been quite large, primarily because America imports far more physical goods than it exports. (The United States typically runs a surplus on trade in services and is close to balance on income payments.)

The 2006 current account deficit of $803 billion was the largest on record and was equivalent to about 6.5 percent of the country's GDP. The deficit has shrunk since then, in response to the economic crisis and prolonged recession of 2008–2009 as much as anything else. Many people find these figures disturbing, the common assumption being that high imports of goods displaces domestic production, causes unemployment, and reduces the growth of the U.S. economy. For example, *The New York Times* responded to the record current account deficit in 2006 by stating:

> A growing trade deficit acts as a drag on overall economic growth. Economists said that they expect that, in light of the new numbers, the government will have to revise its estimate of the nation's fourth quarter gross domestic product to show slightly slower expansion.[46]

TABLE A.1 U.S. Balance-of-Payments Accounts, 2011

Current Account	$ Millions
Exports of goods, services, and income receipts	2,847,988
Goods	1,497,406
Services	605,961
Income receipts	744,621
Imports of goods, services, and income payments	−3,180,861
Goods	−2,235,819
Services	−427,428
Income payments	−517,614
Unilateral current transfers (net)	−133,053
Current account balance	−465,926
Capital Account	
Capital account transactions (net)	−1,212
Financial Account	
U.S.-owned assets abroad (net)	−483,653
U.S. official reserve assets	−15,877
U.S. government assets	−103,666
U.S. private assets	−364,110
Foreign-owned assets in the United States	1,000,990
Foreign official assets in the United States	211,826
Other foreign assets in the United States	14,018
Statistical discrepancy	−89,208

Source: Bureau of Economic Analysis.

However, the issue is somewhat more complex than implied by statements like this. Fully understanding the implications of a large and persistent deficit requires that we look at the rest of the balance-of-payments accounts.

The **capital account** records one-time changes in the stock of assets. As noted earlier, until recently this item was included in the current account. The capital account includes capital transfers, such as debt forgiveness and migrants' transfers (the goods and financial assets that accompany migrants as they enter or leave the country). In the big scheme of things this is a relatively small figure amounting to −$1,212 million in 2011.

The **financial account** (formerly the capital account) records transactions that involve the purchase or sale of assets. Thus, when a German firm purchases stock in a U.S. company or buys a U.S. bond, the transaction enters the U.S. balance of payments as a credit on the capital account. This is because capital is flowing into the country. When capital flows out of the United States, it enters the capital account as a debit.

The financial account is comprised of a number of elements. The net change in U.S.-owned assets abroad includes the change in assets owned by the U.S. government (U.S. official reserve assets and

U.S. government assets) and the change in assets owned by private individuals and corporations. As can be seen from Table A.1, in 2011 there was a –$483 billion reduction in U.S. assets owned abroad due to a fall in the amount of foreign assets owned by the U.S. government and private individuals and corporations. In other words, these entities were selling off foreign assets, such as foreign bonds and currencies, during 2011.

Also included in the financial account are foreign-owned assets in the United States. These are divided into assets owned by foreign governments (foreign official assets) and assets owned by other foreign entities such as corporations and individuals (other foreign assets in the United States). As can be seen, in 2011 foreigners increased their holdings of U.S. assets, including Treasury bills, corporate stocks and bonds, and direct investments in the United States, by $1 trillion. Some $212 billion of this was due to an increase in the holding of U.S. assets by foreign governments, while foreign private corporations and individuals reduced their holdings of U.S. assets by $789 billion.

A basic principle of balance-of-payments accounting is double-entry bookkeeping. Every international transaction automatically enters the balance of payments twice—once as a credit and once as a debit. Imagine that you purchase a car produced in Japan by Toyota for $20,000. Because your purchase represents a payment to another country for goods, it will enter the balance of payments as a debit on the current account. Toyota now has the $20,000 and must do something with it. If Toyota deposits the money at a U.S. bank, Toyota has purchased a U.S. asset—a bank deposit worth $20,000—and the transaction will show up as a $20,000 credit on the financial account. Or Toyota might deposit the cash in a Japanese bank in return for Japanese yen. Now the Japanese bank must decide what to do with the $20,000. Any action that it takes will ultimately result in a credit for the U.S. balance of payments. For example, if the bank lends the $20,000 to a Japanese firm that uses it to import personal computers from the United States, then the $20,000 must be credited to the U.S. balance-of-payments current account. Or the Japanese bank might use the $20,000 to purchase U.S. government bonds, in which case it will show up as a credit on the U.S. balance-of-payments financial account.

Thus, any international transaction automatically gives rise to two offsetting entries in the balance of payments. Because of this, *the sum of the current account balance, the capital account, and the financial account balance should always add up to zero*. In practice, this does not always occur due to the existence of "statistical discrepancies," the source of which need not concern us here (note that in 2011, the statistical discrepancy amounted to –$89 billion).

DOES THE CURRENT ACCOUNT DEFICIT MATTER?

As discussed earlier, there is some concern when a country is running a deficit on the current account of its balance of payments.[47] In recent years, a number of rich countries, including most notably the United States, have run persistent and growing current account deficits. When a country runs a current account deficit, the money that flows to other countries can then be used by those countries to purchase assets in the deficit country. Thus, when the United States runs a trade deficit with China, the Chinese use the money that they receive from U.S. consumers to purchase U.S. assets such as stocks, bonds, and the like. Put another way, a deficit on the current account is financed by selling assets to other countries; that is, by a surplus on the financial account. Thus, the persistent U.S. current account deficit is being financed by a steady sale of U.S. assets (stocks, bonds, real estate, and whole corporations) to other countries. In short, countries that run current account deficits become net debtors.

For example, as a result of financing its current account deficit through asset sales, the United States must deliver a stream of interest payments to foreign bondholders, rents to foreign landowners, and dividends to foreign stockholders. One might argue that such payments to foreigners drain resources from a country and limit the funds available for investment within the country. Since investment within a country is necessary to stimulate economic growth, a persistent current account deficit can choke off a country's future economic growth. This is the basis of the argument that persistent deficits are bad for an economy.

However, things are not this simple. For one thing, in an era of global capital markets money is efficiently directed toward its highest value uses, and over the past quarter of a century many of the highest value uses of capital have been in the United States. So even though capital is flowing out of the United States in the form of payments to foreigners, much of that capital finds its way right back into the country to fund productive investments in the United States. In short, it is not clear that the current account deficit chokes off U.S. economic growth. In fact, notwithstanding the 2008–2009 recession, the U.S. economy has grown substantially over the past 30 years, despite running a persistent current account deficit and despite financing that deficit by selling U.S. assets to foreigners. This is precisely because foreigners reinvest much of the income earned from U.S. assets, and from exports to the United States, right back into the United States. This revisionist view, which has gained in popularity in recent years, suggests that a persistent current account deficit might not be the drag on economic growth it was once thought to be.[48]

Having said this, there is still a nagging fear that at some point the appetite that foreigners have for U.S. assets might decline. If foreigners suddenly reduced their investments in the United States, what would happen? In short, instead of reinvesting the dollars that they earn from exports and investment in the United States back into the country, they would sell those dollars for another currency, European euros, Japanese yen, or Chinese yuan, for example, and invest in euro-, yen-, and yuan-denominated assets instead. This would lead to a fall in the value of the dollar on foreign exchange markets, and that in turn would increase the price of imports, and lower the price of U.S. exports, making them more competitive, which should reduce the overall level of the current account deficit. Thus, in the long run, the persistent U.S. current account deficit could be corrected via a reduction in the value of the U.S. dollar. The concern is that such adjustments may not be smooth. Rather than a controlled decline in the value of the dollar, the dollar might suddenly lose a significant amount of its value in a very short time, precipitating a "dollar crisis."[49] Because the U.S. dollar is the world's major reserve currency, and is held by many foreign governments and banks, any dollar crisis could deliver a body blow to the world economy and at the very least trigger a global economic slowdown. That would not be a good thing.

Endnotes

1. "Transatlantic trading," *The Economist,* February 2, 2013; Andrew Walker, "EU and US free trade talks launched," *BBC News,* February 13, 2013; and Paul Ames, "Parmesan Cheese: Thorn in US-EU free trade deal?" *GlobalPost.com,* February 25, 2013.
2. H. W. Spiegel, *The Growth of Economic Thought* (Durham, NC: Duke University Press, 1991).
3. M. Solis, "The Politics of Self-Restraint: FDI Subsidies and Japanese Mercantilism," *The World Economy* 26 (February 2003), pp. 153–70.
4. A. Browne, "China's Wild Swings Can Roil the Global Economy," *The Wall Street Journal,* October 24, 2005, p. A2; S. H. Hanke, "Stop the Mercantilists," *Forbes,* June 20, 2005, p. 164; G. Dyer and A. Balls, "Dollar Threat as China Signals Shift," *Financial Times,* January 6, 2006, p. 1; Tim Annett, "Righting the Balance," *The Wall Street Journal,* January 10, 2007, p. 15; "China's Trade Surplus Peaks," *Financial Times,* January 12, 2008, p. 1; W. Chong, "China's Trade Surplus to U.S. to Narrow," *China Daily,* December 7, 2009; A. Wang and K. Yao, "China's Trade Surplus Dips, Taking Heat off Yuan," *Reuters,* January 9, 2011; and Aaron Back, "China's Trade Surplus Shrank in '11," *The Wall Street Journal,* January 11, 2012.
5. S. Hollander, *The Economics of David Ricardo* (Buffalo: University of Toronto Press, 1979).
6. D. Ricardo, *The Principles of Political Economy and Taxation* (Homewood, IL: Irwin, 1967, first published in 1817).
7. For example, R. Dornbusch, S. Fischer, and P. Samuelson, "Comparative Advantage: Trade and Payments in a Ricardian Model with a Continuum of Goods," *American Economic Review* 67 (December 1977), pp. 823–39.

8. B. Balassa, "An Empirical Demonstration of Classic Comparative Cost Theory," *Review of Economics and Statistics,* 1963, pp. 231–38.

9. See P. R. Krugman, "Is Free Trade Passé?" *Journal of Economic Perspectives* 1 (Fall 1987), pp. 131–44.

10. P. Samuelson, "Where Ricardo and Mill Rebut and Confirm Arguments of Mainstream Economists Supporting Globalization," *Journal of Economic Perspectives* 18, no. 3 (Summer 2004), pp. 135–46.

11. P. Samuelson, "The Gains from International Trade Once Again," *Economic Journal* 72 (1962), pp. 820–29.

12. S. Lohr, "An Elder Challenges Outsourcing's Orthodoxy," *The New York Times,* September 9, 2004, p. C1.

13. P. Engardio, A. Bernstein, and M. Kripalani, "Is Your Job Next?" *BusinessWeek,* February 3, 2003, pp. 50–60; "America's Pain, India's Gain," *The Economist,* January 11, 2003, p. 57; M. Schroeder and T. Aeppel, "Skilled Workers Mount Opposition to Free Trade, Swaying Politicians," *The Wall Street Journal,* October 10, 2003, pp. A1, A11; D. Clark, "New U.S. Fees on Visas Irk Outsources," *The Wall Street Journal,* August 16, 2010, p. 6; and J. R. Hagerty, "U.S. Loses High Tech Jobs as R&D Shifts to Asia," *The Wall Street Journal,* January 18, 2012, p. B1.

14. Samuelson, "Where Ricardo and Mill Rebut and Confirm Arguments of Mainstream Economists Supporting Globalization," p, 143.

15. D. H. Autor, D. Dorn, and Gordon H. Hanson. "The China Syndrome: Local Labor Market Effects of Import Competition in the United States," *MIT Working Paper,* August 2011.

16. See A. Dixit and G. Grossman, "Samuelson Says Nothing about Trade Policy," Princeton University, 2004, accessed from http://depts.washington.edu/teclass/ThinkEcon/readings/Kalles/Dixit%20and%20Grossman%20on%20Samuelson.pdf

17. J. R. Hagerty, "U.S. Loses High Tech Jobs as R&D Shifts to Asia," *The Wall Street Journal,* January 18, 2012, p. B1.

18. For example, J. D. Sachs and A. Warner, "Economic Reform and the Process of Global Integration," *Brookings Papers on Economic Activity,* 1995, pp. 1–96; J. A. Frankel and D. Romer, "Does Trade Cause Growth?" *American Economic Review* 89, no. 3 (June 1999), pp. 379–99; and D. Dollar and A. Kraay, "Trade, Growth and Poverty," Working Paper, Development Research Group, World Bank, June 2001. Also, for an accessible discussion of the relationship between free trade and economic growth, see T. Taylor, "The Truth about Globalization," *Public Interest,* Spring 2002, pp. 24–44; D. Acemoglu, S. Johnson, and J. Robinson, "The Rise of Europe: Atlantic Trade, Institutional Change and Economic Growth," *American Economic Review* 95, no. 3 (2005), pp. 547–79; and T. Singh, "Does International Trade Cause Economic Growth?" *The World Economy* 33, no. 11 (2010), pp. 1517–64.

19. Sachs and Warner, "Economic Reform and the Process of Global Integration."

20. Ibid., pp. 35–36.

21. R. Wacziarg and K. H. Welch, "Trade Liberalization and Growth: New Evidence," *National Bureau of Economic Research Working Paper Series,* working paper no. 10152, December 2003.

22. Singh, "Does International Trade Cause Economic Growth?"

23. Frankel and Romer, "Does Trade Cause Growth?"

24. A recent skeptical review of the empirical work on the relationship between trade and growth questions these results. See Francisco Rodriguez and Dani Rodrik, "Trade Policy and Economic Growth: A Skeptics Guide to the Cross-National Evidence," *National Bureau of Economic Research Working Paper Series,* working paper no. 7081, April 1999. Even these authors, however, cannot find any evidence that trade hurts economic growth or income levels.

25. B. Ohlin, *Interregional and International Trade* (Cambridge, MA: Harvard University Press, 1933). For a summary, see R. W. Jones and J. P. Neary, "The Positive Theory of International Trade," in *Handbook of International Economics,* R. W. Jones and P. B. Kenen, eds. (Amsterdam: North Holland, 1984).

26. W. Leontief, "Domestic Production and Foreign Trade: The American Capital Position Re-examined," *Proceedings of the American Philosophical Society* 97 (1953), pp. 331–49.

27. R. M. Stern and K. Maskus, "Determinants of the Structure of U.S. Foreign Trade," *Journal of International Economics* 11 (1981), pp. 207–44.

28. See H. P. Bowen, E. E. Leamer, and L. Sveikayskas, "Multicountry, Multifactor Tests of the Factor Abundance Theory," *American Economic Review* 77 (1987), pp. 791–809.

29. D. Trefler, "The Case of the Missing Trade and Other Mysteries," *American Economic Review* 85 (December 1995), pp. 1029–46.

30. D. R. Davis and D. E. Weinstein, "An Account of Global Factor Trade," *American Economic Review,* December 2001, pp. 1423–52.

31. R. Vernon, "International Investments and International Trade in the Product Life Cycle," *Quarterly Journal of Economics,* May 1966, pp. 190–207; and R. Vernon and L. T. Wells, *The Economic Environment of International Business,* 4th ed. (Englewood Cliffs, NJ: Prentice Hall, 1986).

32. For a good summary of this literature, see E. Helpman and P. Krugman, *Market Structure and Foreign Trade: Increasing Returns, Imperfect Competition, and the International Economy* (Boston: MIT Press, 1985). Also see P. Krugman, "Does the New Trade Theory Require a New Trade Policy?" *World Economy* 15, no. 4 (1992), pp. 423–41.

33. M. B. Lieberman and D. B. Montgomery, "First-Mover Advantages," *Strategic Management Journal* 9 (Summer 1988), pp. 41–58; and W. T. Robinson and Sungwook Min, "Is the First to Market the First to Fail?" *Journal of Marketing Research* 29 (2002), pp. 120–28.

34. J. R. Tybout, "Plant and Firm Level Evidence on New Trade Theories," *National Bureau of Economic Research Working Paper Series,* working paper no. 8418, August 2001 (paper available at www.nber.org); and S. Deraniyagala and B. Fine, "New Trade Theory versus Old Trade Policy: A Continuing Enigma," *Cambridge Journal of Economics* 25 (November 2001), pp. 809–25.

35. A. D. Chandler, *Scale and Scope* (New York: Free Press, 1990).

36. Krugman, "Does the New Trade Theory Require a New Trade Policy?"

37. M. E. Porter, *The Competitive Advantage of Nations* (New York: Free Press, 1990). For a good review of this book, see R. M. Grant, "Porter's Competitive Advantage of Nations: An Assessment," *Strategic Management Journal* 12 (1991), pp. 535–48.

38. B. Kogut, ed., *Country Competitiveness: Technology and the Organizing of Work* (New York: Oxford University Press, 1993).

39. Porter, *The Competitive Advantage of Nations,* p. 121.

40. Lieberman and Montgomery, "First-Mover Advantages." See also Robinson and Min, "Is the First to Market the First to Fail?"; W. Boulding and M. Christen, "First Mover Disadvantage," *Harvard Business Review,* October 2001, pp. 20–21; and R. Agarwal and M. Gort, "First Mover Advantage and the Speed of Competitive Entry," *Journal of Law and Economics* 44 (2001), pp. 131–59.

41. C. A. Hamilton, "Building Better Machine Tools," *Journal of Commerce,* October 30, 1991, p. 8; and "Manufacturing Trouble," *The Economist,* October 12, 1991, p. 71.

42. Jain, Arun Kumar, *Corporate Excellence – Growth Strategies under Constraints,* AIMA, 1996.

43. Jain, Arun Kumar, *Competitive Excellence – Critical Success Factors,* Vikas Publishing, 2000 (2nd edition).

44. Adapted from Jain, Arun Kumar, 'Competitive Excellence, Critical Success Factors', Vikas, 2000. (2nd print)

45. H. Timmons, "A Pharmaceutical Future," *The New York Times,* July 7, 2010, pp. B1, B4; K. K. Sharma, "On the World Stage," *Business Today,* January 9, 2011, pp. 116–17; M. Velterop, "The Indian Perspective," *Pharmaceutical Technology Europe,* September 2010, pp. 40–41; and "Pharma Exports Expected to Touch Rs 75,000 in 2012–2013," *Business Standard,* February 27, 2013.

46. J. W. Peters, "U.S. Trade Deficit Grew to Another Record in 06," *The New York Times,* February 14, 2007, p. 1.

47. P. Krugman, *The Age of Diminished Expectations* (Cambridge, MA: MIT Press, 1990).

48. D. Griswold, "Are Trade Deficits a Drag on U.S. Economic Growth?" *Free Trade Bulletin,* March 12, 2007; and O. Blanchard, "Current Account Deficits in Rich Countries," *National Bureau of Economic Research Working Paper Series,* working paper no. 12925, February 2007.

49. S. Edwards, "The U.S. Current Account Deficit: Gradual Correction or Abrupt Adjustment?" *National Bureau of Economic Research Working Paper Series,* working paper no. 12154, April 2006.

Chapter 7
The Political Economy of International Trade

LEARNING OBJECTIVES

After reading this chapter you will be able to:

LO7-1 Identify the policy instruments used by governments to influence international trade flows.

LO7-2 Understand why governments sometimes intervene in international trade.

LO7-3 Summarize and explain the arguments against strategic trade policy.

LO7-4 Describe the development of the world trading system and the current trade issue.

LO7-5 Explain the implications for managers of developments in the world trading system.

CHINA LIMITS EXPORTS OF RARE EARTH METALS

Opening Case

Rare earth metals are a set of 17 chemical elements in the periodic table and include scandium, yttrium, cerium, and lanthanum. Small concentrations of these metals are a crucial ingredient in the manufacture of a wide range of high-technology products, including wind turbines, iPhones, industrial magnets, and the batteries used in hybrid cars. Extracting rare earth metals can be a dirty process due to the toxic acids that are used during the refining process. As a consequence, strict environmental regulations have made it extremely expensive to extract and refine rare earth metals in many countries.

Environmental restrictions in countries such as Australia, Canada, and the United States have opened the way for China to become the world's leading producer and exporter of rare earth metals. In 1990, China accounted for 27 percent of global rare earth production. By 2010, this figure had surged to 97 percent. In 2010, China sent shock waves through the high-tech manufacturing community when it imposed tight quotas on the exports of rare earths. In 2009, it exported around 50,000 tons of rare earths. The 2010 quota limited exports to 30,000 tons. The quota remained in effect for 2011 and was increased marginally to 30,996 tons in 2012.

The reason offered by China for imposing the export quota is that several of its own mining companies didn't meet environmental standards and had to be shut down. The effect, however, was to dramatically increase prices for rare earth metals outside of China, putting foreign manufacturers at a cost disadvantage. Many observers quickly concluded that the imposition of export quotas was an attempt by China to give its domestic manufacturers a cost advantage and to encourage foreign manufacturers to move more production to China so that they could get access to lower-cost supplies of rare earths. As news magazine *The Economist* concluded, "Slashing their exports of rare earth metals has little to do with dwindling supplies or environmental concerns. It's all about moving Chinese manufacturers up the supply chain, so they can sell valuable finished goods to the world rather than lowly raw materials." In other words, China may have been using trade policy to support its industrial policy.

Developed countries cried foul, claiming that the export quotas violate China's obligations under World Trade Organization (WTO) rules. In July 2012 the WTO responded by launching its own investigation. Commenting on the investigation, a U.S. administration official said that the export quotas were part of a "deeply rooted industrial policy aimed at providing substantial competitive advantages for Chinese manufacturers at the expense of non-Chinese manufacturers."

In the meantime, the world is not sitting still. In response to the high prices for rare earth metals, many companies have been redesigning their products to use substitute materials. Toyota, Renault, and Tesla, for example—all major automotive consumers of rare earth products—have stated that they plan to stop using parts that have rare earth elements in their cars. Governments have also tried to encourage private mining companies to expand their production of rare earth metals. By 2012, there were some 350 rare earth mine projects under development outside of China and India. An example, Molycorp, a U.S. mining company is quickly boosting its rare earth production at a California mine and claims that by the end of 2012 its production was at an annual rate of 19,000 tons per year.[1]

INTRODUCTION

The review of the classical trade theories of Smith, Ricardo, and Heckscher-Ohlin in Chapter 6 showed that in a world without trade barriers, trade patterns are determined by the relative productivity of different factors of production in different countries. Countries will specialize in products that they can make most efficiently, while importing products that they can produce less efficiently. Chapter 6 also laid out the intellectual case for free trade. Remember, **free trade** refers to a situation in which a government does not attempt to restrict what its citizens can buy from or sell to another country. As we saw in Chapter 6, the theories of Smith, Ricardo, and Heckscher-Ohlin predict that the consequences of free trade include both static economic gains (because free trade supports a higher level of domestic consumption and more efficient utilization of resources) and dynamic economic gains (because free trade stimulates economic growth and the creation of wealth).

This chapter looks at the political reality of international trade. Although many nations are nominally committed to free trade, they tend to intervene in international trade to protect the interests of politically important groups or promote the interests of key domestic producers. The opening case illustrates one such situation. In 2010, China imposed a quota on exports of rare earth metals, reducing export supply by 40 percent. Because China at the time accounted for 95 percent of global production of rare earth metals, which are a crucial ingredient in many high-tech products, the immediate effect was to drive up the price of rare earths outside of China and, hence, the production costs of foreign manufacturers. In other words, the policy created an environment that gave Chinese manufacturers a competitive advantage over their foreign rivals. Several developed nations have protested this decision, and the World Trade Organization (WTO) initiated an investigation in July 2012. How this dispute plays out remains to be seen (it may be two years before the WTO reports its findings), but it presents us with a clear example of government intervention in international trade that is designed to protect the interests of domestic producers.

This chapter explores the political and economic reasons that governments have for intervening in international trade. When governments intervene, they often do so by restricting imports of goods and services into their nation, while adopting policies that promote domestic production and exports. Normally, their motives are to protect domestic producers. In recent years, social issues have intruded into the decision-making calculus. In the United States, for example, a movement is growing to ban imports of goods from countries that do not abide by the same labor, health, and environmental regulations as the United States.

This chapter starts by describing the range of policy instruments that governments use to intervene in international trade. A detailed review of governments' various political and economic motives for intervention follows. In the third section of this chapter, we consider how the case for free trade stands up in view of the various justifications given for government intervention in international trade. Then we look at the emergence of the modern international trading system, which is based on the General Agreement on Tariffs and Trade (GATT) and its successor, the WTO. The GATT and WTO are the creations of a series of multinational treaties. The final section of this chapter discusses the implications of this material for management practice.

INSTRUMENTS OF TRADE POLICY

Trade policy uses seven main instruments: tariffs, subsidies, import quotas, voluntary export restraints, local content requirements, administrative policies, and antidumping duties. Tariffs are the oldest and simplest instrument of trade policy. As we shall see later in this chapter, they are also the instrument that the GATT and WTO have been most successful in limiting. A fall in tariff barriers in recent decades has been accompanied by a rise in nontariff barriers, such as subsidies, quotas, voluntary export restraints, and antidumping duties.

Tariffs

A **tariff** is a tax levied on imports (or exports). Tariffs fall into two categories. **Specific tariffs** are levied as a fixed charge for each unit of a good imported (e.g., $3 per barrel of oil). **Ad valorem tariffs** are levied as a proportion of the value of the imported good. In most cases, tariffs are placed on imports to protect domestic producers from foreign competition by raising the price of imported goods. However, tariffs also produce revenue for the government. Until the income tax was introduced, for example, the U.S. government received most of its revenues from tariffs.

The important thing to understand about an import tariff is who suffers and who gains. The government gains, because the tariff increases government revenues. Domestic producers gain, because the tariff affords them some protection against foreign competitors by increasing the cost of imported foreign goods. Consumers lose because they must pay more for certain imports. For example, in 2002 the U.S. government placed an ad valorem tariff of 8 to 30 percent on imports of foreign steel. The idea was to protect domestic steel producers from cheap imports of foreign steel. The effect, however, was to raise the price of steel products in the United States between 30 and 50 percent. A number of U.S. steel consumers, ranging from appliance makers to automobile companies, objected that the steel tariffs would raise their costs of production and make it more difficult for them to compete in the global marketplace. Whether the gains to the government and domestic producers exceed the loss to consumers depends on various factors, such as the amount of the tariff, the importance of the imported good to domestic consumers, the number of jobs saved in the protected industry, and so on. In the steel case, many argued that the losses to steel consumers apparently outweighed the gains to steel producers. In November 2003, the World Trade Organization declared that the tariffs represented a violation of the WTO treaty, and the United States removed them in December of that year.

In general, two conclusions can be derived from economic analysis of the effect of import tariffs.[2] First, tariffs are generally pro-producer and anticonsumer. While they protect producers from foreign competitors, this restriction of supply also raises domestic prices. For example, a study by Japanese economists calculated that tariffs on imports of foodstuffs, cosmetics, and chemicals into Japan cost the average Japanese consumer about $890 per year in the form of higher prices. Almost all studies find that import tariffs impose significant costs on domestic consumers in the form of higher prices. Second, import tariffs reduce the overall efficiency of the world economy. They reduce efficiency because a protective tariff encourages domestic firms to produce products at home that, in theory, could be produced more efficiently abroad. The consequence is an inefficient utilization of resources.

Sometimes tariffs are levied on exports of a product from a country. Export tariffs are less common than import tariffs. In general, export tariffs have two objectives: first, to raise revenue for the government, and second, to reduce exports from a sector, often for political reasons. For example, in 2004 China imposed a tariff on textile exports. The primary objective was to moderate the growth in exports of textiles from China, thereby alleviating tensions with other trading partners.

Subsidies

A **subsidy** is a government payment to a domestic producer. Subsidies take many forms, including cash grants, low-interest loans, tax breaks, and government equity participation in domestic firms. By lowering production costs, subsidies help domestic producers in two ways: (1) competing against foreign imports and (2) gaining export markets. Agriculture tends to be one of the largest beneficiaries of subsidies in most countries. The European Union has been paying out about €44 billion annually ($55 billion) in farm subsidies. The farm bill that passed the U.S. Congress in 2007 contained subsidies of $289 billion for the next 10 years. The Japanese also have a long history of supporting inefficient domestic producers with farm subsidies. According to the World Trade Organization, in mid-2000 countries spent some $300 billion on subsidies, $250 billion of which was spent by 21 developed nations.[4] In response to a severe sales slump following the global financial crisis, between mid-2008 and mid-2009, some developed nations gave $45 billion in subsidies to their automobile makers. While the purpose of the subsidies was to help them survive a very difficult economic climate, one of the consequences was to give subsidized companies an unfair competitive advantage in the global auto industry. Somewhat ironically given the government bailouts of U.S. auto companies during the global financial crisis, in 2012 the Obama administration filed a complaint with the WTO arguing that the Chinese were illegally subsidizing exports of autos and auto parts. Details are given in the above Country Focus feature.

The main gains from subsidies accrue to domestic producers, whose international competitiveness is increased as a result. Advocates of strategic trade policy (which, as you will recall from Chapter 6, is an outgrowth of the new trade theory) favor subsidies to help domestic firms achieve a dominant position

Are the Chinese Illegally Subsidizing Auto Exports?

In late 2012, during the presidential election campaign, the Obama administration filed a complaint against China with the World Trade Organization. The complaint claims that China is providing export subsidies to its auto and auto parts industries. The subsidies include cash grants for exporting, grants for R&D, subsidies to pay interest on loans, and preferential tax treatment.

The United States estimates the value of the subsidies to be at least $1 billion between 2009 and 2011. The complaint also points out that in the years 2002 through 2011, the value of China's exports of autos and auto parts increased more than ninefold from $7.4 billion to $69.1 billion. The United States was China's largest market for exports of auto parts during this period. The United States is asserting that, to some degree, this growth may have been helped by subsidies. The complaint goes on to claim that these subsidies have hurt producers of automobiles and auto parts in the United States. This is a large industry in the United States, employing over 800,000 people and generating some $350 billion in sales.

While some in the labor movement applauded the move, the response from U.S. auto companies and auto parts producers was muted. One reason for this is that many U.S. producers do business in China and, in all probability, want to avoid retaliation from the Chinese government. GM, for example, has a joint venture and two wholly owned subsidiaries in China and is doing very well there. In addition, some U.S. producers benefit by purchasing cheap Chinese auto parts, so any retaliatory tariffs imposed on those imports might actually raise their costs.

More cynical observers saw the move as nothing more than political theater. The week before the complaint was filed, the Republican presidential candidate, Mitt Romney, had accused the Obama administration of "failing American workers" by not labeling China a currency manipulator. So perhaps the complaint was in part simply another move on the presidential campaign chessboard. In any event, the WTO does not move fast, so it will be at least a year, if not two, before a ruling is issued.[3]

in those industries in which economies of scale are important and the world market is not large enough to profitably support more than a few firms (aerospace and semiconductors are two such industries). According to this argument, subsidies can help a firm achieve a first-mover advantage in an emerging industry (just as U.S. government subsidies, in the form of substantial R&D grants, allegedly helped Boeing). If this is achieved, further gains to the domestic economy arise from the employment and tax revenues that a major global company can generate. However, government subsidies must be paid for, typically by taxing individuals and corporations.

Whether subsidies generate national benefits that exceed their national costs is debatable. In practice, many subsidies are not that successful at increasing the international competitiveness of domestic producers. Rather, they tend to protect the inefficient and promote excess production. One study estimated that if advanced countries abandoned subsidies to farmers, global trade in agricultural products would be 50 percent higher and the world as a whole would be better off by $160 billion.[5] Another study estimated that removing all barriers to trade in agriculture (both subsidies and tariffs) would raise world income by $182 billion.[6] This increase in wealth arises from the more efficient use of agricultural land.

Import Quotas and Voluntary Export Restraints

An **import quota** is a direct restriction on the quantity of some good that may be imported into a country. The restriction is usually enforced by issuing import licenses to a group of individuals or firms. For example, the United States has a quota on cheese imports. The only firms allowed to import cheese are certain trading companies, each of which is allocated the right to import a maximum number of pounds of cheese each year. In some cases, the right to sell is given directly to the governments of exporting countries. Historically, this was the case for textile imports in the United States. However, the international agreement governing the imposition of import quotas on textiles, the Multi-fiber Agreement, expired on January 1, 2005.

A common hybrid of a quota and a tariff is known as a tariff rate quota. Under a **tariff rate quota,** a lower tariff rate is applied to imports within the quota than those over the quota. For example, as illustrated in Figure 7.1, an ad valorem tariff rate of 10 percent might be levied on 1 million tons of rice imports into South Korea, after which an out-of-quota rate of 80 percent might be applied. Thus, South Korea might import 2 million tons of rice, 1 million at a 10 percent tariff rate and another 1 million at an 80 percent tariff. Tariff rate quotas are common in agriculture, where their goal is to limit imports over quota.

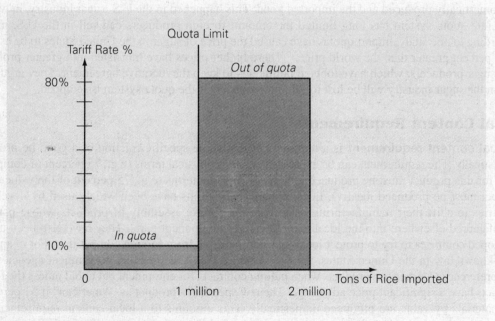

Figure 7.1 *Hypothetical Tariff Rate Quota*

A variant on the import quota is the voluntary export restraint. A **voluntary export restraint (VER)** is a quota on trade imposed by the exporting country, typically at the request of the importing country's government. One of the most famous historical examples is the limitation on auto exports to the United States enforced by Japanese automobile producers in 1981. A response to direct pressure from the U.S. government, this VER limited Japanese imports to no more than 1.68 million vehicles per year. The agreement was revised in 1984 to allow 1.85 million Japanese vehicles per year. The agreement was allowed to lapse in 1985, but the Japanese government indicated its intentions at that time to continue to restrict exports to the United States to 1.85 million vehicles per year.[7] In 2012, Brazil imposed what amounts to voluntary export restraints on shipments of vehicles from Mexico to Brazil. The two countries have a decade-old free trade agreement, but a surge in vehicles heading to Brazil from Mexico prompted Brazil to raise its protectionist walls. Mexico has agreed to quotas on Brazil-bound vehicle exports for the next three years.[8] Foreign producers agree to VERs because they fear more damaging punitive tariffs or import quotas might follow if they do not. Agreeing to a VER is seen as a way to make the best of a bad situation by appeasing protectionist pressures in a country.

As with tariffs and subsidies, both import quotas and VERs benefit domestic producers by limiting import competition. As with all restrictions on trade, quotas do not benefit consumers. An import quota or VER always raises the domestic price of an imported good. When imports are limited to a low percentage of the market by a quota or VER, the price is bid up for that limited foreign supply. The automobile industry VER mentioned earlier increased the price of the limited supply of Japanese imports. According to a study by the U.S. Federal Trade Commission, the automobile VER cost U.S. consumers about $1 billion per year between 1981 and 1985. That $1 billion per year went to Japanese producers in the form of higher prices.[9] The extra profit that producers make when supply is artificially limited by an import quota is referred to as a **quota rent.**

If a domestic industry lacks the capacity to meet demand, an import quota can raise prices for *both* the domestically produced and the imported good. This happened in the U.S. sugar industry, in which a tariff rate quota system has long limited the amount foreign producers can sell in the U.S. market. According to one study, import quotas have caused the price of sugar in the United States to be as much as 40 percent greater than the world price.[10] These higher prices have translated into greater profits for U.S. sugar producers, which have lobbied politicians to keep the lucrative agreement. They argue U.S. jobs in the sugar industry will be lost to foreign producers if the quota system is scrapped.

Local Content Requirements

A **local content requirement** is a requirement that some specific fraction of a good be produced domestically. The requirement can be expressed either in physical terms (e.g., 75 percent of component parts for this product must be produced locally) or in value terms (e.g., 75 percent of the value of this product must be produced locally). Local content regulations have been widely used by developing countries to shift their manufacturing base from the simple assembly of products whose parts are manufactured elsewhere into the local manufacture of component parts. They have also been used in developed countries to try to protect local jobs and industry from foreign competition. For example, a little-known law in the United States, the Buy America Act, specifies that government agencies must give preference to American products when putting contracts for equipment out to bid unless the foreign products have a significant price advantage. The law specifies a product as "American" if 51 percent of the materials by value are produced domestically. This amounts to a local content requirement. If a foreign company, or an American one for that matter, wishes to win a contract from a U.S. government agency to provide some equipment, it must ensure that at least 51 percent of the product by value is manufactured in the United States.

Local content regulations provide protection for a domestic producer of parts in the same way an import quota does: by limiting foreign competition. The aggregate economic effects are also the same; domestic producers benefit, but the restrictions on imports raise the prices of imported components. In turn, higher prices for imported components are passed on to consumers of the final product in the form of higher final prices. So as with all trade policies, local content regulations tend to benefit producers and not consumers.

Administrative Policies

In addition to the formal instruments of trade policy, governments of all types sometimes use informal or administrative policies to restrict imports and boost exports. **Administrative trade policies** are bureaucratic rules designed to make it difficult for imports to enter a country. It has been argued that the Japanese are the masters of this trade barrier. In recent decades, Japan's formal tariff and nontariff barriers have been among the lowest in the world. However, critics charge that the country's informal administrative barriers to imports more than compensate for this. For example, at one point the Netherlands exported tulip bulbs to almost every country in the world except Japan. In Japan, customs inspectors insisted on checking every tulip bulb by cutting it vertically down the middle, and even Japanese ingenuity could not put any back together. Federal Express also initially had a tough time expanding its global express shipping services into Japan because Japanese customs inspectors insist on opening a large proportion of express packages to check for pornography, a process that delayed an "express" package for days. As with all instruments of trade policy, administrative instruments benefit producers and hurt consumers, who are denied access to possibly superior foreign products.

Antidumping Policies

In the context of international trade, **dumping** is variously defined as selling goods in a foreign market at below their costs of production or as selling goods in a foreign market at below their "fair" market value. There is a difference between these two definitions; the fair market value of a good is normally judged to be greater than the costs of producing that good because the former includes a "fair" profit margin. Dumping is viewed as a method by which firms unload excess production in foreign markets. Some dumping may be the result of predatory behavior, with producers using substantial profits from their home markets to subsidize prices in a foreign market with a view to driving indigenous competitors out of that market. Once this has been achieved, so the argument goes, the predatory firm can raise prices and earn substantial profits.

An alleged example of dumping occurred in 1997, when two South Korean manufacturers of semiconductors, LG Semicon and Hyundai Electronics, were accused of selling dynamic random access memory (DRAM) chips in the U.S. market at below their costs of production. This action occurred in the middle of a worldwide glut of chip-making capacity. It was alleged that the firms were trying to unload their excess production in the United States.

Antidumping policies are designed to punish foreign firms that engage in dumping. The ultimate objective is to protect domestic producers from unfair foreign competition. Although antidumping policies vary from country to country, the majority are similar to those used in the United States. If a domestic producer believes that a foreign firm is dumping production in the U.S. market, it can file a petition with two government agencies, the Commerce Department and the International Trade Commission (ITC). In the Korean DRAM case, Micron Technology, a U.S. manufacturer of DRAM chips, filed the petition. The government agencies then investigate the complaint. If a complaint has merit, the Commerce Department may impose an antidumping duty on the offending foreign imports (antidumping duties are often called **countervailing duties**). These duties, which represent a special tariff, can be fairly substantial and stay in place for up to five years. For example, after reviewing Micron's complaint, the Commerce Department imposed 9 percent and 4 percent countervailing duties on LG Semicon and Hyundai DRAM chips, respectively. The accompanying Management Focus discusses another example of how a firm, U.S. Magnesium, used antidumping legislation to gain protection from unfair foreign competitors.

U.S. Magnesium Seeks Protection

In February 2004, U.S. Magnesium, the sole surviving U.S. producer of magnesium, a metal that is primarily used in the manufacture of certain automobile parts and aluminum cans, filed a petition with the U.S. International Trade Commission contending that a surge in imports had caused material damage to the U.S. industry's employment, sales, market share, and profitability. According to U.S. Magnesium, Russian and Chinese producers had been selling the metal at prices significantly below market value. During 2002 and 2003, imports of magnesium into the United States rose 70 percent, while prices fell by 40 percent, and the market share accounted for by imports jumped to 50 percent from 25 percent.

"The United States used to be the largest producer of magnesium in the world," a U.S. Magnesium spokesperson said at the time of the filing. "What's really sad is that you can be state of the art and have modern technology, and if the Chinese, who pay people less than 90 cents an hour, want to run you out of business, they can do it. And that's why we are seeking relief."

During a yearlong investigation, the ITC solicited input from various sides in the dispute. Foreign producers and consumers of magnesium in the United States argued that falling prices for magnesium during 2002 and 2003 simply reflected an imbalance between supply and demand due to additional capacity coming on stream not from Russia or China but from a new Canadian plant that opened in 2001 and from a planned Australian plant. The Canadian plant shut down in 2003, the Australian plant never came on stream, and prices for magnesium rose again in 2004.

Magnesium consumers in the United States also argued to the ITC that imposing antidumping duties on foreign imports of magnesium would raise prices in the United States significantly above world levels. A spokesperson for Alcoa, which mixes magnesium with aluminum to make alloys for cans, predicted that if antidumping duties were imposed, high magnesium prices in the United States would force Alcoa to move some production out of the United States. Alcoa also noted that in 2003, U.S. Magnesium was unable to supply all of Alcoa's needs, forcing the company to turn to imports. Consumers of magnesium in the automobile industry asserted that high prices in the United States would drive engineers to design magnesium out of automobiles, or force manufacturing elsewhere, which would ultimately hurt everyone.

The six members of the ITC were not convinced by these arguments. In March 2005, the ITC ruled that both China and Russia had been dumping magnesium in the United States. The government decided to impose duties ranging from 50 percent to more than 140 percent on imports of magnesium from China. Russian producers faced duties ranging from 19 percent to 22 percent. The duties were to be levied for five years, after which the ITC would revisit the situation. The ITC revoked the antidumping order on Russia in February 2011 but continued the order on China.

According to U.S. Magnesium, the favorable ruling would allow the company to reap the benefits of nearly $50 million in investments made in its manufacturing plant and enable the company to boost its capacity by 28 percent by the end of 2005. Commenting on the favorable ruling, a U.S. Magnesium spokesperson noted, "Once unfair trade is removed from the marketplace we'll be able to compete with anyone." U.S. Magnesium's customers and competitors, however, did not view the situation in the 2002–2003 period as one of unfair trade. While the imposition of antidumping duties no doubt will help to protect U.S. Magnesium and the 400 people it employs from foreign competition, magnesium consumers in the United States are left wondering if they will be the ultimate losers.[11]

THE CASE FOR GOVERNMENT INTERVENTION

Now that we have reviewed the various instruments of trade policy that governments can use, it is time to look at the case for government intervention in international trade. Arguments for government intervention take two paths: political and economic. Political arguments for intervention are concerned with protecting the interests of certain groups within a nation (normally producers), often at the expense of other groups (normally consumers), or with achieving some political objective that lies outside the sphere of economic relationships, such as protecting the environment or human rights. Economic arguments for intervention are typically concerned with boosting the overall wealth of a nation (to the benefit of all, both producers and consumers).

Political Arguments for Intervention

Political arguments for government intervention cover a range of issues, including preserving jobs, protecting industries deemed important for national security, retaliating against unfair foreign competition, protecting consumers from "dangerous" products, furthering the goals of foreign policy, and advancing the human rights of individuals in exporting countries.

Protecting Jobs and Industries

Perhaps the most common political argument for government intervention is that it is necessary for protecting jobs and industries from unfair foreign competition. The tariffs placed on imports of foreign steel by President George W. Bush in 2002 were designed to do this (many steel producers were located in states that Bush needed to win reelection in 2004). A political motive also underlay establishment of the Common Agricultural Policy (CAP) by the European Union. The CAP was designed to protect the jobs of Europe's politically powerful farmers by restricting imports and guaranteeing prices. However, the higher prices that resulted from the CAP have cost Europe's consumers dearly. This is true of many attempts to protect jobs and industries through government intervention. For example, the imposition of steel tariffs in 2002 raised steel prices for American consumers, such as automobile companies, making them less competitive in the global marketplace.

National Security

Countries sometimes argue that it is necessary to protect certain industries because they are important for national security. Defense-related industries often get this kind of attention (e.g., aerospace, advanced electronics, and semiconductors). Although not as common as it used to be, this argument is still made. Those in favor of protecting the U.S. semiconductor industry from foreign competition, for example, argue that semiconductors are now such important components of defense products that it would be dangerous to rely primarily on foreign producers for them. In 1986, this argument helped persuade the federal government to support Sematech, a consortium of 14 U.S. semiconductor companies that accounted for 90 percent of the U.S. industry's revenues. Sematech's mission was to conduct joint research into manufacturing techniques that could be parceled out to members. The government saw the venture as so critical that Sematech was specially protected from antitrust laws. Initially, the U.S. government provided Sematech with $100 million per year in subsidies. By the mid-1990s, however, the U.S. semiconductor industry had regained its leading market position, largely through the personal computer boom and demand for microprocessor chips made by Intel. In 1994, the consortium's board voted to seek an end to federal funding, and since 1996 the consortium has been funded entirely by private money.[12]

Retaliation

Some argue that governments should use the threat to intervene in trade policy as a bargaining tool to help open foreign markets and force trading partners to "play by the rules of the game." The U.S. government has used the threat of punitive trade sanctions to try to get the Chinese government to enforce its intellectual property laws. Lax enforcement of these laws had given rise to massive copyright infringements in China that had been costing U.S. companies such as Microsoft hundreds of millions of dollars per year in lost sales revenues. After the United States threatened to impose 100 percent tariffs on a range of Chinese imports, and after harsh words between officials from the two countries, the Chinese agreed to tighter enforcement of intellectual property regulations.[13]

If it works, such a politically motivated rationale for government intervention may liberalize trade and bring with it resulting economic gains. It is a risky strategy, however. A country that is being pressured may not back down and instead may respond to the imposition of punitive tariffs by raising trade barriers of its own. This is exactly what the Chinese government threatened to do when pressured by the United States, although it ultimately did back down. If a government does not back down, the results could be higher trade barriers all around and an economic loss to all involved.

Protecting Consumers

Many governments have long had regulations to protect consumers from unsafe products. The indirect effect of such regulations often is to limit or ban the importation of such products. For example, in 2003 several countries, including Japan and South Korea, decided to ban imports of American beef after a single case of mad cow disease was found in Washington State. The ban was motivated to protect consumers from what was seen to be an unsafe product. Together, Japan and South Korea accounted for about $2 billion of U.S. beef sales, so the ban had a significant impact on U.S. beef producers. After two years, both countries lifted the ban, although they placed stringent requirements on U.S. beef imports to reduce the risk of importing beef that might be tainted by mad cow disease (e.g., Japan required that all beef must come from cattle under 21 months of age). The accompanying Country Focus describes how the European Union banned the sale and importation of hormone-treated beef. The ban was motivated by a desire to protect European consumers from the possible health consequences of eating meat from animals treated with growth hormones.

Furthering Foreign Policy Objectives

Governments sometimes use trade policy to support their foreign policy objectives.[14] A government may grant preferential trade terms to a country with which it wants to build strong relations. Trade policy has also been used several times to pressure or punish "rogue states" that do not abide by international law or norms. Iraq labored under extensive trade sanctions after the UN coalition defeated the country in the 1991 Gulf War until the 2003 invasion of Iraq by U.S.-led forces. The theory is that such pressure might persuade the rogue state to mend its ways, or it might hasten a change of government. In the case of Iraq, the sanctions were seen as a way of forcing that country to comply with several UN resolutions. The United States has maintained long-running trade sanctions against Cuba. Their principal function is to impoverish Cuba in the hope that the resulting economic hardship will lead to the downfall of Cuba's Communist government and its replacement with a more democratically inclined (and pro-U.S.) regime. The United States has also had trade sanctions in place against Libya and Iran, both of which were

Trade in Hormone-Treated Beef

In the 1970s, scientists discovered how to synthesize certain hormones and use them to accelerate the growth rate of livestock animals, reduce the fat content of meat, and increase milk production. Bovine somatotropin (BST), a growth hormone produced by cattle, was first synthesized by the biotechnology firm Genentech. Injections of BST could be used to supplement an animal's own hormone production and increase its growth rate. These hormones became popular among farmers, who found they could cut costs and help satisfy consumer demands for leaner meat. Although these hormones occurred naturally in animals, consumer groups in several countries soon raised concerns about the practice. They argued that the use of hormone supplements was unnatural and that the health consequences of consuming hormone-treated meat were unknown but might include hormonal irregularities and cancer.

The European Union responded to these concerns in 1989 by banning the importation of hormone-treated meat and the use of growth-promoting hormones in the production of livestock. The ban was controversial because a reasonable consensus existed among scientists that the hormones posed no health risk. Although the EU banned hormone-treated meat, many other countries did not, including big meat-producing countries such as Australia, Canada, New Zealand, and the United States. The use of hormones soon became widespread in these countries. According to trade officials outside the EU, the European ban constituted an unfair restraint on trade. As a result of this ban, exports of meat to the EU fell. For example, U.S. red meat exports to the EU declined from $231 million in 1988 to $98 million in 1994. The complaints of meat exporters were bolstered in 1995 when Codex Alimentarius, the international food standards body of the UN's Food and Agriculture Organization and the World Health Organization, approved the use of growth hormones. In making this decision, Codex reviewed the scientific literature and found no evidence of a link between the consumption of hormone-treated meat and human health problems, such as cancer.

Fortified by such decisions, in 1995 the United States pressed the EU to drop the import ban on hormone-treated beef. The EU refused, citing "consumer concerns about food safety." In response, Canada and the United States filed formal complaints with the World Trade Organization. They were soon joined by a number of other countries, including Australia and New Zealand. The WTO created a trade panel of three independent experts. After reviewing evidence and hearing from a range of experts and representatives of both parties, the panel in May 1997 ruled that the EU ban on hormone-treated beef was illegal because it had no scientific justification.

This ruling left the EU in a difficult position. Legally, the EU had to lift the ban or face punitive sanctions, but the ban had wide public support in Europe. The EU feared that lifting the ban could produce a consumer backlash. Instead the EU did nothing. In February 1999 the United States asked the WTO for permission to impose punitive sanctions on the EU. The WTO responded by allowing the United States to impose punitive tariffs valued at $125 million on EU exports to the United States. The EU decided to accept these tariffs rather than lift the ban on hormone-treated beef. In 2012, the EU struck a deal with the United States that allowed it to keep the ban in place, in return for increasing its import quota of high-quality non-hormone-treated beef from the United States. In response, the U.S. lifted its punitive tariffs on EU food exports, thereby ending one of the longest running trade disputes in history.[15]

accused of supporting terrorist action against U.S. interests and building weapons of mass destruction. In late 2003, the sanctions against Libya seemed to yield some returns when that country announced it would terminate a program to build nuclear weapons. The U.S. government responded by relaxing those sanctions. The U.S. government is now using trade sanctions to try and pressure the Iranian government to halt its alleged nuclear weapons program, with limited success as of 2013.

Other countries can undermine unilateral trade sanctions. The U.S. sanctions against Cuba, for example, have not stopped other Western countries from trading with Cuba. The U.S. sanctions have done little more than help create a vacuum into which other trading nations, such as Canada and Germany, have stepped.

Protecting Human Rights

Protecting and promoting human rights in other countries is an important element of foreign policy for many democracies. Governments sometimes use trade policy to try to improve the human rights policies of trading partners. For example, as discussed in Chapter 5, the U.S. government long had trade sanctions in place against the nation of Myanmar, in no small part due to the poor human rights practices in that nation. In late 2012 the U.S. said that it would ease trade sanctions against Myanmar in response to democratic reforms in that country. Similarly, in the 1980s and 1990s, Western governments used trade sanctions against South Africa as a way of pressuring that nation to drop its apartheid policies, which were seen as a violation of basic human rights.

Economic Arguments for Intervention

With the development of the new trade theory and strategic trade policy (see Chapter 6), the economic arguments for government intervention have undergone a renaissance in recent years. Until the early 1980s, most economists saw little benefit in government intervention and strongly advocated a free trade policy. This position has changed at the margins with the development of strategic trade policy, although as we will see in the next section, there are still strong economic arguments for sticking to a free trade stance.

The Infant Industry Argument

The **infant industry argument** is by far the oldest economic argument for government intervention. Alexander Hamilton proposed it in 1792. According to this argument, many developing countries have a potential comparative advantage in manufacturing, but new manufacturing industries cannot initially compete with established industries in developed countries. To allow manufacturing to get a toehold, the argument is that governments should temporarily support new industries (with tariffs, import quotas, and subsidies) until they have grown strong enough to meet international competition.

This argument has had substantial appeal for the governments of developing nations during the past 50 years, and the GATT has recognized the infant industry argument as a legitimate reason for protectionism. Nevertheless, many economists remain critical of this argument for two main reasons. First, protection of manufacturing from foreign competition does no good unless the protection helps make the industry efficient. In case after case, however, protection seems to have done little more than foster the development of inefficient industries that have little hope of ever competing in the world market. Brazil, for example, built the world's tenth-largest auto industry behind tariff barriers and quotas. Once those barriers were removed in the late 1980s, however, foreign imports soared, and the industry was forced to face up to the fact that after 30 years of protection, the Brazilian auto industry was one of the world's most inefficient.[16]

Second, the infant industry argument relies on an assumption that firms are unable to make efficient long-term investments by borrowing money from the domestic or international capital market. Consequently, governments have been required to subsidize long-term investments. Given the development of global capital markets over the past 20 years, this assumption no longer looks as valid as it once did. Today, if a developing country has a potential comparative advantage in a manufacturing industry, firms in that country should be able to borrow money from the capital markets to finance the required investments. Given financial support, firms based in countries with a potential comparative advantage have an incentive to endure the necessary initial losses in order to make long-run gains without requiring government protection. Many Taiwanese and South Korean firms did this in industries such as textiles, semiconductors, machine tools, steel, and shipping. Thus, given efficient global capital markets, the only industries that would require government protection would be those that are not worthwhile.

Strategic Trade Policy

Some new trade theorists have proposed the strategic trade policy argument.[17] We reviewed the basic argument in Chapter 6 when we considered the new trade theory. The new trade theory argues that in industries in which the existence of substantial economies of scale implies that the world market will profitably support only a few firms, countries may predominate in the export of certain products simply because they have firms that were able to capture first-mover advantages. The long-term dominance of Boeing in the commercial aircraft industry has been attributed to such factors.

The **strategic trade policy** argument has two components. First, it is argued that by appropriate actions, a government can help raise national income if it can somehow ensure that the firm or firms that gain first-mover advantages in an industry are domestic rather than foreign enterprises. Thus, according to the strategic trade policy argument, a government should use subsidies to support promising firms that are active in newly emerging industries. Advocates of this argument point out that the substantial R&D grants that the U.S. government gave Boeing in the 1950s and 1960s probably helped tilt the field of competition in the newly emerging market for passenger jets in Boeing's favor. (Boeing's first commercial jet airliner, the 707, was derived from a military plane.) Similar arguments have been made with regard to Japan's dominance in the production of liquid crystal display screens (used in computers). Although these screens were invented in the United States, the Japanese government, in cooperation with major electronics companies, targeted this industry for research support in the late 1970s and early 1980s. The result was that Japanese firms, not U.S. firms, subsequently captured first-mover advantages in this market.

The second component of the strategic trade policy argument is that it might pay a government to intervene in an industry by helping domestic firms overcome the barriers to entry created by foreign firms that have already reaped first-mover advantages. This argument underlies government support of Airbus, Boeing's major competitor. Formed in 1966 as a consortium of four companies from Great Britain, France, Germany, and Spain, Airbus had less than 5 percent of the world commercial aircraft market when it began production in the mid-1970s. By 2011, it had increased its share to 64 percent, threatening Boeing's long-term dominance of the market. How did Airbus achieve this? According to the U.S. government, the answer is a $15 billion subsidy from the governments of Great Britain, France, Germany, and Spain.[18] Without this subsidy, Airbus would never have been able to break into the world market.

If these arguments are correct, they support a rationale for government intervention in international trade. Governments should target technologies that may be important in the future and use subsidies to support development work aimed at commercializing those technologies. Furthermore, government should provide export subsidies until the domestic firms have established first-mover advantages in the world market. Government support may also be justified if it can help domestic firms overcome the first-mover advantages enjoyed by foreign competitors and emerge as viable competitors in the world market (as in the Airbus and semiconductor examples). In this case, a combination of home-market protection and export-promoting subsidies may be needed.

THE REVISED CASE FOR FREE TRADE   ⬛ LO 7-3 ⬛

The strategic trade policy arguments of the new trade theorists suggest an economic justification for government intervention in international trade. This justification challenges the rationale for unrestricted free trade found in the work of classic trade theorists such as Adam Smith and David Ricardo. In response to this challenge to economic orthodoxy, a number of economists—including some of those responsible for the development of the new trade theory, such as Paul Krugman—point out that although strategic trade policy looks appealing in theory, in practice it may be unworkable. This response to the strategic trade policy argument constitutes the revised case for free trade.[19]

Retaliation and Trade War

Krugman argues that a strategic trade policy aimed at establishing domestic firms in a dominant position in a global industry is a beggar-thy-neighbor policy that boosts national income at the expense of other countries. A country that attempts to use such policies will probably provoke retaliation. In many cases, the resulting trade war between two or more interventionist governments will leave all countries involved worse off than if a hands-off approach had been adopted in the first place. If the U.S. government were to respond to the Airbus subsidy by increasing its own subsidies to Boeing, for example, the result might be that the subsidies would cancel each other out. In the process, both European and U.S. taxpayers would end up supporting an expensive and pointless trade war, and both Europe and the United States would be worse off.

Krugman may be right about the danger of a strategic trade policy leading to a trade war. The problem, however, is how to respond when one's competitors are already being supported by government subsidies; that is, how should Boeing and the United States respond to the subsidization of Airbus? According to Krugman, the answer is probably not to engage in retaliatory action but to help establish rules of the game that minimize the use of trade-distorting subsidies. This is what the World Trade Organization seeks to do.

Domestic Policies

Governments do not always act in the national interest when they intervene in the economy; politically important interest groups often influence them. The European Union's support for the Common Agricultural Policy (CAP), which arose because of the political power of French and German farmers, is an example. The CAP benefits inefficient farmers and the politicians who rely on the farm vote, but not consumers in the EU, who end up paying more for their foodstuffs. Thus, a further reason for not embracing strategic trade policy, according to Krugman, is that such a policy is almost certain to be captured by special-interest groups within the economy, which will distort it to their own ends. Krugman concludes that in the United States,

> To ask the Commerce Department to ignore special-interest politics while formulating detailed policy for many industries is not realistic; to establish a blanket policy of free trade, with exceptions granted only under extreme pressure, may not be the optimal policy according to the theory but may be the best policy that the country is likely to get.[20]

DEVELOPMENT OF THE WORLD TRADING SYSTEM ▮◖07◗4▮

Strong economic arguments support unrestricted free trade. While many governments have recognized the value of these arguments, they have been unwilling to unilaterally lower their trade barriers for fear that other nations might not follow suit. Consider the problem that two neighboring countries, say, Brazil and Argentina, face when deciding whether to lower trade barriers between them. In principle, the government of Brazil might favor lowering trade barriers, but it might be unwilling to do so for fear that Argentina will not do the same. Instead, the government might fear that the Argentineans will take advantage of Brazil's low barriers to enter the Brazilian market while continuing to shut Brazilian products out of their market through high trade barriers. The Argentinean government might believe that it faces the same dilemma. The essence of the problem is a lack of trust. Both governments recognize that their respective nations will benefit from lower trade barriers between them, but neither government is willing to lower barriers for fear that the other might not follow.[21]

Such a deadlock can be resolved if both countries negotiate a set of rules to govern cross-border trade and lower trade barriers. But who is to monitor the governments to make sure they are playing by the trade rules? And who is to impose sanctions on a government that cheats? Both governments could set up an independent body to act as a referee. This referee could monitor trade between the countries, make sure that no side cheats, and impose sanctions on a country if it does cheat in the trade game.

While it might sound unlikely that any government would compromise its national sovereignty by submitting to such an arrangement, since World War II an international trading framework has evolved that has exactly these features. For its first 50 years, this framework was known as the General Agreement on Tariffs and Trade (GATT). Since 1995, it has been known as the World Trade Organization. Here, we look at the evolution and workings of the GATT and WTO.

From Smith to the Great Depression

As noted in Chapter 5, the theoretical case for free trade dates to the late eighteenth century and the work of Adam Smith and David Ricardo. Free trade as a government policy was first officially embraced by Great Britain in 1846, when the British Parliament repealed the Corn Laws. The Corn Laws placed a high tariff on imports of foreign corn. The objectives of the Corn Laws tariff were to raise government revenues and to protect British corn producers. There had been annual motions in Parliament in favor of free trade since the 1820s when David Ricardo was a member. However, agricultural protection was withdrawn only as a result of a protracted debate when the effects of a harvest failure in Great Britain were compounded by the imminent threat of famine in Ireland. Faced with considerable hardship and suffering among the populace, Parliament narrowly reversed its long-held position.

During the next 80 years or so, Great Britain, as one of the world's dominant trading powers, pushed the case for trade liberalization, but the British government was a voice in the wilderness. Its major trading partners did not reciprocate the British policy of unilateral free trade. The only reason Britain kept this policy for so long was that as the world's largest exporting nation, it had far more to lose from a trade war than did any other country.

By the 1930s, the British attempt to stimulate free trade was buried under the economic rubble of the Great Depression. Economic problems were compounded in 1930 when the U.S. Congress passed the Smoot-Hawley tariff. Aimed at avoiding rising unemployment by protecting domestic industries and diverting consumer demand away from foreign products, the **Smoot-Hawley Act** erected an enormous wall of tariff barriers. Almost every industry was rewarded with its "made-to-order" tariff. The Smoot-Hawley Act had a damaging effect on employment abroad. Other countries reacted by raising their own tariff barriers. U.S. exports tumbled in response, and the world slid further into the Great Depression.[22]

1947–1979: GATT, Trade Liberalization, and Economic Growth

Economic damage caused by the beggar-thy-neighbor trade policies that the Smoot-Hawley Act ushered in exerted a profound influence on the economic institutions and ideology of the post–World War II world. The United States emerged from the war both victorious and economically dominant. After the debacle of the Great Depression, opinion in the U.S. Congress had swung strongly in favor of free trade. Under U.S. leadership, the GATT was established in 1947.

The GATT was a multilateral agreement whose objective was to liberalize trade by eliminating tariffs, subsidies, import quotas, and the like. From its foundation in 1947 until it was superseded by the WTO, the GATT's membership grew from 19 to more than 120 nations. The GATT did not attempt to liberalize trade restrictions in one fell swoop; that would have been impossible. Rather, tariff reduction was spread over eight rounds.

In its early years, the GATT was by most measures very successful. For example, the average tariff declined by nearly 92 percent in the United States between the Geneva Round of 1947 and the Tokyo Round of 1973–1979. Consistent with the theoretical arguments first advanced by Ricardo and reviewed in Chapter 5, the move toward free trade under the GATT appeared to stimulate economic growth.

1980–1993: Protectionist Trends

During the 1980s and early 1990s, the trading system erected by the GATT came under strain as pressures for greater protectionism increased around the world. There were three reasons for the rise in such pressures during the 1980s. First, the economic success of Japan during that time strained the world trading system (much as the success of China has created strains today). Japan was in ruins when the GATT was created. By the early 1980s, however, it had become the world's second-largest economy and its largest exporter. Japan's success in such industries as automobiles and semiconductors might have been enough to strain the world trading system. Things were made worse by the widespread perception in the West that despite low tariff rates and subsidies, Japanese markets were closed to imports and foreign investment by administrative trade barriers.

Second, the world trading system was strained by the persistent trade deficit in the world's largest economy, the United States. The consequences of the U.S. deficit included painful adjustments in industries such as automobiles, machine tools, semiconductors, steel, and textiles, where domestic producers steadily lost market share to foreign competitors. The resulting unemployment gave rise to renewed demands in the U.S. Congress for protection against imports.

A third reason for the trend toward greater protectionism was that many countries found ways to get around GATT regulations. Bilateral voluntary export restraints (VERs) circumvent GATT agreements, because neither the importing country nor the exporting country complains to the GATT bureaucracy in Geneva—and without a complaint, the GATT bureaucracy can do nothing. Exporting countries agreed to VERs to avoid more damaging punitive tariffs. One of the best-known examples is the automobile VER between Japan and the United States, under which Japanese producers promised to limit their auto imports into the United States as a way of defusing growing trade tensions. According to a World Bank study, 16 percent of the imports of industrialized countries in 1986 were subjected to nontariff trade barriers such as VERs.[23]

The Uruguay Round and the World Trade Organization

Against the background of rising pressures for protectionism, in 1986 GATT members embarked on their eighth round of negotiations to reduce tariffs, the Uruguay Round (so named because it occurred in Uruguay). This was the most ambitious round of negotiations yet. Until then, GATT rules had applied only to trade in manufactured goods and commodities. In the Uruguay Round, member countries sought to extend GATT rules to cover trade in services. They also sought to write rules governing the protection of intellectual property, to reduce agricultural subsidies, and to strengthen the GATT's monitoring and enforcement mechanisms.

The Uruguay Round dragged on for seven years before an agreement was reached on December 15, 1993. It went into effect July 1, 1995. The Uruguay Round contained the following provisions:

1. Tariffs on industrial goods were to be reduced by more than one-third, and tariffs were to be scrapped on more than 40 percent of manufactured goods.
2. Average tariff rates imposed by developed nations on manufactured goods were to be reduced to less than 4 percent of value, the lowest level in modern history.
3. Agricultural subsidies were to be substantially reduced.
4. GATT fair trade and market access rules were to be extended to cover a wide range of services.
5. GATT rules also were to be extended to provide enhanced protection for patents, copyrights, and trademarks (intellectual property).
6. Barriers on trade in textiles were to be significantly reduced over 10 years.
7. The World Trade Organization was to be created to implement the GATT agreement.

The World Trade Organization

The WTO acts as an umbrella organization that encompasses the GATT along with two new sister bodies, one on services and the other on intellectual property. The WTO's General Agreement on Trade in Services (GATS) has taken the lead to extending free trade agreements to services. The WTO's Agreement on Trade-Related Aspects of Intellectual Property Rights (TRIPS) is an attempt to narrow the gaps in the way intellectual property rights are protected around the world and to bring them under common international rules. WTO has taken over responsibility for arbitrating trade disputes and monitoring the trade policies of member countries. While the WTO operates on the basis of consensus as the GATT did, in the area of dispute settlement, member countries are no longer able to block adoption of arbitration reports. Arbitration panel reports on trade disputes between member countries are automatically adopted by the WTO unless there is a consensus to reject them. Countries that have been found by the arbitration panel to violate GATT rules may appeal to a permanent appellate body, but its verdict is binding. If offenders fail to comply with the recommendations of the arbitration panel, trading partners have the right to compensation or, in the last resort, to impose (commensurate) trade sanctions. Every stage of the procedure is subject to strict time limits. Thus, the WTO has something that the GATT never had—teeth.[24]

WTO: Experience to Date

By 2013, the WTO had 159 members, including China, which joined at the end of 2001, and Russia, which joined in 2012. WTO members collectively account for 98 percent of world trade. Since its formation, the WTO has remained at the forefront of efforts to promote global free trade. Its creators expressed the belief that the enforcement mechanisms granted to the WTO would make it more effective at policing global trade rules than the GATT had been. The great hope was that the WTO might emerge as an effective advocate and facilitator of future trade deals, particularly in areas such as services. The experience so far has been encouraging, although the collapse of WTO talks in Seattle in late 1999, slow progress with the next round of trade talks (the Doha Round), and a shift back toward some limited protectionism following the global financial crisis of 2008–2009 have raised a number of questions about the future direction of the WTO.

WTO as Global Police

The first two decades in the life of the WTO suggests that its policing and enforcement mechanisms are having a positive effect.[25] Between 1995 and 2012, more than 400 trade disputes between member-countries were brought to the WTO.[26] This record compares with a total of 196 cases handled by the GATT over almost half a century. Of the cases brought to the WTO, three-fourths have been resolved by informal consultations between the disputing countries. Resolving the remainder has involved more formal procedures, but these have been largely successful. In general, countries involved have adopted the WTO's recommendations. The fact that countries are using the WTO represents an important vote of confidence in the organization's dispute resolution procedures.

Expanding Trade Agreements

As explained earlier, the Uruguay Round of GATT negotiations extended global trading rules to cover trade in services. The WTO was given the role of brokering future agreements to open up global trade in services. The WTO was also encouraged to extend its reach to encompass regulations governing foreign direct investment, something the GATT had never done. Two of the first industries targeted for reform were the global telecommunication and financial services industries.

In February 1997, the WTO brokered a deal to get countries to agree to open their telecommunication markets to competition, allowing foreign operators to purchase ownership stakes in domestic telecommunication providers and establishing a set of common rules for fair competition. Most of the world's biggest markets—including the United States, European Union, and Japan—were fully liberalized by January 1, 1998, when the pact went into effect. All forms of basic telecommunication service are covered, including voice telephony, data, and satellite and radio communications. Many telecommunication companies responded positively to the deal, pointing out that it would give them a much greater ability to offer their business customers one-stop shopping—a global, seamless service for all their corporate needs and a single bill.

This was followed in December 1997 with an agreement to liberalize cross-border trade in financial services. The deal covered more than 95 percent of the world's financial services market. Under the agreement, which took effect at the beginning of March 1999, 102 countries pledged to open (to varying degrees) their banking, securities, and insurance sectors to foreign competition. In common with the telecommunication deal, the accord covers not just cross-border trade but also foreign direct investment. Seventy countries agreed to dramatically lower or eradicate barriers to foreign direct investment in their financial services sector. The United States and the European Union (with minor exceptions) are fully open to inward investment by foreign banks, insurance, and securities companies. As part of the deal, many Asian countries made important concessions that allow significant foreign participation in their financial services sectors for the first time.

The Future of The WTO: Unresolved Issues and the Doha Round

Since the successes of the 1990s, the World Trade Organization has struggled to make progress on the international trade front. Confronted by a slower growing world economy after 2001, many national governments have been reluctant to agree to a fresh round of policies designed to reduce trade barriers.

Political opposition to the WTO has been growing in many nations. As the public face of globalization, some politicians and nongovernmental organizations blame the WTO for a variety of ills, including high unemployment, environmental degradation, poor working conditions in developing nations, falling real wage rates among the lower paid in developed nations, and rising income inequality. The rapid rise of China as a dominant trading nation has also played a role here. Like sentiments regarding Japan 20 years ago, many perceive China as failing to play by the international trading rules, even as it embraces the WTO.

Against this difficult political backdrop, much remains to be done on the international trade front. Four issues at the forefront of the current agenda of the WTO are antidumping policies, the high level of protectionism in agriculture, the lack of strong protection for intellectual property rights in many nations, and continued high tariff rates on nonagricultural goods and services in many nations. We shall look at each in turn before discussing the latest round of talks between WTO members aimed at reducing trade barriers, the Doha Round, which began in 2001 and is still ongoing.

Antidumping Actions

Antidumping actions proliferated during the 1990s. WTO rules allow countries to impose antidumping duties on foreign goods that are being sold cheaper than at home, or below their cost of production, when domestic producers can show that they are being harmed. Unfortunately, the rather vague definition of what constitutes "dumping" has proved to be a loophole that many countries are exploiting to pursue protectionism.

Between 1995 and mid-2012, WTO members had reported implementation of some 4,125 antidumping actions to the WTO. India initiated the largest number of antidumping actions, some 663; the EU initiated 444 over the same period, and the United States, 465. Antidumping actions seem to be concentrated in certain sectors of the economy, such as basic metal industries (e.g., aluminum and steel), chemicals, plastics, and machinery and electrical equipment.[27] These sectors account for approximately 70 percent of all antidumping actions reported to the WTO. Since 1995, these four sectors have been characterized by periods of intense competition and excess productive capacity, which have led to low prices and profits (or losses) for firms in those industries. It is not unreasonable, therefore, to hypothesize that the high level of antidumping actions in these industries represents an attempt by beleaguered manufacturers to use the political process in their nations to seek protection from foreign competitors, which they claim are engaging in unfair competition. While some of these claims may have merit, the process can become very politicized as representatives of businesses and their employees lobby government officials to "protect domestic jobs from unfair foreign competition," and government officials, mindful of the need to get votes in future elections, oblige by pushing for antidumping actions. The WTO is clearly worried by the use of antidumping policies, suggesting that it reflects persistent protectionist tendencies and pushing members to strengthen the regulations governing the imposition of antidumping duties.

Protectionism in Agriculture

Another focus of the WTO has been the high level of tariffs and subsidies in the agricultural sector of many economies. Tariff rates on agricultural products are generally much higher than tariff rates on manufactured products or services. For example, in mid-2000, the average tariff rates on nonagricultural products among developed nations were around 4 percent. On agricultural products, however, the average tariff rates were 21.2 percent for Canada, 15.9 percent for the European Union, 18.6 percent for

Japan, and 10.3 percent for the United States.[28] The implication is that consumers in these countries are paying significantly higher prices than necessary for agricultural products imported from abroad, which leaves them with less money to spend on other goods and services.

The historically high tariff rates on agricultural products reflect a desire to protect domestic agriculture and traditional farming communities from foreign competition. In addition to high tariffs, agricultural producers also benefit from substantial subsidies. According to estimates from the Organization for Economic Cooperation and Development (OECD), government subsidies on average account for about 17 percent of the cost of agricultural production in Canada, 21 percent in the United States, 35 percent in the European Union, and 59 percent in Japan.[29] OECD countries spend more than $300 billion a year in agricultural subsidies.

Not surprisingly, the combination of high tariff barriers and subsidies introduces significant distortions into the production of agricultural products and international trade of those products. The net effect is to raise prices to consumers, reduce the volume of agricultural trade, and encourage the overproduction of products that are heavily subsidized (with the government typically buying the surplus). Because global trade in agriculture currently amounts to 10.5 percent of total merchandized trade, the WTO argues that removing tariff barriers and subsidies could significantly boost the overall level of trade, lower prices to consumers, and raise global economic growth by freeing consumption and investment resources for more productive uses. According to estimates from the International Monetary Fund, removal of tariffs and subsidies on agricultural products would raise global economic welfare by $128 billion annually.[30] Others suggest gains as high as $182 billion.[31]

The biggest defenders of the existing system have been the advanced nations of the world, which want to protect their agricultural sectors from competition by low-cost producers in developing nations. In contrast, developing nations have been pushing hard for reforms that would allow their producers greater access to the protected markets of the developed nations. Estimates suggest that removing all subsidies on agricultural production alone in OECD countries could return to the developing nations of the world three times more than all the foreign aid they currently receive from the OECD nations.[32] In other words, free trade in agriculture could help jump-start economic growth among the world's poorer nations and alleviate global poverty.

Protecting Intellectual Property

Another issue that has become increasingly important to the WTO has been protecting intellectual property. The 1995 Uruguay agreement that established the WTO also contained an agreement to protect intellectual property (the Trade-Related Aspects of Intellectual Property Rights, or TRIPS, agreement). The TRIPS regulations oblige WTO members to grant and enforce patents lasting at least 20 years and copyrights lasting 50 years. Rich countries had to comply with the rules within a year. Poor countries, in which such protection was generally much weaker, had 5 years' grace, and the very poorest had 10 years. The basis for this agreement was a strong belief among signatory nations that the protection of intellectual property through patents, trademarks, and copyrights must be an essential element of the international trading system. Inadequate protections for intellectual property reduce the incentive for innovation. Because innovation is a central engine of economic growth and rising living standards, the argument has been that a multilateral agreement is needed to protect intellectual property.

Without such an agreement it is feared that producers in a country—let's say, India—might market imitations of patented innovations pioneered in a different country—say, the United States. This can affect international trade in two ways. First, it reduces the export opportunities in India for the original innovator in the United States. Second, to the extent that the Indian producer is able to export its pirated imitation to additional countries, it also reduces the export opportunities in those countries for the U.S. inventor. Also, one can argue that because the size of the total world market for the innovator is reduced, its incentive to pursue risky and expensive innovations is also reduced. The net effect would be less innovation in the world economy and less economic growth.

Market Access for Nonagricultural Goods and Services

Although the WTO and the GATT have made big strides in reducing the tariff rates on nonagricultural products, much work remains. Although most developed nations have brought their tariff rates on industrial products down to an average of 3.8 percent of value, exceptions still remain. In particular, while average tariffs are low, high tariff rates persist on certain imports into developed nations, which limit market access and economic growth. For example, Australia and South Korea, both OECD countries, still have bound tariff rates of 15.1 percent and 24.6 percent, respectively, on imports of transportation equipment (*bound tariff rates* are the highest rate that can be charged, which is often, but not always, the rate that is charged). In contrast, the bound tariff rates on imports of transportation equipment into the United States, EU, and Japan are 2.7 percent, 4.8 percent, and 0 percent, respectively. A particular area for concern is high tariff rates on imports of selected goods from developing nations into developed nations.

In addition, tariffs on services remain higher than on industrial goods. The average tariff on business and financial services imported into the United States, for example, is 8.2 percent, into the EU it is 8.5 percent, and into Japan it is 19.7 percent.[33] Given the rising value of cross-border trade in services, reducing these figures can be expected to yield substantial gains.

The WTO would like to bring down tariff rates still further and reduce the scope for the selective use of high tariff rates. The ultimate aim is to reduce tariff rates to zero. Although this might sound ambitious, 40 nations have already moved to zero tariffs on information technology goods, so a precedent exists. Empirical work suggests that further reductions in average tariff rates toward zero would yield substantial gains. One estimate by economists at the World Bank suggests that a broad global trade agreement coming out of the current Doha negotiations could increase world income by $263 billion annually, of which $109 billion would go to poor countries.[35] Another estimate from the OECD suggests a figure closer to $300 billion annually.[36] See the accompanying Country Focus for estimates of the benefits to the American economy from free trade.

Looking further out, the WTO would like to bring down tariff rates on imports of nonagricultural goods into developing nations. Many of these nations use the infant industry argument to justify the continued imposition of high tariff rates; however, ultimately these rates need to come down for these nations to reap the full benefits of international trade. For example, the bound tariff rates of 53.9 percent on imports of transportation equipment into India and 33.6 percent on imports into Brazil, by raising domestic prices, help protect inefficient domestic producers and limit economic growth by reducing the real income of consumers who must pay more for transportation equipment and related services.

A New Round of Talks: Doha

In 2001, the WTO launched a new round of talks between member states aimed at further liberalizing the global trade and investment framework. For this meeting, it picked the remote location of Doha in the Persian Gulf state of Qatar. The talks were originally scheduled to last three years, although they have already gone on for 12 years and are currently stalled.

The Doha agenda includes cutting tariffs on industrial goods and services, phasing out subsidies to agricultural producers, reducing barriers to cross-border investment, and limiting the use of antidumping

Estimating the Gains from Trade for America

A study published by the Institute for international Economics tried to estimate the gains to the American economy from free trade. According to the study, due to reductions in tariff barriers under the GATT and WTO since 1947, by 2003 the gross domestic product (GDP) of the United States was 7.3 percent higher than would otherwise be the case. The benefits of that amounted to roughly $1 trillion a year, or $9,000 extra income for each American household per year.

The same study tried to estimate what would happen if America concluded free trade deals with all its trading partners, reducing tariff barriers on all goods and services to zero. Using several methods to estimate the impact, the study concluded that additional annual gains of between $450 billion and $1.3 trillion could be realized. This final march to free trade, according to the authors of the study, could safely be expected to raise incomes of the average American household by an additional $4,500 per year.

The authors also tried to estimate the scale and cost of employment disruption that would be caused by a move to universal free trade. Jobs would be lost in certain sectors and gained in others if the country abolished all tariff barriers. Using historical data as a guide, they estimated that 226,000 jobs would be lost every year due to expanded trade, although some two-thirds of those losing jobs would find reemployment after a year. Reemployment, however, would be at a wage that was 13 to 14 percent lower. The study concluded that the disruption costs would total some $54 billion annually, primarily in the form of lower lifetime wages to those whose jobs were disrupted as a result of free trade. Offset against this, however, must be the higher economic growth resulting from free trade, which creates many new jobs and raises household incomes, creating another $450 billion to $1.3 trillion annually in *net* gains to the economy. In other words, the estimated annual gains from trade are far greater than the estimated annual costs associated with job disruption, and more people benefit than lose as a result of a shift to a universal free trade regime.[34]

laws. The talks are currently ongoing. They have been characterized by halting progress punctuated by significant setbacks and missed deadlines. A September 2003 meeting in Cancún, Mexico, broke down, primarily because there was no agreement on how to proceed with reducing agricultural subsidies and tariffs; the EU, United States, and India, among others, proved less than willing to reduce tariffs and subsidies to their politically important farmers, while countries such as Brazil and certain West African nations wanted free trade as quickly as possible. In 2004, both the United States and the EU made a determined push to start the talks again. Since then, however, little progress has been made, and the talks are in deadlock, primarily because of disagreements over how deep the cuts in subsidies to agricultural producers should be. As of early 2013, the goal was to reduce tariffs for manufactured and agricultural goods by 60 to 70 percent and to cut subsidies to half of their current level—but getting nations to agree to these goals was proving exceedingly difficult. In response the apparent failure of the Doha Round negotiations to progress, many nations have pushed forward with bilateral free trade agreements. These include the United States and the EU, which in 2013 launched bilateral talks aimed at reducing trade barriers between them.

■ IMPLICATIONS FOR MANAGERS ▰▰▰▰▰▰ ▮07-5▮

What are the implications of all this for business practice? Why should the international manager care about the political economy of free trade or about the relative merits of arguments for free trade and protectionism? There are two answers to this question. The first concerns the impact of trade barriers on a firm's strategy. The second concerns the role that business firms can play in promoting free trade or trade barriers.

TRADE BARRIERS AND FIRM STRATEGY

To understand how trade barriers affect a firm's strategy, consider first the material in Chapter 6. Drawing on the theories of international trade, we discussed how it makes sense for the firm to disperse its various production activities to those countries around the globe where they can be performed most efficiently. Thus, it may make sense for a firm to design and engineer its product in one country, to manufacture components in another, to perform final assembly operations in yet another country, and then export the finished product to the rest of the world.

Clearly, trade barriers constrain a firm's ability to disperse its productive activities in such a manner. First and most obvious, tariff barriers raise the costs of exporting products to a country (or of exporting partly finished products between countries). This may put the firm at a competitive disadvantage to indigenous competitors in that country. In response, the firm may then find it economical to locate production facilities in that country so that it can compete on an even footing. Second, quotas may limit a firm's ability to serve a country from locations outside of that country. Again, the response by the firm might be to set up production facilities in that country—even though it may result in higher production costs. Such reasoning was one of the factors behind the rapid expansion of Japanese automaking capacity in the United States during the 1980s and 1990s. This followed the establishment of a VER agreement between the United States and Japan that limited U.S. imports of Japanese automobiles.

Third, to conform to local content regulations, a firm may have to locate more production activities in a given market than it would otherwise. Again, from the firm's perspective, the consequence might be to raise costs above the level that could be achieved if each production activity was dispersed to the optimal location for that activity. And finally, even when trade barriers do not exist, the firm may still want to locate some production activities in a given country to reduce the threat of trade barriers being imposed in the future.

All these effects are likely to raise the firm's costs above the level that could be achieved in a world without trade barriers. The higher costs that result need not translate into a significant competitive disadvantage relative to other foreign firms, however, if the countries imposing trade barriers do so to the imported products of all foreign firms, irrespective of their national origin. But when trade barriers are targeted at exports from a particular nation, firms based in that nation are at a competitive disadvantage to firms of other nations. The firm may deal with such targeted trade barriers by moving production into the country imposing barriers. Another strategy may be to move production to countries whose exports are not targeted by the specific trade barrier.

Finally, the threat of antidumping action limits the ability of a firm to use aggressive pricing to gain market share in a country. Firms in a country also can make strategic use of antidumping measures to limit aggressive competition from low-cost foreign producers. For example, the U.S. steel industry has been very aggressive in bringing antidumping actions against foreign steelmakers, particularly in times of weak global demand for steel and excess capacity. In 1998 and 1999, the United States faced a surge in low-cost steel imports as a severe recession in Asia left producers there with excess capacity. The U.S. producers filed several complaints with the International Trade Commission. One argued that Japanese producers of hot rolled steel were selling it at below cost in the United States. The ITC agreed and levied tariffs ranging from

18 percent to 67 percent on imports of certain steel products from Japan (these tariffs are separate from the steel tariffs discussed earlier).[37]

POLICY IMPLICATIONS

As noted in Chapter 6, business firms are major players on the international trade scene. Because of their pivotal role in international trade, firms can and do exert a strong influence on government policy toward trade. This influence can encourage protectionism, or it can encourage the government to support the WTO and push for open markets and freer trade among all nations. Government policies with regard to international trade can have a direct impact on business.

Consistent with strategic trade policy, examples can be found of government intervention in the form of tariffs, quotas, antidumping actions, and subsidies helping firms and industries establish a competitive advantage in the world economy. In general, however, the arguments contained in this chapter and in Chapter 6 suggest that government intervention has three drawbacks. Intervention can be self-defeating because it tends to protect the inefficient rather than help firms become efficient global competitors. Intervention is dangerous; it may invite retaliation and trigger a trade war. Finally, intervention is unlikely to be well executed, given the opportunity for such a policy to be captured by special-interest groups. Does this mean that business should simply encourage government to adopt a laissez-faire free trade policy?

Most economists would probably argue that the best interests of international business are served by a free trade stance, but not a laissez-faire stance. It is probably in the best long-run interests of the business community to encourage the government to aggressively promote greater free trade by, for example, strengthening the WTO. Business probably has much more to gain from government efforts to open protected markets to imports and foreign direct investment than from government efforts to support certain domestic industries in a manner consistent with the recommendations of strategic trade policy.

This conclusion is reinforced by a phenomenon we touched on in Chapter 1—the increasing integration of the world economy and internationalization of production that has occurred over the past two decades. We live in a world where many firms of all national origins increasingly depend for their competitive advantage on globally dispersed production systems. Such systems are the result of freer trade. Freer trade has brought great advantages to firms that have exploited it and to consumers who benefit from the resulting lower prices. Given the danger of retaliatory action, business firms that lobby their governments to engage in protectionism must realize that by doing so they may be denying themselves the opportunity to build a competitive advantage by constructing a globally dispersed production system. By encouraging their governments to engage in protectionism, their own activities and sales overseas may be jeopardized if other governments retaliate. This does not mean a firm should never seek protection in the form of antidumping actions and the like, but it should review its options carefully and think through the larger consequences.

Chapter Summary

This chapter described how the reality of international trade deviates from the theoretical ideal of unrestricted free trade reviewed in Chapter 6. In this chapter, we reported the various instruments of trade policy, reviewed the political and economic arguments for government intervention in international trade, reexamined the economic case for free trade in light of the strategic trade policy argument, and looked at the evolution of the world trading framework. While a policy of free trade may not always be the theoretically optimal policy (given the arguments of the new trade theorists), in practice it is probably the best policy for a government to pursue. In particular, the long-run interests of business and consumers may be best served by strengthening international institutions such as the WTO. Given the danger that isolated protectionism might escalate into a trade war, business probably has far more to gain from government efforts to open protected markets to imports and foreign direct investment (through the WTO) than from government efforts to protect domestic industries from foreign competition. The chapter made the following points:

1. Trade policies such as tariffs, subsidies, antidumping regulations, and local content requirements tend to be pro-producer and anticonsumer. Gains accrue to producers (who are protected from foreign competitors), but consumers lose because they must pay more for imports.

2. There are two types of arguments for government intervention in international trade: political and economic. Political arguments for intervention are concerned with protecting the interests of certain groups, often at the expense of other groups, or with promoting goals with regard to foreign policy, human rights, consumer protection, and the like. Economic arguments for intervention are about boosting the overall wealth of a nation.

3. A common political argument for intervention is that it is necessary to protect jobs. However, political intervention often hurts consumers, and it can be self-defeating. Countries sometimes argue that it is important to protect certain industries for reasons of national security. Some argue that government should use the threat to intervene in trade policy as a bargaining tool to open foreign markets. This can be a risky policy; if it fails, the result can be higher trade barriers.

4. The infant industry argument for government intervention contends that to let manufacturing get a toehold, governments should temporarily support new industries. In practice, however, governments often end up protecting the inefficient.

5. Strategic trade policy suggests that with subsidies, government can help domestic firms gain first-mover advantages in global industries where economies of scale are important. Government subsidies may also help domestic firms overcome barriers to entry into such industries.

6. The problems with strategic trade policy are twofold: (*a*) Such a policy may invite retaliation, in which case all will lose, and (*b*) strategic trade policy may be captured by special-interest groups, which will distort it to their own ends.

7. The GATT was a product of the postwar free trade movement. The GATT was successful in lowering trade barriers on manufactured goods and commodities. The move toward greater free trade under the GATT appeared to stimulate economic growth.

8. The completion of the Uruguay Round of GATT talks and the establishment of the World Trade Organization have strengthened the world trading system by extending GATT rules to services, increasing protection for intellectual property, reducing agricultural subsidies, and enhancing monitoring and enforcement mechanisms.

9. Trade barriers act as a constraint on a firm's ability to disperse its various production activities to optimal locations around the globe. One response to trade barriers is to establish more production activities in the protected country.

10. Business may have more to gain from government efforts to open protected markets to imports and foreign direct investment than from government efforts to protect domestic industries from foreign competition.

Critical Thinking and Discussion Questions

1. Do you think governments should consider human rights when granting preferential trading rights to countries? What are the arguments for and against taking such a position?

2. Whose interests should be the paramount concern of government trade policy—the interests of producers (businesses and their employees) or those of consumers?
3. Given the arguments relating to the new trade theory and strategic trade policy, what kind of trade policy should business be pressuring government to adopt?
4. You are an employee of a U.S. firm that produces personal computers in Thailand and then exports them to the United States and other countries for sale. The personal computers were originally produced in Thailand to take advantage of relatively low labor costs and a skilled workforce. Other possible locations considered at the time were Malaysia and Hong Kong. The U.S. government decides to impose punitive 100 percent ad valorem tariffs on imports of computers from Thailand to punish the country for administrative trade barriers that restrict U.S. exports to Thailand. How should your firm respond? What does this tell you about the use of targeted trade barriers?
5. Reread the Management Focus, "U.S. Magnesium Seeks Protection." Who gains most from the antidumping duties levied by the United States on imports of magnesium from China and Russia? Who are the losers? Are these duties in the best national interests of the United States?

Research Task 🌐 globalEDGE globaledge.msu.edu

The Political Economy of International Trade

Use the globalEDGE website (globaledge.msu.edu) to complete the following exercises:

Exercise 1

You work for a pharmaceuticals company that hopes to provide products and services in New Zealand. Yet management's current knowledge of this country's trade policies and barriers is limited. After searching a resource that summarizes the *import and export regulation,* outline the most important foreign trade barriers your firm's managers must keep in mind while developing a strategy for entry into New Zealand's pharmaceutical market.

Exercise 2

The number of member nations of the World Trade Organization has increased considerably in recent years. In addition, some nonmember countries have observer status in the WTO. Such status requires accession negotiations to begin within five years of attaining this preliminary position. Visit WTO's website to identify a list of current members and observers. Identify the last five countries that joined the WTO as members. Also, examine the list of current observer countries. Do you notice anything in particular about the countries that have recently joined or have observer status?

Closing CASE

U.S. Tariffs on Tire Imports from China

In September 2009, President Obama placed a tariff on tire imports from China. The tariff was a response to a rising tide of imports from China and intense lobbying from the United Steelworkers union, which represents 15,000 workers at 13 tire plants in the United States. Tires imported from China are usually low-end models that sell for half the price of American-made, name-brand tires. In 2008, the

United States imported 46 million tires from China, three times as many as it did in 2004. China's share of the American market leaped from 5 percent to almost 17 percent over the same period, while U.S. employment in the industry fell by more than 5,000 and domestic production slumped from 218 million tires to 160 million tires.

The United Steelworkers petitioned the International Trade Commission, which is a unit of the U.S. Department of Commerce, for protection. After reviewing the case, the commission concluded that the surge in Chinese tire imports was causing significant "market disruption" and recommended imposing a three-year tariff on imports of Chinese tires. The Obama administration agreed and placed a 35 percent tariff for one year on tire imports from China, followed by a 30 percent tariff in the second year and a 25 percent tariff in the final year. These tariffs were placed on top of an existing 4 percent import tariff.

The Chinese quickly objected, calling the tariffs "a serious case of protectionism" and arguing that the United States was violating World Trade Organization rules, of which both countries were members. For its part, the United States argued that the tariffs were allowed under the terms of a special safeguard provision that was part of the U.S. agreement to support China's entry into the WTO in 2001. Under that provision, U.S. companies or workers harmed by imports from China can ask the government for protection simply by demonstrating that American producers have suffered a "market disruption" or have experienced a surge in imports from China.

The WTO's dispute resolution panel quickly took on the case. In December 2010, the panel issued its ruling, finding that the United States "did not fail to comply with its obligations" under world trade agreements and allowing the tariffs to remain. China immediately appealed the ruling. Chinese officials stated the tariff had hurt the interests of both China and the United States. They argued that the tariffs cost jobs in the U.S. sales sector, causing some small and medium-size wholesalers and dealers to go out of business. Moreover, they argued that the tariff has burdened low-income consumers in the United States, with the average price of tires increasing 10 to 20 percent since the tariffs were imposed.

For its part, the United Steelworkers argued that the tariff had been a big success. For the first six months after the tariffs were imposed, U.S. production increased more than 15 percent, and the union claimed that U.S. producers were making plans to add additional capacity. During the same period, tire imports from China fell by 34 percent. However, the union may have been too quick to claim victory. Over the next 18 months, tire imports surged from Thailand, Indonesia, and Mexico, suggesting that low-cost producers in other countries were taking advantage of the tariffs on Chinese tires to increase their exports to the United States. Furthermore, U.S. producers did not add capacity. Indeed, several U.S. tire makers have factories in China and elsewhere and had, for some time, been exporting from them. To complicate matters, China responded to the tariffs on tires by placing tariffs on the export of some U.S. products, such as broiler chickens, to China.[38]

Case Discussion Questions

1. Which groups benefited from the imposition of U.S. tariffs on Chinese tire imports? Which groups suffered? What does this tell you about tariffs in general?
2. How do you think that the United States would have reacted if the Chinese had raised tariff rates on the importation of certain goods from the United States?
3. What does the rise of tire imports from Thailand, Indonesia, and Mexico during 2010 and 2011 tell you about the value of this kind of trade policy?
4. Do you think that the policy was in the best interests of the United States? Justify your answer.

Transfer Pricing Laws in India

Comprehensive transfer pricing regulations (TPRs) were introduced, effective 1st April 2001, with the objective to prevent MNCs from manipulating prices in intra-group transactions, e.g., by transferring their profits outside India.

Indian transfer pricing provisions are generally in line with transfer pricing guidelines for MNCs and tax administrators issued by the Organization for Economic Cooperation and Development (OECD Guidelines). However, there are some significant differences, e.g., these guidelines encompass a wider definition of the term "associated enterprise" and follow the concept of arithmetic mean as opposed to statistical measures of median/arm's length range followed internationally.

Under TPRs, any international transaction (ITN) between two or more associated enterprises (including permanent establishments) must be at arm's length price (ALP). These regulations also apply to cost-sharing arrangements. For computation of ALP, TPRs require the application of the most appropriate among all prescribed methods. The prescribed methods are given below.

- Comparable uncontrolled price method
- Resale price method
- Cost plus method
- Profit split method
- Transactional net margin method
- Any method, which takes into account the price for the same or similar uncontrolled transaction between non-associated enterprises, under similar circumstances, considering all the relevant facts.

However, TPRs do not mandate a hierarchy of methods.

Where more than one ALP is determined, the TPRs mandate that the arithmetic mean of such prices shall be taken to be the ALP. If the variation between the ALP and the price of ITN does not exceed a prescribed percentage of transfer price, the ITN are considered to be at arm's length. The CBDT is yet to notify the prescribed percentages as allowable variations from transfer price. However, the Finance Act 2012 has put an upper ceiling of 3% on the prescribed percentages.

TPRs require taxpayers entering into ITNs to maintain prescribed documents and information and also obtain and furnish an accountant's report, which includes prescribed details related to the ITNs being carried out, to the tax authorities. The due date for filing the accountant's report, both for corporate and non-corporate taxpayers is 30 November following the end of the relevant financial year.

The prescribed documents include details of the ownership structure, description of the functions performed, risks undertaken, assets used by the parties to the relevant transaction, etc. Failure to maintain the documentation required by TPRs or to furnish the report of a Chartered Accountant result in imposition of a penalty.

Nature of default	Possible penalty
Failure to keep and maintain documents and information with respect to an ITN	An amount equal to 2% of the value of the ITN
Failure to furnish the documents or information required by TPRs	An amount equal to 2% of the value of the ITN for each such failure
Failure to report any ITN, which is required to be reported.	An amount equal to 2% of the value of the ITN for each such failure
Maintenance or furnishing of any incorrect information or documents	An amount equal to 2% of the value of the ITN for each such failure
Failure to furnish the report of a Chartered Accountant mandated by TPRs	INR 100,000

According to TPRs, enterprises are considered to be "associated" if there is direct/indirect participation in the management, control or capital of an enterprise or by the same persons in both the enterprises. Further, TPRs suggest certain other deeming provisions, which also trigger an associated enterprise relationship. Some of the important ones among these include:

- Direct/indirect shareholding giving rise to 26% or more of voting power.
- Dependence on source of raw material/consumables as well as on customers in the case of manufactured/processed goods, price and other conditions being influenced by the contracting party.
- Authority to appoint more than 50% of board of directors or one or more of executive directors or members of the governing board of the other enterprise.
- Dependence on borrowings, i.e., advancing loans amounting to not less than 51% of the total assets of the enterprise or providing a guarantee amounting to not less than 10% of the total borrowings.

Definition of International Transaction

TPRs defines ITN to mean a transaction between two or more associated enterprises, either or both of whom are non-residents and have a bearing on the profits, income, losses or assets of such enterprises. Amendments to the Finance Act 2012 have clarifies the meaning of ITN. Accordingly, ITN now covers the following:

- Transactions of business restructuring or reorganization
- Financial transactions such as capital financing, including any type of long-term or short borrowing or lending or provision of guarantee, etc.
- Services related to market research, scientific research, market development, legal or accounting services
- Purchase, sale, transfer, lease or use of tangible property including building, plant and machinery, vehicles or any other article, product or thing
- Purchase, sale, transfer, lease or use of any intangible property; intangible property defined to include marketing, technology artistic activity, goodwill, location, or include customer list, customer contracts, methods, programmes, systems, procedures, campaigns, surveys, studies, forecasts, estimates, customer lists, technical data, etc.

Safe Harbor Rules

According to the amendment of the Finance Act (No. 2) 2009, determination of ALP with respect to ITN is subject to "safe harbor" rules, which the CBDT is empowered to draft. Safe harbor indicates the circumstances under which tax authorities accept a transfer price declared by a taxpayer. Currently, safe harbor rules are yet to be notified by the CBDT.

Specified Domestic Transactions (SDTs)

Finance Act 2012 has brought certain SDTs (not being ITNs) within the ambit of TPRs with effect from 1st April 2013 where the aggregate of such transactions exceeds INR 50 m. The SDTs are as follows:

- Any expenditure incurred in favor of any domestic related party
- Any deductions claimed while computing taxable income, which have related party transactions
- Transactions with related domestic companies or units eligible for tax holiday; the amendments will primarily affect the following taxpayers:
    - Taxpayers with income from SEZ units
    - Developers of SEZ
    - Infrastructure developers
    - Developers of industrial park
    - Telecommunication service providers

- Producers or distributors of power
- Commercial producers of mineral oil/natural gas and refiners of mineral oil
- Eligible housing projects
- Eligible hospitals
- Eligible Hotels and convention centers
- Eligible taxpayers with units in North-eastern states
- Any other transaction as may be specified

Advance Pricing Arrangements (APAs)

Finance Act 2012 has introduced enabling provision effective 1 July 2012 that empowers CBDT to enter into advance pricing arrangements (APAs) with taxpayers to determine the arm's length pricing (ALP) or specifying the manner in which an ALP is to be determined in relation to the ITN to be entered with the taxpayer. Some of the salient features of the provisions are as follows:

- APAs are likely to be applicable only for specific ITN to be entered into.
- APAs will be applicable for a maximum period of five consecutive years.
- An APA will be binding on Income Tax authorities, the taxpayer in respect of the transaction in relation to which the APA has been entered into.
- An APA will be declared void if it is found to be obtained by fraud or misrepresentation of facts.
- Taxpayers are required to modify their returns of income in accordance with the APA within three months from the end of the month of entering into the APA.
- The AO will have to assess or reassess taxpayers in accordance with the APA concluded and the modified returns of income.
- The CBDT, which has already set up a separate team under the Director General of Income Tax, International Taxation (the APA Authority) for negotiating APAs, has recently notified the APA rules. The rules contain procedures for APA applications, information, data and forms that need to be filed, etc.

Changes in Transfer Pricing Regulation

The Finance Act 2012 has made the following amendments in the transfer pricing regulations (TPRs):

- The proviso benefit of the arm's length range of +/- 5% has been amended retrospectively with effect from 1st April 2002 so that the arithmetic mean of ALP will be considered to be the ALP if the difference between the arithmetic mean and the taxpayer's transfer price is greater than five percent. Further, the range is computed from the transfer price and not from the arm's length price.
- Effective 1st June 2002, the TPO is entitled to evaluate and determine ALP of any transaction, which comes to his notice irrespective of whether it has been disclosed in accountant's report filed with the AO.
- Non-furnishing of report in respect of international transaction, which the taxpayer was required to furnish will now be grounds for re-opening assessment proceedings.

Acknowledgement:
Adapted from material at India Brand Equity Fund website. Commons IPR, 2013.

Marketing in India Requires Customization[39]

There is a contrasting story being played out in India's cities compared with its villages. While rural India seems to be on a winning streak, the urban areas are in sharp contrast pessimistic mood.

The festive season raises hopes among policymakers, corporate honchos and stock market traders that individuals and households would begin to splurge on the latest TVs, washing machines, music systems, cars, bikes, smartphones, laptops and even on vacations, at least to the nearest tourist destinations.

What few seem to be clued into, however, is that much of the binge may be happening in our villages, reporting higher sales, while the mood in our cities may be dark and sombre. An excellent monsoon and government programmes, such as employment guarantee schemes will spur rural demand, while layoffs or fear of job losses across the economic spectrum, particularly infrastructure (especially power, oil and telecom), media and stock broking, will restrain spending by city dwellers. First things first, retailers, consumer durables' companies and carmakers seem to have assumed that citizens will continue to splurge, come what may, as they have been doing in the past few years.

The Onam sales in Kerala in September 2013, perhaps the most-anticipated shopping season by retailers, second only to Diwali, saw buoyant spending. Several consumer electronics and durables' companies made double-digit growth. The trend may repeat in North India during Navratri to Diwali (October – November period). Yet, it might be wrong to expect the North to replicate the big Kerala sales story, especially from a stock market investor's point of view.

It is well known that Kerala is an `NRI economy'. The state depends mostly on remittances from non-resident 'Keralites'. In 2013, the massive fall in the rupee value meant 36 percent spike in Forex inflows to the state at INR 75,883 crore, as of June 2013-end. Simply put, the state's higher consumption might have hardly been financed by the local economy. The beneficiaries, too, were multinationals, including Samsung, LG, Sony, Panasonic and carmakers Ford, Hyundai and Volkswagen, all of which are not listed on the Indian stock market. The steep rise in the dollar value converted to higher rupee repatriation by NRKs toiling in West Asia, perhaps, resulting in higher spending during festivals, including not just Onam, but also Eid and Easter.

Why are rural areas doing well? To understand the sentiment in rural areas, Deutsche Bank research analysts, Srinivas Rao and Manish Shukla toured Nashik and two smaller towns in 'rurban' (rural + semi rural) Maharashtra and found that consumer sentiment in the villages remained robust on the back of an exceptionally good monsoons. Further, according to them, farmers make a fairly well-informed consumer segment due to their products finding higher exposure abroad. Thirdly, loans are viewed as a 'stopgap' arrangements with a basic objective of being paid back early. Lastly, tractors (rent/purchase) have become a necessity, due to lack of cheap 'farmhands'.

The economy of Nashik (India's 11th most populous district), the 'wine capital of India', and two other towns that were surveyed, viz., Malegaon and Lasalgaon, is primarily driven by agriculture grapes, pomegranates and vegetables which are the key cash crops. Lasalgaon's wholesale market is the largest onion trading hub in India. Malegaon also has a legacy power-loom textile industry, a major source of local employment. "The region is relatively prosperous and abundant rains (after a gap of two years) are having a positive effect on the local economy.

Deutsche Bank analysts wrote in their report, *"Winning in India — It Takes Two to Tango"*, that while large parts of the region are irrigated, monsoon still plays a key role in shaping expectations and propensity to spend. During the visit, it was observed that the Malegaon (population around 409,000) and Lasalgaon (population around 12,500) branches of Mahindra & Mahindra Finance have witnessed significantly stronger growth compared to Nashik, which has a higher urban profile.

The analysts found significant improvement in access to financial services and quality of retailing. "Despite its size, Malegaon has around 7–8 banks, including those from the private sector. Lasalgaon has 3–4 public sector banks and ICICI Bank. Banking habits have also seen a significant change — Mahindra & Mahindra Finance executives indicated that around 40 percent of customers pay through post-dated cheques (PDC). The signs of development are most visible in automotive dealerships, private multi-specialty hospitals and ongoing construction of commercial space," they noted.

Ambit Capital, an Indian broking outfit, too tried to understand the consumer trend by surveying more than 100 large distributors and unlisted companies, spread across India and across most key consumption segments (white goods, FMCG, footwear, jewelry, watches, paints, light electrical, and kitchenware).

It pointed out that the momentum of rural consumption has remained robust, led by a combination of positive consumer sentiments amongst agri-dependent consumers in anticipation of a good harvest from October onwards, given the strong monsoon (a factor prevalent since July 2013). Also, growth in household incomes of traditionally backward regions like Uttarakhand, Bihar and Madhya Pradesh, as a result of which the labor workforce has 'reverse migrated' from cities to villages (a factor prevalent over last 12–18 months) and continued improvement in distribution network in rural India, thereby supporting consumption.

In another report, Deutsche Bank said that its analysis of foodgrain production estimates of individual states, presented at the recently held national conference on agriculture, showed that India's foodgrain production was likely to sharply exceed the government's initial estimate of 257.8 million tonnes. Based on this analysis, Deutsche Bank believes that actual foodgrain production in FY2014 may grow by close to 7–8 percent YoY with a strong possibility of India recording its highest ever foodgrain output. Record agricultural production will create multilayered benefits for the broader economy, by boosting agricultural GDP and supporting rural demand.

Cities Battered and Shattered

In sharp contrast, for firms depending on sales from India's top cities the story is nothing great to write home about. In fact, the mood is pessimistic.

According to the industry association, ASSOCHAM, new job generation has declined by 28 percent in the first quarter of this fiscal alone. Even Mumbai's share of new jobs generated across India has plummeted from over 14 percent a year ago to just over 10 percent. Further, there has been no hike in salaries in most sectors in the past 2–3 years.

Many hundreds have lost their jobs in media, stock broking and infrastructure sectors (oil and gas, telecom, and power) and are sitting at home. Credit Suisse's Neekanth Mishra, in a note, said salaries for entry-level engineers at Infosys have remained unchanged for the past six years, which may be true for other firms, as well.

"Demand in the urban segment has decelerated further", noted Ambit Capital, adding there will be a moderation in demand from premium/high-ticket/urban consumers. "YoY volume growth across segments (including air conditioners, FMCG, footwear, jewelry, light electrical, and watches) has moderated significantly compared with the YoY growth reported in first quarter FY2014 as well as in FY2013," the brokerage said. Urban India is seeing muted growth on rising interest rates and high inflation, noted the Deutsche Bank analysts.

Endnotes

1. *Sources:* Chuin-Wei Yap, "China Revamps Rare-Earth Exports," *The Wall Street Journal,* December 28, 2011, p. C3; "The Difference Engine: More Precious than Gold," *The Economist,* September 17, 2010; "Of Metals and Market Forces," *The Economist,* February 4, 2012; and J. T. Areddy and C. W. Yap, "China Raises Rare-Earth Export Quota," *The Wall Street Journal,* August 22, 2012.
2. For a detailed welfare analysis of the effect of a tariff, see P. R. Krugman and M. Obstfeld, *International Economics: Theory and Policy* (New York: HarperCollins, 2000), Ch. 8.

3. James Healey, "U.S. Alleges Unfair China Auto Subsidies in WTO Action," *USA Today,* September 17, 2012; and M. A. Memoli, "Obama to Tell WTO That China Illegally Subsidizes Auto Imports," *Los Angeles Times,* September 17, 2012.
4. World Trade Organization, *World Trade Report 2006* (Geneva: WTO, 2006).
5. The study was undertaken by Kym Anderson of the University of Adelaide. See "A Not So Perfect Market," *The Economist; Survey of Agriculture and Technology,* March 25, 2000, pp. 8–10.
6. K. Anderson, W. Martin, and D. van der Mensbrugghe, "Distortions to World Trade: Impact on Agricultural Markets and Farm Incomes," *Review of Agricultural Economics* 28 (Summer 2006), pp. 168–94.
7. R. W. Crandall, *Regulating the Automobile* (Washington, DC: Brookings Institution, 1986).
8. J. B. Teece, "Voluntary Export Restraints Are Back; They Didn't Work the Last Time," *Automotive News,* April 23, 2012.
9. Krugman and Obstfeld, *International Economics.*
10. G. Hufbauer and Z. A. Elliott, *Measuring the Costs of Protectionism in the United States* (Washington, DC: Institute for International Economics, 1993).
11. D. Anderton, "U.S. Magnesium Lands Ruling on Unfair Imports," *Desert News,* October 1, 2004, p. D10; "U.S. Magnesium and Its Largest Consumers Debate before U.S. ITC," *Platt's Metals Week,* February 28, 2005, p. 2; and S. Oberbeck, "U.S. Magnesium Plans Big Utah Production Expansion," *Salt Lake Tribune,* March 30, 2005; "US to keep anti-dumping duty on China pure magnesium," Chinadaily.com, September 13th, 2012.
12. Alan Goldstein, "Sematech Members Facing Dues Increase; 30% Jump to Make Up for Loss of Federal Funding," *Dallas Morning News,* July 27, 1996, p. 2F.
13. N. Dunne and R. Waters, "U.S. Waves a Big Stick at Chinese Pirates," *Financial Times,* January 6, 1995, p. 4.
14. Peter S. Jordan, "Country Sanctions and the International Business Community," *American Society of International Law Proceedings of the Annual Meeting* 20, no. 9 (1997), pp. 333–42.
15. C. Southey, "Hormones Fuel a Meaty EU Row," *Financial Times,* September 7, 1995, p. 2; E. L. Andrews, "In Victory for U.S., European Ban on Treated Beef Is Ruled Illegal," *The New York Times,* May 9, 1997, p. A1; R. Baily, "Food and Trade: EU Fear Mongers' Lethal Harvest," *Los Angeles Times,* August 18, 2002, p. M3; Scott Miller, "EU Trade Sanctions Have Dual Edge," *The Wall Street Journal,* February 26, 2004, p. A3; and G. Reilhac, "Lawmakers Approve Rise in Imports of Hormone Free Beef," Reuters, March 14, 2012.
16. "Brazil's Auto Industry Struggles to Boost Global Competitiveness," *Journal of Commerce,* October 10, 1991, p. 6A.
17. For reviews, see J. A. Brander, "Rationales for Strategic Trade and Industrial Policy," in *Strategic Trade Policy and the New International Economics,* P. R. Krugman, ed. (Cambridge, MA: MIT Press, 1986); P. R. Krugman, "Is Free Trade Passé?" *Journal of Economic Perspectives* 1 (1987), pp. 131–44; and P. R. Krugman, "Does the New Trade Theory Require a New Trade Policy?" *World Economy* 15, no. 4 (1992), pp. 423–41.
18. "Airbus and Boeing: The Jumbo War," *The Economist,* June 15, 1991, pp. 65–66.
19. For details see Krugman, "Is Free Trade Passé?"; and Brander, "Rationales for Strategic Trade and Industrial Policy."
20. Krugman, "Is Free Trade Passé?"
21. This dilemma is a variant of the famous prisoner's dilemma, which has become a classic metaphor for the difficulty of achieving cooperation between self-interested and mutually suspicious entities. For a good general introduction, see A. Dixit and B. Nalebuff, *Thinking Strategically: The Competitive Edge in Business, Politics, and Everyday Life* (New York: W. W. Norton & Co., 1991).
22. Note that the Smoot-Hawley Act did not cause the Great Depression. However, the beggar-thy-neighbor trade policies that it ushered in certainly made things worse. See J. Bhagwati, *Protectionism* (Cambridge, MA: MIT Press, 1988).
23. World Bank, *World Development Report* (New York: Oxford University Press, 1987).
24. Frances Williams, "WTO—New Name Heralds New Powers," *Financial Times,* December 16, 1993, p. 5; and Frances Williams, "GATT's Successor to Be Given Real Clout," *Financial Times,* April 4, 1994, p. 6.
25. W. J. Davey, "The WTO Dispute Settlement System: The First Ten Years," *Journal of International Economic Law,* March 2005, pp. 17–28.
26. Information provided on WTO website, www.wto.org/english/tratop_e/dispu_e/dispu_status_e.htm.
27. Data at www.wto.org/english/tratop_e/adp_e/adp_e.htm.
28. *Annual Report by the Director General 2003* (Geneva: World Trade Organization, 2003).
29. Ibid.
30. Ibid.
31. Anderson, Martin, and van der Mensbrugghe, "Distortions to World Trade."
32. World Trade Organization, *Annual Report 2002* (Geneva: WTO, 2002).
33. S. C. Bradford, P. L. E. Grieco, and G. C. Hufbauer, "The Payoff to America from Global Integration," in *The United States and the World Economy: Foreign Policy for the Next Decade,* C. F. Bergsten, ed. (Washington, DC: Institute for International Economics, 2005).

34. S. C. Bradford, P. L. E. Grieco, and G. C. Hufbauer, "The Payoff to America from Global Integration," in *The United States and the World Economy: Foreign Policy for the Next Decade,* C. F. Bergsten, ed. (Washington, DC: Institute for International Economics, 2005).

35. World Bank, *Global Economic Prospects 2005* (Washington, DC: World Bank, 2005).

36. "Doha Development Agenda," *OECD Observer*, September 2006, pp. 64–67.

37. "Punitive Tariffs Are Approved on Imports of Japanese Steel," *The New York Times,* June 12, 1999, p. A3.

38. S. Chan, "World Trade Organization Upholds American Tariffs on Imports of Tires from China," *The New York Times,* December 14, 2010, p. B3; "WTO Rules US Tariff on Chinese Tire Imports," *China Daily,* December 14, 2010; J. M. Freedman, "WTO Rules US Tariffs on Chinese Tire Imports Legal," *Bloomberg BusinessWeek,* December 27, 2010; and J. Bussey, "Get Tough Policy on Chinese Tires Falls Flat," *The Wall Street Journal,* January 20, 2012.

39. Case study prepared based on article:
http://e.mydigitalfc.com/PUBLICATIONS/DCF/DCF/2013/ 10/14/ArticleHtmls/A-TALE-OF-TWO-INDIAS-141020
13141018.shtml?Mode=undefined Accessed on Oct 15, 2015

Chapter 8
Foreign Direct Investment

LEARNING OBJECTIVES

After reading this chapter, you will be able to:

LO8-1 Recognize current trends regarding foreign direct investment (FDI) in the world economy.

LO8-2 Explain the different theories of FDI.

LO8-3 Understand how political ideology shapes a government's attitudes toward FDI.

LO8-4 Describe the benefits and costs of FDI to home and host countries.

LO8-5 Explain the range of policy instruments that governments use to influence FDI.

LO8-6 Identify the implications for managers of the theory and government policies associated with FDI.

◇◇ **FOREIGN RETAILERS IN INDIA** ◇◇

Opening Case

For years now, there has been intense debate in India about the wisdom of relaxing the country's restrictions on foreign direct investment into its retail sector. The Indian retailing sector is highly fragmented and dominated by small enterprises. Estimates suggest that barely 6 percent of India's almost $500 billion in retail sales takes place in organized retail establishments. The rest takes place in small shops, most of which are unincorporated businesses run by individuals or households. In contrast, organized retail establishments account for more than 20 percent of sales in China, 36 percent of sales in Brazil, and 85 percent of all retail sales in the United States. In total, retail establishments in India employ some 34 million people, accounting for more than 7 percent of the workforce.

Advocates of opening up retailing in India to large foreign enterprises, such as Walmart, Carrefour, IKEA, and Tesco, make a number of arguments. They believe that foreign retailers can be a positive force for improving the efficiency of India's distribution systems. Companies like Walmart and Tesco are experts in supply chain management. Applied to India, such know-how could take significant costs out of the economy. Logistics costs are around 14 percent of GDP in India, much higher than the 8 percent in the United States. While this is partly due to a poor road system, it is also the case that most distribution is done by small trucking enterprises, often with a single truck, that have few economies of scale or scope. Large foreign retailers tend to establish their own trucking operations and can reap significant gains from tight control of their distribution system.

Foreign retailers will also probably make major investments in distribution infrastructure such as cold storage facilities and warehouses. Currently, there is a chronic lack of cold storage facilities in India. Estimates suggest that about 25 to 30 percent of all fruits and vegetables spoil before they reach the market due to inadequate cold storage. Similarly, there is a lack of warehousing capacity. A lot of wheat, for example, is simply stored under tarpaulins, where it is at risk of rotting. Such problems raise foods costs to consumers and impose significant losses on farmers.

Farmers have emerged as significant advocates of reform. This is not surprising, because they stand to benefit from working with foreign retailers. Similarly, reform-minded politicians argue that foreign retailers will help keep food processing in check, which benefits all. Ranged against them is a powerful coalition of small shop owners and left-wing politicians, who argue that the entry of large, well-capitalized foreign retailers will result in significant job losses and force many small retailers out of businesses.

In 1997, it looked as if the reformers had the upper hand when they succeeded in changing the rules to allow foreign enterprises to participate in wholesale trading. Taking advantage of this reform, in 2009 Walmart started to open up wholesale stores in India under the name Best Price. The stores are operated by a joint venture with Bharti, an Indian conglomerate. These stores are only allowed to sell to other businesses, such as hotels, restaurants, and small retailers. By 2012, the venture had 20 stores in India. Customers of these stores note that unlike many local competitors, they always have produce in stock, and they are not constantly changing their prices. Farmers, too, like the joint venture because it has worked closely with farmers to secure consistent supplies and has made investments in warehouses and cold storage. The joint venture also pays farmers better prices—something it can afford to do because far less produce goes to waste in its system.

In 2012 the Indian government passed legislation to allow foreign enterprises like Walmart entry into the retail sector. This occurred despite considerable political opposition and suggests that those promoting economic reform in India are for now in ascendancy.[1]

INTRODUCTION

Foreign direct investment (FDI) occurs when a firm invests directly in facilities to produce or market a product in a foreign country. According to the U.S. Department of Commerce, FDI occurs whenever a U.S. citizen, organization, or affiliated group takes an interest of 10 percent or more in a foreign business entity. Once a firm undertakes FDI, it becomes a *multinational enterprise*. An example of FDI is given in the opening case, which describes Walmart's recent investments in India. Walmart first became a multinational in the early 1990s when it invested in Mexico.

FDI takes on two main forms. The first is a **greenfield investment**, which involves the establishment of a new operation in a foreign country. The second involves acquiring or merging with an existing firm in the foreign country. Acquisitions can be a minority (where the foreign firm takes a 10 to 49 percent interest in the firm's voting stock), majority (foreign interest of 50 to 99 percent), or full outright stake (foreign interest of 100 percent).[2]

This chapter opens by looking at the importance of foreign direct investment in the world economy. Next, it reviews the theories that have been used to explain foreign direct investment. The chapter then moves on to look at government policy toward foreign direct investment and closes with a section on implications for business.

FOREIGN DIRECT INVESTMENT IN THE WORLD ECONOMY

LO8-1

When discussing foreign direct investment, it is important to distinguish between the flow of FDI and the stock of FDI. The **flow of FDI** refers to the amount of FDI undertaken over a given time period (normally a year). The **stock of FDI** refers to the total accumulated value of foreign-owned assets at a given time. We also talk of **outflows of FDI**, meaning the flow of FDI out of a country, and **inflows of FDI**, the flow of FDI into a country.

Trends in FDI

The past 35 years have seen a marked increase in both the flow and stock of FDI in the world economy. The average yearly outflow of FDI increased from $25 billion in 1975 to $1.6 trillion in 2012 (see Figure 8.1).[3] Over the past 30 years the flow of FDI has accelerated faster than the growth in world trade and world output. For example, between 1992 and 2012, the total flow of FDI from all countries increased around ninefold while world trade by value grew fourfold and world output by around 55

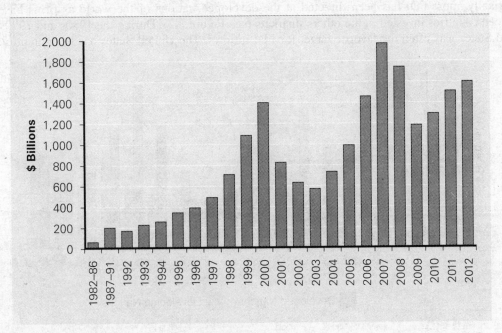

Figure 8.1 *FDI Outflows, 1982–2012 ($ billions)*

Source: Calculted by the author from United Nations *World Investment Report,* various editions.

percent.[4] As a result of the strong FDI flows, by 2011 the global stock of FDI was about $21 trillion. The foreign affiliates of multinationals had more than $27.9 trillion in global sales and accounted for one-third of all cross-border trade in goods and services.[5] The value added by multinationals (revenues less outside purchases of materials and services) reached $7 trillion in 2011, roughly one-tenth of global GDP. Clearly by any measure, FDI is a very important phenomenon.

FDI has grown more rapidly than world trade and world output for several reasons. First, despite the general decline in trade barriers over the past 30 years, firms still fear protectionist pressures. Executives see FDI as a way of circumventing future trade barriers. Second, much of the increase in FDI has been driven by the political and economic changes that have been occurring in many of the world's developing nations. The general shift toward democratic political institutions and free market economies that we discussed in Chapter 3 has encouraged FDI. Across much of Asia, eastern Europe, and Latin America, economic growth, economic deregulation, privatization programs that are open to foreign investors, and removal of many restrictions on FDI have made these countries more attractive to foreign multinationals. According to the United Nations, some 90 percent of the 2,700 changes made worldwide between 1992 and 2009 in the laws governing foreign direct investment created a more favorable environment for FDI.[6]

The globalization of the world economy is also having a positive effect on the volume of FDI. Many firms see the whole world as their market, and they are undertaking FDI in an attempt to make sure they have a significant presence in many regions of the world. For reasons that we explore later in this book, many firms now believe it is important to have production facilities close to their major customers. This too creates pressure for greater FDI.

The Direction of FDI

Historically, most FDI has been directed at the developed nations of the world as firms based in advanced countries invested in the others' markets (see Figure 8.2). During the 1980s and 1990s, the United States was often the favorite target for FDI inflows. The United States has been an attractive

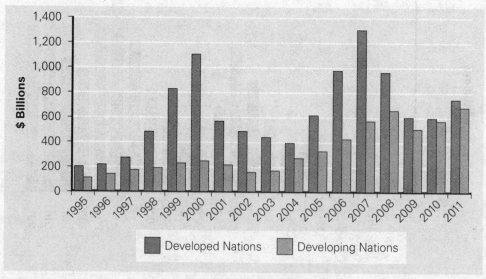

Figure 8.2 *FDI Inflows by Region, 1995–2011 ($ billions)*

Source: Calculated by the author from United Nations *World Investment Report*, various editions.

target for FDI because of its large and wealthy domestic markets, its dynamic and stable economy, a favorable political environment, and the openness of the country to FDI. Investors include firms based in Great Britain, Japan, Germany, Holland, and France. Inward investment into the United States remained high during the 2000s and stood at $227 billion in 2011. The developed nations of the European Union have also been recipients of significant FDI inflows, principally from the United States and other member states of the EU. In 2011, inward investment into the EU was $421 billion. The United Kingdom and France have historically been the largest recipients of inward FDI.[7]

Even though developed nations still account for the largest share of FDI inflows, FDI into developing nations has increased markedly (see Figure 8.2). Most recent inflows into developing nations have been targeted at the emerging economies of Southeast Asia. Driving much of the increase has been the growing importance of China as a recipient of FDI, which attracted about $60 billion of FDI in 2004 and rose steadily to hit a record $124 billion in 2011.[8] The reasons for the strong flow of investment into China are discussed in the accompanying Country Focus. Latin America is the next most important region in the developing world for FDI inflows. In 2011, total inward investments into this region reached $216 billion. Brazil has historically been the top recipient of inward FDI in Latin America. At the other end of the scale, Africa has long received the smallest amount of inward investment, $42.7 billion in 2011. In recent years, Chinese enterprises have emerged as major investors in Africa, particularly in extraction industries where they seem to be trying to ensure future supplies of valuable raw materials. The inability of Africa to attract greater investment is in part a reflection of the political unrest, armed conflict, and frequent changes in economic policy in the region.[9]

The Source of FDI

Since World War II, the United States has consistently been the largest source country for FDI. Other important source countries include the United Kingdom, France, Germany, the Netherlands, and Japan. Collectively, these six countries accounted for 60 percent of all FDI outflows for 1998–2011 (see Figure 8.3). As might be expected, these countries also predominate in rankings of the world's largest multinationals.[10] These nations dominate primarily because they were the most developed nations with

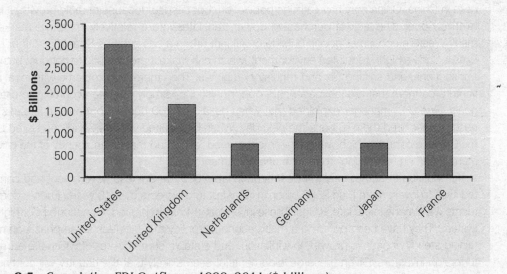

Figure 8.3 *Cumulative FDI Outflows, 1998–2011 ($ billions)*

Source: Calculted by the author from United Nations *World Investment Report,* various editions.

COUNTRY FOCUS

Foreign Direct Investment in China

Beginning in late 1978, China's leadership decided to move the economy away from a centrally planned socialist system to one that was more market driven. The result has been 35 years of sustained high economic growth rates of around 8–10 percent, compounded annually. This growth attracted substantial foreign investment. Starting from a tiny base, foreign investment increased to an annual average rate of $2.7 billion between 1985 and 1990 and then surged to $40 billion annually in the late 1990s, making China the second-biggest recipient of FDI inflows in the world after the United States. The growth has continued, with inward investments into China hitting a record $124 billion in 2011 (with another $83 billion going into Hong Kong). Over the past 20 years, this inflow has resulted in the establishment of more than 300,000 foreign-funded enterprises in China. The total stock of FDI in mainland China grew from almost nothing in 1978 to $712 billion in 2011 (another $1.1 trillion of FDI stock was in Hong Kong).

The reasons for this investment are fairly obvious. With a population of more than 1.3 billion people, China represents the world's largest market. Historically, import tariffs made it difficult to serve this market via exports, so FDI was required if a company wanted to tap into the country's huge potential. China joined the World Trade Organization in 2001. As a result, average tariff rates on imports have fallen from 15.4 percent to about 8 percent today, and reducing the tariff became a motive for investing in China (although at 8 percent, tariffs are still above the average of 3.5 percent found in many developed nations). Notwithstanding tariff rates, many foreign firms believe that doing business in China requires a substantial presence in the country to build *guanxi,* the crucial relationship networks (see Chapter 4 for details). Furthermore, a combination of relatively inexpensive labor and tax incentives, particularly for enterprises that establish themselves in special economic zones, makes China an attractive base from which to serve Asian or world markets with exports (although rising labor costs in China are now making this less important).

Less obvious, at least to begin with, was how difficult it would be for foreign firms to do business in China. China may have a huge population, but despite decades of rapid growth, it is still relatively poor. The lack of purchasing power translates into a relatively immature market for many Western consumer goods outside of affluent urban areas such as Shanghai. Other problems include a highly regulated environment, which can make it problematic to conduct business transactions, and shifting tax and regulatory regimes. Then there are problems with local joint-venture partners that are inexperienced, opportunistic, or simply operate according to different goals. One U.S. manager explained that when he laid off 200 people to reduce costs, his Chinese partner hired them all back the next day. When he inquired why they had been hired back, the Chinese partner, which was government-owned, explained that as an agency of the government, it had an "obligation" to reduce unemployment.

To continue to attract foreign investment, in late 2000 the Chinese government had committed itself to invest more than $800 billion in infrastructure projects over 10 years. Further commitments were made in the late 2000s. These investments have improved the nation's poor highway system. They have been pursuing a macroeconomic policy that includes an emphasis on maintaining steady economic growth, low inflation, and a stable currency—all of which are attractive to foreign investors. Given these developments, it seems likely that the country will continue to be an important magnet for foreign investors well into the future.[11]

the largest economies during much of the postwar period and therefore home to many of the largest and best capitalized enterprises. Many of these countries also had a long history as trading nations and naturally looked to foreign markets to fuel their economic expansion. Thus, it is no surprise that enterprises based there have been at the forefront of foreign investment trends.

That being said, it is noteworthy that Chinese firms have started to emerge as major foreign investors. In 2005, Chinese firms invested some $15 billion internationally. Since then, the figure has risen steadily, reaching $65 billion in 2011. Firms based in Hong Kong accounted for another $81 billion of outward FDI in 2011. Much of the outward investment by Chinese firms has been directed at extractive industries in less developed nations (e.g., China has been a major investor in African countries). A major motive for these investments has been to gain access to raw materials, of which China is one of the world's largest consumers. There are signs, however, that Chinese firms are starting to turn their attention to more advanced nations. In 2012, Chinese firms invested $6.5 billion in the United States, up from $146 million in 2003.[12]

The Form of FDI: Acquisitions Versus Greenfield Investments

FDI can take the form of a greenfield investment in a new facility or an acquisition of or a merger with an existing local firm. UN estimates indicate that some 40 to 80 percent of all FDI inflows were in the form of mergers and acquisitions between 1998 and 2011.[13] However, FDI flows into developed nations differ markedly from those into developing nations. In the case of developing nations, only about one-third or less of FDI is in the form of cross-border mergers and acquisitions. The lower percentage of mergers and acquisitions may simply reflect the fact that there are fewer target firms to acquire in developing nations.

When contemplating FDI, when do firms prefer to acquire existing assets rather than undertake greenfield investments? We consider this question in depth in Chapter 15. For now, we will make a few basic observations. First, mergers and acquisitions are quicker to execute than greenfield investments. This is an important consideration in the modern business world where markets evolve very rapidly. Many firms apparently believe that if they do not acquire a desirable target firm, then their global rivals will. Second, foreign firms are acquired because those firms have valuable strategic assets, such as brand loyalty, customer relationships, trademarks or patents, distribution systems, production systems, and the like. It is easier and perhaps less risky for a firm to acquire those assets than to build them from the ground up through a greenfield investment. Third, firms make acquisitions because they believe they can increase the efficiency of the acquired unit by transferring capital, technology, or management skills (see the next Management Focus on Cemex for an example). However, as we discuss in Chapter 15, there is evidence that many mergers and acquisitions fail to realize their anticipated gains.[14]

THEORIES OF FOREIGN DIRECT INVESTMENT

LO8-2

In this section, we review several theories of foreign direct investment. These theories approach the various phenomena of foreign direct investment from three complementary perspectives. One set of theories seeks to explain why a firm will favor direct investment as a means of entering a foreign market when two other alternatives, exporting and licensing, are open to it. Another set of theories seeks to explain why firms in the same industry often undertake foreign direct investment at the same time and why they favor certain locations over others as targets for foreign direct investment. Put differently, these theories attempt to explain the observed *pattern* of foreign direct investment flows. A third theoretical perspective, known as the **eclectic paradigm**, attempts to combine the two other perspectives into a single holistic explanation of foreign direct investment (this theoretical perspective is *eclectic* because the best aspects of other theories are taken and combined into a single explanation).

Foreign Direct Investment by Cemex

Since the early 1990s, Mexico's largest cement manufacturer, Cemex, has transformed itself from a primarily Mexican operation into the third-largest cement company in the world behind Holcim of Switzerland and Lafarge Group of France. Cemex has long been a powerhouse in Mexico and currently controls more than 60 percent of the market for cement in that country. Cemex's domestic success has been based in large part on an obsession with efficient manufacturing and a focus on customer service that is tops in the industry.

Cemex is a leader in using information technology to match production with consumer demand. The company sells ready-mixed cement that can survive for only about 90 minutes before solidifying, so precise delivery is important. But Cemex can never predict with total certainty what demand will be on any given day, week, or month. To better manage unpredictable demand patterns, Cemex developed a system of seamless information technology—including truck-mounted global positioning systems, radio transmitters, satellites, and computer hardware—that allows it to control the production and distribution of cement like no other company can, responding quickly to unanticipated changes in demand and reducing waste. The results are lower costs and superior customer service, both differentiating factors for Cemex.

Cemex's international expansion strategy was driven by a number of factors. First, the company wished to reduce its reliance on the Mexican construction market, which was characterized by very volatile demand. Second, the company realized there was tremendous demand for cement in many developing countries, where significant construction was being undertaken or needed. Third, the company believed that it understood the needs of construction businesses in developing nations better than the established multinational cement companies, all of which were from developed nations. Fourth, Cemex believed that it could create significant value by acquiring inefficient cement companies in other markets and transferring its skills in customer service, marketing, information technology, and production management to those units.

The company embarked in earnest on its international expansion strategy in the early 1990s. Initially, Cemex targeted other developing nations, acquiring established cement makers in Venezuela, Colombia, Indonesia, the Philippines, Egypt, and several other countries. It also purchased two stagnant companies in Spain and turned them around. Bolstered by the success of its Spanish ventures, Cemex began to look for expansion opportunities in developed nations. In 2000, Cemex purchased Houston-based Southland, one of the largest cement companies in the United States, for $2.5 billion. Following the Southland acquisition, Cemex had 56 cement plants in 30 countries, most of which were gained through acquisitions. In all cases, Cemex devoted great attention to transferring its technological, management and marketing know-how to acquired units, thereby improving their performance.

In 2004, Cemex made another major foreign investment move, purchasing RMC of Great Britain for $5.8 billion. RMC was a huge multinational cement firm with sales of $8 billion, only 22 percent of which were in the United Kingdom, and operations in more than 20 other nations, including many European nations where Cemex had no presence. Finalized in March 2005, the RMC acquisition had transformed Cemex into a global powerhouse in the cement industry with more than $15 billion in annual sales and operations in 50 countries. Only about

15 percent of the company's sales was now generated in Mexico. Following the acquisition of RMC, Cemex found that the RMC plant in Rugby was running at only 70 percent of capacity, partly because repeated production problems kept causing a kiln shutdown. Cemex brought in an international team of specialists to fix the problem and quickly increased production to 90 percent of capacity. Going forward, Cemex has made it clear that it will continue to expand and is eyeing opportunities in the fast-growing economies of China and India where currently it lacks a presence and where its global rivals are already expanding.[15]

Why Foreign Direct Investment?

Why do firms go to the trouble of establishing operations abroad through foreign direct investment when two alternatives, exporting and licensing, are available to them for exploiting the profit opportunities in a foreign market? **Exporting** involves producing goods at home and then shipping them to the receiving country for sale. **Licensing** involves granting a foreign entity (the licensee) the right to produce and sell the firm's product in return for a royalty fee on every unit sold. The question is important, given that a cursory examination of the topic suggests that foreign direct investment may be both expensive and risky compared with exporting and licensing. FDI is expensive because a firm must bear the costs of establishing production facilities in a foreign country or of acquiring a foreign enterprise. FDI is risky because of the problems associated with doing business in a different culture where the rules of the game may be very different. Relative to indigenous firms, there is a greater probability that a foreign firm undertaking FDI in a country for the first time will make costly mistakes due to its ignorance. When a firm exports, it need not bear the costs associated with FDI, and it can reduce the risks associated with selling abroad by using a native sales agent. Similarly, when a firm allows another enterprise to produce its products under license, the licensee bears the costs or risks. So why do so many firms apparently prefer FDI over either exporting or licensing? The answer can be found by examining the limitations of exporting and licensing as means for capitalizing on foreign market opportunities.

Limitations of Exporting

The viability of an exporting strategy is often constrained by transportation costs and trade barriers. When transportation costs are added to production costs, it becomes unprofitable to ship some products over a large distance. This is particularly true of products that have a low value-to-weight ratio and that can be produced in almost any location. For such products, the attractiveness of exporting decreases, relative to either FDI or licensing. This is the case, for example, with cement. Thus, Cemex, the large Mexican cement maker, has expanded internationally by pursuing FDI, rather than exporting (see the accompanying Management Focus). For products with a high value-to-weight ratio, however, transportation costs are normally a minor component of total landed cost (e.g., electronic components, personal computers, medical equipment, computer software, etc.) and have little impact on the relative attractiveness of exporting, licensing, and FDI.

Transportation costs aside, some firms undertake foreign direct investment as a response to actual or threatened trade barriers such as import tariffs or quotas. By placing tariffs on imported goods, governments can increase the cost of exporting relative to foreign direct investment and licensing. Similarly, by limiting imports through quotas, governments increase the attractiveness of FDI and licensing. For example, the wave of FDI by Japanese auto companies in the United States during the 1980s and 1990s was partly driven by protectionist threats from Congress and by quotas on the importation of Japanese cars. For Japanese auto companies, these factors decreased the profitability of exporting and increased that of foreign direct investment. In this context, it is important to understand that trade barriers do not have to be physically in place for FDI to be favored over exporting. Often, the desire to reduce the threat that trade barriers might be imposed is enough to justify foreign direct investment as an alternative to exporting.

Limitations of Licensing

A branch of economic theory known as **internalization theory** seeks to explain why firms often prefer foreign direct investment over licensing as a strategy for entering foreign markets (this approach is also known as the **market imperfections** approach).[16] According to internalization theory, licensing has three major drawbacks as a strategy for exploiting foreign market opportunities. First, *licensing may result in a firm's giving away valuable technological know-how to a potential foreign competitor*. For example, in the 1960s, RCA licensed its leading-edge color television technology to a number of Japanese companies, including Matsushita and Sony. At the time, RCA saw licensing as a way to earn a good return from its technological know-how in the Japanese market without the costs and risks associated with foreign direct investment. However, Matsushita and Sony quickly assimilated RCA's technology and used it to enter the U.S. market to compete directly against RCA. As a result, RCA is now a minor player in its home market, while Matsushita and Sony have a much bigger market share.

A second problem is that *licensing does not give a firm the tight control over manufacturing, marketing, and strategy in a foreign country that may be required to maximize its profitability*. With licensing, control over manufacturing, marketing, and strategy are granted to a licensee in return for a royalty fee. However, for both strategic and operational reasons, a firm may want to retain control over these functions. The rationale for wanting control over the strategy of a foreign entity is that a firm might want its foreign subsidiary to price and market very aggressively as a way of keeping a foreign competitor in check. Unlike a wholly owned subsidiary, a licensee would probably not accept such an imposition, because it would likely reduce the licensee's profit, or it might even cause the licensee to take a loss.

The rationale for wanting control over the operations of a foreign entity is that the firm might wish to take advantage of differences in factor costs across countries, producing only part of its final product in a given country, while importing other parts from elsewhere where they can be produced at lower cost. Again, a licensee would be unlikely to accept such an arrangement, since it would limit the licensee's autonomy. Thus, for these reasons, when tight control over a foreign entity is desirable, foreign direct investment is preferable to licensing.

A third problem with licensing arises when the firm's competitive advantage is based not as much on its products as on the management, marketing, and manufacturing capabilities that produce those products. The problem here is that *such capabilities are often not amenable to licensing*. While a foreign licensee may be able to physically reproduce the firm's product under license, it often may not be able to do so as efficiently as the firm could itself. As a result, the licensee may not be able to fully exploit the profit potential inherent in a foreign market.

For example, consider Toyota, a company whose competitive advantage in the global auto industry is acknowledged to come from its superior ability to manage the overall process of designing, engineering, manufacturing, and selling automobiles—that is, from its management and organizational capabilities. Indeed, Toyota is credited with pioneering the development of a new production process, known as *lean production*, that enables it to produce higher-quality automobiles at a lower cost than its global rivals.[17] Although Toyota could license certain products, its real competitive advantage comes from its management and process capabilities. These kinds of skills are difficult to articulate or codify; they certainly cannot be written down in a simple licensing contract. They are organizationwide and have been developed over the years. They are not embodied in any one individual but instead are widely dispersed throughout the company. Put another way, Toyota's skills are embedded in its organizational culture, and culture is something that cannot be licensed. Thus, if Toyota were to allow a foreign entity to produce its cars under license, the chances are that the entity could not do so as efficiently as could Toyota. In turn, this would limit the ability of the foreign entity to fully develop the market potential of that product. Such reasoning underlies Toyota's preference for direct investment in foreign markets, as opposed to allowing foreign automobile companies to produce its cars under license.

All of this suggests that when one or more of the following conditions holds, markets fail as a mechanism for selling know-how and FDI is more profitable than licensing: (1) when the firm has valuable know-how that cannot be adequately protected by a licensing contract; (2) when the firm needs tight control over a foreign entity to maximize its market share and earnings in that country; and (3) when a firm's skills and know-how are not amenable to licensing.

Advantages of Foreign Direct Investment

It follows that a firm will favor foreign direct investment over exporting as an entry strategy when transportation costs or trade barriers make exporting unattractive. Furthermore, the firm will favor foreign direct investment over licensing (or franchising) when it wishes to maintain control over its technological know-how, or over its operations and business strategy, or when the firm's capabilities are simply not amenable to licensing, as may often be the case.

The Pattern of Foreign Direct Investment

Observation suggests that firms in the same industry often undertake foreign direct investment at about the same time. Also, firms tend to direct their investment activities toward the same target markets. The two theories we consider in this section attempt to explain the patterns that we observe in FDI flows.

Strategic Behavior

One theory is based on the idea that FDI flows are a reflection of strategic rivalry between firms in the global marketplace. An early variant of this argument was expounded by F. T. Knickerbocker, who looked at the relationship between FDI and rivalry in oligopolistic industries.[18] An **oligopoly** is an industry composed of a limited number of large firms (e.g., an industry in which four firms control 80 percent of a domestic market would be defined as an oligopoly). A critical competitive feature of such industries is interdependence of the major players: What one firm does can have an immediate impact on the major competitors, forcing a response in kind. By cutting prices, one firm in an oligopoly can take market share away from its competitors, forcing them to respond with similar price cuts to retain their market share. Thus, the interdependence between firms in an oligopoly leads to imitative behavior; rivals often quickly imitate what a firm does in an oligopoly.

Imitative behavior can take many forms in an oligopoly. One firm raises prices, and the others follow; one expands capacity, and the rivals imitate lest they be left at a disadvantage in the future. Knickerbocker argued that the same kind of imitative behavior characterizes FDI. Consider an oligopoly in the United States in which three firms—A, B, and C—dominate the market. Firm A establishes a subsidiary in France. Firms B and C decide that if successful, this new subsidiary may knock out their export business to France and give a first-mover advantage to firm A. Furthermore, firm A might discover some competitive asset in France that it could repatriate to the United States to torment firms B and C on their native soil. Given these possibilities, firms B and C decide to follow firm A and establish operations in France.

Studies that have looked at FDI by U.S. firms show that firms based in oligopolistic industries tended to imitate each other's FDI.[19] The same phenomenon has been observed with regard to FDI undertaken by

Japanese firms.[20] For example, Toyota and Nissan responded to investments by Honda in the United States and Europe by undertaking their own FDI in the United States and Europe. Research has also shown that models of strategic behavior in a global oligopoly can explain the pattern of FDI in the global tire industry.[21]

Knickerbocker's theory can be extended to embrace the concept of multipoint competition. **Multipoint competition** arises when two or more enterprises encounter each other in different regional markets, national markets, or industries.[22] Economic theory suggests that rather like chess players jockeying for advantage, firms will try to match each other's moves in different markets to try to hold each other in check. The idea is to ensure that a rival does not gain a commanding position in one market and then use the profits generated there to subsidize competitive attacks in other markets.

Although Knickerbocker's theory and its extensions can help explain imitative FDI behavior by firms in oligopolistic industries, it does not explain why the first firm in an oligopoly decides to undertake FDI rather than to export or license. Internalization theory addresses this phenomenon. The imitative theory also does not address the issue of whether FDI is more efficient than exporting or licensing for expanding abroad. Again, internalization theory addresses the efficiency issue. For these reasons, many economists favor internalization theory as an explanation for FDI, although most would agree that the imitative explanation tells an important part of the story.

The Eclectic Paradigm

The eclectic paradigm has been championed by the British economist John Dunning.[23] Dunning argues that in addition to the various factors discussed earlier, location-specific advantages are also of considerable importance in explaining both the rationale for and the direction of foreign direct investment. By **location-specific advantages,** Dunning means the advantages that arise from utilizing resource endowments or assets that are tied to a particular foreign location and that a firm finds valuable to combine with its own unique assets (such as the firm's technological, marketing, or management capabilities). Dunning accepts the argument of internalization theory that it is difficult for a firm to license its own unique capabilities and know-how. Therefore, he argues that combining location-specific assets or resource endowments with the firm's own unique capabilities often requires foreign direct investment. That is, it requires the firm to establish production facilities where those foreign assets or resource endowments are located.

An obvious example of Dunning's arguments are natural resources, such as oil and other minerals, which are by their character specific to certain locations. Dunning suggests that to exploit such foreign resources, a firm must undertake FDI. Clearly, this explains the FDI undertaken by many of the world's oil companies, which have to invest where oil is located in order to combine their technological and managerial capabilities with this valuable location-specific resource. Another obvious example is valuable human resources, such as low-cost, highly skilled labor. The cost and skill of labor varies from country to country. Because labor is not internationally mobile, according to Dunning it makes sense for a firm to locate production facilities in those countries where the cost and skills of local labor are most suited to its particular production processes.

However, Dunning's theory has implications that go beyond basic resources such as minerals and labor. Consider Silicon Valley, which is the world center for the computer and semiconductor industry. Many of the world's major computer and semiconductor companies—such as Apple Computer, Hewlett-Packard, Oracle, Google, and Intel—are located close to each other in the Silicon Valley region of California. As a result, much of the cutting-edge research and product development in computers and semiconductors occurs there. According to Dunning's arguments, knowledge being generated in Silicon Valley with regard to the design and manufacture of computers and semiconductors is available nowhere else in the world. To be sure, that knowledge is commercialized as it diffuses throughout the world, but the leading edge of knowledge generation in the computer and semiconductor industries is to be found in Silicon Valley. In Dunning's language, this means that Silicon Valley has a *location-specific advantage* in the generation of knowledge related to the computer and semiconductor industries. In part, this advantage comes from the sheer concentration of intellectual talent in this area, and in part it arises from a network of informal contacts that allows firms to benefit from each other's knowledge generation. Economists refer to such knowledge "spillovers" as **externalities**, and there is a well-established theory suggesting that firms can benefit from such externalities by locating close to their source.[24]

Insofar as this is the case, it makes sense for foreign computer and semiconductor firms to invest in research and, perhaps, production facilities so they too can learn about and utilize valuable new knowledge before those based elsewhere, thereby giving them a competitive advantage in the global marketplace.[25] Evidence suggests that European, Japanese, South Korean, and Taiwanese computer and semiconductor firms are investing in the Silicon Valley region precisely because they wish to benefit from the externalities that arise there.[26] Others have argued that direct investment by foreign firms in the U.S. biotechnology industry has been motivated by desires to gain access to the unique location-specific technological knowledge of U.S. biotechnology firms.[27] Dunning's theory, therefore, seems to be a useful addition to those outlined previously, because it helps explain how location factors affect the direction of FDI.[28]

POLITICAL IDEOLOGY AND FOREIGN DIRECT INVESTMENT

LO8-3

Historically, political ideology toward FDI within a nation has ranged from a dogmatic radical stance that is hostile to all inward FDI at one extreme to an adherence to the noninterventionist principle of free market economics at the other. Between these two extremes is an approach that might be called *pragmatic nationalism*.

The Radical View

The radical view traces its roots to Marxist political and economic theory. Radical writers argue that the multinational enterprise (MNE) is an instrument of imperialist domination. They see the MNE as a tool for exploiting host countries to the exclusive benefit of their capitalist-imperialist home countries. They argue that MNEs extract profits from the host country and take them to their home country, giving nothing of value to the host country in exchange. They note, for example, that key technology is tightly controlled by the MNE and that important jobs in the foreign subsidiaries of MNEs go to home-country nationals rather than to citizens of the host country. Because of this, according to the radical view, FDI by the MNEs of advanced capitalist nations keeps the less developed countries of the world relatively backward and dependent on advanced capitalist nations for investment, jobs, and technology. Thus, according to the extreme version of this view, no country should ever permit foreign corporations to undertake FDI, because they can never be instruments of economic development, only of economic domination. Where MNEs already exist in a country, they should be immediately nationalized.[29]

From 1945 until the 1980s, the radical view was very influential in the world economy. Until the collapse of communism between 1989 and 1991, the countries of eastern Europe were opposed to FDI. Similarly, Communist countries elsewhere—such as China, Cambodia, and Cuba—were all opposed in principle to FDI (although, in practice, the Chinese started to allow FDI in mainland China in the 1970s). Many socialist countries—particularly in Africa, where one of the first actions of many newly independent states was to nationalize foreign-owned enterprises—also embraced the radical position.

Countries whose political ideology was more nationalistic than socialistic further embraced the radical position. This was true in Iran and India, for example, both of which adopted tough policies restricting FDI and nationalized many foreign-owned enterprises. Iran is a particularly interesting case because its Islamic government, while rejecting Marxist theory, has essentially embraced the radical view that FDI by MNEs is an instrument of imperialism.

By the early 1990s, the radical position was in retreat almost everywhere. There seem to be three reasons for this: (1) the collapse of communism in eastern Europe; (2) the generally abysmal economic performance of those countries that embraced the radical position, and a growing belief by many of these countries that FDI can be an important source of technology and jobs and can stimulate economic growth; and (3) the strong economic performance of those developing countries that embraced capitalism rather than radical ideology (e.g., Singapore, Hong Kong, and Taiwan).

The Free Market View

The free market view traces its roots to classical economics and the international trade theories of Adam Smith and David Ricardo (see Chapter 6). The intellectual case for this view has been strengthened by the internalization explanation of FDI. The free market view argues that international production should be distributed among countries according to the theory of comparative advantage. Countries should specialize in the production of those goods and services that they can produce most efficiently. Within this framework, the MNE is an instrument for dispersing the production of goods and services to the most efficient locations around the globe. Viewed this way, FDI by the MNE increases the overall efficiency of the world economy.

Imagine that Dell decided to move assembly operations for many of its personal computers from the United States to Mexico to take advantage of lower labor costs in Mexico. According to the free market view, moves such as this can be seen as increasing the overall efficiency of resource utilization in the world economy. Mexico, due to its lower labor costs, has a comparative advantage in the assembly of PCs. By moving the production of PCs from the United States to Mexico, Dell frees U.S. resources for use in activities in which the United States has a comparative advantage (e.g., the design of computer software, the manufacture of high value-added components such as microprocessors, or basic R&D). Also, consumers benefit because the PCs cost less than they would if they were produced domestically. In addition, Mexico gains from the technology, skills, and capital that the computer company transfers with its FDI. Contrary to the radical view, the free market view stresses that such resource transfers benefit the host country and stimulate its economic growth. Thus, the free market view argues that FDI is a benefit to both the source country and the host country.

Pragmatic Nationalism

In practice, many countries have adopted neither a radical policy nor a free market policy toward FDI, but instead a policy that can best be described as pragmatic nationalism.[30] The pragmatic nationalist view is that FDI has both benefits and costs. FDI can benefit a host country by bringing capital, skills, technology, and jobs, but those benefits come at a cost. When a foreign company rather than a domestic company produces products, the profits from that investment go abroad. Many countries are also concerned that a foreign-owned manufacturing plant may import many components from its home country, which has negative implications for the host country's balance-of-payments position.

Recognizing this, countries adopting a pragmatic stance pursue policies designed to maximize the national benefits and minimize the national costs. According to this view, FDI should be allowed so long as the benefits outweigh the costs. Japan offers an example of pragmatic nationalism. Until the

1980s, Japan's policy was probably one of the most restrictive among countries adopting a pragmatic nationalist stance. This was due to Japan's perception that direct entry of foreign (especially U.S.) firms with ample managerial resources into the Japanese markets could hamper the development and growth of its own industry and technology.[31] This belief led Japan to block the majority of applications to invest in Japan. However, there were always exceptions to this policy. Firms that had important technology were often permitted to undertake FDI if they insisted that they would neither license their technology to a Japanese firm nor enter into a joint venture with a Japanese enterprise. IBM and Texas Instruments were able to set up wholly owned subsidiaries in Japan by adopting this negotiating position. From the perspective of the Japanese government, the benefits of FDI in such cases—the stimulus that these firms might impart to the Japanese economy—outweighed the perceived costs.

Another aspect of pragmatic nationalism is the tendency to aggressively court FDI believed to be in the national interest by, for example, offering subsidies to foreign MNEs in the form of tax breaks or grants. The countries of the European Union often seem to be competing with each other to attract U.S. and Japanese FDI by offering large tax breaks and subsidies. Britain has been the most successful at attracting Japanese investment in the automobile industry. Nissan, Toyota, and Honda now have major assembly plants in Britain and use the country as their base for serving the rest of Europe—with obvious employment and balance-of-payments benefits for Britain.

Shifting Ideology

Recent years have seen a marked decline in the number of countries that adhere to a radical ideology. Although few countries have adopted a pure free market policy stance, an increasing number of countries are gravitating toward the free market end of the spectrum and have liberalized their foreign investment regime. This includes many countries that less than two decades ago were firmly in the radical camp (e.g., the former Communist countries of eastern Europe, many of the socialist countries of Africa, and India) and several countries that until recently could best be described as pragmatic nationalists with regard to FDI (e.g., Japan, South Korea, Italy, Spain, and most Latin American countries). One result has been the surge in the volume of FDI worldwide, which, as we noted earlier, has been growing twice as fast as the growth in world trade. Another result has been an increase in the volume of FDI directed at countries that have recently liberalized their FDI regimes, such as China, India, and Vietnam.

As a counterpoint, there is some evidence of a shift to a more hostile approach to foreign direct investment in some nations. Venezuela and Bolivia have become increasingly hostile to foreign direct investment. In 2005 and 2006, the governments of both nations unilaterally rewrote contracts for oil and gas exploration, raising the royalty rate that foreign enterprises had to pay the government for oil and gas extracted in their territories. Following his election victory in 2006, Bolivian President Evo Morales nationalized the nation's gas fields and stated that he would evict foreign firms unless they agreed to pay about 80 percent of their revenues to the state and relinquish production oversight. In some developed nations, there is increasing evidence of hostile reactions to inward FDI as well. In Europe in 2006, there was a hostile political reaction to the attempted takeover of Europe's largest steel company, Arcelor, by Mittal Steel, a global company controlled by the Indian entrepreneur Lakshmi Mittal. In mid-2005, China National Offshore Oil Company withdrew a takeover bid for Unocal of the United States after highly negative reaction in Congress about the proposed takeover of a "strategic asset" by a Chinese company. Similarly, as detailed in the accompanying Management Focus, in 2006 a Dubai-owned company withdrew its planned takeover of some operations at six U.S. ports after negative political reactions. So far, these countertrends are nothing more than isolated incidents, but if they become more widespread, the 30-year movement toward lower barriers to cross-border investment could be in jeopardy.

DP World and the United States

In February 2006, DP World, a ports operator with global reach owned by the government of Dubai, a member of the United Arab Emirates and a staunch U.S. ally, paid $6.8 billion to acquire P&O, a British firm that runs a global network of marine terminals. With P&O came the management operations of six U.S. ports: Miami, Philadelphia, Baltimore, New Orleans, New Jersey, and New York. The acquisition had already been approved by U.S. regulators when it suddenly became front-page news. Upon hearing about the deal, several prominent U.S. senators raised concerns about the acquisition. Their objections were twofold. First, they raised questions about the security risks associated with management operations in key U.S. ports being owned by a foreign enterprise that was based in the Middle East. The implication was that terrorists could somehow take advantage of the ownership arrangement to infiltrate U.S. ports. Second, they were concerned that DP World was a state-owned enterprise and argued that foreign governments should not be in a position of owning key "U.S. strategic assets."

The Bush administration was quick to defend the takeover, stating it posed no threat to national security. Others noted that DP World was a respected global firm with an American chief operating officer and an American-educated chairman; the head of the global ports management operation would also be an American. DP World would not own the U.S. ports in question, just manage them, while security issues would remain in the hands of American customs officials and the U.S. Coast Guard. Dubai was also a member of America's Container Security Initiative, which allows American customs officials to inspect cargo in foreign ports before it leaves for the United States. Most of the DP World employees at American ports would be U.S. citizens, and any UAE citizen transferred to DP World would be subject to American visa approval.

These arguments fell on deaf ears. With several U.S. senators threatening to pass legislation to prohibit foreign ownership of U.S. port operations, DP World bowed to the inevitable and announced it would sell off the right to manage the six U.S. ports for about $750 million. Looking forward, however, DP World stated it would seek an initial public offering in 2007, and the then-private firm would in all probability continue to look for ways to enter the United States. In the words of the firm's CEO, "This is the world's largest economy. How can you just ignore it?"[32]

BENEFITS AND COSTS OF FDI

LO8-4

To a greater or lesser degree, many governments can be considered pragmatic nationalists when it comes to FDI. Accordingly, their policy is shaped by a consideration of the costs and benefits of FDI. Here, we explore the benefits and costs of FDI, first from the perspective of a host (receiving) country and then from the perspective of the home (source) country. In the next section, we look at the policy instruments governments use to manage FDI.

Host-Country Benefits

The main benefits of inward FDI for a host country arise from resource-transfer effects, employment effects, balance-of-payments effects, and effects on competition and economic growth.

Resource-Transfer Effects

Foreign direct investment can make a positive contribution to a host economy by supplying capital, technology, and management resources that would otherwise not be available and thus boost that country's economic growth rate (as described in the opening case, the Indian government has come around to this view and has adopted a more permissive attitude to inward investment).[33]

With regard to capital, many MNEs, by virtue of their large size and financial strength, have access to financial resources not available to host-country firms. These funds may be available from internal company sources, or, because of their reputation, large MNEs may find it easier to borrow money from capital markets than host-country firms would.

As for technology, you will recall from Chapter 3 that technology can stimulate economic development and industrialization. Technology can take two forms, both of which are valuable. Technology can be incorporated in a production process (e.g., the technology for discovering, extracting, and refining oil), or it can be incorporated in a product (e.g., personal computers). However, many countries lack the research and development resources and skills required to develop their own indigenous product and process technology. This is particularly true in less developed nations. Such countries must rely on advanced industrialized nations for much of the technology required to stimulate economic growth, and FDI can provide it.

Research supports the view that multinational firms often transfer significant technology when they invest in a foreign country.[34] For example, a study of FDI in Sweden found that foreign firms increased both the labor and total factor productivity of Swedish firms that they acquired, suggesting that significant technology transfers had occurred (technology typically boosts productivity).[35] Also, a study of FDI by the Organization for Economic Cooperation and Development (OECD) found that foreign investors invested significant amounts of capital in R&D in the countries in which they had invested, suggesting that not only were they transferring technology to those countries but they may also have been upgrading existing technology or creating new technology in those countries.[36]

Foreign management skills acquired through FDI may also produce important benefits for the host country. Foreign managers trained in the latest management techniques can often help improve the efficiency of operations in the host country, whether those operations are acquired or greenfield developments. This is one reason the Indian government would like to open up the Indian retail sector to inward investment by foreign firms such as Walmart and Carrefour (see the opening case). Beneficial spin-off effects may also arise when local personnel who are trained to occupy managerial, financial, and technical posts in the subsidiary of a foreign MNE leave the firm and help establish indigenous firms. Similar benefits may arise if the superior management skills of a foreign MNE stimulate local suppliers, distributors, and competitors to improve their own management skills.

Employment Effects

Another beneficial employment effect claimed for FDI is that it brings jobs to a host country that would otherwise not be created there. The effects of FDI on employment are both direct and indirect. Direct effects arise when a foreign MNE employs a number of host-country citizens. Indirect effects arise when jobs are created in local suppliers as a result of the investment and when jobs are created because of increased local spending by employees of the MNE. The indirect employment effects are often as large as, if not larger than, the direct effects. For example, when Toyota decided to open a new auto plant in France, estimates suggested the plant would create 2,000 direct jobs and perhaps another 2,000 jobs in support industries.[37]

Cynics argue that not all the "new jobs" created by FDI represent net additions in employment. In the case of FDI by Japanese auto companies in the United States, some argue that the jobs created by this investment have been more than offset by the jobs lost in U.S.-owned auto companies, which have lost market share to their Japanese competitors. As a consequence of such substitution effects, the net number of new jobs created by FDI may not be as great as initially claimed by an MNE. The issue of the likely net gain in employment may be a major negotiating point between an MNE wishing to undertake FDI and the host government.

When FDI takes the form of an acquisition of an established enterprise in the host economy as opposed to a greenfield investment, the immediate effect may be to reduce employment as the multinational tries to restructure the operations of the acquired unit to improve its operating efficiency. However, even in such cases, research suggests that once the initial period of restructuring is over, enterprises acquired by foreign firms tend to increase their employment base at a faster rate than domestic rivals. An OECD study found that foreign firms created new jobs at a faster rate than their domestic counterparts.[38]

Balance-of-Payments Effects

FDI's effect on a country's balance-of-payments accounts is an important policy issue for most host governments. A country's **balance-of-payments accounts** track both its payments to and its receipts from other countries. Governments normally are concerned when their country is running a deficit on the current account of their balance of payments. The **current account** tracks the export and import of goods and services. A current account deficit, or *trade deficit* as it is often called, arises when a country is importing more goods and services than it is exporting. Governments typically prefer to see a current account surplus than a deficit. The only way in which a current account deficit can be supported in the long run is by selling off assets to foreigners (for a detailed explanation of why this is the case, see the appendix to Chapter 6). For example, the persistent U.S. current account deficit since the 1980s has been financed by a steady sale of U.S. assets (stocks, bonds, real estate, and whole corporations) to foreigners. Because national governments invariably dislike seeing the assets of their country fall into foreign hands, they prefer their nation to run a current account surplus. There are two ways in which FDI can help a country achieve this goal.

First, if the FDI is a substitute for imports of goods or services, the effect can be to improve the current account of the host country's balance of payments. Much of the FDI by Japanese automobile companies in the United States and Europe, for example, can be seen as substituting for imports from Japan. Thus, the current account of the U.S. balance of payments has improved somewhat because many Japanese companies are now supplying the U.S. market from production facilities in the United States, as opposed to facilities in Japan. Insofar as this has reduced the need to finance a current account deficit by asset sales to foreigners, the United States has clearly benefited.

A second potential benefit arises when the MNE uses a foreign subsidiary to export goods and services to other countries. According to a UN report, inward FDI by foreign multinationals has been a major driver of export-led economic growth in a number of developing and developed nations.[39] For example, in China exports increased from $26 billion in 1985 to more than $250 billion by 2001 and $1.9 trillion in 2012. Much of this dramatic export growth was due to the presence of foreign multinationals that invested heavily in China during the 1990s.

Effect on Competition and Economic Growth

Economic theory tells us that the efficient functioning of markets depends on an adequate level of competition between producers. When FDI takes the form of a greenfield investment, the result is to establish a new enterprise, increasing the number of players in a market and thus consumer choice. In turn, this can increase the level of competition in a national market, thereby driving down prices and increasing the economic welfare of consumers. Increased competition tends to stimulate capital investments by firms in plant, equipment, and R&D as they struggle to gain an edge over their rivals. The long-term results may include increased productivity growth, product and process innovations, and greater economic growth.[40] Such beneficial effects seem to have occurred in the South Korean retail sector following the liberalization of FDI regulations in 1996. FDI by large Western discount stores—including Walmart, Costco, Carrefour, and Tesco—seems to have encouraged indigenous discounters such as E-Mart to improve the efficiency of their own operations. The results have included more competition and lower prices, which benefit South Korean consumers.

FDI's impact on competition in domestic markets may be particularly important in the case of services, such as telecommunications, retailing, and many financial services, where exporting is often not an option because the service has to be produced where it is delivered.[41] For example, under a 1997 agreement sponsored by the World Trade Organization, 68 countries accounting for more than 90 percent of world telecommunications revenues pledged to start opening their markets to foreign investment and competition and to abide by common rules for fair competition in telecommunications. Before this agreement, most of the world's telecommunications markets were closed to foreign competitors, and in most countries the market was monopolized by a single carrier, which was often a state-owned enterprise. The agreement has dramatically increased the level of competition in many national telecommunications markets, producing two major benefits. First, inward investment has increased competition and stimulated investment in the modernization of telephone networks around the world, leading to better service. Second, the increased competition has resulted in lower prices.

Host-Country Costs

Three costs of FDI concern host countries. They arise from possible adverse effects on competition within the host nation, adverse effects on the balance of payments, and the perceived loss of national sovereignty and autonomy.

Adverse Effects on Competition

Host governments sometimes worry that the subsidiaries of foreign MNEs may have greater economic power than indigenous competitors. If it is part of a larger international organization, the foreign MNE may be able to draw on funds generated elsewhere to subsidize its costs in the host market, which could drive indigenous companies out of business and allow the firm to monopolize the market. Once the market is monopolized, the foreign MNE could raise prices above those that would prevail in competitive markets, with harmful effects on the economic welfare of the host nation. This concern tends to be greater in countries that have few large firms of their own (generally, less developed countries). It tends to be a relatively minor concern in most advanced industrialized nations.

In general, while FDI in the form of greenfield investments should increase competition, it is less clear that this is the case when the FDI takes the form of acquisition of an established enterprise in the host nation, as was the case when Cemex acquired RMC in Britain (see the Management Focus). Because an acquisition does not result in a net increase in the number of players in a market, the effect on competition may be neutral. When a foreign investor acquires two or more firms in a host country, and subsequently merges them, the effect may be to reduce the level of competition in that market, create monopoly power for the foreign firm, reduce consumer choice, and raise prices. For example, in India, Hindustan Lever Ltd., the Indian subsidiary of Unilever, acquired its main local rival, Tata Oil Mills, to assume a dominant position in the bath soap (75 percent) and detergents (30 percent) markets. Hindustan Lever also acquired several local companies in other markets, such as the ice cream makers Dollops, Kwality, and Milkfood. By combining these companies, Hindustan Lever's share of the Indian ice cream market went from zero in 1992 to 74 percent in 1997.[42] However, although such cases are of obvious concern, there is little evidence that such developments are widespread. In many nations, domestic competition authorities have the right to review and block any mergers or acquisitions that they view as having a detrimental impact on competition. If such institutions are operating effectively, this should be sufficient to make sure that foreign entities do not monopolize a country's markets.

Adverse Effects on the Balance of Payments

The possible adverse effects of FDI on a host country's balance-of-payments position are twofold. First, set against the initial capital inflow that comes with FDI must be the subsequent outflow of earnings from the foreign subsidiary to its parent company. Such outflows show up as capital outflow on balance-of-payments accounts. Some governments have responded to such outflows by restricting the amount of earnings that can be repatriated to a foreign subsidiary's home country. A second concern arises when a foreign subsidiary imports a substantial number of its inputs from abroad, which results in a debit on the current account of the host country's balance of payments. One criticism leveled against Japanese-owned auto assembly operations in the United States, for example, is that they tend to import many component parts from Japan. Because of this, the favorable impact of this FDI on the current account of the U.S. balance-of-payments position may not be as great as initially supposed. The Japanese auto companies responded to these criticisms by pledging to purchase 75 percent of their component parts from U.S.-based manufacturers (but not necessarily U.S.-owned manufacturers). When the Japanese auto company Nissan invested in the United Kingdom, Nissan responded to concerns about local content by pledging to increase the proportion of local content to 60 percent and subsequently raising it to more than 80 percent.

National Sovereignty and Autonomy

Some host governments worry that FDI is accompanied by some loss of economic independence. The concern is that key decisions that can affect the host country's economy will be made by a foreign parent that has no real commitment to the host country, and over which the host country's government has no real control. Most economists dismiss such concerns as groundless and irrational. Political scientist Robert Reich has noted that such concerns are the product of outmoded thinking because they fail to account for the growing interdependence of the world economy.[43] In a world in which firms from all advanced nations are increasingly investing in each other's markets, it is not possible for one country to hold another to "economic ransom" without hurting itself.

Home-Country Benefits

The benefits of FDI to the home (source) country arise from three sources. First, the home country's balance of payments benefits from the inward flow of foreign earnings. FDI can also benefit the home country's balance of payments if the foreign subsidiary creates demands for home-country exports of capital equipment, intermediate goods, complementary products, and the like.

Second, benefits to the home country from outward FDI arise from employment effects. As with the balance of payments, positive employment effects arise when the foreign subsidiary creates demand for home-country exports. Thus, Toyota's investment in auto assembly operations in Europe has benefited both the Japanese balance-of-payments position and employment in Japan, because Toyota imports some component parts for its European-based auto assembly operations directly from Japan.

Third, benefits arise when the home-country MNE learns valuable skills from its exposure to foreign markets that can subsequently be transferred back to the home country. This amounts to a reverse resource-transfer effect. Through its exposure to a foreign market, an MNE can learn about superior management techniques and superior product and process technologies. These resources can then be transferred back to the home country, contributing to the home country's economic growth rate.[44] For example, one reason General Motors and Ford invested in Japanese automobile companies (GM owns part of Isuzu, and Ford owns part of Mazda) was to learn about their production processes. If GM and Ford are successful in transferring this know-how back to their U.S. operations, the result may be a net gain for the U.S. economy.

Home-Country Costs

Against these benefits must be set the apparent costs of FDI for the home (source) country. The most important concerns center on the balance-of-payments and employment effects of outward FDI. The home country's balance of payments may suffer in three ways. First, the balance of payments suffers from the initial capital outflow required to finance the FDI. This effect, however, is usually more than offset by the subsequent inflow of foreign earnings. Second, the current account of the balance of payments suffers if the purpose of the foreign investment is to serve the home market from a low-cost production location. Third, the current account of the balance of payments suffers if the FDI is a substitute for direct exports. Thus, insofar as Toyota's assembly operations in the United States are intended to substitute for direct exports from Japan, the current account position of Japan will deteriorate.

With regard to employment effects, the most serious concerns arise when FDI is seen as a substitute for domestic production. This was the case with Toyota's investments in the United States and Europe. One obvious result of such FDI is reduced home-country employment. If the labor market in the home country is already tight, with little unemployment, this concern may not be that great. However, if the home country is suffering from unemployment, concern about the export of jobs may arise. For example, one objection frequently raised by U.S. labor leaders to the free trade pact among the United States, Mexico, and Canada (see the next chapter) is that the United States would lose hundreds of thousands of jobs as U.S. firms invest in Mexico to take advantage of cheaper labor and then export back to the United States.[45]

International Trade Theory and FDI

When assessing the costs and benefits of FDI to the home country, keep in mind the lessons of international trade theory (see Chapter 6). International trade theory tells us that home-country concerns about the negative economic effects of offshore production may be misplaced. The term **offshore production** refers to FDI undertaken to serve the home market. Far from reducing home-country employment, such FDI may actually stimulate economic growth (and hence employment) in the home country by freeing home-country resources to concentrate on activities where the home country has a comparative advantage. In addition, home-country consumers benefit if the price of the particular product falls as a result of the FDI. Also, if a company were prohibited from making such investments on the grounds of negative employment effects while its international competitors reaped the benefits of low-cost production locations, it would undoubtedly lose market share to its international competitors. Under such a scenario, the adverse long-run economic effects for a country would probably outweigh the relatively minor balance-of-payments and employment effects associated with offshore production.

GOVERNMENT POLICY INSTRUMENTS AND FDI

We have now reviewed the costs and benefits of FDI from the perspective of both home country and host country. We now turn our attention to the policy instruments that home (source) countries and host countries can use to regulate FDI.

Home-Country Policies

Through their choice of policies, home countries can both encourage and restrict FDI by local firms. We look at policies designed to encourage outward FDI first. These include foreign risk insurance, capital assistance, tax incentives, and political pressure. Then we will look at policies designed to restrict outward FDI.

Encouraging Outward FDI

Many investor nations now have government-backed insurance programs to cover major types of foreign investment risk. The types of risks insurable through these programs include the risks of expropriation (nationalization), war losses, and the inability to transfer profits back home. Such programs are particularly useful in encouraging firms to undertake investments in politically unstable countries.[46] In addition, several advanced countries also have special funds or banks that make government loans to firms wishing to invest in developing countries. As a further incentive to encourage domestic firms to undertake FDI, many countries have eliminated double taxation of foreign income (i.e., taxation of income in both the host country and the home country). Last, and perhaps most significant, a number of investor countries (including the United States) have used their political influence to persuade host countries to relax their restrictions on inbound FDI. For example, in response to direct U.S. pressure, Japan relaxed many of its formal restrictions on inward FDI in the 1980s. Now, in response to further U.S. pressure, Japan has moved toward relaxing its informal barriers to inward FDI. One beneficiary of this trend has been Toys "R" Us, which, after five years of intensive lobbying by company and U.S. government officials, opened its first retail stores in Japan in December 1991. By 2011, Toys "R" Us had more 170 stores in Japan, and its Japanese operation, in which Toys "R" Us retained a controlling stake, had a listing on the Japanese stock market.

Restricting Outward FDI

Virtually all investor countries, including the United States, have exercised some control over outward FDI from time to time. One policy has been to limit capital outflows out of concern for the country's balance of payments. From the early 1960s until 1979, for example, Britain had exchange-control regulations that limited the amount of capital a firm could take out of the country. Although the main intent of such policies was to improve the British balance of payments, an important secondary intent was to make it more difficult for British firms to undertake FDI.

In addition, countries have occasionally manipulated tax rules to try to encourage their firms to invest at home. The objective behind such policies is to create jobs at home rather than in other nations. At one time, Britain adopted such policies. The British advanced corporation tax system taxed British companies' foreign earnings at a higher rate than their domestic earnings. This tax code created an incentive for British companies to invest at home.

Finally, countries sometimes prohibit national firms from investing in certain countries for political reasons. Such restrictions can be formal or informal. For example, formal U.S. rules prohibited U.S. firms from investing in countries such as Cuba and Iran, whose political ideology and actions are judged to be contrary to U.S. interests. Similarly, during the 1980s, informal pressure was applied to dissuade

U.S. firms from investing in South Africa. In this case, the objective was to pressure South Africa to change its apartheid laws, which happened during the early 1990s.

Host-Country Policies

Host countries adopt policies designed both to restrict and to encourage inward FDI. As noted earlier in this chapter, political ideology has determined the type and scope of these policies in the past. In the last decade of the twentieth century, many countries moved quickly away from adhering to some version of the radical stance and prohibiting much FDI, and toward a situation where a combination of free market objectives and pragmatic nationalism took hold.

Encouraging Inward FDI

It is common for governments to offer incentives to foreign firms to invest in their countries. Such incentives take many forms, but the most common are tax concessions, low-interest loans, and grants or subsidies. Incentives are motivated by a desire to gain from the resource-transfer and employment effects of FDI. They are also motivated by a desire to capture FDI away from other potential host countries. For example, in the mid-1990s, the governments of Britain and France competed with each other on the incentives they offered Toyota to invest in their respective countries. In the United States, state governments often compete with each other to attract FDI. For example, Kentucky offered Toyota an incentive package worth $147 million to persuade it to build its U.S. automobile assembly plants there. The package included tax breaks, new state spending on infrastructure, and low-interest loans.[47]

Restricting Inward FDI

Host governments use a wide range of controls to restrict FDI in one way or another. The two most common are ownership restraints and performance requirements. Ownership restraints can take several forms. In some countries, foreign companies are excluded from specific fields. They are excluded from tobacco and mining in Sweden and from the development of certain natural resources in Brazil, Finland, and Morocco. In other industries, foreign ownership may be permitted although a significant proportion of the equity of the subsidiary must be owned by local investors. Foreign ownership is restricted to 25 percent or less of an airline in the United States. In India, foreign firms were prohibited from owning media businesses until 2001, when the rules were relaxed, allowing foreign firms to purchase up to 26 percent of an Indian newspaper. As described in the opening case, foreign firms are still restricted from owning retail establishments in India.[48]

The rationale underlying ownership restraints seems to be twofold. First, foreign firms are often excluded from certain sectors on the grounds of national security or competition. Particularly in less developed countries, the feeling seems to be that local firms might not be able to develop unless foreign competition is restricted by a combination of import tariffs and controls on FDI. This is a variant of the infant industry argument discussed in Chapter 7.

Second, ownership restraints seem to be based on a belief that local owners can help maximize the resource-transfer and employment benefits of FDI for the host country. Until the early 1980s, the Japanese government prohibited most FDI but allowed joint ventures between Japanese firms and foreign MNEs if the MNE had a valuable technology. The Japanese government clearly believed such an arrangement would speed up the subsequent diffusion of the MNE's valuable technology throughout the Japanese economy.

Performance requirements can also take several forms. Performance requirements are controls over the behavior of the MNE's local subsidiary. The most common performance requirements are related to local content, exports, technology transfer, and local participation in top management. As with certain ownership restrictions, the logic underlying performance requirements is that such rules help maximize the benefits and minimize the costs of FDI for the host country. Many countries employ some form of performance requirements when it suits their objectives. However, performance requirements tend to be more common in less developed countries than in advanced industrialized nations.[49]

International Institutions and the Liberalization of FDI

Until the 1990s, there was no consistent involvement by multinational institutions in the governing of FDI. This changed with the formation of the World Trade Organization in 1995. The WTO embraces the promotion of international trade in services. Because many services have to be produced where they are sold, exporting is not an option (e.g., one cannot export McDonald's hamburgers or consumer banking services). Given this, the WTO has become involved in regulations governing FDI. As might be expected for an institution created to promote free trade, the thrust of the WTO's efforts has been to push for the liberalization of regulations governing FDI, particularly in services. Under the auspices of the WTO, two extensive multinational agreements were reached in 1997 to liberalize trade in telecommunications and financial services. Both these agreements contained detailed clauses that require signatories to liberalize their regulations governing inward FDI, essentially opening their markets to foreign telecommunications and financial services companies. The WTO has had less success trying to initiate talks aimed at establishing a universal set of rules designed to promote the liberalization of FDI. Led by Malaysia and India, developing nations have so far rejected efforts by the WTO to start such discussions.

■ IMPLICATIONS FOR MANAGERS ■■■■■■■■■■■■■■ ■LO8-6■

Several implications for business are inherent in the material discussed in this chapter. In this section, we deal first with the implications of the theory and then turn our attention to the implications of government policy.

THE THEORY OF FDI

The implications of the theories of FDI for business practice are straightforward. First, the location-specific advantages argument associated with John Dunning does help explain the *direction* of FDI. However, the location-specific advantages argument does not explain *why* firms prefer FDI to licensing or to exporting. In this regard, from both an explanatory and a business perspective, perhaps the most useful theories are those that focus on the limitations of exporting and licensing—that is, internalization theories. These theories are useful because they identify with some precision how the relative profitability of foreign direct investment, exporting, and licensing vary with circumstances. The theories suggest that exporting is preferable to licensing and FDI so long as transportation costs are minor and trade barriers are trivial. As transportation costs or trade barriers increase, exporting becomes unprofitable, and the choice is between FDI and licensing. Because FDI is more costly and more risky than licensing, other things being equal, the theories argue that licensing is preferable to FDI. Other things are seldom equal, however. Although licensing may work, it is not an attractive option when one or more of the following conditions exist: (1) The firm has valuable know-how that cannot be adequately protected by a licensing contract, (2) the firm needs tight control over a foreign entity to maximize its market share and earnings in that country, and (3) a firm's skills and capabilities are not amenable to licensing. Figure 8.4 presents these considerations as a decision tree.

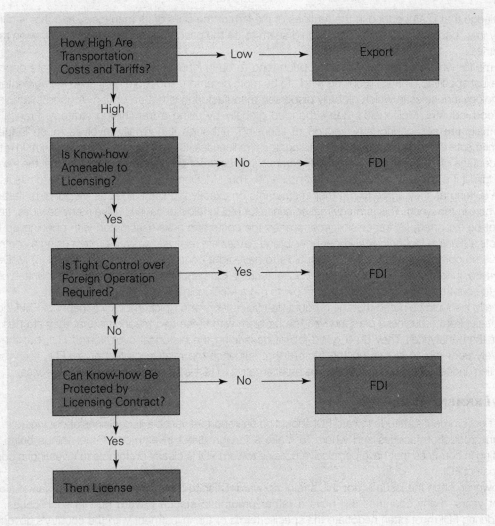

Figure 8.4 *A Decision Framework*

Firms for which licensing is not a good option tend to be clustered in three types of industries:

1. High-technology industries in which protecting firm-specific expertise is of paramount importance and licensing is hazardous.
2. Global oligopolies, in which competitive interdependence requires that multinational firms maintain tight control over foreign operations so that they have the ability to launch coordinated attacks against their global competitors.
3. Industries in which intense cost pressures require that multinational firms maintain tight control over foreign operations (so that they can disperse manufacturing to locations around the globe where factor costs are most favorable in order to minimize costs).

Although empirical evidence is limited, the majority seems to support these conjectures.[50] In addition, licensing is not a good option if the competitive advantage of a firm is based upon managerial or marketing knowledge that is embedded in the routines of the firm or the skills of its managers, and that is difficult to codify in a "book of blueprints." This would seem to be the case for firms based in a fairly wide range of industries.

Firms for which licensing is a good option tend to be in industries whose conditions are opposite to those just specified. That is, licensing tends to be more common, and more profitable, in fragmented, low-technology industries in which globally dispersed manufacturing is not an option. A good example is the fast-food industry. McDonald's has expanded globally by using a franchising strategy. Franchising is essentially the service-industry version of licensing, although it normally involves much longer-term commitments than licensing. With franchising, the firm licenses its brand name to a foreign firm in return for a percentage of the franchisee's profits. The franchising contract specifies the conditions that the franchisee must fulfill if it is to use the franchisor's brand name. Thus, McDonald's allows foreign firms to use its brand name so long as they agree to run their restaurants on exactly the same lines as McDonald's restaurants elsewhere in the world. This strategy makes sense for McDonald's because (1) like many services, fast food cannot be exported; (2) franchising economizes the costs and risks associated with opening up foreign markets; (3) unlike technological know-how, brand names are relatively easy to protect using a contract; (4) there is no compelling reason for McDonald's to have tight control over franchisees; and (5) McDonald's know-how, in terms of how to run a fast-food restaurant, is amenable to being specified in a written contract (e.g., the contract specifies the details of how to run a McDonald's restaurant).

Finally, it should be noted that the product life-cycle theory and Knickerbocker's theory of FDI tend to be less useful from a business perspective. The problem with these two theories is that they are descriptive rather than analytical. They do a good job of describing the historical evolution of FDI, but they do a relatively poor job of identifying the factors that influence the relative profitability of FDI, licensing, and exporting. Indeed, the issue of licensing as an alternative to FDI is ignored by both these theories.

GOVERNMENT POLICY

A host government's attitude toward FDI should be an important variable in decisions about where to locate foreign production facilities and where to make a foreign direct investment. Other things being equal, investing in countries that have permissive policies toward FDI is clearly preferable to investing in countries that restrict FDI.

However, often the issue is not this straightforward. Despite the move toward a free market stance in recent years, many countries still have a rather pragmatic stance toward FDI. In such cases, a firm considering FDI must often negotiate the specific terms of the investment with the country's government. Such negotiations center on two broad issues. If the host government is trying to attract FDI, the central issue is likely to be the kind of incentives the host government is prepared to offer to the MNE and what the firm will commit in exchange. If the host government is uncertain about the benefits of FDI and might choose to restrict access, the central issue is likely to be the concessions that the firm must make to be allowed to go forward with a proposed investment.

To a large degree, the outcome of any negotiated agreement depends on the relative bargaining power of both parties. Each side's bargaining power depends on three factors:

- The value each side places on what the other has to offer.
- The number of comparable alternatives available to each side.
- Each party's time horizon.

From the perspective of a firm negotiating the terms of an investment with a host government, the firm's bargaining power is high when the host government places a high value on what the firm has to offer, the number of comparable alternatives open to the firm is greater, and the firm has a long time in which to complete the negotiations. The converse also holds. The firm's bargaining power is low when the host government places a low value on what the firm has to offer, the number of comparable alternatives open to the firm is fewer, and the firm has a short time in which to complete the negotiations.[51]

Chapter Summary

This chapter reviewed theories that attempt to explain the pattern of FDI between countries and to examine the influence of governments on firms' decisions to invest in foreign countries. The chapter made the following points:

1. Any theory seeking to explain FDI must explain why firms go to the trouble of acquiring or establishing operations abroad when the alternatives of exporting and licensing are available to them.

2. High transportation costs or tariffs imposed on imports help explain why many firms prefer FDI or licensing over exporting.

3. Firms often prefer FDI to licensing when (a) a firm has valuable know-how that cannot be adequately protected by a licensing contract, (b) a firm needs tight control over a foreign entity in order to maximize its market share and earnings in that country, and (c) a firm's skills and capabilities are not amenable to licensing.

4. Knickerbocker's theory suggests that much FDI is explained by imitative behavior by rival firms in an oligopolistic industry.

5. Dunning has argued that location-specific advantages are of considerable importance in explaining the nature and direction of FDI. According to Dunning, firms undertake FDI to exploit resource endowments or assets that are location specific.

6. Political ideology is an important determinant of government policy toward FDI. Ideology ranges from a radical stance that is hostile to FDI to a noninterventionist, free market stance. Between the two extremes is an approach best described as pragmatic nationalism.

7. Benefits of FDI to a host country arise from resource-transfer effects, employment effects, and balance-of-payments effects.

8. The costs of FDI to a host country include adverse effects on competition and balance of payments and a perceived loss of national sovereignty.

9. The benefits of FDI to the home (source) country include improvement in the balance of payments as a result of the inward flow of foreign earnings, positive employment effects when the foreign subsidiary creates demand for home-country exports, and benefits from a reverse resource-transfer effect. A reverse resource-transfer effect arises when the foreign subsidiary learns valuable skills abroad that can be transferred back to the home country.

10. The costs of FDI to the home country include adverse balance-of-payments effects that arise from the initial capital outflow and from the export substitution effects of FDI. Costs also arise when FDI exports jobs abroad.

11. Home countries can adopt policies designed to both encourage and restrict FDI. Host countries try to attract FDI by offering incentives, and try to restrict FDI by dictating ownership restraints and requiring that foreign MNEs meet specific performance requirements.

Critical Thinking and Discussion Questions

1. In 2008, inward FDI accounted for some 63.7 percent of gross fixed capital formation in Ireland, but only 4.1 percent in Japan (*gross fixed capital formation* refers to investments in fixed assets such as factories, warehouses, and retail stores). What do you think explains this difference in FDI inflows into the two countries?

2. Compare and contrast these explanations of FDI: internalization theory and Knickerbocker's theory of FDI. Which theory do you think offers the best explanation of the historical pattern of FDI? Why?

3. What are the strengths of the eclectic theory of FDI? Can you see any shortcomings? How does the eclectic theory influence management practice?

4. Read the Management Focus on Cemex, and then answer the following questions:
   a. Which theoretical explanation, or explanations, of FDI best explains Cemex's FDI?
   b. What is the value that Cemex brings to a host economy? Can you see any potential drawbacks of inward investment by Cemex in an economy?
   c. Cemex has a strong preference for acquisitions over greenfield ventures as an entry mode. Why?

5. You are the international manager of a U.S. business that has just developed a revolutionary new personal computer that can perform the same functions as existing PCs but costs only half as much to manufacture. Several patents protect the unique design of this computer. Your CEO has asked you to formulate a recommendation for how to expand into western Europe. Your options are (*a*) to export from the United States, (*b*) to license a European firm to manufacture and market the computer in Europe, or (*c*) to set up a wholly owned subsidiary in Europe. Evaluate the pros and cons of each alternative, and suggest a course of action to your CEO.

Research Task ◯ globalEDGE globaledge.msu.edu

Foreign Direct Investment

Use the globalEDGE website (globaledge.msu.edu) to complete the following exercises:

Exercise 1

The *World Investment Report* published annually by UNCTAD provides a summary of recent trends in FDI as well as quick access to comprehensive investment statistics. Identify the table of *largest transnational corporations* from developing and transition countries. The ranking is based on the foreign assets each corporation owns. Based only at the top 20 companies, provide a summary of the countries and industries represented. Do you notice any common traits from your analysis? Did any industries or countries in the top 20 surprise you? Why?

Exercise 2

An integral part of successful foreign direct investment is to understand the target market opportunities as well as the nature of the risk inherent in possible investment projects, particularly in developing countries. You work for a company that builds wastewater and sanitation infrastructure in such countries. *The Multilateral Investment Guarantee Agency* (MIGA) provides insurance for risky projects in these markets. Identify the sector brief for the water and wastewater sector, and prepare a report to identify the major risks projects in this sector tend to face and how MIGA can assist in such projects.

India's Retail Sector

With a score of 63, India ranks fourth among the surveyed 30 countries in Global Retail Development Index and ranked sixth in the 2011 Global Apparel Index.[52] India's strong growth fundamentals along with increased urbanization and consumerism opened immense scope for retail expansion for foreign players.[53] The market size in 2010 was estimated at USD 353 billion (Source: IBEF) and is expected to reach USD 543 billion by 2014. Retailing has played a major role the world over in increasing productivity across a wide range of consumer goods and services. In the developed countries, the organized retail industry accounts for almost 80 percent of the total retail trade. In contrast, in India organized retail trade accounts for merely five percent of the total retail trade. This highlights tremendous potential for retail sector growth in India.[54]

India ranks Fourth in the 2011 Global Retail Development Index

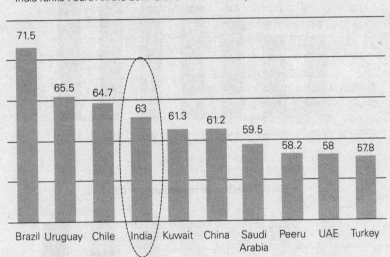

Source: http://www.ibef.org/download/Retail50112.pdf

The sector can be broadly divided into two segments: *Value retailing*, which is typically a low margin-high volume business (primarily food and groceries) and *Lifestyle retailing*, a high margin-low volume business (apparel, footwear, etc). The sector is further divided into various categories, depending on the types of products offered. Food dominates market consumption followed by fashion. The relatively low contribution of other categories indicates opportunity for organized retail growth in these segments, especially with India being one of the world's youngest markets.[55]

Historically, Indians have been conservative spenders, thus food forms a huge chunk of India's consumption needs. Transition from traditional retail to organized retailing is taking place due to changing consumer expectations, demographic mix, etc. With the revival in consumer spending, expansion plans of retailers are back in full swing. The convenience of shopping with multiplicity of choice under one roof (Shop- in Shop), and the increase of mall culture etc. are factors appreciated by the new generation. These are expected to be the growth drivers of organized retailing in India over the long run.[56]

The organized retail segment in India is expected to be nine percent of total retail market by 2015 and 20 percent by 2020. India's grocery retail segment is the most attractive in the world. Hypermarkets would be the largest retail segment, accounting for 21 percent of total retail space by 2013–14.[57]

Foreign retailers are entering into Indian market to share a huge profit. Foreign direct investment (FDI) up to 100 percent is allowed under the automatic route in cash & carry (wholesale). Government is planning to remove the old tax systems to simplify the tax calculation and avoid double taxation in Indian retail. New Goods and Service Tax (GST) will simplify the tax structure.

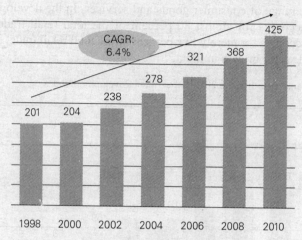

Market size over the past few years (USD billion)

Source: EIU, Euro monitor, Aranca Research

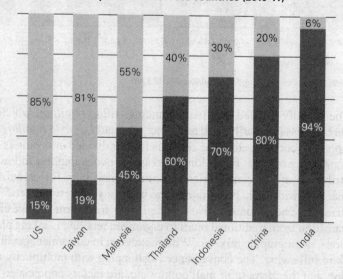

Retail penetration across countries (2010-11)

Source: E&Y report, Aranca Research

Source: http://www.ibef.org/download/Retail50112.pdf

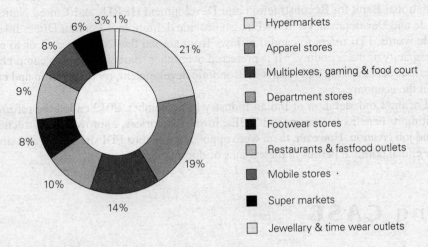

Break-up of all mall space by format (2013-14)

- ☐ Hypermarkets — 21%
- ▨ Apparel stores — 19%
- ■ Multiplexes, gaming & food court — 14%
- ▦ Department stores — 10%
- ■ Footwear stores — 8%
- ▧ Restaurants & fastfood outlets — 8%
- ▨ Mobile stores — 9%
- ■ Super markets — 6%
- ☐ Jewellary & time wear outlets — 3% 1%

Source: Technopak Advisors Pvt Ltd, Cushman & Wakefield Research

Source: http://www.ibef.org/download/Retail50112.pdf

FDI Retail Commencement to India

International Monetary Organization (IMF) and Organization for Economic Cooperation and Development (OECD) define FDI as a category of cross-border investment made by a resident in one economy (the direct investor) with the objective of establishing a 'lasting interest' in an enterprise (the direct investment enterprise) that is resident in an economy other than that of the direct investor. The motive of the direct investor is a strategic long term relationship with the direct investment enterprise

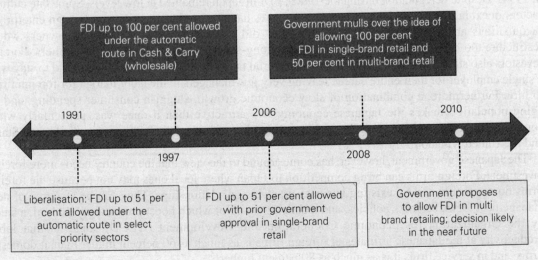

FDI up to 100 per cent allowed under the automatic route in Cash & Carry (wholesale)

Government mulls over the idea of allowing 100 per cent FDI in single-brand retail and 50 per cent in multi-brand retail

1991   1997   2006   2008   2010

Liberalisation: FDI up to 51 per cent allowed under the automatic route in select priority sectors

FDI up to 51 per cent allowed with prior government approval in single-brand retail

Government proposes to allow FDI in multi brand retailing; decision likely in the near future

Source Aranca Research

to ensure significant degree of influence in the management of the direct investment enterprise. Besides, International Bank for Reconstruction and Development (IBRD) and United Nations Conference on Trade and Development (UNCTAD) also provide definition of Foreign Direct Investment. To put in simple words, FDI refers to capital inflows from abroad that is invested in or to enhance the production capacity of the economy.[58] It is preferred over other sources of foreign capital because it is non-volatile, non-debt creating and results in economic development, modernization and employment generation in the economy.[59]

The head of the Confederation of Indian Industry in September, 2012 called the reform "a game-changer", citing its benefits to farmers and SMEs, lower food prices, improved infrastructure and supply chain, and job creation. However, there were oppositions against FDI since 2011 and street protests by several regional political parties in their States of dominance.[60]

Closing CASE

Walmart in Japan

Japan has been a tough market for foreign firms to enter. The level of foreign direct investment (FDI) in Japan is a fraction of that found in many other developed nations. In 2011, for example, the stock of foreign direct investment as a percentage of GDP was 3.9 percent in Japan. In the United States, the comparable figure was 23.5 percent, in Germany 23.4 percent, in France 39 percent, and in the United Kingdom 48.4 percent.

Various reasons account for the lack of FDI in Japan. Until the 1990s, government regulations made it difficult for companies to establish a direct presence in the nation. In the retail sector, for example, the Large Scale Retail Store Law, which was designed to protect politically powerful small retailers, made it all but impossible for foreign retailers to open large-volume stores in the country (the law was repealed in 1994). Despite deregulation during the 1990s, FDI in Japan remained at low levels. Some cite cultural factors in explaining this. Many Japanese companies have resisted acquisitions by foreign enterprises (acquisitions are a major vehicle for FDI). They did so because of fears that new owners would restructure too harshly, cutting jobs and breaking long-standing commitments with suppliers. Foreign investors also state that it is difficult to find managerial talent in Japan. Most managers tend to stay with a single employer for their entire career, leaving very few managers in the labor market for foreign firms to hire. Furthermore, a combination of slow economic growth, sluggish consumer spending, and an aging population makes the Japanese economy less attractive than it once was, particularly when compared to the dynamic and rapidly growing economies of India and China or even the United States and the United Kingdom.

The Japanese government, however, has come around to the view that the country needs more foreign investment. Foreign firms can bring competition to Japan where local ones may not because the foreign firms do not feel bound by existing business practices or relationships. They can be a source of new management ideas, business policies, and technology—all of which boost productivity. Indeed, a study by the Organization for Economic Cooperation and Development (OECD) suggests that labor productivity at the Japanese affiliates of foreign firms is as much as 60 percent higher than at domestic firms, and in service firms it is as much as 80 percent higher.

It was the opportunity to help restructure Japan's retail sector—boosting productivity, gaining market share, and profiting in the process—that attracted Walmart to Japan. The world's largest retailer,

Walmart entered Japan in 2002 by acquiring a stake in Seiyu, which was then the fifth-largest retailer in Japan. Under the terms of the deal, Walmart increased its ownership stake over the next five years, becoming a majority owner by 2006. In 2008 it acquired all the remaining stock in Seiyu. Seiyu was, by all accounts, an inefficient retailer. According to one top officer, "Seiyu is bogged down in old customs that are wasteful. Walmart brings proven skills in managing big supermarkets, which is what we would like to learn to do."

Walmart's goal was to transfer best practices from its U.S. stores and use them to improve the performance of Seiyu. This meant implementing Walmart's cutting-edge information systems, adopting tight inventory control, leveraging its global supply chain to bring low-cost goods into Japan, introducing everyday low prices, retraining employees to improve customer service, extending opening hours, renovating stores, and investing in new ones.

It proved to be more difficult than Walmart had hoped. When Walmart acquired a majority stake in Seiyu, it promptly laid off 1,500 employees at the retailer's headquarters. While this reduced costs, it also created resistance from former and remaining employees, who complained vocally to the press about how Walmart was trying to impose American management practices on a Japanese corporation. This was a public relations setback for Walmart. Walmart also stumbled when it began to stock low-priced (and low-perceived-quality) Chinese goods in its Japanese stores. Japanese consumers did not respond favorably, and Walmart found that it had to alter its merchandising approach, offering more high-value items to match Japanese shopping habits, which were proving to be difficult to change. Walmart's entry also prompted local rivals to change their strategies. They began to make acquisitions and started to cut their prices to match Walmart's discounting strategy. Also, many Japanese suppliers were reluctant to work closely with Walmart due to their belief that Walmart would force them to cut prices to the bone.

Despite such setbacks, Walmart has slowly started to make progress in Japan. The retailer has been adjusting to the Japanese market. For example, it has created special products to cater to the aging Japanese population. "One of its most popular products is a '298-Yen Bento,' a single-serve, freshly prepared meal that sells for about $4 and is tailored to 'someone on a pension with limited funds.'" Walmart has also drawn on its global supply chain to introduce products into Japan that have caught on with local consumers, such as Reese's Pieces peanut butter candies from Hershey Co. The company has also found that by bypassing Japan's traditional multitiered distribution system, and importing food directly from other countries, it can undercut local competitors. For example, grapes imported straight from California can be 20 percent cheaper than those sold by competitors. Due to actions like these, Walmart may ultimately become profitable in Japan. The company is certainly betting on this. In 2012, after a four-year hiatus, Walmart announced that it would open 22 new stores in Japan over the next two years.[61]

Case Discussion Questions

1. Why, historically, has the level of FDI in Japan been so low?
2. What are the potential benefits to the Japanese economy of greater FDI?
3. How might the entry of Walmart into the Japanese retail sector benefit that sector? Who could lose as a result of Walmart's entry?
4. Why has it been so hard for Walmart to make a profit in Japan? What might the company have done differently in its early years in Japan?
5. Why did Walmart announce in late 2012 that it would expand its operations in Japan after opening no new stores in four years?

Endnotes

1. V. Bajaj, "Wal-Mart Debate Rages in India," *The New York Times,* December 6, 2011, pp. B1, B2; S.G. Mozumder, "Walmart Is Not Coming to India Just to Sell," *India Abroad,* December 16, 2011, pp. A18–A19; and R. Kohli and J. Bhaqwati, "Organized Retailing in India: Issues and Outlook," Columbia Program on Indian Economic Policies, working paper no. 2011-1, January 22, 2011. N. Prusty, "Indian Government wins Second Vote on Retail," Reuters, December 7th, 2012.

2. United Nations, *World Investment Report, 2012* (New York and Geneva: United Nations, 2012).

3. United Nations, *World Investment Report, 2012;* and United Nations Conference on Trade and Investment, "Global Flows of Foreign Direct Investment Exceeding Pre-Crisis Levels in 2011," *Global Investment Trends Monitor,* January 24, 2012.

4. World Trade Organization, *International Trade Statistics, 2012* (Geneva: WTO, 2012); and United Nations, *World Investment Report, 2012.*

5. United Nations, *World Investment Report, 2012.*

6. United Nations, *World Investment Report, 2010* (New York and Geneva: United Nations, 2010).

7. United Nations, *World Investment Report, 2012;* and UN Conference on Trade and Investment, "Global Flows of Foreign Direct Investment."

8. Ibid.

9. United Nations, *World Investment Report, 2011* (New York and Geneva: United Nations, 2011).

10. United Nations, *World Investment Report, 2011.*

11. Interviews by the author while in China; United Nations, *World Investment Report, 2012;* Linda Ng and C. Tuan, "Building a Favorable Investment Environment: Evidence for the Facilitation of FDI in China," *The World Economy,* 2002, pp. 1095–114; and S. Chan and G. Qingyang, "Investment in China Migrates Inland," *Far Eastern Economic Review,* May 2006, pp. 52–57.

12. M. Caruso-Cabrera, "Chinese Investment in US May Break Record in 2013," CNBC, January 2, 2013.

13. United Nations, *World Investment Report, 2012.*

14. See D. J. Ravenscraft and F. M. Scherer, *Mergers, Selloffs and Economic Efficiency* (Washington, DC: The Brookings Institution, 1987); and A. Seth, K. P. Song, and R. R. Pettit, "Value Creation and Destruction in Cross-Border Acquisitions," *Strategic Management Journal* 23 (2002), pp. 921–40.

15. C. Piggott, "Cemex's Stratospheric Rise," *Latin Finance,* March 2001, p. 76; J. F. Smith, "Making Cement a Household Word," *Los Angeles Times,* January 16, 2000, p. C1; D. Helft, "Cemex Attempts to Cement Its Future," *The Industry Standard,* November 6, 2000; Diane Lindquist, "From Cement to Services," *Chief Executive,* November 2002, pp. 48–50; "Cementing Global Success," *Strategic Direct Investor,* March 2003, p. 1; M. T. Derham, "The Cemex Surprise," *Latin Finance,* November 2004, pp. 1–2; "Holcim Seeks to Acquire Aggregate," *The Wall Street Journal,* January 13, 2005, p. 1; J. Lyons, "Cemex Prowls for Deals in Both China and India," *The Wall Street Journal,* January 27, 2006, p. C4; and S. Donnan, "Cemex Sells 25 Percent Stake in Semen Gresik," *FT.com,* May 4, 2006, p. 1.

16. For example, see S. H. Hymer, *The International Operations of National Firms: A Study of Direct Foreign Investment* (Cambridge, MA: MIT Press, 1976); A. M. Rugman, *Inside the Multinationals: The Economics of Internal Markets* (New York: Columbia University Press, 1981); D. J. Teece, "Multinational Enterprise, Internal Governance, and Industrial Organization," *American Economic Review* 75 (May 1983), pp. 233–38; C. W. L. Hill and W. C. Kim, "Searching for a Dynamic Theory of the Multinational Enterprise: A Transaction Cost Model," *Strategic Management Journal* 9 (special issue, 1988), pp. 93–104; A. Verbeke, "The Evolutionary View of the MNE and the Future of Internalization Theory," *Journal of International Business Studies* 34 (2003), pp. 498–501; and J. H. Dunning, "Some Antecedents of Internalization Theory," *Journal of International Business Studies* 34 (2003), pp. 108–28.

17. J. P. Womack, D. T. Jones, and D. Roos, *The Machine That Changed the World* (New York: Rawson Associates, 1990).

18. The argument is most often associated with F. T. Knickerbocker, *Oligopolistic Reaction and Multinational Enterprise* (Boston: Harvard Business School Press, 1973).

19. The studies are summarized in R. E. Caves, *Multinational Enterprise and Economic Analysis,* 2nd ed. (Cambridge, UK: Cambridge University Press, 1996).

20. See R. E. Caves, "Japanese Investment in the US: Lessons for the Economic Analysis of Foreign Investment," *The World Economy* 16 (1993), pp. 279–300; B. Kogut and S. J. Chang, "Technological Capabilities and Japanese Direct Investment in the United States," *Review of Economics and Statistics* 73 (1991), pp. 401–43; and J. Anand and B. Kogut, "Technological Capabilities of Countries, Firm Rivalry, and Foreign Direct Investment," *Journal of International Business Studies,* 1997, pp. 445–65.

21. K. Ito and E. L. Rose, "Foreign Direct Investment Location Strategies in the Tire Industry," *Journal of International Business Studies* 33 (2002), pp. 593–602.

22. H. Haveman and L. Nonnemaker, "Competition in Multiple Geographical Markets," *Administrative Science Quarterly* 45 (2000), pp. 232–67; and L. Fuentelsaz and J. Gomez, "Multipoint Competition, Strategic Similarity and Entry into Geographic Markets," *Strategic Management Journal* 27 (2006), pp. 447–57.

23. J. H. Dunning, *Explaining International Production* (London: Unwin Hyman, 1988).

24. P. Krugman. "Increasing Returns and Economic Geography," *Journal of Political Economy* 99, no. 3 (1991), pp. 483–99.

25. J. M. Shaver and F. Flyer, "Agglomeration Economies, Firm Heterogeneity, and Foreign Direct Investment in the United States," *Strategic Management Journal* 21 (2000), pp. 1175–93.

26. J. H. Dunning and R. Narula, "Transpacific Foreign Direct Investment and the Investment Development Path," *South Carolina Essays in International Business,* May 1995.

27. W. Shan and J. Song, "Foreign Direct Investment and the Sourcing of Technological Advantage: Evidence from the Biotechnology Industry," *Journal of International Business Studies,* 1997, pp. 267–84.

28. For some additional evidence, see L. E. Brouthers, K. D. Brouthers, and S. Warner, "Is Dunning's Eclectic Framework Descriptive or Normative?" *Journal of International Business Studies* 30 (1999), pp. 831–44.

29. For elaboration, see S. Hood and S. Young, *The Economics of the Multinational Enterprise* (London: Longman, 1979); and P. M. Sweezy and H. Magdoff, "The Dynamics of U.S. Capitalism," *Monthly Review Press,* 1972.

30. For an example of this policy as practiced in China, see L. G. Branstetter and R. C. Freenstra, "Trade and Foreign Direct Investment in China: A Political Economy Approach," *Journal of International Economics* 58 (December 2002), pp. 335–58.

31. M. Itoh and K. Kiyono, "Foreign Trade and Direct Investment," in *Industrial Policy of Japan,* ed. R. Komiya, M. Okuno, and K. Suzumura (Tokyo: Academic Press, 1988).

32. "Trouble at the Waterfront," *The Economist,* February 25, 2006, p. 48; "Paranoia about Dubai Ports Deals Is Needless," *Financial Times,* February 21, 2006, p. 16; and "DP World: We'll Be Back," *Traffic World,* May 29, 2006, p. 1.

33. R. E. Lipsey, "Home and Host Country Effects of FDI," *National Bureau of Economic Research Working Paper Series,* paper no. 9293, October 2002; and X. Li and X. Liu, "Foreign Direct Investment and Economic Growth," *World Development* 33 (March 2005), pp. 393–413.

34. X. J. Zhan and T. Ozawa, *Business Restructuring in Asia: Cross Border M&As in Crisis Affected Countries* (Copenhagen: Copenhagen Business School, 2000); I. Costa, S. Robles, and R. de Queiroz, "Foreign Direct Investment and Technological Capabilities," *Research Policy* 31 (2002), pp. 1431–43; B. Potterie and F. Lichtenberg, "Does Foreign Direct Investment Transfer Technology across Borders?" *Review of Economics and Statistics* 83 (2001), pp. 490–97; and K. Saggi, "Trade, Foreign Direct Investment and International Technology Transfer," *World Bank Research Observer* 17 (2002), pp. 191–235.

35. K. M. Moden, "Foreign Acquisitions of Swedish Companies: Effects on R&D and Productivity," Research Institute of International Economics, 1998, mimeo.

36. "Foreign Friends," *The Economist,* January 8, 2000, pp. 71–72.

37. A. Jack, "French Go into Overdrive to Win Investors," *Financial Times,* December 10, 1997, p. 6.

38. "Foreign Friends," *The Economist,* January 8, 2000, pp. 71–72.

39. United Nations, *World Investment Report, 2002* (New York and Geneva: United Nations, 2002).

40. R. Ram and K. H. Zang, "Foreign Direct Investment and Economic Growth," *Economic Development and Cultural Change* 51 (2002), pp. 205–25.

41. United Nations, *World Investment Report, 1998* (New York and Geneva: United Nations, 1998).

42. United Nations, *World Investment Report, 2000* (New York and Geneva: United Nations, 2000).

43. R. B. Reich, *The Work of Nations: Preparing Ourselves for the 21st Century* (New York: Alfred A. Knopf, 1991).

44. This idea has been articulated, although not quite in this form, by C. A. Bartlett and S. Ghoshal, *Managing across Borders: The Transnational Solution* (Boston: Harvard Business School Press, 1989).

45. P. Magnusson, "The Mexico Pact: Worth the Price?" *BusinessWeek,* May 27, 1991, pp. 32–35.

46. C. Johnston, "Political Risk Insurance," in *Assessing Corporate Political Risk,* ed. D. M. Raddock (Totowa, NJ: Rowan & Littlefield, 1986).

47. M. Tolchin and S. Tolchin, *Buying into America: How Foreign Money Is Changing the Face of Our Nation* (New York: Times Books, 1988).

48. S. Rai, "India to Ease Limits on Foreign Ownership of Media and Tea," *The New York Times,* June 26, 2002, p. W1.

49. L. D. Qiu and Z. Tao, "Export, Foreign Direct Investment and Local Content Requirements," *Journal of Development Economics* 66 (October 2001), pp. 101–25.

50. See R. E. Caves, *Multinational Enterprise and Economic Analysis* (Cambridge, UK: Cambridge University Press, 1982).

51. For a good general introduction to negotiation strategy, see M. H. Bazerman and M. A. Neale, *Negotiating Rationally* (New York: Free Press, 1992); A. Dixit and B. Nalebuff, *Thinking Strategically: The Competitive Edge in Business, Politics, and*

Everyday Life (New York: W. W. Norton, 1991); and H. Raiffa, *The Art and Science of Negotiation* (Cambridge, MA: Harvard University Press, 1982).

52. http://www.ibef.org/artdisplay.aspx?cat_id=377&art_id=30832
53. Op.cit as 1 above
54. http://www.equitymaster.com/research-it/sector-info/retail/Retailing-Sector-Analysis-Report.asp
55. Op.cit as 3 above
56. http://www.equitymaster.com/research-it/sector-info/retail/Retailing-Sector-Analysis-Report.asp
57. http://www.ibef.org/artdisplay.aspx?cat_id=377&art_id=30832
58. http://cci.gov.in/images/media/ResearchReports/FDI%20in%20Indian%20Retail%20Sector%20Analysis%20of%20Competition%20in%20Agri-Food%20Sector.pdf
59. http://www.legallyindia.com/1468-fdi-in-retailing-sector-in-india-pros-cons-by-hemant-batra
60. http://www.ibef.org/download/Retail50112.pdf
61. D. R. John, "Wal-Mart in Japan: Survival and Future of Its Japanese Business," *ICFAI University Journal of International Business* 3 (2008), pp. 45–67; United Nations, *World Investment Report, 2009* (New York and Geneva: United Nations, 2009); "Challenges Persist in Japan," *MMR,* December 14, 2009, p. 45; J. Matusitz and M. Foster, "Successful Globalization Practices: The Case of Seiyu in Japan," *Journal of Transnational Management,* 2009, pp. 155–76; and S. Banjo, "Wal-Mart Says Time Is Right for Japan," *The Wall Street Journal,* September 27, 2012.

Chapter 9
Regional Economic Integration

LEARNING OBJECTIVES

After reading this chapter, you will be able to:

LO9-1 Describe the different levels of regional economic integration.

LO9-2 Understand the economic and political arguments for regional economic integration.

LO9-3 Understand the economic and political arguments against regional economic integration.

LO9-4 Explain the history, current scope, and future prospects of the world's most important regional economic agreements.

LO9-5 Understand the implications for business that are inherent in regional economic integration agreements.

◇◇◇ **TOMATO WARS** ◇◇◇

Opening Case

When the North America Free Trade Agreement (NAFTA) went into effect in December 1992 and tariffs on imported tomatoes were dropped, U.S. tomato producers in Florida feared that they would lose business to lower-cost producers in Mexico. So they lobbied the government to set a minimum floor price for tomatoes imported from Mexico. The idea was to stop Mexican producers from cutting prices below the floor to gain share in the U.S. market. In 1996 the United States and Mexico agreed on the basic floor price of 21.69 cents a pound. At the time, both sides declared themselves to be happy with the deal.

As it turns out, the deal didn't offer much protection for U.S. tomato growers. In 1992, the year before NAFTA was passed, Mexican producers exported 800 million pounds of tomatoes to the United States. By 2011 they were exporting 2.8 billion pounds of tomatoes, an increase of 3.5-fold. The value of Mexican tomato exports almost tripled to $2 billion during the same period. In contrast, tomato production in Florida has fallen by 41 percent since NAFTA went into effect. Florida growers complained that they could not compete against low wages and lax environmental oversight in Mexico. They also alleged that Mexican growers were dumping tomatoes in the United States market at below the cost of production, with the goal of driving U.S. producers out of business. In 2012, Florida growers petitioned the U.S. Department of Commerce to scrap the 1996 minimum-price agreement, which would then allow them to file an antidumping case against Mexican producers. In September 2012 the Commerce Department announced a preliminary decision to scrap the agreement.

At first glance, it looked as if the Florida growers were going to get their way. It soon became apparent, however, that the situation was more complex than it appeared at first glance. Some 370 business and trade groups in the United States wrote or signed letters to the Commerce Department in favor of continuing the 1996 agreement. Among the letter writers was Kevin Ahern, the CEO of Ahern Agribusiness in San Diego, a company that sells about $20 million a year in tomato seeds and transplants to Mexican farmers. In a letter sent to *The New York Times*, Ahern said, "Yes, Mexico produces their tomatoes on average at a lower cost than Florida; that's what we call competitive advantage." Ahern claimed that without the agreement, his business would suffer. Another U.S. company, NatureSweet Ltd., grows cherry and grape tomatoes under 1,200 acres of greenhouses in Mexico for the U.S. market. It employs 5,000 people, although all but 100 work in Mexico. The CEO, Bryant Ambelang, said that his company couldn't survive without NAFTA. In his view, Mexican-grown tomatoes were more competitive because of lower labor costs, good weather, and more than a decade of investment in greenhouse technology. In a similar vein, Scott DeFife, a representative of the U.S. National Restaurant Association, stated that "people want tomato-based dishes all the time. You plan over the course of the year where you are going to get your supply in the winter, the spring, the fall." De Fife stated that without tomatoes from Mexico, a winter freeze in Florida, for example, would send prices shooting up.

Faced with a potential backlash from U.S. importers and U.S. producers with interests in Mexico, the Commerce Department pulled back from its initial conclusion that the agreement should be scrapped. Instead, in early 2013 it reached an agreement with Mexican growers to raise the minimum floor price from 21.69 cents a pound to 31 cents a pound. The new agreement also established even higher prices for specialty tomatoes and tomatoes grown in controlled environments. This was clearly aimed at Mexican growers, who have invested billions to grow tomatoes in greenhouses. Florida tomatoes are largely picked green and treated with gas to change their color.[1]

INTRODUCTION

This chapter takes a close look at the arguments for regional economic integration through the establishment of trading blocs such as the European Union (EU) and the North American Free Trade Agreement (NAFTA). By **regional economic integration** we mean agreements among countries in a geographic region to reduce, and ultimately remove, tariff and nontariff barriers to the free flow of goods, services, and factors of production between each other. The opening case illustrates some of the issues surrounding the creation of a trading bloc. By creating a single market, NAFTA aimed to lower the price for goods and services in the United States, Canada, and Mexico. Such a policy is good for consumers, because it lowers prices, but it presents challenges to some producers who have to adapt to a more competitive environment. As the opening case explains, while NAFTA has resulted in a surge in tomato imports from Mexico, which has arguably benefited U.S. consumers, food producers, and retailers, it has hurt tomato growers in Florida, who have steadily lost business to Mexican producers.

The past two decades have witnessed an unprecedented proliferation of regional trade blocs that promote regional economic integration. World Trade Organization (WTO) members are required to notify the WTO of any regional trade agreements in which they participate. By 2012, nearly all the WTO's members had notified the organization of participation in one or more regional trade agreements. The total number of regional trade agreements currently in force is more than 500.[2]

Consistent with the predictions of international trade theory and particularly the theory of comparative advantage (see Chapter 6), agreements designed to promote freer trade within regions are believed to produce gains from trade for all member countries. As we saw in Chapter 7, the General Agreement on Tariffs and Trade (GATT) and its successor, the World Trade Organization, also seek to reduce trade barriers. However, the WTO has a global perspective and 159 members, which can make reaching an agreement extremely difficult. By entering into regional agreements, groups of countries aim to reduce trade barriers more rapidly than can be achieved under the auspices of the WTO.

Nowhere has the movement toward regional economic integration been more successful than in Europe. On January 1, 1993, the European Union formally removed many barriers to doing business across borders within the EU in an attempt to create a single market with 340 million consumers. Today, the EU has a population of over 500 million and a gross domestic product of $17.6 trillion, making it larger than the United States in economic terms.

Similar moves toward regional integration are being pursued elsewhere in the world. Canada, Mexico, and the United States have implemented NAFTA. Ultimately, this aims to remove all barriers to the free flow of goods and services among the three countries. While the implementation of NAFTA has resulted in job losses in some sectors of the U.S. economy, in aggregate and consistent with the predictions of international trade theory, most economists argue that the benefits of greater regional trade outweigh any costs (see the Opening Case). South America too has moved toward regional integration. In 1991, Argentina, Brazil, Paraguay, and Uruguay implemented an agreement known as Mercosur to start reducing barriers to trade between each other, and although progress within Mercosur has been halting, the institution is still in place. There are also active attempts at regional economic integration in Central America, the Andean region of South America, Southeast Asia, and parts of Africa.

While the move toward regional economic integration is generally seen as a good thing, some worry that it will lead to a world in which regional trade blocs compete against each other. In this future scenario, free trade will exist within each bloc, but each bloc will protect its market from outside competition with high tariffs. The specter of the EU and NAFTA turning into economic fortresses that shut out foreign producers through high tariff barriers is worrisome to those who believe in unrestricted free trade. If such a situation were to materialize, the resulting decline in trade between blocs could more than offset the gains from free trade within blocs.

With these issues in mind, this chapter explores the economic and political debate surrounding regional economic integration, paying particular attention to the economic and political benefits and costs of integration; review progress toward regional economic integration around the world; and map the important implications of regional economic integration for the practice of international business. Before tackling these objectives, we first need to examine the levels of integration that are theoretically possible.

LEVELS OF ECONOMIC INTEGRATION
LO9-1

Several levels of economic integration are possible in theory (see Figure 9.1). From least integrated to most integrated, they are a free trade area, a customs union, a common market, an economic union, and, finally, a full political union.

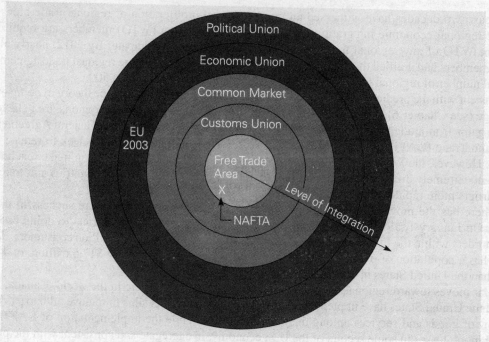

Figure 9.1 *Levels of Economic Integration*

In a **free trade area**, all barriers to the trade of goods and services among member countries are removed. In the theoretically ideal free trade area, no discriminatory tariffs, quotas, subsidies, or administrative impediments are allowed to distort trade between members. Each country, however, is allowed to determine its own trade policies with regard to nonmembers. Thus, for example, the tariffs placed on the products of nonmember countries may vary from member to member. Free trade agreements are the most popular form of regional economic integration, accounting for almost 90 percent of regional agreements.[3]

The most enduring free trade area in the world is the **European Free Trade Association (EFTA)**. Established in January 1960, the EFTA currently joins four countries—Norway, Iceland, Liechtenstein, and Switzerland—down from seven in 1995 (three EFTA members, Austria, Finland, and Sweden, joined the EU on January 1, 1996). The EFTA was founded by those western European countries that initially decided not to be part of the European Community (the forerunner of the EU). Its original members included Austria, Great Britain, Denmark, Finland, and Sweden, all of which are now members of the EU. The emphasis of the EFTA has been on free trade in industrial goods. Agriculture was left out of the arrangement, each member being allowed to determine its own level of support. Members are also free to determine the level of protection applied to goods coming from outside the EFTA. Other free trade areas include the North American Free Trade Agreement, which we discuss in depth later in the chapter.

The customs union is one step farther along the road to full economic and political integration. A **customs union** eliminates trade barriers between member countries and adopts a common external trade policy. Establishment of a common external trade policy necessitates significant administrative machinery to oversee trade relations with nonmembers. Most countries that enter into a customs union desire even greater economic integration down the road. The EU began as a customs union, but it has now moved beyond this stage. Other customs unions include the current version of the Andean Community (formerly known as the Andean Pact) among Bolivia, Colombia, Ecuador, and Peru. The Andean Community established free trade between member countries and imposes a common tariff, of 5 to 20 percent, on products imported from outside.[4]

The next level of economic integration, a **common market**, has no barriers to trade among member countries, includes a common external trade policy, and allows factors of production to move freely among members. Labor and capital are free to move because there are no restrictions on immigration, emigration, or cross-border flows of capital among member countries. Establishing a common market demands a significant degree of harmony and cooperation on fiscal, monetary, and employment policies. Achieving this degree of cooperation has proved very difficult. For years, the European Union functioned as a common market, although it has now moved beyond this stage. Mercosur—the South American grouping of Argentina, Brazil, Paraguay, and Uruguay—hopes to eventually establish itself as a common market. Venezuela was accepted as a full member of Mercosur subject to ratification by the governments of the four existing members. As of early 2013, Paraguay has yet to ratify Venezuela's membership.

An economic union entails even closer economic integration and cooperation than a common market. Like the common market, an **economic union** involves the free flow of products and factors of production among member countries and the adoption of a common external trade policy, but it also requires a common currency, harmonization of members' tax rates, and a common monetary and fiscal policy. Such a high degree of integration demands a coordinating bureaucracy and the sacrifice of significant amounts of national sovereignty to that bureaucracy. The EU is an economic union, although an imperfect one because not all members of the EU have adopted the euro, the currency of the EU; differences in tax rates and regulations across countries still remain; and some markets, such as the market for energy, are still not fully deregulated.

The move toward economic union raises the issue of how to make a coordinating bureaucracy accountable to the citizens of member nations. The answer is through **political union** in which a central political apparatus coordinates the economic, social, and foreign policy of the member states. The EU is on the road toward at least partial political union. The European Parliament, which is playing an ever more important role in the EU, has been directly elected by citizens of the EU countries since the late 1970s. In addition, the Council of Ministers (the controlling, decision-making body of the EU) is composed of government ministers from each EU member. The United States provides an example of even closer political union; in the United States, independent states are effectively combined into a single nation. Ultimately, the EU may move toward a similar federal structure.

THE CASE FOR REGIONAL INTEGRATION   **LO9-2**

The case for regional integration is both economic and political, and it is typically not accepted by many groups within a country, which explains why most attempts to achieve regional economic integration have been contentious and halting. In this section, we examine the economic and political cases for integration and two impediments to integration. In the next section, we look at the case against integration.

The Economic Case for Integration

The economic case for regional integration is straightforward. We saw in Chapter 6 how economic theories of international trade predict that unrestricted free trade will allow countries to specialize in the production of goods and services that they can produce most efficiently. The result is greater world production than would be possible with trade restrictions. That chapter also revealed how opening a country to free trade stimulates economic growth, which creates dynamic gains from trade. Chapter 8 detailed how foreign direct investment (FDI) can transfer technological, marketing, and managerial know-how to host nations. Given the central role of knowledge in stimulating economic growth, opening a country to FDI also is likely to stimulate economic growth. In sum, economic theories suggest that free trade and investment is a positive-sum game, in which all participating countries stand to gain.

Given this, the theoretical ideal is an absence of barriers to the free flow of goods, services, and factors of production among nations. However, as we saw in Chapters 7 and 8, a case can be made for government intervention in international trade and FDI. Because many governments have accepted part or all of the case for intervention, unrestricted free trade and FDI have proved to be only an ideal. Although international institutions such as the WTO have been moving the world toward a free trade regime, success has been less than total. In a world of many nations and many political ideologies, it is very difficult to get all countries to agree to a common set of rules.

Against this background, regional economic integration can be seen as an attempt to achieve additional gains from the free flow of trade and investment between countries beyond those attainable under global agreements such as the WTO. It is easier to establish a free trade and investment regime among a limited number of adjacent countries than among the world community. Coordination and policy harmonization problems are largely a function of the number of countries that seek agreement. The greater the number of countries involved, the more perspectives that must be reconciled, and the harder it will be to reach agreement. Thus, attempts at regional economic integration are motivated by a desire to exploit the gains from free trade and investment.

The Political Case for Integration

The political case for regional economic integration also has loomed large in several attempts to establish free trade areas, customs unions, and the like. Linking neighboring economies and making them increasingly dependent on each other create incentives for political cooperation between the neighboring states and reduce the potential for violent conflict. In addition, by grouping their economies, the countries can enhance their political weight in the world.

These considerations underlay the 1957 establishment of the European Community (EC), the forerunner of the EU. Europe had suffered two devastating wars in the first half of the twentieth century, both arising out of the unbridled ambitions of nation-states. Those who have sought a united Europe have always had a desire to make another war in Europe unthinkable. Many Europeans also believed that after World War II, the European nation-states were no longer large enough to hold their own in world markets and politics. The need for a united Europe to deal with the United States and the politically alien Soviet Union loomed large in the minds of many of the EC's founders.[5] A long-standing joke in Europe is that the European Commission should erect a statue to Joseph Stalin, for without the aggressive policies of the former dictator of the old Soviet Union, the countries of western Europe may have lacked the incentive to cooperate and form the EC.

Impediments to Integration

Despite the strong economic and political arguments in support, integration has never been easy to achieve or sustain for two main reasons. First, although economic integration aids the majority, it has its costs. While a nation as a whole may benefit significantly from a regional free trade agreement, certain groups may lose. Moving to a free trade regime involves painful adjustments. Due to the establishment of NAFTA, some Canadian and U.S. workers in such industries as textiles, which employ low-cost, low-skilled labor, lost their jobs as Canadian and U.S. firms moved production to Mexico. The promise of significant net benefits to the Canadian and U.S. economies as a whole is little comfort to those who lose as a result of NAFTA. Such groups have been at the forefront of opposition to NAFTA and will continue to oppose any widening of the agreement.

A second impediment to integration arises from concerns over national sovereignty. For example, Mexico's concerns about maintaining control of its oil interests resulted in an agreement with Canada and the United States to exempt the Mexican oil industry from any liberalization of foreign investment regulations achieved under NAFTA. Concerns about national sovereignty arise because close economic integration demands that countries give up some degree of control over such key issues as monetary policy, fiscal policy (e.g., tax policy), and trade policy. This has been a major stumbling block in the EU. To achieve full economic union, the EU introduced a common currency, the euro, controlled by a central EU bank. Although most member states have signed on, Great Britain remains an important holdout. A politically important segment of public opinion in that country opposes a common currency on the grounds that it would require relinquishing control of the country's monetary policy to the EU, which many British perceive as a bureaucracy run by foreigners. In 1992, the British won the right to opt out of any single currency agreement, and as of 2013, the British government has yet to reverse its decision—and it does not seem likely to do so, given the sovereign debt crisis in Europe and the strains it has placed on the euro (more on this later).

THE CASE AGAINST REGIONAL INTEGRATION

Although the tide has been running in favor of regional free trade agreements in recent years, some economists have expressed concern that the benefits of regional integration have been oversold, while the costs have often been ignored.[6] They point out that the benefits of regional integration are determined by the extent of trade creation, as opposed to trade diversion. **Trade creation** occurs when high-cost domestic producers are replaced by low-cost producers within the free trade area. It may also occur when higher-cost external producers are replaced by lower-cost external producers within the free trade area. **Trade diversion** occurs when lower-cost external suppliers are replaced by higher-cost suppliers within the free trade area. A regional free trade agreement will benefit the world only if the amount of trade it creates exceeds the amount it diverts.

Suppose the United States and Mexico imposed tariffs on imports from all countries, and then they set up a free trade area, scrapping all trade barriers between themselves but maintaining tariffs on imports from the rest of the world. If the United States began to import textiles from Mexico, would this change be for the better? If the United States previously produced all its own textiles at a higher cost than Mexico, then the free trade agreement has shifted production to the cheaper source. According to the theory of comparative advantage, trade has been created within the regional grouping, and there would be no decrease in trade with the rest of the world. Clearly, the change would be for the better. If, however, the United States previously imported textiles from Costa Rica, which produced them more cheaply than either Mexico or the United States, then trade has been diverted from a low-cost source—a change for the worse.

In theory, WTO rules should ensure that a free trade agreement does not result in trade diversion. These rules allow free trade areas to be formed only if the members set tariffs that are not higher or more restrictive to outsiders than the ones previously in effect. However, as we saw in Chapter 7, GATT and the WTO do not cover some nontariff barriers. As a result, regional trade blocs could emerge whose markets are protected from outside competition by high nontariff barriers. In such cases, the trade diversion effects might outweigh the trade creation effects. The only way to guard against this possibility, according to those concerned about this potential, is to increase the scope of the WTO so it covers nontariff barriers to trade. There is no sign that this is going to occur anytime soon, however, so the risk remains that regional economic integration will result in trade diversion.

REGIONAL ECONOMIC INTEGRATION IN EUROPE   ■LO9-4■

Europe has two trade blocs—the European Union and the European Free Trade Association. Of the two, the EU is by far the more significant, not just in terms of membership (the EU currently has 27 members; the EFTA has 4), but also in terms of economic and political influence in the world economy. Many now see the EU as an emerging economic and political superpower of the same order as the United States. Accordingly, we will concentrate our attention on the EU.[7]

Evolution of the European Union

The **European Union (EU)** is the product of two political factors: (1) the devastation of western Europe during two world wars, and the desire for a lasting peace, and (2) the European nations' desire to hold their own on the world's political and economic stage. In addition, many Europeans were aware of the potential economic benefits of closer economic integration of the countries.

The forerunner of the EU, the European Coal and Steel Community, was formed in 1951 by Belgium, France, West Germany, Italy, Luxembourg, and the Netherlands. Its objective was to remove barriers to intragroup shipments of coal, iron, steel, and scrap metal. With the signing of the **Treaty of Rome** in 1957, the European Community was established. The name changed again in 1993 when the European Community became the European Union following the ratification of the Maastricht Treaty (discussed later).

The Treaty of Rome provided for the creation of a common market. Article 3 of the treaty laid down the key objectives of the new community, calling for the elimination of internal trade barriers and the creation of a common external tariff and requiring member states to abolish obstacles to the free movement of factors of production among the members. To facilitate the free movement of goods, services, and factors of production, the treaty provided for any necessary harmonization of the member states' laws. Furthermore, the treaty committed the EC to establish common policies in agriculture and transportation.

The community grew in 1973, when Great Britain, Ireland, and Denmark joined. These three were followed in 1981 by Greece; in 1986 by Spain and Portugal; and in 1995 by Austria, Finland, and Sweden—bringing the total membership to 15 (East Germany became part of the EC after the reunification of Germany in 1990). Another 10 countries joined the EU on May 1, 2004—8 of them from eastern Europe plus the small Mediterranean nations of Malta and Cyprus. Bulgaria and Romania joined in 2007, bringing the total number of member states to 27 (see Map 9.1). Through these enlargements, the EU has become a global superpower.

Political Structure of the European Union

The economic policies of the EU are formulated and implemented by a complex and still-evolving political structure. The four main institutions in this structure are the European Commission, the Council of the European Union, the European Parliament, and the Court of Justice.[8]

The **European Commission** is responsible for proposing EU legislation, implementing it, and monitoring compliance with EU laws by member states. Headquartered in Brussels, Belgium, it is run

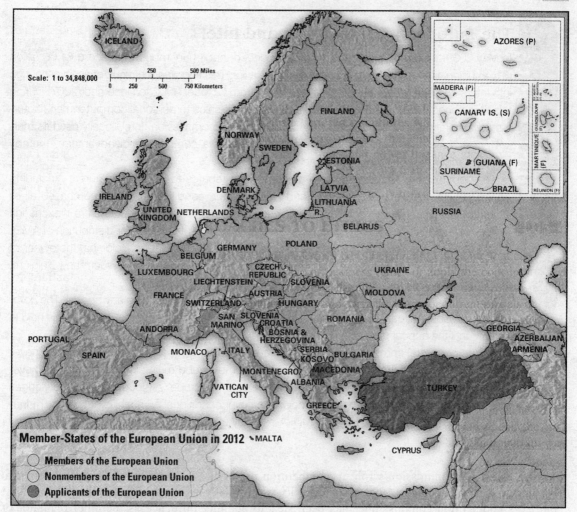

MAP 9.1 Member States of the European Union in 2012

Source: Copyright © European Communities, 1995–2009. Reproduced with permission.

by a group of commissioners appointed by each member country for five-year renewable terms. There are 27 commissioners, one from each member state. A president of the commission is chosen by member states, and the president then chooses other members in consultation with the states. The entire commission has to be approved by the European Parliament before it can begin work. The commission has a monopoly in proposing European Union legislation. The commission makes a proposal, which goes to the Council of the European Union and then to the European Parliament. The council cannot legislate without a commission proposal in front of it. The commission is also responsible for implementing aspects of EU law, although in practice much of this must be delegated to member states. Another responsibility of the commission is to monitor member states to make sure they are complying with EU laws. In this policing role, the commission will normally ask a state to comply with any EU laws that are being broken. If this persuasion is not sufficient, the commission can refer a case to the Court of Justice.

The European Commission and Intel

In May 2009, the European Commission announced that it had imposed a record €1.06 billion ($1.45 billion) fine on Intel for anticompetitive behavior. This fine was the result of an investigation into Intel's competitive conduct during the period from October 2002 to December 2007. During this time period, Intel's market share of microprocessor sales to personal computer manufacturers consistently exceeded 70 percent. According to the commission, Intel illegally used its market power to ensure that its major rival, AMD, was at a competitive disadvantage, thereby harming "millions of European consumers."

The commission charged that Intel granted major rebates to PC manufacturers—including Acer, Dell, Hewlett-Packard, Lenovo, and NEC—on the condition that they purchased all or almost all their supplies from Intel. Intel also made payments to some manufacturers in exchange for them postponing, canceling, or putting restrictions on the introduction or distribution of AMD-based products. Intel also apparently made payments to Media Saturn Holdings, the owner of Media Markt chain of superstores, for only selling Intel-based computers in Germany, Belgium, and other countries.

Under the order, Intel had to change its practices immediately, pending any appeal. The company was also required to write a bank guarantee for the fine, although that guarantee is held in a bank until the appeal process is exhausted.

For its part, Intel immediately appealed the ruling. The company insisted that it had never coerced computer makers and retailers with inducements and maintained that Intel had never paid to stop AMD products from reaching the market in Europe. Although Intel acknowledges that it did offer rebates, it claimed that they were never conditional on specific actions by manufacturers and retailers aimed to limit AMD. As of early 2012, the appeal was still working its way through the judicial process.[9]

The European Commission's role in competition policy has become increasingly important to business in recent years. Since 1990 when the office was formally assigned a role in competition policy, the EU's competition commissioner has been steadily gaining influence as the chief regulator of competition policy in the member nations of the EU. As with antitrust authorities in the United States, which include the Federal Trade Commission and the Department of Justice, the role of the competition commissioner is to ensure that no one enterprise uses its market power to drive out competitors and monopolize markets. In 2009, for example, the commission fined Intel a record €1.06 billion for abusing its market power in the computer chip market. (See the Management Focus for details.) The previous record for a similar abuse was €497 billion imposed on Microsoft in 2004 for blocking competition in markets for server computers and media software. The commissioner also reviews proposed mergers and acquisitions to make sure they do not create a dominant enterprise with substantial market power.[10] For example, in 2000 a proposed merger between Time Warner of the United States and EMI of the United Kingdom, both music recording companies, was withdrawn after the commission expressed concerns that the merger would reduce the number of major record companies from five to four and create a dominant player in the $40 billion global music industry. Similarly, the commission blocked a proposed merger between two U.S. telecommunication companies, WorldCom and Sprint, because their combined holdings of Internet infrastructure in Europe would give the merged companies so much market power that the commission argued the combined company would dominate that market.

The **European Council** represents the interests of member states. It is clearly the ultimate controlling authority within the EU because draft legislation from the commission can become EU law only if the council agrees. The council is composed of one representative from the government of each member state. The membership, however, varies depending on the topic being discussed. When agricultural issues are being discussed, the agriculture ministers from each state attend council meetings; when transportation is being discussed, transportation ministers attend; and so on. Before 1987, all council issues had to be decided by unanimous agreement among member states. This often led to marathon council sessions and a failure to make progress or reach agreement on commission proposals. In an attempt to clear the resulting logjams, the Single European Act formalized the use of majority voting rules on issues "which have as their object the establishment and functioning of a single market." Most other issues, however, such as tax regulations and immigration policy, still require unanimity among council members if they are to become law. The votes that a country gets in the council are related to the size of the country. For example, Britain, a large country, has 29 votes, whereas Denmark, a much smaller state, has 7 votes.

The **European Parliament**, which as of 2012 has 754 members, is directly elected by the populations of the member states. The parliament, which meets in Strasbourg, France, is primarily a consultative rather than legislative body. It debates legislation proposed by the commission and forwarded to it by the council. It can propose amendments to that legislation, which the commission and ultimately the council are not obliged to take up but often will. The power of the parliament recently has been increasing, although not by as much as parliamentarians would like. The European Parliament now has the right to vote on the appointment of commissioners as well as veto some laws (such as the EU budget and single-market legislation).

One major debate waged in Europe during the past few years is whether the council or the parliament should ultimately be the most powerful body in the EU. Some in Europe expressed concern over the democratic accountability of the EU bureaucracy. One side argued that the answer to this apparent democratic deficit lay in increasing the power of the parliament, while others think that true democratic legitimacy lies with elected governments, acting through the Council of the European Union.[11] After significant debate, in December 2007 the member states signed a new treaty, the **Treaty of Lisbon**, under which the power of the European Parliament is increased. When it took effect in December 2009, for the first time in history the European Parliament was the coequal legislator for almost all European laws.[12] The Treaty of Lisbon also creates a new position, a president of the European Council, who serves a 30-month term and represents the nation-states that make up the EU.

The **Court of Justice**, which is comprised of one judge from each country, is the supreme appeals court for EU law. Like commissioners, the judges are required to act as independent officials, rather than as representatives of national interests. The commission or a member country can bring other members to the court for failing to meet treaty obligations. Similarly, member countries, member companies, or member institutions can bring the commission or council to the court for failure to act according to an EU treaty.

The Single European Act

The Single European Act was born of a frustration among members that the community was not living up to its promise. By the early 1980s, it was clear that the EC had fallen short of its objectives to remove barriers to the free flow of trade and investment among member countries and to harmonize the wide range of technical and legal standards for doing business. Against this background, many of the EC's prominent businesspeople mounted an energetic campaign in the early 1980s to end the EC's economic divisions. The EC responded by creating the Delors Commission. Under the chairmanship of Jacques

Delors, the commission proposed that all impediments to the formation of a single market be eliminated by December 31, 1992. The result was the Single European Act, which became EC law in 1987.

The Objectives of the Act

The purpose of the Single European Act was to have one market in place by December 31, 1992. The act proposed the following changes:[13]

- Remove all frontier controls among EC countries, thereby abolishing delays and reducing the resources required for complying with trade bureaucracy.

- Apply the principle of "mutual recognition" to product standards. A standard developed in one EC country should be accepted in another, provided it met basic requirements in such matters as health and safety.

- Institute open public procurement to nonnational suppliers, reducing costs directly by allowing lower-cost suppliers into national economies and indirectly by forcing national suppliers to compete.

- Lift barriers to competition in the retail banking and insurance businesses, which should drive down the costs of financial services, including borrowing, throughout the EC.

- Remove all restrictions on foreign exchange transactions between member countries by the end of 1992.

- Abolish restrictions on cabotage—the right of foreign truckers to pick up and deliver goods within another member state's borders—by the end of 1992. Estimates suggested this would reduce the cost of haulage within the EC by 10 to 15 percent.

All those changes were expected to lower the costs of doing business in the EC, but the single-market program was also expected to have more complicated supply-side effects. For example, the expanded market was predicted to give EC firms greater opportunities to exploit economies of scale. In addition, it was thought that the increase in competitive intensity brought about by removing internal barriers to trade and investment would force EC firms to become more efficient. To signify the importance of the Single European Act, the European Community also decided to change its name to the European Union once the act took effect.

Impact

The Single European Act has had a significant impact on the EU economy.[14] The act provided the impetus for the restructuring of substantial sections of European industry. Many firms have shifted from national to pan-European production and distribution systems in an attempt to realize scale economies and better compete in a single market. The results have included faster economic growth than would otherwise have been the case.

However, 20 years after the formation of a single market, the reality still falls short of the ideal. An example is given in the accompanying Country Focus, which describes the slow progress toward establishing a fully functioning single market for financial services in the EU. Thus, although the EU is undoubtedly moving toward a single marketplace, established legal, cultural, and language differences among nations mean that implementation has been uneven.

The Establishment of the Euro

In February 1992, EC members signed the **Maastricht Treaty**, which committed them to adopting a common currency by January 1, 1999.[15] The euro is now used by 17 of the 27 member states of the

Creating a Single Market in Financial Services

The European Union in 1999 embarked upon an ambitious action plan to create a single market in financial services by January 1, 2005. Launched a few months after the euro, the EU's single currency, the goal was to dismantle barriers to cross-border activity in financial services, creating a continentwide market for banking services, insurance services, and investment products. In this vision of a single Europe, a citizen of France might use a German firm for basic banking services, borrow a home mortgage from an Italian institution, buy auto insurance from a Dutch enterprise, and keep her savings in mutual funds managed by a British company. Similarly, an Italian firm might raise capital from investors across Europe and use a German firm as its lead underwriter to issue stock for sale through stock exchanges in London and Frankfurt.

One main benefit of a single market, according to its advocates, would be greater competition for financial services, which would give consumers more choices, lower prices, and require financial service firms in the EU to become more efficient, thereby increasing their global competitiveness. Another major benefit would be the creation of a single European capital market. The increased liquidity of a larger capital market would make it easier for firms to borrow funds, lowering their cost of capital (the price of money) and stimulating business investment in Europe, which would create more jobs. A European Commission study suggested that the creation of a single market in financial services would increase the EU's gross domestic product by 1.1 percent a year, creating an additional €130 billion in wealth over a decade. Total business investment would increase by 6 percent annually in the long run, private consumption by 0.8 percent, and total employment by 0.5 percent a year.

Creating a single market has been anything but easy. The financial markets of different EU member states have historically been segmented from each other, and each has its own regulatory framework. In the past, EU financial services firms rarely did business across national borders because of a host of different national regulations with regard to taxation, oversight, accounting information, cross-border takeovers, and the like—all of which had to be harmonized. To complicate matters, long-standing cultural and linguistic barriers complicated the move toward a single market. While in theory an Italian might benefit by being able to purchase homeowners insurance from a British company, in practice he might be predisposed to purchase it from a local enterprise, even if the price were higher.

By 2012, the EU had made significant progress. More than 40 measures designed to create a single market in financial services had become EU law, and others were in the pipeline. The new rules embraced issues as diverse as the conduct of business by investment firms, stock exchanges, and banks; disclosure standards for listing companies on public exchanges; and the harmonization of accounting standards across nations. However, there had also been some significant setbacks. Most notably, legislation designed to make it easier for firms to make hostile cross-border acquisitions was defeated, primarily due to opposition from German members of the European Parliament, making it more difficult for financial service firms to build pan-European operations. In addition, national governments have still reserved the right to block even friendly cross-border mergers between financial service firms.

The critical issue now is enforcement of the rules that have been put in place. Some believe that it will be at least another decade before the benefits of the new regulations become apparent. In the meantime, the changes may impose significant costs on financial institutions as they attempt to deal with the new raft of regulations.[16]

European Union; these 17 states are members of what is often referred to as the *euro zone*. It encompasses 330 million EU citizens and includes the powerful economies of Germany and France. Many of the countries that joined the EU on May 1, 2004, and the two that joined in 2007, originally planned to adopt the euro when they fulfilled certain economic criteria—a high degree of price stability, a sound fiscal situation, stable exchange rates, and converged long-term interest rates (the current members had to meet the same criteria). However, the events surrounding the EU sovereign debt crisis of 2010–2012 persuaded many of these countries to put their plans on hold, at least for the time being (further details provided later).

Establishment of the euro was an amazing political feat with few historical precedents. It required participating national governments to give up their own currencies and national control over monetary policy. Governments do not routinely sacrifice national sovereignty for the greater good, indicating the importance that the Europeans attach to the euro. By adopting the euro, the EU has created the second most widely traded currency in the world after that of the U.S. dollar. Some believe that the euro could come to rival the dollar as the most important currency in the world.

Three long-term EU members—Great Britain, Denmark, and Sweden—are still sitting on the sidelines. The countries agreeing to the euro locked their exchange rates against each other January 1, 1999. Euro notes and coins were not actually issued until January 1, 2002. In the interim, national currencies circulated in each participating state. However, in each country the national currency stood for a defined amount of euros. After January 1, 2002, euro notes and coins were issued and the national currencies were taken out of circulation. By mid-2002, all prices and routine economic transactions within the euro zone were in euros.

Benefits of the Euro

Europeans decided to establish a single currency in the EU for a number of reasons. First, they believe that businesses and individuals realize significant savings from having to handle one currency, rather than many. These savings come from lower foreign exchange and hedging costs. For example, people going from Germany to France no longer have to pay a commission to a bank to change German deutsche marks into French francs. Instead, they are able to use euros. According to the European Commission, such savings amount to 0.5 percent of the European Union's GDP, or about $80 billion a year.

Second, and perhaps more important, the adoption of a common currency makes it easier to compare prices across Europe. This has been increasing competition because it has become easier for consumers to shop around. For example, if a German finds that cars sell for less in France than Germany, he may be tempted to purchase from a French car dealer rather than his local car dealer. Alternatively, traders may engage in arbitrage to exploit such price differentials, buying cars in France and reselling them in Germany. The only way that German car dealers will be able to hold onto business in the face of such competitive pressures will be to reduce the prices they charge for cars. As a consequence of such pressures, the introduction of a common currency has led to lower prices, which translates into substantial gains for European consumers.

Third, faced with lower prices, European producers have been forced to look for ways to reduce their production costs to maintain their profit margins. The introduction of a common currency, by increasing competition, has produced long-run gains in the economic efficiency of European companies.

Fourth, the introduction of a common currency has given a boost to the development of a highly liquid pan-European capital market. Over time, the development of such a capital market should lower the cost of capital and lead to an increase in both the level of investment and the efficiency with which investment funds are allocated. This could be especially helpful to smaller companies that have historically had difficulty borrowing money from domestic banks. For example, the capital market of

Portugal is very small and illiquid, which makes it extremely difficult for bright Portuguese entrepreneurs with a good idea to borrow money at a reasonable price. However, in theory, such companies can now tap a much more liquid pan-European capital market.

Finally, the development of a pan-European, euro-denominated capital market will increase the range of investment options open to both individuals and institutions. For example, it will now be much easier for individuals and institutions based in, let's say, Holland to invest in Italian or French companies. This will enable European investors to better diversify their risk, which again lowers the cost of capital, and should also increase the efficiency with which capital resources are allocated.[17]

Costs of the Euro

The drawback, for some, of a single currency is that national authorities have lost control over monetary policy. Thus, it is crucial to ensure that the EU's monetary policy is well managed. The Maastricht Treaty called for establishment of the independent European Central Bank (ECB), similar in some respects to the U.S. Federal Reserve, with a clear mandate to manage monetary policy so as to ensure price stability. The ECB, based in Frankfurt, is meant to be independent from political pressure—although critics question this. Among other things, the ECB sets interest rates and determines monetary policy across the euro zone.

The implied loss of national sovereignty to the ECB underlies the decision by Great Britain, Denmark, and Sweden to stay out of the euro zone. Many in these countries are suspicious of the ECB's ability to remain free from political pressure and to keep inflation under tight control.

In theory, the design of the ECB should ensure that it remains free of political pressure. The ECB is modeled on the German Bundesbank, which historically has been the most independent and successful central bank in Europe. The Maastricht Treaty prohibits the ECB from taking orders from politicians. The executive board of the bank, which consists of a president, vice president, and four other members, carries out policy by issuing instructions to national central banks. The policy itself is determined by the governing council, which consists of the executive board plus the central bank governors from the 17 euro zone countries. The governing council votes on interest rate changes. Members of the executive board are appointed for eight-year nonrenewable terms, insulating them from political pressures to get reappointed. Nevertheless, the jury is still out on the issue of the ECB's independence, and it will take some time for the bank to establish its credentials.

According to critics, another drawback of the euro is that the EU is not what economists would call an optimal currency area. In an **optimal currency area**, similarities in the underlying structure of economic activity make it feasible to adopt a single currency and use a single exchange rate as an instrument of macroeconomic policy. Many of the European economies in the euro zone, however, are very dissimilar. For example, Finland and Portugal have different wage rates, tax regimes, and business cycles, and they may react very differently to external economic shocks. A change in the euro exchange rate that helps Finland may hurt Portugal. Obviously, such differences complicate macroeconomic policy. For example, when euro economies are not growing in unison, a common monetary policy may mean that interest rates are too high for depressed regions and too low for booming regions.

One way of dealing with such divergent effects within the euro zone is for the EU to engage in fiscal transfers, taking money from prosperous regions and pumping it into depressed regions. Such a move, however, opens a political can of worms. Would the citizens of Germany forgo their "fair share" of EU funds to create jobs for underemployed Greece workers? Not surprisingly, there is strong political opposition to such practices.

The Euro Experience: 1999 to the Sovereign Debt Crisis

Since its establishment January 1, 1999, the euro has had a volatile trading history against the world's major currency, the U.S. dollar. After starting life in 1999 at €1 = $1.17, the euro steadily fell until it reached a low of €1 = $0.83 in October 2000, leading critics to claim the euro was a failure. A major reason for the fall in the euro's value was that international investors were investing money in booming U.S. stocks and bonds and taking money out of Europe to finance this investment. In other words, they were selling euros to buy dollars so that they could invest in dollar-denominated assets. This increased the demand for dollars and decreased the demand for the euro, driving the value of the euro down.

The fortunes of the euro began improving in late 2001 when the dollar weakened; the currency stood at a robust all-time high of €1 = $1.54 in early March 2008. One reason for the rise in the value of the euro was that the flow of capital into the United States stalled as the U.S. financial markets fell during 2007 and 2008. Many investors were now taking money out of the United States by selling dollar-denominated assets such as U.S. stocks and bonds and purchasing euro-denominated assets. Falling demand for U.S. dollars and rising demand for euros translated into a fall in the value of the dollar against the euro. Furthermore, in a vote of confidence in both the euro and the ability of the ECB to manage monetary policy within the euro zone, many foreign central banks added more euros to their supply of foreign currencies. In the first three years of its life, the euro never reached the 13 percent of global reserves made up by the deutsche mark and other former euro zone currencies. The euro didn't jump that hurdle until early 2002, but by 2011 it stood at 26.3 percent.[18]

Since 2008 however, the euro has weakened, reflecting persistent concerns over slow economic growth and large budget deficits among several EU member states, particularly Greece, Portugal, Ireland, Italy, and Spain. During the 2000s, all these governments had sharply increased their government debt to finance public spending. Government debt as a percentage of GDP hit record levels in many of these nations. By 2010, private investors became increasingly concerned that these nations would not be able to service their sovereign debt, particularly given the economic slowdown following the 2008–2009 global financial crisis. They sold off government bonds of troubled nations, driving down bond prices and driving up the cost of government borrowing (bond prices and interest rates are inversely related). This led to fears that several national governments, particularly Greece, might default on their sovereign debt, plunging the euro zone into an economic crisis. To try and stave off such a sovereign debt crisis, in May 2010 the euro zone nations and the International Monetary Fund (IMF) agreed to a €110 billion bailout package to help rescue Greece. In November 2010, the EU and IMF agreed to a bailout package for Ireland of €85 billion; in May 2011, euro zone countries and the IMF instituted a €78 billion bailout plan for Portugal. In return for these loans, all three countries had to agree to sharp reductions in government spending, which meant slower economic growth and high unemployment until government debt was reduced to more sustainable levels. While Italy and Spain did not request bailout packages, both countries were forced by falling bond prices to institute austerity programs that required big reductions in government spending. The euro zone nations also set up a permanent bailout fund—the European Stability Mechanism—worth about €500 billion, which was designed to restore confidence in the euro. As detailed in the next Country Focus, by 2012 Greece had been granted two more bailout packages in an attempt to forestall a full-blown default on payment of its sovereign debt.

As might be expected, the economic turmoil led to a decline in the value of the euro. By early 2013, the dollar-euro exchange rate stood at €1 = $1.30, some way below its 2008 level but still significantly better than the exchange rate in early 2000. The euro also declined by 20 to 30 percent against most of the world's other major currencies between late 2008 and early 2013.

More troubling perhaps for the long run success of the euro, many of the newer EU nations that had committed to adopting the euro put their plans on hold. Countries like Poland and the Czech Republic

The Greek Sovereign Debt Crisis

When the euro was established, some critics worried that free-spending countries in the euro zone (such as Italy and Greece) might borrow excessively, running up large public-sector deficits that they could not finance. This would then rock the value of the euro, requiring their more sober brethren, such as Germany or France, to step in and bail out the profligate nation. In 2010, this worry became a reality as a financial crisis in Greece hit the value of the euro.

The financial crisis had its roots in a decade of free spending by the Greek government, which ran up a high level of debt to finance extensive spending in the public sector. Much of the spending increase could be characterized as an attempt by the government to buy off powerful interest groups in Greek society, from teachers and farmers to public-sector employees, rewarding them with high pay and extensive benefits. To make matters worse, the government misled the international community about the level of its indebtedness. In October 2009, a new government took power and quickly announced that the 2009 public-sector deficit, which had been projected to be around 5 percent, would actually be 12.7 percent. The previous government had apparently been cooking the books.

This shattered any faith that international investors might have had in the Greek economy. Interest rates on Greek government debt quickly surged to 7.1 percent, about 4 percentage points higher than the rate on German bonds. Two of the three international rating agencies also cut their ratings on Greek bonds and warned that further downgrades were likely. The main concern now was that the Greek government might not be able to refinance some €20 billion of debt that would mature in April or May 2010. A further concern was that the Greek government might lack the political willpower to make the large cuts in public spending necessary to bring down the deficit and restore investor confidence.

Nor was Greece alone in having large public-sector deficits. Three other euro zone countries—Spain, Portugal, and Ireland—also had large debt loads, and interest rates on their bonds surged as investors sold out. This raised the specter of financial contagion, with large-scale defaults among the weaker members of the euro zone. If this did occur, the EU and IMF would most certainly have to step in and rescue the troubled nations. With this possibility, once considered very remote, investors started to move money out of euros, and the value of the euro started to fall on the foreign exchange market.

Recognizing that the unthinkable might happen—and that without external help, Greece might default on its government debt, pushing the EU and the euro into a major crisis—in May 2010 the euro zone countries, led by Germany, along with the IMF agreed to lend Greece up to €110 billion. These loans were judged sufficient to cover Greece's financing needs for three years. In exchange, the Greek government agreed to implement a series of strict austerity measures. These included tax increases, major cuts in public-sector pay, reductions in benefits enjoyed by public-sector employees (e.g., the retirement age was increased to 65 from 61, and limits were placed on pensions), and reductions in the number of public-sector enterprises from 6,000 to 2,000. However, the Greek economy contracted so fast in 2010 and 2011 that tax revenues plunged. By the end of 2011, the Greek economy was almost 29 percent smaller than it had been in 2005, while unemployment approached 20 percent. The contracting tax base limited the ability of the government to pay down debt. By 2012, yields on 10-year Greek government debt reached 34 percent, indicating that many investors now expected Greece to default on its sovereign debt. This forced the Greek government to seek further aid from the euro zone countries and the IMF. As a condition for a fresh €130 billion bailout plan, the Greek government had to get holders of Greek government bonds to agree to the biggest sovereign debt restructuring in history. In effect, bondholders agreed to write off 53.5 percent of the debt they held. While the Greek government had not technically defaulted on its sovereign debt, to many it seemed as if the EU and IMF had orchestrated an orderly partial default. Whether that might be enough to stave off a complete default in Greece remains to be seen.[19]

had no desire to join the euro zone and then have their taxpayers help bail out the profligate governments of countries like Italy and Greece. To compound matters, the sovereign debt crisis had exposed a deep flaw in the euro zone—it was difficult for fiscally more conservative nations like Germany to limit profligate spending by the governments of other nations that might subsequently create strains and impose costs on the entire euro zone. The Germans in particular found themselves in the unhappy position of having to underwrite loans to bail out the governments of Greece, Portugal, and Ireland. This started to erode support for the euro in the stronger EU states. To try and correct this flaw, 25 of the EU's 27 nations signed a fiscal pact in January 2012 that made it more difficult for member states to break tight new rules on government deficits (the UK and Czech Republic abstained). Whether such actions will be sufficient to get the euro back on track remains to be seen.

Enlargement of the European Union

A major issue facing the EU over the past few years has been that of enlargement. Enlargement of the EU into eastern Europe has been a possibility since the collapse of communism at the end of the 1980s, and by the end of the 1990s, 13 countries had applied to become EU members. To qualify for EU membership, the applicants had to privatize state assets, deregulate markets, restructure industries, and tame inflation. They also had to enshrine complex EU laws into their own systems, establish stable democratic governments, and respect human rights.[20] In December 2002, the EU formally agreed to accept the applications of 10 countries, and they joined May 1, 2004. The new members included the Baltic countries, the Czech Republic, and the larger nations of Hungary and Poland. The only new members not in eastern Europe were the Mediterranean island nations of Malta and Cyprus. Their inclusion in the EU expanded the union to 25 states, stretching from the Atlantic to the borders of Russia; added 23 percent to the landmass of the EU; brought 75 million new citizens into the EU, building an EU with a population of 450 million people; and created a single continental economy with a GDP of close to €11 trillion. In 2007, Bulgaria and Romania joined, bringing total membership to 27 nations.

The new members were not able to adopt the euro until at least 2007 (and 2010 in the case of the latest entrants), and free movement of labor among the new and existing members was prohibited until then (none of them had adopted the euro as of early 2012). Consistent with theories of free trade, the enlargement should create added benefits for all members. However, given the small size of the eastern European economies (together they amount to only 5 percent of the GDP of current EU members), the initial impact will probably be small. The biggest notable change might be in the EU bureaucracy and decision-making processes, where budget negotiations among 27 nations are bound to prove more problematic than negotiations among 15 nations.

Left standing at the door is Turkey. Turkey, which has long lobbied to join the union, presents the EU with some difficult issues. The country has had a customs union with the EU since 1995, and about half its international trade is already with the EU. However, full membership has been denied because of concerns over human rights issues (particularly Turkish policies toward its Kurdish minority). In addition, some on the Turkish side suspect the EU is not eager to let a primarily Muslim nation of 74 million people, which has one foot in Asia, join the EU. The EU formally indicated in December 2002 that it would allow the Turkish application to proceed with no further delay in December 2004 if the country improved its human rights record to the satisfaction of the EU. In December 2004, the EU agreed to allow Turkey to start accession talks in October 2005, but those talks are not moving along rapidly, and at this point, it is unclear when the nation will join.

REGIONAL ECONOMIC INTEGRATION IN THE AMERICAS ◼ L09-4 ◼

No other attempt at regional economic integration comes close to the EU in its boldness or its potential implications for the world economy, but regional economic integration is on the rise in the Americas. The most significant attempt is the North American Free Trade Agreement. In addition to NAFTA, several other trade blocs are in the offing in the Americas (see Map 9.2), the most significant of which appear to be the Andean Community and Mercosur. Also, negotiations are under way to establish a hemispherewide Free Trade Area of the Americas (FTAA), although currently they seem to be stalled.

The North American Free Trade Agreement

The governments of the United States and Canada in 1988 agreed to enter into a free trade agreement, which took effect January 1, 1989. The goal of the agreement was to eliminate all tariffs on bilateral trade between Canada and the United States by 1998. This was followed in 1991 by talks among the United States, Canada, and Mexico aimed at establishing a **North American Free Trade Agreement** for the three countries. The talks concluded in August 1992 with an agreement in principle, and the following year the agreement was ratified by the governments of all three countries. The agreement became law January 1, 1994.[21]

NAFTA'S Contents

The contents of NAFTA include the following:

- Abolition by 2004 of tariffs on 99 percent of the goods traded among Mexico, Canada, and the United States.
- Removal of most barriers on the cross-border flow of services, allowing financial institutions, for example, unrestricted access to the Mexican market by 2000.
- Protection of intellectual property rights.
- Removal of most restrictions on foreign direct investment among the three member countries, although special treatment (protection) will be given to Mexican energy and railway industries, American airline and radio communications industries, and Canadian culture.

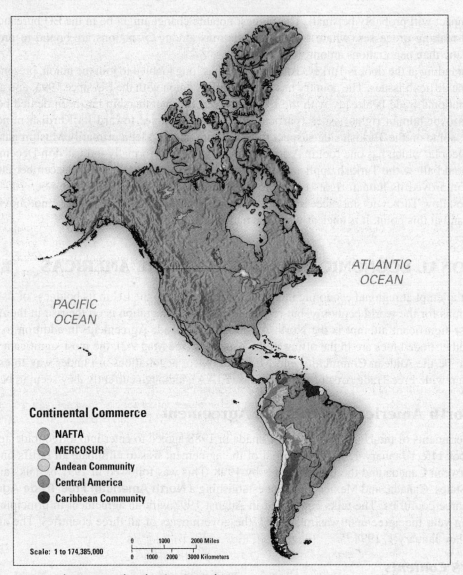

Continental Commerce

- NAFTA
- MERCOSUR
- Andean Community
- Central America
- Caribbean Community

Scale: 1 to 174,385,000

| 0 | 1000 | 2000 Miles |
| 0 | 1000 | 2000 | 3000 Kilometers |

PACIFIC OCEAN

ATLANTIC OCEAN

MAP 9.2   Economic Integration in the Americas

- Application of national environmental standards, provided such standards have a scientific basis. Lowering of standards to lure investment is described as being inappropriate.
- Establishment of two commissions with the power to impose fines and remove trade privileges when environmental standards or legislation involving health and safety, minimum wages, or child labor are ignored.

The Case for NAFTA

Proponents of NAFTA have argued that the free trade area should be viewed as an opportunity to create an enlarged and more efficient productive base for the entire region. Advocates acknowledge that one effect of NAFTA would be that some U.S. and Canadian firms would move production to Mexico to take advantage of lower labor costs. (In 2004, the average hourly labor cost in Mexico was still one-tenth of that in the United States and Canada.) Movement of production to Mexico, they argued, was most likely to occur in low-skilled, labor-intensive manufacturing industries where Mexico might have a comparative advantage. Advocates of NAFTA argued that many would benefit from such a trend. Mexico would benefit from much-needed inward investment and employment. The United States and Canada would benefit because the increased incomes of the Mexicans would allow them to import more U.S. and Canadian goods, thereby increasing demand and making up for the jobs lost in industries that moved production to Mexico. U.S. and Canadian consumers would benefit from the lower prices of products made in Mexico. In addition, the international competitiveness of U.S. and Canadian firms that moved production to Mexico to take advantage of lower labor costs would be enhanced, enabling them to better compete with Asian and European rivals.

The Case against NAFTA

Those who opposed NAFTA claimed that ratification would be followed by a mass exodus of jobs from the United States and Canada into Mexico as employers sought to profit from Mexico's lower wages and less strict environmental and labor laws. According to one extreme opponent, Ross Perot, up to 5.9 million U.S. jobs would be lost to Mexico after NAFTA in what he famously characterized as a "giant sucking sound." Most economists, however, dismissed these numbers as being absurd and alarmist. They argued that Mexico would have to run a bilateral trade surplus with the United States of close to $300 billion for job loss on such a scale to occur—and $300 billion was the size of Mexico's GDP. In other words, such a scenario seemed implausible.

More sober estimates of the impact of NAFTA ranged from a net creation of 170,000 jobs in the United States (due to increased Mexican demand for U.S. goods and services) and an increase of $15 billion per year to the joint U.S. and Mexican GDP, to a net loss of 490,000 U.S. jobs. To put these numbers in perspective, employment in the U.S. economy was predicted to grow by 18 million from 1993 to 2003. As most economists repeatedly stressed, NAFTA would have a small impact on both Canada and the United States. It could hardly be any other way, because the Mexican economy was only 5 percent of the size of the U.S. economy. Signing NAFTA required the largest leap of economic faith from Mexico rather than Canada or the United States. Falling trade barriers would expose Mexican firms to highly efficient U.S. and Canadian competitors that, when compared to the average Mexican firm, had far greater capital resources, access to highly educated and skilled workforces, and much greater technological sophistication. The short-run outcome was likely to be painful economic restructuring and unemployment in Mexico. But advocates of NAFTA claimed there would be long-run dynamic gains in the efficiency of Mexican firms as they adjusted to the rigors of a more competitive marketplace. To the extent that this occurred, they argued, Mexico's economic growth rate would accelerate, and Mexico might become a major market for Canadian and U.S. firms.[22]

Environmentalists also voiced concerns about NAFTA. They pointed to the sludge in the Rio Grande and the smog in the air over Mexico City and warned that Mexico could degrade clean air and toxic waste standards across the continent. They pointed out that the lower Rio Grande was the most polluted river in the United States and that, with NAFTA, chemical waste and sewage would increase along its course from El Paso, Texas, to the Gulf of Mexico.

There was also opposition in Mexico to NAFTA from those who feared a loss of national sovereignty. Mexican critics argued that their country would be dominated by U.S. firms that would not really contribute to Mexico's economic growth, but instead would use Mexico as a low-cost assembly site while keeping their high-paying, high-skilled jobs north of the border.

NAFTA: The Results

Studies of NAFTA's impact suggest its initial effects were at best muted, and both advocates and detractors may have been guilty of exaggeration.[23] On average, studies indicate that NAFTA's overall impact has been small but positive.[24] From 1993 to 2005, trade among NAFTA's partners grew by 250 percent.[25] Canada and Mexico are now among the top three trading partners of the United States (the other is China), suggesting the economies of the three NAFTA nations have become more closely integrated. In 1990, U.S. trade with Canada and Mexico accounted for about a quarter of total U.S. trade. By 2005, the figure was close to one-third. Canada's trade with its NAFTA partners increased from about 70 percent to more than 80 percent of all Canadian foreign trade between 1993 and 2005, while Mexico's trade with NAFTA increased from 66 percent to 80 percent over the same period. All three countries also experienced strong productivity growth over this period. In Mexico, labor productivity has increased by 50 percent since 1993, and the passage of NAFTA may have contributed to this. However, estimates suggest that employment effects of NAFTA have been small. The most pessimistic estimates suggest the United States lost 110,000 jobs per year due to NAFTA between 1994 and 2000—and many economists dispute this figure—which is tiny compared to the more than 2 million jobs a year created in the United States during the same period.

Perhaps the most significant impact of NAFTA has not been economic, but political. Many observers credit NAFTA with helping create the background for increased political stability in Mexico. For most of the post-NAFTA period, Mexico has been viewed as a stable democratic nation with a steadily growing economy, something that is beneficial to the United States, which shares a 2,000-mile border with the country.[26] However, recent events have cast a cloud over Mexico's future. In late 2006, newly elected Mexican President Felipe Calderón initiated a crackdown on Mexico's increasingly powerful drug cartels (whose main business has been the illegal trafficking of drugs across the border into the United States). Calderón sent 6,500 troops into the Mexican state of Michoacan to end escalating drug violence there. The cartels responded by escalating their own violence, and the country is now gripped in what amounts to an all-out war. Fueled by the lucrative business of selling drugs to the United States and armed with guns purchased in the United States, the cartels have been fighting each other and the Mexican authorities in an increasingly brutal conflict that claimed an estimated 57,500 lives between 2007 and 2012 and which some fear could spill over into the United States.[27]

Enlargement

One issue confronting NAFTA is that of enlargement. A number of other Latin American countries have indicated their desire to eventually join NAFTA. The governments of both Canada and the United States are adopting a wait-and-see attitude with regard to most countries. Getting NAFTA approved was a bruising political experience, and neither government is eager to repeat the process soon. Nevertheless, the Canadian, Mexican, and U.S. governments began talks in 1995 regarding Chile's possible entry into NAFTA. As of 2011, however, these talks had yielded little progress, partly because of political opposition in the U.S. Congress to expanding NAFTA. In December 2002, however, the United States and Chile did sign a bilateral free trade pact.

The Andean Community

Bolivia, Chile, Ecuador, Colombia, and Peru signed an agreement in 1969 to create the Andean Pact. The **Andean Community** was largely based on the EU model, but was far less successful at achieving its stated goals. The integration steps begun in 1969 included an internal tariff reduction program, a common external tariff, a transportation policy, a common industrial policy, and special concessions for the smallest members, Bolivia and Ecuador.

By the mid-1980s, the Andean Pact had all but collapsed and had failed to achieve any of its stated objectives. There was no tariff-free trade among member countries, no common external tariff, and no harmonization of economic policies. Political and economic problems seem to have hindered cooperation among member countries. The countries of the Andean Pact have had to deal with low economic growth, hyperinflation, high unemployment, political unrest, and crushing debt burdens. In addition, the dominant political ideology in many of the Andean countries during this period tended toward the radical-socialist end of the political spectrum. Because such an ideology is hostile to the free market economic principles on which the Andean Pact was based, progress toward closer integration could not be expected.

The tide began to turn in the late 1980s when, after years of economic decline, the governments of Latin America began to adopt free market economic policies. In 1990, the heads of the five current members of the Andean Community—Bolivia, Ecuador, Peru, Colombia, and Venezuela—met in the Galápagos Islands. The resulting Galápagos Declaration effectively relaunched the Andean Pact, which was renamed the Andean Community in 1997. The declaration's objectives included the establishment of a free trade area by 1992, a customs union by 1994, and a common market by 1995. This last milestone has not been reached. A customs union was implemented in 1995—although Peru opted out and Bolivia received preferential treatment until 2003. The Andean Community now operates as a customs union. In December 2005, it signed an agreement with Mercosur to restart stalled negotiations on the creation of a free trade area between the two trading blocs. Those negotiations are proceeding at a slow pace. In late 2006, Venezuela withdrew from the Andean Community as part of that country's attempts to join Mercosur.

Mercosur

Mercosur originated in 1988 as a free trade pact between Brazil and Argentina. The modest reductions in tariffs and quotas accompanying this pact reportedly helped bring about an 80 percent increase in trade between the two countries in the late 1980s.[28] This success encouraged the expansion of the pact in March 1990 to include Paraguay and Uruguay. In 2006, the pact was further expanded when Venezuela joined Mercosur, although it may take years for Venezuela to become fully integrated into the pact. As of early 2013, Paraguay had yet to ratify the agreement allowing Venezuela to become a full member of Mercosur.

The initial aim of Mercosur was to establish a full free trade area by the end of 1994 and a common market sometime thereafter. In December 1995, Mercosur's members agreed to a five-year program under which they hoped to perfect their free trade area and move toward a full customs union—something that has yet to be achieved.[29] For its first eight years or so, Mercosur seemed to be making a positive contribution to the economic growth rates of its member states. Trade among the four core members quadrupled between 1990 and 1998. The combined GDP of the four member states grew at an annual average rate of 3.5 percent between 1990 and 1996, a performance that is significantly better than the four attained during the 1980s.[30]

However, Mercosur had its critics, including Alexander Yeats, a senior economist at the World Bank, who wrote a stinging critique.[31] According to Yeats, the trade diversion effects of Mercosur outweigh its trade creation effects. Yeats pointed out that the fastest-growing items in intra-Mercosur trade were cars, buses, agricultural equipment, and other capital-intensive goods that are produced relatively inefficiently in the four member countries. In other words, Mercosur countries, insulated from outside competition by tariffs that run as high as 70 percent of value on motor vehicles, are investing in factories that build products that are too expensive to sell to anyone but themselves. The result, according to Yeats, is that Mercosur countries might not be able to compete globally once the group's external trade barriers come down. In the meantime, capital is being drawn away from more efficient enterprises. In the near term, countries with more efficient manufacturing enterprises lose because Mercosur's external trade barriers keep them out of the market.

Mercosur hit a significant roadblock in 1998 when its member states slipped into recession and intrabloc trade slumped. Trade fell further in 1999 following a financial crisis in Brazil that led to the devaluation of the Brazilian real, which immediately made the goods of other Mercosur members 40 percent more expensive in Brazil, their largest export market. At this point, progress toward establishing a full customs union all but stopped. Things deteriorated further in 2001 when Argentina, beset by economic stresses, suggested the customs union be temporarily suspended. Argentina wanted to suspend Mercosur's tariff so that it could abolish duties on imports of capital equipment, while raising those on consumer goods to 35 percent (Mercosur had established a 14 percent import tariff on both sets of goods). Brazil agreed to this request, effectively halting Mercosur's quest to become a fully functioning customs union.[32] Hope for a revival arose in 2003 when new Brazilian President Lula da Silva announced his support for a revitalized and expanded Mercosur modeled after the EU with a larger membership, a common currency, and a democratically elected Mercosur parliament.[33] As of 2011, however, little progress had been made in moving Mercosur down that road, and critics believed the customs union was, if anything, becoming more imperfect over time.

Central American Common Market, Cafta, and Caricom

Two other trade pacts in the Americas have not made much progress. In the early 1960s, Costa Rica, El Salvador, Guatemala, Honduras, and Nicaragua attempted to set up a **Central American Common Market**. It collapsed in 1969 when war broke out between Honduras and El Salvador after a riot at a soccer match between teams from the two countries. Since then, the member countries have made some progress toward reviving their agreement (the five founding members were joined by the Dominican Republic). The proposed common market was given a boost in 2003 when the United States signaled its intention to enter into bilateral free trade negotiations with the group. These culminated in a 2004 agreement to establish a free trade agreement between the six countries and the United States. Known as the **Central America Free Trade Agreement (CAFTA)**, the aim is to lower trade barriers between the United States and the six countries for most goods and services.

A customs union was to have been created in 1991 between the English-speaking Caribbean countries under the auspices of the Caribbean Community. Referred to as **CARICOM,** it was established in 1973. However, it repeatedly failed to progress toward economic integration. A formal commitment to economic and monetary union was adopted by CARICOM's member states in 1984, but since then little progress has been made. In October 1991, the CARICOM governments failed, for the third consecutive time, to meet a deadline for establishing a common external tariff. Despite this, CARICOM expanded to 15 members by 2005. In early 2006, six CARICOM members established the **Caribbean Single Market and Economy (CSME)**. Modeled on the EU's single market, CSME's goal is to lower trade barriers and harmonize macroeconomic and monetary policy between member states.[34]

Free Trade Area of the Americas

At a hemispherewide Summit of the Americas in December 1994, a Free Trade Area of the Americas (FTAA) was proposed. It took more than three years for the talks to start, but in April 1998, 34 heads of state traveled to Santiago, Chile, for the second Summit of the Americas, where they formally inaugurated talks to establish an FTAA by January 1, 2005—something that didn't occur. The continuing talks have addressed a wide range of economic, political, and environmental issues related to cross-border trade and investment. Although both the United States and Brazil were early advocates of the FTAA, support from both countries seems to be mixed at this point. Because the United States and Brazil have the largest economies in North and South America, respectively, strong U.S. and Brazilian support is a precondition for establishment of the free trade area.

The major stumbling blocks so far have been twofold. First, the United States wants its southern neighbors to agree to tougher enforcement of intellectual property rights and lower manufacturing tariffs, which they do not seem to be eager to embrace. Second, Brazil and Argentina want the United States to reduce its subsidies to U.S. agricultural producers and scrap tariffs on agricultural imports, which the U.S. government does not seem inclined to do. For progress to be made, most observers agree that the United States and Brazil have to first reach an agreement on these crucial issues.[35] If the FTAA is eventually established, it will have major implications for cross-border trade and investment flows within the hemisphere. The FTAA would open a free trade umbrella over 850 million people, who accounted for some $18 trillion in GDP in 2008.

Currently, however, FTAA is very much a work in progress, and the progress has been slow. The most recent attempt to get talks going again, in November 2005 at a summit of 34 heads of state from North and South America, failed when opponents, led by Venezuela's populist President Hugo Chávez, blocked efforts by the Bush administration to set an agenda for further talks on FTAA. In voicing his opposition, Chávez condemned the U.S. free trade model as a "perversion" that would unduly benefit the United States to the detriment of poor people in Latin America, who Chávez claimed have not benefited from free trade details.[36] Such views make it unlikely that there will be much progress establishing an FTAA in the near term.

REGIONAL ECONOMIC INTEGRATION ELSEWHERE ▐ L09-4 ▌

Numerous attempts at regional economic integration have been tried throughout Asia and Africa. However, few exist in anything other than name. Perhaps the most significant is the Association of Southeast Asian Nations (ASEAN). In addition, the Asia-Pacific Economic Cooperation (APEC) forum has recently emerged as the seed of a potential free trade region.

Association of Southeast Asian Nations

Formed in 1967, the **Association of Southeast Asian Nations (ASEAN)** includes Brunei, Cambodia, Indonesia, Laos, Malaysia, Myanmar, Philippines, Singapore, Thailand, and Vietnam. Laos, Myanmar, Vietnam, and Cambodia have all joined recently, creating a regional grouping of 500 million people with a combined GDP of some $740 billion (see Map 9.3). The basic objective of ASEAN is to foster freer trade among member countries and to achieve cooperation in their industrial policies. Progress so far has been limited, however.

Until recently, only 5 percent of intra-ASEAN trade consisted of goods whose tariffs had been reduced through an ASEAN preferential trade arrangement. This may be changing. In 2003, an ASEAN Free Trade Area (AFTA) among the six original members of ASEAN came into full effect. The AFTA has cut tariffs on manufacturing and agricultural products to less than 5 percent. However, there are some significant exceptions to this tariff reduction. Malaysia, for example, refused to bring down tariffs on imported cars until 2005 and then agreed to lower the tariff only to 20 percent, not the 5 percent called for under the AFTA. Malaysia wanted to protect Proton, an inefficient local carmaker, from foreign competition. Similarly, the Philippines has refused to lower tariff rates on petrochemicals, and rice, the largest agricultural product in the region, will remain subject to higher tariff rates until at least 2020.[37]

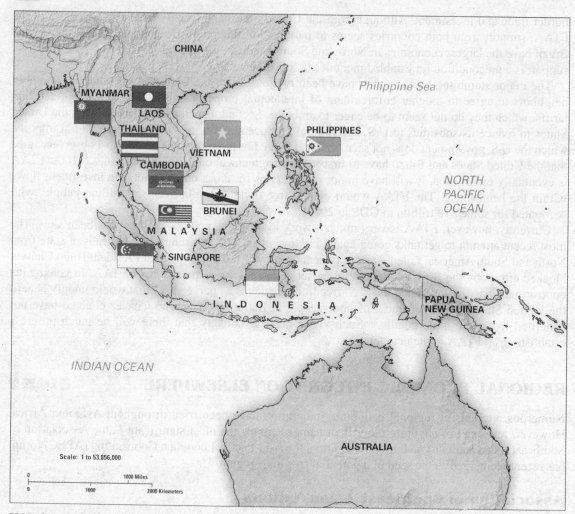

MAP 9.3 ASEAN Countries

Source: Reprinted with permission, www.asean.org.

Notwithstanding such issues, ASEAN and AFTA are at least progressing toward establishing a free trade zone. Vietnam joined the AFTA in 2006, Laos and Myanmar in 2008, and Cambodia in 2010. The goal was to reduce import tariffs among the six original members to zero by 2010 and to do so by 2015 for the newer members (although important exceptions to that goal, such as tariffs on rice, will persist).

ASEAN signed a free trade agreement with China that removes tariffs on 90 percent of traded goods. This went into effect January 1, 2010. Trade between China and ASEAN members more than tripled during the first decade of the twenty-first century, and this agreement should spur further growth.[38]

Asia-Pacific Economic Cooperation

The Asia-Pacific Economic Cooperation (APEC) was founded in 1990 at the suggestion of Australia. APEC currently has 21 member states, including such economic powerhouses as the United States,

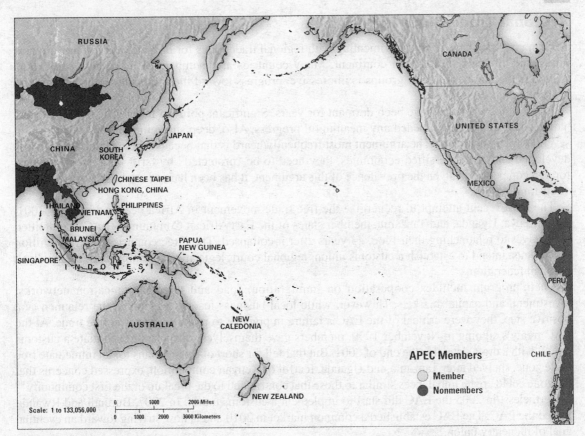

MAP 9.4   APEC Members

Source: From www.apec.org. Reprinted with permission.

Japan, and China (see Map 9.4). Collectively, the member states account for about 55 percent of the world's GNP, 49 percent of world trade, and much of the growth in the world economy. The stated aim of APEC is to increase multilateral cooperation in view of the economic rise of the Pacific nations and the growing interdependence within the region. U.S. support for APEC was also based on the belief that it might prove a viable strategy for heading off any moves to create Asian groupings from which it would be excluded.

Interest in APEC was heightened considerably in November 1993 when the heads of APEC member states met for the first time at a two-day conference in Seattle. Debate before the meeting speculated on the likely future role of APEC. One view was that APEC should commit itself to the ultimate formation of a free trade area. Such a move would transform the Pacific Rim from a geographic expression into the world's largest free trade area. Another view was that APEC would produce no more than hot air and lots of photo opportunities for the leaders involved. As it turned out, the APEC meeting produced little more than some vague commitments from member states to work together for greater economic integration and a general lowering of trade barriers. However, member states did not rule out the possibility of closer economic cooperation in the future.[39] The heads of state have met again on a number of occasions. However, the vague plan committed APEC to doing no more than holding further talks, which is all that has been accomplished to date.

Regional Trade Blocs in Africa

African countries have been experimenting with regional trade blocs for half a century. There are now nine trade blocs on the African continent. Many countries are members of more than one group. Although the number of trade groups is impressive, progress toward the establishment of meaningful trade blocs has been slow.

Many of these groups have been dormant for years. Significant political turmoil in several African nations has persistently impeded any meaningful progress. Also, deep suspicion of free trade exists in several African countries. The argument most frequently heard is that because these countries have less developed and less diversified economies, they need to be "protected" by tariff barriers from unfair foreign competition. Given the prevalence of this argument, it has been hard to establish free trade areas or customs unions.

The most recent attempt to reenergize the free trade movement in Africa occurred in early 2001, when Kenya, Uganda, and Tanzania, member states of the East African Community (EAC), committed themselves to relaunching their bloc, 24 years after it collapsed. The three countries, with 80 million inhabitants, intend to establish a customs union, regional court, legislative assembly, and, eventually, a political federation.

Their program includes cooperation on immigration, road and telecommunication networks, investment, and capital markets. However, while local business leaders welcomed the relaunch as a positive step, they were critical of the EAC's failure in practice to make progress on free trade. At the EAC treaty's signing in November 1999, members gave themselves four years to negotiate a customs union, with a draft slated for the end of 2001. But that fell far short of earlier plans for an immediate free trade zone, shelved after Tanzania and Uganda, fearful of Kenyan competition, expressed concerns that the zone could create imbalances similar to those that contributed to the breakup of the first community.[40] Nevertheless, in 2005 the EAC did start to implement a customs union. In 2007, Burundi and Rwanda joined the EAC. The EAC established a common market in 2010 and is now striving toward an eventual goal of monetary union.

◼ IMPLICATIONS FOR MANAGERS ▰▰▰▰▰▰▰▰▰▰ ▰LO9-5▰

Currently, the most significant developments in regional economic integration are occurring in the EU and NAFTA. Although some of the Latin American trade blocs, ASEAN, and the proposed FTAA may have economic significance in the future, developments in the EU and NAFTA currently have more profound implications for business practice. Accordingly, in this section, we concentrate on the business implications of those two groups. Similar conclusions, however, could be drawn with regard to the creation of a single market anywhere in the world.

OPPORTUNITIES

The creation of a single market through regional economic integration offers significant opportunities because markets that were formerly protected from foreign competition are increasingly open. Additional opportunities arise from the inherent lower costs of doing business in a single market—as opposed to 27 national markets in the case of the EU or 3 national markets in the case of NAFTA. Free movement of goods across borders, harmonized product standards, and simplified tax regimes make it possible for firms based in the EU and the NAFTA countries to realize potentially significant cost economies by centralizing production in those EU and NAFTA locations where the mix of factor costs and skills is optimal. Rather than producing a product in each of the 27 EU countries or the 3 NAFTA countries, a firm may be able to serve the whole EU or North American market from a single location. This location must be chosen carefully, of course, with an eye on local factor costs and skills.

Even after the removal of barriers to trade and investment, enduring differences in culture and competitive practices often limit the ability of companies to realize cost economies by centralizing production in key locations and producing a standardized product for a single multiple-country market. Consider the case of Atag Holdings NV, a Dutch maker of kitchen appliances.[41] Atag thought it was well placed to benefit from the single market, but found it tough going. Atag's plant is just 1 mile from the German border and near the center of the EU's population. The company thought it could cater to both the "potato" and "spaghetti" belts—marketers' terms for consumers in northern and southern Europe—by producing two main product lines and selling these standardized "euro-products" to "euro-consumers." The main benefit of doing so is the economy of scale derived from mass production of a standardized range of products. Atag quickly discovered that the "euro-consumer" was a myth. Consumer preferences vary much more across nations than Atag had thought. Consider ceramic cooktops: Atag planned to market just 2 varieties throughout the EU but found it needed 11. Belgians, who cook in huge pots, require extra-large burners. Germans like oval pots and burners to fit. The French need small burners and very low temperatures for simmering sauces and broths. Germans like oven knobs on the top; the French want them on the front. Most Germans and French prefer black and white ranges; the British demand a range of colors including peach, pigeon blue, and mint green.

THREATS

Just as the emergence of single markets creates opportunities for business, it also presents a number of threats. For one thing, the business environment within each grouping has become more competitive. The lowering of barriers to trade and investment among countries has led to increased price competition throughout the EU and NAFTA. Over time, price differentials across nations will decline in a single market. This is a direct threat to any firm doing business in EU or NAFTA countries. To survive in the tougher single-market environment, firms must take advantage of the opportunities offered by the creation of a single market to rationalize their production and reduce their costs. Otherwise, they will be at a severe disadvantage.

A further threat to firms outside these trading blocs arises from the likely long-term improvement in the competitive position of many firms within the areas. This is particularly relevant in the EU, where many firms have historically been limited by a high-cost structure in their ability to compete globally with North American and Asian firms. The creation of a single market and the resulting increased competition in the EU produced serious attempts by many EU firms to reduce their cost structure by rationalizing production. This transformed many EU companies into more efficient global competitors. The message for non-EU businesses is that they need to respond to the emergence of more capable European competitors by reducing their own cost structures.

Another threat to firms outside of trading areas is the threat of being shut out of the single market by the creation of a "trade fortress." The charge that regional economic integration might lead to a fortress mentality is most often leveled at the EU. Although the free trade philosophy underpinning the EU theoretically argues against the creation of any fortress in Europe, occasional signs indicate the EU may raise barriers to imports and investment in certain "politically sensitive" areas, such as autos. Non-EU firms might be well advised, therefore, to set up their own EU operations. This could also occur in the NAFTA countries, but it seems less likely.

Finally, the emerging role of the European Commission in competition policy suggests the EU is increasingly willing and able to intervene and impose conditions on companies proposing mergers and acquisitions. This is a threat insofar as it limits the ability of firms to pursue the corporate strategy of their choice. The commission may require significant concessions from businesses as a precondition for allowing proposed mergers and acquisitions to proceed. While this constrains the strategic options for firms, it should be remembered that in taking such action, the commission is trying to maintain the level of competition in Europe's single market, which should benefit consumers.

Chapter Summary

This chapter pursued three main objectives: to examine the economic and political debate surrounding regional economic integration; to review the progress toward regional economic integration in Europe, the Americas, and elsewhere; and to distinguish the important implications of regional economic integration for the practice of international business. The chapter made the following points:

1. A number of levels of economic integration are possible in theory. In order of increasing integration, they include a free trade area, a customs union, a common market, an economic union, and full political union.

2. In a free trade area, barriers to trade among member countries are removed, but each country determines its own external trade policy. In a customs union, internal barriers to trade are removed, and a common external trade policy is adopted. A common market is similar to a customs union, except that a common market also allows factors of production to move freely among countries. An economic union involves even closer integration, including the establishment of a common currency and the harmonization of tax rates. A political union is the logical culmination of attempts to achieve ever-closer economic integration.

3. Regional economic integration is an attempt to achieve economic gains from the free flow of trade and investment between neighboring countries.

4. Integration is not easily achieved or sustained. Although integration brings benefits to the majority, it is never without costs for the minority. Concerns over national sovereignty often slow or stop integration attempts.

5. Regional integration will not increase economic welfare if the trade creation effects in the free trade area are outweighed by the trade diversion effects.

6. The Single European Act sought to create a true single market by abolishing administrative barriers to the free flow of trade and investment among EU countries.

7. Seventeen EU members now use a common currency, the euro. The economic gains from a common currency come from reduced exchange costs, reduced risk associated with currency fluctuations, and increased price competition within the EU.

8. Increasingly, the European Commission is taking an activist stance with regard to competition policy, intervening to restrict mergers and acquisitions that it believes will reduce competition in the EU.

9. Although no other attempt at regional economic integration comes close to the EU in terms of potential economic and political significance, various other attempts are being made in the world. The most notable include NAFTA in North America, the Andean Community and Mercosur in Latin America, ASEAN in Southeast Asia, and perhaps APEC.

10. The creation of single markets in the EU and North America means that many markets that were formerly protected from foreign competition are now more open. This creates major investment and export opportunities for firms within and outside these regions.

11. The free movement of goods across borders, the harmonization of product standards, and the simplification of tax regimes make it possible for firms based in a free trade area to realize potentially enormous cost economies by centralizing production in those locations within the area where the mix of factor costs and skills is optimal.

12. The lowering of barriers to trade and investment among countries within a trade group will probably be followed by increased price competition.

Critical Thinking and Discussion Questions

1. NAFTA has produced significant net benefits for the Canadian, Mexican, and U.S. economies. Discuss.

2. What are the economic and political arguments for regional economic integration? Given these arguments, why don't we see more substantial examples of integration in the world economy?

3. What in general was the effect of the creation of a single market and a single currency within the EU on competition within the EU? Why?

4. Do you think it is correct for the European Commission to restrict mergers between American companies that do business in Europe? (For example, the European Commission vetoed the proposed merger between WorldCom and Sprint, both U.S. companies, and it carefully reviewed the merger between AOL and Time Warner, again both U.S. companies.)

5. What were the causes of the 2010–2012 sovereign debt crisis in the EU? What does this crisis tell us about the weaknesses of the euro? Do you think the euro will survive the sovereign debt crisis?

6. How should a U.S. firm that currently exports only to ASEAN countries respond to the creation of a single market in this regional grouping?

7. How should a firm with self-sufficient production facilities in several ASEAN countries respond to the creation of a single market? What are the constraints on its ability to respond in a manner that minimizes production costs?

8. After a promising start, Mercosur, the major Latin American trade agreement, has faltered and made little progress since 2000. What problems are hurting Mercosur? What can be done to solve these problems?

9. Would establishment of a Free Trade Area of the Americas (FTAA) be good for the two most advanced economies in the hemisphere, the United States and Canada? How might the establishment of the FTAA affect the strategy of North American firms?

Research Task ⊙ globalEDGE globaledge.msu.edu

Regional Economic Integration

Use the globalEDGE website (globaledge.msu.edu) to complete the following exercises:

Exercise 1

The World Trade Organization maintains a database of *regional trade agreements*. You can search this database to identify all agreements that a specific country participates in. Search the database to identify the trade agreements that Japan currently participates in. What patterns do you see? Which region(s) of the world does Japan seem to be focusing on in its trade endeavors?

Exercise 2

Your company has assigned you with the task of investigating the various trade blocs in Africa to see if your company can benefit from these trade agreements while expanding into African markets. The first trade bloc you come across is *COMESA*. Prepare a short executive summary for your company, explaining the level of integration the bloc has currently achieved, the level it aspires to accomplish, and the relationships it has with other African trade blocs.

Closing CASE

I Want My Greek TV!

It's now almost two decades since the member states of the European Union (EU) started to implement a treaty calling for the establishment of a single market for goods and services across the union, and yet progress toward this goal is still not complete. A case in point: the TV broadcasts of Premier League soccer. The English Premier League, which is one of the most lucrative broadcasting sports franchises in Europe, if not the world, has for years segmented Europe into different national markets, charging different prices for broadcasting rights depending on local demand. Not surprisingly, the rights are most expensive in the United Kingdom, where the league has contracted with British Sky Broadcasting Group and ESPN to screen games.

Karen Murphy, the owner of the Red, White & Blue pub in Portsmouth, England, didn't want to pay the £7,000 annual subscription fee that Sky demanded for access to the Premier League feed. Instead, she purchased a TV signal decoder card and used it to unscramble the feed from a Greek TV broadcaster, Nova, which had purchased the rights to broadcast Premier League soccer in Greece. This cost her just £800 a year. In 2005, it also brought a lawsuit from the Premier League. The initial judgment in a British court upheld the right of the Premier League to segment the market and charge a higher price to UK subscribers. Murphy was fined £8,000. She appealed the ruling, claiming the practice violated the EU's Single Market Act, which the United Kingdom had signed in 1992.

The case eventually landed in the European Court of Justice, the EU's highest court. The Premier League argued before the court that the EU needs individual national TV markets to satisfy the "cultural preferences" of viewers. The court did not agree. In a bombshell for the Premier League, on February 3, 2011, the court stated, "Territorial exclusivity agreements relating to the transmission of football matches are contrary to European Union law. European law does not make it possible to prohibit the live transmission of Premier League matches in pubs by means of foreign decoder cards." In short, Murphy can continue to purchase her feed from Nova. This decision was a legal opinion prepared by the court's advocate general, so technically it is still possible that the full court might overturn it, but in four out of five cases this does not happen.

This was not the first time the EU court had issued a ruling that affected Premier League soccer. In 1995, the court upheld the right of a Belgian soccer player to play in another EU country, stating athletes had the same freedom of movement as other EU workers. Ironically, this ruling, which also affirmed the principle of a single market, benefited Premier League clubs, enabling them to sign foreign players, rapidly transforming the league into the best in the world. The new ruling, however, creates significant challenges for the league. Revenue from broadcasting is a major source of income for Premier League clubs. The current deal giving British broadcasting rights to Sky and ESPN is worth some £1.782 billion to the league between 2010 and 2013.

In February 2012 the EU court affirms the ruling. Many consumers may now follow Murphy and buy TV decoders so that they can watch lower-cost feeds. If enough do this, the income loss from arbitrage by consumers may force the Premier League to move toward pan-European broadcasting and pricing. This will reduce income to the clubs, which could have a profound impact on the players they can recruit and the wages they can afford. In short, the ruling, while benefiting consumers such as Murphy and her customers at the Red, White & Blue pub, is a dark cloud hanging over the future of British soccer.[42]

Case Discussion Questions

1. Why do you think the English Premier League has historically charged different prices for broadcasting rights in different European markets?
2. Do you think the European Court of Justice was right to rule that the league could not stop people from buying Premier League soccer feeds from other countries? Explain your reasoning?
3. Who benefits from the EU ruling? Who will the losers be?
4. If you were running the English Premier League, what would your strategy be on broadcast rights going forward?

Endnotes

1. E. Malkin, "Mexico Finds Unlikely Allies in Trade Fight," *The New York Times,* December 25, 2012, p. B1; S. Strom, "United States and Mexico Reach Tomato Deal, Averting a Trade War," *The New York Times,* February 3, 2013; and J. Margolis, "NAFTA 20 Years After: Florida's Tomato Growers Struggling," *The World,* December 17, 2012.
2. Information taken from World Trade Organization website and current as of April 2012, www.wto.org.
3. Ibid.
4. The Andean Community has been through a number of changes since its inception. The latest version was established in 1991. See "Free-Trade Free for All," *The Economist,* January 4, 1991, p. 63.
5. D. Swann, *The Economics of the Common Market,* 6th ed. (London: Penguin Books, 1990).
6. See J. Bhagwati, "Regionalism and Multilateralism: An Overview," Columbia University Discussion Paper 603, Department of Economics, Columbia University, New York; A. de la Torre and M. Kelly, "Regional Trade Arrangements," Occasional Paper 93, Washington, DC: International Monetary Fund, March 1992; J. Bhagwati, "Fast Track to Nowhere," *The Economist,* October 18, 1997, pp. 21–24; Jagdish Bhagwati, *Free Trade Today* (Princeton and Oxford: Princeton University Press, 2002); and B. K. Gordon, "A High Risk Trade Policy," *Foreign Affairs* 82 no. 4 (July–August 2003), pp. 105–15.
7. N. Colchester and D. Buchan, *Europower: The Essential Guide to Europe's Economic Transformation in 1992* (London: The Economist Books, 1990); and Swann, *Economics of the Common Market.*
8. Swann, *Economics of the Common Market;* Colchester and Buchan, *Europower;* "The European Union: A Survey," *The Economist,* October 22, 1994; "The European Community: A Survey," *The Economist,* July 3, 1993; and the European Union website at http://europa.eu.int.
9. M. Hachman, "EU Hits Intel with $1.45 Billion Fine for Antitrust Violations," *PCMAG.com,* May 13, 2009; and J. Kanter, "Europe Fines Intel $1.45 billion in Antitrust Case," *The New York Times,* May 14, 2009.
10. E. J. Morgan, "A Decade of EC Merger Control," *International Journal of Economics and Business,* November 2001, pp. 451–73.
11. "The European Community: A Survey," 1993.
12. Tony Barber, "The Lisbon Reform Treaty," *FT.com,* December 13, 2007.
13. "One Europe, One Economy," *The Economist,* November 30, 1991, pp. 53–54; and "Market Failure: A Survey of Business in Europe," *The Economist,* June 8, 1991, pp. 6–10.
14. Alan Riley, "The Single Market Ten Years On," *European Policy Analyst,* December 2002, pp. 65–72.

15. See C. Wyploze, "EMU: Why and How It Might Happen," *Journal of Economic Perspectives* 11 (1997), pp. 3–22; and M. Feldstein, "The Political Economy of the European Economic and Monetary Union," *Journal of Economic Perspectives* 11 (1997), pp. 23–42.

16. C. Randzio-Plath, "Europe Prepares for a Single Financial Market," *Intereconomic,* May–June 2004, pp. 142–46; T. Buck, D. Hargreaves, and P. Norman, "Europe's Single Financial Market," *Financial Times,* January 18, 2005, p. 17; "The Gate-Keeper," *The Economist,* February 19, 2005, p. 79; P. Hofheinz, "A Capital Idea: The European Union Has a Grand Plan to Make Its Financial Markets More Efficient," *The Wall Street Journal,* October 14, 2002, p. R4; and "Banking on McCreevy: Europe's Single Market," *The Economist,* November 26, 2005, p. 91.

17. "One Europe, One Economy;" and Feldstein, "The Political Economy of the European Economic and Monetary Union."

18. "Euro Still the World's Second Reserve Currency," *The Economic Times,* July 22, 2011.

19. "A Very European Crisis," *The Economist,* February 6, 2010, pp. 75–77; L. Thomas, "Is Debt Trashing the Euro?" *The New York Times,* February 7, 2010, pp. 1, 7; "Bite the Bullet," *The Economist,* January 15, 2011, pp. 77–79; and "The Wait Is Over," *The Economist,* March 17, 2012, pp. 83–84.

20. Details regarding conditions of membership and the progression of enlargement negotiations can be found at http://europa.eu.int/comm/enlargement/index.htm.

21. "What Is NAFTA?" *Financial Times,* November 17, 1993, p. 6; and S. Garland, "Sweet Victory," *BusinessWeek,* November 29, 1993, pp. 30–31.

22. "NAFTA: The Showdown," *The Economist,* November 13, 1993, pp. 23–36.

23. N. C. Lustog, "NAFTA: Setting the Record Straight," *The World Economy,* 1997, pp. 605–14; and G. C. Hufbauer and J. J. Schott, *NAFTA Revisited: Achievements and Challenges* (Washington, DC: Institute for International Economics, 2005).

24. W. Thorbecke and C. Eigen-Zucchi, "Did NAFTA Cause a Giant Sucking Sound?" *Journal of Labor Research,* Fall 2002, pp. 647–58; G. Gagne, "North American Free Trade, Canada, and U.S. Trade Remedies: An Assessment after Ten Years," *The World Economy,* 2000, pp. 77–91; Hufbauer and Schott, *NAFTA Revisited;* and J. Romalis, "NAFTA's and Custfa's Impact on International Trade," *Review of Economics and Statistics* 98, no. 3 (2007), pp. 416–35.

25. All trade figures from U.S. Department of Commerce Trade Stat Express website at http://tse.export.gov/.

26. J. Cavanagh et al., "Happy Ever NAFTA?" *Foreign Policy,* September–October 2002, pp. 58–65.

27. "Mexican Daily: Nearly 60,000 Drug War Deaths under Calderon," *Fox News Latino,* November 1, 2012.

28. "The Business of the American Hemisphere," *The Economist,* August 24, 1991, pp. 37–38.

29. "NAFTA Is Not Alone," *The Economist,* June 18, 1994, pp. 47–48.

30. "Murky Mercosur," *The Economist,* July 26, 1997, pp. 66–67.

31. See M. Philips, "South American Trade Pact under Fire," *The Wall Street Journal,* October 23, 1996, p. A2; A. J. Yeats, *Does Mercosur's Trade Performance Justify Concerns about the Global Welfare-Reducing Effects of Free Trade Arrangements? Yes!* (Washington, DC: World Bank, 1996); and D. M. Leipziger et al., "Mercosur: Integration and Industrial Policy," *The World Economy,* 1997, pp. 585–604.

32. "Another Blow to Mercosur," *The Economist,* March 31, 2001, pp. 33–34.

33. "Lula Lays Out Mercosur Rescue Mission," *Latin America Newsletters,* February 4, 2003, p. 7.

34. "CARICOM Single Market Begins," *EIU Views,* February 3, 2006.

35. M. Esterl, "Free Trade Area of the Americas Stalls," *The Economist,* January 19, 2005, p. 1.

36. M. Moffett and J. D. McKinnon, "Failed Summit Casts Shadow on Global Trade Talks," *The Wall Street Journal,* November 7, 2005, p. A1.

37. "Every Man for Himself: Trade in Asia," *The Economist,* November 2, 2002, pp. 43–44.

38. L. Gooch, "Asian Free-Trade Zone Raises Hopes," *The New York Times,* January 1, 2010, p. B3.

39. "Aimless in Seattle," *The Economist,* November 13, 1993, pp. 35–36.

40. M. Turner, "Trio Revives East African Union," *Financial Times,* January 16, 2001, p. 4.

41. T. Horwitz, "Europe's Borders Fade," *The Wall Street Journal,* May 18, 1993, pp. A1, A12; "A Singular Market," *The Economist,* October 22, 1994, pp. 10–16; and "Something Dodgy in Europe's Single Market," *The Economist,* May 21, 1994, pp. 69–70.

42. O. Gibson, "Round One to the Pub Lady," *The Guardian,* February 4, 2011, p. 5; J. W. Miller, "European TV Market for Sports Faces Turmoil from Legal Ruling," *The Wall Street Journal,* February 4, 2011; and J. Wilson, "What the Legal Wrangle Means for Armchair Fans," *The Daily Telegraph,* February 4, 2011, p. 8. "Portsmouth pub landlady Karen Murphy has Premier League TV conviction quashed," *Metro,* February 24th, 2012.

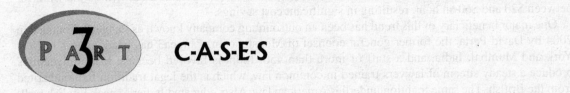

C-A-S-E-S

LEGAL OUTSOURCING

Sacha Baron Cohen, the irreverent British comedian whose fictional characters have included Borat, Ali G, and Bruno, is no stranger to lawsuits, including several from members of the public who claimed they were duped into appearing in his 2006 film, *Borat: Cultural Learnings of America for Make Benefit Glorious Nation of Kazakhstan.* In 2009, Cohen was sued yet again, this time by a woman who claimed Cohen defamed her during a sketch in the *Da Ali G Show,* in which Cohen plays the linguistically challenged rap star Ali G. Like most other suits against Cohen, this one was dismissed. In rendering his opinion, Los Angeles Superior Court Judge Terry Friedman stated, "No reasonable person could consider the statements made by Ali G on the program to be factual. It is obvious that the Ali G character is absurd, and all his statements are gibberish and intended as comedy."

An interesting aspect of this case was that the majority of the preparatory work was done not by lawyers in Los Angeles but by a six-member team of lawyers and legal assistants in Mysore, India. A veteran media lawyer noted that without legal outsourcing to somewhere such as India, mounting a defense against this kind of lawsuit would not have made economic sense. The defendants would have simply paid the plaintiff to go away to avoid paying U.S. legal fees, even though the case had no merit. But with a team of excellent Indian attorneys trained in U.S. law doing a major chunk of the legal work, it was less expensive to fight and win the suit than it was to settle out of court.

Legal outsourcing to places such as India and the Philippines is growing. Although the amounts involved are still small—estimates suggest that of the $180 billion Americans spend on legal services each year only about $1 billion is outsourced—the growth rate is high at 20 to 30 percent annually. The driving force has been spiraling legal fees in the United States. Between 1998 and 2009, hourly rates at big American law firms shot up more than 65 percent, according to industry sources.

Faced with escalating costs, law firms and corporate law departments are exploring outsourcing. Some legal tasks cannot be done cheaply. If the fate of your company hangs on the verdict, you will probably want a brilliant lawyer to argue your case. However, plenty of legal tasks are routine. These include reviewing documents, drafting contracts, and the like. American law firms typically use fresh law graduates to do such grunt work, billing them out at steep rates to generate lots of profit for the firm. The 2008–2009 recession prompted clients to rebel against this practice. Increasingly, clients are pushing their law firms to drive down legal costs through outsourcing. While hourly rates for U.S. lawyers doing grunt work can run from $100 to as high as $500, lawyers in India will do the work for between $20 and $60 an hour, resulting in significant cost savings.

One major beneficiary of this trend has been an outsourcing company known as Pangea3. Founded in 2004 by David Perla, the former general counsel of Monster.com, Pangea3 has headquarters in New York and Mumbai, India, and a staff of more than 450. India is favored because local universities produce a steady stream of lawyers trained in common law, which is the legal tradition India inherited from the British. The same tradition underlies American law. Also, educated Indians speak English well, and the 10- to 12-hour time difference between India and the United States means that work can be done overnight in India, increasing responsiveness to clients.

Pangea3 serves two kinds of clients, corporations and U.S. law firms seeking to outsource routine legal work to low-cost locations. Some 75 percent of its business comes from *Fortune* 1000 companies, while the rest comes from law firms. Pangea3's value proposition is simple: It helps companies and law firms improve their efficiency, and minimize their business and legal risks, by having routine, labor-intensive legal work that requires a low degree of judgment done in India. Most industry experts believe that in the short to medium term, companies such as Pangea3 will see their market opportunity expand from about $1 billion today to $3 billion to $5 billion by decade's end. In anticipation of this rapid growth, Thomson Reuters, one of the world's largest media and information services companies, bought Pangea3 in November 2010.

Case Discussion Questions

1. What are the benefits to a law firm of outsourcing legal services to a foreign country? What are the potential costs and risks?
2. What kind of legal services are most amenable to outsourcing?
3. Which groups gain from the outsourcing of legal services? Which groups lose?
4. On balance, do you think that this kind of outsourcing is a good thing or a bad thing? What are the risks here?
5. Why were the services in this case outsourced to India, as opposed to another country such as China? What does this case tell you about the kinds of factors that are important when a firm is considering whether to outsource a value creation activity, and where to outsource it to?

Sources

"Offshoring Your Lawyer," *The Economist,* December 19, 2010, p. 132; D. Itzkoff, "A Legal Victory for Ali G and Sacha Baron Cohen," *The New York Times,* April 21, 2009; and D. A. Steiger, "The Rise of Global Legal Sourcing," *Business Law Today,* December 2009, pp. 38–43.

THE GLOBAL FINANCIAL CRISIS AND PROTECTIONISM

Two facts have characterized international trade between 1986 and 2007. First, the volume of world trade grew every year, creating an increasingly interdependent global economy, and second, barriers to international trade were progressively reduced. Between 1990 and 2007 international trade grew by 6 percent annually compounded, while import tariffs on goods fell from an average of 26 percent in 1986 to 8.8 percent in 2007. In the wake of the global financial crisis that started in the United States in 2008 and quickly spread around the world, this changed. As global demand slumped and financing for international trade dried up in the wake of tight credit conditions, so did the volume of international trade. The volume of world trade fell by 2 percent in 2008, the first decline since 1982, and then slumped a further 12 percent in 2009.

This contraction was alarming because past sharp declines in trade have been followed by calls for greater protectionism from foreign competition as governments try to protect jobs at home in the wake of declining demand. This is what occurred in the 1930s, when shrinking trade was followed quickly by increases in trade barriers, mostly in the form of higher tariffs. This actually made the situation far worse and contributed to to the Great Depression.

Much has changed since the 1930s. Treaties now in place limit the ability of national governments to raise trade barriers. Most notably, the World Trade Organization rules, in theory, constrain the ability of countries to implement significant increases in trade barriers. But WTO rules are not perfect and there is plenty of evidence that countries are finding ways to raise barriers to international trade. Many developing countries have latitude under WTO rules to raise some tariffs, and according to the World Bank, in 2008 and 2009 they were doing just that. For example, Ecuador raised duties on 600 goods, Russia increased import tariffs on used cars, while India placed them on some sorts of steel imports.

According to the World Bank, however, two-thirds of the protectionist measures taken in 2008 and 2009 were various kinds of "non-tariff barriers that are designed to get around WTO rules." Indonesia, for example, specified that certain kinds of goods, including clothes, shoes, and toys, can be imported only through five ports. Since these ports have limited capacity, this constrains the ability of foreign companies to sell into the Indonesian market. Argentina has imposed discretionary licensing requirements on a range of goods including car parts, textiles, and televisions. If you can't get a license, you can't sell into Argentina. China has stopped a wide range of imports of food and drink products from Europe, citing safety rules and environmental concerns, while India has banned imports of toys from China for safety reasons.

Developed nations in general did not take similar actions, but they sharply increased subsidies to troubled domestic producers, which gave them an advantage against unsubsidized international competitors, and therefore may have distorted trade. The key example of this in 2008 and 2009 was the automobile industry. To protect national producers, hold on to jobs, and stave off bankruptcies, rich countries including the United States, Britain, Canada, France, Germany, Italy, and Sweden gave over $45 billion in subsidies to car companies between mid-2008 and mid-2009. The problem with such subsidies is that they could cause production to switch from more efficient plants to less efficient plants that have an advantage due to state support. Although the WTO has rules against trade-distorting subsidies, its enforcement mechanisms are weaker than in the case of tariffs, and so far countries that have been increasing subsidies have not been challenged.

The volume of international trade has since rebounded strongly, growing by around 14.5 percent on the back of a 3.1 percent increase in the size of the global economy in 2010. As this happened, protectionist pressures abated somewhat. Trade rebounded more strongly in developing nations than in the developed world. China, in particular, saw a massive 28.5 percent leap in the volume of its exports, which created additional trade tensions.

Case Discussion Questions

1. Why do you think calls for protectionism are greater during sharp economic contractions than during boom periods?
2. Despite the sharp economic contraction during 2008–2009, the increase in protectionist measures was fairly modest. Why do you think this was the case?

3. During 2008–2009 many developed nations gave subsidies to their automobile producers. How might this have distorted international trade? Was this a reasonable thing to do given the circumstances?

4. What might occur if a renewed economic slowdown triggered a wave of protectionist measures around the world? Would protectionism actually protect jobs, or would it make things worse?

5. The volume of world trade rebounded sharply in 2010 on the back of a fairly modest growth rate in the world economy. What does this tell you about the nature of international production in today's global economy? What does this tell you about the vulnerability of the world economy to any future trade wars?

Sources

"The Nuts and Bolts Come Apart," *The Economist,* March 28, 2009, pp. 79–81; "Barriers to Entry," *The Economist,* December 20, 2008, p. 121; "Beyond Doha," *The Economist,* October 11, 2008, pp. 30–33; and "Trade Growth to Ease in 2011 but Despite 2010 Record Surge, Crisis Hangover Persists," World Trade Organization press release, April 7, 2011.

NAFTA AND MEXICAN TRUCKING

When the North American Free Trade Agreement (NAFTA) went into effect in 1994, the treaty specified that by 2000 trucks from each nation would be allowed to cross each other's borders and deliver goods to their ultimate destination. The argument was that such a policy would lead to greater efficiencies. Before NAFTA, Mexican trucks stopped at the border, and goods had to be unloaded and reloaded onto American trucks, a process that took time and cost money. It was also argued that greater competition from Mexican trucking firms would lower the price of road transportation within NAFTA. Given that two-thirds of cross-border trade within NAFTA goes by road, supporters argued that the savings could be significant.

This provision was vigorously opposed by the Teamsters Union in the United States, which represents truck drivers. The union argued that Mexican truck drivers had poor safety records and that Mexican trucks did not adhere to the strict safety and environmental standards of the United States. To quote James Hoffa, the president of the Teamsters:

> Mexican trucks are older, dirtier, and more dangerous than American trucks. American truck drivers are taken off the road if they commit a serious traffic violation in their personal vehicle. That's not so in Mexico. Limits on the hours a driver can spend behind the wheel are ignored in Mexico.

Under pressure from the Teamsters, the United States dragged its feet on implementation of the trucking agreement. Ultimately, the Teamsters sued to stop implementation of the agreement. An American court rejected its arguments and stated the country must honor the treaty. So did a NAFTA dispute settlement panel. This panel ruled in 2001 that the United States was violating the NAFTA treaty and gave Mexico the right to impose retaliatory tariffs. Mexico decided not to do that, instead giving the United States a chance to honor its commitment. The Bush administration tried to do just that, but was thwarted by opposition in Congress, which approved a measure setting 22 new safety standards that Mexican trucks would have to meet before entering the United States.

In an attempt to break the stalemate, in 2007 the U.S. government set up a pilot program under which trucks from some 100 Mexican transportation companies could enter the United States, provided they passed American safety inspections. The Mexican trucks were tracked, and after 18 months, the program showed the Mexican carriers had a slightly better safety record than their U.S. counterparts. The Teamsters immediately lobbied Congress to kill the pilot program. In March 2009, an amendment attached to a large spending bill did just that.

This time the Mexican government did not let the United States off the hook. As allowed to under the terms of the NAFTA agreement, Mexico immediately placed tariffs on some $2.4 billion of goods shipped from the United States to Mexico. California, an important exporter of agricultural products to Mexico, was hit hard. Table grapes now faced a 45 percent tariff, while wine, almonds, and juices would pay a 20 percent tariff. Pears, which primarily come from Washington State, faced a 20 percent tariff (4 out of 10 pears that the United States exports go to Mexico). Other products hit with the 20 percent tariff include exports of personal hygiene products and jewelry from New York, tableware from Illinois, and oil seeds from North Dakota. The U.S. Chamber of Commerce has estimated that the situation cost some 25,600 U.S. jobs. The U.S. government said it would try to come up with a new program that both addressed the "legitimate concerns" of Congress and honored its commitment to the NAFTA treaty.

In July 2011, the Obama administration signed an agreement with Mexico designed to end the long-running dispute. The agreement called for Mexican truck emissions to meet U.S. clean air standards and for Mexican drivers to submit to U.S. security checks, to meet U.S. highway safety standards, and to demonstrate competency in English and an understanding of U.S. highway signs. In addition, Mexican truckers are required to purchase U.S. insurance. The Teamsters Union continued to oppose the deal and tried to stop its implementation, but it was unable to do so this time. In October 2011, the first Mexican truck bound for the U.S. interior crossed the international bridge at Laredo, Texas, bound for Dallas and carrying electronic equipment.

Case Discussion Questions

1. What are the potential economic benefits of the trucking provisions in the NAFTA treaty? Who benefits? Who might lose?
2. What do you think motivated the Teamsters to object to the trucking provisions in NAFTA? Are these objections fair? Why did Congress initially align itself with the Teamsters?
3. Did it make economic sense for the United States to bear the costs of punitive tariffs as allowed for under NAFTA, as opposed to letting Mexican trucks enter the United States?
4. Why do you think the Obama administration brokered a deal with Mexico to allow Mexican truck drivers to access the United States? Do you think this is a reasonable deal?

Sources

"Don't Keep on Trucking," *The Economist,* March 21, 2009, p. 39; "Mexico Retaliates," *The Wall Street Journal,* March 19, 2009, p. A14; J. P. Hoffa, "Keep Mexican Trucks Out," *USA Today,* March 1, 2009, p. 10; "The Mexican-American War of 2009," *Washington Times,* March 24, 2009, p. A18; J. Moreno, "In NAFTA Rift, Profits Take a Hit," *Houston Chronical.com,* November 12, 2009; and J. Forsyth, "Years after NAFTA, First Long Haul Mexican Truck Enters U.S.," Reuters, October 21, 2011.

THE RISE OF THE INDIAN AUTOMOBILE INDUSTRY

India is well on its way to becoming a small car manufacturing hub for some of the world's largest automobile companies. Between 2004 and 2011, automobile exports from India jumped from 50,000 to 450,000 per year. Despite a global economic slowdown, exports are predicted to increase, reaching

720,000 vehicles a year by 2016. The leading Indian exporter is the Korean company Hyundai, which committed early to the Indian market. Hyundai began production in India in 1998, when consumers were only purchasing 300,000 cars a year, despite the country's population of almost 1 billion people (in 2011, more than 3 million cars were sold in India). Hyundai invested in a plant in the southern city of Chennai with the capacity to turn out 100,000 cheap small cars a year. It had to train most of the workers from scratch, often giving them two years of on-the-job training before hiring them full time. Soon, Hyundai's early investments were paying off as India's emerging middle class snapped up its cars. Still, the company had excess capacity, so it turned its attention to exports.

By 2004, Hyundai was the country's largest automobile exporter, shipping 70,000 cars a year overseas. Things have only improved for Hyundai since then. By 2008, Hyundai was making 500,000 cars a year in India and exporting more than a third of them. Its smallest cars, the i10, are now produced only in India and are shipped mainly to Europe. In 2005, Hyundai decided to invest around a billion dollars in a second Chennai plant. The plant, which opened in 2010, boosted its Indian output to 650,000 vehicles. Some 250,000 were exported in 2010, making Hyundai the largest exporter of manufactured goods in India. In addition to Europe, Hyundai is now considering selling its Indian-made cars in the United States.

Hyundai's success has not gone unnoticed. Among other automakers, Suzuki and Nissan have also been investing aggressively in Indian factories. Suzuki exported about 50,000 cars from India in 2007 and increased that to around 200,000 in 2010. Nissan also has big plans for India. It has invested some $1.1 billion in a new factory close to Hyundai's in Chennai. Completed in 2010, the factory has the capacity to make some 400,000 cars a year, about half of which will be exported. Ford, BMW, GM, and Toyota are also building, or have already built, car plants in India. A notable local competitor, Tata Motors, launched a low-cost "people's car," priced at $2,500, for the Indian market in 2009.

For all these companies, India has several attractions. For one thing, the rapidly developing country has a potentially large domestic market. Also, labor costs are low compared with many other nations. Nissan, for example, notes that wage rates in India will be one-tenth of those in its Japanese factories. As Hyundai has shown, productivity is high and Indian workers can produce quality automobiles. Hyundai's executives claim that its Indian cars are of comparable quality to those produced in Korea. Nissan's goal is to use the same highly efficient flexible manufacturing processes in India as it uses in Japan. Nissan plans to send Indian workers to its Japanese factories for training on manufacturing processes and quality control.

India produces a large number of engineers every year, providing the professional skill base for designing cars and managing complex manufacturing facilities. Nissan intends to draw on this talent to design a low-cost small car to compete with Tata's "people's car." According to Nissan executives, the great advantage of India's engineers is that they are less likely to have the preconceptions of automobile engineers in developed nations, are more likely to "think outside of the box," and thus may be better equipped to handle the challenges of designing an ultra-low-cost small car.

Establishing manufacturing facilities in India does have problems, however. Nissan executives note that basic infrastructure is still lacking—roads are poor and often clogged with everything from taxis and motorbikes to bullocks and carts—making the Japanese practice of just-in-time delivery hard to implement. It is also proving challenging to find local parts suppliers that can attain the same high-quality standards as those Nissan is used to elsewhere in the world. Nissan's strategy has been to work with promising local companies, helping them raise their standards. For example, under the guidance of teams of engineers from Nissan, the Indian parts supplier Capro, which makes body panels, has built a new factory, using the latest Japanese equipment, near Nissan's Chennai facility. Workers there have also been trained in the Japanese practice of *kaizen,* or continuous process improvement.

Observers see the potential for Chennai to develop into a major auto manufacturing hub, with a cluster of automobile companies and parts suppliers working in the region producing high-quality, low-cost small cars that will not only sell well in the rapidly expanding Indian market but could also sell well worldwide.

Case Discussion Questions

1. What are the attractions of India as a base for producing automobiles both for domestic sale and for export to other nations?
2. Both Hyundai and Nissan made their investments in the southern Indian city of Chennai. What is the advantage to be had by investing in the same region as rivals?
3. What are the drawbacks of basing manufacturing in a country such as India? What other locations might be attractive?
4. If Hyundai, Nissan, their suppliers, and other automobile enterprises continue to make investments in the Chennai region of India, how might this region evolve over time? What does this suggest about manufacturing location strategy?

Sources

E. Bellman, "India Cranks Out Small Cars for Export," *The Wall Street Journal,* October 6, 2008, p. A1; N. Lakshman, "India's Car Market Offers No Relief for Automakers," *BusinessWeek Online,* December 23, 2008; and M. Fackler, "In India, a New Detroit," *The New York Times,* June 26, 2008, pp. C1, C4.

LOGITECH

Best known as one of the world's largest producers of computer mice, Logitech is in many ways the epitome of the modern global corporation. Founded in 1981 in Apples, Switzerland, by two Italians and a Swiss, the company now generates annual sales of over $3.32 billion, mostly from products such as mice, keyboards, and low-cost video cameras that cost less than $100. Logitech made its name as a technological innovator in the highly competitive business of personal computer peripherals. It was the first company to introduce a mouse that used infrared tracking, rather than a tracking ball, and the first to introduce wireless mice and keyboards. Logitech is differentiated from competitors by its continuing innovation, high brand recognition, and strong retail presence. Less obvious to consumers, but equally important, has been the way the company has configured its global value chain to lower production costs while maintaining the value of those assets that lead to differentiation.

Logitech still undertakes basic R&D work (primarily software programming) in Switzerland, where it has several hundred employees. The company is still legally Swiss, but most of the corporate functions are run out of offices in Fremont, California, close to many of America's high-technology enterprises, where it has more than 500 employees. Some R&D work (again, primarily software programming) is also carried out in Fremont. Most significantly, though, Fremont is the headquarters for the company's global marketing, finance, and logistics operations. The ergonomic design of Logitech's products—their look and feel—is done in Ireland by an outside design firm. Most of Logitech's products are manufactured in Asia.

Logitech's expansion into Asian manufacturing began in the late 1980s when it opened a factory in Taiwan. At the time, most of its mice were produced in the United States. Logitech was trying to win two of the most prestigious OEM customers—Apple Computer and IBM. Both bought their mice from Alps, a large Japanese firm that supplied Microsoft. To attract discerning customers such as Apple,

Logitech not only needed the capacity to produce at high volume and low cost but also had to offer a better-designed product. The solution: Manufacture in Taiwan. Cost was a factor in the decision, but it was not as significant as might be expected because direct labor accounted for only 7 percent of the cost of Logitech's mouse. Taiwan offered a well-developed supply base for parts, qualified people, and a rapidly expanding local computer industry. As an inducement to fledgling innovators, Taiwan provided space in its science-based industrial park in Hsinchu for the modest fee of $200,000. Sizing this up as a deal that was too good to miss, Logitech signed the lease. Shortly afterward, Logitech won the OEM contract with Apple. The Taiwanese factory was soon outproducing Logitech's U.S. facility. After the Apple contract, Logitech's other OEM business started being served from Taiwan; the plant's total capacity increased to 10 million mice per year.

By the late 1990s, Logitech needed more production capacity. This time it turned to China. A wide variety of the company's retail products are now made there. A wireless infrared mouse called Wanda, one of Logitech's biggest sellers, is assembled in Suzhou, China, in a Logitech-owned factory. The factory employs 4,000 people, mostly young women such as Wang Yan, an 18-year-old employee from the impoverished rural province of Anhui. She is paid $75 a month to sit all day at a conveyer belt plugging three tiny bits of metal into circuit boards. She does this about 2,000 times each day. The mouse Wang Yan helps assemble sells to American consumers for about $40. Of this, Logitech takes about $8, which is used to fund R&D, marketing, and corporate overhead. What remains after that is the profit attributable to Logitech's shareholders. Distributors and retailers around the world take a further $15. Another $14 goes to the suppliers that make Wanda's parts. For example, a Motorola plant in Malaysia makes the mouse's chips, and another American company, Agilent Technologies, supplies the optical sensors from a plant in the Philippines. That leaves just $3 for the Chinese factory, which is used to cover wages, power, transport, and other overhead costs.

Logitech is not alone in exploiting China to manufacture products. According to China's Ministry of Commerce, foreign companies account for three-quarters of China's high-tech exports. China's top 10 exporters include American companies with Chinese operations, such as Motorola and Seagate Technologies, a maker of disk drives for computers. Intel now produces some 50 million chips a year in China, the majority of which end up in computers and other goods that are exported to other parts of Asia or back to the United States. Yet Intel's plant in Shanghai doesn't really make chips; it tests and assembles chips from silicon wafers made in Intel plants abroad, mostly in the United States. China adds less than 5 percent of the value. The U.S. operations of Intel generate the bulk of the value and profits.

Case Discussion Questions

1. In a world without trade, what would happen to the costs that American consumers would have to pay for Logitech's products?

2. Explain how trade lowers the costs of making computer peripherals such as mice and keyboards.

3. Use the theory of comparative advantage to explain the way in which Logitech has configured its global operations. Why does the company manufacture in China and Taiwan, undertake basic R&D in California and Switzerland, design products in Ireland, and coordinate marketing and operations from California?

4. Who creates more value for Logitech, the 650 people it employees in Fremont and Switzerland or the 4,000 employees at its Chinese factory? What are the implications of this observation for the argument that free trade is beneficial?

5. Why do you think the company decided to shift its corporate headquarters from Switzerland to Fremont?

6. To what extent can Porter's diamond help explain the choice of Taiwan as a major manufacturing site for Logitech?

7. Why do you think China is now a favored location for so much high-technology manufacturing activity? How will China's increasing involvement in global trade help that country? How will it help the world's developed economies? What potential problems are associated with moving work to China?

Sources

V. K. Jolly and K. A. Bechler, "Logitech: The Mouse That Roared," *Planning Review* 20, no. 6 (1992), pp. 20–34; K. Guerrino, "Lord of the Mice," *Chief Executive,* July 2003, pp. 42–44; A. Higgins, "As China Surges, It Also Proves a Buttress to American Strength," *The Wall Street Journal,* January 30, 2004, pp. A1, A8; J. Fox, "Where Is Your Job Going," *Fortune,* November 24, 2003, pp. 84–88; and R. Wray, "Logitech Cuts 500 Jobs and Abandons Targets," *The Guardian,* January 7, 2009, p. 28.

PART 4
The Global Monetary System

Chapter 10
The Foreign Exchange Market

LEARNING OBJECTIVES

After reading this chapter, you will be able to:

LO10-1 Describe the functions of the foreign exchange market.

LO10-2 Understand what is meant by spot exchange rates.

LO10-3 Recognize the role that forward exchange rates play in insuring against foreign exchange risk.

LO10-4 Understand the different theories explaining how currency exchange rates are determined and their relative merits.

LO10-5 Identify the merits of different approaches toward exchange rate forecasting.

LO10-6 Compare and contrast the differences among translation, transaction, and economic exposure, and what managers can do to manage each type of exposure.

◇ THE RISE (AND FALL) OF THE JAPANESE YEN

Opening Case

During the first half of the 2000s, the Japanese yen was relatively weak against the U.S. dollar. This was a boon for Japan's export led economy. On January 1, 2008, it took ¥122 to buy one U.S. dollar. For the next four years, the yen strengthened relentlessly against the dollar, hitting an all-time record high of ¥75.31 to the dollar on October 31, 2011. The reasons for the rise of the yen were complex and had little to do with the strength of the Japanese economy, because there has been very little of that in evidence.

The weakness of the yen during the early to mid-2000s was due to the so-called carry trade. This financial strategy involved borrowing in Japanese yen, where interest rates were close to zero, and investing the loans in higher yielding assets, typically U.S. Treasury bills, which carried interest rates 3 to 4 percentage points greater. Investors made profits from the interest rate differential. At its peak, financial institutions had more than a trillion dollars invested in the carry trade. Because the strategy involved selling borrowed yen to purchase dollar-denominated assets, it drove the value of the yen lower. The interest rate differential existed because the Japanese economy was weak, prices were falling, and the Bank of Japan had been lowering interest rates in an attempt to boost growth and get Japan out of a dangerous deflationary cycle.

When the global financial crisis hit in 2008 and 2009, the Federal Reserve in the United States responded by injecting liquidity into battered financial markets, effectively lowering U.S. interest rates on U.S. Treasury bonds. As these fell, the interest rate differential between Japanese and U.S. assets narrowed sharply, and the carry trade became unprofitable. Financial institutions unwound their positions, selling dollar-denominated assets and buying yen to pay back their original loans. The increased demand drove up the value of the yen.

For Japanese exporters, the 40 percent increase in the value of the yen against the dollar (and the euro) between early 2008 and 2012 was a painful experience. A strong yen hurts the price competitiveness of Japanese exports and reduces the value of profits earned overseas when translated back into yen. Take Toyota as an example: In February 2012, the company stated that its profit for the year ending March 31, 2012, would be about ¥200 billion, 51 percent lower than in the prior year. Toyota makes nearly half of the cars it sells globally at its Japanese plants, so it has been particularly hard hit by a rise in the value of the yen.

In late 2012 things started to change when the pro-business Liberal Democratic Party won national elections, and Shinzo Abe was appointed prime minister. Abe had campaigned on a platform that included taking actions to weaken the value of the yen in order to help Japan's exporters. Even before the election, Japan's central bank had accelerated purchases of government securities, thereby expanding the money supply, and agreed to a higher inflation target. Under Abe's leadership, this policy had explicit government support. One consequence of the policy was to reduce the value of the yen against other currencies. Indeed, between October 2012 and March 2012 the yen lost more than 20 percent of its value against the U.S. dollar. The yen was trading at ¥96 to the U.S. dollar in mid-March 2012. While this helped Japan's exporters, the policy was criticized by other major industrial nations as unilateral action that came dangerously close to precipitating a currency war.[1]

INTRODUCTION

Like many enterprises in the global economy, Toyota is affected by changes in the value of currencies on the foreign exchange market. As described in the opening case, Toyota's profits fell during the year ending March 2012 due to a rise in the value of the Japanese yen against the U.S. dollar. The case illustrates that what happens in the foreign exchange market can have a fundamental impact on the sales, profits, and strategy of an enterprise. Accordingly, it is very important for managers to understand the foreign exchange market, and what the impact of changes in currency exchange rates might be for their enterprise.

This chapter has three main objectives. The first is to explain how the foreign exchange market works. The second is to examine the forces that determine exchange rates and to discuss the degree to which it is possible to predict future exchange rate movements. The third objective is to map the implications for international business of exchange rate movements. This chapter is the first of two that deal with the international monetary system and its relationship to international business. The next chapter explores the institutional structure of the international monetary system. The institutional structure is the context within which the foreign exchange market functions. As we shall see, changes in the institutional structure of the international monetary system can exert a profound influence on the development of foreign exchange markets.

The **foreign exchange market** is a market for converting the currency of one country into that of another country. An **exchange rate** is simply the rate at which one currency is converted into another. For example, Toyota uses the foreign exchange market to convert the dollars it earns from selling cars in the United States into Japanese yen. Without the foreign exchange market, international trade and international investment on the scale that we see today would be impossible; companies would have to resort to barter. The foreign exchange market is the lubricant that enables companies based in countries that use different currencies to trade with each other.

We know from earlier chapters that international trade and investment have their risks. Some of these risks exist because future exchange rates cannot be perfectly predicted. The rate at which one currency is converted into another can change over time. For example, at the start of 2001, one U.S. dollar bought 1.065 euros, but by early 2013 one U.S. dollar only bought 0.76 euro. The dollar had fallen sharply in value against the euro. This made American goods cheaper in Europe, boosting export sales. At the same time, it made European goods more expensive in the United States, which hurt the sales and profits of European companies that sold goods and services to the United States.

One function of the foreign exchange market is to provide some insurance against the risks that arise from such volatile changes in exchange rates, commonly referred to as *foreign exchange risk*. Although the foreign exchange market offers some insurance against foreign exchange risk, it cannot provide complete insurance. It is not unusual for international businesses to suffer losses because of unpredicted changes in exchange rates. Currency fluctuations can make seemingly profitable trade and investment deals unprofitable, and vice versa.

We begin this chapter by looking at the functions and the form of the foreign exchange market. This includes distinguishing among spot exchanges, forward exchanges, and currency swaps. Then we consider the factors that determine exchange rates. We also look at how foreign trade is conducted when a country's currency cannot be exchanged for other currencies, that is, when its currency is not convertible. The chapter closes with a discussion of these things in terms of their implications for business.

THE FUNCTIONS OF THE FOREIGN EXCHANGE MARKET ∎LO10-1∎

The foreign exchange market serves two main functions. The first is to convert the currency of one country into the currency of another. The second is to provide some insurance against **foreign exchange risk**, or the adverse consequences of unpredictable changes in exchange rates.[2]

Currency Conversion

Each country has a currency in which the prices of goods and services are quoted. In the United States, it is the dollar ($); in Great Britain, the pound (£); in France, Germany, and the other 15 members of the euro zone it is the euro (€); in Japan, the yen (¥); and so on. In general, within the borders of a particular country, one must use the national currency. A U.S. tourist cannot walk into a store in Edinburgh, Scotland, and use U.S. dollars to buy a bottle of Scotch whisky. Dollars are not recognized as legal tender in Scotland; the tourist must use British pounds. Fortunately, the tourist can go to a bank and exchange her dollars for pounds. Then she can buy the whisky.

When a tourist changes one currency into another, she is participating in the foreign exchange market. The exchange rate is the rate at which the market converts one currency into another. For example, an exchange rate of €1 = $1.30 specifies that 1 euro buys 1.30 U.S. dollars. The exchange rate allows us to compare the relative prices of goods and services in different countries. Our U.S. tourist wishing to buy a bottle of Scotch whisky in Edinburgh may find that she must pay £30 for the bottle, knowing that the same bottle costs $45 in the United States. Is this a good deal? Imagine the current pound/dollar exchange rate is £1.00 = $2.00 (i.e., one British pound buys $2.00). Our intrepid tourist takes out her calculator and converts £30 into dollars. (The calculation is 30 × 2.) She finds that the bottle of Scotch costs the equivalent of $60. She is surprised that a bottle of Scotch whisky could cost less in the United States than in Scotland (alcohol is taxed heavily in Great Britain).

Tourists are minor participants in the foreign exchange market; companies engaged in international trade and investment are major ones. International businesses have four main uses of foreign exchange markets. First, the payments a company receives for its exports, the income it receives from foreign investments, or the income it receives from licensing agreements with foreign firms may be in foreign currencies. To use those funds in its home country, the company must convert them to its home country's currency. Consider the Scotch distillery that exports its whisky to the United States. The distillery is paid in dollars, but because those dollars cannot be spent in Great Britain, they must be converted into British pounds. Similarly, Toyota sells its cars in the United States for dollars; it must convert the U.S. dollars it receives into Japanese yen to use them in Japan.

Second, international businesses use foreign exchange markets when they must pay a foreign company for its products or services in its country's currency. For example, Dell buys many of the components for its computers from Malaysian firms. The Malaysian companies must be paid in Malaysia's currency, the ringgit, so Dell must convert money from dollars into ringgit to pay them.

Third, international businesses also use foreign exchange markets when they have spare cash that they wish to invest for short terms in money markets. For example, consider a U.S. company that has $10 million it wants to invest for three months. The best interest rate it can earn on these funds in the United States may be 2 percent. Investing in a South Korean money market account, however, may earn 6 percent. Thus, the company may change its $10 million into Korean won and invest it in South Korea. Note, however, that the rate of return it earns on this investment depends not only on the Korean interest rate but also on the changes in the value of the Korean won against the dollar in the intervening period.

Currency speculation is another use of foreign exchange markets. **Currency speculation** typically involves the short-term movement of funds from one currency to another in the hopes of profiting from shifts in exchange rates. Consider again a U.S. company with $10 million to invest for three months. Suppose the company suspects that the U.S. dollar is overvalued against the Japanese yen. That is, the company expects the value of the dollar to depreciate (fall) against that of the yen. Imagine the current dollar/yen exchange rate is $1 = ¥120. The company exchanges its $10 million into yen, receiving ¥1.2 billion ($10 million × 120 = ¥1.2 billion). Over the next three months, the value of the dollar depreciates against the yen until $1 = ¥100. Now the company exchanges its ¥1.2 billion back into dollars and finds that it has $12 million. The company has made a $2 million profit on currency speculation in three months on an initial investment of $10 million! In general, however, companies should beware, for speculation by definition is a very risky business. The company cannot know for sure what will happen to exchange rates. While a speculator may profit handsomely if his speculation about future currency movements turns out to be correct, he can also lose vast amounts of money if he turns out to be wrong.

A kind of speculation that has become more common in recent years is known as the **carry trade** (see the opening case for a discussion). The carry trade involves borrowing in one currency where interest rates are low and then using the proceeds to invest in another currency where interest rates are high. For example, if the interest rate on borrowings in Japan is 1 percent, but the interest rate on deposits in American banks is 6 percent, it can make sense to borrow in Japanese yen, convert the money into U.S. dollars, and deposit it in an American bank. The trader can make a 5 percent margin by doing so, minus the transaction costs associated with changing one currency into another. The speculative element of this trade is that its success is based on a belief that there will be no adverse movement in exchange rates (or interest rates for that matter) that will make the trade unprofitable. However, if the yen were to rapidly increase in value against the dollar, then it would take more U.S. dollars to repay the original loan, and the trade could fast become unprofitable. The dollar/yen carry trade was actually very significant during the mid-2000s, peaking at more than $1 trillion in 2007, when some 30 percent of trade on the Tokyo foreign exchange market was related to the carry trade.[3] This carry trade declined in importance during 2008–2009 because interest rate differentials were falling as U.S. rates came down, making the trade less profitable.

Insuring Against Foreign Exchange Risk LO10-2

A second function of the foreign exchange market is to provide insurance against foreign exchange risk, which is the possibility that unpredicted changes in future exchange rates will have adverse consequences for the firm. When a firm insures itself against foreign exchange risk, it is engaging in *hedging*. To explain how the market performs this function, we must first distinguish among spot exchange rates, forward exchange rates, and currency swaps.

Spot Exchange Rates

When two parties agree to exchange currency and execute the deal immediately, the transaction is referred to as a spot exchange. Exchange rates governing such "on the spot" trades are referred to as spot exchange rates. The **spot exchange rate** is the rate at which a foreign exchange dealer converts one currency into another currency on a particular day. Thus, when our U.S. tourist in Edinburgh goes to a bank to convert her dollars into pounds, the exchange rate is the spot rate for that day.

Spot exchange rates are reported on a real-time basis on many financial websites. An exchange rate can be quoted in two ways: as the amount of foreign currency one U.S. dollar will buy or as the value of a dollar for one unit of foreign currency. Thus, on March 12, 2013 at 12:11 p.m., Eastern Standard Time, one U.S. dollar bought €0.7655, and one euro bought $1.3063.

Spot rates change continually, often on a minute-by-minute basis (although the magnitude of changes over such short periods is usually small). The value of a currency is determined by the interaction between the demand and supply of that currency relative to the demand and supply of other currencies. For example, if lots of people want U.S. dollars and dollars are in short supply, and few people want British pounds and pounds are in plentiful supply, the spot exchange rate for converting dollars into pounds will change. The dollar is likely to appreciate against the pound (or the pound will depreciate against the dollar). Imagine the spot exchange rate is £1 = $2.00 when the market opens. As the day progresses, dealers demand more dollars and fewer pounds. By the end of the day, the spot exchange rate might be £1 = $1.98. Each pound now buys fewer dollars than at the start of the day. The dollar has appreciated, and the pound has depreciated.

Forward Exchange Rates

Changes in spot exchange rates can be problematic for an international business. For example, a U.S. company that imports high-end cameras from Japan knows that in 30 days it must pay yen to a Japanese supplier when a shipment arrives. The company will pay the Japanese supplier ¥200,000 for each camera, and the current dollar/yen spot exchange rate is $1 = ¥120. At this rate, each camera costs the importer $1,667 (i.e., 1,667 = 200,000/120). The importer knows she can sell the camera the day they arrive for $2,000 each, which yields a gross profit of $333 on each ($2,000 − $1,667). However, the importer will not have the funds to pay the Japanese supplier until the cameras are sold. If, over the next 30 days, the dollar unexpectedly depreciates against the yen, say, to $1 = ¥95, the importer will still have to pay the Japanese company ¥200,000 per camera, but in dollar terms that would be equivalent to $2,105 per camera, which is more than she can sell the cameras for. A depreciation in the value of the dollar against the yen from $1 = ¥120 to $1 = ¥95 would transform a profitable deal into an unprofitable one.

To *insure* or *hedge* against this risk, the U.S. importer might want to engage in a forward exchange. A **forward exchange** occurs when two parties agree to exchange currency and execute the deal at some specific date in the future. Exchange rates governing such future transactions are referred to as **forward exchange rates**. For most major currencies, forward exchange rates are quoted for 30 days, 90 days, and 180 days into the future. In some cases, it is possible to get forward exchange rates for several years into the future. Returning to our camera importer example, let us assume the 30-day forward exchange rate for converting dollars into yen is $1 = ¥110. The importer enters into a 30-day forward exchange transaction with a foreign exchange dealer at this rate and is guaranteed that she will have to pay no more than $1,818 for each camera (1,818 = 200,000/110). This guarantees her a profit of $182 per camera ($2,000 − $1,818). She also insures herself against the possibility that an unanticipated change in the dollar/yen exchange rate will turn a profitable deal into an unprofitable one.

In this example, the spot exchange rate ($1 = ¥120) and the 30-day forward rate ($1 = ¥110) differ. Such differences are normal; they reflect the expectations of the foreign exchange market about future currency movements. In our example, the fact that $1 bought more yen with a spot exchange than with a 30-day forward exchange indicates foreign exchange dealers expected the dollar to depreciate against the yen in the next 30 days. When this occurs, we say the dollar is selling at a discount on the 30-day forward market (i.e., it is worth less than on the spot market). Of course, the opposite can also occur. If the 30-day forward exchange rate were $1 = ¥130, for example, $1 would buy more yen with a forward exchange than with a spot exchange. In such a case, we say the dollar is selling at a premium on the 30-day forward market. This reflects the foreign exchange dealers' expectations that the dollar will appreciate against the yen over the next 30 days.

In sum, when a firm enters into a forward exchange contract, it is taking out insurance against the possibility that future exchange rate movements will make a transaction unprofitable by the time that transaction has been executed. Although many firms routinely enter into forward exchange contracts to hedge their foreign exchange risk, there are some spectacular examples of what happens when firms don't take out this insurance. An example is given in the accompanying Management Focus, which explains how a failure to fully insure against foreign exchange risk cost Volkswagen dearly.

Volkswagen's Hedging Strategy

In January 2004, Volkswagen, Europe's largest carmaker, reported a 95 percent drop in 2003 fourth-quarter profits, which slumped from €1.05 billion to a mere €50 million. For all of 2003, Volkswagen's operating profit fell by 50 percent from the record levels attained in 2002. Although the profit slump had multiple causes, two factors were the focus of much attention—the sharp rise in the value of the euro against the dollar during 2003 and Volkswagen's decision to only hedge 30 percent of its foreign currency exposure, as opposed to the 70 percent it had tradition-ally hedged. In total, currency losses due to the dollar's rise are estimated to have reduced Volk-swagen's operating profits by some €1.2 billion ($1.5 billion).

The rise in the value of the euro during 2003 took many companies by surprise. Since its in-troduction January 1, 1999, when it became the currency unit of 12 members of the European Union, the euro had recorded a volatile trading history against the U.S. dollar. In early 1999, the exchange rate stood at €1 = $1.17, but by October 2000 it had slumped to €1 = $0.83. Al-though it recovered, reaching parity of €1 = $1.00 in late 2002, few analysts predicted a rapid rise in the value of the euro against the dollar during 2003. As so often happens in the foreign exchange markets, the experts were wrong; by late 2003, the exchange rate stood at €1 = $1.25. For Volkswagen, which made cars in Germany and exported them to the United States, the fall in the value of the dollar against the euro during 2003 was devastating. To understand what happened, consider a Volkswagen Jetta built in Germany for export to the United States.

Volkswagen could have insured against this adverse movement in exchange rates by entering the foreign exchange market in late 2002 and buying a *forward contract* for dollars at an ex-change rate of around $1 = €1 (a *forward contract* gives the holder the right to exchange one currency for another at some point in the future at a predetermined exchange rate). Called *hedg-ing*, the financial strategy of buying forward guarantees that at some future point, such as 180 days, Volkswagen would have been able to exchange the dollars it got from selling Jettas in the United States into euros at $1 = €1, *irrespective of what the actual exchange rate was at that time*. In 2003, such a strategy would have been good for Volkswagen. However, hedging is not without its costs. For one thing, if the euro had declined in value against the dollar, instead of ap-preciating as it did, Volkswagen would have made even more profit per car in euros by not hedg-ing (a dollar at the end of 2003 would have bought more euros than a dollar at the end of 2002). For another thing, hedging is expensive because foreign exchange dealers will charge a high commission for selling currency forward. Volkswagen decided to hedge just 30 percent of its anticipated U.S. sales in 2003 through forward contracts, rather than the 70 percent it had his-torically hedged. The decision cost the company more than €1 billion. For 2004, the company reverted back to hedging 70 percent of its foreign currency exposure.[4]

Currency Swaps

The preceding discussion of spot and forward exchange rates might lead you to conclude that the option to buy forward is very important to companies engaged in international trade—and you would be right. According to the most recent data, forward instruments account for almost two-thirds of all foreign exchange transactions, while spot exchanges account for about one-third.[5] However, the vast majority of these forward exchanges are not forward exchanges of the type we have been discussing, but rather a more sophisticated instrument known as currency swaps.

A **currency swap** is the simultaneous purchase and sale of a given amount of foreign exchange for two different value dates. Swaps are transacted between international businesses and their banks, between banks, and between governments when it is desirable to move out of one currency into another for a limited period without incurring foreign exchange risk. A common kind of swap is spot against forward. Consider a company such as Apple Computer. Apple assembles laptop computers in the United States, but the screens are made in Japan. Apple also sells some of the finished laptops in Japan. So, like many companies, Apple both buys from and sells to Japan. Imagine Apple needs to change $1 million into yen to pay its supplier of laptop screens today. Apple knows that in 90 days it will be paid ¥120 million by the Japanese importer that buys its finished laptops. It will want to convert these yen into dollars for use in the United States. Let us say today's spot exchange rate is $1 = ¥120 and the 90-day forward exchange rate is $1 = ¥110. Apple sells $1 million to its bank in return for ¥120 million. Now Apple can pay its Japanese supplier. At the same time, Apple enters into a 90-day forward exchange deal with its bank for converting ¥120 million into dollars. Thus, in 90 days Apple will receive $1.09 million (¥120 million/110 = $1.09 million). Because the yen is trading at a premium on the 90-day forward market, Apple ends up with more dollars than it started with (although the opposite could also occur). The swap deal is just like a conventional forward deal in one important respect: It enables Apple to insure itself against foreign exchange risk. By engaging in a swap, Apple knows today that the ¥120 million payment it will receive in 90 days will yield $1.09 million.

THE NATURE OF THE FOREIGN EXCHANGE MARKET

The foreign exchange market is not located in any one place. It is a global network of banks, brokers, and foreign exchange dealers connected by electronic communications systems. When companies wish to convert currencies, they typically go through their own banks rather than entering the market directly. The foreign exchange market has been growing at a rapid pace, reflecting a general growth in the volume of cross-border trade and investment (see Chapter 1). In March 1986, the average total value of global foreign exchange trading was about $200 billion per day. By April 2010, it had hit $4 trillion a day.[6] The most important trading centers are London (37 percent of activity), New York (18 percent of activity), and Zurich, Tokyo, and Singapore (all with around 5 to 6 percent of activity).[7] Major secondary trading centers include Frankfurt, Paris, Hong Kong, and Sydney.

London's dominance in the foreign exchange market is due to both history and geography. As the capital of the world's first major industrial trading nation, London had become the world's largest center for international banking by the end of the nineteenth century, a position it has retained. Today, London's central position between Tokyo and Singapore to the east and New York to the west has made it the critical link between the East Asian and New York markets. Due to the particular differences in time zones, London opens soon after Tokyo closes for the night and is still open for the first few hours of trading in New York.[8]

Two features of the foreign exchange market are of particular note. The first is that the market never sleeps. Tokyo, London, and New York are all shut for only 3 hours out of every 24. During these three hours, trading continues in a number of minor centers, particularly San Francisco and Sydney, Australia. The second feature of the market is the integration of the various trading centers. High-speed computer linkages among trading centers around the globe have effectively created a single market. The integration of financial centers implies there can be no significant difference in exchange rates quoted in the trading centers. For example, if the yen/dollar exchange rate quoted in London at 3 p.m. is ¥120 = $1, the yen/dollar exchange rate quoted in New York at the same time (10 a.m. New York time) will be identical. If the New York yen/dollar exchange rate were ¥125 = $1, a dealer could make a profit through **arbitrage**, buying a currency low and selling it high. For example, if the prices differed in London and New York as given, a dealer in New York could take $1 million and use that to purchase ¥125 million. She could then immediately sell the ¥125 million for dollars in London, where the transaction would yield $1.041666 million, allowing the trader to book a profit of $41,666 on the transaction. If all dealers tried to cash in on the opportunity, however, the demand for yen in New York would rise, resulting in an appreciation of the yen against the dollar such that the price differential between New York and London would quickly disappear. Because foreign exchange dealers are always watching their computer screens for arbitrage opportunities, the few that arise tend to be small, and they disappear in minutes.

Another feature of the foreign exchange market is the important role played by the U.S. dollar. Although a foreign exchange transaction can involve any two currencies, most transactions involve dollars on one side. This is true even when a dealer wants to sell a nondollar currency and buy another. A dealer wishing to sell Korean won for Brazilian real, for example, will usually sell the won for dollars and then use the dollars to buy real. Although this may seem a roundabout way of doing things, it is actually cheaper than trying to find a holder of real who wants to buy won. Because the volume of international transactions involving dollars is so great, it is not hard to find dealers who wish to trade dollars for won or real.

Due to its central role in so many foreign exchange deals, the dollar is a vehicle currency. In 2010, 85 percent of all foreign exchange transactions involved dollars on one side of the transaction. After the dollar, the most important vehicle currencies were the euro (39 percent), the Japanese yen (19 percent), and the British pound (13 percent)—reflecting the historical importance of these trading entities in the world economy.

ECONOMIC THEORIES OF EXCHANGE RATE DETERMINATION

At the most basic level, exchange rates are determined by the demand and supply of one currency relative to the demand and supply of another. For example, if the demand for dollars outstrips the supply of them and if the supply of Japanese yen is greater than the demand for them, the dollar/yen exchange rate will change. The dollar will appreciate against the yen (or the yen will depreciate against the dollar). However, while differences in relative demand and supply explain the determination of exchange rates, they do so only in a superficial sense. This simple explanation does not reveal what factors underlie the demand for and supply of a currency. Nor does it tell us when the demand for dollars will exceed the supply (and vice versa) or when the supply of Japanese yen will exceed demand for them (and vice versa). Neither does it show under what conditions a currency is in demand or under what conditions it is not demanded. In this section, we will review economic theory's answers to these questions. This will give us a deeper understanding of how exchange rates are determined.

If we understand how exchange rates are determined, we may be able to forecast exchange rate movements. Because future exchange rate movements influence export opportunities, the profitability of international trade and investment deals, and the price competitiveness of foreign imports, this is valuable information for an international business. Unfortunately, there is no simple explanation. The forces that determine exchange rates are complex, and no theoretical consensus exists, even among academic economists who study the phenomenon every day. Nonetheless, most economic theories of exchange rate movements seem to agree that three factors have an important impact on future exchange rate movements in a country's currency: the country's price inflation, its interest rate, and market psychology.[9]

Prices and Exchange Rates

To understand how prices are related to exchange rate movements, we first need to discuss an economic proposition known as the law of one price. Then we will discuss the theory of purchasing power parity (PPP), which links changes in the exchange rate between two countries' currencies to changes in the countries' price levels.

The Law of One Price

The **law of one price** states that in competitive markets free of transportation costs and barriers to trade (such as tariffs), identical products sold in different countries must sell for the same price when their price is expressed in terms of the same currency.[10] For example, if the exchange rate between the British pound and the dollar is £1 = $2.00, a jacket that retails for $80 in New York should sell for £40 in London (because $80/2.00 = £40). Consider what would happen if the jacket cost £30 in London ($60 in U.S. currency). At this price, it would pay a trader to buy jackets in London and sell them in New York (an example of *arbitrage*). The company initially could make a profit of $20 on each jacket by purchasing it for £30 ($60) in London and selling it for $80 in New York (we are assuming away transportation costs and trade barriers). However, the increased demand for jackets in London would raise their price in London, and the increased supply of jackets in New York would lower their price there. This would continue until prices were equalized. Thus, prices might equalize when the jacket cost £35 ($70) in London and $70 in New York (assuming no change in the exchange rate of £1 = $2.00).

Purchasing Power Parity

If the law of one price were true for all goods and services, the *purchasing power parity (PPP)* exchange rate could be found from any individual set of prices. By comparing the prices of identical products in different currencies, it would be possible to determine the "real" or PPP exchange rate that would exist if markets were efficient. (An **efficient market** has no impediments to the free flow of goods and services, such as trade barriers.)

A less extreme version of the PPP theory states that given relatively efficient markets—that is, markets in which few impediments to international trade exist—the price of a "basket of goods" should be roughly equivalent in each country. To express the PPP theory in symbols, let P$ be the U.S. dollar price of a basket of particular goods and P¥ be the price of the same basket of goods in Japanese yen. The PPP theory predicts that the dollar/yen exchange rate, E$/¥, should be equivalent to

$$E_{\$/¥} = P_\$/P_¥$$

Thus, if a basket of goods costs $200 in the United States and ¥20,000 in Japan, PPP theory predicts that the dollar/yen exchange rate should be $200/¥20,000 or $0.01 per Japanese yen (i.e., $1 = ¥100).

Every year, the newsmagazine *The Economist* publishes its own version of the PPP theorem, which it refers to as the "Big Mac Index." *The Economist* has selected McDonald's Big Mac as a proxy for a "basket of goods" because it is produced according to more or less the same recipe in about 120 countries. The Big Mac PPP is the exchange rate that would have hamburgers costing the same in each country. According to *The Economist,* comparing a country's actual exchange rate with the one predicted by the PPP theorem based on relative prices of Big Macs is a test of whether a currency is undervalued or not. This is not a totally serious exercise, as *The Economist* admits, but it does provide a useful illustration of the PPP theorem.

Relative currency values according to the Big Mac Index for January 11, 2012, are reproduced in Table 10.1. To calculate the index, *The Economist* converts the price of a Big Mac in a country into dollars at current exchange rates and divides that by the average price of a Big Mac in America (which was $4.20). According to the PPP theorem, the prices

TABLE 10.1 The Big Mac Index, January 11, 2012

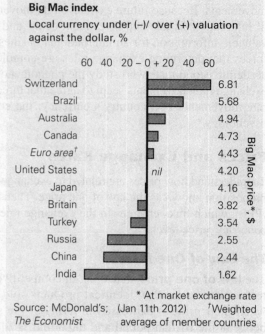

Big Mac index

Local currency under (–)/ over (+) valuation against the dollar, %

	Big Mac price*, $
Switzerland	6.81
Brazil	5.68
Australia	4.94
Canada	4.73
Euro area†	4.43
United States	4.20
Japan	4.16
Britain	3.82
Turkey	3.54
Russia	2.55
China	2.44
India	1.62

* At market exchange rate

Source: McDonald's; (Jan 11th 2012) †Weighted
The Economist average of member countries

Source: *The Economist*, www.economist.com/node/21542808.
Copyright © 2012 The Economist Newspaper Limited, London.

should be the same. If they are not, it implies that the currency is either overvalued against the dollar or undervalued. For example, the average price of a Big Mac in Australia was A$4.94 at the euro/dollar exchange rate prevailing January 11, 2012. Dividing this by the average price of a Big Mac in the United States gives 1.176 (i.e., 4.94/4.20), which suggests that the Australian dollar was overvalued by 17.6 percent against the U.S. dollar.

The next step in the PPP theory is to argue that the exchange rate will change if relative prices change. For example, imagine there is no price inflation in the United States, while prices in Japan are increasing by 10 percent a year. At the beginning of the year, a basket of goods costs $200 in the United States and ¥20,000 in Japan, so the dollar/yen exchange rate, according to PPP theory, should be $1 = ¥100. At the end of the year, the basket of goods still costs $200 in the United States, but it costs ¥22,000 in Japan. PPP theory predicts that the exchange rate should change as a result. More precisely, by the end of the year:

$$E_{\$/¥} = \$200/¥22,000$$

Thus, ¥1 = $0.0091 (or $1 = ¥110). Because of 10 percent price inflation, the Japanese yen has depreciated by 10 percent against the dollar. One dollar will buy 10 percent more yen at the end of the year than at the beginning.

Money Supply and Price Inflation

In essence, PPP theory predicts that changes in relative prices will result in a change in exchange rates. Theoretically, a country in which price inflation is running wild should expect to see its currency depreciate against that of countries in which inflation rates are lower. If we can predict what a country's future inflation rate is likely to be, we can also predict how the value of its currency relative to other currencies—its exchange rate—is likely to change. The growth rate of a country's money supply determines its likely future inflation rate.[11] Thus, in theory at least, we can use information about the growth in money supply to forecast exchange rate movements.

Inflation is a monetary phenomenon. It occurs when the quantity of money in circulation rises faster than the stock of goods and services—that is, when the money supply increases faster than output increases. Imagine what would happen if everyone in the country was suddenly given $10,000 by the government. Many people would rush out to spend their extra money on those things they had always wanted—new cars, new furniture, better clothes, and so on. There would be a surge in demand for goods and services. Car dealers, department stores, and other providers of goods and services would respond to this upsurge in demand by raising prices. The result would be price inflation.

A government increasing the money supply is analogous to giving people more money. An increase in the money supply makes it easier for banks to borrow from the government and for individuals and companies to borrow from banks. The resulting increase in credit causes increases in demand for goods and services. Unless the output of goods and services is growing at a rate similar to that of the money supply, the result will be inflation. This relationship has been observed time after time in country after country.

So now we have a connection between the growth in a country's money supply, price inflation, and exchange rate movements. Put simply, *when the growth in a country's money supply is faster than the growth in its output, price inflation is fueled.* The PPP theory tells us that a country with a high inflation rate will see depreciation in its currency exchange rate. In one of the clearest historical examples, in the mid-1980s, Bolivia experienced *hyperinflation*—an explosive and seemingly uncontrollable price inflation in which money loses value very rapidly. Table 10.2 presents data on Bolivia's money supply, inflation rate, and its peso's exchange rate with the U.S. dollar during the period of hyperinflation. The exchange rate is actually the "black market" exchange rate, because the Bolivian government prohibited converting the peso to other currencies during the period. The data show that the growth in money supply, the rate of price inflation, and the depreciation of the peso against the dollar all moved in step with each other. This is just what PPP theory and monetary economics predict. Between April 1984 and July 1985, Bolivia's money supply increased by 17,433 percent, prices increased by 22,908 percent, and the value of the peso against the dollar fell by 24,662 percent! In October 1985, the Bolivian government instituted a dramatic stabilization plan—which included the introduction of a new currency and tight control of the money supply—and by 1987 the country's annual inflation rate was down to 16 percent.[12]

Another way of looking at the same phenomenon is that an increase in a country's money supply, which increases the amount of currency available, changes the relative demand-and-supply conditions in the foreign exchange market. If the U.S. money supply is growing more rapidly than U.S. output, dollars will be relatively more plentiful than the currencies of countries where monetary growth is closer to output growth. As a result of this relative increase in the supply of dollars, the dollar will depreciate on the foreign exchange market against the currencies of countries with slower monetary growth.

Government policy determines whether the rate of growth in a country's money supply is greater than the rate of growth in output. A government can increase the money supply simply by telling the

TABLE 10.2 Macroeconomic Data for Bolivia, April 1984 to October 1985

Month	Money Supply (billions of pesos)	Price Level Relative to 1982 (average = 1)	Exchange Rate (pesos per dollar)
1984			
April	270	21.1	3,576
May	330	31.1	3,512
June	440	32.3	3,342
July	599	34.0	3,570
August	718	39.1	7,038
September	889	53.7	13,685
October	1,194	85.5	15,205
November	1,495	112.4	18,469
December	3,296	180.9	24,515
1985			
January	4,630	305.3	73,016
February	6,455	863.3	141,101
March	9,089	1,078.6	128,137
April	12,885	1,205.7	167,428
May	21,309	1,635.7	272,375
June	27,778	2,919.1	481,756
July	47,341	4,854.6	885,476
August	74,306	8,081.0	1,182,300
September	103,272	12,647.6	1,087,440
October	132,550	12,411.8	1,120,210

Source: Juan-Antonio Morales, "Inflation Stabilization in Bolivia," in *Inflation Stabilization: The Experience of Israel, Argentina, Brazil, Bolivia, and Mexico,* ed. Michael Bruno et al. (Cambridge, MA: MIT Press, 1988). Reprinted with permission.

country's central bank to issue more money. Governments tend to do this to finance public expenditure (building roads, paying government workers, paying for defense, etc.). A government could finance public expenditure by raising taxes, but because nobody likes paying more taxes and because politicians do not like to be unpopular, they have a natural preference for expanding the money supply. Unfortunately, there is no magic money tree. The result of *excessive* growth in money supply is typically price inflation. However, this has not stopped governments around the world from

COUNTRY FOCUS

Quantitative Easing, Inflation, and the Value of the U.S. Dollar

In fall 2010, the U.S. Federal Reserve decided to expand the U.S. money supply by entering the open market and purchasing $600 billion in U.S. government bonds from bondholders, a technique known as *quantitative easing*. Where did the $600 billion come from? The Fed simply created new bank reserves and used this cash to pay for the bonds. It had, in effect, printed money. The Fed took this action in an attempt to stimulate the U.S. economy, which, in the aftermath of the 2008–2009 global financial crisis, was struggling with low economic growth and high unemployment rates. The Fed had already tried to stimulate the economy by lowering short-term interest rates, but these were already close to zero, so it decided to lower medium- to longer-term rates; its tool for doing this was to pump $600 billion into the economy, increasing the supply of money and lowering its price, the interest rate. The Fed pursued further rounds of quantitative easing in 2011 and 2012, and announced that it would continue to pursue the policy at least through 2014, or until the U.S. unemployment rate fell below 6.5 percent.

Critics were quick to attack the Fed's moves. Many claimed that the policy of expanding the money supply would fuel inflation and lead to a decline in the value of the U.S. dollar on the foreign exchange market. Some even called the policy a deliberate attempt by the Fed to debase the value of the U.S. currency, thereby driving down its value and promoting U.S. exports, which if true would be a form of mercantilism.

However, these charges may be unfounded for two reasons. First, at the time, the core U.S. inflation rate was the lowest in 50 years. In fact, the Fed actually feared the risk of deflation (a persistent fall in prices), which is a very damaging phenomenon. When prices are falling, people hold off their purchases because they know that goods will be cheaper tomorrow than they are today. This can result in a collapse in aggregate demand and high unemployment. The Fed felt that a little inflation—say, 2 percent per year—might be a good thing. Second, U.S. economic growth had been weak, unemployment was high, and there was excess productive capacity in the economy. Consequently, if the injection of money into the economy did stimulate demand, this would not translate into price inflation, because the first response of businesses would be to expand output to utilize their excess capacity. Defenders of the Fed argued that the important point, which the critics seemed to be missing, was that expanding the money supply only leads to higher price inflation when unemployment is relatively low and there is not much excess capacity in the economy, a situation that did not exist in fall 2010. As for the currency market, its reaction was muted. At the beginning of November 2010, just before the Fed announced its policy, the index value of the dollar against a basket of other major currencies stood at 72.0116. At the end of January 2013, it stood at 73.4087—little changed. In short, currency traders did not seem to be selling off the dollar or reflecting worries about high inflation rates.[13]

expanding the money supply, with predictable results. If an international business is attempting to predict future movements in the value of a country's currency on the foreign exchange market, it should examine that country's policy toward monetary growth. If the government seems committed to controlling the rate of growth in money supply, the country's future inflation rate may be low (even if the current rate is high) and its currency should not depreciate too much on the foreign exchange market. If the government seems to lack the political will to control the rate of growth in money supply, the future inflation rate may be high, which is likely to cause its currency to depreciate. Historically, many Latin American governments have fallen into this latter category, including Argentina, Bolivia, and Brazil. More recently, many of the newly democratic states of eastern Europe made the same mistake. In late 2010, when the U.S. Federal Reserve decided to promote growth by expanding the U.S. money supply using a technique known as quantitative easing, critics charged that this too would lead to inflation and a decline in the value of the U.S. dollar on foreign exchange markets, but are they right? For a discussion of this, see the accompanying Country Focus.

Empirical Tests of PPP Theory

PPP theory predicts that exchange rates are determined by relative prices and that changes in relative prices will result in a change in exchange rates. A country in which price inflation is running wild should expect to see its currency depreciate against that of countries with lower inflation rates. This is intuitively appealing, but is it true in practice? There are several good examples of the connection between a country's price inflation and exchange rate position (such as Bolivia). However, extensive empirical testing of PPP theory has yielded mixed results.[14] While PPP theory seems to yield relatively accurate predictions in the long run, it does not appear to be a strong predictor of short-run movements in exchange rates covering time spans of five years or less.[15] In addition, the theory seems to best predict exchange rate changes for countries with high rates of inflation and underdeveloped capital markets. The theory is less useful for predicting short-term exchange rate movements between the currencies of advanced industrialized nations that have relatively small differentials in inflation rates.

The failure to find a strong link between relative inflation rates and exchange rate movements has been referred to as the purchasing power parity puzzle. Several factors may explain the failure of PPP theory to predict exchange rates more accurately.[16] PPP theory assumes away transportation costs and barriers to trade. In practice, these factors are significant, and they tend to create significant price differentials between countries. Transportation costs are certainly not trivial for many goods. Moreover, as we saw in Chapter 7, governments routinely intervene in international trade, creating tariff and nontariff barriers to cross-border trade. Barriers to trade limit the ability of traders to use arbitrage to equalize prices for the same product in different countries, which is required for the law of one price to hold. Government intervention in cross-border trade, by violating the assumption of efficient markets, weakens the link between relative price changes and changes in exchange rates predicted by PPP theory.

PPP theory may not hold if many national markets are dominated by a handful of multinational enterprises that have sufficient market power to be able to exercise some influence over prices, control distribution channels, and differentiate their product offerings between nations.[17] In fact, this situation seems to prevail in a number of industries. In such cases, dominant enterprises may be able to exercise a degree of pricing power, setting different prices in different markets to reflect varying demand conditions. This is referred to as price discrimination. For price discrimination to work, arbitrage must be limited. According to this argument, enterprises with some market power may be able to control distribution channels and therefore limit the unauthorized resale (arbitrage) of products purchased in another national market. They may also be able to limit resale (arbitrage) by differentiating otherwise identical products among nations along some line, such as design or packaging.

For example, even though the version of Microsoft Office sold in China may be less expensive than the version sold in the United States, the use of arbitrage to equalize prices may be limited because few Americans would want a version that was based on Chinese characters. The design differentiation between Microsoft Office for China and for the United States means that the law of one price would not work for Microsoft Office, even if transportation costs were trivial and tariff barriers between the United States and China did not exist. If the inability to practice arbitrage were widespread enough, it would break the connection between changes in relative prices and exchange rates predicted by the PPP theorem and help explain the limited empirical support for this theory.

Another factor of some importance is that governments also intervene in the foreign exchange market in attempting to influence the value of their currencies. We look at why and how they do this in Chapter 11. For now, the important thing to note is that governments regularly intervene in the foreign exchange market, and this further weakens the link between price changes and changes in exchange rates. One more factor explaining the failure of PPP theory to predict short-term movements in foreign exchange rates is the impact of investor psychology and other factors on currency purchasing decisions and exchange rate movements. We discuss this issue in more detail later in this chapter.

Interest Rates and Exchange Rates

Economic theory tells us that interest rates reflect expectations about likely future inflation rates. In countries where inflation is expected to be high, interest rates also will be high, because investors want compensation for the decline in the value of their money. This relationship was first formalized by economist Irvin Fisher and is referred to as the Fisher effect. The **Fisher effect** states that a country's "nominal" interest rate (i) is the sum of the required "real" rate of interest (r) and the expected rate of inflation over the period for which the funds are to be lent (I). More formally,

$$i = r + I$$

For example, if the real rate of interest in a country is 5 percent and annual inflation is expected to be 10 percent, the nominal interest rate will be 15 percent. As predicted by the Fisher effect, a strong relationship seems to exist between inflation rates and interest rates.[18]

We can take this one step further and consider how it applies in a world of many countries and unrestricted capital flows. When investors are free to transfer capital between countries, real interest rates will be the same in every country. If differences in real interest rates did emerge between countries, arbitrage would soon equalize them. For example, if the real interest rate in Japan was 10 percent and only 6 percent in the United States, it would pay investors to borrow money in the United States and invest it in Japan. The resulting increase in the demand for money in the United States would raise the real interest rate there, while the increase in the supply of foreign money in Japan would lower the real interest rate there. This would continue until the two sets of real interest rates were equalized.

It follows from the Fisher effect that if the real interest rate is the same worldwide, any difference in interest rates between countries reflects differing expectations about inflation rates. Thus, if the expected rate of inflation in the United States is greater than that in Japan, U.S. nominal interest rates will be greater than Japanese nominal interest rates.

Because we know from PPP theory that there is a link (in theory at least) between inflation and exchange rates, and because interest rates reflect expectations about inflation, it follows that there must also be a link between interest rates and exchange rates. This link is known as the international Fisher effect (IFE). The **international Fisher effect** states that for any two countries, the spot exchange rate should change in an equal amount but in the opposite direction to the difference in nominal interest rates between the two countries. Stated more formally, the change in the spot exchange rate between the United States and Japan, for example, can be modeled as follows:

$$\frac{S_1 - S_2}{S_2} \times 100 = i_\$ - i_¥$$

where $i_\$$ and $i_¥$ are the respective nominal interest rates in the United States and Japan, S_1 is the spot exchange rate at the beginning of the period, and S_2 is the spot exchange rate at the end of the period. If the U.S. nominal interest rate is higher than Japan's, reflecting greater expected inflation rates, the value of the dollar against the yen should fall by that interest rate differential in the future. So if the interest rate in the United States is 10 percent and in Japan it is 6 percent, we would expect the value of the dollar to depreciate by 4 percent against the Japanese yen.

Do interest rate differentials help predict future currency movements? The evidence is mixed; as in the case of PPP theory, in the long run, there seems to be a relationship between interest rate differentials and subsequent changes in spot exchange rates. However, considerable short-run deviations occur. Like PPP, the international Fisher effect is not a good predictor of short-run changes in spot exchange rates.[19]

Investor Psychology and Bandwagon Effects

Empirical evidence suggests that neither PPP theory nor the international Fisher effect is particularly good at explaining short-term movements in exchange rates. One reason may be the impact of investor psychology on short-run exchange rate movements. Evidence reveals that various psychological factors play an important role in determining the expectations of market traders as to likely future exchange rates.[20] In turn, expectations have a tendency to become self-fulfilling prophecies.

A famous example of this mechanism occurred in September 1992 when the international financier George Soros made a huge bet against the British pound. Soros borrowed billions of pounds, using the assets of his investment funds as collateral, and immediately sold those pounds for German deutsche marks (this was before the advent of the euro). This technique, known as short selling, can earn the speculator enormous profits if he can subsequently buy back the pounds he sold at a much better exchange rate and then use those pounds, purchased cheaply, to repay his loan. By selling pounds and buying deutsche marks, Soros helped to start pushing down the value of the pound on the foreign exchange markets. More importantly, when Soros started shorting the British pound, many foreign exchange traders, knowing Soros's reputation, jumped on the bandwagon and did likewise. This triggered a classic **bandwagon effect** with traders moving as a herd in the same direction at the same time. As the bandwagon effect gained momentum, with more traders selling British pounds and purchasing deutsche marks in expectation of a decline in the pound, their expectations became a self-fulfilling prophecy. Massive selling forced down the value of the pound against the deutsche mark. In other words, the pound declined in value not so much because of any major shift in macroeconomic fundamentals, but because investors followed a bet placed by a major speculator, George Soros.

According to a number of studies, investor psychology and bandwagon effects play an important role in determining short-run exchange rate movements.[21] However, these effects can be hard to predict. Investor psychology can be influenced by political factors and by microeconomic events, such as the investment decisions of individual firms, many of which are only loosely linked to macroeconomic fundamentals, such as relative inflation rates. Also, bandwagon effects can be both triggered and exacerbated by the idiosyncratic behavior of politicians. Something like this seems to have occurred in Southeast Asia during 1997 when, one after another, the currencies of Thailand, Malaysia, South Korea, and Indonesia lost between 50 percent and 70 percent of their value against the U.S. dollar in a few months.

Summary of Exchange Rate Theories

Relative monetary growth, relative inflation rates, and nominal interest rate differentials are all moderately good predictors of long-run changes in exchange rates. They are poor predictors of short-run changes in exchange rates, however, perhaps because of the impact of psychological factors, investor expectations, and bandwagon effects on short-term currency movements. This information is useful for an international business. Insofar as the long-term profitability of foreign investments, export opportunities, and the price competitiveness of foreign imports are all influenced by long-term movements in exchange rates, international businesses would be advised to pay attention to countries' differing monetary growth, inflation, and interest rates. International businesses that engage in foreign exchange transactions on a day-to-day basis could benefit by knowing some predictors of short-term foreign exchange rate movements. Unfortunately, short-term exchange rate movements are difficult to predict.

EXCHANGE RATE FORECASTING

A company's need to predict future exchange rate variations raises the issue of whether it is worthwhile for the company to invest in exchange rate forecasting services to aid decision making. Two schools of thought address this issue. The efficient market school argues that forward exchange rates do the best possible job of forecasting future spot exchange rates, and, therefore, investing in forecasting services would be a waste of money. The other school of thought, the inefficient market school, argues that companies can improve the foreign exchange market's estimate of future exchange rates (as contained in the forward rate) by investing in forecasting services. In other words, this school of thought does not believe the forward exchange rates are the best possible predictors of future spot exchange rates.

The Efficient Market School

Forward exchange rates represent market participants' collective predictions of likely spot exchange rates at specified future dates. If forward exchange rates are the best possible predictor of future spot rates, it would make no sense for companies to spend additional money trying to forecast short-run exchange rate movements. Many economists believe the foreign exchange market is efficient at setting forward rates.[22] An efficient market is one in which prices reflect all available public information. (If forward rates reflect all available information about likely future changes in exchange rates, a company cannot beat the market by investing in forecasting services.)

If the foreign exchange market is efficient, forward exchange rates should be unbiased predictors of future spot rates. This does not mean the predictions will be accurate in any specific situation. It means inaccuracies will not be consistently above or below future spot rates; they will be random. Many empirical tests have addressed the efficient market hypothesis. Although most of the early work seems to confirm the hypothesis (suggesting that companies should not waste their money on forecasting services) some studies have challenged it.[23] There is some evidence that forward rates are not unbiased predictors of future spot rates, and that more accurate predictions of future spot rates can be calculated from publicly available information.[24]

The Inefficient Market School

Citing evidence against the efficient market hypothesis, some economists believe the foreign exchange market is inefficient. An **inefficient market** is one in which prices do not reflect all available information. In an inefficient market, forward exchange rates will not be the best possible predictors of future spot exchange rates.

If this is true, it may be worthwhile for international businesses to invest in forecasting services (as many do). The belief is that professional exchange rate forecasts might provide better predictions of future spot rates than forward exchange rates do. However, the track record of professional forecasting services is not that good.[25] For example, forecasting services did not predict the 1997 currency crisis that swept through Southeast Asia, nor did they predict the rise in the value of the dollar that occurred during late 2008, a period when the United States fell into a deep financial crisis that some thought would lead to a decline in the value of the dollar (it appears that the dollar rose because it was seen as a relatively safe currency in a time when many nations were experiencing economic trouble).

Approaches to Forecasting

Assuming the inefficient market school is correct that the foreign exchange market's estimate of future spot rates can be improved, on what basis should forecasts be prepared? Here again, there are two schools of thought. One adheres to fundamental analysis, while the other uses technical analysis.

Fundamental Analysis

Fundamental analysis draws on economic theory to construct sophisticated econometric models for predicting exchange rate movements. The variables contained in these models typically include those we have discussed, such as relative money supply growth rates, inflation rates, and interest rates. In addition, they may include variables related to balance-of-payments positions.

Running a deficit on a balance-of-payments current account (a country is importing more goods and services than it is exporting) creates pressures that may result in the depreciation of the country's currency on the foreign exchange market.[26] Consider what might happen if the United States was running a persistent current account balance-of-payments deficit (as it has been). Because the United States would be importing more than it was exporting, people in other countries would be increasing their holdings of U.S. dollars. If these people were willing to hold their dollars, the dollar's exchange rate would not be influenced. However, if these people converted their dollars into other currencies, the supply of dollars in the foreign exchange market would increase (as would demand for the other currencies). This shift in demand and supply would create pressures that could lead to the depreciation of the dollar against other currencies.

This argument hinges on whether people in other countries are willing to hold dollars. This depends on such factors as U.S. interest rates, the return on holding other dollar-denominated assets such as stocks in U.S. companies, and, most important, inflation rates. So, in a sense, the balance-of-payments situation is not a fundamental predictor of future exchange rate movements. But what makes financial assets such as stocks and bonds attractive? The answer is prevailing interest rates and inflation rates, both of which affect underlying economic growth and the real return to holding U.S. financial assets. Given this, we are back to the argument that the fundamental determinants of exchange rates are monetary growth, inflation rates, and interest rates.

Technical Analysis

Technical analysis uses price and volume data to determine past trends, which are expected to continue into the future. This approach does not rely on a consideration of economic fundamentals. Technical analysis is based on the premise that there are analyzable market trends and waves and that previous trends and waves can be used to predict future trends and waves. Since there is no theoretical rationale for this assumption of predictability, many economists compare technical analysis to fortune-telling. Despite this skepticism, technical analysis has gained favor in recent years.[27]

CURRENCY CONVERTIBILITY

Until this point, we have assumed that the currencies of various countries are freely convertible into other currencies. Due to government restrictions, a significant number of currencies are not freely convertible into other currencies. A country's currency is said to be **freely convertible** when the country's government allows both residents and nonresidents to purchase unlimited amounts of a foreign currency with it. A currency is said to be **externally convertible** when only nonresidents may convert it into a foreign currency without any limitations. A currency is **nonconvertible** when neither residents nor nonresidents are allowed to convert it into a foreign currency.

Free convertibility is not universal. Many countries place some restrictions on their residents' ability to convert the domestic currency into a foreign currency (a policy of external convertibility). Restrictions range from the relatively minor (such as restricting the amount of foreign currency they may take with them out of the country on trips) to the major (such as restricting domestic businesses' ability to take foreign currency out of the country). External convertibility restrictions can limit domestic companies' ability to invest abroad, but they present few problems for foreign companies wishing to do business in that country. For example, even if the Japanese government tightly controlled the ability of its residents to convert the yen into U.S. dollars, all U.S. businesses with deposits in Japanese banks may at any time convert all their yen into dollars and take them out of the country. Thus, a U.S. company with a subsidiary in Japan is assured that it will be able to convert the profits from its Japanese operation into dollars and take them out of the country.

Serious problems arise, however, under a policy of nonconvertibility. This was the practice of the former Soviet Union, and it continued to be the practice in Russia for several years after the collapse of the Soviet Union. When strictly applied, nonconvertibility means that although a U.S. company doing business in a country such as Russia may be able to generate significant ruble profits, it may not convert those rubles into dollars and take them out of the country. Obviously this is not desirable for international business.

Governments limit convertibility to preserve their foreign exchange reserves. A country needs an adequate supply of these reserves to service its international debt commitments and to purchase imports. Governments typically impose convertibility restrictions on their currency when they fear that free convertibility will lead to a run on their foreign exchange reserves. This occurs when residents and nonresidents rush to convert their holdings of domestic currency into a foreign currency—a phenomenon generally referred to as **capital flight**. Capital flight is most likely to occur when the value of the domestic currency is depreciating rapidly because of hyperinflation or when a country's economic prospects are shaky in other respects. Under such circumstances, both residents and nonresidents tend to believe that their money is more likely to hold its value if it is converted into a foreign currency and invested abroad. Not only will a run on foreign exchange reserves limit the country's ability to service its international debt and pay for imports, but it will also lead to a precipitous depreciation in the exchange rate as residents and nonresidents unload their holdings of domestic currency on the foreign exchange markets (thereby increasing the market supply of the country's currency). Governments fear that the rise in import prices resulting from currency depreciation will lead to further increases in inflation. This fear provides another rationale for limiting convertibility.

Companies can deal with the nonconvertibility problem by engaging in countertrade. **Countertrade** refers to a range of barter-like agreements by which goods and services can be traded for other goods and services. Countertrade can make sense when a country's currency is nonconvertible. For example, consider the deal that General Electric struck with the Romanian government when that country's currency was nonconvertible. When General Electric won a contract for a $150 million generator project in Romania, it agreed to take payment in the form of Romanian goods that could be sold for $150 million on international markets. In a similar case, the Venezuelan government negotiated a contract with Caterpillar under which Venezuela would trade 350,000 tons of iron ore for Caterpillar heavy construction equipment. Caterpillar subsequently traded the iron ore to Romania in exchange for Romanian farm products, which it then sold on international markets for dollars.[28]

How important is countertrade? Twenty years ago, a large number of nonconvertible currencies existed in the world, and countertrade was quite significant. However, in recent years many governments have made their currencies freely convertible, and the percentage of world trade that involves countertrade is probably significantly below 10 percent.[29]

◼ IMPLICATIONS FOR MANAGERS ▬▬▬▬▬ LO10-6

This chapter contains a number of clear implications for business. First, it is critical that international businesses understand the influence of exchange rates on the profitability of trade and investment deals. Adverse changes in exchange rates can make apparently profitable deals unprofitable. As noted, the risk introduced into international business transactions by changes in exchange rates is referred to as foreign exchange risk. Foreign exchange risk is usually divided into three main categories: transaction exposure, translation exposure, and economic exposure.

TRANSACTION EXPOSURE

Transaction exposure is the extent to which the income from individual transactions is affected by fluctuations in foreign exchange values. Such exposure includes obligations for the purchase or sale of goods and services at previously agreed prices and the borrowing or lending of funds in foreign currencies. For example, suppose in 2004 an American airline agreed to purchase 10 Airbus 330 aircraft for €120 million each for a total price of €1.20 billion, with delivery scheduled for 2008 and payment due then. When the contract was signed in 2004 the dollar/euro exchange rate stood at $1 = €1.10, so the American airline anticipated paying $1.09 billion for the 10 aircraft when they were delivered (€1.2 billion/1.1 = $1.09 billion). However, imagine that the value of the dollar depreciates against the euro over the intervening period, so that a dollar only buys €0.80 in 2008 when payment is due ($1 = €0.80). Now the total cost in U.S. dollars is $1.5 billion (€1.2 billion/0.80 = $1.5 billion), an increase of $0.41 billion! The transaction exposure here is $0.41 billion, which is the money lost due to an adverse movement in exchange rates between the time when the deal was signed and when the aircraft were paid for.

TRANSLATION EXPOSURE

Translation exposure is the impact of currency exchange rate changes on the reported financial statements of a company. Translation exposure is concerned with the present measurement of past events.

The resulting accounting gains or losses are said to be unrealized—they are "paper" gains and losses—but they are still important. Consider a U.S. firm with a subsidiary in Mexico. If the value of the Mexican peso depreciates significantly against the dollar, this would substantially reduce the dollar value of the Mexican subsidiary's equity. In turn, this would reduce the total dollar value of the firm's equity reported in its consolidated balance sheet. This would raise the apparent leverage of the firm (its debt ratio), which could increase the firm's cost of borrowing and potentially limit its access to the capital market. Similarly, if an American firm has a subsidiary in the European Union, and if the value of the euro depreciates rapidly against that of the dollar over a year, this will reduce the dollar value of the euro profit made by the European subsidiary, resulting in negative translation exposure. In fact, many U.S. firms suffered from significant negative translation exposure in Europe during 2000, precisely because the euro did depreciate rapidly against the dollar. In 2002–2007, the euro rose in value against the dollar. This positive translation exposure boosted the dollar profits of American multinationals with significant operations in Europe.

ECONOMIC EXPOSURE

Economic exposure is the extent to which a firm's future international earning power is affected by changes in exchange rates. Economic exposure is concerned with the long-run effect of changes in exchange rates on future prices, sales, and costs. This is distinct from transaction exposure, which is concerned with the effect of exchange rate changes on individual transactions, most of which are short-term affairs that will be executed within a few weeks or months. Consider the effect of wide swings in the value of the dollar on many U.S. firms' international competitiveness. The rapid rise in the value of the dollar on the foreign exchange market in the 1990s hurt the price competitiveness of many U.S. producers in world markets. U.S. manufacturers that relied heavily on exports saw their export volume and world market share decline. The reverse phenomenon occurred in 2000–2009, when the dollar declined against most major currencies. The fall in the value of the dollar helped increase the price competitiveness of U.S. manufacturers in world markets.

REDUCING TRANSLATION AND TRANSACTION EXPOSURE

A number of tactics can help firms minimize their transaction and translation exposure. These tactics primarily protect short-term cash flows from adverse changes in exchange rates. We have already discussed two of these tactics at length in the chapter, entering into forward exchange rate contracts and buying swaps. In addition to buying forward and using swaps, firms can minimize their foreign exchange exposure through leading and lagging payables and receivables—that is, paying suppliers and collecting payment from customers early or late depending on expected exchange rate movements. A **lead strategy** involves attempting to collect foreign currency receivables (payments from customers) early when a foreign currency is expected to depreciate and paying foreign currency payables (to suppliers) before they are due when a currency is expected to appreciate. A **lag strategy** involves delaying collection of foreign currency receivables if that currency is expected to appreciate and delaying payables if the currency is expected to depreciate. Leading and lagging involve accelerating payments from weak-currency to strong-currency countries and delaying inflows from strong-currency to weak-currency countries.

Lead and lag strategies can be difficult to implement, however. The firm must be in a position to exercise some control over payment terms. Firms do not always have this kind of bargaining power, particularly when they are dealing with important customers who are in a position to dictate payment terms. Also, because lead and lag strategies can put pressure on a weak currency, many governments limit leads and lags. For example, some countries set 180 days as a limit for receiving payments for exports or making payments for imports.

Dealing with the Rising Euro

Udo Pfeiffer, the CEO of SMS Elotherm, a German manufacturer of machine tools to engineer crankshafts for cars, signed a deal in late November 2004 to supply the U.S. operations of Chrysler with $1.5 million worth of machines. The machines would be manufactured in Germany and exported to the United States. When the deal was signed, Pfeiffer calculated that at the agreed price, the machines would yield a profit of €30,000 each. Within three days, that profit had declined by €8,000! The dollar had slid precipitously against the euro. SMS would be paid in dollars by Chrysler, but when translated back into euros, the price had declined. Because the company's costs were in euros, the declining revenues when expressed in euros were squeezing profit margins.

With the exchange rate standing at €1 = $1.33 in early December 2004, Pfeiffer was deeply worried. He knew that if the dollar declined further to around €1 = $1.50, SMS would be losing money on its sales to America. He could try to raise the dollar price of his products to compensate for the fall in the value of the dollar, but he knew that was unlikely to work. The market for machine tools was very competitive, and manufacturers were constantly pressuring machine tool companies to lower prices, not raise them.

Another small German supplier to U.S. automobile companies, Keiper, was faring somewhat better. In 2001 Keiper, which manufactures metal frames for automobile seats, opened a plant in London, Ontario, to supply the U.S. operations of Chrysler. At the time the investment was made, the exchange rate was €1 = $1. Management at Keiper had agonized over whether the investment made sense. Some in the company believed it was better to continue exporting from Germany. Others argued that Keiper would benefit from being close to a major customer. Now with the euro appreciating every day, it looked like a smart move. Keiper had a real hedge against the rising value of the euro. But the advantages of being based in Canada were tempered by two things; first, the U.S. dollar had also depreciated against the Canadian dollar, although not by as much as its depreciation against the euro. Second, Keiper was still importing parts from Germany, and the euro had also appreciated against the Canadian dollar, raising the costs at Keiper's Ontario plant.[30]

REDUCING ECONOMIC EXPOSURE

Reducing economic exposure requires strategic choices that go beyond the realm of financial management. The key to reducing economic exposure is to distribute the firm's productive assets to various locations so the firm's long-term financial well-being is not severely affected by adverse changes in exchange rates. This is a strategy that firms both large and small sometimes pursue. For example, fearing that the euro will continue to strengthen against the U.S. dollar, some European firms that do significant business in the United States have set up local production facilities in that market to ensure that a rising euro does not put them at a competitive disadvantage relative to their local rivals. Similarly, Toyota has production plants distributed around the world in part to make sure that a rising yen does not price Toyota cars out of local markets. Caterpillar has also pursued this strategy, setting up factories around the world that can act as a hedge against the possibility that a strong dollar will price Caterpillar's exports out of foreign markets. In 2008 and 2009, this real hedge proved to be very useful. The accompanying Management Focus discusses how two German firms tried to reduce economic exposure.

OTHER STEPS FOR MANAGING FOREIGN EXCHANGE RISK

A firm needs to develop a mechanism for ensuring it maintains an appropriate mix of tactics and strategies for minimizing its foreign exchange exposure. Although there is no universal agreement as to the components of this mechanism, a number of common themes stand out.[31] First, central control of exposure is needed to protect resources efficiently and ensure that each subunit adopts the correct mix of tactics and strategies. Many companies have set up in-house foreign exchange centers. Although such centers may not be able to execute all foreign exchange deals—particularly in large, complex multinationals where myriad transactions may be pursued simultaneously—they should at least set guidelines for the firm's subsidiaries to follow.

Second, firms should distinguish between, on one hand, transaction and translation exposure and, on the other, economic exposure. Many companies seem to focus on reducing their transaction and translation exposure and pay scant attention to economic exposure, which may have more profound long-term implications.[32] Firms need to develop strategies for dealing with economic exposure. For example, Stanley Black & Decker, the maker of power tools, has a strategy for actively managing its economic risk. The key to Stanley Black & Decker's strategy is flexible sourcing. In response to foreign exchange movements, Stanley Black & Decker can move production from one location to another to offer the most competitive pricing. Stanley Black & Decker manufactures in more than a dozen locations around the world—in Europe, Australia, Brazil, Mexico, and Japan. More than 50 percent of the company's productive assets are based outside North America. Although each of Stanley Black & Decker's factories focuses on one or two products to achieve economies of scale, there is considerable overlap. On average, the company runs its factories at no more than 80 percent capacity, so most are able to switch rapidly from producing one product to producing another or to add a product. This allows a factory's production to be changed in response to foreign exchange movements. For example, if the dollar depreciates against other currencies, the amount of imports into the United States from overseas subsidiaries can be reduced and the amount of exports from U.S. subsidiaries to other locations can be increased.[33]

Third, the need to forecast future exchange rate movements cannot be overstated, though, as we saw earlier in the chapter, this is a tricky business. No model comes close to perfectly predicting future movements in foreign exchange rates. The best that can be said is that in the short run, forward exchange rates provide the best predictors of exchange rate movements, and in the long run, fundamental economic factors—particularly relative inflation rates—should be watched because they influence exchange rate movements. Some firms attempt to forecast exchange rate movements in-house; others rely on outside forecasters. However, all such forecasts are imperfect attempts to predict the future.

Fourth, firms need to establish good reporting systems so the central finance function (or in-house foreign exchange center) can regularly monitor the firm's exposure positions. Such reporting systems should enable the firm to identify any exposed accounts, the exposed position by currency of each account, and the time periods covered.

Finally, on the basis of the information it receives from exchange rate forecasts and its own regular reporting systems, the firm should produce monthly foreign exchange exposure reports. These reports should identify how cash flows and balance sheet elements might be affected by forecasted changes in exchange rates. The reports can then be used by management as a basis for adopting tactics and strategies to hedge against undue foreign exchange risks.

Surprisingly, some of the largest and most sophisticated firms don't take such precautionary steps, exposing themselves to very large foreign exchange risks. Thus, as we have seen in this chapter, Volkswagen suffered significant losses during the early 2000s due to a failure to adequately hedge its foreign exchange exposure.

Chapter Summary

This chapter explained how the foreign exchange market works, examined the forces that determine exchange rates, and then discussed the implications of these factors for international business. Given that changes in exchange rates can dramatically alter the profitability of foreign trade and investment deals, this is an area of major interest to international business. The chapter made the following points:

1. One function of the foreign exchange market is to convert the currency of one country into the currency of another. A second function of the foreign exchange market is to provide insurance against foreign exchange risk.

2. The spot exchange rate is the exchange rate at which a dealer converts one currency into another currency on a particular day.

3. Foreign exchange risk can be reduced by using forward exchange rates. A forward exchange rate is an exchange rate governing future transactions. Foreign exchange risk can also be reduced by engaging in currency swaps. A swap is the simultaneous purchase and sale of a given amount of foreign exchange for two different value dates.

4. The law of one price holds that in competitive markets that are free of transportation costs and barriers to trade, identical products sold in different countries must sell for the same price when their price is expressed in the same currency.

5. Purchasing power parity (PPP) theory states the price of a basket of particular goods should be roughly equivalent in each country. PPP theory predicts that the exchange rate will change if relative prices change.

6. The rate of change in countries' relative prices depends on their relative inflation rates. A country's inflation rate seems to be a function of the growth in its money supply.

7. The PPP theory of exchange rate changes yields relatively accurate predictions of long-term trends in exchange rates, but not of short-term movements. The failure of PPP theory to predict exchange rate changes more accurately may be due to transportation costs, barriers to trade and investment, and the impact of psychological factors such as bandwagon effects on market movements and short-run exchange rates.

8. Interest rates reflect expectations about inflation. In countries where inflation is expected to be high, interest rates also will be high.

9. The international Fisher effect states that for any two countries, the spot exchange rate should change in an equal amount but in the opposite direction to the difference in nominal interest rates.

10. The most common approach to exchange rate forecasting is fundamental analysis. This relies on variables such as money supply growth, inflation rates, nominal interest rates, and balance-of-payments positions to predict future changes in exchange rates.

11. In many countries, the ability of residents and nonresidents to convert local currency into a foreign currency is restricted by government policy. A government restricts the convertibility of its currency to protect the country's foreign exchange reserves and to halt any capital flight.

12. Nonconvertibility of a currency makes it very difficult to engage in international trade and investment in the country. One way of coping with the nonconvertibility problem is to engage in countertrade—to trade goods and services for other goods and services.

13. The three types of exposure to foreign exchange risk are transaction exposure, translation exposure, and economic exposure.

14. Tactics that insure against transaction and translation exposure include buying forward, using currency swaps, and leading and lagging payables and receivables.

15. Reducing a firm's economic exposure requires strategic choices about how the firm's productive assets are distributed around the globe.

Critical Thinking and Discussion Questions

1. The interest rate on South Korean government securities with one-year maturity is 4 percent, and the expected inflation rate for the coming year is 2 percent. The interest rate on U.S. government securities with one-year maturity is 7 percent, and the expected rate of inflation is 5 percent. The current spot exchange rate for Korean won is $1 = W1,200. Forecast the spot exchange rate one year from today. Explain the logic of your answer.

2. Two countries, Great Britain and the United States, produce just one good: beef. Suppose the price of beef in the United States is $2.80 per pound and in Britain it is £3.70 per pound.
   a. According to PPP theory, what should the dollar/pound spot exchange rate be?
   b. Suppose the price of beef is expected to rise to $3.10 in the United States and to £4.65 in Britain. What should the one-year forward dollar/pound exchange rate be?
   c. Given your answers to parts *a* and *b*, and given that the current interest rate in the United States is 10 percent, what would you expect the current interest rate to be in Britain?

3. Reread the Management Focus on Volkswagen; then answer the following questions:
   a. Why do you think management at Volkswagen decided to hedge only 30 percent of the auto-maker's foreign currency exposure in 2003? What would have happened if it had hedged 70 percent of exposure? What should it do in a country like India with varying demand and supply constraints and unpredictability?
   b. Why do you think the value of the U.S. dollar declined against that of the euro in 2003?
   c. Apart from hedging through the foreign exchange market, what else can Volkswagen do to reduce its exposure to future declines in the value of the U.S. dollar against the euro?

4. You manufacture wine goblets. In mid-June, you receive an order for 10,000 goblets from Japan. Payment of ¥400,000 is due in mid-December. You expect the yen to rise from its present rate of $1 = ¥130 to $1 = ¥100 by December. You can borrow yen at 6 percent a year. What should you do?

5. You are the CFO of a U.S. firm whose wholly owned subsidiary in Mexico manufactures component parts for your U.S. assembly operations. The subsidiary has been financed by bank borrowings in the United States. One of your analysts told you that the Mexican peso is expected to depreciate by 30 percent against the dollar on the foreign exchange markets over the next year. What actions, if any, should you take?

Research Task ☉ globalEDGE globaledge.msu.edu

The Foreign Exchange Market

Use the globalEDGE website (globaledge.msu.edu) to complete the following exercises:

Exercise 1

One of your company's essential suppliers is located in Japan. Your company needs to make a 1 million Japanese yen payment in six months. Considering that your company primarily operates in U.S. dollars, you are assigned the task of deciding on a strategy to minimize your transaction exposure. Identify the spot and *forward exchange rates* between the two currencies. What factors influence your decision to use each? Which one would you choose? How many dollars must you spend to acquire the amount of yen required?

Exercise 2

Sometimes, analysts use the price of specific products in different locations to compare currency valuation and purchasing power. For example, the *Big Mac Index* compares the purchasing-power parity of many countries based on the price of a Big Mac. Locate the latest edition of this index that is accessible. Identify the five countries (and their currencies) with the lowest purchasing-power parity according to this classification. Which currencies, if any, are overvalued?

Closing CASE

Billabong

Billabong is a quintessential Australian company. The maker of "surf wear" from wet suits and board shorts to T-shirts and watches has a powerful brand name that is recognized by surfing enthusiasts around the globe. The company is a major exporter. Some 80 percent of its sales are generated outside of Australia through a network of 11,000 outlets in more than 100 countries. Not surprisingly, given the history of surfing, the largest foreign market for Billabong is the United States, which accounts for about 50 percent of the company's $1.7 billion in annual sales. As a result, Billabong's fortunes are closely linked to the value of the Australian dollar against the U.S. dollar. When the Australian dollar falls against the U.S. dollar, Billabong's products become less expensive in U.S. dollars, and this can drive sales forward. Conversely, if the Australian dollar rises in value, this can raise the price of Billabong's products in terms of U.S. dollars, which affects sales negatively. Billabong's CEO has stated that every 1 cent movement in the U.S. dollar/Australian dollar exchange rate means a 0.6 percent change in profit for Billabong.

During the second half of 2008, it looked as if things were going Billabong's way. The Australian dollar fell rapidly in value against the U.S. dollar. In June 2008, one Australian dollar was worth $0.97. By October 2008, it was worth only $0.60. The fall in the value of the Australian dollar was in part due to a fear among currency traders that as the world slipped into a recession, caused by the 2008–2009 global financial crisis, global demand for many of the raw materials produced in Australia would decline, exports would slump, and Australia's trade balance would deteriorate. In anticipation of this, institutions sold Australian dollars, driving down their value on foreign exchange markets. For Billabong, however, this was something of a blessing. The cheaper Australian dollar would give it a pricing advantage and help to promote sales in the United States and elsewhere. Also, when sales in U.S. dollars were translated back into Australian dollars, their value increased as the Australian dollar fell. Anticipating this, in February 2009, Billabong's CEO affirmed that he expected the company to increase its profits by as much as 10 percent in 2009, despite the weak global retail environment.

Currency markets, however, can be difficult to predict, and sharp reversals do occur. Between March and November 2009, the Australian dollar surged in value, rising all the way back to $0.94 to one Australian dollar. The cause was twofold. First, there was a global sell-off of the American dollar as the full impact of the global financial crisis became apparent and as the scale of debt in the United States became clearer. Second, despite a recession in the United States and Europe, the emerging economies of China and India continued to grow, and this helped support demand for many of the basic commodities that Australia exports, which led to a strengthening of the Australian dollar. For Billabong, the sharp reversal was an embarrassment. The strong Australian dollar eradicated any pricing advantage Billabong might have enjoyed. Now the amount of Australian dollars that the company received for every sale made in U.S. dollars was declining. In February 2009, every $1 earned in U.S. currency could be exchanged for $1.66 in Australian dollars. By October 2009, every $1 earned in U.S. currency could only be exchanged for $1.06 in Australian dollars. In May 2009, with the Australian dollar rising rapidly, the CEO was forced to revise his previously bullish forecast for sales and earnings. Now, he said, a combination of weaker than expected demand in the United States, plus a strengthening Australian dollar, would lead to a 10 percent decline in profits for 2009. Billabong's troubles continued in 2010 as the company experienced further problems related to exchange rates.[34]

Case Discussion Questions

1. Why does a fall in the value of the Australian dollar against the U.S. dollar benefit Billabong?
2. Could the rise in the value of the Australian dollar that occurred in 2009 have been predicted?
3. What might Billabong had done in order to better protect itself against the unanticipated rise in the value of the Australian dollar that occurred in 2009?
4. The Australian dollar continued to rise by another 20 percent against the U.S. dollar in between 2010 and 2012. How would this have affected Billabong? Is there anything that Billabong might have done to limit its long-term economic exposure to changes in the value of the currency in its largest export market?

Endnotes

1. C. Dawson and Y. Takahashi, "Toyota Shows Optimism Despite Gloom," *The Wall Street Journal*, February 8, 2012; Y. Takahashi, "Nissan's CEO Says Yen Still Not Weak Enough," *The Wall Street Journal*, February 27, 2010; "The Yen's 40 Year Win Streak May Be Ending," *The Wall Street Journal*, January 27, 2012; and "U.S., Europe Seek to Cool Currency Jitters," *The Wall Street Journal*, February 11, 2013.

2. For a good general introduction to the foreign exchange market, see R. Weisweiller, *How the Foreign Exchange Market Works* (New York: New York Institute of Finance, 1990). A detailed description of the economics of foreign exchange markets can be found in P. R. Krugman and M. Obstfeld, *International Economics: Theory and Policy* (New York: HarperCollins, 1994).

3. "The Domino Effect," *The Economist*, July 5, 2008, p. 85.

4. Mark Landler, "As Exchange Rates Swing, Car Makers Try to Duck," *The New York Times*, January 17, 2004, pp. B1, B4; N. Boudette, "Volkswagen Posts 95% Drop in Net," *The Wall Street Journal*, February 19, 2004, p. A3; and "Volkswagen's Financial Mechanic," *Corporate Finance*, June 2003, p. 1.

5. Bank for International Settlements, *Tri-annual Central Bank Survey of Foreign Exchange and Derivatives Market Activity, April 2010* (Basle, Switzerland: BIS, September 2010).

6. Ibid.

7. Ibid.

8. M. Dickson, "Capital Gain: How London Is Thriving as It Takes on the Global Competition," *Financial Times*, March 27, 2006, p. 11.

9. For a comprehensive review, see M. Taylor, "The Economics of Exchange Rates," *Journal of Economic Literature* 33 (1995), pp. 13–47.

10. Krugman and Obstfeld, *International Economics*.

11. M. Friedman, *Studies in the Quantity Theory of Money* (Chicago: University of Chicago Press, 1956). For an accessible explanation, see M. Friedman and R. Friedman, *Free to Choose* (London: Penguin Books, 1979), chap. 9.

12. Juan-Antonio Morales, "Inflation Stabilization in Bolivia," in *Inflation Stabilization: The Experience of Israel, Argentina, Brazil, Bolivia, and Mexico*, ed. Michael Bruno et al. (Cambridge, MA: MIT Press, 1988); and *The Economist, World Book of Vital Statistics* (New York: Random House, 1990).

13. P. Wallsten and S. Reddy, "Fed's Bond Buying Plan Ignites Growing Criticism," *The Wall Street Journal*, November 15, 2010; S. Chan, "Under Attack, the Fed Defends Policy of Buying Bonds," *International Herald Tribune*, November 17, 2010; and "What QE Means for the World; Positive Sum Currency Wars," *The Economist*, February 14, 2013.

14. For reviews and various articles, see H. J. Edison, J. E. Gagnon, and W. R. Melick, "Understanding the Empirical Literature on Purchasing Power Parity," *Journal of International Money and Finance* 16 (February 1997), pp. 1–18; J. R. Edison, "Multi-country Evidence on the Behavior of Purchasing Power Parity under the Current Float," *Journal of International Money and Finance* 16 (February 1997), pp. 19–36; K. Rogoff, "The Purchasing Power Parity Puzzle," *Journal of Economic Literature* 34 (1996), pp. 647–68; D. R. Rapach and M. E. Wohar, "Testing the Monetary Model of Exchange Rate Determination: New Evidence from a Century of Data," *Journal of International Economics,* December 2002, pp. 359–85; and M. P. Taylor, "Purchasing Power Parity," *Review of International Economics,* August 2003, pp. 436–56.

15. M. Obstfeld and K. Rogoff, "The Six Major Puzzles in International Economics," *National Bureau of Economic Research Working Paper Series,* paper no. 7777, July 2000.

16. Ibid.

17. See M. Devereux and C. Engel, "Monetary Policy in the Open Economy Revisited: Price Setting and Exchange Rate Flexibility," *National Bureau of Economic Research Working Paper Series,* paper no. 7665, April 2000. See also P. Krugman, "Pricing to Market When the Exchange Rate Changes," in *Real Financial Economics,* ed. S. Arndt and J. Richardson (Cambridge, MA: MIT Press, 1987).

18. For a summary of the evidence, see the survey by Taylor, "The Economics of Exchange Rates."

19. R. E. Cumby and M. Obstfeld, "A Note on Exchange Rate Expectations and Nominal Interest Differentials: A Test of the Fisher Hypothesis," *Journal of Finance,* June 1981, pp. 697–703; and L. Coppock and M. Poitras, "Evaluating the Fisher Effect in Long Term Cross Country Averages," *International Review of Economics and Finance* 9 (2000), pp. 181–203.

20. Taylor, "The Economics of Exchange Rates." See also R. K. Lyons, *The Microstructure Approach to Exchange Rates* (Cambridge, MA: MIT Press, 2002).

21. See H. L. Allen and M. P. Taylor, "Charts, Noise, and Fundamentals in the Foreign Exchange Market," *Economic Journal* 100 (1990), pp. 49–59; T. Ito, "Foreign Exchange Rate Expectations: Micro Survey Data," *American Economic Review* 80 (1990), pp. 434–49; and T. F. Rotheli, "Bandwagon Effects and Run Patterns in Exchange Rates," *Journal of International Financial Markets, Money and Institutions* 12, no. 2 (2002), pp. 157–66.

22. For example, see E. Fama, "Forward Rates as Predictors of Future Spot Rates," *Journal of Financial Economics,* October 1976, pp. 361–77.

23. L. Kilian and M. P. Taylor, "Why Is It So Difficult to Beat the Random Walk Forecast of Exchange Rates?" *Journal of International Economics* 20 (May 2003), pp. 85–103; and R. M. Levich, "The Efficiency of Markets for Foreign Exchange," in *International Finance,* ed. G. D. Gay and R. W. Kold (Richmond, VA: Robert F. Dane, Inc., 1983).

24. J. Williamson, *The Exchange Rate System* (Washington, DC: Institute for International Economics, 1983); and R. H. Clarida, L. Sarno, M. P. Taylor, and G. Valente, "The Out of Sample Success of Term Structure Models as Exchange Rate Predictors," *Journal of International Economics* 60 (May 2003), pp. 61–84.

25. Kilian and Taylor, "Why Is It So Difficult to Beat the Random Walk Forecast of Exchange Rates?" Journal of International Economics, Vol 60(1), pp. 85–107.

26. Rogoff, "The Purchasing Power Parity Puzzle."

27. C. Engel and J. D. Hamilton, "Long Swings in the Dollar: Are They in the Data and Do Markets Know It?" *American Economic Review,* September 1990, pp. 689–713.

28. J. R. Carter and J. Gagne, "The Do's and Don'ts of International Countertrade," *Sloan Management Review,* Spring 1988, pp. 31–37.

29. D. S. Levine, "Got a Spare Destroyer Lying Around?" *World Trade* 10 (June 1997), pp. 34–35; and Dan West, "Countertrade," *Business Credit,* April 2001, pp. 64–67.

30. Adapted from M. Landler, "Dollar's Fall Drains Profit of European Small Business," *The New York Times,* December 2, 2004, p. C1.

31. For details on how various firms manage their foreign exchange exposure, see the articles contained in the special foreign exchange issue of *Business International Money Report,* December 18, 1989, pp. 401–12.

32. Ibid.

33. S. Arterian, "How Black & Decker Defines Exposure," *Business International Money Report,* December 18, 1989, pp. 404, 405, 409.

34. C. Marriott, "Caught in the Impact Zone," *Australian FX,* January 2010, pp. 11–12; R. Donkin, "Billabong Seeks $290 Million, Slashes Forecast, Stores," *The Western Australian,* May 19, 2009; and "Billabong Ready to Ride the Currency Wave," *The Australian,* October 29, 2008, p. 40.

Chapter 11
The International Monetary System

LEARNING OBJECTIVES

After reading this chapter, you will be able to:

LO11-1 Describe the historical development of the modern global monetary system.

LO11-2 Explain the role played by the World Bank and the IMF in the international monetary system.

LO11-3 Compare and contrast the differences between a fixed and a floating exchange rate system.

LO11-4 Identify exchange rate regimes used in the world today and why countries adopt different exchange rate regimes.

LO11-5 Understand the debate surrounding the role of the IMF in the management of financial crises.

LO11-6 Explain the implications of the global monetary system for currency management and business strategy.

◇◇◇ **ICELAND'S ECONOMIC RECOVERY** ◇◇◇

Opening Case

When the global financial crisis hit in 2008, tiny Iceland suffered more than most. The country's three biggest banks had been expanding at a breakneck pace since 2000 when the government privatized the banking sector. With a population of around 320,000, Iceland was too small for the banker sector's ambitions, so the banks started to expand into other Scandinavian countries and the UK. They entered local mortgage markets, purchased foreign financial institutions, and opened foreign branches, attracting depositors by offering high interest rates. The expansion was financed by debt, much of it structured as short-term loans that had to be regularly refinanced. By early 2008, the three banks held debts that amounted to almost six times the value of the entire economy of Iceland! So long as they could periodically refinance this debt, it was not a problem. However, in 2008, global financial markets imploded following the bankruptcy of Lehman Brothers and the collapse of the U.S. housing market. In the aftermath financial markets froze. The Icelandic banks found that they could not refinance their debt, and they faced bankruptcy.

The Icelandic government lacked the funds to bail out the banks, so it decided to let the big three fail. In quick succession the local stock market plunged 90 percent and unemployment increased ninefold. The krona, Iceland's currency, plunged on foreign exchange markets, pushing up the price of imports, and inflation soared to 18 percent. Iceland appeared to be in free fall. The economy shrank by almost 7 percent in 2009 and another 4 percent in 2010.

To stem the decline, the government secured $10 billion in loans from the International Monetary Fund (IMF) and other countries. The Icelandic government stepped in to help local depositors, seizing the domestic assets of the Icelandic banks and using IMF and other loans to backstop deposit guarantees. Far from implementing austerity measures to solve the crisis, the Icelandic government looked for ways to shore up consumer spending. For example, the government provided means-tested subsidies to reduce the mortgage interest expenses of borrowers. The idea was to stop domestic consumer spending from imploding and further depressing the economy.

With the financial system stabilized, thanks to the IMF and other foreign loans, what happened next is an object lesson in the value of having a floating currency. The fall in the value of the krona helped boost Iceland's exports, such as fish and aluminum, while depressing demand for costly imports, such as automobiles. By 2009 the krona was worth half as much against the U.S. dollar and euro as it was in 2007 before the crisis. Iceland's exports surged and imports slumped. While the high cost of imports did stoke inflation, booming exports started to pump money back into the Icelandic economy. In 2011 the economy grew again at a 3.1 percent annual rate. This was followed by 2.7 percent growth in 2012 while unemployment fell from a high of nearly 10 percent to 5.6 percent.[1]

INTRODUCTION

What happened in Iceland goes to the heart of the subject matter covered in this chapter. Here, we look at the international monetary system, and its role in determining exchange rates. The **international monetary system** refers to the institutional arrangements that govern exchange rates. In Chapter 10, we assumed the foreign exchange market was the primary institution for determining exchange rates and the impersonal market forces of demand and supply determined the relative value of any two currencies (i.e., their exchange rate). Furthermore, we explained that the demand and supply of currencies is influenced by their respective countries' relative inflation rates and interest rates. When the foreign exchange market determines the relative value of a currency, we say that the country is adhering to a **floating exchange rate** regime. Four of the world's major trading currencies—the U.S. dollar, the European Union's euro, the Japanese yen, and the British pound—are all free to float against each other. Thus, their exchange rates are determined by market forces and fluctuate against each other day to day, if not minute to minute. As we saw in the opening case, the Icelandic currency, the krona, is also free to float against other currencies, a fact that some claim helped Iceland recover from the 2008 financial crisis in that country. However, the exchange rates of many currencies are not determined by the free play of market forces; other institutional arrangements are adopted.

Many of the world's developing nations peg their currencies, primarily to the dollar or the euro. A **pegged exchange rate** means the value of the currency is fixed relative to a reference currency, such as the U.S. dollar, and then the exchange rate between that currency and other currencies is determined by the reference currency exchange rate.

Other countries, while not adopting a formal pegged rate, try to hold the value of their currency within some range against an important reference currency such as the U.S. dollar, or a "basket" of currencies. This is often referred to as a **dirty float.** It is a float because in theory, the value of the currency is determined by market forces, but it is a dirty float (as opposed to a clean float) because the central bank of a country will intervene in the foreign exchange market to try to maintain the value of its currency if it depreciates too rapidly against an important reference currency. This has been the policy adopted by the Chinese since July 2005. The value of the Chinese currency, the yuan, has been linked to a basket of other currencies—including the dollar, yen, and euro—and it is allowed to vary in value against individual currencies, but only within limits.

Still other countries have operated with a **fixed exchange rate,** in which the values of a set of currencies are fixed against each other at some mutually agreed-on exchange rate. Before the introduction of the euro in 1999, several member states of the European Union operated with fixed exchange rates within the context of the **European Monetary System (EMS).** For a quarter of a century after World War II, the world's major industrial nations participated in a fixed exchange rate system. Although this system collapsed in 1973, some still argue that the world should attempt to reestablish it.

This chapter explains how the international monetary system works and points out its implications for international business. To understand how the system works, we must review its evolution. We begin with a discussion of the gold standard and its breakup during the 1930s. Then we discuss the 1944 Bretton Woods conference. The Bretton Woods conference also created two major international institutions that play a role in the international monetary system—the International Monetary Fund (IMF) and the World Bank. The IMF was given the task of maintaining order in the international monetary system; the World Bank's role was to promote development. Today, both these institutions continue to play major roles in the world economy and in the international monetary system. As we saw in the opening case, the IMF stepped in to help Iceland navigate its way through a financial crisis when its three biggest banks failed in 2008. The Bretton Woods system of fixed exchange rates collapsed in 1973. Since then, the world has operated with a mixed system in which some currencies are allowed to float freely, but many are either managed by government intervention or pegged to another currency.

Finally, we discuss the implications of all this material for international business. We will see how the exchange rate policy adopted by a government can have an important impact on the outlook for business operations in a given country. We also look at how the policies adopted by the IMF can have an impact on the economic outlook for a country and, accordingly, on the costs and benefits of doing business in that country.

THE GOLD STANDARD

The gold standard had its origin in the use of gold coins as a medium of exchange, unit of account, and store of value—a practice that dates to ancient times. When international trade was limited in volume, payment for goods purchased from another country was typically made in gold or silver. However, as the volume of international trade expanded in the wake of the Industrial Revolution, a more convenient means of financing international trade was needed. Shipping large quantities of gold and silver around the world to finance international trade seemed impractical. The solution adopted was to arrange for payment in paper currency and for governments to agree to convert the paper currency into gold on demand at a fixed rate.

Mechanics of the Gold Standard

Pegging currencies to gold and guaranteeing convertibility is known as the **gold standard**. By 1880, most of the world's major trading nations, including Great Britain, Germany, Japan, and the United States, had adopted the gold standard. Given a common gold standard, the value of any currency in units of any other currency (the exchange rate) was easy to determine.

For example, under the gold standard, one U.S. dollar was defined as equivalent to 23.22 grains of "fine" (pure) gold. Thus, one could, in theory, demand that the U.S. government convert that one dollar into 23.22 grains of gold. Because there are 480 grains in an ounce, one ounce of gold cost $20.67 (480/23.22). The amount of a currency needed to purchase one ounce of gold was referred to as the **gold par value**. The British pound was valued at 113 grains of fine gold. In other words, one ounce of gold cost £4.25 (480/113). From the gold par values of pounds and dollars, we can calculate what the exchange rate was for converting pounds into dollars; it was £1 = $4.87 (i.e., $20.67/£4.25).

Strength of the Gold Standard

The great strength claimed for the gold standard was that it contained a powerful mechanism for achieving balance-of-trade equilibrium by all countries.[2] A country is said to be in **balance-of-trade equilibrium** when the income its residents earn from exports is equal to the money its residents pay to other countries for imports (the current account of its balance of payments is in balance). Suppose there are only two countries in the world, Japan and the United States. Imagine Japan's trade balance is in surplus because it exports more to the United States than it imports from the United States. Japanese exporters are paid in U.S. dollars, which they exchange for Japanese yen at a Japanese bank. The Japanese bank submits the dollars to the U.S. government and demands payment of gold in return. (This is a simplification of what would occur, but it will make our point.)

Under the gold standard, when Japan has a trade surplus, there is a net flow of gold from the United States to Japan. These gold flows automatically reduce the U.S. money supply and swell Japan's money supply. As we saw in Chapter 10, there is a close connection between money supply growth and price inflation. An increase in money supply will raise prices in Japan, while a decrease in the U.S. money supply will push U.S. prices downward. The rise in the price of Japanese goods will decrease demand for these goods, while the fall in the price of U.S. goods will increase demand for these goods. Thus, Japan will start to buy more from the United States, and the United States will buy less from Japan, until a balance-of-trade equilibrium is achieved.

This adjustment mechanism seems so simple and attractive that even today, 80 years after the final collapse of the gold standard, some people believe the world should return to a gold standard.

The Period Between the Wars: 1918–1939

The gold standard worked reasonably well from the 1870s until the start of World War I in 1914, when it was abandoned. During the war, several governments financed part of their massive military expenditures by printing money. This resulted in inflation, and by the war's end in 1918, price levels were higher everywhere. The United States returned to the gold standard in 1919, Great Britain in 1925, and France in 1928.

Great Britain returned to the gold standard by pegging the pound to gold at the prewar gold parity level of £4.25 per ounce, despite substantial inflation between 1914 and 1925. This priced British goods out of foreign markets, which pushed the country into a deep depression. When foreign holders of pounds lost confidence in Great Britain's commitment to maintaining its currency's value, they began converting their holdings of pounds into gold. The British government saw that it could not satisfy the demand for gold without seriously depleting its gold reserves, so it suspended convertibility in 1931.

The United States followed suit and left the gold standard in 1933 but returned to it in 1934, raising the dollar price of gold from $20.67 per ounce to $35 per ounce. Because more dollars were needed to buy an ounce of gold than before, the implication was that the dollar was worth less. This effectively amounted to a devaluation of the dollar relative to other currencies. Thus, before the devaluation, the pound/dollar exchange rate was £1 = $4.87, but after the devaluation it was £1 = $8.24. By reducing the price of U.S. exports and increasing the price of imports, the government was trying to create employment in the United States by boosting output (the U.S. government was basically using the exchange rate as an instrument of trade policy—something it now accuses China of doing). However, a number of other countries adopted a similar tactic, and in the cycle of competitive devaluations that soon emerged, no country could win.

The net result was the shattering of any remaining confidence in the system. With countries devaluing their currencies at will, one could no longer be certain how much gold a currency could buy. Instead of holding onto another country's currency, people often tried to change it into gold immediately, lest the country devalue its currency in the intervening period. This put pressure on the gold reserves of various countries, forcing them to suspend gold convertibility. By the start of World War II in 1939, the gold standard was dead.

THE BRETTON WOODS SYSTEM

In 1944, at the height of World War II, representatives from 44 countries met at Bretton Woods, New Hampshire, to design a new international monetary system. With the collapse of the gold standard and the Great Depression of the 1930s fresh in their minds, these statesmen were determined to build an enduring economic order that would facilitate postwar economic growth. There was consensus that fixed exchange rates were desirable. In addition, the conference participants wanted to avoid the senseless competitive devaluations of the 1930s, and they recognized that the gold standard would not ensure this. The major problem with the gold standard as previously constituted was that no multinational institution could stop countries from engaging in competitive devaluations.

The agreement reached at Bretton Woods established two multinational institutions—the International Monetary Fund (IMF) and the World Bank. The task of the IMF would be to maintain order in the international monetary system and that of the World Bank would be to promote general economic development. The Bretton Woods agreement also called for a system of fixed exchange rates that would be policed by the IMF. Under the agreement, all countries were to fix the value of their currency in terms of gold but were not required to exchange their currencies for gold. Only the dollar remained convertible into gold—at a price of $35 per ounce. Each country decided what it wanted its exchange rate to be vis-à-vis the dollar and then calculated the gold par value of the currency based on that selected dollar exchange rate. All participating countries agreed to try to maintain the value of their currencies within 1 percent of the par value by buying or selling currencies (or gold) as needed. For example, if foreign exchange dealers were selling more of a country's currency than demanded, that country's government would intervene in the foreign exchange markets, buying its currency in an attempt to increase demand and maintain its gold par value.

Another aspect of the Bretton Woods agreement was a commitment not to use devaluation as a weapon of competitive trade policy. However, if a currency became too weak to defend, a devaluation of up to 10 percent would be allowed without any formal approval by the IMF. Larger devaluations required IMF approval.

The Role of the IMF

The IMF Articles of Agreement were heavily influenced by the worldwide financial collapse, competitive devaluations, trade wars, high unemployment, hyperinflation in Germany and elsewhere, and general economic disintegration that occurred between the two world wars. The aim of the Bretton Woods agreement, of which the IMF was the main custodian, was to try to avoid a repetition of that chaos through a combination of discipline and flexibility.

Discipline

A fixed exchange rate regime imposes discipline in two ways. First, the need to maintain a fixed exchange rate puts a brake on competitive devaluations and brings stability to the world trade environment. Second, a fixed exchange rate regime imposes monetary discipline on countries, thereby curtailing price inflation. For example, consider what would happen under a fixed exchange rate regime if Great Britain rapidly increased its money supply by printing pounds. As explained in Chapter 10, the increase in money supply would lead to price inflation. Given fixed exchange rates, inflation would make British goods uncompetitive in world markets, while the prices of imports would become more attractive in Great Britain. The result would be a widening trade deficit in Great Britain, with the country importing more than it exports. To correct this trade imbalance under a fixed exchange rate regime, Great Britain would be required to restrict the rate of growth in its money supply to bring price inflation back under control. Thus, fixed exchange rates are seen as a mechanism for controlling inflation and imposing economic discipline on countries.

Flexibility

Although monetary discipline was a central objective of the Bretton Woods agreement, it was recognized that a rigid policy of fixed exchange rates would be too inflexible. It would probably break down just as the gold standard had. In some cases, a country's attempts to reduce its money supply growth and correct a persistent balance-of-payments deficit could force the country into recession and create high unemployment. The architects of the Bretton Woods agreement wanted to avoid high unemployment, so they built limited flexibility into the system. Two major features of the IMF Articles of Agreement fostered this flexibility: IMF lending facilities and adjustable parities.

The IMF stood ready to lend foreign currencies to members to tide them over during short periods of balance-of-payments deficits, when a rapid tightening of monetary or fiscal policy would hurt domestic employment. A pool of gold and currencies contributed by IMF members provided the resources for these lending operations. A persistent balance-of-payments deficit can lead to a depletion of a country's reserves of foreign currency, forcing it to devalue its currency. By providing deficit-laden countries with short-term foreign currency loans, IMF funds would buy time for countries to bring down their inflation rates and reduce their balance-of-payments deficits. The belief was that such loans would reduce pressures for devaluation and allow for a more orderly and less painful adjustment.

Countries were to be allowed to borrow a limited amount from the IMF without adhering to any specific agreements. However, extensive drawings from IMF funds would require a country to agree to increasingly stringent IMF supervision of its macroeconomic policies. Heavy borrowers from the IMF must agree to monetary and fiscal conditions set down by the IMF, which typically included IMF-mandated targets on domestic money supply growth, exchange rate policy, tax policy, government spending, and so on.

The system of adjustable parities allowed for the devaluation of a country's currency by more than 10 percent if the IMF agreed that a country's balance of payments was in "fundamental disequilibrium." The term *fundamental disequilibrium* was not defined in the IMF's Articles of Agreement, but it was intended to apply to countries that had suffered permanent adverse shifts in the demand for their products. Without devaluation, such a country would experience high unemployment and a persistent trade deficit until the domestic price level had fallen far enough to restore a balance-of-payments equilibrium. The belief was that devaluation could help sidestep a painful adjustment process in such circumstances.

The Role of the World Bank

The official name for the World Bank is the International Bank for Reconstruction and Development (IBRD). When the Bretton Woods participants established the World Bank, the need to reconstruct the war-torn economies of Europe was foremost in their minds. The bank's initial mission was to help finance the building of Europe's economy by providing low-interest loans. As it turned out, the World Bank was overshadowed in this role by the Marshall Plan, under which the United States lent money directly to European nations to help them rebuild. So the bank turned its attention to development and began lending money to third-world nations. In the 1950s, the bank concentrated on public-sector projects. Power stations, road building, and other transportation investments were much in favor. During the 1960s, the bank also began to lend heavily in support of agriculture, education, population control, and urban development.

The bank lends money under two schemes. Under the IBRD scheme, money is raised through bond sales in the international capital market. Borrowers pay what the bank calls a market rate of interest—the bank's cost of funds plus a margin for expenses. This "market" rate is lower than commercial banks' market rate. Under the IBRD scheme, the bank offers low-interest loans to risky customers whose credit rating is often poor, such as the governments of underdeveloped nations.

A second scheme is overseen by the International Development Association (IDA), an arm of the bank created in 1960. Resources to fund IDA loans are raised through subscriptions from wealthy members such as the United States, Japan, and Germany. IDA loans go only to the poorest countries. Borrowers have up to 50 years to repay at an interest rate of less than 1 percent a year. The world's poorest nations receive grants and interest-free loans.

THE COLLAPSE OF THE FIXED EXCHANGE RATE SYSTEM

The system of fixed exchange rates established at Bretton Woods worked well until the late 1960s, when it began to show signs of strain. The system finally collapsed in 1973, and since then we have had a managed-float system. To understand why the system collapsed, one must appreciate the special role of the U.S. dollar in the system. As the only currency that could be converted into gold, and as the currency that served as the reference point for all others, the dollar occupied a central place in the system. Any pressure on the dollar to devalue could wreak havoc with the system, and that is what occurred.

Most economists trace the breakup of the fixed exchange rate system to the U.S. macroeconomic policy package of 1965–1968.[3] To finance both the Vietnam conflict and his welfare programs, President Lyndon Johnson backed an increase in U.S. government spending that was not financed by an increase in taxes. Instead, it was financed by an increase in the money supply, which led to a rise in price inflation from less than 4 percent in 1966 to close to 9 percent by 1968. At the same time, the rise in government spending had stimulated the economy. With more money in their pockets, people spent more—particularly on imports—and the U.S. trade balance began to deteriorate.

The increase in inflation and the worsening of the U.S. foreign trade position gave rise to speculation in the foreign exchange market that the dollar would be devalued. Things came to a head in spring 1971 when U.S. trade figures showed that for the first time since 1945, the United States was importing more than it was exporting. This set off massive purchases of German deutsche marks in the foreign exchange market by speculators who guessed that the mark would be revalued against the dollar. On a single day, May 4, 1971, the Bundesbank (Germany's central bank) had to buy $1 billion to hold the dollar/deutsche mark exchange rate at its fixed exchange rate given the great demand for deutsche marks. On the morning of May 5, the Bundesbank purchased another $1 billion during the first hour of foreign exchange trading! At that point, the Bundesbank faced the inevitable and allowed its currency to float.

In the weeks following the decision to float the deutsche mark, the foreign exchange market became increasingly convinced that the dollar would have to be devalued. However, devaluation of the dollar was no easy matter. Under the Bretton Woods provisions, any other country could change its exchange rates against all currencies simply by fixing its dollar rate at a new level. But as the key currency in the system, the dollar could be devalued only if all countries agreed to simultaneously revalue against the dollar. Many countries did not want this, because it would make their products more expensive relative to U.S. products.

To force the issue, President Nixon announced in August 1971 that the dollar was no longer convertible into gold. He also announced that a new 10 percent tax on imports would remain in effect until U.S. trading partners agreed to revalue their currencies against the dollar. This brought the trading partners to the bargaining table, and in December 1971 an agreement was reached to devalue the dollar by about 8 percent against foreign currencies. The import tax was then removed. The problem was not solved, however. The U.S. balance-of-payments position continued to deteriorate throughout 1973, while the nation's money supply continued to expand at an inflationary rate. Speculation continued to grow that the dollar was still overvalued and that a second devaluation would be necessary. In anticipation, foreign exchange dealers began converting dollars to deutsche marks and other currencies. After a massive wave of speculation in February 1973, which culminated with European central banks spending $3.6 billion on March 1 to try to prevent their currencies from appreciating against the dollar, the foreign exchange market was closed. When the foreign exchange market reopened March 19, the currencies of Japan and most European countries were floating against the dollar, although many developing countries continued to peg their currency to the dollar, and many do to this day. At that time, the switch to a floating system was viewed as a temporary response to unmanageable speculation in the foreign exchange market. But it is now more than 40 years since the Bretton Woods system of fixed exchange rates collapsed, and the temporary solution looks permanent.

The Bretton Woods system had an Achilles' heel: The system could not work if its key currency, the U.S. dollar, was under speculative attack. The Bretton Woods system could work only as long as the U.S. inflation rate remained low and the United States did not run a balance-of-payments deficit. Once these things occurred, the system soon became strained to the breaking point.

THE FLOATING EXCHANGE RATE REGIME

The floating exchange rate regime that followed the collapse of the fixed exchange rate system was formalized in January 1976 when IMF members met in Jamaica and agreed to the rules for the international monetary system that are in place today.

The Jamaica Agreement

The Jamaica meeting revised the IMF's Articles of Agreement to reflect the new reality of floating exchange rates. The main elements of the Jamaica agreement include the following:

- Floating rates were declared acceptable. IMF members were permitted to enter the foreign exchange market to even out "unwarranted" speculative fluctuations.
- Gold was abandoned as a reserve asset. The IMF returned its gold reserves to members at the current market price, placing the proceeds in a trust fund to help poor nations. IMF members were permitted to sell their own gold reserves at the market price.
- Total annual IMF quotas—the amount member countries contribute to the IMF—were increased to $41 billion. (Since then, they have been increased to $767 billion, while the membership of the IMF has been expanded to include 188 countries. Non-oil-exporting, less developed countries were given greater access to IMF funds.)

Exchange Rates Since 1973

Since March 1973, exchange rates have become much more volatile and less predictable than they were between 1945 and 1973.[4] This volatility has been partly due to a number of unexpected shocks to the world monetary system, including:

- The oil crisis in 1971, when the Organization of Petroleum Exporting Countries (OPEC) quadrupled the price of oil. The harmful effect of this on the U.S. inflation rate and trade position resulted in a further decline in the value of the dollar.
- The loss of confidence in the dollar that followed a sharp rise in the U.S. inflation rate in 1977–1978.
- The oil crisis of 1979, when OPEC once again increased the price of oil dramatically—this time it was doubled.
- The unexpected rise in the dollar between 1980 and 1985, despite a deteriorating balance-of-payments picture.
- The rapid fall of the U.S. dollar against the Japanese yen and German deutsche mark between 1985 and 1987, and against the yen between 1993 and 1995.
- The partial collapse of the European Monetary System in 1992.
- The 1997 Asian currency crisis, when the Asian currencies of several countries—including South Korea, Indonesia, Malaysia, and Thailand—lost between 50 and 80 percent of their value against the U.S. dollar in a few months.
- The global financial crisis of 2008–2010 and the sovereign debt crisis in the European Union during 2010–2011.

Figure 11.1 summarizes how the value of the U.S. dollar has fluctuated against an index of major trading currencies between January 1973 and March 2013. (The index, which was set equal to 100 in March 1973, is a weighted average of the foreign exchange values of the U.S. dollar against currencies that circulate widely outside the country of issue.) An interesting phenomenon in Figure 11.1 is the rapid rise in the value of the dollar between 1980 and 1985 and its subsequent fall between 1985 and 1988. A similar, though less pronounced, rise and fall in the value of the dollar occurred between 1995 and 2012. We briefly discuss the rise and fall of the dollar during these periods, because this tells us something about how the international monetary system has operated in recent years.[5]

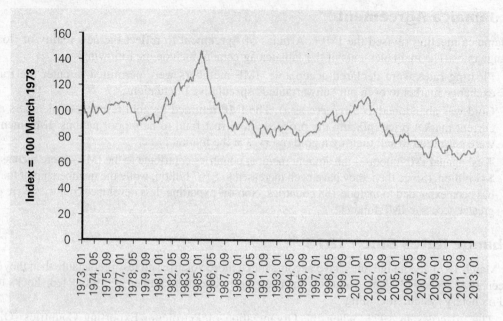

Figure 11.1 *Major Currencies Dollar Index, 1973–2013*

Source: From data at http://www.federalreserve.gov/releases/H10/summary/indexn_m.htm.

The rise in the value of the dollar between 1980 and 1985 occurred when the United States was running a large and growing trade deficit, importing substantially more than it exported. Conventional wisdom would suggest that the increased supply of dollars in the foreign exchange market as a result of the trade deficit should lead to a reduction in the value of the dollar, but as shown in Figure 11.1, it increased in value. Why?

A number of favorable factors overcame the unfavorable effect of a trade deficit. Strong economic growth in the United States attracted heavy inflows of capital from foreign investors seeking high returns on capital assets. High real interest rates attracted foreign investors seeking high returns on financial assets. At the same time, political turmoil in other parts of the world, along with relatively slow economic growth in the developed countries of Europe, helped create the view that the United States was a good place to invest. These inflows of capital increased the demand for dollars in the foreign exchange market, which pushed the value of the dollar upward against other currencies.

The fall in the value of the dollar between 1985 and 1988 was caused by a combination of government intervention and market forces. The rise in the dollar, which priced U.S. goods out of foreign markets and made imports relatively cheap, had contributed to a dismal trade picture. In 1985, the United States posted a then record-high trade deficit of more than $160 billion. This led to growth in demands for protectionism in the United States. In September 1985, the finance ministers and central bank governors of the so-called Group of Five major industrial countries (Great Britain, France, Japan, Germany, and the United States) met at the Plaza Hotel in New York and reached what was later referred to as the Plaza Accord. They announced that it would be desirable for most major currencies to appreciate vis-à-vis the U.S. dollar and pledged to intervene in the foreign exchange markets, selling dollars, to encourage this objective. The dollar had already begun to weaken during summer 1985, and this announcement further accelerated the decline.

The dollar continued to decline until 1987. The governments of the Group of Five began to worry that the dollar might decline too far, so the finance ministers of the Group of Five met in Paris in February 1987 and reached a new agreement known as the Louvre Accord. They agreed that exchange rates had been realigned sufficiently and pledged to support the stability of exchange rates around their current levels by intervening in the foreign exchange markets when necessary to buy and sell currency. Although the dollar continued to decline for a few months after the Louvre Accord, the rate of decline slowed, and by early 1988 the decline had ended.

Except for a brief speculative flurry around the time of the Persian Gulf War in 1991, the dollar was relatively stable for the first half of the 1990s. However, in the late 1990s, the dollar again began to appreciate against most major currencies, including the euro after its introduction, even though the United States was still running a significant balance-of-payments deficit. Once again, the driving force for the appreciation in the value of the dollar was that foreigners continued to invest in U.S. financial assets, primarily stocks and bonds, and the inflow of money drove up the value of the dollar on foreign exchange markets. The inward investment was due to a belief that U.S. financial assets offered a favorable rate of return.

By 2002, however, foreigners had started to lose their appetite for U.S. stocks and bonds, and the inflow of money into the United States slowed. Instead of reinvesting dollars earned from exports to the United States in U.S. financial assets, they exchanged those dollars for other currencies, particularly euros, to invest them in non-dollar-denominated assets. One reason for this was the continued growth in the U.S. trade deficit, which hit a record $791 billion in 2005 (by 2011 it had fallen to $540 billion). Although the U.S. trade deficits had been hitting records for decades, this deficit was the largest ever when measured as a percentage of the country's GDP (6.3 percent of GDP in 2005).

The record deficit meant that even more dollars were flowing out of the United States into foreign hands, and those foreigners were less inclined to reinvest those dollars in the United States at a rate required to keep the dollar stable. This growing reluctance of foreigners to invest in the United States was in turn due to several factors. First, there was a slowdown in U.S. economic activity during 2001–2002. Second, the U.S. government's budget deficit expanded rapidly after 2001. This led to fears that ultimately the budget deficit would be financed by an expansionary monetary policy that could lead to higher price inflation. Third, from 2003 onward, U.S. government officials began to "talk down" the value of the dollar, in part because the administration believed that a cheaper dollar would increase exports and reduce imports, thereby improving the U.S. balance of trade position.[6] Foreigners saw this as a signal that the U.S. government would not intervene in the foreign exchange markets to prop up the value of the dollar, which increased their reluctance to reinvest dollars earned from export sales in U.S. financial assets. As a result of these factors, demand for dollars weakened, and the value of the dollar slid on the foreign exchange markets—hitting an index value of 69.069 in August 2011, the lowest value since the index began in 1973. Some believe that it could resume its fall in coming years, particularly if large holders of U.S. dollars, such as oil-producing states, decide to diversify their foreign exchange holdings (see the accompanying Country Focus for a discussion of this possibility).

Interestingly, from mid-2008 through early 2009, the dollar staged a moderate rally against major currencies, despite the fact that the American economy was suffering from a serious financial crisis. The reason seems to be that despite America's problems, things were even worse in many other countries, and foreign investors saw the dollar as a safe haven and put their money in low-risk U.S. assets, particularly low-yielding U.S. government bonds. This rally faltered in mid-2009 as investors became worried about the level of U.S. indebtedness.

The U.S. Dollar, Oil Prices, and Recycling Petrodollars

Between 2004 and 2008, global oil prices surged. They peaked at $147 a barrel in July 2008, up from about $20 in 2001, before falling sharply back to a $34 to $48 range by early 2009. Since then, they have increased again, rising to around $100 a barrel in early 2013. The rise in oil prices has been due to a combination of greater-than-expected demand for oil, particularly from rapidly developing giants such as China and India; tight supplies; and perceived geopolitical risks in the Middle East, the world's largest oil-producing region.

The surge in oil prices was a windfall for oil-producing countries. Collectively, they earned around $700 billion in oil revenues in 2005, and well over $1 trillion in 2007 and 2008—some 64 percent of which went to members of OPEC. Saudi Arabia, the world's largest oil producer, reaped a major share. Because oil is priced in U.S. dollars, the rise in oil prices has translated into a substantial increase in the dollar holdings of oil producers (the dollars earned from the sale of oil are often referred to as *petrodollars*). In essence, rising oil prices represent a net transfer of dollars from oil consumers in countries such as the United States to oil producers in Russia, Saudi Arabia, and Venezuela. What have they been doing with these dollars?

One option for producing countries was to spend their petrodollars on public-sector infrastructure, such as health services, education, roads, and telecommunications systems. Among other things, this could boost economic growth in those countries and pull in foreign imports, which would help counterbalance the trade surpluses enjoyed by oil producers and support global economic growth. Spending did indeed pick up in many oil-producing countries. However, according to the IMF, OPEC members spent only about 40 percent of their windfall profits from higher oil prices in 2002–2007 (an exception was Venezuela, whose leader, Hugo Chávez, was on a spending spree until his death in early 2013). The last time oil prices increased sharply in 1979, oil producers significantly ramped up spending on infrastructure, only to find themselves saddled with excessive debt when oil prices collapsed a few years later. This time they were more cautious—an approach that seems wise given the rapid fall in oil prices during late 2008.

Another option was for oil producers to invest a good chunk of the dollars they earned from oil sales in dollar-denominated assets, such as U.S. bonds, stocks, and real estate. This did happen. OPEC members in particular funneled dollars back into U.S. assets, mostly low-risk government bonds. The implication is that by recycling their petrodollars, oil producers helped finance the large and growing current account deficit of the United States, enabling it to pay its large oil import bill.

A third possibility for oil producers was to invest in non-dollar-denominated assets, including European and Japanese bonds and stocks. This, too, happened. Also, some OPEC investors had purchased not just small equity positions but entire companies. In 2005, for example, Dubai International Capital purchased the Tussauds Group, a British theme-park firm, and DP World of Dubai purchased P&O, Britain's biggest port and ferries group. Despite examples such as these, between 2005 and 2008 at least, the bulk of petrodollars appear to have been recycled into dollar-denominated assets. In part, this was because U.S. interest rates increased throughout 2004–2007. However, if the flow of petrodollars should dry up, with oil-rich countries investing in other currencies, such as euro-denominated assets, the dollar could fall sharply.[7]

This review tells us that in recent history both market forces and government intervention have determined the value of the dollar. Under a floating exchange rate regime, market forces have produced a volatile dollar exchange rate. Governments have sometimes responded by intervening in the market— buying and selling dollars—in an attempt to limit the market's volatility and to correct what they see as overvaluation (in 1985) or potential undervaluation (in 1987) of the dollar. In addition to direct intervention, statements from government officials have frequently influenced the value of the dollar. The dollar may not have declined by as much as it did in 2004, for example, had not U.S. government officials publicly ruled out any action to stop the decline. Paradoxically, a signal not to intervene can affect the market. The frequency of government intervention in the foreign exchange market explains why the current system is sometimes thought of as a **managed-float system** or a dirty-float system.

FIXED VERSUS FLOATING EXCHANGE RATES

The breakdown of the Bretton Woods system has not stopped the debate about the relative merits of fixed versus floating exchange rate regimes. Disappointment with the system of floating rates in recent years has led to renewed debate about the merits of fixed exchange rates. This section reviews the arguments for fixed and floating exchange rate regimes.[8] We discuss the case for floating rates before studying why many critics are disappointed with the experience under floating exchange rates and yearn for a system of fixed rates.

The Case for Floating Exchange Rates

The case in support of floating exchange rates has three main elements: monetary policy autonomy, automatic trade balance adjustments, and economic recovery following a severe economic crisis.

Monetary Policy Autonomy

It is argued that under a fixed system, a country's ability to expand or contract its money supply as it sees fit is limited by the need to maintain exchange rate parity. Monetary expansion can lead to inflation, which puts downward pressure on a fixed exchange rate (as predicted by the PPP theory; see Chapter 10). Similarly, monetary contraction requires high interest rates (to reduce the demand for money). Higher interest rates lead to an inflow of money from abroad, which puts upward pressure on a fixed exchange rate. Thus, to maintain exchange rate parity under a fixed system, countries were limited in their ability to use monetary policy to expand or contract their economies.

Advocates of a floating exchange rate regime argue that removal of the obligation to maintain exchange rate parity would restore monetary control to a government. If a government faced with unemployment wanted to increase its money supply to stimulate domestic demand and reduce unemployment, it could do so unencumbered by the need to maintain its exchange rate. While monetary expansion might lead to inflation, this would lead to a depreciation in the country's currency. If PPP theory is correct, the resulting currency depreciation on the foreign exchange markets should offset the effects of inflation. Although under a floating exchange rate regime, domestic inflation would have an impact on the exchange rate, it should have no impact on businesses' international cost competitiveness due to exchange rate depreciation. The rise in domestic costs should be exactly offset by the fall in the value of the country's currency on the foreign exchange markets. Similarly, a government could use monetary policy to contract the economy without worrying about the need to maintain parity.

Trade Balance Adjustments

Under the Bretton Woods system, if a country developed a permanent deficit in its balance of trade (importing more than it exported) that could not be corrected by domestic policy, this would require the IMF to agree to currency devaluation. Critics of this system argue that the adjustment mechanism works much more smoothly under a floating exchange rate regime. They argue that if a country is running a trade deficit, the imbalance between the supply and demand of that country's currency in the foreign exchange markets (supply exceeding demand) will lead to depreciation in its exchange rate. In turn, by making its exports cheaper and its imports more expensive, exchange rate depreciation should correct the trade deficit.

Crisis Recovery

Advocates of floating exchange rates also argue that exchange rate adjustments can help a country to deal with economic crises. When a country is hit by a severe economic crisis, such as the banking crisis that hit Iceland in 2008 (see the opening case), its currency typically declines on foreign exchange markets. The reason for this is that investors respond to the crisis by taking their money out of the country, selling the local currency, and driving down its value. At some point, however, the currency becomes so cheap that it starts to stimulate exports. This is what occurred in Iceland after the krona lost 50 percent of its value against the U.S. dollar and euro following the 2008 banking crisis. By 2009 exports of fish and aluminum from Iceland were booming, which helped pull the Icelandic economy out of a recession. A similar process occurred in South Korean after the 1997 Asian banking crisis. The value of the South Korean won plunged to 1,700 per dollar from around 800. In turn, the cheap won helped South Korea increase its exports and resulted in an export-led economic recovery. On the other hand, in both countries the declining value of the currency did raise import prices and led to an increase in inflation, so there is a price that has to be paid for an export-led recovery due to falling currency values.

A contrast can be drawn with the recent situation in Greece, where the economy imploded following the 2008–2009 global financial crisis, and has yet to recover. Part of the problem in Greece is that it gave up its own currency to adopt the euro in 2001, and the euro has remained quite strong—thus Greece cannot rely upon a falling local currency to boost exports and stimulate economic recovery.

The Case for Fixed Exchange Rates

The case for fixed exchange rates rests on arguments about monetary discipline, speculation, uncertainty, and the lack of connection between the trade balance and exchange rates.

Monetary Discipline

We have already discussed the nature of monetary discipline inherent in a fixed exchange rate system when we discussed the Bretton Woods system. The need to maintain fixed exchange rate parity ensures that governments do not expand their money supplies at inflationary rates. While advocates of floating rates argue that each country should be allowed to choose its own inflation rate (the monetary autonomy argument), advocates of fixed rates argue that governments all too often give in to political pressures and expand the monetary supply far too rapidly, causing unacceptably high price inflation. A fixed exchange rate regime would ensure that this does not occur.

Speculation

Critics of a floating exchange rate regime also argue that speculation can cause fluctuations in exchange rates. They point to the dollar's rapid rise and fall during the 1980s, which they claim had nothing to do with comparative inflation rates and the U.S. trade deficit, but everything to do with speculation. They argue that when foreign exchange dealers see a currency depreciating, they tend to sell the currency in the expectation of future depreciation regardless of the currency's longer-term prospects. As more traders jump on the bandwagon, the expectations of depreciation are realized. Such destabilizing speculation tends to accentuate the fluctuations around the exchange rate's long-run value. It can damage a country's economy by distorting export and import prices. Thus, advocates of a fixed exchange rate regime argue that such a system will limit the destabilizing effects of speculation.

Uncertainty

Speculation also adds to the uncertainty surrounding future currency movements that characterizes floating exchange rate regimes. The unpredictability of exchange rate movements in the post–Bretton Woods era has made business planning difficult, and it adds risk to exporting, importing, and foreign investment activities. Given a volatile exchange rate, international businesses do not know how to react to the changes—and often they do not react. Why change plans for exporting, importing, or foreign investment after a 6 percent fall in the dollar this month, when the dollar may rise 6 percent next month? This uncertainty, according to the critics, dampens the growth of international trade and investment. They argue that a fixed exchange rate, by eliminating such uncertainty, promotes the growth of international trade and investment. Advocates of a floating system reply that the forward exchange market ensures against the risks associated with exchange rate fluctuations (see Chapter 10), so the adverse impact of uncertainty on the growth of international trade and investment has been overstated.

Trade Balance Adjustments and Economic Recovery

Those in favor of floating exchange rates argue that floating rates help adjust trade imbalances and can assist with economic recovery after a crisis. Critics question the closeness of the link between the exchange rate, the trade balance and economic growth. They claim trade deficits are determined by the balance between savings and investment in a country, not by the external value of its currency.[9] They argue that depreciation in a currency will lead to inflation (due to the resulting increase in import prices). This inflation, they state, will wipe out any apparent gains in cost competitiveness that arise from currency depreciation. In other words, a depreciating exchange rate will not boost exports and reduce imports, as advocates of floating rates claim; it will simply boost price inflation. In support of this argument, those who favor fixed rates point out that the 40 percent drop in the value of the dollar between 1985 and 1988 did not correct the U.S. trade deficit. In reply, advocates of a floating exchange rate regime argue that between 1985 and 1992, the U.S. trade deficit fell from more than $160 billion to about $70 billion, and they attribute this in part to the decline in the value of the dollar. Moreover, the experience of countries like South Korea and Iceland seems to suggest that floating rates can help a country recover from a severe economic crisis.

Who is Right?

Which side is right in the vigorous debate between those who favor a fixed exchange rate and those who favor a floating exchange rate? Economists cannot agree. Business, as a major player on the international trade and investment scene, has a large stake in the resolution of the debate. Would international business be better off under a fixed regime, or are flexible rates better? The evidence is not clear.

However, a fixed exchange rate regime modeled along the lines of the Bretton Woods system probably will not work. Speculation ultimately broke the system, a phenomenon that advocates of fixed rate regimes claim is associated with floating exchange rates! Nevertheless, a different kind of fixed exchange rate system might be more enduring and might foster the stability that would facilitate more rapid growth in international trade and investment. In the next section, we look at potential models for such a system and the problems with such systems.

EXCHANGE RATE REGIMES IN PRACTICE

Governments around the world pursue a number of different exchange rate policies. These range from a pure "free float" where the exchange rate is determined by market forces to a pegged system that has some aspects of the pre-1973 Bretton Woods system of fixed exchange rates. Some 21 percent of the IMF's members allow their currency to float freely. Another 23 percent intervene in only a limited way (the so-called managed float). A further 5 percent of IMF members now have no separate legal tender of their own (this figure excludes the European Union countries that have adopted the euro). These are typically smaller states, mostly in Africa or the Caribbean, that have no domestic currency and have adopted a foreign currency as legal tender within their borders, typically the U.S. dollar or the euro. The remaining countries use more inflexible systems, including a fixed peg arrangement (43 percent) under which they peg their currencies to other currencies, such as the U.S. dollar or the euro, or to a basket of currencies. Other countries have adopted a system under which their exchange rate is allowed to fluctuate against other currencies within a target zone (an adjustable peg system). In this section, we look more closely at the mechanics and implications of exchange rate regimes that rely on a currency peg or target zone.

Pegged Exchange Rates

Under a pegged exchange rate regime, a country will peg the value of its currency to that of a major currency so that, for example, as the U.S. dollar rises in value, its own currency rises too. Pegged exchange rates are popular among many of the world's smaller nations. As with a full fixed exchange rate regime, the great virtue claimed for a pegged exchange rate is that it imposes monetary discipline on a country and leads to low inflation. For example, if Belize pegs the value of the Belizean dollar to that of the U.S. dollar so that US$1 = B$1.97, then the Belizean government must make sure the inflation rate in Belize is similar to that in the United States. If the Belizean inflation rate is greater than the U.S. inflation rate, this will lead to pressure to devalue the Belizean dollar (i.e., to alter the peg). To maintain the peg, the Belizean government would be required to rein in inflation. Of course, for a pegged exchange rate to impose monetary discipline on a country, the country whose currency is chosen for the peg must also pursue sound monetary policy.

Evidence shows that adopting a pegged exchange rate regime moderates inflationary pressures in a country. An IMF study concluded that countries with pegged exchange rates had an average annual inflation rate of 8 percent, compared with 14 percent for intermediate regimes and 16 percent for floating regimes.[10] However, many countries operate with only a nominal peg and in practice are willing to devalue their currency rather than pursue a tight monetary policy. It can be very difficult for a smaller country to maintain a peg against another currency if capital is flowing out of the country and foreign exchange traders are speculating against the currency. Something like this occurred in 1997 when a combination of adverse capital flows and currency speculation forced several Asian countries, including Thailand and Malaysia, to abandon pegs against the U.S. dollar and let their currencies float freely. Malaysia and Thailand would not have been in this position had they dealt with a number of problems that began to arise in their economies during the 1990s, including excessive private-sector debt and expanding current account trade deficits.

Currency Boards

Hong Kong's experience during the 1997 Asian currency crisis added a new dimension to the debate over how to manage a pegged exchange rate. During late 1997, when other Asian currencies were collapsing, Hong Kong maintained the value of its currency against the U.S. dollar at about $1 = HK$7.80 despite several concerted speculative attacks. Hong Kong's currency board has been given credit for this success. A country that introduces a **currency board** commits itself to converting its domestic currency on demand into another currency at a fixed exchange rate. To make this commitment credible, the currency board holds reserves of foreign currency equal at the fixed exchange rate to at least 100 percent of the domestic currency issued. The system used in Hong Kong means its currency must be fully backed by the U.S. dollar at the specified exchange rate. This is still not a true fixed exchange rate regime, because the U.S. dollar, and by extension the Hong Kong dollar, floats against other currencies, but it has some features of a fixed exchange rate regime.

Under this arrangement, the currency board can issue additional domestic notes and coins only when there are foreign exchange reserves to back it. This limits the ability of the government to print money and, thereby, create inflationary pressures. Under a strict currency board system, interest rates adjust automatically. If investors want to switch out of domestic currency into, for example, U.S. dollars, the supply of domestic currency will shrink. This will cause interest rates to rise until it eventually becomes attractive for investors to hold the local currency again. In the case of Hong Kong, the interest rate on three-month deposits climbed as high as 20 percent in late 1997, as investors switched out of Hong Kong dollars and into U.S. dollars. The dollar peg held, however, and interest rates declined again.

Since its establishment in 1983, the Hong Kong currency board has weathered several storms, including the latest. This success persuaded several other countries in the developing world to consider a similar system. Argentina introduced a currency board in 1991 (but abandoned it in 2002), and Bulgaria, Estonia, and Lithuania have all gone down this road in recent years. Despite interest in the arrangement, however, critics are quick to point out that currency boards have their drawbacks.[11] If local inflation rates remain higher than the inflation rate in the country to which the currency is pegged, the currencies of countries with currency boards can become uncompetitive and overvalued (this is what happened in the case of Argentina, which had a currency board). Also, under a currency board system, government lacks the ability to set interest rates. Interest rates in Hong Kong, for example, are effectively set by the U.S. Federal Reserve. In addition, economic collapse in Argentina in 2001 and the subsequent decision to abandon its currency board dampened much of the enthusiasm for this mechanism of managing exchange rates.

CRISIS MANAGEMENT BY THE IMF

Many observers initially believed that the collapse of the Bretton Woods system in 1973 would diminish the role of the IMF within the international monetary system. The IMF's original function was to provide a pool of money from which members could borrow, short term, to adjust their balance-of-payments position and maintain their exchange rate. Some believed the demand for short-term loans would be considerably diminished under a floating exchange rate regime. A trade deficit would presumably lead to a decline in a country's exchange rate, which would help reduce imports and boost exports. No temporary IMF adjustment loan would be needed. Consistent with this, after 1973, most industrialized countries tended to let the foreign exchange market determine exchange rates in response to demand and supply. Since the early 1970s, the rapid development of global capital markets has generally allowed developed countries such as Great Britain and the United States to finance their deficits by borrowing private money, as opposed to drawing on IMF funds.

Despite these developments, the activities of the IMF have expanded over the past 30 years. By 2012, the IMF had 188 members, 52 of which had some kind of IMF program in place. In 1997, the institution implemented its largest rescue packages until that date, committing more than $110 billion in short-term loans to three troubled Asian countries—South Korea, Indonesia, and Thailand. This was followed by additional IMF rescue packages in Turkey, Russia, Argentina, and Brazil. IMF loans increased again in late 2008 as the global financial crisis took hold. Between 2008 and 2010, the IMF made more than $100 billion in loans to troubled economies such as Latvia, Greece, and Ireland. In April 2009, in response to the growing financial crisis, major IMF members agreed to triple the institution's resources from $250 billion to $750 billion, thereby giving the IMF the financial leverage to act aggressively in times of global financial crisis.

The IMF's activities have expanded because periodic financial crises have continued to hit many economies in the post–Bretton Woods era. The IMF has repeatedly lent money to nations experiencing financial crises, requesting in return that the governments enact certain macroeconomic policies. Critics of the IMF claim these policies have not always been as beneficial as the IMF might have hoped and, in some cases, may have made things worse. Following the IMF loans to several Asian economies, these criticisms reached new levels, and a vigorous debate was waged as to the appropriate role of the IMF. In this section, we discuss some of the main challenges the IMF has had to deal with over the past three decades and review the ongoing debate over the role of the IMF.

Financial Crises in the Post–Bretton Woods Era

A number of broad types of financial crises have occurred over the past 30 years, many of which have required IMF involvement. A **currency crisis** occurs when a speculative attack on the exchange value of a currency results in a sharp depreciation in the value of the currency or forces authorities to expend large volumes of international currency reserves and sharply increase interest rates to defend the prevailing exchange rate. This happened in Brazil in 2002, and the IMF stepped in to help stabilize the value of the Brazilian currency on foreign exchange markets by lending it foreign currency. A **banking crisis** refers to a loss of confidence in the banking system that leads to a run on banks, as individuals and companies withdraw their deposits. This is what happened in Iceland in 2008 (see the opening case). A **foreign debt crisis** is a situation in which a country cannot service its foreign debt obligations, whether private-sector or government debt. This happened to Greece, Ireland, and Portugal in 2010.

These crises tend to have common underlying macroeconomic causes: high relative price inflation rates, a widening current account deficit, excessive expansion of domestic borrowing, high government deficits, and asset price inflation (such as sharp increases in stock and property prices).[13] At times, elements of currency, banking, and debt crises may be present simultaneously, as in the 1997 Asian crisis, the 2000–2002 Argentinean crisis, and the 2010 crisis in Ireland.

To assess the frequency of financial crises, the IMF looked at the macroeconomic performance of a group of 53 countries from 1975 to 1997 (22 of these countries were developed nations, and 31 were developing countries).[14] The IMF found there had been 158 currency crises, including 55 episodes in which a country's currency declined by more than 25 percent. There were also 54 banking crises. The IMF's data suggest that developing nations were more than twice as likely to experience currency and banking crises as developed nations. It is not surprising, therefore, that most of the IMF's loan activities since the mid-1970s have been targeted toward developing nations. The above Country Focus gives a detailed look at the development of one currency crisis, that in Mexico during 1995.

In 1997, several Asian currencies started to fall sharply as international investors came to the realization that there was a speculative investment bubble in the region. They took their money out

The Mexican Currency Crisis of 1995

COUNTRY FOCUS

The Mexican peso had been pegged to the dollar since the early 1980s when the International Monetary Fund made it a condition for lending money to the Mexican government to help bail the country out of a 1982 financial crisis. Under the IMF-brokered arrangement, the peso had been allowed to trade within a tolerance band of plus or minus 3 percent against the dollar. The band was also permitted to "crawl" down daily, allowing for an annual peso depreciation of about 4 percent against the dollar. The IMF believed that the need to maintain the exchange rate within a fairly narrow trading band would force the Mexican government to adopt stringent financial policies to limit the growth in the money supply and contain inflation.

Until the early 1990s, it looked as if the IMF policy had worked. However, the strains were beginning to show by 1994. Since the mid-1980s, Mexican producer prices had risen 45 percent more than prices in the United States, and yet there had not been a corresponding adjustment in the exchange rate. By late 1994, Mexico was running a $17 billion trade deficit, which amounted to some 6 percent of the country's gross domestic product, and there had been an uncomfortably rapid expansion in public- and private-sector debt. Despite these strains, Mexican government officials had been stating publicly they would support the peso's dollar peg at around $1 = 3.5 pesos by adopting appropriate monetary policies and by intervening in the currency markets if necessary. Encouraged by such statements, $64 billion of foreign investment money poured into Mexico between 1990 and 1994 as corporations and money managers sought to take advantage of the booming economy.

However, many currency traders concluded the peso would have to be devalued, and they began to dump pesos on the foreign exchange market. The government tried to hold the line by buying pesos and selling dollars, but it lacked the foreign currency reserves required to halt the speculative tide (Mexico's foreign exchange reserves fell from $6 billion at the beginning of 1994 to less than $3.5 billion at the end of the year). In mid-December 1994, the Mexican government abruptly announced a devaluation. Immediately, much of the short-term investment money that had flowed into Mexican stocks and bonds over the previous year reversed its course as foreign investors bailed out of peso-denominated financial assets. This exacerbated the sale of the peso and contributed to the rapid 40 percent drop in its value.

The IMF stepped in again, this time arm in arm with the U.S. government and the Bank for International Settlements. Together, the three institutions pledged close to $50 billion to help Mexico stabilize the peso and to redeem $47 billion of public- and private-sector debt that was set to mature in 1995. Of this amount, $20 billion came from the U.S. government and another $18 billion came from the IMF (which made Mexico the largest recipient of IMF aid up to that point). Without the aid package, Mexico would probably have defaulted on its debt obligations, and the peso would have gone into free fall. As is normal in such cases, the IMF insisted on tight monetary policies and further cuts in public spending, both of which helped push the country into a deep recession. However, the recession was relatively short-lived, and by 1997 the country was once more on a growth path, had pared down its debt, and had paid back the $20 billion borrowed from the U.S. government ahead of schedule.[12]

of local currencies, changing it into U.S. dollars, and those currencies started to fall precipitously. The currency declines started in Thailand and then, in a process of contagion, quickly spread to other countries in the region. Stabilizing those currencies required massive help from the IMF. In the case of South Korea, local enterprises had built up huge debt loads as they invested heavily in new industrial capacity. By 1997, they found they had too much industrial capacity and could not generate the income required to service their debt. South Korean banks and companies had also made the mistake of borrowing in dollars, much of it in the form of short-term loans that would come due within a year. Thus, when the Korean won started to decline in fall 1997 in sympathy with the problems elsewhere in Asia, South Korean companies saw their debt obligations balloon. Several large companies were forced to file for bankruptcy. This triggered a decline in the South Korean currency and stock market that was difficult to halt.

With its economy on the verge of collapse, the South Korean government requested $20 billion in standby loans from the IMF on November 21. As the negotiations progressed, it became apparent that South Korea was going to need far more than $20 billion. On December 3, 1997, the IMF and South Korean government reached a deal to lend $55 billion to the country. The agreement with the IMF called for the South Koreans to open their economy and banking system to foreign investors. South Korea also pledged to restrain Korea's largest enterprises, the *chaebol,* by reducing their share of bank financing and requiring them to publish consolidated financial statements and undergo annual independent external audits. On trade liberalization, the IMF said South Korea would comply with its commitments to the World Trade Organization to eliminate trade-related subsidies and restrictive import licensing and would streamline its import certification procedures, all of which should open the South Korean economy to greater foreign competition.[15]

Evaluating the IMF's Policy Prescriptions

By 2012, the IMF was committing loans to some 52 countries that were struggling with economic and/or currency crises. All IMF loan packages come with conditions attached. Until very recently, the IMF has insisted on a combination of tight macroeconomic policies, including cuts in public spending, higher interest rates, and tight monetary policy. It has also often pushed for the deregulation of sectors formerly protected from domestic and foreign competition, privatization of state-owned assets, and better financial reporting from the banking sector. These policies are designed to cool overheated economies by reining in inflation and reducing government spending and debt. This set of policy prescriptions has come in for tough criticisms from many observers, and the IMF itself has started to change its approach.[16]

Inappropriate Policies

One criticism is that the IMF's traditional policy prescriptions represent a "one-size-fits-all" approach to macroeconomic policy that is inappropriate for many countries. In the case of the 1997 Asian crisis, critics argue that the tight macroeconomic policies imposed by the IMF were not well suited to countries that are suffering not from excessive government spending and inflation, but from a private-sector debt crisis with deflationary undertones.[17]

In South Korea, for example, the government had been running a budget surplus for years (it was 4 percent of South Korea's GDP in 1994–1996), and inflation was low at about 5 percent. South Korea had the second-strongest financial position of any country in the Organization for Economic Cooperation and Development. Despite this, critics say, the IMF insisted on applying the same policies that it applies to countries suffering from high inflation. The IMF required South Korea to maintain an inflation rate of 5 percent. However, given the collapse in the value of its currency and the subsequent rise in price for imports such as oil, critics claimed inflationary pressures would inevitably increase in South Korea. So to hit a 5 percent inflation rate, the South Koreans would be forced to apply an unnecessarily tight monetary policy. Short-term interest rates in South Korea did jump from 12.5 percent to 21 percent immediately after the country signed its initial deal with the IMF. Increasing interest rates made it even more difficult for companies to service their already excessive short-term debt obligations, and critics used this as evidence to argue that the cure prescribed by the IMF may actually increase the probability of widespread corporate defaults, not reduce them.

At the time the IMF rejected this criticism. According to the IMF, the central task was to rebuild confidence in the won. Once this was achieved, the won would recover from its oversold levels, reducing the size of South Korea's dollar-denominated debt burden when expressed in won, making it easier for companies to service their debt. The IMF also argued that by requiring South Korea to remove restrictions on foreign direct investment, foreign capital would flow into the country to take advantage of cheap assets. This, too, would increase demand for the Korean currency and help improve the dollar/won exchange rate.

South Korea did recover fairly quickly from the crisis, supporting the position of the IMF. While the economy contracted by 7 percent in 1998, by 2000 it had rebounded and grew at a 9 percent rate (measured by growth in GDP). Inflation, which peaked at 8 percent in 1998, fell to 2 percent by 2000, and unemployment fell from 7 percent to 4 percent over the same period. The won hit a low of $1 = W1,812 in early 1998, but by 2000 was back to an exchange rate of around $1 = W1,200, at which it seems to have stabilized.

Moral Hazard

A second criticism of the IMF is that its rescue efforts are exacerbating a problem known to economists as moral hazard. **Moral hazard** arises when people behave recklessly because they know they will be saved if things go wrong. Critics point out that many Japanese and Western banks were far too willing to lend large amounts of capital to overleveraged Asian companies during the boom years of the 1990s. These critics argue that the banks should now be forced to pay the price for their rash lending policies, even if that means some banks must close.[18] Only by taking such drastic action, the argument goes, will banks learn the error of their ways and not engage in rash lending in the future. By providing support to these countries, the IMF is reducing the probability of debt default and in effect bailing out the banks whose loans gave rise to this situation.

This argument ignores two critical points. First, if some Japanese or Western banks with heavy exposure to the troubled Asian economies were forced to write off their loans due to widespread debt default, the impact would have been difficult to contain. The failure of large Japanese banks, for example, could have triggered a meltdown in the Japanese financial markets. That would almost inevitably lead to a serious decline in stock markets around the world, which was the very risk the IMF was trying to avoid by stepping in with financial support. Second, it is incorrect to imply that some banks have not had to pay the price for rash lending policies. The IMF insisted on the closure of banks in South Korea, Thailand, and Indonesia after the 1997 Asian financial crisis. Foreign banks with short-term loans outstanding to South Korean enterprises have been forced by circumstances to reschedule those loans at interest rates that do not compensate for the extension of the loan maturity.

Lack of Accountability

The final criticism of the IMF is that it has become too powerful for an institution that lacks any real mechanism for accountability.[19] The IMF has determined macroeconomic policies in those countries, yet according to critics such as noted economist Jeffrey Sachs, the IMF, with a staff of less than 1,000, lacks the expertise required to do a good job. Evidence of this, according to Sachs, can be found in the fact that the IMF was singing the praises of the Thai and South Korean governments only months before both countries lurched into crisis. Then the IMF put together a draconian program for South Korea without having deep knowledge of the country. Sachs's solution to this problem is to reform the IMF so it makes greater use of outside experts and its operations are open to greater outside scrutiny.

Observations

As with many debates about international economics, it is not clear which side is correct about the appropriateness of IMF policies. There are cases where one can argue that IMF policies had been counterproductive or only had limited success. For example, one might question the success of the IMF's involvement in Turkey given that the country has had to implement some 18 IMF programs since 1958! But the IMF can also point to some notable accomplishments, including its success in containing the Asian crisis, which could have rocked the global international monetary system to its core, and its actions in 2008–2010 to contain the global financial crisis, quickly stepping in to rescue Iceland, Ireland, Greece, and Latvia. Similarly, many observers give the IMF credit for its deft handling of politically difficult situations, such as the Mexican peso crisis, and for successfully promoting a free market philosophy.

Several years after the IMF's intervention, the Asian economy of Asia recovered. Certainly they all averted the kind of catastrophic implosion that might have occurred had the IMF not stepped in, and although some countries still faced considerable problems, it is not clear that the IMF should take much blame for this. The IMF cannot force countries to adopt the policies required to correct economic mismanagement. While a government may commit to taking corrective action in return for an IMF loan, internal political problems may make it difficult for a government to act on that commitment. In such cases, the IMF is caught between a rock and a hard place, because if it decided to withhold money, it might trigger financial collapse and the kind of contagion that it seeks to avoid.

Finally, it is notable that in recent years the IMF has started to change its policies. In response to the global financial crisis of 2008–2009, the IMF began to urge countries to adopt policies that included fiscal stimulus and monetary easing—the direct opposite of what the fund traditionally advocated. Some economists in the fund are also now arguing that higher inflation rates might be a good thing, if the consequence is greater growth in aggregate demand, which would help pull nations out of recessionary conditions. The IMF, in other words, is starting to display the very flexibility in policy responses that its critics claim it lacks. While the traditional policy of tight controls on fiscal policy and tight monetary policy targets might be appropriate for countries suffering from high inflation rates, the Asian economic crisis and the 2008–2009 global financial crisis were caused not by high inflation rates but by excessive debt, and the IMF's "new approach" seems tailored to deal with this.[20]

◼ IMPLICATIONS FOR MANAGERS ▬▬▬▬▬▬ LO11-6

The implications for international businesses of the material discussed in this chapter fall into three main areas: currency management, business strategy, and corporate–government relations.

CURRENCY MANAGEMENT

An obvious implication with regard to currency management is that companies must recognize that the foreign exchange market does not work quite as depicted in Chapter

10. The current system is a mixed system in which a combination of government intervention and speculative activity can drive the foreign exchange market. Companies engaged in significant foreign exchange activities need to be aware of this and to adjust their foreign exchange transactions accordingly. For example, the currency management unit of Caterpillar claims it made millions of dollars in the hours following the announcement of the Plaza Accord by selling dollars and buying currencies that it expected to appreciate on the foreign exchange market following government intervention.

Under the present system, speculative buying and selling of currencies can create very volatile movements in exchange rates (as exhibited by the rise and fall of the dollar during the 1980s and the Asian currency crisis of the late 1990s). Contrary to the predictions of the purchasing power parity theory (see Chapter 10), exchange rate movements during the 1980s and 1990s often did not seem to be strongly influenced by relative inflation rates. Insofar as volatile exchange rates increase foreign exchange risk, this is not good news for business. On the other hand, as we saw in Chapter 10, the foreign exchange market has developed a number of instruments, such as the forward market and swaps, that can help ensure against foreign exchange risk. Not surprisingly, use of these instruments has increased markedly since the breakdown of the Bretton Woods system in 1973.

BUSINESS STRATEGY

The volatility of the current global exchange rate regime presents a conundrum for international businesses. Exchange rate movements are difficult to predict, and yet their movement can have a major impact on a business's competitive position. For a detailed example, see the accompanying Management Focus on Airbus. Faced with uncertainty about the future value of currencies, firms can utilize the forward exchange market, which Airbus has done. However, the forward exchange market is far from perfect as a predictor of future exchange rates (see Chapter 10). It is also difficult if not impossible to get adequate insurance coverage for exchange rate changes that might occur several years in the future. The forward market tends to offer coverage for exchange rate changes a few months—not years—ahead. Given this, it makes sense to pursue strategies that will increase the company's strategic flexibility in the face of unpredictable exchange rate movements—that is, to pursue strategies that reduce the economic exposure of the firm (which we first discussed in Chapter 10).

Maintaining strategic flexibility can take the form of dispersing production to different locations around the globe as a real hedge against currency fluctuations (this seems to be what Airbus has considered). Consider the case of Daimler-Benz, Germany's export-oriented automobile and aerospace company. In June 1995, the company stunned the German business community when it announced it expected to post a severe loss in 1995 of about $720 million. The cause was Germany's strong currency, which had appreciated by 4 percent against a basket of major currencies since the beginning of 1995 and had risen by more than 30 percent against the U.S. dollar since late 1994. By mid-1995, the exchange rate against the dollar stood at $1 = DM1.38. Daimler's management believed it could not make money with an exchange rate under $1 = DM1.60. Daimler's senior managers concluded the appreciation of the mark against the dollar was probably permanent, so they decided to move substantial production outside of Germany and increase purchasing of foreign components. The idea was to reduce the vulnerability of the company to future exchange rate movements. Even before the company's acquisition of Chrysler Corporation in 1998, the Mercedes-Benz division planned to produce 10 percent of its cars outside Germany by 2000, mostly in the United States. Similarly, the move by Japanese automobile companies to expand their productive capacity in the United States and Europe can be seen in the context of the increase in the value of the yen between 1985 and 1995, which raised the price of Japanese exports. For the Japanese companies, building production capacity overseas was a hedge against continued appreciation of the yen (as well as against trade barriers).

Airbus and the Euro

Airbus had reason to celebrate in 2003; for the first time in the company's history, it delivered more commercial jet aircraft than long-time rival Boeing. Airbus delivered 305 planes in 2003, compared to Boeing's 281. The celebration, however, was muted, because the strength of the euro against the U.S. dollar was casting a cloud over the company's future. Airbus, which is based in Toulouse, France, prices planes in dollars, just as Boeing has always done. But more than half of Airbus's costs are in euros. So as the dollar drops in value against the euro—and it dropped by more than 50 percent between 2002 and the end of 2009—Airbus's costs rise in proportion to its revenue, squeezing profits in the process.

In the short run, the fall in the value of the dollar against the euro did not hurt Airbus. The company fully hedged its dollar exposure in 2005 and was mostly hedged for 2006. However, anticipating that the dollar would stay weak against the euro, Airbus started to take other steps to reduce its economic exposure to a strong European currency. Recognizing that raising prices is not an option given the strong competition from Boeing, Airbus decided to focus on reducing its costs. As a step toward doing this, Airbus is giving U.S. suppliers a greater share of work on new aircraft models, such as the A380 superjumbo and the A350. It is also shifting supply work on some of its older models from European to American-based suppliers. This will increase the proportion of its costs that are in dollars, making profits less vulnerable to a rise in the value of the euro and reducing the costs of building an aircraft when they are converted back into euros.

In addition, Airbus is pushing its European-based suppliers to start pricing in U.S. dollars. Because the costs of many suppliers are in euros, the suppliers are finding that to comply with Airbus's wishes, they too have to move more work to the United States, or to countries whose currency is pegged to the U.S. dollar. Thus, one large French-based supplier, Zodiac, has announced that it was considering acquisitions in the United States. Not only is Airbus pushing suppliers to price components for commercial jet aircraft in dollars, but the company is also requiring suppliers to its A400M program, a military aircraft that will be sold to European governments and priced in euros, to price components in U.S. dollars. Beyond these steps, the CEO of EADS, Airbus's parent company, has publicly stated it might be prepared to assemble aircraft in the United States if that helps win important U.S. contracts.[21]

Another way of building strategic flexibility and reducing economic exposure involves contracting out manufacturing. This allows a company to shift suppliers from country to country in response to changes in relative costs brought about by exchange rate movements. However, this kind of strategy may work only for low-value-added manufacturing (e.g., textiles), in which the individual manufacturers have few if any firm-specific skills that contribute to the value of the product. It may be less appropriate for high-value-added manufacturing, in which firm-specific technology and skills add significant value to the product (e.g., the heavy equipment industry) and in which switching costs are correspondingly high. For high-value-added manufacturing, switching suppliers will lead to a reduction in the value that is added, which may offset any cost gains arising from exchange rate fluctuations.

The roles of the IMF and the World Bank in the current international monetary system also have implications for business strategy. Increasingly, the IMF has been acting as the macroeconomic police of the world economy, insisting that countries seeking significant borrowings adopt IMF-mandated macroeconomic policies. These policies typically include anti-inflationary monetary policies and reductions in government spending. In the short run, such policies usually result in a sharp contraction of demand. International businesses selling or producing in such countries need to be aware of this and plan accordingly. In the long run, the kind of policies imposed by the IMF can promote economic growth and an expansion of demand, which create opportunities for international business.

CORPORATE–GOVERNMENT RELATIONS

As major players in the international trade and investment environment, businesses can influence government policy toward the international monetary system. For example, intense government lobbying by U.S. exporters helped convince the U.S. government that intervention in the foreign exchange market was necessary. With this in mind, business can and should use its influence to promote an international monetary system that facilitates the growth of international trade and investment. Whether a fixed or floating regime is optimal is a subject for debate. However, exchange rate volatility such as the world experienced during the 1980s and 1990s creates an environment less conducive to international trade and investment than one with more stable exchange rates. Therefore, it would seem to be in the interests of international business to promote an international monetary system that minimizes volatile exchange rate movements, particularly when those movements are unrelated to long-run economic fundamentals.

Chapter Summary

This chapter explained the workings of the international monetary system and pointed out its implications for international business. The chapter made the following points:

1. The gold standard is a monetary standard that pegs currencies to gold and guarantees convertibility to gold. It was thought that the gold standard contained an automatic mechanism that contributed to the simultaneous achievement of a balance-of-payments equilibrium by all countries. The gold standard broke down during the 1930s as countries engaged in competitive devaluations.

2. The Bretton Woods system of fixed exchange rates was established in 1944. The U.S. dollar was the central currency of this system; the value of every other currency was pegged to its value. Significant exchange rate devaluations were allowed only with the permission of the IMF. The role of the IMF was to maintain order in the international monetary system (*a*) to avoid a repetition of the competitive devaluations of the 1930s and (*b*) to control price inflation by imposing monetary discipline on countries.

3. The fixed exchange rate system collapsed in 1973, primarily due to speculative pressure on the dollar following a rise in U.S. inflation and a growing U.S. balance-of-trade deficit.

4. Since 1973, the world has operated with a floating exchange rate regime, and exchange rates have become more volatile and far less predictable. Volatile exchange rate movements have helped reopen the debate over the merits of fixed and floating systems.

5. The case for a floating exchange rate regime claims (*a*) such a system gives countries autonomy regarding their monetary policy and (*b*) floating exchange rates facilitate smooth adjustment of trade imbalances.

6. The case for a fixed exchange rate regime claims (*a*) the need to maintain a fixed exchange rate imposes monetary discipline on a country; (*b*) floating exchange rate regimes are vulnerable to speculative pressure; (*c*) the uncertainty that accompanies floating exchange rates dampens the growth of international trade and investment; and (*d*) far from correcting trade imbalances, depreciating a currency on the foreign exchange market tends to cause price inflation.

7. In today's international monetary system, some countries have adopted floating exchange rates; some have pegged their currency to another currency such as the U.S. dollar; and some have pegged their currency to a basket of other currencies, allowing their currency to fluctuate within a zone around the basket.

8. In the post–Bretton Woods era, the IMF has continued to play an important role in helping countries navigate their way through financial crises by lending significant capital to embattled governments and by requiring them to adopt certain macroeconomic policies.

9. An important debate is occurring over the appropriateness of IMF-mandated macroeconomic policies. Critics charge that the IMF often imposes inappropriate conditions on developing nations that are the recipients of its loans.

10. The current managed-float system of exchange rate determination has increased the importance of currency management in international businesses.

11. The volatility of exchange rates under the current managed-float system creates both opportunities and threats. One way of responding to this volatility is for companies to build strategic flexibility and limit their economic exposure by dispersing production to different locations around the globe by contracting out manufacturing (in the case of low-value-added manufacturing) and other means.

Critical Thinking and Discussion Questions

1. Why did the gold standard collapse? Is there a case for returning to some type of gold standard? What is it?

2. What opportunities might current IMF lending policies to developing nations create for international businesses? What threats might they create?

3. Do you think the standard IMF policy prescriptions of tight monetary policy and reduced government spending are always appropriate for developing nations experiencing a currency crisis? How might the IMF change its approach? What would the implications be for international businesses?

4. Debate the relative merits of fixed and floating exchange rate regimes 'for a country like India'. From the perspective of an international business, what are the most important criteria in a choice between the systems? Which system is the more desirable for an international business?

5. Imagine that Canada, the United States, and Mexico decide to adopt a fixed exchange rate system. What would be the likely consequences of such a system for (*a*) international businesses and (*b*) the flow of trade and investment among the three countries?

6. Reread the Country Focus on the U.S. dollar, oil prices, and recycling petrodollars; then answer the following questions:

   a. What will happen to the value of the U.S. dollar if oil producers decide to invest most of their earnings from oil sales in domestic infrastructure projects?

   b. What factors determine the relative attractiveness of dollar-, euro-, and yen- denominated assets to oil producers flush with petrodollars? What might lead them to direct more funds toward non-dollar-denominated assets?

    c.   What will happen to the value of the U.S. dollar if OPEC members decide to invest more of their petrodollars toward non-dollar-denominated assets, such as euro-denominated stocks and bonds?

    d.   In addition to oil producers, China is also accumulating a large stock of dollars, currently estimated to total $1.4 trillion. What would happen to the value of the dollar if China and oil-producing nations all shifted out of dollar-denominated assets at the same time? What would be the consequence for the U.S. economy?

Research Task   ○ globalEDGE   globaledge.msu.edu

The International Monetary System

Use the globalEDGE website (globaledge.msu.edu) to complete the following exercises:

Exercise 1

The *Global Financial Stability Report* is a semiannual report published by the International Capital Markets division of the International Monetary Fund (IMF). The report includes an assessment of the risks facing the global financial markets. Locate and download the latest report to get an overview of the most important issues currently under discussion. Also, download a report from five years ago. How do issues from five years ago compare with financial issues identified in the current report?

Exercise 2

An important element to understanding the international monetary system is keeping updated on current growth trends worldwide. A German colleague told you yesterday that *Deutsche Bank Research* provides an effective way to stay informed on important topics in international finance from a European perspective. One area of focus for the site is emerging markets and economic and financial challenges faced by these markets. Find an emerging market research report for analysis. On which emerging market region did you choose to focus? What are the key takeaways from your chosen report?

Closing CASE

Currency Trouble in Malawi

When the former World Bank economist Bingu wa Mutharika became president of the East African nation of Malawi in 2004, it seemed to be the beginning of a new age for one of the world's poorest countries. In landlocked Malawi, most of the population subsists on less than a dollar a day. Mutharika was their champion. He introduced a subsidy program for fertilizer to help poor farmers and gave them seeds. Agricultural output expanded, and the economy boomed, growing by 7 percent per year between 2005 and 2010. International donors loved him, and aid money started to pour in from the United Kingdom and the United States. By 2011, foreign aid was accounting for more than half of Malawi's annual budget.

    In 2009, to no one's surprise, Mutharika was reelected president. Then things started to fall apart. Mutharika became increasingly dictatorial. He pushed aside the country's central bankers and ministers to take full control of economic policy. He called himself "Economist in Chief." Critics at home were harassed and jailed. Independent newspapers were threatened. When a cable from the British ambassador describing Mutharika as "autocratic and intolerant of criticism" was leaked, he expelled the British ambassador. Britain responded by freezing aid worth $550 million over four years. When police in mid-2011 killed 20 antigovernment protestors, other aid donors withdrew their support, including most significantly the United States. Mutharika told the donors they could go to hell. To compound matters, tobacco sales, which usually accounted for 60 percent of foreign currency revenues, plunged on diminishing international demand and the decreasing quality of the local product, which had been hurt by a persistive drought.

By late 2011, Malawi was experiencing a full-blown foreign currency crisis. The International Monetary Fund urged Mutharika to devalue the kwacha, Malawi's currency, to spur tobacco and tea exports. The kwacha was pegged to the U.S. dollar at 170 kwacha to the dollar. The IMF wanted Malawi to adopt an exchange rate of 280 kwacha to the dollar, which was closer to the black market exchange rate. Mutharika refused, arguing that this would cause price inflation and hurt Malawi's poor. He also refused to meet with an IMF delegation, saying that the delegates were "too junior." The IMF put a $79 million loan program it had with Malawi on hold, further exacerbating the foreign currency crisis. Malawi was in a tailspin.

In early April 2012, Mutharika had a massive heart attack. He was rushed to the hospital in the capital Lilongwe, but ironically, the medicines that he needed were out of stock—the hospital lacked the foreign currency to buy them! Mutharika died. Despite considerable opposition from Mutharika supporters who wanted his brother to succeed him, Joyce Banda, the vice president, was sworn in as president. Although no one has stated this publicly, it seems clear that intense diplomatic pressure from the United Kingdom and United States persuaded Mutharika's supporters to relent. Once in power, Banda announced that Malawi would devalue the kwacha by 40 percent. For its part, the IMF unblocked its loan program, while foreign donors, including the UK and United States, stated that they would resume their programs.[22]

Case Discussion Questions

1. What were the causes of Malawi's currency troubles?
2. Why did Mutharika resist IMF calls for currency devaluation? If he had lived and remained in power, what do you think would have happened to the economy of Malawi assuming that he did not change his position?
3. Now that Malawi's currency has been devalued, what do you think the economic consequences will be? Is this good for the economy?

Endnotes

1. Charles Forelle, "In European Crisis, Iceland Emerges as an Island of Recovery," *The Wall Street Journal,* May 19, 2012, pp. A1, A10; "Coming in from the Cold," *The Economist,* December 16, 2010; Charles Duxbury, "Europe Gets Cold Shoulder in Iceland," *The Wall Street Journal,* April 26, 2012; and "Iceland," *The World Factbook 2013* (Washington, DC: Central Intelligence Agency, 2013).
2. The argument goes back to eighteenth-century philosopher David Hume. See D. Hume, "On the Balance of Trade," reprinted in *The Gold Standard in Theory and in History,* ed. B. Eichengreen (London: Methuen, 1985).
3. R. Solomon, *The International Monetary System, 1945–1981* (New York: Harper & Row, 1982).
4. International Monetary Fund, *World Economic Outlook, 2005* (Washington, DC: IMF, May 2005).
5. For an extended discussion of the dollar exchange rate in the 1980s, see B. D. Pauls, "US Exchange Rate Policy: Bretton Woods to the Present," *Federal Reserve Bulletin,* November 1990, pp. 891–908.
6. R. Miller, "Why the Dollar Is Giving Way," *BusinessWeek,* December 6, 2004, pp. 36–37.

7. "Recycling the Petrodollars; Oil Producers' Surpluses," *The Economist,* November 12, 2005, pp. 101–02; S. Johnson, "Dollar's Rise Aided by OPEC Holdings," *Financial Times,* December 5, 2005, p. 17; and "The Petrodollar Puzzle," *The Economist,* June 9, 2007, p. 86.

8. For a feel for the issues contained in this debate, see P. Krugman, *Has the Adjustment Process Worked?* (Washington, DC: Institute for International Economics, 1991); "Time to Tether Currencies," *The Economist,* January 6, 1990, pp. 15–16; P. R. Krugman and M. Obstfeld, *International Economics: Theory and Policy* (New York: HarperCollins, 1994); J. Shelton, *Money Meltdown* (New York: Free Press, 1994); and S. Edwards, "Exchange Rates and the Political Economy of Macroeconomic Discipline," *American Economic Review* 86, no. 2 (May 1996), pp. 159–63.

9. The argument is made by several prominent economists, particularly Stanford's Robert McKinnon. See R. McKinnon, "An International Standard for Monetary Stabilization," *Policy Analyses in International Economics* 8 (1984). The details of this argument are beyond the scope of this book. For a relatively accessible exposition, see P. Krugman, *The Age of Diminished Expectations* (Cambridge, MA: MIT Press, 1990).

10. A. R. Ghosh and A. M. Gulde, "Does the Exchange Rate Regime Matter for Inflation and Growth?" *Economic Issues,* no. 2 (1997).

11. "The ABC of Currency Boards," *The Economist,* November 1, 1997, p. 80.

12. P. Carroll and C. Torres, "Mexico Unveils Program of Harsh Fiscal Medicine," *The Wall Street Journal,* March 10, 1995, pp. A1, A6; and "Putting Mexico Together Again," *The Economist,* February 4, 1995, p. 65.

13. International Monetary Fund, *World Economic Outlook, 1998* (Washington, DC: IMF, 1998).

14. Ibid.

15. T. S. Shorrock, "Korea Starts Overhaul; IMF Aid Hits $55 Billion," *Journal of Commerce,* December 8, 1997, p. 3A.

16. See J. Sachs, "Economic Transition and Exchange Rate Regime," *American Economic Review* 86, no. 92 (May 1996), pp. 147–52; and J. Sachs, "Power unto Itself," *Financial Times,* December 11, 1997, p. 11.

17. Sachs, "Power unto Itself."

18. Martin Wolf, "Same Old IMF Medicine," *Financial Times,* December 9, 1997, p. 12.

19. Sachs, "Power unto Itself."

20. "New Fund, Old Fundamentals," *The Economist,* May 2, 2009, p. 78.

21. D. Michaels, "Airbus Deliveries Top Boeing's; but Several Obstacles Remain," *The Wall Street Journal,* January 16, 2004, p. A9; J. L. Gerondeau, "Airbus Eyes U.S. Suppliers as Euro Gains," *Seattle Times,* February 21, 2004, p. C4; "Euro's Gains Create Worries in Europe," *Houston Chronicle.com,* January 13, 2004, p. 3; and K. Done, "Soft Dollar and A380 Hitches Lead to EADS Losses," *Financial Times,* November 9, 2006, p. 32.

22. P. McGroarty, "Currency Woes Curb Business in Malawi," *The Wall Street Journal,* April 4, 2012; P. McGroarty, "Malawi Hopes New Leader Spurs Recovery," *The Wall Street Journal,* April 8, 2012; J. Herskovitz, "Malawi Paid Price for Ego of Economist in Chief," Reuters, April 16, 2012; and A. R. Martinez and F. Jomo, "Malawi to Devalue Kwacha 40% to Unlock Aid," *Bloomberg BusinessWeek,* April 27, 2012.

Chapter 12
The Global Capital Market

LEARNING OBJECTIVES

After reading this chapter, you will be able to:

LO12-1 Describe the benefits of the global capital market.

LO12-2 Identify why the global capital market has grown so rapidly.

LO12-3 Understand the risks associated with the globalization of capital markets.

LO12-4 Compare and contrast the benefits and risks associated with the Eurocurrency market, the global bond market, and the global equity market.

LO12-5 Understand how foreign exchange risks affect the cost of capital.

DECLINING CROSS-BORDER CAPITAL FLOWS: RETREAT OR RESET?

Opening Case

For decades cross-border capital flows—including lending, foreign direct investment flows, and purchases of equities and bonds—advanced relentlessly, reflecting the increasing integration of national capital markets into one single massive global system. Cross-border capital flows surged from $0.5 trillion in 1980 to a peak of $11.8 trillion in 2007; and then they collapsed. By 2012 cross-border capital flows had retreated to $4.6 trillion, 60 percent below their former peak. The global capital market, it seemed, was in retreat.

To understand why, we have to go back to 2008, when a major crisis swept through the global capital market that very nearly froze the financial pipes that lubricate the wheels of the global economy. Financial institutions and corporations around the world routinely lend and borrow trillions of dollars between themselves. Most banks and corporations issue *unsecured* notes known as *commercial paper* with a fixed maturity of between 1 and 270 days. This is a way for those firms to get access to cash to meet short-term obligations, such as meeting payroll and paying suppliers. Because the notes are unsecured, and not backed by any specific assets, only banks and corporations with excellent credit ratings are able to sell their commercial paper at a reasonable price. This price is set with reference to the London Interbank Offered Rate (LIBOR). The LIBOR is the rate at which banks lend to each other. In normal times, the LIBOR rate is very close to the rate charged by national central banks, such as the U.S. Federal Reserve for the dollar.

Early in 2008 banks in several countries had started to run into trouble as it became clear that the value of the mortgage-backed securities that they held was collapsing. This was due to a fall in housing prices, and rising default rates on mortgages, most notably in the United States and Great Britain, where lenders had written increasingly risky mortgages over the preceding few years. These mortgages were bundled into securities and then sold to other financial institutions. Also, many institutions held complex derivatives, the value of which was tied to the underlying value of mortgage-backed securities. Now these institutions were facing large write-offs on their portfolios of mortgage-backed securities and the associated derivatives. One of these institutions, Lehman Brothers, had taken aggressive positions in the market for mortgage-backed securities. In September 2008 the firm collapsed into bankruptcy after the U.S. government decided not to step in and save the company.

However, the bankruptcy of Lehman sent shock waves through the global financial markets. In effect, the U.S. government had stated it was prepared to let large financial institutions fail. Immediately, banks reduced their short-term loans. They did this for two reasons. First, they felt a need to hoard cash because they no longer knew the value of the mortgage-backed securities they held on their own balance sheets. Second, they were afraid to lend to other banks because those banks might fail and they might not get their money back.

As a result, LIBOR rates quickly spiked. The dollar rate, for example, had been 0.2 percent above the rate on three-month U.S. Treasury bills in 2007, which is a normal spread. However, the spread increased to 3.3 percent by late 2008, raising the cost of short-term borrowing some 16-fold. Many corporations found that they could not raise capital at a reasonable price. Money market funds, which in normal times are large buyers of commercial paper, fled to ultra-safe assets, such as U.S. Treasury bills. This pushed the yield on three-month Treasury bills down to historic lows, and also led to a sharp rise in the value of the U.S. dollar. In essence, the financial plumbing of the global economy was freezing up. If nothing was done about it, many firms could become insolvent and a wave of bankruptcies could sweep around the globe, plunging the world into a serious recession, or even a depression.

At this point several national governments stepped into the breach. The U.S. Federal Reserve entered the commercial paper market, setting up a fund to purchase commercial paper at rates close to the rates for U.S. Treasury bills. Central banks in Japan, Great Britain, and the European Union took similar action. Once participants in the global capital markets saw that national governments were willing to enter the commercial paper market, they too started to ease their lending restrictions, and LIBOR rates started to fall again. The U.S. government established the Troubled Asset Relief Program (TARP), allowing the U.S. Treasury to purchase or insure up to $700 billion in "troubled assets." Under TARP the government began to inject capital into troubled banks by purchasing assets from them that were difficult to value, such as mortgage-backed securities. This signaled there would be no more bankruptcies such as Lehman's. This too helped unfreeze the market for commercial paper. A major crisis had been adverted, but only just. Although the $700 billion price tag for TARP stunned people, most of the money lent to banks under TARP was quickly paid back with interest, and by late 2012 estimates suggest that the total cost to the taxpayer would be close to $24 billion

Five years after the crisis hit, the global capital market has still not fully recovered from its 2007 peak. Does this signal a retreat from the globalization of capital, or merely a reset? Most observers believe the latter is the case. Since 2008 the world economy has grown slowly, and economic troubles persist in many regions, particularly Europe, where several national governments are burdened with unsustainably high levels of sovereign debt that limits their ability to deal with persistently slow growth and high unemployment. Notwithstanding this, the world economy continues to become more integrated, propelled by stronger growth in developing nations, and as this process unfolds, global capital markets will inevitably start to expand again to support cross-border trade in goods and services, as well as cross-border investments.[1]

INTRODUCTION

The opening case illustrates just how interconnected capital markets have become in our global age. Banks and corporations borrow money to meet their short-term needs by issuing commercial paper. The market for commercial paper is a truly global capital market with interest rates set by the London Interbank Offered Rate (LIBOR) and market participants from all over the world entering into exchanges with each other. Its efficient operation is vital for the functioning of the global economy. Without it, banks will stop lending, corporations will not be able to get access to the working capital they need to pay their bills, business will contract, payroll may not be meet, suppliers may not be paid, and international trade will stall.

This chapter looks at the global market for capital. We begin by studying the benefits associated with the globalization of capital markets. This is followed by a more detailed look at the growth of the international capital market and the macroeconomic risks associated with such growth. Next, we review three important segments of the global capital market: the Eurocurrency market, the international bond market, and the international equity market. As usual, we close the chapter by pointing out some of the implications for the practice of international business.

BENEFITS OF THE GLOBAL CAPITAL MARKET　　LO12-1

Although this section is about the global capital market, it opens by discussing the functions of a generic capital market. Then we look at the limitations of domestic capital markets and discuss the benefits of using global capital markets.

Functions of a Generic Capital Market

Capital markets bring together those who want to invest money and those who want to borrow money (see Figure 12.1). Those who want to invest money include corporations with surplus cash, individuals, and nonbank financial institutions (e.g., pension funds, insurance companies). Those who want to borrow money include individuals, companies, and governments. Between these two groups are the

Figure 12.1 *The Main Players in the Generic Capital Market*

market makers. Market makers are the financial service companies that connect investors and borrowers, either directly or indirectly. They include commercial banks (e.g., Citi, U.S. Bank) and investment banks (e.g., Goldman Sachs).

Commercial banks perform an indirect connection function. They take cash deposits from corporations and individuals and pay them a rate of interest in return. They then lend that money to borrowers at a higher rate of interest, making a profit from the difference in interest rates (commonly referred to as the *interest rate spread*). Investment banks perform a direct connection function. They bring investors and borrowers together and charge commissions for doing so. For example, Goldman Sachs may act as a stockbroker for an individual who wants to invest some money. Its personnel will advise her as to the most attractive purchases and buy stock on her behalf, charging a fee for the service.

Capital market loans to corporations are either equity loans or debt loans. An equity loan is made when a corporation sells stock to investors. The money the corporation receives in return for its stock can be used to purchase plants and equipment, fund R&D projects, pay wages, and so on. A share of stock gives its holder a claim to a firm's profit stream. Ultimately, the corporation honors this claim by paying dividends to the stockholders (although many fast-growing young corporations do not start to issue dividends until the business has matured and growth rate slows). The amount of the dividends is not fixed in advance. Rather, it is determined by management based on how much profit the corporation is making. Investors purchase stock both for their dividend yield and in anticipation of gains in the price of the stock, which in theory reflects future dividend yields. Stock prices increase when a corporation is projected to have greater earnings in the future, which increases the probability that it will raise future dividend payments.

A debt loan requires the corporation to repay a predetermined portion of the loan amount (the sum of the principal plus the specified interest) at regular intervals regardless of how much profit it is making. Management has no discretion as to the amount it will pay investors. Debt loans include cash loans from banks and funds raised from the sale of corporate bonds to investors. When an investor purchases a corporate bond, he purchases the right to receive a specified fixed stream of income from the corporation for a specified number of years (i.e., until the bond maturity date). The maturity period of debt loans vary from the very long term, such as 20 years, to extremely short-term loans, including those with a maturity of just one day.

Attractions of the Global Capital Market

A global capital market benefits both borrowers and investors. It benefits borrowers by increasing the supply of funds available for borrowing and by lowering the cost of capital. It benefits investors by providing a wider range of investment opportunities, thereby allowing them to build portfolios of international investments that diversify their risks.

The Borrower's Perspective: Lower Cost of Capital

In a purely domestic capital market, the pool of investors is limited to residents of the country. This places an upper limit on the supply of funds available to borrowers. In other words, the liquidity of the market is limited. A global capital market, with its much larger pool of investors, provides a larger supply of funds for borrowers to draw on.

Perhaps the most important drawback of the limited liquidity of a purely domestic capital market is that the cost of capital tends to be higher than it is in a global market. The cost of capital is the price of borrowing money, which is the rate of return that borrowers must pay investors. This is the interest rate on debt loans and the dividend yield and expected capital gains on equity loans. In a purely domestic market, the limited pool of investors implies that borrowers must pay more to persuade investors to lend them their money. The larger pool of investors in an international market implies that borrowers will be able to pay less.

The argument is illustrated in Figure 12.2, using Deutsche Telekom as an example (see the Management Focus for details). Deutsche Telekom raised over $13 billion by simultaneously offering shares for sales in Frankfurt, New York, London, and Tokyo. The vertical axis in Figure 12.2 is the cost of capital (the price of borrowing money), and the horizontal axis is the amount of money available at varying interest rates. The Deutsche Telekom demand curve for borrowings is DD. Note that the Deutsche Telekom demand for funds varies with the cost of capital; the lower the cost of capital, the more money Deutsche Telekom will borrow. (Money is just like anything else; the lower its price, the more of it people can afford.) The supply curve of funds available in the German capital market is SS_G, and the funds available in the global capital market is represented by SS_I. Note that Deutsche Telekom can borrow more funds more cheaply on the global capital market. As Figure 12.2 illustrates, the greater pool of resources in the global capital market—the greater liquidity—both lowers the cost of capital and increases the amount Deutsche Telekom can borrow. Thus, the advantage of a global capital market to borrowers is that it lowers the cost of capital.

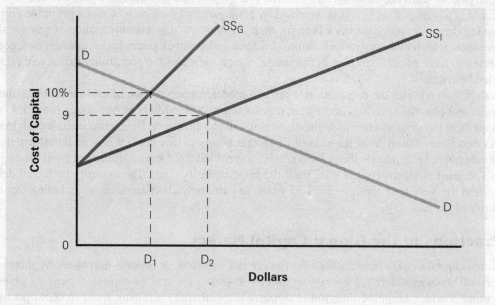

Figure 12.2 *Market Liquidity and the Cost of Capital*

Problems of limited liquidity are not restricted to less developed nations, which naturally tend to have smaller domestic capital markets. In recent decades, even very large enterprises based in some of the world's most advanced industrialized nations have tapped the international capital markets in their search for greater liquidity and a lower cost of capital, such as Germany's Daimler and Deutsche Telekom.[2]

The Investor's Perspective: Portfolio Diversification

By using the global capital market, investors have a much wider range of investment opportunities than in a purely domestic capital market. The most significant consequence of this choice is that investors can diversify their portfolios internationally, thereby reducing their risk to less than what could be

Deutsche Telekom Taps the Global Capital Market

Based in the world's third-largest industrial economy, Deutsche Telekom is one of the world's largest telephone companies. Until late 1996, the German government wholly owned the company. However, in the mid-1990s, the German government formulated plans to privatize the utility, selling shares to the public. The privatization effort was driven by two factors: (1) a realization that state-owned enterprises tend to be inherently inefficient and (2) the impending deregulation of the European Union telecommunications industry in 1998, which promised to expose Deutsche Telekom to foreign competition for the first time. Deutsche Telekom realized that, to become more competitive, it needed massive investments in new telecommunications infrastructure, including fiber optics and wireless, lest it start losing share in its home market to more efficient competitors such as AT&T and British Telecom after 1998. Financing such investments from state sources would have been difficult even under the best of circumstances and almost impossible in the late 1990s, when the German government was trying to limit its budget deficit to meet the criteria for membership in the European monetary union. With the active encouragement of the government, Deutsche Telekom hoped to finance its investments in capital equipment through the sale of shares to the public.

From a financial perspective, the privatization looked anything but easy. In 1996, Deutsche Telekom was valued at about $60 billion. If it maintained this valuation as a private company, it would dwarf all others listed on the German stock market. However, many analysts doubted there was anything close to $60 billion available in Germany for investment in Deutsche Telekom stock. One problem was that there was no tradition of retail stock investing in Germany. In 1996, only 1 in 20 German citizens owned shares, compared with 1 in every 4 or 5 in the United States and Great Britain. This lack of retail interest in stock ownership makes for a relatively illiquid stock market. Nor did banks, the traditional investors in company stocks in Germany, seem enthused about underwriting such a massive privatization effort. A further problem was that a wave of privatizations was already sweeping through Germany and the rest of Europe, so Deutsche Telekom would have to compete with many other state-owned enterprises for investors' attention. Given these factors, probably the only way that Deutsche Telekom could raise $60 billion through the German capital market would have been by promising investors a dividend yield that would raise the company's cost of capital above levels that could be serviced profitably.

Deutsche Telekom managers concluded they had to privatize the company in stages and sell a substantial portion of Deutsche Telekom stock to foreign investors. The company's plans called for an initial public offering (IPO) of 623 million shares of Deutsche Telekom stock, representing 25 percent of the company's total value, for about $18.50 per share. With a total projected value in excess of $13 billion, even this "limited" sale of Deutsche Telekom represented the largest IPO in European history and the second largest in the world after the 1987 sale of shares in Japan's telephone monopoly, NTT, for $15.6 billion. Concluding there was no way the German capital market could absorb even this partial sale of Deutsche Telekom equity, the managers of the company decided to simultaneously list shares and offer them for sale in Frankfurt (where the German stock exchange is located), New York, and Tokyo, attracting investors from all over the world. The IPO was successfully executed in November 1996 and raised $13.3 billion for the company.[3]

achieved in a purely domestic capital market. We consider how this works in the case of stock holdings, although the same argument could be made for bond holdings.

Consider an investor who buys stock in a biotech firm that has not yet produced a new product. Imagine the price of the stock is very volatile—investors are buying and selling the stock in large numbers in response to information about the firm's prospects. Such stocks are risky investments; investors may win big if the firm produces a marketable product; but investors may also lose all their money if the firm fails to come up with a product that sells. Investors can guard against the risk associated with holding this stock by buying other firms' stocks, particularly those weakly or negatively correlated with the biotech stock. By holding a variety of stocks in a diversified portfolio, the losses incurred when some stocks fail to live up to their promise are offset by the gains enjoyed when other stocks exceed their promise.

As an investor increases the number of stocks in her portfolio, the portfolio's risk declines. At first this decline is rapid. Soon, however, the rate of decline falls off and asymptotically approaches the systematic risk of the market. Systematic risk refers to movements in a stock portfolio's value that are attributable to macroeconomic forces affecting all firms in an economy, rather than factors specific to an individual firm. The systematic risk is the level of nondiversifiable risk in an economy. Figure 12.3 illustrates this relationship for the United States using data from a classic study by Solnik.[4] His data suggested that a fully diversified U.S. portfolio is only about 27 percent as risky as a typical individual stock.

By diversifying a portfolio internationally, an investor can reduce the level of risk even further because the movements of stock market prices across countries are not perfectly correlated. For example, one study looked at the correlation between three stock market indexes. The Standard & Poor's 500 (S&P 500) summarized the movement of large U.S. stocks. The Morgan Stanley Capital International Europe, Australia, and Far East Index (EAFE) summarized stock market movements in other developed nations. The third index, the International Finance Corporation Global Emerging Markets Index (IFC), summarized stock market movements in less developed "emerging economies." From 1981 to 1994, the correlation between the S&P 500 and EAFE indexes was 0.45, suggesting they moved together only about 20 percent of the time (i.e., $0.45 \times 0.45 = 0.2025$). The correlation between the S&P 500 and IFC indexes was even lower at 0.32, suggesting they moved together only a little over 10 percent of the time.[5] Other studies have confirmed that despite casual observations, different national stock markets appear to be only moderately correlated. One study found that between 1972 and 2000 the average pair-wise correlation between the world's four largest equity markets in the United States, United Kingdom, Germany, and Japan was 0.475, suggesting that these markets moved in tandem only about 22 percent of the time ($0.475 \times 0.472 = 0.22$ or 22 percent of shared variance).[6]

The relatively low correlation between the movement of stock markets in different countries reflects two basic factors. First, countries pursue different macroeconomic policies and face different economic conditions, so their stock markets respond to different forces and can move in different ways. For example, in 1997, the stock markets of several Asian countries, including South Korea, Malaysia, Indonesia, and Thailand, lost more than 50 percent of their value in response to the Asian financial crisis, while at the same time the S&P 500 increased in value by over 20 percent. Second, different stock markets are still somewhat segmented from each other by capital controls—that is, by restrictions on cross-border capital flows (although as noted earlier, such restrictions are declining rapidly). The most common restrictions include limits on the amount of a firm's stock that a foreigner can own and limits on the ability of a country's citizens to invest their money outside that country. For example, until recently it was difficult for foreigners to own more than 30 percent of the equity of South Korean enterprises. Tight restrictions on capital flows make it very hard for Chinese citizens to take money out of their country and invest it in foreign assets. Such barriers to cross-border capital flows limit the

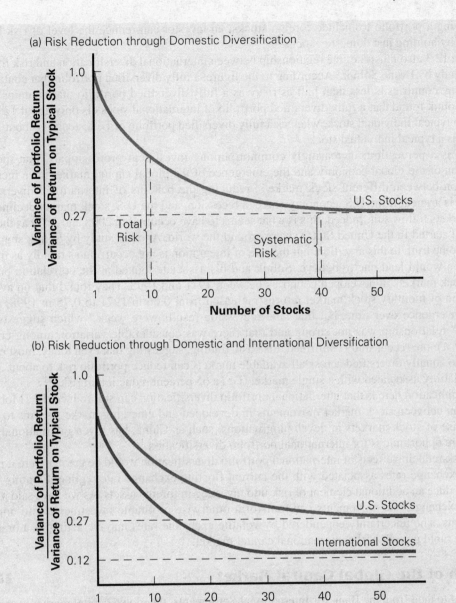

(a) Risk Reduction through Domestic Diversification

(b) Risk Reduction through Domestic and International Diversification

Figure 12.3 *Risk Reduction through Portfolio Diversification*

Source: B. Solnik, "Why Not Diversify Internationally Rather Than Domestically?" Adapted with permission from *Financial Analysts Journal*, July–August 1974, p. 17. Copyright 1974. Financial Analysts Federation, Charlottesville, VA. All rights reserved.

ability of capital to roam the world freely in search of the highest risk-adjusted return. Consequently, at any one time, there may be too much capital invested in some markets and too little in others. This will tend to produce differences in rates of return across stock markets.[7] The implication is that by diversifying a portfolio to include foreign stocks, an investor can reduce the level of risk below that incurred by holding just domestic stocks.

Figure 12.3 also illustrates the relationship between international diversification and risk found in the classic study by Bruno Solnik.[8] According to the figure, a fully diversified portfolio that contains stocks from many countries is less than half as risky as a fully diversified portfolio that contains only U.S. stocks. Solnik found that a fully diversified portfolio of international stocks is only about 12 percent as risky as a typical individual stock, whereas a fully diversified portfolio of U.S. stocks is about 27 percent as risky as a typical individual stock.

There is a perception, increasingly common among investment professionals, that the growing integration of the global economy and the emergence of the global capital market have increased the correlation between different stock markets, reducing the benefits of international diversification.[9] Today, it is argued, if the U.S. economy enters a recession, and the U.S. stock market declines rapidly, other markets follow suit. Indeed, this is what seems to have occurred in 2008 and 2009 as the financial crisis that started in the United States swept around the world. Another study by Solnik suggests there may be some truth to this assertion, but the rate of integration is not occurring as rapidly as the popular perception would lead one to believe. Solnik and his associate looked at the correlation between 15 major stock markets in developed countries between 1971 and 1998. They found that on average, the correlation of monthly stock market returns increased from 0.66 in 1971 to 0.75 in 1998, indicating some convergence over time, but that "the regression results were weak," which suggests that this "average" relationship was not strong and that there was considerable variation among countries.[10] Similarly, a more recent study confirmed this basic finding, suggesting that even today, most of the time a portfolio equally diversified across all available markets can reduce portfolio risk to about 35 percent of the volatility associated with a single market (i.e., a 65 percent reduction in risk).[11]

The implication here is that international portfolio diversification can still reduce risk. Moreover, the correlation between stock market movements in developed and emerging markets seems to be lower, and the rise of stock markets in developing nations, such as China, has given international investors many more opportunities for international portfolio diversification.[12]

The risk-reducing effects of international portfolio diversification would be greater were it not for the volatile exchange rates associated with the current floating exchange rate regime. Floating exchange rates introduce an additional element of risk into investing in foreign assets. As we have said repeatedly, adverse exchange rate movements can transform otherwise profitable investments into unprofitable investments. The uncertainty engendered by volatile exchange rates may be acting as a brake on the otherwise rapid growth of the international capital market.

Growth of the Global Capital Market

According to data from the Bank for International Settlements, the global capital market is growing at a rapid pace.[13] By late 2012 the stock of cross-border bank loans stood at $33,913 billion, compared to $7,859 billion in 2000 and $3,600 billion in 1990. There was $21,979 billion in outstanding international bonds in late 2012, up from $5,908 billion in 2000 and $3,515 billion in 1997. What factors allowed the international capital market to boom in the 1980s, 1990s, and 2000s? There seem to be two answers— advances in information technology and deregulation by governments.

Information Technology

Financial services is an information-intensive industry. It draws on large volumes of information about markets, risks, exchange rates, interest rates, creditworthiness, and so on. It uses this information to make decisions about what to invest where, how much to charge borrowers, how much interest to pay to depositors, and the value and riskiness of a range of financial assets including corporate bonds, stocks, government securities, and currencies.

Because of this information intensity, the financial services industry has been revolutionized more than any other industry by advances in information technology since the 1970s. The growth of international communications technology has facilitated instantaneous communication between any two points on the globe. At the same time, rapid advances in data processing capabilities have allowed market makers to absorb and process large volumes of information from around the world. According to one study, because of these technological developments, the real cost of recording, transmitting, and processing information fell by 95 percent between 1964 and 1990.[14] With the rapid rise of the Internet and the massive increase in computing power that we have seen since 1990, it seems likely that the cost of recording, transmitting, and processing information has fallen by a similar amount since 1990 and is now trivial.

Such developments have facilitated the emergence of an integrated international capital market. It is now technologically possible for financial services companies to engage in 24-hour-a-day trading, whether it is in stocks, bonds, foreign exchange, or any other financial asset. Due to advances in communications and data processing technology, the international capital market never sleeps. San Francisco closes one hour before Tokyo opens, but during this period trading continues in New Zealand.

The integration facilitated by technology has a dark side.[15] "Shocks" that occur in one financial center now spread around the globe very quickly. As discussed in the opening case, the financial crisis that began in the United States in 2008 quickly spread around the globe. However, most market participants would argue that the benefits of an integrated global capital market far outweigh any potential costs. Moreover, despite the fact that shocks in national financial markets do seem to spill over into other markets, on average the correlation between movements in national equity markets remains relatively low, suggesting that such shocks may have a relatively moderate long-term impact outside their home market.[16]

Deregulation

In country after country, financial services has historically been the most tightly regulated of all industries. Governments around the world have traditionally kept other countries' financial service firms from entering their capital markets. In some cases, they have also restricted the overseas expansion of their domestic financial services firms. In many countries, the law has also segmented the domestic financial services industry. In the United States, for example, until the late 1990s commercial banks were prohibited from performing the functions of investment banks, and vice versa. Historically, many countries have limited the ability of foreign investors to purchase significant equity positions in domestic companies. They have also limited the amount of foreign investment that their citizens could undertake. In the 1970s, for example, capital controls made it very difficult for a British investor to purchase American stocks and bonds.

Many of these restrictions have been crumbling since the early 1980s. In part, this has been a response to the development of the Eurocurrency market, which from the beginning was outside national control. (This is explained later in the chapter.) It has also been a response to pressure from financial services companies, which have long wanted to operate in a less regulated environment. Increasing acceptance of the free market ideology associated with an individualistic political philosophy also has a lot to do with the global trend toward the deregulation of financial markets (see Chapter 2). Whatever the reason, deregulation in a number of key countries has undoubtedly facilitated the growth of the international capital market.

The trend began in the United States in the late 1970s and early 80s with a series of changes that allowed foreign banks to enter the U.S. capital market and domestic banks to expand their operations overseas. In Great Britain, the so-called Big Bang of October 1986 removed barriers that had existed between banks and stockbrokers and allowed foreign financial service companies to enter the British stock market. Restrictions on the entry of foreign securities houses have been relaxed in Japan, and Japanese banks are now allowed to open international banking facilities. In France, the "Little Bang" of 1987 opened the French stock market to outsiders and to foreign and domestic banks. In Germany, foreign banks are now allowed to lend and manage foreign euro issues, subject to reciprocity agreements.[17] All of this has enabled financial services companies to transform themselves from primarily domestic companies into global operations with major offices around the world—a prerequisite for the development of a truly international capital market. As we saw in Chapter 8, in late 1997 the World Trade Organization brokered a deal that removed many of the restrictions on cross-border trade in financial services. This deal facilitated further growth in the size of the global capital market.

In addition to the deregulation of the financial services industry, many countries beginning in the 1970s started to dismantle capital controls, loosening both restrictions on inward investment by foreigners and outward investment by their own citizens and corporations. By the 1980s, this trend spread from developed nations to the emerging economies of the world as countries across Latin America, Asia, and eastern Europe started to dismantle decades-old restrictions on capital flows.

The trends toward deregulation of financial services and removal of capital controls were still firmly in place until 2008. However, the global financial crisis of 2008–2009 prompted many to wonder if deregulation had gone too far, and it focused attention on the need for new regulations to govern certain sectors of the financial services industry, including the hedge funds, which operate largely outside of existing regulatory boundaries. (**Hedge funds** are private investment funds that position themselves to make "long bets" on assets that they think will increase in value and "short bets" on assets that they think will decline in value.) Given the benefits associated with the globalization of capital, notwithstanding the current contraction, over the long term the growth of the global capital market can be expected to continue. While most commentators see this as a positive development, some believe the globalization of capital holds inherent serious risks.

Global Capital Market Risks

Some analysts are concerned that due to deregulation and reduced controls on cross-border capital flows, individual nations are becoming more vulnerable to speculative capital flows. They see this as having a destabilizing effect on national economies.[18] Harvard economist Martin Feldstein, for example, has argued that most of the capital that moves internationally is pursuing temporary gains, and it shifts in and out of countries as quickly as conditions change.[19] He distinguishes between this short-term capital, or "hot money," and "patient money" that would support long-term cross-border capital flows. To Feldstein, patient money is still relatively rare, primarily because although capital is free to move internationally, its owners and managers still prefer to keep most of it at home. Feldstein supports his arguments with statistics that demonstrate that although vast amounts of money flows through the foreign exchange markets every day, "when the dust settles, most of the savings done in each country stays in that country."[20] Feldstein argues that the lack of patient money is due to the relative paucity of information that investors have about foreign investments. In his view, if investors had better information about foreign assets, the global capital market would work more efficiently and be less subject to short-term speculative capital flows. Feldstein claims that Mexico's economic problems in the mid-1990s were the result of too much hot money flowing in and out of the country and too little patient money. This example is reviewed in detail in the accompanying Country Focus.

Did the Global Capital Markets Fail Mexico?

In early 1994, soon after passage of the North American Free Trade Agreement (NAFTA), Mexico was widely admired among the international community as a shining example of a developing country with a bright economic future. Since the late 1980s, the Mexican government had pursued sound monetary, budget, tax, and trade policies. By historical standards, inflation was low, the country was experiencing solid economic growth, and exports were booming. This robust picture attracted capital from foreign investors; between 1991 and 1993, foreigners invested more than $75 billion in the Mexican economy, more than in any other developing nation.

If there was a blot on Mexico's economic report card, it was the country's growing current account (trade) deficit. Mexican exports were booming but so were its imports. In the 1989–1990 period, the current account deficit was equivalent to about 3 percent of Mexico's gross domestic product. In 1991 it increased to 5 percent, and by 1994 it was running at an annual rate of over 6 percent. Bad as this might seem, it is not unsustainable and should not bring an economy crashing down. The United States has been running a current account deficit for decades with apparently little in the way of ill effects. A current account deficit will not be a problem for a country as long as foreign investors take the money they earn from trade with that country and reinvest it within the country. This has been the case in the United States for years, and during the early 1990s, it was occurring in Mexico too. Thus, companies such as Ford took the pesos they earned from exports to Mexico and reinvested those funds in productive capacity in Mexico, building auto plants to serve the future needs of the Mexican market and to export elsewhere.

Unfortunately for Mexico, much of the $25 billion annual inflow of capital it received during the early 1990s was not the kind of patient long-term money that Ford was putting into Mexico. Rather, according to economist Martin Feldstein, much of the inflow was short-term capital that could flee if economic conditions changed for the worse. This is what seems to have occurred. In February 1994, the U.S. Federal Reserve began to increase U.S. interest rates. This led to a rapid fall in U.S. bond prices. At the same time, the yen began to appreciate sharply against the U.S. dollar. These events resulted in large losses for many managers of short-term capital, such as hedge fund managers and banks, which had been betting on exactly the opposite happening. Many hedge funds had been betting that interest rates would fall, bond prices would rise, and the dollar would appreciate against the yen.

Faced with large losses, money managers tried to reduce the riskiness of their portfolios by pulling out of risky situations. About the same time, events took a turn for the worse in Mexico. An armed uprising in the southern state of Chiapas, the assassination of the leading candidate in the presidential election campaign, and an accelerating inflation rate all helped produce a feeling that Mexican investments were riskier than had been assumed. Money managers began to pull many of their short-term investments out of the country.

As hot money flowed out, the Mexican government realized it could not continue to count on capital inflows to finance its current account deficit. The government had assumed the inflow was mainly composed of patient, long-term money. In reality, much of it appeared to be short-term money. As money flowed out of Mexico, the Mexican government had to commit more foreign reserves to defending the value of the peso against the U.S. dollar, which was pegged at 3.5 to the dollar. Currency speculators entered the picture and began to bet against the Mexican government by selling pesos short. Events came to a head in December 1994 when the Mexican government was essentially forced by capital flows to abandon its support for the peso. Over the next month, the peso lost 40 percent of its value against the dollar, the government was forced to introduce an economic austerity program, and the Mexican economic boom came to an abrupt end.

According to Martin Feldstein, the Mexican economy was brought down not by currency speculation on the foreign exchange market but by a lack of long-term patient money. He argued that Mexico offered, and still offers, many attractive long-term investment opportunities, but because of the lack of information on long-term investment opportunities in Mexico, most of the capital flowing into the country from 1991 to 1993 was short-term, speculative money, the flow of which could quickly be reversed. If foreign investors had better information, Feldstein argued, Mexico should have been able to finance its current account deficit from inward capital flows because patient capital would naturally gravitate toward attractive Mexican investment opportunities.[22]

A lack of information about the fundamental quality of foreign investments may encourage speculative flows in the global capital market. Faced with a lack of quality information, investors may react to dramatic news events in foreign nations and pull their money out too quickly. Despite advances in information technology, it is still difficult for investors to get access to the same quantity and quality of information about foreign investment opportunities that they can get about domestic investment opportunities. This information gap is exacerbated by different accounting conventions in different countries, which makes the direct comparison of cross-border investment opportunities difficult for all but the most sophisticated investor (see Chapter 19 for details). For example, historically German accounting principles have been different from those found in the United States and presented quite a different picture of the health of a company. Thus, when the Germany company Daimler-Benz translated its German financial accounts into U.S.-style accounts in 1993, as it had to do to be listed on the New York Stock Exchange, it found that while it had made a profit of $97 million under German rules, under U.S. rules it had lost $548 million![21] However, in the 2000s there has been rapid movement toward harmonization of different national accounting standards, which is certainly improving the quality of information available to investors (see Chapter 20 for details).

Given the problems created by differences in the quantity and quality of information, many investors have yet to venture into the world of cross-border investing, and those that do are prone to reverse their decision on the basis of limited (and perhaps inaccurate) information. However, if the international capital market continues to grow, financial intermediaries likely will increasingly provide quality information about foreign investment opportunities. Better information should increase the sophistication of investment decisions and reduce the frequency and size of speculative capital flows. Although concerns about the volume of "hot money" sloshing around in the global capital market increased as a result of the Asian financial crisis, IMF research suggests there has not been an increase in the volatility of financial markets since the 1970s.[23]

THE EUROCURRENCY MARKET

L012-4

A **Eurocurrency** is any currency banked outside of its country of origin. Eurodollars, which account for about two-thirds of all Eurocurrencies, are dollars banked outside the United States. Other important

Eurocurrencies include the Euro-yen, the Euro-pound, and the Euro-euro! The term *Eurocurrency* is actually a misnomer because a Eurocurrency can be created anywhere in the world; the persistent *Euro*-prefix reflects the European origin of the market. The Eurocurrency market has been an important and relatively low-cost source of funds for international businesses.

Genesis and Growth of the Market

The Eurocurrency market was born in the mid-1950s when eastern European holders of dollars, including the former Soviet Union, were afraid to deposit their holdings of dollars in the United States lest they be seized by the U.S. government to settle U.S. residents' claims against business losses resulting from the Communist takeover of eastern Europe.[24] These countries deposited many of their dollar holdings in Europe, particularly in London. Additional dollar deposits came from various western European central banks and from companies that earned dollars by exporting to the United States. These two groups deposited their dollars in London banks, rather than U.S. banks, because they were able to earn a higher rate of interest (which will be explained).

The Eurocurrency market received a major push in 1957 when the British government prohibited British banks from lending British pounds to finance non-British trade, a business that had been very profitable for British banks. British banks began financing the same trade by attracting dollar deposits and lending dollars to companies engaged in international trade and investment. Because of this historical event, London became, and has remained, the leading center of Eurocurrency trading.

The Eurocurrency market received another push in the 1960s when the U.S. government enacted regulations that discouraged U.S. banks from lending to non-U.S. residents. Would-be dollar borrowers outside the United States found it increasingly difficult to borrow dollars in the United States to finance international trade, so they turned to the Eurodollar market to obtain the necessary dollar funds.

The U.S. government changed its policies after the 1973 collapse of the Bretton Woods system (see Chapter 11), removing an important impetus to the growth of the Eurocurrency market. However, another political event, the oil price increases engineered by OPEC in the 1973–74 and 1979–80 periods, gave the market another big shove. As a result of the oil price increases, the Arab members of OPEC accumulated huge amounts of dollars. They were afraid to place their money in U.S. banks or their European branches, lest the U.S. government attempt to confiscate them. (Iranian assets in U.S. banks and their European branches were frozen by President Carter in 1979 after Americans were taken hostage at the U.S. embassy in Tehran; their fear was not unfounded.) Instead, these countries deposited their dollars with banks in London, further increasing the supply of Eurodollars.

Although these various political events contributed to the growth of the Eurocurrency market, they alone were not responsible for it. The market grew because it offered real financial advantages—initially to those who wanted to deposit dollars or borrow dollars and later to those who wanted to deposit and borrow other currencies. We now look at the source of these financial advantages.

Attractions of the Eurocurrency Market

The main factor that makes the Eurocurrency market attractive to both depositors and borrowers is its lack of government regulation. This allows banks to offer higher interest rates on Eurocurrency deposits than on deposits made in the home currency, making Eurocurrency deposits attractive to those who have cash to deposit. The lack of regulation also allows banks to charge borrowers a lower interest rate for Eurocurrency borrowings than for borrowings in the home currency, making Eurocurrency loans attractive for those who want to borrow money. In other words, the spread between the Eurocurrency deposit rate and the Eurocurrency lending rate is less than the spread between the domestic deposit and lending rates (see Figure 12.4). To understand why this is so, we must examine how government regulations raise the costs of domestic banking.

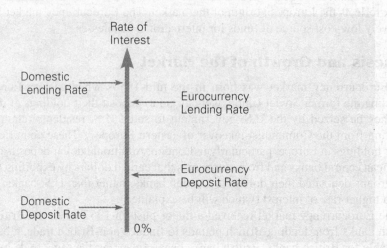

Figure 12.4 *Interest Rate Spreads in Domestic and Eurocurrency Markets*

Domestic currency deposits are regulated in all industrialized countries. Such regulations ensure that banks have enough liquid funds to satisfy demand if large numbers of domestic depositors should suddenly decide to withdraw their money. All countries operate with certain reserve requirements. For example, each time a U.S. bank accepts a deposit in dollars, it must place some fraction of that deposit in a non-interest-bearing account at a Federal Reserve Bank as part of its required reserves. Similarly, each time a British bank accepts a deposit in pounds sterling, it must place a certain fraction of that deposit with the Bank of England.

Banks are given much more freedom in their dealings in foreign currencies, however. For example, the British government does not impose reserve requirement restrictions on deposits of foreign currencies within its borders. Nor are the London branches of U.S. banks subject to U.S. reserve requirement regulations, provided those deposits are payable only outside the United States. This gives Eurobanks a competitive advantage.

For example, suppose a bank based in New York faces a 10 percent reserve requirement. According to this requirement, if the bank receives a $100 deposit, it can lend out no more than $90 of that, and it must place the remaining $10 in a non-interest-bearing account at a Federal Reserve bank. Suppose the bank has annual operating costs of $1 per $100 of deposits and that it charges 10 percent interest on loans. The highest interest the New York bank can offer its depositors and still cover its costs is 8 percent per year. Thus, the bank pays the owner of the $100 deposit (0.08 × $100 =) $8, earns (0.10 × $90 =) $9 on the fraction of the deposit it is allowed to lend, and just covers its operating costs.

In contrast, a Eurobank can offer a higher interest rate on dollar deposits and still cover its costs. The Eurobank, with no reserve requirements regarding dollar deposits, can lend out all of a $100 deposit. Therefore, it can earn 0.10 × $100 = $10 at a loan rate of 10 percent. If the Eurobank has the same operating costs as the New York bank ($1 per $100 deposit), it can pay its depositors an interest rate of 9 percent, a full percentage point higher than that paid by the New York bank, and still cover its costs. That is, it can pay out 0.09 × $100 = $9 to its depositor, receive $10 from the borrower, and be left with $1 to cover operating costs. Alternatively, the Eurobank might pay the depositor 8.5 percent (which is still above the rate paid by the New York bank), charge borrowers 9.5 percent (still less than the New

York bank charges), and cover its operating costs. Thus, the Eurobank has a competitive advantage vis-à-vis the New York bank in both its deposit rate and its loan rate.

Clearly, there are strong financial motivations for companies to use the Eurocurrency market. By doing so, they receive a higher interest rate on deposits and pay less for loans. Given this, the surprising thing is not that the Euromarket has grown rapidly but that it hasn't grown even faster. Why do any depositors hold deposits in their home currency when they could get better yields in the Eurocurrency market?

Drawbacks of the Eurocurrency Market

The Eurocurrency market has two drawbacks. First, when depositors use a regulated banking system, they know that the probability of a bank failure that would cause them to lose their deposits is very low. Regulation maintains the liquidity of the banking system. In an unregulated system such as the Eurocurrency market, the probability of a bank failure that would cause depositors to lose their money is greater (although, in absolute terms, still low). Thus, the lower interest rate received on home-country deposits reflects the costs of insuring against bank failure. Some depositors are more comfortable with the security of such a system and are willing to pay the price.

Second, borrowing funds internationally can expose a company to foreign exchange risk. For example, consider a U.S. company that uses the Eurocurrency market to borrow Euro-pounds—perhaps because it can pay a lower interest rate on Euro-pound loans than on dollar loans. Imagine, however, that the British pound subsequently appreciates against the dollar. This would increase the dollar cost of repaying the Euro-pound loan and thus the company's cost of capital. This possibility can be insured against by using the forward exchange market (as we saw in Chapter 10), but the forward exchange market does not offer perfect insurance. Consequently, many companies borrow funds in their domestic currency to avoid foreign exchange risk, even though the Eurocurrency markets may offer more attractive interest rates.

THE GLOBAL BOND MARKET

The global bond market grew rapidly during the 1980s and 1990s, and has continued to do so in the new century. Bonds are an important means of financing for many companies. The most common kind of bond is a fixed-rate bond. The investor who purchases a fixed-rate bond receives a fixed set of cash payoffs. Each year until the bond matures, the investor gets an interest payment, and then at maturity he gets back the face value of the bond.

International bonds are of two types: foreign bonds and Eurobonds. **Foreign bonds** are sold outside the borrower's country and are denominated in the currency of the country in which they are issued. Thus, when Dow Chemical issues bonds in Japanese yen and sells them in Japan, it is issuing foreign bonds. Many foreign bonds have nicknames; foreign bonds sold in the United States are called Yankee bonds, foreign bonds sold in Japan are Samurai bonds, and foreign bonds sold in Great Britain are bulldogs. Companies will issue international bonds if they believe that it will lower their cost of capital. For example, during the late 1990s and early 2000s many companies issued Samurai bonds in Japan to take advantage of the very low interest rates in Japan. In early 2001, 10-year Japanese government bonds yielded 1.24 percent, compared with 5 percent for comparable U.S. government bonds. Against this background, companies found that they could raise debt at a cheaper rate in Japan than the United States.

Eurobonds are normally underwritten by an international syndicate of banks and placed in countries other than the one in whose currency the bond is denominated. For example, a bond may be issued by a German corporation, denominated in U.S. dollars, and sold to investors outside the United States by an international syndicate of banks. Eurobonds are routinely issued by multinational corporations, large domestic corporations, sovereign governments, and international institutions. They are usually offered simultaneously in several national capital markets, but not in the capital market of the country, nor to residents of the country, in whose currency they are denominated. Historically, Eurobonds accounted for the lion's share of international bond issues, but increasingly they are being eclipsed by foreign bonds.

Attractions of the Eurobond Market

Three features of the Eurobond market make it an appealing alternative to most major domestic bond markets, specifically:

- An absence of regulatory interference.
- Less stringent disclosure requirements than in most domestic bond markets.
- A favorable tax status.

Regulatory Interference

National governments often impose controls on domestic and foreign issuers of bonds denominated in the local currency and sold within their national boundaries. These controls tend to raise the cost of issuing bonds. However, government limitations are generally less stringent for securities denominated in foreign currencies and sold to holders of those foreign currencies. Eurobonds fall outside the regulatory domain of any single nation. As such, they can often be issued at a lower cost to the issuer.

Disclosure Requirements

Eurobond market disclosure requirements tend to be less stringent than those of several national governments. For example, if a firm wishes to issue dollar-denominated bonds within the United States, it must first comply with SEC disclosure requirements. The firm must disclose detailed information about its activities, the salaries and other compensation of its senior executives, stock trades by its senior executives, and the like. In addition, the issuing firm must submit financial accounts that conform to U.S. accounting standards. For non-U.S. firms, redoing their accounts to make them consistent with U.S. standards can be very time-consuming and expensive. Therefore, many firms have found it cheaper to issue Eurobonds, including those denominated in dollars, than to issue dollar-denominated bonds within the United States.

Favorable Tax Status

Before 1984, U.S. corporations issuing Eurobonds were required to withhold for U.S. income tax up to 30 percent of each interest payment to foreigners. This did not encourage foreigners to hold bonds issued by U.S. corporations. Similar tax laws were operational in many countries at that time, and they limited market demand for Eurobonds. U.S. laws were revised in 1984 to exempt from any withholding tax foreign holders of bonds issued by U.S. corporations. As a result, U.S. corporations found it feasible for the first time to sell Eurobonds directly to foreigners. Repeal of the U.S. laws caused other governments—including those of France, Germany, and Japan—to liberalize their tax laws likewise to avoid outflows of capital from their markets. The consequence was an upsurge in demand for Eurobonds from investors who wanted to take advantage of their tax benefits.

THE GLOBAL EQUITY MARKET

Historically substantial regulatory barriers separated national equity markets from each other. Not only was it often difficult to take capital out of a country and invest it elsewhere, but corporations also frequently lacked the ability to list their shares on stock markets outside their home nations. These regulatory barriers made it difficult for a corporation to attract significant equity capital from foreign investors. These barriers tumbled fast during the 1980s and 1990s. The global equity market enabled firms to attract capital from international investors, to list their stock on multiple exchanges, and to raise funds by issuing equity or debt around the world. For example, in 1994, Daimler-Benz, Germany's largest industrial company, raised $300 million by issuing new shares not in Germany but in Singapore.[25] Similarly, in 1996 the German telecommunications provider Deutsche Telekom raised some $13.3 billion by simultaneously listing its shares for sale on stock exchanges in Frankfurt, London, New York, and Tokyo. These German companies elected to raise equity through foreign markets because they reasoned that their domestic capital market was too small to supply the requisite funds at a reasonable cost. To lower their cost of capital, they tapped into the large and highly liquid global capital market.

More recently, many Chinese companies have been raising equity capital through foreign stock issues. In 2010, a record 39 Chinese companies issued stock through the New York Stock Exchange, giving them access to more capital at a lower cost than would have been possible if they had just issued stock in China.[26] Of course, the other side of the coin is that if foreign entities are going to issue stock in New York, London, or another major foreign market, they also have to adhere to the stringent requirements for financial reporting that are common in those markets.

Although we have talked about the growth of the global equity market, strictly speaking there is no international equity market in the sense that there are international currency and bond markets. Rather, many countries have their own domestic equity markets in which corporate stock is traded. The largest of these domestic equity markets are to be found in the United States, Great Britain, and Japan. Although each domestic equity market is still dominated by investors who are citizens of that country and companies incorporated in that country, developments are internationalizing the world equity market. Investors are investing heavily in foreign equity markets to diversify their portfolios. Facilitated by deregulation and advances in information technology, this trend seems to be here to stay.

An interesting consequence of the trend toward international equity investment is the internationalization of corporate ownership. Today it is still generally possible to talk about U.S. corporations, British corporations, and Japanese corporations, primarily because the majority of stockholders (owners) of these corporations are of the respective nationality. However, this is changing. Increasingly, U.S. citizens are buying stock in companies incorporated abroad, and foreigners are buying stock in companies incorporated in the United States. Looking into the future, Robert Reich has mused about "the coming irrelevance of corporate nationality."[27]

A second development internationalizing the world equity market is that companies with historic roots in one nation are broadening their stock ownership by listing their stock in the equity markets of other nations. The reasons are primarily financial. Listing stock on a foreign market is often a prelude to issuing stock in that market to raise capital. The idea is to tap into the liquidity of foreign markets, thereby increasing the funds available for investment and lowering the firm's cost of capital. (The relationship between liquidity and the cost of capital was discussed earlier in the chapter.) Firms also often list their stock on foreign equity markets to facilitate future acquisitions of foreign companies. Other reasons for listing a company's stock on a foreign equity market are that the company's stock and stock options can be used to compensate local management and employees, it satisfies the desire for local ownership, and it increases the company's visibility with local employees, customers, suppliers, and bankers. Although firms based in developed nations were the first to start listing their stock on foreign exchanges, increasingly firms from developing countries who find their own growth limited by an illiquid domestic capital market are exploiting this opportunity.

FOREIGN EXCHANGE RISK AND
THE COST OF CAPITAL

While a firm can borrow funds at a lower cost in the global capital market than in the domestic capital market, foreign exchange risk complicates this picture under a floating exchange rate regime. Adverse movements in foreign exchange rates can substantially increase the cost of foreign currency loans, which is what happened to many Asian companies during the 1997–1998 Asian financial crisis.

Consider a South Korean firm that wants to borrow 1 billion Korean won for one year to fund a capital investment project. The company can borrow this money from a Korean bank at an interest rate of 10 percent, and at the end of the year pay back the loan plus interest, for a total of W1.10 billion. Or the firm could borrow dollars from an international bank at a 6 percent interest rate. At the prevailing exchange rate of $1 = W1,000, the firm would borrow $1 million and the total loan cost would be $1.06 million, or W1.06 billion. By borrowing dollars, the firm could reduce its cost of capital by 4 percent, or W40 million. However, this saving is predicated on the assumption that during the year of the loan, the dollar/won exchange rate stays constant. Instead, imagine that the won depreciates sharply against the U.S. dollar during the year and ends the year at $1 = W1,500. (This occurred in late 1997 when the won declined in value from $1 = 1,000 to $1 = W1,500 in two months.) The firm still has to pay the international bank $1.06 million at the end of the year, but now this costs the company W1.59 billion (i.e., $1.06 million × 1,500). As a result of the depreciation in the value of the won, the cost of borrowing in U.S. dollars has soared from 6 percent to 59 percent, a huge rise in the firm's cost of capital. Although this may seem like an extreme example, it happened to many South Korean firms in 1997 at the height of the Asian financial crisis. Not surprisingly, many of them were pushed into technical default on their loans.

Unpredictable movements in exchange rates can inject risk into foreign currency borrowing, making something that initially seems less expensive ultimately much more expensive. The borrower can hedge against such a possibility by entering into a forward contract to purchase the required amount of the currency being borrowed at a predetermined exchange rate when the loan comes due (see Chapter 10 for details). Although this will raise the borrower's cost of capital, the added insurance limits the risk involved in such a transaction. Unfortunately, many Asian borrowers did not hedge their dollar-denominated short-term debt, so when their currencies collapsed against the dollar in 1997, many saw a sharp increase in their cost of capital.

When a firm borrows funds from the global capital market, it must weigh the benefits of a lower interest rate against the risks of an increase in the real cost of capital due to adverse exchange rate movements. Although using forward exchange markets may lower foreign exchange risk with short-term borrowings, it cannot remove the risk. Most important, the forward exchange market does not provide adequate coverage for long-term borrowings.

▉ IMPLICATIONS **FOR MANAGERS** ▉

The implications of the material discussed in this chapter for international business are quite straightforward but no less important for being obvious. The growth of the global capital market has created opportunities for international businesses that wish to borrow and/or invest money. On the borrowing side, by using the global capital market, firms can often borrow funds at a lower cost than is possible in a purely domestic capital market. This conclusion holds no matter what form of borrowing a firm uses—equity, bonds, or cash loans. The lower cost of capital on the global market reflects its greater liquidity and the general absence of government regulation. Government regulation tends to raise the cost of capital in most domestic capital markets. The global market, being transnational, escapes regulation. Balanced against this, however, is the foreign exchange risk associated with borrowing in a foreign currency.

On the investment side, the growth of the global capital market is providing opportunities for firms, institutions, and individuals to diversify their investments to limit risk. By holding a diverse portfolio of stocks and bonds in different nations, an investor can reduce total risk to a lower level than can be achieved in a purely domestic setting. Once again, however, foreign exchange risk is a complicating factor.

Chapter Summary

This chapter explained the functions and form of the global capital market and defined the implications of these for international business practice. This chapter made the following points:

1. The function of a capital market is to bring those who want to invest money together with those who want to borrow money.

2. Relative to a domestic capital market, the global capital market has a greater supply of funds available for borrowing, and this makes for a lower cost of capital for borrowers.

3. Relative to a domestic capital market, the global capital market allows investors to diversify portfolios of holdings internationally, thereby reducing risk.

4. The growth of the global capital market during recent decades can be attributed to advances in information technology, the widespread deregulation of financial services, and the relaxation of regulations governing cross-border capital flows.

5. A Eurocurrency is any currency banked outside its country of origin. The lack of government regulations makes the Eurocurrency market attractive to both depositors and borrowers. Due to the absence of regulation, the spread between the Eurocurrency deposit and lending rates is less than the spread between the domestic deposit and lending rates. This gives Eurobanks a competitive advantage.

6. The global bond market has two classifications: the foreign bond market and the Eurobond market. Foreign bonds are sold outside of the borrower's country and are denominated in the currency of the country in which they are issued. A Eurobond issue is normally underwritten by an international syndicate of banks and placed in countries other than the one in whose currency the bond is denominated. Eurobonds account for the lion's share of international bond issues.

7. The Eurobond market is an attractive way for companies to raise funds due to the absence of regulatory interference, less stringent disclosure requirements, and Eurobonds' favorable tax status.

8. Foreign investors are investing in other countries' equity markets to reduce risk by diversifying their stock holdings among nations.

9. Many companies are now listing their stock in the equity markets of other nations, primarily as a prelude to issuing stock in those markets to raise additional capital. Other reasons for listing stock in another country's exchange are to facilitate future stock swaps; to enable the company to use its stock and stock options for compensating local management and employees; to satisfy local ownership desires; and to increase the company's visibility among its local employees, customers, suppliers, and bankers.

10. When borrowing funds from the global capital market, companies must weigh the benefits of a lower interest rate against the risks of greater real costs of capital due to adverse exchange rate movements.

11. One major implication of the global capital market for international business is that companies can often borrow funds at a lower cost of capital in the international capital market than they can in the domestic capital market.

12. The global capital market provides greater opportunities for businesses and individuals to build a truly diversified portfolio of international investments in financial assets, which lowers risk.

Critical Thinking and Discussion Questions

1. Why has the global capital market grown so rapidly in recent decades? Do you think this growth will continue throughout the next decade? Why?

2. In 2008–2009, the world economy retrenched in the wake of a global financial crisis. Did the globalization of capital markets contribute to this crisis? If so, what can be done to stop global financial contagion in the future?

3. A firm based in Mexico has found that its growth is restricted by the limited liquidity of the Mexican capital market. List the firm's options for raising money on the global capital market. Discuss the pros and cons of each option, and make a recommendation. How might your recommended options be affected if the Mexican peso depreciates significantly on the foreign exchange markets over the next two years?

4. Happy Company wants to raise $2 million with debt financing. The funds are needed to finance working capital, and the firm will repay them with interest in one year. Happy Company's treasurer is considering three options:
   a. Borrowing U.S. dollars from Security Pacific Bank at 8 percent.
   b. Borrowing British pounds from Midland Bank at 14 percent.
   c. Borrowing Japanese yen from Sanwa Bank at 5 percent.
   If Happy borrows foreign currency, it will not cover it; that is, it will simply change foreign currency for dollars at today's spot rate and buy the same foreign currency a year later at the spot rate then in effect. Happy Company estimates the pound will depreciate by 5 percent relative to the dollar and the yen will appreciate 3 percent relative to the dollar in the next year. From which bank should Happy Company borrow?

Research Task 🌐 globalEDGE globaledge.msu.edu

Global Capital Markets

Use the globalEDGE website (globaledge.msu.edu) to complete the following exercises:

Exercise 1

The top management team of your not-for-profit organization would like to find out more about investing in environmentally responsible companies in Europe. *FTSE* develops various indexes for the global financial markets. A series of indexes, called ESG, cover social, environmental, and good governance standards. One of these is the Environmental Europe 40 Index. Download the index's factsheet for your analysis. Evaluate the top 10 companies, countries, and industries represented in this index. What patterns do you see?

Exercise 2

The *Bureau of Economic Analysis* is an agency of the U.S. Department of Commerce. It lists data about the U.S. economic accounts, including current investment positions and the amount of direct investment by multinational corporations in the United States and abroad. Prepare a brief report regarding the direct investments of other countries in the United States. Include in your report the leading countries in foreign direct investment.

Closing CASE

Industrial and Commercial Bank of China

In October 2006, the Industrial and Commercial Bank of China, or ICBC, successfully completed the world's largest ever initial public offering (IPO), raising some $21 billion. It beat Japan's 1998 IPO of NTT DoCoMo by a wide margin to earn a place in the record books (NTT raised $18.4 billion in its IPO). The ICBC offering followed the IPOs of a number of other Chinese banks and corporations in recent years. Indeed, Chinese enterprises have been regularly tapping global capital markets for the past decade, as the Chinese have sought to fortify the balance sheets of the country's largest companies, to improve corporate governance and transparency, and to give China's industry leaders global recognition. Since 2000, Chinese companies have raised more than $100 billion from the equity markets. About half of that came in 2005 and 2006, largely from the country's biggest banks. Shares sold by Chinese companies are also accounting for a greater share of global equity sales—about 10 percent in 2006 compared to 2.8 percent in 2001, surpassing the total amount raised by companies in the world's then second-largest economy, Japan.

To raise this amount of capital, Chinese corporations have been aggressively courting international investors. In the case of ICBC, it simultaneously listed its IPO shares on the Shanghai stock exchange and the Hong Kong exchange. The rationale for the Hong Kong listing was that regulations in Hong Kong are in accordance with international standards, while those in Shanghai have some way to go. By listing in Hong Kong, ICBC signaled to potential investors that it would adhere to the strict reporting and governance standards expected of the top global companies.

The ICBC listing attracted considerable interest from foreign investors, who saw it as a way to invest in the Chinese economy. ICBC has a nationwide bank network of more than 18,000 branches, the largest in the nation. It claims 2.5 million corporate customers and 150 million personal accounts. Some 1,000 institutions from across the globe reportedly bid for shares in the IPO. Total orders from these institutions were equivalent to 40 times the amount of stock offered for sale. In other words, the offering was massively oversubscribed. Indeed, the issue generated a total demand of some $430 billion, almost twice the value of Citi, the world's largest bank by market capitalization. The listing on Hong Kong attracted some $350 billion in orders from global investors, more than any other offering in Hong Kong's history. The domestic portion of the stock sales, through the Shanghai exchange, attracted some $80 billion in orders. This massive oversubscription enabled ICBC to raise the issuing price for its shares and reap some $2 billion more than planned.[28]

Case Discussion Questions

1. Why did ICBC feel it was necessary to issue equity in markets outside mainland China? What are the advantages of such a move? Can you see any disadvantages?

2. What was the attraction of the ICBC listing to foreign investors? What do you think are the risks for a foreigner associated with investing in ICBC?

Understanding Country Risk—Sistema and Uninor in India[29]

On 2nd February, 2012, the Supreme Court of India delivered judgment on petitions filed by Mr Subramanian Swamy and Center for Public Interest Litigation (CPIL) which had challenged allotment of 2G licenses granted in 2008.[30] The Supreme Court quashed all 122 spectrum licenses granted during the tenure of former communications minister A Raja[31] and described the allocation of 2G spectrum as "unconstitutional and arbitrary"[32]. The bench of Justice GS Singhvi and Justice AK Ganguly imposed fine of INR 5 crore (USD 0.91 million) on Unitech Wireless, Swan telecom and Tata Teleservices and INR 50 lakh (USD 91,000) fine on Loop Telecom, SingTel, Allianz Infratech and Sistema Shyam Tele Services Ltd. The Court's ruling said the current licenses would remain in place for four months, in which time the government should decide fresh norms for issuing licenses. The Court further said in its order that the then telecom minister A. Raja "wanted to favor some companies at the cost of the public exchequer" and listed seven steps he took to ensure this happened.[33] According to the Supreme Court of India the seven steps were as follows.[34]

1. After taking over as telecom minister, Raja directed that all applications received for UAS licenses should be kept pending till receipt of the TRAI's recommendations.

2. The recommendations made by TRAI on 28th August, 2007, were not placed before the full Telecom Commission which would have included the finance secretary. The notice of the meeting of the Telecom Commission was not given to any of the non-permanent members though TRAI's recommendations for allocation of 2G spectrum had serious financial implications and it was, therefore, necessary for DoT to take the finance ministry's opinion under the Government of India (Transaction of Business) Rules, 1961.

3. The DoT officers who attended the Telecom Commission meeting held on 10th October, 2007 had no choice but to approve TRAI's recommendations, since they would otherwise have "incurred" Raja's "wrath".

4. Since Cabinet had approved recommendations made by the Group of Ministers, the DoT had to discuss the issue of spectrum pricing with the finance ministry. But, since Raja knew that the finance secretary had objected to the allocation of 2G spectrum at rates fixed in 2001, he did not consult the finance minister or other officials.

5. Raja brushed aside the law minister's suggestion that the matter should be placed before the empowered group of ministers. Also, within hours of the receipt of the suggestion made by the PM in his letter dated 2nd November, 2007, that keeping in view the inadequacy of spectrum,

transparency and fairness should be maintained in allocation of the spectrum, Raja rejected it saying that it would be unfair, discriminatory, arbitrary and capricious to auction spectrum to new applicants because it would not give them a level-playing field. He also introduced a cut-off date of 25th September, 2007, for considering applications though only the previous day a DoT press release had said 1st October, 2007, would be the last date. This arbitrary action of Raja, "though appears to be innocuous was actually intended to benefit some of the real estate firms who did not have any experience in dealing with telecom services and who had made applications only on 24th September, 2007, i.e., one day before the cut-off date fixed by the C&IT minister on his own".

6. The new cut-off date was not made public till 10th January, 2008, and the first-come-first-served principle followed since 2003 was changed by him at the last moment through a press release dated 10th January, 2008. "This enabled some of the applicants, who had access either to the minister or DoT officers, get bank drafts prepared towards performance guarantee of about INR 1,600 crore".

7. "The manner in which the exercise for grant of LoIs to the applicants was conducted on 10th January, 2008 leaves no room for doubt that everything was stage managed to favor those who were able to know in advance change in the implementation of the first-come-first-served policy." As a result, some firms which had submitted applications in 2004 or 2006 were pushed down in the priority and those who had applied between August and September 2007 succeeded.

After Effects of Supreme Court's Verdict[35]

- Batelcoquitted India —Batelco, the Bahrain telecommunications company holding 42.7 percent stake in SingTel declared that it had agreed to sell its entire holding to Indian partner Sky City Foundation Ltd for 65.8 million Bahraini dinar (USD 174.5 million).[36]
- Telenor terminated agreement and sued Unitech — on 21st February, 2012, Telenor, majority stakeholder in Uninor, terminated its agreement with its Indian partner Unitech and sued it seeking "indemnity and compensation".[37]
- Etisalat sued Shahid Balwa and Vinod Goenka — on 23 February, 2012 Etisalat of the Etasalat-DB Telecom sued Shahid Balwa and Vinod Goenka, promoters of its Indian partner DB Realty for fraud and misrepresentation.[38]

Telenor Group is mostly an international wireless carrier with operations in Scandinavia, Eastern Europe and Asia, working predominantly under the Telenor brand. At the end of 2010, its 203 million subscribers made it one of the largest mobile phone operators in the world. In addition, it has extensive broadband and TV distribution operations in four Nordic Countries, and a 10-year-old research and business line for Machine-to-Machine technology.[39]

Bahrain Telecommunications Company (Batelco) is the principal telecommunications company of Bahrain. The company is headquartered in Bahrain and is listed on the Bahrain Stock Exchange.[40]

Emirates Telecommunications Corporation, branded trade name Etisalatis, a UAE-based telecommunications services provider, currently operating in 18 countries across Asia, the Middle East and Africa. As of February 2012, Etisalat was the 15th largest mobile network operator in the world, with a total customer base of more than 135 million. Etisalat was named the most powerful company in the UAE by Forbes Middle East in 2012.[41]

Unitech Limited is India's second largest real estate investment company, and had claimed to be the largest real estate builder in the country.[42] The company is based in New Delhi and its construction business includes highways, roads, powerhouses, transmission lines, and it has residential projects called Unitech Cities/UniWorld, in cities like Mumbai, Delhi, Kolkata, Chennai, Hyderabad, Bangalore, Kochi, Noida, Greater Noida, Agra, Lucknow, Varanasi, Gurgaon, and Ghaziabad.

Indian Markets Risky: Foreign Investors at lose after 2G license cancellation

Sistema lost USD 700 million, Telenor forfeited USD 680 million and Etisalat wrote off USD 820 million of its investment following the cancellation of 2G licenses by the Supreme Court in February 2012. Uninor and Sistema, better known as MTS, threatened to exit India, in case policies became unfavorable.[43]

Telenor and Unitech JV ended in October 2012

Telenor, held 67.25 percent stake in the joint venture firm Unitech Wireless that offers telecom services under the Uninor brand name.[44] Unitech agreed to dispose off its 33 percent shareholding to Telenor for a nominal amount.[45] The **income-tax department** seized all of Unitech's shares in the joint venture as it had allegedly failed to pay tax of around **INR 700 crore.**[46]

Unitech Ltd, the Indian partner of Norwegian telecommunications group Telenor ASA, later agreed to sell its share of their mobile phone joint venture, the Indian company said, in what it termed as an amicable settlement after months of dispute in October 2012.

Telenor and Unitech were at loggerheads ever since the Supreme Court cancelled Uninor's 22 telecom permits. Telenor wanted to scrap the joint venture and transfer the business to a new firm and get fresh license. Both were engaged in legal battle in courts and the Company Law Board.

With the settlement of disputes with Telenor, Unitech focused on its core business of real estate. In October, 2012, Telenor said it was preparing to participate in the upcoming 2G spectrum auction through a new entity. Unitech and Telenor did not provide further details about the specific terms and conditions of the settlement, citing confidentiality clause.

After its exit from the JV in October 2012 Telenor was preparing itself for the new auction in November 2012 and searching a new partner in India.[47] Telenor planned to bid in **upcoming2G auctions**, will have to subsequently enter into a partnership with a local company as Indian rules do not allow a foreign firm to hold more than **74 percent stake in the telecom sector.**[48]

Sistema Shyam JV still fighting in Indian courts

Sistema owned about 56 percent in Sistema Shyam and the Russian government another 18 percent. The remaining 26 percent was held by the Shyam Group.[49] The Telco operates CDMA technology-based communications services under the brand name MTS has more than 15 million subscribers in the country. The company lost 21 of its 22 telecom licenses after the Supreme Court order in January 2008.

Sistema was considered to be one of two affected companies still interested in participating in India's telecom sector and that was likely to participate in the auction for 2G spectrum till October 2012 but by November 2012 they decided not to participate.[50] They stayed away from the airwaves resale and awaited the outcome of its curative petition filed in the apex court on the grounds that its mobile permits be treated differently as it was allotted CDMA airwaves, which was different from GSM airwaves held by other Telcos.[51]

In November 2012, Sistema was in talks to acquire Aircel, which was the country's seventh-biggest mobile phone operator by customers. But Vsevolod Rozanov, CEO at Sistema-Shyam-TeleServices announced that the company did not expect any deals until the Supreme Court decides on the company's appeal on the order to revoke the permits.

Foreign Government Reactions

In October 2012, Russia said that the dispute over Sistema would have its impact on the foreign investment which could also affect Indo-Russia bilateral cooperation. Russian Ambassodor to India Alexander Kadakin said that if Indian courts failed to resolve Sistema issue, there would be no option left but to take recourse to international arbitration. He said that Russia had expressed its displeasure over the issue many time in the past.[52] The Indo-Russian trade relationship was highly affected by two drawbacks: Sistema's troubles in India and the issue over the new Kudankulam reactors coming under the nuclear liability law.[53] Sistema had invested USD 3.1 billion in telecom venture in India and Russia had already said that it would not let this huge investment go waste.

In May 2012, Norway expressed that any failure of Telenor's USD 3 billion investment in India would have political implications. Norwegian trade and industry minister, Trond Giske said, "Telenor is not just any company. Fifty-four percent of the shares are owned by Norwegian people through state and thus it has political implications. If this investment fails, it will be probably the biggest loss suffered by a Norwegian company in foreign investments ever. I also think it will influence the view of India as an investment country,"[54] Reacting to Giske's statement, Telecom minister, Kapil Sibal said, "There is absolutely no room for concern. The Indian government is committed to protect foreign investments in India and make sure that not just Telenor, but all foreign investors have a robust roadmap ahead."

Conclusion

The lack of policy stability has been a big problem for India. The multiple episodes of corruption (cutting across party lines), political one-upmanship leading to policy logjams, clear evidence of the government losing control by the day, etc., highlight the fact that the investment climate in the country has worsened.[55] Since 2007, both savings and investment have been on a decline. Despite relatively good GDP growth numbers, foreign investors have not rushed to India.

The telecom muddle gave the signal that investment in India can be risky as policies can change over time and can materially affect the existing investment.

Table 11 shows list of companies whose licenses were cancelled:

TABLE 11 Telecom companies affected by cancellation of licenses

Name of company	Parent group	No of licenses cancelled
Uninor	Joint venture between Unitech Group of India and Telenor of Norway Unitech Group	22
Sistema ShyamTele-Services Limited, now MTS India	Joint venture between Shyam group of Indian and Sistema of Russia	21
Loop Mobile formerly BPL Mobile	Owned by Khaitan Holding Group	21
Videocon Telecommunications	Owned by Videocon group of India	21
Etisalat-DB	Joint venture between Swan Telecom of India and Etisalat of UAE	15
Idea Cellular	Aditya Birla Group of India (49.05 percent), Axiata Group Berhad of Malaysia (15 percent) & Providence Equity (10.6 percent) of USA	13

(Continued)

Name of company	Parent group	No of licenses cancelled
S Tel	Joint venture between C Sivasankaran of India and Batelco of Bahrain. After the Supreme Court's decision Batelco sold its 42.7 percent stake to C Sivasankaran company Sky City Foundation Ltd. for $175 million	6
Tata Teleservices	Owned by Tata Group of India	3

References

All website addresses mentioned as endnotes were retrieved on November 22, 2012.

Endnotes

1. Susan Lund et al., "Financial Globalization: Retreat or Reset?" McKinsey Global Institute, March 2013; "Blocked Pipes," *The Economist,* October 4, 2008, pp. 73–75; "On Life Support," *The Economist,* October 4, 2008, pp. 77–78; M. Boyle, "The Fed's Commercial Paper Chase," *BusinessWeek Online,* October 8, 2008, p. 5; and M. Gordon, "TARP Bailout Costs to Taxpayers Expected to Be Lower," *Christian Science Monitor,* December 17, 2012.
2. D. Waller, "Daimler in $250m Singapore Placing," *Financial Times,* May 10, 1994.
3. J. O. Jackson, "The Selling of the Big Pink," *Time,* December 2, 1996, p. 46; S. Ascarelli, "Privatization Is Worrying Deutsche Telekom," *The Wall Street Journal,* February 3, 1995, p. A1; "Plunging into Foreign Markets, *The Economist,* September 17, 1994, pp. 86–87; and A. Raghavan and M. R. Sesit, "Financing Boom: Foreign Firms Raise More and More Money in the U.S. Market," *The Wall Street Journal,* October 5, 1993, p. A1.
4. B. Solnik, "Why Not Diversify Internationally Rather Than Domestically?" *Financial Analysts Journal,* July 1974, p. 17.
5. C. G. Luck and R. Choudhury, "International Equity Diversification for Pension Funds," *Journal of Investing* 5, no. 2 (1996), pp. 43–53.
6. W. N. Goetzmann, L. Li, and K. G. Rouwenhorst, "Long Term Global Market Correlations," *The Journal of Business,* January 2005, pp. 78–126.
7. Ian Domowitz, Jack Glen, and Ananth Madhavan, "Market Segmentation and Stock Prices: Evidence from an Emerging Market," *Journal of Finance* 3, no. 3 (1997), pp. 1059–68.
8. Solnik, "Why Not Diversify Internationally Rather Than Domestically?"
9. A. Lavine, "With Overseas Markets Now Moving in Sync with U.S. Markets, It's Getting Harder to Find True Diversification Abroad," *Financial Planning,* December 1, 2000, pp. 37–40.
10. B. Solnik and J. Roulet. "Dispersion as Cross Sectional Correlation," *Financial Analysts Journal* 56, no. 1 (2000), pp. 54–61.
11. Goetzmann et al., "Long Term Global Market Correlations."
12. Ibid.
13. Bank for International Settlements, *BIS Quarterly Review,* March 2013.
14. T. F. Huertas, "U.S. Multinational Banking: History and Prospects," in *Banks as Multinationals,* ed. G. Jones (London: Routledge, 1990).
15. G. J. Millman, *The Vandals' Crown* (New York: Free Press, 1995).
16. Goetzmann et al., "Long Term Global Market Correlations."
17. P. Dicken, *Global Shift: The Internationalization of Economic Activity* (London: The Guilford Press, 1992).
18. Ibid.
19. Martin Feldstein, "Global Capital Flows: Too Little, Not Too Much," *The Economist,* June 24, 1995, pp. 72–73.
20. Ibid., p. 73.
21. D. Duffy and L. Murry, "The Wooing of American Investors," *The Wall Street Journal,* February 25, 1994, p. A14.
22. Feldstein, "Global Capital Flows"; R. Dornbusch, "We Have Salinas to Thank for the Peso Debacle," *BusinessWeek,* January 16, 1995, p. 20; and P. Carroll and C. Torres, "Mexico Unveils Program of Harsh Fiscal Medicine," *The Wall Street Journal,* March 10, 1995, pp. A1, A6. See also, Martin Feldstein and Charles Horioka, "Domestic Savings and International Capital Flows," *Economic Journal* 90 (1980), pp. 314–29.
23. International Monetary Fund, *World Economic Outlook* (Washington, DC: IMF, 1998).
24. C. Schenk, "The Origins of the Eurodollar Market in London, 1955–1963," *Explorations in Economic History* 35 (1998), pp. 221–39.

25. Waller, "Daimler in $250m Singapore Placing."

26. L. Spears and C. Vannucci, "China's Latest American IPOs Slump as Offerings Increase to Annual Record," *Bloomberg BusinessWeek,* December 6, 2010.

27. R. Reich, *The Work of Nations* (New York: Alfred A. Knopf, 1991).

28. K. Linebaugh, "Record IPO Could Have Been Even Bigger," *The Wall Street Journal,* October 21, 2006, p. B3; "Deals That Changed the Market in 2006: ICBC's Initial Public Offering," *Euromoney,* February 7, 2007, p. 1; and T. Mitchell, ICBC Discovers That Good Things Come to Those Who Wait," *Financial Times,* October 26, 2006, p. 40.

29. http://en.wikipedia.org/wiki/2G_spectrum_scam

30. http://www.dnaindia.com/india/report_supreme-court-quashes-122-2g-licences-awarded-in-2008_1645296

31. Op cit 2 above

32. http://www.ndtv.com/article/india/five-crore-fine-for-unitech-swan-and-tata-teleservices-172607

33. http://timesofindia.indiatimes.com/india/2G-scam-SC-quashes-122-licences-trial-court-to-decide-on-Chidambarams-role-CBI-to-submit-probe-report-to-CVC/articleshow/11724453.cms

34. http://www.indianexpress.com/news/sc-singles-out-raja-says-officers-were-cowed-down/907187/

35. http://en.wikipedia.org/wiki/2G_spectrum_scam

36. http://www.dnaindia.com/money/report_batelco-hangs-up-as-sc-blow-hits-home_1647658

37. http://in.reuters.com/article/2012/02/22/telenor-india-idINDEE81K0FR20120222

38. http://timesofindia.indiatimes.com/business/india-business/Etisalat-sues-Balwa-Goenka/articleshow/12013354.cms

39. http://en.wikipedia.org/wiki/Telenor

40. http://en.wikipedia.org/wiki/Batelco

41. http://en.wikipedia.org/wiki/Emirates_Telecommunications_Corporation

42. http://en.wikipedia.org/wiki/Unitech_Group

43. http://www.expresscomputeronline.com/features/951-2g-spectrum-reauctions-ring-alarm-bells

44. http://www.thehindu.com/todays-paper/tp-business/unitech-to-exit-telecom-joint-venture-with-telenor/article3989682.ece

45. http://insightvas.com/telenor-and-unitech-settles-dispute-transfers-their-joint-venture-to-a-new-compan

46. http://articles.economictimes.indiatimes.com/2012-10-12/news/34389503_1_telenor-plans-top-unitech-executive-sanjay-chandra

47. http://www.reuters.com/article/2012/10/11/unitech-idUSL3E8LB1CU20121011

48. http://insightvas.com/telenor-and-unitech-settles-dispute-transfers-their-joint-venture-to-a-new-company/

49. http://www.livemint.com/Industry/1H5Jdo1rPLtJtlOVxwZrjP/Sistema-asks-why-India-wants-to-delay-arbitration-proceeding.html

50. http://www.telecomtiger.com/Corporate_fullstory.aspx?passfrom=topstory&storyid=16132&section=S162

51. http://economictimes.indiatimes.com/news/news-by-industry/telecom/sistema-shyam-open-to-buyouts-may-bid-for-cdma-airwaves-if-govt-lowers-reserve-price/articleshow/17286239.cms

52. http://www.telecomtiger.com/Corporate_fullstory.aspx?passfrom=topstory&storyid=16132&section=S162

53. http://indrus.in/articles/2012/08/22/business_ties_in_a_neo-liberal_era_17159.html

54. http://www.telegraphindia.com/1120513/jsp/business/story_15483387.jsp#.UK3rweSE3kY

55. http://www.forumdesalternatives.org/en/india-taxing-time-for-foreign-investors

C·A·S·E·S

SOUTH KOREAN CURRENCY CRISIS

In early 1997, South Korea could look back with pride on a 30-year "economic miracle" that had raised the country from the ranks of the poor and given it the world's eleventh-largest economy. By the end of 1997, the Korean currency, the won, had lost a staggering 67 percent of its value against the U.S. dollar, the South Korean economy lay in tatters, and the International Monetary Fund was overseeing a $55 billion rescue package. This sudden turn of events had its roots in investments made by South Korea's large industrial conglomerates, or *chaebol,* during the 1990s, often at the bequest of politicians. In 1993, Kim Young-Sam, a populist politician, became president of South Korea. Kim took office during a mild recession and promised to boost economic growth by encouraging investment in export-oriented industries. He urged the *chaebol* to invest in new factories. South Korea enjoyed an investment-led economic boom in 1994–1995, but at a cost. The *chaebol,* always reliant on heavy borrowing, built up massive debts that were equivalent, on average, to four times their equity.

As the volume of investments ballooned during the 1990s, the quality of many of these investments declined significantly. The investments often were made on the basis of unrealistic projections about future demand conditions. This resulted in significant excess capacity and falling prices. An example is investments made by South Korean *chaebol* in semiconductor factories. Investments in such facilities surged in 1994 and 1995 when a temporary global shortage of dynamic random access memory chips (DRAMs) led to sharp price increases for this product. However, supply shortages had disappeared by 1996, and excess capacity was beginning to make itself felt, just as the South Koreans started to bring new DRAM factories on stream. The results were predictable; prices for DRAMs plunged; and the earnings of South Korean DRAM manufacturers fell by 90 percent, which meant it was difficult for them to make scheduled payments on the debt they had acquired to build the extra capacity. The risk of corporate bankruptcy increased significantly, and not just in the semiconductor industry. South Korean companies were also investing heavily in a wide range of other industries, including automobiles and steel.

Matters were complicated further because much of the borrowing had been in U.S. dollars, as opposed to Korean won. This had seemed like a smart move at the time. The dollar/won exchange rate had been stable at around $1 = W850. Interest rates on dollar borrowings were two to three percentage points lower than rates on borrowings in Korean won. Much of this borrowing was in the form of short-term, dollar-denominated debt that had to be paid back to the lending institution within one year. While the borrowing strategy seemed to make sense, it involved risk. If the won were to depreciate against the dollar, the size of the debt burden that South Korean companies would have to service would increase when measured in the local currency. Currency depreciation would raise borrowing costs, depress corporate earnings, and increase the risk of bankruptcy. This is exactly what happened.

By mid-1997, foreign investors had become alarmed at the rising debt levels of South Korean companies, particularly given the emergence of excess capacity and plunging prices in several areas where the companies had made huge investments, including semiconductors, automobiles, and steel. Given increasing speculation that many South Korean companies would not be able to service their debt payments, foreign investors began to withdraw their money from the Korean stock and bond markets. In the process, they sold Korean won and purchased U.S. dollars. The selling of won accelerated in mid-1997 when two of the smaller *chaebol* filed for bankruptcy, citing their inability to meet scheduled debt payments. The increased supply of won and the increased demand for U.S. dollars pushed down the price of won in dollar terms from around W840 = $1 to W900 = $1.

At this point, the South Korean central bank stepped into the foreign exchange market to try to keep the exchange rate above W1,000 = $1. It used dollars that it held in reserve to purchase won. The idea was to try to push up the price of the won in dollar terms and restore investor confidence in the stability of the exchange rate. This action, however, did not address the underlying debt problem faced by South Korean companies. Against a backdrop of more corporate bankruptcies in South Korea, and the government's stated intentions to take some troubled companies into state ownership, Standard & Poor's, the U.S. credit rating agency, downgraded South Korea's sovereign debt. This caused the Korean stock market to plunge 5.5 percent, and the Korean won to fall to W930 = $1. According to S&P, "The downgrade of . . . ratings reflects the escalating cost to the government of supporting the country's ailing corporate and financial sectors."

The S&P downgrade triggered a sharp sale of the Korean won. In an attempt to protect the won against what was fast becoming a classic bandwagon effect, the South Korean central bank raised short-term interest rates to over 12 percent, more than double the inflation rate. The bank also stepped up its intervention in the currency exchange markets, selling dollars and purchasing won in an attempt to keep the exchange rate above W1,000 = $1. The main effect of this action, however, was to rapidly deplete South Korea's foreign exchange reserves. These stood at $30 billion on November 1, but fell to only $15 billion two weeks later. With its foreign exchange reserves almost exhausted, the South Korean central bank gave up its defense of the won on November 17. Immediately, the price of won in dollars plunged to around W1,500 = $1, effectively increasing by 60 to 70 percent the amount of won heavily indebted Korean companies had to pay to meet scheduled payments on their dollar-denominated debt. These losses, due to adverse changes in foreign exchange rates, depressed the profits of many firms. South Korean firms suffered foreign exchange losses of more than $15 billion in 1997.

Case Discussion Questions

1. What role did the Korean government play in creating the 1997 crisis?
2. What role did Korean enterprises play in creating the 1997 crisis?
3. Why was the Korean central bank unable to stop the decline in the value of the won?
4. In late 1997, the IMF stepped in with a rescue package that included $55 billion in emergency loans to support the currency. These loans had the effect of stabilizing the won, and over the next few years South Korean enjoyed a strong recovery. If the IMF had not stepped in, what might have occurred?

Sources

J. Burton and G. Baker, "The Country That Invested Its Way into Trouble," *Financial Times,* January 15, 1998, p. 8; J. Burton, "South Korea's Credit Rating Is Lowered," *Financial Times,* October 25, 1997, p. 3; J. Burton, "Currency Losses Hit Samsung Electronics," *Financial Times,* March 20, 1998, p. 24; and "Korean Firms' Foreign Exchange Losses Exceed US $15 Billion," *Business Korea,* February 1998, p. 55.

RUSSIAN RUBLE CRISIS AND ITS AFTERMATH

Prelude

In the early 1990s, following the collapse of communism and the dissolution of the Soviet Union, the Russian government implemented an economic reform program designed to transform the country's crumbling centrally planned economy into a dynamic market economy. A central element of this plan was an end to price controls on January 1, 1992. Once controls were removed, however, prices surged. Inflation was soon running at a monthly rate of about 30 percent. For the whole of 1992, the inflation rate in Russia was 3,000 percent. The annual rate for 1993 was approximately 900 percent.

Several factors contributed to the spike in Russia's inflation rate. Prices had been held at artificially low levels by state planners during the Communist era. At the same time there was a shortage of many basic goods, so with nothing to spend their money on, many Russians simply hoarded rubles. After the liberalization of price controls, the country was suddenly awash in rubles chasing a still limited supply of goods. The result was to rapidly bid up prices. The inflationary fires that followed price liberalization were stoked by the Russian government itself. Unwilling to face the social consequences of the massive unemployment that would follow if many state-owned enterprises were quickly privatized, the government continued to subsidize the operations of many money-losing establishments. The result was a surge in the government's budget deficit. In the first quarter of 1992, the budget deficit amounted to 1.5 percent of the country's GDP. By the end of 1992, it had risen to 17 percent. Unable or unwilling to finance this deficit by raising taxes, the government found another solution—it printed money, which added fuel to the inflation fire.

With inflation rising, the ruble tumbled in value against the dollar and other major currencies. In January 1992 the exchange rate stood at $1 = R125. By the end of 1992 it was $1 = R480, and by late 1993, it was $1 = R1,500. As 1994 progressed, it became increasingly evident that due to vigorous political opposition, the Russian government would not be able to bring down its budget deficit as quickly as had been thought. By September the monthly inflation rate was accelerating. October started badly, with the ruble sliding more than 10 percent in value against the U.S. dollar in the first 10 days of the month. On October 11, the ruble plunged 21.5 percent against the dollar, reaching a value of $1 = R3,926 by the time the foreign exchange market closed!

Despite the announcement of a tough budget plan that placed tight controls on the money supply, the ruble continued to slide, and by April 1995 the exchange rate stood at $1 = R5,120. However, by mid-1995 inflation was again on the way down. In June 1995 the monthly inflation rate was at a yearly low of 6.7 percent. Also, the ruble had recovered to stand at $1 = R4,559 by July 6. On that day the Russian government announced it would intervene in the currency market to keep the ruble in a trading range of R4,300 to R4,900 against the dollar. The Russian government believed that it was essential to maintain a relatively stable currency. Government officials announced that the central bank would be able to draw on $10 billion in foreign exchange reserves to defend the ruble against any speculative selling in Russia's relatively small foreign exchange market.

In the world of international finance, $10 billion is small change, and it wasn't long before Russia found that its foreign exchange reserves were being depleted. It was at this point that the Russian government requested IMF loans. In February 1996, the IMF obliged with its second-largest rescue effort ever, a loan of $10 billion. In return for the loan, Russia agreed to limit the growth in its money supply, reduce public-sector debt, increase government tax revenues, and peg the ruble to the dollar. Russia also rebased the value of the ruble, making one ruble equivalent to 1000 old rubles.

Initially the package seemed to have the desired effect. Inflation declined from nearly 50 percent in 1996 to about 15 percent in 1997; the exchange rate stayed within its predetermined band of 4.3 to 4.8

rubles per dollar; and the balance-of-payments situation remained broadly favorable. In 1997, the Russian economy grew for the first time since the breakup of the former Soviet Union, if only by a modest half of 1 percent of GDP. However, the public-sector debt situation did not improve. The Russian government continued to spend more than it agreed to under IMF targets, while government tax revenues were much lower than projected. Low tax revenues were in part due to falling oil prices (the government collected tax on oil sales), in part due to the difficulties of collecting tax in an economy where so much economic activity was in the "underground economy" and partly due to a complex tax system that was peppered with loopholes. In 1997, Russian federal government spending amounted to 18.3 percent of GDP, while revenues were only 10.8 percent of GDP, implying a deficit of 7.5 percent of GDP, which was financed by an expansion in public debt.

Crisis

Dismayed by the failure of Russia to meet its targets, the IMF responded by suspending its scheduled payment to Russia in early 1998, pending reform of Russia's complex tax system and a sustained attempt by the Russian government to cut public spending. This put further pressure on the Russian ruble, forcing the Russian central bank to raise interest rates on overnight loans to 150 percent. In June 1998, the U.S. government indicated it would support a new IMF bailout. The IMF was more circumspect, insisting instead that the Russian government push through a package of corporate tax increases and public spending cuts to balance the budget. The Russian government indicated it would do so, and the IMF released a tranche of $640 million that had been suspended. The IMF followed this with an additional $11.2 billion loan designed to preserve the ruble's stability.

Almost as soon as the funding was announced, however, it began to unravel. The IMF loan required the Russian government to take concrete steps to raise personal tax rates, improve tax collections, and cut government spending. A bill containing the required legislative changes was sent to the Russian parliament, where it was emasculated by antigovernment forces. The IMF responded by withholding $800 million of its first $5.6 billion tranche, undermining the credibility of its own program. The Russian stock market plummeted on the news, closing 6.5 percent down. Selling of rubles accelerated. The central bank began hemorrhaging foreign exchange reserves as it tried to maintain the value of the ruble. Foreign exchange reserves fell by $1.4 billion in the first week of August alone, to $17 billion, while interest rates surged again.

Against this background, on the weekend of August 15–16, top Russian officials huddled to develop a response to the most recent crisis. Their options were limited. The patience of the IMF had been exhausted. Foreign currency reserves were being rapidly depleted. Social tensions in the country were running high. The government faced upcoming redemptions on $18 billion of domestic bonds, with no idea of where the money would come from.

On Monday, August 17, Prime Minister Sergei Kiriyenko announced the results of the weekend's conclave. He said Russia would restructure the domestic debt market, unilaterally transforming short-term debt into long-term debt. In other words, the government had decided to default on its debt commitments. The government also announced a 90-day moratorium on the repayment of private foreign debt and stated it would allow the ruble to decline by 34 percent against the U.S. dollar. In short, Russia had turned its back on the IMF plan. The effect was immediate. Overnight, shops marked up the price of goods by 20 percent. As the ruble plummeted, currency exchange points were only prepared to sell dollars at a rate of 9 rubles per dollar, rather than the new official exchange rate of 6.43 rubles to the dollar. As for Russian government debt, it lost 85 percent of its value in a matter of hours, leaving foreign and Russian holders of debt alike suddenly gaping at a huge black hole in their financial assets.

Aftermath

In the aftermath of Russia's default on government debt, the IMF effectively turned its back on the Russian government, leaving the country to fix its own financial mess. With no more IMF loans in the offing, the government had to find some other way to manage its large public-sector deficit. The government took a two-pronged approach; first, it slashed government spending, and second, it reformed the tax system. With regard to the tax system, the government of Vladimir Putin ignored the advice of the IMF, which wanted Russia to raise tax rates and focus on tougher enforcement. Instead, the government replaced Russia's complex income tax code, which had a top marginal rate of 30 percent, with a 13 percent flat tax. Corporate tax rates were also slashed from 35 percent to 24 percent, and the tax code simplified, closing many loopholes. Paradoxically, the cut in tax rates led to a surge in government revenues as individuals and corporations decided it was easier to pay taxes than go to the trouble of avoiding them—which they had long done.

In addition to these government actions, a sharp rise in commodity prices, and particularly world oil prices, helped the Russian economy enormously. Russia is now the world's largest oil exporter, ahead of even Saudi Arabia. In addition, it exports significant amounts of natural gas, metals, and timber, all of which have seen sharp price increases since 1998. The country now runs a large current account surplus with the rest of the world (in 2004 it hit $46 billion).

As a result of these changes, the Russian economy grew at an average annual rate of 6.5 percent between 1998 and 2004. Foreign debt declined from 90 percent of GDP in 1998 to around 28 percent in 2004, while foreign reserves increased tenfold to $120 billion. The government has been running a budget surplus since 1999. In 2004 it took in some $13.1 billion more than it spent. Moreover, in January 2005 the Russian government repaid its entire obligations to the IMF ahead of schedule.

Despite these positive developments, the Russian economy still has numerous structural weaknesses. The country is now very dependent on commodity prices, and if they should fall, the economy will suffer a sharp pullback. The banking system remains weak, the manufacturing infrastructure is poor, the country is still rife with corruption, there is widespread mistrust in the institutions of government, and foreign investment is relatively low.

Case Discussion Questions

1. What were the causes of the surge in inflation in Russia during the early 1990s? Could these have been avoided? How?
2. What does the decline in the value of the ruble against the dollar between 1992 and 1998 teach you about the relationship between inflation rates and currency values?
3. During the mid-1990s, the IMF wanted Russia to raise tax rates, close loopholes in the tax system, and cut public spending. Russia was unable to do this. Why?
4. In the early 2000s Russia cut tax rates for individuals and corporations, and government tax revenues surged. Why? Does this result suggest that the IMF policy prescriptions were wrong?

Sources

S. Erlanger, "Russia Will Test a Trading Band for the Ruble," *The New York Times,* July 7, 1995, p. 1; C. Freeland, "Russia to Introduce a Trading Band for Ruble against Dollar," *Financial Times,* July 7, 1995, p. 1; J. Thornhill, "Russians Bemused by 'Black Tuesday,'" *Financial Times,* October 12, 1994, p. 4; R. Sikorski, "Mirage of Numbers," *The Wall Street Journal,* May 18, 1994, p. 14; "Can Russia Fight Back?" *The Economist,* June 6, 1998, pp. 47–48; J. Thornhill, "Russia's Shrinking Options," *Financial Times,* August 19, 1998, p. 19; "Russia," *The World Factbook 2005* (Washington, DC: Central Intelligence Agency, 2005); "Change those Light Bulbs: The Russian Economy," *The Economist*, February 8, 2003, p. 43; and "The Kremlin Repents, Maybe: Russia's Economy," *The Economist,* April 9, 2005, p. 32.

CATERPILLAR: COMPETING IN A WORLD OF FLUCTUATING CURRENCIES

Caterpillar has long been one of America's major exporters. The company sells its construction equipment, mining equipment, and engines to some 200 countries worldwide. As a leading exporter, Caterpillar's fate has often been tied to the value of the U.S. dollar. In the 1980s, the U.S. dollar was strong against the Japanese yen. This gave Komatsu, Japan's premier manufacturer of heavy construction equipment, a pricing advantage against Caterpillar. Undercutting Caterpillar's prices by as much as 30 percent, Komatsu grabbed market share in the United States and other markets. For Caterpillar, it was a difficult time. At one point the company was losing a million dollars a day and battling a hostile labor union that was opposed to job restructuring designed to make the company more competitive. The company seemed to be yet another example of a declining business in America's Rust Belt.

Fast forward to the mid-2000s, and Caterpillar was thriving. Much had changed over the previous two decades. Caterpillar had reached deals with its unions and invested in state-of-the-art manufacturing facilities. Its productivity, once abysmal, was now among the best in the industry. Sales, exports, and profits were all rising. There was a worldwide boom in spending on infrastructure, and Caterpillar was reaping the gains, producing record amounts of equipment. Plus, the U.S. dollar, which for years had been strong, weakened significantly during the mid-2000s. This reduced the price of Caterpillar's exports, when translated into many foreign currencies. At this point, Caterpillar was exporting more than half the output of its key U.S. factories near Peoria, Illinois.

Then in 2008, the dollar started to strengthen again. Even though the American economy was stumbling into a financial crisis that would usher in a steep economic recession, foreigners invested strongly in U.S. assets, particularly Treasury bills. Their demand for dollars to purchase these assets pushed up the value of the dollar on the foreign exchange markets. The hunger of foreigners for dollars was based on a belief that even though things were bad in America, they were probably going to be even worse in many other developed economies, and the U.S. government at least would not default on its bonds, making U.S. Treasury bills a safe haven in an economic storm.

Analysts fretted that the stronger dollar would hurt Caterpillar's financial performance because the prices of its exports were rising when converted into many foreign currencies. The reality, however, was somewhat different.

As 2008 progressed, the strong dollar started to negatively affect Caterpillar's revenues, but it had a *favorable* effect on Caterpillar's costs. Over the previous two decades Caterpillar had dramatically expanded its network of foreign manufacturing operations. While still a major exporter, some 102 of its 237 manufacturing facilities were now located outside of North America, many in countries such as China, India, and Brazil that were expanding their infrastructure spending. Although the revenues generated by these operations in local currency, when translated back into dollars, declined as the dollar strengthened, the costs of these operations also fell, since their costs were also priced in local currencies, which reduced the impact on profit margins. Also, although Caterpillar's export revenues from the United States started to fall, because the company now sourced many of its inputs from foreign producers, the price it paid for those inputs also fell, which again moderated the impact of the strong dollar on earnings. Through its globalization strategy, Caterpillar has been able to reduce the impact of fluctuations in the value of the dollar on its profits.

Case Discussion Questions

1. In the 1980s a stronger dollar hurt Caterpillar's competitive position, but in 2008 a stronger dollar did not seem to have the same effect. What had changed?

2. How did Caterpillar use strategy as a "real hedge" to reduce its exposure to foreign exchange risk? What is the downside of its approach?
3. Explain the difference between transaction exposure and translation exposure using the material in the Caterpillar case to illustrate your answer.

Sources

J. B. Kelleher, "U.S. Exporters Can Win from the Strong Dollar," *International Herald Tribune,* May 9, 2008, p. 15; "Caterpillar's Comeback," *The Economist,* June 20, 1998, pp. 7–8; and A. Taylor, "Caterpillar," *Fortune,* July 20, 2007, pp. 48–54.

PART 5
The Strategy and Structure of
International Business

Chapter 13
The Strategy of International Business

◇ FORD'S GLOBAL STRATEGY ◇

Opening Case

When Ford CEO Alan Mulally arrived at the company in 2006 after a long career at Boeing, he was shocked to learn that the company produced one Ford Focus for Europe and a totally different one for the United States. "Can you imagine having one Boeing 737 for Europe and one 737 for the United States?" he said at the time. Due to this product strategy, Ford was unable to buy common parts for the vehicles, could not share development costs, and couldn't use its European Focus plants to make cars for the United States, or vice versa. In a business where economies of scale are important, the result was high costs. Nor were these problems limited to the Ford Focus. The strategy of designing and building different cars for different regions was the standard approach at Ford.

Ford's long-standing strategy of regional models was based on the assumption that consumers in different regions had different tastes and preferences, which required considerable local customization. Americans, it was argued, loved their trucks and SUVs, while Europeans preferred smaller, fuel-efficient cars. Notwithstanding such differences, Mulally still could not understand why small car models like the

Focus, or the Escape SUV, which were sold in different regions, were not built on the same platform and did not share common parts. In truth, the strategy probably had more to do with the autonomy of different regions within Ford's organization, a fact that was deeply embedded in Ford's history as one of the oldest multinational corporations.

When the global financial crisis rocked the world's automobile industry in 2008–2009, and precipitated the steepest drop in sales since the Great Depression, Mulally decided that Ford had to change its long standing practices in order to get its costs under control. Moreover, he felt that there was no way that Ford would be able to compete effectively in the large developing markets of China and India unless Ford leveraged its global scale to produce low cost cars. The result was Mulally's **One Ford** strategy, which aims to create a handful of car platforms that Ford can use everywhere in the world.

Under this strategy new models, such as the 2013 Fiesta, Focus, and Escape, share a common design, are built on a common platform, use the same parts, and are built in identical factories around the world. Ultimately, Ford hopes to have only five platforms to deliver sales of more than 6 million vehicles by 2016. In 2006 Ford had 15 platforms that accounted for sales of 6.6 million vehicles. By pursuing this strategy, Ford can share the costs of design and tooling, and it can attain much greater scale economies in the production of component parts. Ford has stated that it will take about one-third out of the $1 billion cost of developing a new car model and should significantly reduce its $50 billion annual budget for component parts. Moreover, since the different factories producing these cars are identical in all respects, useful knowledge acquired through experience in one factory can quickly be transferred to other factories, resulting in systemwide cost savings.

What Ford hopes is that this strategy will bring down costs sufficiently to enable Ford to make greater profit margins in developed markets and to make good margins at lower price points in hypercompetitive developing nations, such as China, now the world's largest car market, where Ford currently trails its global rivals such as General Motors and Volkswagen. Indeed, the strategy is central to Mulally's goal for increasing Ford's sales from 5.5 million in 2010 to 8 million by mid-decade.[1]

INTRODUCTION

The primary focus thus far in this book has been on aspects of the larger environment in which international businesses compete. As described in the preceding chapters, this environment has included the different political, economic, and cultural institutions found in nations, the international trade and investment framework, and the international monetary system. Now our focus shifts from the environment to the firm itself and, in particular, to the actions managers can take to compete more effectively as an international business. This chapter looks at how firms can increase their profitability by expanding their operations in foreign markets. We discuss the different strategies that firms pursue when competing internationally, consider the pros and cons of these strategies, and study the various factors that affect a firm's choice of strategy.

Ford Motor Company's One Ford strategy, profiled in the opening case, gives a preview of some issues explored in this chapter. Historically Ford pursued a *localization*, selling cars in the different regions that were designed and produced locally (i.e., one design for Europe, another for North America). While this strategy did have the virtue of ensuring that the offering was tailored the tastes and preferences of consumers in different regions, it also generated considerable duplication and high costs. By the late 2000s, Alan Mulally, Ford's CEO, decided that the company could no longer afford the high costs associated with this approach, and he pushed the company to adopt his One Ford strategy. Under this *global standardization strategy* Ford aims to design and sell the same models worldwide. The idea is to reap substantial cost reduction from sharing design costs, building on common platforms, sharing component parts across models, and building cars in identical factories around the world to share tooling costs. To the extent that Ford can do this, the company should be able to lower prices and still make good profits, which should help it not only hold onto its share in developed markets but also gain share in rapidly growing emerging markets such as India and China. While there is a risk that the lack of local customization will lead to some loss of sales at the margin, Mulally clearly feels that the benefits in terms of lower costs and more competitive pricing clearly outweigh those risks. Only time will tell if he is correct. Can we say Mulally was right with us having the benefit of hindsight?

STRATEGY AND THE FIRM

Before we discuss the strategies that managers in the multinational enterprise can pursue, we need to review some basic principles of strategy. A firm's **strategy** can be defined as the actions that managers take to attain the goals of the firm. For most firms, the preeminent goal is to maximize the value of the firm for its owners and its shareholders (subject to the very important constraint that this is done in a legal, ethical, and socially responsible manner—see Chapter 5 for details). To maximize the value of a firm, managers must pursue strategies that increase the *profitability* of the enterprise and its rate of *profit growth* over time (see Figure 13.1). **Profitability** can be measured in a number of ways, but for consistency, we define it as the rate of return that the firm makes on its invested capital (ROIC), which is calculated by dividing the net profits of the firm by total invested capital.[2] **Profit growth** is measured by the percentage increase in net profits over time. In general, higher profitability and a higher rate of profit growth will increase the value of an enterprise and thus the returns garnered by its owners, the shareholders.[3]

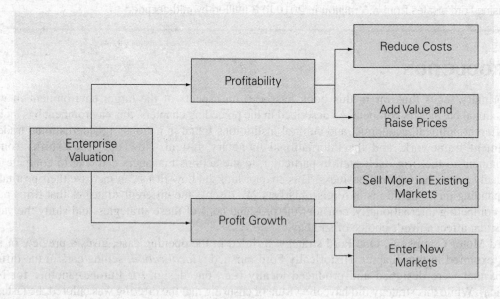

Figure 13.1 *Determinants of Enterprise Value*

Managers can increase the profitability of the firm by pursuing strategies that lower costs or by pursuing strategies that add value to the firm's products, which enables the firm to raise prices. Managers can increase the rate at which the firm's profits grow over time by pursuing strategies to sell more products in existing markets or by pursuing strategies to enter new markets. As we shall see, expanding internationally can help managers boost the firm's profitability *and* increase the rate of profit growth over time.

Value Creation

The way to increase the profitability of a firm is to create more value. The amount of value a firm creates is measured by the difference between its costs of production and the value that consumers perceive in its products. In general, the more value customers place on a firm's products, the higher the price the firm can charge for those products. However, the price a firm charges for a good or service is typically less than the value placed on that good or service by the customer. This is because the customer captures some of that value in the form of what economists call a consumer surplus.[4] The customer is able to do this because the firm is competing with other firms for the customer's business, so the firm must charge a lower price than it could were it a monopoly supplier. Also, it is normally impossible to segment the market to such a degree that the firm can charge each customer a price that reflects that individual's assessment of the value of a product, which economists refer to as a customer's reservation price. For these reasons, the price that gets charged tends to be less than the value placed on the product by many customers.

Figure 13.2 illustrates these concepts. The value of a product to an *average* consumer is V; the average price that the firm can charge a consumer for that product given competitive pressures and its ability to segment the market is P; and the average unit cost of producing that product is C (C comprises all relevant costs, including the firm's cost of capital). The firm's profit per unit sold (p) is equal to $P - C$, while the consumer surplus per unit is equal to $V - P$ (another way of thinking of the consumer surplus is as "value for the money"; the greater the consumer surplus, the greater the value for the money the consumer gets). The firm makes a profit so long as P is greater than C, and its profit will be greater the lower C is *relative* to P. The difference between V and P is in part determined by the intensity of competitive pressure in the marketplace; the lower the intensity of competitive pressure, the higher the price charged relative to V.[5] In general, the higher the firm's profit per unit sold, the greater its profitability, all else being equal.

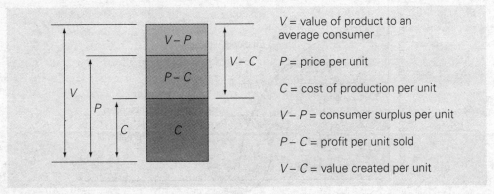

Figure 13.2 *Value Creation*

The firm's **value creation** is measured by the difference between V and C ($V - C$); a company creates value by converting inputs that cost C into a product on which consumers place a value of V. A company can create more value ($V - C$) either by lowering production costs, C, or by making the product more attractive through superior design, styling, functionality, features, reliability, after-sales service, and the like, so that consumers place a greater value on it (V increases) and, consequently, are willing to pay a higher price (P increases). This discussion suggests that *a firm has high profits when it creates more value for its customers and does so at a lower cost.* We refer to a strategy that focuses primarily on lowering production costs as a *low-cost strategy.* We refer to a strategy that focuses primarily on increasing the attractiveness of a product as a *differentiation strategy.*[6]

Michael Porter has argued that *low cost* and *differentiation* are two basic strategies for creating value and attaining a competitive advantage in an industry.[7] According to Porter, superior profitability goes to those firms that can create superior value, and the way to create superior value is to drive down the cost structure of the business and/or differentiate the product in some way so that consumers value it more and are prepared to pay a premium price. Superior value creation relative to rivals does not necessarily require a firm to have the lowest-cost structure in an industry, or to create the most valuable product in the eyes of consumers. However, it does require that the gap between value (V) and cost of production (C) be greater than the gap attained by competitors.

Strategic Positioning

Porter notes that it is important for a firm to be explicit about its choice of strategic emphasis with regard to value creation (differentiation) and low cost, and to configure its internal operations to support that strategic emphasis.[8] Figure 13.3 illustrates his point. The convex curve in Figure 13.3 is what economists refer to as an efficiency frontier. The efficiency frontier shows all of the different positions that a firm can adopt with regard to adding value to the product (V) and low cost (C) assuming that its internal operations are configured efficiently to support a particular position (note that the horizontal axis in Figure 13.3 is reverse scaled—moving along the axis to the right implies lower costs). The efficiency frontier has a convex shape because of diminishing returns. Diminishing returns imply that when a firm already has significant value built into its product offering, increasing value by a relatively small amount requires significant additional costs. The converse also holds, when a firm already has a low-cost structure, it has to give up a lot of value in its product offering to get additional cost reductions.

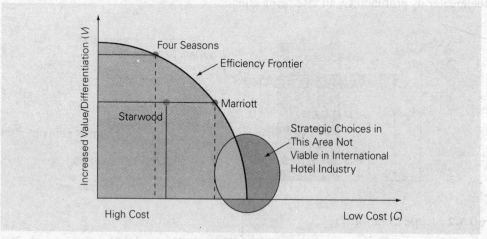

Figure 13.3 *Strategic Choice in the International Hotel Industry*

Figure 13.3 plots three hotel firms with a global presence that cater to international travelers, Four Seasons, Marriott International, and Starwood (Starwood owns the Sheraton and Westin chains). Four

Seasons positions itself as a luxury chain and emphasizes the value of its product offering, which drives up its costs of operations. Marriott and Starwood are positioned more in the middle of the market. Both emphasize sufficient value to attract international business travelers, but are not luxury chains like Four Seasons. In Figure 13.3, Four Seasons and Marriott are shown to be on the efficiency frontier, indicating that their internal operations are well configured to their strategy and run efficiently. Starwood is inside the frontier, indicating that its operations are not running as efficiently as they might be and that its costs are too high. This implies that Starwood is less profitable than Four Seasons and Marriott and that its managers must take steps to improve the company's performance.

Porter emphasizes that it is very important for management to decide where the company wants to be positioned with regard to value (V) and cost (C), to configure operations accordingly, and to manage them efficiently to make sure the firm is operating on the efficiency frontier. However, not all positions on the efficiency frontier are viable. In the international hotel industry, for example, there might not be enough demand to support a chain that emphasizes very low cost and strips all the value out of its product offering (see Figure 13.3). International travelers are relatively affluent and expect a degree of comfort (value) when they travel away from home.

A central tenet of the basic strategy paradigm is that to maximize its profitability, a firm must do three things: (*a*) pick a position on the efficiency frontier that is viable in the sense that there is enough demand to support that choice; (*b*) configure its internal operations, such as manufacturing, marketing, logistics, information systems, human resources, and so on, so that they support that position; and (*c*) make sure that the firm has the right organization structure in place to execute its strategy. *The strategy, operations, and organization of the firm must all be consistent with each other if it is to attain a competitive advantage and garner superior profitability.* By **operations** we mean the different value creation activities a firm undertakes, which we review next.

Operations: the Firm as a Value Chain

The operations of a firm can be thought of as a value chain composed of a series of distinct value creation activities, including production, marketing and sales, materials management, R&D, human resources, information systems, and the firm infrastructure. We can categorize these value creation activities, or operations, as primary activities and support activities (see Figure 13.4).[9] As noted above, if a firm is to implement its strategy efficiently, and position itself on the efficiency frontier shown in Figure 13.3, it must manage these activities effectively and in a manner that is consistent with its strategy.

Primary Activities

Primary activities have to do with the design, creation, and delivery of the product; its marketing; and its support and after-sale service. Following normal practice, in the value chain illustrated in Figure 13.4, the primary activities are divided into four functions: research and development, production, marketing and sales, and customer service.

Research and development (R&D) is concerned with the design of products and production processes. Although we think of R&D as being associated with the design of physical products and production processes in manufacturing enterprises, many service companies also undertake R&D. For example, banks compete with each other by developing new financial products and new ways of delivering those products to customers. Online banking and smart debit cards are two examples of product development in the banking industry. Earlier examples of innovation in the banking industry included automated teller machines, credit cards, and debit cards. Through superior product design, R&D can increase the

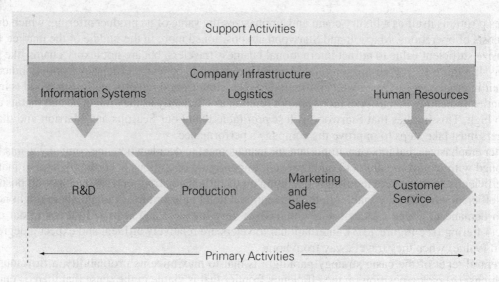

Figure 13.4 *The Value Chain*

functionality of products, which makes them more attractive to consumers (raising *V*). Alternatively, R&D may result in more efficient production processes, thereby cutting production costs (lowering *C*). Either way, the R&D function can create value.

Production is concerned with the creation of a good or service. For physical products, when we talk about production, we generally mean manufacturing. Thus, we can talk about the production of an automobile. For services such as banking or health care, "production" typically occurs when the service is delivered to the customer (for example, when a bank originates a loan for a customer, it is engaged in "production" of the loan). For a retailer such as Walmart, "production" is concerned with selecting the merchandise, stocking the store, and ringing up the sale at the cash register. For MTV, production is concerned with the creation, programming, and broadcasting of content, such as music videos and thematic shows. The production activity of a firm creates value by performing its activities efficiently so lower costs result (lower *C*) and/or by performing them in such a way that a higher-quality product is produced (which results in higher *V*).

The marketing and sales functions of a firm can help create value in several ways. Through brand positioning and advertising, the marketing function can increase the value (*V*) that consumers perceive to be contained in a firm's product. If these create a favorable impression of the firm's product in the minds of consumers, they increase the price that can be charged for the firm's product. For example, Ford produced a high-value version of its Ford Expedition SUV. Sold as the Lincoln Navigator and priced around $10,000 higher, the Navigator has the same body, engine, chassis, and design as the Expedition, but through skilled advertising and marketing, supported by some fairly minor features changes (e.g., more accessories and the addition of a Lincoln-style engine grille and nameplate), Ford has fostered the perception that the Navigator is a "luxury SUV." This marketing strategy has increased the perceived value (*V*) of the Navigator relative to the Expedition and enables Ford to charge a higher price for the car (*P*).

Marketing and sales can also create value by discovering consumer needs and communicating them back to the R&D function of the company, which can then design products that better match those needs. For example, the allocation of research budgets at Pfizer, the world's largest pharmaceutical company, is determined by the marketing function's assessment of the potential market size associated with solving unmet medical needs. Thus, Pfizer is currently directing significant monies to R&D efforts aimed at finding treatments for Alzheimer's disease, principally because marketing has identified the treatment of Alzheimer's as a major unmet medical need in nations around the world where the population is aging.

The role of the enterprise's service activity is to provide after-sale service and support. This function can create a perception of superior value (V) in the minds of consumers by solving customer problems and supporting customers after they have purchased the product. Caterpillar, the U.S.-based manufacturer of heavy earthmoving equipment, can get spare parts to any point in the world within 24 hours, thereby minimizing the amount of downtime its customers have to suffer if their Caterpillar equipment malfunctions. This is an extremely valuable capability in an industry where downtime is very expensive. It has helped to increase the value that customers associate with Caterpillar products and thus the price that Caterpillar can charge.

Support Activities

The support activities of the value chain provide inputs that allow the primary activities to occur (see Figure 13.4). In terms of attaining a competitive advantage, support activities can be as important as, if not more important than, the primary activities of the firm. Consider information systems; these systems refer to the electronic systems for managing inventory, tracking sales, pricing products, selling products, dealing with customer service inquiries, and so on. Information systems, when coupled with the communications features of the Internet, can alter the efficiency and effectiveness with which a firm manages its other value creation activities. Dell, for example, has used its information systems to attain a competitive advantage over rivals. When customers place an order for a Dell product over the firm's website, that information is immediately transmitted, via the Internet, to suppliers, who then configure their production schedules to produce and ship that product so that it arrives at the right assembly plant at the right time. These systems have reduced the amount of inventory that Dell holds at its factories to under two days, which is a major source of cost savings.

The logistics function controls the transmission of physical materials through the value chain, from procurement through production and into distribution. The efficiency with which this is carried out can significantly reduce cost (lower C), thereby creating more value. The combination of logistics systems and information systems is a particularly potent source of cost savings in many enterprises, such as Dell, where information systems tell Dell on a real-time basis where in its global logistics network parts are, when they will arrive at an assembly plant, and thus how production should be scheduled.

The human resource function can help create more value in a number of ways. It ensures that the company has the right mix of skilled people to perform its value creation activities effectively. The human resource function also ensures that people are adequately trained, motivated, and compensated to perform their value creation tasks. In a multinational enterprise, one of the things human resources can do to boost the competitive position of the firm is to take advantage of its transnational reach to identify, recruit, and develop a cadre of skilled managers, regardless of their nationality, who can be groomed to take on senior management positions. They can find the very best, wherever they are in the world. Indeed, the senior management ranks of many multinationals are becoming increasingly diverse, as managers from a variety of national backgrounds have ascended to senior leadership positions. Japan's Sony, for example, is now headed not by a Japanese national, but by Howard Stringer, a Welshman.

The final support activity is the company infrastructure, or the context within which all the other value creation activities occur. The infrastructure includes the organization structure, control systems, and culture of the firm. Because top management can exert considerable influence in shaping these aspects of a firm, top management should also be viewed as part of the firm's infrastructure. Through strong leadership, top management can consciously shape the infrastructure of a firm and through that the performance of all its value creation activities.

GLOBAL EXPANSION, PROFITABILITY, AND PROFIT GROWTH

Expanding globally allows firms to increase their profitability and rate of profit growth in ways not available to purely domestic enterprises.[10] Firms that operate internationally are able to:

1. Expand the market for their domestic product offerings by selling those products in international markets.
2. Realize location economies by dispersing individual value creation activities to those locations around the globe where they can be performed most efficiently and effectively.
3. Realize greater cost economies from experience effects by serving an expanded global market from a central location, thereby reducing the costs of value creation.
4. Earn a greater return by leveraging any valuable skills developed in foreign operations and transferring them to other entities within the firm's global network of operations.

As we will see, however, a firm's ability to increase its profitability and profit growth by pursuing these strategies is constrained by the need to customize its product offering, marketing strategy, and business strategy to differing national conditions, that is, by the imperative of localization.

Expanding the Market: Leveraging Products and Competencies

A company can increase its growth rate by taking goods or services developed at home and selling them internationally. Almost all multinationals started out doing just this. For example, Procter & Gamble developed most of its best-selling products such as Pampers disposable diapers and Ivory soap in the United States, and subsequently then sold them around the world. Likewise, although Microsoft developed its software in the United States, from its earliest days the company has always focused on selling that software in international markets. Automobile companies such as Volkswagen and Toyota also grew by developing products at home and then selling them in international markets. The returns from such a strategy are likely to be greater if indigenous competitors in the nations a company enters lack comparable products. Thus, Toyota increased its profits by entering the large automobile markets of North America and Europe, offering products that were different from those offered by local rivals (Ford and GM) by their superior quality and reliability.

The success of many multinational companies that expand in this manner is based not just upon the goods or services that they sell in foreign nations, but also upon the core competencies that underlie the development, production, and marketing of those goods or services. The term **core competence** refers to skills within the firm that competitors cannot easily match or imitate.[11] These skills may exist in any of the firm's value creation activities—production, marketing, R&D, human resources, logistics, general management, and so on. Such skills are typically expressed in product offerings that other firms find difficult to match or imitate. Core competencies are the bedrock of a firm's competitive advantage. They enable a firm to reduce the costs of value creation and/or to create perceived value in such a way that premium pricing is possible. For example, Toyota has a core competence in the production of cars. It is able to produce high-quality, well-designed cars at a lower delivered cost than any other firm in the world. The competencies that enable Toyota to do this seem to reside primarily in the firm's production and logistics functions.[12] McDonald's has a core competence in managing fast-food operations (it seems to be one of the most skilled firms in the world in this industry). Since core competencies are by definition the source of a firm's competitive advantage, the successful global expansion by manufacturing companies such as Toyota and P&G was based not only on leveraging products and selling them in foreign markets but also on the transfer of core competencies to foreign markets where indigenous competitors lacked them.

Location Economies

Earlier chapters revealed that countries differ along a range of dimensions, including the economic, political, legal, and cultural, and that these differences can either raise or lower the costs of doing business in a country. The theory of international trade also teaches that due to differences in factor costs, certain countries have a comparative advantage in the production of certain products. Japan might excel in the production of automobiles and consumer electronics; the United States in the production of computer software, pharmaceuticals, biotechnology products, and financial services.[13] For a firm that is trying to survive in a competitive global market, this implies that *trade barriers and transportation costs* permitting, the firm will benefit by basing each value creation activity it performs at that location where economic, political, and cultural conditions, including relative factor costs, are most conducive to the performance of that activity.

Firms that pursue such a strategy can realize what we refer to as **location economies**, which are the economies that arise from performing a value creation activity in the optimal location for that activity, wherever in the world that might be (transportation costs and trade barriers permitting). Locating a value creation activity in the optimal location for that activity can have one of two effects. *It can lower the costs of value creation and help the firm achieve a low-cost position, and/or it can enable a firm to differentiate its product offering from those of competitors.* In terms of Figure 13.2, it can lower C and/ or increase V (which in general supports higher pricing), both of which boost the profitability of the enterprise.

For an example of how this works in an international business, consider ClearVision Optical, a manufacturer and distributor of eyewear. Started by David Glassman, the firm now generates annual gross revenues of more than $100 million. Not exactly small, but no corporate giant either, ClearVision is a multinational firm with production facilities on three continents and customers around the world. ClearVision began its move toward becoming a multinational when its sales were still less than $20 million. At the time, the U.S. dollar was very strong, and this made U.S.-based manufacturing expensive. Low-priced imports were taking an ever-larger share of the U.S. eyewear market, and ClearVision realized it could not survive unless it also began to import. Initially the firm bought from independent overseas manufacturers, primarily in Hong Kong. However, the firm became dissatisfied with these suppliers' product quality and delivery. As ClearVision's volume of imports increased, Glassman decided the best way to guarantee quality and delivery was to set up ClearVision's own manufacturing operation overseas. Accordingly, ClearVision found a Chinese partner, and together they opened a manufacturing facility in Hong Kong, with ClearVision being the majority shareholder.

The choice of the Hong Kong location was influenced by its combination of low labor costs, a skilled workforce, and tax breaks given by the Hong Kong government. The firm's objective at this point was to lower production costs by locating value creation activities at an appropriate location. After a few years, however, the increasing industrialization of Hong Kong and a growing labor shortage had pushed up wage rates to the extent that it was no longer a low-cost location. In response, Glassman and his Chinese partner moved part of their manufacturing to a plant in mainland China to take advantage of the lower wage rates there. Again, the goal was to lower production costs. The parts for eyewear frames manufactured at this plant were shipped to the Hong Kong factory for final assembly and then distributed to markets in North and South America. The Hong Kong factory now employs 80 people and the Chinese plant between 300 and 400.

At the same time, ClearVision was looking for opportunities to invest in foreign eyewear firms with reputations for fashionable design and high quality. Its objective was not to reduce production costs but to launch a line of high-quality differentiated, "designer" eyewear. ClearVision did not have the design capability in-house to support such a line, but Glassman knew that certain foreign manufacturers did. As a result, ClearVision invested in factories in Japan, France, and Italy, holding a minority shareholding in each case. These factories now supply eyewear for ClearVision's Status Eye division, which markets high-priced designer eyewear.[14]

Thus, to deal with a threat from foreign competition, ClearVision adopted a strategy intended to lower its cost structure (lower C): shifting its production from a high-cost location, the United States, to a low-cost location, first Hong Kong and later China. Then ClearVision adopted a strategy intended to increase the perceived value of its product (increase V) so it could charge a premium price (P). Reasoning that premium pricing in eyewear depended on superior design, its strategy involved investing capital in French, Italian, and Japanese factories that had reputations for superior design. In sum, ClearVision's strategies included some actions intended to reduce its costs of creating value and other actions intended to add perceived value to its product through differentiation. The overall goal was to increase the value created by ClearVision and thus the profitability of the enterprise. To the extent that these strategies were successful, the firm should have attained a higher profit margin and greater profitability than if it had remained a U.S.-based manufacturer of eyewear.

Creating a Global Web

Generalizing from the ClearVision example, one result of this kind of thinking is the creation of a **global web** of value creation activities, with different stages of the value chain being dispersed to those locations around the globe where perceived value is maximized or where the costs of value creation are minimized.[15] Consider Lenovo's ThinkPad laptop computers (Lenovo is the Chinese computer company that purchased IBM's personal computer operations in 2005).[16] This product is designed in the United States, where marketing and sales are also based. The components are made in Thailand, South Korea, Malaysia, and the United States. They are then manufactured in China.

In theory, a firm that realizes location economies by dispersing each of its value creation activities to its optimal location should have a competitive advantage vis-à-vis a firm that bases all of its value creation activities at a single location. It should be able to better differentiate its product offering (thereby raising perceived value, V) and lower its cost structure (C) than its single-location competitor. In a world where competitive pressures are increasing, such a strategy may become an imperative for survival.

Some Caveats

Introducing transportation costs and trade barriers complicates this picture. Due to favorable factor endowments, New Zealand may have a comparative advantage for automobile assembly operations, but high transportation costs would make it an uneconomical location from which to serve global markets. Another caveat concerns the importance of assessing political and economic risks when making location decisions. Even if a country looks very attractive as a production location when measured against all the standard criteria, if its government is unstable or totalitarian, the firm might be advised not to base production there. (Political risk is discussed in Chapter 2.) Similarly, if the government appears to be pursuing inappropriate economic policies that could lead to foreign exchange risk, that might be another reason for not basing production in that location, even if other factors look favorable.

Experience Effects

The **experience curve** refers to systematic reductions in production costs that have been observed to occur over the life of a product.[17] A number of studies have observed that a product's production costs decline by some quantity about each time *cumulative* output doubles. Figure 13.5 illustrates this experience curve relationship between unit production costs and *cumulative* output (the relationship is for *cumulative* output over time, and *not* output in any one period, such as a year). Two things explain this: learning effects and economies of scale.

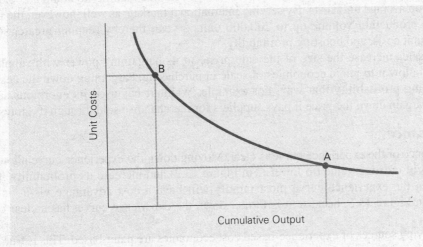

Figure 13.5 *The Experience Curve*

Learning Effects

Learning effects refer to cost savings that come from learning by doing. Labor, for example, learns by repetition how to carry out a task, such as assembling airframes, most efficiently. Labor productivity increases over time as individuals learn the most efficient ways to perform particular tasks. Equally important, in new production facilities management typically learns how to manage the new operation more efficiently over time. Hence, production costs decline due to increasing labor productivity and management efficiency, which increases the firm's profitability. No matter how complex the task, however, learning effects typically disappear after a while. It has been suggested that they are important only during the start-up period of a new process and that they cease after two or three years.[18] Any decline in the experience curve after such a point is due to economies of scale.

Economies of Scale

Economies of scale refer to the reductions in unit cost achieved by producing a large volume of a product. Attaining economies of scale lowers a firm's unit costs and increases its profitability. Economies of scale have a number of sources. One is the ability to spread fixed costs over a large volume.[19] Fixed costs are the costs required to set up a production facility, develop a new product, and the like. They can be substantial. For example, the fixed cost of establishing a new production line to manufacture semiconductor chips now exceeds $1 billion. Similarly, according to one estimate, developing a new drug and bringing it to market costs about $800 million and takes about 12 years.[20] The only way to recoup such high fixed costs may be to sell the product worldwide, which reduces average unit costs by spreading fixed costs over a larger volume. The more rapidly that cumulative sales volume is built up, the more rapidly fixed costs can be amortized over a large production volume, and the more rapidly unit costs will fall.

Second, a firm may not be able to attain an efficient scale of production unless it serves global markets. In the automobile industry, for example, an efficiently scaled factory is one designed to produce about 200,000 units a year. Automobile firms would prefer to produce a single model from each factory since this eliminates the costs associated with switching production from one model to another. If domestic demand for a particular model is only 100,000 units a year, the inability to attain a 200,000-unit output will drive up average unit costs. By serving international markets as well, however, the firm may be able to push production volume up to 200,000 units a year, thereby reaping greater scale economies, lowering unit costs, and boosting profitability.

Finally, as global sales increase the size of the enterprise, so its bargaining power with suppliers increases, which may allow it to attain economies of scale in purchasing, bargaining down the cost of key inputs and boosting profitability that way. For example, Walmart has used its enormous sales volume as a lever to bargain down the price it pays suppliers for merchandise sold through its stores.

Strategic Significance

The strategic significance of the experience curve is clear. Moving down the experience curve allows a firm to reduce its cost of creating value (to lower C in Figure 13.2) and increase its profitability. The firm that moves down the experience curve most rapidly will have a cost advantage vis-à-vis its competitors. Firm A in Figure 13.5, because it is farther down the experience curve, has a clear cost advantage over firm B.

Many of the underlying sources of experience-based cost economies are plant-based. This is true for most learning effects as well as for the economies of scale derived by spreading the fixed costs of building productive capacity over a large output, attaining an efficient scale of output, and utilizing a plant more intensively. Thus, one key to progressing downward on the experience curve as rapidly as possible is to increase the volume produced by a single plant as rapidly as possible. Because global markets are larger than domestic markets, a firm that serves a global market from a single location is likely to build accumulated volume more quickly than a firm that serves only its home market or that serves multiple markets from multiple production locations. Thus, serving a global market from a single location is consistent with moving down the experience curve and establishing a low-cost position. In addition, to get down the experience curve rapidly, a firm may need to price and market aggressively so demand will expand rapidly. It will also need to build sufficient production capacity for serving a global market. Also, the cost advantages of serving the world market from a single location will be even more significant if that location is the optimal one for performing the particular value creation activity.

Once a firm has established a low-cost position, it can act as a barrier to new competition. Specifically, an established firm that is well down the experience curve, such as firm A in Figure 13.5, can price so that it is still making a profit while new entrants, which are farther up the curve, are suffering losses.

The classic example of the successful pursuit of such a strategy concerns the Japanese consumer electronics company Matsushita. Along with Sony and Philips, Matsushita was in the race to develop a commercially viable videocassette recorder in the 1970s. Although Matsushita initially lagged behind

Philips and Sony, it was able to get its VHS format accepted as the world standard and to reap enormous experience curve–based cost economies in the process. This cost advantage subsequently constituted a formidable barrier to new competition. Matsushita's strategy was to build global volume as rapidly as possible. To ensure it could accommodate worldwide demand, the firm increased its production capacity 33-fold from 205,000 units in 1977 to 6.8 million units by 1984. By serving the world market from a single location in Japan, Matsushita realized significant learning effects and economies of scale. These allowed Matsushita to drop its prices 50 percent within five years of selling its first VHS-format VCR. As a result, Matsushita was the world's major VCR producer by 1983, accounting for about 45 percent of world production and enjoying a significant cost advantage over its competitors. The next largest firm, Hitachi, accounted for only 11.1 percent of world production in 1983.[21] Today, firms such as Intel are the masters of this kind of strategy. The costs of building a state-of-the-art facility to manufacture microprocessors are so large (now in excess of $2 billion) that to make this investment pay, Intel *must* pursue experience curve effects, serving world markets from a limited number of plants to maximize the cost economies that derive from scale and learning effects.

Leveraging Subsidiary Skills

Implicit in our earlier discussion of core competencies is the idea that valuable skills are developed first at home and then transferred to foreign operations. However, for more mature multinationals that have already established a network of subsidiary operations in foreign markets, the development of valuable skills can just as well occur in foreign subsidiaries.[22] Skills can be created anywhere within a multinational's global network of operations, wherever people have the opportunity and incentive to try new ways of doing things. The creation of skills that help lower the costs of production, or enhance perceived value and support higher product pricing, is not the monopoly of the corporate center.

Leveraging the skills created within subsidiaries and applying them to other operations within the firm's global network may create value. McDonald's increasingly is finding that its foreign franchisees are a source of valuable new ideas. Faced with slow growth in France, its local franchisees have begun to experiment not only with the menu but also with the layout and theme of restaurants. Gone are the ubiquitous golden arches; gone too are many of the utilitarian chairs and tables and other plastic features of the fast-food giant. Many McDonald's restaurants in France now have hardwood floors, exposed brick walls, and even armchairs. Half of the 1,200 or so outlets in France have been upgraded to a level that would make them unrecognizable to an American. The menu too has been changed to include premier sandwiches, such as chicken on focaccia bread, priced some 30 percent higher than the average hamburger. In France at least, the strategy seems to be working. Following the change, increases in same-store sales rose from 1 percent annually to 3.4 percent. Impressed with the impact, McDonald's executives are considering similar changes at other McDonald's restaurants in markets where same-store sales growth is sluggish, including the United States.[23] Another example of a multinational firm leveraging subsidiary skills is given in the next Management Focus feature.

For the managers of the multinational enterprise, this phenomenon creates important new challenges. First, they must have the humility to recognize that valuable skills that lead to competencies can arise anywhere within the firm's global network, not just at the corporate center. Second, they must establish an incentive system that encourages local employees to acquire new skills. This is not as easy as it sounds. Creating new skills involves a degree of risk. Not all new skills add value. For every valuable idea created by a McDonald's subsidiary in a foreign country, there may be several failures. The management of the multinational must install incentives that encourage employees to take the necessary risks. The company must reward people for successes and not sanction them unnecessarily for taking risks that did not pan out. Third, managers must have a process

MANAGEMENT FOCUS

Leveraging Subsidiary Skills at ArcelorMittal

In the 1990s Lakshmi Mittal began assembling what is now the world's largest steelmaker, ArcelorMittal, with 263,000 employees in 20 countries and 112 steelmaking facilities. Mittal perfected a deceptively simple strategy—buy rundown steel mills, cut costs, lay off excess workers, take actions to improve productivity, particularly through automation, and transform the acquisition into a profitable enterprise. It worked again and again all around the world.

More recently, he has kept the productivity gains coming by pursuing a strategy known in the company as "twinning." Mittal "twins" pairs of mills—usually of a similar size, age, product mix, and output level—against each other. The weaker mill is told to copy the practices of the stronger mill, while the stronger mill is told to keep its edge. Managers are summoned to regular meetings to compare their performance and to look for ways of improving the productivity of the weaker mill.

In one example, a poorly performing plant in Burns Harbor, Indiana, was twinned with a high-performing mill in Gent, Belgium. The Burns Harbor mill had been acquired by ArcelorMittal in 2008. Over 100 engineers and managers were flown from Burns Harbor to Gent and told to look at everything the Belgiums did and copy them. The Belgium mill was one of the most efficient of its kind in the world, with work hours per ton of steel produced coming in at 1.25, versus an industry average of 2.0.

The Americans quickly realized that Gent's high performance was not due to lower pay—in fact, total pay plus benefits was higher in Gent than at Burns Harbor. Rather, the Belgium mill had adopted a number of processes that increased productivity. For example, in Gent a computer coordinates the movement and processing of iron and steel slabs, whereas in Burns Harbor the same work was done by workers relying on phone calls and paper. Employees at Gent had also made a number of modifications to reduce waste. They developed a specially designed nozzle attached to a huge hose that was used to remove flakes from hot steel. Placed at a more efficient angle, the same amount of surface impurities could be removed with less water. Welders at Gent also cut coils of steel to order, which also kept waste to a minimum.

By adopting the improvements pioneered in Gent, employees at Burns Harbor found that they were able to significantly increase productivity. For example, by adopting the same computer software that the Gent workers had developed, employees at Burns Harbor were able to increase the average number of caldrons of molten steel they made each day from 42 to 50. As a result of improvements such as these, employee productivity at Burns Harbor, measured by work hours per ton of steel produced, increased from around 2.0 in 2008 to 1.32 in 2012. By leveraging the skills developed at Gent, and applying them to the Burns Harbor steel mill, ArcelorMittal had boosted the performance of the acquired company, creating considerable value in the process and guaranteeing the future of the Burns Harbor mill.[24]

for identifying when valuable new skills have been created in a subsidiary. And finally, they need to act as facilitators, helping transfer valuable skills within the firm.

Summary

We have seen how firms that expand globally can increase their profitability and profit growth by entering new markets where indigenous competitors lack similar competencies, by lowering costs and adding value to their product offering through the attainment of location economies, by exploiting experience curve effects, and by transferring valuable skills between their global network of subsidiaries. For completeness it should be noted that strategies that increase profitability may also expand a firm's business, and thus enable it to attain a higher rate of profit growth. For example, by simultaneously realizing location economies and experience effects, a firm may be able to produce a more highly valued product at a lower unit cost, thereby boosting profitability. The increase in the perceived value of the product may also attract more customers, thereby increasing revenues and profits as well. Furthermore, rather than raising prices to reflect the higher perceived value of the product, the firm's managers may elect to hold prices low in order to increase global market share and attain greater scale economies (in other words, they may elect to offer consumers better "value for money"). Such a strategy could increase the firm's rate of profit growth even further, since consumers will be attracted by prices that are low relative to value. The strategy might also increase profitability if the scale economies that result from market share gains are substantial. In sum, managers need to keep in mind the complex relationship between profitability and profit growth when making strategic decisions about pricing.

COST PRESSURES AND PRESSURES FOR LOCAL RESPONSIVENESS

LO13-3

Firms that compete in the global marketplace typically face two types of competitive pressure that affect their ability to realize location economies and experience effects, and to leverage products and transfer competencies and skills within the enterprise. They face *pressures for cost reductions* and *pressures to be locally responsive* (see Figure 13.6).[25] These competitive pressures place conflicting demands on a firm. Responding to pressures for cost reductions requires that a firm try to minimize its unit costs. But responding to pressures to be locally responsive requires that a firm differentiate its product offering and marketing strategy from country to country in an effort to accommodate the diverse demands arising

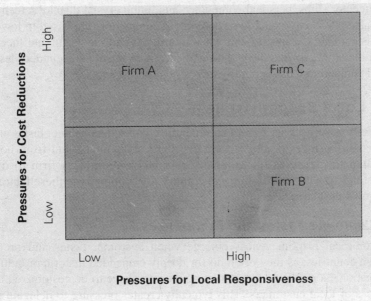

Figure 13.6 *Pressures for Cost Reductions and Local Responsiveness*

from national differences in consumer tastes and preferences, business practices, distribution channels, competitive conditions, and government policies. Because differentiation across countries can involve significant duplication and a lack of product standardization, it may raise costs.

While some enterprises, such as firm A in Figure 13.6, face high pressures for cost reductions and low pressures for local responsiveness, and others, such as firm B, face low pressures for cost reductions and high pressures for local responsiveness, many companies are in the position of firm C. They face high pressures for *both* cost reductions and local responsiveness. Dealing with these conflicting and contradictory pressures is a difficult strategic challenge, primarily because being locally responsive tends to raise costs.

Pressures for Cost Reductions

In competitive global markets, international businesses often face pressures for cost reductions. Responding to pressures for cost reduction requires a firm to try to lower the costs of value creation. A manufacturer, for example, might mass-produce a standardized product at the optimal location in the world, wherever that might be, to realize economies of scale, learning effects, and location economies (this in part is what Ford is trying to achieve with its One Ford strategy—see the opening case for details). Alternatively, a firm might outsource certain functions to low-cost foreign suppliers in an attempt to reduce costs. A service business such as a bank might respond to cost pressures by moving some back-office functions, such as information processing, to developing nations where wage rates are lower.

Pressures for cost reduction can be particularly intense in industries producing commodity-type products where meaningful differentiation on nonprice factors is difficult and price is the main competitive weapon. This tends to be the case for products that serve universal needs. **Universal needs** exist when the tastes and preferences of consumers in different nations are similar if not identical. This is the case for conventional commodity products such as bulk chemicals, petroleum, steel, sugar, and the like. It also tends to be the case for many industrial and consumer products, for example, handheld calculators, semiconductor chips, personal computers, and liquid crystal display screens. Pressures for cost reductions are also intense in industries where major competitors are based in low-cost locations, where there is persistent excess capacity and where consumers are powerful and face low switching costs. The liberalization of the world trade and investment environment in recent decades, by facilitating greater international competition, has generally increased cost pressures.[26]

Pressures for Local Responsiveness

Pressures for local responsiveness arise from national differences in consumer tastes and preferences, infrastructure, accepted business practices, and distribution channels, and from host-government demands. Responding to pressures to be locally responsive requires a firm to differentiate its products and marketing strategy from country to country to accommodate these factors, all of which tends to raise the firm's cost structure.

Differences in Customer Tastes and Preferences

Strong pressures for local responsiveness emerge when customer tastes and preferences differ significantly between countries, as they often do for deeply embedded historic or cultural reasons. In such cases, a multinational's products and marketing message have to be customized to appeal to the tastes and preferences of local customers. This typically creates pressure to delegate production and marketing responsibilities and functions to a firm's overseas subsidiaries.

For example, the automobile industry in the 1980s and early 1990s moved toward the creation of "world cars." The idea was that global companies such as General Motors, Ford, and Toyota would be able to sell the same basic vehicle the world over, sourcing it from centralized production locations. If successful, the strategy would have enabled automobile companies to reap significant gains from global scale economies. However, this strategy frequently ran aground on the hard rocks of consumer reality. Consumers in different automobile markets seem to have different tastes and preferences, and demand different types of vehicles. North American consumers show a strong demand for pickup trucks. This is particularly true in the South and West where many families have a pickup truck as a second or third car. But in European countries, pickup trucks are seen purely as utility vehicles and are purchased primarily by firms rather than individuals. As a consequence, the product mix and marketing message needs to be tailored to consider the different nature of demand in North America and Europe. Interestingly, Ford is now trying to shift back to the "world car" concept with its One Ford strategy (see the opening case). This shift reflects Ford's belief that the differences between tastes and preferences that derailed the world car concept in the 1990s are not as important in the second decade of the twenty-first century.

Some commentators have argued that customer demands for local customization are on the decline worldwide.[28] According to this argument, modern communications and transport technologies have created the conditions for a convergence of the tastes and preferences of consumers from different nations. The result is the emergence of enormous global markets for standardized consumer products. The worldwide acceptance of McDonald's hamburgers, Coca-Cola, Gap clothes, Apple iPhones, and Microsoft's Xbox, all of which are sold globally as standardized products, are often cited as evidence of the increasing homogeneity of the global marketplace.

However, this argument may not hold in many consumer goods markets. Significant differences in consumer tastes and preferences still exist across nations and cultures. Managers in international businesses do not yet have the luxury of being able to ignore these differences, and they may not for a long time to come. For an example of a company that has discovered how important pressures for local responsiveness can still be, read the accompanying Management Focus on MTV Networks.

Differences in Infrastructure and Traditional Practices

Pressures for local responsiveness arise from differences in infrastructure or traditional practices among countries, creating a need to customize products accordingly. Fulfilling this need may require the delegation of manufacturing and production functions to foreign subsidiaries. For example, in North America, consumer electrical systems are based on 110 volts, whereas in some European countries, 240-volt systems are standard. Thus, domestic electric appliances have to be customized for this difference in infrastructure.

Although many national differences in infrastructure are rooted in history, some are quite recent. For example, in the wireless telecommunications industry different technical standards exist in different parts of the world. A technical standard known as GSM is common in Europe, and an alternative standard, CDMA, is more common in the United States and parts of Asia. Equipment designed for GSM will not work on a CDMA network, and vice versa. Thus, companies such as Nokia, Motorola, and Samsung, which manufacture wireless handsets and infrastructure such as switches, need to customize their product offering according to the technical standard prevailing in a given country.

Differences in Distribution Channels

A firm's marketing strategies may have to be responsive to differences in distribution channels among countries, which may necessitate the delegation of marketing functions to national subsidiaries. In the

Local Responsiveness at MTV Networks

MTV Networks has become a symbol of globalization. Established in 1981, the U.S.-based TV network has been expanding outside of its North American base since 1987 when it opened MTV Europe. Today MTV Networks figures that every second of every day over 2 million people are watching MTV around the world, the majority outside the United States. Despite its international success, MTV's global expansion got off to a weak start. In the 1980s, when the main programming fare was still music videos, it piped a single feed across Europe almost entirely composed of American programming with English-speaking veejays. Naively, the network's U.S. managers thought Europeans would flock to the American programming. But while viewers in Europe shared a common interest in a handful of global superstars, their tastes turned out to be surprisingly local. After losing share to local competitors, who focused more on local tastes, MTV changed its strategy in the 1990s. It broke its service into "feeds" aimed at national or regional markets. While MTV Networks exercises creative control over these different feeds, and while all the channels have the same familiar frenetic look and feel of MTV in the United States, a significant share of the programming and content is now local.

Although a lot of programming ideas still originate in the United States, with staples such as the *Real World* having equivalents in different countries, an increasing share of programming is local in conception. In Italy, *MTV Kitchen* combines cooking with a music countdown. *Erotica* airs in Brazil and features a panel of youngsters discussing sex. The Indian channel produces 21 homegrown shows hosted by local veejays who speak "Hinglish," a city-bred version of Hindi and English. Many feeds still feature music videos by locally popular performers. This localization push reaped big benefits for MTV, allowing the network to capture viewers back from local imitators.[27]

pharmaceutical industry, for example, the British and Japanese distribution systems are radically different from the U.S. system. British and Japanese doctors will not accept or respond favorably to a U.S.-style high-pressure sales force. Thus, pharmaceutical companies have to adopt different marketing practices in Britain and Japan compared with the United States—soft sell versus hard sell. Similarly, Poland, Brazil, and Russia all have similar per capita income on a purchasing power parity basis, but there are big differences in distribution systems across the three countries. In Brazil, supermarkets account for 36 percent of food retailing, in Poland for 18 percent, and in Russia for less than 1 percent.[29] These differences in channels require that companies adapt their own distribution and sales strategy.

Host-Government Demands

Economic and political demands imposed by host-country governments may require local responsiveness. For example, pharmaceutical companies are subject to local clinical testing, registration procedures, and pricing restrictions, all of which make it necessary that the manufacturing and marketing of a drug should meet local requirements. Because governments and government agencies control a significant proportion of the health care budget in most countries, they are in a powerful position to demand a high level of local responsiveness.

More generally, threats of protectionism, economic nationalism, and local content rules (which require that a certain percentage of a product should be manufactured locally) dictate that international businesses manufacture locally. For example, consider Bombardier, the Canadian-based manufacturer of railcars, aircraft, jet boats, and snowmobiles. Bombardier has 12 railcar factories across Europe. Critics of the company argue that the resulting duplication of manufacturing facilities leads to high costs and helps explain why Bombardier makes lower profit margins on its railcar operations than on its other business lines. In reply, managers at Bombardier argue that in Europe, informal rules with regard to local content favor people who use local workers. To sell railcars in Germany, they claim, you must manufacture in Germany. The same goes for Belgium, Austria, and France. To try to address its cost structure in Europe, Bombardier has centralized its engineering and purchasing functions, but it has no plans to centralize manufacturing.[30]

CHOOSING A STRATEGY

LO13-4

Pressures for local responsiveness imply that it may not be possible for a firm to realize the full benefits from economies of scale, learning effects, and location economies. It may not be possible to serve the global marketplace from a single low-cost location, producing a globally standardized product, and marketing it worldwide to attain the cost reductions associated with experience effects. The need to customize the product offering to local conditions may work against the implementation of such a strategy.

In addition, pressures for local responsiveness imply that it may not be possible to leverage skills and products associated with a firm's core competencies wholesale from one nation to another. Concessions often have to be made to local conditions. Despite being depicted as "poster child" for the proliferation of standardized global products, even McDonald's has found that it has to customize its product offerings (i.e., its menu) to account for national differences in tastes and preferences.

How do differences in the strength of pressures for cost reductions versus those for local responsiveness affect a firm's choice of strategy? Firms typically choose among four main strategic postures when competing internationally. These can be characterized as a global standardization strategy, a localization strategy, a transnational strategy, and an international strategy.[31] The appropriateness of each strategy varies given the extent of pressures for cost reductions and local responsiveness. Figure 13.7 illustrates the conditions under which each of these strategies is most appropriate.

Global Standardization Strategy

Firms that pursue a **global standardization strategy** focus on increasing profitability and profit growth by reaping the cost reductions that come from economies of scale, learning effects, and location economies; that is, their strategic goal is to pursue a low-cost strategy on a global scale. The production, marketing, and R&D activities of firms pursuing a global standardization strategy are concentrated in a few favorable locations. Firms pursuing a global standardization strategy try not to customize their product offering and marketing strategy to local conditions because customization involves shorter production runs and the duplication of functions, which tend to raise costs. Instead, they prefer to market a standardized product worldwide so that they can reap the maximum benefits from economies of scale and learning effects. They also tend to use their cost advantage to support aggressive pricing in world markets.

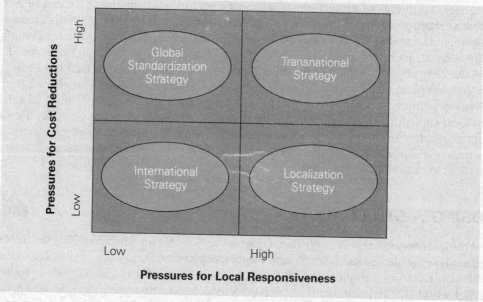

Figure 13.7 *Four Basic Strategies*

This strategy makes most sense when there are strong pressures for cost reductions and demands for local responsiveness are minimal. Increasingly, these conditions prevail in many industrial goods industries, whose products often serve universal needs. In the semiconductor industry, for example, global standards have emerged, creating enormous demands for standardized global products. Accordingly, companies such as Intel, Texas Instruments, and Motorola all pursue a global standardization strategy. However, these conditions are not always found in many consumer goods markets, where demands for local responsiveness remain high. The strategy is inappropriate when demands for local responsiveness can remain high.

Localization Strategy

A **localization strategy** focuses on increasing profitability by customizing the firm's goods or services so that they provide a good match to tastes and preferences in different national markets. Localization is most appropriate when there are substantial differences across nations with regard to consumer tastes and preferences, and where cost pressures are not too intense. By customizing the product offering to local demands, the firm increases the value of that product in the local market. On the downside, because it involves some duplication of functions and smaller production runs, customization limits the ability of the firm to capture the cost reductions associated with mass-producing a standardized product for global consumption. The strategy may make sense, however, if the added value associated with local customization supports higher pricing, which enables the firm to recoup its higher costs, or if it leads to substantially greater local demand, enabling the firm to reduce costs through the attainment of some scale economies in the local market.

At the same time, firms still have to keep an eye on costs. Firms pursuing a localization strategy still need to be efficient and, whenever possible, to capture some scale economies from their global reach. As noted earlier, many automobile companies have found that they have to customize some of their product offerings to local market demands—for example, producing large pickup trucks for U.S.

consumers and small, fuel-efficient cars for Europeans and Japanese. At the same time, these multinationals try to get some scale economies from their global volume by using common vehicle platforms and components across many different models, and manufacturing those platforms and components at efficiently scaled factories that are optimally located. By designing their products in this way, these companies have been able to localize their product offering, yet simultaneously capture some scale economies, learning effects, and location economies.

Transnational Strategy

We have argued that a global standardization strategy makes most sense when cost pressures are intense, and demands for local responsiveness are limited. Conversely, a localization strategy makes most sense when demands for local responsiveness are high, but cost pressures are moderate or low. What happens, however, when the firm simultaneously faces both strong cost pressures and strong pressures for local responsiveness? How can managers balance the competing and inconsistent demands such divergent pressures place on the firm? According to some researchers, the answer is to pursue what has been called a transnational strategy.

Two of these researchers, Christopher Bartlett and Sumantra Ghoshal, argue that in today's global environment, competitive conditions are so intense that to survive, firms must do all they can to respond to pressures for cost reductions and local responsiveness. They must try to realize location economies and experience effects, to leverage products internationally, to transfer core competencies and skills within the company, and to simultaneously pay attention to pressures for local responsiveness.[32] Bartlett and Ghoshal note that in the modern multinational enterprise, core competencies and skills do not reside just in the home country but can develop in any of the firm's worldwide operations. Thus, they maintain that the flow of skills and product offerings should not be all one way, from home country to foreign subsidiary. Rather, the flow should also be from foreign subsidiary to home country and from foreign subsidiary to foreign subsidiary. Transnational enterprises, in other words, must also focus on leveraging subsidiary skills.

In essence, firms that pursue a **transnational strategy** are trying to simultaneously achieve low costs through location economies, economies of scale, and learning effects; differentiate their product offering across geographic markets to account for local differences; and foster a multidirectional flow of skills between different subsidiaries in the firm's global network of operations. As attractive as this may sound in theory, the strategy is not an easy one to pursue since it places conflicting demands on the company. Differentiating the product to respond to local demands in different geographic markets raises costs, which runs counter to the goal of reducing costs. Companies such as 3M and ABB (one of the world's largest engineering conglomerates) have tried to embrace a transnational strategy and found it difficult to implement.

How best to implement a transnational strategy is one of the most complex questions that large multinationals are grappling with today. Few if any enterprises have perfected this strategic posture. But some clues as to the right approach can be derived from a number of companies. For an example, consider the case of Caterpillar. The need to compete with low-cost competitors such as Komatsu of Japan forced Caterpillar to look for greater cost economies. However, variations in construction practices and government regulations across countries mean that Caterpillar also has to be responsive to local demands. Therefore, Caterpillar confronted significant pressures for cost reductions *and* for local responsiveness.

To deal with cost pressures, Caterpillar redesigned its products to use many identical components and invested in a few large-scale component manufacturing facilities, sited at favorable locations, to fill global demand and realize scale economies. At the same time, the company augments the centralized manufacturing of components with assembly plants in each of its major global markets. At these plants, Caterpillar adds local product features, tailoring the finished product to local needs. Thus, Caterpillar is able to realize many of the benefits of global manufacturing while reacting to pressures for local responsiveness by differentiating its product among national markets.[33] Caterpillar started to pursue this strategy in the 1980s and by the 2000s had succeeded in doubling output per employee, significantly reducing its overall cost structure in the process. Meanwhile, Komatsu and Hitachi, which are still wedded to a Japan-centric global strategy, have seen their cost advantages evaporate and have been steadily losing market share to Caterpillar.

Changing a firm's strategic posture to build an organization capable of supporting a transnational strategy is a complex and challenging task. Some would say it is too complex, because the strategy implementation problems of creating a viable organization structure and control systems to manage this strategy are immense.

International Strategy

Sometimes it is possible to identify multinational firms that find themselves in the fortunate position of being confronted with low cost pressures and low pressures for local responsiveness. Many of these enterprises have pursued an **international strategy**, taking products first produced for their domestic market and selling them internationally with only minimal local customization. The distinguishing feature of many such firms is that they are selling a product that serves universal needs, but they do not face significant competitors, and thus unlike firms pursuing a global standardization strategy, they are not confronted with pressures to reduce their cost structure. Xerox found itself in this position in the 1960s after its invention and commercialization of the photocopier. The technology underlying the photocopier was protected by strong patents, so for several years Xerox did not face competitors—it had a monopoly. The product serves universal needs, and it was highly valued in most developed nations. Thus, Xerox was able to sell the same basic product the world over, charging a relatively high price for that product. Since Xerox did not face direct competitors, it did not have to deal with strong pressures to minimize its cost structure.

Enterprises pursuing an international strategy have followed a similar developmental pattern as they expanded into foreign markets. They tend to centralize product development functions such as R&D at home. However, they also tend to establish manufacturing and marketing functions in each major country or geographic region in which they do business. The resulting duplication can raise costs, but this is less of an issue if the firm does not face strong pressures for cost reductions. Although they may undertake some local customization of product offering and marketing strategy, this tends to be rather limited in scope. Ultimately, in most firms that pursue an international strategy, the head office retains fairly tight control over marketing and product strategy.

Other firms that have pursued this strategy include Procter & Gamble and Microsoft. Historically, Procter & Gamble developed innovative new products in Cincinnati and then transferred them wholesale to local markets (see the accompanying Management Focus). Similarly, the bulk of Microsoft's product development work occurs in Redmond, Washington, where the company is headquartered. Although some localization work is undertaken elsewhere, this is limited to producing foreign-language versions of popular Microsoft programs.

The Evolution of Strategy

The Achilles' heel of the international strategy is that over time, competitors inevitably emerge, and if managers do not take proactive steps to reduce their firm's cost structure, it will be rapidly outflanked

Evolution of Strategy at Procter & Gamble

Founded in 1837, Cincinnati-based Procter & Gamble has long been one of the world's most international companies. Today P&G is a global colossus in the consumer products business with annual sales in excess of $80 billion, some 54 percent of which are generated outside the United States. P&G sells more than 300 brands—including Ivory soap, Tide, Pampers, IAMS pet food, Crisco, and Folgers—to consumers in 180 countries. Historically the strategy at P&G was well established. The company developed new products in Cincinnati and then relied on semiautonomous foreign subsidiaries to manufacture, market, and distribute those products in different nations. In many cases, foreign subsidiaries had their own production facilities and tailored the packaging, brand name, and marketing message to local tastes and preferences. For years this strategy delivered a steady stream of new products and reliable growth in sales and profits. By the 1990s, however, profit growth at P&G was slowing.

The essence of the problem was simple; P&G's costs were too high because of extensive duplication of manufacturing, marketing, and administrative facilities in different national subsidiaries. The duplication of assets made sense in the world of the 1960s, when national markets were segmented from each other by barriers to cross-border trade. Products produced in Great Britain, for example, could not be sold economically in Germany due to high tariff duties levied on imports into Germany. By the 1980s, however, barriers to cross-border trade were falling rapidly worldwide and fragmented national markets were merging into larger regional or global markets. Also, the retailers through which P&G distributed its products were growing larger and more global, such as Walmart, Tesco from the United Kingdom, and Carrefour from France. These emerging global retailers were demanding price discounts from P&G.

In the 1990s P&G embarked on a major reorganization in an attempt to control its cost structure and recognize the new reality of emerging global markets. The company shut down some 30 manufacturing plants around the globe, laid off 13,000 employees, and concentrated production in fewer plants that could better realize economies of scale and serve regional markets. It wasn't enough! Profit growth remained sluggish so in 1999 P&G launched its second reorganization of the decade. Named "Organization 2005," the goal was to transform P&G into a truly global company. The company tore up its old organization, which was based on countries and regions, and replaced it with one based on seven self-contained global business units, ranging from baby care to food products. Each business unit was given complete responsibility for generating profits from its products, and for manufacturing, marketing, and product development. Each business unit was told to rationalize production, concentrating it in fewer larger facilities; to try to build global brands wherever possible, thereby eliminating marketing differences between countries; and to accelerate the development and launch of new products. P&G announced that as a result of this initiative, it would close another 10 factories and lay off another 15,000 employees, mostly in Europe where there was still extensive duplication of assets. The annual cost savings were estimated to be about $800 million. P&G planned to use the savings to cut prices and increase marketing spending in an effort to gain market share, and thus further lower costs through the attainment of scale economies. This time the strategy seemed to be working. For most of the 2000s P&G reported strong growth in both sales and profits. Significantly, P&G's global competitors, such as Unilever, Kimberly-Clark, and Colgate-Palmolive, were struggling during the same time period.[34]

by efficient global competitors. This is exactly what happened to Xerox. Japanese companies such as Canon ultimately invented their way around Xerox's patents, produced their own photocopiers in very efficient manufacturing plants, priced them below Xerox's products, and rapidly took global market share from Xerox. In the final analysis, Xerox's demise was not due to the emergence of competitors, for ultimately that was bound to occur, but due to its failure to proactively reduce its cost structure in advance of the emergence of efficient global competitors. The message in this story is that an international strategy may not be viable in the long term, and to survive, firms need to shift toward a global standardization strategy or a transnational strategy in advance of competitors (see Figure 13.8).

The same can be said about a localization strategy. Localization may give a firm a competitive edge, but if it is simultaneously facing aggressive competitors, the company will also have to reduce its cost structure, and the only way to do that may be to shift toward a transnational strategy. This is what Procter & Gamble has been doing (see the accompanying Management Focus). Thus, as competition intensifies, international and localization strategies tend to become less viable, and managers need to direct their companies toward either a global standardization strategy or a transnational strategy.

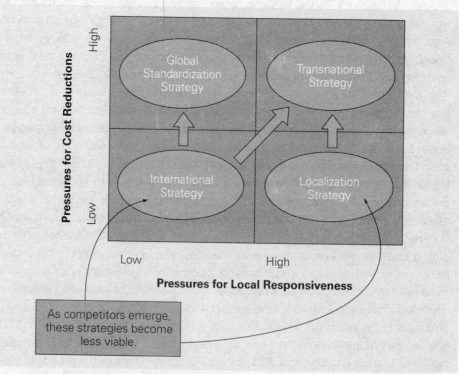

Figure 13.8 *Changes in Strategy over Time*

Chapter Summary

This chapter reviewed basic principles of strategy and the various ways in which firms can profit from global expansion, and it looked at the strategies that firms competing globally can adopt. The chapter made the following points:

1. A strategy can be defined as the actions that managers take to attain the goals of the firm. For most firms, the preeminent goal is to maximize shareholder value. Maximizing shareholder value requires firms to focus on increasing their profitability and the growth rate of profits over time.
2. International expansion may enable a firm to earn greater returns by transferring the product offerings derived from its core competencies to markets where indigenous competitors lack those product offerings and competencies.
3. It may pay a firm to base each value creation activity it performs at that location where factor conditions are most conducive to the performance of that activity. We refer to this strategy as focusing on the attainment of location economies.
4. By rapidly building sales volume for a standardized product, international expansion can assist a firm in moving down the experience curve by realizing learning effects and economies of scale.
5. A multinational firm can create additional value by identifying valuable skills created within its foreign subsidiaries and leveraging those skills within its global network of operations.
6. The best strategy for a firm to pursue often depends on a consideration of the pressures for cost reductions and for local responsiveness.
7. Firms pursuing an international strategy transfer the products derived from core competencies to foreign markets while undertaking some limited local customization.
8. Firms pursuing a localization strategy customize their product offering, marketing strategy, and business strategy to national conditions.
9. Firms pursuing a global standardization strategy focus on reaping the cost reductions that come from experience curve effects and location economies.
10. Many industries are now so competitive that firms must adopt a transnational strategy. This involves a simultaneous focus on reducing costs, transferring skills and products, and boosting local responsiveness. Implementing such a strategy may not be easy.

Critical Thinking and Discussion Questions

1. In a world of zero transportation costs, no trade barriers, and significant differences between nations with regard to factor conditions, firms must expand internationally if they are to survive. Discuss.
2. Plot the position of the following firms on Figure 13.6: Procter & Gamble, IBM, Apple, Coca-Cola, Dow Chemical, Intel, and McDonald's. In each case justify your answer.
3. In what kind of industries does a localization strategy make sense? When does a global standardization strategy make most sense?
4. Reread the Management Focus on Procter & Gamble, and then answer the following questions:
   a. What strategy was Procter & Gamble pursuing when it first entered foreign markets in the period up until the 1980s?
   b. Why do you think this strategy became less viable in the 1990s?

    c.   What strategy does P&G appear to be moving toward? What are the benefits of this strategy? What are the potential risks associated with it?

5.   What do you see as the main organizational problems that are likely to be associated with implementation of a transnational strategy?

Research Task   ◯ globalEDGE   globaledge.msu.edu

The Strategy of International Business

Use the globalEDGE website (globaledge.msu.edu) to complete the following exercises:

Exercise 1

Your company, a white goods manufacturer (primarily major kitchen appliances) based in the United States, has decided to pursue international expansion opportunities in sub-Saharan Africa. In order to achieve some economies of scale, your strategy is to minimize local adaptation. Focusing on a comparison of two sub-Saharan African countries of your choice, prepare an executive summary that features aspects of the product where standardization will simply not be possible and adaptation to local conditions will be essential.

Exercise 2

A. T. Kearney publishes an annual study to help retailers prioritize their global development strategies by ranking the retail expansion attractiveness of emerging countries based on a particular set of criteria. Find the latest version of this *Global Retail Development Index*. What criteria are used to identify the attractiveness of the retail environment in emerging countries? Categorize the top 10 countries by world region. Are there any of these countries that surprise you? Why (or why not)?

Closing CASE

Avon Products

For six years after Andrea Jung became CEO of Avon Products in 1999, revenues for the beauty products company famous for its direct-sales model grew in excess of 10 percent a year. Profits tripled, making Jung a Wall Street favorite. Then in 2005, the success story started to turn ugly. Avon, which derives as much as 70 percent of its revenues from international markets, mostly in developing nations, suddenly began losing sales across the globe. A ban on direct sales had hurt its business in China (the Chinese government had accused companies that used a direct-sales model of engaging in pyramid schemes and of creating "cults"). To compound matters, economic weakness in eastern Europe, Russia, and Mexico, all drivers of Avon's success, stalled growth further. The dramatic turn of events took investors by surprise. In May 2005 Jung had told investors that Avon would exceed Wall Street's targets for the year. By September she was rapidly backpedaling, and the stock fell 45 percent.

    With her job on the line, Jung began to reevaluate Avon's global strategy. Until this point, the company had expanded primarily by replicating its U.S. strategy and organization in other countries. When it entered a nation, it gave country managers considerable autonomy. All used the Avon brand name and adopted the direct-sales model that has been the company's hallmark. The result was an army of 5 million Avon representatives around the world, all independent contractors, who sold the company's skin care and makeup products. However, many country managers also set up their own local manufacturing operations and supply chains, were responsible for local marketing, and developed their own new products. In Jung's words, "they were the king or queen of every decision." The result was a lack of consistency in marketing strategy from nation to nation, extensive duplication of manufacturing operations and supply chains, and a profusion of new products, many of which were not profitable. In Mexico, for example, the roster of products for sale had ballooned to 13,000. The company had 15 layers of management, making accountability and communication problematic. There was also a distinct lack of data-driven analysis of new-product opportunities, with country managers often making decisions based on their intuition or gut feelings.

Jung's turnaround strategy involved several elements. To help transform Avon, she hired seasoned managers from well-known global consumer products companies such as Procter & Gamble and Unilever. She flattened the organization to improve communication, performance visibility, and accountability, reducing the number of management layers to just eight and laying off 30 percent of managers. Manufacturing was consolidated in a number of regional centers, and supply chains were rationalized, eliminating duplication and reducing costs by more than $1 billion a year. Rigorous return on investment criteria were introduced to evaluate product profitability. As a consequence, 25 percent of Avon's products were discontinued. New-product decisions were centralized at Avon's headquarters. Jung also invested in centralized product development. The goal was to develop and introduce blockbuster new products that could be positioned as global brands. And Jung pushed the company to emphasize its value proposition in every national market, which could be characterized as high quality at a low price.

By 2007 this strategy was starting to yield dividends. The company's performance improved and growth resumed. It didn't hurt that Jung, a Chinese-American who speaks Mandarin, was instrumental in persuading Chinese authorities to rescind the ban on direct sales, allowing Avon to recruit 400,000 new representatives in China. Then in 2008 and 2009 the global financial crisis hit. Jung's reaction: This was an opportunity for Avon to expand its business. In 2009, Avon ran ads around the world aimed at recruiting sales representatives. In the ads, female sales representatives talked about working for Avon. "I can't get laid off, I can't get fired," is what one said. Phones started to ring off the hook, and Avon was quickly able to expand its global sales force. Jung also instituted an aggressive pricing strategy, while packaging was redesigned for a more elegant look at no additional cost. The idea was to emphasize the "value for money" that Avon products represented. Media stars were used in ads to help market the company's products, and Avon pushed its representatives to use online social networking sites as a medium for marketing themselves.

The result of all this was initially good: In the difficult years of 2008 and 2009, Avon gained global market share and its financial performance improved. However, the company started to stumble again in 2010 and 2011. The reasons were complex. In many of Avon's important emerging markets, the company found itself increasingly on the defensive against rivals such as Procter & Gamble that were building a strong retail presence there. Meanwhile, sales in developed markets spluttered in the face of persistently slow economic growth. To complicate matters, there were reports of numerous operational mistakes—problems with implementing information systems, for example—that were costly for the company. Avon also came under fire for a possible violation of the Foreign Corrupt Practices Act when it was revealed that some executives in China had been paying bribes to local government officials. Under pressure from investors, in December 2011 Andrea Jung relinquished her CEO role, although she will stay on as chairwoman until at least 2014.[35]

Case Discussion Questions

1. What strategy was Avon pursuing until the mid-2000s? What were the advantages of this strategy? What were the disadvantages?

2. What changes did Andrea Jung make in Avon's strategy after 2005? What were the benefits of these changes? Can you see any drawbacks?

3. In terms of the framework introduced in this chapter, what strategy was Avon pursuing by the late 2000s?

4. Do you think that Avon's problems in 2010 and 2011 were a result of the changes in its strategy, or were there other reasons for this?

Endnotes

1. M. Ramsey, "Ford SUV Marks New World Car Strategy," *The Wall Street Journal,* November 16, 2011; B. Vlasic, "Ford Strategy Will Call for Stepping Up Expansion, Especially in Asia," *The New York Times,* June 7, 2011; and "Global Manufacturing Strategy Gives Ford Competitive Advantage," Ford Motor Company, http://media.ford.com/article_display.cfm?article_id=13633.

2. More formally, ROIC = net profit after tax ÷ capital, where capital includes the sum of the firm's equity and debt. This way of calculating profitability is highly correlated with return on assets.

3. T. Copeland, T. Koller, and J. Murrin, *Valuation: Measuring and Managing the Value of Companies* (New York: John Wiley & Sons, 2000).

4. The concept of consumer surplus is an important one in economics. For a more detailed exposition, see D. Besanko, D. Dranove, and M. Shanley, *Economics of Strategy* (New York: John Wiley & Sons, 1996).

5. However, $P = V$ only in the special case where the company has a perfect monopoly, and where it can charge each customer a unique price that reflects the value of the product to that customer (i.e., where perfect price discrimination is possible). More generally, except in the limiting case of perfect price discrimination, even a monopolist will see most consumers capture some of the value of a product in the form of a consumer surplus.

6. This point is central to the work of M. E. Porter, *Competitive Advantage* (New York: Free Press, 1985). See also chap. 4 in P. Ghemawat, *Commitment: The Dynamic of Strategy* (New York: Free Press, 1991).

7. M. E. Porter, *Competitive Strategy* (New York: Free Press, 1980).

8. M. E. Porter, "What Is Strategy?" *Harvard Business Review,* On-point Enhanced Edition article, February 1, 2000.

9. Porter, *Competitive Advantage.*

10. Empirical evidence does seem to indicate that, on average, international expansion is linked to greater firm profitability. For some examples, see M. A. Hitt, R. E. Hoskisson, and H. Kim, "International Diversification, Effects on Innovation and Firm Performance," *Academy of Management Journal* 40, no. 4 (1997), pp. 767–98; and S. Tallman and J. Li, "Effects of International Diversity and Product Diversity on the Performance of Multinational Firms," *Academy of Management Journal* 39, no. 1 (1996), pp. 179–96.

11. This concept has been popularized by G. Hamel and C. K. Prahalad, *Competing for the Future* (Boston: Harvard Business School Press, 1994). The concept is grounded in the resource-based view of the firm; for a summary, see J. B. Barney, "Firm Resources and Sustained Competitive Advantage," *Journal of Management* 17 (1991), pp. 99–120; and K. R. Conner, "A Historical Comparison of Resource-Based Theory and Five Schools of Thought within Industrial Organization Economics: Do We Have a New Theory of the Firm?" *Journal of Management* 17 (1991), pp. 121–54.

12. J. P. Womack, D. T. Jones, and D. Roos, *The Machine That Changed the World* (New York: Rawson Associates, 1990).

13. M. E. Porter, *The Competitive Advantage of Nations* (New York: Free Press, 1990).

14. Example is based on C. S. Trager, "Enter the Mini-multinational," *Northeast International Business,* March 1989, pp. 13–14.

15. See R. B. Reich, *The Work of Nations* (New York: Alfred A. Knopf, 1991); and P. J. Buckley and N. Hashai, "A Global System View of Firm Boundaries," *Journal of International Business Studies,* January 2004, pp. 33–50.

16. D. Barboza, "An Unknown Giant Flexes Its Muscles," *The New York Times,* December 4, 2004, pp. B1, B3.

17. G. Hall and S. Howell, "The Experience Curve from an Economist's Perspective," *Strategic Management Journal* 6 (1985), pp. 197–212.

18. Hall and Howell, "The Experience Curve from an Economist's Perspective."

19. For a full discussion of the source of scale economies, see D. Besanko, D. Dranove, and M. Shanley, *Economics of Strategy* (New York: John Wiley & Sons, 1996).

20. This estimate was provided by the Pharmaceutical Manufacturers Association.

21. "Matsushita Electrical Industrial in 1987," in *Transnational Management,* eds. C. A. Bartlett and S. Ghoshal (Homewood, IL: Richard D. Irwin, 1992).

22. See J. Birkinshaw and N. Hood, "Multinational Subsidiary Evolution: Capability and Charter Change in Foreign Owned Subsidiary Companies," *Academy of Management Review* 23 (October 1998), pp. 773–95; A. K. Gupta and V. J. Govindarajan, "Knowledge Flows within Multinational Corporations," *Strategic Management Journal* 21 (2000), pp. 473–96; V. J. Govindarajan and A. K. Gupta, *The Quest for Global Dominance* (San Francisco: Jossey Bass, 2001); T. S. Frost, J. M. Birkinshaw, and P. C. Ensign, "Centers of Excellence in Multinational Corporations," *Strategic Management Journal* 23 (2002), pp. 997–1018; and U. Andersson, M. Forsgren, and U. Holm, "The Strategic Impact of External Networks," *Strategic Management Journal* 23 (2002), pp. 979–96.

23. S. Leung, "Armchairs, TVs and Espresso: Is It McDonald's?" *The Wall Street Journal,* August 30, 2002, pp. A1, A6.

24. J. W. Miller, "Indiana Steel Mill Revived with Lessons from Abroad," *The Wall Street Journal,* May 21, 2012.

25. C. K. Prahalad and Yves L. Doz, *The Multinational Mission: Balancing Local Demands and Global Vision* (New York: Free Press, 1987). Also see J. Birkinshaw, A. Morrison, and J. Hulland, "Structural and Competitive Determinants of a Global Integration Strategy," *Strategic Management Journal* 16 (1995), pp. 637–55; and P. Ghemawat, *Redefining Global Strategy* (Boston: Harvard Business School Press, 2007).

26. Prahalad and Doz, *The Multinational Mission.* Prahalad and Doz actually talk about local responsiveness rather than local customization.

27. M. Gunther, "MTV's Passage to India," *Fortune,* August 9, 2004, pp. 117–122; B. Pulley and A. Tanzer, "Sumner's Gemstone," *Forbes,* February 21, 2000, pp. 107–11; K. Hoffman, "Youth TV's Old Hand Prepares for the Digital Challenge," *Financial Times,* February 18, 2000, p. 8; presentation by Sumner M. Redstone, chairman and CEO, Viacom Inc., delivered to Salomon Smith Barney 11th Annual Global Entertainment Media, Telecommunications Conference, Scottsdale, AZ, January 8, 2001, archived at www.viacom.com; and Viacom 10K Statement, 2005.

28. T. Levitt, "The Globalization of Markets," *Harvard Business Review,* May–June 1983, pp. 92–102.

29. W. W. Lewis. *The Power of Productivity*, (Chicago, University of Chicago Press, 2004).

30. C. J. Chipello, "Local Presence Is Key to European Deals," *The Wall Street Journal,* June 30, 1998, p. A15.

31. C. A. Bartlett and S. Ghoshal, *Managing across Borders* (Boston: Harvard Business School Press, 1989).

32. Ibid. Pankaj Ghemawat makes a similar argument, although he does not use the term *transnational*. See Ghemawat, *Redefining Global Strategy.*

33. T. Hout, M. E. Porter, and E. Rudden, "How Global Companies Win Out," *Harvard Business Review,* September–October 1982, pp. 98–108.

34. J. Neff, "P&G Outpacing Unilever in Five-Year Battle," *Advertising Age,* November 3, 2003, pp. 1–3; G. Strauss, "Firm Restructuring into Truly Global Company," *USA Today,* September 10, 1999, p. B2; *Procter & Gamble 10K Report, 2005;* and M. Kolbasuk McGee, "P&G Jump-Starts Corporate Change," *Information Week,* November 1, 1999, pp. 30–34.

35. A. Chang, "Avon's Ultimate Makeover Artist," *MarketWatch,* December 3, 2009; N. Byrnes, "Avon: More Than Cosmetic Change," *BusinessWeek,* March 3, 2007, pp. 62–63; J. Hodson, "Avon 4Q Profit Jumps on Higher Overseas Sales," *The Wall Street Journal* (online), February 4, 2010; and M. Boyle, "Avon Surges after Saying That Andrea Jung Will Step Down as CEO," *Bloomberg BusinessWeek,* December 15, 2011.

Chapter 14
The Organization of International Business

LEARNING OBJECTIVES

After reading this chapter, you will be able to:

LO14-1 Explain what is meant by organizational architecture.

LO14-2 Describe the different organizational choices that can be made in an international business.

LO14-3 Explain how organization can be matched to strategy to improve the performance of an international business.

LO14-4 Discuss what is required for an international business to change its organization so that it better matches its strategy.

◇◇◇ **ORGANIZING SIEMENS TO COMPETE GLOBALLY** ◇◇◇

Opening Case

The German company Siemens is one of the world's great engineering conglomerates manufacturing everything from hearing aids and medical scanners to giant power generation turbines, wind systems, and locomotives. By the late 2000s, however, it was struggling with subpar performance relative to its global rivals such as General Electric, Honeywell, and United Technologies. In July 2007 Siemens hired Peter Löscher as CEO and gave him the task of trying to revitalize the organization. Löscher, an Austrian whose career included major leadership positions at General Electric and Merck, was the first outsider to run Siemens since the company's establishment in 1847.

Löscher inherited a global organization of significant complexity. At the time Siemens had 475,000 employees, revenues of $72 billion, operated in a wide range of industries, and had activities in over 190 countries. Siemens was organized into 12 operating groups, which were further subdivided into 70 business divisions. Although each division had its own product focus, such as wind power or molecular imaging, Siemens worked hard to deliver integrated solutions to customers. This required the divisions to cooperate with each other on large projects.

Siemens also had a strong tradition of local responsiveness. The countries where the company was most active had their own executive manager, known as "Mr./Ms. Siemens." This individual acted as the country manager for all of Siemens businesses in a specific geography, and was also the CEO of the respective local company. The operating group and business division structure was often replicated within the local company. This resulted in a matrix organization, with the head of the power generation business in Argentina, for example, reporting to the local country CEO and to the global head of the business division.

It was the responsibility of Mr./Ms. Siemens and his/her staff to manage relations with local customers, developing bids for projects, and ensure that business divisions cooperated on the delivery of a project. Local companies were given significant discretion over product specifications for local clients. Thus, the local company in Argentina might bid on a subway project in Buenos Aires, tailor that bid to the needs of the local client, and if the bid was accepted, make sure there was sufficient cooperation between the different business divisions in order to successfully complete the project.

Löscher could see the virtue in this organization—it tried to meld together global scale at the business level with local responsiveness at the country level—but it was very complex. In his view, there were too many direct reports to the corporate headquarters, resulting in significant information overload. There was also a serious accountability problem. If the company failed to deliver a project profitably—let's say the subway system in Buenos Aires—who was responsible for that: the local managers or the managers in the business divisions? Löscher believed that country managers had too much power in the structure, and the business divisions had too little and were not accountable enough.

In 2008, he changed the structure to deal with these issues. He consolidated the operating groups into three mains sectors—industry, energy, and health care. The business divisions were placed within their respective sectors. He then organized the 190 country units into 17 regional clusters, and gave them primary responsibility developing a cost-efficient regional infrastructure, focusing on customers and managing local sales organizations. Profit and loss responsibility was assigned to the sectors and business divisions. Previously each operating group and national subsidiary had maintained its own separate profit and loss accounts. This change was a shock to the Mr./Ms. Siemens around the world, who were told that their goal was to contribute toward the global profit and loss accounts for a sector and business division. While not doing away with local responsiveness, Löscher had effectively reduced the power of country managers within Siemens structure, making them directly responsible for boosting the profitability of the global businesses.

Löscher went further, instituting a management review process that led to the replacement of half of the company's top 100 managers. Löscher is now directly involved in the appointment of the top 300 management positions in the company. He also took out two layers of top management that had no operational accountability in the previous structure. His goal in doing all of this seems to have been to replace managers who did not buy into a new way of doing things, and to increase the performance accountability of the people who ran the sectors and business divisions.[1]

INTRODUCTION

The story of Siemens, which is profiled in the opening case, is similar to that of many multinationals over the past four decades. Originally Siemens pursued a localization strategy (see Chapter 13). It implemented this strategy through strong national organizations. By the mid-2000s, however, this organization was not working well. In response, under the leadership of a new CEO, Siemens reorganized in 2008 to give more power, responsibility, and accountability to the global business divisions and to reduce the power of the national organizations. At the same time, Siemens continued to recognize the importance of national organizations for purposes of interfacing with customers and ensuring cooperation between divisions on local projects, but management wanted to make sure that ultimately those organizations served the best interests of the global business divisions. By making these changes, Siemens was trying to reap the gains from globalization, particularly with regard to realizing the scale and location economies that come from optimally configuring the global value chain for a business while continuing to recognize the importance of local responsiveness. In the language of the last chapter, Siemens was shifting its organization to try and become more of a *transnational* enterprise; it was moving from a localization strategy to a transnational strategy, and the change in organization reflected this.

As suggested by the Siemens example, this chapter is concerned with identifying the organizational architecture that international businesses use to manage and direct their global operations. By **organizational architecture** we mean the totality of a firm's organization, including formal organizational structure, control systems and incentives, processes, organizational culture, and people. The core argument outlined in this chapter is that superior enterprise profitability requires three conditions to be fulfilled. First, the different elements of a firm's organizational architecture must be internally consistent. For example, the control and incentive systems used in the firm must be consistent with the structure of the enterprise. Second, the organizational architecture must match or fit the strategy of the firm—strategy and architecture must be consistent.[2] For example, if a firm is pursuing a global standardization strategy but has the wrong kind of organizational architecture in place, it is unlikely that it will be able to execute that strategy effectively and poor performance may result. The strategy and architecture of the firm must not only be consistent with each other but make sense given the competitive conditions prevailing in the firm's markets—strategy, architecture, and competitive environment must all be consistent. For example, a firm pursuing a localization strategy might have the right kind of organizational architecture in place for that strategy. However, if it competes in markets where cost pressures are intense and demands for local responsiveness are low, it will still have inferior performance because a global standardization strategy is more appropriate in such an environment.

To explore the issues illustrated by examples such as Siemens, this chapter opens by discussing in more detail the concepts of organizational architecture and fit. Next it turns to a more detailed exploration of various components of architecture—structure, control systems and incentives, organizational culture, and processes—and explains how these components must be internally consistent. (We discuss the "people" component of architecture in Chapter 19, when we discuss human resource strategy in the multinational firm.) After reviewing the various components of architecture, we look at the ways in which architecture can be matched to strategy and the competitive environment to achieve high performance. The chapter closes with a discussion of organizational change, for as the Siemens example illustrates, periodically firms have to change their organization so that it matches new strategic and competitive realities.

ORGANIZATIONAL ARCHITECTURE

As noted in the introduction, the term *organizational architecture* refers to the totality of a firm's organization, including formal organizational structure, control systems and incentives, organizational culture, processes, and people.[3] Figure 14.1 illustrates these different elements. By **organizational**

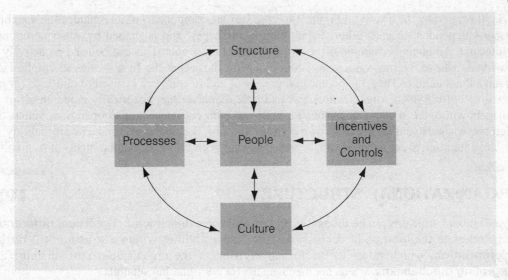

Figure 14.1 *Organizational Architecture*

structure, we mean three things: First, the formal division of the organization into subunits such as product divisions, national operations, and functions (most organizational charts display this aspect of structure); second, the location of decision-making responsibilities within that structure (e.g., centralized or decentralized); and third, the establishment of integrating mechanisms to coordinate the activities of subunits, including cross-functional teams and or pan-regional committees.

Control systems are the metrics used to measure the performance of subunits and make judgments about how well managers are running those subunits. For example, historically Unilever measured the performance of national operating subsidiary companies according to profitability—profitability was the metric. **Incentives** are the devices used to reward appropriate managerial behavior. Incentives are very closely tied to performance metrics. For example, the incentives of a manager in charge of a national operating subsidiary might be linked to the performance of that company. Specifically, she might receive a bonus if her subsidiary exceeds its performance targets.

Processes are the manner in which decisions are made and work is performed within the organization. Examples are the processes for formulating strategy, for deciding how to allocate resources within a firm, or for evaluating the performance of managers and giving feedback. Processes are conceptually distinct from the location of decision-making responsibilities within an organization, although both involve decisions. While the CEO might have ultimate responsibility for deciding what the strategy of the firm should be (i.e., the decision-making responsibility is centralized), the process he or she uses to make that decision might include the solicitation of ideas and criticism from lower-level managers.

Organizational culture refers to the norms and value systems that are shared among the employees of an organization. Just as societies have cultures (see Chapter 4 for details), so do organizations. Organizations are societies of individuals who come together to perform collective tasks. They have their own distinctive patterns of culture and subculture.[4] As we shall see, organizational culture can have a profound impact on how a firm performs. Finally, by **people** we mean not only the employees of the organization but also the strategy used to recruit, compensate, and retain those individuals and the type of people that they are in terms of their skills, values, and orientation (discussed in depth in Chapter 19).

As illustrated by the arrows in Figure 14.1, the various components of an organization's architecture are not independent of each other: Each component shapes, and is shaped by, other components of architecture. An obvious example is the strategy regarding people. This can be used proactively to hire individuals whose internal values are consistent with those that the firm wishes to emphasize in its organizational culture. Thus, the people component of architecture can be used to reinforce (or not) the prevailing culture of the organization. For example, Unilever has historically made an effort to hire managers who were sociable and placed a high value on consensus and cooperation, values that the enterprise wished to emphasize in its own culture.[5] If a firm is going to maximize its profitability, it must pay close attention to achieving internal consistency between the various components of its architecture.

ORGANIZATIONAL STRUCTURE

Organizational structure can be thought of in terms of three dimensions: (1) **vertical differentiation**, which refers to the location of decision-making responsibilities within a structure; (2) **horizontal differentiation**, which refers to the formal division of the organization into subunits; and (3) **integrating mechanisms**, which are mechanisms for coordinating subunits.

Vertical Differentiation: Centralization and Decentralization

A firm's vertical differentiation determines where in its hierarchy the decision-making power is concentrated.[6] Are production and marketing decisions centralized in the offices of upper-level managers, or are they decentralized to lower-level managers? Where does the responsibility for R&D decisions lie? Are important strategic and financial decisions pushed down to operating units, or are they concentrated in the hands of top management? And so on. There are arguments for both centralization and decentralization.

Arguments for Centralization

There are four main arguments for centralization. First, centralization can facilitate coordination. For example, consider a firm that has a component manufacturing operation in Taiwan and an assembly operation in Mexico. The activities of these two operations may need to be coordinated to ensure a smooth flow of products from the component operation to the assembly operation. This might be achieved by centralizing production scheduling at the firm's head office. Second, centralization can help ensure that decisions are consistent with organizational objectives. When decisions are decentralized to lower-level managers, those managers may make decisions at variance with top management's goals. Centralization of important decisions minimizes the chance of this occurring.

Third, by concentrating power and authority in one individual or a management team, centralization can give top-level managers the means to bring about needed major organizational changes. Fourth, centralization can avoid the duplication of activities that occurs when similar activities are carried on by various subunits within the organization. For example, many international firms centralize their R&D functions at one or two locations to ensure that R&D work is not duplicated. Production activities may be centralized at key locations for the same reason.

Arguments for Decentralization

There are five main arguments for decentralization. First, top management can become overburdened when decision-making authority is centralized, and this can result in poor decisions. Decentralization gives top management time to focus on critical issues by delegating more routine issues to lower-level managers. Second, motivational research favors decentralization. Behavioral scientists have long argued that people are willing to give more to their jobs when they have a greater degree of individual freedom and control over their work. Third, decentralization permits greater flexibility—more rapid response to environmental changes—because decisions do not have to be "referred up the hierarchy" unless they are exceptional in nature. Fourth, decentralization can result in better decisions. In a decentralized structure, decisions are made closer to the spot by individuals who (presumably) have better information than managers several levels up in a hierarchy (for an example of decentralization to achieve this goal, see the Management Focus on Walmart's international division). Fifth, decentralization can increase control. Decentralization can be used to establish relatively autonomous, self-contained subunits within an organization. Subunit managers can then be held accountable for subunit performance. The more responsibility subunit managers have for decisions that impact subunit performance, the fewer excuses they have for poor performance.

MANAGEMENT FOCUS

The International Division at Walmart

When Walmart started to expand internationally in the early 1990s, it decided to set up an international division to oversee the process. The international division was based in Bentonville, Arkansas, at the company headquarters. Today the division oversees operations in 27 countries that collectively generate more than $135 billion in sales. In terms of reporting structure, the division is divided into three regions—Europe, Asia, and the Americas—with the CEO of each region reporting to the CEO of the international division, who in turn reports to the CEO of Walmart.

Initially, the senior management of the international division exerted tight centralized control over merchandising strategy and operations in different countries. The reasoning was straightforward; Walmart's managers wanted to make sure that international stores copied the format for stores, merchandising, and operations that had served the company so well in the United States. They believed, naively perhaps, that centralized control over merchandising strategy and operations was the way to make sure this was the case.

By the late 1990s, with the international division approaching $20 billion in sales, Walmart's managers concluded this centralized approach was not serving them well. Country managers had to get permission from their superiors in Bentonville before changing strategy and operations, and this was slowing decision making. Centralization also produced information overload at the headquarters, and led to some poor decisions. Walmart found that managers in Bentonville were not necessarily the best ones to decide on store layout in Mexico, merchandising strategy in Argentina, or compensation policy in the United Kingdom. The need to adapt merchandising strategy and operations to local conditions argued strongly for greater decentralization.

The pivotal event that led to a change in policy at Walmart was the company's 1999 acquisition of Britain's ASDA supermarket chain. The ASDA acquisition added a mature and successful $14 billion operation to Walmart's international division. The company realized that it was not appropriate for managers in Bentonville to be making all-important decisions for ASDA. Accordingly, over the next few months, John Menzer, CEO of the international division, reduced the number of staff located in Bentonville that were devoted to international operations by 50 percent. Country leaders were given greater responsibility, especially in the area of merchandising and operations. In Menzer's own words, "We were at the point where it was time to break away a little bit. . . . You can't run the world from one place. The countries have to drive the business. . . . The change has sent a strong message [to country managers] that they no longer have to wait for approval from Bentonville."

Although Walmart has now decentralized decisions within the international division, it is still struggling to find the right formula for managing global procurement. Ideally, the company would like to centralize procurement in Bentonville so that it could use its enormous purchasing power to bargain down the prices it pays suppliers. As a practical matter, however, this has not been easy to attain given that the product mix in Walmart stores has to be tailored to conditions prevailing in the local market. Currently, significant responsibility for procurement remains at the country and regional level. However, Walmart would like to have a global procurement strategy such that it can negotiate on a global basis with key suppliers and can simultaneously introduce new merchandise into its stores around the world.

As merchandising and operating decisions have been decentralized, the international division has increasingly taken on a new role—that of identifying best practices and transferring them between countries. For example, the division has developed a knowledge management system whereby stores in one country, let's say Argentina, can quickly communicate pictures of items, sales data, and ideas on how to market and promote products to stores in another country, such as Japan. The division is also starting to move personnel between stores in different countries as a way of facilitating the flow of best practices across national borders. Finally, the division is at the cutting edge of moving Walmart away from its U.S.-centric mentality and showing the organization that ideas implemented in foreign operations might also be used to improve the efficiency and effectiveness of Walmart's operations at home.[7]

Strategy and Centralization in an International Business

The choice between centralization and decentralization is not absolute. Frequently it makes sense to centralize some decisions and to decentralize others, depending on the type of decision and the firm's strategy. Decisions regarding overall firm strategy, major financial expenditures, financial objectives, and legal issues are typically centralized at the firm's headquarters. However, operating decisions, such as those relating to production, marketing, R&D, and human resource management, may or may not be centralized depending on the firm's strategy.

Consider firms pursuing a global standardization strategy. They must decide how to disperse the various value creation activities around the globe so location and experience economies can be realized. The head office must make the decisions about where to locate R&D, production, marketing, and so on. In addition, the globally dispersed web of value creation activities that facilitates a global strategy must be coordinated. All of this creates pressures for centralizing some operating decisions.

In contrast, the emphasis on local responsiveness in firms pursuing a localization strategy creates strong pressures for decentralizing operating decisions to foreign subsidiaries. Firms pursuing an international strategy also tend to maintain centralized control over their core competencies and to decentralize other decisions to foreign subsidiaries. Typically, such firms centralize control over R&D in their home country, but decentralize operating decisions to foreign subsidiaries. For example, Microsoft Corporation, which fits the international mode, centralizes its product development activities (where its core competencies lie) at its Redmond, Washington, headquarters and decentralizes marketing activities to various foreign subsidiaries. Thus, while products are developed at home, managers in the various foreign subsidiaries have significant latitude for formulating strategies to market those products in their particular settings.[8]

The situation in firms pursuing a transnational strategy is more complex. The need to realize location and experience curve economies requires some degree of centralized control over global production centers. However, the need for local responsiveness dictates the decentralization of many operating decisions, particularly for marketing, to foreign subsidiaries. Thus, in firms pursuing a transnational strategy, some operating decisions are relatively centralized, while others are relatively decentralized. In addition, global learning based on the multidirectional transfer of skills between subsidiaries, and between subsidiaries and the corporate center, is a central feature of a firm pursuing a transnational strategy. The concept of global learning is predicated on the notion that foreign subsidiaries within a multinational firm have significant freedom to develop their own skills and competencies. Only then can these be leveraged to benefit other parts of the organization. A substantial degree of decentralization is required if subsidiaries are going to have the freedom to do this. For this reason too, the pursuit of a transnational strategy requires a high degree of decentralization.[9]

Horizontal Differentiation: The Design of Structure

Horizontal differentiation is concerned with how the firm decides to divide itself into subunits.[10] The decision is normally made on the basis of function, type of business, or geographic area. In many firms, just one of these predominates, but more complex solutions are adopted in others. This is particularly likely in the case of multinational firms, where the conflicting demands to organize the company around different products (to realize location and experience curve economies) and different national markets (to remain locally responsive) must be reconciled.

The Structure of Domestic Firms

Most firms begin with no formal structure and are run by a single entrepreneur or a small team of individuals. As they grow, the demands of management become too great for one individual or a small team to handle. At this point the organization is split into functions reflecting the firm's value creation activities (e.g., production, marketing, R&D, sales). These functions are typically coordinated and controlled by top management (see Figure 14.2). Decision making in this functional structure tends to be centralized.

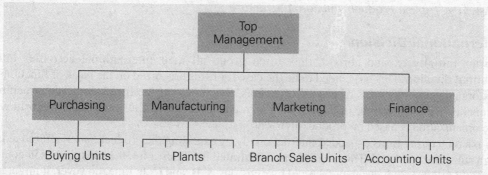

Figure 14.2 *A Typical Functional Structure*

Further horizontal differentiation may be required if the firm significantly diversifies its product offering, which takes the firm into different business areas. For example, Dutch multinational Philips

Electronics NV began as a lighting company, but diversification took the company into consumer electronics (e.g., visual and audio equipment), industrial electronics (integrated circuits and other electronic components), and medical systems (MRI scanners and ultrasound systems). In such circumstances, a functional structure can be too clumsy. Problems of coordination and control arise when different business areas are managed within the framework of a functional structure.[11] For one thing, it becomes difficult to identify the profitability of each distinct business area. For another, it is difficult to run a functional department, such as production or marketing, if it is supervising the value creation activities of several business areas.

To solve the problems of coordination and control, at this stage most firms switch to a product divisional structure (see Figure 14.3). With a product divisional structure, each division is responsible for a distinct product line (business area). Thus, Philips created divisions for lighting, consumer electronics, industrial electronics, and medical systems. Each product division is set up as a self-contained, largely autonomous entity with its own functions. The responsibility for operating decisions is typically decentralized to product divisions, which are then held accountable for their performance. Headquarters is responsible for the overall strategic development of the firm and for the financial control of the various divisions.

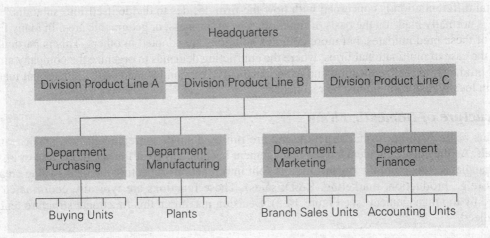

Figure 14.3 *A Typical Product Divisional Structure*

The International Division

When firms initially expand abroad, they often group all their international activities into an **international division**. This has tended to be the case for firms organized on the basis of functions and for firms organized on the basis of product divisions. Regardless of the firm's domestic structure, its international division tends to be organized on geography. Figure 14.4 illustrates this for a firm whose domestic organization is based on product divisions.

Many manufacturing firms expanded internationally by exporting the product manufactured at home to foreign subsidiaries to sell. Thus, in the firm illustrated in Figure 14.4, the subsidiaries in countries 1 and 2 would sell the products manufactured by divisions A, B, and C. In time, however, it might prove viable to manufacture the product in each country, and so production facilities would be added on a country-by-country basis. For firms with a functional structure at home, this might mean replicating the functional structure in every country in which the firm does business. For firms with a divisional

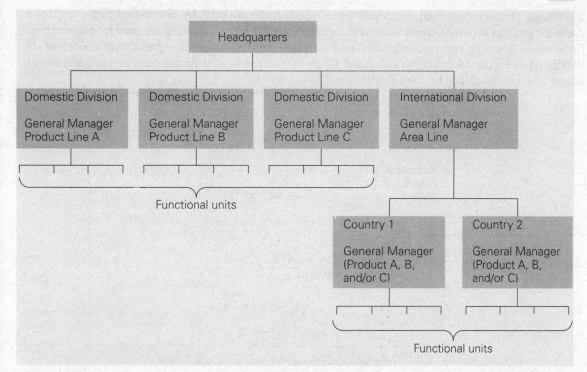

Figure 14.4   *One Company's International Division Structure*

structure, this might mean replicating the divisional structure in every country in which the firm does business.

This structure has been widely used; according to a Harvard study, 60 percent of all firms that have expanded internationally have initially adopted it. A good example of a company that uses this structure is Walmart, which created an international division in 1993 to manage its global expansion (Walmart's international division is profiled in the Management Focus). Despite its popularity, an international division structure can give rise to problems.[12] The dual structure it creates contains inherent potential for conflict and coordination problems between domestic and foreign operations. One problem with the structure is that the heads of foreign subsidiaries are not given as much voice in the organization as the heads of domestic functions (in the case of functional firms) or divisions (in the case of divisional firms). Rather, the head of the international division is presumed to be able to represent the interests of all countries to headquarters. This effectively relegates each country's manager to the second tier of the firm's hierarchy, which is inconsistent with a strategy of trying to expand internationally and build a true multinational organization.

Another problem is the implied lack of coordination between domestic operations and foreign operations, which are isolated from each other in separate parts of the structural hierarchy. This can inhibit the worldwide introduction of new products, the transfer of core competencies between domestic and foreign operations, and the consolidation of global production at key locations so as to realize location and experience curve economies.

As a result of such problems, many firms that continue to expand internationally abandon this structure and adopt one of the worldwide structures discussed next. The two initial choices are a worldwide product divisional structure, which tends to be adopted by diversified firms that have domestic product divisions, and a worldwide area structure, which tends to be adopted by undiversified firms whose domestic structures are based on functions. These two alternative paths of development are illustrated in Figure 14.5. The model in the figure is referred to as the international structural stages model and was developed by John Stopford and Louis Wells.[13]

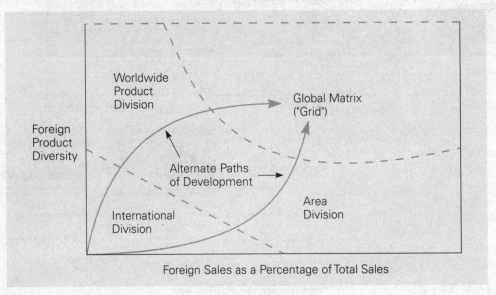

Figure 14.5 *The International Structural Stages Model*

Worldwide Area Structure

A **worldwide area structure** tends to be favored by firms with a low degree of diversification and a domestic structure based on functions (see Figure 14.6). Under this structure, the world is divided into geographic areas. An area may be a country (if the market is large enough) or a group of countries. Each area tends to be a self-contained, largely autonomous entity with its own set of value creation activities

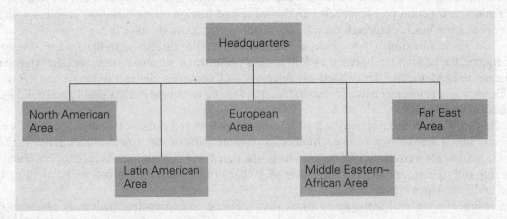

Figure 14.6 *A Worldwide Area Structure*

(e.g., its own production, marketing, R&D, human resources, and finance functions). Operations authority and strategic decisions relating to each of these activities are typically decentralized to each area, with headquarters retaining authority for the overall strategic direction of the firm and financial control.

This structure facilitates local responsiveness. Because decision-making responsibilities are decentralized, each area can customize product offerings, marketing strategy, and business strategy to the local conditions. However, this structure encourages fragmentation of the organization into highly autonomous entities. This can make it difficult to transfer core competencies and skills between areas and to realize location and experience curve economies. In other words, the structure is consistent with a localization strategy, but may make it difficult to realize gains associated with global standardization. Firms structured on this basis may encounter significant problems if local responsiveness is less critical than reducing costs or transferring core competencies for establishing a competitive advantage.

Worldwide Product Divisional Structure

A **worldwide product division structure** tends to be adopted by firms that are reasonably diversified and, accordingly, originally had domestic structures based on product divisions. As with the domestic product divisional structure, each division is a self-contained, largely autonomous entity with full responsibility for its own value creation activities. The headquarters retains responsibility for the overall strategic development and financial control of the firm (see Figure 14.7).

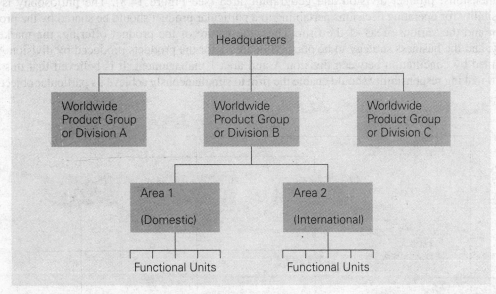

Figure 14.7 *A Worldwide Product Divisional Structure*

Underpinning the organization is a belief that the value creation activities of each product division should be coordinated by that division worldwide. Thus, the worldwide product divisional structure is designed to help overcome the coordination problems that arise with the international division and worldwide area structures. This structure provides an organizational context that enhances the consolidation of value creation activities at key locations necessary for realizing location and experience curve economies. It also facilitates the transfer of core competencies within a division's worldwide operations and the simultaneous worldwide introduction of new products. The main problem with the structure is the limited voice it gives to area or country managers, since they are seen as subservient to product division managers. The result can be a lack of local responsiveness, which, as Chapter 13 showed, can lead to performance problems.

Global Matrix Structure

Both the worldwide area structure and the worldwide product divisional structure have strengths and weaknesses. The worldwide area structure facilitates local responsiveness, but it can inhibit the realization of location and experience curve economies and the transfer of core competencies between areas. The worldwide product division structure provides a better framework for pursuing location and experience curve economies and for transferring core competencies, but it is weak in local responsiveness. Other things being equal, this suggests that a worldwide area structure is more appropriate if the firm is pursuing a localization strategy, while a worldwide product divisional structure is more appropriate for firms pursuing global standardization or international strategies. However, as we saw in Chapter 13, other things are not equal. As Bartlett and Ghoshal have argued, to survive in some industries, firms must adopt a transnational strategy. That is, they must focus simultaneously on realizing location and experience curve economies, on local responsiveness, and on the internal transfer of core competencies (worldwide learning).[14]

Some firms have attempted to cope with the conflicting demands of a transnational strategy by using a matrix structure. In the classic **global matrix structure**, horizontal differentiation proceeds along two dimensions: product division and geographic area (see Figure 14.8). The philosophy is that responsibility for operating decisions pertaining to a particular product should be shared by the product division and the various areas of the firm. Thus, the nature of the product offering, the marketing strategy, and the business strategy to be pursued in area 1 for the products produced by division A are determined by conciliation between division A and area 1 management. It is believed that this dual decision-making responsibility should enable the firm to simultaneously achieve its particular objectives.

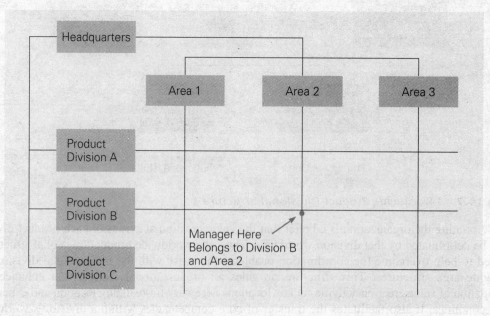

Figure 14.8   *A Global Matrix Structure*

In a classic matrix structure, giving product divisions and geographic areas equal status within the organization reinforces the idea of dual responsibility. Individual managers thus belong to two hierarchies (a divisional hierarchy and an area hierarchy) and have two bosses (a divisional boss and an area boss).

The reality of the global matrix structure is that it often does not work as well as the theory predicts. In practice, the matrix often is clumsy and bureaucratic. It can require so many meetings that it is difficult to get any work done. The need to get an area and a product division to reach a decision can slow decision making and produce an inflexible organization unable to respond quickly to market shifts or to innovate. The dual-hierarchy structure can lead to conflict and perpetual power struggles between the areas and the product divisions, catching many managers in the middle. To make matters worse, it can prove difficult to ascertain accountability in this structure. When all critical decisions are the product of negotiation between divisions and areas, one side can always blame the other when things go wrong. As a manager in one global matrix structure, reflecting on a failed product launch, said to the author, "Had we been able to do things our way, instead of having to accommodate those guys from the product division, this would never have happened." (A manager in the product division expressed similar sentiments.) The result of such finger-pointing can be that accountability is compromised, conflict is enhanced, and headquarters loses control over the organization. (See the accompanying Management Focus on Dow Chemical for an example of the problems associated with a matrix structure.)

The Rise and Fall of Dow Chemical's Matrix Structure

MANAGEMENT FOCUS

A handful of major players compete head to head around the world in the chemical industry. These companies are Dow Chemical and Du Pont of the United States, Great Britain's ICI, and the German trio of BASF, Hoechst AG, and Bayer. The barriers to the free flow of chemical products between nations largely disappeared in the 1970s. This along with the commodity nature of most bulk chemicals has ushered in a prolonged period of intense price competition. In such an environment, the company that wins the competitive race is the one with the lowest costs. Dow Chemical was long among the cost leaders.

For years, Dow's managers insisted that part of the credit should be placed at the feet of its "matrix" organization. Dow's organizational matrix had three interacting elements: functions (e.g., R&D, manufacturing, marketing), businesses (e.g., ethylene, plastics, pharmaceuticals), and geography (e.g., Spain, Germany, Brazil). Managers' job titles incorporated all three elements—for example, plastics marketing manager for Spain—and most managers reported to at least two bosses. The plastics marketing manager in Spain might report to both the head of the worldwide plastics business and the head of the Spanish operations. The intent of the matrix was to make Dow operations responsive to both local market needs and corporate objectives. Thus, the plastics business might be charged with minimizing Dow's global plastics production costs, while the Spanish operation might be charged with determining how best to sell plastics in the Spanish market.

When Dow introduced this structure, the results were less than promising; multiple reporting channels led to confusion and conflict. The large number of bosses made for an unwieldy bureaucracy. The overlapping responsibilities resulted in turf battles and a lack of accountability. Area managers disagreed with managers overseeing business sectors about which plants should be built and where. In short, the structure didn't work. Instead of abandoning the structure, however, Dow decided to see if it could be made more flexible.

Dow's decision to keep its matrix structure was prompted by its move into the pharmaceuticals industry. The company realized that the pharmaceutical business is very different from the bulk chemicals business. In bulk chemicals, the big returns come from achieving economies of scale in production. This dictates establishing large plants in key locations from which regional or global markets can be served. But in pharmaceuticals, regulatory and marketing requirements for drugs vary so much from country to country that local needs are far more important than reducing manufacturing costs through scale economies. A high degree of local responsiveness is essential. Dow realized its pharmaceutical business would never thrive if it were managed by the same priorities as its mainstream chemical operations.

Accordingly, instead of abandoning its matrix, Dow decided to make it more flexible so it could better accommodate the different businesses, each with its own priorities, within a single management system. A small team of senior executives at headquarters helped set the priorities for each type of business. After priorities were identified for each business sector, one of the three elements of the matrix—function, business, or geographic area—was given primary authority in decision making. Which element took the lead varied according to the type of decision and the market or location in which the company was competing. Such flexibility required that all employees understand what was occurring in the rest of the matrix. Although this may seem confusing, for years Dow claimed this flexible system worked well and credited much of its success to the quality of the decisions it facilitated.

By the mid-1990s, however, Dow had refocused its business on the chemicals industry, divesting itself of its pharmaceutical activities where the company's performance had been unsatisfactory. Reflecting the change in corporate strategy, in 1995 Dow decided to abandon its matrix structure in favor of a more streamlined structure based on global business divisions. The change was also driven by the realization that the matrix structure was just too complex and costly to manage in the intense competitive environment of the 1990s, particularly given the company's renewed focus on its commodity chemicals where competitive advantage often went to the low-cost producer. As Dow's then CEO put it in a 1999 interview, "We were an organization that was matrixed and depended on teamwork, but there was no one in charge. When things went well, we didn't know whom to reward; and when things went poorly, we didn't know whom to blame. So we created a global divisional structure, and cut out layers of management. There used to be 11 layers of management between me and the lowest-level employees, now there are five." In short, Dow ultimately found that a matrix structure was unsuited to a company that was competing in very cost-competitive global industries, and it had to abandon its matrix to drive down operating costs.[15]

In light of these problems, many firms that pursue a transnational strategy have tried to build "flexible" matrix structures based more on enterprisewide management knowledge networks, and a shared culture and vision, than on a rigid hierarchical arrangement. Within such companies the informal structure plays a greater role than the formal structure. We discuss this issue when we consider informal integrating mechanisms in the next section.

Integrating Mechanisms

The previous section explained that firms divide themselves into subunits. One way of coordinating these subunits is through centralization. If the coordination task is complex, however, centralization may not be very effective. Higher-level managers responsible for achieving coordination can soon become overwhelmed by the volume of work required to coordinate the activities of various subunits, particularly if the subunits are large, diverse, and/or geographically dispersed. When this is the case, firms look toward integrating mechanisms, both formal and informal, to help achieve coordination. This section introduces the various integrating mechanisms that international businesses can use. But first, we explore the need for coordination in international firms and some impediments to coordination.

Strategy and Coordination in the International Business

The need for coordination between subunits varies with the strategy of the firm.[16] The need for coordination is lowest in firms pursuing a localization strategy, is higher in international companies, higher still in global companies, and highest of all in transnational companies. Firms pursuing a localization strategy are primarily concerned with local responsiveness. Such firms are likely to operate with a worldwide area structure in which each area has considerable autonomy and its own set of value creation functions. Because each area is established as a stand-alone entity, the need for coordination between areas is minimized.

The need for coordination is greater in firms pursuing an international strategy and trying to profit from the transfer of core competencies and skills between units at home and abroad. Coordination is necessary to support the transfer of skills and product offerings between units. The need for coordination is also great in firms trying to profit from location and experience curve economies, that is, in firms pursuing global standardization strategies. Achieving location and experience curve economies involves dispersing value creation activities to various locations around the globe. The resulting global web of activities must be coordinated to ensure the smooth flow of inputs into the value chain, the smooth flow of semifinished products through the value chain, and the smooth flow of finished products to markets around the world.

The need for coordination is greatest in transnational firms, which simultaneously pursue location and experience curve economies, local responsiveness, and the multidirectional transfer of core competencies and skills among all the firm's subunits (referred to as global learning). As with a global standardization strategy, coordination is required to ensure the smooth flow of products through the global value chain. As with an international strategy, coordination is required for ensuring the transfer of core competencies to subunits. However, the transnational goal of achieving multidirectional transfer of competencies requires much greater coordination than in firms pursuing an international strategy. In addition, a transnational strategy requires coordination between foreign subunits and the firm's globally dispersed value creation activities (e.g., production, R&D, marketing) to ensure that any product offering and marketing strategy is sufficiently customized to local conditions.

Impediments to Coordination

Managers of the various subunits have different orientations, partly because they have different tasks. For example, production managers are typically concerned with production issues such as capacity utilization, cost control, and quality control, whereas marketing managers are concerned with marketing issues such as pricing, promotions, distribution, and market share. These differences can inhibit communication between the managers. Quite simply, these managers often do not even "speak the same language." There may also be a lack of respect between subunits (e.g., marketing managers "looking down on" production managers, and vice versa), which further inhibits the communication required to achieve cooperation and coordination.

Differences in subunits' orientations also arise from their differing goals. For example, worldwide product divisions of a multinational firm may be committed to cost goals that require global production of a standardized product, whereas a foreign subsidiary may be committed to increasing its market share in its country, which will require a nonstandard product. These different goals can lead to conflict.

Such impediments to coordination are not unusual in any firm, but they can be particularly problematic in the multinational enterprise with its profusion of subunits at home and abroad. Differences in subunit orientation are often reinforced in multinationals by the separations of time zone, distance, and nationality between managers of the subunits.

Formal Integrating Mechanisms

The formal mechanisms used to integrate subunits vary in complexity from simple direct contact and liaison roles, to teams, to a matrix structure (see Figure 14.9). In general, the greater the need for coordination, the more complex the formal integrating mechanisms need to be.[17]

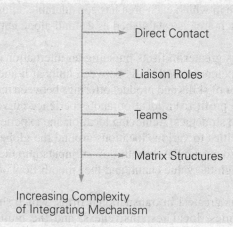

Figure 14.9 *Formal Integrating Mechanisms*

Direct contact between subunit managers is the simplest integrating mechanism. By this "mechanism," managers of the various subunits simply contact each other whenever they have a common concern. Direct contact may not be effective if the managers have differing orientations that act to impede coordination, as pointed out in the previous subsection.

Liaison roles are a bit more complex. When the volume of contacts between subunits increases, coordination can be improved by giving a person in each subunit responsibility for coordinating with another subunit on a regular basis. Through these roles, the people involved establish a permanent relationship. This helps attenuate the impediments to coordination discussed in the previous subsection.

When the need for coordination is greater still, firms tend to use temporary or permanent teams composed of individuals from the subunits that need to achieve coordination. They typically coordinate product development and introduction, but they are useful when any aspect of operations or strategy requires the cooperation of two or more subunits. Product development and introduction teams are typically composed of personnel from R&D, production, and marketing. The resulting coordination aids the development of products that are tailored to consumer needs and that can be produced at a reasonable cost (design for manufacturing).

When the need for integration is very high, firms may institute a matrix structure, in which all roles are viewed as integrating roles. The structure is designed to facilitate maximum integration among subunits. The most common matrix in multinational firms is based on geographic areas and worldwide product divisions. This achieves a high level of integration between the product divisions and the areas so that, in theory, the firm can pay close attention to both local responsiveness and the pursuit of location and experience curve economies.

In some multinationals, the matrix is more complex still, structuring the firm into geographic areas, worldwide product divisions, and functions, all of which report directly to headquarters. Thus, within a company such as Dow Chemical before it abandoned its matrix in the mid-1990s (see the Management Focus), each manager belonged to three hierarchies (e.g., a plastics marketing manager in Spain was a member of the Spanish subsidiary, the plastics product division, and the marketing function). In addition to facilitating local responsiveness and location and experience curve economies, such a matrix fosters the transfer of core competencies within the organization. This occurs because core competencies tend to reside in functions (e.g., R&D, marketing). A structure such as this in theory facilitates the transfer of competencies existing in functions from division to division and from area to area.

However, as discussed earlier, such matrix solutions to coordination problems in multinational enterprises can quickly become bogged down in a bureaucratic tangle that creates as many problems as it solves. Matrix structures tend to be bureaucratic, inflexible, and characterized by conflict rather than the hoped-for cooperation. For such a structure to work, it needs to be somewhat flexible and to be supported by informal integrating mechanisms.[18]

Informal Integrating Mechanism: Knowledge Networks

In attempting to alleviate or avoid the problems associated with formal integrating mechanisms in general, and matrix structures in particular, firms with a high need for integration have been experimenting with an informal integrating mechanism: knowledge networks that are supported by an organizational culture that values teamwork and cross-unit cooperation.[19] A **knowledge network** is a network for transmitting information within an organization that is based not on formal organizational structure, but on informal contacts between managers within an enterprise and on distributed information systems.[20] The great strength of such a network is that it can be used as a nonbureaucratic conduit for knowledge flows within a multinational enterprise.[21] For a network to exist, managers at different locations within the organization must be linked to each other at least indirectly. For example, Figure 14.10 shows the

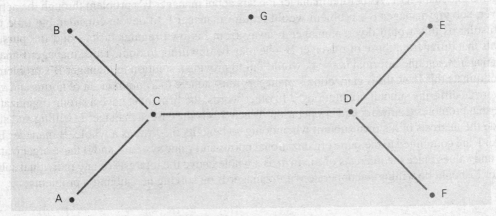

Figure 14.10 *A Simple Management Network*

simple network relationships between seven managers within a multinational firm. Managers A, B, and C all know each other personally, as do managers D, E, and F. Although manager B does not know manager F personally, they are linked through common acquaintances (managers C and D). Thus, we can say that managers A through F are all part of the network, and also that manager G is not.

Imagine manager B is a marketing manager in Spain and needs to know the solution to a technical problem to better serve an important European customer. Manager F, an R&D manager in the United States, has the solution to manager B's problem. Manager B mentions her problem to all of her contacts, including manager C, and asks if they know of anyone who might be able to provide a solution. Manager C asks manager D, who tells manager F, who then calls manager B with the solution. In this way, coordination is achieved informally through the network, rather than by formal integrating mechanisms such as teams or a matrix structure.

For such a network to function effectively, however, it must embrace as many managers as possible. For example, if manager G had a problem similar to manager B's, he would not be able to utilize the informal network to find a solution; he would have to resort to more formal mechanisms. Establishing companywide knowledge networks is difficult, and although network enthusiasts speak of networks as the "glue" that binds multinational companies together, it is far from clear how successful firms have been at building companywide networks. Two techniques being used to establish networks are information systems and management development policies.

Firms are using their distributed computer and telecommunications information systems to provide the foundation for informal knowledge networks.[22] Electronic mail, videoconferencing, high-bandwidth data systems, and web-based search engines make it much easier for managers scattered over the globe to get to know each other, to identify contacts that might help solve a particular problem, and to publicize and share best practices within the organization. Walmart, for example, now uses its intranet system to communicate ideas about merchandising strategy between stores located in different countries.

Firms are also using their management development programs to build informal networks. Tactics include rotating managers through various subunits on a regular basis so they build their own informal network and using management education programs to bring managers of subunits together in a single location so they can become acquainted.

Knowledge networks by themselves may not be sufficient to achieve coordination if subunit managers persist in pursuing subgoals that are at variance with companywide goals. For a knowledge network to function properly—and for a formal matrix structure to work also—managers must share a strong commitment to the same goals. To appreciate the nature of the problem, consider again the case of manager B and manager F. As before, manager F hears about manager B's problem through the network. However, solving manager B's problem would require manager F to devote considerable time to the task. Insofar as this would divert manager F away from his own regular tasks—and the pursuit of subgoals that differ from those of manager B—he may be unwilling to do it. Thus, manager F may not call manager B, and the informal network would fail to provide a solution to manager B's problem.

To eliminate this flaw, the organization's managers must adhere to a common set of norms and values that override differing subunit orientations.[23] In other words, the firm must have a strong organizational culture that promotes teamwork and cooperation. When this is the case, a manager is willing and able to set aside the interests of his own subunit when doing so benefits the firm as a whole. If manager B and manager F are committed to the same organizational norms and value systems, and if these organizational norms and values place the interests of the firm as a whole above the interests of any individual subunit, manager F should be willing to cooperate with manager B on solving her subunit's problems.

Summary

The message contained in this section is crucial to understanding the problems of managing the multinational firm. Multinationals need integration—particularly if they are pursuing global standardization, international, or transnational strategies—but it can be difficult to achieve due to the impediments to coordination discussed. Firms traditionally have tried to achieve coordination by adopting formal integrating mechanisms. These do not always work, however, since they tend to be bureaucratic and do not necessarily address the problems that arise from differing subunit orientations. This is particularly likely with a complex matrix structure, and yet, a complex matrix structure is required for simultaneously achieving location and experience curve economies, local responsiveness, and the multidirectional transfer of core competencies within the organization. The solution to this dilemma seems twofold. First, the firm must try to establish an informal knowledge network that can do much of the work previously undertaken by a formal matrix structure. Second, the firm must build a common culture. Neither of these partial solutions, however, is easy to achieve.[24]

CONTROL SYSTEMS AND INCENTIVES

A major task of a firm's leadership is to control the various subunits of the firm—whether they be defined on the basis of function, product division, or geographic area—to ensure their actions are consistent with the firm's overall strategic and financial objectives. Firms achieve this with various control and incentive systems. In this section, we first review the various types of control systems firms use to control their subunits. Then we briefly discuss incentive systems. Then we look at how the appropriate control and incentive systems vary according to the strategy of the multinational enterprise.

Types of Control Systems

Four main types of control systems are used in multinational firms: personal controls, bureaucratic controls, output controls, and cultural controls. In most firms, all four are used, but their relative emphasis varies with the strategy of the firm.

Personal Controls

Personal control is control by personal contact with subordinates. This type of control tends to be most widely used in small firms, where it is seen in the direct supervision of subordinates' actions. However, it also structures the relationships between managers at different levels in multinational enterprises. For example, the CEO may use a great deal of personal control to influence the behavior of his or her immediate subordinates, such as the heads of worldwide product divisions or major geographic areas. In turn, these heads may use personal control to influence the behavior of their subordinates, and so on down through the organization. Jack Welch, the longtime CEO of General Electric who retired in 2001, had regular one-on-one meetings with the heads of all of GE's major businesses (most of which are international).[25] He used these meetings to probe the managers about the strategy, structure, and financial performance of their operations. In doing so, he essentially exercised personal control over these managers and, undoubtedly, over the strategies that they favored.

Bureaucratic Controls

Bureaucratic control is control through a system of rules and procedures that directs the actions of subunits. The most important bureaucratic controls in subunits within multinational firms are budgets and capital spending rules. Budgets are essentially a set of rules for allocating a firm's financial resources. A subunit's budget specifies with some precision how much the subunit may spend. Headquarters uses budgets to influence the behavior of subunits. For example, the R&D budget normally specifies how much cash the R&D unit may spend on product development. R&D managers know that if they spend too much on one project, they will have less to spend on other projects, so they modify their behavior to stay within the budget. Most budgets are set by negotiation between headquarters management and subunit management. Headquarters management can encourage the growth of certain subunits and restrict the growth of others by manipulating their budgets.

Capital spending rules require headquarters management to approve any capital expenditure by a subunit that exceeds a certain amount. A budget allows headquarters to specify the amount a subunit can spend in a given year, and capital spending rules give headquarters additional control over how the money is spent. Headquarters can be expected to deny approval for capital spending requests that are at variance with overall firm objectives and to approve those that are congruent with firm objectives.

Output Controls

Output controls involve setting goals for subunits to achieve and expressing those goals in terms of relatively objective performance metrics such as profitability, productivity, growth, market share, and quality. The performance of subunit managers is then judged by their ability to achieve the goals.[26] If goals are met or exceeded, subunit managers will be rewarded. If goals are not met, top management will normally intervene to find out why and take appropriate corrective action. Thus, control is achieved by comparing actual performance against targets and intervening selectively to take corrective action. Subunits' goals depend on their role in the firm. Self-contained product divisions or national subsidiaries are typically given goals for profitability, sales growth, and market share. Functions are more likely to be given goals related to their particular activity. Thus, R&D will be given product development goals, production will be given productivity and quality goals, marketing will be given market share goals, and so on.

As with budgets, goals are normally established through negotiation between subunits and headquarters. Generally, headquarters tries to set goals that are challenging but realistic, so subunit managers are forced to look for ways to improve their operations but are not so pressured that they will resort to dysfunctional activities to do so (such as short-run profit maximization). Output controls foster a system of "management by exception," in that so long as subunits meet their goals, they are left alone. If a subunit fails to attain its goals, however, headquarters managers are likely to ask some tough questions. If they don't get satisfactory answers, they are likely to intervene proactively in a subunit, replacing top management and looking for ways to improve efficiency.

Cultural Controls

Cultural controls exist when employees "buy into" the norms and value systems of the firm. When this occurs, employees tend to control their own behavior, which reduces the need for direct supervision. In a firm with a strong culture, self-control can reduce the need for other control systems. We discuss organizational culture later. McDonald's actively promotes organizational norms and values, referring to its franchisees and suppliers as partners and emphasizing its long-term commitment to them. This commitment is not just a public relations exercise; it is backed by actions, including a willingness to help suppliers and franchisees improve their operations by providing capital and/or management assistance when needed. In response, McDonald's franchisees and suppliers are integrated into the firm's culture and thus become committed to helping McDonald's succeed. One result is that McDonald's can devote less time than would otherwise be necessary to controlling its franchisees and suppliers.

Incentive Systems

Incentives refer to the devices used to reward appropriate employee behavior. Many employees receive incentives in the form of annual bonus pay. Incentives are usually closely tied to the performance metrics used for output controls. For example, setting targets linked to profitability might be used to measure the performance of a subunit, such as a global product division. To create positive incentives for employees to work hard to exceed those targets, they may be given a share of any profits above those targeted. If a subunit has set a goal of attaining a 15 percent return on investment and it actually attains a 20 percent return, unit employees may be given a share in the profits generated in excess of the 15 percent target in the form of bonus pay. We return to the topic of incentive systems in Chapter 19 when we discuss human resource strategy in the multinational firm. For now, however, several important points need to be made. First, the type of incentive used often varies depending on the employees and their tasks. Incentives for employees working on the factory floor may be very different from the incentives used for senior managers. The incentives used must be matched to the type of work being performed. The employees on the factory floor of a manufacturing plant may be broken into teams of 20 to 30 individuals, and they may have their bonus pay tied to the ability of their team to hit or exceed targets for output and product quality. In contrast, the senior managers of the plant may be rewarded according to metrics linked to the output of the entire operation. The basic principle is to make sure the incentive scheme for an individual employee is linked to an output target that he or she has some control over and can influence. The individual employees on the factory floor may not be able to exercise much influence over the performance of the entire operation, but they can influence the performance of their team, so incentive pay is tied to output at this level.

Second, the successful execution of strategy in the multinational firm often requires significant cooperation between managers in different subunits. For example, as noted earlier, some multinational firms operate with matrix structures where a country subsidiary might be responsible for marketing and sales in a nation, while a global product division might be responsible for manufacturing and product development. The managers of these different units need to cooperate closely with each other if the firm is to be successful. One way of encouraging the managers to cooperate is to link incentives to performance at a higher level in the organization. Thus, the senior managers of the country subsidiaries and global product divisions might be rewarded according to the profitability of the entire firm. The thinking here is that boosting the profitability of the entire firm requires managers in the country subsidiaries and product divisions to cooperate with each other on strategy implementation, and linking incentive systems to the next level up in the hierarchy encourages this. Most firms use a formula for incentives that links a portion of incentive pay to the performance of the subunit in which a manager or employee works and a portion to the performance of the entire firm, or some other higher-level organizational unit. The goal is to encourage employees to improve the efficiency of their unit and to cooperate with other units in the organization.

Third, the incentive systems used within a multinational enterprise often have to be adjusted to account for national differences in institutions and culture. Incentive systems that work in the United States might not work, or even be allowed, in other countries. For example, Lincoln Electric, a leader in the manufacture of arc welding equipment, has used an incentive system for its employees based on piecework rates in its American factories (under a piecework system, employees are paid according to the amount they produce). While this system has worked very well in the United States, Lincoln has found that the system is difficult to introduce in other countries. In some countries, such as Germany, piecework systems are illegal, while in others the prevailing national culture is antagonistic to a system where performance is so closely tied to individual effort.

Finally, it is important for managers to recognize that incentive systems can have unintended consequences. Managers need to carefully think through exactly what behavior certain incentives encourage. For example, if employees in a factory are rewarded solely on the basis of how many units of output they produce, with no attention paid to the quality of that output, they may produce as many units as possible to boost their incentive pay, but the quality of those units may be poor.

Control Systems, Incentives, and Strategy in the International Business

The key to understanding the relationship between international strategy, control systems, and incentive systems is the concept of performance ambiguity.

Performance Ambiguity

Performance ambiguity exists when the causes of a subunit's poor performance are not clear. This is not uncommon when a subunit's performance is partly dependent on the performance of other subunits, that is, when there is a high degree of interdependence between subunits within the organization. Consider the case of a French subsidiary of a U.S. firm that depends on another subsidiary, a manufacturer based in Italy, for the products it sells. The French subsidiary is failing to achieve its sales goals, and the U.S. management asks the managers to explain. They reply that they are receiving poor-quality goods from the Italian subsidiary. The U.S. management asks the managers of the Italian operation what the problem is. They reply that their product quality is excellent—the best in the industry, in fact—and that the French simply don't know how to sell a good product. Who is right, the French or the Italians? Without more information, top management cannot tell. Because they are dependent on the Italians for their product, the French have an alibi for poor performance. U.S. management needs to have more information to determine who is correct. Collecting this information is expensive and time-consuming and will divert attention away from other issues. In other words, performance ambiguity raises the costs of control.

Consider how different things would be if the French operation were self-contained, with its own manufacturing, marketing, and R&D facilities. The French operation would lack a convenient alibi for its poor performance; the French managers would stand or fall on their own merits. They could not blame the Italians for their poor sales. The level of performance ambiguity, therefore, is a function of the interdependence of subunits in an organization.

Strategy, Interdependence, and Ambiguity

Now let us consider the relationships between strategy, interdependence, and performance ambiguity. In firms pursuing a localization strategy, each national operation is a stand-alone entity and can be judged on its own merits. The level of performance ambiguity is low. In an international firm, the level of interdependence is somewhat higher. Integration is required to facilitate the transfer of core competencies and skills. Since the success of a foreign operation is partly dependent on the quality of the competency transferred from the home country, performance ambiguity can exist.

In firms pursuing a global standardization strategy, the situation is still more complex. Recall that in a pure global firm the pursuit of location and experience curve economies leads to the development of a global web of value creation activities. Many of the activities in a global firm are interdependent. A French subsidiary's ability to sell a product does depend on how well other operations in other countries perform their value creation activities. Thus, the levels of interdependence and performance ambiguity are high in global companies.

The level of performance ambiguity is highest of all in transnational firms. Transnational firms suffer from the same performance ambiguity problems that global firms do. In addition, since they emphasize the multidirectional transfer of core competencies, they also suffer from the problems characteristic of firms pursuing an international strategy. The extremely high level of integration within transnational firms implies a high degree of joint decision making, and the resulting interdependencies create plenty of alibis for poor performance. There is lots of room for finger-pointing in transnational firms.

Implications for Control and Incentives

The arguments of the previous section, along with the implications for the costs of control, are summarized in Table 14.1. The costs of control can be defined as the amount of time top management must devote to monitoring and evaluating subunits' performance. This is greater when the amount of performance ambiguity is greater. When performance ambiguity is low, management can use output controls and a system of management by exception; when it is high, managers have no such luxury. Output controls do not provide totally unambiguous signals of a subunit's efficiency when the performance of that subunit is dependent on the performance of another subunit within the organization. Thus, management must devote time to resolving the problems that arise from performance ambiguity, with a corresponding rise in the costs of control.

TABLE 14.1 Interdependence, Performance Ambiguity, and the Costs of Control for the Four International Business Strategies

Strategy	Interdependence	Performance Ambiguity	Costs of Control
Localization	Low	Low	Low
International	Moderate	Moderate	Moderate
Global	High	High	High
Transnational	Very high	Very high	Very high

Table 14.1 reveals a paradox. We saw in Chapter 13 that a transnational strategy is desirable because it gives a firm more ways to profit from international expansion than do localization, international, and global standardization strategies. But now we see that due to the high level of interdependence, the costs of controlling transnational firms are higher than the costs of controlling firms that pursue other strategies. Unless there is some way of reducing these costs, the higher profitability associated with a transnational strategy could be canceled out by the higher costs of control. The same point, although to a lesser extent, can be made with regard to firms pursuing a global standardization strategy. Although firms pursuing a global standardization strategy can reap the cost benefits of location and experience curve economies, they must cope with a higher level of performance ambiguity, and this raises the costs of control (in comparison with firms pursuing an international or localization strategy).

This is where control systems and incentives come in. When we survey the systems that corporations use to control their subunits, we find that irrespective of their strategy, multinational firms all use output and bureaucratic controls. However, in firms pursuing either global or transnational strategies, the usefulness of output controls is limited by substantial performance ambiguities. As a result, these firms place greater emphasis on cultural controls. Cultural control—by encouraging managers to want to assume the organization's norms and value systems—gives managers of interdependent subunits an incentive to look for ways to work out problems that arise between them. The result is a reduction in finger-pointing and, accordingly, in the costs of control. The development of cultural controls may be a precondition for the successful pursuit of a transnational strategy and perhaps of a global strategy as well.[27] As for incentives, the material discussed earlier suggests that the conflict between different subunits can be reduced and the potential for cooperation enhanced if incentive systems are tied in some way to a higher level in the hierarchy. When performance ambiguity makes it difficult to judge the performance of subunits as stand-alone entities, linking the incentive pay of senior managers to the entity to which both subunits belong can reduce the resulting problems.

PROCESSES

Processes, defined as the manner in which decisions are made and work is performed within the organization, can be found at many different levels within an organization.[28] There are processes for formulating strategy, processes for allocating resources, processes for evaluating new-product ideas, processes for handling customer inquiries and complaints, processes for improving product quality, processes for evaluating employee performance, and so on. Often, the core competencies or valuable skills of a firm are embedded in its processes. Efficient and effective processes can lower the costs of value creation and add additional value to a product. For example, the global success of many Japanese manufacturing enterprises in the 1980s was based in part on their early adoption of processes for improving product quality and operating efficiency, including total quality management and just-in-time inventory systems. Today, the competitive success of General Electric can in part be attributed to a number of processes that have been widely promoted within the company. These include the company's Six Sigma process for quality improvement, its process for "digitalization" of business (using corporate intranets and the Internet to automate activities and reduce operating costs), and its process for idea generation, referred to within the company as "workouts," where managers and employees get together for intensive sessions over several days to identify and commit to ideas for improving productivity.

An organization's processes can be summarized by means of a flow chart, which illustrates the various steps and decision points involved in performing work. Many processes cut across functions, or divisions, and require cooperation between individuals in different subunits. For example, product development processes require employees from R&D, manufacturing, and marketing to work together in a cooperative manner to make sure new products are developed with market needs in mind and designed in such a way that they can be manufactured at a low cost. Because they cut across organizational boundaries, performing processes effectively often requires the establishment of formal integrating mechanisms and incentives for cross-unit cooperation.

A detailed consideration of the nature of processes and strategies for process improvement and reengineering is beyond the scope of this book. However, it is important to make two basic remarks about managing processes, particularly in the context of an international business.[29] The first is that in a multinational enterprise, many processes cut not only across organizational boundaries, embracing several different subunits, but also across national boundaries. Designing a new product may require the cooperation of R&D personnel located in California, production people located in Taiwan, and marketing located in Europe, America, and Asia. The chances of pulling this off are greatly enhanced if the processes are embedded in an organizational culture that promotes cooperation between individuals from different subunits and nations, if the incentive systems of the organization explicitly reward such cooperation, and if formal and informal integrating mechanisms are used to facilitate coordination between subunits.

Second, it is particularly important for a multinational enterprise to recognize that valuable new processes that might lead to a competitive advantage can be developed anywhere within the organization's global network of operations.[30] New processes may be developed by a local operating subsidiary in response to conditions pertaining to its market. Those processes might then have value to other parts of the multinational enterprise. The ability to create valuable processes matters, but it is also important to leverage those processes. This requires both formal and informal integrating mechanisms such as knowledge networks.

ORGANIZATIONAL CULTURE

Chapter 4 applied the concept of culture to nation-states. Culture, however, is a social construct ascribed to societies, including organizations.[31] Thus, we can speak of organizational culture and organizational subculture. The basic definition of culture remains the same, whether we are applying it to a large society such as a nation-state or a small society such as an organization or one of its subunits. Culture refers to a system of values and norms that are shared among people. Values are abstract ideas about what a group believes to be good, right, and desirable. Norms mean the social rules and guidelines that prescribe appropriate behavior in particular situations. Values and norms express themselves as the behavior patterns or style of an organization that new employees are automatically encouraged to follow by their fellow employees. Although an organization's culture is rarely static, it tends to change relatively slowly.

Creating and Maintaining Organizational Culture

An organization's culture comes from several sources. First, there seems to be wide agreement that founders or important leaders can have a profound impact on an organization's culture, often imprinting their own values on the culture.[32] A famous example of a strong founder effect concerns the Japanese firm Matsushita. Konosuke Matsushita's almost Zen-like personal business philosophy was codified in the "Seven Spiritual Values" of Matsushita that all new employees still learn today. These values are (1) national service through industry, (2) fairness, (3) harmony and cooperation, (4) struggle for betterment, (5) courtesy and humility, (6) adjustment and assimilation, and (7) gratitude. A leader does not have to be the founder to have a profound influence on organizational culture. Jack Welch is widely credited with having changed the culture of GE when he first became CEO, primarily by emphasizing a countercultural set of values, such as risk taking, entrepreneurship, stewardship, and boundaryless behavior. It is more difficult for a leader, however forceful, to change an established organizational culture than it is to create one from scratch in a new venture.

Another important influence on organizational culture is the broader social culture of the nation where the firm was founded. In the United States, for example, the competitive ethic of individualism looms large and there is enormous social stress on producing winners. Many American firms find ways of rewarding and motivating individuals so that they see themselves as winners.[33] The values of American firms often reflect the values of American culture. Similarly, the cooperative values found in many Japanese firms have been argued to reflect the values of traditional Japanese society, with its emphasis on group cooperation, reciprocal obligations, and harmony.[34] Thus, although it may be a generalization, there may be something to the argument that organizational culture is influenced by national culture.

A third influence on organizational culture is the history of the enterprise, which over time may come to shape the values of the organization. In the language of historians, organizational culture is the path-dependent product of where the organization has been through time. For example, Philips Electronics NV, the Dutch multinational long operated with a culture that placed a high value on the independence of national operating companies. This culture was shaped by the history of the company. During World War II, Holland was occupied by the Germans. With the head office in occupied territories, power was devolved by default to various foreign operating companies, such as Philips' subsidiaries in the United States and Great Britain. After the war ended, these subsidiaries continued to operate in a highly autonomous fashion. A belief that this was the right thing to do became a core value of the company.

Decisions that subsequently result in high performance tend to become institutionalized in the values of a firm. In the 1920s, 3M was primarily a manufacturer of sandpaper. Richard Drew, who was a young laboratory assistant at the time, came up with what he thought would be a great new product—a glue-covered strip of paper, which he called "sticky tape." Drew saw applications for the product in the automobile industry, where it could be used to mask parts of a vehicle during painting. He presented the idea to the company's president, William McKnight. An unimpressed McKnight suggested that Drew drop the research. Drew didn't; instead he developed the "sticky tape" and then went out and got endorsements from potential customers in the auto industry. Armed with this information, he approached McKnight again. A chastened McKnight reversed his position and gave Drew the go-ahead to start developing what was to become one of 3M's main product lines—sticky tape—a business it dominates to this day.[35] From then on, McKnight emphasized the importance of giving researchers at 3M free rein to explore their own ideas and experiment with product offerings. This soon became a core value at 3M and was enshrined in the company's famous "15 percent rule," which stated that researchers could spend 15 percent of the company time working on ideas of their own choosing. Today, new employees are often told the Drew story, which is used to illustrate the value of allowing individuals to explore their own ideas.

Culture is maintained by a variety of mechanisms. These include (1) hiring and promotional practices of the organization, (2) reward strategies, (3) socialization processes, and (4) communication strategy. The goal is to recruit people whose values are consistent with those of the company. To further reinforce values, a company may promote individuals whose behavior is consistent with the core values of the organization. Merit review processes may also be linked to a company's values, which further reinforces cultural norms.

Socialization can be formal, such as training programs that educate employees in the core values of the organization. Informal socialization may be friendly advice from peers or bosses or may be implicit in the actions of peers and superiors toward new employees. As for communication strategy, many companies with strong cultures devote a lot of attention to framing their key values in corporate mission statements, communicating them often to employees, and using them to guide difficult decisions. Stories and symbols are often used to reinforce important values (e.g., the Drew and McKnight story at 3M).

Organizational Culture and Performance in the International Business

Management authors often talk about "strong cultures."[36] In a strong culture, almost all managers share a relatively consistent set of values and norms that have a clear impact on the way work is performed. New employees adopt these values very quickly, and employees that do not fit in with the core values tend to leave. In such a culture, a new executive is just as likely to be corrected by his subordinates as by his superiors if he violates the values and norms of the organizational culture. Firms with a strong culture are normally seen by outsiders as having a certain style or way of doing things. Lincoln Electric, featured in the accompanying Management Focus, is an example of a firm with a strong culture.

Culture and Incentives at Lincoln Electric

Lincoln Electric is one of the leading companies in the global market for arc welding equipment. Lincoln's success has been based on extremely high levels of employee productivity. The company attributes its productivity to a strong organizational culture and an incentive scheme based on piecework. Lincoln's organizational culture dates back to James Lincoln, who in 1907 joined the company that his brother had established a few years earlier. Lincoln had a strong respect for the ability of the individual and believed that, correctly motivated, ordinary people could achieve extraordinary performance. He emphasized that Lincoln should be a meritocracy where people were rewarded for their individual effort. Strongly egalitarian, Lincoln removed barriers to communication between "workers" and "managers," practicing an open-door policy. He made sure that all who worked for the company were treated equally; for example, everyone ate in the same cafeteria, there were no reserved parking places for "managers," and so on. Lincoln also believed that any gains in productivity should be shared with consumers in the form of lower prices, with employees in the form of higher pay, and with shareholders in the form of higher dividends.

The organizational culture that grew out of James Lincoln's beliefs was reinforced by the company's incentive system. Production workers receive no base salary but are paid according to the number of pieces they produce. The piecework rates at the company enable an employee working at a normal pace to earn an income equivalent to the average wage for manufacturing workers in the area where a factory is based. Workers have responsibility for the quality of their output and must repair any defects spotted by quality inspectors before the pieces are included in the piecework calculation. Since 1934, production workers have been awarded a semiannual bonus based on merit ratings. These ratings are based on objective criteria (such as an employee's level and quality of output) and subjective criteria (such as an employee's attitudes toward cooperation and his or her dependability). These systems give Lincoln's employees an incentive to work hard and to generate innovations that boost productivity, for doing so influences their level of pay. Lincoln's factory workers have been able to earn a base pay that often exceeds the average manufacturing wage in the area by more than 50 percent and receive a bonus on top of this that in good years could double their base pay. Despite high employee compensation, the workers are so productive that Lincoln has a lower cost structure than its competitors.

While this organizational culture and set of incentives works well in the United States, where it is compatible with the individualistic culture of the country, it did not translate easily into foreign operations. In the 1980s and early 1990s, Lincoln expanded aggressively into Europe and Latin America, acquiring a number of local arc welding manufacturers. Lincoln left local managers in place, believing that they knew local conditions better than Americans. However, the local managers had little working knowledge of Lincoln's strong organizational culture and were unable or unwilling to impose that culture on their units, which had their own long-established organizational cultures. Nevertheless, Lincoln told local managers to introduce its incentive systems in acquired companies. They frequently ran into legal and cultural roadblocks.

In many countries, piecework is viewed as an exploitive compensation system that forces employees to work ever harder. In Germany, where Lincoln made an acquisition, it is illegal. In Brazil, a bonus paid for more than two years becomes a legal entitlement! In many other countries, both managers and workers were opposed to the idea of piecework. Lincoln found that many European workers valued extra leisure more highly than extra income and were not prepared to work as hard as their American counterparts. Many of the acquired companies were also unionized, and the local unions vigorously opposed the introduction of piecework. As a result, Lincoln was not able to replicate the high level of employee productivity that it had achieved in the United States, and its expansion pulled down the performance of the entire company.[40]

Strong does not necessarily mean good. A culture can be strong but bad. The culture of the Nazi Party in Germany was certainly strong, but it was most definitely not good. Nor does it follow that a strong culture leads to high performance. One study found that in the 1980s General Motors had a "strong culture," but it was a strong culture that discouraged lower-level employees from demonstrating initiative and taking risks, which the authors argued was dysfunctional and led to low performance at GM.[37] Also, a strong culture might be beneficial at one point, leading to high performance, but inappropriate at another time. The appropriateness of the culture depends on the context. In the 1980s, when IBM was performing very well, several management authors sang the praises of its strong culture, which among other things placed a high value on consensus-based decision making.[38] These authors argued that such a decision-making process was appropriate given the substantial financial investments that IBM routinely made in new technology. However, this process turned out to be a weakness in the fast-moving computer industry of the late 1980s and 1990s. Consensus-based decision making was slow, bureaucratic, and not particularly conducive to corporate risk taking. While this was fine in the 1970s, IBM needed rapid decision making and entrepreneurial risk taking in the 1990s, but its culture discouraged such behavior. IBM found itself outflanked by then-small enterprises such as Microsoft.

One academic study concluded that firms that exhibited high performance over a prolonged period tended to have strong but adaptive cultures. According to this study, in an adaptive culture most managers care deeply about and value customers, stockholders, and employees. They also strongly value people and processes that create useful change in a firm.[39] While this is interesting, it does reduce the issue to a very high level of abstraction; after all, what company would say that it doesn't care deeply about customers, stockholders, and employees? A somewhat different perspective is to argue that the culture of the firm must match the rest of the architecture of the organization, the firm's strategy, and the demands of the competitive environment for superior performance to be attained. All these elements must be consistent with each other. Lincoln Electric provides another useful example (see the Management Focus). Lincoln competes in a business that is very competitive, where cost minimization is a key source of competitive advantage. Lincoln's culture and incentive systems both encourage employees to strive for high levels of productivity, which translates into the low costs that are critical for Lincoln's success. The Lincoln example also demonstrates another important point for international businesses: A culture that leads to high performance in the firm's home nation may not be easy to impose on foreign subsidiaries! Lincoln's culture has clearly helped the firm achieve superior performance in the U.S. market, but this same culture is very "American" in its form and difficult to implement in other countries. The managers and employees of several of Lincoln's European subsidiaries found the culture to be alien to their own values and were reluctant to adopt it. The result was that Lincoln found it very difficult to replicate in foreign markets the success it has had in the United States. Lincoln compounded the problem by acquiring established enterprises that already had their own organizational culture. Thus, in trying to impose its culture on foreign operating subsidiaries, Lincoln had to deal with two problems: how to change the established organizational culture of those units, and how to introduce an organizational culture whose key values might be alien to the values held by members of that society. These problems are not unique to Lincoln; many international businesses have to deal with exactly the same problems.

The solution Lincoln has adopted is to establish new subsidiaries, rather than acquiring and trying to transform an enterprise with its own culture. It is much easier to establish a set of values in a new enterprise than it is to change the values of an established enterprise. A second solution is to devote a lot of time and attention to transmitting the firm's organizational culture to its foreign operations. This was something Lincoln originally omitted. Other firms make this an important part of their strategy for internationalization.

The need for a common organizational culture that is the same across a multinational's global network of subsidiaries probably varies with the strategy of the firm. Shared norms and values can facilitate coordination and cooperation between individuals from different subunits.[41] A strong common culture may lead to goal congruence and can attenuate the problems that arise from interdependence, performance ambiguities, and conflict among managers from different subsidiaries. As noted earlier, a shared culture may help informal integrating mechanisms such as knowledge networks to operate more effectively. As such, a common culture may be of greater value in a multinational that is pursuing a strategy that requires cooperation and coordination between globally dispersed subsidiaries. This suggests that it is more important to have a common culture in firms employing a transnational strategy than a localization strategy, with global and international strategies falling between these two extremes.

SYNTHESIS: STRATEGY AND ARCHITECTURE   LO14-3

Chapter 13 identified four basic strategies that multinational firms pursue: localization, international, global, and transnational. So far in this chapter we have looked at several aspects of organizational architecture, and we have discussed the interrelationships between these dimensions and strategies. Now it is time to synthesize this material.

Localization Strategy

Firms pursuing a localization strategy focus on local responsiveness. Table 14.2 shows that such firms tend to operate with worldwide area structures, within which operating decisions are decentralized to functionally self-contained country subsidiaries. The need for coordination between subunits (areas and country subsidiaries) is low. This suggests that firms pursuing a localization strategy do not have a high need for integrating mechanisms, either formal or informal, to knit together different national operations. The lack of interdependence implies that the level of performance ambiguity in such enterprises is low, as (by extension) are the costs of control. Thus, headquarters can manage foreign operations by relying primarily on output and bureaucratic controls and a policy of management by exception. Incentives can be linked to performance metrics at the level of country subsidiaries. Since the need for integration and coordination is low, the need for common processes and organizational culture is also quite low. Were it not for the fact that these firms are unable to profit from the realization of location and experience curve economies, or from the transfer of core competencies, their organizational simplicity would make this an attractive strategy.

International Strategy

Firms pursuing an international strategy attempt to create value by transferring core competencies from home to foreign subsidiaries. If they are diverse, as most of them are, these firms operate with a

TABLE 14.2 A Synthesis of Strategy, Structure, and Control Systems

Structure and Controls	Strategy			
	Localization	International	Global Standardization	Transnational
Vertical differentiation	Decentralized	Core competency more centralized; rest decentralized	Some centralization	Mixed centralization and decentralization
Horizontal differentiation	Worldwide area structure	Worldwide product divisions	Worldwide product divisions	Informal matrix
Need for coordination	Low	Moderate	High	Very high
Integrating mechanisms	None	Few	Many	Very many
Performance ambiguity	Low	Moderate	High	Very high
Need for cultural controls	Low	Moderate	High	Very high

worldwide product division structure. Headquarters typically maintains centralized control over the source of the firm's core competency, which is most typically found in the R&D and/or marketing functions of the firm. All other operating decisions are decentralized within the firm to subsidiary operations in each country (which in diverse firms report to worldwide product divisions).

The need for coordination is moderate in such firms, reflecting the need to transfer core competencies. Thus, although such firms operate with some integrating mechanisms, they are not that extensive. The relatively low level of interdependence that results translates into a relatively low level of performance ambiguity. These firms can generally get by with output and bureaucratic controls and with incentives that are focused on performance metrics at the level of country subsidiaries. The need for a common organizational culture and common processes is not that great. An important exception to this is when the core skills or competencies of the firm are embedded in processes and culture, in which case the firm needs to pay close attention to transferring those processes and associated culture from the corporate center to country subsidiaries. Overall, although the organization required for an international strategy is more complex than that of firms pursuing a localization strategy, the increase in the level of complexity is not that great.

Global Standardization Strategy

Firms pursuing a global standardization strategy focus on the realization of location and experience curve economies. If they are diversified, as many of them are, these firms operate with a worldwide product division structure. To coordinate the firm's globally dispersed web of value creation activities, headquarters typically maintains ultimate control over most operating decisions. In general, such firms are more centralized than enterprises pursuing a localization or international strategy. Reflecting the need for coordination of the various stages of the firms' globally dispersed value chains, the need for integration in these firms also is high. Thus, these firms tend to operate with an array of formal and informal integrating mechanisms. The resulting interdependencies can lead to significant performance ambiguities. As a result, in addition to output and bureaucratic controls, firms pursuing a global standardization strategy tend to stress the need to build a strong organizational culture that can facilitate coordination and cooperation. They also tend to use incentive systems that are linked to performance metrics at the corporate level, giving the managers of different operations a strong incentive to cooperate with each other to increase the performance of the entire corporation. On average, the organization of such firms is more complex than that of firms pursuing a localization or international strategy.

Transnational Strategy

Firms pursuing a transnational strategy focus on the simultaneous attainment of location and experience curve economies, local responsiveness, and global learning (the multidirectional transfer of core competencies or skills). These firms may operate with matrix-type structures in which both product divisions and geographic areas have significant influence. The need to coordinate a globally dispersed value chain and to transfer core competencies creates pressures for centralizing some operating decisions (particularly production and R&D). At the same time, the need to be locally responsive creates pressures for decentralizing other operating decisions to national operations (particularly marketing). Consequently, these firms tend to mix relatively high degrees of centralization for some operating decisions with relative high degrees of decentralization for other operating decisions.

The need for coordination is high in transnational firms. This is reflected in the use of an array of formal and informal integrating mechanisms, including formal matrix structures and informal management networks. The high level of interdependence of subunits implied by such integration can result in significant performance ambiguities, which raise the costs of control. To reduce these, in addition to output and bureaucratic controls, firms pursuing a transnational strategy need to cultivate a strong culture and to establish incentives that promote cooperation between subunits.

Environment, Strategy, Architecture, and Performance

Underlying the scheme outlined in Table 14.2 is the notion that a "fit" between strategy and architecture is necessary for a firm to achieve high performance. For a firm to succeed, two conditions must be fulfilled. First, the firm's strategy must be consistent with the environment in which the firm operates. We discussed this issue in Chapter 13 and noted that in some industries a global standardization strategy is most viable, in others an international or transnational strategy may be most viable, and in still others a localization strategy may be most viable. Second, the firm's organizational architecture must be consistent with its strategy.

If the strategy does not fit the environment, the firm is likely to experience significant performance problems. If the architecture does not fit the strategy, the firm is also likely to experience performance problems. Therefore, to survive, a firm must strive to achieve a fit of its environment, its strategy, and its organizational architecture. For example, consider Philips NV. For reasons rooted in the history of the firm, Philips operated until recently with an organization typical of an enterprise pursuing localization; operating decisions were decentralized to largely autonomous foreign subsidiaries. Historically, electronics markets were segmented from each other by high trade barriers, so an organization consistent with a localization strategy made sense. However, by the mid-1980s, the industry in which Philips competed had been revolutionized by declining trade barriers, technological change, and the emergence of low-cost Japanese competitors that utilized a global strategy. To survive, Philips needed to adopt a global standardization strategy itself. The firm recognized this and tried to adopt a global posture, but it did little to change its organizational architecture. The firm nominally adopted a matrix structure based on worldwide product divisions and national areas. In reality, however, the national areas continued to dominate the organization, and the product divisions had little more than an advisory role. As a result, Philips' architecture did not fit the strategy, and by the early 1990s Philips was losing money. It was only after four years of wrenching change and large losses that Philips was finally able to tilt the balance of power in its matrix toward the product divisions. By the mid-1990s, the fruits of this effort to realign the company's strategy and architecture with the demands of its operating environment were beginning to show up in improved financial performance.[42]

ORGANIZATIONAL CHANGE

LO14-4

Multinational firms periodically have to alter their architecture so that it conforms to the changes in the environment in which they are competing and the strategy they are pursuing. To be profitable, Philips NV had to alter its strategy and architecture in the 1990s so that both matched the demands of the competitive environment in the electronics industry, which had shifted from localization toward a global industry. While a detailed consideration of organizational change is beyond the scope of this book, a few comments are warranted regarding the sources of organization inertia and the strategies and tactics for implementing organizational change.

Organizational Inertia

Organizations are difficult to change. Within most organizations are strong inertia forces. These forces come from a number of sources. One source of inertia is the existing distribution of power and influence within an organization.[43] The power and influence enjoyed by individual managers are in part a function of their role in the organizational hierarchy, as defined by structural position. By definition, most substantive changes in an organization require a change in structure and, by extension, a change in the distribution of power and influence within the organization. Some individuals will see their power and influence increase as a result of organizational change, and some will see the converse. For example, in the 1990s, Philips increased the roles and responsibilities of its global product divisions and decreased the roles and responsibilities of its foreign subsidiary companies. This meant the managers running the global product divisions saw their power and influence increase, while the managers running the foreign subsidiary companies saw their power and influence decline. As might be expected, some managers of foreign subsidiary companies did not like this change and resisted it, which slowed the pace of change. Those whose power and influence are reduced as a consequence of organizational change can be expected to resist it, primarily by arguing that the change might not work. To the extent that they are successful, this constitutes a source of organizational inertia that might slow or stop change.

Another source of organizational inertia is the existing culture, as expressed in norms and value systems. Value systems reflect deeply held beliefs, and as such, they can be very hard to change. If the formal and informal socialization mechanisms within an organization have been emphasizing a consistent set of values for a prolonged period, and if hiring, promotion, and incentive systems have all reinforced these values, then suddenly announcing that those values are no longer appropriate and need to be changed can produce resistance and dissonance among employees. For example, Philips historically placed a very high value on local autonomy. The changes of the 1990s implied a reduction in the autonomy enjoyed by foreign subsidiaries, which was counter to the established values of the company and thus resisted.

Organizational inertia might also derive from senior managers' preconceptions about the appropriate business model or paradigm. When a given paradigm has worked well in the past, managers might have trouble accepting that it is no longer appropriate. At Philips, granting considerable autonomy to foreign subsidiaries had worked very well in the past, allowing local managers to tailor product and business strategy to the conditions prevailing in a given country. Since this paradigm had worked so well, it was difficult for many managers to understand why it no longer applied. Consequently, they had difficulty accepting a new business model and tended to fall back on their established paradigm and ways of doing things. This change required managers to let go of long-held assumptions about what worked and what didn't work, which was something many of them couldn't do.

Institutional constraints might also act as a source of inertia. National regulations including local content rules and policies pertaining to layoffs might make it difficult for a multinational to alter its global value chain. A multinational might wish to take control for manufacturing away from local subsidiaries, transfer that control to global product divisions, and consolidate manufacturing at a few choice locations. However, if local content rules (see Chapter 7) require some degree of local production and if regulations regarding layoffs make it difficult or expensive for a multinational to close operations in a country, a multinational may find that these constraints make it very difficult to adopt the most effective strategy and architecture.

Implementing Organizational Change

Although all organizations suffer from inertia, the complexity and global spread of many multinationals might make it particularly difficult for them to change their strategy and architecture to match new organizational realities. Yet at the same time, the trend toward globalization in many industries has made it more critical than ever that many multinationals do just that. In industry after industry, declining barriers to cross-border trade and investment have led to a change in the nature of the competitive environment. Cost pressures have increased, requiring multinationals to respond by streamlining their operations to realize economic benefits associated with location and experience curve economies and with the transfer of competencies and skills within the organization. At the same time, local responsiveness remains an important source of differentiation. To survive in this emerging competitive environment, multinationals must change not only their strategy but also their architecture so that it matches strategy in discriminating ways. The basic principles for successful organizational change can be summarized as follows: (1) unfreeze the organization through shock therapy, (2) move the organization to a new state through proactive change in the architecture, and (3) refreeze the organization in its new state.

Unfreezing the Organization

Because of inertia forces, incremental change is often no change. Those whose power is threatened by change can too easily resist incremental change. This leads to the big bang theory of change, which maintains that effective change requires taking bold action early to "unfreeze" the established culture of an organization and to change the distribution of power and influence. Shock therapy to unfreeze the organization might include the closure of plants deemed uneconomic or the announcement of a dramatic structural reorganization. It is also important to realize that change will not occur unless senior managers are committed to it. Senior managers must clearly articulate the need for change so employees understand both why it is being pursued and the benefits that will flow from successful change. Senior managers must also practice what they preach and take the necessary bold steps. If employees see senior managers preaching the need for change but not changing their own behavior or making substantive changes in the organization, they will soon lose faith in the change effort, which then will flounder.

Moving to the New State

Once an organization has been unfrozen, it must be moved to its new state. Movement requires taking action—closing operations; reorganizing the structure; reassigning responsibilities; changing control, incentive, and reward systems; redesigning processes; and letting people go who are seen as an impediment to change. In other words, movement requires a substantial change in the form of a multinational's organizational architecture so that it matches the desired new strategic posture. For movement to be successful, it must be done with sufficient speed. Involving employees in the change effort is an excellent way to get them to appreciate and buy into the needs for change and to help with rapid movement. For example, a firm might delegate substantial responsibility for designing operating processes to lower-level employees. If enough of their recommendations are then acted on, the employees will see the consequences of their efforts and consequently buy into the notion that change is really occurring.

Refreezing the Organization

Refreezing the organization takes longer. It may require that a new culture be established while the old one is being dismantled. Thus, refreezing requires that employees be socialized into the new way of doing things. Companies will often use management education programs to achieve this. At General Electric, where longtime CEO Jack Welch instituted a major change in the culture of the company, management education programs were used as a proactive tool to communicate new values to organization members. On their own, however, management education programs are not enough. Hiring policies must be changed to reflect the new realities, with an emphasis on hiring individuals whose own values are consistent with that of the new culture the firm is trying to build. Similarly, control and incentive systems must be consistent with the new realities of the organization, or change will never take. Senior management must recognize that changing culture takes a long time. Any letup in the pressure to change may allow the old culture to reemerge as employees fall back into familiar ways of doing things. The communication task facing senior managers, therefore, is a long-term endeavor that requires managers to be relentless and persistent in their pursuit of change. One striking feature of Jack Welch's two-decade tenure at GE, for example, is that he never stopped pushing his change agenda. It was a consistent theme of his tenure. He was always thinking up new programs and initiatives to keep pushing the culture of the organization along the desired trajectory.

Chapter Summary

This chapter identified the organizational architecture that can be used by multinational enterprises to manage and direct their global operations. A central theme of the chapter was that different strategies require different architectures; strategy is implemented through architecture. To succeed, a firm must match its architecture to its strategy in discriminating ways. Firms whose architecture does not fit their strategic requirements will experience performance problems. It is also necessary for the different components of architecture to be consistent with each other. The chapter made the following points:

1. Organizational architecture refers to the totality of a firm's organization, including formal organizational structure, control systems and incentives, processes, organizational culture, and people.
2. Superior enterprise profitability requires three conditions to be fulfilled: the different elements of a firm's organizational architecture must be internally consistent, the organizational architecture must fit the strategy of the firm, and the strategy and architecture of the firm must be consistent with competitive conditions prevailing in the firm's markets.
3. Organizational structure means three things: the formal division of the organization into subunits (horizontal differentiation), the location of decision-making responsibilities within that structure (vertical differentiation), and the establishment of integrating mechanisms.

4. Control systems are the metrics used to measure the performance of subunits and make judgments about how well managers are running those subunits.

5. Incentives refer to the devices used to reward appropriate employee behavior. Many employees receive incentives in the form of annual bonus pay. Incentives are usually closely tied to the performance metrics used for output controls.

6. Processes refer to the manner in which decisions are made and work is performed within the organization. Processes can be found at many different levels within an organization. The core competencies or valuable skills of a firm are often embedded in its processes. Efficient and effective processes can help lower the costs of value creation and add additional value to a product.

7. Organizational culture refers to a system of values and norms that is shared among employees. Values and norms express themselves as the behavior patterns or style of an organization that new employees are automatically encouraged to follow by their fellow employees.

8. Firms pursuing different strategies must adopt a different architecture to implement those strategies successfully. Firms pursuing localization, global, international, and transnational strategies all must adopt an organizational architecture that matches their strategy.

9. While all organizations suffer from inertia, the complexity and global spread of many multinationals might make it particularly difficult for them to change their strategy and architecture to match new organizational realities. At the same time, the trend toward globalization in many industries has made it more critical than ever that many multinationals do just that.

Critical Thinking and Discussion Questions

1. "The choice of strategy for a multinational firm must depend on a comparison of the benefits of that strategy (in terms of value creation) with the costs of implementing it (as defined by organizational architecture necessary for implementation). On this basis, it may be logical for some firms to pursue a localization strategy, others a global or international strategy, and still others a transnational strategy." Is this statement correct?

2. Discuss this statement: "An understanding of the causes and consequences of performance ambiguity is central to the issue of organizational design in multinational firms."

3. Describe the organizational architecture a transnational firm might adopt to reduce the costs of control.

4. What is the most appropriate organizational architecture for a firm that is competing in an industry where a global strategy is most appropriate?

5. If a firm is changing its strategy from an international to a transnational strategy, what are the most important challenges it is likely to face in implementing this change? How can the firm overcome these challenges?

6. Reread the Management Focus on Walmart's international division, and answer the following questions:

    a. Why did the centralization of decisions at the headquarters on Walmart's international division create problems for the company's different national operations? Has Walmart's response been appropriate?

    b. Do you think that having an international division is the best structure for managing Walmart's foreign operations? What problems might arise with this structure? What other structure might work?

7. Reread the Management Focus on the rise and fall of the matrix structure at Dow Chemical; then answer the following questions:

   a. Why did Dow first adopt a matrix structure? What were the problems with this structure? Do you think these problems are typical of matrix structures?

   b. What drove the shift away from the matrix structure in the late 1990s? Does Dow's structure now make sense given the nature of its businesses and the competitive environment it competes in?

8. Reread the Management Focus on Lincoln Electric; then answer the following questions:

   a. To what extent are the organizational culture and incentive systems of Lincoln Electric aligned with the firm's strategy?

   b. How was the culture at Lincoln Electric created and nurtured over time?

   c. Why did the culture and incentive systems work well in the United States? Why did it not take in other nations?

Research Task ⚙ globalEDGE   globaledge.msu.edu

The Organization of International Business

Use the globalEDGE website (globaledge.msu.edu) to complete the following exercises:

Exercise 1

Fortune conducts an annual survey and publishes the rankings of the *world's most admired companies*. Locate the most recent ranking available, and focus on the factors used to determine which companies are most admired. Prepare an executive summary of the strategic and organizational success factors for a company of your choice.

Exercise 2

You work at a European-based pharmaceutical company that is planning to expand operations to other parts of the world. To design the structure of the organization as it expands internationally, management has requested additional information on the pharmaceutical sector worldwide. Use the *Industry Profiles* section on the globalEDGE site to prepare a risk assessment of the food and beverage industry that can help management gain a better understanding of the external environment in foreign markets.

Closing CASE

Philips NV

Established in 1891 in Holland, Philips Electronics NV is one of the world's oldest multinationals. The company began making lighting products and over time diversified into a range of businesses that included domestic appliances, consumer electronics, and health care products. From the beginning, Holland's small domestic market created pressures for Philips to look to foreign markets for growth. By the start of World War II, Philips already had a global presence. During the war, Holland was occupied by Germany. By necessity, the company's national organizations in countries such as Britain, Australia, Brazil, Canada, and the United States gained considerable autonomy during this period.

After the war, a structure based on strong national organizations remained in place. Each national organization was in essence a self-contained entity that was responsible for much of its own manufacturing, marketing, and sales. Most R&D activities, however, were centralized at Philips' headquarters in Eindhoven, Holland. Reflecting this, several product divisions were created. Based in Eindhoven, the product divisions developed technologies and products, which were then made and sold by the different national organizations. During this period, the career track of most senior managers at Philips involved significant postings in various national organizations around the world.

For several decades this organizational arrangement worked well. It allowed Philips to customize its product offerings, sales, and marketing efforts to the conditions that existed in different national markets. By the 1970s, however, flaws were appearing in the approach. The structure involved significant duplication of activities around the world, particularly in manufacturing, which created an intrinsically high-cost structure. When trade barriers were high, this did not matter so much, but by the 1970s trade barriers were starting to fall and competitors, including Sony and Matsushita from Japan, General Electric from the United States, and Samsung from Korea, were gaining market share by serving increasingly global markets from centralized production facilities where they could achieve greater scale economies and hence lower costs.

Philips' response was to try to tilt the balance of power in its structure away from national organizations and toward the product divisions. International production centers were established under the direction of the product divisions. The national organizations, however, remained responsible for local marketing and sales, and they often maintained control over some local production facilities. One problem Philips faced in trying to change its structure at this time was that most senior managers had come up through the national organizations. Consequently, they were loyal to them and tended to protect their autonomy.

Despite several reorganization efforts, the national organizations remained a strong influence at Philips until the 1990s. In the mid-1990s Cor Boonstra became CEO. He famously described the company's organizational structure as a "plate of spaghetti" and asked how Philips could compete when the company had 350 subsidiaries around the world and significant duplication of manufacturing and marketing efforts across nations. Boonstra instituted a radical reorganization. He replaced the company's 21 product divisions with just 7 global business divisions, making them responsible for global product development, production, and marketing. The heads of the divisions reported directly to him, while the national organizations reported to the divisions. The national organizations remained responsible for local sales and local marketing efforts, but after this reorganization they finally lost their historic sway on the company.

Philips, however, continued to underperform its global rivals. By 2008, Gerard Kleisterlee, who succeeded Boonstra as CEO in 2001, decided Philips was still not sufficiently focused on global markets. He reorganized yet again, this time around just three global divisions, health care, lighting, and consumer lifestyle (which included the company's electronics businesses). The divisions were responsible for product strategy, global marketing, and shifting production to low-cost locations (or outsourcing production). The divisions also took over some sales responsibilities, particularly dealing with global retail chains such as Walmart, Tesco, and Carrefour. To accommodate national differences, however, some sales and marketing activities remained located at the national organizations.[44]

Case Discussion Questions

1. Why did Philips' organizational structure make sense in the 1950s and 1970s? Why did this structure start to create problems for the company in the 1980s?

2. What was Philips trying to achieve by tilting the balance of power in its structure away from national organizations and toward the product divisions? Why was this hard to achieve?
3. What was the point of the organizational changes made by Cor Boonstra? What was he trying to achieve?
4. In 2008 Philips reorganized yet again. Why do you think it did this? What is it trying to achieve?

Walmart India in Scandal Before Launch

The Bribery scandal of Walmart was busted in April, 2012 with a series of allegations that the company engaged in systematic bribery in Mexico for several years and then covered it up[*]. The share price was also hampered after these allegations. Walmart then, did not deny the allegations. Rather, it said it is once again investigating them—the way it did several years ago, before it shoved them under the rug. According to David Barstow of The New York Times (NYT), who reported the story, the bribes were directed by the man who went on to become Vice-Chairman and the head of Walmart's US division, Eduardo Castro-Wright. At the time, Castro-Wright was head of the company's Mexico unit, and was praised and promoted for the astonishing growth he delivered there—growth that the NYT said was directly the result of bribes paid by the company.

The essence of the allegations was that the head of Walmart in Mexico and his chief lieutenants, including the Mexican General Counsel and Chief Auditor, knowingly orchestrated bribes of Mexican officials to obtain building permits, zoning variances, and environmental clearances, and that they also falsified records to hide the payments. When the lawyer in Mexico, directly responsible for bribery payments, had a change of heart and reported the scheme to Walmart lawyers in the US, those lawyers hired an independent firm which recommended a major inquiry. This was rejected by the Walmart management which instead told an internal Walmart investigative unit to look into it.[45]

In November, 2012, an internal probe of Walmart's actions in developing markets has extended beyond the company's Mexican subsidiary to Brazil, China and India. The expansion comes only a year after Walmart revealed Justice Department and SEC investigations of whether it bribed officials to spur the growth of its Mexican subsidiary.[46] "Walmart disclosed on November 15, 2012 that it has expanded an internal investigation into bribery accusations in Mexico to Brazil, China and India, "Stephanie Clifford wrote in New York Times.[47]

The disclosure came in the retail giant's third-quarter earnings filing of 2012 with the United States Securities and Exchange Commission, which said:

Inquiries or investigations regarding allegations of potential FCPA violations were commenced in a number of foreign markets where they operated, including but not limited to Brazil, China and India. The FCPA is the Foreign Corrupt Practices Act, an American anti-bribery law. The New York Times reported in April that seven years ago, Wal-Mart had found credible evidence that its Mexican subsidiary had paid bribes, a violation of the law, and that executives had suppressed an internal investigation into the matter.

The company was one of several big global retailers expected to expand into India under new, less strict foreign direct investment rules for retailers introduced in year 2012. Shortly thereafter, Walmart was the subject of an informal investigation into potential violations of foreign investment rules. Its legal team came under special scrutiny because they had the maximum amount of dealings with government departments that issue licenses and assorted real estate permissions, areas flagged up by

---

[*]This portion is based in article published in various sources including New York Times, http://finance.yahoo.com/blogs/daily-ticker/busted-wal-mart-caught-massive-bribery-scandal-goes-150100011.html.

investigators as potential violation-prone areas.[48] The Indian unit of Walmart suspended its chief financial officer and entire legal team in the country as part of a high-profile, global investigation into potential violations of America's anti-bribery laws on November 23, 2012. Bharti Walmart commented that it did not tolerate non-compliance of the FCPA anywhere or at any level of the company, and it's "expectation is that each and every one of our associates will adhere not only to the letter of the law, but also to the highest standards of personal integrity".

In the first week of November 2012, an anti-corruption squad consisting of auditors from KPMG and US-based Law Company Greenberg Traurig separately summoned five members of the legal team and told them not to enter the Bharti Walmart office until the investigations are concluded. These five included the CFO, who doubled up as the firm's acting legal counsel, a senior manager, manager, assistant manager and retainer. The five, whose job was to procure licenses required for stores and other real estate approvals, taxation and logistics, were told not to attend office until the FCPA-related investigations were over.

The bribery investigations surrounding Walmart have provided additional ammunition to opponents of the policy allowing global retailers into the country. In the past few months, the anti-FDI in retail lobby has burned effigies of Walmart and filed cases against it.

Indian law requires retailers to secure dozens of permissions involving multiple government departments—the Retailers Association of India lists as many as 51 different approvals required for opening even a single store. Many retailers privately admit that it is very difficult to obtain all those permissions in India without greasing the palms of officials at the 32 different agencies involved.

Bharti Walmart, the 50:50 Joint Venture of Bharti and Walmart in India, decided in November 2012 to go slow on planned rollouts of its cash-and-carry stores, B2B wholesale cash-and-carry stores and back-end supply chain management operations[49] in India until the investigation into violations of the US Foreign Corruption Practice Act (FCPA) reaches a conclusion.

In November 2012, the company was also the subject of an investigation by the Enforcement Directorate, which was probing whether Walmart flouted India's foreign exchange regulations when it invested about $100 million into the holding company of Bharti Enterprises-owned Bharti Retail Ltd.

Retail Chain of Bharti Walmart

Ignoring political opposition to foreign direct investment (FDI) in retail, Bharti Enterprises began talks with Walmart in September 2012 to set up a retail chain in the country.

Bharti Enterprises Vice-Chairman and MD Rajan Bharti Mittal clarified that like in their wholesale joint venture; here too, Walmart will not be allowed to have a majority stake in the partnership. Mr Mittal said, "Talks have started. All I am trying to say is when they had an opportunity to go 100 percent, they went 50-50 with Bharti. Now with the opening of the front end, discussions are on the table and hopefully the relationship that we have enjoyed in the last five years will continue".

In September 2012, Walmart was firming up plans to open its first store in India in about 18 months, boosted by the government's move to allow foreign direct investment (FDI) in retail. "It normally takes 12 to 18 months after you start planning opening a retail store. Our thinking is that it will take 18 months for us to be able to do that," Raj said, after launching a Bharti Walmart Best Price store in Hyderabad. "I think there are enough (eight) states which have agreed. Big states like Maharashtra and Andhra Pradesh have expressed their willingness to allow FDI. I think these states are big enough to start our operations," he added. Further he expressed, "The government is asking companies like us to demonstrate that we can make a meaningful difference to the lives of consumers and farmers. It is a good challenge. We accept that challenge. Once we demonstrate that it has no negative impact on small shop owners, other states will open as well." He also indicated that their first retail store could come up in Andhra Pradesh. "Andhra is a progressive state. It is a very large market and a large agrarian society. We will invest in backend in Andhra, will integrate back with farmers and manufacturers and bring their products both in retail and wholesale stores," he said. Mr. Mittal denied that they were unhappy with the government's condition of bringing USD 100 million fresh FDI in the first three years, half of it into back-end infrastructure.[50]

On the government's conditional retail sales outlets be set up only in cities with a population of more than 10 lakh, the company admitted that this would restrict them to few cities in every state. Huge cost of real estate in large cities, inefficient supply chain and training people were identified as the three major challenges for the retail industry.

Endnotes

1. B. Kammel and R. Weiss, "How Siemens Got Its Mojo Back," *Bloomberg BusinessWeek,* January 27, 2011; V. J. Racanelli, "The Culture Changer," *Barron's,* March 10, 2012; S. G. Leslie and J. Sorensen, "Siemens: Building a Structure to Drive Performance and Responsibility (A)," Stanford Business School Case, October 7, 2010.

2. This has long been a central theme of the strategic management literature. See, for example, C. W. L. Hill and R. E. Hoskisson, "Strategy and Structure in the Multiproduct Firm," *Academy of Management Review,* 1987, pp. 331–41. Also see J. Wolf and W. G. Egelhoff, "A Reexamination and Extension of International Strategy Structure Theory," *Strategic Management Journal* 23 (2002), pp. 181–90.

3. D. Naidler, M. Gerstein, and R. Shaw, *Organization Architecture* (San Francisco: Jossey-Bass, 1992).

4. G. Morgan, *Images of Organization* (Beverly Hills, CA: Sage Publications, 1986).

5. "Unilever: A Networked Organization," *Harvard Business Review,* November–December 1996, p. 138.

6. The material in this section draws on John Child, *Organizations* (London: Harper & Row, 1984).

7. M. Troy, "Wal-Mart Braces for International Growth with Personnel Moves," *DSN Retailing Today,* February 9, 2004, pp. 5–7; "Division Heads Let Numbers Do the Talking," *DSN Retailing Today,* June 21, 2004, pp. 26–28; "The Division That Defines the Future," *DSN Retailing Today,* June 2001, pp. 4–7; and Walmart 2013 annual report.

8. Allan Cane, "Microsoft Reorganizes to Meet Market Challenges," *Financial Times,* March 16, 1994, p. 1. Interviews by Charles Hill.

9. For research evidence that is related to this issue, see J. Birkinshaw, "Entrepreneurship in the Multinational Corporation: The Characteristics of Subsidiary Initiatives," *Strategic Management Journal* 18 (1997), pp. 207–29; J. Birkinshaw, N. Hood, and S. Jonsson, "Building Firm Specific Advantages in Multinational Corporations: The Role of Subsidiary Initiatives," *Strategic Management Journal* 19 (1998), pp. 221–41; and I. Bjorkman, W. Barner-Rasussen, and L. Li, "Managing Knowledge Transfer in MNCs: The Impact of Headquarters Control Mechanisms," *Journal of International Business* 35 (2004), pp. 443–60.

10. For more detail, see S. M. Davis, "Managing and Organizing Multinational Corporations," in C. A. Bartlett and S. Ghoshal, *Transnational Management* (Homewood, IL: Richard D. Irwin, 1992). Also see Wolf and Egelhoff, "A Reexamination and Extension of International Strategy Structure Theory."

11. A. D. Chandler, *Strategy and Structure: Chapters in the History of the Industrial Enterprise* (Cambridge, MA: MIT Press, 1962).

12. Davis, "Managing and Organizing Multinational Corporations."

13. J. M. Stopford and L. T. Wells, *Strategy and Structure of the Multinational Enterprise* (New York: Basic Books, 1972).

14. C. A. Bartlett and S. Ghoshal, *Managing across Borders* (Boston: Harvard Business School Press, 1989).

15. "Dow Draws Its Matrix Again, and Again, and Again," *The Economist,* August 5, 1989, pp. 55–56; "Dow Goes for Global Structure," *Chemical Marketing Reporter,* December 11, 1995, pp. 4–5; and R. M. Hodgetts, "Dow Chemical CEO William Stavropoulos on Structure and Decision Making," *Academy of Management Executive,* November 1999, pp. 29–35.

16. C. A. Bartlett and S. Ghoshal, *Managing across Borders;* and A. McDonnell, P. Gunnigle, and J. Lavelle, "Learning Transfer in Multinational Companies," *Human Resource Management Journal,* 2010, pp. 23–43.

17. See J. R. Galbraith, *Designing Complex Organizations* (Reading, MA: Addison-Wesley, 1977).

18. M. Goold and A. Campbell, "Structured Networks: Towards the Well Designed Matrix," *Long Range Planning,* October 2003, pp. 427–60.

19. Bartlett and Ghoshal, *Managing across Borders;* F. V. Guterl, "Goodbye, Old Matrix," *Business Month,* February 1989, pp. 32–38; Bjorkman, Barner-Rasussen, and Li, "Managing Knowledge Transfer in MNCs;" and M. T. Hansen and B. Lovas, "How Do Multinational Companies Leverage Technological Competencies?" *Strategic Management Journal,* 2004, pp. 801–22.

20. M. S. Granovetter, "The Strength of Weak Ties," *American Journal of Sociology* 78 (1973), pp. 1360–80.

21. A. K. Gupta and V. J. Govindarajan, "Knowledge Flows within Multinational Corporations," *Strategic Management Journal* 21, no. 4 (2000), pp. 473–96; V. J. Govindarajan and A. K. Gupta, *The Quest for Global Dominance.* (San Francisco: Jossey-Bass, 2001); and U. Andersson, M. Forsgren, and U. Holm, "The Strategic Impact of External Networks: Subsidiary Performance and Competence Development in the Multinational Corporation," *Strategic Management Journal* 23 (2002), pp. 979–96.

22. For examples, see W. H. Davidow and M. S. Malone, *The Virtual Corporation* (New York: HarperCollins, 1992).

23. W. G. Ouchi, "Markets, Bureaucracies, and Clans," *Administrative Science Quarterly* 25 (1980), pp. 129–44.

24. For some empirical work that addresses this issue, see T. P. Murtha, S. A. Lenway, and R. P. Bagozzi, "Global Mind Sets and Cognitive Shift in a Complex Multinational Corporation," *Strategic Management Journal* 19 (1998), pp. 97–114.

25. J. Welch and J. Byrne, *Jack: Straight from the Gut* (Warner Books: New York, 2001).

26. C. W. L. Hill, M. E. Hitt, and R. E. Hoskisson, "Cooperative versus Competitive Structures in Related and Unrelated Diversified Firms," *Organization Science* 3 (1992), pp. 501–21.

27. Murtha, Lenway, and Bagozzi, "Global Mind Sets."

28. M. Hammer and J. Champy, *Reengineering the Corporation* (New York: Harper Business, 1993).

29. T. Kostova, "Transnational Transfer of Strategic Organizational Practices: A Contextual Perspective," *Academy of Management Review* 24, no. 2 (1999), pp. 308–24.

30. Andersson, Forsgren, and Holm, "The Strategic Impact of External Networks."

31. E. H. Schein, "What Is Culture?" in P. J. Frost et al., *Reframing Organizational Culture* (Newbury Park, CA: Sage, 1991).

32. E. H. Schein, *Organizational Culture and Leadership,* 2nd ed. (San Francisco: Jossey-Bass, 1992).

33. G. Morgan, *Images of Organization* (Beverly Hills, CA: Sage, 1986).

34. R. Dore, *British Factory, Japanese Factory* (London: Allen & Unwin, 1973).

35. M. Dickson, "Back to the Future," *Financial Times,* May 30, 1994, p. 7.

36. See J. P. Kotter and J. L. Heskett, *Corporate Culture and Performance* (New York: Free Press, 1992); and M. L. Tushman and C. A. O'Reilly, *Winning through Innovation* (Boston: Harvard Business School Press, 1997).

37. Kotter and Heskett, *Corporate Culture and Performance.*

38. The classic song of praise was produced by T. Peters and R. H. Waterman, *In Search of Excellence* (New York: Harper & Row, 1982). Ironically, IBM's decline began shortly after Peters and Waterman's book was published.

39. Kotter and Heskett, *Corporate Culture and Performance.*

40. J. O'Connell, "Lincoln Electric: Venturing Abroad," Harvard Business School Case No. 9-398-095, April 1998; and www.lincolnelectric.com.

41. Bartlett and Ghoshal, *Managing across Borders.*

42. See F. J. Aguilar and M. Y. Yoshino, "The Philips Group: 1987," Howard Business School Case No. 388-050, 1987; "Philips Fights Flab," *The Economist,* April 7, 1990, pp. 73–74; and R. Van de Krol, "Philips Wins Back Old Friends," *Financial Times,* July 14, 1995, p. 14.

43. J. Pfeffer, *Managing with Power: Politics and Influence within Organizations* (Boston: Harvard Business School Press, 1992).

44. C. A. Bartlett, "Philips versus Matsushita: The Competitive Battle Continues," Harvard Business School Case, December 11, 2009; and "Philips Communicates Vision 2010 Strategic Plan," Philips press release, September 10, 2007.

45. http://www.theatlantic.com/business/archive/2012/04/walmarts-massive-bribery-scandal-what-happens-now/256206/

46. http://www.forbes.com/sites/abrambrown/2012/11/15/probe-into-wal-mart-bribery-past-mexico-to-brazil-china-and-india/

47. http://india.blogs.nytimes.com/2012/11/15/wal-marts-foreign-bribery-investigation-expands-to-india/

48. This portion is based in article published in various sources including http://economictimes.indiatimes.com/news/news-by-industry/services/retail/bharti-walmart-suspends-cfo-legal-team-due-to-fcpa-bribery-probe/articleshow/17329816.cms?curpg=2

49. http://www.bharti-walmart.in/AboutUs.aspx

50. This portion is based in article published in various sources including http://businesstoday.intoday.in/story/fdi-in-retail-walmart-to-open-first-india-store-in-18-months/1/188481.html

Chapter 15
Entry Strategy and Strategic Alliances

LEARNING OBJECTIVES

After reading this chapter you will be able to:

LO15-1 Explain the three basic decisions that firms contemplating foreign expansion must make: which markets to enter, when to enter those markets, and on what scale.

LO15-2 Compare and contrast the different modes that firms use to enter foreign markets.

LO15-3 Identify the factors that influence a firm's choice of entry mode.

LO15-4 Recognize the pros and cons of acquisitions versus greenfield ventures as an entry strategy.

LO15-5 Evaluate the pros and cons of entering into strategic alliances.

◇ JCB IN INDIA ◇

Opening Case

JCB, the venerable British manufacturer of construction equipment, has long been a relatively small player in a global market that is dominated by the likes of Caterpillar and Komatsu, but there is one exception to this: India. While the company is present in 150 countries, of the 69,100 machines it sold globally in 2012, around a third were in India. For JCB, India is truly the jewel in the crown.

The story of JCB in India dates back to 1979 when the company entered into a joint venture with Escorts, an Indian engineering conglomerate, to manufacture backhoe loaders for sale in India. Escorts held a majority 60 percent stake in the venture, and JCB 40 percent. The joint venture was a first for

JCB, which historically had exported as much as two-thirds of its production from Britain to a wide range of nations. However, high tariff barriers made direct exports to India difficult.

JCB would probably have preferred to go it alone in India, but government regulations at the time required foreign investors to create joint ventures with local companies. JCB believed the Indian construction market was ripe for growth and could become very large. The company's managers believed that it was better to get a foothold in the nation, thereby gaining an advantage over global competitors, rather than wait until the growth potential was realized.

By the end of the 1990s the joint venture was selling some 2,000 backhoes in India, and had an 80 percent share of the Indian market. After years of deregulation, the Indian economy was booming. However, JCB felt that the joint venture limited its ability to expand. For one thing, much of JCB's global success was based upon the utilization of leading-edge manufacturing technologies and relentless product innovation, but the company was very hesitant about transferring this know-how to a venture where it did not have a majority stake and therefore lacked control. The last thing JCB wanted was for these valuable technologies to leak out of the joint venture into Escorts, which was one of the largest manufacturers of tractors in India and might conceivably become a direct competitor in the future. Moreover, JCB was unwilling to make the investment in India required to take the joint venture to the next level unless it could capture more of the long-run returns.

In 1999 JCB took advantages of changes in government regulations to renegotiate the terms of the venture with Escorts, purchasing 20 percent of its partner's equity to give JCB majority control. In 2003, JCB took this to its logical end when it responded to further relaxation of government regulations on foreign investment to purchase all of Escorts' remaining equity, transforming the joint venture into a wholly owned subsidiary.

Having gained full control, in early 2005 JCB increased its investment in India, announcing it would build a second factory in Pune that it would use to serve the Indian market. In 2007, in what represented a bold bet on future demand in the Indian market in the face of a global economic slowdown, JCB embarked on a major overhaul and expansion of its original India factory in Ballabgarh. To sell the additional Indian output, JCB rapidly expanded its dealer network, doubling the number of outlets in six years to reach 400 by 2011. The company also localized production for more than 80 percent of the parts used in its best-selling backhoe loader. This was done both to keep costs low, and to make sure dealers had immediate access to spare parts. The strategy worked; between 2001 and 2012 JCB's Indian revenues increased tenfold and the company is now the leading manufacturer of backhoes in the country.[1]

INTRODUCTION

This chapter is concerned with three closely related topics: (1) the decision of which foreign markets to enter, when to enter them, and on what scale; (2) the choice of entry mode; and (3) the role of strategic alliances. Any firm contemplating foreign expansion must first struggle with the issue of which foreign markets to enter and the timing and scale of entry. The choice of which markets to enter should be driven by an assessment of relative long-run growth and profit potential. For example, as discussed in the opening case, JCB was an early entrant into India's market for heavy construction equipment. This commitment was a strategic bet on the long-term growth potential of the market—a bet that turned out to be correct. Leveraging its early-mover advantage, by 2011 JCB was the largest heavy construction equipment manufacturer in India.

The choice of mode for entering a foreign market is another major issue with which international businesses must wrestle. The various modes for serving foreign markets are exporting, licensing or franchising to host-country firms, establishing joint ventures with a host-country firm, setting up a new wholly owned subsidiary in a host country to serve its market, and acquiring an established enterprise in the host nation to serve that market. Each of these options has advantages and disadvantages. The magnitude of the advantages and disadvantages associated with each entry mode is determined by a number of factors, including transport costs, trade barriers, political risks, economic risks, business risks, costs, and firm strategy. The optimal entry mode varies by situation, depending on these factors. Thus, whereas some firms may best serve a given market by exporting, other firms may better serve the market by setting up a new wholly owned subsidiary or by acquiring an established enterprise. In the case of JCB, its initial choice of entry mode, a joint venture with an Indian company, was dictated by circumstances at the time (Indian government regulations made a joint venture the only practical alternative).

The final topic of this chapter is strategic alliances. **Strategic alliances** are cooperative agreements between potential or actual competitors. The term is often used to embrace a variety of agreements between actual or potential competitors including cross-shareholding deals, licensing arrangements, formal joint ventures, and informal cooperative arrangements. The motives for entering strategic alliances are varied, but they often include market access, hence the overlap with the topic of entry mode.

BASIC ENTRY DECISIONS

A firm contemplating foreign expansion must make three basic decisions: which markets to enter, when to enter those markets, and on what scale.[2]

Which Foreign Markets?

The 196 nation-states in the world do not all hold the same profit potential for a firm contemplating foreign expansion. Ultimately, the choice must be based on an assessment of a nation's long-run profit potential. This potential is a function of several factors, many of which we have studied in earlier chapters. Chapters 2 and 3 looked in detail at the economic and political factors that influence the potential attractiveness of a foreign market. The attractiveness of a country as a potential market for an international business depends on balancing the benefits, costs, and risks associated with doing business in that country.

Chapters 2 and 3 also noted that the long-run economic benefits of doing business in a country are a function of factors such as the size of the market (in terms of demographics), the present wealth (purchasing power) of consumers in that market, and the likely future wealth of consumers, which depends on economic growth rates. While some markets are very large when measured by number of consumers (e.g., China, India, and Indonesia), one must also look at living standards and economic growth. On this basis, China and India, while relatively poor, are growing so rapidly that they are attractive targets for inward investment (hence JCB's decision to make major additional investments in India in the mid-2000s). Alternatively, weak growth in Indonesia implies that this populous nation is a far less attractive target for inward investment. As we saw in Chapters 2 and 3, likely future economic growth rates appear to be a function of a free market system and a country's capacity for growth (which may be greater in less developed nations). Also, the costs and risks associated with doing business in a foreign country are typically lower in economically advanced and politically stable democratic nations, and they are greater in less developed and politically unstable nations.

The discussion in Chapters 2 and 3 suggests that, other things being equal, the benefit–cost–risk trade-off is likely to be most favorable in politically stable developed and developing nations that have free market systems, and where there is not a dramatic upsurge in either inflation rates or private-sector debt. The trade-off is likely to be least favorable in politically unstable developing nations that operate with a mixed or command economy or in developing nations where speculative financial bubbles have led to excess borrowing.

Another important factor is the value an international business can create in a foreign market. This depends on the suitability of its product offering to that market and the nature of indigenous competition.[3] If the international business can offer a product that has not been widely available in that market and that satisfies an unmet need, the value of that product to consumers is likely to be much greater than if the international business simply offers the same type of product that indigenous competitors and other foreign entrants are already offering. Greater value translates into an ability to charge higher prices and/or to build sales volume more rapidly. By considering such factors, a firm can rank countries in terms of their attractiveness and long-run profit potential. Preference is then given to entering markets that rank highly. For example, Tesco, the large British grocery chain, has been aggressively expanding its foreign operations, primarily by focusing on emerging markets that lack strong indigenous competitors (see the accompanying Management Focus).

Timing of Entry

Once attractive markets have been identified, it is important to consider the **timing of entry**. Entry is early when an international business enters a foreign market before other foreign firms and late when it enters after other international businesses have already established themselves. The advantages frequently associated with entering a market early are commonly known as **first-mover advantages**.[4] One first-mover advantage is the ability to preempt rivals and capture demand by establishing a strong brand name. This desire has driven the rapid expansion by Tesco into developing nations (see the Management Focus). A second advantage is the ability to build sales volume in that country and ride down the experience curve ahead of rivals, giving the early entrant a cost advantage over later entrants. One could argue that this factor motivated JCB to enter the Indian market in 1979 when it was still tiny (the Indian market is now among the world's largest; see the opening case). This cost advantage may enable the early entrant to cut prices below that of later entrants, thereby driving them out of the market. A third advantage is the ability of early entrants to create switching costs that tie customers into their products or services. Such switching costs make it difficult for later entrants to win business.

There can also be disadvantages associated with entering a foreign market before other international businesses. These are often referred to as **first-mover disadvantages**.[6] These disadvantages may give rise to **pioneering costs**, costs that an early entrant has to bear that a later entrant can avoid. Pioneering costs arise when the business system in a foreign country is so different from that in a firm's home market that the enterprise has to devote considerable effort, time, and expense to learning the rules of the game. Pioneering costs include the costs of business failure if the firm, due to its ignorance of the foreign environment, makes major mistakes. A certain liability is associated with being a foreigner, and this liability is greater for foreign firms that enter a national market early.[7] Research seems to confirm that the probability of survival increases if an international business enters a national market after several other foreign firms have already done so.[8] The late entrant may benefit by observing and learning from the mistakes made by early entrants.

Pioneering costs also include the costs of promoting and establishing a product offering, including the costs of educating customers. These can be significant when the product being promoted is unfamiliar to local consumers. In contrast, later entrants may be able to ride on an early entrant's investments in learning and customer education by watching how the early entrant proceeded in the

Tesco's International Growth Strategy

Tesco is the largest grocery retailer in the United Kingdom, with a 25 percent share of the local market. In its home market, the company's strengths are reputed to come from strong competencies in marketing and store site selection, logistics and inventory management, and its own label product offerings. By the early 1990s, these competencies had already given the company a leading position in the United Kingdom. The company was generating strong free cash flows, and senior managers had to decide how to use that cash. One strategy they settled on was overseas expansion. As they looked at international markets, they soon concluded the best opportunities were not in established markets, such as those in North America and western Europe, where strong local competitors already existed, but in the emerging markets of eastern Europe and Asia where there were few capable competitors but strong underlying growth trends.

Tesco's first international foray was into Hungary in 1995, when it acquired an initial 51 percent stake in Global, a 43-store, state-owned grocery chain. By 2012, Tesco was the market leader in Hungary, with some 118 hypermarkets and 98 smaller stores. In 1996, Tesco acquired 31 stores in Poland from Stavia; a year later it added 13 stores purchased from Kmart in the Czech Republic and Slovakia; and the following year it entered the Republic of Ireland.

Tesco's Asian expansion began in 1998 in Thailand when it purchased 75 percent of Lotus, a local food retailer with 13 stores. Building on that base, Tesco had more than 1,400 stores in Thailand by 2012. In 1999, the company entered South Korea when it partnered with Samsung to develop a chain of hypermarkets. This was followed by entry into Taiwan in 2000, Malaysia in 2002, and China in 2004. The move into China came after three years of careful research and discussions with potential partners. Like many other Western companies, Tesco was attracted to the Chinese market by its large size and rapid growth. In the end, Tesco settled on a fifty-fifty joint venture with Hymall, a hypermarket chain that is controlled by Ting Hsin, a Taiwanese group, which had been operating in China for six years. By 2012 Tesco had 131 stores in China. Ting Hsin is a well-capitalized enterprise in its own right, and it has matched Tesco's investments, reducing the risks Tesco faced in China.

As a result of these moves, by 2012 Tesco generated sales of £22.4 billion outside the United Kingdom (its UK annual revenues were £43 billion excluding VAT). The addition of international stores has helped make Tesco the third-largest company in the global grocery market behind Walmart and Carrefour of France. Of the three, however, Tesco may be the most successful internationally. By 2012, all its foreign ventures except for a small U.S. operation that it is planning to divest were making money.

In explaining the company's success, Tesco's managers have detailed a number of important factors. First, the company devotes considerable attention to transferring its core capabilities in retailing to its new ventures. At the same time, it does not send in an army of expatriate managers to run local operations, preferring to hire local managers and support them with a few operational experts from the United Kingdom. Second, the company believes that its partnering strategy in Asia has been a great asset. Tesco has teamed up with good companies that have a deep understanding of the markets in which they are participating but that lack Tesco's financial strength and retailing capabilities. Consequently, both Tesco and its partners have brought useful assets to the venture, increasing the probability of success. As the venture becomes established, Tesco has typically increased its ownership stake in its partner. By 2010, Tesco owned 99 percent of Homeplus, its South Korean hypermarket chain. When the venture was established, Tesco owned 51 percent. Third, the company has focused on markets with good growth potential but that lack strong indigenous competitors, which provides Tesco with ripe ground for expansion.[5]

market, by avoiding costly mistakes made by the early entrant, and by exploiting the market potential created by the early entrant's investments in customer education. For example, KFC introduced the Chinese to American-style fast food, but a later entrant, McDonald's, has capitalized on the market in China.

An early entrant may be put at a severe disadvantage, relative to a later entrant, if regulations change in a way that diminishes the value of an early entrant's investments. This is a serious risk in many developing nations where the rules that govern business practices are still evolving. Early entrants can find themselves at a disadvantage if a subsequent change in regulations invalidates prior assumptions about the best business model for operating in that country.

Scale of Entry and Strategic Commitments

Another issue that an international business needs to consider when contemplating market entry is the scale of entry. Entering a market on a large scale involves the commitment of significant resources. Entering a market on a large scale implies rapid entry. Consider the entry of the Dutch insurance company ING into the U.S. insurance market in 1999. ING had to spend several billion dollars to acquire its U.S. operations. Not all firms have the resources necessary to enter on a large scale, and even some large firms prefer to enter foreign markets on a small scale and then build slowly as they become more familiar with the market.

The consequences of entering on a significant scale—entering rapidly—are associated with the value of the resulting strategic commitments.[9] A strategic commitment has a long-term impact and is difficult to reverse. Deciding to enter a foreign market on a significant scale is a major strategic commitment. Strategic commitments, such as rapid large-scale market entry, can have an important influence on the nature of competition in a market. For example, by entering the U.S. financial services market on a significant scale, ING signaled its commitment to the market. This will have several effects. On the positive side, it will make it easier for the company to attract customers and distributors (such as insurance agents). The scale of entry gives both customers and distributors reasons for believing that ING will remain in the market for the long run. The scale of entry may also give other foreign institutions considering entry into the United States pause; now they will have to compete not only against indigenous institutions in the United States but also against an aggressive and successful European institution. On the negative side, by committing itself heavily to one country, the United States, ING may have fewer resources available to support expansion in other desirable markets, such as Japan. The commitment to the United States limits the company's strategic flexibility.

As suggested by the ING example, significant strategic commitments are neither unambiguously good nor bad. Rather, they tend to change the competitive playing field and unleash a number of changes, some of which may be desirable and some of which will not be. It is important for a firm to think through the implications of large-scale entry into a market and act accordingly. Of particular relevance is trying to identify how actual and potential competitors might react to large-scale entry into a market. Also, the large-scale entrant is more likely than the small-scale entrant to be able to capture first-mover advantages associated with demand preemption, scale economies, and switching costs.

The value of the commitments that flow from rapid large-scale entry into a foreign market must be balanced against the resulting risks and lack of flexibility associated with significant commitments. But strategic inflexibility can also have value. A famous example from military history illustrates the value of inflexibility. When Hernán Cortés landed in Mexico, he ordered his men to burn all but one of his ships. Cortés reasoned that by eliminating their only method of retreat, his men had no choice but to fight hard to win against the Aztecs—and ultimately they did.[10]

Balanced against the value and risks of the commitments associated with large-scale entry are the benefits of a small-scale entry. Small-scale entry allows a firm to learn about a foreign market while limiting the firm's exposure to that market. Small-scale entry is a way to gather information about a foreign market before deciding whether to enter on a significant scale and how best to enter. By giving the firm time to collect information, small-scale entry reduces the risks associated with a subsequent large-scale entry. But the lack of commitment associated with small-scale entry may make it more difficult for the small-scale entrant to build market share and to capture first-mover or early-mover advantages. The risk-averse firm that enters a foreign market on a small scale may limit its potential losses, but it may also miss the chance to capture first-mover advantages.

Summary

There are no "right" decisions here, just decisions that are associated with different levels of risk and reward. Entering a large developing nation such as China or India before most other international businesses in the firm's industry, and entering on a large scale, will be associated with high levels of risk. In such cases, the liability of being foreign is increased by the absence of prior foreign entrants whose experience can be a useful guide. At the same time, the potential long-term rewards associated with such a strategy are great. The early large-scale entrant into a major developing nation may be able to capture significant first-mover advantages that will bolster its long-run position in that market.[11] This was what JCB hoped to do when it entered India in 1994, and as of 2012 it seemed as if JCB had captured a significant first-mover, or at least early-mover, advantage (see opening case). In contrast, entering developed nations such as Australia or Canada after other international businesses in the firm's industry, and entering on a small scale to first learn more about those markets, will be associated with much lower levels of risk. However, the potential long-term rewards are also likely to be lower because the firm is essentially forgoing the opportunity to capture first-mover advantages and because the lack of commitment signaled by small-scale entry may limit its future growth potential.

This section has been written largely from the perspective of a business based in a developed country considering entry into foreign markets. Christopher Bartlett and Sumantra Ghoshal have pointed out the ability that businesses based in developing nations have to enter foreign markets and become global players.[12] Although such firms tend to be late entrants into foreign markets, and although their resources may be limited, Bartlett and Ghoshal argue that such late movers can still succeed against well-established global competitors by pursuing appropriate strategies. In particular, Bartlett and Ghoshal argue that companies based in developing nations should use the entry of foreign multinationals as an opportunity to learn from these competitors by benchmarking their operations and performance against them. Furthermore, they suggest the local company may be able to find ways to differentiate itself from a foreign multinational, for example, by focusing on market niches that the multinational ignores or is unable to serve effectively if it has a standardized global product offering. Having improved its performance through learning and

MANAGEMENT FOCUS

The Jollibee Phenomenon—A Philippine Multinational

Jollibee is one of the Philippines' phenomenal business success stories. Jollibee, which stands for "Jolly Bee," began operations in 1975 as a two-branch ice cream parlor. It later expanded its menu to include hot sandwiches and other meals. Encouraged by early success, Jollibee Foods Corporation was incorporated in 1978, with a network that had grown to seven outlets. In 1981, when Jollibee had 11 stores, McDonald's began to open stores in Manila. Many observers thought Jollibee would have difficulty competing against McDonald's. However, Jollibee saw this as an opportunity to learn from a very successful global competitor. Jollibee benchmarked its performance against that of McDonald's and started to adopt operational systems similar to those used at McDonald's to control its quality, cost, and service at the store level. This helped Jollibee improve its performance.

As it came to better understand McDonald's business model, Jollibee began to look for a weakness in McDonald's global strategy. Jollibee executives concluded that McDonald's fare was too standardized for many locals and that the local firm could gain share by tailoring its menu to local tastes. Jollibee's hamburgers were set apart by a secret mix of spices blended into the ground beef to make the burgers sweeter than those produced by McDonald's, appealing more to Philippine tastes. It also offered local fare, including various rice dishes, pineapple burgers, and banana *langka* and peach mango pies for desserts. By pursuing this strategy, Jollibee maintained a leadership position over the global giant. By 2012, Jollibee had over 740 stores in the Philippines, a market share of more than 60 percent, and revenues in excess of $600 million. McDonald's, in contrast, had about 250 stores.

In the mid-1980s, Jollibee had gained enough confidence to expand internationally. Its initial ventures were into neighboring Asian countries such as Indonesia, where it pursued the strategy of localizing the menu to better match local tastes, thereby differentiating itself from McDonald's. In 1987, Jollibee entered the Middle East, where a large contingent of expatriate Filipino workers provided a ready-made market for the company. The strategy of focusing on expatriates worked so well that in the late 1990s Jollibee decided to enter another foreign market where there was a large Filipino population—the United States. Between 1999 and 2012, Jollibee opened 25 stores in the United States, 20 of which are in California. Even though many believe the U.S. fast-food market is saturated, the stores have performed well. While the initial clientele was strongly biased toward the expatriate Filipino community, where Jollibee's brand awareness is high, non-Filipinos increasingly are coming to the restaurant. In the San Francisco store, which has been open the longest, more than half the customers are now non-Filipino. Today, Jollibee has 75 international stores that operate under the Jollibee name and a potentially bright future as a niche player in a market that has historically been dominated by U.S. multinationals.[13]

differentiated its product offering, the firm from a developing nation may then be able to pursue its own international expansion strategy. Even though the firm may be a late entrant into many countries, by benchmarking and then differentiating itself from early movers in global markets, the firm from the developing nation may still be able to build a strong international business presence. A good example of how this can work is given in the accompanying Management Focus, which looks at how Jollibee, a

Philippines-based fast-food chain, has started to build a global presence in a market dominated by U.S. multinationals such as McDonald's and KFC.

ENTRY MODES

Once a firm decides to enter a foreign market, the question arises as to the best mode of entry. Firms can use six different modes to enter foreign markets: exporting, turnkey projects, licensing, franchising, establishing joint ventures with a host-country firm, or setting up a new wholly owned subsidiary in the host country. Each entry mode has advantages and disadvantages. Managers need to consider these carefully when deciding which to use.[14]

Exporting

Many manufacturing firms begin their global expansion as exporters and only later switch to another mode for serving a foreign market. We take a close look at the mechanics of exporting in Chapter 16. Here we focus on the advantages and disadvantages of exporting as an entry mode.

Advantages

Exporting has two distinct advantages. First, it avoids the often substantial costs of establishing manufacturing operations in the host country. Second, exporting may help a firm achieve experience curve and location economies (see Chapter 13). By manufacturing the product in a centralized location and exporting it to other national markets, the firm may realize substantial scale economies from its global sales volume. This is how many Japanese automakers made inroads into the U.S. market.

Disadvantages

Exporting has a number of drawbacks. First, exporting from the firm's home base may not be appropriate if lower-cost locations for manufacturing the product can be found abroad (i.e., if the firm can realize location economies by moving production elsewhere). Thus, particularly for firms pursuing global or transnational strategies, it may be preferable to manufacture where the mix of factor conditions is most favorable from a value creation perspective and to export to the rest of the world from that location. This is not so much an argument against exporting as an argument against exporting from the firm's home country. Many U.S. electronics firms have moved some of their manufacturing to the Far East because of the availability of low-cost, highly skilled labor there. They then export from that location to the rest of the world, including the United States.

A second drawback to exporting is that high transport costs can make exporting uneconomical, particularly for bulk products. One way of getting around this is to manufacture bulk products regionally. This strategy enables the firm to realize some economies from large-scale production and at the same time to limit its transport costs. For example, many multinational chemical firms manufacture their products regionally, serving several countries from one facility.

Another drawback is that tariff barriers can make exporting uneconomical. Similarly, the threat of tariff barriers by the host-country government can make it very risky. A fourth drawback to exporting arises when a firm delegates its marketing, sales, and service in each country where it does business to another company. This is a common approach for manufacturing firms that are just beginning to expand internationally. The other company may be a local agent, or it may be another multinational with extensive international distribution operations. Local agents often carry the products of competing firms and so have divided loyalties. In such cases, the local agent may not do as good a job as the firm would if it managed its marketing itself. Similar problems can occur when another multinational takes on distribution.

The way around such problems is to set up wholly owned subsidiaries in foreign nations to handle local marketing, sales, and service. By doing this, the firm can exercise tight control over marketing and sales in the country while reaping the cost advantages of manufacturing the product in a single location or a few choice locations.

Turnkey Projects

Firms that specialize in the design, construction, and start-up of turnkey plants are common in some industries. In a **turnkey project**, the contractor agrees to handle every detail of the project for a foreign client, including the training of operating personnel. At completion of the contract, the foreign client is handed the "key" to a plant that is ready for full operation—hence, the term *turnkey.* This is a means of exporting process technology to other countries. Turnkey projects are most common in the chemical, pharmaceutical, petroleum-refining, and metal-refining industries, all of which use complex, expensive production technologies.

Advantages

The know-how required to assemble and run a technologically complex process, such as refining petroleum or steel, is a valuable asset. Turnkey projects are a way of earning great economic returns from that asset. The strategy is particularly useful where foreign direct investment (FDI) is limited by host-government regulations. For example, the governments of many oil-rich countries have set out to build their own petroleum-refining industries, so they restrict FDI in their oil-refining sectors. But because many of these countries lack petroleum-refining technology, they gain it by entering into turnkey projects with foreign firms that have the technology. Such deals are often attractive to the selling firm because without them, they would have no way to earn a return on their valuable know-how in that country. A turnkey strategy can also be less risky than conventional FDI. In a country with unstable political and economic environments, a longer-term investment might expose the firm to unacceptable political and/or economic risks (e.g., the risk of nationalization or of economic collapse).

Disadvantages

Three main drawbacks are associated with a turnkey strategy. First, the firm that enters into a turnkey deal will have no long-term interest in the foreign country. This can be a disadvantage if that country subsequently proves to be a major market for the output of the process that has been exported. One way around this is to take a minority equity interest in the operation. Second, the firm that enters into a turnkey project with a foreign enterprise may inadvertently create a competitor. For example, many of the Western firms that sold oil-refining technology to firms in Saudi Arabia, Kuwait, and other Gulf states now find themselves competing with these firms in the world oil market. Third, if the firm's process technology is a source of competitive advantage, then selling this technology through a turnkey project is also selling competitive advantage to potential and/or actual competitors.

Licensing

A **licensing agreement** is an arrangement whereby a licensor grants the rights to intangible property to another entity (the licensee) for a specified period, and in return, the licensor receives a royalty fee from the licensee.[15] Intangible property includes patents, inventions, formulas, processes, designs, copyrights, and trademarks. For example, to enter the Japanese market, Xerox, inventor of the photocopier, established a joint venture with Fuji Photo that is known as Fuji Xerox. Xerox then licensed its xerographic know-how to Fuji Xerox. In return, Fuji Xerox paid Xerox a royalty fee equal to 5 percent of the net sales revenue that Fuji Xerox earned from the sales of photocopiers based on Xerox's patented know-how. In the Fuji Xerox case, the license was originally granted for 10 years, and it has been renegotiated and extended several times since. The licensing agreement between Xerox and Fuji Xerox also limited Fuji Xerox's direct sales to the Asian Pacific region (although Fuji Xerox does supply Xerox with photocopiers that are sold in North America under the Xerox label).[16]

Advantages

In the typical international licensing deal, the licensee puts up most of the capital necessary to get the overseas operation going. Thus, a primary advantage of licensing is that the firm does not have to bear the development costs and risks associated with opening a foreign market. Licensing is very attractive for firms lacking the capital to develop operations overseas. In addition, licensing can be attractive when a firm is unwilling to commit substantial financial resources to an unfamiliar or politically volatile foreign market. Licensing is also often used when a firm wishes to participate in a foreign market but is prohibited from doing so by barriers to investment. This was one of the original reasons for the formation of the Fuji Xerox joint venture. Xerox wanted to participate in the Japanese market but was prohibited from setting up a wholly owned subsidiary by the Japanese government. So Xerox set up the joint venture with Fuji and then licensed its know-how to the joint venture.

Finally, licensing is frequently used when a firm possesses some intangible property that might have business applications, but it does not want to develop those applications itself. For example, Bell Laboratories at AT&T originally invented the transistor circuit in the 1950s, but AT&T decided it did not want to produce transistors, so it licensed the technology to a number of other companies, such as Texas Instruments. Similarly, Coca-Cola has licensed its famous trademark to clothing manufacturers, which have incorporated the design into clothing.

Disadvantages

Licensing has three serious drawbacks. First, it does not give a firm the tight control over manufacturing, marketing, and strategy that is required for realizing experience curve and location economies. Licensing typically involves each licensee setting up its own production operations. This severely limits the firm's ability to realize experience curve and location economies by producing its product in a centralized location. When these economies are important, licensing may not be the best way to expand overseas.

Second, competing in a global market may require a firm to coordinate strategic moves across countries by using profits earned in one country to support competitive attacks in another. By its very nature, licensing limits a firm's ability to do this. A licensee is unlikely to allow a multinational firm to use its profits (beyond those due in the form of royalty payments) to support a different licensee operating in another country.

A third problem with licensing is one that we encountered in Chapter 8 when we reviewed the economic theory of FDI. This is the risk associated with licensing technological know-how to foreign companies. Technological know-how constitutes the basis of many multinational firms' competitive advantage. Most firms wish to maintain control over how their know-how is used, and a firm can quickly lose control over its technology by licensing it. Many firms have made the mistake of thinking they could maintain control over their know-how within the framework of a licensing agreement. RCA Corporation, for example, once licensed its color TV technology to Japanese firms including Matsushita and Sony. The Japanese firms quickly assimilated the technology, improved on it, and used it to enter the U.S. market, taking substantial market share away from RCA.

There are ways of reducing this risk. One way is by entering into a cross-licensing agreement with a foreign firm. Under a cross-licensing agreement, a firm might license some valuable intangible property to a foreign partner, but in addition to a royalty payment, the firm might also request that the foreign partner license some of its valuable know-how to the firm. Such agreements are believed to reduce the risks associated with licensing technological know-how, since the licensee realizes that if it violates the licensing contract (by using the knowledge obtained to compete directly with the licensor), the licensor can do the same to it. Cross-licensing agreements enable firms to hold each other hostage, which reduces the probability that they will behave opportunistically toward each other.[17] Such cross-licensing agreements are increasingly common in high-technology industries.

Another way of reducing the risk associated with licensing is to follow the Fuji Xerox model and link an agreement to license know-how with the formation of a joint venture in which the licensor and licensee take important equity stakes. Such an approach aligns the interests of licensor and licensee, because both have a stake in ensuring that the venture is successful. Thus, the risk that Fuji Photo might appropriate Xerox's technological know-how, and then compete directly against Xerox in the global photocopier market, was reduced by the establishment of a joint venture in which both Xerox and Fuji Photo had an important stake.

Franchising

Franchising is similar to licensing, although franchising tends to involve longer-term commitments than licensing. **Franchising** is basically a specialized form of licensing in which the franchiser not only sells intangible property (normally a trademark) to the franchisee but also insists that the franchisee agree to abide by strict rules as to how it does business. The franchiser will also often assist the franchisee to run the business on an ongoing basis. As with licensing, the franchiser typically receives a royalty payment, which amounts to some percentage of the franchisee's revenues. Whereas licensing is pursued primarily by manufacturing firms, franchising is employed primarily by service firms.[18] McDonald's is a good example of a firm that has grown by using a franchising strategy. McDonald's strict rules as to how franchisees should operate a restaurant extend to control over the menu, cooking methods, staffing policies, and design and location. McDonald's also organizes the supply chain for its franchisees and provides management training and financial assistance.[19]

Advantages

The advantages of franchising as an entry mode are very similar to those of licensing. The firm is relieved of many of the costs and risks of opening a foreign market on its own. Instead, the franchisee typically assumes those costs and risks. This creates a good incentive for the franchisee to build a profitable operation as quickly as possible. Thus, using a franchising strategy, a service firm can build a global presence quickly and at a relatively low cost and risk, as McDonald's has.

Disadvantages

The disadvantages are less pronounced than in the case of licensing. Since franchising is often used by service companies, there is no reason to consider the need for coordination of manufacturing to achieve experience curve and location economies. But franchising may inhibit the firm's ability to take profits out of one country to support competitive attacks in another. A more significant disadvantage of franchising is quality control. The foundation of franchising arrangements is that the firm's brand name conveys a message to consumers about the quality of the firm's product. Thus, a business traveler checking in at a Four Seasons hotel in Hong Kong can reasonably expect the same quality of room, food, and service that she would receive in New York. The Four Seasons name is supposed to guarantee consistent product quality. This presents a problem in that foreign franchisees may not be as concerned about quality as they are supposed to be, and the result of poor quality can extend beyond lost sales in a particular foreign market to a decline in the firm's worldwide reputation. For example, if the business traveler has a bad experience at the Four Seasons in Hong Kong, she may never go to another Four Seasons hotel and may urge her colleagues to do likewise. The geographic distance of the firm from its foreign franchisees can make poor quality difficult to detect. In addition, the sheer numbers of franchisees—in the case of McDonald's, tens of thousands—can make quality control difficult. Due to these factors, quality problems may persist.

One way around this disadvantage is to set up a subsidiary in each country in which the firm expands. The subsidiary might be wholly owned by the company or a joint venture with a foreign company. The subsidiary assumes the rights and obligations to establish franchises throughout the particular country or region. McDonald's, for example, establishes a master franchisee in many countries. Typically, this master franchisee is a joint venture between McDonald's and a local firm. The proximity and the smaller number of franchises to oversee reduce the quality control challenge. In addition, because the subsidiary (or master franchisee) is at least partly owned by the firm, the firm can place its own managers in the subsidiary to help ensure that it is doing a good job of monitoring the franchises. This organizational arrangement has proven very satisfactory for McDonald's, KFC, and others.

Joint Ventures

A **joint venture** entails establishing a firm that is jointly owned by two or more otherwise independent firms. Fuji Xerox, for example, was set up as a joint venture between Xerox and Fuji Photo. Establishing a joint venture with a foreign firm has long been a popular mode for entering a new market. The most typical joint venture is a fifty-fifty venture, in which there are two parties, each of which holding a 50 percent ownership stake and contributing a team of managers to share operating control. This was the case with the Fuji–Xerox joint venture until 2001; it is now a 25:75 venture with Xerox holding 25 percent. The GM SAIC venture in China was a fifty-fifty venture until 2010, which it became a 51:49 venture, with SAIC holding the 51 percent stake. Some firms, however, have sought joint ventures in which they have a majority share and thus tighter control.[20]

Advantages

Joint ventures have a number of advantages. First, a firm benefits from a local partner's knowledge of the host country's competitive conditions, culture, language, political systems, and business. Thus, for many U.S. firms, joint ventures have involved the U.S. company providing technological know-how and products and the local partner providing the marketing expertise and the local knowledge necessary for competing in that country. Second, when the development costs and/or risks of opening a foreign market are high, a firm might gain by sharing these costs and or risks with a local partner. Third, in many countries, political considerations make joint ventures the only feasible entry mode. Research suggests joint ventures with local partners face a low risk of being subject to nationalization or other forms of adverse government interference.[21] This appears to be because local equity partners, who may have some influence on host-government policy, have a vested interest in speaking out against nationalization or government interference.

Disadvantages

Despite these advantages, there are major disadvantages with joint ventures. First, as with licensing, a firm that enters into a joint venture risks giving control of its technology to its partner. Thus, a proposed joint venture in 2002 between Boeing and Mitsubishi Heavy Industries to build a new wide-body jet (the 787) raised fears that Boeing might unwittingly give away its commercial airline technology to the Japanese. However, joint-venture agreements can be constructed to minimize this risk. One option is to hold majority ownership in the venture. This allows the dominant partner to exercise greater control over its technology. But it can be difficult to find a foreign partner who is willing to settle for minority ownership. Another option is to "wall off" from a partner technology that is central to the core competence of the firm, while sharing other technology.

A second disadvantage is that a joint venture does not give a firm the tight control over subsidiaries that it might need to realize experience curve or location economies. Nor does it give a firm the tight control over a foreign subsidiary that it might need for engaging in coordinated global attacks against its rivals. Consider the entry of Texas Instruments (TI) into the Japanese semiconductor market. When TI established semiconductor facilities in Japan, it did so for the dual purpose of checking Japanese manufacturers' market share and limiting their cash available for invading TI's global market. In other words, TI was engaging in global strategic coordination. To implement this strategy, TI's subsidiary in Japan had to be prepared to take instructions from corporate headquarters regarding competitive strategy. The strategy also required the Japanese subsidiary to run at a loss if necessary. Few if any potential joint-venture partners would have been willing to accept such conditions, since it would have necessitated a willingness to accept a negative return on investment. Indeed, many joint ventures establish a degree of autonomy that would make such direct control over strategic decisions all but impossible to establish.[22] Thus, to implement this strategy, TI set up a wholly owned subsidiary in Japan.

A third disadvantage with joint ventures is that the shared ownership arrangement can lead to conflicts and battles for control between the investing firms if their goals and objectives change or if they take different views as to what the strategy should be. This was apparently not a problem with the Fuji Xerox joint venture. According to Yotaro Kobayashi, the former chairman of Fuji Xerox, a primary reason is that both Xerox and Fuji Photo adopted an arm's-length relationship with Fuji Xerox, giving the venture's management considerable freedom to determine its own strategy.[23] However, much research indicates that conflicts of interest over strategy and goals often arise in joint ventures. These conflicts tend to be greater when the venture is between firms of different nationalities, and they often end in the dissolution of the venture.[24] Such conflicts tend to be triggered by shifts in the relative bargaining power of venture partners. For example, in the case of ventures between a foreign firm and a local firm, as a foreign partner's knowledge about local market conditions increases, it depends less on the expertise of a local partner. This increases the bargaining power of the foreign partner and ultimately leads to conflicts over control of the venture's strategy and goals.[25] Some firms have sought to limit such problems by entering into joint ventures in which one partner has a controlling interest.

Wholly Owned Subsidiaries

In a **wholly owned subsidiary**, the firm owns 100 percent of the stock. Establishing a wholly owned subsidiary in a foreign market can be done two ways. The firm either can set up a new operation in that country, often referred to as a greenfield venture, or it can acquire an established firm in that host nation and use that firm to promote its products.[26] For example, ING's strategy for entering the U.S. insurance market was to acquire established U.S. enterprises, rather than try to build an operation from the ground floor.

Advantages

There are several clear advantages of wholly owned subsidiaries. First, when a firm's competitive advantage is based on technological competence, a wholly owned subsidiary will often be the preferred entry mode because it reduces the risk of losing control over that competence. (See Chapter 8 for more details.) Many high-tech firms prefer this entry mode for overseas expansion (e.g., firms in the semiconductor, electronics, and pharmaceutical industries). Second, a wholly owned subsidiary gives a firm tight control over operations in different countries. This is necessary for engaging in global strategic coordination (i.e., using profits from one country to support competitive attacks in another).

Third, a wholly owned subsidiary may be required if a firm is trying to realize location and experience curve economies (as firms pursuing global and transnational strategies try to do). As we saw in Chapter 11, when cost pressures are intense, it may pay a firm to configure its value chain in such a way that the value added at each stage is maximized. Thus, a national subsidiary may specialize in manufacturing only part of the product line or certain components of the end product, exchanging parts and products with other subsidiaries in the firm's global system. Establishing such a global production system requires a high degree of control over the operations of each affiliate. The various operations must be prepared to accept centrally determined decisions as to how they will produce, how much they will produce, and how their output will be priced for transfer to the next operation. Because licensees or joint-venture partners are unlikely to accept such a subservient role, establishing wholly owned subsidiaries may be necessary. Finally, establishing a wholly owned subsidiary gives the firm a 100 percent share in the profits generated in a foreign market.

Disadvantage

Establishing a wholly owned subsidiary is generally the most costly method of serving a foreign market from a capital investment standpoint. Firms doing this must bear the full capital costs and risks of setting up overseas operations. The risks associated with learning to do business in a new culture are less if the firm acquires an established host-country enterprise. However, acquisitions raise additional problems, including those associated with trying to marry divergent corporate cultures. These problems may more than offset any benefits derived by acquiring an established operation. Because the choice between greenfield ventures and acquisitions is such an important one, we discuss it in more detail later in the chapter.

SELECTING AN ENTRY MODE

As the preceding discussion demonstrated, all the entry modes have advantages and disadvantages, as summarized in Table 15.1. Thus, trade-offs are inevitable when selecting an entry mode. For example, when considering entry into an unfamiliar country with a track record for discriminating against foreign-owned enterprises when awarding government contracts, a firm might favor a joint venture with a local enterprise. Its rationale might be that the local partner will help it establish operations in an unfamiliar environment and will help the company win government contracts. However, if the firm's core competence is based on proprietary technology, entering a joint venture might risk losing control of that technology to the joint-venture partner, in which case the strategy may seem unattractive. Despite the

TABLE 15.1 Advantages and Disadvantages of Entry Modes

Entry Mode	Advantages	Disadvantages
Exporting	Ability to realize location and experience curve economies	High transport costs Trade barriers Problems with local marketing agents
Turnkey contracts	Ability to earn returns from process technology skills in countries where FDI is restricted	Creating efficient competitors Lack of long-term market presence
Licensing	Low development costs and risks	Lack of control over technology Inability to realize location and experience curve economies Inability to engage in global strategic coordination
Franchising	Low development costs and risks	Lack of control over quality Inability to engage in global strategic coordination
Joint ventures	Access to local partner's knowledge Sharing development costs and risks Politically acceptable	Lack of control over technology Inability to engage in global strategic coordination Inability to realize location and experience economies
Wholly owned subsidiaries	Protection of technology Ability to engage in global strategic coordination Ability to realize location and experience economies	High costs and risks

existence of such trade-offs, it is possible to make some generalizations about the optimal choice of entry mode.[27]

Core Competencies and Entry Mode

We saw in Chapter 13 that firms often expand internationally to earn greater returns from their core competencies, transferring the skills and products derived from their core competencies to foreign markets where indigenous competitors lack those skills. The optimal entry mode for these firms depends to some degree on the nature of their core competencies. A distinction can be drawn between firms whose core competency is in technological know-how and those whose core competency is in management know-how.

Technological Know-How

As was observed in Chapter 8, if a firm's competitive advantage (its core competence) is based on control over proprietary technological know-how, licensing and joint-venture arrangements should be avoided if possible to minimize the risk of losing control over that technology. Thus, if a high-tech firm sets up operations in a foreign country to profit from a core competency in technological know-how, it will probably do so through a wholly owned subsidiary. This rule should not be viewed as hard and fast, however. Sometimes a licensing or joint-venture arrangement can be structured to reduce the risk of licensees or joint-venture partners expropriating technological know-how. Another exception exists when a firm perceives its technological advantage to be only transitory, when it expects rapid imitation of its core technology by competitors. In such cases, the firm might want to license its technology as rapidly as possible to foreign firms to gain global acceptance for its technology before the imitation occurs.[28] Such a strategy has some advantages. By licensing its technology to competitors, the firm may deter them from developing their own, possibly superior, technology. Further, by licensing its technology, the firm may establish its technology as the dominant design in the industry. This may ensure a steady stream of royalty payments. However, the attractions of licensing are frequently outweighed by the risks of losing control over technology, and if this is a risk, licensing should be avoided.

Management Know-How

The competitive advantage of many service firms is based on management know-how (e.g., McDonald's, Starbucks). For such firms, the risk of losing control over the management skills to franchisees or joint-venture partners is not that great. These firms' valuable asset is their brand name, and brand names are generally well protected by international laws pertaining to trademarks. Given this, many of the issues arising in the case of technological know-how are of less concern here. As a result, many service firms favor a combination of franchising and master subsidiaries to control the franchises within particular countries or regions. The master subsidiaries may be wholly owned or joint ventures, but most service firms have found that joint ventures with local partners work best for the master controlling subsidiaries. A joint venture is often politically more acceptable and brings a degree of local knowledge to the subsidiary.

Pressures for Cost Reductions and Entry Mode

The greater the pressures for cost reductions, the more likely a firm will want to pursue some combination of exporting and wholly owned subsidiaries. By manufacturing in those locations where factor conditions are optimal and then exporting to the rest of the world, a firm may be able to realize substantial location and experience curve economies. The firm might then want to export the finished product to marketing subsidiaries based in various countries. These subsidiaries will typically be wholly owned and have the responsibility for overseeing distribution in their particular countries. Setting up wholly owned marketing subsidiaries is preferable to joint-venture arrangements and to using foreign marketing agents because it gives the firm tight control that might be required for coordinating a globally dispersed value chain. It also gives the firm the ability to use the profits generated in one market to improve its competitive position in another market. In other words, firms pursuing global standardization or transnational strategies tend to prefer establishing wholly owned subsidiaries.

GREENFIELD VENTURE OR ACQUISITION?   LO15-4

A firm can establish a wholly owned subsidiary in a country by building a subsidiary from the ground up, the so-called greenfield strategy, or by acquiring an enterprise in the target market.[29] The volume of cross-border acquisitions has been growing at a rapid rate for two decades. Over most of the past two decades, between 40 and 80 percent of all FDI inflows have been in the form of mergers and acquisitions.[30]

Pros and Cons of Acquisitions

Acquisitions have three major points in their favor. First, they are quick to execute. By acquiring an established enterprise, a firm can rapidly build its presence in the target foreign market. When the German automobile company Daimler-Benz decided it needed a bigger presence in the U.S. automobile market, it did not increase that presence by building new factories to serve the United States, a process that would have taken years. Instead, it acquired the third-largest U.S. automobile company, Chrysler, and merged the two operations to form DaimlerChrysler (Daimler spun off Chrysler into a private equity firm in 2007). When the Spanish telecommunications service provider Telefónica wanted to build a service presence in Latin America, it did so through a series of acquisitions, purchasing telecommunications companies in Brazil and Argentina. In these cases, the firms made acquisitions because they knew that was the quickest way to establish a sizable presence in the target market.

Second, in many cases firms make acquisitions to preempt their competitors. The need for preemption is particularly great in markets that are rapidly globalizing, such as telecommunications, where a combination of deregulation within nations and liberalization of regulations governing cross-border foreign direct investment has made it much easier for enterprises to enter foreign markets through acquisitions. Such markets may see concentrated waves of acquisitions as firms race each other to attain global scale. In the telecommunications industry, for example, regulatory changes triggered what can be called a feeding frenzy, with firms entering each other's markets via acquisitions to establish a global presence. These included the $56 billion acquisition of AirTouch Communications in the United States by the British company Vodafone, which was the largest acquisition ever; the $13 billion acquisition of One 2 One in Britain by the German company Deutsche Telekom; and the $6.4 billion acquisition of Excel Communications in the United States by Teleglobe of Canada, all of which occurred in 1998 and 1999.[31] A similar wave of cross-border acquisitions occurred in the global automobile industry over the same time period, with Daimler acquiring Chrysler, Ford acquiring Volvo, and Renault acquiring Nissan.

Third, managers may believe acquisitions to be less risky than greenfield ventures. When a firm makes an acquisition, it buys a set of assets that are producing a known revenue and profit stream. In contrast, the revenue and profit stream that a greenfield venture might generate is uncertain because it does not yet exist. When a firm makes an acquisition in a foreign market, it not only acquires a set of tangible assets, such as factories, logistics systems, customer service systems, and so on, but also acquires valuable intangible assets, including a local brand name and managers' knowledge of the business environment in that nation. Such knowledge can reduce the risk of mistakes caused by ignorance of the national culture.

Despite the arguments for making acquisitions, acquisitions often produce disappointing results.[32] For example, a study by Mercer Management Consulting looked at 150 acquisitions worth more than $500 million each.[33] The Mercer study concluded that 50 percent of these acquisitions eroded shareholder value, while another 33 percent created only marginal returns. Only 17 percent were judged to be successful. Similarly, a study by KPMG, an accounting and management consulting company, looked at 700 large acquisitions. The study found that while some 30 percent of these actually created value for the acquiring company, 31 percent destroyed value, and the remainder had little impact.[34] A similar study by McKinsey & Company estimated that some 70 percent of mergers and acquisitions failed to achieve expected revenue synergies.[35] In a seminal study of the postacquisition performance of acquired companies, David Ravenscraft and Mike Scherer concluded that on average the profits and market shares of acquired companies declined following acquisition.[36] They also noted that a smaller but substantial subset of those companies experienced traumatic difficulties, which ultimately led to their being sold by the acquiring company. Ravenscraft and Scherer's evidence suggests that many acquisitions destroy rather than create value. While most research has looked at domestic acquisitions, the findings probably also apply to cross-border acquisitions.[37]

Why Do Acquisitions Fail?

Acquisitions fail for several reasons. First, the acquiring firms often overpay for the assets of the acquired firm. The price of the target firm can get bid up if more than one firm is interested in its purchase, as is often the case. In addition, the management of the acquiring firm is often too optimistic about the value that can be created via an acquisition and is thus willing to pay a significant premium over a target firm's market capitalization. This is called the "hubris hypothesis" of why acquisitions fail. The hubris hypothesis postulates that top managers typically overestimate their ability to create value from an acquisition, primarily because rising to the top of a corporation has given them an exaggerated sense of their own capabilities.[38] For example, Daimler acquired Chrysler in 1998 for $40 billion, a premium of 40 percent over the market value of Chrysler before the takeover bid. Daimler paid this much because it thought it could use Chrysler to help it grow market share in the United States. At the time, Daimler's management issued bold announcements about the "synergies" that would be created from combining the operations of the two companies. However, within a year of the acquisition, Daimler's German management was faced with a crisis at Chrysler, which was suddenly losing money due to weak sales in the United States. In retrospect, Daimler's management had been far too optimistic about the potential for future demand in the U.S. auto market and about the opportunities for creating value from "synergies." Daimler acquired Chrysler at the end of a multiyear boom in U.S. auto sales and paid a large premium over Chrysler's market value just before demand slumped (and in 2007, in an admission of failure, Daimler sold its Chrysler unit to a private equity firm).[39]

Second, many acquisitions fail because there is a clash between the cultures of the acquiring and acquired firms. After an acquisition, many acquired companies experience high management turnover, possibly because their employees do not like the acquiring company's way of doing things.[40] This happened at DaimlerChrysler; many senior managers left Chrysler in the first year after the merger. Apparently, Chrysler executives disliked the dominance in decision making by Daimler's German managers, while the Germans resented that Chrysler's American managers were paid two to three times as much as their German counterparts. These cultural differences created tensions, which ultimately exhibited themselves in high management turnover at Chrysler.[41] The loss of management talent and expertise can materially harm the performance of the acquired unit.[42] This may be particularly problematic in an international business, where management of the acquired unit may have valuable local knowledge that can be difficult to replace.

Third, many acquisitions fail because attempts to realize gains by integrating the operations of the acquired and acquiring entities often run into roadblocks and take much longer than forecast. Differences in management philosophy and company culture can slow the integration of operations. Differences in national culture may exacerbate these problems. Bureaucratic haggling between managers also complicates the process. Again, this reportedly occurred at DaimlerChrysler, where grand plans to integrate the operations of the two companies were bogged down by endless committee meetings and by simple logistical considerations such as the six-hour time difference between Detroit and Germany. By the time an integration plan had been worked out, Chrysler was losing money, and Daimler's German managers suddenly had a crisis on their hands.

Finally, many acquisitions fail due to inadequate preacquisition screening.[43] Many firms decide to acquire other firms without thoroughly analyzing the potential benefits and costs. They often move with undue haste to execute the acquisition, perhaps because they fear another competitor may preempt them. After the acquisition, however, many acquiring firms discover that instead of buying a well-run business, they have purchased a troubled organization. This may be a particular problem in cross-border acquisitions because the acquiring firm may not fully understand the target firm's national culture and business system.

Reducing the Risks of Failure

These problems can all be overcome if the firm is careful about its acquisition strategy.[44] Screening of the foreign enterprise to be acquired, including a detailed auditing of operations, financial position, and management culture, can help to make sure the firm (1) does not pay too much for the acquired unit, (2) does not uncover any nasty surprises after the acquisition, and (3) acquires a firm whose organization culture is not antagonistic to that of the acquiring enterprise. It is also important for the acquirer to allay any concerns that management in the acquired enterprise might have. The objective should be to reduce unwanted management attrition after the acquisition. Finally, managers must move rapidly after an acquisition to put an integration plan in place and to act on that plan. Some people in both the acquiring and acquired units will try to slow or stop any integration efforts, particularly when losses of employment or management power are involved, and managers should have a plan for dealing with such impediments before they arise.

Pros and Cons of Greenfield Ventures

The big advantage of establishing a greenfield venture in a foreign country is that it gives the firm a much greater ability to build the kind of subsidiary company that it wants. For example, it is much easier to build an organization culture from scratch than it is to change the culture of an acquired unit. Similarly, it is much easier to establish a set of operating routines in a new subsidiary than it is to convert the operating routines of an acquired unit. This is a very important advantage for many international businesses, where transferring products, competencies, skills, and know-how from the established operations of the firm to the new subsidiary are principal ways of creating value. For example, when Lincoln Electric, the U.S. manufacturer of arc welding equipment, first ventured overseas in the mid-1980s, it did so by acquisitions, purchasing arc welding equipment companies in Europe. However, Lincoln's competitive advantage in the United States was based on a strong organizational culture and a unique set of incentives that encouraged its employees to do everything possible to increase productivity. Lincoln found through bitter experience that it was almost impossible to transfer its organizational culture and incentives to acquired firms, which had their own distinct organizational cultures and incentives. As a result, the firm switched its entry strategy in the mid-1990s and began to enter foreign countries by establishing greenfield ventures, building operations from the ground up. While this strategy takes more time to execute, Lincoln has found that it yields greater long-run returns than the acquisition strategy.

Set against this significant advantage are the disadvantages of establishing a greenfield venture. Greenfield ventures are slower to establish. They are also risky. As with any new venture, a degree of uncertainty is associated with future revenue and profit prospects. However, if the firm has already been successful in other foreign markets and understands what it takes to do business in other countries, these risks may not be that great. For example, having already gained great knowledge about operating internationally, the risk to McDonald's of entering yet another country is probably not that great. Also, greenfield ventures are less risky than acquisitions in the sense that there is less potential for unpleasant surprises. A final disadvantage is the possibility of being preempted by more aggressive global competitors who enter via acquisitions and build a big market presence that limits the market potential for the greenfield venture.

Greenfield Venture or Acquisition?

The choice between acquisitions and greenfield ventures is not an easy one. Both modes have their advantages and disadvantages. In general, the choice will depend on the circumstances confronting the firm. If the firm is seeking to enter a market where there are already well-established incumbent enterprises, and where global competitors are also interested in establishing a presence, it may pay the firm to enter via an acquisition. In such circumstances, a greenfield venture may be too slow to establish a sizable presence. However, if the firm is going to make an acquisition, its management should be cognizant of the risks associated with acquisitions that were discussed earlier and consider these when determining which firms to purchase. It may be better to enter by the slower route of a greenfield venture than to make a bad acquisition.

If the firm is considering entering a country where there are no incumbent competitors to be acquired, then a greenfield venture may be the only mode. Even when incumbents exist, if the competitive advantage of the firm is based on the transfer of organizationally embedded competencies, skills, routines, and culture, it may still be preferable to enter via a greenfield venture. Things such as skills and organizational culture, which are based on significant knowledge that is difficult to articulate and codify, are much easier to embed in a new venture than they are in an acquired entity, where the firm may have to overcome the established routines and culture of the acquired firm. Thus, as our earlier examples suggest, firms such as McDonald's and Lincoln Electric prefer to enter foreign markets by establishing greenfield ventures.

STRATEGIC ALLIANCES

LO15-5

Strategic alliances refer to cooperative agreements between potential or actual competitors. In this section, we are concerned specifically with strategic alliances between firms from different countries. Strategic alliances run the range from formal joint ventures, in which two or more firms have equity stakes (e.g., Fuji Xerox), to short-term contractual agreements, in which two companies agree to cooperate on a particular task (such as developing a new product). Collaboration between competitors is fashionable; recent decades have seen an explosion in the number of strategic alliances.

The Advantages of Strategic Alliances

Firms ally themselves with actual or potential competitors for various strategic purposes.[45] First, strategic alliances may facilitate entry into a foreign market. For example, many firms believe that if they are to successfully enter the Chinese market, they need a local partner who understands business conditions and who has good connections (or *guanxi*—see Chapter 4). Thus, in 2004 Warner Brothers entered into a joint venture with two Chinese partners to produce and distribute films in China. As a foreign film company, Warner found that if it wanted to produce films on its own for the Chinese market, it had to go through a complex approval process for every film, and it had to farm out distribution to a local company, which made doing business in China very difficult. Due to the participation of Chinese firms, however, the joint-venture films will go through a streamlined approval process, and the venture will be able to distribute any films it produces. Also, the joint venture will be able to produce films for Chinese TV, something that foreign firms are not allowed to do.[46]

Second, strategic alliances also allow firms to share the fixed costs (and associated risks) of developing new products or processes. An alliance between Boeing and a number of Japanese companies to build Boeing's latest commercial jetliner, the 787, was motivated by Boeing's desire to share the estimated $8 billion investment required to develop the aircraft.

Third, an alliance is a way to bring together complementary skills and assets that neither company could easily develop on its own.[47] In 2003, for example, Microsoft and Toshiba established an alliance aimed at developing embedded microprocessors (essentially tiny computers) that can perform a variety of entertainment functions in an automobile (e.g., run a backseat DVD player or a wireless Internet connection). The processors run a version of Microsoft's Windows CE operating system. Microsoft brought its software engineering skills to the alliance and Toshiba its skills in developing microprocessors.[48] The alliance between Cisco and Fujitsu was also formed to share know-how.

Fourth, it can make sense to form an alliance that will help the firm establish technological standards for the industry that will benefit the firm. For example, in 2011 Nokia, one of the leading makers of smartphones, entered into an alliance with Microsoft under which Nokia agreed to license and use Microsoft's Windows Mobile operating system in Nokia's phones. The motivation for the alliance was in part to help establish Windows Mobile as the industry standard for smartphones as opposed to the rival operating systems such as Apple's iPhone and Google's Android.

The Disadvantages of Strategic Alliances

The advantages we have discussed can be very significant. Despite this, some commentators have criticized strategic alliances on the grounds that they give competitors a low-cost route to new technology and markets.[49] For example, 25 years ago some commentators argued that many strategic alliances between U.S. and Japanese firms were part of an implicit Japanese strategy to keep high-paying, high-value-added jobs in Japan while gaining the project engineering and production process skills that underlie the competitive success of many U.S. companies.[50] They argued that Japanese success in the machine tool and semiconductor industries was built on U.S. technology acquired through strategic alliances. And they argued that U.S. managers were aiding the Japanese by entering alliances that channel new inventions to Japan and provide a U.S. sales and distribution network for the resulting products. Although such deals may generate short-term profits, so the argument goes, in the long run the result is to "hollow out" U.S. firms, leaving them with no competitive advantage in the global marketplace.

These critics have a point; alliances have risks. Unless a firm is careful, it can give away more than it receives. But there are so many examples of apparently successful alliances between firms—including alliances between U.S. and Japanese firms—that the critics' position seems extreme. It is difficult to see how the Microsoft–Toshiba alliance, the Boeing–Mitsubishi alliance for the 787, and the Fuji–Xerox alliance fit the critics' thesis. In these cases, both partners seem to have gained from the alliance. Why do some alliances benefit both firms while others benefit one firm and hurt the other? The next section provides an answer to this question.

Making Alliances Work

The failure rate for international strategic alliances seems to be high. One study of 49 international strategic alliances found that two-thirds run into serious managerial and financial troubles within two years of their formation, and that although many of these problems are solved, 33 percent are ultimately rated as failures by the parties involved.[51] The success of an alliance seems to be a function of three main factors: partner selection, alliance structure, and the manner in which the alliance is managed.

Partner Selection

One key to making a strategic alliance work is to select the right ally. A good ally, or partner, has three characteristics. First, a good partner helps the firm achieve its strategic goals, whether they are market access, sharing the costs and risks of product development, or gaining access to critical core competencies. The partner must have capabilities that the firm lacks and that it values. Second, a good partner shares the firm's vision for the purpose of the alliance. If two firms approach an alliance with radically different agendas, the chances are great that the relationship will not be harmonious, will not flourish, and will end in divorce. Third, a good partner is unlikely to try to opportunistically exploit the alliance for its own ends, that is, to expropriate the firm's technological know-how while giving away little in return. In this respect, firms with reputations for "fair play" probably make the best allies. For example, companies such as General Electric are involved in so many strategic alliances that it would not pay the company to trample over individual alliance partners.[52] This would tarnish GE's reputation of being a good ally and would make it more difficult for GE to attract alliance partners.

To select a partner with these three characteristics, a firm needs to conduct comprehensive research on potential alliance candidates. To increase the probability of selecting a good partner, the firm should:

1. Collect as much pertinent, publicly available information on potential allies as possible.
2. Gather data from informed third parties. These include firms that have had alliances with the potential partners, investment bankers that have had dealings with them, and former employees.
3. Get to know the potential partner as well as possible before committing to an alliance. This should include face-to-face meetings between senior managers (and perhaps middle-level managers) to ensure that the chemistry is right.

Alliance Structure

A partner having been selected, the alliance should be structured so that the firm's risks of giving too much away to the partner are reduced to an acceptable level. First, alliances can be designed to make it difficult (if not impossible) to transfer technology not meant to be transferred. The design, development, manufacture, and service of a product manufactured by an alliance can be structured so as to wall off sensitive technologies to prevent their leakage to the other participant. In a long-standing alliance between General Electric and Snecma to build commercial aircraft engines for single-aisle commercial jet aircraft, for example, GE reduced the risk of excess transfer by walling off certain sections of the production process. The modularization effectively cut off the transfer of what GE regarded as key competitive technology, while permitting Snecma access to final assembly. Formed in 1974, the alliance has been remarkably successful, and today it dominates the market for jet engines used on the Boeing 737 and Airbus 320.[53] Similarly, in the alliance between Boeing and the Japanese to build the 767, Boeing walled off research, design, and marketing functions considered central to its competitive position, while allowing the Japanese to share in production technology. Boeing also walled off new technologies not required for 767 production.[54]

Second, contractual safeguards can be written into an alliance agreement to guard against the risk of opportunism by a partner. (Opportunism includes the theft of technology and/or markets.) For example, TRW Automotive has three strategic alliances with large Japanese auto component suppliers to produce seat belts, engine valves, and steering gears for sale to Japanese-owned auto assembly plants in the United States. TRW has clauses in each of its alliance contracts that bar the Japanese firms from competing with TRW to supply U.S.-owned auto companies with component parts. By doing this, TRW protects itself against the possibility that the Japanese companies are entering into the alliances merely to gain access to the North American market to compete with TRW in its home market.

Third, both parties to an alliance can agree in advance to swap skills and technologies that the other covets, thereby ensuring a chance for equitable gain. Cross-licensing agreements are one way to achieve this goal. Fourth, the risk of opportunism by an alliance partner can be reduced if the firm extracts a significant credible commitment from its partner in advance. The long-term alliance between Xerox and Fuji to build photocopiers for the Asian market perhaps best illustrates this. Rather than enter into an informal agreement or a licensing arrangement (which Fuji Photo initially wanted), Xerox insisted that Fuji invest in a fifty-fifty joint venture to serve Japan and East Asia. This venture constituted such a significant investment in people, equipment, and facilities that Fuji Photo was committed from the outset to making the alliance work in order to earn a return on its investment. By agreeing to the joint venture, Fuji essentially made a credible commitment to the alliance. Given this, Xerox felt secure in transferring its photocopier technology to Fuji.[55]

Managing the Alliance

Once a partner has been selected and an appropriate alliance structure has been agreed on, the task facing the firm is to maximize its benefits from the alliance. As in all international business deals, an important factor is sensitivity to cultural differences (see Chapter 4). Many differences in management style are attributable to cultural differences, and managers need to make allowances for these in dealing with their partner. Beyond this, maximizing the benefits from an alliance seems to involve building trust between partners and learning from partners.[56]

Managing an alliance successfully requires building interpersonal relationships between the firms' managers, or what is sometimes referred to as *relational capital*.[57] This is one lesson that can be drawn from a successful strategic alliance between Ford and Mazda. Ford and Mazda set up a framework of meetings within which their managers not only discuss matters pertaining to the alliance but also have time to get to know each other better. The belief is that the resulting friendships help build trust and facilitate harmonious relations between the two firms. Personal relationships also foster an informal management network between the firms. This network can then be used to help solve problems arising in more formal contexts (such as in joint committee meetings between personnel from the two firms).

Academics have argued that a major determinant of how much knowledge a company gains from an alliance is its ability to learn from its alliance partner.[58] For example, in a five-year study of 15 strategic alliances between major multinationals, Gary Hamel, Yves Doz, and C. K. Prahalad focused on a number of alliances between Japanese companies and Western (European or American) partners.[59] In every case in which a Japanese company emerged from an alliance stronger than its Western partner, the Japanese company had made a greater effort to learn. Few Western companies studied seemed to want to learn from their Japanese partners. They tended to regard the alliance purely as a cost-sharing or risk-sharing device, rather than as an opportunity to learn how a potential competitor does business.

Consider the alliance between General Motors and Toyota constituted in 1985 to build the Chevrolet Nova. This alliance was structured as a formal joint venture, called New United Motor Manufacturing, Inc., and each party had a 50 percent equity stake. The venture owned an auto plant in Fremont, California. According to one Japanese manager, Toyota quickly achieved most of its objectives from the alliance: "We learned about U.S. supply and transportation. And we got the confidence to manage U.S. workers."[60] All that knowledge was then transferred to Georgetown, Kentucky, where Toyota opened its own plant in 1988. Possibly all GM got was a new product, the Chevrolet Nova. Some GM managers complained that the knowledge they gained through the alliance with Toyota has never been put to good use inside GM. They believe they should have been kept together as a team to educate GM's engineers and workers about the Japanese system. Instead, they were dispersed to various GM subsidiaries.

To maximize the learning benefits of an alliance, a firm must try to learn from its partner and then apply the knowledge within its own organization. It has been suggested that all operating employees should be well briefed on the partner's strengths and weaknesses and should understand how acquiring particular skills will bolster their firm's competitive position. Hamel, Doz, and Prahalad note that this is already standard practice among Japanese companies. They made this observation:

> We accompanied a Japanese development engineer on a tour through a partner's factory. This engineer dutifully took notes on plant layout, the number of production stages, the rate at which the line was running, and the number of employees. He recorded all this despite the fact that he had no manufacturing responsibility in his own company, and that the alliance did not encompass joint manufacturing. Such dedication greatly enhances learning.[61]

For such learning to be of value, it must be diffused throughout the organization (as was seemingly not the case at GM after the GM–Toyota joint venture). To achieve this, the managers involved in the alliance should educate their colleagues about the skills of the alliance partner.

Chapter Summary

The chapter made the following points:

1. Basic entry decisions include identifying which markets to enter, when to enter those markets, and on what scale.
2. The most attractive foreign markets tend to be found in politically stable developed and developing nations that have free market systems and where there is not a dramatic upsurge in either inflation rates or private-sector debt.
3. There are several advantages associated with entering a national market early, before other international businesses have established themselves. These advantages must be balanced against the pioneering costs that early entrants often have to bear, including the greater risk of business failure.
4. Large-scale entry into a national market constitutes a major strategic commitment that is likely to change the nature of competition in that market and limit the entrant's future strategic flexibility. Although making major strategic commitments can yield many benefits, there are also risks associated with such a strategy.
5. There are six modes of entering a foreign market: exporting, creating turnkey projects, licensing, franchising, establishing joint ventures, and setting up a wholly owned subsidiary.
6. Exporting has the advantages of facilitating the realization of experience curve economies and of avoiding the costs of setting up manufacturing operations in another country. Disadvantages include high transport costs, trade barriers, and problems with local marketing agents.
7. Turnkey projects allow firms to export their process know-how to countries where FDI might be prohibited, thereby enabling the firm to earn a greater return from this asset. The disadvantage is that the firm may inadvertently create efficient global competitors in the process.
8. The main advantage of licensing is that the licensee bears the costs and risks of opening a foreign market. Disadvantages include the risk of losing technological know-how to the licensee and a lack of tight control over licensees.
9. The main advantage of franchising is that the franchisee bears the costs and risks of opening a foreign market. Disadvantages center on problems of quality control of distant franchisees.

10. Joint ventures have the advantages of sharing the costs and risks of opening a foreign market and of gaining local knowledge and political influence. Disadvantages include the risk of losing control over technology and a lack of tight control.

11. The advantages of wholly owned subsidiaries include tight control over technological know-how. The main disadvantage is that the firm must bear all the costs and risks of opening a foreign market.

12. The optimal choice of entry mode depends on the firm's strategy. When technological know-how constitutes a firm's core competence, wholly owned subsidiaries are preferred, since they best control technology. When management know-how constitutes a firm's core competence, foreign franchises controlled by joint ventures seem to be optimal. When the firm is pursuing a global standardization or transnational strategy, the need for tight control over operations to realize location and experience curve economies suggests wholly owned subsidiaries are the best entry mode.

13. When establishing a wholly owned subsidiary in a country, a firm must decide whether to do so by a greenfield venture strategy or by acquiring an established enterprise in the target market.

14. Acquisitions are quick to execute, may enable a firm to preempt its global competitors, and involve buying a known revenue and profit stream. Acquisitions may fail when the acquiring firm overpays for the target, when the cultures of the acquiring and acquired firms clash, when there is a high level of management attrition after the acquisition, and when there is a failure to integrate the operations of the acquiring and acquired firm.

15. The advantage of a greenfield venture in a foreign country is that it gives the firm a much greater ability to build the kind of subsidiary company that it wants. For example, it is much easier to build an organization culture from scratch than it is to change the culture of an acquired unit.

16. Strategic alliances are cooperative agreements between actual or potential competitors. The advantage of alliances are that they facilitate entry into foreign markets, enable partners to share the fixed costs and risks associated with new products and processes, facilitate the transfer of complementary skills between companies, and help firms establish technical standards.

17. The disadvantage of a strategic alliance is that the firm risks giving away technological know-how and market access to its alliance partner.

18. The disadvantages associated with alliances can be reduced if the firm selects partners carefully, paying close attention to the firm's reputation and the structure of the alliance so as to avoid unintended transfers of know-how.

19. Two keys to making alliances work seem to be building trust and informal communications networks between partners and taking proactive steps to learn from alliance partners.

Critical Thinking and Discussion Questions

1. Review the Management Focus on Tesco. Then answer the following questions:
   a. Why did Tesco's initial international expansion strategy focus on developing nations?
   b. How does Tesco create value in its international operations?
   c. In Asia, Tesco has a history of entering into joint-venture agreements with local partners. What are the benefits of doing this for Tesco? What are the risks? How are those risks mitigated?
   d. In March 2006 Tesco announced it would enter the United States. This represented a departure from its historic strategy of focusing on developing nations. Why do you think Tesco

made this decision? How is the U.S. market different from others Tesco has entered? What are the risks here?

2. Licensing proprietary technology to foreign competitors is the best way to give up a firm's competitive advantage. Discuss.

3. Discuss how the need for control over foreign operations varies with firms' strategies and core competencies. What are the implications for the choice of entry mode?

4. A small Canadian firm that has developed valuable new medical products using its unique biotechnology know-how is trying to decide how best to serve the European Union market. Its choices are given below. The cost of investment in manufacturing facilities will be a major one for the Canadian firm, but it is not outside its reach. If these are the firm's only options, which one would you advise it to choose? Why?

   a. Manufacture the products at home, and let foreign sales agents handle marketing.

   b. Manufacture the products at home, and set up a wholly owned subsidiary in Europe to handle marketing.

   c. Enter into an alliance with a large European pharmaceutical firm. The products would be manufactured in Europe by the fifty-fifty joint venture and marketed by the European firm.

Research Task ◯ globalEDGE globaledge.msu.edu

Entry Strategy and Strategic Alliances

Use the globalEDGE website (globaledge.msu.edu) to complete the following exercises:

Exercise 1

The *Entrepreneur* annually publishes a ranking of the *top global franchises*. Provide a list of the top 25 companies that pursue franchising as their preferred mode of international expansion. Study one of these companies in detail, and describe its business model, its international expansion pattern, desirable qualifications in possible franchisees, and the support and training the company typically provides.

Exercise 2

The U.S. Commercial Service prepares reports known as the *Country Commercial Guide* for countries of interest to U.S. investors. Utilize the *Country Commercial Guide* for Russia to gather information on this country's energy and mining industry. Considering that your company has plans to enter Russia in the foreseeable future, select the most appropriate entry method. Be sure to support your decision with the information collected.

Closing CASE

General Motors in China

The late 2000s were not kind to General Motors. Hurt by a deep recession in the United States and plunging vehicle sales, GM capped off the decade, where it had progressively lost market share to foreign rivals such as Toyota, by entering Chapter 11 bankruptcy. Between 1980, when it dominated the

U.S. market, and 2009, when it entered bankruptcy protection, GM saw its U.S. market share slip from 44 percent to just 19 percent. The troubled company emerged from bankruptcy a few months later a smaller enterprise with fewer brands, and yet going forward some believe that the new GM could be a much more profitable enterprise. One major reason for this optimism was the success of its joint ventures in China.

GM entered China in 1997 with a $1.6 billion investment to establish a joint venture with the state-owned Shanghai Automotive Industry Corporation (SAIC) to build Buick sedans. At the time the Chinese market was tiny (fewer than 400,000 cars were sold in 1996), but GM was attracted by the enormous potential in a country of more than 1 billion people that was experiencing rapid economic growth. GM forecast that by the late 2000s some 3 million cars a year might be sold in China. While it explicitly recognized that it had much to learn about the Chinese market, and would probably lose money for years to come, GM executives believed it was crucial to establish a beachhead and to team up with SAIC (one of the early leaders in China's emerging automobile industry) before its global rivals did. The decision to enter a joint venture was not a hard one. Not only did GM lack knowledge and connections in China, but Chinese government regulations made it all but impossible for a foreign automaker to go it alone in the country.

While GM was not alone in investing in China—many of the world's major automobile companies entered into some kind of Chinese joint venture during this time period—it was among the largest investors. Only Volkswagen, whose management shared GM's view, made a similar-size investment. Other companies adopted a more cautious approach, investing smaller amounts and setting more limited goals.

By 2007 GM had expanded the range of its partnership with SAIC to include vehicles sold under the names of Chevrolet, Cadillac, and Wuling. The two companies had also established the Pan-Asian Technical Automotive center to design cars and components not just for China but also for other Asian markets. At this point it was already clear that both the Chinese market and the joint venture were exceeding GM's initial expectations. Not only was the venture profitable, but it was also selling more than 900,000 cars and light trucks in 2007, an 18 percent increase over 2006, placing it second only to Volkswagen in the market among foreign nameplates. Equally impressive, some 8 million cars and light trucks were sold in China in 2007, making China the second-largest car market in the world, ahead of Japan and behind the United States.

Much of the venture's success could be attributed to its strategy of designing vehicles explicitly for the Chinese market. For example, together with SAIC it produced a tiny minivan, the Wuling Sunshine. The van costs $3,700, has a 0.8-liter engine, hits a top speed of 60 mph, and weighs less than 1000 kilograms—a far cry from the heavy SUVs GM was known for in the United States. For China, the vehicle was perfect, and some 460,000 were sold in 2007, making it the best seller in the light truck sector.

It is the future, however, that has people excited. In 2008 and 2009, while the U.S. and European automobile markets slumped, China's market registered strong growth. In 2009 some 13.8 million vehicles were sold in the country, surpassing the United States to become the largest automobile market in the world. In 2012 the figure was 19.4 million. By 2012, GM and its local partners had a 15 percent share of the Chinese market, and its annual sales in China surpassed those in the United States. On the back of this strong growth, GM continues to make aggressive investments in China. In 2013 it announced that it would expand its Chinese dealer network to 5,100 from 3,800, and it plans to have 17 assembly plants in China by mid-decade, more than the 12 it has in the United States. Driving this expansion are forecasts from GM that demand in China will reach 35 million vehicles a year by 2022. Underlying these forecasts are the still relatively low vehicle penetration rates in China. In 2012 China had 85 vehicles per 1000 people, compared to around 800 vehicles for every 1,000 people in the United States.[62]

Case Discussion Questions

1. GM entered the Chinese market at a time when demand was very limited. Why? What was the strategic rationale?
2. Why did GM enter through a joint venture with SAIC? What are the benefits of this approach? What are the potential risks here?
3. Why did GM not simply license its technology to SAIC? Why did it not export cars from the United States?
4. Why has the joint venture been so successful to date?
5. As of 2013 GM appears to be increasing its strategic commitments to China, building more factories and opening more dealers. Why is the company making these bets? Do you think it is doing the right thing? What are the potential risks here?

Jain Irrigation's Global Growth through M&As

Micro-irrigation systems are basically segmented on the basis of applications such as agriculture micro-irrigation, landscaping micro-irrigation, and greenhouse micro-irrigation systems.[63] The micro-irrigation system market includes Drip micro-irrigation systems and Sprinkler micro-irrigation systems.

Sprinkler micro-irrigation systems primarily consist of micro-sprinkler irrigation system and micro-jet irrigation system. Sprinkler micro-irrigation systems currently hold 72 percent of the global micro-irrigation system market. Drip irrigation systems are used mostly for greenhouse irrigation and water scarce areas and are expected to grow faster.

Rising water scarcity and cost effectiveness of fertigation and chemigation in micro-irrigation systems over other crop protection and fertilizer application methods are driving the demand for micro-irrigation system market in the near future. Increasing population and water scarcity are another driving factors for this market. However, high initial and maintenance cost is major constraint for the rapid development of the market.[64]

Worldwide spread of Micro Irrigation

Region	No of countries	Available irrigated area (Mha)	Sprinkler irrigated area (Mha)	Drip irrigated area (Mha)	Total micro irrigated area	% of available irrigated area
Americas	35	41.9	13.3	1.9	15.2	36.3
Europe	35	24.2	10.1	1.8	11.9	47.2
Asia	46	194	6.8	1.8	8.6	4.4
Africa	53	12.5	1.9	0.4	2.3	18.4
Oceania	5	2.6	0.9	0.2	1.1	42.3
Total	174	276.2	33	6.1	39.1	14.2
India	—	140	5	5	3.6	

Source: Company, PINC Research

Source: *www.business-standard.com/content/.../jain_051111_01.pdf*

Jain Irrigation Systems (also known as **Jain Irrigation or JISL**) is a multinational with presence in 120 countries based in Jalgaon, Maharashtra, India. JISL employs over 10,500 workers, has 24 manufacturing plants, and manufactures a number of products including drip and sprinkler irrigation systems and components, integrated irrigation automation systems, PVC and PE piping systems, plastic sheets, greenhouses, bio-fertilizers, solar water-heating systems, biogas plant on turnkey basis, wind hybrid energy and photovoltaic system. JISL also processes dehydrated, concentrated and frozen fruits and vegetables.[65]

JISL operates in two major segments and enjoys a leadership position in all its products and services, viz.[66]

(a) **Hi-tech Agri-Input Products**: Micro-irrigation Systems, polyvinyl chloride (PVC) pipes and bio-tech tissue culture.

(b) **Industrial Products**: PVC and Polycarbonate (PC) sheets, (PE) pipes, onion and vegetable dehydration, and fruit processing.

JISL is also:

- Globally second and India's largest (55 perecent market share) micro-irrigation company
- Largest manufacturer of plastic pipes and PVC and PC sheets in India
- Largest manufacturer of Mango pulp, puree, and concentrate
- Globally the second largest manufacturer of dehydrated onion

Mergers and Acquisitions at Jain Irrigation[67]

Jain Irrigation Systems Ltd. emerged as one big company after merging with various Jain Group Companies, such as Jain Plastic & Chemicals Ltd., Jain Kemira Fertilizers Ltd., Jain Rahan Biotech Ltd, Jain Brothers Industries, and Jain Pipe.[68] Its global acquisitions include:

- **2006:** JISL acquired Chapin Watermatic,[69] US pioneer in irrigation systems
- **2006:** JISL acquired NuCedar Mills, a US company in the custom homebuilding market.[70]
- **December 2006:** JISL acquired a majority stake in the US-based Cascade Specialties, Inc., which specializes in natural low-bacteria onion products and organic dehydrated onion. With this acquisition, Jain Irrigation became the third-largest dehydrated onion producer in the world, with a combined capacity in excess of 25,000 MTS.[71]
- **February 2007:** Acquired US-based Aquarius Brands for USD 21.5 million in an all-cash deal.[72]
- **June 2007:** Jain Irrigation Acquired 50.001% stake in NaanDan. Following the transaction, which includes a USD 30 million investment, NaanDan and Jain became the second largest irrigation company worldwide.[73]
- **November 2010:** By acquiring controlling stake in Sleaford Quality Foods Limited ("SQFL" or "Sleaford Quality Foods"), a UK-based Industrial Food Ingredients Supplier Jain Irrigation got direct access to a large market with value added products with this acquisition.[74]
- **May 2012:** Jain acquired the remaining 50% of NaanDan Jain Ltd. from Kibbutz Na'an in Israel for an estimated USD 35 million.[75]

What Jain Irrigation Looks Forward in any Acquisitions

The company has a wide range of micro-irrigation products, carefully built through a string of acquisitions. Five of its eight overseas acquisitions have been in the micro-irrigation space, including the 2006 buyout of Chapin Watermatics, which pioneered flat drip irrigation systems in the US in 1963, and NaanDan Irrigation in Israel, which pioneered the sprinkler system in 1956. "Our acquisitions have always been for market entry, technology or R&D skills that can be leveraged to build new products," says Ajit Jain, Director (marketing) of JISL.[76]

They aim to be among the top global players in each of their major business segments and become an international brand in the agricultural business. In addition to organic growth, JISL evaluates on a case-by-case basis potential acquisition targets that can grow their business, provide new technology, increase production capacity and/or expand their capabilities or geographic reach. For example, Chapin Watermatics Inc., a USA Company, was purchased to incorporate their subsoil irrigation technology. Investment in NaanDan Jain an Israeli irrigation Company, was done to incorporate their controlled irrigation technology and micro-sprinkler products; THE Machines, a Swiss Company, to adopt their equipment and machine manufacturing expertise, and more recently Sleaford (UK), a UK food distribution Company, to have direct access to a large market with value-added new food products. JISL plans to acquire the minority stakes from past acquisitions to further integrate these businesses into its operations. Acquisitions are pursued that are related to their key strengths, are synergistic and in their assessment, have manageable integration risks.

Jain Irrigation NaanDan Israeli Acquisition

NaanDan was formed in 2001 by a merger of two well-established and prominent irrigation companies. Naan, was established in 1937, while Dan was established in 1970. NaanDan develops, manufactures and markets advanced irrigation technologies, covering an extensive range of applications in open fields, orchards and plantations, greenhouses and nurseries, residential and landscape areas and industry.[77] Kibbutz Naan of Israel is one of the largest and better managed kibbutz in Israel. Kibbutz is a kind of cooperative society with members contributing and sharing the economic benefits from kibbutz assets and management.[78]

Jain Irrigation, signed an agreement with Kibbutz Naan for its acquisition. The agreement ensures that the scope of the company's activity will remain in Israel until 2020, with the aim of expanding it in the future. Since signing the first agreement in 2007, NaanDan Jain has increased its sales turnover more than 25 percent. In the past five years, more than NIS 125 million (INR 125 crore) had been invested in the joint venture company in innovative drip irrigation and sprinklers equipment both in Israel and in NaanDan Jain subsidiaries worldwide. Investments in research and development have also increased.[79]

NaanDan has six production sites, including two located in Israel (Kibbutz Naan and Kibbutz Dan). The cooperation between Jain and NaanDan Jain opened new markets for the company, and both companies together offer the widest range of products and services in the world—thus realizing the one-stop-shop concept. JISL introduced the latest technology in NaanDan Jain in drip lines-tapes and NaanDan Jain offered world's best sprinklers and dripper products to the Indian partner.

NaanDan's global network includes manufacturing companies in the USA, Spain, Mexico, Brazil, Chile and Australia and marketing subsidiaries in France and Italy. NaanDan has exclusive distributors in over 50 countries and employs 550 people worldwide. NaanDan has achieved a USD 75 million revenue for 2006 and is a profit making company.[80]

2009–2012: The road NaanDan Jain Traveled

- Powerful presence at international and Israeli exhibitions
- Strengthening relationships with the foreign and national media
- Many visits by delegations, ministers, potential customers and other VIPs
- Deep and ongoing relationships with the relevant government agencies
- Extensive branding process with BBDO[81] which is a worldwide advertising agency network, with headquarters in New York. The agency began in 1891 with George Batten's Batten Company, and later in 1928, through a merger of BDO (Barton, Durstine & Osborn) and Batten Co. the agency

became BBDO Worldwide. The agency has been named the "Most Awarded Agency Network in the World" by *The Gunn Report* for 5 consecutive years beginning 2005.

In effect, through its aggressive acquisitions strategy, JISL has become the second largest drip irrigation company in the world. It operates in the entire agri-value chain, thus enhancing its appeal to farmers around the world. It serves millions of farmers around the world, and is the first true multinational Company from an emerging market to become a leader in developed markets.[82]

Jain Irrigation Managing Director and NaanDan Jain Chairman Anil B Jain says that the acquisition of NaanDan is "a significant step in the strengthening of ties between Israel and India. This is an immense opportunity to expand our activity in the world in areas that provide solutions to the growing global climate change, water, food and energy crises. Jain's response to this challenge in the fields of agriculture and irrigation will be expressed upon the conclusion of the agreement, and we foresee new possibilities for growth of our Company in these areas. NaanDan Jain provides much added value to Jain, and we are proud and excited with this opportunity to preserve and develop it for the benefit of our clients around the world. Together, we expect to become the world's leading agro-industrial concern."

NaanDan Jain's CEO Avner Hermoni stated: "Jain's large investment is an expression of faith in NaanDan Jain. The agreement will ensure the expansion of NaanDan Jain in the coming years".[83]

According to Mr. B. H. Jain, Chairman of JISL, "this is a historic deal where Jain Irrigation which is the fastest growing irrigation company in the world, has joined hands with NaanDan, which is one of the earliest pioneers of the irrigation technology having global presence. We will be able to leverage their technology to improve productivity of Indian agriculture and use their access to global markets to increase exports from both the countries."

Secretary General of Kibbutz Naan, Mrs. Smadar Shavit said, "the JV Company will reap economic and strategic benefits of the synergies the two companies enjoy in drip/sprinkler business, to become a worldwide leader in the irrigation business."

A New Land Acquisition Act[84]

Throughout world history, whenever nations have embarked on the path of industrial growth, the process of land reforms and land acquisition has been tumultuous. The transition from an old economy to a new economy is complex, as it brings with itself a change in the socio-economic structures.

Conflict is bound to arise and this is what necessitates involvement of the state in detailing policies which are governed by the principle of what is good for the nation and its citizens, and are at the same time dynamic in nature. The process of land acquisition is critical for India, something which the Indian government has been cognizant off. As the government seeks greater private sector participation, including investment from overseas Indians and foreign players, to develop infrastructure and industrialize the economy, it has simultaneously embarked on the process to ensure that land acquisition is fast, timely and transparent, with fair and equitable compensation to those from whom land has been acquired.

The Group of Ministers (GoM) of the Indian Government approved the draft Land Acquisition Bill, paving way for the bill to be introduced in the Indian Parliament. The bill now named as "The Right to Fair Compensation, Resettlement, Rehabilitation and Transparency in Land Acquisition Bill", was introduced in the Indian Parliament in November 2012. However, the bill was referred to a Standing Committee as some quarters of the Government felt that it could become a hurdle in infrastructure development and lower investor sentiment.

The draft bill, which has been passed in the Parliament, now proposes consent of two-thirds of land owners for a private sector projects and joint private-public partnerships. The original bill required consent from 80 percent of project affected parties, which not only included land owners but also those whose livelihood depended on the area, to acquire the land.

From a scope perspective, the new law gives State governments the discretion to set the limit for application of Resettlement and Rehabilitation (R&R) provisions. The original avatar of the bill had set more than 100 acres in rural areas and more than 50 acres in urban areas as the limits from which R&R provisions would apply. State governments also get the flexibility to fix compensation in rural areas between two to four times the market value depending on the distance from urban areas, as opposed to the fixed four times market value compensation proposed in the original version.

Furthermore, the government will be able to acquire land for about 40 infrastructure-related sectors, which includes special economic zone, hotels outside urban areas as well as hospitals and educational institutions.

Land Acquisition, Rehabilitation and Resettlement Bill, 2011—An Insight into Some Key Issues

The Bill seeks to balance the need for facilitating land acquisition for various public purposes including infrastructure development, industrialization and urbanization, while at the same time, addressing the concerns of farmers and those whose livelihoods are dependent on the land being acquired. Some of the new changes made in the Bill include:

- Mandatory and better compensation for landowners and livelihood losers (compared to the 1894 Act)
- Inclusion of definition of "Landowners" and "Livelihood losers"
- Comprehensive Rehabilitation & Resettlement package for all private purchases through private negotiations if the land purchased is over 100 acres in rural areas or 50 acres in urban areas
- Need for consent of 80 percent of landowners for acquisition of land for Private projects for Public purposes and Private Public Partnership (PPP) projects,
- Provisions for Social Impact Assessment (SIA) before acquisition,
- Restrictions on acquiring multi- crop and agricultural land,
- Involvement of local authorities like Gram Sabha, Panchayats, etc., among others.

The Bill provides for a better and increased compensation package along with certain other allowances as compared to the erstwhile Act of 1894, which is likely to benefit the affected landowners and livelihood losers. But, at the same time, this is also likely to have an impact on the operating cost for the private and smaller players in the Real Estate market.

Although the Bill provides for a higher compensation package to the affected landowners and livelihood losers, a more practical and rational means of calculating the price of the land by linking it to the prevalent land prices or by a mechanism to determine prices through auctions might have served the purpose better.

Impact on FDI

The mandatory provisions of Rehabilitation and Resettlement reflects the socialistic approach of the Bill, but one concern which may arise is whether this is likely to create unplanned urbanization, disorganized human displacement and creation of slums. Another issue is whether the mandatory provisions of R&R for private players on acquisition of 100 acres of land in rural areas and 50 acres of land in urban areas will have any impact on the size of projects in order to save on the cost for R&R.

Considering the sentimental value of lands in India, the sensitivity of the issue of land acquisition and keeping in view the recent incidents witnessed in Singur (West Bengal) for Tata-Nano project, and other parts of the country, the mandatory provision for 80 percent consent of the affected people has been incorporated in the Bill which seeks to protect the interests of land-owners and also of those whose livelihoods depend on the land. But, on the flipside, this could raise a debate whether such a requirement has the potential to make the setting up of medium to large scale industries cumbersome and long drawn because of tedious transactional negotiations with large numbers of land owners.

Critics argue that the term 'public purpose' could have been better defined in the Bill without leaving it open ended for multiple interpretations. It has further been argued that the vagueness attached to the phrases "provisions of public service" and "production of public goods" in relation to public private partnerships and acquisition by private companies leaves a lot of discretionary powers with the government to determine the purpose of the acquisition.

The Bill also suggests that under no circumstances should multi-cropped and irrigated land be acquired for private and PPP projects, which is also appreciable. But since most lands available in the country are agricultural lands, it remains to be seen how the developers deal with the issue of availability of lands for their projects.

In conclusion, the new Bill is a much improved version of the erstwhile Act of 1894 as it seeks to strengthen the rights of landowners and potential livelihood losers. Only time will tell how it effectively balances the needs of the poor rural landowners and farmers and the aspirations of millions of Indians for affordable housing and infrastructure.

Acknowledgement

Adapted from material at India Brand Equity Fund website. Commons IPR, 2013.

Endnotes

1. P. Marsh, "Partnerships Feel the Indian Heat," *Financial Times,* June 22, 2006, p. 11; P. Marsh, "JCB Targets Asia to Spread Production," *Financial Times,* March 16, 2005, p. 26; D. Jones, "Profits Jump at JCB," *Daily Post,* June 20, 2006, p. 21; R. Bentley, "Still Optimistic about Asia," *Asian Business Review,* October 1, 1999, p. 1; "JCB Launches India-Specific Heavy Duty Crane," *The Hindu,* October 18, 2008; P. M. Thomas, "JCB Hits Pay Dirt in India," Forbes.com, December 6, 2011; and J. Moulds, "JCB Unearths Record Sales and Profits," *The Guardian,* April 17, 2012.

2. For interesting empirical studies that deal with the issues of timing and resource commitments, see T. Isobe, S. Makino, and D. B. Montgomery, "Resource Commitment, Entry Timing, and Market Performance of Foreign Direct Investments in Emerging Economies," *Academy of Management Journal* 43, no. 3 (2000), pp. 468–84; and Y. Pan and P. S. K. Chi, "Financial Performance and Survival of Multinational Corporations in China," *Strategic Management Journal* 20, no. 4 (1999), pp. 359–74. A complementary theoretical perspective on this issue can be found in V. Govindarjan and A. K. Gupta, *The Quest for Global Dominance* (San Francisco: Jossey-Bass, 2001). Also see F. Vermeulen and H. Barkeme, "Pace, Rhythm and Scope: Process Dependence in Building a Profitable Multinational Corporation," *Strategic Management Journal* 23 (2002), pp. 637–54.

3. This can be reconceptualized as the resource base of the entrant, relative to indigenous competitors. For work that focuses on this issue, see W. C. Bogner, H. Thomas, and J. McGee, "A Longitudinal Study of the Competitive Positions and Entry Paths of European Firms in the U.S. Pharmaceutical Market," *Strategic Management Journal* 17 (1996), pp. 85–107; D. Collis, "A Resource-Based Analysis of Global Competition," *Strategic Management Journal* 12 (1991), pp. 49–68; and S. Tallman, "Strategic Management Models and Resource-Based Strategies among MNEs in a Host Market," *Strategic Management Journal* 12 (1991), pp. 69–82.

4. For a discussion of first-mover advantages, see M. Lieberman and D. Montgomery, "First-Mover Advantages," *Strategic Management Journal* 9 (Summer Special Issue, 1988), pp. 41–58.

5. P. N. Child, "Taking Tesco Global," *The McKenzie Quarterly,* no. 3 (2002); H. Keers, "Global Tesco Sets Out Its Stall in China," *Daily Telegraph,* July 15, 2004, p. 31; K. Burgess, "Tesco Spends Pounds 140m on Chinese Partnership," *Financial Times,* July 15, 2004, p. 22; J. McTaggart, "Industry Awaits Tesco Invasion," *Progressive Grocer,* March 1, 2006, pp. 8–10; Tesco's annual reports, archived at www.tesco.com; P. Sonne, "Five Years and $1.6 Billion later, Tesco Decides to Quit US," *The Wall Street Journal,* December 6, 2012; and "Tesco Set to Push Ahead in the United States," *The Wall Street Journal,* October 6, 2010, p. 19.

6. J. M. Shaver, W. Mitchell, and B. Yeung, "The Effect of Own Firm and Other Firm Experience on Foreign Direct Investment Survival in the United States, 1987–92," *Strategic Management Journal* 18 (1997), pp. 811–24.

7. S. Zaheer and E. Mosakowski, "The Dynamics of the Liability of Foreignness: A Global Study of Survival in the Financial Services Industry," *Strategic Management Journal* 18 (1997), pp. 439–64.

8. Shaver, Mitchell, and Yeung, "The Effect of Own Firm and Other Firm Experience."

9. P. Ghemawat, *Commitment: The Dynamics of Strategy* (New York: Free Press, 1991).

10. R. Luecke, *Scuttle Your Ships before Advancing* (Oxford: Oxford University Press, 1994).

11. Isobe, Makino, and Montgomery, "Resource Commitment, Entry Timing, and Market Performance"; Pan and Chi, "Financial Performance and Survival of Multinational Corporations in China"; and Govindarjan and Gupta, *The Quest for Global Dominance.*

12. Christopher Bartlett and Sumantra Ghoshal, "Going Global: Lessons from Late Movers," *Harvard Business Review,* March–April 2000, pp. 132–45.

13. "Jollibee Battles Burger Giants in US Market," *Philippine Daily Inquirer,* July 13, 2000; M. Ballon, "Jollibee Struggling to Expand in U.S.," *Los Angeles Times,* September 16, 2002, p. C1; J. Hookway, "Burgers and Beer," *Far Eastern Economic Review,* December 2003, pp. 72–74; S. E. Lockyer, "Coming to America," *Nation's Restaurant News,* February 14, 2005, pp. 33–35; Erik de la Cruz, "Jollibee to Open 120 New Stores This Year, Plans India," *Inquirer Money,* July 5, 2006 (business.inquirer.net); and www.jollibee.com.ph.

14. This section draws on numerous studies, including C. W. L. Hill, P. Hwang, and W. C. Kim, "An Eclectic Theory of the Choice of International Entry Mode," *Strategic Management Journal* 11 (1990), pp. 117–28; C. W. L. Hill and W. C. Kim, "Searching for a Dynamic Theory of the Multinational Enterprise: A Transaction Cost Model," *Strategic Management Journal* 9 (Special Issue on Strategy Content, 1988), pp. 93–104; E. Anderson and H. Gatignon, "Modes of Foreign Entry: A Transaction Cost Analysis and Propositions," *Journal of International Business Studies* 17 (1986), pp. 1–26; F. R. Root, *Entry Strategies for International Markets* (Lexington, MA: D. C. Heath, 1980); A. Madhok, "Cost, Value and Foreign Market Entry: The Transaction and the Firm," *Strategic Management Journal* 18 (1997), pp. 39–61; K. D. Brothers and L. B. Brothers, "Acquisition or Greenfield Start-Up?" *Strategic Management Journal* 21, no. 1 (2000), pp. 89–97; X. Martin and R. Salmon, "Knowledge Transfer Capacity and Its Implications for the Theory of the Multinational Enterprise," *Journal of International Business Studies,* July 2003, p. 356; and A. Verbeke, "The Evolutionary View of the MNE and the Future of Internalization Theory," *Journal of International Business Studies,* November 2003, pp. 498–515.

15. For a general discussion of licensing, see F. J. Contractor, "The Role of Licensing in International Strategy," *Columbia Journal of World Business,* Winter 1982, pp. 73–83.

16. See E. Terazono and C. Lorenz, "An Angry Young Warrior," *Financial Times,* September 19, 1994, p. 11; and K. McQuade and B. Gomes-Casseres, "Xerox and Fuji-Xerox," Harvard Business School Case No. 9-391-156.

17. O. E. Williamson, *The Economic Institutions of Capitalism* (New York: Free Press, 1985).

18. J. H. Dunning and M. McQueen, "The Eclectic Theory of International Production: A Case Study of the International Hotel Industry," *Managerial and Decision Economics* 2 (1981), pp. 197–210.

19. Andrew E. Serwer, "McDonald's Conquers the World," *Fortune,* October 17, 1994, pp. 103–16.

20. For an excellent review of the basic theoretical literature of joint ventures, see B. Kogut, "Joint Ventures: Theoretical and Empirical Perspectives," *Strategic Management Journal* 9 (1988), pp. 319–32. More recent studies include T. Chi, "Option to Acquire or Divest a Joint Venture," *Strategic Management Journal* 21, no. 6 (2000), pp. 665–88; H. Merchant and D. Schendel, "How Do International Joint Ventures Create Shareholder Value?" *Strategic Management Journal* 21, no. 7 (2000), pp. 723–37; H. K. Steensma and M. A. Lyles, "Explaining IJV Survival in a Transitional Economy though Social Exchange and Knowledge Based Perspectives," *Strategic Management Journal* 21, no. 8 (2000), pp. 831–51; and J. F. Hennart and M. Zeng, "Cross Cultural Differences and Joint Venture Longevity," *Journal of International Business Studies,* December 2002, pp. 699–717.

21. D. G. Bradley, "Managing against Expropriation," *Harvard Business Review,* July–August 1977, pp. 78–90.

22. J. A. Robins, S. Tallman, and K. Fladmoe-Lindquist, "Autonomy and Dependence of International Cooperative Ventures," *Strategic Management Journal,* October 2002, pp. 881–902.

23. Speech given by Tony Kobayashi at the University of Washington Business School, October 1992.

24. A. C. Inkpen and P. W. Beamish, "Knowledge, Bargaining Power, and the Instability of International Joint Ventures," *Academy of Management Review* 22 (1997), pp. 177–202; and S. H. Park and G. R. Ungson, "The Effect of National Culture, Organizational Complementarity, and Economic Motivation on Joint Venture Dissolution," *Academy of Management Journal* 40 (1997), pp. 279–307.

25. Inkpen and Beamish, "Knowledge, Bargaining Power, and the Instability of International Joint Ventures."

26. See Brothers and Brothers, "Acquisition or Greenfield Start-Up?"; and J. F. Hennart and Y. R. Park, "Greenfield versus Acquisition: The Strategy of Japanese Investors in the United States," *Management Science,* 1993, pp. 1054–70.

27. This section draws on Hill, Hwang, and Kim, "An Eclectic Theory of the Choice of International Entry Mode."
28. C. W. L. Hill, "Strategies for Exploiting Technological Innovations: When and When Not to License," *Organization Science* 3 (1992), pp. 428–41.
29. See Brouthers and Brouthers, "Acquisition or Greenfield Start-Up?"; and J. Anand and A. Delios, "Absolute and Relative Resources as Determinants of International Acquisitions," *Strategic Management Journal,* February 2002, pp. 119–34.
30. United Nations, *World Investment Report, 2010* (New York and Geneva: United Nations, 2010).
31. Ibid.
32. For evidence on acquisitions and performance, see R. E. Caves, "Mergers, Takeovers, and Economic Efficiency," *International Journal of Industrial Organization* 7 (1989), pp. 151–74; M. C. Jensen and R. S. Ruback, "The Market for Corporate Control: The Scientific Evidence," *Journal of Financial Economics* 11 (1983), pp. 5–50; R. Roll, "Empirical Evidence on Takeover Activity and Shareholder Wealth," in *Knights, Raiders and Targets,* ed. J. C. Coffee, L. Lowenstein, and S. Rose (Oxford: Oxford University Press, 1989); A. Schleifer and R. W. Vishny, "Takeovers in the 60s and 80s: Evidence and Implications," *Strategic Management Journal* 12 (Winter 1991 Special Issue), pp. 51–60; T. H. Brush, "Predicted Changes in Operational Synergy and Post-acquisition Performance of Acquired Businesses," *Strategic Management Journal* 17 (1996), pp. 1–24; and A. Seth, K. P. Song, and R. R. Pettit, "Value Creation and Destruction in Cross-Border Acquisitions," *Strategic Management Journal* 23 (October 2002), pp. 921–40.
33. J. Warner, J. Templeman, and R. Horn, "The Case against Mergers," *BusinessWeek,* October 30, 1995, pp. 122–34.
34. "Few Takeovers Pay Off for Big Buyers," *Investor's Business Daily,* May 25, 2001, p. 1.
35. S. A. Christofferson, R. S. McNish, and D. L. Sias, "Where Mergers Go Wrong," *The McKinsey Quarterly* 2 (2004), pp. 92–110.
36. D. J. Ravenscraft and F. M. Scherer, *Mergers, Selloffs, and Economic Efficiency* (Washington, DC: Brookings Institution, 1987).
37. See P. Ghemawat and F. Ghadar, "The Dubious Logic of Global Mega-Mergers," *Harvard Business Review,* July–August 2000, pp. 65–72.
38. R. Roll, "The Hubris Hypothesis of Corporate Takeovers," *Journal of Business* 59 (1986), pp. 197–216.
39. "Marital Problems," *The Economist,* October 14, 2000.
40. See J. P. Walsh, "Top Management Turnover Following Mergers and Acquisitions," *Strategic Management Journal* 9 (1988), pp. 173–83.
41. B. Vlasic and B. A. Stertz, *Taken for a Ride: How Daimler-Benz Drove Off with Chrysler* (New York: HarperCollins, 2000).
42. See A. A. Cannella and D. C. Hambrick, "Executive Departure and Acquisition Performance," *Strategic Management Journal* 14 (1993), pp. 137–52.
43. P. Haspeslagh and D. Jemison, *Managing Acquisitions* (New York: Free Press, 1991).
44. Ibid.
45. See K. Ohmae, "The Global Logic of Strategic Alliances," *Harvard Business Review,* March–April 1989, pp. 143–54; G. Hamel, Y. L. Doz, and C. K. Prahalad, "Collaborate with Your Competitors and Win!" *Harvard Business Review,* January–February 1989, pp. 133–39; W. Burgers, C. W. L. Hill, and W. C. Kim, "Alliances in the Global Auto Industry," *Strategic Management Journal* 14 (1993), pp. 419–32; and P. Kale, H. Singh, and H. Perlmutter, "Learning and Protection of Proprietary Assets in Strategic Alliances: Building Relational Capital," *Strategic Management Journal* 21 (2000), pp. 217–37.
46. L. T. Chang, "China Eases Foreign Film Rules," *The Wall Street Journal,* October 15, 2004, p. B2.
47. B. L. Simonin, "Transfer of Marketing Know-How in International Strategic Alliances," *Journal of International Business Studies,* 1999, pp. 463–91; and J. W. Spencer, "Firms' Knowledge Sharing Strategies in the Global Innovation System," *Strategic Management Journal* 24 (2003), pp. 217–33.
48. C. Souza, "Microsoft Teams with MIPS, Toshiba," *EBN,* February 10, 2003, p. 4.
49. Kale, Singh, and Perlmutter, "Learning and Protection of Proprietary Assets."
50. R. B. Reich and E. D. Mankin, "Joint Ventures with Japan Give Away Our Future," *Harvard Business Review,* March–April 1986, pp. 78–90.
51. J. Bleeke and D. Ernst, "The Way to Win in Cross-Border Alliances," *Harvard Business Review,* November–December 1991, pp. 127–35.
52. C. H. Deutsch, "The Venturesome Giant," *The New York Times*, October 5, 2007, pp. C1, C8.
53. "Odd Couple: Jet Engines," *The Economist*, May 5, 2007, pp. 79–80.
54. W. Roehl and J. F. Truitt, "Stormy Open Marriages Are Better," *Columbia Journal of World Business,* Summer 1987, pp. 87–95.
55. McQuade and Gomes-Casseres, "Xerox and Fuji-Xerox."

56. See T. Khanna, R. Gulati, and N. Nohria, "The Dynamics of Learning Alliances: Competition, Cooperation, and Relative Scope," *Strategic Management Journal* 19 (1998), pp. 193–210; and Kale, Singh, and Perlmutter, "Learning and Protection of Proprietary Assets."

57. Kale, Singh, Perlmutter, "Learning and Protection of Proprietary Assets."

58. Hamel, Doz, and Prahalad, "Collaborate with Your Competitors"; Khanna, Gulati, and Nohria, "The Dynamics of Learning Alliances"; and E. W. K. Tang, "Acquiring Knowledge by Foreign Partners from International Joint Ventures in a Transition Economy: Learning by Doing and Learning Myopia," *Strategic Management Journal* 23 (2002), pp. 835–54.

59. Hamel, Doz, and Prahalad, "Collaborate with Your Competitors."

60. B. Wysocki, "Cross-Border Alliances Become Favorite Way to Crack New Markets," *The Wall Street Journal,* March 4, 1990, p. A1.

61. Hamel, Doz, and Prahalad, "Collaborate with Your Competitors," p. 138.

62. S. Schifferes, "Cracking China's Car Market,*" BBC News,* May 17, 2007; N. Madden, "Led by Buick, Carmaker Learning Fine Points of Regional China Tastes," *Automotive News,* September 15, 2008, pp. 186–90; "GM Posts Record Sales in China," *Toronto Star,* January 5, 2010, p. B4; "GM's Sales in China Top US," *Investor's Business Daily,* January 25, 2011, p. A1; and K. Naughton, "GM's China Bet Mimics Toyota's Bet on U.S. Last Century," Bloomberg.com, April 29, 2013.

63. http://www.marketsandmarkets.com/Market-Reports/micro-irrigation-system-market-566.html

64. Op. cit. 1

65. http://corporate.indbankonline.com/documents/JainIrrigationSystemsLtd.pdf

66. http://stockshastra.moneyworks4me.com/jain-irrigation-drip-systems-agri-green-cleantech-investment-opportunity-for-future/

67. http://en.wikipedia.org/wiki/Jain_Irrigation_Systems#cite_note-8

68. http://economictimes.indiatimes.com/jain-irrigation-systems-ltd/infocompanyhistory/companyid-13532.cms

69. http://www.newaginternational.com/news/news108/news108.html

70. http://www.capitalmarket.com/CMEdit/story2-0.asp?SNo=116382

71. http://www.domain-b.com/management/m_a/20061120_acquires.html

72. http://www.jains.com/Company/News/Aquarius%20brands%20acquistion.htm

73. http://www.business-standard.com/india/news/jain-irrigation-buys-50-in-israel-firm/285911/

74. http://www.vccircle.com/news/others/2010/11/03/jain-irrigation-acquires-80-uk-based-sleaford

75. http://www.globes.co.il/serveen/globes/docview.asp?did=1000748674&fid=1725

76. http://business.outlookindia.com/article.aspx?282315

77. http://excelpest.in/Company/News/Jain%20Irrigation%20to%20acquire%2050%20stake%20in%20NaanDan.htm

78. Op. cit above

79. NaanDanhttp://www.indiawaterreview.in/Story/News/jain-irrigation-to-buy-out-israeli-partner-in-NaanDanjain/671/1#.ULyL5-SE1n4

80. http://excelpest.in/Company/News/Jain%20Irrigation%20to%20acquire%2050%20stake%20in%20NaanDan.htm

81. http://en.wikipedia.org/wiki/BBDO

82. India Water Review : May 16, 2012

83. Source: NaanDanhttp://www.indiawaterreview.in/Story/News/jain-irrigation-to-buy-out-israeli-partner-in-NaanDanjain/671/1#.ULyL5-SE1n4

84. Based on article by **Souvik Mukherjee,** Associate Corporate Professionals, Advocates & Solicitors, on Nov 14, 2012 http://www.oifc.in/Investing-in-India/Investment-Info/Insight/Land-Acquisition-Rehabilitation-and-Resettlement-Bill-2011-An-Insight-into-some-key-Issues

C-A-S-E-S

THE EVOLVING STRATEGY OF IBM

IBM's former CEO, Sam Palmisano, liked to talk about the evolution of global strategy at one of the world's largest computer enterprises. According to Palmisano, when IBM first started to expand internationally, it did so in the classic "international" pattern of many enterprises, undertaking most of its activities at home and selling its products internationally through overseas sales offices. By the time Palmisano joined IBM in 1972, the company had already moved away from this model and was a classic "multinational" enterprise, with mini-IBM's in major national markets around the world. This structure made sense for IBM in the 1970s, given that many markets were still segmented from each other by high barriers to cross-border trade and given that national differences in business practices often required considerable localization.

In recent decades, IBM has moved away from this model and towards one that Palmisano characterizes as a "globally integrated enterprise." In his words:

> We are locating work and operations anywhere in the world based on economics, expertise, and the right business environment. We are integrating those operations horizontally and globally. We used to have separate supply chains in different markets. Now we have one supply chain, a global one. Our R&D has been global for many years, with research and software development carried out in labs around the world. But in our professional services businesses, where we used to think about our human capital—our people—in terms of countries, and regions, and business units, we now manage and deploy them as one global asset.

Thus today's IBM locates its semiconductor R&D and manufacturing operation in upstate New York and Vermont and its global procurement center in China. Global services delivery is in India, while many of the services that support IBM's external and internal websites are in places like Ireland and Brazil. The people at each of these centers are not focused on their national markets; they are leading integrated global operations.

This strategic shift was a response to three things: the globalization of the world economy; the global nature of many of IBM's customers, who were themselves shifting towards a global integration strategy; and the emergence of fierce competition from enterprises in emerging markets such as China and India. Take India as an example; in the 1990s a trio of Indian outsourcing firms, Tata Consulting Services, Infosys, and Wipro started to take share away from IBM in its core information technology services business. The Indians enjoyed an advantage based on a large supply of highly educated but relative inexpensive engineering and managerial talent. IBM felt that to compete, it had to adopt the low-cost model being pioneered in India. So in 2004, it bought Daksh, an Indian firm that was a smaller version of India's big three information technology services firms. IBM has invested heavily in its Indian unit, building it into a large global business with leading market share that now competes effectively on cost and quality against its Indian rivals. While Palmisano notes that the original motivation for expanding in India was to gain access to low-cost labor, he now argues that the skill base in India is just as important, if not more so. IBM can find a large supply of highly skilled people in India who can staff its global services operations and move seamlessly around the world. It doesn't hurt that most Indians have a good command of the English language, which has become the de facto language of business in much of the world.

Palmisano stresses that IBM has some way to go in its journey to become a fully integrated global enterprise. The big thrust going forward will be on developing the human capital of the enterprise—helping produce managers and engineers who see themselves as global professionals, and global citizens, who are able to move effortlessly around the world, and do business effectively in wide range of national contexts.

Case Discussion Questions

1. In the 1970s and 1980s Palmisano states that IBM was organized as a classic multinational enterprise. What does this mean? Why do you think IBM was organized that way? What were the advantages of this kind of strategic orientation?
2. By the 1990s the classic multinational strategic orientation was no longer working well for IBM. Why not?
3. What are the strategic advantages to IBM of its globally integrated enterprise strategy? What kind of organizational changes do you think had to be made at IBM to make this strategy a reality?
4. In terms of the strategic choice framework introduced in this chapter, what strategy do you think IBM is pursuing today?

Sources

"The Empire Fights Back," *The Economist,* September 30, 2008, pp. 12–16; S. Palmisano, "The Globally Integrated Enterprise," *Vital Speeches of the Day,* October 2007, pp. 449–53; and S. Hamm, "IBM vs. Tata: Which Is More American?" *BusinessWeek,* October 5, 2008, p. 28.

IKEA in 2013: Furniture Retailer to the World

Introduction

IKEA is one of the world's most successful global retailers. By 2012 IKEA had 320 home-furnishing superstores in 40 countries and was visited by some 776 million shoppers. IKEA's low-priced, elegantly designed merchandise, displayed in large warehouse stores, generated sales of €27.5 billion in 2012, up from €4.4 billion in 1994, and €4.2 billion in net profit. Although the privately held company refuses to publish detailed financial data, its net profit margins were rumored to be around 10 percent, high for a retailer. The founder, Ingvar Kamprad, now in his 80s but still an active "adviser" to the company, is rumored to be one of the world's richest men.

Company Background

IKEA was established by Ingvar Kamprad in Sweden in 1943 when he was 17 years old. The fledgling company sold fish, Christmas magazines, and seeds from his family farm. It wasn't his first business—that had been selling matches, which the enterprising Kamprad had purchased wholesale in 100-box lots (with help from his grandmother who financed the enterprise) and then resold them individually at a higher markup. The name IKEA is an acronym, *I* and *K* being his initials, while *E* stood for Elmtaryd, the name of the family farm, and *A* stood for Agunnaryd, the name of the village in southern Sweden where the farm was located. Before long Kamprad had added ballpoint pens to his list and was selling his products via mail order. His warehouse was a shed on the family farm. The customer fulfillment system utilized the local milk truck, which picked up goods daily and took them to the train station.

In 1948 Kamprad added furniture to his product line, and in 1949 he published his first catalog, distributed then, as now, for free. In 1953 Kamprad found himself struggling with another problem, the milk tuck had changed its route, and he could no longer use it to take goods to the train station. Kamprad's solution was to buy an idle factory in nearby Almhult and convert it into his warehouse. With business now growing rapidly, Kamprad hired a 22-year-old designer, Gillis Lundgren. Lundgren originally helped Kamprad do photo shoots for the early IKEA catalogs, but over time he started to design more and more furniture for IKEA, eventually designing as many as 400 pieces, including many best sellers.

IKEA's goal as it emerged over time was to provide stylish, functional designs with minimalist lines that could be manufactured cost efficiently under contract by suppliers and priced low enough to allow most people to afford them. Kamprad's theory was that "good furniture could be priced so that the man with that flat wallet would make a place for it in his spending and could afford it."[1] Kamprad was struck by the fact that furniture in Sweden was expensive at the time, something that he attributed to a fragmented industry dominated by small retailers. Furniture was also often considered a family heirloom, passed down across the generations. He wanted to change this: to make it possible for people of modest means to buy their own furniture. Ultimately, this led to the concept of what IKEA calls "democratic design"—a design that, according to Kamprad, "was not just good, but also from the start adapted to machine production and thus cheap to assemble."[2] Gillis Lundgren was instrumental in the implementation of this concept. Time and time again he would find ways to alter the design of furniture to save on manufacturing costs.

Gillis Lundgren also stumbled on what was to become a key feature of IKEA furniture: self-assembly. Trying to efficiently pack and ship a long-legged table, he hit upon the idea of taking the legs off and mailing them packed flat under the tabletop. Kamprad quickly noticed that flat-packed furniture reduced transport and warehouse costs, and also reduced damage (IKEA had been having a lot of problems with furniture damaged during the shipping process). Moreover, customers seemed willing to take on the task of assembly in return for lower prices. By 1956, self-assembly was integral to the IKEA concept.

In 1957 IKEA started to exhibit and sell its products at home-furnishing fairs in Sweden. By cutting retailers out of the equation and using the self-assembly concept, Kamprad could undercut the prices of established retail outlets, much to their chagrin. Established retailers responded by prohibiting IKEA from taking orders at the annual furniture trade in Stockholm. Established outlets claimed that IKEA was imitating their designs. This was to no avail, however, so the retailers went further, pressuring furniture manufacturers not to sell to IKEA. This had two unintended consequences. First, without access to the designs of many manufacturers, IKEA was forced to design more of its products

---

[1]Quoted in R. Heller, "Folk Fortune," *Forbes,* September 4, 2000, p. 67.
[2]B. Torekull, *Leading by Design: The IKEA Story* (New York: Harper Collins, 1998), p. 53.

in-house. Second, Kamprad looked for a manufacturer who would produce the IKEA-designed furniture. Ultimately he found one in Poland.

To his delight, Kamprad discovered that furniture manufactured in Poland was as much as 50 percent cheaper than furniture made in Sweden, allowing him to cut prices even further. Kamprad also found that doing business with the Poles required the consumption of considerable amounts of vodka to celebrate business transactions, and for the next 40 years his drinking was legendary. Alcohol consumption apart, the relationship that IKEA established with the Poles was to become the archetype for future relationships with suppliers. According to one of the Polish managers, there were three advantages of doing business with IKEA:

> One concerned the decision making; it was always one man's decision, and you could rely upon what had been decided. We were given long-term contracts, and were able to plan in peace and quiet. . . . A third advantage was that IKEA introduced new technology. One revolution for instance, was a way of treating the surface of wood. They also mastered the ability to recognize cost savings that could trim the price.[3]

By the early 1960s, Polish-made goods were to be found on over half the pages of the IKEA catalog.

By 1958, an expanded facility at the Almhult location became the first IKEA store. The original idea behind the store was to have a location where customers could come and see IKEA furniture set up. It was a supplement to IKEA's main mail-order business; but it very quickly became an important sales point in its own right. The store soon started to sell car roof racks so that customers could leave with flat-packed furniture loaded on top. Noticing that a trip to an IKEA store was something of an outing for many shoppers (Almhult was not a major population center, and people often drove in from long distances), Kamprad experimented with adding a restaurant to the Almhult store so that customers could relax and refresh themselves while shopping. The restaurant was a hit, and it became an integral feature of all IKEA stores.

The response of IKEA's competitors to its success was to argue that IKEA products were of low quality. In 1964, just after 800,000 IKEA catalogs had been mailed to Swedish homes, the widely read Swedish magazine *Allt i Hemmet* (*Everything for the Home*) published a comparison of IKEA furniture to that sold in traditional Swedish retailers. The furniture was tested for quality in a Swedish design laboratory. The magazine's analysis, detailed in a 16-page spread, was that not only was IKEA's quality as good if not better than that from other Swedish furniture manufacturers but also the prices were much lower. For example, the magazine concluded that a chair bought at IKEA for 33 kroner ($4) was better than a virtually identical one bought in a more expensive store for 168 kroner ($21). The magazine also showed how a living room furnished with IKEA products was as much as 65 percent less expensive than one furnished with equivalent products from four other stores. This publicity made IKEA acceptable in middle-class households, and sales began to take off.

In 1965, IKEA opened its first store in Stockholm, Sweden's capital. By now, IKEA was generating the equivalent of €25 million and had already opened a store in neighboring Norway. The Stockholm store, its third, was the largest furniture store in Europe and had an innovative circular design that was modeled on the famous Guggenheim Art Museum in New York. The location of the store was to set the pattern at IKEA for decades. The store was situated on the outskirts of the city, rather than downtown, and there was ample space for parking and good access roads. The new store generated a large amount of traffic, so much so that employees could not keep up with customer orders, and long lines formed at the checkouts and merchandise pickup areas. To try and reduce the lines, IKEA experimented with a self-service pickup solution, allowing shoppers to enter the warehouse, load flat-packed furniture onto trolleys, and then take them through the checkout. It was so successful that this soon became the norm in all stores.

---

[3]Ibid., pp. 61–62.

International Expansion

By 1973 IKEA was the largest furniture retailer in Scandinavia with nine stores. The company enjoyed a market share of 15 percent in Sweden. Kamprad, however, felt that growth opportunities were limited. Starting with a single store in Switzerland, over the next 15 years the company expanded rapidly in western Europe. IKEA meet with considerable success, particularly in West Germany where it had 15 stores by the late 1980s. As in Scandinavia, western European furniture markets were largely fragmented and served by high-cost retailers located in expensive downtown stores and selling relatively expensive furniture that was not always immediately available for delivery. IKEA's elegant functional designs with their clean lines, low prices, and immediate availability were a breath of fresh air, as was the self-service store format. The company was met with almost universal success even though, as one former manager put it: "We made every mistake in the book, but money nevertheless poured in. We lived frugally, drinking now and again, yes perhaps too much, but we were on our feet bright and cheery when the doors were open for the first customers, competing in good Ikean spirit for the cheapest solutions."[4]

The man in charge of the European expansion was Jan Aulino, Kamprad's former assistant, who was just 34 years old when the expansion started. Aulino surrounded himself with a young team. Aulino recalled that the expansion was so fast-paced that the stores were rarely ready when IKEA moved in. Moreover, it was hard to get capital out of Sweden due to capital controls, so the trick was to make a quick profit and get a positive cash flow going as soon as possible. In the haste to expand, Aulino and his team did not always pay attention to detail, and he reportedly clashed with Kamprad on several occasions and considered himself fired at least four times, although he never was. Eventually the European business was reorganized and tighter controls were introduced.

IKEA was slow to expand in the UK, however, where the locally grown company Habitat had built a business that was similar in many respects to IKEA, offering stylish furniture and at a relatively low price. IKEA also entered North America, opening seven stores in Canada between 1976 and 1982. Emboldened by this success, in 1985 the company entered the United States. It proved to be a challenge of an entirely different nature.

On the face of it, America looked to be fertile territory for IKEA. As in western Europe, furniture retailing was a very fragmented business in the United States. At the low end of the market were the general discount retailers, such as Walmart, Costco, and Office Depot, which sold a limited product line of basic furniture, often at a very low price. This furniture was very functional, lacked the design elegance associated with IKEA, and was generally of a fairly low quality. Then there were higher-end retailers, such as Ethan Allen, which offered high-quality, well-designed, and high-priced furniture. It sold this furniture in full-service stores staffed by knowledgeable salespeople. High-end retailers would often sell ancillary services as well, such as interior design. Typically these retailers would offer home delivery service, including setup in the home, either for free or for a small additional charge. Since it was expensive to keep large inventories of high-end furniture, much of what was on display in stores was not readily available, and the client would often have to wait a few weeks before it was delivered.

IKEA opened its first U.S. store in 1985 in Philadelphia. The company had decided to locate on the coasts. Surveys of American consumers suggested that IKEA buyers were more likely to be people who had traveled abroad, who considered themselves risk takers, and who liked fine food and wine. These people were concentrated on the coasts. As one manager put it, "there are more Buicks driven in the middle than on the coasts."[5]

---

[4]Ibid., p. 109.

[5]J. Leland, "How the Disposable Sofa Conquered America," *The New York Times Magazine,* October 5, 2005, p. 45.

Although IKEA initially garnered favorable reviews, and enough sales to persuade it to start opening additional stores, by the early 1990s it was clear that things were not going well in America. The company found that its European-style offerings didn't always resonate with American consumers. Beds were measured in centimeters, not the king, queen, and twin sizes with which Americans are familiar. American sheets didn't fit on IKEA beds. Sofas weren't big enough, wardrobe drawers were not deep enough, glasses were too small, curtains too short, and kitchens didn't fit U.S.-size appliances. In a story often repeated at IKEA, managers noted that customers were buying glass vases and using them to drink out of, rather than the small glasses for sale at IKEA. The glasses were apparently too small for Americans who like to add liberal quantities of ice to their drinks. To make matters worse, IKEA was sourcing many of the goods from overseas, and they were priced in Swedish kroner, which was strengthening against the U.S. dollar. This drove up the price of goods in IKEA's American stores. Moreover, some of the stores were poorly located, and the stores were not large enough to offer the full IKEA experience familiar to Europeans.

Turning around its American operations required IKEA to take some decisive actions. Many products had to be redesigned to fit with American needs. Newer and larger store locations were chosen. To bring prices down, goods were sourced from lower-cost locations and priced in dollars. IKEA also started to source some products from factories in the United States to reduce both transport costs and dependency on the value of the dollar. At the same time, IKEA was noticing a change in American culture. Americans were becoming more concerned with design and more open to the idea of disposable furniture. It used to be said that Americans changed their spouses about as often as they changed their dining room table, about 1.5 times in a lifetime, but something was shifting in American culture. Younger people were more open to risks and more willing to experiment, and there was a thirst for design elegance and quality. Starbucks was tapping into this, as was Apple Computer, and so did IKEA. According to one manager at IKEA, "ten or 15 years ago, travelling in the United States, you couldn't eat well. You couldn't get good coffee. Now you can get good bread in the supermarket, and people think that is normal. I like that very much. That is more important to good life than the availability of expensive wines. That is what IKEA is about."[6]

To tap into America's shifting culture, IKEA reemphasized design, and it started promoting itself with a series of quirky hip advertisements aimed at a younger demographic: young married couples, college students, and twenty- to thirty-something singles. One IKEA commercial, called "Unboring," made fun of the reluctance of Americans to part with their furniture. One famous ad featured a discard lamp, forlorn and forsaken in some rainy American city. A man turns to the camera sympathetically. "Many of you feel bad for this lamp," he says in thick Swedish accent. "That is because you are crazy." Hip people, the commercial implied, bought furniture at IKEA. Hip people didn't hang onto their furniture either; after a while they discarded it and replaced it with something else from IKEA.

The shift in tactics worked. IKEA's revenues doubled in a four-year period to $1.27 billion in 2001, up from $600 million in 1997. By 2012 the United States was IKEA's largest market after Germany, with 44 stores accounting for 14 percent of the global total revenues.

Having learnt vital lessons about competing in foreign countries outside of continental western Europe, IKEA continued to expand internationally in the 1990s and 2000s. It first entered the UK in 1987 and by 2012 had 18 stores in the country. IKEA also acquired Britain's Habitat in the early 1990s, and continued to run it under the Habitat brand name. In 1998, IKEA entered China, where it had 14 stores by 2012, followed by Russia in 2000 (14 stores by 2012), and in 2006 Japan, a country where it had failed miserably 30 years earlier (by 2012 IKEA had 6 stores in Japan). In total, by 2012 there were 320 IKEA stores in 40 countries

---

[6]Ibid., p. 45.

and territories. The company's plans call for continued global expansion, opening 20–25 stores per year, funded by an investment of around €20 billion.

IKEA's latest target market is India, where it has plans to invest €1.5 billion and ultimately open 25 stores. In late 2012 India's foreign investment board approved IKEA's plans to open stores in the country. However, the approval came with strings attached. The board denied IKEA offering products in areas that the government thinks are politically sensitive and where it wants to protect local retailers. These include food and beverage outlets, which are a standard feature of IKEA stores around the world, and 18 of the 30 product categories it had initially applied for. Those 18 categories include gift items, fabrics, books, toys, and consumer electronics. It remains to be seen how IKEA will adapt to these retractions.[7]

As with the United States, some local customization has been the order of the day. In China, for example, the store layout reflects the layout of many Chinese apartments, and since many Chinese apartments have balconies, IKEA's Chinese

Exhibit 1   IKEA by the Numbers in 2012

IKEA stores	238 in 40 countries
IKEA sales	€27.5 billion
IKEA suppliers	1,030 in 54 countries*
The IKEA range	9,500 products
IKEA coworkers	154,000 in 40 countries

Source: Company website.

*The supplier figures are for 2008. IKEA has not published detailed data on suppliers in recent years.

Exhibit 2   Sales and Suppliers

Top Five Sales Countries		Top Five Supplying Countries	
Germany	15%	China	21%
USA	12%	Poland	17%
France	10%	Italy	8%
US	7%	Sweden	6%
Sweden	6%	Germany	6%

Source: Company website.

stores include a balcony section. IKEA also has had to adapt its locations in China, where car ownership is still not widespread. In the West, IKEA stores are generally located in suburban areas and have lots of parking space. In China, stores are located near public transportation, and IKEA offers delivery services so that Chinese customers can get their purchases home. IKEA has also adopted a deep price discounting model in China, pricing some items as much as 70 percent below their price in IKEA stores outside China. To make this work, IKEA has sourced a large percentage of its products sold in China from local suppliers.

On thing that IKEA has refused to adapt to, however, are business practices that clash with its values. The company prides itself on its "clean" image and is willing to halt investment in order to protect that. In the mid 2000s it put investment in Russia on hold as a protest against endemic corruption. It subsequently fired two senior executives in the country for allegedly turning a bribe to a subcontractor to secure electricity supply for its St Petersburg outlets.[8]

Senior executives at IKEA have been know to complain that they could expand the business faster, were it not for administrative "red tape" in many countries that slows down the rate of expansion. According to the current CEO, Mikael Ohlsson, the amount of time it takes to open a store has roughly doubled to 5 or 6 years since the 1990s. Ohlsson singled out German local authorities as having planning restrictions designed to protect local city center shops that are detrimental to IKEA's expansion plans.

---

[7]Manu Kaushik, "Conditions Apply," *Business Today,* December 23, 2010.
[8]"The Secret of IKEA's Success," *The Economist,* February 24, 2011.

Ohlsson argues that such regulations are holding back investment by IKEA, and thus job creation, across the European Union.[9]

The IKEA Concept and Business Model

IKEA's target market is the young upwardly mobile global middle class who are looking for low-priced but attractively designed furniture and household items. This group is targeted with somewhat wacky offbeat advertisements that help drive traffic into the stores. The stores themselves are large warehouses festooned in the blue and yellow colors of the Swedish flag that offer 8,000 to 10,000 items, from kitchen cabinets to candlesticks. There is plenty of parking outside, and the stores are located with good access to major roads.

The interior of the stores is configured almost as a maze that requires customers to pass through each department to get to the checkout. The goal is simple; to get customers to make more impulse purchases as they wander through the IKEA wonderland. Customers who enter the store planning to buy a $40 coffee table can end up spending $500 on everything from storage units to kitchenware. The flow of departments is constructed with an eye to boosting sales. For example, when IKEA managers noticed that men would get bored while their wives stopped in the home textile department, they added a tool section just outside the textile department, and sales of tools skyrocketed. At the end of the maze, just before the checkout, is the warehouse where customers can pick up their flat-packed furniture. IKEA stores also have restaurants (located in the middle of the store) and child-care facilities (located at the entrance for easy drop-off) so that shoppers stay as long as possible.

Products are designed to reflect the clean Swedish lines that have become IKEA's trademark. IKEA has a product strategy council, which is a group of senior managers who establish priorities for IKEA's product lineup. Once a priority is established, product developers survey the competition, and then set a price point that is 30–50 percent below that of rivals. As IKEA's website states, "we design the price tag first, then the product." Once the price tag is set, designers work with a network of suppliers to drive down the cost of producing the unit. The goal is to identify the appropriate suppliers and least costly materials, a trial-and-error process that can take as long as three years. In 2008 IKEA had 1,380 suppliers in 54 countries. The top sourcing countries were China (21 percent of supplies), Poland (17 percent), Italy (8 percent), Sweden (6 percent), and Germany (6 percent).

IKEA devotes considerable attention to finding the right supplier for each item. Consider the company's best-selling Klippan love seat. Designed in 1980, the Klippan, with its clean lines, bright colors, simple legs, and compact size, has sold over 1.5 million units by 2010. IKEA originally manufactured the product in Sweden but soon transferred production to lower-cost suppliers in Poland. As demand for the Klippan grew, IKEA then decided that it made more sense to work with suppliers in each of the company's big markets to avoid the costs associated with shipping the product all over the world. In 2010 there were five suppliers of the frames in Europe, plus three in the United States and two in China. To reduce the cost of the cotton slipcovers, IKEA concentrated production in four core suppliers in China and Europe. The resulting efficiencies from these global sourcing decisions enabled IKEA to reduce the price of the Klippan by some 40 percent between 1999 and 2005.

Although IKEA contracts out manufacturing for most of its products, since the early 1990s a certain proportion of goods have been made internally (today around 90 percent of all products are sourced from independent suppliers, with 10 percent being produced internally). The integration into manufacturing was born out of the collapse of Communist governments in eastern Europe after the fall of the Berlin Wall in 1989. By 1991 IKEA was sourcing some 25 percent of its goods from eastern European

[9]Richard Milne, "Red Tape Frustrates IKEA's Plans for Growth," *Financial Times,* January 25, 2013.

manufacturers. It had invested considerable energy in building long-term relationships with these suppliers, and had often helped them to develop and purchase new technology so that they could make IKEA products at a lower cost. As communism collapsed and new bosses came in to the factories, many did not feel bound by the relationships with IKEA. They effectively tore up contracts, tried to raise prices, and underinvested in new technology.

With its supply base at risk, IKEA purchased a Swedish manufacturer, Swedwood. IKEA then used Swedwood as the vehicle to buy and run furniture manufacturers across eastern Europe, with the largest investments being made in Poland. IKEA invested heavily in its Swedwood plants, equipping them with the most modern technology. Beyond the obvious benefits of given IKEA a low-cost source of supply, Swedwood has also enabled IKEA to acquire knowledge about manufacturing processes that are useful both in product design and in relationships with other suppliers, giving IKEA the ability to help suppliers adopt new technology and drive down their costs.

For illustration, consider IKEA's relationship with suppliers in Vietnam. IKEA has expanded its supply base here to help support its growing Asian presence. IKEA was attracted to Vietnam by the combination of low-cost labor and inexpensive raw materials. IKEA drives a tough bargain with its suppliers, many of whom say that they make thinner margins on their sales to IKEA than they do with other foreign buyers. IKEA demands high quality at a low price. But there is an upside; IKEA offers the prospect of forging a long-term, high-volume business relationship. Moreover, IKEA regularly advises its Vietnamese suppliers on how to seek out the best and cheapest raw materials, how to set up and expand factories, what equipment to purchase, and how to boost productivity through technology investments and management process.

Organization and Management

In many ways IKEA's organization and management practices reflect the personal philosophy of its founder. A 2004 article in *Fortune* describes Kamprad, then one of the world's richest men, as an informal and frugal man who "insists on flying coach, takes the subway to work, drives a ten year old Volvo, and avoids suits of any kind. It has long been rumored in Sweden that when his self-discipline fails and he drinks an overpriced Coke out of a hotel mini bar, he will go down to a grocery store to buy a replacement."[10] Kamprad's thriftiness is attributed to his upbringing in Smaland, a traditionally poor region of Sweden. Kamprad's frugality is now part of IKEA's DNA. Managers are forbidden to fly first class and expected to share hotel rooms.

Under Kamprad, IKEA became mission-driven. He had a cause, and those who worked with him adopted it too. It was to make life better for the masses, to democratize furniture. Kamprad's management style was informal, nonhierarchical, and team-based. Titles and privileges are taboo at IKEA. There are no special perks for senior managers. Pay is not particularly high, and people generally work there because they like the atmosphere. Suits and ties have always been absent, from the head office to the loading docks. The culture is egalitarian. Offices are open plan, furnished with IKEA furniture, and private offices are rare. Everyone is called a "coworker," and first names are used throughout. IKEA regularly stages antibureaucracy weeks during which executives work on the store floor or tend to registers. In a *BusinessWeek* article then CEO, Andres Dahlvig, described how he spent sometime earlier in the year unloading trucks and selling beds and mattresses.[11] Creativity is highly valued, and the company is replete with stories of individuals taking the initiative; from Gillis Lundgren's pioneering of the self-assemble concept to the store manager in the Stockhom store who let customers go into the

[10]C. Daniels and A. Edstrom, "Create IKEA, Make Billions, Take a Bus," *Fortune*, May 3, 2006, p. 44.
[11]K. Capell et al., "Ikea," *BusinessWeek*, November 14, 2005, pp. 96–106.

warehouse to pick up their own furniture. To solidify this culture, IKEA had a preference for hiring younger people who had not worked for other enterprises and then promoting from within. IKEA has historically tended to shy away from hiring the highly educated status-oriented elite because they often adapted poorly to the company.

Kamprad seems to have viewed his team as extended family. Back in 1957 he bankrolled a weeklong trip to Spain for all 80 employees and their families as reward for hard work. The early team of employees all lived near each other. They worked together, played together, drank together, and talked about IKEA around the clock. When asked by an academic researcher what was the fundamental key to good leadership, Kamprad replied, "Love." Recollecting the early days, he noted that "when we were working as a small family in Almhult, we were as if in love. Nothing whatsoever to do with eroticism. We just liked each other so damn much."[12] Another manager noted that "we who wanted to join IKEA did so because the company suits our way of life. To escape thinking about status, grandeur and smart clothes."[13]

As IKEA grew, the question of taking the company public arose. While there were obvious advantages associated with doing so, including access to capital, Kamprad decided against it. His belief was that the stock market would impose short-term pressures on IKEA that would not be good for the company. The constant demands to produce profits, regardless of the business cycle, would in Kamprad's view, make it more difficult for IKEA to take bold decisions. At the same time, as early as 1970 Kamprad stared to worry about what would happen if he died. He decided that he did not want his sons to inherit the business. His worry was that they would either sell the company, or they might squabble over control of the company, and thus destroy it. All three of his sons, it should be noted, went to work at IKEA as managers.

The solution to this dilemma created one of the most unusual corporate structures in the world. In 1982 Kamprad transferred his interest in IKEA to a Dutch-based charitable foundation, Stichting Ingka Foundation. This is a tax-exempt, nonprofit legal entity that in turn owns Ingka Holding, a private Dutch firm that is the legal owner of IKEA. A five-person committee chaired by Kamprad and which includes his wife runs the foundation. In addition, the IKEA trademark and concept was transferred to IKEA Systems, another private Dutch company, whose parent company, Inter-IKEA, is based in Luxembourg. The Luxembourg company is in turn owned by an identically named company in the Netherlands Antilles, whose beneficial owners remain hidden from public view, but they are almost certainly the Kamprad family. Inter-IKEA earns its money from a franchise agreement it has with each IKEA store. The largest franchisee is none other than Ingka Holdings. IKEA states that franchisees pay 3 percent of sales to Inter-IKEA. Thus, Kamprad has effectively moved ownership of IKEA out of Sweden, although the company's identity and headquarters remains there, and established a mechanism for transferring funds to himself and his family from the franchising of the IKEA concept. Kamprad himself moved to Switzerland in the 1980s to escape Sweden's high taxes, and he has lived there ever since.

In 1986, Kamprad gave up day-to-day control of IKEA to Andres Moberg, a 36–year-old Swede who had dropped out of college to join IKEA's mail-order department. Despite relinquishing management control, Kamprad continued to exert influence over the company as an adviser to senior management and an ambassador for IKEA, a role he was still pursuing with vigor in 2012, despite being in his mid-80s.

---

[12]B. Torekull, *Leading by Design: The IKEA Story,* p. 82.
[13]Ibid., p. 83.

Looking Forward

In its half-century, IKEA had established an enviable position for itself. It had become one of the most successful retail establishments in the world. It had expanded into numerous foreign markets, learning from its failures and building on its successes. It had brought affordable, well-designed, functional furniture to the masses, helping them to, in Kamprad's words, achieve a better everyday life. IKEA's goal is to continue to grow, opening 25 stores by 2020. Achieving that growth would mean continued expansion into non-Western markets, including most notably China and India. Could the company continue to do so? Is its competitive advantage secure?

Case Discussion Questions

1. By the early 1970s IKEA had established itself as the largest furniture retailer in Sweden. What was the source of its competitive advantage at that time?
2. Why do you think IKEA's expansion into Europe went so well? Why did the company subsequently stumble in North America? What lessons did IKEA learn from this experience? How is the company now applying these lessons?
3. How would you characterize IKEA's strategy prior to its missteps in North America? How would you characterize its strategy today?
4. What is IKEA's strategy toward its suppliers? How important is this strategy to IKEA's success?
5. What is the source of IKEA's success today? Can you see any weaknesses in the company? What might it do to correct these?

Sources

"Furnishing the World," *The Economist,* November 19, 1995, pp. 79–80; "Flat Pack Accounting," *The Economist,* May 13, 2006, pp. 69–70; K. Capell, A. Sains, C. Lindblad, and A. T. Palmer, "IKEA," *BusinessWeek,* November 14, 2005, pp. 96–101; K. Capell et al., "What a Sweetheart of a Love Seat," *BusinessWeek,* November 14, 2005, p. 101; C. Daniels, "Create IKEA, Make Billions, Take Bus," *Fortune,* May 3, 2004, p. 44; J. Flynn and L. Bongiorno, "IKEA's new game plan," *BusinessWeek,* October 6, 1997, pp. 99–102; R. Heller, "Folk Fortune," *Forbes,* September 4, 2000, p. 67; IKEA documents at www.ikea.com; J. Leland, "How the Disposable Sofa Conquered America," *New York Times Magazine,* October 5, 2005, pp. 40–50; P. M. Miller, "IKEA with Chinese Characteristics," *Chinese Business Review,* July–August 2004, pp. 36–69; B. Torekull, *Leading by Design: The IKEA Story* (New York: Harper Collins, 1998); and "The Secret of IKEA's Success," *The Economist,* February 24, 2011.

PEUGEOT'S STRATEGIC ENTRY CHOICES AND DILEMMAS[1]

'There is no decision on India and no timetable for a decision'
—Pierre-Olivier Salmon, Peugeot spokesman in Paris

The Indian passenger car market was heating up to booming consumer demand and competition amongst the world's leading car makers. All of them were reporting robust sales by the end of June 2010.

The result was the rapidly growing economy at the rate of more than eight percent per annum for last many years. There was a huge emerging middle class which were moving up from two-wheelers to four-wheelers and thus required an economic (low fuel consumption and low maintenance) car. The

[1]Case by Professor Arun Kumar JAIN at Indian Institute of Management – Lucknow. The case is based on discussions with different stakeholders as well as from secondary data for the purpose of classroom teaching rather than to judge the decision-making. ©Author 2010. No part can be reproduced or printed without written permission of the author.

property prices in the suburbs of major cities were making the local farmers millionaires overnight and they were buying the heavy-duty SUVs and upscale models as status symbols in the villages.

Companies were devising innovative strategies to attract new customers and achieve geographic spread. They knew that after China, this was their biggest opportunity in terms of market size and emerging opportunities. India is a nation which has almost 54 percent of its population below the age of 20. This amounted to more than 500 million people (more than the combined population of entire Europe). Each young man had seen a quality of life which his or her parent had never a chance to experience. They were healthier, literate and conscious of the opportunities galore in the world. The IT and call-center employment opportunities had seen young people leaving homes and farms to work in air-conditioned offices. They all wanted the good things in life, including cars.

These growth prospect sentiments were echoed by Mayank Pareek, Managing Executive Officer (sales) at Maruti Suzuki: 'the economy is growing and salaries are rising. Sentiment remains strong and this should help tide over negative effects like inflation or rising rates.' According to him, 'young population incomes are rising and they are willing to spend. The rural markets have been growing rapidly. For example, while these markets contributed just 3.5 percent to Maruti's sales in 2008, this number now stood at 16.5 percent.'

Business Environment

Fundamentals for new car sales remain strong and demand is unlikely to slow down in the near future, said officials at the country's top three car makers — Maruti Suzuki, Hyundai and Tata Motors. 'We believe that the fundamentals are strong. If the economy continues to grow as it is, there should not be any impact on demand,' according to Carl Peter Forster, CEO of Tata Motors.

When is Peugeot Citroën Entering India?

Given all this background, could PSA continue to stand at the sidewalls and just watching? There were multiple and confusing news coming from various sources about PSA Peugeot Citroen (henceforth PSA) re-entry into India. PSA has spoken to many Indian biggies for a possible manufacturing and marketing tie-up, but things did not work out to its satisfaction. Now that almost every big global carmaker is looking into India, PSA could no longer afford to ignore the market.

In 2008, news came that after testing the market for a few months; PSA was ready to begin working towards establishing a component sourcing base in India for its global operations. The French company had then set up a dedicated office in India, through which it aimed to conduct all its sourcing activity in the country. The company was working towards sourcing auto components from India for its global operations but any car launches from the company will be done only after setting up the manufacturing base in the country.

Later another piece of news was that PSA was returning to India for manufacturing of passenger cars and begun re-staffing its operations in the country. PSA Peugeot Citroen was scouting for land in one of the two south Indian states to set up a greenfield plant. Andhra Pradesh government had reportedly offered 800 acres of land to the company to set up its plant.

The third news that were emerging were that following cues from global auto giants like General Motors, Renault-Nissan, Ford, Toyota, Mitsubishi, Hyundai *et al.*, PSA Peugeot- Citroën was chalking out robust plans to roll out low cost cars for emerging markets like India. This car, which was expected to be introduced by 2011, accommodated up to five people and still has sufficient space for luggage and stowage.

PSA appeared keen to grow the brand name in India and not repeat either its earlier mistakes or flip-flops made by Renault—fellow French company—on setting up manufacturing plants in India. Renault pulled out of a partnership with Mahindra & Mahindra, India's biggest sport-utility maker, in April 2010 after sales of the Logan car plunged due to non-competitiveness of the car against aggressive Japanese, Korean and Indian car makers.

Rajesh Nellore, Vice-President, PSA Peugeot Citroen (India), denied any plans to begin manufacturing in India but admitted his brief was to set-up, 'a complete integrated chain of manufacturing and sourcing in India'. He had also indicated that PSA could well take the JV route in the country. There have been reports of PSA scouting for a contract manufacturing alliance or a partner for assembly operations in India.

In the Russian market, for example, PSA works through a joint venture with Mitsubishi.

Regarding sourcing, Jean-Christophe Quémard, Executive Vice-President (Programmes), mentioned that PSA had an agent in India to help develop the country as a major component sourcing base. Quemard said PSA was targeting sourcing of machine parts to the tune of 200 million euros by end-2010. Nellore had also made it clear that if it made economic sense, 'there could be big investments coming India's way. We were actively sourcing in India through our partners Magna Steyr but we're looking at taking a more direct approach'.

Once Bitten Twice Shy

PSA's renewed interest in India was sobered on the back of an unsuccessful stint in the mid-nineties when it partnered Premier Automobiles, and this may explain its rather cautious approach this time around. 'Peugeot was still studying opportunities in India. There is no decision on India and no timetable for a decision', said Pierre-Olivier Salmon, a spokesman in Paris.

This indecision stems from a legacy that haunts Peugeot even today. It is possibly for this reason that the PSA group would be more comfortable about opting for the Citroen range first so that there are no uncomfortable past negative issues associated with brand Peugeot in India. The general perception was of Peugeot being far too Europe-centric with little idea of the world beyond.

The company's decision about FDI was further delayed because of hiccups in relationship with Mitsubishi. Peugeot Citroen's Executive Vice-President, Gregoire Olivier said that the carmaker shelved its plans for India as it was negotiating with Mitsubishi Motors about a tie-up. Later, Peugeot broke off talks over a share swap with Mitsubishi with which it has facility sharing and marketing arrangements in Eastern Europe.

PSA Peugeot-Citroen was expected to take a call on entering the Indian market by end-2010. Indications were that Peugeot will go ahead with the India plan but tread cautiously. Numbers will be modest to begin with and could be ramped up gradually depending on the market acceptance of the products on offer. Cars could begin rolling out by end-2011 if things went according to schedule.

Peugeot's Indian expansion plan would intensify competition in Asia's third largest passenger car market, where Maruti Suzuki India dominates with a 50% share. Toyota and Nissan are introducing new models in the country as car sales expanded at the fastest pace in six years. Toyota and Volkswagen AG announced plans to spend more than USD 6 billion to expand in India, where sales may reach three million units by 2015, according to a forecast by the government. Toyota will spend INR 500 crore (USD 106 million) on a facility at its local unit to build engines and transmissions for the new Etios (compact car) model.

The state of Tamil Nadu has a strong component base, critical from the viewpoint of localization. The state of Andhra Pradesh was also pitching aggressively for the FDI. There were near misses earlier of

Volkswagen and Proton plants. This time around, the Government was pulling out all stops to offer the best incentive package.

A report said that Peugeot may spend around Euro 700 million (USD 881 million) on the factory with annual production capacity of 1,00,000 cars in the southern state of Andhra Pradesh. An investment, at a time when rising disposable incomes boost demand for cars in the world's third-fastest growing major economy, would mark Peugeot's re-entry in India more than a decade after the carmaker exited a local venture. Rival Renault had resumed selling cars in India from a factory it's building in Chennai in south India. "There is enough space for manufacturers to grow as the Indian economy expands and aspirations rise," said Ammar Master, a Bangkok-based analyst at JD Power & Associates. "It is a good thing if PSA enters the market as it's the last major global automaker left to come to India."[2]

The Cluttered Compact Segment—21 Models but Only Few Winners

Consumers have a vast choice in the passenger car market in India. More so, if it the compact car segment, popularly known as the A2 segment! This segment had 21 models and variants on offer. However, the fact was that just five top performing variants of the 21 cumulatively sold almost 64 percent of all small cars. Addedly, only two—Maruti Suzuki and Hyundai—among the 14 global car manufacturers present in the category corner three-fourths of the total sales.

Surprisingly, Maruti and Hyundai between them have 10 variants on offer in compacts. Where does that leave the rest of the models? About 1.1 million compact cars were sold in 2009–10 in India. Despite a big recession and global slowdown, overall car sales rose by 25.10 per cent to over 1.5 million in 2009–10 from 1.2 million in the 2008–09. The compact segment, thus, accounts for 72 percent of the total sales in the country.

The Society of Indian Automobile Manufacturers (SIAM) forecast that car sales will grow by between 12 and 13 percent during 2010–11 reaching 1.70 million cars. What was absolutely clear is that despite the fancy of Indian consumer for compacts, and entry of almost all major Indian and foreign manufacturers, only a handful of brands could make the survival grade. India's highest selling brand is the Alto from Maruti Suzuki, with an average sale of 22,000 cars per month. Hyundai's i10 is the second largest selling car with average monthly sales of 12,700 cars per month. Maruti's Swift is third, with average sales of 11,800 per month; Tata Motors' Indica is fourth, with an average of 11,700 cars per month and Maruti's Wagon-R is fifth with sales of 11,000 per month. This implied that five models account for about 64 percent of all sales in the compact segment.

This raised the billion-dollar question. If five models are primarily driving small car sales in India, is there scope for 21 others? The consumer choice is crystal clear. The market leader itself has seven models (Alto K-10, Alto, Wagon-R, Swift, Estillo, Ritz and A-Star) and only three of them actually sell well. Purists would ascribe this to the flotilla management theory, which prescribes creation of smaller ships to prevent the competition from directly reaching the big ship (the Alto in this case).

The potential for growth and profit in the small-car sector is high. It is estimated that India has a vehicle density of only seven cars per thousand people, compared to the US which already has 477 per thousand. In 2006 alone, an astonishing one million cars were sold in India, with the annual growth rate of sales pegged at 16 percent.

New Market Penetrations

There has been a lot of excitement in the rural markets too with new and aggressive launches and sustained efforts from the automakers. They had been building dealerships network in the largely

---

[2]Based on report in The Hindu Business Line: http://www.thehindubusinessline.com/2009/06/25/stories/2009062552410100.htm

untapped rural market and offering great discounts and promotional schemes including free insurance and easy finance to promote growth. Rural consumers- mostly agriculture based economy-could afford cars as income levels were rising partly because of good monsoon and better farm outputs. According to Vishnu Mathur, Director General of SIAM, 'The festival season will generate additional demand.'

Abdul Majeed, an auto analyst at consultancy firm PwC, felt that "demand for compact and sub-compact cars was increasing in rural areas because affordability is increasing and banks are offering easy finance. I expect the growth to continue in the coming months and even a percentage rise in car loan rates won't deter growth".

With these figures, it is no wonder carmakers were jumping eagerly onto the bandwagon. Nissan-Renault revealed that it was strategizing on offering a 'USD 3000 car', while India's Hero Group, the world's largest motorcycle manufacturer, was reported to be collaborating with a Canadian company on a mini-car. Maruti-Suzuki was busy with what they call a "competitively-priced" 660cc vehicle; South India's Bajaj Auto will introduce their entry-level model during next year's national Auto Expo. Even Xenetis, India's low-cost computer maker, intends to develop a low-cost car.

Ford Motor India will begin exporting its compact Figo to 50 new markets from India starting next year, according to Joe Hinrichs, President, Asia Pacific and Africa. He also said that it would be export Figo to North African countries and the UAE markets. Ford launched its compact Figo car in India in early 2010 and it has become a best-seller for the company. **Nissan** registered also has seen impressive sales since launch of its small car Micra in July 2010. Within just two months of its launch, the fully automated Micra has driven Nissan sails though the roof. Nissan's sales are a clear indication of the Micra's domination in comparison to Nissan's luxury offerings including sedan and lifestyle SUV offerings. Heralding the early success of Nissan's first small car in India, Kiminobu Tokuyama, Managing Director & CEO, Nissan Motors, "yes, indeed we are happy and delighted at the initial response the Nissan Micra has received from the Indian customers so far. However, this is just the beginning. The Micra has been successful because of its value proposition combined with a complete package of good features including comfort, safety and fuel efficiency. This apart, the look and feel effect of Micra has also attracted customers."

The Luxury Car Segment

The last two years have seen entry of large number of foreign automakers, primarily in the premium segment. These include Nissan, Audi, Bentley and Porsche. Ferrari and Maserati, too, were planning to come to the lucrative market. Honda and Toyota are already here. The reason, of course, lies in the growing number of people in the high-income category in the country. Surveys have pointed out that number of millionaires in the country is increasing at a steady rate and so is the appetite for luxury cars. Incidentally, while the Porsche range in India is available for between Rs 4.5 million and Rs 10 million, the Bentley range is priced at over INR 15 million.

Tata Motors was expected to open a Land Rover assembly facility in India within a year, apart from the one coming up in China. Tata Motors also planned to revamp the Jaguar-Land Rover (JLR) range by adding a station wagon, a roadster and an entry-level model. The company proposed to hire 'around 1,000 engineers, including experts and freshers', said Ralph Speth, chief executive officer of JLR. The company was the maker of world-attention gathering under USD 2500 Nano car. It was increasing the capacity of Tata Nano plant at Sanand in Gujarat.

Peugeot's Previous Indian Legacy

'We burnt our fingers there'
—Paul Alvarez, Peugeot spokesperson on company's Indian experience.

In October 1994, Europe's then fourth largest automobile major, Peugeot of France (Peugeot), entered the Indian automobile market through a joint venture with Premier Automobiles Ltd. (PAL), christened as PAL-Peugeot Ltd. Each company had a 32% stake each in the joint venture.

As Peugeot was one of the first automobile MNCs to enter India, the early mover advantage was expected to help the company make its mark in the Indian automobile market. Peugeot planned to achieve cash breakeven within two years and generating profits by 1998. Peugeot decided to enter the Indian market with its passenger car model, Peugeot 309, as the car was believed to be the best suited for Indian terrain. Production began at the Kalyan (near Mumbai) plant and the car was launched in 1995, positioned in the mid-size segment, against Daewoo's Cielo and Maruti Suzuki's Esteem. The initial response to the car was positive, with the company selling around 10,000 units in the first year of the launch.

Three Became a Crowd

Despite the impressive 10,000 unit sales in its first year, Peugeot recorded a loss of INR 920 million for the year 1995–96 (12 months). The company's problems could by and large be traced back to PAL's association with Fiat. In the early 1950s, PAL entered into a technical agreement with the Italian automobile major Fiat for manufacturing Fiat 500 in India.

Later PAL entered into a fresh technical agreement for assembly of Fiat Uno at its Kurla (near Mumbai) plant. This technical agreement was changed into a joint venture in 1997. PAL was manufacturing the Premier Padmini and the Premier 118NE at the Kurla plant (later the Uno and Siena models as well) and the Peugeot 309 and the 118NE at the Kalyan plant. The June 1996 production slowdown at the Kalyan plant had its roots in the problems at PAL's Kurla plant where the workers had gone on strike over issues related to wages, incentives and voluntary retirement scheme. The Kurla and Kalyan plants were dependent on each other as the former was the sole supplier of components such as gearboxes and rear axles to the latter.

PAL was reportedly unhappy with Peugeot over the level of indigenization of the 309 which was at the time of closure only 24 percent. This made the spare parts very expensive and the company was unable to reduce the price of the car. PAL accused that Peugeot was just not interested in increasing the indigenization level of the vehicle.

There were reports of disagreements over the high price of the CKD from Peugeot as well. Due to 1996 labor problems, the company had to bear heavy inventory carrying costs. To compensate for this, PAL reportedly asked Peugeot to cut down the CKD prices and release funds as loan to the joint venture. PAL sources said that Peugeot could have advanced loans to the company by treating CKD and other equipment with the venture as security for the loan. PAL even requested Peugeot to use its name to raise bank loans abroad for the joint venture, where the cost of funds was much lower than in India.

By 1997, the company's accumulated losses touched over INR 3 billion. In November 1997, Peugeot announced its decision to exit from the joint venture and leave the Indian market. The news came as no surprise, as there had been several media reports about how Peugeot was finding it difficult to survive in the Indian market. Peugeot of course claimed that it was moving out of India only because of a policy decision by its parent company to concentrate only on European markets. Pegueot's exit from the Indian market opened up a debate on a host of issues including the company's blunders, and more importantly, the survival prospects of MNC players in the newly-liberalized Indian economy.

The French company was, ironically, among the earlier entrants to India way back in 1993–94 with its 309 model. Peugeot's first entry was a disaster as they failed to impress the consumer with outdated products.

Finally a legal spat with its local partner which had to be resolved in court. Peugeot won the case but then stunned industry circles by deciding to call it quits in November 1997. It was a move that left a bitter taste in everyone's mouth right from financiers and dealers to suppliers and customers since dues had not been squared with most of them.

Peugeot's topsy-turvy past in India has seen alliance with Tata Motors for the 307 project which never took-off. In January 2001, Peugeot Citroen and Tata Motors began discussions for introducing a luxury car in India. The Peugeot-Mitsubishi alliance was supposed to be interesting as both the companies were contemplating a cross-holding of equity but which eventually never happened. There were also reports of Peugeot planning a tie-up with the Indian two-wheeler major Hero Honda to enter the motorcycle segment in India. Interestingly enough, some Indian banks were reported to be planning to approach the Foreign Investment Promotion Board (FIPB) to protest at that time against the possible re-entry of Peugeot because of their bad loans and outstandings. However, in July 2001, after completion of various feasibility studies, the two companies decided against going ahead with the project for the time being.

About PSA

PSA Peugeot Citroën (previously Peugeot Société Anonyme) is a French automobile and motorcycle manufacturer; and sells these under Peugeot and Citroën marquees. The PSA Peugeot Citroën is owned by Peugeot S.A. company. The two brands retained their separate sales and marketing structures, but have benefited from a common technology, development and assembling assets.

PSA Peugeot Citroën, Europe's No. 2 Manufacturer

To ensure its growth and profitability, PSA Peugeot Citroën needed to step up its international development to become a more global group. In 2009, sales outside Europe accounted for one-third of the Group total or 1,055,000 vehicles. The global automotive industry is in the throes of major change. In 2009, China became the world's biggest automotive market, ahead of North America. The emerging countries account for the bulk of growth in automotive markets. Historically based in Western Europe, PSA Peugeot Citroën started deploying its production base and products in South America from the start of the 1980s, and in China from 1992.

PSA in China, South America and Russia

Being more global means achieving critical mass in market share in these regions, particularly through vehicles and subsystems better tailored to the specific requirements of local customers and local energy resources: automatic or other types of gearbox, hatchbacks or sedans, diesel, petrol or flex-fuel engines, etc. But being more global also means developing and showcasing a wider variety of cultures and profiles within the company, primarily at management level.

Peugeot and Citroën brands successfully pursued their international expansion in 2009, building primarily on the launch of new vehicles. In 2010, the Group's international growth received new impetus with the opening of the Kaluga plant in Russia and the launch of new body styles, such as the Peugeot 408 in China, and the Peugeot Hoggar pick-up and Citroën C3 Aircross in South America.

Vision of PSA was to be a Global Player

After the merger between PSA Peugeot and Citroen in 2007, the company operates both brands within and outside Europe in passenger car and light commercial vehicle segments. Its vision was now to become a major player in global markets. The Group's first priority was to reach critical mass in Latin America and Asia, especially China. It was felt by the PSA Management Board that the Group's market shares in Latin America and Asia were currently too low to amortize local product and network development costs. To reach critical mass, PSA Peugeot Citroën will have to focus on sustaining organic growth with new model launches.

As part of the plan, PSA Peugeot Citroën decided to accelerate the adaptation of its cars to the needs of non-European customers. In this area, the Group will benefit from the investment it is making in its R&D centers in Shanghai and Sao Paolo. Even though 50 percent of the cars sold by Peugeot and Citroën are equipped with gasoline engines, yet there was a need to further improve the Group's offer. The Group was also expanding its automatic gearbox offer. To minimize the added cost of these developments, the Group thought it made sense to enhance its current co-operations. To succeed in these efforts, PSA Peugeot Citroën was making its management teams more international.

The Decision Point

Peugeot Citroen has identified three focused markets for future expansion, yet they could also not ignore the burgeoning Indian market. Given all the background, the agenda on board was to put a comprehensive business model in place. This included entry strategy mode, investments plans, location choices, products and geographies, local and global integration, employment levels, financials, etc. The company had several entry options to choose from:

- Bring the small car in SKD or CKD condition from Turkey or Thailand
- Invest in India in a manufacturing facility, and which then caters to global markets as in the cae of Suzuki, Fiat, Ford, etc.
- Assemble the car in India and bring cars in SKD or CKD conditions
- Launch the high-margin Citroen top-end and luxury models, and forget the low-cost high margin economy small car models
- Go only for global sourcing of auto components

Case Questions

Each option had an array of difficult critical success factors. High volume markets meant appointing dealers and service stations throughout the country and providing spare parts at cheap and economical prices; the high end model required styling, branding and image in a market where Audi, BMW, Volkswagen, Mercedes, Honda, and Toyota were already jostling for space and sales.

Many analysts felt that PSA was already late into India by at least three years, and any further delay may permanently close the doors to the market.

- What is your recommendation to the Board? What should it do? How do they take the call in terms of entry strategy, business models, and investments?
- Which theories can explain the dilemma and give us road for decision?
- In case it decided to go ahead, what product range should it go for?

GENERAL ELECTRIC'S JOINT VENTURES

Historically at General Electric, if you wanted to enter a foreign market, you either acquired an established firm in that market or you went alone, establishing a greenfield subsidiary. Joint ventures with a local company were almost never considered. The prevailing philosophy was that if GE didn't have full control, you didn't do the deal. However, times have changed. Since the early 2000s joint ventures have become one of the most powerful strategic tools in GE's arsenal. To enter the South Korean market, for example, GE Money, the retail lending arm of GE's financial services business, formed joint ventures with Hyundai to offer auto loans, mortgages, and credit cards. GE has a 43 percent stake in these ventures. Similarly, in Spain it has formed several joint ventures with local banks to provide consumer loans and credit cards to Spanish residents, and in Central America it has a joint venture with BAC-Credomatic, the largest bank in the region.

There are several reasons for the switch in strategy. For one thing, GE used to be able to buy its way into majority ownership in almost any business, but prices for acquisitions have been bid so high that GE is reluctant to acquire for fear of overpaying. Better to form a joint venture, so the thinking goes, than risk paying too much for a company that turns out to have problems that are discovered only after the acquisition. Just as importantly, GE now sees joint ventures as a great way to dip its toe into foreign markets where it lacks local knowledge. Also, in certain nations, China being an example, economic, political, legal, and cultural considerations make joint ventures an easier option than either acquisitions or greenfield ventures. GE believes it can often benefit from the political contacts, local expertise, and business relationships that the local partner brings to the table, to say nothing of the fact that in certain sectors of the Chinese economy and some others, local laws prohibit other entry modes. GE also sees joint ventures as a good way to share the risk of building a business in a nation where it lacks local knowledge. Finally, under the leadership of CEO Jeffrey Immelt, GE has adopted aggressive growth goals, and it feels that entering via joint ventures into nations where it lacks a presence is the only way of attaining those goals. Fueled by its large number of joint ventures, GE has rapidly expanded its international presence over the past decade. For the first time, in 2007 the company derived the majority of its revenue from foreign operations.

Of course, General Electric has done joint ventures in the past. For example, it has a long-standing fifty-fifty joint venture with the French company Snecma to make engines for commercial jet aircraft, another with Fanuc of Japan to make controls for electric equipment, and a third with Sea Containers of the United Kingdom, which has become one of the world's largest companies leasing shipping containers. But all these ventures came about only after GE had explored other ways to gain access to particular markets or technology. While GE formerly used joint ventures as the last option, they are now often the preferred entry strategy.

GE managers also note that there is no shortage of partners willing to enter into a joint venture with the company. The company has a well-earned reputation for being a good partner to work with. GE is well known for its innovative management techniques and excellent management development programs. Many partners are only too happy to team up with GE to get access to this know-how. The knowledge flow, therefore, goes both ways, with GE acquiring access to knowledge about local markets and partners learning cutting-edge management techniques from GE that can be used to boost their own productivity.

Nevertheless, joint ventures are no panacea. GE's agreements normally give even the minority partner in a joint venture veto power over major strategic decisions, and control issues can scuttle some ventures. In January 2007, for example, GE announced it would enter into a venture with Britain's Smiths Group to make aerospace equipment. However, nine months later, GE ended talks aimed at establishing the venture, stating they could not reach an agreement over the vision for the joint venture. GE has also found that as much as it would like majority ownership, or even a fifty-fifty split, sometimes it has to settle for a minority stake to gain access to a foreign market. In 2003, when GE entered into a joint venture with Hyundai to offer auto loans, it did so as a minority partner even though it would have preferred a majority position. Hyundai had refused to cede control over to GE.

Case Discussion Questions

1. GE used to prefer acquisitions or greenfield ventures as an entry mode rather than joint ventures. Why do you think this was the case?
2. Why do you think that GE has come to prefer joint ventures in recent years? Do you think that the global economic crisis of 2008–2009 might have affected this preference in any way? If so, how?
3. What are the risks that GE must assume when it enters into a joint venture? Is there any way for GE to reduce those risks?
4. The case mentions that GE has a well-earned reputation for being a good partner. What are the likely benefits of this reputation to GE? If GE were to tarnish its reputation by, for example, opportunistically taking advantage of a partner, how might this affect the company going forward?
5. In addition to its reputation for being a good partner, what other assets do you think GE brings to the table that make it an attractive joint-venture partner?

Sources

C. H. Deutsch, "The Venturesome Giant," *The New York Times,* October 5, 2007, pp. C1, C8; "Odd Couple: Jet Engines," *The Economist,* May 5, 2007, p. 72; and "GE, BAC Joint Venture to Buy Banco Mercantil," *Financial Wire,* January 11, 2007, p. 1.

THE GLOBALIZATION OF STARBUCKS

Thirty years ago, Starbucks was a single store in Seattle's Pike Place Market selling premium-roasted coffee. Today it is a global roaster and retailer of coffee with more than 16,000 stores, 40 percent of which are in 50 countries outside of the United States. Starbucks set out on its current course in the 1980s when the company's director of marketing, Howard Schultz, came back from a trip to Italy enchanted with the Italian coffeehouse experience. Schultz, who later became CEO, persuaded the company's owners to experiment with the coffeehouse format—and the Starbucks experience was born. The strategy was to sell the company's own premium-roasted coffee and freshly brewed espresso-style coffee beverages, along with a variety of pastries, coffee accessories, teas, and other products, in a tastefully designed coffeehouse setting. From the outset, the company focused on selling "a third place between work and home," rather than just the coffee. The formula led to spectacular success in the United States, where Starbucks went from obscurity to one of the best-known brands in the country in a decade. Thanks to Starbucks, coffee stores became places for relaxation, chatting with friends, reading the newspaper, holding business meetings, or (more recently) browsing the web.

In 1995, with 700 stores across the United States, Starbucks began exploring foreign opportunities. The first target market was Japan. The company established a joint venture with a local retailer, Sazaby Inc. Each company held a 50 percent stake in the venture, Starbucks Coffee of Japan. Starbucks initially invested $10 million in this venture, its first foreign direct investment. The Starbucks format was then licensed to the venture, which was charged with taking over responsibility for increasing Starbucks' presence in Japan.

To make sure the Japanese operations replicated the "Starbucks experience" in North America, Starbucks transferred some employees to the Japanese operation. The licensing agreement required all Japanese store managers and employees to attend training classes similar to those given to U.S. employees. The agreement also required that stores adhere to the design parameters established in the United States. In 2001, the company introduced a stock option plan for all Japanese employees, making it the first company in Japan to do so. Skeptics doubted that Starbucks would be able to replicate its North American success overseas, but by the end of 2009 Starbucks had some 850 stores and a profitable business in Japan.

After Japan, the company embarked on an aggressive foreign investment program. In 1998, it purchased Seattle Coffee, a British coffee chain with 60 retail stores, for $84 million. An American couple, originally from Seattle, had started Seattle Coffee with the intention of establishing a Starbucks-like chain in Britain. In the late 1990s, Starbucks opened stores in Taiwan, China, Singapore, Thailand, New Zealand, South Korea, and Malaysia. In Asia, Starbucks' most common strategy was to license its format to a local operator in return for initial licensing fees and royalties on store revenues. As in Japan, Starbucks insisted on an intensive employee-training program and strict specifications regarding the format and layout of the store.

By 2002, Starbucks was pursuing an aggressive expansion in mainland Europe. As its first entry point, Starbucks chose Switzerland. Drawing on its experience in Asia, the company entered into a joint venture with a Swiss company, Bon Appetit Group, Switzerland's largest food service company. Bon Appetit was to hold a majority stake in the venture, and Starbucks would license its format to the Swiss company using a similar agreement to those it had used successfully in Asia. This was followed by a joint venture in other countries.

As it has increased its global footprint, Starbucks has also embraced ethical sourcing policies and environmental responsibility. Now one of the world's largest buyers of coffee, in 2000 Starbucks started to purchase Fair Trade Certified coffee. The goal was to empower small-scale farmers organized in cooperatives to invest in their farms and communities, to protect the environment, and to develop the business skills necessary to compete in the global marketplace. In short, Starbucks was trying to use its influence to change not only the way people consumed coffee around the world but also the way coffee was produced in a manner that benefited the farmers and the environment. By 2010, some 75 percent of the coffee Starbucks purchased was Fair Trade Certified, and the company has a goal of increasing that to 100 percent by 2015.

Case Discussion Questions

1. Where did the original idea for the Starbucks' format come from? What lesson for international business can be drawn from this?
2. What drove Starbucks to start expanding internationally? How is the company creating value for its shareholders by pursuing an international expansion strategy?
3. Why do you think Starbucks decided to enter the Japanese market via a joint venture with a Japanese company? What lesson can you draw from this?
4. Is Starbucks a force for globalization? Explain your answer.
5. When it comes to purchasing coffee beans, Starbucks adheres to a "fair trade" program. What do you think is the difference between fair trade and free trade? How might a fair trade policy benefit Starbucks?

Sources

Starbucks 10K, various years; C. McLean, "Starbucks Set to Invade Coffee-Loving Continent," *Seattle Times,* October 4, 2000, p. E1; J. Ordonez, "Starbucks to Start Major Expansion in Overseas Market," *The Wall Street Journal,* October 27, 2000, p. B10; S. Homes and D. Bennett, "Planet Starbucks", *BusinessWeek,* September 9, 2002, pp. 99–110; "Starbucks Outlines International Growth Strategy," *Business Wire,* October 14, 2004; A. Yeh, "Starbucks Aims for New Tier in China," *Financial Times,* February 14, 2006, p. 17; and C. Matlack, "Will Global Growth Help Starbucks?" *BusinessWeek,* July 2, 2008.

COCA-COLA'S STRATEGY

Coca-Cola, the iconic American soda maker, has long been among the most international of enterprises. The company made its first move outside the United States in 1902, when it entered Cuba. By 1929, Coke was marketed in 76 countries. In World War II, Coca-Cola struck a deal to supply the U.S. military with Coca-Cola wherever in the world it went. During this era, the company built 63 bottling plants around the world. Its global push continued after the war, fueled in part by the belief that the U.S. market would eventually reach maturity and by the perception that huge growth opportunities lay overseas. Today more than 59,000 of the company's 71,000 employees are located in 200 countries outside of the United States, and over 70 percent of Coca-Cola's case volume is in international markets.

Until the 1980s, Coca-Cola's strategy was one of considerable localization. Local operations were granted a high degree of independence to manage their own operations. This all changed in the 1980s and 1990s under the leadership of Roberto Goizueta, a talented Cuban immigrant who became the CEO in 1981. Goizueta placed renewed emphasis on the company's flagship brands, which were extended with the introduction of Diet Coke, Cherry Coke, and the like. His prime belief was that the main difference between the United States and international markets was the lower level of penetration in the latter, where consumption per capita of colas was only 10 to 15 percent of the U.S. figure. Goizueta pushed Coca-Cola to become a global company, centralizing a great deal of management and marketing activities at the corporate headquarters in Atlanta, focusing on core brands, and taking equity stakes in foreign bottlers so that the company could exert more strategic control over them. This one-size-fits-all strategy was built around standardization and the realization of economies of scale by, for example, using the same advertising message worldwide.

Goizueta's global strategy was adopted by his successor, Douglas Ivester, but by the late 1990s the drive toward a one-size-fits-all strategy was running out of steam, as smaller, more nimble local competitors marketing local beverages began to halt the Coke growth engine. With Coca-Cola failing to hit its financial targets for the first time in a generation, Ivester resigned in 2000 and was replaced by Douglas Daft. Daft instituted a 180-degree shift in strategy. Daft's belief was that Coca-Cola needed to put more power back in the hands of local country managers. He thought that strategy, product development, and marketing should be tailored to local needs. He laid off 6,000 employees, many of them in Atlanta, and granted country managers much greater autonomy. In a striking move for a marketing company, he announced the company would stop making global advertisements, and he placed advertising budgets and control over creative content back in the hands of country managers. Ivester's move was in part influenced by the experience of Coca-Cola in Japan, the company's second most profitable market, where the best-selling Coca-Cola product is not a carbonated beverage, but a canned cold coffee drink, Georgia, that is sold in vending machines. The Japanese experience seemed to signal that products should be customized to local tastes and preferences, and that Coca-Cola would do well to decentralize more decision-making authority to local managers.

However, the shift toward localization didn't produce the growth that had been expected, and by 2002 the pendulum was swinging back toward more central coordination, with Atlanta exercising oversight over marketing and product development in different nations. But this time it was not the one-size-fits-all ethos of the Goizueta era. Under the leadership of Neville Isdell, who became CEO in March 2004 and retired in July 2008, Coca-Cola reviewed and guided local marketing and product development but adopted the belief that strategy, including pricing, product offerings, and marketing message, should be varied from market to market to match local conditions. Isdell's position represented a midpoint between the strategy of Goizueta and that of Daft. Moreover, Isdell stressed the importance of leveraging good ideas across nations. An example is Georgia coffee. Having seen the success of this beverage in Japan, in October 2007 Coca-Cola entered into a strategic alliance with Illycaffe, one of Italy's premier coffee makers, to build a global franchise for canned or bottled cold coffee beverages. Similarly, in 2003 the Coca-Cola subsidiary in China developed a low-cost noncarbonated orange-based drink that rapidly became one of the best-selling drinks in that nation. Seeing the potential of the drink, Coca-Cola rolled it out in other Asian countries. It has been a huge hit in Thailand, where it was launched in 2005, and seems to be gaining traction in India, where it was launched in 2007.

Case Discussion Questions

1. Why do you think that Roberto Goizueta switched from a strategy that emphasized localization toward one that empathized global standardization? What were the benefits of such a strategy?
2. What were the limitations of Goizueta's strategy that persuaded his successor, Daft, to shift away from it? What was Daft trying to achieve? Daft's strategy also did not produce the desired results. Why do you think this was the case?
3. How would you characterize the strategy pursued by Coca-Cola under Isdell's leadership? What is the enterprise trying to do? How is this different from the strategies of both Goizueta and Daft? What are the benefits? What are the potential costs and risk?
4. What does the evolution of Coca-Cola's strategy tell you about the convergence of consumer tastes and preference in today's global economy?

Sources

"Orange Gold," *The Economist,* March 3, 2007, p. 68; P. Bettis, "Coke Aims to Give Pepsi a Routing in Cold Coffee War," *Financial Times,* October 17, 2007, p. 16; P. Ghemawat, *Redefining Global Strategy* (Boston: Harvard Business School Press, 2007); and D. Foust, "Queen of Pop," *BusinessWeek,* August 7, 2006, pp. 44–47.

PART 6
International Business Functions

Chapter 16
Exporting, Importing, and Countertrade

LEARNING OBJECTIVES

After reading this chapter, you will be able to:

LO16-1   Explain the promises and risks associated with exporting.

LO16-2   Identify the steps managers can take to improve their firm's export performance.

LO16-3   Identify information sources and government programs that exist to help exporters.

LO16-4   Recognize the basic steps involved in export financing.

LO16-5   Describe how countertrade can be used to facilitate exporting.

◇ STEELMASTER BUILDINGS ◇

Opening Case

SteelMaster Buildings designs, manufactures, and supplies prefabricated arched steel structures that are used for anything from basic residential storage facilities to complex aircraft hangers. A small private company, SteelMaster first ventured into the export market in 2006. Its motivations were straightforward. Domestic competition was intense, and SteelMaster saw foreign markets as the best way of expanding sales. The company believed that its expertise in designing high-quality arched steel structures would serve it well in foreign markets where there were few indigenous competitors with the same capabilities. Moreover, by optimizing its manufacturing systems and logistics chain, SteelMaster would be able to lower its cost structure and be competitive on pricing. The combination of high quality, the ability to produce customized designs, and competitive pricing helped create demand for the company's products.

Today, export sales account for 15 percent of the company's revenues. The Virginia Beach company estimates that it has sold more than 40,000 buildings worldwide in more than 40 countries. Much of the growth is through a distribution network that now encompasses 50 countries. Not only do the distributors work to drive sales, but they also provide in-country customer service and technical assistance. In addition, they are key to providing SteelMaster with feedback in specific markets.

One thing that helped SteelMaster increase its export business was to have someone who was dedicated to developing the international businesses. To fill this role, the company hired Emma Granada, whose fluency in Spanish and French has been a strong attribute. It also helped that the U.S. dollar has been relatively weak for some years now, increasing SteelMaster's price competitiveness.

To navigate its foray into the world of exporting, SteelMaster drew on a variety of resources, including the Virginia Economic Development Partnership and the U.S. Commercial Service. The U.S. Commercial Service invited the company to events where company executives met representatives from U.S. embassies around the world. SteelMaster quickly realized that there was a strong network in place to help small businesses export. According to the company, this resource helped the company better understand the markets it was targeting for exports. Without such help, it would have been limited to cold-calling prospects.

On the marketing side, to supplement its in-country distributors, SteelMaster has used a website to reach more international prospects. In addition to English, the company has a Spanish language website and introductory pages in Arabic, French, Portuguese, Romanian, and Korean, among others. By bidding for key words on search engines such as Google and Bing, SteelMaster has been able to drive traffic to its website—and that enhances people's understanding of the product and can ultimately translate into sales.[1]

INTRODUCTION

The previous chapter reviewed exporting from a strategic perspective. We considered exporting as just one of a range of strategic options for profiting from international expansion. This chapter is more concerned with the nuts and bolts of exporting (and importing). It looks at how to export. As the opening case makes clear, exporting is not just for large enterprises; many small firms such as SteelMaster have benefited significantly from the moneymaking opportunities of exporting.

The volume of export activity in the world economy has increased as exporting has become easier. The gradual decline in trade barriers under the umbrella of GATT and now the WTO (see Chapter 7) along with regional economic agreements such as the European Union and the North American Free Trade Agreement (see Chapter 9) have significantly increased export opportunities. At the same time, modern communication and transportation technologies have alleviated the logistical problems associated with exporting. Over the last two decades firms have increasingly used the Internet, toll-free phone numbers, and international air express services to reduce the costs of exporting. Consequently, it is not unusual to find thriving exporters among small companies.

Nevertheless, exporting remains a challenge for many firms. Smaller enterprises can find the process intimidating. The firm wishing to export must identify foreign market opportunities, avoid a host of unanticipated problems that are often associated with doing business in a foreign market, familiarize itself with the mechanics of export and import financing, learn where it can get financing and export credit insurance, and learn how it should deal with foreign exchange risk. The process can be made more problematic by currencies that are not freely convertible. Arranging payment for exports to countries with weak currencies can be a problem. Countertrade allows payment for exports to be made through goods and services rather than money. This chapter discusses all these issues with the exception of foreign exchange risk, which was covered in Chapter 10. The chapter opens by considering the promise and pitfalls of exporting.

THE PROMISE AND PITFALLS OF EXPORTING

LO16-1

The great promise of exporting is that large revenue and profit opportunities are to be found in foreign markets for most firms in most industries. This was true for SteelMaster, which was profiled in the opening case. The international market is normally so much larger than the firm's domestic market that exporting is nearly always a way to increase the revenue and profit base of a company. By expanding the size of the market, exporting can enable a firm to achieve economies of scale, thereby lowering its unit costs. Firms that do not export often lose out on significant opportunities for growth and cost reduction.[2]

Consider the case of Marlin Steel Wire Products, a Baltimore manufacturer of wire baskets and fabricated metal items with revenues of about $5 million. Among its products are baskets to hold dedicated parts for aircraft engines and automobiles. Its engineers design custom wire baskets for the assembly lines of companies such as Boeing and Toyota. It has a reputation for producing high-quality products for these niche markets. Like many small businesses, Marlin did not have a history of exporting. However, in the mid-2000s, Marlin dipped its toe in the export market, shipping small numbers of products to Mexico and Canada. Marlin CEO Drew Greenblatt soon realized that export sales could be the key to growth. In 2008, when the global financial crisis hit and America slid into a serious recession, Marlin was exporting only 5 percent of its orders to foreign markets. Greenblatt's strategy for dealing with weak demand from the United States was to aggressively expand international sales. By 2010, exports accounted for 17 percent of sales, and the company has set a goal of exporting half its output.[3]

Despite examples such as SteelMaster and Marlin, studies have shown that while many large firms tend to be proactive about seeking opportunities for profitable exporting—systematically scanning foreign markets to see where the opportunities lie for leveraging their technology, products, and marketing skills in foreign countries—many medium-size and small firms are very reactive.[4] Typically, such reactive firms do not even consider exporting until their domestic market is saturated and the emergence of excess productive capacity at home forces them to look for growth opportunities in foreign markets. Also, many small and medium-size firms tend to wait for the world to come to them, rather than going out into the world to seek opportunities. Even when the world does come to them, they may not respond. An example is MMO Music Group, which makes sing-along tapes for karaoke machines. Foreign sales accounted for about 15 percent of MMO's revenues of $8 million, but the firm's CEO admits this figure would probably have been much higher had he paid attention to building international sales. Unanswered e-mails and phone messages from Asia and Europe often piled up while he was trying to manage the burgeoning domestic side of the business. By the time MMO did turn its attention to foreign markets, competitors had stepped into the breach, and MMO found it tough going to build export volume.[5]

MMO's experience is common, and it suggests a need for firms to become more proactive about seeking export opportunities. One reason more firms are not proactive is that they are unfamiliar with foreign market opportunities; they simply do not know how big the opportunities actually are or where they might lie. Simple ignorance of the potential opportunities is a huge barrier to exporting.[6] Also, many would-be exporters, particularly smaller firms, are often intimidated by the complexities and mechanics of exporting to countries where business practices, language, culture, legal systems, and currency are very different from the home market.[7] This combination of unfamiliarity and intimidation probably explains why exporters still account for only a tiny percentage of U.S. firms, less than 5 percent of firms with fewer than 500 employees, according to the Small Business Administration.[8]

To make matters worse, many neophyte exporters run into significant problems when first trying to do business abroad, and this sours them on future exporting ventures. Common pitfalls include poor market analysis, a poor understanding of competitive conditions in the foreign market, a failure to customize the product offering to the needs of foreign customers, a lack of an effective distribution program, a poorly executed promotional campaign, and problems securing financing.[9] Novice exporters tend to underestimate the time and expertise needed to cultivate business in foreign countries.[10] Few realize the amount of management resources that have to be dedicated to this activity. Many foreign customers require face-to-face negotiations on their home turf. An exporter may have to spend months learning about a country's trade regulations, business practices, and more before a deal can be closed. The accompanying Management Focus, which documents the experience of FCX Systems in China, suggests that it may take years before foreigners are comfortable enough to purchase in significant quantities.

MANAGEMENT FOCUS

FCX Systems

Founded with the help of a $20,000 loan from the Small Business Administration, FCX Systems is an exporting success story. FCX makes power converters for the aerospace industry. These devices convert common electric utility frequencies into the higher frequencies used in aircraft systems and are primarily used to provide power to aircraft while they are on the ground. Today, the West Virginia enterprise generates more than half its annual sales from exports to more than 70 countries. FCX's prowess in opening foreign markets has earned the company several awards for export excellence, including a presidential award for achieving extraordinary growth in export sales.

FCX initially got into exporting because it found that foreigners were often more receptive to the company's products than potential American customers. According to Don Gallion, president of FCX, "In the overseas market, they were looking for a good technical product, preferably made in the U.S., but they weren't asking questions about 'How long have you been in business? Are you still going to be here tomorrow?' They were just anxious to get the product."

In 1989, shortly after it had been founded, FCX signed on with an international distribution company to help with exporting, but Gallion became disillusioned with that company, and in 1994 FCX started to handle the exporting process on its own. At the time, exports represented 12 percent of sales, but by 1997 they had jumped to more than 50 percent of the total, where they have stayed since.

In explaining the company's export success, Gallion cites a number of factors. One was the extensive assistance that FCX has received over the years from a number of federal and state agencies, including the U.S. Department of Commerce and the Development Office of West Virginia. These agencies demystified the process of exporting and provided good contacts for FCX. Finding a good local representative to help work through local regulations and customs is another critical factor, according to Gallion, who says, "A good rep will keep you out of trouble when it comes to customs and what you should and shouldn't do." Persistence is also very important, says Gallion, particularly when trying to break into markets where personal relationships are crucial, such as China.

China has been an interesting story for FCX. Recently, the company has been booking $2 million to $3 million in sales to China, but it took years to get to this point. China had been on Gallion's radar screen since the early 1990s, primarily because of the country's rapid modernization and its plans to build or remodel some 179 airports between 1998 and 2008. This constituted a potentially large market opportunity for FCX, particularly compared with the United States, where perhaps only three new airports would be built during the same period. Despite the scale of the opportunity, progress was very slow. The company had to identify airports and airline projects, government agencies, customers, and decision makers, as well as work through different languages—and make friends. According to Gallion, "Only after they consider you a friend will they buy a product. They believe a friend would never cheat you." To make friends in China, Gallion estimates he had to make more than 100 trips to China since the early 1990s, but now that the network has been established, it is starting to pay dividends.[12]

Exporters often face voluminous paperwork, complex formalities, and many potential delays and errors. According to a UN report on trade and development, a typical international trade transaction may involve 30 parties, 60 original documents, and 360 document copies, all of which have to be checked, transmitted, reentered into various information systems, processed, and filed. The United Nations has calculated that the time involved in preparing documentation, along with the costs of common errors in paperwork, often amounts to 10 percent of the final value of goods exported.[11]

IMPROVING EXPORT PERFORMANCE   LO16-2

Inexperienced exporters have a number of ways to gain information about foreign market opportunities and avoid common pitfalls that tend to discourage and frustrate novice exporters.[13] In this section, we look at information sources for exporters to increase their knowledge of foreign market opportunities, we consider the pros and cons of using export management companies (EMCs) to assist in the export process, and we review various exporting strategies that can increase the probability of successful exporting. We begin, however, with a look at how several nations try to help domestic firms export.

An International Comparison

One big impediment to exporting is the simple lack of knowledge of the opportunities available. Often, there are many markets for a firm's product, but because they are in countries separated from the firm's home base by culture, language, distance, and time, the firm does not know of them. Identifying export opportunities is made even more complex because more than 200 countries with widely differing cultures compose the world of potential opportunities. Faced with such complexity and diversity, firms sometimes hesitate to seek export opportunities.

The way to overcome ignorance is to collect information. In Germany—one of the   LO16-3 world's most successful exporting nations—trade associations, government agencies, and commercial banks gather information, helping small firms identify export opportunities. A similar function is provided by the Japanese Ministry of International Trade and Industry (**MITI**), which is always on the lookout for export opportunities. In addition, many Japanese firms are affiliated in some way with the *sogo shosha*, Japan's great trading houses. The *sogo shosha* have offices all over the world, and they proactively, continuously seek export opportunities for their affiliated companies large and small.[14]

German and Japanese firms can draw on the large reservoirs of experience, skills, information, and other resources of their respective export-oriented institutions. Unlike their German and Japanese competitors, many U.S. firms are relatively blind when they seek export opportunities; they are information-disadvantaged. In part, this reflects historical differences. Both Germany and Japan have long made their living as trading nations, whereas until recently the United States has been a relatively self-contained continental economy in which international trade played a minor role. This is changing; both imports and exports now play a greater role in the U.S. economy than they did 20 years ago. However, the United States has not yet evolved an institutional structure for promoting exports similar to that of either Germany or Japan.

Information Sources

Despite institutional disadvantages, U.S. firms can increase their awareness of export opportunities. The most comprehensive source of information is the U.S. Department of Commerce and its district offices all over the country. Within that department are two organizations dedicated to providing businesses with intelligence and assistance for attacking foreign markets: the International Trade Administration and the U.S. Commercial Service.

Those agencies provide the potential exporter with a "best prospects" list, which gives the names and addresses of potential distributors in foreign markets along with businesses they are in, the products they handle, and their contact person. In addition, the Department of Commerce has assembled a "comparison shopping service" for 14 countries that are major markets for U.S. exports. For a small fee, a firm can receive a customized market research survey on a product of its choice. This survey provides information on marketability, the competition, comparative prices, distribution channels, and names of potential sales representatives. Each study is conducted on-site by an officer of the Department of Commerce.

The Department of Commerce also organizes trade events that help potential exporters make foreign contacts and explore export opportunities. The department organizes exhibitions at international trade fairs, which are held regularly in major cities worldwide. The department also has a matchmaker program, in which department representatives accompany groups of U.S. businesspeople abroad to meet with qualified agents, distributors, and customers.

Another government organization, the Small Business Administration (SBA), can help potential exporters (see the accompanying Management Focus for examples of the SBA's work). The SBA employs 76 district international trade officers and 10 regional international trade officers throughout the United States as well as a 10-person international trade staff in Washington, D.C. Through its Service Corps of Retired Executives (SCORE) program, the SBA also oversees some 11,500 volunteers with international trade experience to provide one-on-one counseling to active and new-to-export businesses. The SBA also coordinates the Export Legal Assistance Network (ELAN), a nationwide group of international trade attorneys who provide free initial consultations to small businesses on export-related matters.

In addition to the Department of Commerce and SBA, nearly every state and many large cities maintain active trade commissions whose purpose is to promote exports. Most of these provide business counseling, information gathering, technical assistance, and financing. Unfortunately, many have fallen victim to budget cuts or to turf battles for political and financial support with other export agencies.

A number of private organizations are also beginning to provide more assistance to would-be exporters. Commercial banks and major accounting firms are more willing to assist small firms in starting export operations than they were a decade ago. In addition, large multinationals that have been

Exporting with a Little Government Help

Exporting can seem like a daunting prospect, but the reality is that in the United States, as in many other countries, many small enterprises have built profitable export businesses. For example, Landmark Systems of Virginia had virtually no domestic sales before it entered the European market. Landmark had developed a software program for IBM mainframe computers and located an independent distributor in Europe to represent its product. In the first year, 80 percent of sales were attributed to exporting. In the second year, sales jumped from $100,000 to $1.4 million—with 70 percent attributable to exports. Landmark is not alone; government data suggest that in the United States, more than 97 percent of the 240,000 firms that export are small or medium-size businesses that employ fewer than 500 people. Their share of total U.S. exports has grown steadily and is around 30 percent today.

To help jump-start the exporting process, many small companies have drawn on the expertise of government agencies, financial institutions, and export management companies. Consider the case of Novi Inc., a California-based business. Company President Michael Stoff tells how he utilized the services of the U.S. Small Business Administration (SBA) Office of International Trade to start exporting:

"When I began my business venture, Novi Inc., I knew that my Tune-Tote (a stereo system for bicycles) had the potential to be successful in international markets. Although I had no prior experience in this area, I began researching and collecting information on international markets. I was willing to learn, and by targeting key sources for information and guidance, I was able to penetrate international markets in a short period of time. One vital source I used from the beginning was the SBA. Through SBA I was directed to a program that dealt specifically with business development—the Service Corps of Retired Executives (SCORE). I was assigned an adviser who had run his own import/export business for 30 years. The services of SCORE are provided on a continual basis and are free."

"As I began to pursue exporting, my first step was a thorough marketing evaluation. I targeted trade shows with a good presence of international buyers. I also went to DOC [Department of Commerce] for counseling and information about the rules and regulations of exporting. I advertised my product in *Commercial News USA,* distributed through United States embassies to buyers worldwide. I utilized DOC's World Traders Data Reports to get background information on potential foreign buyers. As a result, I received 60–70 inquiries about Tune-Tote from around the world. Once I completed my research and evaluation of potential buyers, I decided which ones would be most suitable to market my product internationally. Then I decided to grant exclusive distributorship. In order to effectively communicate with my international customers, I invested in a fax. I chose a U.S. bank to handle international transactions. The bank also provided guidance on methods of payment and how best to receive and transmit money. This is essential know-how for anyone wanting to be successful in foreign markets."

In just one year of exporting, export sales at Novi topped $1 million and increased 40 percent in the second year of operations. Today, Novi Inc. is a large distributor of wireless intercom systems that exports to more than 10 countries.[15]

successful in the global arena are typically willing to discuss opportunities overseas with the owners or managers of small firms.[16]

Utilizing Export Management Companies   LO16-2

One way for first-time exporters to identify the opportunities associated with exporting and to avoid many of the associated pitfalls is to hire an **export management company (EMC)**. EMCs are export specialists that act as the export marketing department or international department for their client firms. EMCs normally accept two types of export assignments. They start exporting operations for a firm with the understanding that the firm will take over operations after they are well established. In another type, start-up services are performed with the understanding that the EMC will have continuing responsibility for selling the firm's products. Many EMCs specialize in serving firms in particular industries and in particular areas of the world. Thus, one EMC may specialize in selling agricultural products in the Asian market, while another may focus on exporting electronics products to eastern Europe.

In theory, the advantage of EMCs is that they are experienced specialists that can help the neophyte exporter identify opportunities and avoid common pitfalls. A good EMC will have a network of contacts in potential markets, have multilingual employees, have a good knowledge of different business mores, and be fully conversant with the ins and outs of the exporting process and with local business regulations. However, the quality of EMCs varies.[17] While some perform their functions very well, others appear to add little value to the exporting company. Therefore, an exporter should review carefully a number of EMCs and check references. One drawback of relying on EMCs is that the company can fail to develop its own exporting capabilities.

Export Strategy   LO16-2

In addition to using EMCs, a firm can reduce the risks associated with exporting if it is careful about its choice of export strategy.[18] A few guidelines can help firms improve their odds of success. For example, one of the most successful exporting firms in the world, 3M (originally, Minnesota Mining & Manufacturing Company), has built its export success on three main principles—enter on a small scale to reduce risks, add additional product lines once the exporting operations start to become successful, and hire locals to promote the firm's products (3M's export strategy is profiled in the accompanying Management Focus). Another successful exporter, Red Spot Paint & Varnish Company, emphasizes the importance of cultivating personal relationships when trying to build an export business.

The probability of exporting successfully can be increased dramatically by taking a handful of simple strategic steps. First, particularly for the novice exporter, it helps to hire an EMC or at least an experienced export consultant to identify opportunities and navigate the paperwork and regulations so often involved in exporting. Second, it often makes sense to initially focus on one market or a handful of markets. Learn what is required to succeed in those markets before moving to other markets. The firm that enters many markets at once runs the risk of spreading its limited management resources too thin. The result of such a shotgun approach to exporting may be a failure to become established in any one market. Third, as with 3M, it often makes sense to enter a foreign market on a small scale to reduce the costs of any subsequent failure. Most important, entering on a small scale provides the time and opportunity to learn about the foreign country before making significant capital commitments to that market. Fourth, the exporter needs to recognize the time and managerial commitment involved in building export sales and should hire additional personnel to oversee this activity. Fifth, in many countries, it is important to devote a lot of attention to building strong and enduring relationships with local distributors and/or customers. Sixth, as 3M often does, it is important to hire local personnel to

Export Strategy at 3M

3M, which makes more than 40,000 products including tape, sandpaper, medical products, and the ever-present Post-it notes, is one of the world's great multinational operations. Today, more than 60 percent of the firm's revenues are generated outside the United States. Although the bulk of these revenues came from foreign-based operations, 3M remains a major exporter with more than $2 billion in exports. The company often uses its exports to establish an initial presence in a foreign market, only building foreign production facilities once sales volume rises to a level that justifies local production.

The export strategy is built around simple principles. One is known as "FIDO," which stands for *first in* (to a new market) *defeats others*. The essence of FIDO is to gain an advantage over other exporters by getting into a market first and learning about that country and how to sell there before others do. A second principle is "make a little, sell a little," which is the idea of entering on a small scale with a very modest investment and pushing one basic product, such as reflective sheeting for traffic signs in Russia or scouring pads in Hungary. Once 3M believes it has learned enough about the market to reduce the risk of failure to reasonable levels, it adds additional products.

A third principle at 3M is to hire local employees to sell the firm's products. The company normally sets up a local sales subsidiary to handle its export activities in a country. It then staffs this subsidiary with local hires because it believes they are likely to have a much better idea than American expatriates of how to sell in their own country. Because of the implementation of this principle, fewer than 200 of 3M's 40,000-plus foreign employees are U.S. expatriates.

Another common practice at 3M is to formulate global strategic plans for the export and eventual overseas production of its products. Within the context of these plans, 3M gives local managers considerable autonomy to find the best way to sell the product within their country. Thus, when 3M first exported its Post-it notes, it planned to "sample the daylights" out of the product, but it also told local managers to find the best way of doing this. Local managers hired office cleaning crews to pass out samples in Great Britain and Germany; in Italy, office products distributors were used to pass out free samples; while in Malaysia, local managers employed young women to go from office to office handing out samples of the product. In typical 3M fashion, when the volume of Post-it notes was sufficient to justify it, exports from the United States were replaced by local production. Thus, after several years, 3M found it worthwhile to set up production facilities in France to produce Post-it notes for the European market.[19]

help the firm establish itself in a foreign market. Local people are likely to have a much greater sense of how to do business in a given country than a manager from an exporting firm who has previously never set foot in that country. Seventh, several studies have suggested the firm needs to be proactive about seeking export opportunities.[20] Armchair exporting does not work! The world will not normally beat a pathway to your door. Finally, it is important for the exporter to retain the option of local production. Once exports reach a sufficient volume to justify cost-efficient local production, the exporting firm should consider establishing production facilities in the foreign market. Such localization helps foster good relations with the foreign country and can lead to greater market acceptance. Exporting is often not an end in itself, but merely a step on the road toward establishment of foreign production (again, 3M provides an example of this philosophy).

EXPORT AND IMPORT FINANCING

LO16-4

Mechanisms for financing exports and imports have evolved over the centuries in response to a problem that can be particularly acute in international trade: the lack of trust that exists when one must put faith in a stranger. In this section, we examine the financial devices that have evolved to cope with this problem in the context of international trade: the letter of credit, the draft (or bill of exchange), and the bill of lading. Then we trace the 14 steps of a typical export-import transaction.[21]

Lack of Trust

Firms engaged in international trade have to trust someone they may have never seen, who lives in a different country, who speaks a different language, who abides by (or does not abide by) a different legal system, and who could be very difficult to track down if he or she defaults on an obligation. Consider a U.S. firm exporting to a distributor in France. The U.S. businessman might be concerned that if he ships the products to France before he receives payment from the French businesswoman, she might take delivery of the products and not pay him. Conversely, the French importer might worry that if she pays for the products before they are shipped, the U.S. firm might keep the money and never ship the products or might ship defective products. Neither party to the exchange completely trusts the other. This lack of trust is exacerbated by the distance between the two parties—in space, language, and culture—and by the problems of using an underdeveloped international legal system to enforce contractual obligations.

Due to the (quite reasonable) lack of trust between the two parties, each has his or her own preferences as to how the transaction should be configured. To make sure he is paid, the manager of the U.S. firm would prefer the French distributor to pay for the products before he ships them (see Figure 16.1). Alternatively, to ensure she receives the products, the French distributor would prefer not to pay for them until they arrive (see Figure 16.2). Thus, each party has a different set of preferences. Unless there is some way of establishing trust between the parties, the transaction might never occur.

The problem is solved by using a third party trusted by both—normally a reputable bank—to act as an intermediary. What happens can be summarized as follows (see Figure 16.3). First, the French importer obtains the bank's promise to pay on her behalf, knowing the U.S. exporter will trust the bank.

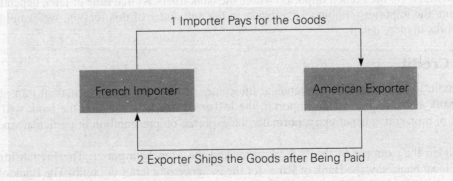

Figure 16.1 *Preference of the U.S. Exporter*

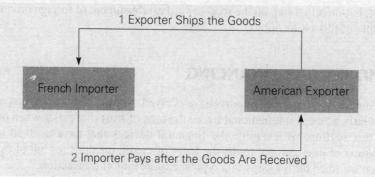

1 Exporter Ships the Goods

French Importer

American Exporter

2 Importer Pays after the Goods Are Received

Figure 16.2 *Preference of the French Importer*

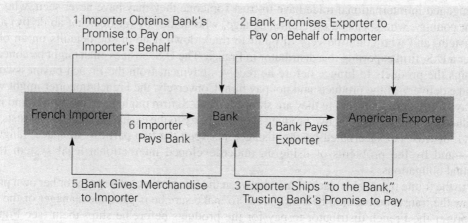

1 Importer Obtains Bank's Promise to Pay on Importer's Behalf

2 Bank Promises Exporter to Pay on Behalf of Importer

French Importer

6 Importer Pays Bank

Bank

4 Bank Pays Exporter

American Exporter

5 Bank Gives Merchandise to Importer

3 Exporter Ships "to the Bank," Trusting Bank's Promise to Pay

Figure 16.3 *The Use of a Third Party*

This promise is known as a letter of credit. Having seen the letter of credit, the U.S. exporter now ships the products to France. Title to the products is given to the bank in the form of a document called a bill of lading. In return, the U.S. exporter tells the bank to pay for the products, which the bank does. The document for requesting this payment is referred to as a draft. The bank, having paid for the products, now passes the title on to the French importer, whom the bank trusts. At that time or later, depending on their agreement, the importer reimburses the bank. In the remainder of this section, we examine how this system works in more detail.

Letter of Credit

A letter of credit, abbreviated as L/C, stands at the center of international commercial transactions. Issued by a bank at the request of an importer, the **letter of credit** states that the bank will pay a specified sum of money to a beneficiary, normally the exporter, on presentation of particular, specified documents.

Consider again the example of the U.S. exporter and the French importer. The French importer applies to her local bank, say, the Bank of Paris, for the issuance of a letter of credit. The Bank of Paris then undertakes a credit check of the importer. If the Bank of Paris is satisfied with her creditworthiness, it will issue a letter of credit. However, the Bank of Paris might require a cash deposit or some other form of collateral from her first. In addition, the Bank of Paris will charge the importer a fee for this service. Typically this amounts to between 0.5 and 2 percent of the value of the letter of credit, depending on the importer's creditworthiness and the size of the transaction. (As a rule, the larger the transaction, the lower the percentage.)

Assume the Bank of Paris is satisfied with the French importer's creditworthiness and agrees to issue a letter of credit. The letter states that the Bank of Paris will pay the U.S. exporter for the merchandise as long as it is shipped in accordance with specified instructions and conditions. At this point, the letter of credit becomes a financial contract between the Bank of Paris and the U.S. exporter. The Bank of Paris then sends the letter of credit to the U.S. exporter's bank, say, the Bank of New York. The Bank of New York tells the exporter that it has received a letter of credit and that he can ship the merchandise. After the exporter has shipped the merchandise, he draws a draft against the Bank of Paris in accordance with the terms of the letter of credit, attaches the required documents, and presents the draft to his own bank, the Bank of New York, for payment. The Bank of New York then forwards the letter of credit and associated documents to the Bank of Paris. If all the terms and conditions contained in the letter of credit have been complied with, the Bank of Paris will honor the draft and will send payment to the Bank of New York. When the Bank of New York receives the funds, it will pay the U.S. exporter.

As for the Bank of Paris, once it has transferred the funds to the Bank of New York, it will collect payment from the French importer. Alternatively, the Bank of Paris may allow the importer some time to resell the merchandise before requiring payment. This is not unusual, particularly when the importer is a distributor and not the final consumer of the merchandise, since it helps the importer's cash flow. The Bank of Paris will treat such an extension of the payment period as a loan to the importer and will charge an appropriate rate of interest.

The great advantage of this system is that both the French importer and the U.S. exporter are likely to trust reputable banks, even if they do not trust each other. Once the U.S. exporter has seen a letter of credit, he knows that he is guaranteed payment and will ship the merchandise. Also, an exporter may find that having a letter of credit will facilitate obtaining pre-export financing. For example, having seen the letter of credit, the Bank of New York might be willing to lend the exporter funds to process and prepare the merchandise for shipping to France. This loan may not have to be repaid until the exporter has received his payment for the merchandise. As for the French importer, she does not have to pay for the merchandise until the documents have arrived and unless all conditions stated in the letter of credit have been satisfied. The drawback for the importer is the fee she must pay the Bank of Paris for the letter of credit. In addition, because the letter of credit is a financial liability against her, it may reduce her ability to borrow funds for other purposes.

Draft

A draft, sometimes referred to as a **bill of exchange**, is the instrument normally used in international commerce to effect payment. A **draft** is simply an order written by an exporter instructing an importer, or an importer's agent, to pay a specified amount of money at a specified time. In the example of the U.S. exporter and the French importer, the exporter writes a draft that instructs the Bank of Paris, the French importer's agent, to pay for the merchandise shipped to France. The person or business initiating the draft is known as the maker (in this case, the U.S. exporter). The party to whom the draft is presented is known as the drawee (in this case, the Bank of Paris).

International practice is to use drafts to settle trade transactions. This differs from domestic practice in which a seller usually ships merchandise on an open account, followed by a commercial invoice that specifies the amount due and the terms of payment. In domestic transactions, the buyer can often obtain possession of the merchandise without signing a formal document acknowledging his or her obligation to pay. In contrast, due to the lack of trust in international transactions, payment or a formal promise to pay is required before the buyer can obtain the merchandise.

Drafts fall into two categories, sight drafts and time drafts. A **sight draft** is payable on presentation to the drawee. A **time draft** allows for a delay in payment—normally 30, 60, 90, or 120 days. It is presented to the drawee, who signifies acceptance of it by writing or stamping a notice of acceptance on its face. Once accepted, the time draft becomes a promise to pay by the accepting party. When a time draft is drawn on and accepted by a bank, it is called a *banker's acceptance.* When it is drawn on and accepted by a business firm, it is called a *trade acceptance.*

Time drafts are negotiable instruments; that is, once the draft is stamped with an acceptance, the maker can sell the draft to an investor at a discount from its face value. Imagine the agreement between the U.S. exporter and the French importer calls for the exporter to present the Bank of Paris (through the Bank of New York) with a time draft requiring payment 120 days after presentation. The Bank of Paris stamps the time draft with an acceptance. Imagine further that the draft is for $100,000.

The exporter can either hold onto the accepted time draft and receive $100,000 in 120 days or sell it to an investor, say, the Bank of New York, for a discount from the face value. If the prevailing discount rate is 7 percent, the exporter could receive $97,700 by selling it immediately (7 percent per year discount rate for 120 days for $100,000 equals $2,300, and $100,000 − $2,300 = $97,700). The Bank of New York would then collect the full $100,000 from the Bank of Paris in 120 days. The exporter might sell the accepted time draft immediately if he needed the funds to finance merchandise in transit and/or to cover cash flow shortfalls.

Bill of Landing

The third key document for financing international trade is the bill of lading. The **bill of lading** is issued to the exporter by the common carrier transporting the merchandise. It serves three purposes: it is a receipt, a contract, and a document of title. As a receipt, the bill of lading indicates that the carrier has received the merchandise described on the face of the document. As a contract, it specifies that the carrier is obligated to provide a transportation service in return for a certain charge. As a document of title, it can be used to obtain payment or a written promise of payment before the merchandise is released to the importer. The bill of lading can also function as collateral against which funds may be advanced to the exporter by its local bank before or during shipment and before final payment by the importer.

A Typical International Trade Transaction

Now that we have reviewed the elements of an international trade transaction, let us see how the process works in a typical case, sticking with the example of the U.S. exporter and the French importer. The typical transaction involves 14 steps (see Figure 16.4).

1. The French importer places an order with the U.S. exporter and asks the American if he would be willing to ship under a letter of credit.
2. The U.S. exporter agrees to ship under a letter of credit and specifies relevant information such as prices and delivery terms.
3. The French importer applies to the Bank of Paris for a letter of credit to be issued in favor of the U.S. exporter for the merchandise the importer wishes to buy.

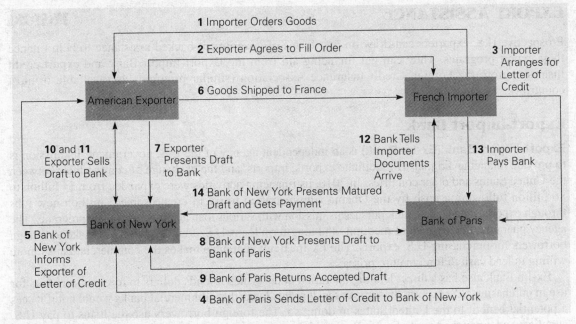

Figure 16.4 *A Typical International Trade Transaction*

4. The Bank of Paris issues a letter of credit in the French importer's favor and sends it to the U.S. exporter's bank, the Bank of New York.
5. The Bank of New York advises the exporter of the opening of a letter of credit in his favor.
6. The U.S. exporter ships the goods to the French importer on a common carrier. An official of the carrier gives the exporter a bill of lading.
7. The U.S. exporter presents a 90-day time draft drawn on the Bank of Paris in accordance with its letter of credit and the bill of lading to the Bank of New York. The exporter endorses the bill of lading so title to the goods is transferred to the Bank of New York.
8. The Bank of New York sends the draft and bill of lading to the Bank of Paris. The Bank of Paris accepts the draft, taking possession of the documents and promising to pay the now-accepted draft in 90 days.
9. The Bank of Paris returns the accepted draft to the Bank of New York.
10. The Bank of New York tells the U.S. exporter that it has received the accepted bank draft, which is payable in 90 days.
11. The exporter sells the draft to the Bank of New York at a discount from its face value and receives the discounted cash value of the draft in return.
12. The Bank of Paris notifies the French importer of the arrival of the documents. She agrees to pay the Bank of Paris in 90 days. The Bank of Paris releases the documents so the importer can take possession of the shipment.
13. In 90 days, the Bank of Paris receives the importer's payment, so it has funds to pay the maturing draft.
14. In 90 days, the holder of the matured acceptance (in this case, the Bank of New York) presents it to the Bank of Paris for payment. The Bank of Paris pays.

EXPORT ASSISTANCE

Prospective U.S. exporters can draw on two forms of government-backed assistance to help finance their export programs. They can get financing aid from the Export-Import Bank and export credit insurance from the Foreign Credit Insurance Association (similar programs are available in most countries).

Export-Import Bank

Export-Import Bank (Ex-Im Bank) is an independent agency of the U.S. government. Its mission is to provide financing aid that will facilitate exports, imports, and the exchange of commodities between the United States and other countries. In 2010, its financing activities were expanded from $4 billion to $6 billion following a push by the Obama administration to try to create some 2 million new jobs through exports. The Ex-Im Bank pursues its mission with various loan and loan-guarantee programs. The agency guarantees repayment of medium- and long-term loans U.S. commercial banks make to foreign borrowers for purchasing U.S. exports. The Ex-Im Bank guarantee makes the commercial banks more willing to lend cash to foreign enterprises.

Ex-Im Bank also has a direct lending operation under which it lends dollars to foreign borrowers for use in purchasing U.S. exports. In some cases, it grants loans that commercial banks would not if it sees a potential benefit to the United States in doing so. The foreign borrowers use the loans to pay U.S. suppliers and repay the loan to Ex-Im Bank with interest.

Export Credit Insurance

For reasons outlined earlier, exporters clearly prefer to get letters of credit from importers. However, sometimes an exporter who insists on a letter of credit will lose an order to one who does not require a letter of credit. Thus, when the importer is in a strong bargaining position and able to play competing suppliers against each other, an exporter may have to forgo a letter of credit.[22] The lack of a letter of credit exposes the exporter to the risk that the foreign importer will default on payment. The exporter can insure against this possibility by buying export credit insurance. If the customer defaults, the insurance firm will cover a major portion of the loss.

In the United States, export credit insurance is provided by the Foreign Credit Insurance Association (FCIA), an association of private commercial institutions operating under the guidance of the Export-Import Bank. The FCIA provides coverage against commercial risks and political risks. Losses due to commercial risk result from the buyer's insolvency or payment default. Political losses arise from actions of governments that are beyond the control of either buyer or seller. Marlin, the small Baltimore manufacturer of wire baskets discussed earlier, credits export credit insurance with giving the company the confidence to push ahead with export sales. For a premium of roughly half a percent of the price of a sale, Marlin has been able to insure itself against the possibility of nonpayment by a foreign buyer.[23]

COUNTERTRADE

Countertrade is an alternative means of structuring an international sale when conventional means of payment are difficult, costly, or nonexistent. We first encountered countertrade in Chapter 10's discussion of currency convertibility. A government may restrict the convertibility of its currency to preserve its foreign exchange reserves so they can be used to service international debt commitments and purchase crucial imports.[24] This is problematic for exporters. Nonconvertibility implies that the exporter may not be paid in his or her home currency, and few exporters would desire payment in a currency that is not convertible. Countertrade is a common solution.[25] **Countertrade** denotes a range of barterlike agreements; its principle is to trade goods and services for other goods and services when they cannot be traded for money. Some examples of countertrade are:

- An Italian company that manufactures power-generating equipment, ABB SAE Sadelmi SpA, was awarded a 720 million baht ($17.7 million) contract by the Electricity Generating Authority of Thailand. The contract specified that the company had to accept 218 million baht ($5.4 million) of Thai farm products as part of the payment.
- Saudi Arabia agreed to buy ten 747 jets from Boeing with payment in crude oil, discounted at 10 percent below posted world oil prices.
- General Electric won a contract for a $150 million electric generator project in Romania by agreeing to market $150 million of Romanian products in markets to which Romania did not have access.
- The Venezuelan government negotiated a contract with Caterpillar under which Venezuela would trade 350,000 tons of iron ore for Caterpillar earthmoving equipment.
- Albania offered such items as spring water, tomato juice, and chrome ore in exchange for a $60 million fertilizer and methanol complex.
- Philip Morris ships cigarettes to Russia, for which it receives chemicals that can be used to make fertilizer. Philip Morris ships the chemicals to China, and in return, China ships glassware to North America for retail sale by Philip Morris.[26]

The Popularity of Countertrade

In the modern era, countertrade arose in the 1960s as a way for the Soviet Union and the Communist states of eastern Europe, whose currencies were generally nonconvertible, to purchase imports. During the 1980s, the technique grew in popularity among many developing nations that lacked the foreign exchange reserves required to purchase necessary imports. Today, reflecting their own shortages of foreign exchange reserves, some successor states to the former Soviet Union and the eastern European Communist nations periodically engage in countertrade to purchase their imports. Estimates of the percentage of world trade covered by some sort of countertrade agreement range from highs of 8 and 10 percent by value to lows of around 2 percent.[27] The precise figure is unknown, but it is probably at the low end of these estimates, given the increasing liquidity of international financial markets and wider currency convertibility. However, a short-term spike in the volume of countertrade can follow periodic financial crises. For example, countertrade activity increased notably after the Asian financial crisis of 1997. That crisis left many Asian nations with little hard currency to finance international trade. In the tight monetary regime that followed the crisis in 1997, many Asian firms found it very difficult to get access to export credit to finance their own international trade. Thus, they turned to the only option available to them—countertrade.

Given that countertrade is a means of financing international trade, albeit a relatively minor one, prospective exporters may have to engage in this technique from time to time to gain access to certain international markets. The governments of developing nations sometimes insist on a certain amount of countertrade.[28] For example, all foreign companies contracted by Thai state agencies for work costing more than 500 million baht ($12.3 million) are required to accept at least 30 percent of their payment in Thai agricultural products. Between 1994 and mid-1998, foreign firms purchased 21 billion baht ($517 million) in Thai goods under countertrade deals.[29]

Types of Countertrade

With its roots in the simple trading of goods and services for other goods and services, countertrade has evolved into a diverse set of activities that can be categorized as five distinct types of trading arrangements: barter, counterpurchase, offset, switch trading, and compensation or buyback.[30] Many countertrade deals involve not just one arrangement, but elements of two or more.

Barter

Barter is the direct exchange of goods and/or services between two parties without a cash transaction. Although barter is the simplest arrangement, it is not common. Its problems are twofold. First, if goods are not exchanged simultaneously, one party ends up financing the other for a period. Second, firms engaged in barter run the risk of having to accept goods they do not want, cannot use, or have difficulty reselling at a reasonable price. For these reasons, barter is viewed as the most restrictive countertrade arrangement. It is primarily used for one-time-only deals in transactions with trading partners who are not creditworthy or trustworthy.

Counterpurchase

Counterpurchase is a reciprocal buying agreement. It occurs when a firm agrees to purchase a certain amount of materials back from a country to which a sale is made. Suppose a U.S. firm sells some products to China. China pays the U.S. firm in dollars, but in exchange, the U.S. firm agrees to spend some of its proceeds from the sale on textiles produced by China. Thus, although China must draw on its foreign exchange reserves to pay the U.S. firm, it knows it will receive some of those dollars back because of the counterpurchase agreement. In one counterpurchase agreement, Rolls-Royce sold jet parts to Finland. As part of the deal, Rolls-Royce agreed to use some of the proceeds from the sale to purchase Finnish-manufactured TV sets that it would then sell in Great Britain.

Offset

An **offset** is similar to a counterpurchase insofar as one party agrees to purchase goods and services with a specified percentage of the proceeds from the original sale. The difference is that this party can fulfill the obligation with any firm in the country to which the sale is being made. From an exporter's perspective, this is more attractive than a straight counterpurchase agreement because it gives the exporter greater flexibility to choose the goods that it wishes to purchase.

Switch Trading

The term **switch trading** refers to the use of a specialized third-party trading house in a countertrade arrangement. When a firm enters a counterpurchase or offset agreement with a country, it often ends up with what are called counterpurchase credits, which can be used to purchase goods from that country. Switch trading occurs when a third-party trading house buys the firm's counterpurchase credits and sells them to another firm that can better use them. For example, a U.S. firm concludes a counterpurchase agreement with Poland for which it receives some number of counterpurchase credits for purchasing Polish goods. The U.S. firm cannot use and does not want any Polish goods, however, so it sells the credits to a third-party trading house at a discount. The trading house finds a firm that can use the credits and sells them at a profit.

In one example of switch trading, Poland and Greece had a counterpurchase agreement that called for Poland to buy the same U.S.-dollar value of goods from Greece that it sold to Greece. However, Poland could not find enough Greek goods that it required, so it ended up with a dollar-denominated counterpurchase balance in Greece that it was unwilling to use. A switch trader bought the right to 250,000 counterpurchase dollars from Poland for $225,000 and sold them to a European sultana (grape) merchant for $235,000, who used them to purchase sultanas from Greece.

Compensation or Buybacks

A **buyback** occurs when a firm builds a plant in a country—or supplies technology, equipment, training, or other services to the country—and agrees to take a certain percentage of the plant's output as partial payment for the contract. For example, Occidental Petroleum negotiated a deal with Russia under which Occidental would build several ammonia plants in Russia and as partial payment receive ammonia over a 20-year period.

Pros and Cons of Countertrade

Countertrade's main attraction is that it can give a firm a way to finance an export deal when other means are not available. Given the problems that many developing nations have in raising the foreign exchange necessary to pay for imports, countertrade may be the only option available when doing business in these countries. Even when countertrade is not the only option for structuring an export transaction, many countries prefer countertrade to cash deals. Thus, if a firm is unwilling to enter a countertrade agreement, it may lose an export opportunity to a competitor that is willing to make a countertrade agreement.

In addition, a countertrade agreement may be required by the government of a country to which a firm is exporting goods or services. Boeing often has to accept to counterpurchase agreements to capture orders for its commercial jet aircraft. For example, in exchange for gaining an order from Air India, Boeing may be required to purchase certain component parts, such as aircraft doors, from an Indian company. Taking this one step further, Boeing can use its willingness to enter into a counterpurchase agreement as a way of winning orders in the face of intense competition from its global rival, Airbus. Thus, countertrade can become a strategic marketing weapon.

However, the drawbacks of countertrade agreements are substantial. Other things being equal, firms would normally prefer to be paid in hard currency. Countertrade contracts may involve the exchange of unusable or poor-quality goods that the firm cannot dispose of profitably. For example, a few years ago, one U.S. firm got burned when 50 percent of the television sets it received in a countertrade agreement with Hungary were defective and could not be sold. In addition, even if the goods it receives are of high quality, the firm still needs to dispose of them profitably. To do this, countertrade requires the firm to invest in an in-house trading department dedicated to arranging and managing countertrade deals. This can be expensive and time-consuming.

Given these drawbacks, countertrade is most attractive to large, diverse multinational enterprises that can use their worldwide network of contacts to dispose of goods acquired in countertrading. The masters of countertrade are Japan's giant trading firms, the *sogo shosha,* which use their vast networks of affiliated companies to profitably dispose of goods acquired through countertrade agreements. The trading firm of Mitsui & Company, for example, has about 120 affiliated companies in almost every sector of the manufacturing and service industries. If one of Mitsui's affiliates receives goods in a countertrade agreement that it cannot consume, Mitsui & Company will normally be able to find another affiliate that can profitably use them. Firms affiliated with one of Japan's *sogo shosha* often have a competitive advantage in countries where countertrade agreements are preferred.

Western firms that are large, diverse, and have a global reach (e.g., General Electric, Philip Morris, and 3M) have similar profit advantages from countertrade agreements. Indeed, 3M has established its own trading company—3M Global Trading Inc.—to develop and manage the company's international countertrade programs. Unless there is no alternative, small and medium-size exporters should probably try to avoid countertrade deals because they lack the worldwide network of operations that may be required to profitably utilize or dispose of goods acquired through them.[31]

Chapter Summary

This chapter examined the steps that firms must take to establish themselves as exporters. The chapter made the following points:

1. One big impediment to exporting is ignorance of foreign market opportunities.

2. Neophyte exporters often become discouraged or frustrated with the exporting process because they encounter many problems, delays, and pitfalls.

3. The way to overcome ignorance is to gather information. In the United States, a number of institutions, the most important of which is the Department of Commerce, can help firms gather information in the matchmaking process. Export management companies can also help identify export opportunities.

4. Many of the pitfalls associated with exporting can be avoided if a company hires an experienced export management company, or export consultant, and if it adopts the appropriate export strategy.

5. Firms engaged in international trade must do business with people they cannot trust and people who may be difficult to track down if they default on an obligation. Due to the lack of trust, each party to an international transaction has a different set of preferences regarding the configuration of the transaction.

6. The problems arising from lack of trust between exporters and importers can be solved by using a third party that is trusted by both, normally a reputable bank.

7. A letter of credit is issued by a bank at the request of an importer. It states that the bank promises to pay a beneficiary, normally the exporter, on presentation of documents specified in the letter.

8. A draft is the instrument normally used in international commerce to effect payment. It is an order written by an exporter instructing an importer, or an importer's agent, to pay a specified amount of money at a specified time.

9. Drafts are either sight drafts or time drafts. Time drafts are negotiable instruments.

10. A bill of lading is issued to the exporter by the common carrier transporting the merchandise. It serves as a receipt, a contract, and a document of title.

11. U.S. exporters can draw on two types of government-backed assistance to help finance their exports: loans from the Export-Import Bank and export credit insurance from the FCIA.

12. Countertrade includes a range of barterlike agreements. It is primarily used when a firm exports to a country whose currency is not freely convertible and may lack the foreign exchange reserves required to purchase the imports.

13. The main attraction of countertrade is that it gives a firm a way to finance an export deal when other means are not available. A firm that insists on being paid in hard currency may be at a competitive disadvantage vis-à-vis one that is willing to engage in countertrade.

14. The main disadvantage of countertrade is that the firm may receive unusable or poor-quality goods that cannot be disposed of profitably.

Critical Thinking and Discussion Questions

1. A firm based in Washington State wants to export a shipload of finished lumber to the Philippines. The would-be importer cannot get sufficient credit from domestic sources to pay for the shipment but insists that the finished lumber can quickly be resold in the Philippines for a profit. Outline the steps the exporter should take to effect this export to the Philippines.

2. You are the assistant to the CEO of a small textile firm that manufactures quality, premium-priced, stylish clothing. The CEO has decided to see what the opportunities are for exporting and has asked you for advice as to the steps the company should take. What advice would you give the CEO?

3. An alternative to using a letter of credit is export credit insurance. What are the advantages and disadvantages of using export credit insurance rather than a letter of credit for exporting (a) a luxury yacht from California to Canada and (b) machine tools from New York to Ukraine?

4. How do you explain the use of countertrade? Under what scenarios might its use increase further by 2020? Under what scenarios might its use decline?

5. How might a company make strategic use of countertrade schemes as a marketing weapon to generate export revenues? What are the risks associated with pursuing such a strategy?

Research Task ⚓ globalEDGE   globaledge.msu.edu

Exporting, Importing, and Countertrade

Use the globalEDGE website (globaledge.msu.edu) to complete the following exercises:

Exercise 1

One way that exporters analyze conditions in emerging markets is through the use of macroeconomic indicators. The *Market Potential Index* (MPI) is a yearly study conducted by the Michigan State University Center for International Business Education and Research (MSU-CIBER) to compare the market potential of emerging markets for U.S. exporters. Provide a description of the dimensions used in the index. Which of the dimensions would have greater importance for a company that markets wireless devices? What about a company that sells clothing?

Exercise 2

You work in the sales department of a company that manufactures and sells medical implants. An Indian company contacted your department and expressed interest in purchasing a large quantity of your products. The Brazilian company requested an FOB price quote. One of your colleagues mentioned to you that FOB is part of a collection of international shipping terms called "Incoterms," but that was all he knew. Find the *Export Tutorials* on the globalEDGE site, and find a more detailed explanation of Incoterms. For an FOB quote, what line items will you need to include in your price quote, in addition to the price your company will charge for the products?

Closing CASE

Vellus Products

Sharon Doherty founded Vellus Products in 1991 in Columbus, Ohio, to sell pet shampoo. Doherty's original insight was that shampoos for people don't work well on pets because the skin of most animals is more sensitive than that of humans and becomes easily irritated. A competitive dog exhibitor, she knew that most existing pet shampoo left dog hair unmanageable and lacking the glamour needed for a dog show. Working with her nephew, who had a PhD in chemistry, Doherty developed salon-type formulas that were specially suited to dogs (shampoo for horses was added later).

Doherty booked Vellus's first export sales in 1993 when a Taiwanese businessman, who had picked up Vellus shampoo in the United States, ordered $25,000 worth of products he wanted to try to sell through dog shows in Taiwan. Before long, Doherty was getting calls from people around the world—most of whom heard about Vellus Products at dog shows—and a thriving export business was born.

As the volume of inquiries grew, Doherty realized she needed a better understanding of foreign markets, export potential, and financing options, so she contacted the U.S. Department of Commerce's Commercial Service offices in Columbus. "As business has grown, I have gone from ordering country profiles to requesting customized exporting and financing strategies tailored to maximize export potential," she says. Today, Vellus exports to 32 nations, although the bulk of the firm's international business operates through distributors in Sweden, Finland, Britain, Germany, Australia, New Zealand, Canada, and Iceland, where the products are marketed at pet shows and exhibitions. The company has registered its trademark in 15 European countries, and international sales account for more than half the firm's total. "I credit the U.S. Commercial Service for helping me to expand my exports, as it would have been much more difficult on my own," says Doherty.

Reflecting on her international success, Doherty has some advice for others who might want to go down the same road. First she says, relationships are important to successful exporting. Doherty says she goes out of her way to give advice and guidance to her distributors, sharing her knowledge and helping them to be successful. Second, know whom you are dealing with. Having been duped by a man who claimed he knew the pet market when he didn't, she advocates doing background checks on potential business partners. "Gather as much information as you can," she says. "Don't make any assumptions; the wrong choice can cost your business valuable time and money." Third, Doherty believes that it is important to learn the local culture. Vellus products are adapted to best suit different grooming techniques in different countries, something that she believes has helped make the company more successful. Finally, Doherty says, enjoy the ride! "I love exporting because it has enabled me to meet so many people from other cultures. Exporting has made me more broad-minded, and I have developed a great appreciation for other cultures and the way others live their lives."[32]

Case Discussion Questions

1. Why does Vellus export through local distributors rather than set up its own sales force in country? What are the risks associated with using local distributors? How can these risks be reduced?
2. Vellus's original entry into exporting was both reactive and serendipitous. Do you think this is the exception or the rule for small businesses? What might be done to make small firms more proactive with regard to exporting?
3. What lessons about successful exporting can be derived from the Vellus case?

4. How important has government assistance been to Vellus Products? Do you think helping firms such as Vellus represents good use of taxpayer money?

Endnotes

1. L. L. Sowinski, "And the Winner Is . . . ," *World Trade,* January 2011, pp. 40–42; "Virginia Based Company Wins SBA/VISA Export Video Contest," *U.S. Newswire,* November 7, 2011; and "UPS Honors SteelMaster with Global Trade Award," *Business Wire,* January 12, 2011.
2. R. A. Pope, "Why Small Firms Export: Another Look," *Journal of Small Business Management* 40 (2002), pp. 17–26.
3. M. C. White "Marlin Steel Wire Products," *Slate Magazine,* November 10, 2010.
4. S. T. Cavusgil, "Global Dimensions of Marketing," in *Marketing,* ed. P. E. Murphy and B. M. Enis (Glenview, IL: Scott, Foresman, 1985), pp. 577–99.
5. S. M. Mehta, "Enterprise: Small Companies Look to Cultivate Foreign Business," *The Wall Street Journal,* July 7, 1994, p. B2.
6. P. A. Julien and C. Ramagelahy, "Competitive Strategy and Performance of Exporting SMEs," *Entrepreneurship Theory and Practice,* 2003, pp. 227–94.
7. W. J. Burpitt and D. A. Rondinelli, "Small Firms' Motivations for Exporting: To Earn and Learn?" *Journal of Small Business Management,* October 2000, pp. 1–14; and J. D. Mittelstaedt, G. N. Harben, and W. A. Ward, "How Small Is Too Small?" *Journal of Small Business Management* 41 (2003), pp. 68–85.
8. Small Business Administration, "The State of Small Business 1999–2000: Report to the President," 2001; and D. Ransom, "Obama's Math: More Exports Equals More Jobs," *The Wall Street Journal,* February 6, 2010.
9. A. O. Ogbuehi and T. A. Longfellow, "Perceptions of U.S. Manufacturing Companies Concerning Exporting," *Journal of Small Business Management,* October 1994, pp. 37–59; and U.S. Small Business Administration, "Guide to Exporting," www.sba.gov/oit/info/Guide-to-Exporting/index.html.
10. R. W. Haigh, "Thinking of Exporting?" *Columbia Journal of World Business* 29 (December 1994), pp. 66–86.
11. F. Williams, "The Quest for More Efficient Commerce," *Financial Times,* October 13, 1994, p. 7.
12. J. Sparshott, "Businesses Must Export to Compete," *The Washington Times,* September 1, 2004, p. C8; "Entrepreneur of the Year 2001: Donald Gallion, FCX Systems," *The State Journal,* June 18, 2001, p. S10; and T. Pierro, "Exporting Powers Growth of FCX Systems," *The State Journal,* April 6, 1998, p. 1.
13. See Burpitt and Rondinelli, "Small Firms' Motivations for Exporting"; and C. S. Katsikeas, L. C. Leonidou, and N. A. Morgan, "Firm Level Export Performance Assessment," *Academy of Marketing Science* 28 (2000), pp. 493–511.
14. M. Y. Yoshino and T. B. Lifson, *The Invisible Link* (Cambridge, MA: MIT Press, 1986).
15. Small Business Administration Office of International Trade, "Guide to Exporting," www.sba.gov/oit/info/Guide-ToExporting/index.html; U.S. Department of Commerce, "A Profile of U.S. Exporting Companies, 2000–2001," February 2003, report available at www.census.gov/foreign-trade/aip/index.html#profile; and *The 2007 National Exporting Strategy* (Washington, DC: U.S. International Trade Commission, 2007).
16. L. W. Tuller, *Going Global* (Homewood, IL: Business One–Irwin, 1991).
17. Haigh, "Thinking of Exporting?"
18. M. A. Raymond, J. Kim, and A. T. Shao. "Export Strategy and Performance," *Journal of Global Marketing* 15 (2001), pp. 5–29; and P. S. Aulakh, M. Kotabe, and H. Teegen, "Export Strategies and Performance of Firms from Emerging Economies," *Academy of Management Journal* 43 (2000), pp. 342–61.
19. R. L. Rose, "Success Abroad," *The Wall Street Journal,* March 29, 1991, p. A1; T. Eiben, "US Exporters Keep On Rolling," *Fortune,* June 14, 1994, pp. 128–31; 3M Company, *A Century on Innovation,* 3M, 2002; and 2005 10K form archived at 3M's website at www.3m.com.
20. J. Francis and C. Collins-Dodd, "The Impact of Firms' Export Orientation on the Export Performance of High-Tech Small and Medium Sized Enterprises," *Journal of International Marketing* 8, no. 3 (2000), pp. 84–103.
21. J. Koch, "Integration of U.S. Small Businesses into the Export Trade Sector Using Available Financial Tools and Resources," *Business Credit* 109, no. 10 (2007), pp. 64–68.
22. For a review of the conditions under which a buyer has power over a supplier, see M. E. Porter, *Competitive Strategy* (New York: Free Press, 1980).
23. White, "Marlin Steel Wire Products."
24. *Exchange Agreements and Exchange Restrictions* (Washington, DC: International Monetary Fund, 1989).
25. It's also sometimes argued that countertrade is a way of reducing the risks inherent in a traditional money-for-goods transaction, particularly with entities from emerging economies. See C. J. Choi, S. H. Lee, and J. B. Kim, "A Note of Counter-

trade: Contractual Uncertainty and Transactional Governance in Emerging Economies," *Journal of International Business Studies* 30, no. 1 (1999), pp. 189–202.

26. J. R. Carter and J. Gagne, "The Do's and Don'ts of International Countertrade," *Sloan Management Review,* Spring 1988, pp. 31–37; and W. Maneerungsee, "Countertrade: Farm Goods Swapped for Italian Electricity," *Bangkok Post,* July 23, 1998.

27. Estimate from the American Countertrade Association at www.countertrade.org/index.htm. See also D. West, "Countertrade," *Business Credit* 104, no. 4 (2001), pp. 64–67; and B. Meyer, "The Original Meaning of Trade Meets the Future of Barter," *World Trade* 13 (January 2000), pp. 46–50.

28. Carter and Gagne, "The Do's and Don'ts of International Countertrade."

29. Maneerungsee, "Countertrade."

30. For details, see Carter and Gagne, "Do's and Don'ts of International Countertrade"; J. F. Hennart, "Some Empirical Dimensions of Countertrade," *Journal of International Business Studies,* 1990, pp. 240–60; and West, "Countertrade."

31. D. J. Lecraw, "The Management of Counter-Trade: Factors Influencing Success," *Journal of International Business Studies,* Spring 1989, pp. 41–59.

32. U.S. Department of Commerce, "Vellus Products Inc.," www.export.gov; C. K. Cultice, "Best in Show: Vellus Products," *World Trade,* January 2007, pp. 70–73; and C. K. Cultice, "Lathering up World Markets," *Business America,* July 1997, p. 33.

Chapter 17
Global Production, Outsourcing, and Logistics

LEARNING OBJECTIVES

After reading this chapter, you will be able to:

LO17-1 Explain why production and logistics decisions are of central importance to many multinational businesses.

LO17-2 Explain how country differences, production technology, and product features all affect the choice of where to locate production activities.

LO17-3 Recognize how the role of foreign subsidiaries in production can be enhanced over time as they accumulate knowledge.

LO17-4 Identify the factors that influence a firm's decision of whether to source supplies from within the company or from foreign suppliers.

LO17-5 Describe what is required to efficiently coordinate a globally dispersed production system.

DID BOEING OUTSOURCE TOO MUCH WORK ON THE 787?

Opening Case

Back in the early 2000s it looked as if the Boeing 787 was going to be a triumph for the company. The wide-bodied long-haul jet built out of carbon fiber and capable of carrying 250 people had captured a record number of orders in the year after its launch. The big selling point: The two-engine 787 weighs considerably less than comparable aircraft and, as a result, uses 20 percent less fuel. As a bonus, the 787 is estimated to be 30 percent cheaper to maintain. Moreover, Boeing was three years ahead of its rival Airbus in the race to develop this type of jet.

As the 787 program progressed, however, things started to go seriously wrong for Boeing. Problems kept cropping up in the manufacture and testing of the plane. Small wrinkles were found in parts of the carbon fiber fuselage that required extensive rework. There was a weakness in the region where the wings attached to the fuselage, necessitating a redesign. Bottlenecks kept cropping up in the supply chain. Parts were frequently not delivered on time, bringing production to a halt. The delivery schedule was pushed back at least seven times. The first planes were delivered three years late. Even then, the problems didn't stop. First there was a windshield crack, then minor fuel leaks, and in early 2013, there were two incidents of overheating in lithium-ion batteries used on the plane, which grounded the entire 787 fleet for three months.

Many observers were quick to point out that Boeing had outsourced production of the 787 by as much as 70 percent to suppliers around the world. The implication was that this had resulted in many of the problems. The outsourcing was driven by two factors. First, there was a drive to reduce production costs, with a belief that foreign suppliers could perform the work at a lower cost. Second, some outsourcing to foreign countries may have been motivated by a desire to gain orders for the 787 from airlines in those countries. Most notably, 35 percent of the 787's airframe structure was made in Japan. Japan's two largest airlines, JAL and ANA, are major Boeing customers.

Boeing's critics claim that the company's outsourcing strategy was naive. The company outsourced not only much of the component part manufacturing for the 787 but also the design engineering of those components. This was particularly risky with a plane as innovative as the 787, which was the first jet airliner to be built entirely out of composites. As time progressed, it became increasingly clear that some key suppliers lacked the requisite design engineering skills. Moreover, there were multiple tiers of outsourced companies that were supposed to be making their designs consistent so that the parts all fitted together—and they didn't. There was a gross lack of coordination between design engineers at different part in the supply chain, principally because no one company owned the overall design process. Boeing, the critics argue, should *not* have outsourced design engineering. Instead it should have had subcontractors make parts in strict accordance with Boeing's design requirements.

In short, Boeing did not look at the total costs of outsourcing when it made its initial decision to farm out large chunks of the 787 program to foreign suppliers. While it clearly did look at basic manufacturing costs, it did not look adequately at the implicit costs of outsourcing design engineering, including the cost overruns that resulted from poor design decisions by companies upstream in the global supply chain. In 2009, Boeing spent more than a billion dollars to acquire some of the worst-performing suppliers and bring them in-house in a belated effort to gain control over the design and production process. In an admission that serious mistakes had been made, Jim Albaugh, who ran the 787 program from 2009 through 2012, stated, "We spent a lot more money in trying to recover than we ever would have spent if we'd tried to keep the key technologies closer to home."[1]

INTRODUCTION

As trade barriers fall and global markets develop, many firms increasingly confront a set of interrelated issues. First, where in the world should production activities be located? Should they be concentrated in a single country, or should they be dispersed around the globe, matching the type of activity with country differences in factor costs, tariff barriers, political risks, and the like to minimize costs and maximize value added? Second, what should be the long-term strategic role of foreign production sites? Should the firm abandon a foreign site if factor costs change, moving production to another more favorable location, or is there value to maintaining an operation at a given location even if underlying economic conditions change? Third, should the firm own foreign production activities, or is it better to outsource those activities to independent vendors? Fourth, how should a globally dispersed supply chain be managed, and what is the role of Internet-based information technology in the management of global logistics? Fifth, should the firm manage global logistics itself, or should it outsource the management to enterprises that specialize in this activity?

The example of Boeing's 787 program discussed in the opening case touches on some of these issues. Like many modern products, different components for the 787 are manufactured in different locations to produce a low-cost product. In choosing which company should make which components, Boeing was guided by the need to keep the cost of the airplane low so that it could price aggressively and gain market share from its global rival, Airbus. However, as the case demonstrates, Boeing may have miscalculated when it decided to outsource not only manufacturing but also design engineering, particularly for a product as innovative as the 787. In this case, serious problems arose in Boeing's globally dispersed supply chain that led to delays and billions of dollars in cost overruns. As the Boeing example illustrates, companies need to be very careful when deciding to outsource production to foreign suppliers, and they need to think about the *total costs* of outsourcing, not just basic differentials in production cost.

STRATEGY, PRODUCTION, AND LOGISTICS   IOITSI

Chapter 13 introduced the concept of the value chain and discussed a number of value creation activities, including production, marketing, logistics, R&D, human resources, and information systems. This chapter focuses on two of these activities—**production** and **logistics**—and attempts to clarify how they might be performed internationally to (1) lower the costs of value creation and (2) add value by better serving customer needs. We discuss the contributions of information technology to these activities, which has become particularly important in the era of the Internet. The remaining chapters in this text look at other value creation activities in this international context (marketing, R&D, and human resource management).

In Chapter 13, we defined *production* as "the activities involved in creating a product." We used the term *production* to denote both service and manufacturing activities, because one can produce a service or produce a physical product. Although in this chapter we focus more on the production of physical goods, we should not forget that the term can also be applied to services. This has become more evident in recent years, with the trend among U.S. firms to outsource the "production" of certain service activities to developing nations where labor costs are lower (e.g., the trend among many U.S. companies to outsource customer care services to places such as India, where English is widely spoken and labor costs are much lower). Logistics is the activity that controls the transmission of physical materials through the value chain, from procurement through production and into distribution. Production and logistics are closely linked because a firm's ability to perform its production activities efficiently depends on a timely supply of high-quality material inputs, for which logistics is responsible.

The production and logistics functions of an international firm have a number of important strategic objectives.[2] One is to lower costs. Dispersing production activities to various locations around the globe where each activity can be performed most efficiently can lower costs. Costs can also be cut by managing the global supply chain efficiently so as to better match supply and demand. Efficient supply chain management reduces the amount of inventory in the system and increases inventory turnover, which means the firm has to invest less working capital in inventory and is less likely to find excess inventory on hand that cannot be sold and has to be written off.

A second strategic objective shared by production and logistics is to increase product quality by eliminating defective products from both the supply chain and the manufacturing process.[3] (In this context,

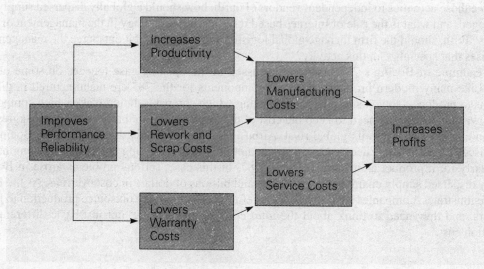

Figure 17.1   *The Relationship between Quality and Costs*

quality means *reliability*, implying that the product has no defects and performs well.) The objectives of reducing costs and increasing quality are not independent of each other. As illustrated in Figure 17.1, the firm that improves its quality control will also reduce its costs of value creation. Improved quality control reduces costs by:

- Increasing productivity because time is not wasted producing poor-quality products that cannot be sold, leading to a direct reduction in unit costs.
- Lowering rework and scrap costs associated with defective products.
- Reducing the warranty costs and time associated with fixing defective products.

The effect is to lower the costs of value creation by reducing both production and after-sales service costs.

The principal tool that most managers now use to increase the reliability of their product offering is the Six Sigma quality improvement methodology. The Six Sigma methodology is a direct descendant of the **total quality management (TQM)** philosophy that was widely adopted, first by Japanese companies and then American companies, during the 1980s and early 1990s.[4] The TQM philosophy was developed by a number of American consultants such as W. Edward Deming, Joseph Juran, and A. V. Feigenbaum.[5] Deming identified a number of steps that should be part of any TQM program. He argued that management should embrace the philosophy that mistakes, defects, and poor-quality materials are not acceptable and should be eliminated. He suggested that the quality of supervision should be improved by allowing more time for supervisors to work with employees and by providing them with the tools they need to do the job. Deming recommended that management should create an environment in which employees will not fear reporting problems or recommending improvements. He believed that work standards should not only be defined as numbers or quotas but also include some notion of quality to promote the production of defect-free output. He argued that management has the responsibility to train employees in new skills to keep pace with changes in the workplace. In addition, he believed that achieving better quality requires the commitment of everyone in the company.

Six Sigma, the modern successor to TQM, is a statistically based philosophy that aims to reduce defects, boost productivity, eliminate waste, and cut costs throughout a company. Six Sigma programs have been adopted by several major corporations, such as Motorola, General Electric, and Honeywell. Sigma comes from the Greek letter that statisticians use to represent a standard deviation from a mean; the higher the number of "sigmas," the smaller the number of errors. At six sigmas, a production process would be 99.99966 percent accurate, creating just 3.4 defects per million units. While it is almost impossible for a company to achieve such perfection, Six Sigma quality is a goal to strive toward. Increasingly, companies are adopting Six Sigma programs to try to boost their product quality and productivity.[6]

The growth of international standards has also focused greater attention on the importance of product quality. In Europe, for example, the European Union requires that the quality of a firm's manufacturing processes and products be certified under a quality standard known as **ISO 9000** before the firm is allowed access to the EU marketplace. Although the ISO 9000 certification process has proved to be somewhat bureaucratic and costly for many firms, it does focus management attention on the need to improve the quality of products and processes.[7]

In addition to lowering costs and improving quality, two other objectives have particular importance in international businesses. First, production and logistics functions must be able to accommodate demands for local responsiveness. As we saw in Chapter 13, demands for local responsiveness arise from national differences in consumer tastes and preferences, infrastructure, distribution channels, and host-government demands. Demands for local responsiveness create pressures to decentralize production activities to the major national or regional markets in which the firm does business or to implement flexible manufacturing processes that enable the firm to customize the product coming out of a factory according to the market in which it is to be sold.

Second, production and logistics must be able to respond quickly to shifts in customer demand. In recent years, time-based competition has grown more important.[8] When consumer demand is prone to large and unpredictable shifts, the firm that can adapt most quickly to these shifts will gain an advantage.[9] As we shall see, both production and logistics play critical roles here.

WHERE TO PRODUCE

An essential decision facing an international firm is where to locate its production activities to best minimize costs and improve product quality. For the firm contemplating international production, a number of factors must be considered. These factors can be grouped under three broad headings: country factors, technological factors, and product factors.[10]

Country Factors

We reviewed country-specific factors in some detail earlier in the book. Political economy, culture, and relative factor costs differ from country to country. In Chapter 6, we saw that due to differences in factor costs, some countries have a comparative advantage for producing certain products. In Chapters 2, 3, and 4 we saw how differences in political economy and national culture influence the benefits, costs, and risks of doing business in a country. Other things being equal, a firm should locate its various manufacturing activities where the economic, political, and cultural conditions—including relative factor costs—are conducive to the performance of those activities (for an example, see the accompanying Management Focus, which looks at the Philips investment in China). In Chapter 13, we referred to the benefits derived from such a strategy as location economies. We argued that one result of the strategy is the creation of a global web of value creation activities.

Philips in China

The Dutch consumer electronics, lighting, semiconductor, and medical equipment conglomerate Philips Electronics NV has been operating factories in China since 1985, when the country first opened its markets to foreign investors. When Philips initially entered China, it had dreams of Chinese consumers snapping up its products by the millions. However, the company soon found out that the reason it liked China—low wage rates—also meant that few Chinese workers could afford to buy its products. So Philips hit on a new strategy: Keep the factories in China, but export most of the goods to developed nations.

The initial attractions of China to Philips included low wage rates, an educated workforce, a robust Chinese economy, a stable exchange rate that is linked to the U.S. dollar through a managed float, a rapidly expanding industrial base that includes many other Western and Chinese companies that Philips uses as suppliers, and easier access to world markets given China's entry into the WTO in 2001. By the early 2000s Philips employed some 30,000 people in China either directly, or indirectly at joint ventures. Philips exported nearly two-thirds of the $7 billion in products that its Chinese factories were producing. At this point, 25 percent of everything that Philips made worldwide came from China.

As time passed, Philips started to give its Chinese factories a greater role in product development. In the TV business, for example, basic development used to occur in Holland but was moved to Singapore in the early 1990s. In the early 2000s Philips transferred TV development work to a new R&D center in Suzhou near Shanghai. Similarly, basic product development work on LCD screens for cell phones was shifted to Shanghai. In 2011, in a testament to just how important China had become to Philips, the company moved the global headquarters of its domestic appliances business from Amsterdam to Shanghai. By this point, China was far more than just an export base. Demand in China had accelerated rapidly, and the country was now the second-largest market for Philips.

Some worry that Philips and companies pursuing a similar strategy might be overdoing it. Too much dependence on China could be dangerous if political, economic, or other problems disrupt production and the company's ability to supply global markets. Some observers believe that it might be better if the manufacturing facilities of companies were more geographically diverse as a hedge against problems in China. These fears have taken on added importance recently as labor costs have accelerated in China due to labor shortages. According to estimates, labor costs have been growing by 20 percent per year since the 2000s. On the other hand, there is a silver lining to this cloud: Chinese consumption of many of the products that Philips makes there is now rising rapidly.[11]

Also important in some industries is the presence of global concentrations of activities at certain locations. In Chapter 8, we discussed the role of location externalities in influencing foreign direct investment decisions. Externalities include the presence of an appropriately skilled labor pool and supporting industries.[12] Such externalities can play an important role in deciding where to locate production activities. For example, because of a cluster of semiconductor manufacturing plants in Taiwan, a pool of labor with experience in the semiconductor business has developed. In addition, the plants have attracted a number of supporting industries, such as the manufacturers of semiconductor capital equipment and silicon, which have established facilities in Taiwan to be near their customers. This implies that there are real benefits to locating in Taiwan, as opposed to another location that lacks such externalities. Other things being equal, the externalities make Taiwan an attractive location for semiconductor manufacturing facilities. The same process is now under way in two Indian cities, Hyderabad and Bangalore, where both Western and Indian information technology companies have established operations. For example, locals refer to a section of Hyderabad as "Cyberabad," where Microsoft, IBM, Infosys, and Qualcomm (among others) have major facilities.

Of course, other things are not equal. Differences in relative factor costs, political economy, culture, and location externalities are important, but other factors also loom large. Formal and informal trade barriers obviously influence location decisions (see Chapter 7), as do transportation costs and rules and regulations regarding foreign direct investment (see Chapter 8). For example, although relative factor costs may make a country look attractive as a location for performing a manufacturing activity, regulations prohibiting foreign direct investment may eliminate this option. Similarly, a consideration of factor costs might suggest that a firm should source production of a certain component from a particular country, but trade barriers could make this uneconomical.

Another important country factor is expected future movements in its exchange rate (see Chapters 10 and 11). Adverse changes in exchange rates can quickly alter a country's attractiveness as a manufacturing base. Currency appreciation can transform a low-cost location into a high-cost location. Many Japanese corporations had to grapple with this problem during the 1990s and early 2000s. The relatively low value of the yen on foreign exchange markets between 1950 and 1980 helped strengthen Japan's position as a low-cost location for manufacturing. More recently, however, the yen's steady appreciation against the dollar increased the dollar cost of products exported from Japan, making Japan less attractive as a manufacturing location. In response, many Japanese firms moved their manufacturing offshore to lower-cost locations in East Asia.

Technological Factors

The type of technology a firm uses to perform specific manufacturing activities can be pivotal in location decisions. For example, because of technological constraints, in some cases it is necessary to perform certain manufacturing activities in only one location and serve the world market from there. In other cases, the technology may make it feasible to perform an activity in multiple locations. Three characteristics of a manufacturing technology are of interest here: the level of fixed costs, the minimum efficient scale, and the flexibility of the technology.

Fixed Costs

As noted in Chapter 12, in some cases the fixed costs of setting up a production plant are so high that a firm must serve the world market from a single location or from a very few locations. For example, it now costs up to $5 billion to set up a state-of-the-art plant to manufacture semiconductor chips. Given this, other things being equal, serving the world market from a single plant sited at a single (optimal) location can make sense.

Conversely, a relatively low level of fixed costs can make it economical to perform a particular activity in several locations at once. This allows the firm to better accommodate demands for local responsiveness. Manufacturing in multiple locations may also help the firm avoid becoming too dependent on one location. Being too dependent on one location is particularly risky in a world of floating exchange rates. Many firms disperse their manufacturing plants to different locations as a "real hedge" against potentially adverse moves in currencies.

Minimum Efficient Scale

The concept of economies of scale tells us that as plant output expands, unit costs decrease. The reasons include the greater utilization of capital equipment and the productivity gains that come with specialization of employees within the plant.[13] However, beyond a certain level of output, few additional scale economies are available. Thus, the "unit cost curve" declines with output until a certain output level is reached, at which point further increases in output realize little reduction in unit costs. The level of output at which most plant-level scale economies are exhausted is referred to as the **minimum efficient scale** of output. This is the scale of output a plant must operate to realize all major plant-level scale economies (see Figure 17.2).

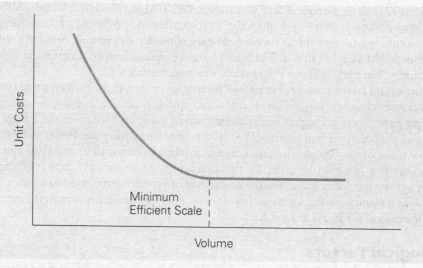

Figure 17.2 *A Typical Unit Cost Curve*

The implications of this concept are as follows: The larger the minimum efficient scale of a plant relative to total global demand, the greater the argument for centralizing production in a single location or a limited number of locations. Alternatively, when the minimum efficient scale of production is low relative to global demand, it may be economical to manufacture a product at several locations. For example, the minimum efficient scale for a plant to manufacture personal computers is about 250,000 units a year, while the total global demand exceeds 35 million units a year. The low level of minimum efficient scale in relation to total global demand makes it economically feasible for a company such as Dell to assemble PCs in six locations.

As in the case of low fixed costs, the advantages of a low minimum efficient scale include allowing the firm to accommodate demands for local responsiveness or to hedge against currency risk by manufacturing the same product in several locations.

Flexible Manufacturing and Mass Customization

Central to the concept of economies of scale is the idea that the best way to achieve high efficiency, and hence low unit costs, is through the mass production of a standardized output. The trade-off implicit in this idea is between unit costs and product variety. Producing greater product variety from a factory implies shorter production runs, which in turn implies an inability to realize economies of scale. That is, wide product variety makes it difficult for a company to increase its production efficiency and thus reduce its unit costs. According to this logic, the way to increase efficiency and drive down unit costs is to limit product variety and produce a standardized product in large volumes.

This view of production efficiency has been challenged by the rise of flexible manufacturing technologies. The term **flexible manufacturing technology**—or **lean production,** as it is often called—covers a range of manufacturing technologies designed to (1) reduce setup times for complex equipment, (2) increase the utilization of individual machines through better scheduling, and (3) improve quality control at all stages of the manufacturing process.[14] Flexible manufacturing technologies allow the company to produce a wider variety of end products at a unit cost that at one time could be achieved only through the mass production of a standardized output. Research suggests the adoption of flexible manufacturing technologies may actually increase efficiency and lower unit costs relative to what can be achieved by the mass production of a standardized output while enabling the company to customize its product offering to a much greater extent than was once thought possible. The term **mass customization** has been coined to describe the ability of companies to use flexible manufacturing technology to reconcile two goals that were once thought to be incompatible—low cost and product customization.[15] Flexible manufacturing technologies vary in their sophistication and complexity.

One of the most famous examples of a flexible manufacturing technology, Toyota's production system, has been credited with making Toyota the most efficient auto company in the world. (Despite Toyota's recent problems with sudden uncontrolled acceleration, the company continues to be an efficient producer of high-quality automobiles, according to J.D. Power, which produces an annual quality survey. Toyota's Lexus models continue to top J.D. Power's quality rankings.)[16] Toyota's flexible manufacturing system was developed by one of the company's engineers, Taiichi Ohno. After working at Toyota for five years and visiting Ford's U.S. plants, Ohno became convinced that the mass production philosophy for making cars was flawed. He saw numerous problems with mass production.

First, long production runs created massive inventories that had to be stored in large warehouses. This was expensive, both because of the cost of warehousing and because inventories tied up capital in unproductive uses. Second, if the initial machine settings were wrong, long production runs resulted in the production of a large number of defects (i.e., waste). Third, the mass production system was unable to accommodate consumer preferences for product diversity.

In response, Ohno looked for ways to make shorter production runs economical. He developed a number of techniques designed to reduce setup times for production equipment (a major source of fixed costs). By using a system of levers and pulleys, he reduced the time required to change dies on stamping equipment from a full day in 1950 to three minutes by 1971. This made small production runs economical, which allowed Toyota to respond better to consumer demands for product diversity. Small production runs also eliminated the need to hold large inventories, thereby reducing warehousing costs. Plus, small product runs and the lack of inventory meant that defective parts were produced only in small numbers and entered the assembly process immediately. This reduced waste and helped trace defects back to their source to fix the problem. In sum, these innovations enabled Toyota to produce a more diverse product range at a lower unit cost than was possible with conventional mass production.[17]

Flexible machine cells are another common flexible manufacturing technology. A flexible machine cell is a grouping of various types of machinery, a common materials handler, and a centralized cell controller (computer). Each cell normally contains four to six machines capable of performing a variety of operations. The typical cell is dedicated to the production of a family of parts or products. The settings on machines are computer-controlled, which allows each cell to switch quickly between the production of different parts or products.

Improved capacity utilization and reductions in work in progress (i.e., stockpiles of partly finished products) and in waste are major efficiency benefits of flexible machine cells. Improved capacity utilization arises from the reduction in setup times and from the computer-controlled coordination of production flow between machines, which eliminates bottlenecks. The tight coordination between machines also reduces work-in-progress inventory. Reductions in waste are due to the ability of computer-controlled machinery to identify ways to transform inputs into outputs while producing a minimum of unusable waste material. While freestanding machines might be in use 50 percent of the time, the same machines when grouped into a cell can be used more than 80 percent of the time and produce the same end product with half the waste. This increases efficiency and results in lower costs.

The effects of installing flexible manufacturing technology on a company's cost structure can be dramatic. The Ford Motor Company has been introducing flexible manufacturing technologies into its automotive plants around the world. These new technologies should allow Ford to produce multiple models from the same line and to switch production from one model to another much more quickly than in the past, allowing Ford to take $2 billion out of its cost structure.[18]

Besides improving efficiency and lowering costs, flexible manufacturing technologies enable companies to customize products to the demands of small consumer groups—at a cost that at one time could be achieved only by mass-producing a standardized output. Thus, the technologies help a company achieve mass customization, which increases its customer responsiveness. Most important for international business, flexible manufacturing technologies can help a firm customize products for different national markets. The importance of this advantage cannot be overstated. When flexible manufacturing technologies are available, a firm can manufacture products customized to various national markets at a single factory sited at the optimal location. And it can do this without absorbing a significant cost penalty. Thus, firms no longer need to establish manufacturing facilities in each major national market to provide products that satisfy specific consumer tastes and preferences, part of the rationale for a localization strategy (Chapter 12).

Summary

A number of technological factors support the economic arguments for concentrating production facilities in a few choice locations or even in a single location. Other things being equal, when fixed costs are substantial, the minimum efficient scale of production is high, and/or flexible manufacturing technologies are available, the arguments for concentrating production at a few choice locations are strong. This is true even when substantial differences in consumer tastes and preferences exist between national markets because flexible manufacturing technologies allow the firm to customize products to national differences at a single facility. Alternatively, when fixed costs are low, the minimum efficient scale of production is low, and flexible manufacturing technologies are not available, the arguments for concentrating production at one or a few locations are not as compelling. In such cases, it may make more sense to manufacture in each major market in which the firm is active if this helps the firm better respond to local demands. This holds only if the increased local responsiveness more than offsets the cost disadvantages of not concentrating manufacturing. With the advent of flexible manufacturing technologies and mass customization, such a strategy is becoming less attractive. In sum, technological factors are making it feasible, and necessary, for firms to concentrate manufacturing facilities at optimal locations. Trade barriers and transportation costs are major brakes on this trend.

Product Factors

Two product features affect location decisions. The first is the product's *value-to-weight* ratio because of its influence on transportation costs. Many electronic components and pharmaceuticals have high value-to-weight ratios; they are expensive and they do not weigh very much. Thus, even if they are shipped halfway around the world, their transportation costs account for a very small percentage of total costs. Given this, other things being equal, there is great pressure to produce these products in the optimal location and to serve the world market from there. The opposite holds for products with low value-to-weight ratios. Refined sugar, certain bulk chemicals, paint, and petroleum products all have low value-to-weight ratios; they are relatively inexpensive products that weigh a lot. Accordingly, when they are shipped long distances, transportation costs account for a large percentage of total costs. Thus, other things being equal, there is great pressure to make these products in multiple locations close to major markets to reduce transportation costs.

The other product feature that can influence location decisions is whether the product serves universal needs, needs that are the same all over the world. Examples include many industrial products (e.g., industrial electronics, steel, bulk chemicals) and modern consumer products (e.g., handheld calculators, personal computers, video-game consoles). Because there are few national differences in consumer taste and preference for such products, the need for local responsiveness is reduced. This increases the attractiveness of concentrating production at an optimal location.

Locating Production Facilities

There are two basic strategies for locating production facilities: concentrating them in a centralized location and serving the world market from there, or decentralizing them in various regional or national locations that are close to major markets. The appropriate strategic choice is determined by the various country-specific, technological, and product factors discussed in this section and summarized in Table 17.1.

As can be seen, concentration of production makes most sense when:

- Differences among countries in factor costs, political economy, and culture have a substantial impact on the costs of manufacturing in various countries.
- Trade barriers are low.
- Externalities arising from the concentration of like enterprises favor certain locations.

TABLE 17.1 Location Strategy and Production

	Concentrated Production Favored	Decentralized Production Favored
Country Factors		
Differences in political economy	Substantial	Few
Differences in culture	Substantial	Few
Differences in factor costs	Substantial	Few
Trade barriers	Few	Substantial
Location externalities	Important in industry	Not important in industry
Exchange rates	Stable	Volatile
Technological Factors		
Fixed costs	High	Low
Minimum efficient scale	High	Low
Flexible manufacturing technology	Available	Not available
Product Factors		
Value-to-weight ratio	High	Low
Serves universal needs	Yes	No

- Important exchange rates are expected to remain relatively stable.
- The production technology has high fixed costs and high minimum efficient scale relative to global demand, or flexible manufacturing technology exists.
- The product's value-to-weight ratio is high.
- The product serves universal needs.

Alternatively, decentralization of production is appropriate when:

- Differences among countries in factor costs, political economy, and culture do not have a substantial impact on the costs of manufacturing in various countries.
- Trade barriers are high.
- Location externalities are not important.
- Volatility in important exchange rates is expected.
- The production technology has low fixed costs and low minimum efficient scale, and flexible manufacturing technology is not available.
- The product's value-to-weight ratio is low.
- The product does not serve universal needs (i.e., significant differences in consumer tastes and preferences exist among nations).

In practice, location decisions are seldom clear-cut. For example, it is not unusual for differences in factor costs, technological factors, and product factors to point toward concentrated production, while a combination of trade barriers and volatile exchange rates points toward decentralized production. This seems to be the case in the world automobile industry. Although the availability of flexible manufacturing and cars' relatively high value-to-weight ratios suggest concentrated manufacturing, the combination of formal and informal trade barriers and the uncertainties of the world's current floating exchange rate regime (see Chapter 10) have inhibited firms' ability to pursue this strategy. For these reasons, several automobile companies have established "top-to-bottom" manufacturing operations in three major regional markets: Asia, North America, and western Europe.

The Hidden Costs of Foreign Locations

There may be some "hidden costs" to basing production in a foreign location. Numerous anecdotes suggest that high employee turnover, shoddy workmanship, poor product quality, and low productivity are significant issues in some outsourcing locations.[19] Microsoft, for example, established a major facility in Hyderabad, India, for four very good reasons: (1) The wage rate of software programmers in India is one-third of that in the United States. (2) India has an excellent higher education system that graduates a lot of computer science majors every year. (3) There was already a high concentration of information technology companies and workers in Hyderabad. (4) Many of Microsoft's highly skilled Indian employees, after spending years in the United States, wanted to return home, and Microsoft saw the Hyderabad facility as a way of holding on to this valuable human capital.

However, the company has found that the turnover rate among its Indian employees is higher than in the United States. Demand for software programmers in India is high, and many employees are prone to switch jobs to get better pay. Although Microsoft has tried to limit turnover by offering good benefits and long-term incentive pay, such as stock grants to high performers who stay with the company, many of the Indians who were hired locally apparently place little value on long-term incentives and prefer higher current pay. High employee turnover, of course, has a negative impact on productivity. One Microsoft manager in India noted that 40 percent of his core team had left within the past 12 months, making it very difficult to stay on track with development projects.[20]

Microsoft is not alone in experiencing this problem. The manager of an electronics company that outsourced the manufacture of wireless headsets to China noted that after four years of frustrations with late deliveries and poor quality, his company decided to move production *back* to the United States. In his words: "On the face of it, labor costs seemed so much lower in China that the decision to move production there was a very easy one. In retrospect, I wish we had looked much closer at productivity and workmanship. We have actually lost market share because of this decision."[21] Another example of this phenomenon is given in the next Management Focus, which looks at the decision by General Electric to move some production from China back to the United States. The lesson here is that it is important to look beyond pay rates and make judgments about employee productivity before deciding whether to outsource activities to foreign locations.

MANAGEMENT FOCUS

GE Moves Manufacturing, from China to the United States

For decades General Electric has been at the forefront of the move to shift production offshore from high-cost locations inside the United States to cheaper locations, such as China. But there are now some signs that the relentless flow of production offshore may be slowing down and, in some cases, starting to reverse. There are several reasons for this. Wage rates in China and some other developing nations have been rising fast, closing the differential between costs in the United States and overseas. In dollar terms, wage rates in China were some five times higher in 2012 than they were in 2000, and they are still rising fast. Labor productivity has also increased significantly in the United States, further closing the gap in labor costs. Meanwhile, high oil prices have raised the cost of shipping products across oceans, while the abundance of cheap natural gas in the United States is helping to lower production costs. If this were not enough, there are signs that there are benefits to having product design and manufacturing co-located, and in some cases, this is driving a shift in production back to the United States.

A case in point is GE's GeoSpring water heater. This was originally designed in the United States and manufactured in China. The finished product was then shipped back across the ocean for sale in the United States. In 2010, given the macro trends in labor productivity and energy prices, GE decided to see what would happen if it brought some of its appliance products back to the United States. The GeoSpring was one of its first attempts at this. GE established a team of engineers and production workers at its appliance plant in Louisville, Kentucky, to see what they could do with the GeoSpring. The team quickly concluded that the GeoSpring was not easy to manufacture due to poor design. They redesigned the product for ease of assembly, eliminating one out of every five parts and cutting material costs by 25 percent. As a result, GE cut the time required to assemble the product from 10 hours in China to 2 hours in Louisville.

The end result: Material costs went down, labor requirement went down, and product quality went up. Indeed, the cost savings were so big that GE was able to reduce the price of the GeoSpring 20 percent below that of the Chinese manufactured product and still make a decent margin. Time to market also improved greatly. It used to take five weeks to get a GeoSpring from China into a U.S. retail store—now GE can do that in a matter of days, which improves inventory management.

Having learned from experiences like this, GE is now planning to ramp up production of other appliance products at Louisville. It has recently doubled the workforce there to 3,700, and has also hired 500 new designers and engineers to redesign many of its products for ease of manu-facture. A few years ago less than half of the revenues of the appliance business came from products made in the United States. By mid-decade, GE plans to have 75 percent of the revenue of the appliance business to come from American-made products.[22]

THE STRATEGIC ROLE OF FOREIGN PRODUCTION SITES

LO17-3

Whatever the rationale behind establishing a foreign production facility, the strategic role of foreign sites can evolve over time.[23] Initially, many foreign sites are established where labor costs are low. Typically, their strategic role is to produce labor-intensive products at as low a cost as possible. For example, beginning in the 1970s, many U.S. firms in the computer and telecommunication equipment businesses established factories across Southeast Asia to manufacture electronic components, such as circuit boards and semiconductors, at the lowest possible cost. They located their factories in countries such as Malaysia, Thailand, and Singapore precisely because each of these countries offered an attractive combination of low labor costs, adequate infrastructure, and a favorable tax and trade regime. Initially, the components produced by these factories were designed elsewhere, and the final product was assembled elsewhere. Over time, however, the strategic role of some of these factories has expanded; they have become important centers for the design and final assembly of products for the global marketplace. For example, Hewlett-Packard's operation in Singapore was established as a low-cost location for the production of circuit boards, but the facility has become the center for the design and final assembly of portable ink-jet printers for the global marketplace (see the accompanying Management Focus).

MANAGEMENT FOCUS

Hewlett-Packard in Singapore

In the late 1960s, Hewlett-Packard was looking around Asia for a low-cost location to produce electronic components that were to be manufactured using labor-intensive processes. The company settled on Singapore, opening its first factory there in 1970. Although Singapore did not have the lowest labor costs in the region, costs were low relative to North America. Plus, Singapore had several important benefits that could not be found at many other locations in Asia. The education level of the local workforce was high. English was widely spoken. The government of Singapore seemed stable and committed to economic development, and the city-state had one of the better infrastructures in the region, including good communication and transportation networks and a rapidly developing industrial and commercial base. HP also extracted favorable terms from the Singapore government with regard to taxes, tariffs, and subsidies.

At its start, the Singapore unit manufactured only basic components. The combination of low labor costs and a favorable tax regime helped make this plant profitable early. In 1973, HP transferred the manufacture of one of its basic handheld calculators from the United States to Singapore. The objective was to reduce manufacturing costs, which the Singapore factory was quickly able to do. Increasingly confident in the capability of the Singapore factory to handle entire products, as opposed to just components, HP's management transferred other products to Singapore over the next few years, including keyboards, solid-state displays, and integrated circuits. However, all these products were still designed, developed, and initially produced in the United States.

The unit's status shifted in the early 1980s when HP embarked on a worldwide campaign to boost product quality and reduce costs. HP transferred the production of its HP41C handheld calculator to Singapore. The managers in Singapore were given the goal of substantially reducing manufacturing costs. They argued that this could be achieved only if they were allowed to redesign the product so it could be manufactured at a lower overall cost. HP's central management agreed, and 20 engineers from the Singapore facility were transferred to the United States for one year to learn how to design application-specific integrated circuits. They then brought this expertise back to Singapore and set about redesigning the HP41C.

The results were a huge success. By redesigning the product, the Singapore engineers reduced manufacturing costs for the HP41C by 50 percent. Using this newly acquired capability for product design, the Singapore facility then set about redesigning other products it produced. HP's corporate managers were so impressed with the progress made that they transferred production of the entire calculator line to Singapore in 1983. This was followed by the partial transfer of ink-jet production to Singapore in 1984 and keyboard production in 1986. In all cases, the facility redesigned the products and often reduced unit manufacturing costs by more than 30 percent. The initial development and design of all these products, however, still occurred in the United States.

In the late 1980s and 1990s, the Singapore operation assumed added responsibilities, particularly in the ink-jet printer business. The unit was given the job of redesigning an HP ink-jet printer for the Japanese market. Although the initial product redesign was a market failure, the managers in Singapore pushed to be allowed to try again. They were given the job of redesigning HP's DeskJet 505 printer for the Japanese market. This time, the redesigned product was a success, garnering significant sales in Japan. Emboldened by this success, the Singapore operation has continued to take on additional design responsibilities. Today, it is viewed as a "lead plant" within HP's global network, with primary responsibility not only for manufacturing but also for the development and design of many products targeted at the Asian market. In 2010, the role of Singapore was further enhanced when HP opened a basic research lab there. Currently, the lab is focused on developing a cloud-computing platform for enterprises.[24]

Such upward migration in the strategic role of foreign production sites arises because many foreign sites upgrade their own capabilities.[25] This improvement comes from two sources. First, pressure from the center to improve a site's cost structure and/or customize a product to the demands of consumers in a particular nation can start a chain of events that ultimately leads to the development of additional capabilities at that factory. For example, to meet centrally mandated directions to drive down costs, engineers at HP's Singapore factory argued that they needed to redesign products so they could be manufactured at a lower cost. This led to the establishment of a design center in Singapore. As this design center proved its worth, HP executives realized the importance of co-locating design and manufacturing operations. They increasingly transferred more design responsibilities to the Singapore factory. In addition, the Singapore factory ultimately became the center for the design of products tailored to the needs of the Asian market. This made good strategic sense because it meant products were being designed by engineers who were close to the Asian market and probably had a good understanding of the needs of that market, as opposed to engineers located in the United States.

A second source of improvement in the capabilities of a foreign site can be the increasing abundance of advanced factors of production in the nation in which the factory is located. Many nations that were considered economic backwaters a generation ago have been experiencing rapid economic development during the past 20 years. Their communication and transportation infrastructures and the education level of the population have improved. While these countries once lacked the advanced infrastructure required to support sophisticated design, development, and manufacturing operations, this is often no longer the case. This has made it much easier for factories based in these nations to take on a greater strategic role.

Because of such developments, many international businesses are moving away from a system in which their foreign facilities were viewed as nothing more than low-cost production facilities and toward one in which they are viewed as globally dispersed centers of excellence.[26] In this new model, foreign sites may take the lead role for the design and manufacture of products to serve important national or regional markets or even the global market. The development of such dispersed centers of excellence is consistent with the concept of a transnational strategy, introduced in Chapter 13. A major aspect of a transnational strategy is a belief in **global learning**—the idea that valuable knowledge does not reside just in a firm's domestic operations; it may also be found in its foreign subsidiaries. Foreign factories that upgrade their capabilities over time are creating valuable knowledge that might benefit the whole corporation.

Managers of international businesses need to remember that foreign factories can improve their capabilities over time, and this can be of immense strategic benefit to the firm. Rather than viewing foreign factories simply as sweatshops where unskilled labor churns out low-cost goods, managers need to see them as potential centers of excellence and to encourage and foster attempts by local managers to upgrade the capabilities of their factories and, thereby, enhance their strategic standing within the corporation.

Such a process does imply that once a foreign factory has been established and valuable skills have been accumulated, it may not be wise to switch production to another location simply because some underlying variable, such as wage rates, has changed.[27] HP has kept its facility in Singapore, rather than switching production to a location where wage rates are now much lower, such as Vietnam, because it recognizes that the Singapore operation has accumulated valuable skills that boost productivity and more than make up for the higher wage rates. Thus, when reviewing the location of production facilities, the international manager must consider the valuable skills that may have been accumulated at various locations and the impact of those skills on factors such as productivity and product design.

OUTSOURCING PRODUCTION: MAKE-OR-BUY DECISIONS

LO17-4

International businesses frequently face **make-or-buy decisions,** decisions about whether they should perform a certain value creation activity themselves or outsource it to another entity.[28] Historically, most outsourcing decisions have involved the manufacture of physical products. Most manufacturing firms have done their own final assembly but have had to decide whether to vertically integrate and manufacture their own component parts or outsource the production of such parts, purchasing them from independent suppliers. Such make-or-buy decisions are an important aspect of the strategy of many firms. In the automobile industry, for example, the typical car contains more than 10,000 components, so automobile firms constantly face make-or-buy decisions. Toyota produces less than 30 percent of the value of cars that roll off its assembly lines. The remaining 70 percent, mainly accounted for by component parts and complex subassemblies, comes from independent suppliers. In the athletic shoe industry, the make-or-buy issue has been taken to an extreme with companies such as Nike and Reebok having no involvement in manufacturing; all production has been outsourced, primarily to manufacturers based in low-wage countries.

In recent years, the outsourcing decision has gone beyond the manufacture of physical products to embrace the production of service activities. For example, many U.S.-based companies, from credit card issuers to computer companies, have outsourced their customer call centers to India. They are "buying" the customer call center function while "making" other parts of the product in-house. Similarly, many information technology companies have been outsourcing some parts of the software development process, such as testing computer code written in the United States, to independent providers based in India. Such companies are "making" (writing) most of the code in-house but "buying," or outsourcing, part of the production process—testing—to independent companies. India is often the focus of such outsourcing because English is widely spoken there; the nation has a well-educated workforce, particularly in engineering fields; and the pay is much lower than in the United States (a call center worker in India earns about $200 to $300 a month, about one-tenth of the comparable U.S. wage).[29]

Outsourcing decisions pose plenty of problems for purely domestic businesses but even more problems for international businesses. These decisions in the international arena are complicated by the volatility of countries' political economies, exchange rate movements, changes in relative factor costs, and the like. In this section, we examine the arguments for making products in-house and for buying them, and we consider the trade-offs involved in such a decision. Then we discuss strategic alliances as an alternative to producing all or part of a product within the company.

The Advantages of Make

The arguments that support making all or part of a product in-house—vertical integration—are fivefold. In-house production may be associated with lower costs, facilitate investments in highly specialized assets, protect proprietary product technology, enable the firm to accumulate valuable skills and capabilities, and ease the scheduling of adjacent processes.

Lowering Costs

It may pay a firm to continue manufacturing a product or component part in-house if the firm is more efficient at that production activity than any other enterprise.

Facilitating Specialized Investments

Sometimes firms have to invest in specialized assets in order to do business with another enterprise.[30] A **specialized asset** is one whose value is contingent on a particular relationship persisting. For example, imagine Ford of Europe has developed a new, high-performance, high-quality, and uniquely designed fuel injection system. The increased fuel efficiency will help sell Ford cars. Ford must decide whether to make the system in-house or to contract out the manufacturing to an independent supplier. Manufacturing these uniquely designed systems requires investments in equipment that can be used only for this purpose; it cannot be used to make fuel injection systems for any other automaker. Thus, investment in this equipment constitutes an investment in specialized assets. When, as in this situation, one firm must invest in specialized assets to supply another, mutual dependency is created. In such circumstances, each party might fear the other will abuse the relationship by seeking more favorable terms.

To appreciate this, let us first examine this situation from the perspective of an independent supplier who has been asked by Ford to make this investment. The supplier might reason that once it has made the investment, it will become dependent on Ford for business because Ford is the only possible customer for the output of this equipment. The supplier perceives this as putting Ford in a strong bargaining position and worries that once the specialized investment has been made, Ford might use this to squeeze down prices for the systems. Given this risk, the supplier declines to make the investment in specialized equipment.

Now take the position of Ford. Ford might reason that if it contracts out production of these systems to an independent supplier, it might become too dependent on that supplier for a vital input. Because specialized equipment is required to produce the fuel injection systems, Ford cannot easily switch its orders to other suppliers that lack that equipment. (It would face high switching costs.) Ford perceives this as increasing the bargaining power of the supplier and worries that the supplier might use its bargaining strength to demand higher prices.

Thus, the mutual dependency that outsourcing would create makes Ford nervous and scares away potential suppliers. The problem here is lack of trust. Neither party completely trusts the other to play fair. Consequently, Ford might reason that the only safe way to get the new fuel injection systems is to manufacture them itself. It may be unable to persuade any independent supplier to manufacture them. Thus, Ford decides to make rather than buy.

In general, we can predict that when substantial investments in specialized assets are required to manufacture a component, the firm will prefer to make the component internally rather than contract it out to a supplier. Substantial empirical evidence supports this prediction.[31]

Protecting Proprietary Product Technology

Proprietary product technology is unique to a firm. If it enables the firm to produce a product containing superior features, proprietary technology can give the firm a competitive advantage. The firm would not want competitors to get this technology. If the firm outsources the production of entire products or components containing proprietary technology, it runs the risk that those suppliers will expropriate the technology for their own use or that they will sell it to the firm's competitors. Thus, to maintain control over its technology, the firm might prefer to make such products or component parts in-house.

Accumulating Dynamic Capabilities

Competitive advantage is not a static concept. The capability to effectively and efficiently produce goods and services is one that evolves over time. Firms can learn through their experience how to lower cost, design better products, increase product reliability, and so on. Their capabilities (skills), in other words, are *dynamic;* they are learned through experience (the term **dynamic capabilities** is used to describe skills that become more valuable over time through learning).[32] Also, the experience learned producing one kind of product might create a capability that is then useful for producing another kind of product.

For example, in the late 1990s under the leadership of CEO Steven Jobs, Apple developed some very valuable design capabilities. Under Jobs's direction, Apple hired talented industrial designers and gave them a *major* say in product development. Originally, these designers worked on Apple's line of desktop and laptop computers. They produced computers that were differentiated by superior design elegance from those produced by its rivals. Through this process, over time the design team built up considerable capabilities in industrial design as applied to computing devices for consumers. Subsequently, Apple has been able to leverage these capabilities to produce a range of elegantly designed products that have been very successful, including the iPod, iPhone, and iPad.

Now imagine if in an effort to save costs, instead of hiring its own designers, Apple had outsourced design to an independent design firm (such firms do exist). If it had done so, Apple may never have acquired the capabilities that subsequently enabled it to design products like the iPhone and iPad. Instead, those capabilities would have resided in the design firm. Put differently, Apple would have missed out on the opportunity to establish a competitive advantage based on a capability in industrial design.

The Apple example points to one of the problems with outsourcing. Firms that outsource activities to gain a short-term cost advantage may miss out on the opportunity to subsequently build important capabilities in that activity. Critics claim that the rush by American firms to outsource activities during the 1990s and 2000s to low-cost foreign suppliers has had just this effect.[33] Although each decision may have seemed reasonable in isolation when it was taken, the cumulative effect of outsourcing may be to pass up on the opportunity to develop capabilities in that activity—capabilities that might subsequently lead to a competitive advantage. When Amazon was deciding which source should make the display screen for the Kindle, for example, it had to go to a Taiwanese firm. All American enterprises had exited the LCD industry in the 1990s, but none now had the capability to make what Amazon required.

The key point here is that firms should be very careful about what they outsource. They should not outsource activities for a short-term cost saving if those activities are potentially important for the long-term competitive advantage of the enterprise. Some would argue that Boeing made this mistake when it outsourced the production of wings for its 787 jet aircraft. Although the decision may have seemed reasonable when judged from a pure cost perspective, Boeing is no longer accumulating capabilities in the design of a key component in large commercial jet aircraft, and this may hurt the company down the road.

Improving Scheduling

Another argument for producing all or part of a product in-house is that production cost savings result because it makes planning, coordination, and scheduling of adjacent processes easier.[34] This is particularly important in firms with just-in-time inventory systems (discussed later in the chapter). In the 1920s, for example, Ford profited from tight coordination and scheduling made possible by backward vertical integration into steel foundries, iron ore shipping, and mining. Deliveries at Ford's foundries on the Great Lakes were coordinated so well that ore was turned into engine blocks within 24 hours. This substantially reduced Ford's production costs by eliminating the need to hold excessive ore inventories.

For international businesses that source worldwide, scheduling problems can be exacerbated by the time and distance between the firm and its suppliers. This is true whether the firms use their own subunits as suppliers or use independent suppliers. However, ownership of upstream production facilities is not the issue here. By using information technology, firms can attain tight coordination between different stages in the production process.

The Advantages of Buy

Buying component parts, or an entire product, from independent suppliers can give the firm greater flexibility, can help drive down the firm's cost structure, and may help the firm capture orders from international customers.

Strategic Flexibility

The great advantage of buying component parts, or even an entire product, from independent suppliers is that the firm can maintain its flexibility, switching orders between suppliers as circumstances dictate. This is particularly important internationally, where changes in exchange rates and trade barriers can alter the attractiveness of supply sources. One year, Hong Kong might offer the lowest cost for a particular component; the next year, Mexico may have the lowest cost. Many firms source the same products from suppliers based in two countries primarily as a hedge against adverse movements in factor costs, exchange rates, and the like.

Sourcing products from independent suppliers can also be advantageous when the optimal location for manufacturing a product is beset by political risks. Under such circumstances, foreign direct investment to establish a component manufacturing operation in that country would expose the firm to political risks. The firm can avoid many of these risks by buying from an independent supplier in that country, thereby maintaining the flexibility to switch sourcing to another country if a war, revolution, or other political change alters that country's attractiveness as a supply source.

However, maintaining strategic flexibility has its downside. If a supplier perceives the firm will change suppliers in response to changes in exchange rates, trade barriers, or general political circumstances, that supplier might not be willing to make investments in specialized plants and equipment that would ultimately benefit the firm.

Lower Costs

Although making a product or component part in-house—vertical integration—is often undertaken to lower costs, it may have the opposite effect. When this is the case, outsourcing may lower the firm's cost structure. Making all or part of a product in-house increases an organization's scope, and the resulting increase in organizational complexity can raise a firm's cost structure. There are three reasons for this.

First, the greater the number of subunits in an organization, the more problems coordinating and controlling those units. Coordinating and controlling subunits require top management to process large amounts of information about subunit activities. The greater the number of subunits, the more information top management must process and the harder it is to do well. Theoretically, when the firm becomes involved in too many activities, headquarters management will be unable to effectively control all of them, and the resulting inefficiencies will more than offset any advantages derived from vertical integration.[35] This can be particularly serious in an international business, where the problem of controlling subunits is exacerbated by distance and differences in time, language, and culture.

Second, the firm that vertically integrates into component part manufacture may find that because its internal suppliers have a captive customer in the firm, they lack an incentive to reduce costs. The fact that they do not have to compete for orders with other suppliers may result in high operating costs. The managers of the supply operation may be tempted to pass on cost increases to other parts of the firm in the form of higher transfer prices, rather than looking for ways to reduce those costs.

Third, vertically integrated firms have to determine appropriate prices for goods transferred to subunits within the firm. This is a challenge in any firm, but it is even more complex in international businesses. Different tax regimes, exchange rate movements, and headquarters' ignorance about local conditions all increase the complexity of transfer pricing decisions. This complexity enhances internal suppliers' ability to manipulate transfer prices to their advantage, passing cost increases downstream rather than looking for ways to reduce costs.

The firm that buys its components from independent suppliers can avoid all these problems and the associated costs. The firm that sources from independent suppliers has fewer subunits to control. The incentive problems that occur with internal suppliers do not arise when independent suppliers are used. Independent suppliers know they must continue to be efficient if they are to win business from the firm. Also, because independent suppliers' prices are set by market forces, the transfer pricing problem does not exist. In sum, the bureaucratic inefficiencies and resulting costs that can arise when firms vertically integrate backward and produce their own components are avoided by buying component parts from independent suppliers.

Offsets

Another reason for outsourcing some manufacturing to independent suppliers based in other countries is that it may help the firm capture more orders from that country. Offsets are common in the commercial aerospace industry. For example, before Air India places a large order with Boeing, the Indian government might ask Boeing to push some subcontracting work toward Indian manufacturers. This is not unusual in international business. Representatives of the U.S. government have repeatedly urged Japanese automobile companies to purchase more component parts from U.S. suppliers to partially offset the large volume of automobile exports from Japan to the United States.

Trade-Offs

Clearly, make-or-buy decisions involve trade-offs. The benefits of making all or part of a product in-house seem to be greatest when highly specialized assets are involved, when in-house production is necessary for protecting proprietary technology, when the firm may build valuable capabilities over time if it continues to perform an activity in-house, or when the firm is simply more efficient than external suppliers at performing a particular activity. When these conditions are not present, the risk of strategic inflexibility and organizational problems suggest it may be better to contract out some or all production to independent suppliers. Because issues of strategic flexibility and organizational control loom even larger for international businesses than purely domestic ones, an international business should be particularly wary of vertical integration into component part manufacture. In addition, some outsourcing in the form of offsets may help a firm gain larger orders in the future.

Strategic Alliances With Suppliers

Several international businesses have tried to reap some benefits of vertical integration without the associated organizational problems by entering strategic alliances with essential suppliers. For example, there was an alliance between Kodak and Canon, under which Canon built photocopiers for sale by Kodak; an alliance between Microsoft and Flextronics, under which Flextronics built the Xbox for Microsoft; and an alliance between Boeing and several Japanese companies to build its jet aircraft, including the 787. By these alliances, Kodak, Microsoft, and Boeing committed themselves to long-term relationships with these suppliers, which have encouraged the suppliers to undertake specialized investments. Strategic alliances build trust between the firm and its suppliers. Trust is built when a firm makes a credible commitment to continue purchasing from a supplier on reasonable terms. For example, the firm may invest money in a supplier—perhaps by taking a minority shareholding—to signal its intention to build a productive, mutually beneficial long-term relationship.

This kind of arrangement between the firm and its parts suppliers was pioneered in Japan by large auto companies such as Toyota. Many Japanese automakers have cooperative relationships with their suppliers that go back decades. In these relationships, the auto companies and their suppliers collaborate on ways to increase value added by, for example, implementing just-in-time inventory systems or cooperating in the design of component parts to improve quality and reduce assembly costs. These relationships have been formalized when the auto firms acquired minority shareholdings in many of their essential suppliers to symbolize their desire for long-term cooperative relationships with them. At the same time, the relationship between the firm and each essential supplier remains market-mediated and terminable if the supplier fails to perform. By pursuing such a strategy, the Japanese automakers capture many of the benefits of vertical integration, particularly those arising from investments in specialized assets, without suffering the organizational problems that come with formal vertical integration. The parts suppliers also benefit from these relationships because they grow with the firm they supply and share in its success.[36]

Alliances are not all good. Like formal vertical integration, a firm that enters long-term alliances may limit its strategic flexibility by the commitments it makes to its alliance partners. As we saw in Chapter 15 when we considered alliances between competitors, a firm that allies itself with another firm risks giving away key technological know-how to a potential competitor.

MANAGING A GLOBAL SUPPLY CHAIN

Logistics encompasses the activities necessary to get materials from suppliers to a manufacturing facility, through the manufacturing process, and out through a distribution system to the end user.[37] In the international business, the logistics function manages the global supply chain. The twin objectives of logistics are to manage a firm's global supply chain at the lowest possible cost and in a way that best serves customer needs, thereby lowering the costs of value creation and helping the firm establish a competitive advantage through superior customer service.

The potential for reducing costs through more efficient logistics is enormous. For the typical manufacturing enterprise, material costs account for between 50 and 70 percent of revenues, depending on the industry. Even a small reduction in these costs can have a substantial impact on profitability. According to one estimate, for a firm with revenues of $1 million, a return on investment rate of 5 percent, and materials costs that are 50 percent of sales revenues, a $15,000 increase in total profits could be achieved either by increasing sales revenues 30 percent or by reducing materials costs by 3 percent.[38] In a saturated market, it would be much easier to reduce materials costs by 3 percent than to increase sales revenues by 30 percent.

The Role of Just-In-Time Inventory

Pioneered by Japanese firms during that country's remarkable economic transformation during the 1960s and 1970s, just-in-time inventory systems now play a major role in most manufacturing firms. The basic philosophy behind **just-in-time (JIT) inventory** systems is to economize on inventory holding costs by having materials arrive at a manufacturing plant just in time to enter the production process and not before. The major cost savings comes from speeding up inventory turnover. This reduces inventory holding costs, such as warehousing and storage costs. It means the company can reduce the amount of working capital it needs to finance inventory, freeing capital for other uses and/or lowering the total capital requirements of the enterprise. Other things being equal, this will boost the company's profitability as measured by return on capital invested. It also means the company is less likely to have excess unsold inventory that it has to write off against earnings or price low to sell.

In addition to the cost benefits, JIT systems can also help firms improve product quality. Under a JIT system, parts enter the manufacturing process immediately; they are not warehoused. This allows defective inputs to be spotted right away. The problem can then be traced to the supply source and fixed before more defective parts are produced. Under a more traditional system, warehousing parts for weeks before they are used allows many defective parts to be produced before a problem is recognized.

The drawback of a JIT system is that it leaves a firm without a buffer stock of inventory. Although buffer stocks are expensive to store, they can help a firm respond quickly to increases in demand and tide a firm over shortages brought about by disruption among suppliers. Such a disruption occurred after the September 11, 2001, attacks on the World Trade Center and Pentagon, when the subsequent shutdown of international air travel and shipping left many firms that relied upon globally dispersed suppliers and tightly managed "just-in-time" supply chains without a buffer stock of inventory. A less pronounced but similar situation occurred again in April 2003, when the outbreak of the pneumonia-like SARS (severe acute respiratory syndrome) virus in China resulted in the temporary shutdown of several plants operated by foreign companies and disrupted their global supply chains. Similarly, in late 2004, record imports into the United States left several major West Coast shipping ports clogged with too many ships from Asia that could not be unloaded fast enough, which disrupted the finely tuned supply chains of several major U.S. enterprises.[39]

There are ways of reducing the risks associated with a global supply chain that operates on just-in-time principles. To reduce the risks associated with depending on one supplier for an important input, some firms source these inputs from several suppliers located in different countries. While this does not help in the case of an event with global ramifications, such as September 11, 2001, it does help manage country-specific supply disruptions, which are more common.

The Role of Information Technology and the Internet

Web-based information systems play a crucial role in modern materials management. By tracking component parts as they make their way across the globe toward an assembly plant, information systems enable a firm to optimize its production scheduling according to when components are expected to arrive. By locating component parts in the supply chain precisely, good information systems allow the firm to accelerate production when needed by pulling key components out of the regular supply chain and having them flown to the manufacturing plant.

Firms now typically use electronic data interchange (EDI) via the Internet to coordinate the flow of materials into manufacturing, through manufacturing, and out to customers. Sometimes, customers also are integrated into the system. These electronic links are then used to place orders with suppliers, to register parts leaving a supplier, to track them as they travel toward a manufacturing plant, and to register their arrival. Suppliers typically use an EDI link to send invoices to the purchasing firm. One consequence of an EDI system is that suppliers, shippers, and the purchasing firm can communicate with each other with no time delay, which increases the flexibility and responsiveness of the whole global supply system. A second consequence is that much of the paperwork between suppliers, shippers, and the purchasing firm is eliminated. Good EDI systems can help a firm decentralize materials management decisions to the plant level by giving corporate-level managers the information they need for coordinating and controlling decentralized materials management groups.

Before the emergence of the Internet as a major communication medium, firms and their suppliers normally had to purchase expensive proprietary software solutions to implement EDI systems. The ubiquity of the Internet and the availability of web-based applications have made most of these proprietary solutions obsolete. Less expensive web-based systems that are much easier to install and manage now dominate the market for global supply chain management software. These web-based systems have transformed the management of globally dispersed supply chains, allowing even small firms to achieve a much better balance between supply and demand, thereby reducing the inventory in their systems and reaping the associated economic benefits. With many firms now using these systems, those that do not will find themselves at a competitive disadvantage.

MNCs STRATEGIZING IN RURAL BACKYARDS

MNC's in the rural market (Oral/Toothpaste category)

Chhattisgarh is one of the emerging states with relatively high growth rates of Net State Domestic Product (NSDP) of 8.2 percent compared to 7.1 percent average and per capita NSDP of 6.2 percent vs. 5.4 percent for All-India over 2002–2008 period. Thus it appears that Chhattisgarh is rapidly catching up with other states in respect of growth and per capita income. However, Chhattisgarh still has low levels of per capita income as compared to the other states. The demographic profile shows that about 80 percent of the total population lives in rural areas making it a prime target for all MNCs in the FMCG sector.

Chhattisgarh is the largest market for LUP (least unit point) pack size in TP (Toothpaste) category in the country. Colgate Palmolive (CP) faces stiff competition in this segment. For leadership in this segment it is important to get a complete understanding of the INR 5 price point and come up with ideas and strategies to ensure its distribution and demand.

Colgate has divided Chhattisgarh into 3 zones namely, Raipur, Bhilai and Bilaspur. These zones are under supervision of Customer Development Officer (CDO). Under CDO, there are Product Sales Representatives (PSR) and Salesman who travel regularly to take orders, execute activations, visibility and schemes to the customers (Wholesalers and Retailers).

Go-to Market Strategy

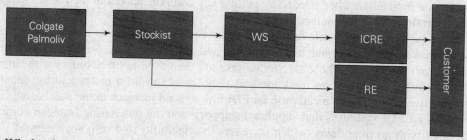

WS – Wholesaler   ICRE – Indirectly Catered Retail Environment   RE – Retail Environment

Alternate Channel of Distribution

Other than recognized wholesalers and retailers, hawkers also sold toothpastes in remotely located villages. They generally buy cheap products from either a wholesaler and sell it on a motor bike.

Scenario for INR 10 Close-up and INR 5 Babool

The major competitor at this price point is Dabur's Babool. Other brands like Dabur's Red toothpaste and HUL's Pepsodent does not have a significant presence in the market. It has almost five to six times the market share of Colgate Dental Cream 5.

Babool enjoys are distinct first movers' advantage as it had started in this market years before Colgate came in.

The following key factors differentiate Babool from Colgate:

- Higher Retailer margins
- Small sub-dealers cover areas which leads to better relationship with most stores
- Higher value for money (in volume)
- Bigger packaging

In INR 10 segment, Close-up is a market leader but the INR 10 Colgate MaxFresh is fast catching up with the improved distribution strategy and heavy investments in the same. MaxFresh with their new campaign in 2009 had started gaining share.

Differentiation for the Brand in Terms of Consumer Brand

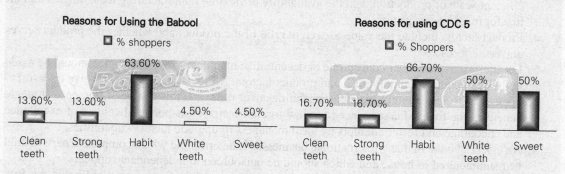

Future of the Brand – Colgate

Colgate in INR 5 segment is trying to topple Babool since four years, but the first mover advantage of Babool is consistent. Colgate INR 5 unit is far behind in terms of market share in rural areas. With new activations like selling toothpaste in Jar, they are constantly trying to innovate but in vain.

Questions:

- What are the main issues of concern for Colgate in terms of opportunities and challenges?
- Is the purchasing power of rural population adequate for companies to invest in this region?
- How are they deploying the distribution network and what are their margins?
- How does one decide the number of distribution partners?
- Can the learnings be leveraged by the MNCs in other markets, say Africa?

Case prepared by Professor Arun Kumar Jain in 2013 based on student inputs on their summer training.

Chapter Summary

This chapter explained how efficient production and logistics functions can improve the competitive position of an international business by lowering the costs of value creation and by performing value creation activities in such ways that customer service is enhanced and value added is maximized. We looked closely at three issues central to international production and logistics: where to produce, what to make and what to buy, and how to coordinate a globally dispersed manufacturing and supply system. The chapter made the following points:

1. The choice of an optimal production location must consider country factors, technological factors, and product factors.
2. Country factors include the influence of factor costs, political economy, and national culture on production costs, along with the presence of location externalities.

3. Technological factors include the fixed costs of setting up production facilities, the minimum efficient scale of production, and the availability of flexible manufacturing technologies that allow for mass customization.

4. Product factors include the value-to-weight ratio of the product and whether the product serves universal needs.

5. Location strategies either concentrate or decentralize manufacturing. The choice should be made in light of country, technological, and product factors. All location decisions involve trade-offs.

6. Foreign factories can improve their capabilities over time, and this can be of immense strategic benefit to the firm. Managers need to view foreign factories as potential centers of excellence and encourage and foster attempts by local managers to upgrade factory capabilities.

7. An essential issue in many international businesses is determining which component parts should be manufactured in-house and which should be outsourced to independent suppliers.

8. Making components in-house facilitates investments in specialized assets and helps the firm protect its proprietary technology. It may improve scheduling between adjacent stages in the value chain also. In-house production also makes sense if the firm is an efficient, low-cost producer of a technology.

9. Buying components from independent suppliers facilitates strategic flexibility and helps the firm avoid the organizational problems associated with extensive vertical integration. Outsourcing might also be employed as part of an "offset" policy, which is designed to win more orders for the firm from a country by pushing some subcontracting work to that country.

10. Several firms have tried to attain the benefits of vertical integration and avoid its associated organizational problems by entering long-term strategic alliances with essential suppliers.

11. Although alliances with suppliers can give a firm the benefits of vertical integration without dispensing entirely with the benefits of a market relationship, alliances have drawbacks. The firm that enters a strategic alliance may find its strategic flexibility limited by commitments to alliance partners.

12. Logistics encompasses all the activities that move materials to a production facility, through the production process, and out through a distribution system to the end user. The logistics function is complicated in an international business by distance, time, exchange rates, custom barriers, and other things.

13. Just-in-time systems generate major cost savings by reducing warehousing and inventory holding costs and by reducing the need to write off excess inventory. In addition, JIT systems help the firm spot defective parts and remove them from the manufacturing process quickly, thereby improving product quality.

14. Information technology, particularly Internet-based electronic data interchange, plays a major role in materials management. EDI facilitates the tracking of inputs, allows the firm to optimize its production schedule, lets the firm and its suppliers communicate in real time, and eliminates the flow of paperwork between a firm and its suppliers.

Critical Thinking and Discussion Questions

1. An electronics firm is considering how best to supply the world market for microprocessors used in consumer and industrial electronic products. A manufacturing plant costs about $500 million to construct and requires a highly skilled workforce. The total value of the world market for this product over the next 10 years is estimated to be between $10 billion and $15 billion. The tariffs prevailing in this industry are currently low. Should the firm adopt a concentrated or

decentralized manufacturing strategy? What kind of location(s) should the firm favor for its plant(s)?

2. A chemical firm is considering how best to supply the world market for sulfuric acid. A manufacturing plant costs about $20 million to construct and requires a moderately skilled workforce. The total value of the world market for this product over the next 10 years is estimated to be between $20 billion and $30 billion. The tariffs prevailing in this industry are moderate. Should the firm favor concentrated manufacturing or decentralized manufacturing? What kind of location(s) should the firm seek for its plant(s)?

3. A firm must decide whether to make a component part in-house or to contract it out to an independent supplier. Manufacturing the part requires a nonrecoverable investment in specialized assets. The most efficient suppliers are located in countries with currencies that many foreign exchange analysts expect to appreciate substantially over the next decade. What are the pros and cons of *(a)* manufacturing the component in-house and *(b)* outsourcing manufacturing to an independent supplier? Which option would you recommend? Why?

4. Reread the Management Focus on Philips in China and then answer the following questions:
   a. What are the benefits to Philips of shifting so much of its global production to China?
   b. What are the risks associated with a heavy concentration of manufacturing assets in China?
   c. What strategies might Philips adopt to maximize the benefits and mitigate the risks associated with moving so much product?

5. Explain how an efficient logistics function can help an international business compete more effectively in the global marketplace.

Research Task ⊘ globalEDGE globaledge.msu.edu

Global Production, Outsourcing, and Logistics

Use the globalEDGE website (globaledge.msu.edu) to complete the following exercises:

Exercise 1

The globalization of production makes many people aware of the differences in manufacturing costs worldwide. The U.S. Department of Labor's Bureau of International Labor Affairs publishes the *Chartbook of International Labor Comparisons*. Locate the latest edition of this report, and identify the hourly compensation costs for manufacturing workers in China, Brazil, Mexico, Turkey, Germany, and the United States.

Exercise 2

The World Bank's *Logistics Performance Index* (LPI) assesses the trade logistics environment and performance of countries. Locate the most recent LPI ranking. What components for each country are examined to construct the index? Identify the top 10 logistics performers. Prepare an executive summary highlighting the key findings from the LPI. How are these findings helpful for companies trying to build a competitive supply chain network?

Closing **CASE**

Making the Amazon Kindle

When online retailer Amazon.com invented its revolutionary e-book reader, the Kindle, the company had to decide where to have it made. Guiding the decision was an understanding that if the Kindle was going to be successful, it had to have that magic combination of low price, high functionality, high reliability, and design elegance. Over time, this has only become more important as competitors have emerged. These have included Sony with various readers, Barnes & Noble with its Nook, and, most notably, Apple with its multipurpose iPad, which can function as a digital reader among other things. Amazon's goal has been to aggressively reduce the price of the Kindle so that it both has an edge over competitors and becomes feasible to have a couple Kindles lying around the house as a sort of digital library.

Amazon designed the Kindle in a lab in California, precisely because this is where the key R&D expertise was located. One of the Kindle's crucial components, the "ink" (the tiny microcapsule beads used in its display) were designed and are made by E Ink, a company based in Cambridge, Massachusetts. Much of the rest of the value of the Kindle, however, is outsourced to manufacturing enterprises in Asia.

The market research firm iSuppli estimates that when it was introduced in 2009, the total manufacturing cost for the Kindle 2 ran about $185. The most expensive single component was the display, which cost about $60. Although the display used E Ink's technology, there were no American firms with the expertise required to manufacture a bistable electrophoretic display that will show an image even when it is not drawing on battery power. This technology is central to the Kindle because it allows very long battery life. Ultimately, Amazon contracted with a Taiwanese firm, Prime View International, to make the display. Prime View had considerable expertise in the manufacture of LCDs and was known as an efficient and reliable manufacturer. Estimates suggest that 40 to 50 percent of the value of the display is captured by E Ink, with the rest going to Prime View.

After the display, the next most expensive component is the wireless card that allows the Kindle to connect to Amazon's digital bookstore through a wireless link. The card costs about $40. Novatel Wireless, a South Korean enterprise that has developed considerable expertise in making wireless chipsets for cell phone manufacturers, produces this component. The card includes a $13 chip that was designed by Qualcomm of San Diego. This too is manufactured in Asia. The brain of the Kindle is an $8.64 microprocessor chip designed by Texas-based Freescale Semiconductor. Freescale outsources its chip making to foundries in Taiwan and China. Another key component, the lithium polymer battery, costs about $7.50 and is manufactured in China. In sum, out of a total manufacturing cost of about $185, perhaps $40 to $50 is accounted for by activities undertaken in the United States by E Ink, Qualcomm, and Freescale, with the remainder being outsourced to manufacturers in Taiwan, China, and South Korea.[40]

Case Discussion Questions

1. What criteria drove Amazon's decision of where to produce the different components that go into the Kindle? Were these the right criteria?
2. Some have argued that the fact that only $40–$50 of the value associated with manufacturing the Kindle goes to U.S. companies is a sign of the decline of American competitiveness. Do you agree with this assessment?
3. If Amazon had decided to design and manufacture the Kindle and all its components in the United States, what do you think the consequences would have been for Amazon?

India's Globally Competitive Two-Wheeler Industry

Indian two-wheeler industry is undergoing a churning. There has been a consolidation in the mass-market with three main players, while other players are trying for very niche markets. Within the mass players, Hero, Bajaj, and Honda are becoming increasingly aggressive to attain the dominant position.

That India is critical to global Honda Motor's fortunes became evident at the close of financial year 2012–13. The Japanese company had forecast that it would sell 15.52 million motorcycles and all-terrain vehicles (ATVs), and ended up falling marginally short (15.494 million) but that it was even able to get so close to the target was because its Indian unit grew at a cracking 30 percent pace.

The numbers pretty much tell the story of what has been achieved by Honda Motorcycle and Scooter India (HMSI) since its parent broke up with the Hero Group about three years ago. Already, HMSI accounts for 17–18 percent of Honda Motor's global motorcycle and ATV business. Of the 1.96 million additional bikes and ATVs that the Japanese company is looking to sell in year 2013, more than half —1.18 million —will be from HMSI, which has forecast a sharp acceleration in growth to 43 percent, taking sales to 3.93 million units. If these targets are achieved, then HMSI's share of its parent's volume could rise to 22.58%.

Dream Run

What's apparent is that the Hero-Honda split freed up HMSI to undertake a wide-ranging offensive aimed at grabbing market share. In three years or so, HMSI's market share has jumped about nine percentage points to almost 23 percent at the end of September 2013. Along the way, it overtook Bajaj Auto and TVS Motor to become the second-largest two-wheeler maker in India in FY13, though still a fair distance behind Hero. Bajaj Auto boss Rajiv Bajaj, however, says the company's sales numbers are coming closer to those of HMSI.

The Key: Pace of Transformation   How did HMSI do this? The simple answer—by putting key elements of the process chain in close proximity to each other to respond rapidly to market needs and trends, widening the product range to cover more market segments, deepening its presence to cover smaller markets better and increasing the number of dealerships, among other things. Most importantly, doing all this quickly.

"It has been a multi-pronged approach but the key has been the pace of change (after the break-up), be it in terms of reworking strategy, expanding scooter capacity, new model line-up, fresh line of communication, expanding network into the interiors of the country or even strengthening technical centre in India, which is more agile than before," said YS Guleria, Vice-President of sales and marketing at HMSI.

The Honda R&D India unit was relocated inside the factory so that the group could work closely with the marketing and the sourcing team to develop future product portfolio strategy. Honda regards this as a significant strategic step.

"The lifecycle of products is getting shorter by the day, customers are getting more demanding, and we need to quickly react to the changing needs in terms of refreshes and facelifts," Guleria said. "With R&D moving in, sales, engineering and design and purchase are all in sync with each other. These things should help us immensely going ahead and you will see new products at regular frequency from Honda going ahead."

On the marketing front, the company hired a brand ambassador —Bollywood star Akshay Kumar. In order to strengthen its presence, it set up nine zonal offices with training centres across the country, apart from its five regional centers. In 2012, zonal offices have been opened at Ahmedabad, Chennai, Bhopal, Mohali and Bhubaneswar for gathering local market intelligence in order to strategize and implement a regional approach faster. HMSI plans another four-five zonal offices.

The sales and service network was expanded to more than 1,950 outlets across India. This includes 654 dealers, 670 branches/subdealers and 626 service stations across India. HMSI entered the mass market 100 cc space with the Dream series of bikes within two years of the break-up. The Dream Yuga took on Hero's Passion in 2012 and in early part of 2013, it introduced Splendor competitor Dream Neo. The company plans to sell 6 lakh Dream motorcycles in FY14, and 1.2 million in the fiscal after that.

While entering the mass market widened coverage of the motorcycle market to 95% from 45%, the revamped scooter range with fuel-efficient engines also played a key role in HMSI's growth over the last two years, Guleria said.

Incremental volumes are coming from unrepresented areas (new dealerships) with the right products (100 cc bikes), Guleria said. It may take HMSI another three–five years, however, to have the same kind of network as the leaders.

The numbers indicate that Honda Motorcycle and Scooter has taken a bite of the market share of Bajaj Auto and TVS Motor rather than just its erstwhile partner.

"It's a multi-player race and the competition is intense. Honda has eaten into the shares of all the players and not just Hero," said Pradeep Saxena, executive director at marketing research firm TNS Auto. "As a consequence, Hero has lost 2% market share and Honda has gained 3% market share in the last one year."This suggests that Honda still has a lot of ground to cover," he said.

Hero and Bajaj are pushing hard to shore up their positions against the HMSI onslaught. Both the companies are planning to take the marketing fight to the rival camp during the festive season.

Since the break up at the end of FY11, Honda's share in the overall two-wheeler market has grown to 22.23 per cent from 13.2 per cent at the expense of rivals. In motorcycles, Honda saw its market share almost double to 14.53 per cent, while that of the others has dropped. In scooters, the shares of both HMSI and Hero MotoCorp have risen.

Hero has been engaged in establishing its independent brand, besides setting up its own R&D centre and reaching out to more export markets."Since the time we have gone on our own, our annual volumes have increased by a million units, our network has increased by a thousand touch points and we are holding on to our huge motorcycle market share and in fact we have gained more than 2 per cent in scooter market," said Anil Dua, Senior Vice-President, sales and marketing at Hero MotoCorp. "And this is without our new line of products, which will hit the market this festive season."

Bajaj Auto has been cutting stocks to make way for a series of new models it plans to launch. Does that mean Bajaj could re-enter the scooter space? "Our strategy is to be the best motorcycle maker in the world, not a maker of all kinds of two-wheelers for India alone," Bajaj said categorically. Bajaj Auto has six new products coming up, ranging from 100 cc to the premium segment.

What Next?

Clearly, HMSI will face tough competition in its bid to sell four million vehicles this fiscal year, especially if the economic gloom persists. Hero will be launching about 12–15 new models across the portfolio, largely refreshes and facelifts, ahead of its new range of vehicles hitting the market in 2014–15.

HMSI is preparing to launch a new 125 cc scooter to strengthen its 50% market share in the executive segment, according to people aware of the plan. It also has a new 125 cc Shine motorcycle in the works, to strengthen its position in the segment.

Experts wonder whether HMSI has grown too much, too fast, to the extent that finding an upside from here on in may be difficult."All this growth for Honda came from expansion of the distribution network and the latent demand for its mass market motorcycle —two core strategies they have already utilized," said Saxena of TNS Auto. "It will be interesting to watch what will be the new growth

Honda Sales Figures

	FY12	Share	FY13	Share	Q1 volumes	Share	FY14 Forecast	Share
Global Sales	15.06 mn	100.00%	15.49 mn	100%	4.05 mn	100%	17.4 mn	100%
Total Asia Sales	12.41 mn	82.41%	13.03 mn	84.12%	3.47 mn	85.81%	NA	–
India	2.10 mn	13.99%	2.75 mn	17.77%	0.74 mn	18.27%	3.93 mn	22.58%

Two-Wheeler Sales in India

	Volumes				Market Share (%)			
	2010–11	2011–12	2012–13	FY14*	2010–11	2011–12	2012–13	FY14*
Bajaj Auto	2,414,633	2,566,757	2,463,863	875,817	20.5	19.1	17.86	15.23
Hero MotoCorp	5,269,381	6,069,280	5,912.538	2,455,321	44.8	45.2	42.85	42.69
HMSI	1,551,378	1,996,320	2,606,841	1,278,609	13.2	14.9	18.89	22.23

*(April to August)

Motorcycle Sales in India

	Volumes				Market Share			
	2010–11	2011–12	2012–13	FY14*	2010–11	2011–12	2012–13	FY14*
Bajaj Auto	2,414,606	2,566,757	2,463,863	875,817	26.8	25.4	24.43	21.21
Hero MotoCorp	4,926,390	5,651,056	5,362,730	2,180,123	54.7	56.0	53.17	52.80
HMSI	658.043	771.721	1,186,726	599,752	7.3	7.6		

*(April to August)

strategy." HMSI retains its goal of becoming number one in India by 2020, but clearly, getting there won't be easy, given that the competition will give it a long, hard fight.

The Luxury Motorcycle Segment

Meanwhile in the niche luxury space, Volkswagen was also changing gears with Ducati added to its portfolio. Ducati, which was launched in India two years ago, has still not 'settled down' in the country. Buyers complain of late deliveries, booking goof-ups and lack of servicing-related infrastructure. The company has shut down showrooms in Gurgaon and Bangalore, two of the biggest bike markets in India. The German auto major Audi — from the Volkswagen (VW) stable —took over Ducati Worldwide for USD 1.1 billion. One customer who was hoping to get his first Ducati in next few months, felt that "maybe now, they will get their delivery timing and their pricing right." Experts and industry watchers are not so hopeful. "Nothing will change for the next three years or so. Both Audi and Ducati have limited penetration here. While Audi sources parts from India, Ducati does not, so there is no immediate visible change expected," says Deepesh Rathore, MD, IHS Automotive India.

The structure might change if one of the premier brands decides to manufacture in India, says Rathore. For example, Porsche (which is launching an SUV) or Ducati, might start local sourcing or manufacturing to bring in more affordable products in a few years. "After a couple of years, Volkswagen's financial muscle might help push innovation and distribution in the form of relatively low-cost superbikes which will do well in India and China," adds Rathore.

Post the acquisition of Ducati from Invest industrial, the company issued a release that said: "Ducati is a globally active company and has manufacturing operations at its headquarters in Bologna and at its own factory in Thailand. It maintains a series of importer companies in strategic markets. Experts predict that the motorcycle market will enjoy strong growth over the next few years, especially in Asia." Ducati India had ambitious plans hoping to sell more than 1,000 bikes every year by mid-decade through at least 11 dealerships spread across the country. "We started in India in December 2009 and we have sold close to 300 bikes till now," said the official spokesperson. Globally, Ducati sold 42,200 units, resulting in 11% global market share in 2011. According to a TechSci Research report, the Indian superbike (above 750 cc) market, pegged at about 3,000 units, exploded with a growth rate of 324% between 2009 and 2011. "The growth could be higher as the base is smaller," says Rathore. Going by the figures, Ducati is barely 10% of the market; a number, which is expected to go up with the launch of new variants, say company officials.

Crash Price

A Ducati low-cost bike is already available in India and is generating a lot of excitement in the biker community. The Ducati Monster 795 was launched in 2012 at INR 7 lakhs. The price is only for the Chinese and Indian markets. "It's a stripped down version of the bike. Other brands give much powerful bikes at the same price," says Dhiman.

Yet, those who want to own the brand cannot wait. Informal estimates put the booking queue for this one more than 200 long. Meanwhile, competitors like Harley-Davidson, Triumph, Suzuki and even BMW have jumped the fray making 1,600 cc bikes available at under INR 10 lakh.

Adapted from article by Ketan Thakkar, ET Bureau, *Economic Times*, Oct 7. Available at 2013http://economictimes.indiatimes.com/news/news-by-industry/auto/two-wheelers/post-separ; Accessed on Oct 17, 2013

The Ducati portion is based on article by*YaminiDhallin Economic Times dated April 28, 2012* http://epaper.timesofindia.com/APD26302/PrintArt.asp?SkinFolder=ET&artType=Article

Endnotes

1. S. Denning, "The Boeing Debacle: Seven Lessons Every CEO Must Learn," *Forbes*, January 17, 2013; J. Surowiecki, "Requiem for a Dreamliner," *The New Yorker*, February 4, 2013; and J. N. Stewart, "Japan's Role in Making Batteries for Boeing," *The New York Times*, January 25, 2013.

2. B. C. Arntzen, G. G. Brown, T. P. Harrison, and L. L. Trafton, "Global Supply Chain Management at Digital Equipment Corporation," *Interfaces* 25 (1995), pp. 69–93; and Diana Farrell, "Beyond Offshoring," *Harvard Business Review*, December 2004, pp. 1–8.

3. D. A. Garvin, "What Does Product Quality Really Mean," *Sloan Management Review* 26 (Fall 1984), pp. 25–44.

4. See the articles published in the special issue of the *Academy of Management Review on Total Quality Management* 19, no. 3 (1994). The following article provides a good overview of many of the issues involved from an academic perspective: J. W. Dean and D. E. Bowen, "Management Theory and Total Quality," *Academy of Management Review* 19 (1994), pp. 392–

418. Also see T. C. Powell, "Total Quality Management as Competitive Advantage," *Strategic Management Journal* 16 (1995), pp. 15–37; and S. B. Han et al., "The Impact of ISO 9000 on TQM and Business Performance," *Journal of Business and Economic Studies* 13, no. 2 (2007), pp. 1–25.

5. For general background information, see "How to Build Quality," *The Economist,* September 23, 1989, pp. 91–92; A. Gabor, *The Man Who Discovered Quality* (New York: Penguin, 1990); P. B. Crosby, *Quality Is Free* (New York: Mentor, 1980); and M. Elliot et al., "A Quality World, a Quality Life," *Industrial Engineer,* January 2003, pp. 26–33.

6. G. T. Lucier and S. Seshadri, "GE Takes Six Sigma beyond the Bottom Line," *Strategic Finance,* May 2001, pp. 40–46; and U. D. Kumar et al., "On the Optimal Selection of Process Alternatives in a Six Sigma Implementation," *International Journal of Production Economics* 111, no. 2 (2008), pp. 456–70.

7. M. Saunders, "U.S. Firms Doing Business in Europe Have Options in Registering for ISO 9000 Quality Standards," *Business America,* June 14, 1993, p. 7; and Han et al. "The Impact of ISO 9000."

8. G. Stalk and T. M. Hout, *Competing against Time* (New York: Free Press, 1990).

9. N. Tokatli, "Global Sourcing: Insights from the Global Clothing Industry—The Case of Zara, a Fast Fashion Retailer," *Journal of Economic Geography* 8, no. 1 (2008), pp. 21–39.

10. Diana Farrell, "Beyond Offshoring," *Harvard Business Review,* December 2004, pp. 1–8; and M. A. Cohen and H. L. Lee, "Resource Deployment Analysis of Global Manufacturing and Distribution Networks," *Journal of Manufacturing and Operations Management* 2 (1989), pp. 81–104.

11. B. Einhorn, "Philips' Expanding Asia Connections," *BusinessWeek Online,* November 27, 2003; K. Leggett and P. Wonacott, "The World's Factory: A Surge in Exports from China Jolts the Global Industry," *The Wall Street Journal,* October 10, 2002, p. A1; J. Blau, "Philips Tears Down Eindhoven R&D Fence," *Research Technology Management* 50, no. 6 (2007), pp. 9–11; L. Baijia, "Philips Elevates China's Market Status," *China Daily,* May 26, 2011; and information on Philips NV website, www.philips.com/shared/assets/Downloadablefile/Investor/2011_05_26_Frans_van_Houten_Morgan_Stanley.pdf.

12. P. Krugman, "Increasing Returns and Economic Geography," *Journal of Political Economy* 99, no. 3 (1991), pp. 483–99; J. M. Shaver and F. Flyer, "Agglomeration Economies, Firm Heterogeneity, and Foreign Direct Investment in the United States," *Strategic Management Journal* 21 (2000), pp. 1175–93; and R. E. Baldwin and T. Okubo, "Heterogeneous Firms, Agglomeration Economies, and Economic Geography," *Journal of Economic Geography* 6, no. 3 (2006), pp. 323–50.

13. For a review of the technical arguments, see D. A. Hay and D. J. Morris, *Industrial Economics: Theory and Evidence* (Oxford, UK: Oxford University Press, 1979). See also C. W. L. Hill and G. R. Jones, *Strategic Management: An Integrated Approach* (Boston: Houghton Mifflin, 2004).

14. See P. Nemetz and L. Fry, "Flexible Manufacturing Organizations: Implications for Strategy Formulation," *Academy of Management Review* 13 (1988), pp. 627–38; N. Greenwood, *Implementing Flexible Manufacturing Systems* (New York: Halstead Press, 1986); J. P. Womack, D. T. Jones, and D. Roos, *The Machine That Changed the World* (New York: Rawson Associates, 1990); and R. Parthasarthy and S. P. Seith, "The Impact of Flexible Automation on Business Strategy and Organizational Structure," *Academy of Management Review* 17 (1992), pp. 86–111.

15. B. J. Pine, *Mass Customization: The New Frontier in Business Competition* (Boston: Harvard Business School Press, 1993); S. Kotha, "Mass Customization: Implementing the Emerging Paradigm for Competitive Advantage," *Strategic Management Journal* 16 (1995), pp. 21–42; J. H. Gilmore and B. J. Pine II, "The Four Faces of Mass Customization," *Harvard Business Review,* January–February 1997, pp. 91–101; and M. Zerenler and D. Ozilhan, "Mass Customization Manufacturing: The Drivers and Concepts," *Journal of American Academy of Business* 12, no. 1 (2007), pp. 230–262.

16. "Toyota Motor Corporation Captures Ten Segment Awards," J. D. Power press release, March 19, 2009, http://businesscenter.jdpower.com/news/pressrelease.aspx?ID=2009043.

17. M. A. Cusumano, *The Japanese Automobile Industry* (Cambridge, MA: Harvard University Press, 1989); T. Ohno, *Toyota Production System* (Cambridge, MA: Productivity Press, 1990); and Womack, Jones, and Roos, *The Machine That Changed the World.*

18. P. Waurzyniak, "Ford's Flexible Push," *Manufacturing Engineering,* September 2003, pp. 47–50.

19. "The Boomerang Effect," *The Economist,* April 21, 2012; and Charles Fishman, "The Insourcing Boom," *The Atlantic,* December 2012.

20. This anecdote was told to the author by a Microsoft manager while the author was visiting Microsoft facilities in Hyderabad, India.

21. Interview by author. The manager was a former executive MBA student of the author.

22. Charles Fishman, "The Insourcing Boom"; and J. R. Immelt, "Sparking an American Manufacturing Renewal," *Harvard Business Review,* March 2012.

23. K. Ferdows, "Making the Most of Foreign Factories," *Harvard Business Review,* March–April 1997, pp. 73–88.

24. Sources: K. Ferdows, "Making the Most of Foreign Factories," *Harvard Business Review,* March–April 1997, pp. 73–88; and "Hewlett-Packard: Singapore," Harvard Business School, Case No. 694–035.

25. This argument represents a simple extension of the dynamic capabilities research stream in the strategic management literature. See D. J. Teece, G. Pisano, and A. Shuen, "Dynamic Capabilities and Strategic Management," *Strategic Management Journal* 18 (1997), pp. 509–33.

26. T. S. Frost, J. M. Birkinshaw, and P. C. Ensign, "Centers of Excellence in Multinational Corporations," *Strategic Management Journal* 23 (November 2002), pp. 997–1018.

27. C. W. L. Hill, "Globalization, the Myth of the Nomadic Multinational Enterprise, and the Advantages of Location Persistence," Working Paper, School of Business, University of Washington, 2001.

28. Anne Parmigiani, "Why Do Firms Both Make and Buy?" *Strategic Management Journal* 29, no. 3 (2007), pp. 285–303.

29. J. Solomon and E. Cherney, "A Global Report: Outsourcing to India Sees a Twist," *The Wall Street Journal,* April 1, 2004, p. A2.

30. The material in this section is based primarily on the transaction cost literature of vertical integration; for example, O. E. Williamson, *The Economic Institutions of Capitalism* (New York: The Free Press, 1985).

31. For a review of the evidence, see Williamson, *The Economic Institutions of Capitalism.* See also L. Poppo and T. Zenger, "Testing Alternative Theories of the Firm: Transaction Cost, Knowledge Based, and Measurement Explanations for Make or Buy Decisions in Information Services," *Strategic Management Journal* 19 (1998), pp. 853–78; and R. Carter and G. M. Hodgson, "The Impact of Empirical Tests to Transaction Cost Economics on the Debate on the Nature of the Firm," *Strategic Management Journal* 27, no. 5 (2006), pp. 461–80.

32. Teece, Pisano, and Shuen, "Dynamic Capabilities and Strategic Management."

33. G. P. Pisano and W. C. Shih, "Restoring American Competitiveness," *Harvard Business Review,* July–August 2009, pp. 114–26.

34. A. D. Chandler, *The Visible Hand* (Cambridge, MA: Harvard University Press, 1977).

35. For a review of these arguments, see C. W. L. Hill and R. E. Hoskisson, "Strategy and Structure in the Multiproduct Firm," *Academy of Management Review* 12 (1987), pp. 331–41.

36. C. W. L. Hill, "Cooperation, Opportunism, and the Invisible Hand," *Academy of Management Review* 15 (1990), pp. 500–13.

37. See R. Narasimhan and J. R. Carter, "Organization, Communication and Coordination of International Sourcing," *International Marketing Review* 7 (1990), pp. 6–20; and Arntzen, Brown, Harrison, and Trafton, "Global Supply Chain Management."

38. H. F. Busch, "Integrated Materials Management," *IJPD & MM* 18 (1990), pp. 28–39.

39. T. Aeppel, "Manufacturers Cope with the Costs of Strained Global Supply Lines," *The Wall Street Journal,* December 8, 2004, p. A1.

40. M. Muro, "Amazon's Kindle: Symbol of American Decline?" Brookings Institute, February 25, 2010, www.brookings.edu; and Pisano and Shih, "Restoring American Competitiveness."

Chapter 18
Global Marketing and R&D

LEARNING OBJECTIVES

After reading this chapter, you will be able to:

LO18-1 Explain why it might make sense to vary the attributes of a product from country to country.

LO18-2 Recognize why and how a firm's distribution strategy might vary among countries.

LO18-3 Identify why and how advertising and promotional strategies might vary among countries.

LO18-4 Explain why and how a firm's pricing strategy might vary among countries.

LO18-5 Describe how the globalization of the world economy is affecting new-product development within the international business firm.

BURBERRY'S GLOBAL BRAND STRATEGY

Opening Case

Burberry, the icon British luxury apparel retailer famed for its trench coats and plaid-patterned accessories, has been on a roll in recent years. In the late 1990s, one critic described Burberry as "an outdated business with a fashion cache of almost zero." By 2012, Burberry was widely recognized as one of the planet's premier luxury brands with a strong presence in many of the world's richest cities, more than 560 retail stores, and revenues in excess of $2.2 billion.

Two successive American CEOs have been behind Burberry's transformation. The first, Rose Marie Bravo, joined the company in 1997 from Saks Fifth Avenue. Bravo saw immense hidden value in the Burberry brand. One of her first moves was to hire world-class designers to reenergize the brand. The company also shifted its orientation toward a younger hipper demographic, perhaps best exemplified by the ads featuring supermodel Kate Moss that helped to reposition the brand. By the time Bravo retired in 2006, she had transformed Burberry into what one commentator called an "achingly hip," high-end fashion brand whose raincoats, clothes, handbags, and other accessories were must-have items for younger, well-heeled, fashion-conscious consumers worldwide.

Bravo was succeeded by Angela Ahrendts, whose career had taken her from a small town in Indiana and a degree at Ball State University, through Warnaco and Liz Claiborne, to become the CEO of Burberry at age 46. Ahrendts realized that for all of Bravo's success, Burberry still faced significant problems. The company had long pursued a licensing strategy, allowing partners in other countries to design and sell their own offerings under the Burberry label. This lack of control over the offering was hurting its brand equity. The Spanish partner, for example, was selling casual wear that bore no relationship to what was being designed in London. So long as this state of affairs continued, Burberry would struggle to build a unified global brand.

Ahrendts's solution was to start acquiring partners and/or buying licensing rights back in order to regain control over the brand. Hand in hand with this, she pushed for an aggressive expansion of the company's retail store strategy. The company's core demographics under Ahrendts remained the well-heeled, younger, fashion-conscious set. To reach this demographic, Burberry has focused on 25 of the world's wealthier cities. Key markets include New York, London, and Beijing, which according to Burberry, account for more than half the global luxury fashion trade. As a result of this strategy, the number of retail stores increased from 211 in 2007 to 563 in 2011.

Another aspect of Burberry's strategy has been to embrace digital marketing tools to reach its tech-savvy customer base. Indeed, there are few luxury brand companies that have utilized digital technology as aggressively as Burberry. Burberry has simulcast its runway shows in 3-D in New York, Los Angeles, Dubai, Paris, and Tokyo. Viewers at home can stream the shows over the Internet and post comments in real time. Outerwear and bags are made available through "click and buy" technology, with delivery several months before they reach the stores. Burberry had more than 10 million Facebook fans as of early 2012. At "The Art of the Trench," a company-run social media site, people can submit photos of themselves in the company's icon rainwear.

The global marketing strategy seems to be working. Between 2007 and 2011, revenues at Burberry increased from £859 million to £1,501 million, and this against the background of a global economic slowdown. Over the same period, retail sales increased from 48 percent of the total to 64 percent of the total. By March 2012, 72 percent of Burberry's sales came through retail establishments.[1]

INTRODUCTION

The previous chapter looked at the roles of global production and logistics in an international business. This chapter continues our focus on specific business functions by examining the roles of marketing and research and development (R&D) in an international business. We focus on how marketing and R&D can be performed so they will reduce the costs of value creation and add value by better serving customer needs.

In Chapter 13, we spoke of the tension existing in most international businesses between the need to reduce costs and, at the same time, respond to local conditions, which tends to raise costs. This tension continues to be a persistent theme in this chapter. A global marketing strategy that views the world's consumers as similar in their tastes and preferences is consistent with the mass production of a standardized output. By mass-producing a standardized output, whether it be soap, semiconductor chips, or high-end apparel, the firm can realize substantial unit cost reductions from experience curve and other economies of scale. However, ignoring country differences in consumer tastes and preferences can lead to failure. Thus, an international business's marketing function needs to determine when product standardization is appropriate and when it is not, and to adjust the marketing strategy accordingly. Even if product standardization is appropriate, the way in which a product is positioned in a market and the promotions and messages used to sell that product may still have to be customized so that they resonate with local consumers.

As described in the opening case, the luxury fashion retailer Burberry has been dealing with these issues. Burberry's core demographic has been the affluent, younger, fashion-conscious set. Burberry has come to view this demographic as sharing a lot of the same tastes and preferences worldwide. Accordingly, it has devoted considerable attention to building a unified global brand with a consistent marketing message and the same product offering worldwide. As part of this strategy, Burberry has bought back licensing rights from partners around the world in order to regain control over its brand, and it has aggressively expanded its own retail presence in many of the world's richer cities, where the company's core target demographic lives. The global marketing strategy has worked for Burberry, but it might not work for others. It depends on the extent to which consumer tastes and preferences are homogeneous, and as we will see, they are often not.

We consider marketing and R&D within the same chapter because of their close relationship. A critical aspect of the marketing function is identifying gaps in the market so that the firm can develop new products to fill those gaps. Developing new products requires R&D—thus the linkage between marketing and R&D. A firm should develop new products with market needs in mind, and only marketing can define those needs for R&D personnel. Also, only marketing can tell R&D whether to produce globally standardized or locally customized products. Research has long maintained that a major contributor to the success of new-product introductions is a close relationship between marketing and R&D.[2]

In this chapter, we begin by reviewing the debate on the globalization of markets. Then we discuss the issue of market segmentation. Next, we look at four elements that constitute a firm's marketing mix: product attributes, distribution strategy, communication strategy, and pricing strategy. The **marketing mix** is the set of choices the firm offers to its targeted markets. Many firms vary their marketing mix from country to country, depending on differences in national culture, economic development, product standards, distribution channels, and so on.

The chapter closes with a look at new-product development in an international business and at the implications of this for the organization of the firm's R&D function.

THE GLOBALIZATION OF MARKETS AND BRANDS

In a now-classic *Harvard Business Review* article, the late Theodore Levitt wrote lyrically about the globalization of world markets. Levitt's arguments have become something of a lightning rod in the debate about the extent of globalization. According to Levitt,

> A powerful force drives the world toward a converging commonalty, and that force is technology. It has proletarianized communication, transport, and travel. The result is a new commercial reality—the emergence of global markets for standardized consumer products on a previously unimagined scale of magnitude.
>
> Gone are accustomed differences in national or regional preferences. The globalization of markets is at hand. With that, the multinational commercial world nears its end, and so does the multinational corporation. The multinational corporation operates in a number of countries and adjusts its products and practices to

each—at high relative costs. The global corporation operates with resolute consistency—at low relative cost—as if the entire world were a single entity; it sells the same thing in the same way everywhere.

Commercially, nothing confirms this as much as the success of McDonald's from the Champs Élysées to the Ginza, of Coca-Cola in Bahrain and Pepsi-Cola in Moscow, and of rock music, Greek salad, Hollywood movies, Revlon cosmetics, Sony television, and Levi's jeans everywhere.

Ancient differences in national tastes or modes of doing business disappear. The commonalty of preference leads inescapably to the standardization of products, manufacturing, and the institutions of trade and commerce.[3]

This is eloquent and evocative writing, but is Levitt correct? The rise of the global media phenomenon from CNN to MTV, and the ability of such media to help shape a global culture, would seem to lend weight to Levitt's argument. If Levitt is correct, his argument has major implications for the marketing strategies pursued by international businesses. However, many academics feel that Levitt overstates his case.[4] Although Levitt may have a point when it comes to many basic industrial products, such as steel, bulk chemicals, and semiconductor chips, globalization in the sense used by Levitt seems to be the exception rather than the rule in many consumer goods markets and industrial markets. Even a firm such as McDonald's, which Levitt holds up as the archetypal example of a consumer products firm that sells a standardized product worldwide, modifies its menu from country to country in light of local consumer preferences. In the Middle East, for example, McDonald's sells the McArabia, a chicken sandwich on Arabian-style bread, and in France, the Croque McDo, a hot ham and cheese sandwich.[5]

On the other hand, Levitt is probably correct to assert that modern transportation and communications technologies are facilitating a convergence of certain tastes and preferences among consumers in the more advanced countries of the world, and this has become even more prevalent since he wrote. In the long run, such technological forces may lead to the evolution of a global culture. At present, however, the continuing persistence of cultural and economic differences between nations acts as a brake on any trend toward the standardization of consumer tastes and preferences across nations. Indeed, that may never occur. Some writers have argued that the rise of global culture doesn't mean that consumers share the same tastes and preferences.[6] Rather, people in different nations, often with conflicting viewpoints, are increasingly participating in a shared "global" conversation, drawing upon shared symbols that include global brands from Nike and Dove to Coca-Cola and Sony. But the way in which these brands are perceived, promoted, and used still varies from country to country, depending on local differences in tastes and preferences. Furthermore, trade barriers and differences in product and technical standards also constrain a firm's ability to sell a standardized product to a global market using a standardized marketing strategy. We discuss the sources of these differences in subsequent sections when we look at how products must be altered from country to country. In short, Levitt's globally standardized market is some way off in many industries.

MARKET SEGMENTATION

Market segmentation refers to identifying distinct groups of consumers whose purchasing behavior differs from others in important ways. Markets can be segmented in numerous ways: by geography, demography (sex, age, income, race, education level, etc.), sociocultural factors (social class, values, religion, lifestyle choices), and psychological factors (personality). Because different segments exhibit different patterns of purchasing behavior, firms often adjust their marketing mix from segment to segment. Thus, the precise design of a product, the pricing strategy, the distribution channels used, and the choice of communication strategy may all be varied from segment to segment. The goal is to

Marketing to Black Brazil

Brazil is home to the largest black population outside of Nigeria. Nearly half of the 195 million people in Brazil are of African or mixed race origin. Despite this, until recently businesses have made little effort to target this numerically large segment of the population. Part of the reason is rooted in economics. Black Brazilians have historically been poorer than Brazilians of European origin and thus have not received the same attention as whites. But after a decade of relatively strong economic performance in Brazil, an emerging black middle class is beginning to command the attention of consumer product companies. To take advantage of this, companies such as Unilever have introduced a range of skin care products and cosmetics aimed at black Brazilians, and Brazil's largest toy company introduced a black Barbie-like doll, Susi Olodum, sales of which quickly caught up with sales of a similar white doll.

But there is more to the issue than simple economics. Unlike the United States, where a protracted history of racial discrimination gave birth to the civil rights movement, fostered black awareness, and produced an identifiable subculture in U.S. society, the history of blacks in Brazil has been very different. Although Brazil did not abolish slavery until 1888, racism in Brazil has historically been much subtler than in the United States. Brazil has never excluded blacks from voting nor had a tradition of segregating the races. Historically, too, the government encouraged intermarriage between whites and blacks. Partly due to this more benign history, Brazil has not had a black rights movement similar to that in the United States, and racial self-identification is much weaker. Surveys routinely find that African Brazilian consumers decline to categorize themselves as either black or white; instead, they choose one of dozens of skin tones and see themselves as being part of a culture that transcends race. Indeed, only 7.4 percent of Brazil's population classify themselves as "Afro-Brazilian," while 42.6 percent classify themselves as "pardo" or brown Brazilians of mixed race ancestry including white, African, and Amerindian descent.

This subtler racial dynamic has important implications for market segmentation and tailoring the marketing mix in Brazil. Unilever had to face this issue when launching a Vaseline Intensive Care lotion for black consumers in Brazil. The company learned in focus groups that for the product to resonate with nonwhite women, its promotions had to feature women of different skin tones, excluding neither whites nor blacks. The campaign Unilever devised features three women with different skin shades at a fitness center. The bottle says the lotion is for "tan and black skin," a description that could include many white women considering that much of the population lives near the beach. Unilever learned that the segment exists, but it is more difficult to define and requires more subtle marketing messages than the African American segment in the United States or middle-class segments in Africa.[8]

optimize the fit between the purchasing behavior of consumers in a given segment and the marketing mix, thereby maximizing sales to that segment. Automobile companies, for example, use a different marketing mix to sell cars to different socioeconomic segments. Thus, Toyota uses its Lexus division to sell high-priced luxury cars to high-income consumers while selling its entry-level models, such as the Toyota Corolla, to lower-income consumers. Similarly, personal computer manufacturers will offer different computer models, embodying different combinations of product attributes and price points, to appeal to consumers from different market segments (e.g., business users and home users).

When managers in an international business consider market segmentation in foreign countries, they need to be cognizant of two main issues: the differences between countries in the structure of market segments and the existence of segments that transcend national borders. The structure of market segments may differ significantly from country to country. An important market segment in a foreign country may have no parallel in the firm's home country, and vice versa. The firm may have to develop a unique marketing mix to appeal to the purchasing behavior of a certain segment in a given country. An example of such a market segment is given in the accompanying Management Focus, which looks at the African Brazilian market segment in Brazil, which as you will see is very different from the African American segment in the United States. In another example, a research project identified a segment of consumers in China in the 50-to-60 age range that has few parallels in other countries.[7] This group came of age during China's Cultural Revolution in the late 1960s and early 1970s. This group's values have been shaped by their experiences during the Cultural Revolution. They tend to be highly sensitive to price and respond negatively to new products and most forms of marketing. Thus, firms doing business in China may need to customize their marketing mix to address the unique values and purchasing behavior of the group. The existence of such a segment constrains the ability of firms to standardize their global marketing strategy.

In contrast, the existence of market segments that transcend national borders clearly enhances the ability of an international business to view the global marketplace as a single entity and pursue a global strategy—selling a standardized product worldwide and using the same basic marketing mix to help position and sell that product in a variety of national markets. For a segment to transcend national borders, consumers in that segment must have some compelling similarities along important dimensions—such as age, values, lifestyle choices—and those similarities must translate into similar purchasing behavior. Although such segments clearly exist in certain industrial markets, they are somewhat rarer in consumer markets. As the opening case illustrates, however, they do exist. Thus, Burberry has been successful by gearing its offering toward a young, affluent, fashion-conscious, tech-savvy demographic. Burberry believes that consumers in this target segment clearly have much in common with each other, whether they live in Beijing, London, or New York.

One emerging global segment that is attracting the attention of international marketers of consumer goods is the so-called global youth segment. Global media are paving the way for a global youth segment. Evidence that such a segment exists comes from a study of the cultural attitudes and purchasing behavior of more than 6,500 teenagers in 26 countries.[9] The findings suggest that teens and young adults around the world are increasingly living parallel lives that share many common values. It follows that they are likely to purchase the same kind of consumer goods and for the same reasons.

PRODUCT ATTRIBUTES

A product can be viewed as a bundle of attributes.[10] For example, the attributes that make up a car include power, design, quality, performance, fuel consumption, and comfort; the attributes of a hamburger include taste, texture, and size; a hotel's attributes include atmosphere, quality, comfort, and service. Products sell well when their attributes match consumer needs (and when their prices are appropriate). BMW cars sell well to people who have high needs for luxury, quality, and performance, precisely because BMW builds those attributes into its cars. If consumer needs were the same the world over, a firm could simply sell the same product worldwide. However, consumer needs vary from country to country, depending on culture and the level of economic development. A firm's ability to sell the same product worldwide is further constrained by countries' differing product standards. This section reviews each of these issues and discusses how they influence product attributes.

Cultural Differences

We discussed countries' cultural differences in Chapter 4. Countries differ along a whole range of dimensions, including social structure, language, religion, and education. These differences have important implications for marketing strategy. For example, "hamburgers" do not sell well in Islamic countries, where the consumption of ham is forbidden by Islamic law (the name is changed). The most important aspect of cultural differences is probably the impact of tradition. Tradition is particularly important in foodstuffs and beverages. For example, reflecting differences in traditional eating habits, the Findus frozen food division of Nestlé, the Swiss food giant, markets fish cakes and fish fingers in Great Britain, but beef bourguignon and coq au vin in France and vitéllo con funghi and braviola in Italy. In addition to its normal range of products, Coca-Cola in Japan markets Georgia, a cold coffee in a can, and Aquarius, a tonic drink, both of which appeal to traditional Japanese tastes.

For historical and idiosyncratic reasons, a range of other cultural differences exist among countries. For example, scent preferences differ from one country to another. SC Johnson, a manufacturer of waxes and polishes, encountered resistance to its lemon-scented Pledge furniture polish among older consumers in Japan. Careful market research revealed the polish smelled similar to a latrine disinfectant used widely in Japan. Sales rose sharply after the scent was adjusted.[11]

There is some evidence of the trends Levitt talked about. Tastes and preferences are becoming more cosmopolitan. Coffee is gaining ground against tea in Japan and Great Britain, while American-style frozen dinners have become popular in Europe (with some fine-tuning to local tastes). Taking advantage of these trends, Nestlé has found that it can market its instant coffee, spaghetti bolognese, and Lean Cuisine frozen dinners in essentially the same manner in both North America and western Europe. However, there is no market for Lean Cuisine dinners in most of the rest of the world, and there may not be for years or decades. Although some cultural convergence has occurred, particularly among the advanced industrial nations of North America and western Europe, Levitt's global culture characterized by standardized tastes and preferences is still a long way off.

Economic Development

Just as important as differences in culture are differences in the level of economic development. We discussed the extent of country differences in economic development in Chapter 3. Consumer behavior is influenced by the level of economic development of a country. Firms based in highly developed countries such as the United States tend to build a lot of extra performance attributes into their products. These extra attributes are not usually demanded by consumers in less developed nations, where the preference is for more basic products. Thus, cars sold in less developed nations typically lack many of the features found in developed nations, such as air-conditioning, power steering, power windows, radios, and CD players. For most consumer durables, product reliability may be a more important attribute in less developed nations, where such a purchase may account for a major proportion of a consumer's income, than it is in advanced nations.

Contrary to Levitt's suggestions, consumers in the most developed countries are often not willing to sacrifice their preferred attributes for lower prices. Consumers in the most advanced countries often shun globally standardized products that have been developed with the lowest common denominator in mind. They are willing to pay more for products that have additional features and attributes customized to their tastes and preferences. For example, demand for top-of-the-line four-wheel-drive sport utility vehicles—such as Chrysler's Jeep, Ford's Explorer, and Toyota's Land Cruiser—has been largely restricted to the United States. This is due to a combination of factors, including the high income level of U.S. consumers, the country's vast distances, the relatively low cost of gasoline, and the culturally grounded "outdoor" theme of American life.

Product and Technical Standards

Even with the forces that are creating some convergence of consumer tastes and preferences among advanced, industrialized nations, Levitt's vision of global markets may still be a long way off because of national differences in product and technological standards.

Differing government-mandated product standards can rule out mass production and marketing of a standardized product. Differences in technical standards also constrain the globalization of markets. Some of these differences result from idiosyncratic decisions made long ago, rather than from government actions, but their long-term effects are profound. For example, DVD equipment manufactured for sale in the United States will not play DVDs recorded on equipment manufactured for sale in Great Britain, Germany, and France (and vice versa). Different technical standards for television signal frequency emerged in the 1950s that require television and video equipment to be customized to prevailing standards. RCA stumbled in the 1970s when it failed to account for this in its marketing of TVs in Asia. Although several Asian countries adopted the U.S. standard, Singapore, Hong Kong, and Malaysia adopted the British standard. People who bought RCA TVs in those countries could receive a picture but no sound![12]

DISTRIBUTION STRATEGY

LO18-2

A critical element of a firm's marketing mix is its distribution strategy: the means it chooses for delivering the product to the consumer. The way the product is delivered is determined by the firm's entry strategy, discussed in Chapter 15. This section examines a typical distribution system, discusses how its structure varies between countries, and looks at how appropriate distribution strategies vary from country to country.

Figure 18.1 illustrates a typical distribution system consisting of a channel that includes a wholesale distributor and a retailer. If the firm manufactures its product in the particular country, it can sell directly to the consumer, to the retailer, or to the wholesaler. The same options are available to a firm that manufactures outside the country. Plus, this firm may decide to sell to an import agent, which then deals with the wholesale distributor, the retailer, or the consumer. Later in the chapter we consider the factors that determine the firm's choice of channel.

Differences Between Countries

The four main differences between distribution systems are retail concentration, channel length, channel exclusivity, and channel quality.

Retail Concentration

In some countries, the retail system is very concentrated, but it is fragmented in others. In a **concentrated retail system**, a few retailers supply most of the market. A **fragmented retail system** is one in which there are many retailers, none of which has a major share of the market. Many of the

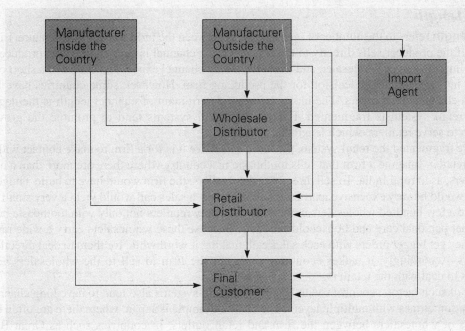

Figure 18.1   *A Typical Distribution System*

differences in concentration are rooted in history and tradition. In the United States, the importance of the automobile and the relative youth of many urban areas have resulted in a retail system centered on large stores or shopping malls to which people can drive. This has facilitated system concentration. Japan, with a much greater population density and a large number of urban centers that grew up before the automobile, has a more fragmented retail system, with many small stores serving local neighborhoods and to which people frequently walk. In addition, the Japanese legal system protects small retailers. Small retailers can try to block the establishment of a large retail outlet by petitioning their local government.

There is a tendency for greater retail concentration in developed countries. Three factors that contribute to this are the increases in car ownership, the number of households with refrigerators and freezers, and the number of two-income households. All these factors have changed shopping habits and facilitated the growth of large retail establishments sited away from traditional shopping areas. The last decade has seen consolidation in the global retail industry, with companies such as Walmart and Carrefour attempting to become global retailers by acquiring retailers in different countries. This has increased retail concentration.

In contrast, retail systems are very fragmented in many developing countries, which can make for interesting distribution challenges. In rural China, large areas of the country can be reached only by traveling rutted dirt roads. In India, Unilever has to sell to retailers in 600,000 rural villages, many of which cannot be accessed via paved roads, which means products can reach their destination only by bullock, bicycle, or cart. In neighboring Nepal, the terrain is so rugged that even bicycles and carts are not practical, and businesses rely on yak trains and the human back to deliver products to thousands of small retailers.

Channel Length

Channel length refers to the number of intermediaries between the producer (or manufacturer) and the consumer. If the producer sells directly to the consumer, the channel is very short. If the producer sells through an import agent, a wholesaler, and a retailer, a long channel exists. The choice of a short or long channel is, in part, a strategic decision for the producing firm. However, some countries have longer distribution channels than others. The most important determinant of channel length is the degree to which the retail system is fragmented. Fragmented retail systems tend to promote the growth of wholesalers to serve retailers, which lengthens channels.

The more fragmented the retail system, the more expensive it is for a firm to make contact with each individual retailer. Imagine a firm that sells toothpaste in a country where there are more than a million small retailers, as in rural India. To sell directly to the retailers, the firm would have to build a huge sales force. This would be very expensive, particularly because each sales call would yield a very small order. But suppose a few hundred wholesalers in the country supply retailers not only with toothpaste but also with all other personal care and household products. Because these wholesalers carry a wide range of products, they get bigger orders with each sales call, making it worthwhile for them to deal directly with the retailers. Accordingly, it makes economic sense for the firm to sell to the wholesalers and the wholesalers to deal with the retailers.

Because of such factors, countries with fragmented retail systems also tend to have long channels of distribution, sometimes with multiple layers. The classic example is Japan, where there are often two or three layers of wholesalers between the firm and retail outlets. In countries such as Great Britain, Germany, and the United States, where the retail systems are far more concentrated, channels are much shorter. When the retail sector is very concentrated, it makes sense for the firm to deal directly with retailers, cutting out wholesalers. A relatively small sales force is required to deal with a concentrated retail sector, and the orders generated from each sales call can be large. Such circumstances tend to prevail in the United States, where large food companies may sell directly to supermarkets rather than going through wholesale distributors.

Another factor that is shortening channel length in some countries is the entry of large discount superstores, such as Carrefour, Walmart, and Tesco. The business model of these retailers is, in part, based on the idea that in an attempt to lower prices, they cut out wholesalers and instead deal directly with manufacturers. Thus, when Walmart entered Mexico, its policy of dealing directly with manufacturers, instead of buying merchandise through wholesalers, helped shorten distribution channels in that nation. Similarly, Japan's historically long distribution channels are now being shortened by the rise of large retailers, some of them foreign-owned, such as Toys "R" Us and Walmart, and some of them indigenous enterprises that are imitating the American model, all of which are progressively cutting out wholesalers and dealing directly with manufacturers.

Channel Exclusivity

An **exclusive distribution channel** is one that is difficult for outsiders to access. For example, it is often difficult for a new firm to get access to shelf space in supermarkets. This occurs because retailers tend to prefer to carry the products of established manufacturers of foodstuffs with national reputations rather than gamble on the products of unknown firms. The exclusivity of a distribution system varies among countries. Japan's system is often held up as an example of a very exclusive system. In Japan, relationships among manufacturers, wholesalers, and retailers often go back decades. Many of these relationships are based on the understanding that distributors will not carry the products of competing firms. In return, the distributors are guaranteed an attractive markup by the manufacturer. As many U.S. and European manufacturers have learned, the close ties that result from this arrangement can make access to the Japanese market difficult.

However, it is possible to break into the Japanese market with a new consumer product. Procter & Gamble did during the 1990s with its Joy brand of dish soap. P&G was able to overcome a tradition of exclusivity for two reasons. First, after two decades of lackluster economic performance, Japan is changing. In their search for profits, retailers are far more willing than they have been historically to violate the old norms of exclusivity. Second, P&G has been in Japan long enough and has a broad enough portfolio of consumer products to give it considerable leverage with distributors, enabling it to push new products out through the distribution channel.

Channel Quality

Channel quality refers to the expertise, competencies, and skills of established retailers in a nation and their ability to sell and support the products of international businesses. Although the quality of retailers is good in most developed nations, in emerging markets and less developed nations from Russia to Indonesia, channel quality is variable at best. The lack of a high-quality channel may impede market entry, particularly in the case of new or sophisticated products that require significant point-of-sale assistance and after-sales services and support. When channel quality is poor, an international business may have to devote considerable attention to upgrading the channel, for example, by providing extensive education and support to existing retailers and, in extreme cases, by establishing its own channel. Thus, after pioneering its Apple retail store concept in the United States, Apple opened retail stores in several nations—including the United Kingdom, France, Germany, Japan, and China—to provide point-of-sales education, service, and support for its popular iPod, iPad, iPhone, and iMac products. Apple believes that this strategy will help it gain market share in these nations.

Choosing a Distribution Strategy

A choice of distribution strategy determines which channel the firm will use to reach potential consumers. Should the firm try to sell directly to the consumer? Or should it go through retailers, go through a wholesaler, use an import agent, or invest in establishing its own channel? The optimal strategy is determined by the relative costs and benefits of each alternative, which vary from country to country, depending on the four factors we have just discussed: retail concentration, channel length, channel exclusivity, and channel quality.

Because each intermediary in a channel adds its own markup to the products, there is generally a critical link among channel length, the final selling price, and the firm's profit margin. The longer a channel, the greater the aggregate markup, and the higher the price that consumers are charged for the final product. To ensure that prices do not get too high as a result of markups by multiple intermediaries, a firm might be forced to operate with lower profit margins. Thus, if price is an important competitive weapon, and if the firm does not want to see its profit margins squeezed, other things being equal, the firm would prefer to use a shorter channel.

However, the benefits of using a longer channel may outweigh these drawbacks. As we have seen, one benefit of a longer channel is that it cuts selling costs when the retail sector is very fragmented. Thus, it makes sense for an international business to use longer channels in countries where the retail sector is fragmented and shorter channels in countries where the retail sector is concentrated. Another benefit of using a longer channel is market access—the ability to enter an exclusive channel. Import agents may have long-term relationships with wholesalers, retailers, or important consumers and thus be better able to win orders and get access to a distribution system. Similarly, wholesalers may have long-standing relationships with retailers and be better able to persuade them to carry the firm's product than the firm itself would.

Import agents are not limited to independent trading houses; any firm with a strong local reputation could serve as well. For example, to break down channel exclusivity and gain greater access to the Japanese market, when Apple Computer originally entered Japan, it signed distribution agreements with five large Japanese firms, including business equipment giant Brother Industries, stationery leader Kokuyo, Mitsubishi, Sharp, and Minolta. These firms use their own long-established distribution relationships with consumers, retailers, and wholesalers to push Apple computers through the Japanese distribution system. Today, Apple has supplemented this strategy with its own stores in the country.

If such an arrangement is not possible, the firm might want to consider other, less traditional alternatives to gaining market access. Frustrated by channel exclusivity in Japan, some foreign manufacturers of consumer goods have attempted to sell directly to Japanese consumers using direct mail and catalogs. Finally, if channel quality is poor, a firm should consider what steps it could take to upgrade the quality of the channel, including establishing its own distribution channel.

COMMUNICATION STRATEGY

LO18-3

Another critical element in the marketing mix is communicating the attributes of the product to prospective customers. A number of communication channels are available to a firm, including direct selling, sales promotion, direct marketing, and advertising. A firm's communication strategy is partly defined by its choice of channel. Some firms rely primarily on direct selling, others on point-of-sale promotions or direct marketing, and others on mass advertising; still others use several channels simultaneously to communicate their message to prospective customers. This section looks first at the barriers to international communication. Then, we survey the various factors that determine which communication strategy is most appropriate in a particular country. After that, we discuss global advertising.

Barriers to International Communication

International communication occurs whenever a firm uses a marketing message to sell its products in another country. The effectiveness of a firm's international communication can be jeopardized by three potentially critical variables: cultural barriers, source effects, and noise levels.

Cultural Barriers

Cultural barriers can make it difficult to communicate messages across cultures. We discussed some sources and consequences of cultural differences between nations in Chapter 4 and in the previous section of this chapter. Because of cultural differences, a message that means one thing in one country may mean something quite different in another. Benetton, the Italian clothing manufacturer and retailer, ran into cultural problems with its advertising. The company launched a worldwide advertising campaign with the theme "United Colors of Benetton" that had won awards in France. One of its ads featured a black woman breast-feeding a white baby, and another one showed a black man and a white man handcuffed together. Benetton was surprised when the ads were attacked by U.S. civil rights groups for promoting white racial domination. Benetton withdrew its ads and fired its advertising agency, Eldorado of France.

The best way for a firm to overcome cultural barriers is to develop cross-cultural literacy (see Chapter 4). In addition, it should use local input, such as a local advertising agency, in developing its marketing message. If the firm uses direct selling rather than advertising to communicate its message, it should develop a local sales force whenever possible. Cultural differences limit a firm's ability to use the same marketing message and selling approach worldwide. What works well in one country may be offensive in another.

Source and Country of Origin Effects

Source effects occur when the receiver of the message (the potential consumer in this case) evaluates the message on the basis of status or image of the sender. Source effects can be damaging for an international business when potential consumers in a target country have a bias against foreign firms. For example, a wave of "Japan bashing" swept the United States in the early 1990s. Worried that U.S. consumers might view its products negatively, Honda responded by creating ads that emphasized the U.S. content of its cars to show how "American" the company had become.

Many international businesses try to counter negative source effects by deemphasizing their foreign origins. When the French antiglobalization protester José Bové was hailed as a hero by some in France for razing a partly built McDonald's in 1999, the French franchisees of McDonald's responded with an ad depicting a fat, ignorant American who could not understand why McDonald's France used locally produced food that wasn't genetically modified. The edgy ad worked, and McDonald's French operations are now among the most robust in the company's global network.[13]

A subset of source effects is referred to as **country of origin effects**, or the extent to which the place of manufacturing influences product evaluations. Research suggests that the consumer may use country of origin as a cue when evaluating a product, particularly if he or she lacks more detailed knowledge of the product. For example, one study found that Japanese consumers tended to rate Japanese products more favorably than U.S. products across multiple dimensions, even when independent analysis showed that they were actually inferior.[14] When a negative country of origin effect exists, an international business may have to work hard to counteract this effect by, for example, using promotional messages that stress the positive performance attributes of its product

Source effects and country of origin effects are not always negative. French wine, Italian clothes, and German luxury cars benefit from nearly universal positive source effects. In such cases, it may pay a firm to emphasize its foreign origins.

Noise Levels

Noise tends to reduce the probability of effective communication. **Noise** refers to the amount of other messages competing for a potential consumer's attention, and this too varies across countries. In highly developed countries such as the United States, noise is extremely high. Fewer firms vie for the attention of prospective customers in developing countries; thus the noise level is lower.

Push Versus Pull Strategies

The main decision with regard to communications strategy is the choice between a push strategy and a pull strategy. A **push strategy** emphasizes personal selling rather than mass media advertising in the promotional mix. Although effective as a promotional tool, personal selling requires intensive use of a sales force and is relatively costly. A **pull strategy** depends more on mass media advertising to communicate the marketing message to potential consumers.

Although some firms employ only a pull strategy and others only a push strategy, still other firms combine direct selling with mass advertising to maximize communication effectiveness. Factors that determine the relative attractiveness of push and pull strategies include product type relative to consumer sophistication, channel length, and media availability.

Unilever—Selling to India's Poor

One of the world's largest and oldest consumer products companies, Unilever has long had a substantial presence in many of the world's poorer nations, such as India. Outside major urban areas, low income, unsophisticated consumers, illiteracy, fragmented retail distribution systems, and the lack of paved roads have made for difficult marketing challenges. Despite this, Unilever has built a significant presence among impoverished rural populations by adopting innovative selling strategies.

India's large rural population is dispersed among some 600,000 villages, more than 500,000 of which cannot be reached by a motor vehicle. Some 91 percent of the rural population lives in villages of fewer than 2,000 people, and of necessity, rural retail stores are very small and carry limited stock. The population is desperately poor, making perhaps a dollar a day, and two-thirds of that income is spent on food, leaving about 30 cents a day for other items. Literacy levels are low, and TVs are rare, making traditional media ineffective. Despite these drawbacks, Hindustan Lever, Unilever's Indian subsidiary, has made a concerted effort to reach the rural poor. Although the revenues generated from rural sales are small, Unilever hopes that as the country develops and income levels rise, the population will continue to purchase the Unilever brands that they are familiar with, giving the company a long-term competitive advantage.

To contact rural consumers, Hindustan Lever tries to establish a physical presence wherever people frequently gather in numbers. This means ensuring that advertisements are seen in places where people congregate and make purchases, such as at village wells and weekly rural markets, and where they consume products, such as at riverbanks where people gather to wash their clothes using (the company hopes) Unilever soap. It is not uncommon to see the village well plastered with advertisements for Unilever products. The company also takes part in weekly rural events, such as market day, at which farm produce is sold and family provisions purchased. Hindustan Lever salespeople will visit these gatherings, display their products, explain how they work, give away some free samples, make a few sales, and seed the market for future demand.

The backbone of Hindustan Lever's selling effort, however, is a rural distribution network that encompasses 100 factories, 7,500 distributors, and an estimated 3 million retail stores, many of which are little more than a hole in a wall or a stall at a market. The total stock of Unilever products in these stores may be no more than a few sachets of shampoo and half a dozen bars of soap. A depot in each of India's states feeds products to major wholesalers, which then sell directly to retailers in thousands of small towns and villages that can be reached by motor vehicles. If access via motor vehicles is not possible, the major wholesalers sell to smaller second-tier wholesalers, which then handle distribution to India's 500,000 inaccessible rural villages, reaching them by bicycle, bullock cart, or baskets carried on a human back.[15]

Product Type and Consumer Sophistication

Firms in consumer goods industries that are trying to sell to a large segment of the market generally favor a pull strategy. Mass communication has cost advantages for such firms; thus they rarely use direct selling. Exceptions can be found in poorer nations with low literacy levels, where direct selling may be the only way to reach consumers (see the Management Focus on Unilever). Firms that sell industrial products or other complex products favor a push strategy. Direct selling allows the firm to educate potential consumers about the features of the product. This may not be necessary in advanced nations where a complex product has been in use for some time, where the product's attributes are well understood, where consumers are sophisticated, and where high-quality channels exist that can provide point-of-sale assistance. However, customer education may be important when consumers have less sophistication toward the product, which can be the case in developing nations or in advanced nations when a new complex product is being introduced, or where high-quality channels are absent or scarce.

Channel Length

The longer the distribution channel, the more intermediaries there are that must be persuaded to carry the product for it to reach the consumer. This can lead to inertia in the channel, which can make entry difficult. Using direct selling to push a product through many layers of a distribution channel can be expensive. In such circumstances, a firm may try to pull its product through the channels by using mass advertising to create consumer demand—once demand is created, intermediaries will feel obliged to carry the product.

In Japan, products often pass through two, three, or even four wholesalers before they reach the final retail outlet. This can make it difficult for foreign firms to break into the Japanese market. Not only must the foreign firm persuade a Japanese retailer to carry its product, but it may also have to persuade every intermediary in the chain to carry the product. Mass advertising may be one way to break down channel resistance in such circumstances. However, in countries such as India, which has a very long distribution channel to serve its massive rural population, mass advertising may not work because of low literacy levels, in which case the firm may need to fall back on direct selling or rely on the goodwill of distributors (see the Management Focus on Unilever).

Media Availability

A pull strategy relies on access to advertising media. In the United States, a large number of media are available, including print media (newspapers and magazines), broadcasting media (television and radio), and the Internet. The rise of cable television in the United States has facilitated extremely focused advertising (e.g., MTV for teens and young adults, Lifetime for women, ESPN for sports enthusiasts). The same is true of the Internet, with different websites attracting different kinds of users, and companies such as Google transforming the ability of companies to do targeted advertising. While this level of media sophistication is now found in many other developed countries, it is still not universal. Even many advanced nations have far fewer electronic media available for advertising than the United States. In Scandinavia, for example, no commercial television or radio stations existed until recently; all electronic media were state-owned and carried no commercials, although this has now changed with the advent of satellite television deregulation. In many developing nations, the situation is even more restrictive because mass media of all types are typically more limited. A firm's ability to use a pull strategy is limited in some countries by media availability. In such circumstances, a push strategy is more attractive. For example, Unilever uses a push strategy to sell consumer products in rural India, where few mass media are available (see the Management Focus).

Media availability is limited by law in some cases. Few countries allow advertisements for tobacco and alcohol products on television and radio, though they are usually permitted in print media. When the leading Japanese whiskey distiller, Suntory, entered the U.S. market, it had to do so without television, its preferred medium. The firm spends about $50 million annually on television advertising in Japan. Similarly, while advertising pharmaceutical products directly to consumers is allowed in the United States, it is prohibited in many other advanced nations. In such cases, pharmaceutical firms must rely heavily on advertising and direct-sales efforts focused explicitly at doctors to get their products prescribed.

The Push–Pull Mix

The optimal mix between push and pull strategies depends on product type and consumer sophistication, channel length, and media sophistication. Push strategies tend to be emphasized:

- For industrial products or complex new products.
- When distribution channels are short.
- When few print or electronic media are available.

Pull strategies tend to be emphasized:

- For consumer goods.
- When distribution channels are long.
- When sufficient print and electronic media are available to carry the marketing message.

Global Advertising

In recent years, largely inspired by the work of visionaries such as Theodore Levitt, there has been much discussion about the pros and cons of standardizing advertising worldwide.[16] One of the most successful standardized campaigns in history was Philip Morris's promotion of Marlboro cigarettes. The campaign was instituted in the 1950s, when the brand was repositioned, to assure smokers that the flavor would be unchanged by the addition of a filter. The campaign theme of "Come to where the flavor is: Come to Marlboro country" was a worldwide success. Marlboro built on this when it introduced "the Marlboro man," a rugged cowboy smoking his Marlboro while riding his horse through the great outdoors. This ad proved successful in almost every major market around the world, and it helped propel Marlboro to the top of the world market.

For Standardized Advertising

The support for global advertising is threefold. First, it has significant economic advantages. Standardized advertising lowers the costs of value creation by spreading the fixed costs of developing the advertisements over many countries. For example, Coca-Cola's advertising agency, McCann Erickson, claims to have saved Coca-Cola more than $100 million over 20 years by using certain elements of its campaigns globally.

Second, there is the concern that creative talent is scarce, so one large effort to develop a campaign will produce better results than 40 or 50 smaller efforts. A third justification for a standardized approach is that many brand names are global (Burberry being a good example; see the opening case). With the substantial amount of international travel today and the considerable overlap in media across national borders, many international firms want to project a single brand image to avoid confusion caused by local campaigns. This is particularly important in regions such as western Europe, where travel across borders is almost as common as travel across state lines in the United States.

Against Standardized Advertising

There are two main arguments against globally standardized advertising. First, as we have seen repeatedly in this chapter and in Chapter 4, cultural differences among nations are such that a message that works in one nation can fail miserably in another. Cultural diversity makes it extremely difficult to develop a single advertising theme that is effective worldwide. Messages directed at the culture of a given country may be more effective than global messages.

Second, advertising regulations may block implementation of standardized advertising. For example, Kellogg could not use a television commercial it produced in Great Britain to promote its cornflakes in

Dove's Global "Real Beauty" Campaign

In 2003, Dove was not a beauty brand; it was a bar of soap that was positioned and sold differently in different markets. Unilever, the company that marketed Dove, was a storied consumer product multinational with global reach, had a strong position in fast-growing developing nations, and had a reputation for customizing products to conditions prevailing in local markets. In India, for example, women often oil their hair before washing it, so Western shampoos that do not remove the oil have not sold well. Unilever reformulated its shampoo for India and was rewarded with market leadership. But sometimes Unilever went too far. It used different formulations for shampoo in Hong Kong and mainland China, for example, even though hair and washing habits were very similar in both markets. Unilever would also often vary the packaging and marketing message in similar products, even for its most commoditized products. The company tended to exaggerate complexity, and by 2003 its financial performance was suffering.

A decade later, Unilever's financial performance has improved, in no small part because it has shifted toward a more global emphasis, and the Dove brand has led the way. The Dove story dates to 2003 when the global brand director, Silvia Lagnado, who was based in New York, decided to move the positioning of Dove from one based on the product to one of an entire beauty brand. The basic message: The brand should stand for the real beauty of all women. Dove's mission was to make women feel more beautiful every day by widening the stereotypical definition of beauty and inspiring them to take care of themselves.

But how was this mission to be executed? Following a series of workshops held around the globe that asked brand managers and advertising agency partners to find ways to communicate an inclusive definition of beauty, the Canadian brand manager asked 67 female photographers to submit work that best reflects real beauty. The photographs are stunning portraits not of models, but of women from all walks of life that come in all shapes, sizes, and ages. It led to a coffee table book and traveling exhibition, called the Dove Photo Tour, which garnered a lot of positive press in Canada. Silvia Lagnado realized that the Canadians were on to something. Around the same time, the German office of Unilever's advertising agency, Ogilvy and Mather Worldwide, came up with a concept for communicating "real beauty" based on photographs showing, instead of skinny models, ordinary women in their underwear. The original German advertisements quickly made their way to the United Kingdom, where a London newspaper article stated the campaign was not advertising; it was politics. Lagnado was not surprised by this. She had commissioned research that revealed only 2 percent of women worldwide considered themselves beautiful, and that half thought their weight was too high.

In 2004, the "Dove Campaign for Real Beauty" was launched globally. This was a radical shift for Unilever and the Dove brand, which until then had left marketing in the hands of local brand managers. The Real Beauty campaign was tweaked to take local sensibilities into account. For example, it was deemed better not to show women touching each other in America, while in Latin America tactile women do not shock anybody, so touching was seen as OK.

In 2005, the campaign was followed by the launch of the Dove "self-esteem fund," a worldwide campaign to persuade girls and young women to embrace a more positive image of themselves. Unilever also made an online video, loaded onto YouTube, called *Onslaught,* which was critical of the beauty industry and ended with the slogan, "Talk to your daughter before the beauty industry does." Another video, *Evolution,* showed how the face of a girl can be changed, partly through computer graphics, to create an image of beauty. The video ended with the tag line, "No wonder our perception of beauty is distorted." Made for very little money, the YouTube videos created a viral buzz around the campaign that helped transform Dove into one of Unilever's leading brands. By its use of such techniques, the campaign has become a model for how to revitalize and build a new global brand.[18]

many other European countries. A reference to the iron and vitamin content of its cornflakes was not permissible in the Netherlands, where claims relating to health and medical benefits are outlawed. A child wearing a Kellogg T-shirt had to be edited out of the commercial before it could be used in France, because French law forbids the use of children in product endorsements. The key line "Kellogg's makes their cornflakes the best they have ever been" was disallowed in Germany because of a prohibition against competitive claims.[17]

Dealing with Country Differences

Some firms are experimenting with capturing some benefits of global standardization while recognizing differences in countries' cultural and legal environments. A firm may select some features to include in all its advertising campaigns and localize other features. By doing so, it may be able to save on some costs and build international brand recognition and yet customize its advertisements to different cultures.

Nokia, the Finnish cell phone manufacturer, has tried to do this. Historically, Nokia had used a different advertising campaign in different markets. In 2004, however, the company launched a global advertising campaign that used the slogan "1001 reasons to have a Nokia imaging phone." Nokia did this to reduce advertising costs, capture some economies of scale, and establish a consistent global brand image. At the same time, Nokia tweaked the advertisements for different cultures. The campaign used actors from the region where the ad ran to reflect the local population, though they said the same lines. Local settings were also modified when showcasing the phones by, for example, using a marketplace when advertising in Italy or a bazaar when advertising in the Middle East.[19] Another example of this process is given in the accompanying Management Focus, which looks at how Unilever built a global brand for its Dove products while still tweaking the message to consider local sensibilities.

PRICING STRATEGY   LO18-4

International pricing strategy is an important component of the overall international marketing mix.[20] This section looks at three aspects of international pricing strategy. First, we examine the case for pursuing price discrimination, charging different prices for the same product in different countries. Second, we look at what might be called strategic pricing. Third, we review regulatory factors, such as government-mandated price controls and antidumping regulations, that limit a firm's ability to charge the prices it would prefer in a country.

Price Discrimination

Price discrimination exists whenever consumers in different countries are charged different prices for the same product, or for slightly different variations of the product.[21] Price discrimination involves charging whatever the market will bear; in a competitive market, prices may have to be lower than in a market where the firm has a monopoly. Price discrimination can help a company maximize its profits. It makes economic sense to charge different prices in different countries.

Two conditions are necessary for profitable price discrimination. First, the firm must be able to keep its national markets separate. If it cannot do this, individuals or businesses may undercut its attempt at price discrimination by engaging in arbitrage. Arbitrage occurs when an individual or business capitalizes on a price differential for a firm's product between two countries by purchasing the product in the country where prices are lower and reselling it in the country where prices are higher. For example, many automobile firms have long practiced price discrimination in Europe. A Ford Escort once cost $2,000 more in Germany than it did in Belgium. This policy broke down when car dealers bought Escorts in Belgium and drove them to Germany, where they sold them at a profit for slightly less than Ford was selling Escorts in Germany. To protect the market share of its German auto dealers, Ford had to bring its German prices into line with those being charged in Belgium. Ford could not keep these markets separate, unlike in Britain where the need for right-hand-drive cars keep the market separate from the rest of Europe.

The second necessary condition for profitable price discrimination is different price elasticities of demand in different countries. The **price elasticity of demand** is a measure of the responsiveness of demand for a product to change in price. Demand is said to be **elastic** when a small change in price produces a large change in demand; it is said to be **inelastic** when a large change in price produces only a small change in demand. Figure 18.2 illustrates elastic and inelastic demand curves. Generally, a firm can charge a higher price in a country where demand is inelastic.

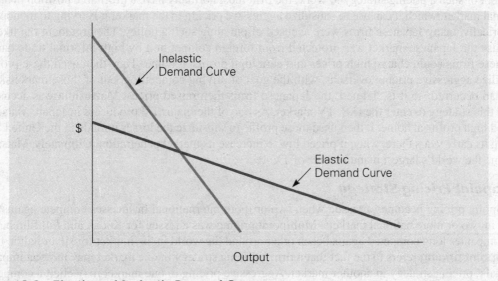

Figure 18.2 *Elastic and Inelastic Demand Curves*

The elasticity of demand for a product in a given country is determined by a number of factors, of which income level and competitive conditions are the two most important. Price elasticity tends to be greater in countries with low income levels. Consumers with limited incomes tend to be very price conscious; they have less to spend, so they look much more closely at price. Thus, price elasticity for products such as personal computers is greater in countries such as India, where a PC is still a luxury item, than in the United States, where it is now considered a necessity. The same is true of the software that resides on those PCs; thus, to sell more software in India, Microsoft has had to introduce low-priced versions of its products into that market, such as Windows Starter Edition.

In general, the more competitors there are, the greater consumers' bargaining power will be and the more likely consumers will be to buy from the firm that charges the lowest price. Thus, many competitors cause high elasticity of demand. In such circumstances, if a firm raises its prices above those of its competitors, consumers will switch to the competitors' products. The opposite is true when a firm faces few competitors. When competitors are limited, consumers' bargaining power is weaker, and price is less important as a competitive weapon. Thus, a firm may charge a higher price for its product in a country where competition is limited than in one where competition is intense.

Strategic Pricing

The concept of **strategic pricing** has three aspects, which we refer to as predatory pricing, multipoint pricing, and experience curve pricing. Both predatory pricing and experience curve pricing may violate antidumping regulations. After we review predatory and experience curve pricing, we will look at antidumping rules and other regulatory policies.

Predatory Pricing

Predatory pricing is the use of price as a competitive weapon to drive weaker competitors out of a national market. Once the competitors have left the market, the firm can raise prices and enjoy high profits. For such a pricing strategy to work, the firm must normally have a profitable position in another national market, which it can use to subsidize aggressive pricing in the market it is trying to monopolize. Historically, many Japanese firms were accused of pursuing such a policy. The argument ran like this: Because the Japanese market was protected from foreign competition by high informal trade barriers, Japanese firms could charge high prices and earn high profits at home. They then used these profits to subsidize aggressive pricing overseas, with the goal of driving competitors out of those markets. Once this had occurred, so it is claimed, the Japanese firms then raised prices. Matsushita was accused of using this strategy to enter the U.S. TV market. As one of the major TV producers in Japan, Matsushita earned high profits at home. It then used these profits to subsidize the losses it made in the United States during its early years there, when it priced low to increase its market penetration. Ultimately, Matsushita became the world's largest manufacturer of TVs.[22]

Multipoint Pricing Strategy

Multipoint pricing becomes an issue when two or more international businesses compete against each other in two or more national markets. Multipoint pricing was an issue for Kodak and Fujifilm because the companies long competed against each other around the world in the market for silver halide film.[23] **Multipoint pricing** refers to the fact that a firm's pricing strategy in one market may have an impact on its rivals' pricing strategy in another market. Aggressive pricing in one market may elicit a competitive response from a rival in another market. For example, Fuji launched an aggressive competitive attack against Kodak in the U.S. company's home market in January 1997, cutting prices on multiple-roll packs of 35mm film by as much as 50 percent.[24] This price cutting resulted in a 28 percent increase in shipments of Fuji color film during the first six months of 1997, while Kodak's shipments dropped by 11 percent. This attack created a dilemma for Kodak; the company did not want to start price discounting in its largest and most profitable market. Kodak's response was to aggressively cut prices in Fuji's largest market, Japan. This strategic response recognized the interdependence between Kodak and Fuji and the fact that they compete against each other in many different nations. Fuji responded to Kodak's counterattack by pulling back from its aggressive stance in the United States.

The Kodak story illustrates an important aspect of multipoint pricing: Aggressive pricing in one market may elicit a response from rivals in another market. The firm needs to consider how its global rivals will respond to changes in its pricing strategy before making those changes. A second aspect of multipoint pricing arises when two or more global companies focus on particular national markets and launch vigorous price wars in those markets in an attempt to gain market dominance. In Brazil's market for disposable diapers, two U.S. companies, Kimberly-Clark and Procter & Gamble, entered a price war as each struggled to establish dominance in the market.[25] As a result, over three years the cost of disposable diapers fell from $1 per diaper to 33 cents per diaper, while several other competitors, including indigenous Brazilian firms, were driven out of the market. Kimberly-Clark and Procter & Gamble are engaged in a global struggle for market share and dominance, and Brazil is one of their battlegrounds. Both companies can afford to engage in this behavior, even though it reduces their profits in Brazil, because they have profitable operations elsewhere in the world that can subsidize these losses.

Pricing decisions around the world need to be centrally monitored. It is tempting to delegate full responsibility for pricing decisions to the managers of various national subsidiaries, thereby reaping the benefits of decentralization. However, because pricing strategy in one part of the world can elicit a competitive response in another, central management needs to at least monitor and approve pricing decisions in a given national market, and local managers need to recognize that their actions can affect competitive conditions in other countries.

Experience Curve Pricing

We first encountered the experience curve in Chapter 13. As a firm builds its accumulated production volume over time, unit costs fall due to experience effects. Learning effects and economies of scale underlie the experience curve. Price comes into the picture because aggressive pricing (along with aggressive promotion and advertising) can build accumulated sales volume rapidly and thus move production down the experience curve. Firms farther down the experience curve have a cost advantage vis-à-vis those farther up the curve.

Many firms pursuing an **experience curve pricing** strategy on an international scale will price low worldwide in attempting to build global sales volume as rapidly as possible, even if this means taking large losses initially. Such a firm believes that in several years, when it has moved down the experience curve, it will be making substantial profits and have a cost advantage over its less aggressive competitors.

Regulatory Influences on Prices

The ability to engage in either price discrimination or strategic pricing may be limited by national or international regulations. Most important, a firm's freedom to set its own prices is constrained by antidumping regulations and competition policy.

Antidumping Regulations

Both predatory pricing and experience curve pricing can run afoul of antidumping regulations. Dumping occurs whenever a firm sells a product for a price that is less than the cost of producing it. Most regulations, however, define dumping more vaguely. For example, a country is allowed to bring antidumping actions against an importer under Article 6 of GATT as long as two criteria are met: sales at "less than fair value" and "material injury to a domestic industry." The problem with this terminology is that it does not indicate what a fair value is. The ambiguity has led some to argue that selling abroad at prices below those in the country of origin, as opposed to below cost, is dumping.

Such logic led the Bush administration to place a 20 percent duty on imports of foreign steel in 2001. Foreign manufacturers protested that they were not selling below cost. Admitting that their prices were lower in the United States than some other countries, they argued that this simply reflected the intensely competitive nature of the U.S. market (i.e., different price elasticities).

Antidumping rules set a floor under export prices and limit firms' ability to pursue strategic pricing. The rather vague terminology used in most antidumping actions suggests that a firm's ability to engage in price discrimination also may be challenged under antidumping legislation.

Competition Policy

Most developed nations have regulations designed to promote competition and to restrict monopoly practices. These regulations can be used to limit the prices a firm can charge in a given country. For example, at one time the Swiss pharmaceutical manufacturer Hoffmann–La Roche had a monopoly on the supply of Valium and Librium tranquilizers. The company was investigated by the British Monopolies and Mergers Commission, which is responsible for promoting fair competition in Great Britain. The commission found that Hoffmann–La Roche was overcharging its tranquilizers and ordered the company to reduce its prices 50 to 60 percent and repay excess profit of $30 million. Hoffmann–La Roche maintained unsuccessfully that it was merely engaging in price discrimination. Similar actions were later brought against Hoffmann–La Roche by the German cartel office and by the Dutch and Danish governments.[26]

CONFIGURING THE MARKETING MIX

A firm might vary aspects of its marketing mix from country to country to take into account local differences in culture, economic conditions, competitive conditions, product and technical standards, distribution systems, government regulations, and the like. Such differences may require variation in product attributes, distribution strategy, communication strategy, and pricing strategy. The cumulative effect of these factors makes it rare for a firm to adopt the same marketing mix worldwide. A detailed example is given in the accompanying Management Focus, which looks at how Levi Strauss now varies its marketing mix from country to country. This is a particularly interesting example because Theodore Levitt held up Levi Strauss as an example of global standardization, but as the Management Focus makes clear, the opposite now seems to be the case.

The financial services industry is often thought of as one in which global standardization of the marketing mix is the norm. However, while a financial services company such as American Express may sell the same basic charge card service worldwide, utilize the same basic fee structure for that product, and adopt the same basic global advertising message ("don't leave home without it"), differences in national regulations still mean that it has to vary aspects of its communication strategy from country to country. Similarly, while McDonald's is often thought of as the quintessential example of a firm that sells the same basic standardized product worldwide, in reality it varies one important aspect of its marketing mix—its menu—from country to country. McDonald's also varies its distribution strategy. In Canada and the United States, most McDonald's are located in areas that are easily accessible by car, whereas in more densely populated and less automobile-reliant societies of the world, such as Japan and Great Britain, location decisions are driven by the accessibility of a restaurant to pedestrian

Levi Strauss Goes Local

It's been tough going for Levi Strauss, the iconic manufacturer of blue jeans. The company—whose 501 jeans became the global symbol of the baby boom generation and were sold in more than 100 countries—saw its sales drop from a peak of $7.1 billion in 1996 to under $4.0 billion in 2004. Fashion trends had moved on, its critics charged, and Levi Strauss, hamstrung by high costs and a stagnant product line, was looking more faded than a well-worn pair of 501s. Perhaps so, but the second half of the decade brought signs that a turnaround was in progress. Sales increased after several years of decline, and after a string of losses, the company started to register profits again.

There were three parts to this turnaround. First, there were cost reductions at home. Levi Strauss closed its last remaining American factories and moved production offshore where jeans could be produced more cheaply. Second, the company broadened its product line, introducing the Levi's Signature brand that could be sold through lower-priced outlets in markets that were more competitive, including the core American market where Walmart had driven down prices. Third, there was a decision in the late 1990s to give more responsibility to national managers, allowing them to better tailor the product offering and marketing mix to local conditions. Before this, Levi Strauss had basically sold the same product worldwide, often using the same advertising message. The old strategy was designed to enable the company to realize economies of scale in production and advertising, but it wasn't working.

Under the new strategy, variations between national markets have become more pronounced. Jeans have been tailored to different body types. In Asia, shorter leg lengths are common, whereas in South Africa, more room is needed for the backside of women's jeans, so Levi Strauss has customized the product offering to account for these physical differences. Then there are sociocultural differences: In Japan, tight-fitting black jeans are popular; in Islamic countries, women are discouraged from wearing tight-fitting jeans, so Levi Strauss offerings in countries such as Turkey are roomier. Climate also has an effect on product design. In northern Europe, standard-weight jeans are sold, whereas in hotter countries lighter denim is used, along with brighter colors that are not washed out by the tropical sun.

Levi's ads, which used to be global, have also been tailored to regional differences. In Europe, the ads now talk about the cool fit. In Asia, they talk about the rebirth of an original. In the United States, the ads show real people who are themselves originals: ranchers, surfers, great musicians. There are also differences in distribution channels and pricing strategy. In the fiercely competitive American market, prices are as low as $25, and Levi's are sold through mass-market discount retailers, such as Walmart. In India, strong sales growth is being driven by Levi's low-priced Signature brand. In Spain, jeans are seen as higher fashion items and are being sold for $50 in higher-quality outlets. In the United Kingdom too prices for 501s are much higher than in the United States, reflecting a more benign competitive environment.

This variation in marketing mix seems to be reaping dividends; although demand in the United States and Europe remains sluggish, growth in many other countries is strong. Turkey, South Korea, and South Africa all recorded growth rates in excess of 20 percent a year following the introduction of this strategy in 2005. Looking forward, Levi Strauss expects 60 percent of its growth to come from emerging markets.[27]

traffic. Because countries typically still differ along one or more of the dimensions discussed earlier, some customization of the marketing mix is normal.

However, there are often significant opportunities for standardization along one or more elements of the marketing mix.[28] Firms may find that it is possible and desirable to standardize their global advertising message or core product attributes to realize substantial cost economies. They may find it desirable to customize their distribution and pricing strategy to take advantage of local differences. In reality, the "customization versus standardization" debate is not an all or nothing issue; it frequently makes sense to standardize some aspects of the marketing mix and customize others, depending on conditions in various national marketplaces.

NEW-PRODUCT DEVELOPMENT

LO18-5

Firms that successfully develop and market new products can earn enormous returns. Examples include DuPont, which has produced a steady stream of successful innovations such as cellophane, nylon, Freon, and Teflon (nonstick pans); Sony, whose successes include the Walkman, the compact disc, the PlayStation, and the Blu-ray high-definition DVD player; Pfizer, the drug company that during the 1990s produced several major new drugs, including Viagra; 3M, which has applied its core competency in tapes and adhesives to developing a wide range of new products; Intel, which has consistently managed to lead in the development of innovative microprocessors to run personal computers; and Apple with its string of hits, including the iPod, iPhone, and iPad.

In today's world, competition is as much about technological innovation as anything else. The pace of technological change has accelerated since the Industrial Revolution in the eighteenth century, and it continues to do so today. The result has been a dramatic shortening of product life cycles. Technological innovation is both creative and destructive.[29] An innovation can make established products obsolete overnight. But an innovation can also make a host of new products possible. Witness changes in the electronics industry. For 40 years before the early 1950s, vacuum tubes were a major component in radios and then in record players and early computers. The advent of transistors destroyed the market for vacuum tubes, but at the same time it created new opportunities connected with transistors. Transistors took up far less space than vacuum tubes, creating a trend toward miniaturization that continues today. The transistor held its position as the major component in the electronics industry for just a decade. Microprocessors were developed in the 1970s, and the market for transistors declined rapidly. The microprocessor created yet another set of new-product opportunities: handheld calculators (which destroyed the market for slide rules), compact disc players (which destroyed the market for analog record players), personal computers (which destroyed the market for typewriters), and cell phones (which are replacing landline phones).

This "creative destruction" unleashed by technological change makes it critical that a firm stay on the leading edge of technology, lest it lose out to a competitor's innovations. As explained in the next subsection, this not only creates a need for the firm to invest in R&D but also requires the firm to establish R&D activities at those locations where expertise is concentrated. As we shall see, leading-edge technology on its own is not enough to guarantee a firm's survival. The firm must also apply that technology to developing products that satisfy consumer needs, and it must design the product so that it can be manufactured in a cost-effective manner. To do that, the firm needs to build close links between R&D, marketing, and manufacturing. This is difficult enough for the domestic firm, but it is even more problematic for the international business competing in an industry where consumer tastes and preferences differ from country to country.[30] With all of this in mind, we move on to examine locating R&D activities and building links between R&D, marketing, and manufacturing.

The Location of R&D

Ideas for new products are stimulated by the interactions of scientific research, demand conditions, and competitive conditions. Other things being equal, the rate of new-product development seems to be greater in countries where:

- More money is spent on basic and applied research and development.
- Underlying demand is strong.
- Consumers are affluent.
- Competition is intense.[31]

Basic and applied research and development discovers new technologies and then commercializes them. Strong demand and affluent consumers create a potential market for new products. Intense competition among firms stimulates innovation as the firms try to beat their competitors and reap potentially enormous first-mover advantages that result from successful innovation.

For most of the post–World War II period, the country that ranked highest on these criteria was the United States. The United States devoted a greater proportion of its gross domestic product to R&D than any other country did. Its scientific establishment was the largest and most active in the world. U.S. consumers were the most affluent, the market was large, and competition among U.S. firms was brisk. Due to these factors, the United States was the market where most new products were developed and introduced. Accordingly, it was the best location for R&D activities; it was where the action was.

Over the past 20 years, things have been changing quickly. The U.S. monopoly on new-product development has weakened considerably. Although U.S. firms are still at the leading edge of many new technologies, Asian and European firms are also strong players, with companies such as Sony, Sharp, Samsung, Ericsson, Nokia, and Philips driving product innovation in their respective industries. In addition, both Japan and the European Union are large, affluent markets, and the wealth gap between them and the United States is closing.

As a result, it is often no longer appropriate to consider the United States as the lead market. In video games, for example, Japan is often the lead market, with companies such as Sony and Nintendo introducing their latest video-game players in Japan some six months before they introduce them in the United States. However, it often is questionable whether any developed nation can be considered the lead market. To succeed in today's high-technology industries, it is often necessary to simultaneously introduce new products in all major industrialized markets. When Intel introduces a new microprocessor, for example, it does not first introduce it in the United States and then roll it out in Europe a year later. It introduces it simultaneously around the world. The same is true of Microsoft with new versions of its Windows operating systems.

Because leading-edge research is now carried out in many locations around the world, the argument for centralizing R&D activity in the United States is not as strong as it was three decades ago. (It used to be argued that centralized R&D eliminated duplication.) Much leading-edge research is now occurring in Asia and Europe. Dispersing R&D activities to those locations allows a firm to stay close to the center of leading-edge activity to gather scientific and competitive information and to draw on local scientific resources.[32] This may result in some duplication of R&D activities, but the cost disadvantages of duplication are outweighed by the advantages of dispersion.

For example, to expose themselves to the research and new-product development work being done in Japan, many U.S. firms have set up satellite R&D centers in Japan. U.S. firms that have established R&D facilities in Japan include Corning, Texas Instruments, IBM, Procter & Gamble, Pfizer, DuPont, Monsanto, and Microsoft.[33] The National Science Foundation (NSF) has documented a sharp increase in the proportion of total R&D spending by U.S. firms that is now done abroad.[34] For example,

Bristol-Myers Squibb has 12 facilities in five countries. At the same time, to internationalize their own research and gain access to U.S. talent, many European and Asian firms are investing in U.S.-based research facilities, according to the NSF.

Integrating R&D, Marketing, and Production

Although a firm that is successful at developing new products may earn enormous returns, new-product development has a high failure rate. One study of product development in 16 companies in the chemical, drug, petroleum, and electronics industries suggested that only about 20 percent of R&D projects result in commercially successful products or processes.[35] Another in-depth case study of product development in three companies (one in chemicals and two in drugs) reported that about 60 percent of R&D projects reached technical completion, 30 percent were commercialized, and only 12 percent earned an economic profit that exceeded the company's cost of capital.[36] Along the same lines, another study concluded that one in nine major R&D projects, or about 11 percent, produced commercially successful products.[37] In sum, the evidence suggests that only 10 to 20 percent of major R&D projects give rise to commercially successful products. Well-publicized product failures include Apple Computer's Newton personal digital assistant, Sony's Betamax format in the video player and recorder market, and Sega's Dreamcast video-game console.

The reasons for such high failure rates are various and include development of a technology for which demand is limited, failure to adequately commercialize promising technology, and inability to manufacture a new product cost effectively. Firms can reduce the probability of making such mistakes by insisting on tight cross-functional coordination and integration among three core functions involved in the development of new products: R&D, marketing, and production.[38] Tight cross-functional integration between R&D, production, and marketing can help a company ensure that:

1. Product development projects are driven by customer needs.
2. New products are designed for ease of manufacture.
3. Development costs are kept in check.
4. Time to market is minimized.

Close integration between R&D and marketing is required to ensure that product development projects are driven by the needs of customers. A company's customers can be a primary source of new-product ideas. Identification of customer needs, particularly unmet needs, can set the context within which successful product innovation occurs. As the point of contact with customers, the marketing function of a company can provide valuable information in this regard. Integration of R&D and marketing is crucial if a new product is to be properly commercialized. Without integration of R&D and marketing, a company runs the risk of developing products for which there is little or no demand.

Integration between R&D and production can help a company design products with manufacturing requirements in mind. Designing for manufacturing can lower costs and increase product quality. Integrating R&D and production can also help lower development costs and speed products to market. If a new product is not designed with manufacturing capabilities in mind, it may prove too difficult to build. Then the product will have to be redesigned, and both overall development costs and the time it takes to bring the product to market may increase significantly. Making design changes during product planning could increase overall development costs by 50 percent and add 25 percent to the time it takes to bring the product to market.[39] Many quantum product innovations require new processes to manufacture them, which makes it all the more important to achieve close integration between R&D and production. Minimizing time to market and development costs may require the simultaneous development of new products and new processes.[40]

Cross-Functional Teams

One way to achieve cross-functional integration is to establish cross-functional product development teams composed of representatives from R&D, marketing, and production. Because these functions may be located in different countries, the team will sometimes have a multinational membership. The objective of a team should be to take a product development project from the initial concept development to market introduction. A number of attributes seem to be important for a product development team to function effectively and meet all its development milestones.[41]

First, the team should be led by a "heavyweight" project manager who has high status within the organization and who has the power and authority required to get the financial and human resources the team needs to succeed. The leader should be dedicated primarily, if not entirely, to the project. He or she should be someone who believes in the project (a champion) and who is skilled at integrating the perspectives of different functions and at helping personnel from different functions and countries work together for a common goal. The leader should also be able to act as an advocate of the team to senior management.

Second, the team should be composed of at least one member from each key function. The team members should have a number of attributes, including an ability to contribute functional expertise, high standing within their function, a willingness to share responsibility for team results, and an ability to put functional and national advocacy aside. It is generally preferable if core team members are 100 percent dedicated to the project for its duration. This ensures their focus on the project, not on the ongoing work of their function.

Third, the team members should physically be in one location if possible to create a sense of camaraderie and to facilitate communication. This presents problems if the team members are drawn from facilities in different nations. One solution is to transfer key individuals to one location for the duration of a product development project. Fourth, the team should have a clear plan and clear goals, particularly with regard to critical development milestones and development budgets. The team should have incentives to attain those goals, such as receiving pay bonuses when major development milestones are hit. Fifth, each team needs to develop its own processes for communication and conflict resolution. For example, one product development team at Quantum Corporation, a California-based manufacturer of hard drives for personal computers, instituted a rule that all major decisions would be made and conflicts resolved at meetings that were held every Monday afternoon. This simple rule helped the team meet its development goals. In this case, it was also common for team members to fly in from Japan, where the product was to be manufactured, to the U.S. development center for the Monday morning meetings.[42]

Building Global R&D Capabilities

The need to integrate R&D and marketing to adequately commercialize new technologies poses special problems in the international business because commercialization may require different versions of a new product to be produced for various countries.[43] To do this, the firm must build close links between its R&D centers and its various country operations. A similar argument applies to the need to integrate R&D and production, particularly in those international businesses that have dispersed production activities to different locations around the globe in consideration of relative factor costs and the like.

Integrating R&D, marketing, and production in an international business may require R&D centers in North America, Asia, and Europe that are linked by formal and informal integrating mechanisms with marketing operations in each country in their regions and with the various manufacturing facilities. In addition, the international business may have to establish cross-functional teams whose members are dispersed around the globe. This complex endeavor requires the company to utilize formal and informal integrating mechanisms to knit its far-flung operations together so they can produce new products in an effective and timely manner.

While there is no one best model for allocating product development responsibilities to various centers, one solution adopted by many international businesses involves establishing a global network of R&D centers. Within this model, fundamental research is undertaken at basic research centers around the globe. These centers are normally located in regions or cities where valuable scientific knowledge is being created and where there is a pool of skilled research talent (e.g., Silicon Valley in the United States, Cambridge in England, Kobe in Japan, Singapore). These centers are the innovation engines of the firm. Their job is to develop the basic technologies that become new products.

These technologies are picked up by R&D units attached to global product divisions and are used to generate new products to serve the global marketplace. At this level, commercialization of the technology and design for manufacturing are emphasized. If further customization is needed so the product appeals to the tastes and preferences of consumers in individual markets, such redesign work will be done by an R&D group based in a subsidiary in that country or at a regional center that customizes products for several countries in the region.

Hewlett-Packard has seven basic research centers located in Palo Alto, California; Bristol, England; Haifa, Israel; Beijing, China; Singapore; Bangalore, India; and St. Petersburg, Russia.[44] These labs are the seedbed for technologies that ultimately become new products and businesses. They are the company's innovation engines. The Palo Alto center, for example, pioneered HP's thermal ink-jet technology. The products are developed by R&D centers associated with HP's global product divisions. Thus, HP's Consumer Products Group, which has its worldwide headquarters in San Diego, California, designs, develops, and manufactures a range of imaging products using HP-pioneered thermal ink-jet technology. Subsidiaries might then customize the product so that it best matches the needs of important national markets. HP's subsidiary in Singapore, for example, is responsible for the design and production of thermal ink-jet printers for Japan and other Asian markets. This subsidiary takes products originally developed in San Diego and redesigns them for the Asian market. In addition, the Singapore subsidiary has taken the lead from San Diego in the design and development of certain portable thermal ink-jet printers. HP delegated this responsibility to Singapore because this subsidiary has acquired important competencies in the design and production of thermal ink-jet products, so it has become the best place in the world to undertake this activity.

Chapter Summary

This chapter discussed the marketing and R&D functions in international business. A persistent theme of the chapter is the tension that exists between the need to reduce costs and the need to be responsive to local conditions, which raises costs. The chapter made the following points:

1. Theodore Levitt argued that due to the advent of modern communications and transport technologies, consumer tastes and preferences are becoming global, which is creating global markets for standardized consumer products. However, this position is regarded as extreme by many commentators, who argue that substantial differences still exist between countries.

2. Market segmentation refers to the process of identifying distinct groups of consumers whose purchasing behavior differs from each other in important ways. Managers in an international

business need to be aware of two main issues relating to segmentation: the extent to which there are differences between countries in the structure of market segments, and the existence of segments that transcend national borders.

3. A product can be viewed as a bundle of attributes. Product attributes need to be varied from country to country to satisfy different consumer tastes and preferences.

4. Country differences in consumer tastes and preferences are due to differences in culture and economic development. In addition, differences in product and technical standards may require the firm to customize product attributes from country to country.

5. A distribution strategy decision is an attempt to define the optimal channel for delivering a product to the consumer.

6. Significant country differences exist in distribution systems. In some countries, the retail system is concentrated; in others, it is fragmented. In some countries, channel length is short; in others, it is long. Access to distribution channels is difficult to achieve in some countries, and the quality of the channel may be poor.

7. A critical element in the marketing mix is communication strategy, which defines the process the firm will use in communicating the attributes of its product to prospective customers.

8. Barriers to international communication include cultural differences, source effects, and noise levels.

9. A communication strategy is either a push strategy or a pull strategy. A push strategy emphasizes personal selling, and a pull strategy emphasizes mass media advertising. Whether a push strategy or a pull strategy is optimal depends on the type of product, consumer sophistication, channel length, and media availability.

10. A globally standardized advertising campaign, which uses the same marketing message all over the world, has economic advantages, but it fails to account for differences in culture and advertising regulations.

11. Price discrimination exists when consumers in different countries are charged different prices for the same product. Price discrimination can help a firm maximize its profits. For price discrimination to be effective, the national markets must be separate and their price elasticities of demand must differ.

12. Predatory pricing is the use of profit gained in one market to support aggressive pricing in another market to drive competitors out of that market.

13. Multipoint pricing refers to the fact that a firm's pricing strategy in one market may affect rivals' pricing strategies in another market. Aggressive pricing in one market may elicit a competitive response from a rival in another market that is important to the firm.

14. Experience curve pricing is the use of aggressive pricing to build accumulated volume as rapidly as possible to quickly move the firm down the experience curve.

15. New-product development is a high-risk, potentially high-return activity. To build a competency in new-product development, an international business must do two things: disperse R&D activities to those countries where new products are being pioneered, and integrate R&D with marketing and manufacturing.

16. Achieving tight integration among R&D, marketing, and manufacturing requires the use of cross-functional teams.

Critical Thinking and Discussion Questions

1. Imagine you are the marketing manager for a U.S. manufacturer of disposable diapers. Your firm is considering entering the Brazilian market. Your CEO believes the advertising message that has been effective in the United States will suffice in Brazil. Outline some possible objections to this. Your CEO also believes that the pricing decisions in Brazil can be delegated to local managers. Why might she be wrong?

2. Within 20 years, we will have seen the emergence of enormous global markets for standardized consumer products. Do you agree with this statement? Justify your answer.

3. You are the marketing manager of a food products company that is considering entering the Indian market. The retail system in India tends to be very fragmented. Also, retailers and wholesalers tend to have long-term ties with Indian food companies; these ties make access to distribution channels difficult. What distribution strategy would you advise the company to pursue? Why?

4. Price discrimination is indistinguishable from dumping. Discuss the accuracy of this statement.

5. You work for a company that designs and manufactures personal computers. Your company's R&D center is in North Dakota. The computers are manufactured under contract in Taiwan. Marketing strategy is delegated to the heads of three regional groups: a North American group (based in Chicago), a European group (based in Paris), and an Asian group (based in Singapore). Each regional group develops the marketing approach within its region. In order of importance, the largest markets for your products are North America, Germany, Great Britain, China, and Australia. Your company is experiencing problems in its product development and commercialization process. Products are late to market, the manufacturing quality is poor, costs are higher than projected, and market acceptance of new products is less than hoped for. What might be the source of these problems? How would you fix them?

6. Reread the Management Focus on Levi Strauss, and then answer the following questions:
   a. What marketing strategy was Levi Strauss using until the early 2000s? Why did this strategy appear to work for decades? Why was it not working by 2004?
   b. How would you characterize Levi Strauss's current strategy? What elements of the marketing mix are now changed from nation to nation?
   c. What are the benefits of the company's new marketing strategy? Is there a downside?
   d. What does the Levi Strauss story tell you about the "globalization of markets"?

Research Task ⟲ globalEDGE globaledge.msu.edu

Global Marketing and R&D

Use the globalEDGE website (globaledge.msu.edu) to complete the following exercises:

Exercise 1

The consumer purchase of specific brands is an indication of the relationship that develops over time between a company and its customers. Locate and retrieve the most current ranking of *best global brands*. Identify the criteria used. Which countries appear to dominate the top 100 global brands list? Why do you think this is the case? Now look at which sectors appear to dominate the list, and try to identify the reasons. Prepare a short report identifying the countries that possess global brands and the potential reasons for success.

Exercise 2

Part of developing a long-term R&D strategy is to locate facilities in countries which are widely known to be competitive. Your company seeks to develop R&D facilities in India to counter recent competitor responses. A publication which evaluates economies based on their competitiveness is the *Global Competitiveness Report*. Locate this report, and develop a presentation for the top management team that presents the benefits and drawbacks for the top five Asian economies listed.

Closing **CASE**

Domino's Pizza

Domino's Pizza made its name by pioneering home delivery service in the United States. In recent years, however, the growth story has been overseas. With the U.S. fast-food market saturated and consumer demand weak, Domino's is looking to international markets for growth opportunities. The company is no newcomer to international business—it opened its first international store in Canada in 1983—but today, almost all new store openings are outside the United States. In 2012 the company had 4,835 stores internationally and 4,907 domestic stores. Its plans call for opening another 350 to 450 international stores a year for the next few years.

As it expands its international businesses, there are some things that Domino's has kept the same as in the United States, and there are some things that are very different. What is the same is the basic business model of home delivery. This sets it apart from many of its U.S. rivals, which changed their basic offering when they entered foreign markets. For example, when Yum Brands Inc. introduced Pizza Hut into China, it radically altered the format, establishing Pizza Hut Casual Dining, a chain that offers a vast selection of American fare—including ribs, spaghetti, and steak—in a full-service setting. Pizza Hut adopted this format because table service was what the locals were used to, but Domino's isn't interested. "We go in there with a tried-and-true business model of delivery and carry-out pizza that we deploy around the world," states Domino's international president, Richard Allison. "In emerging markets, we've got more tables than you would find in the U.S., but we have no plans to lean toward a casual dining model where the server comes out and takes an order."

On the other hand, there are things that vary from country to country. In the United States, pizza is viewed as casual food, frequently mentioned in the same breath as beer and football. In Japan, it's viewed as more upscale fare. This is reflected in the offering. Japanese pizzas come with toppings that the average American couldn't fathom. Domino's has sold a $50 pizza in Japan featuring foie gras. Other premium toppings include snow crab, Mangalitsa pork with Bordeaux sauce, and beef stew with fresh mozzarella. Japanese consumers value aesthetics and really care about the look of food, so presentation is key. Patrons expect every slice to have precisely the same amount of toppings, which must be uniformly spaced. Shrimp, for example, are angled with the tails pointing the same way.

Pizza consumption is low in Japan—the average Japanese pizza customer only consumes the product four times a year. To boost this, Domino's has been working to create more occasions to enjoy it. For example, on Valentine's Day, its Japanese stores deliver heart-shaped pizzas in pink boxes. Heart-shaped pizzas also appear on Mother's Day.

To promote the offering in Japan, rather than spending money on commercials, Domino's tries to create news, like topics that people talk about. If the topic is fun and hot, Domino's believes that people will talk about it, which ultimately translates into better sales. One promotion in particular received heavy coverage. The chain offered 2.5 million yen (about $31,000) for one hour's work at a Domino's store. In all, about 12,000 people applied for the "job." The lucky winner was a rural housewife who had never eaten pizza. She flew to a small island to deliver pizza to schoolchildren, who were also new to pizza. The event received heavy news coverage—free advertising in other words.

In India, where Domino's has more than 400 stores and has plans for 1,000 more, 50 percent of the menu is vegetarian in order to match the preferences of the large Hindu population. For delivery, Domino's has a fleet of mopeds, which makes sense in large cities like Mumbai where traffic congestion is awful. Because Indians like things spicy, instead of including Parmesan cheese packets, Domino's includes an "Oregano SpiceMix." In general, the toppings have far more spice than in the United States. Although Indians are used to full service in restaurants, Domino's doesn't use servers or busboys in their stores, even though each store typically has a few tables in for those who want to eat on premises. Instead, it is educating customers to clean up after themselves, with in-store trashcans that say "Use Me" in big bold letters.[45]

Case Discussion Questions

1. Do you think it is wise for Domino's to stick to its traditional "home delivery" business model, even when that is not the norm in a country and when its international rivals have changed their format?

2. What do you think Domino's does from an organizational perspective to make sure that it accommodates local differences in consumer tastes and preferences?

3. How does the marketing mix for Domino's Pizza in Japan differ from that in the United States? How does that in India differ from the U.S. marketing mix?

4. What lessons can we draw from the Domino's case study that might be useful for other international businesses selling consumer goods?

ORACLE In India[46]

Introduction

About Oracle Corporation

Oracle Corporation, the world's leading enterprise software company, provides the world's most complete, open, and integrated business software and hardware systems to more than 370,000 customers—including 100 of the Fortune 100—that represent a variety of sizes and industries in more than 145 countries around the globe. The combination of Oracle and Sun means that customers can benefit from fully integrated systems —the entire stack, from applications to disk—that are faster, more reliable, and lower cost. The company mainly operates in the US. It is headquartered in Redwood City, California and employs about 105,000 people.

Oracle is a global market leader with number one in database, middleware, CRM, HCM, EPM and financial services.

Oracle India Private Limited

Business in India

Oracle India provides the Asian continent with enterprise software for managing business data, supporting business operations, and facilitating collaboration and application development. Companies use its database management software to store and access data across numerous platforms. The company also offers business applications for data warehousing, customer relationship management, and supply chain management. Oracle opened its first office in India in 1991, and formed its first Indian subsidiary in 1993. Oracle's other Indian operations include the India Development Center, which is its largest research facility outside the US.

Oracle's Entry into India

More than 20 years ago, before India became recognized as the dynamic force in information technology that is known to be today, Oracle was one of the first multinational software companies to set up operations in India. Beginning with a distributorship through Tata Consultancy Services in 1987, the company established direct operations with a liaison office in 1991. Oracle established its Indian subsidiary in August 1993 with less than 10 people focusing on sales and marketing of Oracle software in India. Shortly afterwards, in 1994, it became the first major US software company to establish an India Development Center in Bangalore to support its product development strategy for global markets.

Oracle has been a significant player in the Information Technology (IT) industry in India. Presently, Oracle has seven development and solution centers:

- Asia R&D Center
- Partner Solution Center
- E-governance Center
- Retail Center of Excellence
- Three Global Development Centers in Bangalore, Hyderabad, and Noida

With continuous investments, Oracle is one of the largest MNC software employers in India, with over 4000 employees across the country and a technology community which has hundreds of thousands of Indian software developers, besides significant sales and marketing operations, product development, global support and consulting and internal BPO services.

The Bangalore and Hyderabad Development Centers develop best-in-class products for Oracle's global customers. The firm enhanced its commitment to India with the establishment of a global consulting group in Bangalore and global product support centers in Bangalore and Hyderabad. It plans to expand Hyderabad center for total of 6000 employees.

Currently, the Oracle Technology Park in Bangalore, is hosting three major Oracle divisions: Oracle's India Development Center (IDC), the company's International Support Center (ISC) and Oracle Solution Services India (OSSI). The three divisions comprise a 'Center of Excellence' supporting the company's global operations. India is the only country to have three different business units of this size and scope outside of the company's main headquarters in Redwood Shores, California. Many Asian customers are leveraging the capabilities of Oracle's development, support, and consulting groups in India. It is also the hub for financial service operations.

Through its extensive network of more than 500 channel and alliance partners under the Oracle PartnerNetwork, Oracle India markets the complete range of Oracle products and services across India. Oracle India has more than 7000 customers in the telecommunications, banking, insurance, manufacturing and utilities industries, across the government and private sector.

Competitive Landscape

The US-economy heavily influences business spending for software products. The success of programming companies depends heavily on strong technical expertise. The success of packaged software companies depends on technical expertise and good marketing. Small software companies compete mainly by developing packaged products in small niches or producing custom products for individuals. Many small companies form alliances with larger ones to market their products. The packaged software industry is capital-intensive: average annual revenue per worker is about USD 360,000. The custom programming industry is relatively labor-intensive: average annual revenue per worker is about USD 175,000.

India had been Oracle's favorite hunting ground. The company has found that Indian parameters are extremely conducive to the growth of Oracle; that, in turn, led to growth of economy and IT industry in the nation, forming a virtuous circle.

Market in India

Since coming to India, Oracle has played a key role in shaping the IT industry inside the country and has established a footprint unmatched by most of its multinational competitors. Today, India is Oracle's fourth largest market in Asia-Pacific in terms of revenue, up from tenth a few years ago, and boasts the largest research and development investment outside the US.

The Oracle Database 10g supports transactions and interfaces in 13 major Indian languages including Assamese, Bengali, Gujarati, Hindi, Kannada, Malayalam, Marathi, Oriya, Punjabi, Telugu, and Tamil. Oracle has 6000 technology and over 600 applications customers in India, and counts some of the most important government and private organizations amongst those using Oracle software and services to reduce costs, increase productivity and innovate business operations. Oracle network includes companies such as i-Flex, Infosys, Satyam, Sonata, Tata Consultancy Services, and Wipro.

India holds great promise as a domestic market for Oracle software solutions. The mid–market segment makes up 40 percent of Oracle's current customer base in India. Oracle thinks that small, local companies in the region to drive the future growth of Oracle's business. As Indian companies seek to expand their businesses to new markets in and outside of India, they will need to invest in information technology, including databases, e-business technologies and applications that provide real business value —the core competency of Oracle.

To address this opportunity, Oracle has charted an aggressive growth plan to rapidly expand its presence in India. Known as the "Emerald India" initiative, the plan is intended to fully leverage the potential of the highly skilled Indian workforce to take advantage of new opportunities in a variety of industries. From this commitment to and investment in the Indian market, the company expects to dramatically grow its domestic business while contributing further to the burgeoning Indian economy and the advancement of the IT industry.

Turning Point

Because of presence of significant pool of highly educated software development engineers based in India, Oracle opened its India Development Center (IDC) in Bangalore in 1994. This early commitment to the country marked Oracle's vision for India as both a domestic market and a center for research and development. The company became the first multinational company to establish core software development operations in India to support its global product development strategy and to address the needs of the local market. Initially, the India Development Center took on development work on a project basis for different development divisions as determined by the company's headquarters located at Redwood Shores (California). As word spread throughout the company of the India team's record delivery time of development projects that met the highest standards of quality, the IDC was tasked with more strategic projects and increasingly demanding requirements.

In 1996, when India development team was challenged with taking on a strategic research and development project, it marked a turning point in the history of IDC. The India team was given three months to develop the first version of what would become the basis of Oracle's Internet computing technology, driving the shift to simplified, low–cost computing machines which could access information stored on larger, professionally managed servers. With no additional resources, the IDC, having been asked only to show version one of the technology, delivered instead a second–generation version three months to the day from the start of the project. Concurrently, the team also met all deadlines and quality standards for the other 16 projects with which the IDC was tasked with at that time. The world-class development abilities of the India development team were impressed upon the highest levels of the company, garnering praise and recognition from Oracle founder and CEO, Larry Ellison. This transformed the India Development Center into a growth engine, integral to the future and vision of the world's largest enterprise software company. The team's success on the project propelled the IDC into the development spotlight at Oracle. From that point forward, the India Development Center was integrated into Oracle's global software development organization, working on the latest technology for Oracle customers around the world. At the same time, Oracle's increasing success in the country established the company as the dominant provider of database and enterprise software to the government and corporate sectors in India.

In year 2002, when Oracle was looking to expand its facility by four times in India, its Executive Vice-President for Asia-Pacific, Derek Williams said, "India is a jewel in Oracle's crown. We have invested well in expanding our presence in India and plan to continue to do so." It has expanded development facilities in Bangalore and is in the process of acquiring over seven acres of land in Hyderabad for expansion of its India Development Center (IDC). Williams said Oracle valued the Indian capability and, "We anticipate that the coming years will add strength and luster to the ever-expanding commitment demonstrated by Oracle."

The combined resources of the India Development Center in Bangalore and Hyderabad contribute to core software development across the entire Oracle product family, including Oracle Database 10g, Oracle Application Server 10g, Oracle Collaboration Suite and Oracle E-Business Suite. The work carried out in India includes new product design, development, technology and feature enhancements, quality engineering, documentation, curriculum for instructor-led and online training, integration, as well as support and maintenance of existing products. The IDC has made major contributions to the research and development of key focus areas for the company including the future of grid computing, technology and applications deployment on Linux, security, Java application development, XML, and Warehouse Management Systems, to name a few. The IDC also contributes significantly to Oracle's online developer community, Oracle Technology Network, showcasing new technology, best practices, sample applications, discussion forums, and through participation in global events.

In addition to providing software development for the entire Oracle product family for Indian and global markets, Oracle India has become host to a number of other functions critical to Oracle's operations as a global company. Through the six facilities of Oracle India Private Ltd., headed out of Gurgaon near New Delhi, the company offers sales, marketing, consulting, education and support to local customers. Additionally, Oracle India hosts a number of global operations that make it possible for the company to conduct 24 by 7 consulting, finance and administration, support and sales operations, in addition to software development.

Oracle India represents the only organization outside Oracle's headquarters in California to represent so many divisions and lines of business, effectively mirroring Oracle's global operations.

Competitors

Oracle's Main Competitors

Oracle competes head on with IBM across the full stack of software and hardware offerings, especially after its Sun Microsystems acquisition. Its major competition with Microsoft is in the space of Database & File Management Software and that with SAP is for Business Applications.

Products and Services Offered

Oracle started with Database product, but has grown into all-pervasive software products/solutions provider. Oracle has become total solution provider competing against IBM in all domains. Only IBM and Oracle can claim to be Integrated Stack providers, capable of supplying end-to-end IT solution.

Whichever way the IT Business is sliced and diced, Oracle has products/solutions for every bit. Over the past four years, through some major acquisitions as well as internal product transformations, Oracle has been offering solutions all the way up the HW/SW stack, from hardware and operating systems to middleware to applications. Only IBM is in a comparable position.

There has been a major push into service oriented architecture during this time, with the software giant providing and promoting a whole range of solutions in this space.

The essence of Oracle's strategy going forward revolves around convincing CIOs to buy into the entire stack:

- "Expand and accelerate—dramatically—the potentially massive global market for highly optimized and integrated hardware-software systems, and then dominate that market."
- "Convince CIOs that a complete IT stack purchased from Oracle will deliver not only sufficient openness to avoid the dreaded vendor lock-in, but also superior performance compared with heterogeneous combinations."
- "Convince CIOs that the combination of above will lower the costs of assembling, setting up, testing, tuning, managing, integrating, trouble-shooting, fixing, upgrading, and running those systems."
- "Complete that infrastructure with ultra-modern Fusion applications that can run with existing enterprise apps, from Oracle or anyone else."

- "Win in vertical markets like retail, healthcare, and telecom by complementing the broad horizontal apps with deep industry knowledge and functionality."

Industry-wise Categorization of Oracle Products

Oracle has customized its business products to match each and every Industry Vertical:
- Aerospace
- Automotive
- Chemicals
- Consumer Goods, Distribution
- Education and Research
- Public Sector, Government
- Engineering and construction
- Financial Sector
- HealthCare
- Industrial manufacturing, Oil and Gas, Utilities
- Media and entertainment

Oracle Products for Value-Chain activities

With strong applications in each of Horizontal segments of Value-chain, Oracle straddles across the Whole Value-Chain:
- Supply-Chain management (SCM)
- Enterprise Resource Planning (ERP)
- Customer relationship management (CRM)

Oracle Presence in all vertical Levels of IT-Architecture

- Hardware systems: Sparc-microProcessors (up to 64-cores), Sun servers, Storage systems; Network servers
- Operating system: Linux(lower-end) , Solaris(high-performance systems)
- Database and Middleware: Oracle-DB, Application-development
- High-end Applications and Tools: SCM, ERP, CRM, Data warehouse, Business-Intelligence

Oracle Products for 3-tier Architecture and Web-Ecommerce

Oracle products were developed for traditional 2-tier and 3-tier architectures, such as application logic and DBMS. However, Oracle products enable development of tiers of Web-development/ deployment, and E-commerce activities. Oracle has become a dominant player in Internet with products like Sun-Java, BEA-Web Logic, Middleware and SOA products.
- Oracle's presence in the 3-tier architecture:
- Presentation tier: Java-based clients and servers, Web servers
- Business Logic tier (Middleware): WebLogic Application Server, JavaEE and EJB based applications
- DataSource tier: Oracle DBMS

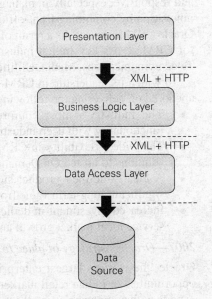

Growth Strategy

"Today, only Oracle can offer a robust, integrated information architecture comprising both database and applications, which is based on open standards."

Oracle strategy is to capitalize on this integrated offering across industries and verticals in India.

Journey so far… (Some clippings given below)

2005 -Oracle Defines Three-Pronged Strategy to Capture Indian HCM market

With an aim to capture a larger share of the Human Capital Management (HCM) market in India, Oracle has defined a three-pronged market strategy to meet customer requirements and address new opportunities in HCM. By focusing on product alignment to meet the needs of the Indian market, coupled with partner empowerment and targeted marketing programs, Oracle aims to reach out to Indian customers more effectively. This expanded network of partners and programs positions Oracle strongly to lead in Indian market.

New CRM Strategy and SMB Offering to Further Oracle's Leadership in India

Oracle CRM-On-Demand is Oracle's fastest growing application worldwide. The SaaS CRM market in India is projected to grow at >30%+ over the next four years, and by 2014, India will be the largest market for SaaS CRM. With over 50 customers using Oracle CRM applications in India, Oracle is the clear market leader in the local CRM market. These include well-known names such as Tata Motors Ltd, IFFCO Tokio, Bharti Airtel, Bank of Maharashtra, UTI Bank, Genpact, Tata Sky, Hutch, and Tata Consultancy Services.

Indian organizations are competing in a global marketplace that requires them to be extremely agile and responsive, especially in managing distributed customer information. Oracle is leading the way in innovation by combining front-office and back-office, as well as industry-specific solutions within the Oracle CRM footprint. As a result of this, Oracle is gaining significant customer success and momentum for CRM across key Indian industries —Banking, Insurance, Manufacturing, Consumer Products, Telecommunications, Media, Utilities, and the Public Sector.

To widen its leadership in CRM in India and across Asia-Pacific, Oracle's CRM growth strategy is anchored on delivering the following:

- The industry's most comprehensive CRM portfolio — combining 'best-of-breed' CRM functionality with deep industry capabilities;
- The widest flexibility in CRM solution and deployment options — from on-premise enterprise solutions to hosted On Demand solutions;
- A clearly-defined product support and development roadmap to enable customers to derive significant long-term value from their CRM investments; and,
- Increased investment in dedicated CRM sales, services, consulting and marketing resources to service local market growth and ensure positive customer outcomes.

2007—Oracle's strategy in place to tap retail opportunities

Oracle, the world's largest enterprise software company, has put in place strategy to tap the huge opportunities in Indian retail market. Oracle have a dedicated India team, that employs over 200 retail experts with competencies in all aspects of retailing at its Bangalore-based Retail Center of Excellence.

In 2007, then, the size of Indian retail industry was at USD 320 billion. Organized retail accounted for just four percent of the total business but increased to about 15 per cent 2013. Organized retail invests four to five percent of its revenues on IT, which provides huge opportunities in retail. Oracle retail solutions are used by 17 of the top 20 global retailers. To name, LifeKen, a leading retail pharmaceutical chain, Aditya Birla Retail Limited, HomeCare Retail Marts Pvt Ltd (HomeCare) are few Oracle retail customers in India. Globally Oracle Retail customers include WalMart, Zale Corporation, Dress Barn, Orscheln Farm and Home, Perry Ellis International, and Goody's Family Clothing.

2010 —Oracle Apps penetrate Indian Insurance sector

Oracle India witnesses strong momentum in the insurance sector in India. According to IDC, Oracle is refining its strategy in the financial applications market through a number of product enhancements that aim to boost the global appeal and usability factor for both PeopleSoft Enterprise and Oracle E-Business Suite customers.

HR Policies

Oracle HR policies are very strong and have been customized for Indian context. Previously, one came to India because the work was cheap. Now, the company admits, it is in India because of high-quality work and talent. The fact that it is also cheap allows one to go beyond. Basically, Oracle looks for innovative geeks, who also have strong soft skills that are very much required for future emerging third elephant economy. It becomes a virtuous cycle whereby the people are trained to contribute further to the economy and Oracle provides an excellent platform, at the same time benefitting itself, leading to a win–win situation.

Oracle places great stress upon hiring the right talent. First of all, it makes sure it hires the best people. The interview process is designed to reduce the tension involved for both the parties, without losing out on quality candidates. In general, the caliber of the people working at Oracle is very high. Being a results oriented organization, Oracle encourages its employees to set their goals, encourages them to be aggressive in their targets, allows them the freedom to achieve their goals and gives them the best tools, training and infrastructure. Naturally, every employee ends up giving his or her best to the organization.

The interview tests the candidate not only for technical competency but also for personality, communication skills, initiative, and aptitude, and probably more of the softer skills than the technical ones. Technical questions are designed to elicit what we are looking for—not merely knowledge but the ability to think around problems.

Oracle India concentrates on growth of the employees. With its huge portfolio of products, technology and worldwide operations, it offers its employees opportunities to broaden and deepen their experience and to grow horizontally and vertically.

Training (technical as well as soft skill) is of importance at Oracle. A person is well traced as far as what he needs, gets and should get. His own desires are also taken into account. Managers are kept updated to what the people need and what they are taught. Employees at Oracle have probably the best opportunity to regularly sharpen their saws and keep themselves at the cutting edge of knowledge.

Rather than consciously think of retaining a particular person or a group of people, the approach is to look at what the people want to do, and need to do, and what does the company want to do and needs to do. End result – Oracle India probably has the lowest attrition rate in the country! While it may not necessarily imply that everybody is happy with what he/she does, but definitely that he/she can talk to the supervisor and HR. Open communication does not mean satisfying everyone's whims and fancies but saying this is what has to be done and why it has to be done.

The drivers for retention have changed a lot in past decade—today people do not stay for things like car policies but because of what they are learning, how they are growing and because they enjoy what they are doing. Some of the things that people have described about Oracle are as follows:

- Oracle's penchant to be in the leading edge of technology and products
- Dynamism that exists at Oracle
- Clear and strong long-term strategy
- Tactically very adaptable to change based on business needs
- Diversity of opportunities that Oracle provides to its employees
- Company of the people/colleagues

Educating the Customer

Oracle educates its customers through the following ways:

- Product training
- Classroom
- Live virtual
- Self-study CD-ROM
- Self-paced online programmes
- Training by job role

Educators worldwide transform education through personalized learning, improved teacher development and performance, enhanced access to information, and more efficient management of the processes that facilitate teaching, learning, and research.

- Oracle delivers database, middleware, hardware, and applications based on open industry standards
- Oracle offers complete, integrated, market-leading solutions that enable education institutions and jurisdictions to adapt to the changing needs and demands of all their constituents-students, teachers, parents, faculty, researchers, staff, graduates and alumni, governance bodies, and the extended community of supporters and stakeholders
- Oracle delivers the most comprehensive, adaptable solutions to meet the needs of small institutions as well as large, multi-location school districts and university systems

Oracle is committed in helping schools around the world address today's challenging educational environment. Oracle runs two courses to support informed decision-making and transparency.

Higher Education and Research	Primary and Secondary Education (K-12)
Oracle Business Intelligence Applications	Oracle Crystal Ball
Oracle's PeopleSoft Enterprise Performance Management	Oracle's PeopleSoft CRM for Higher Education
Oracle Master Data Management	Oracle Accelerate Solutions for Education and Research
Oracle's Human Capital Management Solutions	Oracle's PeopleSoft Enterprise Campus Solutions
Oracle's Sun Servers and Storage	Oracle's PeopleSoft Enterprise Student Administration Integration Pack
Oracle's Financial Management Solutions	Oracle's Higher Education Constituent Hub
Oracle's Procurement Applications	Oracle Business Intelligence Applications
Oracle Hyperion Planning and Budgeting	Oracle's PeopleSoft Enterprise Performance Management

Oracle Identity and Access Management Suite	Oracle Master Data Management
PeopleSoft Campus Solutions Complete	Oracle's Human Capital Management Solutions
Oracle Content Management	Oracle's Financial Management Solutions
Oracle Database 11g	Oracle's Procurement Applications
Oracle Fusion Middleware	Oracle Hyperion Planning and Budgeting
Oracle Open Office	Oracle Identity and Access Management Suite
Oracle's PeopleSoft Enterprise Campus Solutions	Oracle Content Management
Oracle's PeopleSoft Enterprise Student	Oracle Fusion Middleware
	View All Oracle Education Products

Benefits Oracle Offers to Customers

Oracle, the global leader in Customer Relationship Management (CRM) helped Indian organizations to transform into 'customer-centric' organizations, and achieve increased competitiveness, profitability and shareholder value through improved customer satisfaction, customer loyalty, as well as by attracting new customers. Oracle strategy for continued growth and leadership is simple – #1 position in CRM by helping customers – across large, medium and small businesses – transform into truly 'customer-centric' organizations. Oracle helps its customers to optimize their strategies, people, processes and technology around their customers. Oracle Database has extended the productivity and business revenue by offering best needed solution to users. Oracle's CRM solutions for SMBs are developed expressly to meet the unique needs of SMBs as they seek to improve customer satisfaction and loyalty, as well as attract new customers.

Oracle also has an Oracle Partner Solution Center for technical assistance, training, lead generation opportunities and access to state-of-the-art infrastructure. This center is tightly integrated with the Oracles research and development centers in China and Singapore and gives partners in India access to Oracles product expertise, which will allow them to stay ahead of competition by developing compelling IT solutions for industries and governments. Oracle Partner Network provides the following:

- Skills enablement through focused training roadmaps, discounted courses, free online training
- Marketing opportunities through demand generation activities
- Selling incentives and support through referral and influence incentives
- Technical support, both online and by phone, to help partners with migration, development and implementation of solutions built on or integrated with Oracle technology

Challenges and Road Ahead

Powering India's economic growth requires a mix of software rights solutions, not proprietary ones alone.

–Scott McNealy

Today, nearly every corner of the world faces the challenge of a stagnant or shrinking economy. Bleak economic forecasts, shrinking budgets and increasing pressure on businesses and governments to meet the needs of their customers and constituents—often with fewer resources to do so—are becoming commonplace. Technology and innovation drive global economic progress, and therefore the remedy for many of these challenges is in our hands.

India is, of course, not immune to these challenges. But the country is very well positioned to meet them. India is one of the world's fastest growing tech economies and one of the leading participants in the global shift towards free and open source technologies—those eschew the dependencies of cost and barriers to access that often "come standard" with proprietary technologies. As such, India can play a central role in fostering and adopting the innovations driving its own economic and social growth as well as positioning itself for a larger role on the global economic and technological stage.

The major challenge faced by Oracle India at this point in time is to cater to the increasing and diverse demands of its customers (across diverse industry backgrounds- some known and some unknown) where they have a great bargaining power, owing to a number of small and large players, in a cost-effective manner, and to provide holistic integrated solutions to retain their competitive advantage.

Looking ahead, Oracle's intent is to focus on acquisitions based growth and providing private cloud to enterprises.

Oracle's Growth Strategy: Buy, Buy, Buy

Oracle is expanding into new business areas to protect market share, with more than USD 42 billion already spent on acquisitions since the beginning of 2005.

Some of major companies acquired by Oracle:
- BEA WebLogic: Middleware, Application servers
- Siebel: CRM
- PeopleSoft: ERP
- JD Edwards: Enterprise systems
- Sun: Microprocessors, servers, network servers, Storage systems, Java
- Primavera: Project management systems for Enterprises
- Hyperion: Business intelligence and Decision-support systems
- iFlex: Banking and finance applications
- Communication: Net4call , Netsure telecom, telephony@work
- ATG: SCM & ecommerce for Retail industry

Oracle on Cloud

Cloud offers compelling benefits such as high availability of resources, efficiency, scalability and savings but has serious security concerns too. According to Forrester Research's Cloud Computing study 2009, about 44 percent of large enterprises are interested in building an internal cloud. Enterprises are more attracted to private cloud compared to public, due to security concerns about mission critical applications and data.

Oracle's cloud computing strategy is to ensure that cloud computing is fully enterprise grade and supports both public and private cloud computing as per customers' choice. Oracle's focus in next 5–10 years is to build private cloud for enterprises. Oracle had been doing cloud for many years with Oracle On demand CRM solution, and the acquisition of Sun Microsystems has strengthened it.

Oracle has been a late entrant in this field and has a long way to go before it can match sales foce. com. However, it has recognized the need for enterprises to have a private cloud offering owing to sensitivity of data and aims to capture the market share in that space.

Conclusion

Having captured major share of Database market by 2000, oracle realized that it has to expand into new products to continue its growth. Oracle has, subsequently, followed Diversification strategy to fuel its aggressive growth. It has become Integrated IT solutions provider from hardware and operating systems to middleware to business applications. Oracle has launched its products range in most of countries of world using strategies of Internationalization and localization/customizations.

Oracle has achieved this by large number of acquisitions. It has acquired leading products in various segments. As Oracle has acquired these companies, it has retained the Indian operations of the acquired companies (Sun, Hyperion, BEA systems). Oracle has continued to expand the India development center making it a key part of its global strategy.

As Indian economy expands, Oracle is well positioned to capture significant Enterprise application's market. Oracle has major presence in India's Banking and Insurance, Government and public sectors. Oracle now has complete suite of products to provide any Enterprise's full IT needs. In each of the categories, it has best-in-class products. In its ability to deliver integrated solution, only IBM is in comparable position. Hence, Oracle is challenging IBM as provider of integrated stack.

SAP is market leader in Business Applications. With its acquisitions of ERP/CRM/SCM companies, Oracle may soon be able to challenge SAP in Business applications space. Oracle has developed/customized its products for every Industry vertical.

Oracle can deliver the cloud computing in-a-box. Hence, it is in a position to dominate the expanding cloud computing market.

Questions

1. Why has Oracle found India to be a very lucrative market for its global strategy?
2. How does one explain India's competitive advantage in providing end-to-end as well as customized IT solutions?
3. What does the presence of companies like Oracle or Adobe or Microsoft mean for Indian IT companies such as Wipro, Infy, and TCS? And for Indian IT industry overall?
4. How is Oracle's Indian strategy linked to its global strategy?

Endnotes

1. Nancy Hass, "Earning Her Stripes," *The Wall Street Journal*, September 9, 2010; "Burberry Shines as Aquascutum Fades," *The Wall Street Journal*, April 17, 2010; Peter Evans, "Burberry Sales Ease from Blistering Pace," *The Wall Street Journal*, April 17, 2010; and "Burberry Case Study," *Market Line*, www.marketline.com, January 2012.
2. See R. W. Ruekert and O. C. Walker, "Interactions between Marketing and R&D Departments in Implementing Different Business-Level Strategies," *Strategic Management Journal* 8 (1987), pp. 233–48; and K. B. Clark and S. C. Wheelwright, *Managing New Product and Process Development* (New York: Free Press, 1993).
3. T. Levitt, "The Globalization of Markets," *Harvard Business Review*, May–June 1983, pp. 92–102. Reprinted by permission of *Harvard Business Review*, an excerpt from "The Globalization of Markets," by Theodore Levitt, May–June 1983. Copyright © 1983 by the President and Fellows of Harvard College. All rights reserved.
4. For example, see S. P. Douglas and Y. Wind, "The Myth of Globalization," *Columbia Journal of World Business*, Winter 1987, pp. 19–29; C. A. Bartlett and S. Ghoshal, *Managing across Borders: The Transnational Solution* (Boston: Harvard Business School Press, 1989); V. J. Govindarajan and A. K. Gupta, *The Quest for Global Dominance* (San Francisco: Jossey Bass, 2001); J. Quelch, "The Return of the Global Brand," *Harvard Business Review*, August 2003, pp. 1–3; and P. J. Ghemawat, *Redefining Global Strategy* (Boston: Harvard Business School Press, 2007).
5. J. Tagliabue, "U.S. Brands Are Feeling Global Tension," *The New York Times*, March 15, 2003, p. C3.
6. D. B. Holt, J. A. Quelch, and E. L. Taylor, "How Global Brands Compete," *Harvard Business Review*, September 2004.
7. J. T. Landry, "Emerging Markets: Are Chinese Consumers Coming of Age?" *Harvard Business Review*, May–June 1998, pp. 17–20.
8. M. Jordan, "Marketers Discover Black Brazil," *The Wall Street Journal*, November 24, 2000, pp. A11, A14. Copyright 2000 by Dow Jones & Co. Inc. Reproduced with permission from Dow Jones & Co. Inc. in the format textbook by the Copyright Clearance Center.
9. C. Miller, "Teens Seen as the First Truly Global Consumers," *Marketing News*, March 27, 1995, p. 9.
10. This approach was originally developed in K. Lancaster, "A New Approach to Demand Theory," *Journal of Political Economy* 74 (1965), pp. 132–57.

11. V. R. Alden, "Who Says You Can't Crack Japanese Markets?" *Harvard Business Review,* January–February 1987, pp. 52–56.

12. "RCA's New Vista: The Bottom Line," *BusinessWeek,* July 4, 1987, p. 44.

13. C. Matlack and P. Gogoi, "What's This? The French Love McDonald's?" *BusinessWeek,* January 13, 2003, pp. 50–51.

14. Z. Gurhan-Cvanli and D. Maheswaran, "Cultural Variation in Country of Origin Effects," *Journal of Marketing Research,* August 2000, pp. 309–17.

15. K. Merchant, "Striving for Success—One Sachet at a Time," *Financial Times,* December 11, 2000, p. 14; M. Turner, "Bicycle Brigade Takes Unilever to the People," *Financial Times,* August 17, 2000, p. 8; "Brands Thinking Positively," *Brand Strategy,* December 2003, pp. 28–29; and "The Legacy That Got Left on the Shelf," *The Economist,* February 2, 2008, pp. 77–79.

16. See M. Laroche, V. H. Kirpalani, F. Pons, and L. Zhou, "A Model of Advertising Standardization in Multinational Corporations," *Journal of International Business Studies* 32 (2001), pp. 249–66; and D. A. Aaker and E. Joachimsthaler, "The Lure of Global Branding," *Harvard Business Review,* November–December 1999, pp. 137–44.

17. "Advertising in a Single Market," *The Economist,* March 24, 1990, p. 64.

18. "The Legacy That Got Left on the Shelf," *The Economist,* February 2, 2008, pp. 77–79; R. Rothenberg, "Dove Effort Gives Package-Goods Marketers Lessons for the Future," *Advertising Age,* March 5, 2007, p. 18; J. Neff, "A Real Beauty: Dove's Viral Makes Big Splash for No Cash," *Advertising Age,* 2006, pp. 1–2; and K. Mazurkewich, "Dove Story: You Know the Name, and Some of the Story," *Strategy,* January 2007, pp. 37–39.

19. R. G. Matthews and D. Pringle, "Nokia Bets One Global Message Will Ring True in Many Markets," *The Wall Street Journal,* September 27, 2004, p. B6.

20. R. J. Dolan and H. Simon, *Power Pricing* (New York: Free Press, 1999).

21. B. Stottinger, "Strategic Export Pricing: A Long Winding Road," *Journal of International Marketing* 9 (2001), pp. 40–63; S. Gil-Pareja "Export Process Discrimination in Europe and Exchange Rates," *Review of International Economics,* May 2002, pp. 299–312; and G. Corsetti and L. Dedola, "A Macro Economic Model of International Price Discrimination," *Journal of International Economics,* September 2005, pp. 129–40.

22. These allegations were made on a PBS *Frontline* documentary telecast in the United States in May 1992.

23. Y. Tsurumi and H. Tsurumi, "Fujifilm-Kodak Duopolistic Competition in Japan and the United States," *Journal of International Business Studies* 30 (1999), pp. 813–30.

24. G. Smith and B. Wolverton, "A Dark Moment for Kodak," *BusinessWeek,* August 4, 1997, pp. 30–31.

25. R. Narisette and J. Friedland, "Disposable Income: Diaper Wars of P&G and Kimberly-Clark Now Heat Up in Brazil," *The Wall Street Journal,* June 4, 1997, p. A1.

26. J. F. Pickering, *Industrial Structure and Market Conduct* (London: Martin Robertson, 1974).

27. "How Levi Strauss Rekindled the Allure of Brand America," *World Trade,* March 2005, p. 28; "Levi Strauss Walks with a Swagger into New Markets," *Africa News,* March 17, 2005; "Levi's Adaptable Standards," *Strategic Direction,* June 2005, pp. 14–16; A. Benady, "Levi's Looks to the Bottom Line," *Financial Times,* February 15, 2005, p. 14; and R. A. Smith, "At Levi Strauss Dockers Are In," *The Wall Street Journal,* February 14, 2007, p. A14.

28. S. P. Douglas, C. Samuel Craig, and E. J. Nijissen, "Integrating Branding Strategy across Markets," *Journal of International Marketing* 9, no. 2 (2001), pp. 97–114.

29. The phrase was first used by economist Joseph Schumpeter in *Capitalism, Socialism, and Democracy* (New York: Harper Brothers, 1942).

30. S. Kotabe, S. Srinivasan, and P. S. Aulakh. "Multinationality and Firm Performance: The Moderating Role of R&D and Marketing," *Journal of International Business Studies* 33 (2002), pp. 79–97.

31. See D. C. Mowery and N. Rosenberg, *Technology and the Pursuit of Economic Growth* (Cambridge, UK: Cambridge University Press, 1989); and M. E. Porter, *The Competitive Advantage of Nations* (New York: Free Press, 1990).

32. W. Kuemmerle, "Building Effective R&D Capabilities Abroad," *Harvard Business Review,* March–April 1997, pp. 61–70; and C. Le Bas and C. Sierra, "Location versus Home Country Advantages in R&D Activities," *Research Policy* 31 (2002), pp. 589–609.

33. "When the Corporate Lab Goes to Japan," *The New York Times,* April 28, 1991, sec. 3, p. 1.

34. D. Shapley, "Globalization Prompts Exodus," *Financial Times,* March 17, 1994, p. 10.

35. E. Mansfield, "How Economists See R&D," *Harvard Business Review,* November–December 1981, pp. 98–106.

36. Ibid.

37 G. A. Stevens and J. Burley, "Piloting the Rocket of Radical Innovation," *Research Technology Management* 46 (2003), pp. 16–26.

38. K. B. Clark and S. C. Wheelwright, *Managing New Product and Process Development* (New York: Free Press, 1993); and M. A. Shilling and C. W. L. Hill, "Managing the New Product Development Process," *Academy of Management Executive* 12, no. 3 (1998), pp. 67–81.

39. O. Port, "Moving Past the Assembly Line," *BusinessWeek Special Issue: Reinventing America,* 1992, pp. 177–80.

40. K. B. Clark and T. Fujimoto, "The Power of Product Integrity," *Harvard Business Review,* November–December 1990, pp. 107–18; Clark and Wheelwright, *Managing New Product and Process Development;* S. L. Brown and K. M. Eisenhardt, "Product Development: Past Research, Present Findings, and Future Directions," *Academy of Management Review* 20 (1995), pp. 348–78; and G. Stalk and T. M. Hout, *Competing against Time* (New York: Free Press, 1990).

41. Shilling and Hill, "Managing the New Product Development Process."

42. C. Christensen. "Quantum Corporation—Business and Product Teams," Harvard Business School case no. 9-692-023.

43. R. Nobel and J. Birkinshaw, "Innovation in Multinational Corporations: Control and Communication Patterns in International R&D Operations," *Strategic Management Journal* 19 (1998), pp. 479–96.

44. Information comes from the company's website; also see K. Ferdows, "Making the Most of Foreign Factories," *Harvard Business Review,* March–April 1997, pp. 73–88.

45. A. Gasparro, "Domino's Sticks to Its Ways Abroad," *The Wall Street Journal,* April 17, 2012, p. B10; A. C. Beattie, "In Japan, Pizza Is Recast as a Meal for Special Occasions," *Advertising Age,* April 2, 2012, p. 16; A. Gasparro, "Domino's Sees Bigger Slice Overseas," *The Wall Street Journal,* February 29, 2012, p. B7; and R. Shah, "How Domino's Pizza Is Taking a Bite Out of India," *Getting More Awesome,* www.gettingmoreawesome.com/2012/02/08/how-dominos-is-taking-a-bite-out-of-india/.

46. (i) www.oracle.com
    (ii) http://360.datamonitor.com
    (iii) http://www.hoovers.com/company/Oracle_India_Private_Limited/ryxycif-1-1njdap.html
    (iv) http://www.siliconindia.com/shownews/Oracle_apps_penetrate_Indian_insurance_sector_-nid-65154.html
    (v) http://www.oracle.com/global/in/pressroom/StrategytoExtendCRMLeadership.html

Chapter 19
Global Human Resource Management

LEARNING OBJECTIVES

After reading this chapter, you will be able to:

LO19-1 Summarize the strategic role of human resource management in the international business.

LO19-2 Identify the pros and cons of different approaches to staffing policy in the international business.

LO19-3 Explain why managers may fail to thrive in foreign postings.

LO19-4 Recognize how management development and training programs can increase the value of human capital in the international business firm.

LO19-5 Explain how and why performance appraisal systems might vary across nations.

LO19-6 Understand how and why compensation systems might vary across nations.

LO19-7 Understand how organized labor can influence strategic choices in international business firms.

⬦ **THE STRATEGIC ROLE OF HUMAN RESOURCES AT IBM** ⬦

Opening Case

Back in the early 2000s IBM's new CEO, Sam Palmisano, set out to recreate IBM as a globally integrated enterprise that would provide its customers IBM products and services—software, hardware, business processing, consulting and more—wherever and whenever they needed it. Underpinning Palmisano's vision was a realization that globalization was proceeding rapidly, and that many of IBM's customers were themselves increasingly global enterprises. Global customers wanted to deal with one IBM, not many different national units. Palmisano also understood that for IBM to build a sustained competitive advantage in this new world, it would have to have world-class human capital. People and their acquired skills, he realized, were the foundation of competitive advantage. Companies that rely on technological or manufacturing innovations alone cannot be expected to dominate their markets indefinitely. Competitors can and do catch up. In Palmisano's view, the quality and strategic deployment of human capital is what separates winners from also-rans. This was particularly true for a company like IBM, which increasingly relied on its people to build and deliver world-class services.

To execute his strategy, Palmisano created global product divisions, but that alone was not enough. He realized that IBM's existing human resource systems were not aligned with the new strategy. Much of the hiring, training, and staffing functions of HR were still based in national units. The company lacked a global approach to managing and deploying its human capital, and executing Palmisano's vision required this.

That insight was the genesis for what became known as the Workforce Management Initiative (WMI) at IBM. Established by the global human resource group, the purpose of this initiative was to create for the first time a single, integrated approach to hiring, managing, and deploying IBM's global workforce. The ultimate goal was to enable the company to find and deploy the best people within the company to help solve client problems or respond to their requests. For this to work, HR had to become intimately involved in understanding the business strategy of different IBM units and the implications that business strategy holds for human resource deployment. Unless HR had a seat at the strategy table, it could not properly identify and provide the right people to execute a unit's strategy.

As it progressed, the WMI involved investing more than $100 million to create a companywide database to document the skills of more than 400,000 employees at IBM, measure the supply and demand for different skills and capabilities, and seek to match human capital with specific projects. The goal was to get the right person, with the right skills, at the right time, place, and cost. For example, when a health care client needed a consultant with a clinical background, a search using the WMI database immediately targeted a former registered nurse who was now an IBM consultant. By improving the efficiency of its internal labor market and leveraging its global workforce, IBM estimates that the WMI database saved the company as much as $1.4 billion in its first four years in operation.

The WMI database has a number of other benefits. It helps employees make career decisions, as by accessing it they can see which skills are in demand. Moreover, by identifying potential mismatches between the supply and demand of skills, it drives decisions about internal management development and training programs, enabling IBM to identify with precision which skills its employees need to acquire for the company to maintain its competitive edge going forward.[1]

INTRODUCTION

This chapter continues our survey of specific functions within an international business by looking at international human resource management. **Human resource management (HRM)** refers to the activities an organization carries out to use its human resources effectively.[2] These activities include determining the firm's human resource strategy, staffing, performance evaluation, management development, compensation, and labor relations. None of these activities is performed in a vacuum; all are related to the strategy of the firm. As we will see, HRM has an important strategic component.[3] Through its influence on the character, development, quality, and productivity of the firm's human resources, the HRM function can help the firm achieve its primary strategic goals of reducing the costs of value creation and adding value by better serving customers. A good example of this is given in the opening case, which looks at how IBM uses human resources in a highly strategic way to build and sustain a competitive advantage over rivals.

Irrespective of the desire of managers in multinationals such as IBM to build a truly global enterprise with a global workforce, the reality is that HRM practices still have to be modified to national context. The strategic role of HRM is complex enough in a purely domestic firm, but it is more complex in an international business, where staffing, management development, performance evaluation, and compensation activities are complicated by profound differences between countries in labor markets, culture, legal systems, economic systems, and the like (see Chapters 2, 3, and 4). For example,

- Compensation practices may vary from country to country, depending on prevailing management customs.
- Labor laws may prohibit union organization in one country and mandate it in another.
- Equal employment legislation may be strongly pursued in one country and not in another.

If it is to build a cadre of managers capable of managing a multinational enterprise, the HRM function must deal with a host of issues. It must decide how to staff key management posts in the company, how to develop managers so that they are familiar with the nuances of doing business in different countries, how to compensate people in different nations, and how to evaluate the performance of managers based in different countries. HRM must also deal with a host of issues related to expatriate managers. (An **expatriate manager** is a citizen of one country who is working abroad in one of the firm's subsidiaries.) It must decide when to use expatriates, determine whom to send on expatriate postings, be clear about the reasons why, compensate expatriates appropriately, and make sure that they are adequately debriefed and reoriented once they return home.

This chapter looks closely at the role of HRM in an international business. It begins by briefly discussing the strategic role of HRM. Then we turn our attention to four major tasks of the HRM function: staffing policy, management training and development, performance appraisal, and compensation policy. We point out the strategic implications of each task. The chapter closes with a look at international labor relations and the relationship between the firm's management of labor relations and its overall strategy.

THE STRATEGIC ROLE OF INTERNATIONAL HRM

A large and expanding body of academic research suggests that a strong fit between human resource practices and strategy is required for high profitability.[4] You will recall from Chapter 14 that superior performance requires not only the right strategy, but the strategy must also be supported by the right organizational architecture. Strategy is implemented through organization. As shown in Figure 19.1, people are the linchpin of a firm's organizational architecture. For a firm to outperform its rivals in the global marketplace, it must have the right people in the right postings (see the opening case on IBM for an example). Those people must be trained appropriately so that they have the skill sets required to perform their jobs effectively and so that they behave in a manner that is congruent with the desired culture of the firm. Their compensation packages must create incentives for them to take actions that are consistent with the strategy of the firm, and the performance appraisal system the firm uses must measure the behavior that the firm wants to encourage.

As indicated in Figure 19.1, the HRM function, through its staffing, training, compensation, and performance appraisal activities, has a critical impact on the people, culture, incentive, and control system elements of the firm's organizational architecture (performance appraisal systems are part of the control systems in an enterprise). Thus, HRM professionals have a critically important strategic role. It is incumbent on them to shape these elements of a firm's organizational architecture in a manner that is consistent with the strategy of the enterprise, so that the firm can effectively implement its strategy.

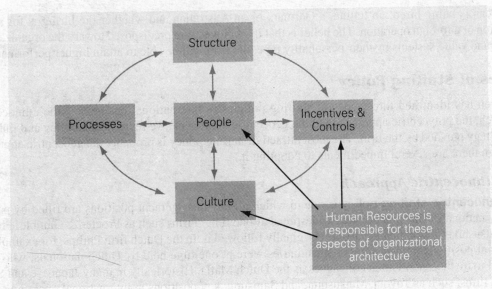

Figure 19.1 *The Role of Human Resources in Shaping Organizational Architecture*

In short, superior human resource management can be a sustained source of high productivity and competitive advantage in the global economy. At the same time, research suggests that many international businesses have room for improving the effectiveness of their HRM function. In one study of competitiveness among 326 large multinationals, the authors found that human resource management was one of the weakest capabilities in most firms, suggesting that improving the effectiveness of international HRM practices might have substantial performance benefits.[5]

In Chapter 13, we examined four strategies pursued by international businesses: localization strategy, international strategy, global standardization strategy, and transnational strategy. In this chapter, we will see that success also requires HRM policies to be congruent with the firm's strategy. For example, a transnational strategy imposes different requirements for staffing, management development, and compensation practices from a localization strategy. Firms pursuing a transnational strategy need to build a strong corporate culture and an informal management network for transmitting information and knowledge within the organization. Through its employee selection, management development, performance appraisal, and compensation policies, the HRM function can help develop these things. Thus, as we have noted, HRM has a critical role to play in implementing strategy. In each section that follows, we review the strategic role of HRM in some detail.

STAFFING POLICY

LO19-2

Staffing policy is concerned with the selection of employees for particular jobs. At one level, this involves selecting individuals who have the skills required to do particular jobs. At another level, staffing policy can be a tool for developing and promoting the desired corporate culture of the firm.[6] By **corporate culture,** we mean the organization's norms and value systems. A strong corporate culture can help a firm implement its strategy. General Electric, for example, is not just concerned with hiring people who have the skills required for performing particular jobs; it wants to hire individuals whose behavioral styles, beliefs, and value systems are consistent with those of GE. This is true whether an

American is being hired, an Italian, a German, or an Australian and whether the hiring is for a U.S. operation or a foreign operation. The belief is that if employees are predisposed toward the organization's norms and value systems by their personality type, the firm will be able to attain higher performance.

Types of Staffing Policy

Research has identified three types of staffing policies in international businesses: the ethnocentric approach, the polycentric approach, and the geocentric approach.[7] We review each policy and link it to the strategy pursued by the firm. The most attractive staffing policy is probably the geocentric approach, although there are several impediments to adopting it.

The Ethnocentric Approach

An **ethnocentric staffing policy** is one in which all key management positions are filled by parent-country nationals. This practice was widespread at one time. Firms such as Procter & Gamble, Philips, and Matsushita (now called Panasonic) originally followed it. In the Dutch firm Philips, for example, all important positions in most foreign subsidiaries were at one time held by Dutch nationals, who were referred to by their non-Dutch colleagues as the Dutch Mafia. Historically in many Japanese and South Korean firms, such as Toyota, Matsushita, and Samsung, key positions in international operations have often been held by home-country nationals. For example, according to the Japanese Overseas Enterprise Association, only 29 percent of foreign subsidiaries of Japanese companies had presidents who were not Japanese. In contrast, 66 percent of the Japanese subsidiaries of foreign companies had Japanese presidents.[8] Today, there is evidence that as Chinese enterprises are expanding internationally, they too are using an ethnocentric staffing policy in their foreign operations.[9]

Firms pursue an ethnocentric staffing policy for three reasons. First, the firm may believe the host country lacks qualified individuals to fill senior management positions. This argument is heard most often when the firm has operations in less developed countries. Second, the firm may see an ethnocentric staffing policy as the best way to maintain a unified corporate culture. Many Japanese firms, for example, have traditionally preferred their foreign operations to be headed by expatriate Japanese managers because these managers will have been socialized into the firm's culture while employed in Japan.[10] Procter & Gamble until fairly recently preferred to staff important management positions in its foreign subsidiaries with U.S. nationals who had been socialized into P&G's corporate culture by years of employment in its U.S. operations. Such reasoning tends to predominate when a firm places a high value on its corporate culture.

Third, if the firm is trying to create value by transferring core competencies to a foreign operation, as firms pursuing an international strategy are, it may believe that the best way to do this is to transfer parent-country nationals who have knowledge of that competency to the foreign operation. Imagine what might occur if a firm tried to transfer a core competency in marketing to a foreign subsidiary without a corresponding transfer of home-country marketing management personnel. The transfer would probably fail to produce the anticipated benefits because the knowledge underlying a core competency cannot easily be articulated and written down. Such knowledge often has a significant tacit dimension; it is acquired through experience. Just like the great tennis player who cannot instruct others how to become great tennis players simply by writing a handbook, the firm that has a core competency in marketing, or anything else, cannot just write a handbook that tells a foreign subsidiary how to build the firm's core competency anew in a foreign setting. It must also transfer management personnel to the foreign operation to show foreign managers how to become good marketers, for example. The need to transfer managers overseas arises because the knowledge that underlies the firm's core competency resides in the heads of its domestic managers and was acquired through years of experience, not by reading a handbook. Thus, if a firm is to transfer a core competency to a foreign subsidiary, it must also transfer the appropriate managers.

Despite this rationale for pursuing an ethnocentric staffing policy, the policy is now on the wane in most international businesses for two reasons. First, an ethnocentric staffing policy limits advancement opportunities for host-country nationals. This can lead to resentment, lower productivity, and increased turnover among that group. Resentment can be greater still if, as often occurs, expatriate managers are paid significantly more than home-country nationals.

Second, an ethnocentric policy can lead to *cultural myopia,* the firm's failure to understand host-country cultural differences that require different approaches to marketing and management. The adaptation of expatriate managers can take a long time, during which they may make major mistakes. For example, expatriate managers may fail to appreciate how product attributes, distribution strategy, communications strategy, and pricing strategy should be adapted to host-country conditions. The result may be costly blunders. They may also make decisions that are ethically suspect simply because they do not understand the culture in which they are managing.[11] In one highly publicized case in the United States, Mitsubishi Motors was sued by the federal Equal Employment Opportunity Commission for tolerating extensive and systematic sexual harassment in a plant in Illinois. The plant's top management, all Japanese expatriates, denied the charges. The Japanese managers may have failed to realize that behavior that would be viewed as acceptable in Japan was not acceptable in the United States.[12]

The Polycentric Approach

A **polycentric staffing policy** requires host-country nationals to be recruited to manage subsidiaries, while parent-country nationals occupy key positions at corporate headquarters. In many respects, a polycentric approach is a response to the shortcomings of an ethnocentric approach. One advantage of adopting a polycentric approach is that the firm is less likely to suffer from cultural myopia. Host-country managers are unlikely to make the mistakes arising from cultural misunderstandings to which expatriate managers are vulnerable. A second advantage is that a polycentric approach may be less expensive to implement, reducing the costs of value creation. Expatriate managers can be expensive to maintain.

A polycentric approach has its drawbacks. Host-country nationals have limited opportunities to gain experience outside their own country and thus cannot progress beyond senior positions in their own subsidiary. As in the case of an ethnocentric policy, this may cause resentment. Perhaps the major drawback with a polycentric approach, however, is the gap that can form between host-country managers and parent-country managers. Language barriers, national loyalties, and a range of cultural differences may isolate the corporate headquarters staff from the various foreign subsidiaries. The lack of management transfers from home to host countries, and vice versa, can exacerbate this isolation and lead to a lack of integration between corporate headquarters and foreign subsidiaries. The result can be a "federation" of largely independent national units with only nominal links to the corporate headquarters. Within such a federation, the coordination required to transfer core competencies or to pursue experience curve and location economies may be difficult to achieve. Thus, although a polycentric approach may be effective for firms pursuing a localization strategy, it is inappropriate for other strategies.

The federation that may result from a polycentric approach can also be a force for inertia within the firm. After decades of pursuing a polycentric staffing policy, food and detergents giant Unilever found that shifting from a strategic posture that emphasized localization to a transnational posture was very difficult. Unilever's foreign subsidiaries had evolved into quasi-autonomous operations, each with its own strong national identity. These "little kingdoms" objected strenuously to corporate headquarters' attempts to limit their autonomy and to rationalize global manufacturing.[13]

The Geocentric Approach

A **geocentric staffing policy** seeks the best people for key jobs throughout the organization, regardless of nationality. This policy has a number of advantages. First, it enables the firm to make the best use of its human resources. Second, and perhaps more important, a geocentric policy enables the firm to build a cadre of international executives who feel at home working in a number of cultures. Creation of such a cadre may be a critical first step toward building a strong unifying corporate culture and an informal management network, both of which are required for global standardization and transnational strategies.[14] Firms pursuing a geocentric staffing policy may be better able to create value from the pursuit of experience curve and location economies and from the multidirectional transfer of core competencies than firms pursuing other staffing policies. In addition, the multinational composition of the management team that results from geocentric staffing tends to reduce cultural myopia and to enhance local responsiveness.

In sum, other things being equal, a geocentric staffing policy seems the most attractive. Indeed, in recent years there has been a sharp shift toward adoption of a geocentric staffing policy by many multinationals. For example, India's Tata Group, now a $100 billion global conglomerate, runs several of its companies with American and British executives. Japan's Sony Corporation broke 60 years of tradition in 2005 when it installed its first non-Japanese chairman and CEO, Howard Stringer, a former CBS president and a U.S. citizen who was born and raised in Wales. American companies increasingly draw their managerial talent from overseas. One study found that by mid-2005, 24 percent of the managers among the top 100 to 250 people in U.S. companies were from outside the United States. For European companies, the average was 40 percent.[15]

However, a number of problems limit the firm's ability to pursue a geocentric policy. Many countries want foreign subsidiaries to employ their citizens. To achieve this goal, they use immigration laws to require the employment of host-country nationals if they are available in adequate numbers and have the necessary skills. Most countries, including the United States, require firms to provide extensive documentation if they wish to hire a foreign national instead of a local national. This documentation can be time-consuming, expensive, and at times futile. A geocentric staffing policy also can be expensive to implement. Training and relocation costs increase when transferring managers from country to country. The company may also need a compensation structure with a standardized international base pay level higher than national levels in many countries. In addition, the higher pay enjoyed by managers placed on an international fast track may be a source of resentment within a firm.

Summary

The advantages and disadvantages of the three approaches to staffing policy are summarized in Table 19.1. Broadly speaking, an ethnocentric approach is compatible with an international strategy, a polycentric approach is compatible with a localization strategy, and a geocentric approach is compatible with both global standardization and transnational strategies. (See Chapter 13 for details of the strategies.)

While the staffing policies described here are well known and widely used among both practitioners and scholars of international businesses, some critics have claimed that the typology is too simplistic and that it obscures the internal differentiation of management practices within international businesses. The critics claim that within some international businesses, staffing policies vary significantly from national subsidiary to national subsidiary; while some are managed on an ethnocentric basis, others are managed in a polycentric or geocentric manner.[16] Other critics note that the staffing policy adopted by a firm is primarily driven by its geographic scope, as opposed to its strategic orientation. Firms that have a broad geographic scope are the most likely to have a geocentric mind-set.[17]

TABLE 19.1   Comparison of Staffing Approaches

Staffing Approach	Strategic Appropriateness	Advantages	Disadvantages
Ethnocentric	International	Overcomes lack of qualified managers in host nation Unified culture Helps transfer core competencies	Produces resentment in host country Can lead to cultural myopia
Polycentric	Localization	Alleviates cultural myopia Inexpensive to implement	Limits career mobility Isolates headquarters from foreign subsidiaries
Geocentric	Global standardization and transnational	Uses human resources efficiently Helps build strong culture and informal management networks	National immigration policies may limit implementation Expensive

Expatriate Managers

LO19-3

Two of the three staffing policies we have discussed—the ethnocentric and the geocentric—rely on extensive use of expatriate managers. As defined earlier, expatriates are citizens of one country who are working in another country. Sometimes the term *inpatriates* is used to identify a subset of expatriates who are citizens of a foreign country working in the home country of their multinational employer.[18] Thus, a citizen of Japan who moves to the United States to work at Microsoft would be classified as an inpatriate (Microsoft has large numbers of inpatriates working at its main U.S. location near Seattle). With an ethnocentric policy, the expatriates are all home-country nationals who are transferred abroad. With a geocentric approach, the expatriates need not be home-country nationals; the firm does not base transfer decisions on nationality. A prominent issue in the international staffing literature is **expatriate failure**—the premature return of an expatriate manager to his or her home country.[19] Here, we briefly review the evidence on expatriate failure before discussing a number of ways to minimize the failure rate.

Expatriate Failure Rates

Expatriate failure represents a failure of the firm's selection policies to identify individuals who will not thrive abroad.[20] The consequences include premature return from a foreign posting and high resignation rates, with expatriates leaving their company at about twice the rate of domestic managers.[21] Research suggests that between 16 and 40 percent of all American employees sent abroad to developed nations return from their assignments early, and almost 70 percent of employees sent to developing nations return home early.[22] Although detailed data are not available for most nationalities, one suspects that high expatriate failure is a universal problem. Some 28 percent of British expatriates, for example, are estimated to fail in their overseas postings.[23] The costs of expatriate failure are high. One estimate is that the average cost per failure to the parent firm can be as high as three times the expatriate's annual domestic salary plus the cost of relocation (which is affected by currency exchange rates and location of assignment). Estimates of the costs of each failure run between $40,000 and $1 million.[24] In addition, approximately 30 to 50 percent of American expatriates, whose average annual compensation package runs to $250,000, stay at their international assignments but are considered ineffective or marginally effective by their firms.[25] In a seminal study, R. L. Tung surveyed a number of U.S., European, and Japanese multinationals.[26] Her results, summarized in Table 19.2, show that 76 percent of U.S. multinationals experienced expatriate failure rates of 10 percent or more, and 7 percent experienced a failure rate of more than 20 percent. Tung's work also suggests that U.S.-based multinationals experience a much higher expatriate failure rate than either European or Japanese multinationals.

TABLE 19.2 Expatriate Failure Rates

Recall Rate Percent	Percent of Companies
U.S. multinationals	
20–40	7
10–20	69
<10	24
European multinationals	
11–15	3
6–10	38
<5	59
Japanese multinationals	
11–19	14
6–10	10
<5	76

Source: Data from R. L. Tung, "Selection and Training Procedures of U.S., European, and Japanese Multinationals," *California Management Review* 25 (1982), pp. 51–71.

Tung asked her sample of multinational managers to indicate reasons for expatriate failure. For U.S. multinationals, the reasons, in order of importance, were:

1. Inability of spouse to adjust.
2. Manager's inability to adjust.
3. Other family problems.
4. Manager's personal or emotional maturity.
5. Inability to cope with larger overseas responsibilities.

Managers of European firms gave only one reason consistently to explain expatriate failure: the inability of the manager's spouse to adjust to a new environment. For the Japanese firms, the reasons for failure were:

1. Inability to cope with larger overseas responsibilities.
2. Difficulties with new environment.
3. Personal or emotional problems.
4. Lack of technical competence.
5. Inability of spouse to adjust.

The most striking difference between these lists is that "inability of spouse to adjust" was the top reason for expatriate failure among U.S. and European multinationals but only the fifth reason among Japanese multinationals. Tung comments that this difference was not surprising, given the role and status to which Japanese society traditionally relegates the wife and the fact that most of the Japanese expatriate managers in the study were men.

Since Tung's study, a number of other studies have consistently confirmed that the inability of a spouse to adjust, the inability of the manager to adjust, or other family problems remain major reasons for continuing high levels of expatriate failure.[27] One study by International Orientation Resources, an HRM consulting firm, found that 60 percent of expatriate failures occur due to these three reasons.[28] Another study found that the most common reason for assignment failure is lack of partner (spouse) satisfaction, which was listed by 27 percent of respondents.[29] The inability of expatriate managers to adjust to foreign postings seems to be caused by a lack of cultural skills on the part of the manager being transferred. According to one HRM consulting firm, this is because the expatriate selection process at many firms is fundamentally flawed: "Expatriate assignments rarely fail because the person cannot accommodate to the technical demands of the job. Typically, the expatriate selections are made by line managers based on technical competence. They fail because of family and personal issues and lack of cultural skills that haven't been part of the selection process."[30]

The failure of spouses to adjust to a foreign posting seems to be related to a number of factors. Often, spouses find themselves in a foreign country without the familiar network of family and friends. Language differences make it difficult for them to make new friends. While this may not be a problem for the manager, who can make friends at work, it can be difficult for the spouse, who might feel trapped at home. The problem is often exacerbated by immigration regulations prohibiting the spouse from taking employment. With the recent rise of two-career families in many developed nations, this issue has become much more important. One survey found that 69 percent of expatriates are married, with spouses accompanying them 77 percent of the time. Of those spouses, 49 percent were employed before an assignment and only 11 percent were employed during an assignment.[31] Research suggests that a main reason managers now turn down international assignments is concern over the impact such an assignment might have on their spouse's career.[32] The accompanying Management Focus examines how one large multinational company, Royal Dutch Shell, has tried to come to grips with this issue.

Expatriate Selection

One way to reduce expatriate failure rates is by improving selection procedures to screen out inappropriate candidates. In a review of the research on this issue, Mendenhall and Oddou state that a major problem in many firms is that HRM managers tend to equate domestic performance with overseas performance potential.[33] Domestic performance and overseas performance potential are *not* the same thing. An executive who performs well in a domestic setting may not be able to adapt to managing in a different cultural setting. From their review of the research, Mendenhall and Oddou identified four dimensions that seem to predict success in a foreign posting: self-orientation, others-orientation, perceptual ability, and cultural toughness.

1. *Self-orientation.* The attributes of this dimension strengthen the expatriate's self-esteem, self-confidence, and mental well-being. Expatriates with high self-esteem, self-confidence, and mental well-being were more likely to succeed in foreign postings. Mendenhall and Oddou concluded that such individuals were able to adapt their interests in food, sport, and music; had interests outside of work that could be pursued (e.g., hobbies); and were technically competent.

Managing Expatriates at Royal Dutch Shell

Royal Dutch Shell is a global petroleum company with joint headquarters in both London and The Hague in the Netherlands. The company employs more than 80,000 people, approximately 5,500 of whom are at any one time living and working as expatriates. The expatriates at Shell are a diverse group, made up of more than 70 nationalities and located in more than 100 countries. Shell, as a global corporation, has long recognized that the international mobility of its workforce is essential to its success. By the 1990s, however, Shell was finding it harder to recruit key personnel for foreign postings. To discover why, the company interviewed more than 200 expatriate employees and their spouses to determine their biggest concerns. The data were then used to construct a survey that was sent to 17,000 current and former expatriate employees, expatriates' spouses, and employees who had declined international assignments.

The survey registered a phenomenal 70 percent response rate, clearly indicating that many employees thought this was an important issue. According to the survey, five issues had the greatest impact on the willingness of an employee to accept an international assignment. In order of importance, these were (1) separation from children during their secondary education (the children of British and Dutch expatriates were often sent to boarding schools in their home countries while their parents worked abroad), (2) harm done to a spouse's career and employment, (3) failure to recognize and involve a spouse in the relocation decision, (4) failure to provide adequate information and assistance regarding relocation, and (5) health issues. The underlying message was that the family is the basic unit of expatriation, not the individual, and Shell needed to do more to recognize this.

To deal with these issues, Shell implemented a number of programs designed to address some of these problems. To help with the education of children, Shell built elementary schools for Shell employees where there was a heavy concentration of expatriates. As for secondary school education, it worked with local schools, often providing grants, to help them upgrade their educational offerings. It also offered an education supplement to help expatriates send their children to private schools in the host country.

Helping spouses with their careers is a more vexing problem. According to the survey data, half the spouses accompanying Shell staff on assignment were employed until the transfer. When expatriated, only 12 percent were able to secure employment, while a further 33 percent wished to be employed. Shell set up a spouse employment center to address the problem. The center provides career counseling and assistance in locating employment opportunities both during and immediately after an international assignment. The company also agreed to reimburse up to 80 percent of the costs of vocational training, further education, or reaccreditation, up to $4,400 per assignment.

Shell also set up a global information and advice network known as "The Outpost" to provide support for families contemplating a foreign posting. The Outpost has its headquarters in The Hague and now runs 45 to 55 local offices around the world (depending on the business). The center recommends schools and medical facilities and provides housing advice and up-to-date information on employment, study, self-employment, and volunteer work.[34]

2. *Others-orientation.* The attributes of this dimension enhance the expatriate's ability to interact effectively with host-country nationals. The more effectively the expatriate interacts with host-country nationals, the more likely he or she is to succeed. Two factors seem to be particularly important here: relationship development and willingness to communicate. Relationship development refers to the ability to develop long-lasting friendships with host-country nationals. Willingness to communicate refers to the expatriate's willingness to use the host-country language. Although language fluency helps, an expatriate need not be fluent to show willingness to communicate. Making the effort to use the language is what is important. Such gestures tend to be rewarded with greater cooperation by host-country nationals.

3. *Perceptual ability.* This is the ability to understand why people of other countries behave the way they do, that is, the ability to empathize. This dimension seems critical for managing host-country nationals. Expatriate managers who lack this ability tend to treat foreign nationals as if they were home-country nationals. As a result, they may experience significant management problems and considerable frustration. As one expatriate executive from Hewlett-Packard observed, "It took me six months to accept the fact that my staff meetings would start 30 minutes late, and that it would bother no one but me." According to Mendenhall and Oddou, well-adjusted expatriates tend to be nonjudgmental and nonevaluative in interpreting the behavior of host-country nationals and willing to be flexible in their management style, adjusting it as cultural conditions warrant.

4. *Cultural toughness.* This dimension refers to the relationship between the country of assignment and how well an expatriate adjusts to a particular posting. Some countries are much tougher postings than others because their cultures are more unfamiliar and uncomfortable. For example, many Americans regard Great Britain as a relatively easy foreign posting, and for good reason— the two cultures have much in common. But many Americans find postings in non-Western cultures, such as India, Southeast Asia, and the Middle East, to be much tougher.[35] The reasons are many, including poor health care and housing standards, inhospitable climate, lack of Western entertainment, and language difficulties. Also, many cultures are extremely male-dominated and may be particularly difficult postings for female Western managers.

The Global Mind-Set

Some researchers suggest that a global mind-set, one characterized by cognitive complexity and a cosmopolitan outlook, is the fundamental attribute of a global manager. Such managers can deal with high levels of complexity and ambiguity and are open to the world. How do you develop these attributes? Often they are gained in early life, from a family that is bicultural, lives in foreign countries, or learns foreign languages as a regular part of family life.

Mendenhall and Oddou note that standard psychological tests can be used to assess the first three of these dimensions, whereas a comparison of cultures can give managers a feeling for the fourth dimension. They contend that these four dimensions, in addition to domestic performance, should be considered when selecting a manager for foreign posting. However, practice does not often conform to Mendenhall and Oddou's recommendations. Tung's research, for example, showed that only 5 percent of the firms in her sample used formal procedures and psychological tests to assess the personality traits and relational abilities of potential expatriates.[36] Research by International Orientation Resources suggests that when selecting employees for foreign assignments, only 10 percent of the 50 *Fortune* 500 firms surveyed tested for important psychological traits such as cultural sensitivity, interpersonal skills, adaptability, and flexibility. Instead, 90 percent of the time employees were selected on the basis of their technical expertise, not their cross-cultural fluency.[37]

Mendenhall and Oddou do not address the problem of expatriate failure due to a spouse's inability to adjust. According to a number of other researchers, a review of the family situation should be part of the expatriate selection process (see the Management Focus on Royal Dutch Shell for an example).[38] A survey by Windam International, another international HRM consulting firm, found that spouses were included in preselection interviews for foreign postings only 21 percent of the time and that only half of them received any cross-cultural training. The rise of dual-career families has added an additional and difficult dimension to this long-standing problem.[39] Increasingly, spouses wonder why they should have to sacrifice their own career to further that of their partner.[40]

TRAINING AND MANAGEMENT DEVELOPMENT LO19-4

Selection is just the first step in matching a manager with a job. The next step is training the manager to do the specific job. For example, an intensive training program might be used to give expatriate managers the skills required for success in a foreign posting. However, management development is a much broader concept. It is intended to develop the manager's skills over his or her career with the firm. Thus, as part of a management development program, a manager might be sent on several foreign postings over a number of years to build his or her cross-cultural sensitivity and experience. At the same time, along with other managers in the firm, the person might attend management education programs at regular intervals. The thinking behind job transfers is that broad international experience will enhance the management and leadership skills of executives. Research suggests this may be the case.[41]

Historically, most international businesses have been more concerned with training than with management development. Plus, they tended to focus their training efforts on preparing home-country nationals for foreign postings. Recently, however, the shift toward greater global competition and the rise of transnational firms have changed this. It is increasingly common for firms to provide general management development programs in addition to training for particular posts. In many international businesses, the explicit purpose of these management development programs is strategic. Management development is seen as a tool to help the firm achieve its strategic goals, not only by giving managers the required skill set but also by helping reinforce the desired culture of the firm and by facilitating the creation of an informal network for sharing knowledge within the multinational enterprise.

With this distinction between training and management development in mind, we first examine the types of training managers receive for foreign postings. Then we discuss the connection between management development and strategy in the international business.

Training for Expatriate Managers

Earlier in the chapter, we saw that the two most common reasons for expatriate failure were the inability of a manager's spouse to adjust to a foreign environment and the manager's own inability to adjust to a foreign environment. Training can help the manager and spouse cope with both these problems. Cultural training, language training, and practical training all seem to reduce expatriate failure. We discuss each of these kinds of training here.[42] Despite the usefulness of the training, evidence suggests that many managers receive no training before they are sent on foreign postings. One study found that only about 30 percent of managers sent on one- to five-year expatriate assignments received training before their departure.[43]

Cultural Training

Cultural training seeks to foster an appreciation for the host country's culture. The belief is that understanding a host country's culture will help the manager empathize with the culture, which will enhance his or her effectiveness in dealing with host-country nationals. It has been suggested that expatriates should receive training in the host country's culture, history, politics, economy, religion, and social and business practices.[44] If possible, it is also advisable to arrange for a familiarization trip to the host country before the formal transfer, because this seems to ease culture shock. Given the problems related to spouse adaptation, it is important that the spouse, and perhaps the whole family, be included in cultural training programs.

Language Training

English is the language of world business; it is quite possible to conduct business all over the world using only English. Notwithstanding the prevalence of English, however, an exclusive reliance on English diminishes an expatriate manager's ability to interact with host-country nationals. As noted earlier, a willingness to communicate in the language of the host country, even if the expatriate is far from fluent, can help build rapport with local employees and improve the manager's effectiveness. Despite this, one study of 74 executives of U.S. multinationals found that only 23 believed knowledge of foreign languages was necessary for conducting business abroad.[45] Those firms that did offer foreign language training for expatriates believed it improved their employees' effectiveness and enabled them to relate more easily to a foreign culture, which fostered a better image of the firm in the host country.

Practical Training

Practical training is aimed at helping the expatriate manager and family ease themselves into day-to-day life in the host country. The sooner a routine is established, the better are the prospects that the expatriate and his or her family will adapt successfully. One critical need is for a support network of friends for the expatriate. Where an expatriate community exists, firms often devote considerable effort to ensuring the new expatriate family is quickly integrated into that group. The expatriate community can be a useful source of support and information and can be invaluable in helping the family adapt to a foreign culture.

Repatriation of Expatriates

A largely overlooked but critically important issue in the training and development of expatriate managers is to prepare them for reentry into their home-country organization.[46] Repatriation should be seen as the final link in an integrated, circular process that connects good selection and cross-cultural training of expatriate managers with completion of their term abroad and reintegration into their national organization. However, instead of having employees come home to share their knowledge and encourage other high-performing managers to take the same international career track, expatriates too often face a different scenario.[47]

Often when they return home after a stint abroad—where they have typically been autonomous, well-compensated, and celebrated as a big fish in a little pond—they face an organization that doesn't know what they have done for the past few years, doesn't know how to use their new knowledge, and doesn't particularly care. In the worst cases, reentering employees have to scrounge for jobs, or firms will create standby positions that don't use the expatriate's skills and capabilities and fail to make the most of the business investment the firm has made in that individual.

Research illustrates the extent of this problem. According to one study of repatriated employees, 60 to 70 percent didn't know what their position would be when they returned home. Also, 60 percent said their organizations were vague about repatriation, about their new roles, and about their future career progression within the company; 77 percent of those surveyed took jobs at a lower level in their home organization than in their international assignments.[48] Not surprisingly, 15 percent of returning expatriates leave their firms within a year of arriving home, and 40 percent leave within three years.[49]

Monsanto's Repatriation Program

Monsanto is a global provider of agricultural products with 20,000 employees. At any one time, the company will have 100 mid- and higher-level managers on extended postings abroad. Two-thirds of these are Americans posted overseas; the remainder are foreign nationals employed in the United States. At Monsanto, managing expatriates and their repatriation begins with a rigorous selection process and intensive cross-cultural training, both for the managers and for their families. As at many other global companies, the idea is to build an internationally minded cadre of highly capable managers who will lead the organization in the future.

One of the strongest features of this program is that employees and their sending and receiving managers, or sponsors, develop an agreement about how this assignment will fit into the firm's business objectives. The focus is on why employees are going abroad to do the job and what their contribution to Monsanto will be when they return. Sponsoring managers are expected to be explicit about the kind of job opportunities the expatriates will have once they return home.

Once they arrive back in their home country, expatriate managers meet with cross-cultural trainers during debriefing sessions. They are also given the opportunity to showcase their experiences to their peers, subordinates, and superiors in special information exchanges.

However, Monsanto's repatriation program focuses on more than just business; it also attends to the family's reentry. Monsanto has found that difficulties with repatriation often have more to do with personal and family-related issues than with work-related issues. But the personal matters obviously affect an employee's on-the-job performance, so it is important for the company to pay attention to such issues.

This is why Monsanto offers returning employees an opportunity to work through personal difficulties. About three months after they return home, expatriates meet for three hours at work with several colleagues of their choice. The debriefing session is a conversation aided by a trained facilitator who has an outline to help the expatriate cover all the important aspects of the repatriation. The debriefing allows the employee to share important experiences and to enlighten managers, colleagues, and friends about his or her expertise so others within the organization can use some of the global knowledge. According to one participant, "It sounds silly, but it's such a hectic time in the family's life, you don't have time to sit down and take stock of what's happening. You're going through the move, transitioning to a new job, a new house, and the children may be going to a new school. This is a kind of oasis; a time to talk and put your feelings on the table." Apparently it works; since the program was introduced, the attrition rate among returning expatriates has dropped sharply.[50]

The key to solving this problem is good human resource planning. Just as the HRM function needs to develop good selection and training programs for its expatriates, it also needs to develop good programs for reintegrating expatriates back into work life within their home-country organization, for preparing them for changes in their physical and professional landscape, and for utilizing the knowledge they acquired while abroad. For an example of the kind of program that might be used, see the accompanying Management Focus that looks at the repatriation program developed by Monsanto.

Management Development and Strategy

Management development programs are designed to increase the overall skill levels of managers through a mix of ongoing management education and rotations of managers through a number of jobs within the firm to give them varied experiences. They are attempts to improve the overall productivity and quality of the firm's management resources.

International businesses are increasingly using management development as a strategic tool. This is particularly true in firms pursuing a transnational strategy, as increasing numbers are. Such firms need a strong unifying corporate culture and informal management networks to assist in coordination and control. In addition, transnational firm managers need to be able to detect pressures for local responsiveness—and that requires them to understand the culture of a host country.

Management development programs help build a unifying corporate culture by socializing new managers into the norms and value systems of the firm. In-house company training programs and intense interaction during off-site training can foster esprit de corps—shared experiences, informal networks, perhaps a company language or jargon—as well as develop technical competencies. These training events often include songs, picnics, and sporting events that promote feelings of togetherness. These rites of integration may include "initiation rites" wherein personal culture is stripped, company uniforms are donned (e.g., T-shirts bearing the company logo), and humiliation is inflicted (e.g., a pie in the face). All these activities aim to strengthen a manager's identification with the company.[51]

Bringing managers together in one location for extended periods and rotating them through different jobs in several countries help the firm build an informal management network. Such a network can then be used as a conduit for exchanging valuable performance-enhancing knowledge within the organization.[52] Consider the Swedish telecommunications company Ericsson. Interunit cooperation is extremely important at Ericsson, particularly for transferring know-how and core competencies from the parent to foreign subsidiaries, from foreign subsidiaries to the parent, and between foreign subsidiaries. To facilitate cooperation, Ericsson transfers large numbers of people back and forth between headquarters and subsidiaries. Ericsson sends a team of 50 to 100 engineers and managers from one unit to another for a year or two. This establishes a network of interpersonal contacts. This policy is effective for both solidifying a common culture in the company and coordinating the company's globally dispersed operations.[53]

PERFORMANCE APPRAISAL

LO9-5

Performance appraisal systems are used to evaluate the performance of managers against some criteria that the firm judges to be important for the implementation of strategy and the attainment of a competitive advantage. A firm's performance appraisal systems are an important element of its control systems, and control systems are a central component of organizational architecture. A particularly thorny issue in many international businesses is how best to evaluate the performance of expatriate managers.[54] This section looks at this issue and considers guidelines for appraising expatriate performance.

Performance Appraisal Problems

Unintentional bias makes it difficult to evaluate the performance of expatriate managers objectively. In many cases, two groups evaluate the performance of expatriate managers—host-nation managers and home-office managers—and both are subject to bias. The host-nation managers may be biased by their own cultural frame of reference and expectations. For example, Oddou and Mendenhall report the case of a U.S. manager who introduced participative decision making while working in an Indian subsidiary.[55] The manager subsequently received a negative evaluation from host-country managers because in India, the strong social stratification means managers are seen as experts who should not have to ask subordinates for help. The local employees apparently viewed the U.S. manager's attempt at participatory management as an indication that he was incompetent and did not know his job.

Home-country managers' appraisals may be biased by distance and by their own lack of experience working abroad. Home-office managers are often not aware of what is going on in a foreign operation. Accordingly, they tend to rely on hard data in evaluating an expatriate's performance, such as the subunit's productivity, profitability, or market share. Such criteria may reflect factors outside the expatriate manager's control (e.g., adverse changes in exchange rates, economic downturns). Also, hard data do not take into account many less visible soft variables that are also important, such as an expatriate's ability to develop cross-cultural awareness and to work productively with local managers. Due to such biases, many expatriate managers believe that headquarters management evaluates them unfairly and does not fully appreciate the value of their skills and experience. This could be one reason many expatriates believe a foreign posting does not benefit their careers. In one study of personnel managers in U.S. multinationals, 56 percent of the managers surveyed stated that a foreign assignment is either detrimental or immaterial to one's career.[56]

Guidelines for Performance Appraisal

Several things can reduce bias in the performance appraisal process.[57] First, most expatriates appear to believe more weight should be given to an on-site manager's appraisal than to an off-site manager's appraisal. Due to proximity, an on-site manager is more likely to evaluate the soft variables that are important aspects of an expatriate's performance. The evaluation may be especially valid when the on-site manager is of the same nationality as the expatriate, since cultural bias should be alleviated. In practice, home-office managers often write performance evaluations after receiving input from on-site managers. When this is the case, most experts recommend that a former expatriate who served in the same location should be involved in the appraisal to help reduce bias. Finally, when the policy is for foreign on-site managers to write performance evaluations, home-office managers should be consulted before an on-site manager completes a formal termination evaluation. This gives the home-office manager the opportunity to balance what could be a very hostile evaluation based on a cultural misunderstanding.

COMPENSATION

LO19-6

Two issues are raised in every discussion of compensation practices in an international business. One is how compensation should be adjusted to reflect national differences in economic circumstances and compensation practices. The other issue is how expatriate managers should be paid. From a strategic perspective, the important point is that whatever compensation system is used, it should reward managers for taking actions that are consistent with the strategy of the enterprise.

National Differences in Compensation

Differences exist in the compensation of executives at the same level in various countries. The results of a survey undertaken by Towers Watson, for example, suggest that U.S. CEOs earn, on average, roughly double the pay of non-U.S. CEOs.[58]

National differences in compensation raise a perplexing question for an international business: Should the firm pay executives in different countries according to the prevailing standards in each country, or should it equalize pay on a global basis? The problem does not arise in firms pursuing ethnocentric or polycentric staffing policies. In ethnocentric firms, the issue can be reduced to that of how much home-country expatriates should be paid (which we consider later). As for polycentric firms, the lack of managers' mobility among national operations implies that pay can and should be kept country-specific. There would seem to be no point in paying executives in Great Britain the same as U.S. executives if they never work side by side.

However, this problem is very real in firms with geocentric staffing policies. A geocentric staffing policy is consistent with a transnational strategy. One aspect of this policy is the need for a cadre of international managers that may include many different nationalities. Should all members of such a cadre be paid the same salary and the same incentive pay? For a U.S.-based firm, this would mean raising the compensation of foreign nationals to U.S. levels, which could be expensive. If the firm does not equalize pay, it could cause considerable resentment among foreign nationals who are members of the international cadre and work with U.S. nationals. If a firm is serious about building an international cadre, it may have to pay its international executives the same basic salary irrespective of their country of origin or assignment. Currently, however, this practice is not widespread.

Over the past decade many firms have moved toward a compensation structure that is based on consistent global standards, with employees being evaluated by the same grading system and having access to the same bonus pay and benefits structure irrespective of where they work. Some 85 percent of the companies in a survey by Mercer Management Consulting stated they now have a global compensation strategy in place.[60] McDonald's, which is featured in the accompanying Management Focus, is one such enterprise. Another survey found that two-thirds of multinationals now exercise central control over the benefit plans offered in different nations.[61] However, except for a relative small cadre of internationally mobile executives, base pay in most firms is set with regard to local market conditions.

Expatriate Pay

The most common approach to expatriate pay is the balance sheet approach. According to Organizational Resources Consulting, some 80 percent of the 781 companies it surveyed used this approach.[62] This approach equalizes purchasing power across countries so employees can enjoy the same living standard in their foreign posting that they enjoyed at home. In addition, the approach provides financial incentives to offset qualitative differences between assignment locations.[63] Figure 19.2 shows a typical balance sheet. Note that home-country outlays for the employee are designated as income taxes, housing expenses, expenditures for goods and services (food, clothing, entertainment, etc.), and reserves (savings, pension contributions, etc.). The balance sheet approach attempts to provide expatriates with the same standard of living in their host countries as they enjoy at home plus a financial inducement (i.e., premium, incentive) for accepting an overseas assignment.

The components of the typical expatriate compensation package are a base salary, a foreign service premium, allowances of various types, tax differentials, and benefits. We briefly review each of these components.[64] An expatriate's total compensation package may amount to three times what he or she would cost the firm in a home-country posting. Because of the high cost of expatriates, many firms have reduced their use of them in recent years. However, a firm's ability to reduce its use of expatriates may be limited, particularly if it is pursuing an ethnocentric or geocentric staffing policy.

MANAGEMENT FOCUS

Global Compensation Practices at McDonald's

With more than 400,000 managers and senior staff employees in 119 countries around the world, by the early 2000s McDonald's realized it had to develop a consistent global compensation and performance appraisal strategy. After months of consultation with managers all over the world, the company began to roll out its new global compensation program in 2004.

One important element of this program calls for the corporate head office to provide local country managers with a menu of business principles to focus on in the coming year. These principles include areas such as customer service, marketing, and restaurant re-imaging. Each country manager then picks three to five areas to focus on for success in the local market. For example, if France is introducing a new menu item, it might create business targets around that for the year. Human resource managers then submit their business cases and targets to senior executives at headquarters for approval. At the end of the year, the country's annual incentive pool is based on how the region met its targets, as well as on the business unit's operating income. A portion of an individual employee's annual bonus is based on that mix.

The other portion of an employee's annual incentive is based on individual performance. McDonald's has always had a performance rating system, but in 2004 the company introduced global guidelines that suggest 20 percent of employees receive the highest rating, 70 percent the middle, and 10 percent the bottom. By giving guidelines rather than forced ranking, McDonald's hopes to encourage differentiation of performance while allowing for some local flexibility nuances. By providing principles and guidance, and yet allowing local managers to customize their compensation programs to meet local market demands, McDonald's also claims it has seen a reduction in turnover. The company's own internal surveys suggest more employees now believe that their compensation is fair and reflects local market conditions.[59]

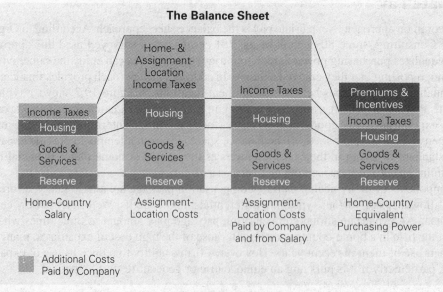

Figure 19.2 *The Balance Sheet Approach to Expatriate Pay*

Base Salary

An expatriate's base salary is normally in the same range as the base salary for a similar position in the home country. The base salary is normally paid in either the home-country currency or in the local currency.

Foreign Service Premium

A foreign service premium is extra pay the expatriate receives for working outside his or her country of origin. It is offered as an inducement to accept foreign postings. It compensates the expatriate for having to live in an unfamiliar country isolated from family and friends, having to deal with a new culture and language, and having to adapt to new work habits and practices. Many firms pay foreign service premiums as a percentage of base salary, ranging from 10 to 30 percent after tax, with 16 percent being the average premium.[65]

Allowances

Four types of allowances are often included in an expatriate's compensation package: hardship, housing, cost of living, and education. A hardship allowance is paid when the expatriate is being sent to a difficult location, usually defined as one where such basic amenities as health care, schools, and retail stores are grossly deficient by the standards of the expatriate's home country. A housing allowance is normally given to ensure that the expatriate can afford the same quality of housing in the foreign country as at home. In locations where housing is expensive (e.g., London, Tokyo), this allowance can be substantial— as much as 10 to 30 percent of the expatriate's total compensation package. A cost-of-living allowance ensures that the expatriate will enjoy the same standard of living in the foreign posting as at home. An education allowance ensures that an expatriate's children receive adequate schooling (by home-country standards). Host-country public schools are sometimes not suitable for an expatriate's children, in which case they must attend a private school.

Taxation

Unless a host country has a reciprocal tax treaty with the expatriate's home country, the expatriate may have to pay income tax to both the home- and host-country governments. When a reciprocal tax treaty is not in force, the firm typically pays the expatriate's income tax in the host country. In addition, firms normally make up the difference when a higher income tax rate in a host country reduces an expatriate's take-home pay.

Benefits

Many firms also ensure that their expatriates receive the same level of medical and pension benefits abroad that they received at home. This can be costly for the firm, because many benefits that are tax-deductible for the firm in the home country (e.g., medical and pension benefits) may not be deductible out of the country.

INTERNATIONAL LABOR RELATIONS   LO19-7

The HRM function of an international business is typically responsible for international labor relations. From a strategic perspective, the key issue in international labor relations is the degree to which organized labor can limit the choices of an international business. A firm's ability to integrate and consolidate its global operations to realize experience curve and location economies can be limited by organized labor, constraining the pursuit of a transnational or global standardization strategy. Prahalad and Doz cite the example of General Motors, which gained peace with labor unions in Germany by agreeing not to integrate and consolidate operations in the most efficient manner.[66] General Motors made substantial investments in Germany—matching its new investments in Austria and Spain—at the demand of the German metalworkers' unions.

One task of the HRM function is to foster harmony and minimize conflict between the firm and organized labor. With this in mind, this section is divided into three parts. First, we review organized labor's concerns about multinational enterprises. Second, we look at how organized labor has tried to deal with these concerns. And third, we look at how international businesses manage their labor relations to minimize labor disputes.

The Concerns of Organized Labor

Labor unions generally try to get better pay, greater job security, and better working conditions for their members through collective bargaining with management. Unions' bargaining power is derived largely from their ability to threaten to disrupt production, either by a strike or some other form of work protest (e.g., refusing to work overtime). This threat is credible, however, only insofar as management has no alternative but to employ union labor.

A principal concern of domestic unions about multinational firms is that the company can counter its bargaining power with the power to move production to another country. Ford, for example, clearly threatened British unions with a plan to move manufacturing to continental Europe unless British workers abandoned work rules that limited productivity, showed restraint in negotiating for wage increases, and curtailed strikes and other work disruptions.[67]

Another concern of organized labor is that an international business will keep highly skilled tasks in its home country and farm out only low-skilled tasks to foreign plants. Such a practice makes it relatively easy for an international business to switch production from one location to another as economic conditions warrant. Consequently, the bargaining power of organized labor is once more reduced.

A final union concern arises when an international business attempts to import employment practices and contractual agreements from its home country. When these practices are alien to the host country, organized labor fears the change will reduce its influence and power. This concern has surfaced in response to Japanese multinationals that have been trying to export their style of labor relations to other countries. For example, much to the annoyance of the United Auto Workers (UAW), many Japanese auto plants in the United States are not unionized. As a result, union influence in the auto industry is declining.

The Strategy of Organized Labor

Organized labor has responded to the increased bargaining power of multinational corporations by taking three actions: (1) trying to establish international labor organizations, (2) lobbying for national legislation to restrict multinationals, and (3) trying to achieve international regulations on multinationals through such organizations as the United Nations. These efforts have not been very successful.

In the 1960s, organized labor began to establish international trade secretariats (ITSs) to provide worldwide links for national unions in particular industries. The long-term goal was to be able to bargain transnationally with multinational firms. Organized labor believed that by coordinating union action across countries through an ITS, it could counter the power of a multinational corporation by threatening to disrupt production on an international scale. For example, Ford's threat to move production from Great Britain to other European locations would not have been credible if the unions in various European countries had united to oppose it.

However, the ITSs have had virtually no real success. Although national unions may want to cooperate, they also compete with each other to attract investment from international businesses, and hence jobs for their members. For example, in attempting to gain new jobs for their members, national unions in the auto industry often court auto firms that are seeking locations for new plants. One reason Nissan chose to build its European production facilities in Great Britain rather than Spain was that the British unions agreed to greater concessions than the Spanish unions did. As a result of such competition between national unions, cooperation is difficult to establish.

A further impediment to cooperation has been the wide variation in union structure. Trade unions developed independently in each country. As a result, the structure and ideology of unions tend to vary significantly from country to country, as does the nature of collective bargaining. For example, in Great Britain, France, and Italy, many unions are controlled by left-wing socialists, who view collective bargaining through the lens of "class conflict." In contrast, most union leaders in Germany, the Netherlands, Scandinavia, and Switzerland are far more moderate politically. The ideological gap between union leaders in different countries has made cooperation difficult. Divergent ideologies are reflected in radically different views about the role of a union in society and the stance unions should take toward multinationals.

Organized labor has also met with only limited success in its efforts to get national and international bodies to regulate multinationals. Such international organizations as the International Labor Organization (ILO) and the Organization for Economic Cooperation and Development (OECD) have adopted codes of conduct for multinational firms to follow in labor relations. However, these guidelines are not as far-reaching as many unions would like. They also do not provide any enforcement mechanisms. Many researchers report that such guidelines are of only limited effectiveness.[68]

Approaches to Labor Relations

International businesses differ markedly in their approaches to international labor relations. The main difference is the degree to which labor relations activities are centralized or decentralized. Historically, most international businesses have decentralized international labor relations activities to their foreign subsidiaries because labor laws, union power, and the nature of collective bargaining varied so much from country to country. It made sense to decentralize the labor relations function to local managers. The belief was that there was no way central management could effectively handle the complexity of simultaneously managing labor relations in a number of different environments.

Although this logic still holds, the trend is toward greater centralized control. This trend reflects international firms' attempts to rationalize their global operations. The general rise in competitive pressure in industry after industry has made it more important for firms to control their costs. Because labor costs account for such a large percentage of total costs, some firms are now using the threat to move production to another country in their negotiations with unions to change work rules and limit wage increases (as Ford did in Europe). Because such a move would involve major new investments and plant closures, this bargaining tactic requires the input of headquarters management. Thus, the level of centralized input into labor relations is increasing.

In addition, the realization is growing that the way work is organized within a plant can be a major source of competitive advantage. Much of the competitive advantage of Japanese automakers, for example, has been attributed to the use of self-managing teams, job rotation, cross-training, and the like in their Japanese plants.[69] To replicate their domestic performance in foreign plants, the Japanese firms have tried to replicate their work practices there. This often brings them into direct conflict with traditional work practices in those countries, as sanctioned by the local labor unions, so the Japanese firms have often made their foreign investments contingent on the local union accepting a radical change in work practices. To achieve this, the headquarters of many Japanese firms bargains directly with local unions to get union agreement to changes in work rules before committing to an investment. For example, before Nissan decided to invest in northern England, it got a commitment from British unions to agree to a change in traditional work practices. By its very nature, pursuing such a strategy requires centralized control over the labor relations function.

Chapter Summary

This chapter focused on human resource management in international businesses. HRM activities include human resource strategy, staffing, performance evaluation, management development, compensation, and labor relations. None of these activities is performed in a vacuum; all must be appropriate to the firm's strategy. The chapter made the following points:

1. Firm success requires HRM policies to be congruent with the firm's strategy and with its formal and informal structure and controls.

2. Staffing policy is concerned with selecting employees who have the skills required to perform particular jobs. Staffing policy can be a tool for developing and promoting a corporate culture.

3. An ethnocentric approach to staffing policy fills all key management positions in an international business with parent-country nationals. The policy is congruent with an international strategy. A drawback is that ethnocentric staffing can result in cultural myopia.

4. A polycentric staffing policy uses host-country nationals to manage foreign subsidiaries and parent-country nationals for the key positions at corporate headquarters. This approach can minimize the dangers of cultural myopia, but it can create a gap between home- and host-country operations. The policy is best suited to a localization strategy.

5. A geocentric staffing policy seeks the best people for key jobs throughout the organization, regardless of their nationality. This approach is consistent with building a strong unifying culture and informal management network and is well suited to both global standardization and transnational strategies. Immigration policies of national governments may limit a firm's ability to pursue this policy.

6. A prominent issue in the international staffing literature is expatriate failure, defined as the premature return of an expatriate manager to his or her home country. The costs of expatriate failure can be substantial.

7. Expatriate failure can be reduced by selection procedures that screen out inappropriate candidates. The most successful expatriates seem to be those who have high self-esteem and self-confidence, can get along well with others, are willing to attempt to communicate in a foreign language, and can empathize with people of other cultures.

8. Training can lower the probability of expatriate failure. It should include cultural training, language training, and practical training, and it should be provided to both the expatriate manager and the spouse.

9. Management development programs attempt to increase the overall skill levels of managers through a mix of ongoing management education and rotation of managers through different jobs within the firm to give them varied experiences. Management development is often used as a strategic tool to build a strong unifying culture and informal management network, both of which support transnational and global standardization strategies.

10. It can be difficult to evaluate the performance of expatriate managers objectively because of unintentional bias. A firm can take a number of steps to reduce this bias.

11. Country differences in compensation practices raise a difficult question for an international business: Should the firm pay executives in different countries according to the standards in each country or equalize pay on a global basis?

12. The most common approach to expatriate pay is the balance sheet approach. This approach aims to equalize purchasing power so employees can enjoy the same living standard in their foreign posting that they had at home.

13. A key issue in international labor relations is the degree to which organized labor can limit the choices available to an international business. A firm's ability to pursue a transnational or global standardization strategy can be significantly constrained by the actions of labor unions.

14. A principal concern of organized labor is that the multinational can counter union bargaining power with threats to move production to another country.

15. Organized labor has tried to counter the bargaining power of multinationals by forming international labor organizations. In general, these efforts have not been effective.

India's Global Leadership in the BPO-ITeS Industry*

The Economic Benefits of Offshoring

Offshoring, in addition to helping overcome the expected domestic labor shortfall, will also continue to provide other significant benefits to the US economy. For every USD 100 offshored to a low-cost location, USD 130–USD 145 will be reinvested in the US economy. The benefits will be realized through the creation of larger global markets for US-based goods and services. For example, offshore firms require substantial technical and communications infrastructure. US based companies and their subsidiaries often provide this infrastructure. Further, the resulting prosperity of the offshore labor force and their surrounding communities will create additional markets for US goods and services (including entertainment, transportation, financial and insurance services, consumer goods, and high-technology products).

According to a research by META Group Inc., 80 percent of global organizations will outsource at least one function by 2005, while 70 percent of that group will renew their outsourcing contracts, many will reduce both the scope and the duration of the original agreement[70]. With an increased focus to integrate business functions with an intended IT strategy and architecture, combined with the emerging trend of asset-leasing arrangements provided by third party vendors, there was a possibility that firms might go for curtailing their outsourcing engagements. However, despite reduced scope and duration of outsourcing, it still seems to be a viable option for firms seeking to remain competitive. Immediate market growth lies in application development and maintenance (20 percent). The offshore outsourcing market was expected to continue to grow by nearly 20 percent annually through 2008.

Strategic Review of India's BPO Industry

Outsourcing has its conceptualization roots in the David Ricardo's comparative advantage theory. However, the definition of outsourcing has undergone a sea change in the past few decades. What started off as

---

*Case prepared and updated by Professor Arun Kumar Jain, Indian Institute of Management - Lucknow in 2013 for the purpose of classroom discussion on International Business and Industry Evolution.

This case is to be used for: a) understanding various international trade theories and making a comparison between them. Please look at chart that highlights the supporting nature of Competitive Advantage of Nation and Global Competitiveness Alignment Matrix in Chapter 6; and, b) for Human Resource Management; and, c) Global Supply Chains.

a shift of manufacturing to countries with cheap labor during the Industrial Revolution, has taken a new connotation in the post-Industrial Society scenario. Essentially, Business Process Outsourcing is the act of transferring some of an organization's repeated non-core and core business processes to an outside provider to achieve cost reductions while improving service quality and increasing shareholder value. According to the Gartner Group[71], Business Process Outsourcing is the delegation of one or more *business processes* to an *external provider* who, in turn, *owns, administers, and manages* the selected process(es), based upon *defined and measurable* performance metrics to *improve overall business performance*.

In the face of the volatility in economic environment and currency, 2011 recorded steady growth for the technology and related services sector, with worldwide spending exceeding USD 1.7 trillion, a growth of 5.4 percent over 2010. Software products, IT and BPO services continued to lead, accounting for over USD 1 trillion – 63 percent of the total spend. The year saw renewed demand for overall global sourcing which recorded a healthy growth driven by record contracting activity in small size deals, as clients aim to conserve cash flows and, at the same time, try out new models and service offerings.

New networking technologies had made it possible for global companies to seek the lowest cost solutions from anywhere in the world for all the activities that could be digitized. Companies could outsource their non-core functions such as human resources, finance and accounting, customer relationship management, IT services, etc., to a third party mainly to be able to focus their resources on their core activities and, hence, reduce their operational costs.

Although used interchangeably, there is a marked difference between BPO and IT services outsourcing. BPO involves an entire end-to-end process, not just a task, as is often the case with IT outsourcing. The business rationale behind BPO was that outsourcing saves money and focuses scarce management time and resources on a few core competencies. Another reason behind the surge in BPO was that companies were becoming increasingly demanding towards value-added services. The ultimate goal was to link business performance to increased business value.

The Changed Thinking in 21st Century—the Pressures on MNCs

The quick rise of the global BPO industry is a classic case of globalization and technology feeding each other into a virtuous cycle. The more the companies globalized, the more technology they required; and the more technology requirement meant focusing on the core and outsourcing the rest from any part of the world to achieve the desired efficiencies and productivity standards (Figure 1). The globalized logistics value-chain and Internet technologies meant that global companies could efficiently access resources from any part of the world.

Classifying the Industry

IT Enabled Services-Business Process Outsourcing, (ITeS-BPO) could broadly be categorized into two major components, viz.

i. The sectors or verticals (manufacturing, ICT, energy, financial services, technology, energy, government and public sector, retail and transportation, leisure and tourism, health sector), and
ii. The service lines or process areas or horizontals. These are primarily categorized into three main subcategories and subprocesses (Figure 2)[72]:

BPO – Transforming the Value Chain

To understand the various value-generating activities in the entire business processes, so as to develop insights of the industry-level critical success factors, we borrow the value chain concept of the previous century.

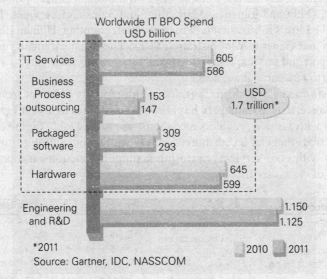

Figure 1 *Worldwide spend on offshoring*

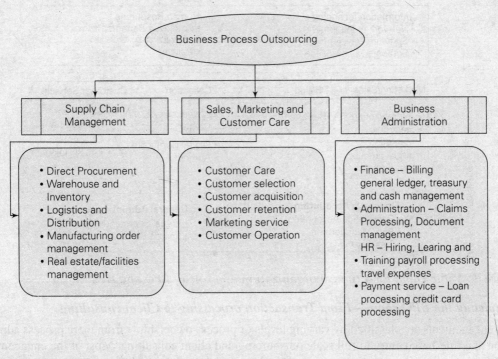

Figure 2 *BPO service lines*

A typical value chain for any industry comprises of traditional primary functions such as inbound logistics, Operations, Outbound logistics, Marketing, and Sales and Services. In addition, there are 'support' functions like Firm's Infrastructure, Finance and Accounting, Human Resource Management, Information Systems and General Administration tasks. The usual extended functions like training, billing, customer support and service, were undertaken by the firms internally — now the technological advances allow firms to outsource these as well.

The new and transformed value-chain, thus, looks substantially different from the traditional one. The convergence of voice, data and imagery has allowed companies to hive off entire departments and enter in relationships with service providers anywhere across the globe. Figure 3 provides a template for the potential functions that can be outsourced in a typical manufacturing firm. The BPO and ITeS work in conjunction with core services, performing support functions and providing base for the successful execution of core activities.

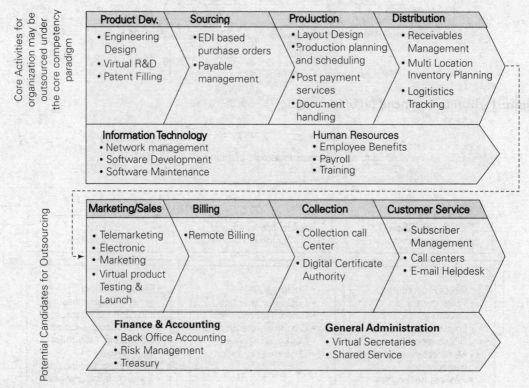

Figure 3 *Value chain for a typical organization and role of BPO and ITeS*[4]

Completing the BPO chain—From Transaction processing to Client consulting

BPO engagements are classified by varying levels of process ownership – from mere process administration and rule-based entry to full scale outsourcing and client consulting. Most of the engagements, till today, are primarily in the lower rung of the ladder and the output is also quite homogeneous. The industry was moving towards commoditization where the key business driver here was pure cost reduction.

Some firms created a unique and differentiated positioning in the BPO space, by gradually moving over to full process outsourcing and becoming a consulting partner to the client. The service offerings like customer care, billing, administration, accounts and receivables, etc., come under the lower end while processes like process reengineering, technology services, quality improvement, etc., are part of the higher end services (Figure 4).[73]

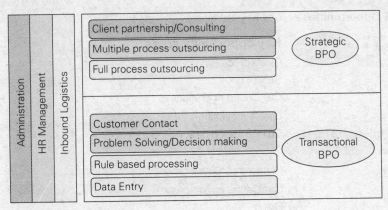

Figure 4 *BPO value chain*

Service lines and revenue projections

IT enabled services (BPO) in India has grown significantly over the last few years and is expected to reach anywhere between $21-$24 Billion by 2008

Service line	NASSCOM Estimates	Rationale
HR	3.5–4.0	• Globally the biggest opportunity • Service line yet to take off in India • Very strong BPO players, who have not locked at India
Customer Care	8.0–8.5	• Proven robust business model • Constitutes bulk of current ITES activity • Strong presence of third party and global BPO majors
Payment Services	3.0–3.5	• Heightened activity around credit card and cheque processing • Big processors at pilot stage
Content Development and Others	2.5–3.0	• Engineering and design services well established with multiple third party and capative vendors • Intense competition from other hubs for animation
Administration	1.5–2.0	• Several pilots in advanced stages • High quality and necessary talent available
Finance	2.5–3.0	• Has emerged much faster than expected • Very high-quality and low-cost manpower available
Total	21-24	

Source: Nasscom-McKinsey analysis

Figure 5 *BPO service Offerings*

Top three service lines: Customer Care, HR and Administration constitute about 70 percent of the long term ITeS potential. Banking and insurance (within financial services) were likely to provide the maximum opportunity driven by the high cost base and high extent of offshorable processes in these verticals. Medical BPO too was emerging as an attractive opportunity and large healthcare companies have set up Medical BPO facilities. In addition, the verticals offer large opportunities (Table 1):

TABLE 1 ITeS Opportunities Across Key Verticals

Vertical	Key opportunity areas
Insurance	Claim processing
	Servicing
	Call Centre operations
Retail Financial Services/Retail Banking Services	Loan Processing
	Call Centre operations
Pharmaceuticals	Research & Development
Telecom	Call Centre operations
	Billing
Automotive	Engineering and Design
	Accounts Payable/ Receivable
Airlines	Revenue Accounting
	Call Centre Operations
	Frequent Flyer programmes

The Indian BPO Industry

The IT industry in India began as a domestic industry and eventually spread to international markets. The BPO business, on the other hand, started with a strong export focus. While this industry began with a few key foreign investments in Bangalore around IC design, the real momentum arose from the immigration patterns of individuals and the offering of skilled labor via "body shopping" to firms in the US. The driver of this — consistent with the constraints of software development — was not labor cost, but access to skilled labor.

Declining enrollments by US citizens within engineering professions, the increasing expansion of foreign enrollments at US universities, the growth of US demand, and the limits on Indian domestic industry opportunities combined to create a demand for new sources of skilled labor for the US software industry.

With the rise in quality of the offshore environment, improved management capabilities and new government policies tailored specifically for software, the shackles towards foreign investments in India were loosened. Global firms began to locate development centers within India to access the highest quality labor at the lowest search and employment cost. The combination of these trends — maximization of cost savings, access to labor at the source, and the benefits of agglomerated production — underpinned the emergence of new regional sites of software within India.

The mid-1990s witnessed the rise of new centers of software development beyond Bangalore, most importantly Hyderabad, and Andhra Pradesh. Successful BPO companies understood the need to invest in quality and consistency at early stages using tools such as Six Sigma, COPC, and ISO. India became world class with respect to many of these operational measures.

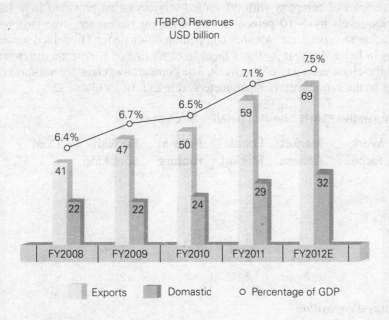

Source: NASSCOM

Figure 6 *IT/ITeS growth*

Source: *www.nasscom.org* website

The ITeS-BPO sector steadily increased its share in total revenue of India's IT software and services industry, rising from 6.5 percent in 1998–99 to an estimated 29 percent by 2004. It grew by 46 percent in 2003–04 to USD 3.6 billion and currently employs around 250,000 professionals. It was expected to contribute 37 percent to the revenues of Indian IT software and services industry by 2007. Global clients save costs in the range of 40–60 percent depending on the process 'offshored'.

India's Advantages

India surpasses other competitors in terms of employment, number of companies sourcing ITeS and the spectrum of verticals and services lines it offers. India is the largest ITeS player in the world in terms of manpower and has the potential to generate direct employment for one million by 2008. India, in particular, is witnessing rapid growth due to its cost advantage, the early success achieved by the reference of light house customers and government initiatives implemented to improve location attractiveness.

The manpower cost in India is around 70–80 percent less than in US and UK. Salaries in the US are still, on an average, nearly 10 times higher than those in India (USD 80,286 versus USD 8,593).

India's proposition was based on the availability of a significant pool of appropriately skilled and trained resources at a competitive price. Mainly the advantage was driven by

- Availability of appropriately skilled resources
- Lower cost of manpower (1/5th to 1/10th) and
- Ability to generate better quality of work, more efficiently

There are examples of company with off-shored services being provided from India which have improved service levels by 5–10 percent across different parameters like customer satisfaction, response time, accuracy, speed, etc. Another compelling rationale for IT-enabled service companies to base operations in India was that it allows them to capitalize on time zone differences and provide services round-the-clock each day of the week. The comparative chart for various countries and the relative ranking on the various relevant parameters were as follows (Table 2):

TABLE 2 Comparative Matrix Showing Relative Strengths

Country	Work force	Market Access	Local Market	Infra-st ructure	English speaking	Cost	
New Zealand	2	2	2	2	3	2	Ratings are based on a scale of 1 to 3, with 1 being lowest and 3 being highest
Cambodia	1	2	2	2	2	2	
Japan	1	2	1	3	1	3	
Hong Kong	1	2	2	2	2	2	
India	3	2	2	2	3	1	
UK	1	2	2	3	2	3	

The Indian Value-Proposition

Apart from savings in manpower and allied costs, Indian companies offer 20 percent higher productivity in comparison to other competing countries like Philippines, Canada and Australia. In terms of quality of services offered, India ranks 30 percent higher than any other region. India has maintained its global competitiveness, offering the best combination of cost-quality-scalability as compared to other off-shore destinations like Philippines and China. Indian productivity-quality-cost model has emerged as an optimal value proposition for the software and service industry. Indian ITeS-BPO companies were adopting global quality standards like Six-sigma, COPC and ISO 9001.

India had quickly emerged as a leader in the field of IT-enabled or remote services. The country's competitive advantage in providing these services is well known: cost effectiveness, world-class quality, high reliability, and rapid delivery, all of it powered by state-of-the-art technologies. The following map gives a diagrammatic representation of India's advantages vis-à-vis other countries (Figure 7).

Major Worries for the Indian BPO-ITeS Industry

- **Reckless Start-ups**

  Although the BPO Industry promises huge profits and potential yet a vast majority of the 310 start-ups are headed for a dead-end was alarming news. According to industry research, the capacity utilization of these firms was less than one of the three shifts. These companies have driven down prices to grab business, but have failed to deliver. Moreover they do not show much acumen towards people, processes or technologies- the three key elements of the BPO business.

- **Poor Infrastructure**

  Another major concern was poor infrastructure. Although state of art technology was used for telecom networks, yet getting a connection still takes up to three months. Unreliable power supply was forcing units to create their own back-ups. In terms of roads and airports also, there was a dire need of repairs and upgrades.

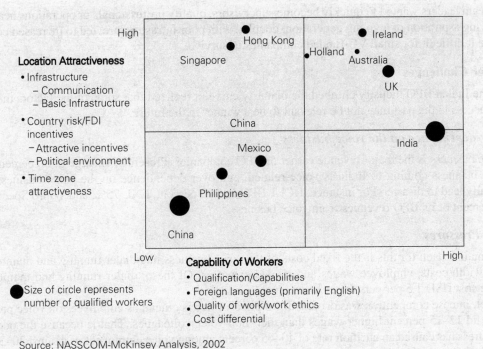

Location Attractiveness
- Infrastructure
  – Communication
  – Basic Infrastructure
- Country risk/FDI incentives
  – Attractive incentives
  – Political environment
- Time zone attractiveness

● Size of circle represents number of qualified workers

Capability of Workers
- Qualification/Capabilities
- Foreign languages (primarily English)
- Quality of work/work ethics
- Cost differential

Source: NASSCOM-McKinsey Analysis, 2002

Figure 7 *Location/Capability of workers*

- ## High Attrition Rates and Rising Aspirations

  A major problem was the high attrition and growth aspirations of the workforce. At the end of March 2004, Indian BPO industry employed around 245,100 people compared to 171,000 last year. The industry witnessed a hiring growth rate of 40–42 percent. At least 60,000 of the 171,000 workforce changed jobs within one year. Thus, such an attrition rate clubbed with the high hiring growth rate seemed a matter of concern. Looking at the value chain, attrition rates were much higher at the lower end of value chain (like call centers) compared to the higher end (like engineering). Similarly, attrition rates in non-voice based processing was much lesser compared to voice based processing.

TABLE 3 Attrition Rates in BPO-ITeS Industry Across the Globe

Attrition rates	%
US	42
Australia	29
Europe	24
India	18
Global Average	24

*Source-*Times News*, New York

Team leaders wanted to quickly become supervisors, quality professionals or operations heads. The growing aspiration of a young generation, coupled with poor infrastructure, led to increased costs and made it difficult for small VC-funded companies to survive.

Other Challenges

As the Indian BPO industry climbed the maturity curve, it realized that some of the factors that led to its success in the past may not be relevant to be a winner in the future.

Over-dependence on the voice business

Voice business is the major revenue earner of BPO companies. Presently, upsurge of 60 percent of the BPO business coming to India is voice-related, and over-dependence on the voice business could actually lead to disaster. For instance, HCLT BPO had 90 percent, EXL 75%, and Wipro Spectramind 80 percent of its BPO revenues from voice business.

Cost Pressures

The main reason for this is the fixed costs of the voice business like dialer running and maintenance, bandwidth costs, employee wages and related expenses. Of these, dialer running and maintenance alone cost USD 1.5 per person per hour.

Yet, intense competition was driving down prices. Price is crucial as employees on voice processes are paid 12–15 percent higher wages than their non-voice colleagues. That is because the odd hours and stress has caused an attrition rate of 40–45 percent among voice employees as against 30–35% for non-voice work. This increases recruitment and training costs. An estimate of INR 45,000–50,000 is spent on training an agent and if he leaves within three to five months, it increases overall costs of operations.

Second, the overall costs of BPO operations are rising rapidly. Unless Indian firms graduate to more value-added business — or contain costs — they will become financially unviable given the rock-bottom prices in the business.

For non-voice work like transactions processing, a company billing below USD 6 will be unable to recover costs. So, if small players desperate for deals want to survive, price cutting will only lead to a quicker end.

The weakening dollar added to cost pressure. Added to this, for some companies especially the ones into technology help-desk operations, customer acquisition costs run to about 10–15 percent of the revenues.

Lack of Managerial Expertise

The third factor is the lack of managerial experience in dealing with large USD 100-million contracts. In fact, for the dozen-odd big Indian players, getting to the USD 100-million club will depend on their ability to ramp up operations rapidly. Here, the 40 percent average attrition rate is the biggest hurdle. More importantly, firms will need to consolidate business within a few clients. Ideally, for a 10,000-people center, there should be only 25 clients. Otherwise, the management will be stretched too thin. Relationship building will be a problem and companies will start losing control.

But ramping up operations with just a handful of clients will, in turn, depend on how quickly Indian BPO companies were able to capture more business from the same clients. The winners will be those who can convince their clients to trust them with more end-to-end processes. Most companies were doing business task outsourcing — data entry, staffing, payroll processing or call centre work. These are subsets of large processes.

Government Initiatives

As a part of the National Electronics Policy, the Government of India is planning to set-up 15 new laboratories under public-private-partnership (PPP) model for hardware and software testing. The labs will facilitate registration and testing of IT products before they are launched in the market. FDI up to 100 percent under the automatic route is allowed in Data processing, software development and computer consultancy services; software supply services; business and management consultancy services, market research services, technical testing and analysis services.

In the 12th Five Year Plan (2012–17), the Department of Information Technology proposes to strengthen and extend the existing core infrastructure projects to provide more horizontal connectivity, build redundancy connectivity, undertake energy audits of State Data Centers (SDCs), etc. The core infrastructure including fiber optic-based connectivity will be leveraged and additional 150,000 Common Service Centers (CSCs) will be set-up to create the right Governance and service delivery ecosystem at the Panchayats.

Some of the major initiatives taken by the Government to promote IT and ITeS sector in India are:

- Fast-track process for setting up of centers of National Institute of Electronics and Information Technology (NIELIT) in Northeast India
- Liberalized issue of short term work visas, a move which will make it easier for Indian IT professionals to take up assignments in Brazil
- India and Vietnam signing two memorandums of understanding (MoU) for partnership in the field of information, communications and technology (ICT)
- Approval of the National Policy on Information Technology 2012. The policy aims to increase revenues of IT and ITES industry from USD 100 billion to USD 300 billion by 2020 and expand exports from USD 69 billion to USD 200 billion by 2020
- Plans for setting up 15 new laboratories for testing hardware and software products under public-private partnership (PPP) model

Road Ahead

As IT is increasingly gaining traction in small and medium business activities, the sector offers impressive growth opportunities and is estimated at approximately USD 230 billion–USD 250 billion by 2020. In a bid to reduce cost, governments across the world are exploring outsourcing and global sourcing options.

Technologies, such as telemedicine, mHealth (mobile), remote monitoring solutions and clinical information systems, would continue to boost demand for IT service across the globe. IT sophistication in the utilities segment and the need for standardization of the process are expected to drive demand.

Digitization of content and increased connectivity is leading to a rise in IT adoption by media. Emerging technologies present an entire new gamut of opportunities for IT firms in India. Social, mobility, analytics and cloud (SMAC) provide USD 1 trillion opportunity. Cloud represents the largest opportunity under SMAC, increasing at a CAGR of approximately 30 percent to around USD 650 billion–USD 700 billion by 2020. Social media is the second most lucrative segment for IT firms, offering a USD 250 billion market opportunity by 2020.

(Exchange Rate Used: INR 1 = USD 0.0148 as on August 29, 2013)

References: *Media Reports, Press Releases, Department of Industrial Policy and Promotion (DIPP) statistics, Department of Information and Technology*

http://www.ibef.org/industry/information-technology-india.aspx

Top 10 players in IT Services in India*

S.No	Company Name
1	Tata Consultancy Services Ltd
2	Infosys Ltd
3	Wipro Ltd
4	HCL Technologies Ltd
5	Mahindra IT & Business Services
6	MphasiS Ltd
7	iGate
8	Larsen & Toubro Infotech Ltd
9	Syntel Ltd
10	CSC, India

*Source: www.nasscom.org Website accessed on Feb 12, 2013.

Note: This list does not include some companies whose corporate headquarters are located outside India, but have significant India-centric delivery capabilities, and have not shared their India-centric revenue figures. Had they been ranked based on their India revenues, companies such as Accenture, Cognizant, HP, Capgemini, Oracle and IBM and would also have appeared in this ranking.

Appendix A: Differences between ITeS and BPO

Feature	BPO	ITeS
Time Frame	BPO is a continuous process. This makes it more involving with the client. However, this also entails subtle relationship management with the client.	ITeS is project to project. Therefore the involvement with the client is temporary.
Margins	Margins are higher compared to ITeS.	Margins are lower
Stability	BPO is more stable. The cost of changing the vendor is huge for the client. Also, the revenue flow is more uniform.	ITeS is less stable as it is project to project. Also the clients are temporary.
Offshoreability	The BPO business is more offshoreable. This implies that cost of providing is lower. The cost of under-utilization of capacity is also lower.	The ITeS business is less offshoreable.
Access to manpower	Training burden is high as lot of effort goes into converting raw manpower to effective workforce.	Access to manpower is easy as fresh recruits from engineering colleges are near-ready to commence job straightaway.

Appendix B[74]

Key Facts about IT Hubs in India

- **Bangalore**
  - Is the silicon valley of India
  - Took the lead in the mid 90's to become the IT hub of India
  - Most global IT organizations have their offices in Bangalore

- **Hyderabad**
  - Developed as a late entrant in the field
  - Primarily due to the impetus of their state Chief Minister – C Naidu
  - Is at par with Bangalore today
  - Boasts of a huge talent pool of IT employees
  - One of the fastest growing cities in the country

- **Delhi**
  - Mainly a center for Back Office and BPO organizations
  - Is expected to grow in the future
  - Suburbs (Eg. Gurgaon) are seeing more activity than proper Delhi

- **Mumbai (Bombay)**
  - Has become a natural IT Hub due to its financial Importance
  - State government is eccouraging IT Enabled Service organizations
  - Cost of operations is high

- **Pune**
  - In close proximity to Mumbai (Bombay)
  - May replace Mumbai as the IT hub in the west

Summary

The rapid rise of the global Business Process Outsourcing and IT Enabled Services (BPO-ITeS) industry highlights theoretical and conceptualization issues, such as

- How an industry globalizes suddenly from nowhere
- How countries can leverage knowledge-based yet inherent advantages
- The challenges of sustaining a country's leadership position in an industry.

Critical Thinking and Discussion Questions

1. What are the main advantages and disadvantages of the ethnocentric, polycentric, and geocentric approaches to staffing policy? When is each approach appropriate?
2. Research suggests that many expatriate employees encounter problems that limit both their effectiveness in a foreign posting and their contribution to the company when they return home. What are the main causes and consequences of these problems, and how might a firm reduce the occurrence of such problems?
3. What is the link between an international business's strategy and its human resource management policies, particularly with regard to the use of expatriate employees and their pay scale?
4. In what ways can organized labor constrain the strategic choices of an international business? How can an international business limit these constraints?
5. Reread the Management Focus on McDonald's global compensation practices. How does the McDonald's approach help the company take local differences into account when reviewing the performance of different country managers and awarding bonus pay?

Research Task ⚡globalEDGE globaledge.msu.edu

Global Human Resource Management

Use the globalEDGE website (globaledge.msu.edu) to complete the following exercises:

Exercise 1

The impact of strikes and lockouts on business activities can be substantial. Since your manufacturing company is planning to expand its operations in the Asian markets, you have to identify the countries where strikes and lockouts could introduce interruptions to your operations. Using *labor statistics* from the International Labour Organization (ILO) to develop your report, identify the three Asian countries with the highest number of strikes and lockouts, as well as the total number of lost worker days. What types of precautions can your company take to prevent interruptions from occurring in these markets?

Exercise 2

You work in the human resource department at the headquarters of a multinational corporation. Your company is about to send a number of managers overseas as expatriates (or expats) to France and New Zealand. You need to create an executive summary evaluating, comparing, and contrasting the possible issues expats may encounter in these two countries. Your manager tells you that a tool called *Expat Explorer* created by HSBC can assist you in your task.

Closing CASE

MMC China

It had been a very bad morning for John Ross, the general manager of MMC's Chinese joint venture. He had just gotten off the phone with his boss in St Louis, Phil Smith, who was demanding to know why the joint venture's return on investment was still in the low single digits four years after Ross had taken over the top post in the operation. "We had expected much better performance by now," Smith said, "particularly given your record of achievement; you need to fix this John! Our patience is not infinite. You know the corporate goal is for a 20 percent return on investment for operating units, and your unit is not even close to that." John Ross had a very bad feeling that Smith had just fired a warning shot across his bow. There was an implicit threat underlying Smith's demands for improved performance. For the first time in his 20-year career at MMC, Ross felt that his job was on the line.

MMC was a U.S.-based multinational electronics enterprise with sales of $2 billion and operations in more than 10 countries. MMC China specialized in the mass production of printed circuit boards for companies in the cell phone and computer industries. MMC was a joint venture with Shanghai Electronic Corporation, a former state-owned enterprise that held 49 percent of the joint-venture equity (MMC held the rest). While MMC held a majority of the equity, the company had to consult with its partner before making major investments or changing employment levels.

John Ross had been running MMC China for the past four years. He had arrived at MMC China after a very successful career at MMC, which included extended postings in Mexico and Hungary. When he took the China position, Ross thought that if he succeeded, he would probably be in line for one of the top jobs at corporate headquarters within a few years. Ross had known that he was taking on a challenge with MMC China, but nothing prepared him for what he found there. The joint venture was a mess. Operations were horribly inefficient. Despite low wages, productivity was being killed by poor product quality, lax inventory controls, and high employee turnover. The venture probably employed too many people, but MMC's Chinese partner seemed to view the venture as a job-creation program and repeatedly objected to any plans for cutting the workforce. To make matters worse, MMC China had failed to keep up with the latest developments in manufacturing technology, and it was falling behind competitors. Ross was determined to change this, but it had not been easy.

To improve operations, Ross had put in a request to corporate HR for two specialists from the United States to work with the Chinese production employees. It had been a disaster. One had lasted three months before requesting a transfer home for personal reasons. Apparently, his spouse hated China. The other had stayed for a year, but he had interacted so poorly with the local Chinese employees that he had to be sent back to the United States. Ross wished that MMC's corporate HR department had done a better job of selecting and then training these employees for a difficult foreign posting, but in retrospect he had to admit that he wasn't surprised at the lack of training; he had never been given any.

After this failure, Ross had taken a different tack. He had picked four of his best Chinese production employees and sent them to MMC's U.S. operations, along with a translator, for a two-month training program focusing on the latest production techniques. This had worked out much better. The Chinese had visited efficient MMC factories in the United States, Mexico, and Brazil and had seen what was possible. They had returned home fired up to improve operations at MMC China. Within a year they had introduced a Six Sigma quality control program and improved the flow of inventory through MMC's factory. Ross could now walk through the factory without being appalled by the sight of large quantities of inventory stacked on the floor or bins full of discarded circuit boards that had failed postassembly quality tests. Productivity had improved as a result, and after three tough years, MMC China had finally turned a profit.

Apparently this was not good enough for corporate headquarters. Ross knew that improving performance further would be tough. The market in China was very competitive. MMC was vying with many other enterprises to produce printed circuit boards for large multinational customers that had assembly operations in China. The customers were constantly demanding lower prices, and it seemed to Ross that prices were falling almost as fast as MMC's costs. Also, Ross was limited in his ability to cut the workforce by the demands of his Chinese joint-venture partner. Ross had tried to explain all this to Phil Smith, but Smith didn't seem to get it. "The man is just a number cruncher," thought Ross. "He has no sense of the market in China. He has no idea how hard it is to do business here. I have worked damn hard to turn this operation around, and I am getting no credit for it, none at all."[75]

Case Discussion Questions

1. Is it right for MMC to hold Ross to the same performance goals as managers of units in other countries? What other approach might it adopt?
2. Why had bringing in specialists from the United States not worked at MMC? Why did Ross's strategy of sending Chinese employees over to the United States for training produce better results? What are the lessons here?
3. What changes could the HR department at MMC make to improve its utilization of human capital and facilitate knowledge transfers within the company?

Endnotes

1. G. Jones, "IBM: Pinpointing Inside Up and Comers," *BusinessWeek*, October 9, 2005; J. Smerd, "IBM Optimas Award Winner for Financial Impact," *Workforce Management*, October 24, 2008; and R. J. Grossman, "IBM's HR Takes a Risk," *HR Magazine*, April 1, 2007.

2. P. J. Dowling and R. S. Schuler, *International Dimensions of Human Resource Management* (Boston: PSW-Kent, 1990).

3. J. Millman, M. A. von Glinow, and M. Nathan, "Organizational Life Cycles and Strategic International Human Resource Management in Multinational Companies," *Academy of Management Review* 16 (1991), pp. 318–39; A. Bird and S. Beechler, "Links between Business Strategy and Human Resource Management," *Journal of International Business Studies* 26 (1995), pp. 23–47; B. A. Colbert, "The Complex Resource Based View: Implications for Theory and Practice of Strategic Human Resource Management," *Academy of Management Review* 29 (2004), pp. 341–60; and C. J. Collins and K. D. Clark, "Strategic Human Resource Practices, Top Management Team Social Networks, and Firm Performance," *Academy of Management Journal* 46 (2003), pp. 740–60.

4. See Peter Bamberger and Ilan Meshoulam, *Human Resource Strategy: Formulation, Implementation, and Impact* (Thousand Oaks, CA: Sage, 2000); P. M. Wright and S. Snell, "Towards a Unifying Framework for Exploring Fit and Flexibility in Human Resource Management," *Academy of Management Review* 23 (October 1998), pp. 756–72; Colbert, "The Complex Resource-Based View"; and R. S. Schuler and S. E. Jackson, "A Quarter Century Review of Human Resource Management in the US: The Growth in Importance of the International Perspective," *Management Review* 16 (2005), pp. 1–25.

5. R. Colman, "HR Management Lags behind at World Class Firms," *CMA Management,* July–August 2002, p. 9.

6. E. H. Schein, *Organizational Culture and Leadership* (San Francisco: Jossey-Bass, 1985).

7. H. V. Perlmutter, "The Tortuous Evolution of the Multinational Corporation," *Columbia Journal of World Business* 4 (1969), pp. 9–18; D. A. Heenan and H. V. Perlmutter, *Multinational Organizational Development* (Reading, MA: Addison-Wesley, 1979); D. A. Ondrack, "International Human Resources Management in European and North American Firms," *International Studies of Management and Organization* 15 (1985), pp. 6–32; and T. Jackson, "The Management of People across Cultures: Valuing People Differently," *Human Resource Management* 41 (2002), pp. 455–75.

8. V. Reitman and M. Schuman, "Men's Club: Japanese and Korean Companies Rarely Look Outside for People to Run Their Overseas Operations," *The Wall Street Journal,* September 26, 1996, p. 17.

9. E. Wong, "China's Export of Labor Faces Growing Scorn," *The New York Times,* December 21, 2009, p. A1.

10. S. Beechler and J. Z. Yang, "The Transfer of Japanese Style Management to American Subsidiaries," *Journal of International Business Studies* 25 (1994), pp. 467–91. See also R. Konopaske, S. Warner, and K. E. Neupert, "Entry Mode Strategy and Performance: The Role of FDI Staffing," *Journal of Business Research,* September 2002, pp. 759–70.

11. M. Banai and L. M. Sama, "Ethical Dilemma in MNCs' International Staffing Policies," *Journal of Business Ethics,* June 2000, pp. 221–35.

12. V. Reitman and M. Schuman, "Men's Club: Japanese and Korean Companies Rarely Look Outside for People to Run Their Overseas Operations," *The Wall Street Journal,* September 26, 1996, p. 17.

13. C. A. Bartlett and S. Ghoshal, *Managing across Borders: The Transnational Solution* (Boston: Harvard Business School Press, 1989).

14. S. J. Kobrin, "Geocentric Mindset and Multinational Strategy," *Journal of International Business Studies* 25 (1994), pp. 493–511.

15. F. Hansen, "International Business Machine," *Workforce Management,* July 2005, pp. 36–44.

16. P. M. Rosenzweig and N. Nohria, "Influences on Human Resource Management Practices in Multinational Corporations," *Journal of International Business Studies* 25 (1994), pp. 229–51.

17. Kobrin, "Geocentric Mindset and Multinational Strategy."

18. M. Harvey and H. Fung, "Inpatriate Managers: The Need for Realistic Relocation Reviews," *International Journal of Management* 17 (2000), pp. 151–59.

19. S. Black, M. Mendenhall, and G. Oddou, "Toward a Comprehensive Model of International Adjustment," *Academy of Management Review* 16 (1991), pp. 291–317; J. Shay and T. J. Bruce, "Expatriate Managers," *Cornell Hotel & Restaurant Administration Quarterly,* February 1997, p. 30–40; and Y. Baruch and Y. Altman, "Expatriation and Repatriation in MNCs—A Taxonomy," *Human Resource Management* 41 (2002), pp. 239–59.

20. M. G. Harvey, "The Multinational Corporation's Expatriate Problem: An Application of Murphy's Law," *Business Horizons* 26 (1983), pp. 71–78.

21. J. Barbian, "Return to Sender," *Training,* January 2002, pp. 40–43.

22. Shay and Bruce, "Expatriate Managers." Also see J. S. Black and H. Gregersen, "The Right Way to Manage Expatriates," *Harvard Business Review,* March–April 1999, pp. 52–63; and Baruch and Altman, "Expatriation and Repatriation in MNCs."

23. N. Foster, "The Persistent Myth of High Expatriate Failure Rates," *Journal of Human Resource Management* 8 (1997), pp. 177–205.

24. Barbian, "Return to Sender"; and K. Yeaton and N. Hall, "Expatriates: Reducing Failure Rates," *Journal of Corporate Accounting and Finance,* March–April 2008, pp. 75–78.

25. Black, Mendenhall, and Oddou, "Toward a Comprehensive Model of International Adjustment."

26. R. L. Tung, "Selection and Training Procedures of U.S., European, and Japanese Multinationals," *California Management Review* 25 (1982), pp. 57–71.

27. H. W. Lee, "Factors That Influence Expatriate Failure," *International Journal of Management* 24 (2007), pp. 403–15.

28. C. M. Solomon, "Success Abroad Depends upon More Than Job Skills," *Personnel Journal,* April 1994, pp. 51–58.

29. C. M. Solomon, "Unhappy Trails," *Workforce,* August 2000, pp. 36–41.

30. Solomon, "Success Abroad."

31. Solomon, "Unhappy Trails."

32. M. Harvey, "Addressing the Dual-Career Expatriation Dilemma," *Human Resource Planning* 19, no. 4 (1996), pp. 18–32.

33. M. Mendenhall and G. Oddou, "The Dimensions of Expatriate Acculturation: A Review," *Academy of Management Review* 10 (1985), pp. 39–47.

34. E. Smockum, "Don't Forget the Trailing Spouse," *Financial Times,* May 6, 1998, p. 22; V. Frazee, "Tearing Down Roadblocks," *Workforce* 77, no. 2 (1998), pp. 50–54; C. Sievers, "Expatriate Management," *HR Focus* 75, no. 3 (1998), pp. 75–76; J. Barbian, "Return to Sender," *Training,* January 2002, pp. 40–43; and J. Mainwaring, "Shell Schools: Supporting Expat Families," *Rigzone,* June 21, 2012.

35. I. Torbiorin, *Living Abroad: Personal Adjustment and Personnel Policy in the Overseas Setting* (New York: John Wiley & Sons, 1982).

36. R. L. Tung, "Selection and Training of Personnel for Overseas Assignments," *Columbia Journal of World Business* 16 (1981), pp. 68–78.

37. Solomon, "Success Abroad."

38. S. Ronen, "Training and International Assignee," in *Training and Career Development,* ed. I. Goldstein (San Francisco: Jossey-Bass, 1985); and Tung, "Selection and Training of Personnel for Overseas Assignments."

39. Solomon, "Success Abroad."

40. Harvey, "Addressing the Dual-Career Expatriation Dilemma"; and J. W. Hunt, "The Perils of Foreign Postings for Two," *Financial Times,* May 6, 1998, p. 22.

41. C. M. Daily, S. T. Certo, and D. R. Dalton, "International Experience in the Executive Suite: A Path to Prosperity?" *Strategic Management Journal* 21 (2000), pp. 515–23.

42. Dowling and Schuler, *International Dimensions.*

43. Ibid.

44. G. Baliga and J. C. Baker, "Multinational Corporate Policies for Expatriate Managers: Selection, Training, and Evaluation," *Advanced Management Journal,* Autumn 1985, pp. 31–38.

45. J. C. Baker, "Foreign Language and Departure Training in U.S. Multinational Firms," *Personnel Administrator,* July 1984, pp. 68–70.

46. A 1997 study by the Conference Board looked at this in depth. For a summary, see L. Grant, "That Overseas Job Could Derail Your Career," *Fortune,* April 14, 1997, p. 166. Also see J. S. Black and H. Gregersen, "The Right Way to Manage Expatriates," *Harvard Business Review,* March–April 1999, pp. 52–63.

47. J. S. Black and M. E. Mendenhall, *Global Assignments: Successfully Expatriating and Repatriating International Managers* (San Francisco: Jossey-Bass, 1992); and K. Vermond, "Expatriates Come Home," *CMA Management,* October 2001, pp. 30–33.

48. Ibid.

49. Figures from the Conference Board study. For a summary, see Grant, "That Overseas Job Could Derail Your Career."

50. C. M. Solomon, "Repatriation: Up, Down, or Out?" *Personnel Journal,* January 1995, pp. 28–34; and J. Schaefer, E. Hannibal, and J. O'Neill, "How Strategy, Culture and Improved Service Delivery Reshape Monsanto's International Assignment Program," *Journal of Organizational Excellence* 22, no. 3 (2003), pp. 35–40.

51. S. C. Schneider, "National vs. Corporate Culture: Implications for Human Resource Management," *Human Resource Management* 27 (Summer 1988), pp. 231–46.

52. I. M. Manve and W. B. Stevenson, "Nationality, Cultural Distance and Expatriate Status," *Journal of International Business Studies* 32 (2001), pp. 285–303; and D. Minbaeva et al., "MNC Knowledge Transfer, Subsidiary Absorptive Capacity, and HRM," *Journal of International Business Studies* 34, no. 6 (2003), pp. 586–604.

53. Bartlett and Ghoshal, *Managing across Borders.*

54. See G. Oddou and M. Mendenhall, "Expatriate Performance Appraisal: Problems and Solutions," in *International Human Resource Management,* ed. M. Mendenhall and G. Oddou (Boston: PWS-Kent, 1991); Dowling and Schuler, *International*

Dimensions; R. S. Schuler and G.W. Florkowski, "International Human Resource Management," in *Handbook for International Management Research,* ed. B. J. Punnett and O. Shenkar (Oxford: Blackwell, 1996); and K. Roth and S. O'Donnell, "Foreign Subsidiary Compensation Strategy: An Agency Theory Perspective," *Academy of Management Journal* 39, no. 3 (1996), pp. 678–703.

55. Oddou and Mendenhall, "Expatriate Performance Appraisal."

56. "Expatriates Often See Little Benefit to Careers in Foreign Stints, Indifference at Home," *The Wall Street Journal,* December 11, 1989, p. B1.

57. Oddou and Mendenhall, "Expatriate Performance Appraisal"; and Schuler and Florkowski, "International Human Resource Management."

58. Towers Perrin, *Towers Perrin Worldwide Total Remuneration Study, 2005–2006,* www.towerswatson.com. Note all researchers agree with this conclusion; see for example N. Fernandes et al., "Are US CEOs Paid More? New International Evidence," *The Review of Financial Studies,* in press, 2013.

59. J. Marquez, "McDonald's Rewards Program Leaves Some Room for Local Flavor," *Workforce Management,* April 10, 2006, p. 26.

60. J. Cummings and L. Brannen, "The New World of Compensation," *Business Finance,* June 2005, p. 8.

61. "Multinationals Tighten Control of Benefit Plans," *Workforce Management,* May 2005, p. 5.

62. Organizational Resource Counselors, *2002 Survey of International Assignment Policies and Practices,* March 2003.

63. C. Reynolds, "Compensation of Overseas Personnel," in *Handbook of Human Resource Administration,* ed. J. J. Famularo (New York: McGraw-Hill, 1986).

64. M. Helms, "International Executive Compensation Practices," in *International Human Resource Management,* ed. M. Mendenhall and G. Oddou (Boston: PWS-Kent, 1991).

65. G. W. Latta, "Expatriate Incentives," *HR Focus* 75, no. 3 (March 1998), p. S3.

66. C. K. Prahalad and Y. L. Doz, *The Multinational Mission* (New York: Free Press, 1987).

67. Ibid.

68. Schuler and Florkowski, "International Human Resource Management."

69. See J. P. Womack, D. T. Jones, and D. Roos, *The Machine That Changed the World* (New York: Rawson Associates, 1990).

70. See Aug 06, 2004 http://www.sharedxpertise.org/modules.php?op=modload&name=News&file=article&sid=1785&mode=thread&order=0&thold=0

71. Ravi Datar, *Business Process Outsourcing in India: A Fact Book* (Executive Summary), 26 June 2002.

72. Figure adapted from a white paper on *"BPO-destination India"* by Patni Computer systems, Sep. 2003.

73. Figure adapted from http://www.renodis.com/about/market_overview/value_chain.html

74. http://www.newhorizonsonline.com/NHC_Healthcare_BPO_ITeS_Industry_India.pdf
Accsessed on 26 Dec 2004.

75. This is a disguised case history based on interviews undertaken by the author.

Chapter 20
Accounting and Finance in the International Business

LEARNING OBJECTIVES

After reading this chapter, you will be able to:

LO20-1 Discuss the national differences in accounting standards.

LO20-2 Explain the implications of the rise of international accounting standards.

LO20-3 Explain how accounting systems affect control systems within the multinational enterprise.

LO20-4 Discuss how operating in different nations impacts investment decisions within the multinational enterprise.

LO20-5 Discuss the different financing options available to the foreign subsidiary of a multinational enterprise.

LO20-6 Understand how money management in the international business can be used to minimize cash balances, transaction costs, and taxation.

LO20-7 Understand the basic techniques for global money management.

◇ TAX STRATEGY AT GOOGLE ◇

Opening Case

In early 2013 the Internet search firm Google found itself under sharp attack from politicians in Europe when it was revealed that the company had adopted strategies to avoiding paying corporate income tax on the bulk of its earnings outside the United States, the majority of which was generated in Europe. Estimates suggest that in 2011 Google avoided about $2 billion in worldwide corporate income tax by shifting $9.8 billion in revenues into a shell company in Bermuda where there is no income tax. Google's tax rate on profits earned overseas was just 3.2 percent, even though most of its foreign sales were made in European countries with corporate income tax rates ranging from 26 percent to 34 percent.

Politicians in Britain, where Google has a major presence, called the strategy "deeply immoral." Google generated revenues of £2.5 billion in the UK in 2011, but ended up paying just £6 million in corporate income tax. For its part, Google insists that it has done nothing wrong, and is playing by the rules that the politicians themselves have written. In a British radio interview on the matter, Google's chairman, stated: "You're describing the way taxes work globally. And the fact of the matter is these are the way taxes are done globally. The same is true for British firms operating in the U.S., for example." Schmidt went on to defend Google's operations in the UK, noting, "We empower literally billions of pounds of start-ups through our advertising network (in the UK). And we're a key part of the electronic commerce expansion of Britain, which is driving a lot of economic growth for the country. So from our perspective you have to look at it in totality."

So how does Google minimize its overseas tax liability? The company starts with a tactic known as the "Double Irish." First, the U.S. parent creates an Irish subsidiary and gives that subsidiary the rights to all of Google's intangible property. In return, the new subsidiary agrees to help market and promote Google's products in Europe. Thus all European income that previously would have been taxed in the United States is now taxed in Ireland instead. This in itself is advantageous, since Ireland's corporate income tax rate is just 12.5 percent, compared to 35 percent in the United States. Second, the new Irish subsidiary then changes its headquarters to Bermuda, a true tax haven of no corporate income tax. Third, Google forms another Irish subsidiary. The first Irish subsidiary (now headquartered in Bermuda) then licenses company products to the second Irish company in exchange for royalties. The second Irish subsidiary books sales in Europe and pays Irish corporate income tax of 12.5 percent on any profits earned on those sales, as opposed to higher rates in places like the UK and France. Now the tax rate in Ireland can be reduced below the 12.5 percent level, since the royalties paid to the Bermuda-based company are treated as an expense, and can be deducted against earnings in Ireland.

If this were not enough, Google has added another twist to the strategy, known as the "Dutch Sandwich." This involves creating a third subsidiary in the Netherlands. Instead of licensing the parent's products directly to the second Irish subsidiary, the Bermuda-based subsidiary grants them to the Dutch subsidiary, which in turn licenses them to the second Irish subsidiary. The Irish subsidiary pays royalties to the Dutch subsidiary, which in turn passes them to the Bermuda subsidiary. The key to all this is that Ireland does not tax money as it moves between other members of the European Union, and authorities in the Netherlands only take a tiny fee on money going from a Netherlands company to one in Bermuda. By using this stratagem, Google has effectively reduced its corporate income tax on money earned in Europe to almost zero. All this, it should be noted, is perfectly legal and simply takes advantage of corporate tax rules as they are written in the different countries. Whether it is immoral, as some British politicians have claimed, is another question, of course.[1]

INTRODUCTION

This chapter deals with two related topics, accounting and finance in the international business. These are both highly specialized topics, and a full review is beyond the scope of an introductory textbook. The goal of this chapter is to provide the reader with a high-level nontechnical overview of some of the main issues in accounting and finance that confront the manager in an international business.

Accounting has often been referred to as "the language of business."[2] This language finds expression in profit and loss statements, balance sheets, budgets, investment analysis, and tax analysis. Accounting information is the means by which firms communicate their financial position to the providers of capital, enabling them to assess the value of their investments and make decisions about future resource allocations. Accounting information is also the means by which firms report their income to the government, so the government can assess how much tax the firm owes. It is also the means by which the firm can evaluate its performance, control its internal expenditures, and plan for future expenditures and income. Thus, a good accounting function is critical to the smooth running of the firm and to a nation's financial system. In this regard, international businesses face a number of accounting problems that do not confront purely domestic businesses—most notably, the lack of consistency in the accounting standards of different countries.

Financial management in an international business includes three sets of related decisions: (1) investment decisions, decisions about what activities to finance, (2) financing decisions, decisions about how to finance those activities, and (3) money management decisions, decisions about how to manage the firm's financial resources most efficiently. In an international business, investment, financing, and money management decisions are complicated by the fact that countries have different currencies, different tax regimes, different regulations concerning the flow of capital across their borders, different norms regarding the financing of business activities, different levels of economic and political risk, and so on. Financial managers must consider all these factors when deciding which activities to finance, how best to finance those activities, how best to manage the firm's financial resources, and how best to protect the firm from political and economic risks (including foreign exchange risk).

As we shall see, one of the money management goals that financial managers try to achieve in an international business is to minimize global tax liability. The opening case looks at how Google manages flow of money between different subsidiaries in order to attain this goal. What Google does may seem somewhat convoluted, and some argue it is ethically suspect, but it is entirely consistent with national and international laws. Moreover, Google is hardly alone in doing this. Most multinationals try to manage the flow of funds within the enterprise in order to minimize the global tax burden.

This chapter begins by looking at country differences in accounting standards and current attempts aimed at harmonizing accounting standards across nations. Next we discuss the issues that can arise when managers in the international business use accounting systems to control foreign subsidiaries. Then we move on to look at investment decisions in an international business. We discuss how such factors as political and economic risk complicate investment decisions. This is followed by a review of financing decisions in an international business. Finally, we examine money management decisions in an international business, including decisions aimed at reducing tax liabilities.

NATIONAL DIFFERENCES IN ACCOUNTING STANDARDS   LO20-1

Accounting is shaped by the environment in which it operates. Just as different countries have different political systems, economic systems, and cultures, historically they have also had different accounting systems.[3] These differences had a number of sources. For example, in countries where there were well-developed capital markets, such as the United States and Britain, firms typically raised capital by issuing stock or bonds to investors. Investors in these countries demanded detailed accounting disclosures so that they could better assess the risk and likely return on their investments. The accounting system evolved to accommodate these requests. In contrast, in Germany and Switzerland the banks emerged as the main providers of capital to enterprises. Bank officers often sat on the boards of these companies and were privy to detailed information about their operations and financial position. As a consequence, there were fewer demands for detailed accounting disclosures, and public accounts tended to reveal less information. Another important influence has been the political or economic ties between nations. U.S.-style accounting systems were adopted in the Philippines, which was once a U.S. protectorate. Similarly, the vast majority of former colonies of the British Empire have accounting practices modeled after Great Britain's, while former French colonies followed the French system.

Diverse accounting practices were enshrined in national accounting and auditing standards. **Accounting standards** are rules for preparing financial statements; they define what is useful accounting information. **Auditing standards** specify the rules for performing an audit—the technical process by which an independent person (the auditor) gathers evidence for determining if financial accounts conform to required accounting standards and if they are also reliable.

One result of national differences in accounting and auditing standards was a general lack of comparability of financial reports from one country to another (something that is now changing). For example, (1) Dutch standards favored the use of current values for replacement assets; Japanese law generally prohibited revaluation and prescribed historic cost; (2) capitalization of financial leases was required practice in Great Britain, but not practiced in France; (3) research and development costs must be written off in the year they are incurred in the United States, but in Spain they could be deferred as an asset and need not be amortized as long as benefits that will cover them are expected to arise in the future; and (4) German accountants treated depreciation as a liability, whereas British companies deducted it from assets.

Such differences would not matter much if there were little need for a firm headquartered in one country to report its financial results to citizens of another country. However, one striking development of the past two decades has been the development of global capital markets. We have seen the growth of both transnational financing and transnational investment. Transnational financing occurs when a firm based in one country enters another country's capital market to raise capital from the sale of stocks or bonds. Transnational investment occurs when an investor based in one country enters the capital market of another nation to invest in the stocks or bonds of a firm based in that country.

The rapid expansion of transnational financing and investment has been accompanied by a corresponding growth in transnational financial reporting. However, the lack of comparability between accounting standards in different nations caused some confusion. For example, the German firm that issued two sets of financial reports, one set prepared under German standards and the other under U.S. standards, may have found that its financial position looked significantly different in the two reports, and its investors may have had difficulty identifying the firm's true worth.

In an example of the confusion that can arise from different accounting standards, in 2000, British Airways reported a loss under British accounting rules of £21 million, but under U.S. rules, its loss was £412 million. Most of the difference could be attributed to adjustments for a number of relatively small items such as depreciation and amortization, pensions, and deferred taxation. The largest adjustment was due to a reduction in revenue reported in the U.S. accounts of £136 million. This reduced revenue was related to frequent flyer miles, which under U.S. rules have to be deferred until the miles are redeemed. Apparently, this is not the case under British rules.

In addition to the problems lack of comparability gives investors, it can give the firm major headaches. The firm has to explain to its investors why its financial position looks so different in the two accountings. Also, an international business may find it difficult to assess the financial positions of important foreign customers, suppliers, and competitors.

INTERNATIONAL ACCOUNTING STANDARDS

Substantial efforts have been made in recent years to harmonize accounting standards across countries.[4] The rise of global capital markets during the past three decades has added urgency to this endeavor.

Chinese Accounting

Over the past decade, more and more Chinese companies have been tapping global capital markets, and more foreigners have been investing in Chinese companies through the Shanghai Stock Exchange. Foreign investors want to be assured that the financial picture they are getting of Chinese enterprises is reliable. That has not always been the case. In December 2003, for example, China Life Insurance successfully listed its stock on the Hong Kong and New York stock exchanges, raising some $3.4 billion. However, in January 2004, the head of China's National Audit Office let it slip that a routine audit of China Life's state-owned parent company had uncovered $652 million in financial irregularities in 2003. The stock immediately fell, and China Life found itself the target of a class action lawsuit on behalf of U.S. investors claiming financial fraud. Soon afterward, plans to list China Minsheng Banking Corp., China's largest private bank, on the New York Stock Exchange were put on hold after the company admitted it had faked a shareholder meeting in 2000. The stock of another successful Chinese offering in New York, Semiconductor Manufacturing International, slid in 2004 when its chief financial officer made statements that contradicted those contained in filings with the U.S. Securities and Exchange Commission.

The core of the problem is that accounting rules in China are not consistent with international standards, making it difficult for investors to accurately value Chinese companies. Accounting in China has traditionally been rooted in information gathering and compliance reporting designed to measure the government's production and tax goals. The Chinese system was based on the old Soviet system, which had little to do with profit. Although the system has been changing rapidly, many problems associated with the old order still remain. Indeed, it is often said, only half in jest, that Chinese firms keep several sets of books—one for the government, one for company records, one for foreigners, and one to report what is actually going on.

To bring its rules into closer alignment with international standards, China has signaled that it will move toward adopting standards developed by the International Accounting Standards Board (IASB). In 2001, China adopted a new regulation, called the Accounting System for Business Enterprises, that was largely based on IASB standards. The system is now used to regulate both local and foreign companies operating in China. In 2005, the Chinese went further still, mandating that on January 1, 2007, the largest 1,200 firms listed on the Shanghai and Shenzhen exchanges adopt a broad set of accounting rules that are based on, but not identical to, IASB standards. It remains to be seen whether adoption of these new rules will make the financial performance of Chinese companies more transparent.

At present, many large public Chinese companies are now reporting results according to two sets of rules, Chinese accounting standards and IASB standards. The differences between the two are instructive. In mid-2008 China Eastern, one of the largest airlines in China, said its net profit fell 29 percent from a year earlier to 41.6 million yuan ($6.1 million) under Chinese accounting rules. Based on international standards, however, the airline incurred a net loss of 212.5 million yuan, over five times as great![6]

Today, many companies raise money from providers of capital outside their national borders. Those providers are demanding consistency in the way financial results are reported so they can make more informed investment decisions. Also, there is a realization that the adoption of common accounting standards will facilitate the development of global capital markets because more investors will be willing to invest across borders, and the end result will be to lower the cost of capital and stimulate economic growth. It is increasingly accepted that the standardization of accounting practices across national borders is in the best interests of all participants in the world economy.

The International Accounting Standards Board (IASB) has emerged as a major proponent of standardization. The IASB was formed in March 2001 to replace the International Accounting Standards Committee (IASC), which had been established in 1973. The IASB has 16 members who are responsible for the formulation of new international financial reporting standards. To issue a new standard, 75 percent of the 16 members of the board must agree. It can be difficult to get three-quarters agreement, particularly since members come from different cultures and legal systems. To get around this problem, most IASB statements provide two acceptable alternatives. As Arthur Wyatt, former chairman of the IASB, once said, "It's not much of a standard if you have two alternatives, but it's better than having six. If you can get agreement on two alternatives, you can capture the 11 required votes and eliminate some of the less used practices."[5]

Another hindrance to the development of international accounting standards is that compliance is voluntary; the IASB has no power to enforce its standards. Despite this, support for the IASB and recognition of its standards has been growing. Increasingly, the IASB is regarded as an effective voice for defining acceptable worldwide accounting principles. Japan, for example, began requiring financial statements to be prepared on a consolidated basis after the IASB issued its initial standards on the topic, and in 2004 Japanese accounting authorities started working closely with the IASB to try to harmonize standards. Japan set 2008 as a target date to achieve harmonization—after meeting this, it set 2012 as a date for mandatory adoption of International Financial Reporting Standards (IFRS). Russia and China have also stated their intention to adopt emerging international standards (see the next Management Focus for a discussion of accounting practices in China). By 2012 more than 100 nations had either adopted the IASB standards or permitted their use to report financial results, including three quarters of the G20, the world's 20 largest economies.

To date, the impact of the IASB standards has probably been least noticeable in the United States because most of the standards issued by the IASB have been consistent with opinions already articulated by the U.S. Financial Accounting Standards Board (FASB). The FASB writes the generally accepted accounting principles (GAAP) by which the financial statements of U.S. firms must be prepared. Nevertheless, differences between IASB and FASB standards remain, although the IASB and FASB have a goal of convergence. The U.S. Securities and Exchange Commission has been considering whether to allow U.S. public companies to use IASB standards, rather than GAAP, to report their results, a move that some believe could ultimately spell the end of GAAP.[7]

Another body that is having a substantial influence on the harmonization of accounting standards is the European Union. In accordance with its plans for closer economic and political union, the EU has mandated harmonization of the accounting principles of its member countries. The EU does this by issuing directives that the member states are obligated to incorporate into their own national laws. Because EU directives have the power of law, the EU might have a better chance of achieving harmonization than the IASB does. The EU has required that since January 1, 2005, financial accounts issued by some 7,000 publicly listed companies in the EU were to be in accordance with IASB standards. The Europeans hope that this requirement, by making it easier to compare the financial position of companies from different EU member states, will facilitate the development of a pan-European capital market and ultimately lower the cost of capital for EU firms.

Given the harmonization in the EU, and given that countries including Japan, China, and Russia are following suit, there could soon be only two major accounting bodies with dominant influence on global reporting: FASB in the United States and IASB elsewhere. Under an agreement reached in 2002, these two bodies are trying to align their standards, suggesting that differences in accounting standards across countries may disappear eventually.

In a move that indicates the trend toward adoption of acceptable international accounting standards is accelerating, the IASB has developed accounting standards for firms seeking stock listings in global markets. Also, the FASB has joined forces with accounting standard setters in Canada, Mexico, and Chile to explore areas in which the four countries can harmonize their accounting standards (Canada, Mexico, and the United States are members of NAFTA, and Chile would like to join). The SEC has also dropped many of its objections to international standards, which could accelerate their adoption.

ACCOUNTING ASPECTS OF CONTROL SYSTEMS

One role of corporate headquarters in large complex enterprises is to control subunits within the organization to ensure they achieve the best possible performance. In the typical firm, the control process is annual and involves three main steps: (1) Head office and subunit management jointly determine subunit goals for the coming year; (2) throughout the year, the head office monitors subunit performance against the agreed goals; (3) if a subunit fails to achieve its goals, the head office intervenes in the subunit to learn why the shortfall occurred, taking corrective action when appropriate.

The accounting function plays a critical role in this process. Most of the goals for subunits are expressed in financial terms and are embodied in the subunit's budget for the coming year. The budget is the main instrument of financial control. The budget is typically prepared by the subunit, but it must be approved by headquarters management. During the approval process, headquarters and subunit managers debate the goals that should be incorporated in the budget. One function of headquarters management is to ensure a subunit's budget contains challenging but realistic performance goals. Once a budget is agreed to, accounting information systems are used to collect data throughout the year so a subunit's performance can be evaluated against the goals contained in its budget.

In most international businesses, many of the firm's subunits are foreign subsidiaries. The performance goals for the coming year are thus set by negotiation between corporate management and the managers of foreign subsidiaries. According to one survey of control practices within multinational enterprises, the most important criterion for evaluating the performance of a foreign subsidiary is the subsidiary's actual profits compared to budgeted profits.[8] This is closely followed by a subsidiary's actual sales compared to budgeted sales and its return on investment. The same criteria are also useful in evaluating the performance of the subsidiary managers. We discuss this point later in this section. First, however, we examine two factors that can complicate the control process in an international business: exchange rate changes and transfer pricing practices.

Exchange Rate Changes and Control Systems

Most international businesses require all budgets and performance data within the firm to be expressed in the "corporate currency," which is normally the home currency. Thus, the Malaysian subsidiary of a U.S. multinational would probably submit a budget prepared in U.S. dollars, rather than Malaysian ringgit, and performance data throughout the year would be reported to headquarters in U.S. dollars.

This facilitates comparisons between subsidiaries in different countries, and it makes things easier for headquarters management. However, it also allows exchange rate changes during the year to introduce substantial distortions. For example, the Malaysian subsidiary may fail to achieve profit goals not because of any performance problems, but merely because of a decline in the value of the ringgit against the dollar. The opposite can occur, also, making a foreign subsidiary's performance look better than it actually is.

The Lessard-Lorange Model

According to research by Donald Lessard and Peter Lorange, a number of methods are available to international businesses for dealing with this problem.[9] Lessard and Lorange point out three exchange rates that can be used to translate foreign currencies into the corporate currency in setting budgets and in the subsequent tracking of performance:

- The initial rate, the spot exchange rate when the budget is adopted.
- The projected rate, the spot exchange rate forecast for the end of the budget period (i.e., the forward rate).
- The ending rate, the spot exchange rate when the budget and performance are being compared.

These three exchange rates imply nine possible combinations (see Figure 20.1). Lessard and Lorange ruled out four of the nine combinations as illogical and unreasonable; Figure 20.1 shows the four in color. For example, it would make no sense to use the ending rate to translate the budget and the initial rate to translate actual performance data. Any of the remaining five combinations might be used for setting budgets and evaluating performance.

With three of these five combinations—II, PP, and EE—the same exchange rate is used for translating both budget figures and performance figures into the corporate currency. All three combinations have the advantage that a change in the exchange rate during the year does not distort the control process.

		Rate Used to Translate Actual Performance for Comparison with Budget		
		Initial (I)	Projected (P)	Ending (E)
Rate Used for Translating Budget	Initial (I)	(II) Budget at Initial Actual at Initial	Budget at Initial Actual at Projected	(IE) Budget at Initial Actual at Ending
	Projected (P)	Budget at Projected Actual at Initial	(PP) Budget at Projected Actual at Projected	(PE) Budget at Projected Actual at Ending
	Ending (E)	Budget at Ending Actual at Initial	Budget at Ending Actual at Projected	(EE) Budget at Ending Actual at Ending

Figure 20.1 *Possible Combinations of Exchange Rates in the Control Process*

This is not true for the other two combinations, IE and PE. In those cases, exchange rate changes can introduce distortions. The potential for distortion is greater with IE; the ending spot exchange rate used to evaluate performance against the budget may be quite different from the initial spot exchange rate used to translate the budget. The distortion is less serious in the case of PE because the projected exchange rate considers future exchange rate movements.

Of the five combinations, Lessard and Lorange recommend that firms use the projected spot exchange rate to translate both the budget and performance figures into the corporate currency, combination PP. The projected rate in such cases will typically be the forward exchange rate as determined by the foreign exchange market (see Chapter 10 for the definition of *forward rate*) or some company-generated forecast of future spot rates, which Lessard and Lorange refer to as the **internal forward rate**. The internal forward rate may differ from the forward rate quoted by the foreign exchange market if the firm wishes to bias its business in favor of, or against, the particular foreign currency.

Transfer Pricing and Control Systems

Chapter 13 reviewed the various strategies that international businesses pursue. Two of these strategies, the global strategy and the transnational strategy, give rise to a globally dispersed web of productive activities. Firms pursuing these strategies disperse each value creation activity to its optimal location in the world. Thus, a product might be designed in one country, some of its components manufactured in a second country, other components manufactured in a third country, all assembled in a fourth country, and then sold worldwide.

The volume of intrafirm transactions in such firms is very high. The firms are continually shipping component parts and finished goods between subsidiaries in different countries. This poses a very important question: How should goods and services transferred between subsidiary companies in a multinational firm be priced? The price at which such goods and services are transferred is referred to as the *transfer price.*

The choice of transfer price can critically affect the performance of two subsidiaries that exchange goods or services. Consider this example: A French manufacturing subsidiary of a U.S. multinational imports a major component from Brazil. It incorporates this part into a product that it sells in France for the equivalent of $230 per unit. The product costs $200 to manufacture, of which $100 goes to the Brazilian subsidiary to pay for the component part. The remaining $100 covers costs incurred in France. Thus, the French subsidiary earns $30 profit per unit.

	Before Change in Transfer Price	After 20 Percent Increase in Transfer Price
Revenues per unit	$230	$230
Cost of component per unit	100	120
Other costs per unit	100	100
Profit per unit	$ 30	$ 10

See what happens if corporate headquarters decides to increase transfer prices by 20 percent ($20 per unit). The French subsidiary's profits will fall by two-thirds from $30 per unit to $10 per unit. Thus, the performance of the French subsidiary depends on the transfer price for the component part imported from Brazil, and the transfer price is controlled by corporate headquarters. When setting budgets and reviewing a subsidiary's performance, corporate headquarters must keep in mind the distorting effect of transfer prices.

How should transfer prices be determined? We discuss this issue in detail later in the chapter. International businesses often manipulate transfer prices to minimize their worldwide tax liability, minimize import duties, and avoid government restrictions on capital flows. For now, however, it is enough to note that the transfer price must be considered when setting budgets and evaluating a subsidiary's performance.

Separation of Subsidiary and Manager Performance

In many international businesses, the same quantitative criteria are used to assess the performance of both a foreign subsidiary and its managers. Many accountants, however, argue that although it is legitimate to compare subsidiaries against each other on the basis of return on investment (ROI) or other indicators of profitability, it may not be appropriate to use these for comparing and evaluating the managers of different subsidiaries. Foreign subsidiaries do not operate in uniform environments; their environments have widely different economic, political, and social conditions, all of which influence the costs of doing business in a country and hence the subsidiaries' profitability. Thus, the manager of a subsidiary in an adverse environment that has an ROI of 5 percent may be doing a better job than the manager of a subsidiary in a benign environment that has an ROI of 20 percent. Although the firm might want to pull out of a country where its ROI is only 5 percent, it may also want to recognize the manager's achievement.

Accordingly, it has been suggested that the evaluation of a subsidiary should be kept separate from the evaluation of its manager.[10] The manager's evaluation should consider how hostile or benign the country's environment is for that business. Further, managers should be evaluated in local currency terms after making allowances for those items over which they have no control (e.g., interest rates, tax rates, inflation rates, transfer prices, exchange rates).

FINANCIAL MANAGEMENT: THE INVESTMENT DECISION   LO20-4

One role of the financial manager in an international business is to try to quantify the various benefits, costs, and risks that are likely to flow from an investment in a given location. A decision to invest in activities in a given country must consider many economic, political, cultural, and strategic variables. We have been discussing this issue throughout much of this book. Chapters 2, 3, and 4 touched on it when we discussed how the political, economic, legal, and cultural environment of a country can influence the benefits, costs, and risks of doing business there and thus its attractiveness as an investment site. We returned to the issue in Chapter 8 with a discussion of the economic theory of foreign direct investment. We identified a number of factors that determine the economic attractiveness of a foreign investment opportunity. We also looked at the political economy of foreign direct investment in Chapter 7 and we considered the role that government intervention can play in foreign investment. In Chapter 13, we pulled much of this material together when we considered how a firm can reduce its costs of value creation and/ or increase its value added by investing in productive activities in other countries. We returned to the issue again in Chapter 15 when we considered the various modes for entering foreign markets.

Capital Budgeting

Capital budgeting is the technique financial managers use to try to quantify the benefits, costs, and risks of an investment. This enables top managers to compare, in a reasonably objective fashion, different investment alternatives within and across countries so they can make informed choices about where the firm should invest its scarce financial resources. Capital budgeting for a foreign project uses the same theoretical framework that domestic capital budgeting uses; that is, the firm must first estimate the cash flows associated with the project over time. In most cases, the cash flows will be negative at first, because the firm will be investing heavily in production facilities. After some initial period, however, the cash flows will become positive as investment costs decline and revenues grow. Once the cash flows have been estimated, they must be discounted to determine their net present value using an appropriate discount rate. The most commonly used discount rate is either the firm's cost of capital or some other required rate of return. If the net present value of the discounted cash flows is greater than zero, the firm should go ahead with the project.[11]

Although this might sound quite straightforward, capital budgeting is in practice a very complex and imperfect process. Among the factors complicating the process for an international business are these:

1. A distinction must be made between cash flows to the project and cash flows to the parent company.
2. Political and economic risks, including foreign exchange risk, can significantly change the value of a foreign investment.
3. The connection between cash flows to the parent and the source of financing must be recognized.

We look at the first two of these issues in this section. Discussion of the connection between cash flows and the source of financing is postponed until the next section, where we discuss the source of financing.

Project and Parent Cash Flows

A theoretical argument exists for analyzing any foreign project from the perspective of the parent company because cash flows to the project are not necessarily the same thing as cash flows to the parent company. The project may not be able to remit all its cash flows to the parent for a number of reasons. For example, cash flows may be blocked from repatriation by the host-country government, they may be taxed at an unfavorable rate, or the host government may require that a certain percentage of the cash flows generated from the project be reinvested within the host nation. While these restrictions don't affect the net present value of the project itself, they do affect the net present value of the project to the parent company because they limit the cash flows that can be remitted to it from the project.

When evaluating a foreign investment opportunity, the parent should be interested in the cash flows it will receive—as opposed to those the project generates—because those are the basis for dividends to stockholders, investments elsewhere in the world, repayment of worldwide corporate debt, and so on. Stockholders will not perceive blocked earnings as contributing to the value of the firm, and creditors will not count them when calculating the parent's ability to service its debt.

But the problem of blocked earnings is not as serious as it once was. The worldwide move toward greater acceptance of free market economics (discussed in Chapters 2 and 3) has reduced the number of countries in which governments are likely to prohibit the affiliates of foreign multinationals from remitting cash flows to their parent companies. In addition, as explained later in the chapter, firms have a number of options for circumventing host-government attempts to block the free flow of funds from an affiliate.

Black Sea Oil and Gas Ltd.

In 1996, Black Sea Oil and Gas Ltd., of Calgary, Canada, formed a fifty-fifty joint venture with the Tyumen Oil Company, then Russia's sixth-largest integrated oil company. The objective of the venture, known as the Tura Petroleum Company, was to explore the Tura oil field in western Siberia. At the time, Tyumen was 90 percent owned by the Russian government; consequently Black Sea negotiated directly with representatives of the Russian government when establishing the joint venture. The agreement called for both parties to contribute more than $40 million to the formation of the venture, Black Sea in the form of cash, technology, and expertise, and Tyumen in the form of infrastructure and the licenses for oil exploration and production that it held in the region.

From an operational perspective, the venture proved to be a success. Following the injection of cash and technology from Black Sea, production at the Tura field went from 4,000 barrels a day to nearly 12,000. However, Black Sea did not capture any of the economic profits flowing from this investment. In 1997, the Moscow-based Alfa Group, one of Russia's largest private companies, purchased a controlling stake in Tyumen from the Russian government. The new owners of Tyumen quickly concluded the Tura joint venture was not fair to them, and they wanted it canceled. Their argument was that the value of the assets contributed by Tyumen to the joint venture was far in excess of $40 million, while the value of the technology and expertise contributed by Black Sea was significantly less than $40 million. The new owners also found some conflicting legislation that seemed to indicate the licenses held by Tura were owned by Tyumen and that Black Sea therefore had no right to the resulting production. Tyumen took the issue to court in Russia and won, despite the fact that the original deal had been negotiated by the Russian government. Black Sea had little choice but to walk away from the deal. According to Black Sea, by legal maneuvering, Tyumen expropriated Black Sea's investment in the Tura venture. In contrast, the management of Tyumen claimed it had behaved in a perfectly legal manner.[13]

Adjusting for Political and Economic Risk

When analyzing a foreign investment opportunity, the company must consider the political and economic risks that stem from the foreign location.[12] We discuss these before looking at how capital budgeting methods can be adjusted to take risks into account.

Political Risk

The concept of political risk was introduced in Chapter 2. There we defined it as the likelihood that political forces will cause drastic changes in a country's business environment that hurt the profit and other goals of a business enterprise. Political risk tends to be greater in countries experiencing social unrest or disorder and in countries where the underlying nature of the society makes the likelihood of social unrest high. When political risk is high, there is a high probability that a change will occur in the country's political environment that will endanger foreign firms there.

In extreme cases, political change may result in the expropriation of foreign firms' assets. This occurred to U.S. firms after the Iranian revolution of 1979. In recent decades, the risk of outright expropriations has become almost zero. However, a lack of consistent legislation and proper law enforcement and no willingness on the part of the government to enforce contracts and protect private property rights can result in the de facto expropriation of the assets of a foreign multinational. An example of this, which occurred in Russia, is given in the accompanying Management Focus.

Political and social unrest may also result in economic collapse, which can render worthless a firm's assets. In less extreme cases, political changes may result in increased tax rates, the imposition of exchange controls that limit or block a subsidiary's ability to remit earnings to its parent company, the imposition of price controls, and government interference in existing contracts. The likelihood of any of these events impairs the attractiveness of a foreign investment opportunity.

Many firms devote considerable attention to political risk analysis and to quantifying political risk. *Euromoney* magazine publishes an annual "country risk rating," which incorporates assessments of political and other risks and is widely used by businesses. The problem with all attempts to forecast political risk, however, is that they try to predict a future that can only be guessed at—and in many cases, the guesses are wrong. Few people foresaw the 1979 Iranian revolution, the collapse of communism in eastern Europe, the dramatic breakup of the Soviet Union, the terrorist attack on the World Trade Center in September 2001; yet all these events had a profound impact on the business environments of many countries. This is not to say that political risk assessment is without value, but it is more art than science.

Economic Risk

The concept of economic risk was also introduced in Chapter 3. It was defined as the likelihood that economic mismanagement will cause drastic changes in a country's business environment that hurt the profit and other goals of a business enterprise. In practice, the biggest problem arising from economic mismanagement has been inflation. Historically, many governments have expanded their domestic money supply in misguided attempts to stimulate economic activity. The result has often been too much money chasing too few goods, resulting in price inflation. As we saw in Chapter 10, price inflation is reflected in a drop in the value of a country's currency on the foreign exchange market. This can be a serious problem for a foreign firm with assets in that country because the value of the cash flows it receives from those assets will fall as the country's currency depreciates on the foreign exchange market. The likelihood of this occurring decreases the attractiveness of foreign investment in that country.

There have been many attempts to quantify countries' economic risk and long-term movements in their exchange rates. (*Euromoney*'s annual country risk rating also incorporates an assessment of economic risk in its calculation of each country's overall level of risk.) As we saw in Chapter 11, there have been extensive empirical studies of the relationship between countries' inflation rates and their currencies' exchange rates. These studies show there is a long-run relationship between a country's relative inflation rates and changes in exchange rates. However, the relationship is not as close as theory would predict; it is not reliable in the short run and is not totally reliable in the long run. So as with political risk, any attempts to quantify economic risk must be tempered with some healthy skepticism.

Risk and Capital Budgeting

In analyzing a foreign investment opportunity, the additional risk that stems from its location can be handled in at least two ways. The first method is to treat all risk as a single problem by increasing the discount rate applicable to foreign projects in countries where political and economic risks are perceived as high. Thus, for example, a firm might apply a 6 percent discount rate to potential investments in Great Britain, the United States, and Germany, reflecting those countries' economic and political stability, and it might use a 12 percent discount rate for potential investments in Russia, reflecting the greater perceived political and economic risks in that country. The higher the discount rate, the higher the projected net cash flows must be for an investment to have a positive net present value.

Adjusting discount rates to reflect a location's riskiness seems to be fairly widely practiced. For example, several studies of large U.S. multinationals have found that many of them routinely add a premium percentage for risk to the discount rate they used in evaluating potential foreign investment projects.[14] However, critics of this method argue that it penalizes early cash flows too heavily and does not penalize distant cash flows enough.[15] They point out that if political or economic collapse were expected in the near future, the investment would not occur anyway. So for any investment decisions, the political and economic risk being assessed is not of immediate possibilities but at some distance in the future. Accordingly, it can be argued that rather than using a higher discount rate to evaluate such risky projects, which penalizes early cash flows too heavily, it is better to revise future cash flows from the project downward to reflect the possibility of adverse political or economic changes sometime in the future. Surveys of actual practice within multinationals suggest that the practice of revising future cash flows downward is almost as popular as that of revising the discount rate upward.[16]

FINANCIAL MANAGEMENT: THE FINANCING DECISION

When considering its options for financing, an international business must consider how the foreign investment will be financed. If external financing is required, the firm must decide whether to tap the global capital market for funds or borrow from sources in the host country. If the firm is going to seek external financing for a project, it will want to borrow funds from the lowest-cost source of capital available. As we saw in Chapter 12, firms increasingly are turning to the global capital market to finance their investments. The cost of capital is typically lower in the global capital market, by virtue of its size and liquidity, than in many domestic capital markets, particularly those that are small and relatively illiquid. Thus, for example, a U.S. firm making an investment in Denmark may finance the investment by borrowing through the London-based Eurobond market rather than the Danish capital market.

However, despite the trends toward deregulation of financial services, in some cases host-country government restrictions may rule out this option. The governments of some countries require, or at least prefer, foreign multinationals to finance projects in their country by local debt financing or local sales of equity. In countries where liquidity is limited, this raises the cost of capital used to finance a project. Thus, in capital budgeting decisions, the discount rate must be adjusted upward to reflect this. However, this is not the only possibility. In Chapter 8, we saw that some governments court foreign investment by offering foreign firms low-interest loans, lowering the cost of capital. Accordingly, in capital budgeting decisions, the discount rate should be revised downward in such cases.

In addition to the impact of host-government policies on the cost of capital and financing decisions, the firm may wish to consider local debt financing for investments in countries where the local currency is expected to depreciate on the foreign exchange market. The amount of local currency required to meet interest payments and retire principal on local debt obligations is not affected when a country's currency depreciates. However, if foreign debt obligations must be served, the amount of local currency required to do this will increase as the currency depreciates, and this effectively raises the cost of capital. Thus, although the initial cost of capital may be greater with local borrowing, it may be better to borrow locally if the local currency is expected to depreciate on the foreign exchange market.

FINANCIAL MANAGEMENT: GLOBAL MONEY MANAGEMENT

Money management decisions attempt to manage the firm's global cash resources—its working capital—most efficiently. This involves minimizing cash balances, reducing transaction costs, and minimizing the corporate tax burden.

Minimizing Cash Balances

LO20-6

Every business needs to hold some cash balances for servicing accounts that must be paid and for insuring against unanticipated negative variation from its projected cash flows. The critical issue for an international business is whether each foreign subsidiary should hold its own cash balances or whether cash balances should be held at a centralized depository. In general, firms prefer to hold cash balances at a centralized depository for three reasons.

First, by pooling cash reserves centrally, the firm can deposit larger amounts. Cash balances are typically deposited in liquid accounts, such as overnight money market accounts. Because interest rates on such deposits normally increase with the size of the deposit, by pooling cash centrally, the firm should be able to earn a higher interest rate than it would if each subsidiary managed its own cash balances.

Second, if the centralized depository is located in a major financial center (e.g., London, New York, or Tokyo), it should have access to information about good short-term investment opportunities that the typical foreign subsidiary would lack. Also, the financial experts at a centralized depository should be able to develop investment skills and know-how that managers in the typical foreign subsidiary would lack. Thus, the firm should make better investment decisions if it pools its cash reserves at a centralized depository.

Third, by pooling its cash reserves, the firm can reduce the total size of the cash pool it must hold in highly liquid accounts, which enables the firm to invest a larger amount of cash reserves in longer-term, less liquid financial instruments that earn a higher interest rate. For example, a U.S. firm has three foreign subsidiaries—one in Korea, one in China, and one in Japan. Each subsidiary maintains a cash balance that includes an amount for dealing with its day-to-day needs plus a precautionary amount for dealing with unanticipated cash demands. The firm's policy is that the total required cash balance is equal to three standard deviations of the expected day-to-day needs amount. The three-standard-deviation requirement reflects the firm's estimate that, in practice, there is a 99.87 percent probability that the subsidiary will have sufficient cash to deal with both day-to-day and unanticipated cash demands. Cash needs are assumed to be normally distributed in each country and independent of each other (e.g., cash needs in Japan do not affect cash needs in China).

The individual subsidiaries' day-to-day cash needs and the precautionary cash balances they should hold are as follows (in millions of dollars):

	Day-to-Day Cash Needs (A)	One Standard Deviation (B)	Required Cash Balance (A + 3 × B)
Korea	$10	$1	$13
China	6	2	12
Japan	12	3	21
Total	$28	$6	$46

Thus, the Korean subsidiary estimates that it must hold $10 million to serve its day-to-day needs. The standard deviation of this is $1 million, so it is to hold an additional $3 million as a precautionary amount. This gives a total required cash balance of $13 million. The total of the required cash balances for all three subsidiaries is $46 million.

Now consider what might occur if the firm decided to maintain all three cash balances at a centralized depository in Tokyo. Because variances are additive when probability distributions are independent of each other, the standard deviation of the combined precautionary account would be

$$\text{Standard deviation} = \sqrt{\$1{,}000{,}000^2 + \$2{,}000{,}000^2 + \$3{,}000{,}000^2}$$
$$= \sqrt{\$14{,}000{,}000}$$
$$= \$3{,}741{,}657$$

Therefore, if the firm used a centralized depository, it would need to hold $28 million for day-to-day needs plus ($3 × $3,741,657) as a precautionary amount, or a total cash balance of $39,224,971. In other words, the firm's total required cash balance would be reduced from $46 million to $39,224,971, a saving of $6,775,029. This is cash that could be invested in less liquid, higher-interest accounts or in tangible assets. The saving arises simply due to the statistical effects of summing the three independent, normal probability distributions.

However, a firm's ability to establish a centralized depository that can serve short-term cash needs might be limited by government-imposed restrictions on capital flows across borders (e.g., controls put in place to protect a country's foreign exchange reserves). Also, the transaction costs of moving money into and out of different currencies can limit the advantages of such a system. Despite this, many firms hold at least their subsidiaries' precautionary cash reserves at a centralized depository, having each subsidiary hold its own cash balance for day-to-day needs. The globalization of the world capital market and the general removal of barriers to the free flow of cash across borders (particularly among advanced industrialized countries) are two trends likely to increase the use of centralized depositories.

Reducing Transaction Costs

Transaction costs are the cost of exchange. Every time a firm changes cash from one currency into another currency it must bear a transaction cost—the commission fee it pays to foreign exchange dealers for performing the transaction. Most banks also charge a **transfer fee** for moving cash from one location to another; this is another transaction cost. The commission and transfer fees arising from intrafirm transactions can be substantial; according to the United Nations, 40 percent of international trade involves transactions between the different national subsidiaries of transnational corporations. The volume of such transactions is likely to be particularly high in a firm that has a globally dispersed web of interdependent value creation activities. Multilateral netting allows a multinational firm to reduce the transaction costs that arise when many transactions occur between its subsidiaries by reducing the number of transactions.

Multilateral netting is an extension of **bilateral netting**. Under bilateral netting, if a French subsidiary owes a Mexican subsidiary $6 million and the Mexican subsidiary simultaneously owes the French subsidiary $4 million, a bilateral settlement will be made with a single payment of $2 million from the French subsidiary to the Mexican subsidiary, the remaining debt being canceled.

Under **multilateral netting**, this simple concept is extended to the transactions between multiple subsidiaries within an international business. Consider a firm that wants to establish multilateral netting among four Asian subsidiaries based in Korea, China, Japan, and Taiwan. These subsidiaries all trade with each other, so at the end of each month a large volume of cash transactions must be settled. Figure 20.2 shows how the payment schedule might look at the end of a given month. Figure 20.3 is a payment matrix that summarizes the obligations among the subsidiaries. Note that $43 million needs to flow among the subsidiaries. If the transaction costs (foreign exchange commissions plus transfer fees) amount to 1 percent of the total funds to be transferred, this will cost the parent firm $430,000. However, this amount can be reduced by multilateral netting. Using the payment matrix (Figure 20.3), the firm can determine the payments that need to be made among its subsidiaries to settle these obligations. Figure 20.4 shows the results. By multilateral netting, the transactions depicted in Figure 20.2 are reduced to just three; the Korean subsidiary pays $3 million to the Taiwanese subsidiary, and the Chinese subsidiary pays $1 million to the Japanese subsidiary and $1 million to the Taiwanese subsidiary. The total funds that flow among the subsidiaries are reduced from $43 million to just $5 million, and the transaction costs are reduced from $430,000 to $50,000, a savings of $380,000 achieved through multilateral netting.

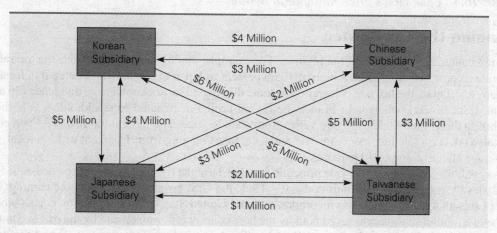

FIGURE 20.2 *Cash Flows before Multilateral Netting*

Paying Subsidiary

Receiving Subsidiary	Korea	China	Japan	Taiwan	Total Receipts	Net Receipts (payments)
Korean	—	$ 3	$4	$5	$12	($3)
Chinese	$ 4	—	2	3	9	(2)
Japanese	5	3	—	1	9	1
Taiwanese	6	5	2	—	13	4
Total payments	$15	$11	$8	$9	$43	$5

FIGURE 20.3 *Calculation of Net Receipts (all amounts in millions)*

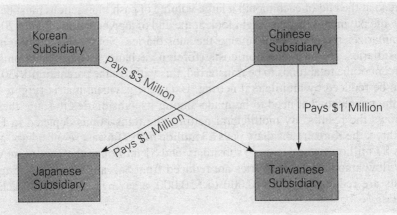

FIGURE 20.4 *Cash Flows after Multilateral Netting*

Managing the Tax Burden

Different countries have different tax regimes. For example, among developed nations the top rates for corporate income tax varies from a high of 40.69 percent in Japan to a low of 12.5 percent in Ireland. In Germany and Japan, the tax rate is lower on income distributed to stockholders as dividends (36 and 35 percent, respectively), whereas in France the tax on profits distributed to stockholders is higher (42 percent). In the United States, the rate varies from state to state. The federal top rate is 35 percent, but states also tax corporate income, with state and local taxes ranging from 1 percent to 12 percent, hence the average effective rate of 40 percent.

Many nations follow the worldwide principle that they have the right to tax income earned outside their boundaries by entities based in their country.[17] Thus, the U.S. government can tax the earnings of the German subsidiary of an enterprise incorporated in the United States. Double taxation occurs when the income of a foreign subsidiary is taxed both by the host-country government and by the parent company's home government. However, double taxation is mitigated by tax credits, tax treaties, and the deferral principle.

A **tax credit** allows an entity to reduce the taxes paid to the home government by the amount of taxes paid to the foreign government. A **tax treaty** between two countries is an agreement specifying which items of income will be taxed by the authorities of the country where the income is earned. For example, a tax treaty between the United States and Germany may specify that a U.S. firm need not pay tax in Germany on any earnings from its German subsidiary that are remitted to the United States in the form of dividends. A **deferral principle** specifies that parent companies are not taxed on foreign source income until they actually receive a dividend.

For the international business with activities in many countries, the various tax regimes and the tax treaties have important implications for how the firm should structure its internal payments system among the foreign subsidiaries and the parent company. The opening case provides an example of how one firm, Google, has done this in order to reduce its effective tax rate on foreign earnings to nearly zero. As we will see in the next section, the firm can use transfer prices and fronting loans to minimize its global tax liability. In addition, the form in which income is remitted from a foreign subsidiary to the parent company (e.g., royalty payments versus dividend payments) can be structured to minimize the firm's global tax liability.

Some firms use **tax havens** such as the Bahamas and Bermuda to minimize their tax liability (Google uses Bermuda—see the opening case). A tax haven is a country with an exceptionally low, or even no, income tax. International businesses avoid or defer income taxes by establishing a wholly owned, nonoperating subsidiary in the tax haven. The tax haven subsidiary owns the common stock of the operating foreign subsidiaries. This allows all transfers of funds from foreign operating subsidiaries to the parent company to be funneled through the tax haven subsidiary. The tax levied on foreign source income by a firm's home government, which might normally be paid when a dividend is declared by a foreign subsidiary, can be deferred under the deferral principle until the tax haven subsidiary pays the dividend to the parent. This dividend payment can be postponed indefinitely if foreign operations continue to grow and require new internal financing from the tax haven affiliate.

Many U.S. multinationals maintain large tax balances in foreign tax havens because they do not want to pay U.S. corporate taxes when those earnings are repatriated to the U.S. In early 2013, estimates suggest that American multinationals had as much as $1.9 trillion in accumulated foreign earnings parked in foreign tax havens such as Bermuda. Companies with large cash holdings in tax-sheltered subsidiaries include Apple, Cisco Systems, Microsoft, and Google (see the opening case). Apple alone had roughly $140 billion in cash and short-term securities on its balance sheet in the first quarter of 2013, of which 70 percent was held overseas. Microsoft had $74.5 billion, of which 88 percent was held in subsidiaries located in tax havens.[18]

Some argue that holding such large cash balances overseas to avoid tax is counterproductive, and that shareholders would benefit more if the cash was repatriated to the United States, tax paid on it, and the remaining funds returned to shareholders in the form of dividend payouts and stock buybacks. Due to tax credits, for example, Microsoft would probably pay a U.S. corporate tax rate of about 30 percent on the money held overseas if it decided to send it back to the United States. This would still leave the company with around $46 billion after taxes that could be used to buy back stock, which could increase the share price by around 25 percent, assuming that valuations remain the same.

Moving Money Across Borders

Pursuing the objectives of utilizing the firm's cash resources most efficiently and minimizing the firm's global tax liability requires the firm to be able to transfer funds from one location to another around the globe. International businesses use a number of techniques to transfer liquid funds across borders. These include dividend remittances, royalty payments and fees, transfer prices, and fronting loans. Some firms rely on more than one of these techniques to transfer funds across borders—a practice known as *unbundling.* By using a mix of techniques to transfer liquid funds from a foreign subsidiary to the parent company, unbundling allows an international business to recover funds from its foreign subsidiaries without piquing host-country sensitivities with large "dividend drains."

A firm's ability to select a particular policy is severely limited when a foreign subsidiary is part-owned either by a local joint-venture partner or by local stockholders. Serving the legitimate demands of the local co-owners of a foreign subsidiary may limit the firm's ability to impose the kind of dividend policy, royalty payment schedule, or transfer pricing policy that would be optimal for the parent company.

Dividend Remittances

Payment of dividends is the most common method by which firms transfer funds from foreign subsidiaries to the parent company. The dividend policy typically varies with each subsidiary depending on such factors as tax regulations, foreign exchange risk, the age of the subsidiary, and the extent of local equity participation. For example, the higher the rate of tax levied on dividends by the host-country government, the less attractive this option becomes relative to other options for transferring liquid funds. With regard to foreign exchange risk, firms sometimes require foreign subsidiaries based in "high-risk" countries to speed up the transfer of funds to the parent through accelerated dividend payments. This moves corporate funds out of a country whose currency is expected to depreciate significantly. The age of a foreign subsidiary influences dividend policy in that older subsidiaries tend to remit a higher proportion of their earnings in dividends to the parent, presumably because a subsidiary has fewer capital investment needs as it matures. Local equity participation is a factor because local co-owners' demands for dividends must be recognized.

Royalty Payments and Fees

Royalties represent the remuneration paid to the owners of technology, patents, or trade names for the use of that technology or the right to manufacture and/or sell products under those patents or trade names. It is common for a parent company to charge its foreign subsidiaries royalties for the technology, patents, or trade names it has transferred to them. Royalties may be levied as a fixed monetary amount per unit of the product the subsidiary sells or as a percentage of a subsidiary's gross revenues.

A fee is compensation for professional services or expertise supplied to a foreign subsidiary by the parent company or another subsidiary. Fees are sometimes differentiated into "management fees" for general expertise and advice and "technical assistance fees" for guidance in technical matters. Fees are usually levied as fixed charges for the particular services provided.

Royalties and fees have certain tax advantages over dividends, particularly when the corporate tax rate is higher in the host country than in the parent's home country. Royalties and fees are often tax-deductible locally (because they are viewed as an expense), so arranging for payment in royalties and fees will reduce the foreign subsidiary's tax liability. If the foreign subsidiary compensates the parent company by dividend payments, local income taxes must be paid before the dividend distribution, and withholding taxes must be paid on the dividend itself. Although the parent can often take a tax credit for the local withholding and income taxes it has paid, part of the benefit can be lost if the subsidiary's combined tax rate is higher than the parent's.

Transfer Prices

Any international business normally involves a large number of transfers of goods and services between the parent company and foreign subsidiaries and between foreign subsidiaries. This is particularly likely in firms pursuing global and transnational strategies because these firms are likely to have dispersed their value creation activities to various "optimal" locations around the globe (see Chapter 13). As noted earlier, the price at which goods and services are transferred between entities within the firm is referred to as the transfer price.[19]

Transfer prices can be used to position funds within an international business. For example, funds can be moved out of a particular country by setting high transfer prices for goods and services supplied to a subsidiary in that country and by setting low transfer prices for the goods and services sourced from that subsidiary. Conversely, funds can be positioned in a country by the opposite policy: setting low transfer prices for goods and services supplied to a subsidiary in that country and setting high transfer prices for the goods and services sourced from that subsidiary. This movement of funds can be between the firm's subsidiaries or between the parent company and a subsidiary.

At least four gains can be derived by adjusting transfer prices:

1. The firm can reduce its tax liabilities by using transfer prices to shift earnings from a high-tax country to a low-tax one.

2. The firm can use transfer prices to move funds out of a country where a significant currency devaluation is expected, thereby reducing its exposure to foreign exchange risk.
3. The firm can use transfer prices to move funds from a subsidiary to the parent company (or a tax haven) when financial transfers in the form of dividends are restricted or blocked by host-country government policies.
4. The firm can use transfer prices to reduce the import duties it must pay when an ad valorem tariff is in force—a tariff assessed as a percentage of value. In this case, low transfer prices on goods or services being imported into the country are required. Since this lowers the value of the goods or services, it lowers the tariff.

However, significant problems are associated with pursuing a transfer pricing policy.[20] Few governments like it.[21] When transfer prices are used to reduce a firm's tax liabilities or import duties, most governments feel they are being cheated of their legitimate income. Similarly, when transfer prices are manipulated to circumvent government restrictions on capital flows (e.g., dividend remittances), governments perceive this as breaking the spirit—if not the letter—of the law. Many governments now limit international businesses' ability to manipulate transfer prices in the manner described. The United States has strict regulations governing transfer pricing practices. According to Section 482 of the Internal Revenue Code, the Internal Revenue Service (IRS) can reallocate gross income, deductions, credits, or allowances between related corporations to prevent tax evasion or to reflect more clearly a proper allocation of income. Under the IRS guidelines and subsequent judicial interpretation, the burden of proof is on the taxpayer to show that the IRS has been arbitrary or unreasonable in reallocating income. The correct transfer price, according to the IRS guidelines, is an arm's-length price—the price that would prevail between unrelated firms in a market setting. Such a strict interpretation of what is a correct transfer price theoretically limits a firm's ability to manipulate transfer prices to achieve the benefits we have discussed. Many other countries have followed the U.S. lead in emphasizing that transfer prices should be set on an arm's-length basis.

Another problem associated with transfer pricing is related to management incentives and performance evaluation.[22] Transfer pricing is inconsistent with a policy of treating each subsidiary in the firm as a profit center. When transfer prices are manipulated by the firm and deviate significantly from the arm's-length price, the subsidiary's performance may depend as much on transfer prices as it does on other pertinent factors, such as management effort. A subsidiary told to charge a high transfer price for a good supplied to another subsidiary will appear to be doing better than it actually is, while the subsidiary purchasing the good will appear to be doing worse. Unless this is recognized when performance is being evaluated, serious distortions in management incentive systems can occur. For example, managers in the selling subsidiary may be able to use high transfer prices to mask inefficiencies, while managers in the purchasing subsidiary may become disheartened by the effect of high transfer prices on their subsidiary's profitability.

Despite these problems, research suggests that not all international businesses use arm's-length pricing but instead use some cost-based system for pricing transfers among their subunits (typically cost plus some standard markup). A survey of 164 U.S. multinational firms found that 35 percent of the firms used market-based prices, 15 percent used negotiated prices, and 65 percent used a cost-based pricing method. (The figures add up to more than 100 percent because some companies use more than one method.)[23] Only market and negotiated prices could reasonably be interpreted as arm's-length prices. The opportunity for price manipulation is much greater with cost-based transfer pricing. Other more sophisticated research has uncovered indirect evidence that many corporations do manipulate transfer prices in order to reduce global tax liabilities.[24]

Although a firm may be able to manipulate transfer prices to avoid tax liabilities or circumvent government restrictions on capital flows across borders, this does not mean the firm should do so. Since the practice often violates at least the spirit of the law in many countries, the ethics of engaging in transfer pricing are dubious at best. Also, there are clear signs that tax authorities in many countries are increasing their scrutiny of this practice in order to stamp out abuses. A survey of some 600 multinationals undertaken by accountants at Ernst & Young found that 75 percent of them believed they would be the subject of a transfer pricing audit by tax authorities in the next two years.[25] Some 61 percent of the multinationals in the survey stated that transfer pricing was the top tax issue that they faced.

Fronting Loans

A fronting loan is a loan between a parent and its subsidiary channeled through a financial intermediary, usually a large international bank. In a direct intrafirm loan, the parent company lends cash directly to the foreign subsidiary, and the subsidiary repays it later. In a fronting loan, the parent company deposits funds in an international bank, and the bank then lends the same amount to the foreign subsidiary. Thus, a U.S. firm might deposit $100,000 in a London bank. The London bank might then lend that $100,000 to an Indian subsidiary of the firm. From the bank's point of view, the loan is risk-free because it has 100 percent collateral in the form of the parent's deposit. The bank "fronts" for the parent, hence the name. The bank makes a profit by paying the parent company a slightly lower interest rate on its deposit than it charges the foreign subsidiary on the borrowed funds.

Firms use fronting loans for two reasons. First, fronting loans can circumvent host-country restrictions on the remittance of funds from a foreign subsidiary to the parent company. A host government might restrict a foreign subsidiary from repaying a loan to its parent in order to preserve the country's foreign exchange reserves, but it is less likely to restrict a subsidiary's ability to repay a loan to a large international bank. To stop payment to an international bank would hurt the country's credit image, whereas halting payment to the parent company would probably have a minimal impact on its image. Consequently, international businesses sometimes use fronting loans when they want to lend funds to a subsidiary based in a country with a fairly high probability of political turmoil that might lead to restrictions on capital flows (i.e., where the level of political risk is high).

A fronting loan can also provide tax advantages. For example, a tax haven (Bermuda) subsidiary that is 100 percent owned by the parent company deposits $1 million in a London-based international bank at 8 percent interest. The bank lends the $1 million to a foreign operating subsidiary at 9 percent interest. The country where the foreign operating subsidiary is based taxes corporate income at 50 percent (see Figure 20.5).

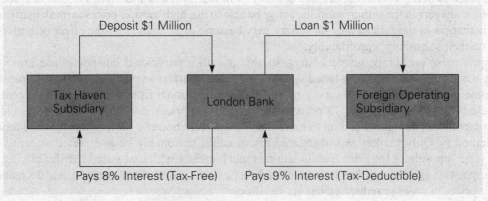

FIGURE 20.5   *An Example of the Tax Aspects of a Fronting Loan*

Under this arrangement, interest payments net of income tax will be as follows:

1. The foreign operating subsidiary pays $90,000 interest to the London bank. Deducting these interest payments from its taxable income results in a net after-tax cost of $45,000 to the foreign operating subsidiary.
2. The London bank receives the $90,000. It retains $10,000 for its services and pays $80,000 interest on the deposit to the Bermuda subsidiary.
3. The Bermuda subsidiary receives $80,000 interest on its deposit tax-free.

The net result is that $80,000 in cash has been moved from the foreign operating subsidiary to the tax haven subsidiary. Because the foreign operating subsidiary's after-tax cost of borrowing is only $45,000, the parent company has moved an additional $35,000 out of the country by using this arrangement. If the tax haven subsidiary had made a direct loan to the foreign operating subsidiary, the host government may have disallowed the interest charge as a tax-deductible expense by ruling that it was a dividend to the parent disguised as an interest payment.

Chapter Summary

This chapter focused on accounting and financial management in the international business. It explained why accounting practices and standards differ from country to country and surveyed the efforts under way to harmonize countries' accounting practices. We reviewed several issues related to the use of accounting-based control systems within international businesses. We discussed how investment decisions, financing decisions, and money management decisions are complicated by the fact that different countries have different currencies, different tax regimes, different levels of political and economic risk, and so on. This chapter made the following points:

1. Each country's accounting system evolved in response to the local demands for accounting information. National differences in accounting and auditing standards resulted in a general lack of comparability in countries' financial reports.
2. This lack of comparability has become a problem as transnational financing and transnational investment have grown rapidly in recent decades (a consequence of the globalization of capital markets). Due to the lack of comparability, a firm may have to explain to investors why its financial position looks very different on financial reports that are based on different accounting practices.
3. The most significant push for harmonization of accounting standards across countries has come from the International Accounting Standards Board (IASB).
4. In most international businesses, the annual budget is the main instrument by which headquarters controls foreign subsidiaries. Throughout the year, headquarters compares a subsidiary's performance against the financial goals incorporated in its budget, intervening selectively in its operations when shortfalls occur.
5. Most international businesses require all budgets and performance data within the firm to be expressed in the corporate currency. This enhances comparability, but it distorts the control process if the relevant exchange rates change between the time a foreign subsidiary's budget is set and the time its performance is evaluated. According to the Lessard-Lorange model, the best way

to deal with this problem is to use a projected spot exchange rate to translate both budget figures and performance figures into the corporate currency.

6. Transfer prices can introduce significant distortions into the control process and thus must be considered when setting budgets and evaluating a subsidiary's performance.

7. When using capital budgeting techniques to evaluate a potential foreign project, the firm needs to recognize the specific risks arising from its foreign location. These include political risks and economic risks (including foreign exchange risk). Political and economic risks can be incorporated into the capital budgeting process by using a higher discount rate to evaluate risky projects or by forecasting lower cash flows for such projects.

8. The cost of capital is lower in the global capital market than in domestic markets. Consequently, other things being equal, firms prefer to finance their investments by borrowing from the global capital market.

9. Borrowing from the global capital market may be restricted by host-government regulations or demands. In such cases, the discount rate used in capital budgeting must be revised upward to reflect this.

10. The firm may want to consider local debt financing for investments in countries where the local currency is expected to depreciate.

11. The principal objectives of global money management are to utilize the firm's cash resources in the most efficient manner and to minimize the firm's global tax liabilities.

12. By holding cash at a centralized depository, the firm may be able to invest its cash reserves more efficiently. It can reduce the total size of the cash pool that it needs to hold in highly liquid accounts, thereby freeing cash for investment in higher-interest-bearing (less liquid) accounts or in tangible assets.

13. Firms use a number of techniques to transfer funds across borders, including dividend remittances, royalty payments and fees, transfer prices, and fronting loans. Dividend remittances are the most common method used for transferring funds across borders, but royalty payments and fees have certain tax advantages over dividend remittances.

14. The manipulation of transfer prices may be used by firms to move funds out of a country to minimize tax liabilities, hedge against foreign exchange risk, circumvent government restrictions on capital flows, and reduce tariff payments. However, manipulating transfer prices in this manner runs counter to government regulations in many countries, it may distort incentive systems within the firm, and it has ethically dubious foundations.

15. Fronting loans involves channeling funds from a parent company to a foreign subsidiary through a third party, normally an international bank. Fronting loans can circumvent host-government restrictions on the remittance of funds and provide certain tax advantages.

Critical Thinking and Discussion Questions

1. Why do the accounting systems of different countries differ? Why do these differences matter?

2. Why might an accounting-based control system provide headquarters management with biased information about the performance of a foreign subsidiary? How can these biases best be corrected?

3. You are the CFO of a U.S. firm whose wholly owned subsidiary in Mexico manufactures component parts for your U.S. assembly operations. The subsidiary has been financed by bank borrowings in the United States. One of your analysts told you that the Mexican peso is expected to

depreciate by 30 percent against the dollar on the foreign exchange markets over the next year. What actions, if any, should you take?

4. You are the CFO of a Canadian firm that is considering building a $10 million factory in Russia to produce milk. The investment is expected to produce net cash flows of $3 million each year for the next 10 years, after which the investment will have to close because of technological obsolescence. Scrap values will be zero. The cost of capital will be 6 percent if financing is arranged through the Eurobond market. However, you have an option to finance the project by borrowing funds from a Russian bank at 12 percent. Analysts tell you that due to high inflation in Russia, the Russian ruble is expected to depreciate against the Canadian dollar. Analysts also rate the probability of violent revolution occurring in Russia within the next 10 years as high. How would you incorporate these factors into your evaluation of the investment opportunity? What would you recommend the firm do?

Research Task ○ globalEDGE | globaledge.msu.edu

Accounting and Finance in the International Business

Use the globalEDGE website (globaledge.msu.edu) to complete the following exercises:

Exercise 1

The inflation rate of a country can affect financial planning in multinational corporations since the value of receivables in each country can face significant devaluation if the inflation rates are high. Your company has operations in the following countries: Belarus, Costa Rica, Finland, Iceland, Paraguay, Thailand, and Zimbabwe. Use the *Country Comparator* on the globalEDGE site to rank the risk of devaluation of your company's receivables from highest to lowest, based on the most recent data available for each country. What precautions can your company take in the countries at the top of this list to minimize the risk?

Exercise 2

The top management of your company has requested information on the tax policies of Argentina. Using the country guide for Argentina on *Deloitte International Tax and Business Guides*—a resource that provides information on the investment climate, operating conditions, and tax systems of major trading countries—prepare a short report summarizing your findings on business taxation in Argentina.

Closing **CASE**

Microsoft's Acquisition of Skype

In May 2011 Microsoft announced that it would be purchasing the Luxembourg-based Internet communications company Skype in an all-cash deal worth $8.5 billion. The acquisition was the largest in Microsoft's history. Skype had been purchased by eBay in 2005 for $3.1 billion, but eBay took a $1.4 billion accounting charge in 2007 after the acquisition failed to realize hoped-for synergies. In 2009, eBay sold a 70 percent stake in Skype to a group of investors led by the U.S. private equity firm Silver Lake Partners. The sale to Silver Lake valued Skype at $2.75 billion. Many observers were surprised that only 18 months later Microsoft was prepared to pay $8.5 billion. Microsoft's stated goal was to integrate Skype's voice and video communications offerings into Microsoft's suite of products, in order to bolster sales of those products and make Microsoft more relevant in the age of digital devices, mobile communications, and cloud computing.

To finance the acquisition, Microsoft used cash held overseas in foreign subsidiaries located in countries with very low corporate tax rates, such as Ireland, Singapore, and Bermuda. At the end of Microsoft's 2010 financial year, the company stated in its annual report that it had $29.5 billion in "permanently reinvested earnings" outside the United States. This figure represents the accumulated net proceeds from foreign sales. Under U.S. law, Microsoft does not pay taxes on those earnings until they are repatriated to the United States. In theory at least, they can be held indefinitely overseas. Microsoft also noted that the tax cost of repatriating those earning to the United States would be $9.2 billion, representing an effective tax rate of 31 percent. The U.S. corporate tax rate is actually 35 percent. Microsoft stated that the reduction to 31 percent would come from foreign tax credits, implying that the taxes the company paid on earnings retained overseas amounts to just 4 percent, nine times lower than the top U.S. rate. Microsoft stated that by using foreign cash to acquire Skype, it was being tax-efficient.

Microsoft wasn't the only company involved in the acquisition that reaped tax benefits. Skype itself was incorporated in Luxemburg, a country with a corporate income tax rate of just 0.4 percent. At the time of the acquisition the U.S. private equity firm Silver Lake owned 39 percent of Skype. Two of the three Silver Lake entities that owned shares in Skype were based in the Caribbean tax havens of the Cayman Islands and George Town, suggesting that Silver Lake would not be paying much in the way of U.S. capital gains tax on the profits made from its investments in Skype. In addition, 30 percent of Skype was owned by eBay. Despite being an American company, eBay's Skype shareholding was held by eBay International AG, which is based in Switzerland where corporate tax rates are between 13 percent and 25 percent.

Despite paying $8.5 billion for Skype, Microsoft's foreign cash hoard has continued to grow. As of March 31, 2013, the company held $66 billion of cash in foreign subsidiaries, representing 89 percent of all the company's cash holdings. In its regulatory filings, the company noted that this cash would be subject to material repatriation tax effects if returned to the United States.[26]

Case Discussion Questions

1. What were the benefits to Microsoft's shareholders of using cash held overseas to purchase Skype?
2. Microsoft's effective tax rate on foreign earnings retained overseas appears to be only 4 percent. How is this possible given that the corporate tax rate in most developed nations where Microsoft earns profits from foreign sales are considerably higher?
3. Why does Microsoft continue to hold so much cash overseas, rather than returning it to the United States? What do you think are the opportunity costs of holding tens of billions of dollars of cash in foreign locations? What potential benefits might accrue to Microsoft shareholders if it returned some of that cash to the United States?
4. Do you think it is ethical for companies like Microsoft to continue to hold cash overseas in order to avoid paying U.S. corporate income taxes? Is this practice always in the best interests of the company's shareholders?

Endnotes

1. J. Drucker, "Google Revenues Sheltered in No-Tax Bermuda Soar to $10 billion," *Bloomberg,* December 9, 2012; R. W.Wood, "Facebook Mirrors Google's Offshore Tax Scheme," *Forbes,* December 27, 2012; and C. Arthur, "Google Chairman Eric Schmidt Defends Tax Avoidance Policies," *The Guardian,* April 22, 2013.

2. G. G. Mueller, H. Gernon, and G. Meek, *Accounting: An International Perspective* (Burr Ridge, IL: Richard D. Irwin, 1991).

3. S. J. Gary, "Towards a Theory of Cultural Influence on the Development of Accounting Systems Internationally," *Abacus* 3 (1988), pp. 1–15; and R. S. Wallace, O. Gernon, and H. Gernon, "Frameworks for International Comparative Financial Accounting," *Journal of Accounting Literature* 10 (1991), pp. 209–64.

4. R. G. Barker, "Global Accounting Is Coming," *Harvard Business Review,* April 2003, pp. 2–3.

5. P. D. Fleming, "The Growing Importance of International Accounting Standards," *Journal of Accountancy,* September 1991, pp. 100–106.

6. P. Practer, "Emerging Trends," *Accountancy,* May 2001, p. 1293; E. Yiu, "China Sees Benefits of Global Standards," *South China Morning Post,* November 20, 2004, p. 3; J. Baglole, "China's Listings Lose Steam," *The Wall Street Journal,* April 26, 2004, p. A13; "Skills Shortage a Hurdle to IAS," *The Standard,* December 2, 2003; E. McDonald, "Shanghai Surprise," *Forbes,* March 26, 2007, pp. 62–63; "Cultural Revolution: Chinese Accounting," *The Economist,* January 13, 2007, p. 63; and S. Hong and J. Ng, "Two Chinese Airlines Post Declines in Profit," *The Wall Street Journal,* August 27, 2008, p. B9.

7. D. Reilly, "SEC to Consider Letting Companies Use International Accounting Rules," *The Wall Street Journal,* April 25, 2007, p. C3.

8. F. Choi and I. Czechowicz, "Assessing Foreign Subsidiary Performance: A Multinational Comparison," *Management International Review* 4, 1983, pp. 14–25.

9. D. Lessard and P. Lorange, "Currency Changes and Management Control: Resolving the Centralization/Decentralization Dilemma," *Accounting Review,* July 1977, pp. 628–37.

10. Mueller, Gernon, and Meek, *Accounting: An International Perspective.*

11. For details of capital budgeting techniques, see R. A. Brealy and S. C. Myers, *Principles of Corporate Finance* (New York: McGraw-Hill, 1988).

12. D. J. Feils and F. M. Sabac, "The Impact of Political Risk on the Foreign Direct Investment Decision: A Capital Budgeting Analysis," *The Engineering Economist* 45 (2000), pp. 129–34.

13. Ibid.; Simon Kukes, "Letters to the Editor: Tura Joint Venture," *The Wall Street Journal,* June 14, 1999, p. A21; and M. Whitehouse, "US Export-Import Bank Agrees to give Russia's Tyumen Oil Loan Guarantee," *The Wall Street Journal,* May 25, 1999, p. A21.

14. See S. Block, "Integrating Traditional Capital Budgeting Concepts into an International Decision Making Environment," *The Engineering Economist* 45 (2000), pp. 309–25; and J. C. Backer and L. J. Beardsley, "Multinational Companies' Use of Risk Evaluation and Profit Measurement for Capital Budgeting Decisions," *Journal of Business Finance,* Spring 1973, pp. 34–43.

15. For example, see D. K. Eiteman, A. I. Stonehill, and M. H. Moffett, *Multinational Business Finance* (Reading, MA: Addison-Wesley, 1992).

16. M. Stanley and S. Block, "An Empirical Study of Management and Financial Variables Influencing Capital Budgeting Decisions for Multinational Corporations in the 1980s," *Management International Review* 23 (1983), pp. 61–71.

17. "Taxing Questions," *The Economist,* May 22, 1993, p. 73.

18. J. Sommer, "How to Unlock That Stashed Foreign Cash," *The New York Times,* March 23, 2013.

19. S. Crow and E. Sauls, "Setting the Right Transfer Price," *Management Accounting,* December 1994, pp. 41–47.

20. V. H. Miesel, H. H. Higinbotham, and C. W. Yi, "International Transfer Pricing: Practical Solutions for Inter-company Pricing," *International Tax Journal* 28 (Fall 2002), pp. 1–22.

21. J. Kelly, "Administrators Prepare for a More Efficient Future," *Financial Times Survey: World Taxation,* February 24, 1995, p. 9.

22. Crow and Sauls, "Setting the Right Transfer Price."

23. M. F. Al-Eryani, P. Alam, and S. Akhter, "Transfer Pricing Determinants of U.S. Multinationals," *Journal of International Business Studies,* September 1990, pp. 409–25.

24. D. L. Swenson. "Tax Reforms and Evidence of Transfer Pricing," *National Tax Journal,* March 2001, pp. 7–25.

25. "Transfer Pricing Survey Shows Multinationals Face Greater Scrutiny," *The CPA Journal,* March 2000, p. 10.

26. E. D. Kleinbard, "Stateless Income," *Florida Tax Review,* 11, no. 9 (2011); R. Jilani, "Microsoft Structured Acquisition of Skype to Avoid US Taxes," *Think Progress,* May 13, 2011; N. Wingfield, "Microsoft Dials Up Change," *The Wall Street Journal,* May 11, 2011; and Microsoft 2010 10K report and Q3 2013 10Q form.

C-A-S-E-S

TAXATION REGIME IN INDIA—2013

Customs Duty

Custom duty is levied by the Government on import of goods into India and is typically payable by the importer of goods. It is also levied on export of certain goods.

Custom duty rates depend on the classification under the Customs Tariff, which is aligned with the International Harmonized System of Nomenclature—generic rate being 28.85%.

Customs duty generally comprises the following components:

- Basic Customs Duty (BCD)
- Additional Customs Duty (CVD)
- in lieu of excise duty
- Education cess/Secondary and Higher education cess
- Special Additional Customs Duty (SAD)

The CVD paid on import of goods is allowed as credit against the output excise/service tax liability, subject to conditions. Whereas, SAD paid on import of goods is allowed as credit only to a manufacturer against the output excise duty, and not to an output service provider, subject to conditions.

In case of import from related parties, the matter is typically referred to the Special Valuation Branch authorities by the customs authorities prima facie to determine if the assessable/transaction value is at arm's length. Accordingly, the relevant customs-related procedures would need to be fulfilled.

Excise Duty

Excise duty is applicable on the manufacture of goods within India and is payable by the manufacturer.

Most products attract a uniform rate of 12% plus education cess at 3% of the excise duty, making the effective excise duty at 12.36%, i.e., excise duty of 12% and education cess of 0.36% (3% on excise duty).

Excise duty is generally levied on an ad valorem basis, either expressed as a percentage of the transaction value or maximum retail price (for certain specified goods). Goods manufactured in India can be exported without payment of excise duty, subject to specified conditions.

Similarly, inputs used in the manufacture of goods to be exported can be procured without payment of excise duty, subject to conditions.

The Cenvat Credit Rules, 2004 (Credit Rules) allow manufacturers to take credit for specified duties, including excise duty. CVD, SAD on varied inputs and capital goods imported, as well as service tax paid on input services used in the manufacture of excisable goods. The manufacturer can utilize such credit to pay the excise duty applicable on the final goods manufactured. Further, credit of duty paid on capital goods will be available to the extent of 50% during the first financial year of its receipt and the balance in the subsequent period.

A lower excise duty of 2% has been provided on 131 specified (for which CENVAT credit would not be available), which were hitherto fully exempt or chargeable to zero excise duty. Alternatively, an option to avail CENVAT credit by charging a duty of 6% on specified 68 items is also available

Service Tax

Service tax is applicable on the provision of services in India. It is also applicable on import of services in India where service recipient is required to discharge service tax liability in cash (under reverse charge mechanism). The present rate of service tax is 12.36%, i.e., 12% service tax and education cess of 0.36% (3% on service tax).

The GoI has introduced negative list-based taxation of services with effect from 1st July, 2012. In view of this, except 17 negative services (mainly provided by or to GoI or state governments, health care services, agriculture, trading, etc.) and 39 specifically exempt services, all other services are taxable unless it is:

- Sale/purchase of goods (including deemed sale)
- Transfer or gift of immovable property
- Transaction in money or actionable claim

Service provided by employee to employer in the course of employment. For certain specified services, the onus of paying service tax is partly on service provider and partly on service recipient. Currently, this provision will apply for hiring of motor vehicle, supply of manpower and works contract services when provided by an individual, HUF, partnership firm or AOP to a body corporate.

Services provided outside India will not be liable to service tax: Such services will be deemed as exports subject to fulfillment of conditions. In respect of services, which qualify as exports, a mechanism has been provided, which prescribes an option for the exporter to claim rebate/ refund of excise duty/ CVD/service tax paid on input/input services used for export of service.

Place of Provision of Services Rules, 2012 (PPOS), have been introduced with effect from 1st July, 2012 to determine the place where a service shall be deemed to be provided. A service shall be taxable only when inter alia it is provided in the taxable territory (i.e., India excluding J&K). In other words, the taxability of a service will be determined based on its place of provision according to PPOS.

According to the Point of Taxation Rules, 2011, the point of taxation for payment of service tax shall be the date of issue of the invoice or the date of receipt of payment for service by the service provider, whichever is earlier. However, where the invoice is not raised within 30 days of completion of provision of service, the point of taxation shall be the date of such completion. In case of services provided continuously or on recurrent basis for a period exceeding three months, under a contract and with an obligation for periodic payment, the date of completion shall be the date of completion of each event under such contract. Further, where the service recipient is required to pay service tax under reverse charge mechanism (i.e., as the importer of service), the point of taxation shall be the date on which such payment is made (provided that payment is made within six months from the invoice date).

The Credit Rules allow the service provider to take credit of duties, including excise duty, CVD paid on inputs and capital goods and service tax paid on input services used to provide taxable output services, subject to conditions. Also, a service recipient is allowed to take credit of the service tax paid on import of services in cash against its output excise or service tax liability.

Credit of SAD paid on import of goods is not available to offset output service tax liability. There is no credit of duty/tax paid on input/input services that are used exclusively to provide non-taxable or exempt services.

VAT/CST

VAT is an intra-state multi-point tax system administered at the state level and is levied on sale of goods at each stage of sale. Currently, all the states in India have replaced their erstwhile sales tax regime with VAT.

The basic rate slabs under VAT are as follows:

- 0% for natural and unprocessed products and other essential goods
- 1% to 2% for special goods such as gold, bullion, silver, etc.
- 4%/5% for agricultural and industrial input, IT products, capital goods and intangible goods, i.e., patents and others, as well as items of basic necessity
- 12.5% to 15% for all other goods that do not fall under any of the categories mentioned above

Interstate sales continue to be liable to Central Sales Tax (CST), which is imposed by the GoI and administered by state governments. The rate of CST is 2%, subject to provision of prescribed declaration form by the purchaser. In the absence of a prescribed declaration form, the VAT rate as applicable in the selling state will apply (i.e., ranging from 4%/5%– 12.5%/15%). Declaration forms are only issued when the goods are procured for (i) resale, (ii) for use in manufacture or processing of goods for sale, (iii) a telecommunications network, (iv) for use in mining or (v) for use in generation or distribution of electricity or any other form of power.

It is proposed that CST will be phased out on introduction of Goods and Service Tax (GST).

Further, a sale involving import of goods from outside India is not liable to VAT/CST, subject to the prescribed conditions. Moreover, sale of goods (including penultimate sale) involving export of goods from India is also not liable to VAT/CST.

Input tax credit is available with respect to VAT paid on locally procured goods, including capital goods (other than the "negative list" of goods provided under respective state VAT laws). The credit can be set off against output VAT liability, including output CST. However, no input credit is available in respect of CST paid on procurements and hence, it is a cost to the purchaser.

Octroi/Entry Tax

Entry tax/Octroi is levied by state/local authorities on the entry of goods within its jurisdiction, for use, consumption or sale on the purchase value of the goods. For this purpose, the state is divided into different local areas. The value of the entry tax levied on different products can vary from state to state. It is relevant to note that the constitutional validity of entry tax laws is currently a subject of dispute. The applicability and status of the dispute needs to be examined on a state-to-state basis.

Octroi is applicable in the state of Maharashtra at various local municipal jurisdictions. The rate varies from 2% to 7%. Octroi paid is a cost as no credit is available.

Research and Development Cess

The Research and Development Cess is levied by the Government at 5% on import of technology by an industrial concern into India in terms of a foreign collaboration or other specified cases. This cess is required to be paid by the importer of technology on payments made for such imports.

"Technology" has been defined to mean special or technical knowledge or special service required by an industrial concern under any foreign collaboration including designs, drawings, publications and technical personnel.

The service tax legislation exempts the taxable service involving import of technology, from so much of the service tax leviable thereon, as is equivalent to the amount of cess paid on the said import of technology.

Other Significant Indirect Taxes

Stamp Duty

Stamp duty is paid for a transaction executed by way of a document or instrument under the provisions of the Indian Stamp Act or the State Acts. Stamp duty is applicable on purchase of immovable property and also on various other transactions, e.g., lease, conveyance, mortgage, partitions, transfers, etc. Levy of stamp duty is generally dependent on the state where the agreement is executed. Typically, for immovable property, this duty is payable in the state where the property is located. Payment of accurate stamp duty on instruments gives them legality. Such instruments have evidentiary value and can be admitted as evidence in a court of law. Instruments that are not properly stamped are not admitted as evidence in a court of law. The rates of stamp duty on instruments related to the transfer of immovable property vary from state to state from 3% to 10% on fair/true market value of the property. Stamp duty can be paid by using stamp paper, adhesive stamps or by franking.

The rate of duty is generally calculated on an ad valorem basis, depending on the nature of the instrument and the state where it is executed. Further, stamp duty can be levied at a flat rate on a certain document, irrespective of the amount involved.

Profession Tax

Profession tax is a state levy on professions, trades, a calling or employment in a state. Thus, every person who is engaged in any of the activities mentioned above is liable to pay profession tax. Not all the state governments levy profession tax currently.

In states where such a levy exists, every enterprise and every employee earning salaries is required to register and pay profession tax. In case of salaried employees, the employer is required to deduct profession tax from the salary paid to its employees at specified rates and deposit it into the Government treasury. The employer is liable to pay the requisite amount of profession tax on such salaries or wages, irrespective of whether it has deducted an equivalent amount from the salaries paid.

Further, employers/businessmen/professionals, etc., are also required to pay profession tax at specified rates in their own capacity.

STT

STT is levied on the value of a taxable securities transaction, as depicted below:

Transaction	Rates	Payable by
Purchase/sale of equity shares, units of equity- oriented mutual funds (delivery-based)	0.1%	Purchaser/seller (both)
Sale of equity shares, units of equity-oriented mutual funds (non-delivery based)	0.025%	Seller
Sale of an option in securities	0.017%	Seller

Sale of an option in securities, where an option is exercised	0.125%	Purchaser
Sale of futures in securities	0.017%	Seller
Sale of units of equity- oriented funds to a mutual fund	0.25%	Seller
Sale of unlisted equity shares under an offer for sale to the public included in an initial public offer and where such shares are subsequently listed on a recognized stock exchange	0.2%	Seller

Luxury Tax

Luxury tax is a state levy on certain specified luxuries and certain facilities, services, enjoyments, utilities, etc. Generally, luxury tax is levied on specific accommodation and services provided in hotels and clubs of a specific kind and on certain commodities.

Property Tax

The owner of a property (usually real estate) is liable to pay property tax. The amount of tax is estimated on the value of the property being taxed (ad valorem tax) at applicable rates. Property tax is levied on residents by local municipal authorities in India, to sustain basic civic services in the city.

Entertainment Tax

State and local governments levy entertainment tax on various entertainment and amusement activities. Traditionally, film exhibition, cable/DTH subscriptions, video games, amusement parks, and events have been subject to entertainment tax. Some of the states also consider entertainment provided through telecom and the internet to be subject to entertainment tax. Entertainment tax rates are fairly high as compared to taxes levied on other luxury goods and services and depend on the relevant state and the entertainment activity. For example, the entertainment tax rate for movie exhibition in Mumbai is as high as 45%, while in Rajasthan, there is an exemption from entertainment tax. Further, many states offer benefits to new multiplexes, sports events and certain films subject to specific conditions.

Goods and Services Tax Legislation (GST)

The GoI has proposed that the indirect tax regime in India be replaced by a comprehensive dual GST, to be levied concurrently by the Centre (CGST) and the states (SGST). It is anticipated that the base for the GST will be comprehensive, including virtually all goods and services, with minimum exemptions. The GST structure will follow the destination principle, i.e., imports will be included in the tax base, while exports will be zero-rated. In the case of inter-state transactions within India, the state tax will apply in the state of destination as opposed to that of origin.

The following are the key taxes proposed to be subsumed under the GST:

Central taxes	State taxes
Central Excise Duty (including additional excise duties)	VAT/sales tax
Service tax	Entry tax not in lieu of Octroi
Additional customs duty	Entertainment tax (other than entertainment tax levied by local bodies)
Special additional customs duty	Stamp duty
	Taxes on Vehicles

Central taxes	**State taxes**
Surcharges and cesses	Taxes on Goods and Passengers
	Taxes and duties on electricity
	Luxury tax
	State cesses and surcharges
CST	Taxes on lottery, betting and gambling

The following are the key taxes not to be subsumed under the proposed GST:

Central taxes	**State taxes**
Customs and export duties	Excise duty on alcohol
Duties of excise on specified petroleum products, natural gas and tobacco	

Full input credit system will operate in parallel for CGST and SGST. GST paid on the procurement of goods and services will be available for credit against that payable on the supply of goods or services. The consumer, being the last person in the supply chain, will bear the tax, with no right of input tax credit. Cross utilization of input tax credit between CGST and SGST will not be permitted.

GST has been envisaged as a more efficient tax system that will widen the tax base, do away with the multiplicity of taxes and their cascading effects, minimize competitive distortions, and encourage better compliance.

The new tax structure will have a significant impact on all businesses —manufacturers, traders and service providers — and on all aspects of their activities, including supply chains and logistics, product pricing, dealer margins, and IT and accounting systems.

Many of the design features of the GST are yet to be finalized. They are being discussed by the GOI and the states.

On 16th March, 2011, the Constitution (One Hundred and Fifteenth Amendment), Bill, 2011 (GST Bill) was introduced in the Parliament, which seeks to introduce articles effecting the introduction of the GST and the introduction of the GST Council. According to the existing structure of indirect taxation, the Parliament has the power to make laws on the manufacture of goods and the provision of services while the State Legislatures have the power to make laws on the sale and purchase of goods within their respective states. The Parliament has retained the exclusivity to make laws pertaining to sale of goods in the course of inter-state trade or commerce.

The highlights of the GST bill are as under:

- Article 246A introduced for enabling concurrent powers to levy GST.
- GST has been defined to mean any tax on supply of goods or services or both except taxes on supply of—petroleum crude, high speed diesel (HSD), petrol, natural gas, Aviation Turbine Fuel (ATF) and alcoholic liquor for human consumption.
- State governments will have the power to levy tax on sale of petroleum crude, HSD, petrol, natural gas, ATF and alcoholic liquor for human consumption. Municipalities or Panchayats shall have the powers to levy tax on entry of goods into local area for consumption, use or sale therein and tax on entertainment and amusement.
- Parliament will be given exclusive power to levy GST on interstate trade imports, exports, apportion revenues between states and the Centre, constitute GST Council, to constitute GST Dispute Settlement Authority etc.

The GoI had expressed its intention to introduce a national-level GST by 1st April, 2012. However, keeping in mind the current state of affairs, the expected date of implementation of GST is still uncertain and a clear roadmap for implementation of GST is still awaited.

However, the GoI is taking other positive and concrete steps toward the introduction of GST and to ensure a smooth transition from the current system. For the said purpose, the Finance Minister of India while presenting the Union Budget 2012 had proposed to make GST Network (GSTN) operational from August 2012 — to implement common PAN-based registrations, returns, and payments processing for all states on a shared platform.

Acknowledgement

Adapted from material at India Brand Equity Fund website. Commons IPR, 2013.

BRAZIL'S GOL AIRLINES

Brazil's Gol Linhas aéreas Inteligentes is a tropical version of JetBlue Airways and Ryanair, the low-cost, no-frills carriers in the United States and Europe. Established in 2001, Gol adopted the low-cost model pioneered by Southwest Airlines and refined by the likes of JetBlue and Ryanair. Gol sells discount tickets, mainly over the Internet. It targets price-sensitive business travelers, who account for 70 percent of all traffic in Brazil's rapidly growing market for air travel (demand for air travel in Brazil is growing at roughly twice the rate of growth in the country's gross domestic product). Gol is also going after Brazil's large bus market; in 2001 some 130 million people in Brazil traveled by interstate bus companies. Gol has standardized its fleet on a single aircraft model, Boeing's 737 series. There are no airport clubs or frequent flyer programs, cabins are a single class, and light snacks and beverages replace meals. The airline also offers Internet check-in and delivers a reliable product, with 95 percent of flights arriving on time. Gol's service has elicited a remarkable response from customers, with an independent market research survey finding that more than 90 percent of customers would continue to use the airline and recommend it to others.

From a standing start in January 2001, this business model enabled Gol to capture a 22 percent share of the Brazilian market by mid-2004. By then, Gol had a fleet of 25 aircraft and was already ranked as one of the fastest-growing and most profitable airlines in the world, but its aspirations were much bigger. Gol wanted to be the low-cost carrier in South America. To get to that point, it planned to expand its fleet to some 69 aircraft by 2010.

To help finance this expansion, Gol decided to tap into the global capital market. In mid-2004, the privately held company offered nonvoting preferred stock to investors on the São Paulo Bovespa and the New York Stock Exchange. The simultaneous offering was oversubscribed, with the underwriters lifting the offering price twice, and raised some $322 million. In explaining the decision to offer stock through the New York Stock Exchange, Gol's chief financial officer noted:

> We wanted to get a solid group of long-term investors that understood the business. We've got that. We also wanted to get a group of research analysts that understood this sector, and we now have seven analysts covering the stock. Southwest, JetBlue, Ryanair, and Westjet are considered the tier one in terms of operating profitability and successes. We were able to put Gol right up in that group. Doing both the NYSE and Bovespa was part of our strategy to sell shares to investors that have familiarity with low-cost carriers. The strategy works. If you look at the list of major investors in the company, the majority of them have high positions in trade of the equities of JetBlue, Southwest, and Ryanair. For them, it was a very easy analysis to understand Gol's business model and how it makes money.

Aided by the financing, Gol was able to expand rapidly. By early 2007 it already had 65 aircraft and was operating 600 daily flights to 55 destinations, including seven international routes to five South American countries. Gol had a market share of 36 percent for routes within Brazil and 13 percent on international routes originating in Brazil. Its planes were 74 percent full on average, the best in Brazil, and it was the most punctual airline in Brazil. By early 2011, Gol surpassed its local rival, TAM, to become the largest airline in Brazil, accounting for 40 percent of the domestic market.

Case Discussion Questions

1. What were the benefits to Gol of a listing on the New York Stock Exchange in addition to the São Paulo Bovespa?
2. Why do you think the Gol stock offering was oversubscribed?
3. Do you think Gol would have raised as much money if it had just listed on the São Paulo exchange?
4. How might the joint listing of the New York and São Paulo stock exchanges affect Gol's ability to raise additional capital in the future?

Sources

E. P. Lima, "Winning Gol!" *Air Transport World,* October 2004, pp. 22–26; G. Samor, "Brazil's Gol Faces Hurdles," *The Wall Street Journal,* August 9, 2004, p. C3; "Gol Launches $322 Million Flotation," *Airfinance Journal,* June 2004, p. 1; "Gol Commemorates Sixth Anniversary," *PR Newswire,* January 15, 2007; and G. Hill, "TAM Loses No. 1 Ranking in Market Share in Brazil," Reuters, March 17, 2011.

FOREIGN INVESTMENT FRAMEWORK IN INDIA

The Foreign Direct Investment (FDI) regime has been progressively liberalized during the course of the 1990s and continues to do so in the 2000s, with most restrictions on foreign investment being removed and procedures simplified. With limited exceptions, foreigners can invest directly in India, either on their own or as a joint venture.

Today, there are very few industries where foreign investment is prohibited. Moreover, investment ceilings, which are applicable in certain cases, are gradually being removed or phased out.

With the intent and objective to promote foreign direct investment through a policy framework, which is transparent, predictable, simple, and reduces regulatory burden, the GoI has formulated, on a yearly basis, a consolidated FDI Policy.

Features of the GoI's consolidated FDI Policy and incentives offered by it

- With the issue of consolidated FDI policy, all earlier press notes/ press releases/clarifications on FDI issued by the Department of Industrial Policy and Promotion, Ministry of Commerce and Industry (DIPP) stand rescinded and subsumed in the consolidated FDI Policy.
- Policy pronouncement on FDI by press notes/press releases take effect from the date of issue of press notes/press releases regardless of the procedural instructions, which shall be issued by the RBI vide relevant A.P. DIR series circulars to amend Foreign Exchange Management (Transfer or Issue of Security by a Person Resident Outside India) Regulations, 2000.
- Indian companies are permitted to issue equity shares, fully, compulsorily and mandatorily convertible debentures (FCD's) and compulsorily and mandatorily convertible preference shares (CCPS) to the non-residents subject to pricing guidelines/valuation norms prescribed under FEMA.

- Issue of warrants, partly paid shares, etc., require prior approval of FIPB. Issue of non-convertible, optionally convertible or partially convertible preference shares/debentures needs to comply with the external commercial borrowing (ECB) guidelines of RBI.
- Foreign investment is calculated on the basis of ownership and control of the Indian company.
- No government approval is required for FDI in virtually all the sectors/activities, except for a small negative list formulated by the GoI.
- FIPB considers proposals for foreign participation that do not qualify for automatic approval.
- Decisions on all foreign investment proposals are usually taken within four to six weeks of submitting an application.
- Free repatriation of capital investment is permitted, provided the original investment (on a repatriable basis) was made in convertible foreign exchange. Further, free repatriation of profits on capital investment is permitted, subject to payment of taxes and other specified conditions.
- Use of foreign brand names/trademarks is permitted for the sale of goods in India.
- All royalty payments, lump sum fee for transfer of technology and for use of trademark/brand name are permitted under the automatic route without any monetary/duration limits.
- "Single window" clearance facilities and "investor escort services" are available in various states to simplify the approval process for new ventures.

Foreign Investment Promotion Board

The FIPB is specially empowered and chaired by the Secretary, Department of Economic Affairs of the Ministry of Finance (MoF). It has been specifically set up to expedite the approval process for foreign investment proposals.

Proposals for FDI are mandatorily required to be submitted online followed by the hard copy of the proposal. The FIPB has the flexibility to examine all the proposals in their totality, free from predetermined parameters or procedures.

The recommendations of the FIPB with respect to proposals under the ambit of the non-automatic route, involving an investment of USD 266.67 million (equivalent of INR 12 billion) or less are considered and approved by the Finance Minister. Projects at an investment greater than this value are submitted by the FIPB to the Cabinet Committee on Economic Affairs for further approval.

Foreign investment in India

Foreign direct investment

The GoI permits FDI on an automatic basis, except with respect to a small negative list, which includes the following:

- Proposals falling under the list of activities/sectors prohibited for FDI by the GoI
- Proposals falling outside the ambit of notified sectoral policy/caps
- For a list of the sectors in which FDI is prohibited/permitted with condition or sectoral cap, refer to Appendix 4.

Foreign portfolio investment

Foreign institutional investors (FIIs) must register themselves with SEBI and comply with RBI's exchange control regulations.

Foreign pension funds, mutual funds, investment trusts, asset management companies, insurance or reinsurance companies, nominee companies and incorporated/institutional portfolio managers (or their power of attorney holders) are allowed to register as FIIs. FIIs can invest in securities traded in primary and secondary capital markets in India under the portfolio investment scheme. These securities include shares, debentures, warrants, units of mutual funds, government securities, treasury bills and derivative instruments.

Certain investment limits are prescribed in FII guidelines and RBI's regulations to regulate investments made by FIIs. However, these restrictions do not apply to the investments made by an FII through offshore funds, GDRs or Euro-convertible bonds.

Registration eligibility

FII guidelines require FIIs to meet certain qualifying conditions for registration. SEBI also examines whether the grant of registration is in the interest of the development of the Indian securities market.

Registration of sub-accounts

Apart from entities that are entitled to be FIIs, other foreign investors are also eligible for registration as sub-accounts. The sub-accounts can be categorized as (i) collective investment funds and institutions, (ii) proprietary funds, or (iii) foreign corporations and nationals.

Foreign Venture Capital Investment Route

A SEBI-registered Foreign Venture Capital Investor (FVCI) with specific approval from the RBI under FEMA regulations can invest in Indian Venture Capital Undertaking (IVCU) or Indian Venture Capital Fund (IVCF) or in a scheme floated by such IVCFs, subject to the condition that the VCF should also be registered with the SEBI.

FVCIs can purchase equity/equity-linked instruments, debt/debt instruments, the debentures of an IVCU, or of a VCF, through an IPO or private placement or by way of private arrangement or purchase from third party. Further, FVCIs are also allowed to invest in securities on a recognized stock exchange subject to the provisions of the SEBI (FVCI) Regulations 2000, and are amended from time to time.

Investment by NRIs

NRIs can invest in the shares or convertible debentures of an Indian company on a non-repatriable basis apart from investment in the form of FDI. These investments do not require FIPB approval and are not construed as FDI. NRIs cannot invest in companies that are engaged in certain financial service or agricultural/plantation activities. While the capital is non-repatriable, the dividends and interest income from such investments can be remitted as current account transactions.

Foreign exchange controls

Foreign exchange policy

Since 1991, the country's foreign exchange reserves have gone up from US$5b to approximately USD 286.749b as on 13th July 2012.

Prior to 1999, India had stringent exchange control regulations under the Foreign Exchange Regulation Act, 1973 (FERA). In 1999, the GoI replaced controls under FERA with regulations under the FEMA.

With the introduction of FEMA in 1999, the objective of the GoI shifted from the conservation of foreign exchange to promoting orderly development and management of the foreign exchange market in India.

Current account transactions

The rupee is fully convertible for trade and current account purposes. Except for certain specified restrictions where RBI approval is required, foreign currency may be freely purchased for trade and current account purposes.

Capital account transactions

These transactions are not permitted unless they are specifically allowed and prescribed conditions are satisfied. Transactions specifically allowed include the following:
- Investment in India by a person resident outside India
- Acquisition and transfer of immovable property in India guaranteed by a person resident outside India, in favor of or on behalf of a person resident in India
- Import and export of currency/currency notes into/from India by a person resident outside India
- Foreign currency accounts in India of a person resident outside the country
- Remittance outside India of the capital assets (held in India) of a person resident outside India

Regional and international trade agreements

Overview

Over the years, India has entered numerous bilateral and regional trade agreements with key trading partners. Apart from offering preferential tariff rates on the trading of goods among member countries, these agreements also enable increased economic cooperation in the fields of trade in services as well as investment and intellectual property, resulting in enhanced trade liberalization.

Existing trade agreements and regulatory scenario

Some of the existing key trade agreements entered into by India include:
- Comprehensive Economic Partnership Agreement (CEPA) with Japan
- Comprehensive Economic Co-operation Agreement (CECA) with Malaysia
- Comprehensive Economic Partnership Agreement (CEPA) with the Republic of Korea
- India-ASEAN Trade in Goods Agreement
- Comprehensive Economic Co-operation Agreement (CECA) with Singapore
- Free Trade Agreement with Sri Lanka (Trade in Goods)
- Agreement on South Asia Free Trade Area executed by India, Bangladesh, Bhutan, Maldives, Nepal, Pakistan and Sri Lanka
- Framework Agreement with Thailand
- Preferential Trade Agreement with MERCOSUR countries
- Preferential Trade Agreement with Chile
- Asia-Pacific Trade Agreement with Bangladesh, Republic of Korea, China, and Sri Lanka
- Preferential Trade Agreement with Afghanistan
- Global System of Trade Preference with 46 countries
- India Bhutan Trade Agreement – India Nepal Trade Treaty
- Economic co-operation agreement with Finland

Recent developments and outlook

India is attempting to fast track its trade agreement negotiations with the EU.

Trade Agreements under negotiation

Some of India's key prospective trade agreements that are currently under negotiation include:
- India-European Union FTA
- India-ASEAN (Services and Investment) CECA
- India-Thailand Comprehensive Economic Cooperation Agreement
- India-New Zealand FTA
- India-European Free Trade Association FTA
- India Canada Comprehensive Economic Cooperation Agreement
- India-Mauritius Comprehensive Economic Cooperation and Partnership Agreement
- India-South African Customs Union PTA
- India-Sri Lanka FTA (to be expanded to include services and investment)
- Bay of Bengal Initiative for Multi-Sectoral Technical and Economic Cooperation
- India-Gulf Cooperation Council FTA
- India-Australia Comprehensive Economic Cooperation Agreement
- India-Israel FTA
- India-MERCOSUR PTA (scope to be expanded)
- India-Chile PTA (scope to be expanded)

Free Trade Agreements under feasibility study

A feasibility study for prospective Free Trade Agreements (FTAs) between two countries is undertaken on the basis of bilateral trade potential. Primarily, the key objectives of conducting a "feasibility study" for a FTA are:
- Identifying the benefits, which the countries entering into FTA is likely to derive under FTA
- Assessing the feasibility of a comprehensive FTA covering goods, services, investment and intellectual property rights
- Assessing prospects for expansion of trade in goods and services through liberalization of tariffs and non-tariff measures
- Creating a favorable environment for investment

Listed below are the Free Trade Agreements under Feasibility Study:
- India–Peru
- India–Russia
- India–Egypt
- India–Turkey

Major trading partners and leading imports and exports

Foreign trade in India

India accounts for 1.8%[1] of global trade in goods and services worldwide. In 2010, India's share of trade in commercial services reached 4.3% of global trade, compared with 2.8% five years ago. India's exports grew by 33% in 2010, making it the country with the most dynamic growth[2]. Moreover, India's

---

[1]"Foreign Trade Policy 2009-14", Directorate General of Foreign Trade website, http:// dgft.gov.in, accessed 15 September 2009
[2]Source: World Trade Organization (WTO) International Trade Statistics 2011

exports accounted for 1.5% of World Merchandise Exports, whereas India's imports accounted for 2.2% of World Merchandise Imports in 2010. Foreign trade in the country is regulated by the Foreign Trade (Development and Regulation) Act, 1992. The Ministry of Commerce and Industry is the foremost body responsible for promoting and regulating foreign trade in India.

Foreign Trade Policy (FTP)

India's FTP covers policies related to fiscal incentives, rationalized procedures, institutional changes, increased access to global markets and diversification of its export market.

To generate employment opportunities and increase India's share in global trade, the FTP lays special emphasis on key sectors including agriculture, handicrafts, leather, gems and jewelry, marine products, handlooms, electronics, IT hardware, sports goods and toys.

The policy focuses on market expansion and diversification to markets in Africa, Oceania, Latin America and some parts of Asia.

Exports: USD 251b (FY11)

Most goods can be freely exported from India, except for a small number of prohibited items. India's key exports include gems and jewelry, petroleum, engineering goods, textiles and drugs and pharmaceuticals. The country also accounts for approximately 4.3% of the global export of commercial services.

Principal export destinations: The UAE continues to be the top-most export destination for India's products ahead of the US consecutively in FY11, FY10 and FY09. Other countries include the US, China, Singapore, the Netherlands, the UK, Germany and Hong Kong.

The cumulative value of exports for FY12 was USD 304.62b as against USD 251.13b in FY11 registering a growth of 21.3% in dollar terms.

Acknowledgement

Adapted from material at India Brand Equity Fund website. Commons IPR, 2013

STAFFING POLICY AT ASTRAZENECA

AstraZeneca is one of the world's largest pharmaceutical companies. Headquartered in London, the company has 65,000 employees, 51 percent of whom are in Europe, 32 percent in the Americas, and 17 percent in Asia, Africa, and Australia. The company is active in more than 100 nations and has sales in excess of $30 billion. A key strategic imperative for this multinational is to build a talented global workforce, led by managers who have a global perspective and are comfortable moving around the world, interacting with people from other cultures and doing business in different nations. It is not easy.

To help build international bench strength, the company moves managers to another country for up to three years. Such assignments are not cheap; the company estimates that it can cost two to four times an employee's annual salary to cover expenses. Expenses can include a child's school tuition, tax equalization, cultural training, and subsidized housing. Because of this expense, AstraZeneca focuses its international assignments only on its most promising "high-potential" employees—those who are scheduled for advancement and leadership positions within the company. In every case, the human resource staff will assess whether the investment in a person is worth making. Simply posting an employee to a foreign country is not enough. To get promoted, employees must also learn to work in international teams and to manage across borders. If a person is judged to lack the capability to do this, he or she will not get a foreign posting. If the employee fails to do this effectively when on the posting, advancement prospects will be reduced.

To ease the transition to another country, AstraZeneca offers employees and their spouses help with moving, locating schools for children, learning a language, and understanding cultural differences. The company also offers repatriation training for employees coming home after extended postings abroad. It does this because experience has shown that many expatriates and their families have problems readjusting to their old life after extended time in a different culture.

Another problem that the human resource function at AstraZeneca has to grapple with is how to raise the talent base of employees in emerging markets where AstraZeneca has been making big investments in recent years. An example is China, where until recently, there was very little in the way of professional management education (this is now changing rapidly). In 2003 the company had a little more than 1,000 employees in China. Now it has more than 3,500. AstraZeneca has been trying to raise the skill level of key Chinese employees as fast as possible. With regard to key managerial talent, the company has been sending them abroad to get exposure to other cultures and to acculturate them into the way in which AstraZeneca does business. It wants them to understand what it is like to be part of a global business. Each expatriate will have a host-country line manager assigned to him or her, as well as a home-country line manager who monitors the expatriate's progress. After a period, the majority of them return to China where the most successful are targeted for future leadership positions within the Chinese subsidiary. The most talented, however, may go beyond this and ultimately move into senior management positions at the corporate level.

Case Discussion Questions

1. What international staffing policy is AstraZeneca pursuing with regard to its high-potential employees?
2. Why does AstraZeneca limit this policy to just high-potential employees? Can you see a drawback in doing this?
3. What staffing policy is AstraZeneca adopting with regard to its subsidiaries in places such as China? Is this an appropriate policy?
4. Do you think the company is doing enough to limit the well-known risks and costs associated with high expatriate failure rates? Is there anything else it might do?

Sources

S. Stern, "AstraZeneca's Long March to China," *Daily Telegraph*, September 7, 2006, p. 3; J. M. Von Bergen, "More U.S. Workers Getting Global Assignments," *Tribune News Service*, August 12, 2008; and T. Mohn, "The Long Trip Home," *The New York Times*, March 10, 2009, p. B6.

Glossary

A

absolute advantage   A country has an absolute advantage in the production of a product when it is more efficient than any other country at producing it.

accounting standards   Rules for preparing financial statements.

ad valorem tariff   A tariff levied as a proportion of the value of an imported good.

administrative trade policies   Administrative policies, typically adopted by government bureaucracies, that can be used to restrict imports or boost exports.

Andean Community   A 1969 agreement between Bolivia, Chile, Ecuador, Colombia, and Peru to establish a customs union.

antidumping policies   Designed to punish foreign firms that engage in dumping and thus protect domestic producers from unfair foreign competition.

arbitrage   The purchase of securities in one market for immediate resale in another to profit from a price discrepancy.

Association of South East Asian Nations (ASEAN)   Formed in 1967, an attempt to establish a free trade area between Brunei, Cambodia, Indonesia, Laos, Malaysia, Myanmar, the Philippines, Singapore, Vietnam, and Thailand.

auditing standards   Rules for performing an audit.

B

balance-of-payments accounts   National accounts that track both payments to and receipts from foreigners.

balance-of-trade equilibrium   Reached when the income a nation's residents earn from exports equals money paid for imports.

bandwagon effect   Movement of traders like a herd, all in the same direction and at the same time, in response to each other's perceived actions.

banking crisis   A loss of confidence in the banking system that leads to a run on banks, as individuals and companies withdraw their deposits.

barter   The direct exchange of goods or services between two parties without a cash transaction.

bilateral netting   Settlement in which the amount one subsidiary owes another can be canceled by the debt the second subsidiary owes the first.

bill of exchange   An order written by an exporter instructing an importer, or an importer's agent, to pay a specified amount of money at a specified time.

bill of lading   A document issued to an exporter by a common carrier transporting merchandise. It serves as a receipt, a contract, and a document of title.

Bretton Woods   A 1944 conference in which representatives of 40 countries met to design a new international monetary system.

bureaucratic controls   Achieving control through establishment of a system of rules and procedures.

business ethics   The accepted principles of right or wrong governing the conduct of businesspeople.

buyback   Agreement to accept a percentage of a plant's output as payment for contract to build a plant.

C

capital account In the balance of payments, records transactions involving one-time changes in the stock of assets.

capital flight Converting domestic currency into a foreign currency.

Caribbean Single Market and Economy (CSME) The six CARICOM members that agreed to lower trade barriers and harmonize macroeconomic and monetary policies.

CARICOM An association of English-speaking Caribbean states that are attempting to establish a customs union.

carry trade A kind of speculation that involves borrowing in one currency where interest rates are low, and then using the proceeds to invest in another currency where interest rates are high.

caste system A system of social stratification in which social position is determined by the family into which a person is born, and change in that position is usually not possible during an individual's lifetime.

Central American Common Market A trade pact among Costa Rica, El Salvador, Guatemala, Honduras, and Nicaragua, which began in the early 1960s but collapsed in 1969 due to war.

Central America Free Trade Agreement (CAFTA) The agreement of the member states of the Central American Common Market joined by the Dominican Republic to trade freely with the United States.

channel length The number of intermediaries that a product has to go through before it reaches the final consumer.

channel quality The expertise, competencies, and skills of established retailers in a nation, and their ability to sell and support the products of international businesses.

civil law system A system of law based on a very detailed set of written laws and codes.

class consciousness A tendency for individuals to perceive themselves in terms of their class background.

class system A system of social stratification in which social status is determined by the family into which a person is born and by subsequent socioeconomic achievements. Mobility between classes is possible.

code of ethics A formal statement of the ethical priorities of a business or organization.

collectivism An emphasis on collective goals as opposed to individual goals.

command economy An economic system where the allocation of resources, including determination of what goods and services should be produced, and in what quantity, is planned by the government.

common law A system of law based on tradition, precedent, and custom. When law courts interpret common law, they do so with regard to these characteristics.

common market A group of countries committed to (1) removing all barriers to the free flow of goods, services, and factors of production between each other and (2) the pursuit of a common external trade policy.

Communist totalitarianism A version of collectivism advocating that socialism can be achieved only through a totalitarian dictatorship.

Communists Those who believe socialism can be achieved only through revolution and totalitarian dictatorship.

concentrated retail system A retail system in which a few retailers supply most of the market.

Confucian dynamism Theory that Confucian teachings affect attitudes toward time, persistence, ordering by status, protection of face, respect for tradition, and reciprocation of gifts and favors.

constant returns to specialization The units of resources required to produce a good are assumed to remain constant no matter where one is on a country's production possibility frontier.

contract Document that specifies conditions of an exchange and details rights and obligations of involved parties.

contract law Body of law that governs contract enforcement.

control systems Metrics used to measure performance of subunits.

Convention on Combating Bribery of Foreign Public Officials in International Business Transactions OECD agreement to make the bribery of foreign public officials a criminal offense.

copyright Exclusive legal rights of authors, composers, playwrights, artists, and publishers to publish and dispose of their work as they see fit.

core competence Firm skills that competitors cannot easily match or imitate.

corporate culture   The organization's norms and value systems.

counterpurchase   A reciprocal buying agreement.

countertrade   The trade of goods and services for other goods and services.

countervailing duties   Antidumping duties.

country of origin effects   A subset of source effects, or the extent to which the place of manufacturing influences product evaluations.

Court of Justice   Supreme appeals court for EU law.

cross-cultural literacy   Understanding how the culture of a country affects the way business is practiced.

cultural controls   Achieving control by persuading subordinates to identify with the norms and value systems of the organization (self-control).

cultural relativism   Belief that ethics are culturally determined, and a firm should adopt the ethics of the culture in which it is operating.

culture   The complex whole that includes knowledge, belief, art, morals, law, custom, and other capabilities acquired by a person as a member of society.

currency board   Means of controlling a country's currency.

currency crisis   Occurs when a speculative attack on the exchange value of a currency results in a sharp depreciation in the value of the currency or forces authorities to expend large volumes of international currency reserves and sharply increase interest rates to defend the prevailing exchange rate.

currency speculation   Involves short-term movement of funds from one currency to another in hopes of profiting from shifts in exchange rates.

currency swap   Simultaneous purchase and sale of a given amount of foreign exchange for two different value dates.

current account   In the balance of payments, records transactions involving the export or import of goods and services.

current account deficit   The current account of the balance of payments is in deficit when a country imports more goods and services than it exports.

current account surplus   The current account of the balance of payments is in surplus when a country exports more goods and services than it imports.

customs union   A group of countries committed to (1) removing all barriers to the free flow of goods and services between each other and (2) the pursuit of a common external trade policy.

D

deferral principle   Parent companies are not taxed on the income of a foreign subsidiary until they actually receive a dividend from that subsidiary.

democracy   Political system in which government is by the people, exercised either directly or through elected representatives.

deregulation   Removal of government restrictions concerning the conduct of a business.

dirty-float system   A system under which a country's currency is nominally allowed to float freely against other currencies, but in which the government will intervene, buying and selling currency, if it believes that the currency has deviated too far from its fair value.

draft   An order written by an exporter telling an importer what and when to pay.

dumping   Selling goods in a foreign market for less than their cost of production or below their "fair" market value.

dynamic capabilities   Skills that become more valuable over time through learning.

E

eclectic paradigm   Argument that combining location-specific assets or resource endowments and the firm's own unique assets often requires FDI; it requires the firm to establish production facilities where those foreign assets or resource endowments are located.

economic exposure   The extent to which a firm's future international earning power is affected by changes in exchange rates.

economic risk   The likelihood that events, including economic mismanagement, will cause drastic changes in a country's business environment that adversely affect the profit and other goals of a particular business enterprise.

economic union   A group of countries committed to (1) removing all barriers to the free flow of goods, services, and factors of production between each other, (2) the adoption of a common currency, (3) the harmonization of tax rates, and (4) the pursuit of a common external trade policy.

economies of scale Cost advantages associated with large-scale production.

efficient market A market where prices reflect all available information.

elastic A small change in price produces a large change in demand.

entrepreneurs Those who first commercialize innovations.

ethical dilemma Situation in which no available alternative seems ethically acceptable.

ethical strategy A course of action that does not violate business ethics.

ethical systems Cultural beliefs about what is proper behavior and conduct.

ethnocentric staffing policy A staffing approach within the MNE in which all key management positions are filled by parent-country nationals.

ethnocentrism Belief in the superiority of one's own ethnic group or culture.

Eurobonds A bond placed in countries other than the one in whose currency the bond is denominated.

Eurocurrency Any currency banked outside its country of origin.

European Commission Responsible for proposing EU legislation, implementing it, and monitoring compliance.

European Council The heads of state of EU members and the president of the European Commission.

European Free Trade Association (EFTA) A free trade association including Norway, Iceland, and Switzerland.

European Monetary System (EMS) EU system designed to create a zone of monetary stability in Europe, control inflation, and coordinate exchange rate policies of EU countries.

European Parliament Elected EU body that provides consultation on issues proposed by European Commission.

European Union (EU) An economic group of 25 European nations. Established as a customs union, it is now moving toward economic union. (Formerly the European Community.)

exchange rate The rate at which one currency is converted into another.

exclusive distribution channel A distribution channel that outsiders find difficult to access.

expatriate failure The premature return of an expatriate manager to the home country.

expatriate manager A national of one country appointed to a management position in another country.

experience curve Systematic production cost reductions that occur over the life of a product.

experience curve pricing Aggressive pricing designed to increase volume and help the firm realize experience curve economies.

export management company (EMC) Export specialists who act as an export marketing department for client firms.

Export–Import Bank (Ex-Im Bank) Agency of the U.S. government whose mission is to provide aid in financing and facilitate exports and imports.

exporting Sale of products produced in one country to residents of another country.

externalities Knowledge spillovers.

externally convertible currency Limitations on the ability of residents to convert domestic currency, though nonresidents can convert their holdings of domestic currency into foreign currency.

external stakeholders All other individuals and groups, other than internal stakeholders, that have some claim on the business.

F

factor endowments A country's endowment with resources such as land, labor, and capital.

factors of production Inputs into the productive process of a firm, including labor, management, land, capital, and technological know-how.

financial account In balance of payments, transactions that involve the purchase or sale of assets.

first-mover advantages Advantages accruing to the first to enter a market.

first-mover disadvantages Disadvantages associated with entering a foreign market before other international businesses.

Fisher effect Nominal interest rates (i) in each country equal the required real rate of interest (r) and the expected rate of inflation over the period of time for which the funds are to be lent (I). That is, $i = r + I$.

fixed exchange rate   A system under which the exchange rate for converting one currency into another is fixed.

flexible machine cells   Flexible manufacturing technology in which a grouping of various machine types, a common materials handler, and a centralized cell controller produces a family of products.

flexible manufacturing technologies or lean production
Manufacturing technologies designed to improve job scheduling, reduce setup time, and improve quality control.

floating exchange rate   A system under which the exchange rate for converting one currency into another is continuously adjusted depending on the laws of supply and demand.

flow of FDI   The amount of foreign direct investment undertaken over a given time period (normally one year).

folkways   Routine conventions of everyday life.

foreign bonds   Bonds sold outside the borrower's country and denominated in the currency of the country in which they are issued.

Foreign Corrupt Practices Act   U.S. law regulating behavior regarding the conduct of international business in the taking of bribes and other unethical actions.

foreign debt crisis   Situation in which a country cannot service its foreign debt obligations, whether private-sector or government debt.

foreign direct investment (FDI)   Direct investment in business operations in a foreign country.

foreign exchange market   A market for converting the currency of one country into that of another country.

foreign exchange risk   The risk that changes in exchange rates will hurt the profitability of a business deal.

forward exchange   When two parties agree to exchange currency and execute a deal at some specific date in the future.

forward exchange rate   The exchange rates governing forward exchange transactions.

fragmented retail system   A retail system in which there are many retailers, no one of which has a major share of the market.

franchising   A specialized form of licensing in which the franchiser sells intangible property to the franchisee and insists on rules to conduct the business.

free trade   The absence of barriers to the free flow of goods and services between countries.

free trade area   A group of countries committed to removing all barriers to the free flow of goods and services between each other, but pursuing independent external trade policies.

freely convertible currency   A country's currency is freely convertible when the government of that country allows both residents and nonresidents to purchase unlimited amounts of foreign currency with the domestic currency.

G

G20   Established in 1999, the G20 comprises the finance ministers and central bank governors of the 19 largest economies in the world, plus representatives from the European Union and the European Central Bank.

General Agreement on Tariffs and Trade (GATT)
International treaty that committed signatories to lowering barriers to the free flow of goods across national borders and led to the WTO.

geocentric staffing policy   A staffing policy where the best people are sought for key jobs throughout an MNE, regardless of nationality.

global learning   The flow of skills and product offerings from foreign subsidiary to home country and from foreign subsidiary to foreign subsidiary.

global matrix structure   Horizontal differentiation proceeds along two dimensions: product divisions and areas.

global standardization strategy   Strategy focusing on increasing profitability by reaping cost reductions from experience curve and location economies.

global web   When different stages of the value chain are dispersed to those locations around the globe where value added is maximized or where costs of value creation are minimized.

globalization   Trend away from distinct national economic units and toward one huge global market.

globalization of markets   Moving away from an economic system in which national markets are distinct entities, isolated by trade barriers and barriers of distance, time, and culture, and toward a system in which national markets are merging into one global market.

globalization of production   Trend by individual firms to disperse parts of their productive processes to different locations around the globe to take advantage of differences in cost and quality of factors of production.

gold par value   The amount of currency needed to purchase one ounce of gold.

gold standard   The practice of pegging currencies to gold and guaranteeing convertibility.

greenfield investment   Establishing a new operation in a foreign country.

gross national income (GNI)   Measures the total annual income received by residents of a nation.

group   An association of two or more individuals who have a shared sense of identity and who interact with each other in structured ways on the basis of a common set of expectations about each other's behavior.

H

hedge fund   Investment fund that not only buys financial assets (stocks, bonds, currencies) but also sells them short.

horizontal differentiation   The division of the firm into subunits.

Human Development Index (HDI)   An attempt by the United Nations to assess the impact of a number of factors on the quality of human life in a country.

human resource management (HRM)   Activities an organization conducts to use its human resources effectively.

I

import quota   A direct restriction on the quantity of a good that can be imported into a country.

incentives   Devices used to reward managerial behavior.

individualism   An emphasis on the importance of guaranteeing individual freedom and self-expression.

individualism versus collectivism   Theory focusing on the relationship between the individual and his or her fellows. In individualistic societies, the ties between individuals are loose and individual achievement is highly valued. In societies where collectivism is emphasized, ties between individuals are tight, people are born into collectives, such as extended families, and everyone is supposed to look after the interests of his or her collective.

inelastic   When a large change in price produces only a small change in demand.

inefficient market   One in which prices do not reflect all available information.

infant industry argument   New industries in developing countries must be temporarily protected from international competition to help them reach a position where they can compete on world markets with the firms of developed nations.

inflows of FDI   Flow of foreign direct investment into a country.

innovation   Development of new products, processes, organizations, management practices, and strategies.

integrating mechanisms   Mechanisms for achieving coordination between subunits within an organization.

intellectual property   Products of the mind, ideas (e.g., books, music, computer software, designs, technological know-how). Intellectual property can be protected by patents, copyrights, and trademarks.

internal forward rate   A company-generated forecast of future spot rates.

internal stakeholders   Individuals or groups who work for or own the business.

internalization theory   Marketing imperfection approach to foreign direct investment.

international business   Any firm that engages in international trade or investment.

international division   Division responsible for a firm's international activities.

international Fisher effect   For any two countries, the spot exchange rate should change in an equal amount but in the opposite direction to the difference in nominal interest rates between countries.

International Monetary Fund (IMF)   International institution set up to maintain order in the international monetary system.

international monetary system Institutional arrangements countries adopt to govern exchange rates.

international strategy Trying to create value by transferring core competencies to foreign markets where indigenous competitors lack those competencies.

international trade Occurs when a firm exports goods or services to consumers in another country.

ISO 9000 Certification process that requires certain quality standards that must be met.

J

joint venture A cooperative undertaking between two or more firms.

just distribution One that is considered fair and equitable.

just-in-time (JIT) inventory Logistics systems designed to deliver parts to a production process as they are needed, not before.

K

Kantian ethics Belief that people should be treated as ends and never purely as means to the ends of others.

knowledge network Network for transmitting information within an organization that is based on informal contacts between managers within an enterprise and on distributed information systems.

L

lag strategy Delaying the collection of foreign currency receivables if that currency is expected to appreciate, and delaying payables if that currency is expected to depreciate.

late-mover advantages Benefits enjoyed by a company that is late to enter a new market, such as consumer familiarity with the product or knowledge gained about a market.

late-mover disadvantages Handicap that late entrants to a market suffer.

law of one price In competitive markets free of transportation costs and barriers to trade, identical products sold in different countries must sell for the same price when their price is expressed in the same currency.

lead strategy Collecting foreign currency receivables early when a foreign currency is expected to depreciate, and paying foreign currency payables before they are due when a currency is expected to appreciate.

learning effects Cost savings from learning by doing.

legal risk The likelihood that a trading partner will opportunistically break a contract or expropriate intellectual property rights.

legal system System of rules that regulate behavior and the processes by which the laws of a country are enforced and through which redress of grievances is obtained.

letter of credit Issued by a bank, indicating that the bank will make payments under specific circumstances.

licensing Occurs when a firm (the licensor) licenses the right to produce its product, use its production processes, or use its brand name or trademark to another firm (the licensee). In return for giving the licensee these rights, the licensor collects a royalty fee on every unit the licensee sells.

licensing agreement Arrangement in which a licensor grants the rights to intangible property to a licensee for a specified period and receives a royalty fee in return.

local content requirement A requirement that some specific fraction of a good be produced domestically.

localization strategy Plan focusing on increasing profitability by customizing the goods or services to match tastes in national markets.

location economies Cost advantages from performing a value creation activity at the optimal location for that activity.

location-specific advantages Advantages that arise from using resource endowments or assets that are tied to a particular foreign location and that a firm finds valuable to combine with its own unique assets (such as the firm's technological, marketing, or management know-how).

logistics The procurement and physical transmission of material through the supply chain, from suppliers to customers.

M

Maastricht Treaty Treaty agreed to in 1992, but not ratified until January 1, 1994, that committed the

12 member states of the European Community to a closer economic and political union.

make-or-buy decisions   Decisions a company makes about whether to perform a value creation activity itself or outsource it to another entity.

managed-float system   System under which some currencies are allowed to float freely, but the majority are either managed by government intervention or pegged to another currency.

market economy   The allocation of resources is determined by the invisible hand of the price system.

market imperfections   Imperfections in the operation of the market mechanism.

market segmentation   Identifying groups of consumers whose purchasing behavior differs from others in important ways.

marketing mix   Choices about product attributes, distribution strategy, communication strategy, and pricing strategy that a firm offers its targeted markets.

masculinity versus femininity   Theory of the relationship between gender and work roles. In masculine cultures, sex roles are sharply differentiated and traditional "masculine values" such as achievement and the effective exercise of power determine cultural ideals. In feminine cultures, sex roles are less sharply distinguished, and little differentiation is made between men and women in the same job.

mass customization   The production of a wide variety of end products at a unit cost that could once be achieved only through mass production of a standardized output.

mercantilism   An economic philosophy advocating that countries should simultaneously encourage exports and discourage imports.

Mercosur   Pact between Argentina, Brazil, Paraguay, and Uruguay to establish a free trade area.

minimum efficient scale   The level of output at which most plant-level scale economies are exhausted.

MITI   Japan's Ministry of International Trade and Industry.

money management   Managing a firm's global cash resources efficiently.

Moore's law   The power of microprocessor technology doubles and its costs of production fall in half every 18 months.

moral hazard   Arises when people behave recklessly because they know they will be saved if things go wrong.

mores   Norms seen as central to the functioning of a society and to its social life.

multilateral netting   A technique used to reduce the number of transactions between subsidiaries of the firm, thereby reducing the total transaction costs arising from foreign exchange dealings and transfer fees.

multinational enterprise (MNE)   A firm that owns business operations in more than one country.

multipoint competition   Arises when two or more enterprises encounter each other in different regional markets, national markets, or industries.

multipoint pricing   Occurs when a pricing strategy in one market may have an impact on a rival's pricing strategy in another market.

N

naive immoralist   Approach that accepts ignoring ethical norms if others do so too.

new trade theory   The observed pattern of trade in the world economy may be due in part to the ability of firms in a given market to capture first-mover advantages.

noise   The amount of other messages competing for a potential consumer's attention.

nonconvertible currency   A currency is not convertible when both residents and nonresidents are prohibited from converting their holdings of that currency into another currency.

norms   Social rules and guidelines that prescribe appropriate behavior in particular situations.

North American Free Trade Agreement (NAFTA)   Free trade area between Canada, Mexico, and the United States.

O

offset   Agreement to purchase goods and services with a specified percentage of proceeds from an original sale in that country from any firm in the country.

offshore production   FDI undertaken to serve the home market.

oligopoly   An industry composed of a limited number of large firms.

One Ford   Business strategy of minimizing the number of business platforms to those that can be used everywhere in the world.

operations   The different value creation activities a firm undertakes.

optimal currency area   Region in which similarities in economic activity make a single currency and exchange rate feasible instruments of macroeconomic policy.

organizational architecture   Totality of a firm's organization.

organizational culture   Norms and values shared by employees.

organizational structure   Determined by the formal division into subunits, the location of decision making, and the coordination of activities of subunits.

outflows of FDI   Flow of foreign direct investment out of a country.

output controls   Achieving control by setting goals for subordinates, expressing these goals in terms of objective criteria, and then judging performance by a subordinate's ability to meet these goals.

P

Paris Convention for the Protection of Industrial Property   International agreement to protect intellectual property; signed by 96 countries.

patent   Grants the inventor of a new product or process exclusive rights to the manufacture, use, or sale of that invention.

pegged exchange rate   Currency value is fixed relative to a reference currency.

people   Part of the organizational architecture that includes strategy used to recruit, compensate, and retain employees.

performance ambiguity   Occurs when the causes of good or bad performance are not clearly identifiable.

personal controls   Achieving control by personal contact with subordinates.

pioneering costs   Costs an early entrant bears that later entrants avoid, such as the time and effort in learning the rules, failure due to ignorance, and the liability of being a foreigner.

political economy   The study of how political factors influence the functioning of an economic system.

political risk   The likelihood that political forces will cause drastic changes in a country's business environment that will adversely affect the profit and other goals of a particular business enterprise.

political system   System of government in a nation.

political union   A central political apparatus coordinates economic, social, and foreign policy.

polycentric staffing policy   A staffing policy in an MNE in which host-country nationals are recruited to manage subsidiaries in their own country, while parent-country nationals occupy key positions at corporate headquarters.

power distance   Theory of how a society deals with the fact that people are unequal in physical and intellectual capabilities. High power distance cultures are found in countries that let inequalities grow over time into inequalities of power and wealth. Low power distance cultures are found in societies that try to play down such inequalities as much as possible.

predatory pricing   Reducing prices below fair market value as a competitive weapon to drive weaker competitors out of the market ("fair" being cost plus some reasonable profit margin).

price elasticity of demand   A measure of how responsive demand for a product is to changes in price.

private action   Violation of property rights through theft, piracy, blackmail, and the like by private individuals or groups.

privatization   The sale of state-owned enterprises to private investors.

processes   Manner in which decisions are made and work is performed.

product liability   Involves holding a firm and its officers responsible when a product causes injury, death, or damage.

product safety laws   Set certain safety standards to which a product must adhere.

production   Activities involved in creating a product.

profit growth   The percentage increase in net profits over time.

profitability   A rate of return concept.

property rights   Bundle of legal rights over the use to which a resource is put and over the use made of any income that may be derived from that resource.

public action Violation of property rights when public officials extort income, resources, or the property itself from property holders.

pull strategy A marketing strategy emphasizing mass media advertising as opposed to personal selling.

purchasing power parity (PPP) An adjustment in gross domestic product per capita to reflect differences in the cost of living.

push strategy A marketing strategy emphasizing personal selling rather than mass media advertising.

Q

quota rent Extra profit producers make when supply is artificially limited by an import quota.

R

regional economic integration Agreements among countries in a geographic region to reduce and ultimately remove tariff and nontariff barriers to the free flow of goods, services, and factors of production between each other.

religion A system of shared beliefs and rituals concerned with the sacred.

representative democracy A political system in which citizens periodically elect individuals to represent them in government.

righteous moralist Approach that one's own ethics are appropriate in all cultures.

rights theories Ethical approaches that recognize that humans have fundamental rights that transcend national boundaries.

right-wing totalitarianism A political system in which political power is monopolized by a party, group, or individual that generally permits individual economic freedom but restricts individual political freedom, including free speech, often on the grounds that it would lead to the rise of communism.

S

sight draft A draft payable on presentation to the drawee.

Six Sigma Statistically based philosophy to reduce defects, boost productivity, eliminate waste, and cut costs.

Smoot-Hawley Act Enacted in 1930 by the U.S. Congress, this act erected a wall of tariff barriers against imports into the United States.

social democrats Those committed to achieving socialism by democratic means.

social mobility The extent to which individuals can move out of the social strata into which they are born.

social responsibility Concept that businesspeople should consider the social consequences of economic actions when making business decisions.

social strata Hierarchical social categories.

social structure The basic social organization of a society.

Socialists Those who believe in public ownership of the means of production for the common good of society.

society Group of people who share a common set of values and norms.

sogo shosha Japanese trading companies; a key part of the *keiretsu,* the large Japanese industrial groups.

source effects Effects that occur when the receiver of the message (i.e. a potential consumer) evaluates the message on the basis of status or image of the sender.

specialized asset An asset designed to perform a specific task, whose value is significantly reduced in its next-best use.

specific tariff Tariff levied as a fixed charge for each unit of good imported.

spot exchange rate The exchange rate at which a foreign exchange dealer will convert one currency into another that particular day.

staffing policy Strategy concerned with selecting employees for particular jobs.

stakeholders Individuals or groups that have an interest, claim, or stake in the company, in what it does, and in how well it performs.

stock of FDI The total accumulated value of foreign-owned assets at a given time.

strategic alliances Cooperative agreements between potential or actual competitors.

strategic pricing The concept containing the three aspects: predatory pricing, multipoint pricing, and experience curve pricing.

strategic trade policy Government policy aimed at improving the competitive position of a domestic industry and/or domestic firm in the world market.

strategy   Actions managers take to attain the firm's goals.

subsidy   Government financial assistance to a domestic producer.

switch trading   Use of a specialized third-party trading house in a countertrade arrangement.

T

tariff   A tax levied on imports.

tariff rate quota   Lower tariff rates applied to imports within the quota than those over the quota.

tax credit   Allows a firm to reduce the taxes paid to the home government by the amount of taxes paid to the foreign government.

tax haven   A country with exceptionally low, or even no, income taxes.

tax treaty   Agreement between two countries specifying what items of income will be taxed by the authorities of the country where the income is earned.

theocratic law system   A system of law based on religious teachings.

theocratic totalitarianism   A political system in which political power is monopolized by a party, group, or individual that governs according to religious principles.

time draft   A promise to pay by the accepting party at some future date.

timing of entry   Entry is early when a firm enters a foreign market before other foreign firms and late when a firm enters after other international businesses have established themselves.

total quality management (TQM)   Management philosophy that takes as its central focus the need to improve the quality of a company's products and services.

totalitarianism   Form of government in which one person or political party exercises absolute control over all spheres of human life and opposing political parties are prohibited.

trade creation   Trade created due to regional economic integration; occurs when high-cost domestic producers are replaced by low-cost foreign producers within a free trade area.

trade deficit   See **current account deficit.**

trade diversion   Trade diverted due to regional economic integration; occurs when low-cost foreign suppliers outside a free trade area are replaced by higher-cost suppliers within a free trade area.

trade surplus   See **current account surplus.**

trademark   Designs and names, officially registered, by which merchants or manufacturers designate and differentiate their products.

transaction costs   The costs of exchange.

transaction exposure   The extent to which income from individual transactions is affected by fluctuations in foreign exchange values.

transfer fee   A bank charge for moving cash from one location to another.

translation exposure   The extent to which the reported consolidated results and balance sheets of a corporation are affected by fluctuations in foreign exchange values.

transnational strategy   Plan to exploit experience-based cost and location economies, transfer core competencies within the firm, and pay attention to local responsiveness.

Treaty of Lisbon   A European Union–sanctioned treaty that will allow the European Parliament to become the co-equal legislator for almost all European laws.

Treaty of Rome   The 1957 treaty that established the European Community.

tribal totalitarianism   A political system in which a party, group, or individual that represents the interests of a particular tribe (ethnic group) monopolizes political power.

turnkey project   A project in which a firm agrees to set up an operating plant for a foreign client and hand over the "key" when the plant is fully operational.

U

uncertainty avoidance   Extent to which cultures socialize members to accept ambiguous situations and to tolerate uncertainty.

United Nations   International institution with 191 member countries created to preserve peace.

United Nations Convention on Contracts for the International Sale of Goods (CIGS)   Agreement establishing a uniform set of rules governing contracts between businesses in different nations.

Universal Declaration of Human Rights   An agreement that establishes basic principles that should be adhered to irrespective of the culture.

universal needs   Needs that are the same all over the world, such as steel, bulk chemicals, and industrial electronics.

utilitarian approach   Ethical approach that holds that the moral worth of actions is determined by their consequences.

V

value creation   Performing activities that increase the value of goods or services to consumers.

values   Abstract ideas about what a society believes to be good, right, and desirable.

vertical differentiation   The centralization and decentralization of decision-making responsibilities.

voluntary export restraint (VER)   A quota on trade imposed from the exporting country's side, instead of the importer's; usually imposed at the request of the importing country's government.

W

wholly owned subsidiary   A subsidiary in which the firm owns 100 percent of the stock.

World Bank   International institution set up to promote general economic development in the world's poorer nations.

World Intellectual Property Organization   Group of 185 countries that have signed international treaties designed to protect intellectual property.

World Trade Organization (WTO)   The organization that succeeded the General Agreement on Tariffs and Trade (GATT) as a result of the successful completion of the Uruguay round of GATT negotiations.

worldwide area structure   Business organizational structure under which the world is divided into areas.

worldwide product division structure   Business organizational structure based on product divisions that have worldwide responsibility.

Z

zero-sum game   A situation in which an economic gain by one country results in an economic loss by another.

Name Index

Organization Index

Subject Index